Brief Contents

Organizational Behaviour

Second European Edition

Robert Kreitner
Arizona State University, USA

Angelo Kinicki
Arizona State University, USA

Marc Buelens
De Vlerick School of Management, Belgium

Mcgraw Hill Publishing Company

London   Boston   Burr Ridge, IL   Dubuque, IA   Madison, WI   New York   San Francisco
St. Louis   Bangkok   Bogotá   Caracas   Lisbon   Madrid   Mexico City   Milan
New Delhi   Seoul   Singapore   Sydney   Taipei   Toronto

Organizational Behaviour, Second European Edition

Kreitner, Kinicki and Buelens

ISBN 0077098285

Published by McGraw-Hill Education
Shoppenhangers Road
Maidenhead
Berkshire
SL6 2QL
Telephone: 44 (0) 1628 502 500
Fax: 44 (0) 1628 770 224
Website: www.mcgraw-hill.co.uk

British Library Cataloguing in Publication Data

A catalogue record for this book is available from the British Library

Library of Congress Cataloguing in Publication Data

The Library of Congress data for this book has been applied for

Acquisitions Editor: Kate Mason
Senior Development Editor: Caroline Howell
Editorial Assistant: Catriona Watson
Senior Marketing Manager: Petra Skytte
Senior Production Editorial Manager: Max Elvey
New Media Designer/Developer: Douglas Greenwood

Produced for McGraw-Hill by Gecko Limited
Text design by Gecko Limited
Cover design by Kate Hyberts Design
Printed and bound in Spain by Mateu Cromo
Cover illustration reproduced by permission of Image Select International Ltd

Contents

Chapter Three

Organizational Culture 56

Chapter Four

International OB: Managing
Across Cultures 84

Preface

This second European edition of **Organizational Behaviour** is intended to serve as a guide to the theory and practice of OB for European students who do not have an extensive background in this exciting field. As explained in the preface to the first edition, the aim of this book is not to give an overview of European OB. This would result in a slim volume with too many blank pages. We want to offer a European student-friendly OB book, with recognisable examples, quotes and case studies drawn from a broad European context. OB has become a fusion kitchen, with ever-increasing influences from different parts of the world. We added some typical European flavours with references to European research and quotes from European OB scholars.

This second European edition builds on the fifth edition of Bob Kreitner & Angelo Kinicki's **Organizational Behaviour**. Standing on a giant's shoulders has one major advantage: one can see further than standing on the ground. One can especially notice that OB theory is not evolving rapidly; in some fields (e.g. motivation theory) one can even use the word 'standstill'. Applications, however, are more and more widespread. Modern organizations, more than ever, behave as well-documented experimental laboratories for all aspects of OB: leadership, motivation, communication, decision-making, and conflict management.

The process of writing and preparing this second European edition reflected the major trends in modern organizations:

- A virtual team beyond boundaries of time and space: Phoenix, New York, Barcelona, London, Ghent.

- A small, very dedicated core team, with Steven Mestdagh at the very core. Steven has developed a 'knack' for the right example, the relevant article, the most important source. And, hard to believe for such a creative person, he delivers on time. Without Steven, there would be no second European Edition. hank you, Steven. Thank you, Herman Van den Broeck for managing our departmental budget so skillfully that Steven could concentrate on this priority.

- Knowledge management. We could build on Fannie Debussche's wisdom and 'surviving the first edition'.

- Experience. Once more, she skilfully crafted her favourite topic: managing diversity.

- Leadership. When things run smoothly, a leader has an easy task–he only has to sign the preface–and that's what I gladly do.

Marc Buelens

Acknowledgements

Our special thanks also to the manuscript reviewers, who for this second European edition were:

Sue Bathmaker, University of Luton

Wendy Bloisi, University of North London

Nicola Bown, University of Leeds

Mary Brown, Robert Gordon University

Finian Buckley, Dublin City University

Irene Greenwood, University of Luton

Jim Grieves, University of Teesside

Anders Hytter, Vaxjo University

Ann-Marie Kelly, Waterford Institute of Technology

Ian Kirkpatrick, University of Leeds

Samantha Lynch, University of Greenwich

Paul McGrath, University College Dublin

Gertjan Nooij, University of Groningen

Doug Pitt, University of Strathclyde

Hugo Prein, University of Rotterdam

James Redmond, Waterford Institute of Technology

John Taylor, Robert Gordon University

Antonie van Nistelrooij, Vrije University Amsterdam

For permission to reproduce material in this book, the publishers would like to thank the following:

Permission to translate 'Als collega's vrienden worden', M Vandersmissen, 21 Spetember 2000, De Standard, Belgium.

'Why your colleagues should be behind bars', FT, 16 August 2000.

'Life is Capital on this side of the pond', FT, 16 August 2000.

'Getting to Grips', Neil Merrick, People Management, 10 December 1998.

Permission to translate 'De psychologie van het e-mailen', Heleen Peverelli, Psychologie Magazine, Amsterdam, The Netherlands, October 2000.

CHANGES TO THE SECOND EDITION

This new edition has been fully revised and updated with new data and references to reflect developments in OB theory, and new demonstrations of the application of OB in real-life organizations across Europe. The Guided Tour on pages xvii to xiv highlights the learning and design features to help you navigate through the book. In addition to these new features and updates, you will find:

- Brand new case material at the opening of every chapter bringing each OB topic to life. New case studies from across Europe, including organizations from the UK, Belgium, Finland, France, and Germany introduce the ideas and topics to be covered in each chapter. Examples include cases examining the parallels between office behaviour and the 'Big Brother' TV phenomenon in Europe, the 'can-do' mentality at Nokia, the cultural and communications challenges encountered during the merger of Daimler and Chrysler, and the teamwork and co-operation required to finish the BT Global Challenge Yacht Race.

- New International OB examples throughout the book. These boxes integrate the impact of globalisation on organizational behaviour, and examine different business practices across cultures. Vignettes include outsiders' perceptions of the social culture of the City of London, the challenges of communicating across continents and time zones from the Netherlands to the USA at Shell, and an insight into Zeneca Pharmaceuticals' policy of helping UK employees to manage stress in the workplace.

- New chapters featuring increased coverage of the topics of conflict, power and politics. A full chapter is devoted to 'Managing Conflict and Negotiation' in this edition, and a further chapter has been developed to focus on 'Influence, Power and Politics' in the workplace.

- New and emerging OB topics integrated in the book. This edition has been developed to integrate a number of hot topics in OB today, with special emphasis on managing diversity, ethics and values in organizational culture, European theories on behaviour modification, and the impact of technology in twenty-first century organizations.

- Increased learning and assessment material. The book is punctuated with many OB Exercises for students to test their own perceptions and develop their ethical awareness and skills. In addition to these exercises, and the summaries of Key Concepts, Personal Awareness and Growth Exercises, and Group Exercises at the end of each chapter, this edition also includes brand new Internet Exercises to encourage students to continue learning and researching on the web. All URLs were correct at the time of going to press.

ONLINE RESOURCES

With this new edition we have improved and expanded the range, currency and quality of resources to support students in their learning and lecturers in their planning, delivery amd assessment of courses. For access to these resources, please visit www.mcgraw-hill.co.uk/textbooks/buelens

For lecturers

Lecturers adopting Organizational Behaviour have access to a range of password-protected supplements to assist them in the delivery of their course using this book. The following resources are available to download at www.mcgraw-hill.co.uk/textbooks/buelens

- Lecturer's Teaching Manual: including chapter overviews, ideas for presenting the material in each chapter, guides to using the case materials and discussion questions, and suggestions for making use of the end-of-chapter team exercises in class.

- PowerPoint lecture plans: a series of PowerPoint slides which can be used to present material from the text, edited to suit the course syllabus.

- On-line testbank of multiple choice and true–false questions for use in automated tests and assessments, or as a resource for examination questions.

- Lecturers adopting this text can create their own website using PageOut, a free and easily accessible course-builder application.

For students

- Chapter-by-chapter self-test questions with automated marking that allow students to test their knowledge on-line as they progress through the book.

- Student OB questionnaires with feedback provide students with a range of facilities to test their skills, perceptions and personality types in on-line quizzes.

- Chapter-by-chapter URLs providing students with a web directory of useful sites for research and further information on companies mentioned in the text.

- Glossary of key terms provides a full list of all of the terms and concepts used in the text with definitions for revision.

- Chapter-by-chapter Revision Notes provide students with learning objectives, figures from the text, and helpful summaries of the important theories and debates in each chapter.

- Updated Internet Exercises – new exercises for on-line research, and updates from the Internet Exercises in the text.

- Extra case studies are provided on-line to supplement the cases in the text, providing students with new, up-to-date, and relevant examples to demonstrate OB theory in action.

GUIDED TOUR

Organizational Behaviour, Second European Edition has been designed for clarity and ease of use. Below is a tour through the text, showing the learning features, examples and exercises included in this edition.

Learning Objectives
Each chapter begins with learning objectives that pinpoint the key concepts that you should understand and be able to apply when you have completed the chapter.

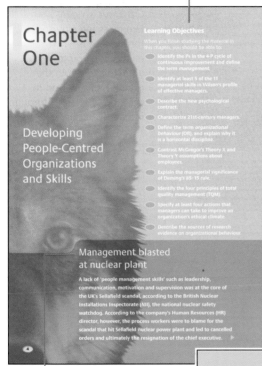

Case Study
A brand new case study provides an interesting and relevant European example that introduces and applies the theories of OB you will learn about in the chapter.

For discussion
Questions at the end of each case focus on new concepts that you should explore, and help you to think about the application of OB theory to practical situations.

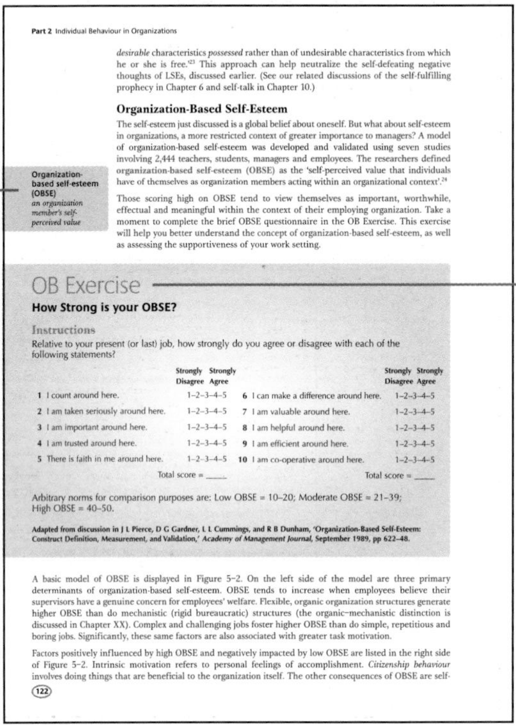

Sample page (top):

desirable characteristics *possessed* rather than of undesirable characteristics from which he or she is free.[42] This approach can help neutralize the self-defeating negative thoughts of LSEs, discussed earlier. (See our related discussions of the self-fulfilling prophecy in Chapter 6 and self-talk in Chapter 10.)

Organization-Based Self-Esteem

The self-esteem just discussed is a global belief about oneself. But what about self-esteem in organizations, a more restricted context of greater importance to managers? A model of organization-based self-esteem was developed and validated using seven studies involving 2,444 teachers, students, managers and employees. The researchers defined organization-based self-esteem (OBSE) as the 'self-perceived value that individuals have of themselves as organization members acting within an organizational context'.[24]

Organization-based self-esteem (OBSE)
an organization member's self-perceived value

Those scoring high on OBSE tend to view themselves as important, worthwhile, effectual and meaningful within the context of their employing organization. Take a moment to complete the brief OBSE questionnaire in the OB Exercise. This exercise will help you better understand the concept of organization-based self-esteem, as well as assessing the supportiveness of your work setting.

OB Exercise

How Strong is your OBSE?

Instructions

Relative to your present (or last) job, how strongly do you agree or disagree with each of the following statements?

	Strongly Disagree	Strongly Agree			Strongly Disagree	Strongly Agree
1 I count around here.	1–2–3–4–5		6 I can make a difference around here.		1–2–3–4–5	
2 I am taken seriously around here.	1–2–3–4–5		7 I am valuable around here.		1–2–3–4–5	
3 I am important around here.	1–2–3–4–5		8 I am helpful around here.		1–2–3–4–5	
4 I am trusted around here.	1–2–3–4–5		9 I am efficient around here.		1–2–3–4–5	
5 There is faith in me around here.	1–2–3–4–5		10 I am co-operative around here.		1–2–3–4–5	

Total score = _____   Total score = _____

Arbitrary norms for comparison purposes are: Low OBSE = 10–20; Moderate OBSE = 21–39; High OBSE = 40–50.

Adapted from discussion in J L Pierce, D G Gardner, L L Cummings, and R B Dunham, 'Organization-Based Self-Esteem: Construct Definition, Measurement, and Validation,' *Academy of Management Journal*, September 1989, pp 622–48.

A basic model of OBSE is displayed in Figure 5-2. On the left side of the model are three primary determinants of organization-based self-esteem. OBSE tends to increase when employees believe their supervisors have a genuine concern for employees' welfare. Flexible, organic organization structures generate higher OBSE than do mechanistic (rigid bureaucratic) structures (the organic–mechanistic distinction is discussed in Chapter XX). Complex and challenging jobs foster higher OBSE than do simple, repetitious and boring jobs. Significantly, these same factors are also associated with greater task motivation.

Factors positively influenced by high OBSE and negatively impacted by low OBSE are listed in the right side of Figure 5-2. Intrinsic motivation refers to personal feelings of accomplishment. *Citizenship behaviour* involves doing things that are beneficial to the organization itself. The other consequences of OBSE are self-

Callout — left:

Key terms
Each new term that is used in the book is highlighted in the text, and a margin box provides a concise definition to aid revision.

Callout — right:

OB Exercise
Exercises interspersed throughout the text encourage you to think analytically about the practice of OB, and to develop your skills through interactive tasks.

Sample page (bottom):

Figure 1-3 illustrates three major sources of influence on the individual's role expectations. People play many roles in life, including those of employee or manager. Their expectations of how those roles should be played are shaped by cultural, organizational and general environmental factors. The International OB describes the cultural differences, between China and Western societies, that influence role expectations and ethical behaviour. This example illustrates how a single behaviour such as hiring relatives can be viewed as both ethical and unethical by people with varying cultural backgrounds.

International OB

http://chineseculture.miningo.com

Religious and Cultural Differences between China and the West Influence Ethical Behavior

By Western standards, China is a secular society; most Chinese do not 'belong' to a faith in the sense of being a Christian, Jew, or Muslim. Little thought is given to supreme beings, other than venerated ancestors, or to such matters as holiness or life after death. There is a dearth of universal ethical principles or moral absolutes other than maintaining the security and well-being of the family and living up to one's Confucian obligations. These remain the primary normative prescriptions for correct behavior. Because maintaining social harmony and order is the highest ideal, minimization of conflict is essential and absolutes are seen as sources of conflict . . .

Confucianism makes no pretence to be a religion. Rather, it is a system of values that govern interpersonal behavior with an eye toward building a civil society. It does not speak to humanity's relationship with any supreme being...

Chinese religion has evolved in ways that support and advance the maintenance of social harmony. In contrast, Judaism and Christianity (and Islam as well) prescribe behavioral and ethical standards to allow the faithful an opportunity to please and prove their worthiness to their Creator and Supreme Being. While banning behavior detrimental to maintaining a civil society (though perhaps one not quite as well-mannered as China's), these religions also prescribe how the Supreme Being should be worshiped and require followers to hold certain beliefs, make certain expressions of faith, and participate in various rituals.

Secular authorities in the West, particularly the Romans building on the precedent set by the ancient Greeks, extended ecclesiastical law into a natural law that dealt with practices, abstract principles, and beliefs beyond the spiritual domain. From natural law, greatly elaborated during the Enlightenment, were derived such notions as liberty, justice, equity, fairness, the binding contract, and ultimately, the social contract between people and their governments. These important social and political virtues, binding governments as well as citizens, acquired the force of principle as important to

many—and perhaps more so to some—as the tenets of sacred scripture. Though Westerners might disagree on what is 'fair' in any set of circumstances, few would argue against the worth of 'fairness'.

The Chinese, like most human beings, will recognize the evil of a wanton crime, but they

will have trouble responding to the invocation of abstractions such as 'fair trade'. What is fair to the Chinese is whatever works, whatever action or manner of speech is necessary to execute a transaction satisfactorily for both parties. Westerners are taught to place the principle of honesty above the nicety of harmony; for them, constructive criticism is the 'right' thing to do, even if painful. For the Chinese, this threat to harmony is antisocial. Likewise, most Westerners would be appalled that a manager could be so unprincipled as to show favoritism in hiring a relative. A Chinese would be equally appalled by any reluctance to do so.

SOURCE: Excerpt from J Scarborough, 'Comparing Chinese and Western Cultural Roots: Why "East Is East and . . .,"' *Business Horizons*, November–December 1998, pp 19–20. Reprinted with permission of *Business Horizons*. Copyright © 1998 by the Board of Trustees at Indiana University Kelley School of Business.

Callout — left:

International OB
These boxes provide examples from around the globe, focusing on the differences in perceptions, cultures and beliefs that affect behaviour in the workplace, providing relevant and interesting insights and an international outlook on OB.

Summary of Key Concepts
At the end of the chapter, a short recap reinforces and clarifies the chapter Learning Objectives to ensure that you have acquired an understanding of the key topics.

Discussion Questions
These end of chapter questions test understanding of core theories and can be used in class or as an assessment. As well as checking comprehension, the questions require you to demonstrate your analytical abilities by citing examples and applications of the concepts in the chapter.

Internet Exercise
New Internet Exercises guide you in making full use of the web as a research tool. The tasks are set to help you develop your on-line research skills and enable you to broaden your OB knowledge through examining real organisations and companies.

Personal Awareness and Growth Exercise
The chapter concludes with an in-depth exercise that prepares you for the decisions you may face in the world of work. These organizational problems aim to develop your ethical awareness and transferable skills, for instance in communication, negotiation or dealing with conflict.

Chapter One Developing People-Centred Organizations and Skills

Summary of Key Concepts

1 **Identify the P's in the 4-P cycle of continuous improvement and define the term management.** The 4 Ps are people, products, processes and productivity. Management is the process of working with and through others to achieve organizational objectives in an efficient and ethical manner.

2 **Identify at least 5 of the 11 managerial skills in Wilson's profile of effective managers.** According to the Wilson skills profile, an effective manager: clarifies goals and objectives; encourages participation; plans and organizes; has technical and administrative expertise; facilitates work through team building and coaching; provides feedback; keeps things moving; controls details; applies reasonable pressure for goals accomplishment; empowers and delegates; and recognizes and rewards good performance.

3 **Describe the new psychological contract.** It is a transactional contract in which employees are expected to be both flexible self-starters and team players with multiple skills. The new contract pays employees for results, not for time spent on the job, and makes employees responsible for their own careers. The company's side of the bargain, in well-managed and ethical organizations, involves giving each employee the opportunity to 'grow' and acquire marketable skills.

4 **Characterize 21st-century managers.** They will be team players who will get things done cooperatively by relying on: joint decision-making; their knowledge instead of formal authority; and their multicultural skills. They will engage in life-long learning and be compensated on the basis of their skills and results. They will facilitate rather than resist change; share rather than hoard power and key information; and be multidirectional communicators. Ethics will be a forethought instead of an afterthought. They will be generalists with multiple specialties.

5 **Define the term organizational behaviour and explain why OB is a horizontal discipline.** Organizational behaviour (OB) is an interdisciplinary field dedicated to better understanding and management of people at work. It is both research and application oriented. Except for teaching and research positions, one does not normally get a job in OB. Rather, because OB is a horizontal discipline, its concepts and lessons are applicable to virtually every job category, business function and professional specialty.

6 **Contrast McGregor's Theory X and Theory Y assumptions about employees.** Theory X employees, according to traditional thinking, dislike work, require close supervision and are primarily interested in security. According to the modern Theory Y, employees are capable of self-direction, seeking responsibility, and of being creative.

7 **Explain the managerial significance of Deming's 85–15 rule.** Deming claimed that about 85 per cent of organizational failures are due to system breakdowns involving factors such as management, machinery, or work rules. He believed the workers themselves are responsible for failures for only about 15 per cent of the time. Consequently, Deming criticized the standard practice of blaming and punishing individuals for what are typically system failures beyond their immediate control.

8 **Identify the four principles of total quality management (TQM).** The four principles are:
a Do it right the first time to eliminate costly rework.
b Listen to, and learn from, customers and employees.
c Make continuous improvement an everyday matter.
d Build teamwork, trust and mutual respect.

9 **Specify at least four actions that managers can take to improve an organization's ethical climate.** They can bring about an improvement by: (a) behaving ethically themselves, (b) screening potential employees, (c) developing a code of ethics, (d) providing ethics training, (e) reinforcing and rewarding ethical behaviour, and (f) creating positions and structural mechanisms to deal with ethical issues.

10 **Describe the sources of research evidence on organizational behaviour.** Five sources of OB research evidence are: meta-analyses (statistically pooled evidence from several studies); field studies (evidence from real-life situations); laboratory studies (evidence from contrived situations); sample surveys (questionnaire data); and case studies (observation of a single person, group, or organization).

Discussion Questions

1 Why view the typical employee as a human resource?
2 In your opinion, what are the three or four most important strategic results in Figure 1–1? Why?
3 How would you respond to a fellow student who says, 'I have a hard time getting along with other people, but I think I could be a good manager'?
4 Based on either personal experience as a manager or on your observation of managers at work, do you consider the 11 skills in Table 1–1 to be a realistic portrayal of what managers do?
5 How willing and able are you to work under the new psychological contract?
6 What is your personal experience of Theory X and Theory Y managers (see Table 1–3)? Which did you prefer? Why?
7 How would you respond to a new manager who made this statement? 'TQM is about statistical process control, not about people.'
8 Do you use the contingency approach in your daily affairs? Explain the circumstances.
9 What 'practical' theories have you formulated to achieve the things you want in life (such as graduating, keeping fit, getting a good job, meeting that special someone)? From a manager's standpoint, which use of research is better: instrumental or conceptual? Explain your rationale.

(27)

Part 1 The World of Organizational Behaviour

Internet Exercise
http://home.sprintmail.comm/~debflanagan/
www.hp.com

Part 1 (Note: This part is for those with little or no Internet experience; those who need to polish their Internet research skills; and experienced Internet users who want to explore a lot of free business information and company profiles.) A free and useful business-oriented tutorial for novice web surfers can be found at http://home.sprintmail.com/~debflanagan/. From the home page of this site – Researching Companies Online – select 'locate high-level company information' and learn how you can find anything you want to know about companies around the world. Also take a look at 'locate company home pages' and 'research company financial information'.

practices discussed at the beginning of this chapter (go back and review them to refresh your memory). On the Internet, go to Hewlett-Packard's home page (www.hp.com), and select Company Information from the main menu. Next, under About HP, select History and Facts and then click corporate objectives on the right side of your screen. Read the Corporate Objectives statement, focusing particularly on the sections Our People, Citizenship and Management as you scroll down. Also try to take a look at diversity@hp, which you'll

Questions
1 What useful online research tips did you discover?
2 What useful business-related information sources did you discover?
3 What useful information did you acquire?
Note: If you know of a better free online research tutorial than this one, please tell your instructor and fellow students.
Part 2 The purpose of this exercise is to focus on one well-known company with a good general reputation (Hewlett-Packard) and look for evidence of the seven people-centred

Questions
1 On a scale of 1 (low) to 10 (high), how people-centred is HP?
2 What specific evidence of each of the seven people-centred practices did you find?
3 Which of the seven practices appears to be HP's strongest suit?
4 Do HP's culture and values give it a strategic competitive advantage? Explain.
5 Would you like to work for HP? Why or why not?

Personal awareness and growth exercise
How Strong Is Your Motivation to Manage?

Objectives
1 To introduce a psychological determinant of managerial success.
2 To assess your readiness to manage.
3 To discuss the implications of motivation to manage, from the standpoint of global competitiveness.

Introduction
By identifying personal traits which are positively correlated with both rapid movement up the career ladder and managerial effectiveness, John B. Miner developed a psychometric test for measuring what he calls 'motivation to manage'. The questionnaire assesses the strength of

seven factors relating to the temperament (or psychological make-up) needed to manage others. One word of caution. The following instrument is a shortened and modified version of Miner's original. Our version is for instructional and discussion purposes only. Although we believe it can indicate the general strength of your motivation to manage, it is not a precise measuring tool.

Instructions
Assess the strength of each of the seven dimensions of your own motivation to manage by circling the appropriate numbers on the 1 to 7 scales. Then add the seven circled numbers to get your total 'motivation to manage' score.

Factor	Description	Scale
1 Authority figures	A desire to meet managerial role requirements in terms of positive relationships with superiors.	Weak 1–2–3–4–5–6–7 Strong
2 Competitive games	A desire to engage in competition with peers involving games or sports and thus meet managerial role requirements in this regard.	Weak 1–2–3–4–5–6–7 Strong
3 Competitive situations	A desire to engage in competition with peers involving occupational or work-related activities and thus meet managerial role requirements in this regard.	Weak 1–2–3–4–5–6–7 Strong

(28)

Part One

1

The World of Organizational Behaviour

Chapter One

Developing People-Centred Organizations and Skills

Learning Objectives

When you finish studying the material in this chapter, you should be able to:

- Identify the Ps in the 4-P cycle of continuous improvement and define the term *management*.

- Identify at least 5 of the 11 managerial skills in Wilson's profile of effective managers.

- Describe the new psychological contract.

- Characterize 21st-century managers.

- Define the term *organizational behaviour* (OB), and explain why it is a horizontal discipline.

- Contrast McGregor's Theory X and Theory Y assumptions about employees.

- Explain the managerial significance of Deming's 85–15 rule.

- Identify the four principles of total quality management (TQM).

- Specify at least four actions that managers can take to improve an organization's ethical climate.

- Describe the sources of research evidence on organizational behaviour.

Management blasted at nuclear plant

A lack of 'people management skills' such as leadership, communication, motivation and supervision was at the core of the UK's Sellafield scandal, according to the British Nuclear Installations Inspectorate (NII), the national nuclear safety watchdog. According to the company's Human Resources (HR) director, however, the process workers were to blame for the scandal that hit Sellafield nuclear power plant and led to cancelled orders and ultimately the resignation of the chief executive. ▷

What had happened at Sellafield? An inspection at the plant revealed that workers had falsified some important quality control data of an experimental, mixed plutonium and uranium fuel. The falsified data involved a test ordered by a Japanese customer, power company Kansai. Workers had to check the diameters of random samples of fuel pellets. Instead of testing each sample, several workers had simply copied old figures from previous batches. A major scandal broke out and five workers were sacked.

But this was not the end: a report by the NII discovered a lack of high-quality safety systems and improper management across the plant. 'In a plant with a proper safety culture, the events that caused the scandal could not have happened', one of the inspectors said. While HR director Roger Leek admitted that there had 'probably not been enough investment in training', he insisted that operators, rather than senior managers, were responsible for practices that had jeopardized safety: 'You rely on the operators to do what is expected of them, rather than stand over them day and night. There are a lot of jobs in this industry that are rather technical, but people still do them,' he said.

There had been a perception at the plant that nothing more than the dismissal of those process workers involved in the affair, along with a tightening up of procedures, would be necessary. After it was revealed that they had falsified the quality check, many thought that it was only the process workers who would be criticized.

However, the report from the UK's nuclear watchdog sent shockwaves through the plant's senior management. It focused on how the nature of the job, lack of supervision and poor training had contributed largely to the procedural failures. The workers' actions were 'not at all surprising' given the 'tedious' nature of the tasks involved, the report said.

Trade unions were quick to blame the crisis on a lack of 'people skills' among middle managers. John Kane, site convenor for the GMB (General and Municipal Boilermakers) union, claimed that managers at the plant rarely talked to staff. 'We have this treacle layer of middle managers who, although highly qualified in certain tasks, have very few people-management skills,' he said. But key figures in personnel believe the problem runs deeper.

The data check was part of a quality assurance inspection and had never been connected with safety, although the use of substandard pellets could have safety implications, according to recent press reports. But the significance of the check, even for quality control, was not emphasized to staff. As a result, falsifying the data became a way of avoiding what was seen as a pointless task. The NII report warned that allowing this attitude towards dull and monotonous work to develop, by failing to explain its significance, could lead to more serious errors in future. Sellafield's initial response was simply to promise improvements. But the Government indicated that this was not enough and that more serious action was required.

The NII report criticized almost every aspect of Sellafield's management structure. It condemned reductions in staff numbers made in response to the Government's plans to prepare British Nuclear Fuels (BNFL) for partial privatization, and warned that health and safety arrangements were unclear, with safety managers overworked and safety training poor.

There was no excuse for falsifying records, the report said, but 'inadequacies' in the working environment were a major factor. Because supervision of the inspection was 'virtually non-existent', managers had sent out 'entirely the wrong message regarding the importance of the task and acted as a demotivator'. Awareness training had been 'ineffective', leaving workers with no idea of the significance of their job. Consequently, staff were 'unlikely to appreciate the importance of the task or take ownership of it'.

The task itself had been poorly conceived, the report said. Other than the prospect of an eventual quality-control stamp and payment for completing the work, there was no recognition of diligent performance. Other workstations at Sellafield, which employs 10,000 people, were also badly designed, according to the report.

Job structures would now be reviewed, Leek said, but the incident had created apprehension among managers about the security of their jobs. 'The ramifications of a few people not following operating procedures has damaged this company. There comes a point where you train people, you give them responsibilities and you expect them to fulfil them correctly—even if the job is boring', he said.

Tom Cannon, chief executive of the Management and Enterprise National Training Organization, also blamed the management at Sellafield. 'As a nation, we are deeply confused about technology. On the one hand, we are technophobes; on the other, we believe that technology will solve everything. There is an implication that, if you get the science right, the people will fit around it. But all the evidence shows that this simply isn't true,' he said.

'The Sellafield managers thought the maths would do the job—and that the more people acted like machines, the better. They didn't seem to be aware of the people—development strategies you'd expect to have in a company that's not short of money.'[1]

For discussion
Sellafield's HR director and the British Nuclear Installations Inspectorate have rather contrasting views on who's to blame for the nuclear scandal. What do you think caused the problems?

True or false? People are the key to success in today's highly competitive global economy. It is nearly a century since Henry Ford said: 'You can destroy my factories and offices, but give me my people and I will build the business right back up again.'[2] Every day, business magazines come up with new stories reporting famous chief executive officers' (CEOs) claims that their employees are their main source of competitive advantage. For example Virgin boss, Richard Branson, said:

There is only one thing that keeps your company alive, that is: the people you work with. All the rest is secondary. You have to motivate people, and attract the best. Every single employee can make a difference. For instance, the girl who opened the best bridal boutique in Europe worked as a stewardess at the airline. She came to me with an idea and I encouraged her to put it into practice. She did, and so Virgin Bride was originated. Because she was free to prove herself, she has been able to use all her talents optimally. The people you hire are so important. If you support the idea that every operator can excel in what he's doing, then that will eventually happen. People often make mistakes but you need to give them space even for that. You have to confirm people in what they're doing and make sure they have fun doing their job. You have to make them feel their work is important and give them the chance to do the things they like. At Virgin, of course, we're lucky that there are so many different functions. Everybody can develop in whatever way he or she wants to. If people see a former stewardess running her own company, people become inspired. Some people who are now working on the Eurostar were also those who helped get the airline off the ground. Some of them are already dreaming of new projects and this keeps the work exciting. People are the essence of an organization and nothing else.[3]

But wait a minute. Dilbert cartoonist Scott Adams, who humorously documents managerial lapses of sanity, sees it differently. Adams rates the oft heard statement: 'Employees are our most valuable asset', as top of his list of Great Lies of Management.[4] This raises serious questions. Is Branson an exception, a manager who actually acts on the idea that people are the most valuable resource? Does the typical manager merely pay lip service to the critical importance of people? If so, what are the implications of this hypocrisy for organizational productivity and employee well-being?

A number of recent studies have been enlightening. Generally, they show that there is a substantial and rapidly expanding body of evidence—some of it based on quite sophisticated methodology—of the strong connection between how firms manage their people and the economic results they achieve.[5]

Jean-Claude Larréché, Professor at the Insead Institute, France, investigated which were the most 'healthy' companies in 1998 and 1999. In both reports, Hewlett-Packard, Unilever, Crédit Suisse, L'Oréal and Whitbread came out as the five healthiest of the largest European and American organizations. Larréché analysed the companies with a system called 'Market effectiveness capabilities assessment'. Over 800 senior managers from 263 organizations were to evaluate the competitiveness of their companies on 150 determinants, clustered in 12 fundamental capacities. It turned out that the most healthy companies differed from the rest in particular aspects such as organizational culture, customer orientation and human resources. On the other hand, according to Larréché, 'the most harmful thing for competitive organizations is that top managers are often unable to relate to their employees and customers'.[6]

A study by the University of Sheffield's Institute of Work Psychology, based on extensive examination of over 100 medium-sized manufacturing companies over a seven-year period, revealed that people management is not only critical to business performance: it also far outstrips emphasis on quality, technology, competitive strategy, and research and development in its influence on the bottom line. The study, known as the Sheffield Effectiveness Programme, also showed that half the firms have no individual in charge of human resources and that more than two-thirds have no written personnel strategy. One researcher said: 'Managers placed considerable emphasis on strategy and technology, but our research suggests that these areas account for only a small part of the differences in financial performance.'[7]

Jeffrey Pfeffer and his colleagues from Stanford University reviewed evidence from companies in both the United States and Germany that 'people-centred practices' were strongly associated with much higher profits and significantly lower employee turnover. Further analysis uncovered the following seven people-centred practices in successful companies.

1   Job security (to eliminate fear of lay-offs).
2   Careful hiring (emphasizing a good fit with the company culture).
3   Power to the people (via decentralization and self-managed teams).
4   Generous pay for performance.
5   Lots of training.
6   Less emphasis on status (to build a 'we' feeling).
7   Trust-building (through the sharing of critical information).[8]

It is vital that these factors form a package deal—they need to be installed in a co-ordinated and systematic manner rather than in bits and pieces.

The dark side of this study is that Scott Adams's cynical assessment is too often true. Managers tend to act counter to their declarations that people are their most important asset. Pfeffer and his colleagues blame a number of modern management trends and practices. For example, undue emphasis on short-term profit precludes long-term efforts to nurture human resources. Also, excessive lay-offs—when managers view people as a cost rather than an asset—erode trust, commitment and loyalty.[9] 'Only 12 per cent of today's organizations', according to Pfeffer, 'have the systematic approaches and persistence to qualify as true people-centred organizations, thus giving them a competitive advantage.'[10] The studies at Insead and the Sheffield Effectiveness Programme seem to confirm this trend.

To us, an 88 per cent shortfall in the quest for people-centred organizations represents a tragic loss, both to society and to the global economy. Toward that end, the aim of this book is to help increase the number of people-centred managers and organizations around the world.

Our starting point is the 4-P model of strategic results as shown in Figure 1–1, which focuses on people, products, processes and productivity. The 4-P model emphasizes the larger, strategic context for managing people. Although people are, indeed, the key to organizational success today, other factors such as planning, technology and finance also require good management. Furthermore, the 4-P model stresses the importance of day-to-day continuous improvement in all aspects of organizational endeavour to cope with more demanding customers and stiffer competition.

The purpose of this first chapter is to explore the manager's job; to define and examine organizational behaviour and its evolution; and to consider the importance of ethics in organizational behaviour. The chapter concludes by presenting the means by which we can learn more about organizational behaviour. Also, a topical model for the balance of OB is introduced.

Figure 1-1 *Strategic Results: The 4-P Cycle of Continuous Improvement*

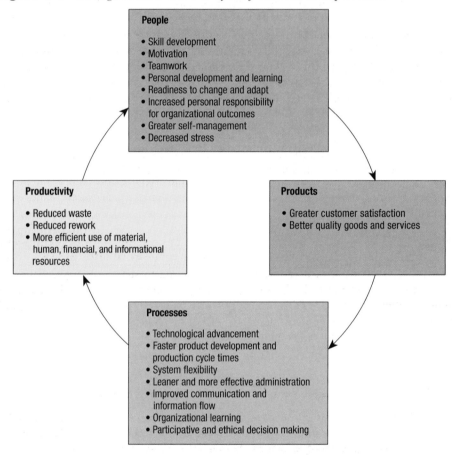

THE MANAGER'S JOB: GETTING THINGS DONE

Whether we like it or not, managers touch our lives in many ways. Schools, hospitals, government agencies, and large and small businesses all require systematic management. Formally defined, management is the process of working with and through others to achieve organizational objectives in an efficient and ethical manner. From the standpoint of organizational behaviour, the central feature of this definition is 'working with and through others'.

Management
process of working with and through others to achieve organizational objectives efficiently and ethically

Managers play a constantly evolving role. Today's successful managers are no longer the I've-got-everything-under-control order givers of yesteryear. Rather, they need to creatively envision and actively sell bold new directions in an ethical and sensitive manner. Effective managers are team players, empowered by the willing and active support of others who are driven by conflicting self-interests. Each of us has a huge stake in how well managers carry out their evolving role. Henry Mintzberg, a respected management scholar, observed: 'No job is more vital to our society than that of the manager. It is the manager who determines whether our social institutions serve us well or whether they squander our talents and resources.'[11] However, to many people, it is far from clear what managers actually do.

Extending our managerial focus, let us take a closer look at the skills that managers need to perform, the evolving relationship between employer and employee, and the future direction of management.

What Do Managers Do? A Skills Profile

Observational studies by, among others, Rosemary Stewart in Europe and Henry Mintzberg in the USA, have found the typical manager's day to be a fragmented collection of brief episodes.[12] Interruptions are commonplace, while large blocks of time for planning and reflective thinking are not. In one particular study, four top-level managers spent 63 per cent of their time on activities lasting less than nine minutes each. Only 5 per cent of the managers' time was devoted to activities lasting more than a hour.[13] But what specific skills do effective managers perform during their hectic and fragmented workdays?

Many attempts have been made over the years to paint a realistic picture of what managers do.[14] Diverse and confusing lists of managerial functions and roles have been suggested. Fortunately, a stream of research over the past 20 years, by Clark Wilson and others, has given us a practical and statistically validated profile of managerial *skills*[15] (see Table 1–1).

Wilson's managerial skills profile focuses on 11 observable categories of managerial behaviour. This is very much in tune with today's emphasis on managerial competency.[16] Wilson's unique skills-assessment technique goes beyond the usual self-report approach with its natural bias. In addition to surveying a given manager about his or her 11 skills, the Wilson approach asks those who report directly to the manager about their boss's skills. According to Wilson and his colleagues, the result is an assessment of skill *mastery*, not simply skill awareness.[17] The logic behind this approach is both simple and compelling. Who better to assess a manager's skills than the people who experience those behaviours on a day-to-day basis–those who report directly to the manager?

The Wilson managerial skills research yields the following three useful lessons.

▼ **Dealing effectively with people is what management is all about. The 11 skills in Table 1–1 constitute a cycle of goal creation, commitment, feedback, reward and accomplishment, which has human interaction at every turn.**

▼ **Managers with high skills mastery tend to have better sub-unit performance and employee morale than managers with low skills mastery.**[18]

▼ **Effective female and male managers do not have significantly different skill profiles,**[19] **contrary to claims in the popular business press in recent years.**[20]

Table 1–1

Skills Exhibited by an Effective Manager*

1. **Clarifies goals and objectives** for everyone involved.
   (See Chapters 6, 8, 11, 16, and 18)

2. **Encourages participation,** upward communication, and suggestions.
   (See Chapters 2, 11, 12, 15 and 16)

3. **Plans and organizes** for an orderly work flow.
   (See Chapters 18 and 19)

4. Has **technical and administrative expertise** to answer organization-related questions.
   (See Chapters 1, 2, 9, 11 and 19)

5. **Facilitates work** through team building, training, coaching, and support.
   (See Chapters 3, 4, 7, 9, 11, 12, 15, 16, and 17)

6. **Provides feedback** honestly and constructively.
   (See Chapters 9, 10, 11, 12, 15 and 16)

7. **Keeps things moving** by relying on schedules, deadlines, and helpful reminders.
   (See Chapters 7, 8, 9, 10, 11, 12, 13, 15 and 16)

8. **Controls details** without being overbearing.
   (See Chapters 2, 4, 5, 6, 9, 11, 14, 16 and 17)

9. Applies reasonable **pressure for goal accomplishment.**
   (See Chapters 1, 4, 5, 6, 7, 8, 9, 10, 12, 13, 15, 16, and 18)

10. **Empowers and delegates** key duties to others while maintaining goal clarity and commitment.
    (See Chapters 2, 3, 14, 15, 16, and 18)

11. **Recognizes good performance** with rewards and positive reinforcement.
    (See Chapters. 7, 8, 9, 10, 11, 15 and 16)

*Annotated with relevant chapters in this textbook.

SOURCE: Adapted from material in C Wilson, 'Identify Needs with Costs in Mind,' *Training and Development Journal*, July 1980, pp 58–62; and F Shipper, 'A Study of the Psychometric Properties of the Managerial Skill Scales of the Survey of Management Practices,' *Educational and Psychological Measurement*, June 1995, pp 468–79.

The New Psychological Contract: A Cautionary Tale

> **Psychological contract**
> *can be defined as the written and implied expectations between employer and employee*

Just imagine you work for a large international company and just woke up from a 20-year nap—you would be shocked and worried. Your **psychological contract**, would have been completely rewritten (without your input or consent).[21] When you went to sleep, your employer expected you to be loyal, hard working, and obedient. In return, you expected to get a steady stream of salary increases and promotions and the proverbial gold watch upon your retirement from the company. In short, the company was like a nurturing parent who knew what was best for you and your career. You loved and trusted the company.

Now your head spins as you hear things about the so-called new psychological contract. 'Everyone is self-employed.' 'You own your own employability.' 'Build a portable career.' 'You're paid to add value.' 'Be willing to stay but ready to leave.' According to this new psychological contract, your employer expects you to be both a creative self-starter and a team player capable of doing a variety of jobs with a diverse array of people. Your pay will be tied to results, not to years on the job. Moreover, your company expects you to take charge of your own career and act more like a partner than an employee. Complaints and comments by co-workers tell you they don't love and trust the company as before. You turn to one of them and whisper, 'What's a stock option? And what on earth is email?' You certainly would have a lot to learn.

The new psychological contract, although couched in terms of Europe's economy in this tale, has immense implications for both individuals and organizations in advanced economies worldwide.

Implications for the Individual

Jean Marie Hiltrop, Professor at the University of Lausanne, Switzerland, and one of Europe's leading writers on the subject, characterizes the new psychological contract as follows.

> *There is no job security. The employee will be employed as long as he or she adds value to the organization, and is personally responsible for finding new ways to add value. In return, the employee has the right to demand interesting and important work, has the*

freedom and resources to perform it well, receives pay that reflects his or her contribution and gets experience and training needed to be employed here or elsewhere.[22]

For employees committed to life-long learning, working smarter rather than harder and making their own opportunities, the new psychological contract is a positive situation. Organizational life will give them more opportunities to develop and be rewarded for creating value for internal and external customers. Promotions will be fewer and slower than under the old psychological contract because of flatter organizations with fewer layers. But lateral moves from one project or function to another will provide lots of challenges for those who get results. The skills profile for an effective manager in Table 1–1 is a good measuring stick for personal growth and success under the new contract.

Meanwhile, the new psychological contract is not good news for employees with an entitlement mentality. They are the ones who believe the company owes them pay rises and promotions just for showing up at work. They also tend to be inflexible and resistant to change.

Implications for Organizations

According to one management writer, there has been a shift from a 'relational contract' to a 'transactional contract'.[23] Unfortunately, so far corporations have done a better job of defining the employees' end of the bargain than it has its own. It is one thing to say everyone is self-employed—but what are the company's obligations in the new transactional environment? How eager are companies to train employees who might turn around and go to work for a competitor? Employees who feel they are sky-diving without a parachute are unlikely to express the loyalty and trust of yesteryear. Yet many executives seem to want it both ways: 21st-century staff flexibility and 1950s-style employee loyalty. After attending a meeting of human resource professionals in 1996, one observer noted that the biggest complaint was that 'high-tech workers have zero company loyalty'.[24]

As some kind of warning to employers, Brousseau and Driver point out that, as a result of the emerging psychological contract, a large proportion of the 21st-century workers will increasingly resemble the characters that cult-author Douglas Coupland describes in Generation X.

The members from Generation X do not appear to have any particular interest in climbing corporate ladders or in spending their careers in one type of work or job. Instead, they want to explore and do different kinds of work in order to learn about themselves and to express their individual values. . . . Generation X employees don't care about fancy titles, are unimpressed with the need to do specific tasks in specific ways merely because their boss wishes them to, and want their work to have meaning. Since one worker's meaning is another one's drudgery, organizations will have to adopt creative, unorthodox methods if they are to benefit from the energy and efforts of the new generation.[25]

21st-Century Managers

Today's workplace is undergoing immense and permanent changes.[26] Organizations are being 're-engineered' for greater speed, efficiency and flexibility.[27] Teams are pushing aside the individual as the primary building block of organizations.[28] Command-and-control management is giving way to participative management and empowerment.[29] Ego-centred leaders are being replaced by customer-centred leaders. Employees are being increasingly viewed as internal customers. All this creates a mandate for a new kind of manager in the 21st century. Table 1–2 contrasts the characteristics of past and future managers. As the balance of this book will demonstrate, the managerial shift in Table 1–2 is not just a good idea, it is an absolute necessity in the new workplace.

Table 1–2

Evolution of the 21st-century Manager

	Past Managers	Future Managers
Primary role	Order-giver, privileged elite, manipulator, controller	Facilitator, team member, teacher, advocate, sponsor, coach
Learning and knowledge	Periodic learning, narrow specialist	Continuous life-long learning, generalist with multiple specialties
Compensation criteria	Time, effort, rank	Skills, results
Cultural orientation	Monocultural, monolingual	Multicultural, multilingual
Primary source of influence	Formal authority	Knowledge (technical and interpersonal)
View of people	Potential problem	Primary resource
Primary communication pattern	Vertical	Multidirectional
Decision-making style	Limited input for individual decisions	Broad-based input for joint decisions
Ethical considerations	Afterthought	Forethought
Nature of interpersonal relationships	Competitive (win–lose)	Co-operative (win–win)
Handling of power and key information	Hoard and restrict access	Share and broaden access
Approach to change	Resist	Facilitate

THE FIELD OF ORGANIZATIONAL BEHAVIOUR: PAST AND PRESENT

Organizational behaviour
interdisciplinary field dedicated to better understanding of management of people at work

By definition, organizational behaviour is both research and application orientated. The three basic levels of analysis in OB are individual, group, and organizational. OB draws upon a diverse array of disciplines—including psychology, management, sociology, organization theory, social psychology, statistics, anthropology, general systems theory, economics, information technology, political science, vocational counselling, human stress management, psychometrics, ergonomics, decision theory and ethics. This rich heritage has spawned many competing perspectives and theories about human work behaviour. By the mid-1980s, one researcher had identified 110 distinct theories about behaviour within the field of OB.[30]

Organizational behaviour is an academic designation. With the exception of teaching and research positions, OB is not an everyday job category such as accounting, marketing or finance. Students of OB typically do not get jobs in organizational behaviour, *per se*. This reality in no way demeans OB or lessens its importance in effective organizational management. OB is a *horizontal* discipline that cuts across virtually every job category, business function and professional specialty. Anyone who plans to make a living in a large or small, public or private, organization needs to study organizational behaviour. Moreover, according to a recent *Management Review* article, more and more CEOs have become 'self-made psychologists'.

Freudian disciples, they're not. But in their own commonsense way, CEOs have turned their attention to issues of human behaviour and psychology. In coming down from the mountain, they have discarded the old reliance on organization and process and become much more directly involved with people and psychological issues. They've adopted a strong 'show me' approach to employee behaviour. It's all very well to create mission statements and articulate corporate values, but CEOs want to see concrete evidence of behaviour that reflects those values. That's why we see IBM's Lou Gerstner spending more than a third of his time visiting and interacting with customers, and Heinrich von Pierer from Germany's Siemens stating that his most important task in directing a change programme was to stimulate people to think differently. The fact is, the previous generation of CEOs placed too high a priority on ivory tower [academic] strategizing. Nowadays they're spending much more time on people issues and learning as they go; in that sense they are getting into applied psychology.[31]

A historical perspective of the study of people at work helps in studying organizational behaviour. According to a management history expert, this is important because it sharpens one's vision of the present not the past.[32] In other words, we can better understand where the field of OB is today and where it appears to be aiming, by appreciating where it has been. Let us examine three significant landmarks in the evolution of understanding and managing people:

▼ **The human relations movement.**

▼ **The total quality management movement.**

▼ **The contingency approach to management.**

The Human Relations Movement

A unique combination of factors during the 1930s fostered the human relations movement. First, following legalization of union-management collective bargaining in the United States in 1935, management began looking for new ways of handling employees. Second, behavioural scientists conducting on-the-job research started calling for more attention to be paid to the 'human' factor. Managers who had lost the battle to keep unions out of their factories heeded the call for better human relations and improved working conditions. One such study, conducted at Western Electric's Hawthorne plant, Chicago was a prime stimulus for the human relations movement. Ironically, many of the Hawthorne findings have turned out to be more myth than fact.

The Hawthorne Legacy

Interviews conducted decades later with three subjects of the Hawthorne studies, and a reanalysis of the original data using modern statistical techniques, do not support the initial conclusions about the positive effect of supportive supervision. Specifically, money, fear of unemployment during the Great Depression, managerial discipline, and high-quality raw materials—not supportive supervision—turned out to be responsible for high output in the relay assembly test room experiments.[33] Nonetheless, the human relations movement gathered momentum through the 1950s, as academics and managers alike made stirring claims about the powerful effect that individual needs, supportive supervision and group dynamics apparently had on job performance.

The Writings of Mayo and Follett

Essential to the human relations movement were the writings of Elton Mayo and Mary Parker Follett. Australian-born Mayo, who headed the Harvard researchers at Hawthorne, advised managers to attend to employees' emotional needs in his 1933 classic, The Human Problems of an Industrial Civilization. Follett was a true pioneer, not only as a woman management consultant in the male-dominated industrial world of the 1920s, but also as a writer who saw employees as complex combinations of attitudes, beliefs, and needs. Mary Parker Follett was far ahead of her time in telling managers to motivate job performance instead of merely demanding it: a 'pull' rather than 'push' strategy. She also built a logical bridge between political democracy and a co-operative spirit in the workplace.[34]

McGregor's Theory Y

In 1960, Douglas McGregor wrote a book entitled *The Human Side of Enterprise*, which has become an important philosophical base for the modern view of people at work.[35] Drawing upon his experience as a management consultant, McGregor formulated two sharply contrasting sets of assumptions about human nature (see Table 1–3). His Theory X assumptions were pessimistic and negative and, according to McGregor's interpretation, typical of how managers traditionally perceived employees. To help managers break with this negative tradition, McGregor formulated his **Theory Y**, a modern and positive set of assumptions about people.

Theory Y
McGregor's modern and positive assumptions about employees being responsible and creative

McGregor believed managers could accomplish more through others by viewing them as self-energized, committed, responsible and creative beings. Forty years ago, motivation at work tended to be tackled as single-issue psychology. Typical advice was 'people will work harder if you give them more attention'. Today, research in Britain revealed that if, for example, a company gives its people a chance to express themselves, it might feel that the organization is a safe environment in which they can become personally involved. This, in turn, might make them more committed to their work so that they produce a larger quantity of better-quality work.[36] According to a study among employees of a Dutch hospital experiencing a tight labour market, job characteristics other than wages, such as labour relations and work content, were found to play a major role in the individuals' choices to resign or stay.[37]

Table 1–3

McGregor's Theory X and Theory Y

Outdated (Theory X) Assumptions about People at Work	Modern (Theory Y) Assumptions about People at Work
1. Most people dislike work; they avoid it when they can.	1. Work is a natural activity, like play or rest.
2. Most people must be coerced and threatened with punishment before they will work. People require close direction when they are working.	2. People are capable of self-direction and self-control if they are committed to objectives.
3. Most people actually prefer to be directed. They tend to avoid responsibility and exhibit little ambition. They are interested only in security.	3. People generally become committed to organizational objectives if they are rewarded for doing so.
	4. The typical employee can learn to accept and seek responsibility.
	5. The typical member of the general population has imagination, ingenuity and creativity.

SOURCE: Adapted from D McGregor, *The Human Side of Enterprise* (New York: McGraw-Hill, 1960), Ch 4.

New Assumptions about Human Nature

Unfortunately, unsophisticated behavioural research methods caused the human relations theorists (human relationists) to embrace some naive and misleading conclusions. For example, they believed in the axiom, 'A satisfied employee is a hardworking employee.' Subsequent research, as discussed later in this book, shows the satisfaction–performance linkage to be more complex than originally thought. A study into how Europeans feel about jobs revealed that, whereas a good salary remains the most important aspect, the weight attached to quality of work has increased. Job certainty, on the other hand, has decreased in importance.[38] Table 1–4 represents the evolution in the job-related values in Europe.

Despite its shortcomings, the human relations movement opened the door to more progressive thinking about human nature. Rather than continuing to view employees as passive economic beings, managers began to see them as active social beings and took steps to create more humane work environments. In the above-mentioned study, quality of work included the job's social aspects and job content.[39]

Characteristic	1990%	1981%
good wages	71%	66%
nice colleagues	65%	62%
interesting job	58%	52%
job security	55%	57%
job that corresponds to capabilities	54%	47%
job with which you can achieve something	49%	42%
job which encourages initiative	45%	40%
job in which you interact with other people	44%	40%
good working hours	42%	41%
responsible job	40%	36%
valued job	37%	31%
reasonable promotion prospects	35%	33%
much leisure time	28%	28%
not much stress	28%	28%

Table 1–4

Job-Related Values in Europe

SOURCE: J Kerkhofs, *The Europeans and their Values* (Leuven, Davidfonds, 1997), pp 51–52. This book was published in Dutch as *De Europeanen en hun waarden*.

The Total Quality Management Movement

A great deal has been written and said about quality in recent years. So much, in fact, that total quality management (TQM) has been dismissed by some as just another fad. Yet TQM programmes are alive and well in the workplace. The European Foundation for Quality Management (EFQM) aims at promoting quality as the fundamental process in total quality. The EFQM-model in Figure 1–2 is designed to assist companies on their way to excellence. The model tells us that customer satisfaction, employee satisfaction and an impact on society are achieved through leadership, which drives policy and strategy, people management, resources and processes on to excellence in business results. Each of the nine elements, therefore, is a criterion that can be used to assess the organization's progress along the path to excellence. The 'results' indicate what the company has achieved and is achieving; the 'enablers' indicate how those results are being achieved.[40]

Training magazine's 1995 survey of US companies with 100 or more employees found 58 per cent of them pursuing TQM initiatives (more than any other type of programme).[41] Disregarding the underlying principles of TQM because of apparent faddishness, would be as unwise as ignoring sound nutrition and exercise guidelines because of endless discussions about dieting. TQM principles have profound practical implications for managing people today.

What Is TQM?

Experts on the subject offer the following definition of total quality management.

TQM means that the organization's culture is defined by, and supports the constant attainment of, customer satisfaction through an integrated system of tools, techniques and training. This involves the continuous improvement of organizational processes, resulting in high-quality products and services.[42]

Total quality management
an organizational culture dedicated to training, continuous improvement and customer satisfaction

Figure 1–2

The EFQM Model

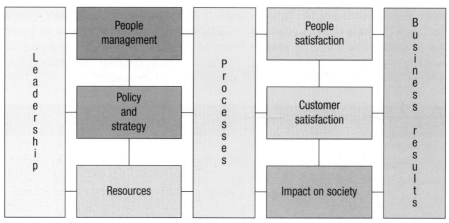

SOURCE: EFQM-homepage: http://www.efqm.org.

Quality consultant Richard J Schonberger sums up TQM as 'continuous, customer-centred, employee-driven improvement'.[43] TQM is necessarily employee-driven because product/service quality cannot be continuously improved without the active learning and participation of every employee. Thus, in successful quality improvement programmes, TQM principles are embedded in the organization's culture.[44]

The Deming Legacy

TQM is firmly established today thanks in large part to the pioneering work of W Edwards Deming.[45] Ironically, the mathematician credited with Japan's post-Second World War quality revolution rarely talked in terms of quality. He instead preferred to discuss 'good management' during the hard-hitting seminars he delivered right up until his death at 93, in 1993.[46] Although Deming's passion was the statistical measurement and reduction of variations in industrial processes, he had much to say about how employees should be treated. Regarding the human side of quality improvement, Deming called for:

▼ **formal training in statistical process control techniques and teamwork**

▼ **helpful leadership, rather than order-giving and punishment**

▼ **the elimination of fear, so employees will feel free to ask questions**

▼ **an emphasis on continuous process improvements rather than on numerical quotas**

▼ **teamwork**

▼ **an elimination of barriers to good workmanship.**[47]

One of Deming's most enduring lessons for managers is his 85–15 rule.[48] Specifically, when things go wrong, there is roughly an 85 per cent chance that the system (including management, machinery and rules) is at fault. Only about 15 per cent of the time is the individual employee at fault. Unfortunately, as Deming observed, the typical manager spends most of his or her time wrongly blaming and punishing individuals for system failures. Statistical analysis is required to uncover system failures.

Principles of TQM

Despite variations in the language and scope of TQM programmes, it is possible to identify four common TQM principles.

▼ **Do it right the first time to eliminate costly rework.**

▼ **Listen to, and learn from, customers and employees.**

▼ **Make continuous improvement an everyday matter.**

▼ **Build teamwork, trust and mutual respect.**[49]

Deming's influence is clearly evident in this list.[50] Once again, as with the human relations movement, we see people as the key factor in organizational success.

In summary, TQM advocates have made a valuable contribution to the field of OB by providing a *practical* context for managing people. When people are managed according to TQM principles, everyone is more likely to get the employment opportunities and high-quality goods and services they demand.[51]

The Contingency Approach

Scholars have wrestled for years with the problem of how best to apply the diverse and growing collection of management tools and techniques. One answer is the **contingency approach**. The contingency approach calls for the use of management techniques in a situationally appropriate manner, instead of trying to rely on 'one best way'. According to a pair of contingency theorists:

> [Contingency theories] developed and their acceptance grew largely because they responded to criticisms that the classical theories advocated 'one best way' of organizing and managing. Contingency theories, on the other hand, proposed that the appropriate organizational structure and management style were dependent upon a set of 'contingency' factors, usually the uncertainty and instability of the environment.[52]

The contingency approach encourages managers to view organizational behaviour within a situational context. According to this modern perspective, evolving situations, not hard-and-fast rules, determine when and where various management techniques are appropriate. For example, as will be discussed in Chapter 17, contingency researchers have determined that there is no single best style of leadership. Organizational behaviour specialists embrace the contingency approach because it helps them realistically interrelate individuals, groups and organizations. Moreover, the contingency approach sends a clear message to managers in today's global economy: 'Carefully read the situation and then be flexible enough to adapt.'[53] (see International OB on next page).

Now that we have outlined what OB is and reviewed its evolution, we need to address another aspect that is inextricably intertwined with any human behaviour in general, and organizational behaviour in particular, namely: the 'moral funding' or ethical basis of this behaviour. Therefore, in this next section, we present some topics on the importance of ethics in OB.

Contingency approach
using management tools and techniques in a situationally appropriate manner; avoiding the one-best-way mentality

International OB

www.coca-cola.com

Three Coca-Cola Executives Address the Issue of a Globally Appropriate Management Style

Lynn Oliver, from the United Kingdom, is responsible for the company's training and development in Western Europe. Kees van Langen, from the Netherlands, works with corporate and Asian managers. David Veale, based in the US, is manager of training and development for Coca-Cola Foods. Mr. Veale posed the questions mostly by email, occasionally commenting himself in the responses.

Veale: Do you see a homogenization of management practices down the road?

Is there one best set of practices that everyone will eventually use?

Oliver: No, I don't because so much is dictated by cultural, political and religious beliefs. Who owns the business also has an impact. The common trends I see are toward a more people-focused management style. Technology requires skilled, thoughtful people with higher education levels. Higher living standards and the increased mobility of these people give them more of a choice of where to work.

Veale: Okay, then. Who has the better or most appropriate management style: Japan, Europe, Great Britain or the US?

Oliver: I don't think any one style is best; there is value in different approaches depending on the market. If you subscribe to the school of thought that the most successful businesses of the future will be those with the ability to learn and respond to new and uncharted environments, there may be some evidence that points to the Japanese systems of developing learning ability in people.

van Langen: The burning question is how to foster industry and commerce in a way that promotes collaboration from the strength of expressive individualism. None of the countries has found the answer as yet, so a discussion of who is best begs the question.

Veale: I have to agree with both of you. I can't see a 'best' style. I don't really see much difference. Being fast, focused, and flexible in working with customers and producing and distributing great products efficiently are challenges for everyone. Lynn, you are correct in identifying learning as the key. Kees is right as well in that managing a balance between society, the individual and commerce is something that businesses face no matter what their country of origin. If anything, perhaps we in the US could learn to be more collaborative as opposed to adversarial in our approach to addressing social and individual needs. It might make the learning happen more quickly.

Excerpted from D Veale, L Oliver, and K van Langen, 'Three Coca-Cola Perspectives on International Management Styles', *Academy of Management Executive*, August 1995, pp 74–77.

ETHICS AND ORGANIZATIONAL BEHAVIOUR

The issue of ethics and ethical behaviour is receiving greater attention today. This interest is partly due to reported cases of questionable or potentially unethical behaviour and the associated costs. The Dutch economist Ann van Bergen, gives the following reasons for the growing consideration for ethical concerns.

Industry has an increasing impact on our society. Companies become larger and larger. Social control, which was self-evident in small companies, is disappearing. Values and norms are no longer anchored in religion or national culture. Many managerial decisions entail high environmental, social and societal risks. Consumers are critical. Employees are emancipated and stand on their rights. People want to feel at home with their employer and be proud of their work.[54]

Unethical behaviour is a relevant issue for all employees. It occurs from the bottom to the top of an organization. For example, a survey of 1,000 senior-level executives revealed that as many as one-third lied on their CVs.[55] Maybe this result should not be surprising because there are more benefits to lying, such as negotiating a higher salary and stock options, and beating the fierce competition for senior management positions.

As you will learn, there are a variety of individual and organizational characteristics that contribute to unethical behaviour. OB is an excellent vantage point for viewing better understanding and improving workplace ethics. If OB can provide insights about managing human work behaviour, then it can teach us something about avoiding *misbehaviour*.

Also important is having a corporate ethical policy which is good for business. As companies like the UK-based Body Shop can testify, people are attracted to working for companies with stated ethical principals. The Body Shop's campaigns against animal testing and the fashion industry's obsession with anorexic models have given the company a positive image, making it easier to attract staff, to sell their products and to gain world-wide familiarity.[56]

Ethics involves the study of moral issues and choices. It is concerned with right versus wrong, good versus bad, and the many shades of grey in supposedly black-

Ethics
study of moral issues and choices

and-white issues. Moral implications spring from virtually every decision, both inside and outside the workplace. Managers are challenged to have more imagination and the courage to do the right thing. Consider what occurred to these male and female human resource management professionals as they attempted to ethically perform their jobs.

'This was a lily-white organization when I joined it,' he says. 'The only diversity was in the lower-end jobs. I brought in two minority managers and, shortly thereafter, started receiving some pressure from the board along some stereotypical lines: 'We don't hire people like that. You're not from here. You don't understand.' They wanted me to fire them. I refused, and it ultimately cost me my job.'

Another HR professional lost her job . . . because, she says, she refused to sit back and do things she considered wrong. What kind of things? Allowing a pay inequality to persist between a male employee whose salary was more than double that of two female colleagues; testing new applicants for HIV and basing hiring decisions on the results; screening out female applicants in their 30s based on the boss's fear that they would miss a lot of work due to child-care issues.[57]

Are you amazed that these individuals were fired for making the decisions they did? What do you think you would have done in these situations? To enhance your understanding about the causes of ethical and unethical behaviour, we present a conceptual framework for making ethical decisions.

A Model of Ethical Behaviour

Ethical and unethical conduct is the product of a complex combination of influences (see Figure 1–3). At the centre of the model in Figure 1–3 is the individual decision-maker. He or she has a unique combination of personality characteristics, values, and moral principles, leaning towards or away from ethical behaviour. Personal experience of being rewarded or reinforced for certain behaviours and punished for others also shapes the individual's tendency to act ethically or unethically. Finally, gender plays an important role in explaining ethical behaviour. Men and women have significantly different moral orientations toward organizational behaviour.[58] This issue will be discussed again in more detail later.

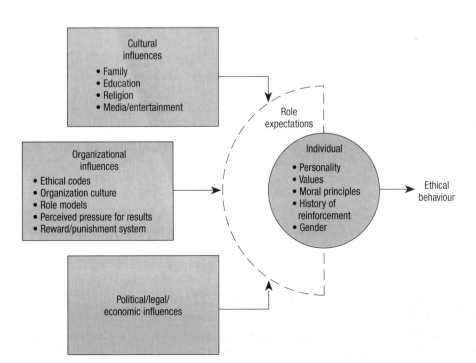

Figure 1–3

A Model of Ethical Behaviour in the Workplace

Figure 1–3 illustrates three major sources of influence on the individual's role expectations. People play many roles in life, including those of employee or manager. Their expectations of how those roles should be played are shaped by cultural, organizational and general environmental factors. The International OB describes the cultural differences, between China and Western societies, that influence role expectations and ethical behaviour. This example illustrates how a single behaviour such as hiring relatives can be viewed as both ethical and unethical by people with varying cultural backgrounds.

International OB

http://chineseculture.miningco.com

Religious and Cultural Differences between China and the West Influence Ethical Behavior

By Western standards, China is a secular society; most Chinese do not 'belong' to a faith in the sense of being a Christian, Jew, or Muslim. Little thought is given to supreme beings, other than venerated ancestors, or to such matters as holiness or life after death. There is a dearth of universal ethical principles or moral absolutes other than maintaining the security and well-being of the family and living up to one's Confucian obligations. These remain the primary normative prescriptions for correct behavior. Because maintaining social harmony and order is the highest ideal, minimization of conflict is essential and absolutes are seen as sources of conflict . . .

Confucianism makes no pretence to be a religion. Rather, it is a system of values that govern interpersonal behavior with an eye toward building a civil society. It does not speak to humanity's relationship with any supreme being . . . .

Chinese religion has evolved in ways that support and advance the maintenance of social harmony. In contrast, Judaism and Christianity (and Islam as well) prescribe behavioral and ethical standards intended to allow the faithful an opportunity to please and prove their worthiness to their Creator and Supreme Being. While banning behavior detrimental to maintaining a civil society (though perhaps one not quite as well-mannered as China's), these religions also prescribe how the Supreme Being should be worshipped and require followers to hold certain beliefs, make certain expressions of faith, and participate in various rituals.

Secular authorities in the West, particularly the Romans building on the precedent set by the ancient Greeks, extended ecclesiastical law into a natural law that dealt with practices, abstract principles, and beliefs beyond the spiritual domain. From natural law, greatly elaborated during the Enlightenment, were derived such notions as liberty, justice, equity, fairness, the binding contract, and ultimately, the social contract between people and their governments. These important social and political virtues, binding governments as well as citizens, acquired the force of principle as important to many—and perhaps more so to some—as the tenets of sacred scripture. Though Westerners might disagree on what is 'fair' in any set of circumstances, few would argue against the worth of 'fairness'.

The Chinese, like most human beings, will recognize the evil of a wanton crime, but they will have trouble responding to the invocation of abstractions such as 'fair trade'. What is fair to the Chinese is whatever works, whatever action or manner of speech is necessary to execute a transaction satisfactorily for both parties. Westerners are taught to place the principle of honesty above the nicety of harmony; for them, constructive criticism is the 'right' thing to do, even if painful. For the Chinese, this threat to harmony is antisocial. Likewise, most Westerners would be appalled that a manager could be so unprincipled as to show favoritism in hiring a relative. A Chinese would be equally appalled by any reluctance to do so.

SOURCE: Excerpt from J Scarborough, 'Comparing Chinese and Western Cultural Roots: Why "East Is East and . . .,"' *Business Horizons*, **November–December 1998, pp 19–20. Reprinted with permission of** *Business Horizons*. **Copyright © 1998 by the Board of Trustees at Indiana University Kelley School of Business.**

Focusing on one troublesome source of organizational influence, many studies have found a tendency among middle- and lower-level managers to act unethically in the face of perceived pressure for results. By fostering a pressure-cooker atmosphere for results, managers can unwittingly set the stage for unethical shortcuts by employees who seek to please and be loyal to the company. Downsizing, business process re-engineering and empowerment may all be necessary steps towards creating the lean, mean organization of the new millenium. But according to accountants at KPMG these management-inspired change programmes also heighten the risk of financial fraud.[59]

Thus, an organization's reward/punishment system can compound the problem of pressure for results. Worse yet, according to a study of 385 managers, those supervisors who were considered by their subordinates to be consistently ethical tended to have lower salaries than their less ethical peers.[60]

Because ethical or unethical behaviour is the result of person–situation interactions, we need to discuss both the decision maker's moral principles and the organization's ethical climate.[61]

General Moral Principles

Management consultant and writer Kent Hodgson has helpfully taken managers a step closer to ethical decisions by identifying seven general moral principles (see Table 1–5). Hodgson calls them 'the magnificent seven' to emphasize their timeless and worldwide relevance. Both the justice and care perspectives are clearly evident in the magnificent seven, which are more detailed and hence more practical. Importantly, according to Hodgson, there are no absolute ethical answers for decision makers. The goal for managers should be to rely on moral principles so their decisions are principled, appropriate, and defensible.[62] Managers require a supportive organizational climate that translates general moral principles into specific do's and don'ts and fosters ethical decisions.

1. *Dignity of human life: The lives of people are to be respected.* Human beings, by the fact of their existence, have value and dignity. We may not act in ways that directly intend to harm or kill an innocent person. Human beings have a right to live; we have an obligation to respect that right to life. Human life is to be preserved and treated as sacred.
2. *Autonomy: All persons are intrinsically valuable and have the right to self-determination.* We should act in ways that demonstrate each person's worth, dignity, and right to free choice. We have a right to act in ways that assert our own worth and legitimate needs. We should not use others as mere "things" or only as means to an end. Each person has an equal right to basic human liberty, compatible with a similar liberty for others.
3. *Honesty: The truth should be told to those who have a right to know it.* Honesty is also known as integrity, truth telling, and honor. One should speak and act so as to reflect the reality of the situation. Speaking and acting should mirror the way things really are. There are times when others have the right to hear the truth from us; there are times when they do not.
4. *Loyalty: Promises, contracts, and commitments should be honored.* Loyalty includes fidelity, promise keeping, keeping the public trust, good citizenship, excellence in quality of work, reliability, commitment, and honoring just laws, rules, and policies.
5. *Fairness: People should be treated justly.* One has the right to be treated fairly, impartially, and equitably. One has the obligation to treat others fairly and justly. All have the right to the necessities of life—especially those in deep need and the helpless. Justice includes equal, impartial, unbiased treatment. Fairness is the toleration of diversity and acceptance differences in people and their ideas.

Table 1–5

The Magnificent Seven: General Moral Principles for Managers

6. *Humaneness.* There are two parts: (1) *Our actions ought to accomplish good,* and (2) *we should avoid doing evil.* We should do good to others and to ourselves. We should have concern for the well-being of others; usually, we show this concern in the form of compassion, giving, kindness, serving, and caring.

7. *The common good:* Actions should accomplish the 'greatest good for the greatest number' of *people.* One should act and speak in ways that benefit the welfare of the largest number of people, while trying to protect the rights of individuals.

SOURCE: *A Rock and a Hard Place: How to Make Ethical Business Decisions When the Choices Are Tough,* © 1992 Kent Hodgson, pp 69–73. Published by AMACOM, a division of the American Management Association. Used with permission.

How to Improve the Organization's Ethical Climate

A team of management researchers recommended the following actions for improving ethics at work.[63]

▼ **Behave ethically yourself. Managers are potent role models whose habits and actual behaviour send clear signals about the importance of ethical conduct. Ethical behaviour is a top-to-bottom proposition.**

▼ **Screen potential employees. Surprisingly, employers are generally lax when it comes to checking references, credentials, transcripts, and other information on applicant résumés. More diligent action in this area can screen out those given to fraud and misrepresentation. Integrity testing is fairly valid but is no panacea.[64]**

▼ **Develop a meaningful code of ethics. Codes of ethics can have a positive impact if they satisfy the following four criteria.**

  ▼ **They are distributed to every employee.**

  ▼ **They are firmly supported by top management.**

  ▼ **They refer to specific practices and ethical dilemmas likely to be encountered by target employees (such as salespersons paying kickbacks, purchasing agents receiving pay-offs, laboratory scientists doctoring data, or accountants 'cooking the books').**

  ▼ **Their enforcement is balanced, with rewards for compliance and strict penalties for non-compliance.**

▼ **Provide ethics training. Employees can be trained to identify and deal with ethical issues during orientation and through seminar and video training sessions.**

▼ **Reinforce ethical behaviour. Behaviour that is reinforced tends to be repeated, whereas behaviour that is not reinforced tends to disappear. Too often, ethical conduct is punished while unethical behaviour is rewarded.**

▼ **Provide mechanisms to deal with ethics. Ethics needs to be an everyday affair, not a one-time announcement of a new ethical code that gets filed away and forgotten. The Body Shop and US-based Ben & Jerry's both use social or ethical audits to assess how well the company is living up to its ethical standards. Organizational changes are then made on the basis of the audit results.[65]**

LEARNING ABOUT OB FROM THEORY, RESEARCH AND PRACTICE

As a human being with years of interpersonal experience to draw upon, you already know a good deal about people at work. But more systematic and comprehensive understanding is possible and desirable. A working knowledge of current OB theory, research and practice can help you develop a tightly integrated understanding of why organizational contributors think and act as they do. In order for this to happen, however, prepare yourself for some intellectual surprises from theoretical models, research results or techniques that may run counter to your current thinking. For instance, one important reason why stress and satisfaction remain popular concepts is the belief that happy, satisfied workers are necessarily more productive workers. Hence, improving the 'feel-good factor' is believed to produce improvements in work performance. This argument has great superficial appeal. But on closer inspection it makes a great deal less sense. For example, feeling particularly happy may make it difficult to concentrate on a complex task, while a person's performance in a repetitive, machine-paced job may not depend on how they feel. In addition, there is little research evidence that supports such links.[66]

Therefore, research surprises can not only make learning fun, as mentioned earlier, they can also improve the quality of our lives both in and out of the workplace. Let us examine the dynamic relationship between, and the value of, OB theory, research and practice.

Figure 1–4 illustrates how theory, research and practice are related. Throughout the balance of this book, we focus primarily on the central portion, where all three areas overlap. Knowledge of why people behave as they do and what managers can do to improve performance is greatest within this area of maximum overlap. For each major topic, we build a foundation for understanding with generally accepted theory. This theoretical foundation is then tested and expanded by reviewing the latest relevant research findings. After interpreting the research, we discuss the nature and effectiveness of related practical applications.

Sometimes, depending on the subject matter, it is necessary to venture into the large areas outside the central portion of Figure 1–4. For example, an insightful theory supported by convincing research evidence might suggest an untried or different way of managing. In other instances, an innovative management technique might call for an explanatory theoretical model and exploratory research. Each area–theory, research and practice–supports and, in turn, is supported by the other two. Each area makes a valuable contribution to our understanding of, and ability to manage, organizational behaviour.

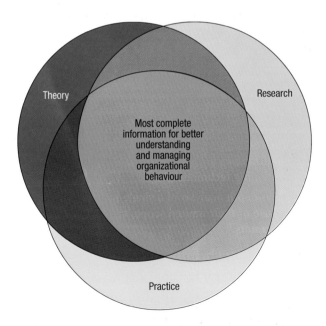

Figure 1–4

Learning about OB through a Combination of Theory, Research, and Practice

Learning from Theory

Theory
a story defining key terms, providing a conceptual framework and explaining why something occurs

A respected behavioural scientist, Kurt Lewin, once said there is nothing as practical as a good **theory**. According to one management researcher, a theory is a story that explains 'why'.[67] Another calls well-constructed theories 'disciplined imagination'.[68] A good OB theory, then, is a story that effectively explains why individuals and groups behave as they do. Moreover, a good theoretical model:

▼ **defines key terms**

▼ **constructs a conceptual framework that explains how important factors are interrelated (graphic models are often used to achieve this end)**

▼ **provides a departure point for research and practical application.**

Indeed, good theories are a fundamental contributor to improved understanding and management of organizational behaviour.[69]

Learning from Research

Because of unfamiliar jargon and complicated statistical procedures, many current and future managers are put off by behavioural research.[70] This is unfortunate because practical lessons can be learned as OB researchers steadily push back the frontier of knowledge. Let us examine the various sources and uses of OB research evidence.

Five Sources of OB Research Insights

To enhance the instructional value of our coverage of major topics, we systematically cite 'hard' evidence from five different categories. Worthwhile evidence was obtained by drawing upon the prioritized research methodologies, namely meta-analyses, field studies, laboratory studies, sample surveys and case studies.

Meta-analysis
pools the results of many studies through statistical procedure

Field study
examination of variables in real-life settings

Laboratory study
manipulation and measurement of variables in contrived situations

Sample survey
questionnaire responses from a sample of people

Case study
in-depth study of a single person, group or organization

▼ **A meta-analysis is a statistical pooling technique that permits behavioural scientists to draw general conclusions about certain variables from many different studies.[71] It typically encompasses a vast number of subjects, often reaching the thousands. Meta-analyses are instructive because they focus on general patterns of research evidence, not fragmented bits and pieces or isolated studies.[72]**

▼ **In OB, a field study probes individual or group processes in an organizational setting. Because field studies involve real-life situations, their results often have immediate and practical relevance for managers.**

▼ **In a laboratory study, variables are manipulated and measured in contrived situations. College students are commonly used as subjects. The highly controlled nature of laboratory studies enhances research precision. But generalizing the results to organizational management requires caution.[73]**

▼ **In a sample survey, samples of people from specified populations respond to questionnaires. The researchers then draw conclusions about the relevant population. Generalizability of the results depends on the quality of the sampling and questioning techniques.**

▼ **A case study is an in-depth analysis of a single individual, group or organization. Because of their limited scope, case studies yield realistic but not very generalizable results.[74]**

Three Uses of OB Research Findings

Organizational scholars point out that managers can put relevant research findings to use in three different ways.[75]

▼ *Instrumental use.* **This involves directly applying research findings to practical problems. For example, a manager experiencing high stress tries a relaxation technique after reading a research report about its effectiveness.**

▼ *Conceptual use.* Research is put to conceptual use when managers derive general enlightenment from its findings. The effect here is less specific and more indirect than with instrumental use. For example, after reading a meta-analysis showing a negative correlation between absenteeism and age,[76] a manager might develop a more positive attitude towards hiring older people.

▼ *Symbolic use.* Symbolic use occurs when research results are relied upon to verify or legitimize stances that are already held. Negative forms of symbolic use involve self-serving bias, prejudice, selective perception, and distortion. For example, tobacco industry spokespersons routinely deny any link between smoking and lung cancer because researchers are largely, but not 100 per cent, in agreement about the negative effects of smoking. A positive example would be managers maintaining their confidence in setting performance goals after reading a research report about the favorable impact of goal setting on job performance.

By systematically reviewing and interpreting research relevant to key topics, this book provides instructive insights about OB.

Learning from Practice

Relative to learning more about how to effectively manage people at work, one might be tempted to ask, 'Why bother with theory and research; let's get right down to *how to do it*.' Our answer lies in the contingency approach, discussed earlier. The effectiveness of specific theoretical models or management techniques is contingent on the situations in which they are applied.

For example, one cross-cultural study of a large multinational corporation's employees working in 50 countries, led the Dutch researcher Geert Hofstede to conclude that most made-in-America management theories and techniques are inappropriate in the context of other cultures.[77] Many otherwise well-intentioned, performance-improvement programmes based on American cultural values have failed in other cultures because of naive assumptions about transferability.

In France, the most common medical complaint is *crise de foie* (liver crisis) while in Germany it is *herzinsufficienz* (heart insufficiency). Prescriptions to soothe the digestive system are higher in France, while in Germany digitalis is prescribed six times more frequently to stimulate the heart. These differences have been attributed to the French cultural obsession with food, and the German cultural quest for romanticism. In other words, different countries have very different approaches to medicine. If the practice of medicine is shaped by its cultural origins, why should the practice of management be any different?[78] (International cultures are discussed in greater detail in Chapter 4.) Fortunately, systematic research is available that tests our 'common sense' assumptions about what works where. Management 'cookbooks' that provide only how-to-do-it advice with no underlying theoretical models or supporting research virtually guarantee misapplication. As mentioned earlier, the three elements of theory, research, and practice mutually reinforce one another.

The theory → research → practice sequence discussed in this section will help you to better understand each of the major topics addressed later in the book. Attention now turns to a topical model that sets the stage for what lies ahead.

A TOPICAL MODEL FOR UNDERSTANDING AND MANAGING OB

Figure 1–5 is a map for our journey through this book, indicating the topics through which we pass. Our destination is organizational effectiveness via continuous improvement. Four different criteria for determining whether or not an organization is effective are discussed in Chapter 18. The study of OB can be a wandering and pointless trip if we overlook the need to translate OB lessons into effective and efficient organized endeavour.

At the far left of our 'topical road map' are managers, those who are responsible for accomplishing organizational results with and through others. The three circles at the centre of the map correspond to Parts Two, Three, and Four of this book. Logically, the flow of topical coverage in this book (following the introductory Part One) goes from individuals, to group processes, to organizational processes and problems, to organizations. Around the core of our topical road map in Figure 1–5, is the organization. Hence, we end our journey with organization-related material in Part Five. Organizational structure and design are covered there, in Chapter 18, to establish and develop the organizational context of organizational behaviour. Completing our organizational context is a discussion of organizational change in Chapter 19. Chapters 3 and 4 provide a cultural context for OB.

The broken line represents a permeable boundary between the organization and its environment. Energy and influence flow both ways across this permeable boundary. Truly, no organization is an island in today's highly interactive and interdependent world. Relative to the *external* environment, international cultures are explored in Chapter 4. Organization–environment contingencies are examined in Chapter 19.

Chapter 2 examines the OB implications of significant demographic and social trends, and Chapter 3 explores important ethical considerations. These discussions provide a realistic context for studying and managing people at work.

Bon voyage! Enjoy your trip through the challenging, interesting, and often surprising world of OB.

Figure 1–5

A Topical Model for What Lies Ahead

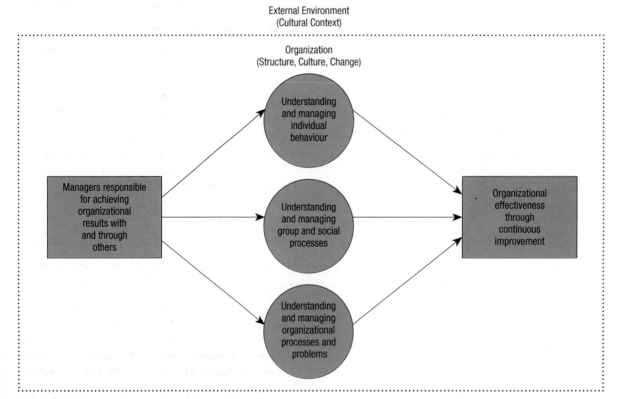

Summary of Key Concepts

1 Identify the P's in the 4-P cycle of continuous improvement and define the term management.
The 4 Ps are people, products, processes and productivity. Management is the process of working with and through others to achieve organizational objectives in an efficient and ethical manner.

2 Identify at least 5 of the 11 managerial skills in Wilson's profile of effective managers.
According to the Wilson skills profile, an effective manager: clarifies goals and objectives; encourages participation; plans and organizes; has technical and administrative expertise; facilitates work through team building and coaching; provides feedback; keeps things moving; controls details; applies reasonable pressure for goals accomplishment; empowers and delegates; and recognizes and rewards good performance.

3 Describe the new psychological contract.
It is a transactional contract in which employees are expected to be both flexible self-starters and team players with multiple skills. The new contract pays employees for results, not for time spent on the job, and makes employees responsible for their own careers. The company's side of the bargain, in well-managed and ethical organizations, involves giving each employee the opportunity to 'grow' and acquire marketable skills.

4 Characterize 21st-century managers.
They will be team players who will get things done cooperatively by relying on: joint decision-making; their knowledge instead of formal authority; and their multicultural skills. They will engage in life-long learning and be compensated on the basis of their skills and results. They will facilitate rather than resist change; share rather than hoard power and key information; and be multidirectional communicators. Ethics will be a forethought instead of an afterthought. They will be generalists with multiple specialties.

5 Define the term organizational behaviour and explain why OB is a horizontal discipline.
Organizational behaviour (OB) is an interdisciplinary field dedicated to better understanding and management of people at work. It is both research and application oriented. Except for teaching and research positions, one does not normally get a job in OB. Rather, because OB is a horizontal discipline, its concepts and lessons are applicable to virtually every job category, business function and professional specialty.

6 Contrast McGregor's Theory X and Theory Y assumptions about employees.
Theory X employees, according to traditional thinking, dislike work, require close supervision and are primarily interested in security. According to the modern Theory Y, employees are capable of self-direction, seeking responsibility, and of being creative.

7 Explain the managerial significance of Deming's 85–15 rule.
Deming claimed that about 85 per cent of organizational failures are due to system breakdowns involving factors such as management, machinery, or work rules. He believed the workers themselves are responsible for failures for only about 15 per cent of the time. Consequently, Deming criticized the standard practice of blaming and punishing individuals for what are typically system failures beyond their immediate control.

8 Identify the four principles of total quality management (TQM). The four principles are:
a Do it right the first time to eliminate costly rework.
b Listen to, and learn from, customers and employees.
c Make continuous improvement an everyday matter.
d Build teamwork, trust and mutual respect.

9 Specify at least four actions that managers can take to improve an organization's ethical climate.
They can bring about an improvement by: (a) behaving ethically themselves, (b) screening potential employees, (c) developing a code of ethics, (d) providing ethics training, (e) reinforcing and rewarding ethical behaviour, and (f) creating positions and structural mechanisms to deal with ethical issues.

10 Describe the sources of research evidence on organizational behaviour.
Five sources of OB research evidence are: meta-analyses (statistically pooled evidence from several studies); field studies (evidence from real-life situations); laboratory studies (evidence from contrived situations); sample surveys (questionnaire data); and case studies (observation of a single person, group, or organization).

Discussion Questions

1 Why view the typical employee as a human resource?

2 In your opinion, what are the three or four most important strategic results in Figure 1–1? Why?

3 How would you respond to a fellow student who says, 'I have a hard time getting along with other people, but I think I could be a good manager'?

4 Based on either personal experience as a manager or on your observation of managers at work, do you consider the 11 skills in Table 1–1 to be a realistic portrayal of what managers do?

5 How willing and able are you to work under the new psychological contract?

6 What is your personal experience of Theory X and Theory Y managers (see Table 1–3)? Which did you prefer? Why?

7 How would you respond to a new manager who made this statement? 'TQM is about statistical process control, not about people.'

8 Do you use the contingency approach in your daily affairs? Explain the circumstances.

9 What 'practical' theories have you formulated to achieve the things you want in life (such as graduating, keeping fit, getting a good job, meeting that special someone)? From a manager's standpoint, which use of research is better: instrumental or conceptual? Explain your rationale.

Internet Exercise

http://home.sprintmail.com/~debflanagan/
www.hp.com

Part 1 (Note: This part is for those with little or no Internet experience; those who need to polish their Internet research skills; and experienced Internet users who want to explore a lot of free business information and company profiles.) A free and useful business-oriented tutorial can be found at **http://home.sprintmail.com/~debflanagan/**. From the homepage of this site—Researching Companies Online—select 'locate high-level company information' and learn how you can find anything you want to know about companies around the world. Also, take a look at 'locate company home pages' and 'research company financial information'.

Questions

1 What useful online research tips did you discover?

2 What useful business-related information sources did you discover?

3 What useful information did you acquire?

Note: If you know of a better free online research tutorial than this one, please tell your instructor and fellow students.

Part 2 The purpose of this exercise is to focus on one well-known company with a good general reputation (Hewlett-Packard) and look for evidence of the seven people-centred practices discussed at the beginning of this chapter (go back and review them to refresh your memory). On the Internet, go to Hewlett-Packard's home page (www.hp.com), and select *Company Information* from the main menu. Next, under *About HP*, select *History and Facts* and then click *corporate objectives* on the right side of your screen. Read the Corporate Objectives statement, focusing particularly on the sections *Our People, Citizenship* and *Management* as you scroll down. Also try to take a look at *diversity@hp*, which you'll find under the heading of 'history and facts'.

Questions

1 On a scale of 1 (low) to 10 (high), how people-centred is HP?

2 What specific evidence do you find to conclude this?

3 Do HP's culture and values, as expressed in the corporate objectives, give it a strategic competitive advantage? Explain.

4 Would you like to work for HP? Why or why not?

Personal awareness and growth exercise

How Strong Is Your Motivation to Manage?

Objectives

1 To introduce a psychological determinant of managerial success.

2 To assess your readiness to manage.

3 To discuss the implications of motivation to manage, from the standpoint of global competitiveness.

Introduction

By identifying personal traits which are positively correlated with both rapid movement up the career ladder and managerial effectiveness, John B. Miner developed a psychometric test for measuring what he calls 'motivation to manage'. The questionnaire assesses the strength of seven factors relating to the temperament (or psychological make-up) needed to manage others. One word of caution. The following instrument is a shortened and modified version of Miner's original. Our version is for instructional and discussion purposes only. Although we believe it can indicate the *general* strength of your motivation to manage, it is *not* a precise measuring tool.

Instructions

Assess the strength of each of the seven dimensions of *your own* motivation to manage by circling the appropriate numbers on the 1 to 7 scales. Then add the seven circled numbers to get your total 'motivation to manage' score.

Factor	Description	Scale
1 Authority figures	A desire to meet managerial role requirements in terms of positive relationships with superiors.	Weak 1–2–3–4–5–6–7 Strong
2 Competitive games	A desire to engage in competition with peers involving games or sports and thus meet managerial role requirements in this regard.	Weak 1–2–3–4–5–6–7 Strong
3 Competitive situations	A desire to engage in competition with peers involving occupational or work-related activities and thus meet managerial role requirements in this regard.	Weak 1–2–3–4–5–6–7 Strong

4 Assertive role	A desire to behave in an active and assertive manner involving activities that in this society are often viewed as predominantly masculine and thus to meet managerial role requirements.	Weak 1–2–3–4–5–6–7 Strong
5 Imposing wishes	A desire to tell others what to do and to utilize sanctions in influencing others, thus indicating a capacity to fulfill managerial role requirements in relationships with subordinates.	Weak 1–2–3–4–5–6–7 Strong
6 Standing out from group	A desire to assume a distinctive position of a unique and highly visible nature in a manner that is role-congruent for managerial jobs.	Weak 1–2–3–4–5–6–7 Strong
7 Routine administrative functions	A desire to meet managerial role requirements regarding activities often associated with managerial work, that are of a day-to-day administrative nature.	Weak 1–2–3–4–5–6–7 Strong
		Total = _____

Scoring and Interpretation

Arbitrary norms for comparison purposes are as follows: Total score of 7–21 = Relatively low motivation to manage; 22–34 = Moderate; 35–49 = Relatively high. How do you measure up? Remember, though, high motivation to manage is only part of the formula for managerial success. The right combination of ability and opportunity is also necessary.

Years of motivation-to-manage research by Miner and others has serious implications for America's future global competitiveness. Generally, in recent years, college students in the United States have not scored highly on motivation to manage.[79] Indeed, compared with samples of US college students, samples of students from Japan, China, Mexico, Korea, and Taiwan consistently scored higher on motivation to manage.[80] Miner believes the United States may consequently lag in developing sufficient managerial talent for a tough global marketplace.[81]

In a study by other researchers, MBA students with higher motivation-to-manage scores tended to earn more money after graduation. But students with a higher motivation to manage did not earn better grades or complete their degree program any sooner than those with a lower motivation to manage.[82]

Questions for discussion

1 Do you believe our adaptation of Miner's motivation to manage instrument accurately assessed your potential as a manager? Explain.

2 Which of the seven dimensions do you think is probably the best predictor of managerial success? Which the least predictive? Why?

3 Miner puts heavy emphasis on competitiveness by anchoring two of the seven dimensions of 'motivation to manage' to the desire to compete. Some observers believe the traditional (win–lose) competitive attitude is being pushed aside in favor of a less competitive (win–win) attitude today, thus making Miner's instrument out of date. What is your position on this competitiveness debate? Explain.

4 Do you believe Miner is correct in saying that low motivation to manage hurts the United States's global competitiveness? Explain.

Group Exercise
Timeless Advice

Objectives

1 To get to know some of your fellow students.

2 To put the management of people into a lively and interesting historical context.

3 To begin to develop your teamwork skills.

Introduction

Your creative energy, willingness to see familiar things in unfamiliar ways, and ability to have fun while learning are keys to the success of this warm-up exercise. A 20-minute, small-group session will be followed by brief oral presentations and a general class discussion. Total time required is approximately 40 to 45 minutes.

Instructions

Your instructor will divide your class randomly into groups of four to six people each. Acting as a team, with everyone offering ideas and one person serving as official recorder, each group will be responsible for writing a one-page memo to your current class. Subject matter of your group's memo will be 'My advice for managing people today is . . .' The fun part of this exercise (and its creative element) involves writing the memo from the viewpoint of the person assigned to your group by your instructor.

Among the memo viewpoints your instructor may assign are the following:

- Anita Roddick (The Body Shop)
- an ancient Egyptian slave master (building the great pyramids)
- Mary Parker Follett
- Douglas McGregor
- a Theory X supervisor of a construction crew (see McGregor's Theories X and Y in Table 1–3)
- W. Edwards Deming
- a TQM co-ordinator at IKEA (Finland-based international furniture business)
- a contingency management theorist
- a Japanese auto company executive
- the chief executive officer of ABB (Asean Brown Bovery, one of the world's leading enterprises in the field of electrical engineering) in the year 2030
- Commander of the *Starship Enterprise II* in the year 3001
- others, as indicated by your instructor.

Use your imagination, make sure everyone participates, and try to be true to any historical facts you've encountered. Attempt to be as specific and realistic as possible. Remember, the idea is to provide advice about managing people from another point in time (or from a particular point of view at the present time).

Make sure you manage your 20-minute time limit carefully. A recommended approach is to spend 2 to 3 minutes putting the exercise into proper perspective. Next, take about 10 to 12 minutes brainstorming ideas for your memo, with your recorder jotting down key ideas and phrases. Have your recorder use the remaining time to write your group's one-page memo, with constructive comments and help from the others. Pick a spokesperson to read your group's memo to the class.

Questions for discussion

1 What valuable lessons about managing people have you heard?

2 What have you learned about how NOT to manage people?

3 From the distant past to today, what significant shifts in the management of people seem to have taken place?

4 Where does the management of people appear to be headed?

5 All things considered, what mistakes are today's managers typically making when managing people?

6 How well did your group function as a 'team'?

Chapter Two

Managing Diversity: Releasing Every Employee's Potential Learning Objectives

Learning Objectives

When you finish studying the material in this chapter, you should be able to:

- Define diversity.
- Discuss the four layers of diversity.
- Explain the differences between affirmative action, valuing diversity and managing diversity
- Review the five reasons why managing diversity gives a competitive advantage.
- Identify the barriers and challenges to managing diversity.
- Discuss the organizational practices used to effectively manage diversity as identified by R. Roosevelt Thomas, Jr, and Ann Morrison.

BAOBAB Catering wins an award for promoting equal opportunities

In early 2000, the work of Belgium's BAOBAB Catering in promoting equal opportunities for refugees in the Belgian labour market, was recognised by the presentation of the Award for Equality of Opportunities by the Ministry for Equal Opportunities Policy. Previous awards received by BAOBAB include a prize, from the Baudouin Foundation, for entrepreneurs who create employment opportunities for underprivileged people. This story of success began in January ▶

1998 when Peter De Roo, a co-ordinator of a Red Cross reception centre in Menen, Belgium, noticed that asylum seekers receiving refugee status found it very difficult to enter the labour market. He decided to create a small catering business in order to give jobs to refugees and migrants and, in so doing, to help them to integrate into Belgian society.

At the start of the project he hired five people including three refugees. Now there are nine employees from all over the world (Cambodia, Iran, India, Congo, Senegal, Morocco, the Philippines, Laos and Burundi) and two Flemish staff. Most of the foreigners working in BAOBAB are recognised refugees. The catering business supplies private companies, public institutions and schools, and also caters for special receptions. The motto of the enterprise is 'The World on Your Table' and, in keeping with this, offers a range of foods from all over the world which is served at receptions by employees dressed in their traditional clothes.

For Peter De Roo, his employees' know-how is a key asset to his business. He believes that, as an outsider, you cannot really assess foreigners' qualifications, know their motivation or potential unless you work with them. Peter De Roo thinks that every business should *dare* to hire at least one recognised refugee, so as to benefit from their enthusiasm and motivation to do a job well: this is certainly proving a key strength for BAOBAB.

The recruiting procedure for BAOBAB is the same for both Flemish applicants and foreigners: comprising both interviews and a practical test. In addition, foreigners are required to be able to speak Dutch so that they can more readily adapt to each new situation; and to be open to other cultures so that they can work well in a multi-cultural environment. In the Ministry's decision to give the award for equal opportunity to BAOBAB, it recognised that the concept of equality as demonstrated by the enterprise went beyond equality between the sexes to that between different races and cultures.[1]

For discussion

In your opinion, how can organizations benefit, in the way that BAOBAB has done, from an ethnically diverse workforce?

Managers are increasingly being asked to boost productivity, quality and customer satisfaction whilst also reducing costs. These goals can only be met, however, through the co-operation and effort of all employees. By creating positive work environments, where people feel valued and appreciated, organizations are more likely to foster the employee commitment and performance necessary for organizational success.

Consider the following examples, which are in contrast with this, taken from three different work environments.

Ade Arogundad, a finance manager with Springboard Southwark Trust has received racist literature telling him he's not wanted at the organization and he has been the subject of anonymous petitions sent to managers demanding that all black employees be removed from the workforce. [2]

A report revealed appalling behaviour in the Dutch police force: 79 per cent of female employees had been confronted with pin-ups, 55 per cent with 'dirty gestures', 38 per cent with blue films and 44 per cent had had the feeling of male colleagues 'undressing them with their eyes'. [3]

When Sarah Locker, a woman police officer, received pornographic magazines on her desk and literature making derogatory reference to her Turkish background, she decided to take her complaints to court. She won her case—but met even more hostility on her return to work. The episode finally ended in a serious suicide attempt. [4]

Sandra Valentine, a woman pilot claimed that she was told by a male colleague, 'Women should not be let loose with anything more technical than a knife and fork'. Once a senior pilot had announced to passengers, 'The first officer is Ms Valentine and yes, ladies and gentlemen, she is a woman. We have them in the front as well as the back these days, so don't blame me.' [5]

As you will learn in this chapter, managing diversity entails much more than creating policies and procedures.

Managing diversity is a sensitive, potentially volatile, and sometimes uncomfortable issue. In Europe, as well as in the USA, creating a diverse workforce is increasingly considered a necessity. Jiten Patel, race equality manager with HSBC, a major UK bank, declares 'For us, the ideal is true diversity, which means that we value every individual for who and what they are, and we provide them with the opportunities to meet their full potential within the organization.' [6]

Nevertheless, a considerable number of organizations do not realize its importance. A Dutch study revealed that 37 out of 94 companies, have no diversity policy at all. Two main reasons are cited: either they do not think that it is necessary or that, when recruiting new entrants, they only consider people's individual qualities regardless of gender, origin or age.[7] Yet managers are required to deal with it in the name of organizational survival. The purpose of this chapter, therefore, is to help you get a better understanding of this important context for organizational behaviour. We begin by defining diversity. Then we build the business case for diversity and next, discuss the barriers and challenges associated with managing diversity. The chapter concludes by describing the organizational practices used to manage diversity effectively.

DEFINING DIVERSITY

Diversity
the host of individual differences that makes people different from, and similar to, each other

Diversity represents the multitude of individual differences and similarities that exist between people. This definition underscores three important issues about managing diversity.[8] Firstly, there are many different dimensions or components of diversity. This implies that diversity pertains to everybody. It is not an issue of age, race or gender. It is not an issue of whether one is heterosexual, gay or lesbian; or, indeed, Catholic, Jewish, Protestant or Muslim. Diversity also does not pit 'white males' against all other groups of people. Diversity pertains to the host of individual differences that makes all of us unique and different from others. Secondly, diversity is not synonymous with 'differences'. Rather, it encompasses both differences and similarities. This means that managing diversity entails dealing with both simultaneously. Finally, diversity comprises a collective mixture of differences and similarities, not just individual pieces within it. Dealing with diversity requires managers to integrate the collective mixture of differences and similarities that exist within an organization.

This section begins our journey into managing diversity by first reviewing the key dimensions of diversity. Because many people associate diversity with 'affirmative action', this section compares affirmative action, valuing diversity and managing diversity. They are not the same.

Layers of Diversity

Like pebbles on the beach, people come in a variety of shapes, sizes and colours. This variety represents the essence of diversity. Lee Gardenswartz and Anita Rowe, both diversity experts, identified four layers of diversity to help distinguish the important ways in which people differ (see Figure 2–1). Taken together, these layers define your personal identity and influence how you see the world.[9]

Figure 2–1 shows that personality is at the centre of the diversity wheel. Personality is at the centre because it represents the stable set of characteristics responsible for a person's identity. The dimensions of personality are discussed later in Chapter 5. The OB Exercise that follows, is a brief self-assessment of your personality profile. It can help you more fully understand how similarities and differences between your personality and those of co-workers, influence your interactions. Take a short break from your reading to complete the OB exercise. Then assess your reaction to the exercise. Are you surprised to see how similarities and differences in personality influence your relationship with someone else? How might you improve your working relationship with this particular person based on results of this exercise?

Figure 2–1

The Four Layers of Diversity

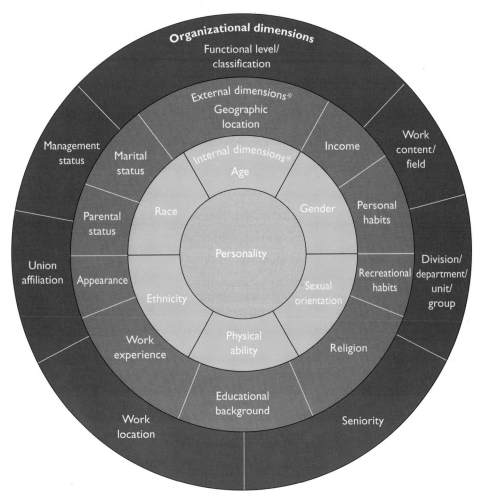

*Internal Dimensions and External Dimensions are adapted from Loden and Rosener, *Workforce America!* (Homewood, IL: Business One Irwin, 1991).

SOURCE: L Gardenswartz and A Rowe, *Diverse Teams at Work: Capitalizing on the Power of Diversity* (New York: McGraw-Hill, 1994), p 33.
© 1994. Reproduced with permission of The McGraw-Hill Companies.

OB Exercise

Drawing Your Personality Profile

Instructions

First, evaluate the extent to which each of the following personality characteristics fits your image of yourself by marking an 'x' along each continuum. There are no right or wrong evaluations. Then connect your 'x's vertically to form your personality profile. Once completed, answer the questions that follow.

Patient	_____	Impatient
Introvert	_____	Extrovert
Doer	_____	Thinker
Assertive	_____	Non-assertive
Competitive	_____	Collaborative
Leader	_____	Follower
Listener	_____	Talker
Fast-paced	_____	Slow-paced
Serious	_____	Humorous
Spontaneous	_____	Scheduled
Flexible	_____	Rigid
Relaxed	_____	Intense
Optimist	_____	Pessimist
Realist	_____	Idealist
Rational	_____	Emotional

1 Which characteristics are likely to make you a good team player when working with others?

2 Which characteristics may cause problems when working with others?

3 Which characteristics are most important to your identity?

We now want you to take this assessment one step further by marking each continuum to form the profile of someone you have a difficult time getting along with. This can be someone that you currently or previously worked with, another student, a friend or family member. Vertically connect the 'x's for this individual's profile and consider the following questions.

1 What personality characteristics of others are hardest for you to deal with?

2 Where are the biggest gaps between the two profiles?

3 What similarities or differences seem to be at the heart of your difficulty in getting along with this individual?

SOURCE: This exercise was adapted from one contained in L Gardenswartz and A Rowe, *Diverse Teams at Work: Capitalizing on the Power of Diversity* (New York: McGraw-Hill, 1994), pp 34–35.

The next layer of diversity consists of a set of internal dimensions that are referred to as 'the primary dimensions of diversity'.[10] These dimensions, for the most part, are not within our control, but strongly influence our attitudes, expectations and assumptions about others, which, in turn, influence our behaviour. Consider the following encounter experienced by a 'black woman' in middle management, while vacationing at a resort.

> While she was sitting by the pool, 'a large 50-ish white male approached me and demanded that I get him extra towels. I said, "Excuse me?" He then said, "Oh, you don't work here", with no shred of embarrassment or apology in his voice.'[11]

Stereotypes, regarding one or more of the primary dimensions of diversity, most likely influenced this man's behaviour towards the woman.

Figure 2–1 reveals that the next layer of diversity is composed of external influences, which are referred to as 'secondary dimensions of diversity'. They represent individual differences over which we have a greater influence or control. Examples include where we grew up and where we live today, our religious affiliation, whether we are married and have children, and our work experiences. These dimensions also exert a significant influence on our perceptions, behaviour and attitudes.

Consider religion as an illustration. A Dutch cleaning service in Amsterdam employing more than 90 per cent of its staff members from ethnic minorities, persisted in putting wine and pork in its Christmas box, states Rahma El Mouden, the companies' present director.[12] Similarly, a lack of sensitivity regarding the Muslim faith led US-based Nike to recall a shoe line in 1997. The shoe was imprinted with a logo that looked like the Arabic script for Allah. Nike paid refunds for returned shoes, issued a public apology, sent employees to sensitivity training, and donated money to a Muslim elementary school in the USA.[13]

A lack of awareness about the external layer of diversity can they cause bad feelings among both employees and customers. The final layer of diversity includes organizational dimensions such as seniority, job title and function, and work location.

Affirmative Action and Valuing Diversity

Valuing diversity and managing diversity require organizations to adopt a new way of thinking about differences between people. Rather than pitting one group against another, both valuing diversity and managing diversity strive to recognize the unique contribution each and every employee can make. This philosophy is different by far from that of affirmative action. This section highlights the differences among affirmative action, valuing diversity, and managing diversity. Table 2–1 compares these three approaches to managing employee differences.

Table 2–1

Comparison of Affirmative Action, Valuing Diversity and Managing Diversity

Affirmative Action	Valuing Diversity	Managing Diversity
Quantitative. Emphasizes achieving equality of opportunity in the work environment through the changing of organizational demographics. Monitored by statistical reports and analysis.	*Qualitative.* Emphasizes the appreciation of differences and creating an environment in which everyone feels valued and accepted. Monitored by organizational surveys focused on attitudes and perceptions.	*Behavioural.* Emphasizes the building of specific skills and creating policies which get the best from every employee. Monitored by progress toward achieving goals and objectives.
Legally driven. Written plans and statistical goals for specific groups are utilized. Reports are mandated by EEO laws and consent decrees.	*Ethically driven.* Moral and ethical imperatives drive this culture change.	*Strategically driven.* Behaviours and policies are seen as contributing to organizational goals and objectives such as profit and productivity and are tied to reward and results.
Remedial. Specific target groups benefit as past wrongs are remedied. Previously excluded groups have an advantage.	*Idealistic.* Everyone benefits. Everyone feels valued and accepted in an inclusive environment.	*Pragmatic.* The organization benefits; morale, profit, and productivity increase.
Assimilation model. Assumes that groups brought into system will adapt to existing organizational norms.	*Diversity model.* Assumes that groups will retain their own characteristics and shape the organization as well as be shaped by it, creating a common set of values.	*Synergy model.* Assumes that diverse groups will create new ways of working together effectively in a pluralistic environment.
Opens doors in the organization. Affects hiring and promotion decisions.	*Opens attitudes, minds, and the culture.* Affects attitudes of employees.	*Opens the system.* Affects managerial practices and policies.

Table 2–1 continued

Affirmative Action	Valuing Diversity	Managing Diversity
Resistance due to perceived limits to autonomy in decision making and perceived fears of reverse discrimination.	*Resistance due to* fear of change, discomfort with differences, and desire for return to "good old days."	*Resistance due to* denial of demographic realities, the need for alternative approaches, and/or benefits associated with change; and the difficulty in learning new skills, altering existing systems, and/or finding time to work toward synergistic solutions.

SOURCE: L Gardenswartz and A Rowe, *Managing Diversity: A Complete Desk Reference and Planning Guide* (Homewood, IL: Business One Irwin, 1993), p 405. Reprinted with permission of The McGraw-Hill Companies.

Affirmative Action

Affirmative action
focuses on achieving equality of opportunity in an organization

As shown in Table 2–1, **affirmative action** focuses on achieving equality of opportunity in an organization and is often mandated by national or supranational laws. There are over 20 countries worldwide that have specific laws mandating affirmative action for employment on the basis of race, sex or disability, and many others that permit it.[14] On 1 May 1999, the European Commission (EU) launched a package of measures to combat discrimination at work, which are the first to emerge from the EC's social and employment affairs directorate under the new leadership of Anna Diamantopoulou. The first directive bans workplace discrimination on the grounds of race, ethnic origin, religion, beliefs, disability, age or sexual orientation. Race and ethnic discrimination in employment, health, education and other areas form the focus of the second directive. The package of proposals contained in the directives is more comprehensive than existing laws even in member states such as the UK, which leads Europe on discrimination legislation.[15] Affirmative action on equalising opportunities is an artificial intervention aimed at giving management a chance to correct an imbalance, an injustice, a mistake or outright discrimination. In some countries the concept is well accepted in the fight against sex discrimination, but women are not the only beneficiaries: Norway's Ordinance N° 622 on the special treatment of men, adopted on 17 July 1998, provides for action to favour men in occupations where they are under-represented, such as education and child care, through training and job opportunities, together with procedural rules for enforcement. The Fair Employment Act 1989 (Northern Ireland) promotes equal opportunities for religious groups. This is the most radical equal opportunities legislation in the UK. It follows North American, rather than British practice in requiring affirmative action.[16] It is also important to note that under no circumstances does affirmative action require companies to hire unqualified people.

Although affirmative action creates tremendous opportunities for women and minorities, it does not foster the type of thinking that is needed to effectively manage diversity.[17] For example, affirmative action is resisted more by white males than women and minorities because it is perceived as involving preferential hiring and treatment based on group membership. Affirmative action plans are more successful when employees view them as fair and equitable.[18]

Affirmative action programmes were also found to *negatively* affect the women and minorities expected to benefit from them. Research demonstrated that women and minorities, supposedly hired on the basis of affirmative action, felt negatively stigmatized as unqualified or incompetent. They also experienced lower job satisfaction and more stress than employees supposedly selected on the basis of merit.[19] A recent study, however, showed that these negative consequences were reduced for women when a merit criterion was included in hiring decisions. In other words, women hired under affirmative action programmes felt better about themselves and exhibited higher performance when they believed they were hired because of their competence rather than their gender.[20] An increasing number of people and institutions now question the positive action programmes, and their doubts were affirmed by the European Court of Justice. The all-male court ruled that the use of quotas is sex discrimination against men and is, therefore, unlawful under the equal treatment directive. This landmark ruling throws into doubt all the systems of positive action giving priority to job applications from women that are favoured by many European states, especially Germany. The ruling was the result of a claim brought by Eckhard Kalanke, a gardener in the Bremen (Germany) parks department. He claimed that a female colleague had been promoted above him because of a law operating in Germany's public sector which requires women with qualifications equal to those of male applicants to be preferred if they are under-represented in certain jobs.[21]

Consider Linda Dickens', a scholar at Warwick Business School, statement on equality legislation.

> *It is important not to overestimate what equality legislation can achieve. But legal regulation can play an effective role in, for example, setting and broadening employer quality agendas; in shaping the climate within which employer decisions are taken (a 'symbolic' function of law); in providing universal standards and minima, thus generalising and underpinning good practice; and in altering the costs of discrimination and employer inaction.*[22]

Valuing Diversity

Table 2–1 indicates that **valuing diversity** emphasizes the awareness, recognition, understanding and appreciation of human differences. It revolves around creating an environment in which everyone feels valued and accepted. In essence, valuing diversity entails a cultural change geared towards viewing employee differences as a valuable resource that can contribute to organizational success.[23] This generally takes place through a series of management education and training programmes that attempt to improve interpersonal relationships between diverse employees and to minimize blatant expressions of sexism and racism.[24] The importance of valuing diversity is stressed by Chris Verheye, HR manager at the pharmaceutical giants, DuPont Europe when he says 'knowing someone else's background seriously influences people's personal value source: a good-looking, boyish person is highly appreciated until it becomes clear that that person is a lesbian woman; the rough appearance of a motor freak is not appreciated until he seems to be the graphic designer for Harley Davidson's'.[25] Consider, for example, the British Crown Prosecution Service's HR director, Indi Seehra's plan for diversity training for all staff, which is by way of a response to an interim report revealing strong evidence of race discrimination and 'institutional racism'.[26]

Valuing diversity
text to go here?

people in general employee publics

finger work

Managing Diversity

Managing diversity entails enabling people to perform up to their maximum potential. It focuses on changing an organization's culture and infrastructure such that people provide the highest productivity possible. Ann Morrison, a diversity expert, conducted a study of 16 organizations that successfully managed diversity. Her results uncovered three key strategies for success:

▼ **education**

▼ **enforcement**

▼ **exposure.**

Managing diversity
creating organizational changes that enable all people to perform up to their maximum potential

She describes them as follows.

The education component of the strategy has two thrusts: one is to prepare less-traditional managers for increasingly responsible posts; the other to help traditional managers overcome their prejudice by thinking about and interacting with people of a different sex or ethnicity. The enforcement component of the strategy puts teeth in diversity goals and encourages behaviour change. The final component, exposure to people with different backgrounds and characteristics, adds a more personal approach to diversity by helping managers get to know and respect others who are different.[27]

In summary, both consultants and academics believe that organizations should strive to manage diversity rather than simply valuing it or using affirmative action. More is said about managing diversity later in this chapter.

BUILDING THE BUSINESS CASE FOR MANAGING DIVERSITY

The rationale for managing diversity goes well beyond legal, social, and moral reasons. Quite simply, the primary reason for managing diversity is the ability to develop and maintain a business in an increasingly competitive marketplace. Organizations cannot use diversity as a strategic advantage if employees fail to contribute their full talents, abilities, motivation and commitment. Thus, it is essential for an organization to create an environment or culture that allows all employees to reach their full potential. This belief is shared by Saji Butt, policy officer of the Black Training and Enterprise group who states that 'targets for recruitment are fair enough. But we need to get people to the top on merit. That means proving that having them there and ensuring that they progress is good business.'[28] Managing diversity is a critical component of creating such an organization.

This section explores the business need to manage diversity by first reviewing the demographic trends that are creating an increasingly diverse workforce. We then review the key reasons why effective management of diversity creates a competitive advantage.

Increasing Diversity in the Workforce

Workforce demographics
statistical profiles of adult workers

Workforce demographics, which are statistical profiles of the characteristics and composition of the adult working population, are an invaluable human-resource planning aid. They enable managers to anticipate and adjust for surpluses or shortages of appropriately skilled individuals. For example, the decline and ageing of Europe's population will see the number of people of working age decline by five per cent in the next 25 years. According to António Vitorino, the European Union's (EU's) commissioner for justice and home affairs, this situation implies that 'we should review the longer term needs of the EU as a whole, estimating how far these can be met from existing resources, and defining a policy for the admission of third country nationals to meet whatever shortage remains'.[29]

Moreover, general population demographics give managers a preview of the values and motives of future employees. This section explores three demographic trends that are creating an increasingly diverse workforce:

▼ **women continue to enter the workforce in increasing numbers**

▼ **ethnic minorities in the European labour force**

▼ **the workforce is ageing.**

Women Entering the Workforce

Women and men benefited equally from the decline in unemployment at the last count [1998] in the EU, so that the overall unemployment rate for women is still some three per cent higher than for men. The gender gap in the employment rate, however, still mounts to just under 20 per cent. Table 2–2 shows serious differences in unemployment rates between men and women. Particularly in Spain, Greece, Italy, Belgium and France, the difference was considerable. Only in the UK, was the unemployment rate for women much less than for men. Denmark has the highest percentage of women in business in the European Union.[30]

In spite of the fact that women constituted 42 per cent of the EU labour force in 1998, they continue to encounter the 'glass ceiling'.[31] This **glass ceiling** represents an invisible barrier separating both women and minorities from advancing into top management positions. It can be particularly demotivating because employees can look up and see coveted top management positions, through the transparent ceiling, yet are unable to obtain them. A variety of statistics support the existence of a glass ceiling.

> **Glass ceiling**
> *invisible barrier blocking women and minorities from top management positions*

Historically, female employment was concentrated in relatively low-paying and low-level occupations. As of 1998, women were still paid less than men: women tended to earn less than men in all EU member states. A disproportionate number of those in the lowest paid 10 per cent of wage earners are women, while a disproportionate number of those in the highest paid 10 per cent are men. The dispersion of men's earnings, moreover, is wider than that of women in nearly all member states. The gap between men's and women's earnings for the higher paid was more than that for the lower paid in all member states.[32]

According to the Industrial Society, the pay gap does not generally result from direct discrimination against women. Instead it has arisen from deeply held views about womens' abilities, why women work, and the value of their work.[33] One female investment banker in the City, London's financial centre, says the main reason for the disparity in earnings between the sexes is that men are more confident when demanding bonuses–part of the traditional City ritual.[34]

Women have still not broken into the highest echelon of corporate Europe to any significant extent. In Britain, women hold a mere five per cent of board seats in its top 200 companies. And, while women hold 40 per cent of all management positions in America, in Europe it is only 20 to 30 per cent.[35] A recent survey conducted by Reuters revealed that female analysts, brokers, economists and fund managers believed they were still hitting ceilings on pay and promotion. Women reported being first in line for redundancies, while pregnancy was considered 'career suicide'.[36]

Consider Sari Baldauf's experience related below.

> When Sari Baldauf took her first line job at Nokia, she visited the German operations. There, the workers would 'look at me and say, "Fine, the secretary's come. Where is the boss?" Bad question. Now 43, Baldauf is a top executive and board member of the hot Finnish tech company that's killing Motorola in the mobile-phone game and that makes her a rarity.[37]

As detailed in the following International OB, the glass ceiling also exists around the world. The glass ceiling has been credited as one reason why women are increasingly starting their own businesses, says Anna Moffat, founder of 'Women in Docklands', a London business organization for women. 'Many women have told me that they worked twice as hard as their male colleagues to eventually earn less and to receive fewer promotion opportunities.[38] For example, in Belgium the number of women-owned businesses has grown from one in four to one in three within 10 years.[39]

International OB

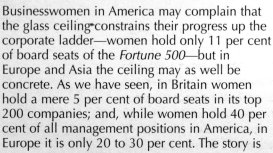

www.now.org

The Glass Ceiling Exists Around the World

Businesswomen in America may complain that the glass ceiling constrains their progress up the corporate ladder—women hold only 11 per cent of board seats of the *Fortune 500*—but in Europe and Asia the ceiling may as well be concrete. As we have seen, in Britain women hold a mere 5 per cent of board seats in its top 200 companies; and, while women hold 40 per cent of all management positions in America, in Europe it is only 20 to 30 per cent. The story is much the same in Asia. Despite China's two decades of formal commitment to sexual equality, there are no female business leaders of note. In Japan, the rigidity of the corporate culture keeps women out of the executive suite. The famed 'salaryman style' can only exist with a full-time homemaker for support.

SOURCE: C Daniels, 'The Global Glass Ceiling: And Ten Women Who Broke Through It', *Fortune*, October 12, 1998, p 102.

OB Exercise

What Are the Strategies for Breaking the Glass Ceiling?

Instructions

Read the 13 career strategies shown below that may be used to break the glass ceiling. Next, rank each strategy in order of its importance in contributing to the advancement of a woman to a senior management position. Rank the strategies from 1 (most important) to 13 (least important). Once this is completed, compute the gap between your rankings and those provided by the women executives who participated in this research. Their rankings are presented at the end of the chapter. In computing the gaps, use the absolute value of the gap. (Absolute values are always positive, so just ignore the sign of your gap.) Finally, compute your total gap score. The larger the gap, the greater the difference in opinion between you and the women executives. What does your total gap score indicate about your recommended strategies?

Strategy	My Rating	Survey Rating	Gap (Your Rating – Survey Rating)
1 Develop leadership outside office			
2 Gain line management experience			
3 Network with influential colleagues			
4 Change companies			
5 Be able to relocate			
6 Seek difficult or high visibility assignments			
7 Upgrade educational credentials			
8 Consistently exceed performance expectations			
9 Move from one functional area to another			
10 Initiate discussion regarding career aspirations			
11 Have an influential mentor			
12 Develop style that men are comfortable with			
13 Gain international experience.			

SOURCE: Strategies and data were taken from B R Ragins, B Townsend, and M Mattis, 'Gender Gap in the Executive Suite: CEOs and Female Executives Report on Breaking the Glass Ceiling', *The Academy of Management Executive*, February 1998, pp 28–42.

Ethnic Minorities in the European Workforce

At least 20 per cent of the populations of Europe's major cities come from minority or migrant communities. Within ten years, 25 per cent of the labour force in London will be from ethnic minority groups. In Copenhagen, 25 per cent of the current school population are from minority groups. Seven out of ten French immigrants live in and around Paris.[40] By 2020, The Netherlands will probably record twice as many immigrants as in 1997.[41]

Unfortunately, three additional trends suggest that ethnic minorities are experiencing their own glass ceiling. First, ethnic minorities are advancing even less in the managerial and professional ranks than women. Second, ethnic minorities also tend to earn less than 'whites'. Finally, a recent study detailing the extent of racism in the UK building industry has revealed that more than half of the potential ethnic minority recruits in the survey thought they would not have the same chance of job success and get the same pay as a white person, and there were serious concerns about promotion prospects. Of those respondents already working in construction, 44 per cent had been subjected to racist comments and 57 per cent felt that there were differences between the opportunities open to them and those available to their white colleagues.[42] These findings are consistent with previous studies that indicated that ethnic minorities have more negative career experiences, lower upward mobility, lower career satisfaction, decreased job involvement, and greater turnover rates than their white counterparts.[43]

Makbool Javaid, a partner at DLA, a UK employment law firm, said that companies such as Coca-Cola are very good when it comes to having equal opportunities policies and setting themselves targets as to the number of individuals they ought to be recruiting. 'But although you get people from ethnic minorities coming in, the company does not change its culture enough to be able to receive them. Such policies raise expectations among ethnic minority recruits, who become frustrated when they find that the company is not as egalitarian as it seems.'[44]

Major mistakes reported in a recent report on racism in the UK Metropolitan Police include the following.

> ▼ **Local police stations are not setting recruitment targets for ethnic minority staff.**
> ▼ **Line managers are insensitive to the needs of ethnic minority staff.**
> ▼ **Staff lack faith in grievance procedures.**
> ▼ **Job descriptions and person specifications vary too much.**
> ▼ **There is too little monitoring of career progression among minorities.**

The race relations training programme by-passed a thorough needs analysis, is unclear over who is responsible and lacks common standards and an in-built evaluation strategy.

Major policies on 'stop and search' and recording racist incidents are not reaching grass-roots level. Local officers are not being brought on board.[45]

It is, however, remarkable to notice that, while ethnic minorities are faced with blatant racism and fewer opportunities than their white colleagues, Europe is heading towards an imminent shortage of labour. According to Jean-Pierre Chevènement, France's interior minister, the EU would need to admit 50 to 75 million immigrants in the next 50 years to fill empty jobs.[46]

Moreover, diverse sources indicate that the contribution of ethnic minority small businesses to the economy is considerable: in the UK alone their contribution amounts to £37bn.[47] In Stockholm, small businesses owned by ethnic minorities are the greatest creators of jobs.[48]

Mr Livingstone, the Lord Major of London, is making the expansion of the ethnic minority business sector one of the policy centrepieces of his mayoralty. A quarter of

London's residents belong to ethnic minority groups, and almost half Britain's total ethnic minority population lives in the capital. Ethnic minority business development is therefore a significant issue for London's economy.[49]

Mr Livingstone stated the following.

Glass ceilings for women and discrimination against Asian and black businesses weaken the potential prosperity of every Londoner. Every citizen of the capital must find that the only limit to their achievement is their own talent, energy and determination.[50]

The Ageing Workforce

Declining birth rates have accompanied rising life expectancy since the mid-1980s, leading to both slowing population growth and an ageing population. Indeed, during the 1990s, population has continued to grow in a number of countries only because of net immigration, and across the EU as a whole, this has been responsible for some two-thirds of the small overall growth (well under 0.5 per cent a year). The scale of inward migration will be the major determinant of how long the numbers of people of working age in the EU will continue to grow in future years before the strong demographic trends cause the almost inevitable decline.

Over the 1990s, the number of young people under 15 has fallen by around 0.5 per cent a year, while the number of those aged 65 and over has risen by some 1.5 per cent a year. In 1998, almost a third of men aged 55 to 59 in the EU were economically inactive, and almost half in Belgium, Italy and Luxemburg. For those aged 60 to 64, still under the official age of retirement in most countries, the figure for the EU was over 70 per cent; and for France and Austria, almost 90 per cent. For women, under 40 per cent of those aged 55 to 59 in the EU were still in the labour force in 1998, as were only just over 10 per cent of those aged 60 to 64.[51] It is astonishing to realize that the age at which employees are classed 'old' is declining continuously. Even in information technology, ageism is becoming a serious problem, despite severe skill shortages. Eastern Europe is also expected to encounter significant economic and political problems due to an ageing population. The following are some examples of this.

- ▼ Margaret Hodge, the UK's equal opportunities minister was 'shocked' by statistics showing that only two-thirds of men over 50 were in work today, compared to 85 per cent in 1979.[52]

- ▼ Research by the UK-based Employers' Forum on Age indicates that nearly half the respondents aged between 18 and 30 believed that they have been held back at work because of their age.[53]

- ▼ In a survey of nearly 1,400 professionals in the IT sector, a quarter said IT people became classified as 'older workers' at 40, and more than one in five said the defining age was 35.[54]

- ▼ Attempts by Eastern European firms to modernize their workforces by recruiting young graduates and contract staff, has left older employees on the shelf in Hungary where half the unemployed are over 40 and destined never to rejoin the labour market.[55]

Managing Diversity—A Competitive Advantage

Some consultants, academics and business leaders believe that effectively managing diversity is a competitive advantage. This advantage stems from the process by which the management of diversity affects organizational behaviour and effectiveness. Effectively managing diversity can influence organizational costs and employee attitudes, recruitment of human resources, sales and market share (see International OB), creativity and innovation, and group problem-solving and productivity. This section explores the relationship between managing diversity and each of these outcomes.

Lower Costs and Improved Employee Attitudes

Turnover and absenteeism were found to be higher for women and ethnic minorities than for whites. Lorraine Paddison, director of consultants TMS Equality and Diversity (UK) suggested that where staff turnover can be tracked, it is noticeably higher among ethnic minorities.[56]

Diversity was also related to employee attitudes. Past research revealed that people who were different from their work units in racial or ethnic background were less psychologically committed to their organizations, less satisfied with their careers, and perceived less autonomy to make decisions on their jobs. Employees' mental and physical abilities and characteristics is another dimension of diversity that needs to be effectively managed. Government research has shown that disabled people in the UK are six times more likely to be unemployed than non-disabled people. And even when they have jobs, these are likely to be low-status.[57]

Improved Recruiting Efforts

Attracting and retaining competent employees is a competitive advantage. This is particularly true given the workforce demographics discussed in the preceding section. Organizations that effectively manage diversity are more likely to meet this challenge because women and ethnic minorities are attracted to such companies. Moreover, recruiting diverse employees helps organizations to provide better customer service.

To improve its access to employment, British Telecom (BT) always participates in the UK's 'Take our daughters to work' initiative. In 1997 it was estimated that 4,500 BT employees and their daughters took part. The focus is on technical jobs with BT—a traditional male preserve—and is said to have both presented a positive image of BT to prospective non-traditional applicants and to raise awareness among employees of the barriers to access and girls' interest and competence in technical areas.[58]

Kamaljeet Jandu wants to increase the number of female, ethnic-minority and disabled workers at Ford Europe by reforming Ford's graduate recruitment scheme.[59] The existence of informal processes of selection—for example, for international postings—is one aspect of organizational culture that seems to weigh against women. In theory, women should focus on international skills in the now well-established list of criteria for effective international managers. Yet women represent between 2 and 15 per cent of the 'overseas' manager population.[60]

Increased Sales, Market Share and Corporate Profits

Workforce diversity is the mirror image of consumer diversity. It is thus important for companies to market their products so that they appeal to diverse customers and markets. Researchers are beginning to examine the effects of a top management team's (TMT's) demographic characteristics on an organization's financial performance. For example, a study of over 1,000 companies suggested that a diverse TMT can contribute to corporate profits. Results revealed that sales growth averaged 22.9 per cent, 20.2 per cent and 13 per cent respectively for companies who's senior management team contained a majority of women; included people from ethnic minorities; and consisted of a majority of white men.[61] Given these impressive results, other researchers are trying to identify the exact process or manner in which a TMT's diversity positively impacts on corporate success. The current thinking is that diversity promotes the sharing of unique ideas and a variety of perspectives, which in turn, leads to more effective decision-making.[62]

Increased Creativity and Innovation

Preliminary research supports the idea that workforce diversity promotes creativity and innovation. This occurs through the sharing of diverse ideas and perspectives. Rosabeth Moss-Kanter, a management expert, was one of the first to investigate this relationship.

Her results indicate that innovative companies deliberately use heterogeneous teams to solve problems, and they employ more women and people of colour than less innovative companies. She also noted that innovative companies do a better job of eliminating racism, sexism and classism.[63] A recent summary of 40 years of diversity research supported Moss-Kanter's conclusion that diversity can promote creativity and improve a team's decision making.[64] British Telecom (BT) is said to benefit from women's creativity and communication skills, which are particularly well suited to the global marketplace.[65]

Increased Group Problem Solving and Productivity

Because diverse groups possess a broader base of experience and perspective from which to analyse a problem, they can potentially improve problem solving and performance. Research findings based on short-term groups that varied in terms of values, attitudes, educational backgrounds, and experience, supported this conclusion. Heterogeneous groups produced better-quality decisions and demonstrated higher productivity than homogeneous groups. Nevertheless, these results must be interpreted cautiously because the experimental samples, tasks, time frames, and environmental situations bear very little resemblance to actual ongoing organizational settings.[66]

More recent studies do not clearly support the proposed benefits of diversity. A study of culturally homogeneous and diverse groups over a period of 17 weeks, showed higher performance among homogeneous groups for the first 9 weeks—due to the fact that heterogeneous groups experience less effective group processes than homogeneous groups. Over weeks 10 to 17, however, homogeneous and heterogeneous groups demonstrated similar performance. Additional studies found that work-group diversity was significantly associated with increased absenteeism, turnover, and less psychological commitment and intention to stay in the organization.[67]

In summary, research shows that diversity can improve creativity and innovation but that these positive benefits may not influence productivity because diverse groups generally experience more negative group dynamics. How then do managers capitalize on the positive benefits of diversity? One lesson seems to be that organizations should not simply assemble a diverse group and then let group dynamics take care of themselves. Rather, training should be used to help group members become aware of the other members' cultural and attitudinal differences. This training should be conducted at the beginning of a group's formation because conflict is likely to be highest at this point and this conflict would otherwise negatively influences subsequent group processes.[68]

A second lesson revolves around the fact that both the group processes and the performance of diverse groups are enhanced when group members share common values and norms that promote the pursuit of common goals.[69] Managers and organizations are thus encouraged to identify ways of enhancing group members' sense of shared values and a common fate. Increasing shared values can be facilitated through an organization's culture, which is discussed in Chapter 3, and common fate can be created by making group members accountable for group or team-level performance goals. Team goals and team rewards are discussed in Chapter 12.

BARRIERS AND CHALLENGES TO MANAGING DIVERSITY

We introduced this chapter by noting that diversity is a sensitive, potentially volatile and sometimes uncomfortable issue. It is therefore not surprising that organizations encounter significant barriers when trying to move forward with managing diversity. The following is a list of the most common barriers to implementing successful diversity programmes.[70]

1 *Inaccurate stereotypes and prejudice.* This barrier manifests itself in the belief that differences are viewed as weaknesses. In turn, this promotes the view that diversity hiring will mean sacrificing competence and quality.

2   *Ethnocentrism.* The barrier of ethnocentrism represents the feeling that one's cultural rules and norms are superior or more appropriate than the rules and norms of another culture.[71] This barrier is thoroughly discussed in Chapter 4.

3   *Poor career planning.* This barrier is associated with the lack of opportunities for diverse employees to get the type of work assignments that qualify them for senior management positions.

4   *An unsupportive and hostile working environment for diverse employees.* Diverse employees are frequently excluded from social events and the friendly camaraderie that takes place in most offices.

5   *Lack of political knowledge on the part of diverse employees.* Diverse employees may not get promoted because they do not know how to 'play the game' of getting along and getting ahead in an organization. Research reveals that women and people of colour are excluded from organizational networks.[72]

6   *Difficulty in balancing career and family issues.* Women still assume the majority of the responsibilities associated with raising children. This makes it harder for women to work evenings and weekends or to frequently travel once they have children. Even without children in the picture, household chores take more of a woman's time than a man's.

7   *Fears of reverse discrimination.* Some employees believe that managing diversity is a smoke screen for reverse discrimination. This belief leads to very strong resistance because people feel that one person's gain is another's loss.

8   *Diversity is not seen as an organizational priority.* This leads to subtle resistance that shows up in the form of complaints and negative attitudes. Employees may complain about the time, energy and resources devoted to diversity that could have been spent doing 'real work.'

9   *The need to revamp the organization's performance appraisal and reward system.* Performance appraisals and reward systems must reinforce the need to effectively manage diversity. This means that success will be based on a new set of criteria. Employees are likely to resist changes that adversely affect their promotions and financial rewards.

10 *Resistance to change.* Effectively managing diversity entails significant organizational and personal change. As discussed in Chapter 19, people resist change for many different reasons.

In summary, managing diversity is a critical component of organizational success. Case studies and limited research inform us that this effort is doomed to failure unless top management is truly committed to managing diversity. The next section examines the variety of ways organizations are attempting to manage diversity.

ORGANIZATIONAL PRACTICES USED TO EFFECTIVELY MANAGE DIVERSITY

Many organizations are unsure of what it takes to effectively manage diversity. This is partly due to the fact that top management only recently became aware of the combined need and importance of this issue.

So what are organizations doing to effectively manage diversity? Answering this question requires that we provide a framework for categorizing organizational initiatives. Researchers and practitioners have developed relevant frameworks. One was developed by R. Roosevelt Thomas, Jr, a diversity expert. He identified eight generic action options that can be used to address any type of diversity issue. A second was proposed by another diversity expert, Ann Morrison. She empirically identified the specific diversity initiatives used by 16 organizations that successfully managed diversity. This section reviews these frameworks in order to provide you with both a broad and specific understanding about how organizations are effectively managing diversity.

R. Roosevelt Thomas, Jr's Generic Action Options

Thomas identified eight basic responses for handling any diversity issue. After describing each option, we discuss relationships among them.[73]

Option 1: Include/Exclude

This choice is an outgrowth of affirmative action programmes. Its primary goal is to either increase or decrease the number of diverse people at all levels of the organizations. BAOBAB Catering, the Belgian organization referred to in the opening to this chapter, represents a good example of an organization that attempts to include diverse employees.

Option 2: Deny

People using this option deny that differences exist. Denial may manifest itself in proclamations that all decisions are colour, gender, and age blind and that success is solely determined by merit and performance. 'Eventually, we want the best applicant, regardless of his of her ethnic origin, gender or age', states Gust Godts, HR Director at Dupont.[74]

Option 3: Assimilate

The basic premise behind this alternative is that all diverse people will learn to fit in, or become like, the dominant group. It only takes time and reinforcement for people 'to see the light'. Organizations initially assimilate employees through their recruitment practices and the use of company orientation programmes. Fresh recruits are generally put through orientation programmes that aim to provide employees with the organization's preferred values and a set of standard operating procedures. Employees are then encouraged to refer to the policies and procedure manual whenever they are confused about what to do in a specific situation. These practices create homogeneity among employees.

Option 4: Suppress

Differences are quashed or discouraged when using this approach. This can be done by telling or reinforcing others to 'quit whining and complaining' about issues. The old 'you've got to pay your dues' line is another frequently used way to promote the status quo.

Option 5: Isolate

This option maintains the current way of doing things by setting the diverse person off to the side. In this way the individual is unable to influence organizational change. Managers can isolate people by putting them on special projects. Entire work groups or departments are isolated by creating functionally independent entities, frequently referred to as 'silos'.

Option 6: Tolerate

'Toleration' entails acknowledging differences but not valuing or accepting them. It represents a live-and-let-live approach that superficially allows organizations to give lip service to the issue of managing diversity. Toleration is different from isolation in that it allows for the inclusion of diverse people. However, differences are not really valued or accepted when an organization uses this approach.

Option 7: Build Relationships

This approach is based on the premise that good relationships can overcome differences. It addresses diversity by fostering quality relationships—characterized by acceptance and understanding—among diverse groups.

Option 8: Foster Mutual Adaptation

In this option, people recognize and accept differences and, most importantly, agree that everyone and everything is free to change. Mutual adaptation allows the greatest accommodation of diversity because it allows for change even when diversity is being effectively managed.

Conclusions about Action Options

Although the action options can be used alone or in combination, some are clearly better than others. Exclusion, denial, assimilation, suppression, isolation and toleration are among the least preferred options. Inclusion, building relationships, and mutual adaptation are the preferred strategies. That said, Thomas reminds us that mutual adaptation is the only approach that unquestionably endorses the philosophy behind managing diversity. In closing this discussion, it is important to note that choosing how best to manage diversity is a dynamic process that is determined by the context. For instance, some organizations are not ready for mutual adaptation. The best one might hope for in this case is the inclusion of diverse people.

Ann Morrison Identifies Specific Diversity Initiatives

As previously mentioned, Ann Morrison conducted a landmark study of the diversity practices used by 16 organizations that successfully managed diversity. Her results uncovered 52 different practices, 20 of which were used by the majority of the companies sampled. She classified the 52 practices into three main types: accountability, development and recruitment.[75] The top 10 practices associated with each type are shown in Table 2–3. They are discussed next in order of their relative importance.

Accountability practices relate to managers' responsibility to treat diverse employees fairly. Table 2–3 reveals that companies predominantly accomplish this objective by creating administrative procedures aimed at integrating diverse employees into the management ranks (practices number 3, 4, 5, 6, 8, 9, and 10). In contrast, work and family policies, practice 7, focuses on creating an environment that fosters employee commitment and productivity. The desire for a decent balance between work and personal life appears to be widespread. A Gemini Consulting survey of workers in 13 industrialized countries found it was rated more highly than a good salary everywhere but in Russia.[76] Marion Lorman, deputy director of HR at the South London Health Trust confirms this by the following statement.

> **Accountability practices**
> *Focus on treating diverse employees fairly*

If we are to be able to meet our staffing needs, we are going to have to turn to a more diverse population—and that includes people who don't want traditional work patterns.[77]

Consider the work and family practices at the following companies. Wendy Jeffreys' mother, Phyllis Hollyoak (87), attends Britain's first workplace eldercare day centre, or 'granny crèche', as it has been labelled. 'I can concentrate on my work because I don't have to ring to make sure she's all right', says Jeffrey, a 55-years-old pensions administrator at the Peugeot car factory in Coventry.[78]

Since Amanda Bridge, operations controller at Littlewoods, returned from having a baby and nine months' career break, she has been working, first one day a week, then two and a half, and finally four days a week. When she asked if starting at 7 a.m. and leaving at 3 p.m. would be a problem, they said no, as long as she agreed it with her manager and the personnel department. 'It really is a flexible firm', she says.[79]

At Origin Nederland, all 6,500 employees may compose their own package of working conditions. Some want more money, others prefer more holidays or simply more leisure time. An automatic simulator calculates the consequences of a person's preferences in terms of their salary.[80]

In Norway each couple has one year parental leave, four weeks of which have to be taken by the father.[81]

Table 2–2 *Common Diversity Practices*

Accountability Practices	Development Practices	Recruitment Practices
1. Top management's personal intervention	1. Diversity training programs	1. Targeted recruitment of non-managers
2. Internal advocacy groups	2. Networks and support groups	2. Key outside hires
3. Emphasis on EEO statistics, profiles	3. Development programs for all high-potential managers	3. Extensive public exposure on diversity (AA)
4. Inclusion of diversity in performance evaluation goals, ratings	4. Informal networking activities	4. Corporate image as liberal, progressive, or benevolent
5. Inclusion of diversity in promotion decisions, criteria	5. Job rotation	5. Partnerships with educational institutions
6. Inclusion of diversity in management succession planning	6. Formal mentoring program	6. Recruitment incentives such as cash supplements
7. Work and family policies	7. Informal mentoring program	7. Internships (such as INROADS)
8. Policies against racism, sexism	8. Entry development programs for all high-potential new hires	8. Publications or PR products that highlight diversity
9. Internal audit or attitude survey	9. Internal training (such as personal safety or language)	9. Targeted recruitment of managers
10. Active AA/EEO committee, office	10. Recognition events, awards	10. Partnership with non-traditional groups

SOURCE: Abstracted from Tables A.10, A.11, and A.12 in A M Morrison, *The New Leaders: Guidelines on Leadership Diversity in America* (San Francisco: Jossey-Bass, 1992).

Development Practices

Development practices
Focus on preparing diverse employees for greater responsibility and advancement.

The use of **development practices** to manage diversity is relatively new compared to the historical use of accountability and recruitment practices. Development practices focus on preparing diverse employees for greater responsibility and advancement. These activities are needed because most non-traditional employees have not been exposed to the type of activities and job assignments that develop effective leadership and social networks.[82] At Ford Europe, training is introduced to enable all employees to progress to supervisory positions.[83] Table 2–2 indicates that diversity training programmes, networks and support groups, and mentoring programmes are among the most frequently used developmental practices.

Recruitment Practices

Recruitment practices
attempts to attract qualified, diverse employees at all levels

Recruitment practices focus on attracting job applicants at all levels who are willing to accept challenging work assignments. This focus is critical because people learn the leadership skills needed for advancement by successfully accomplishing increasingly challenging and responsible work assignments. As shown in Table 2–2, targeted recruitment of nonmanagers (practice 1) and managers (practice 9) are commonly used to identify and recruit women and people of colour. Boeing Company relies on targeted recruiting: at Boeing Co., the Human Resources team launched a slick, advertising campaign aimed at women and ethnic minorities who feel under-utilized in their current jobs.[84]

Summary of Key Concepts

1 Define diversity.

Diversity represents the host of individual differences that make people different from and similar to each other. Diversity pertains to everybody. It is not simply an issue of age, race, gender, or sexual orientation.

2 Discuss the four layers of diversity.

The layers of diversity define an individual's personal identity and constitute a perceptual filter that influences how we interpret the world. Personality is at the centre of the diversity wheel. The second layer of diversity consists of a set of internal dimensions that are referred to as the 'primary dimensions of diversity'. The third layer is composed of external influences and are called 'secondary dimensions of diversity'. The final layer of diversity includes organizational dimensions.

3 Explain the differences between affirmative action, valuing diversity and managing diversity.

Affirmative action focuses on achieving equality of opportunity in an organization. It represents an artificial intervention aimed at giving management a chance to correct an imbalance, an injustice, a mistake, or outright discrimination. Valuing diversity emphasizes an awareness, recognition, understanding and appreciation of human differences. Training programmes are the dominant method used to accomplish this objective. Managing diversity entails creating a host of organizational changes that enable all people to perform up to their maximum potential.

4 Review the five reasons managing diversity is a competitive advantage.

Managing diversity can:

a lower costs and improve employee attitudes

b improve an organization's recruiting efforts

c increase sales, market share, and corporate profits

d increase creativity and innovation

e increase group problem solving and productivity.

5 Identify the barriers and challenges to managing diversity.

There are 10 barriers to successfully implementing diversity initiatives:

a inaccurate stereotypes and prejudice

b ethnocentrism

c poor career planning

d an unsupportive and hostile working environment for diverse employees

e lack of political savvy on the part of diverse employees

f difficulty in balancing career and family issues

g fears of reverse discrimination

h diversity is not seen as an organizational priority

i the need to revamp the organization's performance appraisal and reward system

j resistance to change.

6 Discuss the organizational practices used to effectively manage diversity as identified by R. Roosevelt Thomas, Jr, and Ann Morrison.

There are many different practices that organizations can use to manage diversity. R. Roosevelt Thomas, Jr, identified eight basic responses for handling any diversity issue: include/exclude, deny, assimilate, suppress, isolate, tolerate, build relationships, and foster mutual adaptation. Exclusion, denial, assimilation, suppression, isolation and toleration are among the least preferred options. Inclusion, building relationships and mutual adaptation are the preferred strategies. Ann Morrison's study of diversity practices identified three main types or categories of activities. Accountability practices relate to a manager's responsibility to treat diverse employees fairly. Development practices focus on preparing diverse employees for greater responsibility and advancement. Recruitment practices emphasize attracting job applicants at all levels who are willing to accept challenging work assignments. Table 2–2 presents a list of activities that are used to accomplish each main type.

Discussion Questions

1 Whom do you think would be most resistant to accepting the value or need to manage diversity? Explain.

2 What role does communication play in effectively managing diversity?

3 Does diversity suggest that managers should follow the rule 'Do unto others as you would have them do unto you'?

4 What can be done to break the glass ceiling for women and ethnic minorities?

5 What can be done to facilitate the career success of the disabled? Explain.

6 Why is underemployment a serious human resource management problem? If you have ever been underemployed, what were your feelings about it?

7 How can interpersonal conflict be caused by diversity? Explain your rationale.

8 Have you seen any examples that support the proposition that diversity is a competitive advantage?

9 Which of the barriers to managing diversity would be most difficult to reduce? Explain.

10 How can Thomas's generic action options and Morrison's specific diversity initiatives be helpful in overcoming the barriers and challenges to managing diversity?

Internet Exercise

In this chapter, a number of topics concerning the challenge of managing a diverse workforce were discussed, such as layers of diversity, barriers and challenges to managing diversity, organizational practices and some demographic trends. The purpose of this exercise is to view diversity from a specific European angle. Go to the European Institute for Managing Diversity (EIMD) homepage (www.iegd.org). The EIMD is an umbrella organization for a network of local institutions devoted to tackling the diversity theme. After reading the home page and the sections where the EIMD is presented, select Europe in the left margin. A map of Europe will appear on your screen on which you can select specific information on different countries. Next, select 'products' and also read the scheme under 'process'.

Questions

1 Explain why diversity is such an important theme in the EU. (Maybe you can complete your answer with the charts accompanying the map.)

2 Is there a local diversity organization in your country our region? What does it do? Are there any specific problems in your area?

3 According to the EIMD, which aspects should be considered when implementing a diversity plan? What steps should be followed?

Personal Awareness and Growth Exercise

How Does Your Diversity Profile Affect Your Relationships with Other People?

Objectives

1 To identify the diversity profile of yourself and others.

2 To consider the implications of similarities and differences across diversity profiles.

Introduction

People vary along four layers of diversity: personality, internal dimensions, external dimensions, and organizational dimensions. Differences across these four layers are likely to influence interpersonal relationships and the ability or willingness to work with others. You will be asked to compare yourself with a group of other people with whom you interact and then to examine the quality of the relationships between yourself and these individuals. This enables you to gain a better understanding of how similarities and differences among people influence attitudes and behaviour.

Instructions

Complete the diversity profile by first selecting five current or past co-workers, work associates or fellow students.[85] Alternatively, you can select five people you interact with in order to accomplish your personal goals (such as team members on a class project). Write their names on the diagonal lines at the top of the worksheet. Next, determine whether each person is similar to or different from you with respect to each diversity dimension. Mark an 'S' if the person is the same as yourself or a 'D' if the person is different. Finally, answer the questions for discussion.

Questions for Discussion

1 To whom are you most similar and to whom different?

2 Which diversity dimensions have the greatest influence with respect to who you are drawn to and who you like the best?

3 Which dimensions of diversity seem relatively unimportant with respect to the quality of the interpersonal relationships?

4 Consider the individual that you have the most difficult time working with or getting along with. Which dimensions are similar and which different? Which dimensions seem to be the source of your difficulty?

5 If you choose co-workers for this exercise, discuss the management actions, policies, and/or programs that could be used to increase inclusiveness, reduce turnover, and increase job satisfaction.

Diversity Worksheet

Diversity Dimensions					
Personality					
e.g., Loyalty					
Internal Dimensions					
Age					
Gender					
Sexual orientation					
Physical ability					
Ethnicity					
Race					
External Dimensions					
Geographic location					
Income					
Personal habits					
Recreational habits					
Religion					
Educational background					
Work experience					
Appearance					
Parental status					
Marital status					
Organizational Dimensions					
Functional level/classification					
Work content/field					
Division/department/unit/group					
Seniority					
Work location					
Union affiliation					
Management status					

Group Exercise
Managing Diversity-Related Interactions

Objectives

1 To improve your ability to manage diversity-related interactions more effectively.

2 To explore different approaches for handling diversity interactions.

Introduction

The interpersonal component of managing diversity can be awkward and uncomfortable. This is partly due to the fact that resolving diversity interactions requires us to deal with situations we may never have encountered before. The purpose of this exercise is to help you manage diversity-related interactions more effectively. To do so, you will be asked to read three scenarios and then decide how you will handle each situation.

Instructions

Presented here are three scenarios depicting diversity-related interactions. Please read the first scenario, and then answer the three questions that follow it. Follow the same procedure for the next two scenarios. Next, divide into groups of three. One at a time, each person should present his or her responses to the three questions for the first scenario. Each group should then discuss the various approaches that were proposed to resolve the diversity interaction; and try to arrive at a consensus recommendation. Follow the same procedure for the next two scenarios.

Scenario 1

Dave, who directly reports to you, comes to you and says that he and Scott are having a special commitment ceremony to celebrate the beginning of their lives together. He has invited you to the ceremony. Normally the department has a party and cake for special occasions. Mary, who is one of Dave's peers, has just walked into your office and asks you whether you intend to have a party for Dave.

a How would you respond?

_____
_____
_____

b What is the potential impact of your response?

_____
_____
_____

c If you choose not to respond, what is the potential impact of your behaviour?

_____
_____
_____

Scenario 2

You have an open position for a supervisor, and your top two candidates are an African female and a white female. Both candidates are equally qualified. The job-holder will be responsible for five white team leaders. You hire the white female because the work group likes her. The team leaders said that they felt more comfortable with the white female. The vice president of human resources has just called you on the phone and asks you to explain why you hired the white female.

a How would you respond?

_____
_____
_____

b What is the potential impact of not hiring the African candidate?

_____
_____
_____

c What is the potential impact of hiring the African candidate?

_____
_____
_____

Scenario 3

While attending an off-site business meeting, you are waiting in line with a group of team leaders to get your lunch at a buffet. Without any forewarning, one of your peers in the line loudly says, 'Thank goodness Terry is at the end of the line. With his size and appetite there wouldn't be any food left for the rest of us'. You believe Terry may have heard this comment, and you feel the comment was more of a 'weight-related' slur than a joke.

a How would you respond?

_____

_____

_____

b What is the potential impact of your response?

_____

_____

_____

c If you choose not to respond, what is the potential impact of your behaviour?

_____

_____

_____

Questions for discussion

1 What was the recommended response for each scenario?

2 Which scenario generated the most emotion and disagreement? Explain why this occurred.

3 What is the potential impact of a manager's lack of response to Scenarios 1 and 3? Explain.

Ranking for OB Exercise 'What Are the Strategies for Breaking the Glass Ceiling?'

Here are the ranks for each career strategy: Strategy 1 = 12; Strategy 2 = 6; Strategy 3 = 5; Strategy 4 = 11; Strategy 5 = 9; Strategy 6 = 3; Strategy 7 = 10; Strategy 8 = 1; Strategy 9 = 7; Strategy 10 = 8; Strategy 11 = 4; Strategy 12 = 13.

Chapter Three

Organizational Culture

Learning Objectives

When you finish studying the material in this chapter, you should be able to:

- Discuss the difference between espoused and enacted values.

- Explain the typology of organizational values.

- Describe the manifestations of an organization's culture and the four functions of organizational culture.

- Discuss the three general types of organizational culture and their associated normative beliefs.

- Discuss the process of developing an adaptive culture.

- Summarize the methods used by organizations to embed their cultures.

- Describe the three phases in Feldman's model of organizational socialization.

- Discuss the two basic functions of mentoring and summarize the phases of mentoring.

St Luke's rewrites the DNA-structure of a company

Cynics often refer to the London advertising agency St Luke's by the nickname 'Utopia'. But Andy Law, the founder of the company, just wants the workplace to fit as closely as possible to what employees really want. 'Our prime question was: what do people find important in their lives? That is respect, honesty, freedom and growth. On those values we built our company. And later on, it turned out to be a successful formula.' ▶

A profitable company without rigid rules in the highly competitive world of advertising? It looks a bit like an anarchical experiment, destined for a short life. St Luke's, however, proves the contrary.

Over the last few years, the number of company employees has tripled. Or rather, the number of fellow owners has tripled, because everyone who starts to work at St Luke's gets to own a part of the company. A share option scheme was chosen to make clear to the employees that participation was not a fake promise. Every employee at St Luke's, from the secretary to the creative director, gets an equal say in every major decision. Everyone is considered co-responsible for the organization. This premise turned out to be the key to the company's success and has brought about a different style of working at St Luke's.

'We count on the sense of responsibility that's inherent in every employee', says Andy Law. 'That's our basic rule. You can compare it to raising teenagers: you impose one or two basic rules that are not to be broken, such as: take your schoolwork seriously and respect your parents. In all other cases you don't impose any rules but you look for solutions together and try to encourage your children in so doing. I also find this approach very useful in the workplace: we set some basic rules and explicit core values; and then employees are free to act as they want to, within the borders of these values. This method leaves plenty of space for the individual contribution and creativity of each employee.

Picking up a friend at Heathrow Airport on Tuesday afternoon or reading a book to relax? According to Law, this is all possible. 'If you have an appointment with three people for a meeting, it doesn't matter where you have your meeting: at the office, at home or even in a pub [bar]. What matters is that you stick to your appointment and be there on time.' St Luke's proves that it's not necessary for companies to anxiously formulate rules and prescriptions to keep the place under control. Their free approach seems to work out very well.

The free, informal and value-driven culture of St Luke's, plus their adherence to basic ethical standards, also seems to pay off when it comes to recruiting new employees. When the company started their first foreign agency in Stockholm, they received over 1,000 emails from candidates in just two days. 'It's not easy, especially with a growing organization, to check whether applicants really support the values and approach that are propagated by St Luke's, Andy Law says. 'If candidates say the right things, are they also really behind what they're saying?'

The approach of the advertising agency seems attractive but not everyone can readily handle it. Law gives the example of somebody who left because she missed the way things were done in a traditional agency. 'There, you enter and immediately you are put on the most important project to see if you can cope with it or go down. That's not the way we work here. We want to guide our people to find out together what they like to do and what they can do best.'

Being recruited by St Luke's means you went through a tough selection procedure. Appointing a new employee happens on a basis of consensus and everybody who works at St Luke's gets their say. A new member of the sales team also has to be approved by people of the creative or the administrative department. The fact that the selection is so severe is self-evident to Andy Law. 'The new person becomes a co-owner. If you give a part of your company to somebody, you want to be sure he will succeed.'[1]

This opening case highlights how companies increasingly try to influence and make explicit the values, norms and beliefs they strive for. The core principles of St Luke's provide a sort of ideological background that directs all processes in the company, determining how employees greet each other; how work is organized; new employees recruited; meetings held; people dress; communication takes place and how the organization is structured. It is often said that corporate culture is to an organization what personality is to an individual, that is: a guideline that predicts its behaviour and the way others perceive it. And according to Andy Law, the specific 'way things are done' there enhances morale, productivity, commitment and creates a certain image, all of which is responsible for the company's success.

Much has been written and said about organizational culture, values and ethics in recent years. The results of this activity can be arranged on a continuum of academic rigour. At the low end of the continuum are simplistic typologies and exaggerated claims about the benefits of imitating successful corporate cultures and values. Here the term *corporate culture* is little more than a pop psychology buzzword. At the other end of the continuum is a growing body of theory and research with valuable insights, but one plagued by definitional and measurement inconsistencies.[2] By systematically sifting this diverse collection of material, we find that an understanding of organizational culture is central to learning how to manage people at work in both domestic and international operations.

This chapter will help you to understand better how managers can use organizational culture as a competitive advantage. We discuss: the foundation of organizational culture; the development of a high-performance culture; the organization socialization process; and the role of mentoring in socialization.

FOUNDATIONS OF ORGANIZATIONAL CULTURE

Organizational culture
shared values and beliefs that underlie a company's identity

Organizational culture is 'the set of shared, taken-for-granted implicit assumptions that a group holds and that determines how it perceives, thinks about and reacts to its various environments'.[3] This definition highlights three important characteristics of organizational culture. First, organizational culture is passed on to new employees through the process of socialization, a topic discussed later in this chapter. Second, organizational culture influences our behaviour at work. Finally, organizational culture operates at two different levels. Each level varies in terms of outward visibility and resistance to change.[4]

At the more visible level, culture represents artefacts. Artefacts consist of the physical manifestation of an organization's culture. Organizational examples include acronyms, manner of dress, awards, titles, myths and stories told about the organization, published lists of values, observable rituals and ceremonies, special parking spaces, decorations and so on. This level also includes visible behaviours exhibited by people and groups.

Consider the various artefacts in the following two examples.

Bosses in high-tech, Internet and consultancy firms no longer want to be known as the chief executives. Everyone who is in the vanguard of the new economy wants a wacky or futuristic job title. One British firm that has given its staff funky job titles is The Fourth Room, a consulting agency. There, Piers Schmidt, who would otherwise be called chief executive is called 'The Pacesetter'.

Another example is to be found in the telecommunications company Orange, where Kurt Hirschhorn has the title 'Director of Strategy, Imagineering and Futurology' on his business card. 'A lot of people see my business card and they say "now there's a title". They're not sure what it means, but they know it's something different', Hirschhorn says. His team members range from 'Ambassadors of Knowledge' to 'Senior

Imagineers'. 'With these titles, I knowingly try to express our vision of innovativeness and our culture', he adds. Further, the London law firm Mishcon de Reya appointed a 'Manager of Mischief' to emphasize their customer-oriented culture. Although this trend is becoming more common in Europe, the strangest job titles are nevertheless still found in the USA: for example, the boss of AC-Television is called 'The Keeper of the Magic', the Internet company, Encoding, has a 'Minister of Order and Reason' in its rungs and even Bill Gates, formerly known as the chairman of Microsoft changed his name to 'Chief Software Architect'.[5]

At DHL, the international courier service company, a number of activities are organized to create a feeling of togetherness among its employees. Although mostly organized on a regional basis, this also happens on a national and international basis: for instance, every year *Eurosoccer* is held, where the different parts of DHL worldwide play against each other. In total, 48 DHL teams from over the world gather together for a two-day period during soccer tournament. It is said that these matches really bring out the spirit of DHL.[6]

Artefacts are easier to change than the less visible aspects of organizational culture. At the less visible level, culture reflects the values and beliefs shared by organizational members. These values tend to persist over time and are more resistant to change. Each level of culture influences the other. For example, if a company truly values providing high-quality service, employees are more likely to adopt the behaviour of responding faster to customer complaints. Similarly, causality can flow in the other direction. Employees can come to value high-quality service based on their experiences as they interact with customers.

To gain a better understanding of how organizational culture is formed and used by employees, this section begins by discussing organizational values—the foundation of organizational culture. It then reviews the manifestations of organizational culture, a model for interpreting organizational culture, the four functions of organizational culture and research on the subject.

Organizational Values: the Foundation of Organizational Culture

Organizational **values** and beliefs constitute the foundation of an organization's culture. They also play a key role in influencing ethical behaviour. Values possess five key components, they:

Values
enduring belief in a mode of conduct or end-state

- ▼ **are concepts or beliefs**
- ▼ **pertain to desirable results or behaviours**
- ▼ **transcend situations**
- ▼ **guide selection or evaluation of behaviour and events**
- ▼ **are ordered by relative importance.'**[7]

It is important to distinguish between values that are espoused versus those that are enacted.[8]

Espoused values represent the explicitly stated values and norms that are preferred by an organization. Often they are referred to as 'corporate glue'. They are generally established by the founder of a new or small company or by the top management team in a larger organization. For example, Nokia, the Finnish telecom giant states four worldwide core values, named 'customer satisfaction', 'respect for the individual', 'achievement' and 'continuous learning'. Folke Rosengard, the Nokia Networks director explains.

Espoused values
the stated values and norms preferred by an organization

Respect for the individual is about openness and honesty and goes against the rigid structures and the slavish 'yes sir mentality' that often kills contemporary companies: it destroys innovativeness and development. We need creative, 'almost-anarchists' as, without them, we would be back where we started producing toilet paper. Openness is necessary when, for instance, we set up new offices elsewhere in the world: if there are problems, they have to be communicated to headquarters. If not, we in Helsinki become isolated from the rest of the world. Here in Helsinki, the creative heart of the company beats and people from all over the world come together here. It often takes me more than half an hour just to walk through the canteen, simply because you know everybody. But I'd like to emphasize that it's not our philosophy to print our values on every wall, coffee mug or mousepad in the company. Of course they are useful in interviews and recruitment conversations, but the most important thing is that our people develop a feeling of what it's all about. We walk the talk.[9]

Enacted values
the values and norms that are exhibited by employees

Enacted values, on the other hand, represent the values and norms that actually are exhibited or converted into employee behaviour. Let us consider the difference between these two types of values. A company might espouse that it values integrity. If employees display integrity by following through on their commitments, then the espoused value is enacted and individual behaviour is being influenced by the value of integrity. In contrast, if employees do not follow through on their commitments, then the value of integrity is simply a 'stated' aspiration that does not influence behaviour. Gareth Jones, a professor of organization development at Britain's Henley Management College, warns that many companies exert lots of efforts to make explicit their values in all kinds of ways, but very often they remain dead letter.

'In most cases, some analysis and plenty of workshops follow as the company goes in search of its soul. It draws up a document specifying the right values, and the chief executive delivers an exciting speech to rally the troops, ending with the exhortation, 'Now we know what we stand for, let's go for it'. And very often, that's the end of it. The values wallchart gathers dust along with the other culture-change literature. Managers may pay lots of lip service to new values, without ever really practising them or demonstrating how they can benefit the organization. You know, there's an established technical term for values that look good on the wall but don't add value to the business. That term is bullshit.'[10]

The gap between espoused and enacted values is important because it can significantly influence an organization's culture and employee attitudes. A study of 312 British Rail train drivers, supervisors and senior managers, revealed that the creation of a safety culture was negatively affected by large gaps between senior management's espoused and enacted values. Employees were more cynical about safety when they believed that senior managers' behaviours were inconsistent with the stated values regarding safety.[11]

If we look back at the Nokia example, there this enactment seems to work out pretty well. For example, the British Lynn Rutten, who has been working at the Nokia headquarters in Helsinki (called Nokia House) for about three years, states: 'They do exert a lot of effort to make sure everybody walks the line. Me, personally, I have become a Nokiasaurus.'[12]

Value system
pattern of values within an organization

It also is important to consider how an organization's value system influences organizational culture because companies subscribe to *multiple* values. An organization's **value system** reflects the patterns of conflict and compatibility between values, not the relative importance of each.[13] This definition highlights the point that organizations endorse a constellation of values that contain both conflicting and compatible values. For example, management scholars believe that organizations have two fundamental value systems that naturally conflict with each other. One system relates to the manner in which tasks are accomplished; the other includes values related to maintaining internal cohesion and solidarity. The central issue underlying this value conflict revolves around identifying the main goal being pursued by an organization. Is the organization predominantly interested in financial performance, relationships, or a combination of the two?[14] To help you understand how organizational values influence organizational culture, we present a typology of organizational values and review the relevant research.

A Typology of Organizational Values

SOURCE: Adapted from B Kabanoff and J Holt, 'Changes in the Espoused Values of Australian Organizations 1986–1990', *Journal of Organizational Behavior*, May 1996, pp 201–19.

Figure 3–1 presents a typology of organizational values that is based on crossing organizational reward norms and organization power structures.[15] Organizational reward norms reflect a company's fundamental belief about how rewards should be allocated. According to the equitable reward norm, they should be proportionate to contributions. In contrast, an egalitarian-oriented value system calls for rewarding all employees' equally, regardless of their comparative contributions. Organization power structures reflect a company's basic belief about how power and authority should be shared and distributed. These beliefs range from the extreme of being completely unequal or centralized, to equal or completely decentralized.

Figure 3–1 identifies four types of value systems: elite, meritocratic, leadership and collegial. Each type of value system contains a positive and a negative set of responses to values: some values are reinforced or endorsed by the system while others are seen as inconsistent or discouraged. For example, an elite value system endorses values related to acceptance of authority, high performance and equitable rewards. This value system, however, does not encourage values related to teamwork, participation, commitment or affiliation. In contrast, a collegial value system supports values associated with teamwork, participation, commitment and affiliation whilst discouraging values of authority, high performance and equitable rewards.

Practical Application of Research

Organizations subscribe to a constellation of values rather than to simply one and can be profiled according to their values.[16] This, in turn, enables managers to determine whether an organization's values are consistent and supportive of its corporate goals and initiatives. Organizational change is unlikely to succeed if it is based on a set of values that is highly inconsistent with employees' individual values.[17] Finally, a longitudinal study of 85 Australian organizations revealed four interesting trends about the typology of organizational values, presented in Figure 3–1.[18]

1 Organizational values were quite stable over four years. This result supports the contention that values are relatively stable and resistant to change.

2 There was not a universal movement to one type of value system. The 85 organizations represented all four value systems. This finding reinforces the earlier conclusion that there is no 'one best' organizational culture or value system.

3 Organizations with elite value systems experienced the greatest amount of change over the four-year period. Elite organizations tended to become more collegial.

4 There was an overall increase in the number of organizations that endorsed the individual value of employee commitment. This trend is consistent with the notion that organizational success is partly dependent on the extent to which employees are committed to their organizations.

Manifestations of Organizational Culture

When is an organization's culture most apparent? In addition to the physical artifacts of organizational culture that were previously discussed, cultural assumptions assert themselves through socialization of new employees, subculture clashes and top management behaviour. Consider these three situations, for example:

▼ **A newcomer who shows up late for an important meeting is told a story about someone who was fired for repeated tardiness.**

▼ **Conflict between product design engineers who emphasize a product's function and marketing specialists who demand a more stylish product reveals an underlying clash of subculture values.**

▼ **Top managers, through the behaviour they model and the administrative and reward systems they create, prompt a significant improvement in the quality of a company's products.**

Figure 3–2

A model for Observing and Interpreting General Manifestations of Organizational Culture

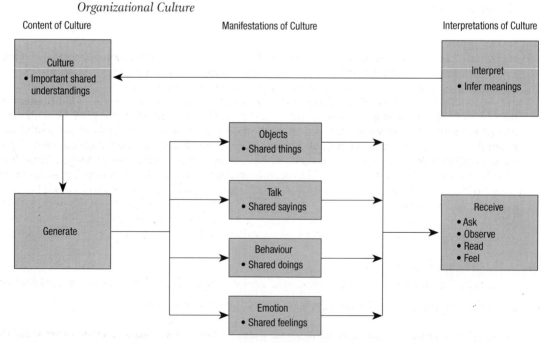

A Model for Interpreting Organizational Culture

A useful model for observing and interpreting organizational culture was developed by Vijay Sathe, a Harvard University researcher (see Figure 3–2). The four general manifestations or evidence of organizational culture in his model are shared things (objects), shared sayings (talk), shared doings (behaviour) and shared feelings (emotion). One can begin collecting cultural information within the organization by asking, observing, reading and feeling. The following OB Exercise provides you with the opportunity to practice identifying the manifestations of organizational culture at the Ritz-Carlton and McDonald's by using the model presented in Figure 3–2. These examples highlight different manifestations of organizational culture.

OB Exercise

Manifestations of Organizational Culture at the Ritz-Carlton and McDonald's

Instructions

Read the following descriptions and answer the discussion questions. Answers can be found following the Notes at the end of this chapter.

Ritz-Carlton

The Ritz-Carlton has created 'a climate and culture that allows them to succeed as an ever-expanding, upscale hotel chain in a very competitive market. At Ritz-Carlton, each hotel employee is part of a team whose members are empowered to do whatever it takes to satisfy a customer. These employees are guided by a credo, called the 'Gold Standards,' that specifies desired behaviours. More importantly, there are policies, practices, procedures and routines designed to support and reward employees engaging in these desired behaviours. Ritz-Carlton makes every employee feel like a valued person. The employee motto is 'We are ladies and gentlemen serving ladies and gentlemen.' Guests and employees alike are treated the right way; there are no mixed messages in Ritz-Carlton's climate and culture.

McDonald's

McDonald's vision is to provide customers with quality, service, convenience and value (QSCV). Ray Kroc, the founder, wanted a restaurant system known for its consistently high quality and uniform methods of preparation. He created Hamburger University, which offers a degree in Hamburgerology, to help create this culture. Franchisees, managers and assistant managers are indoctrinated into McDonald's culture and associated policies and procedures at the University. McDonald's policies and procedures meticulously spell out desired employee behaviours and job responsibilities. For example, they specify how often the bathroom should be cleaned and what colour of nail polish to wear. McDonald's culture is reinforced by using contests and ceremonies to reward those franchisees who best meet their goals. McDonald's recently implemented a set of business practices known as Franchising 2000. Two key components are as follows: franchisees must submit annual financial goals for approval; and a single pricing strategy is established for all products. Franchisees who fail to adhere to the policies and procedures risk losing their franchises when they expire. McDonald's likes to hire executives who have strong traditional values such as loyalty, dedication and service.

Discussion Questions

1 Identify the shared things, sayings, doings and feelings at both the Ritz-Carlton and McDonald's.

2 Which organization is based more on control and/or competition?

The Ritz-Carlton description was excerpted from B Schneider, A P Brief and R A Guzzo, 'Creating a Climate and Culture for Sustainable Organizational Change,' *Organizational Dynamics*, Spring 1996, p 16. Material about McDonald's was obtained from R Gibson, 'A Bit of Heartburn: Some Franchisees Say Moves by McDonald's Hurt Their Operations', *The Wall Street Journal*, April 17, 1996, pp A1, A8; and M A Salva-Ramirez, 'McDonald's: A Prime Example of Corporate Culture', *Public Relations Quarterly*, Winter 1995/96, pp 30–31.

Four Functions of Organizational Culture

As illustrated in Figure 3–3, an organization's culture fulfils four functions.[19] To help bring these four functions to life, let us consider how each of them has taken shape in the US-based 3M Corporation. 3M is a particularly instructive example because it has a long history of being an innovative company.

1 *Give members an organizational identity.*
   3M is known as being an innovative company that relentlessly pursues new-product development. One way of promoting innovation is to encourage the research and development of new products and services. For example, 3M regularly sets future sales targets based on the percentage of sales that must come from new products. In one year, the senior management decreed that 30 per cent of its sales must come from products introduced within the past four years. The old standard was 25 per cent in five years. This identity is reinforced by creating rewards that reinforce innovation. For example, 'The 3M Corporation has its version of a Nobel Prize for innovative employees. The prize is the Golden Step award, whose trophy is a winged foot. Several Golden Steps are given out each year to employees whose new products have reached significant revenue and profit levels.'[20]

2 *Facilitate collective commitment.*
   One of 3M's corporate values is to be 'a company that employees are proud to be a part of'. People who like 3M's culture tend to stay employed there for long periods of time. Approximately 24,000 of its employees have more than 15 years of tenure with the company while 19,600 have stayed more than 20 years. Consider the commitment and pride expressed by Kathleen Stanislawski, a staffing manager. 'I'm a 27-year 3Mer because, quite frankly, there's no reason to leave. I've had great opportunities to do different jobs and to grow a career. It's just a great company.'[21]

3 *Promote social system stability.*
   Social system stability reflects the extent to which the work environment is perceived as positive and reinforcing and conflict and change are managed effectively. Consider how 3M dealt with its financial problems in 1998. 'Even in tough times, which have now arrived because of the upheavals in Asia, 3M hasn't become a mean, miserly or miserable place to work. It's shedding about 4,500 jobs, but slowly and mostly by attrition.'[22] This strategy helped to maintain a positive work environment in the face of adversity. The company also attempts to promote stability through a promote-from-within culture, a strategic hiring policy that ensures that capable college graduates are hired in a timely manner and a redundancy policy that provides displaced workers with six months to find another job at 3M before their employment there is terminated.

4 *Shape behaviour by helping members make sense of their surroundings.*
   This function of culture helps employees understand why the organization does what it does and how it intends to accomplish its long-term goals. 3M sets expectations for innovation in a variety of ways. For example, the company employs an 'internship and co-op programme'. 3M also shapes expectations and behaviour by providing detailed career feedback to its employees. Fresh recruits are measured and evaluated against a career growth standard during their first six months to three years of employment.

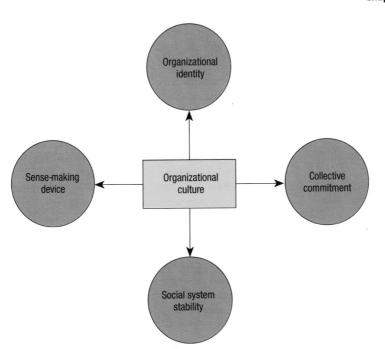

Figure 3–3

Four Functions of Organizational Culture

SOURCE: Adapted from discussion in L Smircich, 'Concepts of Culture and Organizational Analysis', *Administrative Science Quarterly*, September 1983, pp 339–58. Reproduced by permission of John Wiley & Sons, Limited.

Types of Organizational Culture

Table 3–1 *Types of Organizational Culture*

General Types of Culture	Normative Beliefs	Organizational Characteristics
Constructive	Achievement	Organizations that do things well and value members who set and accomplish their own goals. Members are expected to set challenging but realistic goals, establish plans to reach these goals, and pursue them with enthusiasm. (Pursuing a standard of excellence)
Constructive	Self-actualizing	Organizations that value creativity, quality over quantity, and both task accomplishment and individual growth. Members are encouraged to gain enjoyment from their work, develop themselves, and take on new and interesting activities. (Thinking in unique and independent ways)
Constructive	Humanistic-encouraging	Organizations that are managed in a participative and person-centered way. Members are expected to be supportive, constructive, and open to influence in their dealings with one another. (Helping others to grow and develop)
Constructive	Affiliative	Organizations that place a high priority on constructive interpersonal relationships. Members are expected to be friendly, open, and sensitive to the satisfaction of their work group. (Dealing with others in a friendly way)
Passive–defensive	Approval	Organizations in which conflicts are avoided and interpersonal relationships are pleasant—at least superficially. Members feel that they should agree with, gain the approval of, and be liked by others. ('Going along' with others)

General Types of Culture	Normative Beliefs	Organizational Characteristics
Passive–defensive	Conventional	Organizations that are conservative, traditional, and bureaucratically controlled. Members are expected to conform, follow the rules, and make a good impression. (Always following policies and practices)
Passive–defensive	Dependent	Organizations that are hierarchically controlled and nonparticipative. Centralized decision making in such organizations leads members to do only what they are told and to clear all decisions with superiors. (Pleasing those in positions of authority)
Passive–defensive	Avoidance	Organizations that fail to reward success but nevertheless punish mistakes. This negative reward system leads members to shift responsibilities to others and avoid any possibility of being blamed for a mistake. (Waiting for others to act first)
Aggressive–defensive	Oppositional	Organizations in which confrontation and negativism are rewarded. Members gain status and influence by being critical and thus are reinforced to oppose the ideas of others. (Pointing out flaws)
Aggressive–defensive	Power	Nonparticipative organizations structured on the basis of the authority inherent in members' positions. Members believe they will be rewarded for taking charge, controlling subordinates and, at the same time, being responsive to the demands of superiors. (Building up one's power base)
Aggressive–defensive	Competitive	Winning is valued and members are rewarded for outperforming one another. Members operate in a 'win-lose' framework and believe they must work against (rather than with) their peers to be noticed. (Turning the job into a contest)
Aggressive–defensive	Perfectionistic	Organizations in which perfectionism, persistence, and hard work are valued. Members feel they must avoid any mistake, keep track of everything, and work long hours to attain narrowly defined objectives. (Doing things perfectly)

SOURCE: Reproduced with permission of authors and publisher from R A Cooke and J L Szumal, 'Measuring Normative Beliefs and Shared Behavioral Expectations in Organizations: The Reliability and Validity of the Organizational Culture Inventory', *Psychological Reports*, 1993, 72, 1299–1330. © *Psychological Reports*, 1993.

Researchers have attempted to identify and measure various types of organizational culture in order to study the relationship between types of culture and organizational effectiveness. This pursuit was motivated by the possibility that certain cultures were more effective than others. Unfortunately, research has not uncovered a universal typology of cultural styles that everyone accepts.[23] Just the same, there is value in providing an example of various types of organizational culture. Table 3–1 is thus presented as an illustration rather than a definitive conclusion about the types of organizational culture that exist. Awareness of these types provides you with greater understanding about the manifestations of culture.

Table 3–1 shows that there are three general types of organizational culture: constructive; passive–defensive; and aggressive–defensive, and also that each type is associated with a different set of normative beliefs.[24] **Normative beliefs** represent an individual's thoughts and beliefs about how members of a particular group or organization are expected to approach their work and interact with others.

Normative beliefs
thoughts and beliefs about expected behaviour and modes of conduct

A *constructive culture* is one in which employees are encouraged to interact with others and to work on tasks and projects in ways that will assist them in satisfying their needs to grow and develop. This type of culture endorses normative beliefs associated with achievement, self-actualizing, humanistic-encouraging and affiliative. St Luke's, the company discussed in the opening case, could well be classified in this category. Another example is Ericsson, the Swedish manufacturer of cellular phones.

'We have a very sexy image', says Petra Remans, a regional human resource manager for the company. According to her, this is due to various factors: 'Of course the telecom-sector itself has a sexy image. It's a rapidly changing industry that brings you very close to the people. Our employees find it very important that they don't spend too much time on the same thing. They have a continuous need for new challenges. Besides being innovative, the company gives the humane aspect an important role. We attach great importance to open and 'genuine' people. Everybody at Ericsson gets the chance to develop himself and evolve in the direction he or she chooses, but they have to be team players. Development means more than just gathering knowledge for yourself. You also have to learn how to co-operate with other people and work constructively. That's also why our recruitment is very selective: we first see if the person fits into our company and only then will we look at technical abilities.'[25]

In contrast, a *passive-defensive culture* is characterized by an overriding belief that employees must interact with others in ways that do not threaten their own job security. This culture reinforces the normative beliefs associated with approval, conventionalism, dependence and avoidance (see Table 3–1).

Finally, companies with an *aggressive–defensive culture* encourage employees to approach tasks in forceful ways in order to protect their status and job security. This type of culture is more characteristic of normative beliefs reflecting opposition, power, competition and perfectionism.

Although an organization may predominately represent one cultural type, it can still manifest normative beliefs and characteristics from the others. Research demonstrates that organizations can have functional subcultures, hierarchical subcultures based on one's level in the organization, geographical subcultures, occupational subcultures based on one's title or position, social subcultures derived from social activities like a tennis or a reading club.

Different Organizations, Different Cultures

In Europe, important additions to the existing theory on organizational culture were recently made by Gareth Jones and Rob Goffee. In their book *The Character of a Corporation*, they come to an alternative conceptualization, distinguishing four organizational types, each of which reflect their own typical culture, namely the:

▼ **networked organization**

▼ **mercenary organization**

▼ **fragmented organization**

▼ **communal organization**

Further analysis of the various existing types and structures of organizations will be presented in chapter 18: Organizational Design and Effectiveness).

Jones and Goffee suggest that we can use two dimensions of social relationship to analyse culture. The first is *sociability*: affective, non-instrumental relations between individuals who may see one another as friends. A relationship is valued for its own sake and is frequently sustained through continuing face-to-face contact in which people help each other. The second dimension is *solidarity*. This describes task-centred co-operation between unlike individuals and groups. It does not depend upon close friendships or even personal acquaintance, nor is it necessarily sustained by continuous face-to-face interaction. The relationship is instrumental, arising when individuals or groups perceive a shared interest and it occurs when the need arises.

According to these professors, the combination of the above dimensions leads to four different types of organizations.

The networked organization: high sociability, low solidarity. Many employees report that working in such an environment is enjoyable. Moreover, it stimulates creativity because it fosters teamwork, information sharing and a spirit of openness to new ideas. It also encourages people to go beyond the limits of their job if they can find ways of helping their colleagues. But there are also drawbacks: poor performance may be tolerated—it's hard to discipline someone whom you see as a friend. In addition, highly sociable environments are often characterized by an exaggerated concern for consensus. In order to ensure that everyone is on board, they search for the best compromise and not necessarily the best solution. Networked companies place a high importance on recruiting comparable people—individuals who are predisposed to like each other. And training is as much about reinforcing shared norms as it is about developing people's skills.

Examples of this type include Heineken, Philips and Unilever. The industrial giant, Unilever, for instance, is internally characterized by people's willingness to work around the formal system—to get things done through informal networks. Often, these networks were cultivated by colleagues over a number of years. Moreover, it is said that the strength of Unilever's social network was in its predisposition to help colleagues to share information informally and to fit with the existing norms and values.

The mercenary organization: high solidarity, low sociability. Gareth Jones summarizes this organizational type as a culture in which the first rule of survival can be summed up in the phrase 'get to work on Sunday'. Few companies want to be seen as mercenaries, but this culture does have considerable benefits, giving organizations a high degree of strategic focus, rapid response to competitive threats and an intolerance of poor performance. Their competitors sometimes view them as tough and aggressive counterparts, known for their fighting spirit. 'If the underlying strategy of such an organization is basically sound, this degree of focus can be ruthlessly effective', says Gareth. While the networked culture tends to dwell on the ways that goals can be achieved, the mercenary culture is about getting things done—right now.

Immediate action is possible because everyone involved shares the same goal: winning. Mercenary organizations strive to achieve this external goal by setting themselves specific internal targets. They aim not to 'increase customer retention' but 'to increase customer retention by 30 per cent'.

Drawbacks of this type of organization are expressed in the fact that co-operation only occurs when an immediate advantage to all individuals and groups involved is clear. Calls for co-operation are greeted with: 'what's in it for me?' Also, roles tend to be so clearly defined that there may be persistent battles over futilities while critical tasks fall somewhere between the existing job definitions. Lastly, a dangerous aspect of mercenary cultures is that people stay only for as long as it suits them. When the going gets tough or a better offer comes along, individuals will leave. They become, in the most literal sense of the word, mercenaries. Examples of this type include Citicorp., Pepsi and Mars.

The fragmented organization: low sociability, low solidarity. This form is best suited to businesses where there are low levels of interdependence within the work process. Everybody has his or her own projects or responsibilities. Fragmented organizations often have highly detailed organization charts with many departments in which employees know exactly what is expected of them; but communication between departments is in many cases non-existent. In practice, fragmented organizations are almost anti-social, in that its members compete relentlessly against each other. On the other hand, this culture offers employees high levels of personal freedom, a major attraction for those who like control over their own time. Also, there's no other type of organization that holds so much individual top talent. You can become among the best in your industry by having the best individuals who may not cooperate with each other very much. Therefore, the greatest obsession of HR strategies in such a culture is often the recruitment and retention of the best in the relevant field. Examples of this type of organization include some academic institutions, law firms, consultancies and some newspapers.

The communal organization: high sociability, high solidarity. According to Jones and Goffee, communal organizations are sociable, like networked organizations, but far more cohesive and focused on a single goal. Yet, unlike those in mercenary organizations, people don't ask 'What's in it for me?' The communal organization is obsessed with shared values, which are sometimes written down in powerful statements but, more often, are deeply embedded in the organizational process. At the top there's mostly a strong, charismatic leader who actively promotes the vision and values throughout the company. Moreover, such firms have proved themselves to be excellent training grounds for future corporate leaders. On the negative side, communal organizations require more maintenance than other forms. For example, considerable effort and time must be taken to indoctrinate each new employee into the organization's culture. Also, the cohesiveness of such organizations can become a weakness if it makes them inattentive and thus vulnerable to changes outside their boundaries. Typical examples include Hewlett-Packard, IBM and Johnson & Johnson.[26]

Research on Organizational Cultures

Because the concept of organizational culture is a relatively recent addition to OB, the research base is incomplete. Studies to date are characterized by inconsistent definitions and varied methodologies. Quantitative treatments are sparse because there is little agreement on how to measure cultural variables.

So, what have we learned to date? First, financial performance was higher among companies that had adaptive and flexible cultures.[27] The explanation for this important relationship is discussed in the next section on developing high-performance cultures. Second, studies of mergers indicated that they frequently failed due to incompatible cultures.[28]

Due to the increasing number of corporate mergers around the world and the conclusion that seven out of ten mergers and acquisitions failed to meet their financial promise, managers within merged companies would be well advised to consider the role of organizational culture in creating a new organization.[29] The following International OB provides an example of how the management structure and culture at Deutsche Bank changed after the company merged with Bankers Trust. Once you have read the example, consider how you think the employees at Deutsche Bank will respond to Mr Breuer's proposed changes.

International OB

The Merger between Deutsche Bank and Bankers Trust Requires Cultural and Structural Change

Deutsche Bank is now run by a managing board, or Vorstand, in which a handful of executives make all the decisions by consensus. Responsibility is shared, and assigning blame is difficult. Deutsche Bank Chairman Rolf Breuler says that won't work following the merger with Bankers Trust. Instead, he is implementing what he calls 'a virtual holding company' approach, meaning a structure where different divisions are run almost like separate entities, with their own bottom lines and management boards.

'I have said that there is now an end to the Soviet Union behaviour of the central committee, where everyone is present but no-one is accountable', he says.

SOURCE: Excerpted from J L Hiday, A Raghavan, and J Sapsford, 'Sizing Up: BNP Bid Raises Issue of How Large a Bank Can Get, or Should', *The Wall Street Journal*, March 11, 1999, p A6.

Third, several studies demonstrated that organizational culture was significantly correlated with employee behaviour and attitudes. For example, a constructive culture was positively related with job satisfaction, intentions to stay at the company and innovation and was negatively associated with work avoidance. In contrast, passive–defensive and aggressive–defensive cultures were negatively correlated with job satisfaction and intentions to stay at the company.[30]

These results suggest that employees seem to prefer organizations that encourage people to interact and work with others in ways that assist them in satisfying their needs to grow and develop. Finally, results from several studies revealed that the congruence between an individual's values and the organization's values was significantly associated with organizational commitment, job satisfaction, intention to quit and turnover.[31]

These research results underscore the significance of organizational culture. They also reinforce the need to learn more about the process of cultivating and changing an organization's culture. An organization's culture is not determined by fate. It is formed and shaped by the combination and integration of everyone who works in the organization. As a case in point, a longitudinal study of 322 employees working in a US governmental organization revealed that managerial intervention successfully shifted the organizational culture toward greater participation and employee involvement. This change in organizational culture was associated with improved job satisfaction and communication across all hierarchical levels.[32]

This study further highlights the interplay between organizational culture and organizational change. Successful organizational change is highly dependent on an organization's culture.[33] A change-resistant culture, for instance, can undermine the effectiveness of any type of organizational change. Although it is not an easy task to change an organization's culture, the next section provides a preliminary overview of how this might be done.

DEVELOPING HIGH-PERFORMANCE CULTURES

An organization's culture may be strong or weak, depending on variables such as cohesiveness, value consensus and individual commitment to collective goals. Contrary to what one might suspect, a strong culture is not necessarily a good thing. The nature of the culture's central values is more important than its strength. For example, a strong but change-resistant culture may be worse, from the standpoint of profitability and competitiveness, than a weak but innovative culture. IBM is a prime example: its strong culture, coupled with a dogged determination to continually pursue a strategic plan that was out of step with the market, led to its failure to maintain its leadership in the personal computer market. This strategy ultimately costed the company about 90 billion dollars.[34]

This section discusses the types of organizational culture that enhance an organization's financial performance and the process by which cultures are embedded in an organization and learned by employees.

What Type of Cultures Enhance an Organization's Financial Performance?

Strength perspective
assumes that the strength of corporate culture is related to a firm's financial performance

Three perspectives have been proposed to explain the type of cultures that enhance an organization's economic performance. They are referred to as the strength, fit and adaptive perspectives.

1 The **strength perspective** predicts a significant relationship between strength of corporate culture and long-term financial performance. The idea is that strong cultures create goal alignment, employee motivation and the necessary structure

and controls to improve organizational performance. Critics of this perspective believe that companies with a strong culture can become arrogant, inwardly focused and bureaucratic after they achieve financial success because financial success reinforces the strong culture. This reinforcement can blind senior managers to the need for new strategic plans and may result in a general resistance to change.[35]

2   The **fit perspective** is based on the premise that an organization's culture must align with its business or strategic context. For example, a culture that promotes standardization and planning might work well in a slow-growing industry but be totally inappropriate for Internet companies that work in a highly volatile and changing environment. Likewise, a culture in which individual performance is valued might help a sales organization but would undermine performance in an organization where people work in teams. There is therefore no 'one best' culture. A culture is predicted to facilitate economic performance only if it 'fits' its context.[36]

> **Fit perspective**
> *assumes that culture must align with its business or strategic context*

3   The **adaptive perspective** assumes that the most effective cultures help organizations anticipate and adapt to environmental changes. A team of management experts defined this culture as follows.

> **Adaptive perspective**
> *assumes that adaptive cultures enhance a firm's financial performance*

An adaptive culture entails a risk-taking, trusting and proactive approach to organizational as well as individual life. Members actively support one another's efforts to identify all problems and implement workable solutions. There is a shared feeling of confidence: the members believe, without a doubt, that they can effectively manage whatever new problems and opportunities come their way. There is widespread enthusiasm, a spirit of doing whatever it takes to achieve organizational success. The members are receptive to change and innovation.[37]

This proactive adaptability is expected to enhance long-term financial performance.

A Test of the Three Perspectives

John Kotter and James Heskett tested the three perspectives on a sample of 207 companies from 22 industries for the period 1977 to 1988. After correlating results from a cultural survey and three different measures of financial performance, results partially supported the strength and fit perspectives. However, findings were completely consistent with the adaptive culture perspective. Long-term financial performance was highest for organizations with an adaptive culture.[38]

Developing an Adaptive Culture

Figure 3–4 illustrates the process of developing and preserving an adaptive culture. The process begins with leadership; that is, leaders must create and implement a business vision and associated strategies that fit the organizational context. A **vision** represents a long-term goal that describes 'what' an organization wants to become. Kevin Jenkins, former CEO of Canadian Airlines International Ltd, correctly noted, however, that the existence of a corporate vision does not guarantee organizational success.

> **Vision**
> *long-term goal describing what an organization wants to become*

'A vision held only by its leadership is not enough to create any real change,' indicated Jenkins. 'To ensure success, management must continuously—and creatively—articulate the company's vision and goals. This is achieved through open communication systems that encourage employee feedback and facilitate a two-way flow of information. Because the company's ultimate goal must be to satisfy the customer, it is imperative that employees understand what is expected of them as well as their responsibility for achieving results.'[39]

As noted by Jenkins, adaptability is promoted over time by a combination of organizational success and a specific leadership focus. Leaders must get employees to buy into a timeless philosophy or set of values that emphasizes service to the organization's key constituents—customers, stockholders and employees—and also emphasizes the improvement of leadership. An infrastructure must then be created to preserve the organization's adaptability. Management does this by consistently reinforcing and supporting the organization's core philosophy or values of satisfying constituency needs and improving leadership.

Figure 3–4

Developing and Preserving an Adaptive Culture

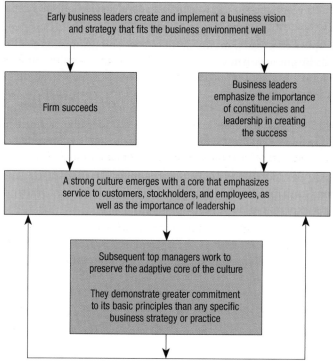

SOURCE: Adapted with permission of **The Free Press**, a division of Simon and Schuster, from *Corporate Culture and Performance* by J P Kotter and J L Heskett. Copyright © 1992 by Kotter Associates, Inc and James L Heskett.

How Cultures Are Embedded in Organizations

An organization's initial culture is an outgrowth of the founder's philosophy. For example, an achievement culture is likely to develop if the founder is an achievement-oriented individual driven by success. Over time, the original culture is either embedded as is or modified to fit the current environmental situation. Johnson & Johnson, for example, has formally documented its cherished corporate values and ideals, as conceived over four decades ago by the founder's son. The resulting Credo has helped J&J become a role model for corporate ethics.[40] Edgar Schein, a well-known OB scholar, notes that embedding a culture involves a teaching process. That is, organizational members teach each other about the organization's preferred values, beliefs, expectations and behaviours. This is accomplished by using one or more of the following mechanisms.[41]

1 *Formal statements of organizational philosophy, mission, vision, values and materials used for recruiting, selection and socialization.* Philips, for example, published a list of five corporate values, listed together with some practical ideas on how to put them into everyday practice. The five values are: delight customers ; value people as our greatest resources, deliver quality and excellence in all actions, achieve premium returns on equity and encourage entrepreneurial behaviour at all levels.[42]

2 *The design of physical space, work environments and buildings.* Consider the use of a new alternative workplace design called 'hotelling'.

   As in the other shared-office options, 'hotel' work spaces are furnished, equipped and supported with typical office services. Employees may have mobile cubbies, file cabinets or lockers for personal storage; and a computer system routes phone calls and email as necessary. But 'hotel' work spaces are reserved by the hour, by the day or by the week instead of being permanently assigned. In addition, a 'concierge' may provide employees with travel and logistic support. At its most advanced, 'hotel' work space is customized with the individuals' personal photos and memorabilia, which are stored electronically, retrieved and 'placed' on the occupants' desktops just before they arrive and then removed as soon as they leave.[43]

3 *Slogans, language, acronyms and sayings.* Philips, or example, emphasizes its concern for delivering top quality products through the slogan 'Let's make things better'. Employees are encouraged to continuously innovate to design products that are among the best and that can improve the quality of our lives. Philips's invention of the CD-player is a good illustration of this mentality. Also slogans used in job advertisements reflect the corporate culture. For instance, the Disney Corporation offers you 'dreams and imagination' and IKEA promises you 'innovation and simplicity'.[44]

4 *Deliberate role modelling, training programmes, teaching and coaching by managers and supervisors.*

5 *Explicit rewards, status symbols (such as titles) and promotion criteria.* Consider the following reward system: over a period of 31 years, Heiko H̦berle, a bodywork painter at Opel in Wanne-Eickel, Germany, was granted DM 50,000 as a result of 150 recommendations for innovations he introduced.[45]

6 *Stories, legends and myths about key people and events.* The stories in the following International OB box, for instance, are used within Tesco PLC, a leading food retailer in England, Scotland and Wales, to embed the value of providing outstanding customer service.

7 *The organizational activities, processes or outcomes that leaders pay attention to, measure and control.* Employees are much more likely to pay attention to the amount of on-time deliveries when senior management uses on-time deliveries as a measure of quality or customer service.

8 *Leader reactions to critical incidents and organizational crises.*

9 *The workflow and organizational structure.* Hierarchical structures are more likely to embed an orientation toward control and authority than a flatter organization.

10 *Organizational systems and procedures.* An organization can promote achievement and competition through the use of sales contests.

11 *Organizational goals and the associated criteria used for employee recruitment, selection, development, promotion, layoffs and retirement of people.*

International OB

Stories of Outstanding Customer Service at Tesco PLC

There was somebody who got hold of one of our assistant managers in one of our stores on a Sunday, and said 'You've got the *Sunday Times* but you haven't got the Customer Service supplement'. They went through all the *Sunday Times* and there was no Customer Service supplement. So they said, 'No problem, we'll get hold of one and get it to you'. She said 'Well I don't live that nearby and I am going out'. They took her name and address and promised to sort it out.

They rang around a few stores and eventually found one. Sure enough, when this person came in that night, there were two *Sunday Times* sitting on her doormat. She wrote to the chairman and said this was fantastic service!

SOURCE: Excerpted from T Mason, 'The Best Shopping Trip? How Tesco Keeps the Customer Satisfied', *Journal of the Market Research Society*, January 1998, p 10.

THE ORGANIZATIONAL SOCIALIZATION PROCESS

**Organizational
Socialization**

*process by which
employees learn an
organization's values,
norms and required
behaviours*

Organizational socialization is defined as 'the process by which a person learns the values, norms and required behaviours which permit him to participate as a member of the organization'.[46] As previously discussed, organization socialization is a key mechanism used by organizations to embed their organizational cultures. In short, organizational socialization turns outsiders into fully functioning insiders by promoting and reinforcing the organization's core values and beliefs. For example, at IKEA, seminars are organized to explain the company's roots and values and where the name IKEA comes from. To enhance involvement, trips are organized to the founder's birthplace in Sweden, where everything began.[47] Consider the following example of the socialization process at AZG, the Academic Hospital of Groningen, Holland.

Every month, an average of 45 'freshmen' began a new job at the Academic Hospital. From the first day of, every new employee is seen as a potential 'carrier of culture' of the AZG. An introduction programme makes them fully aware of what that means in practice. On the 'introduction day', the new employee is made aware of what is expected of him and taught important aspects of the hospital's culture, for example how patients are dealt with and how communication between doctors and nurses takes place. The hospital's main behavioural rules are outlined in the form of four principles: co-operation, customer orientation, initiative and effort. Furthermore, this introduction provides a certain amount of confidence, in that it tries to eliminate existing fears and uncertainties in the new employees. Also, it tries to create an immediate involvement with the organization: for example, a large part of the day is dedicated to making new people feel immediately at home and to know that they are welcome. Finally, this introduction day is an ideal moment for new employees to get to know each other.[48]

This section introduces a three-phase model of organizational socialization and examines the practical application of socialization research.

A Three-Phase Model of Organizational Socialization

One's first year in a complex organization can be confusing. There is a constant swirl of new faces, strange jargon, conflicting expectations and apparently unrelated events. Some organizations treat new members in a rather haphazard, sink-or-swim manner. More typically, though, the socialization process is characterized by a sequence of identifiable steps.[49]

Organizational behaviour researcher, Daniel Feldman, has proposed a three-phase model of organizational socialization that promotes deeper understanding of this important process. As illustrated in Figure 3–5, the three phases are:

▼ **anticipatory socialization**

▼ **encounter**

▼ **change and acquisition.**

Each phase has its associated perceptual and social processes. Feldman's model also specifies behavioural and affective outcomes that can be used to judge how well an individual has been socialized. The entire three-phase sequence may take from a few weeks to a year to complete, depending on individual differences and the complexity of the situation.

Phase 1: Anticipatory Socialization

Organizational socialization begins *before* the individual actually joins the organization. Anticipatory socialization information comes from many sources. Widely circulated stories about IBM being the 'white shirt' company probably deter from applying those people who would prefer to work in jeans.

Figure 3–5 *A Model of Organizational Socialization*

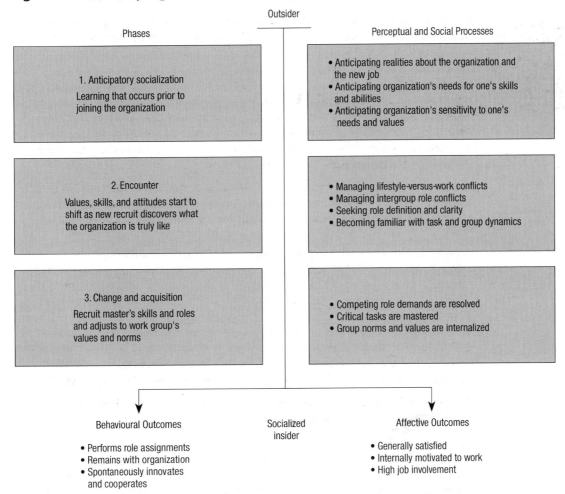

SOURCE: Adapted from material in D C Feldman, ' The Multiple Socialization of Organization Members'. *Academy of Management Review*, April 1981, pp 309–18.

All of this information—whether formal or informal, accurate or inaccurate—helps the individual anticipate organizational realities. Unrealistic expectations about the nature of the work, pay and promotions are often formulated during Phase I. Because employees with unrealistic expectations are more likely to quit their jobs in the future, organizations may want to use realistic job previews.

A **realistic job preview** (RJP) involves giving recruits a realistic idea of what lies ahead by presenting both positive and negative aspects of the job. RJPs may be verbal, in booklet form, audiovisual or hands-on. Research supports the practical benefits of using RJPs. A recent meta-analysis of 40 studies revealed that RJPs were related to higher performance and to lower attrition from the recruitment process. Results also demonstrated that RJPs lowered the initial expectations of job applicants and led to lower turnover among those who were hired.[50]

A modern trend used in many large organizations to seduce young, recently graduated people is to organize all kinds of flashy events. At these events, the company displays its mastery in its field, but at the same time, potential job applicants get a glimpse of the corporate culture. Consider the example of Barco Displays, a member of the Barco Group, manufacturing television and cinema screens.

To attract new engineers, Barco invited 500 final-year students to their own in-house movie halls. The students were shown a live show, where a famous national television

Realistic job preview
presents both positive and negative aspects of a job

presenter, complete with a microphone and a camera team, jogged through the various departments and offices of the company, shooting pictures of people at work and giving short interviews with unsuspecting employees. To convince the students that everything was live, some were given a cellular phone by which they could directly ask questions to the interviewed employees. This way, Barco could show off its technical expertise and products, but the students also got a glimpse of the company's culture. 'With this initiative, Barco has proven that its innovativeness goes way beyond the technological aspect', says the company's HR-manager. 'Also, I often hear from students that they don't really know what we're doing here. With this event, we tried to fill that gap and at the same time show them what being a Barco-employee is all about.'[51]

Phase 2: Encounter

This second phase begins once the employment contract has been signed. It is a time of surprises as the newcomer tries to make sense of unfamiliar territory. Behavioural scientists warn that reality shock can occur during the encounter phase.

> **Reality shock**
> *a newcomer's feeling of surprise after experiencing unexpected situations or events*

Becoming a member of an organization will upset the everyday order of even the most well-informed newcomer. Matters concerning such aspects as friendships, time, purpose, demeanor, competence and the expectations the person holds of the immediate and distant future are suddenly made problematic. The newcomer's most pressing task is to build a set of guidelines and interpretations to explain and make meaningful the myriad of activities observed in the organization.[52]

During the encounter phase, the individual is challenged to resolve any conflicts between the job and outside interests. If the hours prove too long, for example, family duties may require the individual to quit and find a more suitable work schedule. Also, as indicated in Figure 3–5, role conflict stemming from competing demands of different groups needs to be confronted and resolved.

Phase 3: Change and Acquisition

Mastery of important tasks and resolution of role conflict signals the beginning of this final phase of the socialization process. Those who do not make the transition to phase 3 leave voluntarily or involuntarily or become isolated from social networks within the organization. Senior executives frequently play a direct role in the change and acquisition phase.

Practical Application of Socialization Research

Past research suggests five practical guidelines for managing organizational socialization.[53]

1   Managers should avoid a haphazard, sink-or-swim approach to organizational socialization because formalized socialization tactics positively influence new recruits. Formalized socialization enhanced the manner in which newcomers adjusted to their jobs over a 10-month period and reduced role ambiguity, role conflict, stress symptoms and intentions to quit while simultaneously increasing job satisfaction and organizational commitment for a sample of 295 recently graduated students.[54]

2   The encounter phase of socialization is particularly important. Studies of newly hired accountants demonstrated that the frequency and type of information obtained during their first six months of employment significantly affected their job performance, their role clarity, their understanding of the organizational culture and the extent to which they were socially integrated.[55] Managers play a key role during the encounter phase. A recent study of 205 new college graduates further revealed that their manager's task- and relationship-oriented input during the socialization process significantly helped them to adjust to their new jobs.[56]

In summary, managers need to help new recruits to become integrated in the organizational culture.

3 Support for stage models is mixed. Although there are different stages of socialization, they are not identical in order, length or content for all people or jobs.[57] Managers are advised to use a contingency approach toward organizational socialization. In other words, different techniques are appropriate for different people at different times.

4 The organization can benefit by training new employees to use proactive socialization behaviours. A study of 154 entry-level professionals showed that effectively using proactive socialization behaviours influenced the newcomers' general anxiety and stress during the first month of employment and their motivation and anxiety six months later.[58]

5 Managers should pay attention to the socialization of diverse employees. Research demonstrated that diverse employees, particularly those with disabilities, experienced different socialization activities than other newcomers. In turn, these different experiences affected their long-term success and job satisfaction.[59]

SOCIALIZATION THROUGH MENTORING

Mentoring is defined as the process of forming and maintaining an intensive and lasting developmental relationship between a senior person (the mentor) and a junior person (the protégé, if male; or protégée, if female). The modern word *mentor* derives from Mentor, the name of a wise and trusted counsellor in Greek mythology. Terms typically used in connection with mentoring are *teacher*, *coach*, *godfather* and *sponsor*.

> **Mentoring**
> *process of forming and maintaining developmental relationships between a mentor and a junior person*

Mentoring is an important part of developing a high-performance culture for three reasons. First, mentoring contributes to the creation of a sense of oneness by promoting the acceptance of the organization's core values throughout the organization. Second, the socialization aspect of mentoring also promotes a sense of membership. Finally, mentoring increases interpersonal exchanges among organizational members.

Functions of Mentoring

Kathy Kram, a Boston University researcher, conducted in-depth interviews with both members of 18 pairs of senior and junior managers. As a by-product of this study, Kram identified two general functions—career and psychosocial—of the mentoring process (see Figure 3–6). Five *career functions* that enhanced career development were sponsorship, exposure-and-visibility, coaching, protection, and challenging assignments. Four *psychosocial functions* were role modelling, acceptance-and-confirmation, counselling and friendship. The psychosocial functions clarified the participants' identities and enhanced their feelings of competence.[60] An article in *The Guardian* described the process of socialization through mentoring as follows.

> *The first day of a new job is always the most memorable and usually the most terrifying. The best you can hope for is that someone recognizes this, takes you under his wing and patiently provides answers to your endless questions. If you're really lucky, you might even get the odd bit of sound advice as well: 'be more confident. Don't bother that guy unless you have to.'*[61]

Darryl Hartley-Leonard's experience at Hyatt Hotels exemplifies how important the career and psychosocial functions of mentoring can be to your career. Darryl started as a desk clerk at Hyatt in 1964 and rose to the position of CEO. In an interview with *The Wall Street Journal*, Hartley-Leonard indicated that his relationship with Pat Foley, the general manager who originally hired him, changed his life.

The shy Englishman, Darryl, copied his gregarious boss's style and mannerisms. He learnt from Mr Foley how to treat employees. 'People would walk through walls for him,' he says.

As Mr Foley's career prospered, so did Mr Hartley-Leonard's. When Mr Foley became the resident manager at Hyatt's first big hotel in Atlanta, he hired Mr Hartley-Leonard as a front-office supervisor. Mr Foley eventually became president and installed his protégé as executive vice president. Not surprisingly, Mr Hartley-Leonard considers mentoring a critical element in his ascent. 'If you get five people of equal ability, the one who gets mentoring will have the edge,' he says.[62]

This example also highlights the fact that both members of the mentoring relationship can benefit from these career and psychosocial functions. Mentoring is not strictly a top-down proposition, as many mistakenly believe.

Figure 3–6 *The Career and Psychosocial Functions of Mentoring*

SOURCE: Adapted from discussion in K E Kram, *Mentoring of Work: Developmental Relationships in Organizational Life* (Glenview, IL: Scott, Foresman, 1985), pp 22–39

Phases of Mentoring

In addition to identifying the functions of mentoring, Kram's research revealed four phases of the mentoring process:

▼ **initiation**

▼ **cultivation**

▼ **separation**

▼ **redefinition.**

As indicated in Table 3–2, the phases involve *variable* rather than fixed time periods. Tell-tale turning points signal the evolution from one phase to the next. For example, when a junior manager begins to resist guidance and strives to work more autonomously, the separation phase begins. The mentoring relationships in Kram's sample lasted an average of five years.

Research Evidence on Mentoring

Research findings uncovered both individual and organizational benefits of mentoring programmes. Individuals with mentors received more promotions, were more mobile, had greater career satisfaction and earned more than those without mentors.[63] The impact of mentoring on income was even more pronounced when employees were mentored by white men. For example, a study of 1,018 US MBA graduates revealed that graduates who were mentored by white men obtained an average annual compensation advantage of USD16,840 over those with mentors possessing other

Table 3–2 *Phases of the Mentor Relationship*

Phase	Definition	Turning Points*
Initiation	A period of six months to a year during which time the relationship gets started and begins to have importance for both managers.	Fantasies become concrete expectations. Expectations are met; senior manager provides coaching, challenging work, visibility; junior manager provides technical assistance, respect, and desire to be coached. There are opportunities for interaction around work tasks.
Cultivation	A period of two to five years during which time the range of career and psychosocial functions provided expand to a maximum.	Both individuals continue to benefit from the relationship. Opportunities for meaningful and more frequent interaction increase. Emotional bond deepens and intimacy increases.
Separation	A period of six months to two years after a significant change in the structural role relationship and/or the emotional experience of the relationship.	Junior manager no longer wants guidance but rather the opportunity to work more autonomously. Senior manager faces midlife crisis and is less available to provide mentoring functions. Job rotation or promotion limits opportunities for continued interaction; career and psychosocial functions can no longer be provided. Blocked opportunity creates resentment and hostility that disrupts positive interaction.
Redefinition	An indefinite period after the separation phase, during which time the relationship is ended or takes on significantly different characteristics, making it a more peerlike friendship.	Stresses of separation diminish, and new relationships are formed. The mentor relationship is no longer needed in its previous form. Resentment and anger diminish; gratitude and appreciation increase. Peer status is achieved.

*Examples of the most frequently observed psychological and organizational factors that cause movement into the current relationship phase.

SOURCE: K E Kram, 'Phases of the Mentor Relationship', *Academy of Management Journal*, December 1983, p 622. Used with permission.

demographic characteristics.[64] The same trend was found for people of colour. A sample of 170 male and female African-Americans, who graduated with either an undergraduate or MBA degree, revealed that graduates who subsequently established mentoring relationships with white males earned US$9,794 more than those without mentoring relationships. On a positive note, there were no gender-based pay differences found in this sample.[65] Mentoring inconsistently affected performance. Research revealed that ability and past experience impacted performance more than career and psychosocial mentoring.[66]

Research also supports the organizational benefits of mentoring. In addition to the obvious benefit of employee development, mentoring enhances the effectiveness of organizational communication. Specifically, mentoring increases the amount of vertical communication both up and down an organization and it provides a mechanism for modifying or reinforcing organizational culture.[67]

Research also investigated the dynamics associated with the establishment of mentoring relationships. Two key findings were uncovered. First, mentoring relationships were more likely to form when the mentor and protégé/protégée possessed similar attitudes, philosophies, personalities, interests, background and education.[68] Second, the most common cross-gender mentor relationship involved a male mentor and female protégée. This trend occurred for three reasons:

▼ **there is an under-representation of women in executive-level positions**

▼ **women perceived more negative drawbacks to becoming mentors than did men**

▼ **there are a number of individual, group and organizational barriers that inhibit mentoring relationships for diverse employees.** [69]

Getting the Most Out of Mentoring

A team of mentoring experts offered the following guidelines for implementing effective organizational mentoring programmes.[70]

1 Train mentors and protégés/protégées on how best to use career and psychosocial mentoring.

2 Use both formal and informal mentoring but do not dictate mentoring relationships.

3 Diverse employees should be informed about the benefits and drawbacks associated with establishing mentoring relationships with individuals of similar and different gender and race.

4 Women should be encouraged to mentor others but perceived barriers need to be addressed and eliminated for this to occur.

5 Increase the number of 'diverse' mentors in high-ranking positions.

Summary of Key Concepts

1 Discuss the difference between espoused and enacted values.

Espoused values represent the explicitly stated values and norms that are preferred by an organization. Enacted values, in contrast, reflect the values and norms that are actually exhibited or converted into employee behaviour. Employees become cynical when management espouses one set of values and norms and then behaves in an inconsistent fashion.

2 Explain the typology of organizational values.

The typology of organizational values identifies four types of organizational value systems. It is based on crossing organizational reward norms and organization power structures. The types of value systems include elite, meritocratic, leadership and collegial. Each type of value system contains a set of values that are both consistent and inconsistent with the underlying value system.

3 Describe the manifestations of an organization's culture and the four functions of organizational culture.

General manifestations of an organization's culture are shared objects, talk, behaviour and emotion. Four functions of organization culture are organizational identity, collective commitment, social system stability and sense-making device.

4 Discuss the three general types of organizational culture and their associated normative beliefs.

The three general types of organizational culture are constructive, passive–defensive and aggressive–defensive. Each type is grounded in different normative beliefs. Normative beliefs represent an individual's thoughts and beliefs about how members of a particular group or organization are expected to approach their work and interact with others. A constructive culture is associated with the beliefs of achievement, self-actualizing, humanistic-encouraging and affiliative. Passive–defensive organizations tend to endorse the beliefs of approval, conventional, dependent and avoidance. Aggressive–defensive cultures tend to endorse the beliefs of oppositional, power, competitive and the perfectionist.

5 Discuss the process of developing an adaptive culture.

The process begins with charismatic leadership that creates a business vision and strategy. Over time, adaptiveness is created by a combination of organizational success and the leaders' ability to get employees to buy into a philosophy or set of values of satisfying constituency needs and improving leadership. Finally, an infrastructure is created to preserve the organization's adaptiveness.

6 Summarize the methods used by organizations to embed their cultures.

Embedding a culture amounts to teaching employees about the organization's preferred values, beliefs, expectations and behaviours. This is accomplished by using one or more of the following 11 mechanisms: (a) formal statements of organizational philosophy, mission, vision, values and materials used for recruiting, selection and socialization; (b) the design of physical space, work environments and buildings; (c) slogans, language, acronyms and sayings; (d) deliberate role modelling, training programmes, teaching and coaching by managers and supervisors; (e) explicit rewards, status symbols and promotion criteria; (f) stories, legends and myths about key people and events; (g) the organizational activities, processes or outcomes that leaders pay attention to, measure and control; (h) leader reactions to critical incidents and organizational crises; (i) the workflow and organizational structure; (j) organizational systems and procedures; and (k) organizational goals and the associated criteria used for employer recruitment, selection, development, promotion, layoffs and retirement.

7 Describe the three phases in Feldman's model of organizational culture.

The three phases of Feldman's model are anticipatory socialization, encounter, and change and acquisition. Anticipatory socialization begins before an individual actually joins the organization. The encounter phase begins when the employment contract has been signed. Phase 3 involves the period in which employees master important tasks and resolve any role conflicts.

8 Discuss the two basic functions of mentoring and summarize the phases of mentoring.

Mentors help protégés in two basic functions: career and psychosocial functions. For career functions, mentors provide advice and support in regard to sponsorship, exposure and visibility, coaching, protection and challenging assignments. Psychosocial functions entail role modelling, acceptance and confirmation, counselling and friendship. There are four phases of the mentoring process: (a) initiation, (b) cultivation, (c) separation and (d) redefinition. Each phase involves variable rather than fixed periods of time and there are key activities that occur during each phase.

Discussion Questions

1 How would you respond to someone who made the following statement? 'Organizational cultures are not important as far as managers are concerned.'

2 What type of organizational culture exists within your current or most recent employer? Explain.

3 Can you think of any organizational heroes who have influenced your work behaviour? Describe them and explain how they affected your behaviour.

4 Do you know of any successful companies that do not have a positive adaptive culture? Why do you think they are successful?

5 Why is socialization essential to organizational success?

6 Have you ever had a mentor? Explain how things turned out.

7 What type of value system exists within your study group? Provide examples to support your evaluation.

Internet Exercise

This chapter focused on the role of values and beliefs in forming an organization's culture. We also discussed how cultures are embedded and reinforced through socialization and mentoring. The topic of organizational culture is big business on the Internet. Many companies use their Web pages to describe their mission, vision and corporate values and beliefs. There also are many consulting companies that advertise how they help organizations to change their cultures. The purpose of this exercise is for you to obtain information pertaining to the organizational culture of two different companies. You can go about this task by simply searching on the key words 'organizational culture' or 'corporate vision and values.' This search will identify numerous companies for you to use in answering the following questions. You may want to select a company for this exercise that you would like to work for in the future.

Questions

1 What are the organization's espoused values and beliefs?

2 Using Table 3–1 as a guide, how would you classify the organization's culture? Be sure to provide supporting evidence.

3 To what extent does the company engage in socially responsible actions?

Personal Awareness and Growth Exercise

How Does Your Current Employer Socialize Employees?

Objectives

1 To promote deeper understanding of organizational socialization processes.

2 To provide you with a useful tool for analyzing and comparing organizations.

Introduction

Employees are socialized in many different ways in today's organizations. Some organizations, such as IBM, have made an exact science out of organizational socialization. Others leave things to chance in the hope that collective goals will somehow be achieved. The questionnaire in this exercise is designed to help you gauge how widespread and systematic the socialization process is in a particular organization.

Instructions

If you are presently employed and have a good working knowledge of your organization, you can complete this questionnaire yourself. If not, identify a manager or professional (such as a corporate lawyer, engineer or nurse) and have that individual complete the questionnaire for his or her organization.

Respond to the items below as they apply to the handling of professional employees (including managers). Upon completion, compute the total score by adding up your responses. For comparison, scores for a number of strong, intermediate and weak culture firms are provided.

	Not True Of This Company		Very True Of This Company		
1 Recruiters receive at least one week of intensive training.	1	2	3	4	5
2 Recruitment forms identify severalkey traits deemed crucial to the firm's success; traits are defined in concrete terms and the interviewer records specific evidence of each trait.	1	2	3	4	5
3 Recruits are subjected to at least four in-depth interviews.	1	2	3	4	5
4 Company actively facilitates deselection during the recruiting process by revealing minuses as well as pluses.	1	2	3	4	5
5 New recruits work long hours, are exposed to intensive training of considerable difficulty and/or perform relatively menial tasks in the first months.	1	2	3	4	5
6 The intensity of entry-level experience builds cohesiveness among peers in each entering class.	1	2	3	4	5
7 All professional employees in a particular discipline begin in entry-level positions regardless of experience or advanced degrees.	1	2	3	4	5
8 Reward systems and promotion criteria require mastery of a core discipline as a precondition of advancement.	1	2	3	4	5

	Not True Of This Company		Very True Of This Company		

9 The career path for professional employees is relatively consistent over the first 6 to 10 years with the company. 1 2 3 4 5

10 Reward systems, performance incentives, promotion criteria and other primary measures of success reflect a high degree of congruence. 1 2 3 4 5

11 Virtually all professional employees can identify and articulate the firm's shared values (i.e., the purpose or mission that ties the firm to society, the customer or its employees). 1 2 3 4 5

12 There are very few instances when the actions of management appear to violate the firm's espoused values. 1 2 3 4 5

13 Employees frequently make personal sacrifices for the firm out of commitment to the firm's shared values. 1 2 3 4 5

14 When confronted with trade-offs between systems measuring short-term results and doing what's best for the company in the long term, the firm usually decides in favour of the long term. 1 2 3 4 5

15 This organization fosters mentor-protégé(e) relationships. 1 2 3 4 5

16 There is considerable similarity among high potential candidates in each particular discipline. 1 2 3 4 5

Total score = _____

For Comparative Purposes, some US examples:

Scores

Strongly socialized firms	65–80	IBM, P&G, Morgan Guaranty
	55–64	AT&T, Morgan Stanley, Delta Airlines
	45–54	United Airlines, Coca-Cola
	35–44	General Foods, PepsiCo
	25–34	United Technologies, ITT
Weakly socialized firms	Below 25	Atari

Questions for discussion

1 How strongly socialized is the organization in question? What implications does this degree of socialization have for satisfaction, commitment and turnover?

2 In examining the 16 items in the preceding questionnaire, what evidence of realistic job previews and behaviour modelling can you find? Explain.

3 What does this questionnaire say about how organizational norms are established and enforced? Frame your answer in terms of specific items in the questionnaire.

4 Using this questionnaire as a gauge, would you rather work for a strongly, moderately or weakly socialized organization?

Chapter Four

International OB: Managing Across Cultures

www.chryslercars.com

Even the best-kept corporate secrets eventually break out into the open. For Stefan Buchner, a 39-year-old purchasing director at Daimler-Benz headquarters in Stuttgart, the news came during an afternoon strategy meeting. That's when a colleague rushed in to say German radio had just reported that Daimler, the German manufacturer of Mercedez-Benz luxury cars, was on the verge of a merger with Chrysler, America's third largest car-maker. Six time zones away at Chrysler headquarters, Louise Linder's phone rang. Her contacts at Chrysler's suppliers had heard the same news and wanted the inside scoop. ▷

'Hey, I know as much as you do', she told them. Late that afternoon Linder's vice president called her into his office. Assemble your staff in the auditorium, he said. Prepare for a big announcement.

Mergers are traditionally assessed by the amount of money involved, but beneath those piles of cash are several thousand people whose lives are often up-ended when two companies put themselves together. For top executives, mergers can bring incredible riches; for bottom-rung workers toiling in plants or behind counters, changes may be imperceptible. Probably, the people in the middle face the biggest challenges. Mid-level managers are often axed to cut costs after deals; those who remain are pushed to find savings, work through culture clashes and integrate two companies into one.

While chairmen Robert Eaton and Jürgen Schrempp make grand plans for the new Daimler-Chrysler, it's up to managers like Buchner and Linder, who perform identical tasks on different sides of the Atlantic, to make the deal work. As the anniversary of their merger nears, *Newsweek* asked them to reconstruct their first year in the trenches together.

For Linder and Buchner, there are reasons for optimism. They have considerable responsibility. Each ranks one rung below vice president and together they oversee 140 employees who buy seats, steering wheels and other interior components. But unlike top officers, they haven't had to battle to preserve power or joust for the upper hand as jobs consolidate. Says Linder: 'I haven't felt any stress or anxiety about whether they're going to choose between Stefan or I.' Their careers are still on the upswing and both believe the merger puts their performance in the spotlight. 'It's a huge chance to develop my career', Buchner says. Even if they're tempted to complain, they're probably too busy. Mergers breed countless committee assignments and brutally long days. Says Linder, 'It almost feels like a second job.'

In the past year, their teams have become well acquainted. The process began at a distance. Linder spent the early summer reading up on Daimler and quizzing suppliers who'd been through mergers. In August, Buchner's team traveled to Detroit, USA where they discussed big-picture issues: how their departments are organized, how they work with suppliers to reduce prices. Until the deal was sealed in November, 'the really interesting questions were taboo', Buchner says. 'For example, what does an airbag cost here, what does it cost there?' Since then they've begun comparing and brainstorming ways to consolidate and save.

Linder and her American colleagues praise their German counterparts' skill with English (though they try to cut out slang to simplify speech when the Germans are in town). To reciprocate, many Americans are taking German lessons. They can also tick off cultural eccentricities: the Germans eat hamburgers with knives and forks and call their cell phones 'handies'. At a Detroit piano bar one night last summer, Linder's team got its biggest surprise: the Germans know all the lyrics to rock-and-roll oldies. Back in Stuttgart, the Germans have been experimenting with business casual dress. They've taken classes on cultural awareness (key points: Americans shake hands less and aren't allowed to compliment women).

As they've begun meeting with Americans more often, they're learning to understand their different decision-making style. Americans favour fast-paced, trial-and-error experimentation; Germans lay painstaking plans and implement them precisely. The potential result: 'The Americans think the Germans are stubborn militarists and the Germans think the Americans are totally chaotic', says Edith Meissner, an executive at the Sindelfingen plant. To foster compromise, Americans are encouraged to make more specific plans and Germans are urged to begin experimenting more quickly. Both sides surround workers with their sister culture. Whether this giant marriage will meet the high expectations is not certain yet but it is promised to rock the global auto industry for sure . . . .[1]

For discussion
Based on what you have just read here (and perhaps elsewhere), do you think Daimler-Chrysler will be able to blend its German and US units into a successful global competitor? Explain.

Globalization of the economy challenges virtually all employees to become more internationally aware and cross-culturally adept. The path to the top, these days, typically winds through one or more foreign assignments. A prime example is Maurits Barendrecht, one the executives of the Dutch Rabobank, who is now based at Curaçao. Barendrecht signed a 'mobility contract' for life: the bank 'kicks' him, for an ample salary, from one country to the next. In a period of eleven years, he changed his residence up to five times: moving to Madrid (starting a new branch), Montevideo (management support), Amsterdam (supervision on foreign offices) and Milan (executive officer), and finally ending up in Curaçao.[2]

Even managers and employees who stay in their native country will find it hard to escape today's global economy. Many will be thrust into international relationships by working for foreign-owned companies or by dealing with foreign suppliers, customers and co-workers. Jonathan Fenby, editor of *Business Europe*, presents the following amusing viewpoint.

Nationality means less and less in a world of unprecedented mobility where British Airways is run by an Australian; France's biggest beauty products firm by a Welshman; where Daimler embraces Chrysler; and a French-Brazilian flies off to tell Nissan how to run it's car business—and where Orange bounces between Asian, German and French ownership under the stewardship of an entrepreneur born to a British father in Germany, brought up in Canada, trained in Hong Kong and married to a Chinese wife . . . .[3]

The global economy is a rich mix of cultures, with different ideas, different ways of social conduct and different methods of organizing work. It's easy to think that people who have lived abroad or who are multilingual have global brains, while those who still live in their hometowns are parochial. But both notions are fallacies. Employees who have never left their home countries can have global brains if they are interested in the wider world around them, make an effort to learn about other people's perspectives and integrate those perspectives into their own way of thinking.[4]

Accordingly, the purpose of this chapter is to help you take a step in that direction by exploring the impacts of culture in today's increasingly internationalized organization. This chapter draws upon the area of cultural anthropology. We begin with a model that shows how societal culture and organizational culture (covered in Chapter 3) combine to influence work behaviour, followed by a fundamental cultural distinction. Next, we examine key dimensions of international OB with the goal of enhancing cross-cultural awareness. Practical lessons from cross-cultural management research are then reviewed. The chapter concludes by exploring the challenge of accepting a foreign assignment.

CULTURE AND ORGANIZATIONAL BEHAVIOUR

How would you, as a manager, interpret the following situations?

▼ **An Asian executive for a multinational company, transferred from Taiwan to the US, appears aloof and autocratic to his peers.**[5]

▼ **In Saudi Arabia, an invitation kindly asked that dogs and women be kept at home.**[6]

▼ **In Germany, an employee only wants to stay and do overtime if it's paid for and if a deadline is to be met.**[7]

If you attribute the behaviour in these situations to personalities, three descriptions come to mind: arrogant, unfriendly and disloyal to the company. These are reasonable conclusions. Unfortunately, they are probably wrong, being based more on prejudice and stereotypes than on actual fact. However, if you attribute the behavioural outcomes to *cultural* differences, you stand a better chance of making the following more valid interpretations. As it turns out:

▼ **Asian culture encourages a more distant management style.**[8]

▼ **In Muslim countries, women going out are seen as prostitutes.**[9]

▼ **In Germany overtime is exceptional as the company is seen as having no right to interfere with your private time.**[10]

One cannot afford to overlook relevant cultural contexts when trying to understand and manage organizational behaviour.

Culture is Complex and Multilayered

While noting that cultures exist in social units of all sizes (from civilizations through to countries to ethnic groups, organizations and work groups), Edgar Schein defined culture as follows.

A pattern of basic assumptions—invented, discovered or developed by a given group as it learns to cope with its problems of external adaptation and internal integration—that has worked well enough to be considered valid and, therefore, to be taught to new members as the correct way to perceive, think and feel in relation to those problems.[11]

> **Culture**
> *socially derived, taken-for-granted assumptions about how to think and act*

The word *taught* needs to be interpreted carefully because it implies formal education or training. While cultural lessons may indeed be taught in schools, religious settings and in the workplace, formal inculcation is secondary. Most cultural lessons are learned by observing and imitating role models as they go about their daily affairs, or from those observed in the media.[12]

Culture is difficult to grasp because it is multilayered. International management experts, Fons Trompenaars (from the Netherlands) and Charles Hampden-Turner (from Britain), offer the following instructive analogy in their landmark book, *Riding the Waves of Culture*.

Culture comes in layers, like an onion. To understand it you have to unpeel it layer by layer.

On the outer layer are the products of culture, like the soaring skyscrapers of Manhattan, pillars of private power, with congested public streets between them. These are expressions of deeper values and norms, in a society, that are not directly visible (values such as upward mobility, 'the more-the-better,' status, material success). The layers of values and norms are deeper within the 'onion,' and are more difficult to identify.[13]

Culture is a Subtle but Pervasive Force

Culture generally remains below the threshold of conscious awareness because it involves *taken-for-granted assumptions* about how one should perceive, think, act and feel. Cultural anthropologist Edward T. Hall put it the following way.

Since much of culture operates outside our awareness, frequently we don't even know what we know. We pick [expectations and assumptions] up in the cradle. We unconsciously learn what to notice and what not to notice, how to divide time and space, how to walk and talk and use our bodies, how to behave as men or women, how to relate to other people, how to handle responsibility, whether experience is seen as whole or fragmented. This applies to all people. The Chinese, Japanese or Arabs are each as unaware of their assumptions as we are of our own. We each assume that they're part of human nature. What we think of as 'mind' is really internalized culture.[14]

In sum, it has been said that, 'you are your culture and your culture is you'. As part of the growing sophistication of marketing practices in the global economy, companies are realizing that from this perspective, consumers from different countries need to be approached differently, or as Lucas Brenninkmeijer, CEO of the European clothes-giant C&A states: 'making clothes for a whole continent is a hard job. When it's hot enough for a bikini in Barcelona, you might need a raincoat in Rotterdam. But the weather is not really what bothers us. The real problem are all these little differences: a T-shirt of the Flintstones might be very hip for a fourteen year old in München, but completely ridiculous at a playground in Manchester.'[15]

A Model of Societal and Organizational Cultures

As illustrated in Figure 4–1, culture influences organizational behaviour in two ways. Employees bring their societal culture to work with them in the form of customs and language. Organizational culture, a by-product of societal culture, in turn affects the individual's values and ethics, attitudes, assumptions and expectations.[16]

Figure 4–1 *Cultural Influences on Organizational Behavior*

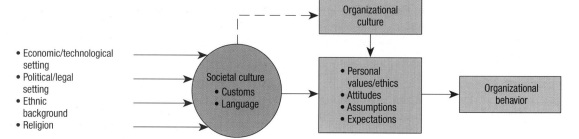

SOURCE: Adapted in part from B J Punnett and S Withane, 'Hofstede's Value Survey Module: To Embrace or Abandon?' in *Advances in International Comparative Management*, vol 5, ed S B Prasad (Greenwich, CT: JAI Press, 1990), pp 69–89.

The term societal culture is used here instead of national culture because the boundaries of many modern nation-states were not drawn along cultural lines. The former Soviet Union, for example, included 15 republics and more than 100 ethnic nationalities, many with their own distinct language.[17] Meanwhile, English-speaking Canadians in Vancouver are culturally closer to Americans in Seattle than to their French-speaking compatriots in Quebec. Societal culture is shaped by the various environmental factors listed in the left-hand side of Figure 4–1.

Once inside the organization's sphere of influence, the individual is further affected by the *organization's* culture. Mixing of societal and organizational cultures can produce interesting dynamics in multinational companies. For example, with French and American employees working side by side at General Electric's medical imaging production facility in Waukesha, Wisconsin, unit head Claude Benchimol has witnessed some culture shock.

The French are surprised that the American parking lots empty out as early as 5 p.m.; the Americans are surprised the French don't start work at 8 a.m. Benchimol feels the French are more talkative and candid. Americans have more of a sense of hierarchy and are less likely to criticize. But they may be growing closer to the French. Says Benchimol, 'It's taken a year to get across the idea that we are all entitled to say what we don't like, to become more productive and to work better.'[18]

Same company, same company culture, yet GE's French and American co-workers have different attitudes about time, hierarchy and communication. They are the products of different societal cultures.[19]

When managing people at work, the individual's societal culture, the organizational culture and any interaction between the two need to be taken into consideration.

'If buyers don't do their homework properly, you're sure to end up with a cultural catastrophe', says Valerie Lachman of M&A International, a German consulting agency

specialized in advising companies during a take-over. 'For example, when a US group bought a 180 year old, family-owned small company, it didn't take long for the deal to turn sour. The Americans used first names with everybody, spoke English and closed the canteen in the belief that staff could eat sandwiches on the run. They did not, Germans like hot lunches.' Finally, there was even a morning cheerleader session, where German staff were expected to take part and sing 'we are the best'. They did not . . . .[20]

International OB

Why your colleagues should be behind bars

In 'the City', the financial district of London, employees have a very specific way of sharing information, discussing projects or just spreading company gossip. Never mind secret memos and discrete lunches: You'll never know what's really going on in a company in 'the City' unless you frequently go to the local pub or bar with your colleges.

The many different nationalities working in London, however, have different attitudes towards this custom. Britons, Australians and Americans like to say they lead the pack when it comes to catching a pint. Some Europeans, however, prefer to stay at the office a bit longer or go straight home, even if it means losing out on the gossip.

'This pub-culture just isn't French', says Christian Lengelle from Crédit Lyonnais. 'We are not used to going to the café after work to have a drink with colleagues. But I do know some French bachelors who will join their British colleagues for a dinner of beer and peanuts.' Lengelle believes it is easier for Britons to negotiate with their partners to be allowed at least one weekly drink with workmates, because this is a part of the British culture. 'German and French employees have to struggle through lenghty conversations to convince their partners that a night at the pub is as vital for their careers as showing up on time for their meetings', he says.

'The French and the Germans like to keep their work and private lives separate', says a British analyst working at a German bank. 'They don't like contacts outside the office very much.' Americans, on the other hand, like to boast that they are good at organizing dinners with their colleagues. 'I invite the entire team for a dinner at my home to celebrate the closing of a deal', says Jeff Lubin from New York. 'This enhances trust and loyalty.'

However, drinking during working hours is another matter. London 'City' veterans often brag about the fact that they can handle a bottle of wine during a business lunch and still achieve wonders at work afterwards; but Americans pride themselves on not drinking anything during working hours, although some of them can purposefully 'let themselves go', just to be part of the group. 'Americans have a strong desire to be accepted, even if this means drinking alcohol during lunchtime, something which is not natural for them', says Jeff Lubin. 'Recently, I had lunch in "the City" with an American. He apologized to me saying 'I really can't drink a bottle of wine today'. But he quickly added that he was still recovering from his '"wet lunch" the other day.'

Keith Nelson is a manager at Matson, Driscoll & Damico, an international consulting firm. Moving from Los Angeles in the US to London proved a rough transition for him—but he would do it again if he had his life over again. 'I really don't miss the riots, the earthquakes, being shot at, you know that kind of thing.' He's been living in London for over three years now and feels comfortable there. He works longer hours in London but says the atmosphere is a lot more relaxed than 'on the other side of the pond'. He says, 'people here are less aggressive and have a lot more interests besides work.' His only complaint about working in the City is the pubs' opening hours. 'For a city the size of London, the 11 p.m. closing time is a bit antiquated.'

SOURCE: adapted from Astrid Wendlandt, 'Why your colleagues should be behind bars', *The Financial Times*, August 15, 2000 and Astrid Wendlandt, 'Life is capital on this side of the pond', *The Financial Times*, August 16, 2000.

Ethnocentrism: A Cultural Roadblock in the Global Economy

Ethnocentrism
belief that one's native country, culture, language and behaviour are superior

Ethnocentrism, the belief that one's native country, culture, language and modes of behaviour are superior to all others, has its roots in the dawn of civilization. First identified as a behavioural science concept in 1906, involving the tendency of groups to reject outsiders,[21] the term *ethnocentrism* generally has a more encompassing (national or societal) meaning today. Worldwide evidence of ethnocentrism is plentiful. For example, ethnocentrism led to deadly 'ethnic cleansing' in Bosnia and Kosovo and genocide in the African nations of Rwanda and Burundi. Less dramatic, but still troublesome, is ethnocentrism within managerial and organizational contexts. Experts on the subject framed the problem in the following way.

[Ethnocentric managers have] a preference for putting home-country people in key positions anywhere in the world and rewarding them more handsomely for work, along with a tendency to feel that this group is more intelligent, more capable or more reliable .... Ethnocentrism is often not attributable to prejudice as much as to inexperience or lack of knowledge about foreign persons and situations. This is not too surprising, since most executives know far more about employees from their home environments. As one executive put it, 'At least I understand why our own managers make mistakes. With our foreigners, I never know. The foreign managers may be better. But if I can't trust a person, should I hire him or her just to prove we're multinational?'[22]

Also, many of today's top executives are getting increasingly careful with their international contacts, in order to avoid ethnocentrism. For example, Goran Lindahl, the former chief executive of the ABB Group, who has been nominated *Industry Week's* CEO of the Year, in 1999, stated in an interview, 'In some cultures, you're not allowed to talk about interest on borrowed money. And you can say, "They are wrong", "They are crazy." They may be, or they may not be, but that's not the issue. The issue is how you can include that value in your way of managing.'[23]

And indeed, as recent research suggests, ethnocentrism is bad for business. A survey of 918 companies with home offices in the United States (272 companies), Japan (309) and Europe (337) found ethnocentric staffing and human resource policies to be associated with increased personnel problems. Those problems included recruiting difficulties, high turnover rates and lawsuits over personnel policies. Among the three regional samples, Japanese companies had the most ethnocentric human resource practices and the most international human resource problems.[24]

Current and future managers can effectively deal with ethnocentrism through education, greater cross-cultural awareness, a conscious effort to value cultural diversity and, of course, international experience. 'You go to America or Asia and you simply learn a whole lot of things you would only read about if you stayed here', says Alison Clarke, head of an Asian division of Shandwick, a British public relations group. 'We like to think that we're the centre of the universe in Britain, but we're not. I find a lot of my colleagues here are way behind in their thinking. The trouble is that they don't realise it.'[25]

High-Context and Low-Context Societal Cultures

Cultural anthropologists believe interesting and valuable lessons can be learned by comparing one culture with another. Many models have been proposed for distinguishing between the world's rich variety of cultures. One general distinction contrasts high-context and low-context cultures[26] (see Figure 4–2). Managers in multicultural settings need to know the difference if they are to communicate and interact effectively.

Figure 4-2 *Contrasting High-Context and Low-Context Cultures*

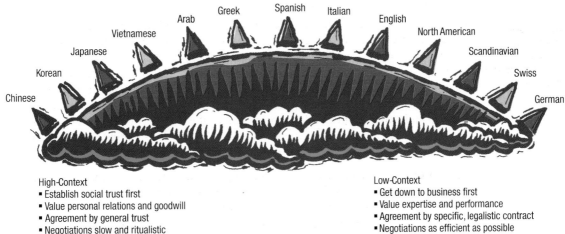

High-Context
- Establish social trust first
- Value personal relations and goodwill
- Agreement by general trust
- Negotiations slow and ritualistic

Low-Context
- Get down to business first
- Value expertise and performance
- Agreement by specific, legalistic contract
- Negotiations as efficient as possible

SOURCE: M Munter, 'Cross-Cultural Communication for Managers'. Reprinted with permission from *Business Horizons*, May–June 1993, Figure 3, p 72. Copyright © 1993 by the Board of Trustees at Indiana University, Kelley School of Business.

Reading Between the Lines in High-Context Cultures

People from high-context cultures rely heavily on situational cues for meaning, when perceiving and communicating with another person. Non-verbal cues such as one's official position or status conveys messages more powerfully than do spoken words. Thus, we come to better understand the ritual of exchanging *and reading* business cards in Japan. Japanese culture is relatively high-context. One's business card, listing employer and official position, conveys vital silent messages to members of Japan's homogeneous society. An intercultural communications authority explains:

> *Nearly all communication in Japan takes place within an elaborate and vertically organized social structure. Everyone has a distinct place within this framework. Rarely do people converse without knowing, or determining, who is above and who is below them. Associates are always older or younger, male or female, subordinate or superior. And these distinctions all carry implications for the form of address, choice of words, physical distance and demeanor. As a result, conversation tends to reflect this formal hierarchy.*[27]

Verbal and written communication in high-context cultures such as China, Korea and Japan are secondary to taken-for-granted cultural assumptions about other people.[28] In eastern Europe, business practices are more formal and decision making more hierarchical and lengthy. Titles and honorifics are important. Letters are answered late, if at all.[29]

High-context cultures
primary meaning derived from non-verbal situational cues

Reading the Fine Print in Low-Context Cultures

In low-context cultures, written and spoken words carry the burden of shared meaning. True, people in low-context cultures read non-verbal messages from body language, dress, status and belongings. However, they tend to double-check their perceptions and assumptions verbally. To do so in China or Japan would be to gravely insult the other person, thus causing them to 'lose face'.[30] Their positions on the continuum in Figure 4-2 indicate the German preoccupation with written rules for even the finest details of behaviour and the North American preoccupation with precise legal documents.[31] In high-context cultures, agreements tend to be made on the basis of someone's word or a handshake, after a rather prolonged trust-building period. European-Americans, who have been taught from birth not to take anything for granted, see the handshake as a prelude to demanding a signature on a detailed, lawyer-approved, iron-clad contract.

Low context cultures
primary meaning derived from written and spoken words

For example, this distinction between high- and low-context cultures also provides insight into the mechanisms that make negotiations between Western and Asian businesspeople so difficult and for us Europeans, often unnecessarily long-winded and boring. The Western negotiator will try to seek a rather fast agreement on the basis of an impersonal set of promises written down in a contract, whereas the Asian party would prefer to explore more fully the nature of the relationship, being distrustful of legalistic approaches to complex problems, before agreeing to commit time and resources to the venture. The Asian will rely more on the trust that grows over time so that mutual confidence can grow.[32]

In his book, *We Europeans*,[33] Richard Hill presents his Ethnic Map of Europe, which divides the continental western Europeans into two main groups, the Germanics and the Latins. Latins are identified as high context, whereas Germanics are rather low context. This implies that the Latins need no in-depth, background information because they keep themselves informed about everything through friends, family, colleagues and clients. Hence, their professional and private lives are interrelated. Germanics, on the other hand, have no informal networks and need more solid information before they go on. Their approach to life is generally segmented and compartmentalized. In eastern Europe, family and friends come first as well: rather than going through official channels to get something done, they will first network their families, friends and any personal contacts who owe them a favour.[34]

Generally speaking, one can say that in southern Europe a working day starts early in the morning and ends at lunch time, whereas a working day in northern Europe starts between 8 and 9 a.m. and end between 5 and 6 p.m.

A good indicator as to whether a country is high or low context is to check how their meetings are held.[35]

Figure 4–3 *Hill's Ethnic map of Europe*

SOURCE: R Hill, *We Europeans* (Brussels: Europublications, 1995), p 320.

- ▼ France: detailed agenda, briefing and co-ordination, interaction between the members through the boss, 15 minutes delay is acceptable.
- ▼ Germany: very formal, agenda and minutes, co-ordination and briefing, communication through a senior person, it is very important to be punctual.
- ▼ Italy: unstructured and informal, people may come and people may go, difficult to impose an agenda, free for all opinions, delay is accepted.
- ▼ Netherlands: informality of manner but nevertheless keep to the basic protocols of keeping an agenda, speaking through the chairman.
- ▼ Spain: no meetings culture, only to communicate instructions, delay is endemic.
- ▼ United Kingdom: most important and time-consuming tool, very serious, unpunctuality is the rule!

Toward Greater Cross-cultural Awareness and Competence

Aside from being high- or low-context, cultures stand apart in other ways as well.[36] Let us briefly review the following basic factors that vary from culture to culture: individualism, time, interpersonal space, language and communication.[37] This list is intended to be indicative rather than exhaustive. Separately or together these factors can foster huge cross-cultural gaps. Effective multicultural management often depends on whether or not these gaps can be bridged.

A qualification needs to be offered at this juncture. It is important to view all of the cultural differences in this chapter and elsewhere as *tendencies* and *patterns*, rather than as absolutes. As soon as one falls into the trap of assuming *all* Germans are this, *all* British are that and so on, potentially instructive generalizations become mindless stereotypes.[38]

Well-founded cultural generalizations are fundamental to successfully doing business in other cultures. But one needs to be constantly alert to individuals who are exceptions to the local cultural rule. 'People are, in practice, far more diverse than the cultural labelling allows for', warns professor Maurice Cleasby in the *British Journal of Administrative Management*.[39] For instance, it is possible to encounter talkative and aggressive Japanese people and quiet and deferential Americans neither of whom fit their respective cultural moulds. Also, tipping the scale against clear, cultural differences are space-age transportation; global telecommunications, television and computer networks; tourism; global marketing; and music and entertainment. These areas are 'homogenizing' the peoples of the world. The result, according to experts on the subject, is an emerging 'world culture' in which, someday, people may be more alike than different.[40]

Individualism versus Collectivism

Have you ever been torn between what you personally wanted and what the group, organization or society expected of you? If so, you have first-hand experience of a fundamental and important cultural distinction: individualism versus collectivism. Awareness of this distinction, as we will soon see, can spell the difference between success and failure in cross-cultural business dealings.

Individualistic cultures, characterized as 'I' and 'me' cultures, give priority to individual freedom and choice. Collectivist cultures, characterised instead as 'we' and 'us' cultures, rank shared goals higher than individual desires and goals. People in collectivist cultures are expected to subordinate their own wishes and goals to those of the relevant social unit. A worldwide survey of 30,000 managers by Trompenaars and Hampden-Turner, who prefer the term *communitarianism* to collectivism, found the

Individualistic culture
primary emphasis on personal freedom and choice

Collectivist culture
personal goals less important than community goals and interests

highest degree of individualism in Israel, Romania, Nigeria, Canada and the United States. Countries ranking lowest in individualism—thus qualifying as collectivist cultures—were Egypt, Nepal, Mexico, India and Japan. Brazil, China and France also ended up toward the collectivist end of the scale.[41]

A Business Success Factor

In our multicultural Western society, one can of course expect to encounter both individualists and collectivists. For example, imagine the frustration of Dave Murphy, an American salesperson who tried to get Navajo Indians interested in saving money for their retirement. After several fruitless meetings with groups of Navajo employees, he was given this cultural insight by a local official, 'If you come to this environment, you have to understand that money is different. It's there to be spent. If you have some, you help your family.'[42] To traditional Navajos, enculturated as collectivists, saving money is an unworthy act of selfishness. Subsequently, the sales pitch was tailored to emphasize the family benefits of individual retirement savings plans.

Allegiance to Whom?

The Navajo example raises an important point about collectivist cultures. Specifically, which unit of society predominates? For the Navajos, family is the key reference group. But, as Trompenaars and Hampden-Turner observe, important differences exist even between collectivist (or communitarian) cultures.

For each society, it is necessary to determine the group with which individuals have the closest identification. They could be keen to identify with either their trade union, family, corporation, religion, profession, nation or the state apparatus. The French tend to identify with *la France, la famille, le cadre*; the Japanese with the corporation; the former Eastern Bloc with the Communist Party; and the Irish with their Church. Communitarian goals may be good or bad for industry depending on the community concerned, its attitude and relevance to business development.[43]

Cultural Perceptions of Time

In North American and northern European cultures, time seems to be a simple matter. It is linear, relentlessly marching forward, never backward, in standardized chunks. To the German who received a watch for his or her third birthday, time is like money. It is spent, saved or wasted.[44] Americans are taught to show up 10 minutes early for appointments. When working across cultures, however, time becomes a very complex matter.[45] Imagine a Swiss person's chagrin when left in a waiting room for 45 minutes, only to find a Latin-American government official then deals with him and three other people all at once. The Swiss person resents the lack of prompt and undivided attention. The Latin-American official resents the Swiss person's impatience and apparent self-centredness.[46] This vicious cycle of resentment can be explained by the distinction between monochronic time and polychronic time.

Monochronic time
preference for doing one thing at a time because time is limited, precisely segmented and schedule driven

> *The former is revealed in the ordered, precise, schedule-driven use of public time that typifies and even caricatures efficient northern Europeans and North Americans. The latter is seen in the multiple and cyclical activities and concurrent involvement with different people in the Mediterranean, Latin American and especially Arab cultures.*[47]

A Matter of Degree

Polychronic time
preference for doing more than one thing at a time because time is flexible and multidimensional

Monochronic and polychronic are relative rather than absolute concepts. Generally, the more things a person tends to do at once, the more polychronic that person is.[48] Thanks to computers and advanced telecommunications systems, highly polychronic managers can engage in 'multitasking.'[49] For instance, it is possible to talk on the telephone, read and respond to computer email messages, print a report, check a pager message and eat a stale sandwich all at the same time. Unfortunately, this extreme polychronic behaviour is too often not as efficient as hoped and can be very stressful.

> *In a European context, we can say that, using our categories, Latins are polychronic whereas Germanics are monochronic. In other words, the first are schedule-independent and the latter schedule-dependent. In Italy, for example, if something intervenes to make you late—a meeting running overtime, a surprise meeting with someone important or an unexpected telephone call—then it is understandable. While it is impolite to arrive late for a meeting, it is even more impolite to break off the previous one because it is overrunning.*[50]

Monochronic people prefer to do one thing at a time. What is your attitude toward time? (You can find out by completing the Polychronic Attitude Index in the next OB Exercise).

Practical Implications

Low-context cultures, such as those of Northern America and northern Europe, tend to run on monochronic time while high-context cultures, such as those of Latin America and southern Europe, tend to run on polychronic time. People in polychronic cultures view time as flexible, fluid and multidimensional. The Germans and Swiss have made an exact science of monochronic time. In fact, a new radio-controlled watch made by a German company, Junghans, is 'guaranteed to lose no more than one second in 1 million years'.[51] Many a visitor has been a minute late for a Swiss train, only to see its tail lights leaving the station. Time is more elastic in polychronic cultures. During the Islamic holy month of Ramadan in the Middle East, for example, the faithful fast during daylight hours and the general pace of things markedly slows. Managers need to reset their mental clocks when doing business across cultures.

OB Exercise

The Polychronic Attitude Index

Please consider how you feel about the following statements. Circle your choice on the scale provided, showing whether you: strongly agree, agree, are neutral, disagree or strongly disagree.

	Strongly Disagree	Disagree	Neutral	Agree	Strongly Agree
I do not like to juggle several activities at the same time.	5	4	3	2	1
People should not try to do many things at once.	5	4	3	2	1
When I sit down at my desk, I work on one project at a time.	5	4	3	2	1
I am not comfortable doing several things at the same time.	5	4	3	2	1

Add up your points, and divide the total by 4. Then plot your score on the scale below.

1.0	1.5	2.0	2.5	3.0	3.5	4.0	4.5	5.0
Monochronic								Polychronic

The lower your score (below 3.0), the more monochronic your orientation; and the higher your score (above 3.0), the more polychronic.

SOURCE: A C Bluedorn, C F Kaufman, and P M Lane, 'How Many Things Do You Like to Do at Once? An Introduction to Monochronic and Polychronic Time', *Academy of Management Executive*, November 1992, Exhibit 2, p 20.

Interpersonal Space

Anthropologist Edward T. Hall noticed a connection between culture and preferred interpersonal distance. People from high-context cultures were observed standing close when talking to someone. Low-context cultures appeared to dictate a greater amount of interpersonal space. Hall applied the term **proxemics** to the study of cultural expectations about interpersonal space.[52] He specified four interpersonal distance zones. Some call them space bubbles. These distances are referred to as:

Proxemics

Hall's term for the cultural expectations about interpersonal space

▼ **intimate**

▼ **personal**

▼ **social**

▼ **public.**

Ranges for the four interpersonal distance zones are illustrated in Figure 4–3, along with selected cultural differences.

In North America or northern Europe, business conversations are normally conducted at about a metre (three to four foot) distance, within the personal zone in Figure 4–3. A range of approximately a third of a metre (one foot) is common in Latin American and Asian cultures, which is uncomfortably close for northern Europeans and North Americans. Arabs like to get even closer. Mismatches in culturally dictated interpersonal space zones can prove very distracting for the unprepared. Hall explains:

> *Arabs tend to get very close and breathe on you. It's part of the high sensory involvement of a high-context culture.*

> *The Briton on the receiving end can't identify all the sources of his discomfort but feels that the Arab is pushy. The Arab comes close, the Brit backs away. The Arab follows, because he can only interact at certain distances. Once the Briton learns that Arabs handle space differently and that breathing on people is a form of communication, the situation can sometimes be redefined so the Briton relaxes.*[53]

Asian and Middle-Eastern hosts grow weary of having to seemingly chase their low-context guests around at social gatherings to maintain what they feel is proper conversational range. Backing away all evening to keep conversational partners at a proper distance is an awkward experience as well. Awareness of cultural differences, along with skilful accommodation, are essential to productive intercultural business dealings.

Norwegians, by comparison, can be very jealous of their bubbles of space—to an extent that they even astonished an American visitor. 'One of the first things I noticed when I moved to Norway was that Norwegians need a lot of personal space', he remarked to an interviewer. 'Once I went into someone's office for an informal chat and sat down on the edge of his desk, some two metres from him! I had the direct impression that I was on his territory. Also, I have found that if one reaches out to another during a conversation, there will almost immediately be a recoil from the listener.'[54]

Language and Cross-Cultural Communication

More than 3,000 different languages are spoken worldwide. What is the connection between these languages and information processing and behaviour? There is an ongoing debate among anthropologists concerning the extent to which language influences perception and behaviour. On one side of the argument, the *relativists* claim each language fosters unique perceptions. On the other side, *universalists* state that all languages share common elements and thus foster common thought processes and perceptions.

A study involving subjects from eight countries attempted to resolve this debate. Subjects from the United States, Britain, Italy, Greece, former Yugoslavia, Pakistan, Hong Kong and Vietnam were shown 15 flash cards, each printed with three pairs of words. Language experts certified the various translations as accurate. The idea was to see if adults from different cultures, speaking different languages, would perceive the

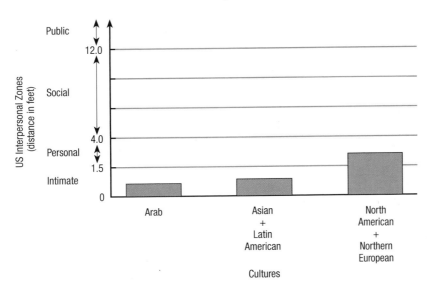

Figure 4-4

Interpersonal Distance Zones for Business Conversations Vary from Culture to Culture

same semantic elements in the paired words. Illustrative semantic elements or basic language building blocks, are as follows: opposite = alive/dead; similar = furniture/bed. The researchers found 'considerable cross-cultural agreement on the meaning and use of semantic relations'.[55] Greatest agreement was found for semantic opposites (such as alive/dead). These findings tip the scale in favor of the universalists. We await additional research evidence for a definitive answer.

If we take a closer look at language knowledge in Europe, Table 4-1 reveals that English is still the best known language throughout Europe (42 per cent). Surprisingly, however, more people know German (31 per cent) than French (29 per cent); although French is still the main second language in many schools in Europe. However, these data do not imply that those speaking one or more of the above-mentioned languages should not make any effort to learn other languages, as 58 per cent of the European population still does not understand English, with 69 per cent and 71 per cent not speaking German and French respectively. According to Nigel Brockman, human resource manager of the publishing arm of the Thomson Corporation, language skills account for part of the success of managers of smaller countries such as Belgium or Switzerland.[56]

	Bel	Dk	Ger	Gr	Sp	Fr	Ire	It	Lux	NL	Por	UK	EU12
Danish	0	100	2	0	0	0	0	0	2	0	0	0	2
Greek	0	0	0	100	0	0	0	0	2	1	0	1	3
Portuguese	1	0	0	0	2	2	0	0	4	1	100	0	3
Dutch	68	1	1	0	0	0	0	0	4	100	0	1	7
Spanish	3	2	2	0	98	10	1	2	4	3	7	3	14
Italian	3	1	1	2	1	4	1	100	15	1	1	2	18
French	70	8	9	4	9	100	14	17	90	90	16	21	29
German	16	47	99	5	1	8	4	3	90	60	1	8	31
English	34	68	35	25	13	30	100	19	46	72	20	100	42
Other	3	5	6	3	25	6	20	1	94	9	1	6	7

SOURCE: *Eurobarometer*, 1994.

Table 4-1

Percentage of People in 12 Former EC Countries Who Can Take Part in a Conversation in Another Language

Three Cross-Cultural Communication Options

Those attempting to communicate across cultures have three options:

▼ **stick to their own language**

▼ **rely on translators**

▼ **learn the local language.**

The first option, preferred by those who insist English has become the language of global business, are at a serious competitive disadvantage. Ignorance of the local language means missing subtle yet crucial meanings, risking unintended insult and jeopardizing the business transaction. For example, according to one well-travelled business writer, 'In Asia, a "yes" answer to a question simply means the question is understood. It's the beginning of negotiations. In the Middle East, the response will probably be some version of "God willing".'[57] Live translations, translations of written documents and advertisements, and computer email translations are helpful but plagued by accuracy problems.[58]

Bad translations might often be amusing, but they're potentially damaging to business. In *Management Today*, Jonah Bloom gives this example from a hotel brochure advertising holidays in the French Alps: 'The hotel has a heated of course swimming pool. Thus even by thunder weather dare to dive in and in case of likely congestion, the barmaid owning proper diplomas will help.' All very funny, until it's your brochure being read.

In business, a lack of linguistic ability can be fatal, Bloom continues, 'the most poignant story involves a UK manufacturer that went bust. When the official receivers looked through the paperwork, they found a letter in a filing cabinet, written in German. No-one at the firm had understood it, so it had been filed away with other miscellaneous correspondence. It turned out to be a purchase big enough to have saved the firm from insolvency.'[59]

Successful international managers, especially the ones from smaller countries, tell us there is no adequate substitute for knowing the local language. However, language skills account for only part of their success: linguistic skills, although important, are not the only skill needed by a cross-cultural manager. 'We have had some people from the UK who go to a continental subsidiary with hardly any knowledge of the language, but who manage to communicate', says Nicole Huyghens, a Belgian born-manager who works in Marks & Spencer's Paris office. 'It is an attitude of mind. Humility is an important quality', she says. 'You have to accept you are not going to be as confident or competent as you are in your own environment.'[60]

'In fact, every culture has its own manual', states Belle Van der Linden, a Dutch adviser specialized in attracting and selecting migrant employees. 'If you want to be successful, you have to know how people in other cultures communicate with each other. For example, if you want to hire Moroccan or Turkish girls to work in the health sector, the permission of each girl's father is essential. If you want to attract personnel from the Chinese minority in our country, you have to approach the daughters. Generally, the parents only speak Chinese and the daughters are often the key person [or link with the non-Chinese community] in a family. They are the ones that can introduce you to others in the community.'[61]

Very often, communication difficulties arise in the numerous 'marriages' between Dutch and British companies, such as Reed and Elsevier, Shell, P&O Nedlloyd and so on. The discussions between British Airways and KLM, the Dutch airways, came to nothing partly due to communication troubles. The Britons have a rather indirect style during meetings, they don't want to say things in a negative way, because this would mean loss of face for the other one. The Dutch, on the other hand, have some kind of a 'you're an idiot but don't take it personally' attitude, their style is more direct. They want to make decisions during meetings and transform them into actions; but the English do that before and after the meetings, in a private atmosphere.

'That's why diplomatic missions at Shell were always assigned to the English. For the tougher business part, the Dutch were engaged', says cross-cultural expert Fons Trompenaars. 'Britons and the Dutch have a radically different style of communicating. It's the English *stiff upper lip* versus the Dutch openness. At Shell, this caused enormous problems during meetings', he concludes.[62] (An overview of Trompenaar's main theories will be briefly given later in the chapter.)

General Guidelines for Effective Cross-Cultural Communication

Regardless of which cross-cultural communication option is used, the following four guidelines from international management scholars Philip R. Harris and Robert T. Moran are useful.

1 *No matter how hard one tries, one cannot avoid communicating.* All behaviour in human interaction has a message and communicates something. Body language communicates as well as our activity or inactivity, the colour of our skin, the colour of our clothes or the gift we give. All behaviour is communication because all behaviour contains a message, whether intended or not.

2 *Communication does not necessarily mean understanding.* Even when two individuals agree that they are communicating or talking to each other, it does not mean that they have understood each other. Understanding occurs when the two individuals have the same interpretation of the symbols being used in the communication process, whether the symbols be words or gestures.

3 *Communication is irreversible.* One cannot take back one's communication (although sometimes one wishes that one could). However, one can explain, clarify or re-state the message. Once one has communicated, it is part of his or her experience and it influences present and future meanings. Disagreeing with a Saudi Arabian in the presence of others is an 'impoliteness' in the Arab world and may be difficult to remedy.

4 *Communication occurs in a context.* One cannot ignore the context of communication that occurs at a certain time, in a certain place, using certain media. Such factors have message value and give meaning to the communicators. For example, a business conversation with a French manager in France during an evening meal may be inappropriate.[63]

Practical Insights from Cross-Cultural Management Research

Nancy Adler, an international OB specialist at Canada's McGill University, has offered the following introductory definition. '**Cross-cultural management** studies the behaviour of people in organizations around the world and trains people to work in organizations with employee and client populations from several cultures.'[64] Inherent in this definition are three steps. First, understand cultural differences; second, identify culturally appropriate management practices; and third, teach cross-cultural management lessons. The cross-cultural studies discussed in this section contribute to all three.

Cross-cultural management
understanding and teaching behavioural patterns in different cultures

The Hofstede–Bond Stream of Research

Instructive insights surfaced in the mid-1980s when the results of two very different cross-cultural management studies were merged. The first study was conducted under the guidance of Dutch researcher, Geert Hofstede. The tremendous impact his research had on the contemporary cultural thinking is reflected by the fact that Hofstede is currently the world's most cited living author in the entire area of the social sciences. Canadian Michael Harris Bond, at the Chinese University of Hong Kong, was a key researcher in the second study. What follows is a brief overview of each study, a discussion of the combined results and a summary of important practical implications.

The Two Studies

Hofstede's study is a classic in the annals of cross-cultural management research.[65] He drew his data for that study from a collection of 116,000 attitude surveys administered to IBM employees worldwide between 1967 and 1973. Respondents to the attitude survey, which also asked questions on cultural values and beliefs, included IBM employees from 72 countries. Fifty-three cultures were eventually analyzed and contrasted according to four cultural dimensions. Hofstede's database was unique, not only because of its large size, but also because it allowed him to isolate cultural effects. If his subjects had not performed similar jobs in different countries for the same company, no such control would have been possible. Cross-cultural comparisons were made along the first four dimensions listed in Table 4–2, power distance, individualism–collectivism, masculinity–femininity and uncertainty avoidance.

Bond's study was much smaller, involving a survey of 100 (50 per cent women) students from 22 countries and 5 continents. The survey instrument was the Chinese Value Survey (CVS), based on the Rokeach Value Survey.[66] The CVS also tapped four cultural dimensions. Three corresponded with Hofstede's first three in Table 4–2. Hofstede's fourth cultural dimension, uncertainty avoidance, was not measured by the CVS. Instead, Bond's study isolated the fifth cultural dimension in Table 4–2. It eventually was renamed *long-term versus short-term orientation* to reflect how strongly a person believes in the long-term thinking promoted by the teachings of the Chinese philosopher Confucius (551–479 BC). According to an update by Hofstede, 'On the long-term side one finds values oriented towards the future, like thrift (saving) and persistence. On the short-term side one finds values rather more oriented towards the past and present, like respect for tradition and fulfilling social obligations.'[67] Importantly, one may embrace Confucian long-term values without knowing a thing about Confucius.[68]

Table 4–2

Key Cultural Dimensions in the Hofstede–Bond Studies

Power distance: How much do people expect inequality in social institutions (e.g., family, work organizations, government)?
Individualism–collectivism: How loose or tight is the bond between individuals and societal groups?
Masculinity–femininity: To what extent do people embrace competitive masculine traits (e.g., success, assertiveness and performance) or nurturing feminine traits (e.g., solidarity, personal relationships, service, quality of life)?
Uncertainty avoidance: To what extent do people prefer structured versus unstructured situations?
Long-term versus short-term orientation (Confucian values): To what extent are people oriented toward the future by saving and being persistent versus being oriented toward the present and past by respecting tradition and meeting social obligations?

SOURCE: Adapted from discussion in G Hofstede, 'Cultural Constraints in Management Theories', *Academy of Management Executive*, February 1993, pp 81–94.

East Meets West

By merging the two studies, a serious flaw in each was corrected. Namely, Hofstede's study had an inherent Anglo-European bias and Bond's study had a built-in Asian bias. How would cultures compare if viewed through the overlapping lenses of the two studies? Hofstede and Bond were able to answer that question because 18 countries in Bond's study overlapped the 53 countries in Hofstede's sample.[69] Table 4–3 lists the countries scoring highest on each of the five cultural dimensions. (Countries earning between 67 and 100 points on a 0 to 100 relative ranking scale, qualified as 'high' for Table 4–2.) The United States, for example, scored the highest in individualism, moderate in power distance, masculinity and uncertainty avoidance and low in long-term orientation.

High Power Distance	High Individualism	High Masculinity	High Uncertainty Avoidance	High Long-Term Orientation*
Philippines	United States	Japan	Japan	Hong Kong***
India	Australia		Korea	Taiwan
Singapore	Great Britain		Brazil	Japan
Brazil	Netherlands		Pakistan	Korea
Hong Kong***	Canada		Taiwan	
	New Zealand			
	Sweden			
	Germany**			

Table 4–3

Countries Scoring the Highest in the Hofstede–Bond Studies

*Originally called **Confucian Dynamism.**

Former **West Germany.

***Reunited with **China.**

SOURCE: Adapted from Exhibit 2 in G Hofstede and M H Bond, 'The Confucius Connection: From Cultural Roots to Economic Growth', *Organizational Dynamics*, Spring 1988, pp 12–13.

Practical Lessons

Individually and together, the Hofstede and Bond studies yielded the following useful lessons for international managers.

1 Due to varying cultural values, management theories and practices need to be adapted to the local culture. This is particularly true for made-in-America management theories (such as Maslow's need hierarchy theory, see Chapter 7) and Japanese management practices.[70] There is no 'one best way' to manage across cultures.

2 High long-term orientation was the only one of the five cultural dimensions to correlate positively with national economic growth.

3 Industrious cultural values are a necessary but insufficient condition for economic growth. Markets and a supportive political climate are also required to create the right mix.[71]

4 Cultural arrogance is a luxury individuals and nations can no longer afford in a global economy.

Trompenaars's forms of relating to other people

In his study on cultural differences between 28 countries, Fons Trompenaars has developed five relevant dimensions[72]: universalism–particularism; individualism–collectivism; neutral–emotional; specific–diffuse; and achievement–ascription.

Universalism–Particularism

Universalism implies that what is good and right can be applied everywhere (abstract societal codes). Typical rule-based cultures are, for example, Anglo-Saxon and Scandinavian countries like the Netherlands, Germany and Switzerland. Particularist cultures, on the other hand, are more friendship-based. What counts here are relationships and unique circumstances. 'I must protect the people around me, no matter what the rules say.' Typical particularist countries are, for example, Russia, Spain and France.

In practice, we will need both judgements. For example, sometimes universalist rules have no answers to particularist problems. Hence, co-operation between people from both cultures will sometimes cause serious problems: univeralists will, for example, accuse particularists of corruption when they 'help' a friend or a family member, whereas universalists will be said to be selfish if they refuse to help an acquaintance. A very detailed contract, drawn by a universalist specifying every legal detail, is seen by the particularist as if 'he does not trust me as a business partner'. The particularist will first build a relationship with his business partner. Once mutual trust is established, a particularist considers it is not necessary to draw up a detailed contract: the relationship is the guarantee. (See table 4-4)

Table 4-4

Business Areas Affected by Universalism/ Particularism

UNIVERSALISM	PARTICULARISM
Focus is more on rules than on relationships	Focus is more on relationships than on rules
Legal contracts are readily drawn up	Legal contracts are readily modified
A trustworthy person is one who honours his or her 'word' or contract	A trustworthy person is the one who honours changing circumstances
There is only one truth or reality, that which has been agreed to	There are several perspectives on reality relative to each participant
A deal is a deal	Relationships evolve

Individualism-Collectivism

Individualist countries, such as the Netherlands and Sweden, are oriented on one's self. Collectivist countries are rather group-oriented. Think about the typical family-minded Frenchman.

Regarding oneself as an individual or as part of a group has serious influences on negotiations, on decision-making and on motivation. Pay-for-performance, for example, is welcomed in the USA, the Netherlands and the UK. More collectivist cultures, such as France, most parts of Asia and Germany, are very reluctant to follow the Anglo-Saxon pay-for-performance systems. They take offence at the idea that one's performance is related to another's deficiencies. In negotiations and decision-making, collectivists will take no decision without prior and elaborate discussions with the home front. Individualists, however, will usually take a decision on their own without the prior consent of their colleagues or bosses. As to motivation, too, individualism and collectivism play an important role. Individualists work for money rewards, collectivists rather more for positive reward and support from their colleagues (see Table 4-5) .

Table 4-5

Business Areas Affected by Individualism/ Collectivism

INDIVIDUALISM	COLLECTIVISM
More frequent use of 'I' and 'me'	More frequent use of 'we'
In negotiations, decisions typically made on the spot by a representative	Decisions typically referred back by delegate to the organization
People ideally achieve alone and assume personal responsibility	People ideally achieve in groups which assume joint responsibility
Holidays taken in pairs, or even alone	Holiday taken in organized groups or extended family

Neutral-emotional

Showing or not showing our emotion is culturally embedded. People from countries such as North America, Europe and Japan will hardly express their feelings in a first business contact, whereas people from southern countries, like Italy and France are very affective and open. Business contacts between the cultures may cause numerous misunderstandings. Neutral people are considered as having no feelings, emotional people are considered as being out of control (see Table 4-6).

EMOTIONAL	NEUTRAL
Show immediate reactions either verbally or non-verbally	Opaque emotional state
Express face and body signals	Do not readily express what they think or feel
At ease with physical contact	Embarrassed or awkward at public displays of emotions
Raise voice readily	Discomfort with physical contact outside 'private' circle
	Subtle in verbal and non-verbal expressions

Table 4–6

Business Areas Affected by Neutral/Affective Relationships

Specific–diffuse

In specific cultures home and business are strictly separated, contacts are on a contractual basis. In more diffuse cultures both worlds are interrelated, the entire person is involved. In specific-oriented cultures, the relationship you have with a person depends on the common ground you have with that person at that moment. If you are specialized in a certain area you will have 'the advantage' in that subject. If, on the other hand, the other person has more knowledge in another area, the roles will be reversed. In diffuse countries, like France, one's authority permeates each area of life. In such cultures, everything is connected to everything. In negotiations, for example, your business partner may ask for your personal background (see Table 4–7).

SPECIFIC	DIFFUSE
More 'open' public space, more closed 'private' space	More 'closed' public space but, once in, more 'open' private space
Appears direct, open and extravert	Appears indirect, closed and introvert
'To the point' and often appears abrasive Highly mobile	Often evades issues and 'beats about the bush'
Separates work and private life	Low mobility
Varies approach to fit circumstances especially with use of titles (e.g., Herr Doktor Müller at work is Hans in social environments or in certain business meetings)	Work and private life are closely linked Consistent in approach, especially with use of titles (e.g., Herr Doktor Müller remains Herr Doktor Müller in any setting)

Table 4–7

Business Areas Affected by Specific/Diffuse Relationships

Achievement–ascription

In achievement-oriented cultures, such as France, emphasis is put on what you have accomplished; in ascription-oriented cultures, your personality counts. Different countries confer status on individuals in different ways. Anglo-Saxons, for example, will ascribe status to reasons for achievement.

The following situation illustrates that cultural differences can lead to serious misunderstandings in business. A Danish paint manufacturing company wanted a large English firm to represent it in Britain. Having received encouraging signals on a first visit, the Danish managers came over a second time and were surprised by the complete lack of interest. Yet they were still not turned down. The British 'no' was finally received in a telex of three lines after a total of three visits and much wasted advance planning from the Danish end. Why didn't the English say 'no' at the start?[73]

A Contingency Model for Cross-Cultural Leadership

If a manager has a favourite leadership style in his or her own culture, will that style be equally appropriate in another culture? According to a model that built upon Hofstede's work, the answer is 'not necessarily'.[74] Four leadership styles—directive, supportive, participative and achievement—were matched with variations of three of Hofstede's cultural dimensions. The dimensions used were power distance, individualism–collectivism and uncertainty avoidance.

By combining this model with Hofstede's and Bond's findings, we derived the useful contingency model for cross-cultural leadership as set out in Table 4–8. Participative leadership turned out to be culturally appropriate for all 18 countries. Importantly, this does *not* mean that the participative style is necessarily the *best* style of leadership in cross-cultural management. It simply has broad applicability. One exception surfaced in a more recent study in Russia's largest textile mill. The researchers found that both rewarding good performance with American-made goods and motivating performance with feedback and positive reinforcement improved output. But an employee participation programme actually made performance *worse*. This may have been due to the Russians' lack of faith in participative schemes, which were found to be untrustworthy in the past.[75]

Also of note, with the exception of France, the directive or autocratic style appears to be culturally *inappropriate* in North America, northern Europe, Australia and New Zealand. Some locations, such as Hong Kong and the Philippines, require great leadership versatility. Leadership needs to be matched to the prevailing cultural climate.

Table 4–8

A Contingency Model for Cross-Cultural Leadership

Most Culturally Appropriate Leadership Behaviours

COUNTRY	DIRECTIVE	SUPPORTIVE	PARTICIPATIVE	ACHIEVEMENT
Australia		X	X	X
Brazil	X		X	
Canada		X	X	X
France	X		X	
Germany*		X	X	X
Great Britain		X	X	X
Hong Kong	X	X	X	X
India	X		X	X
Italy	X	X	X	
Japan	X	X	X	
Korea	X	X	X	
Netherlands		X	X	X
New Zealand			X	X
Pakistan	X	X	X	
Philippines	X	X	X	X
Sweden			X	X
Taiwan	X	X	X	
United States		X	X	X

*Former West Germany.

Source: Adapted in part from C A Rodrigues, 'The Situation and National Culture as Contingencies for Leadership Behaviour: Two Conceptual Models', in *Advances in International Comparative Management* vol 5, ed S B Prasad (Greenwich, CT: JAI Press, 1990), pp 51–68; and G Hofstede and M H Bond, 'The Confucius Connection: From Cultural Roots to Economic Growth', *Organizational Dynamics*, Spring 1988, pp 4–21.

Although many researchers have focused their attention on leadership differences between countries with greater cultural distance, a recent study was conducted in the United States and Germany, two close international allies and business partners. It was found that both countries differed in the transformational leadership dimensions of charisma and inspirational motivation (see Chapter 8). In this study, US employees reported a greater frequency of leadership focused on vision, a desired future, and optimism and enthusiasm in its attainability. These findings suggest that the primary difference between these two countries lies in the stronger use of charisma and inspirational leadership among US plant populations.[76] However, if we relate these findings to our Daimler-Chrysler opening case, the leadership styles of Jürgen Schrempp and Robert Eaton–the two respective chairmen of the German and the American division at that time–seem rather contrary to these results. 'Eaton was a rather introvert, silent thinker, not a consensus builder. Schrempp was a man who revelled in hearty discussions; a man who valued relationships', write Bill Vlasic and Bradley Stertz in their book *Taken for a Ride*. 'At the merger celebration, nobody sang louder, longer and more exuberantly than Schrempp. He was leading the company and the chorus, raising the rafters in song.'[77] As this example makes clear, leadership is influenced by a variety of factors of which national culture is only one: personality characteristics are also of overriding importance. (We will discuss Leadership further in Chapter 16 and Personality in Chapter 5.)

National culture and leadership profiles in Europe: some results from the GLOBE study

Today, probably the largest cross-cultural study ever on leadership profiles is the GLOBE project. Using data gathered over the last 10 years, the GLOBE team discusses similarities and differences on culture and leadership dimensions all over the world. GLOBE has evolved into a project in which some 170 investigators over 60 nations are represented. In Europe, some 21 countries are involved.

The results from their European study show that two broad clusters or patterns of leadership profiles can be distinguished, contrasting north-western and south-eastern Europe. Within these clusters, differences in leadership prototypes mirror differences in culture to a certain extent. One thing that is clear from their research is that it is hardly possible to speak of a single, typically European culture or one distinct European management style.

For example, managers in the countries of south and east Europe show high scores on the following aspects in the GLOBE: administrative competence, autocratic, conflict inducing, diplomatic, face-saving, non-participative, procedural oriented, self-centred and status conscious. In the countries of north and west Europe, the categories showing high scores, and therefore thought of as most important are: inspirational, charismatic and integrity.

The researchers place these results in the context of recent history. Managers from central and eastern Europe show a considerably less negative attitude towards autocratic management styles than do western European managers. Also, perhaps as a result of their long experience in a command economy that fostered formal and obedient behaviour through its highly bureaucratic practices and traditions, managers from this part of Europe developed a more positive attitude towards administrative skills and procedural behaviours. Furthermore, managers from south and east Europe value diplomacy in leaders more than do the European managers from the north and west.[78]

Preparing employees for successful foreign assignments

As mentioned in the opening to this chapter, foreign experience has become a necessary stepping stone in one's career development. As the reach of global companies continues to grow, many opportunities for living and working in foreign countries will arise. For example, one company who in its striving to become a worldwide force, makes increasing use of international assignments, is British Airways. 'We knew we had to globalize our company and that centred entirely on how we develop people in the business', says Fran Spencer, HR manager at the airline. 'We will know when we have got there: a third of graduate recruits will be from outside the UK, a quarter of the board will be non-UK nationals; and our own top 100 managers will have spent at least half a year of their working life outside the country'.[79]

Why Do So Many Expatriates Fail On Foreign Assignments?

Expatriate
anyone living or working in a foreign country

As we use the term here, **expatriate** refers to anyone living or working outside their home country. Hence, they are said to be expatriated when transferred to another country and repatriated when transferred back home. A recent article described European expatriates strikingly well as 'Euronomads'. According to Kevin Martin, a Scot working in Brussels, 'Euronomads are like mercenaries. They don't have a fixed spot to live, all they need is a decent laptop, the will to wander and a schedule of the Eurostar.'[80]

As an example, David Best, who works for the pan-European company Motor Care, does business all over Europe. He's been everywhere, to Sweden, Ireland, Germany and France. He does more international than national conversations—has six retirement plans running. He noticed that he's not so much appreciated for his knowledge and his managerial skills as his ability to readily adapt to different European cultures. 'There's a difference between talking French and acting French', he explains. 'The boss needs me, sometimes to play interpreter, sometimes just to inform him about specific sensitivities in certain cultures'.[81]

However, expatriate managers are usually characterized as culturally inept and prone to failure on international assignments. Sadly, research supports this view. A pair of international management experts recently offered the following assessment.

Over the past decade, we have studied the management of expatriates at about 750 US, European and Japanese companies. We asked both the expatriates themselves, and the executives who sent them abroad, to evaluate their experiences. In addition, we looked at what happened after expatriates returned home.

Overall, the results of our research were alarming. We found that between 10 and 20 per cent of all managers sent abroad returned early because of job dissatisfaction or difficulties in adjusting to a foreign country. Of those who stayed for the duration, nearly a third did not perform up to the expectations of their superiors. And perhaps most problematic, a fourth of those who completed an assignment left their company, often to join a competitor, within a year of repatriation. That turnover rate is double that of managers who did not go abroad.[82]

Because of the high cost of sending employees and their families to foreign countries for extended periods, significant improvement is needed. Research has uncovered specific reasons for the failure of expatriates. Listed in decreasing order of frequency, are the following seven most common reasons.

1   The expatriate's spouse cannot adjust to new physical or cultural surroundings.
2   The expatriate cannot adapt to new physical or cultural surroundings.
3   Family problems.
4   The expatriate is emotionally immature.
5   The expatriate cannot cope with foreign duties.
6   The expatriate is not technically competent.
7   The expatriate lacks the proper motivation for a foreign assignment.[83]

Collectively, family and personal adjustment problems, not technical competence, provide the main stumbling block for people working in foreign countries.

This conclusion is reinforced by the results of a survey that asked 72 human resource managers, at multinational corporations, to identify the most important success factor in a foreign assignment. 'Nearly 35 per cent said cultural adaptability: patience, flexibility and tolerance for others' beliefs. Only 22 per cent of them listed technical and management skills.[84] Consider what happened to Gabriëlle Rosenbaum.

In the beginning, she was thrilled with the idea of her husband's foreign assignment for Philips. As for many Dutchmen and women, a foreign assignment was equal to exotic resorts, sunshine, swimming pools, parties and recreation. The good life was in store for her and her family. Until she, her husband and their three sons left for Pakistan, where they were confronted with the everyday life of another, Islamic, culture. Others' habits, norms and values lead to serious misunderstandings. How could she reprimand her children in a public place like a restaurant? Her three sons were a gift from God, weren't they? In their next assignment, the impoverished metropolis of Bombay, misunderstanding after misunderstanding again occurred. At home, in The Netherlands, she had treated people equally, regardless of their position. Why hadn't she realized how confusing such an attitude could be in India, where society is based on castes and contrasts? 'In Bombay in particular I realized how badly I had been prepared for this assignement. For my husband it was an enormous challenge to go abroad. He had his job to do, whereas I was left on my own, nobody had cared about how I would manage with the three children.'[85]

The Global Manager

On any given day in today's global economy, a manager can interact with colleagues from several different countries or cultures. For instance, at PolyGram, the British music company, the top 33 managers are from 15 different countries.[86] If they are to be effective, managers in such multicultural situations need to develop *global* skills (see Table 4–9). Developing skilled managers who move comfortably from culture to culture takes time. Consider, for example, this comment by the head of Gillette, who wants twice as many global managers on the payroll. 'We could try to hire the best and the brightest but it's the experience with Gillette that we need. About half our [expatriates] are now on their fourth country—that kind of experience. It takes 10 years to make the kind of Gillette manager I'm talking about.'[87]

Importantly, these global skills will help managers in culturally diverse countries do a more effective job on a day-to-day basis.

Table 4–9

Global Skills for Global Managers

Skill	Description
Global perspective	Broaden focus from one or two countries to a global business perspective
Cultural responsiveness	Become familiar with many cultures
Appreciate cultural synergies	Learn the dynamics of multicultural situations
Cultural adaptability	Be able to live and work effectively in many different cultures
Cross-cultural communication	Engage in cross-cultural interaction every day, whether at home or in a foreign country
Cross-cultural collaboration	Work effectively in multicultural teams where everyone is equal
Acquire broad foreign experience	Move up the career ladder by going from one foreign country to another, instead of taking frequent home-country assignments

SOURCE: Adapted from N J Adler and S Bartholomew, 'Managing Globally Competent People', *Academy of Management Executive*, August 1992, Table 1, pp 52–65.

Avoiding OB Trouble Spots in Foreign Assignments

Finding the right person (usually along with a supportive and adventurous family) for a foreign position is a complex, time-consuming and costly process.[88] For our purposes, it is sufficient to narrow the focus to common OB trouble spots in the foreign assignment cycle. As illustrated in Figure 4–4, the first and last stages of the cycle occur at home. The middle two stages occur in the foreign or host country. Each stage hides an OB-related trouble spot that needs to be anticipated and neutralized. Otherwise, the bill for another failed foreign assignment will grow.

Figure 4–5

The Foreign Assignment Cycle (with OB Trouble Spots)

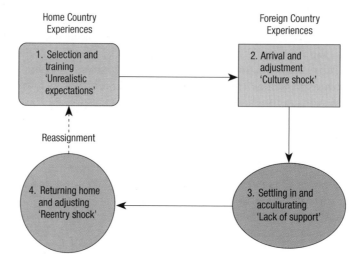

Avoiding Unrealistic Expectations with Cross-Cultural Training

Realistic job previews (RJPs) have proven effective at bringing people's unrealistic expectations about a pending job assignment down to earth by providing a realistic balance of good and bad news. People with realistic expectations tend to quit less often and be more satisfied than those with unrealistic expectations. RJPs are a must for future expatriates. In addition, cross-cultural training is required.

Cross-cultural training
structured experiences to help people adjust to a new culture or country

Cross-cultural training is any type of structured experience designed to help departing employees adjust to a foreign culture. As documented in the case at the end of the chapter, the trend is toward more such training. Although costly, companies believe cross-cultural training is less expensive than failed foreign assignments. Programmes vary widely in type and in rigour.[89] Of course, the greater the difficulty, the greater the time and expense.

▼ **Easiest:** pre-departure training is limited to informational materials, including books, lectures, films, videos and internet searches.

▼ **Moderately difficult:** experiential training is conducted through case studies, role playing, assimilators (simulated intercultural incidents) and introductory language instruction.

▼ **Most difficult:** departing employees are given some combination of the preceding methods plus comprehensive language instruction and field experience in the target culture.[90]

As an example, when a Dutch manager was assigned to start up a new Philips plant in Skierniewice, Poland, he and his wife went through an intensive 'country information-programme'. Some managers who formerly worked in Poland, such as the head of Unilever's eastern Europe division, were invited. At first, the couple could ask them some simple practical questions, such as: 'What do I have to do with a drunk employee?

Where can I find an interpreter? Why are the rents in Warschau that high? Is it safe to drink tap water?' Then they were taught some basic aspects of behaviour in Poland, such as the dos and don'ts of conversations, meetings and so on and an introduction to the Polish language.[91]

Avoiding Culture Shock

Have you ever been in a totally unfamiliar situation and felt disoriented and perhaps a bit frightened? If so, you already know something about culture shock. According to anthropologists, **culture shock** involves anxiety and doubt caused by an overload of unfamiliar expectations and social cues.[92] First year students often experience a variation of culture shock. An expatriate manager or family member may be thrown off-balance by an avalanche of strange sights, sounds and behaviours. Among them may be unreadable road signs, strange-tasting food, an inability to use your left hand for social activities (in Islamic countries, the left hand is the toilet hand) or failure to get a laugh with your sure-fire joke. For the expatriate manager trying to concentrate on the fine details of a business negotiation, culture shock is more than an embarrassing inconvenience. It is a disaster! Like the confused first-year student who quits and goes home, culture-shocked employees often panic and go home early.

> **Culture shock**
> *anxiety and doubt caused by an overload of new expectations and cues*

Even people moving to a country where they speak the same language sometimes have trouble adapting, as this British woman working in Kentucky, USA, describes: 'You never know when culture shock will bite. There you are, thinking you've got the measure of a country, you're turning out of side roads onto the proper side of the main one, you've mastered the use of "y'all" and learned not to fear doggy bags and suddenly some tiny detail turns everything on its head, reminds you that you are, after all, a stranger in a foreign country.'[93]

The best defense against culture shock is comprehensive cross-cultural training, including intensive language study. Once again, the only way to pick up subtle—yet important—social cues is via the local language.

Support During the Foreign Assignment

Especially during the first six months, when everything is so new to the expatriate, a support system needs to be in place.[94] Host-country sponsors, assigned to individual managers or families, are recommended. In a foreign country, where even the smallest errand can turn into an utterly exhausting production, sponsors can get things done quickly because they know the cultural and geographical territory.

> *Dutch Royal Shell founded two organizations which are charged with providing practical information on the living conditions abroad: a network of Shell-families for Shell-families. There is Outpost, which tries to introduce new expats to existing expats in the same area. A Spouse Employment Consultant provides information on the working conditions, recognition of degrees, work permits, and so forth.*[95]

Avoiding Re-entry Shock

Before reading on, consider the following case of Trevor Doust.

> *Trevor Doust is not angry or resentful, just a bit bewildered. Last year he was the high-flying executive vice-president of a joint venture company set up in Japan by John Crane International, the world's leading manufacturer of engineered sealing products. Today, at 50, he is back in the UK and unemployed. He didn't do anything wrong. His only mistake was being out of touch on the other side of the world when his company decided to rationalize and make changes at the top. 'If you are reasonably high up the tree,' says Doust, 'then even in a very large corporation there's a very small group back at the ranch who can be of any use to you. If they change while you're away the new guys don't know you and if at the same time they retrench a bit, you have got a real problem.'*[96]

Strange as it may seem, many otherwise successful expatriate managers encounter their first major difficulty only *after* their foreign assignment is over. Why? Returning to one's native culture is taken for granted because it seems so routine and ordinary. But having adjusted to another country's way of doing things for an extended period of time can result in putting one's own culture and surroundings in a strange new light. Three areas for potential re-entry shock are work, social activities and general environment (such as politics, climate, transportation, food).

Work-related adjustments were found to be a major problem for samples of repatriated Finnish, Japanese and American employees.[97] Upon being repatriated, a 12-year veteran of one US company said, 'Our organizational culture was turned upside down. We now have a different strategic focus, different 'tools' to get the job done and different buzzwords to make it happen. I had to learn a whole new corporate "language".[98] Re-entry shock can be reduced through employee career counselling and home-country sponsors. Simply being aware of the problem of re-entry shock is a big step toward effectively dealing with it.[99]

Overall, the key to a successful foreign assignment is making it a well-integrated link in a career chain rather than treating it as an isolated adventure.

Summary of Key Concepts

1 Explain how societal culture and organizational culture combine to influence on-the-job behaviour.

Culture involves the taken-for-granted assumptions that collections of people have about how they should think, act and feel. Key aspects of societal culture, such as customs and language, are brought to work by the individual. Working together, societal and organizational culture influence the person's values, ethics, attitudes and expectations.

2 Define ethnocentrism and distinguish between high-context and low-context cultures.

Ethnocentrism is the belief that one's native culture, language and ways of doing things are superior to all others. People from low-context cultures infer relatively less from situational cues and extract more meaning from spoken and written words. In high-context cultures, such as China and Japan, managers prefer slow negotiations and trust-building meetings, which tends to frustrate low-context northern Europeans and North Americans who prefer to get straight down to business.

3 Draw a distinction between individualistic cultures and collectivist cultures.

People in individualistic cultures think primarily in terms of 'I' and 'me' and place a high value on freedom and personal choice. Collectivist cultures teach people to be 'we' and 'us' oriented and to subordinate personal wishes and goals to the interests of the relevant social unit (such as family, group, organization or society).

4 Explain the difference between monochronic and polychronic cultures.

People in monochronic cultures are schedule-driven and prefer to do one thing at a time. To them, time is like money; it is spent wisely or wasted. In polychronic cultures, there is a tendency to do many things at once and to perceive time as flexible and multidimensional. Polychronic people view monochronic people as being too preoccupied with time.

5 Discuss the cultural implications of interpersonal space, language and religion.

Anthropologist Edward Hall coined the term *proxemics* to refer to the study of cultural expectations about interpersonal space. Asians and Latin Americans like to stand close (six inches to a foot) during business conversations, while North Americans and northern Europeans prefer a larger interpersonal distance (three to four feet). Conflicting expectations about proper interpersonal distance can create awkward cross-cultural situations. Research uncovered a high degree of agreement about semantic elements across eight cultures. Another study found no agreement about the primary work value across five different religious preference groups.

6 Describe the practical lessons from the Hofstede–Bond cross-cultural studies.

According to the Hofstede–Bond cross-cultural management studies, caution needs to be exercised when transplanting management theories and practices from one culture to another. Also, long-term orientation was the only one of five cultural dimensions in the Hofstede–Bond studies to correlate positively with national economic growth.

7 Explain what cross-cultural studies have found about leadership styles.

One cross-cultural management study suggests the need to vary leadership styles from one culture to another. The participative style turned out to be the only leadership style applicable to all 18 countries studied. Still, the participative style has its limitations and is not universally effective.

8 Specify why expatriates have a high failure rate in foreign assignments and identify the skills needed by today's global managers.

Many expatriates are troubled by family and personal adjustment problems. Experts say global managers need the following skills: a global perspective, cultural responsiveness, appreciation of cultural synergies, cultural adaptability, cross-cultural communication, cross-cultural collaboration and broad foreign experience.

9 Discuss the importance of cross-cultural training relative to the foreign assignment cycle.

The foreign assignment cycle has four stages: selection and training, arrival and adjustment, settling in and acculturating and returning home and adjusting. Cross-cultural training, preferably combining informational and experiential sessions before departure, can help expatriates avoid two OB trouble spots: unrealistic expectations and culture shock. There are no adequate substitutes for knowing the local language and culture.

Discussion Questions

1 Regarding your cultural awareness, how would you describe the prevailing culture in your country to a stranger from another land?

2 What are your personal experiences with ethnocentrism and cross-cultural dealings? What lessons have you learned?

3 Why are people from high-context cultures such as China and Japan likely to be misunderstood by low-context Westerners?

4 Culturally speaking, are you individualistic or collectivist? How does that cultural orientation affect how you run your personal and/or business affairs?

5 Based on your score on the Polychronic Attitude Index, are you relatively monochronic or polychronic? What difficulties do you encounter because of this cultural tendency?

6 In your view, what is the most important lesson for global managers from the Hofstede–Bond studies? Explain.

7 Based on your personal experience with one or more of the countries listed in Table 4–8, do you agree or disagree with the leadership profiles? Explain.

8 What needs to be done to improve the success rate of US managers in foreign assignments?

9 Which of the global manager skills in Table 4–9 do you need to develop? Explain.

10 What is your personal experience with culture shock? Which of the OB trouble spots in Figure 4–4 do you believe is the greatest threat to expatriate employee success? Explain.

Internet Exercise

www.lonelyplanet.com

Thanks to the power of the Internet, you can take a trip to a far-flung corner of the world without ever leaving your chair. The purpose of this exercise is to enhance your cross-cultural awareness by using the Internet to learn about a foreign country of your choice. Our primary resource is the Internet site www.lonelyplanet.com based on the popular, highly readable and somewhat off-beat Lonely Planet travel guides, available in bookstores. (This is our favourite but if you prefer another online travel guide, use it and tell others.) At the Lonely Planet Online home page, select *Worldguide* from the main menu. Use the geographic menus on this page to select a foreign country where your native language is not the primary language. Explore the map of your selected country and then read the material in the 'Facts at a Glance' and 'Culture' sections. If you have the time and interest, read some of the other relevant sections such as 'History,' 'Economy,' and 'Facts for the Traveller.'

A second important stop on your Internet trip is www.travlang.com to start building your language skills for your selected country. At the home page, select *travlang's*

foreign language for travellers. Then follow steps 1 and 2. Next, select *Basic Words* from the language page you picked in step 2. Practice essential words such as 'hello, yes, no, and thank you', and any others you deem necessary. Take the language quiz if you have time.

Questions

1 How strong is your interest in taking a foreign assignment in your selected country? Explain.

2 Culturally, does your focus country seem to be high-context or low-context, individualistic or collectivist and monochronic or polychronic? Cite specific clues from your Internet research.

3 How do you say 'hello' and 'thank you' in the primary language of your chosen country? (Perhaps you have a fellow student who can help you with your pronunciation.)

4 What is the likelihood of experiencing 'culture shock' in your selected country? How could you avoid or minimize it?

Personal Awareness and Growth Exercise

How Do Your Work Goals Compare Internationally?

Objectives

1 To increase your cross-cultural awareness.

2 To see how your own work goals compare internationally.

Introduction

In today's multicultural global economy, it is a mistake to assume everyone wants the same things from the job as you do. This exercise provides a 'window' on the world of work goals.

Instructions

Below is a list of 11 goals potentially attainable in the workplace. In terms of your own personal preferences, rank the goals from 1 to 11 (1 = most important; 11 = least important). After you have ranked all 11 work goals, compare your list with the national samples under the heading *Survey Results* below. These national samples represent cross sections of employees from all levels and all major occupational groups. (Please complete your ranking now, before looking at the national samples.)

How important are the following in your work life?

Rank	Work Goals
_____	A lot of opportunity to learn new things
_____	Good interpersonal relations (supervisors, co-workers)
_____	Good opportunity for upgrading or promotion
_____	Convenient work hours
_____	A lot of variety
_____	Interesting work (work that you really like)
_____	Good job security
_____	A good match between your job requirements and your abilities and experience
_____	Good pay
_____	Good physical working conditions (such as light, temperature, cleanliness, low noise level)
_____	A lot of autonomy (you decide how to do your work).**

Questions for Discussion

1 Which national profile of work goals most closely matches your own? Is this what you expected or not?

2 Are you surprised by any of the rankings in the four national samples? Explain.

3 What sorts of motivational/leadership adjustments would a manager have to make when moving among the four countries?

Survey Results**; Ranking of Work Goals by Country (1 = most important; 11 = least important)

Work Goals	United States	Britain	Germany*	Japan
Interesting work	1	1	3	2
Pay	2	2	1	5
Job security	3	3	2	4
Match between person and job	4	6	5	1
Opportunity to learn	5	8	9	7
Variety	6	7	6**	9
Interpersonal relations	7	4	4	6
Autonomy	8	10	8	3
Convenient work hours	9	5	6**	8
Opportunity for promotion	10	11	10	11
Working conditions	11	9	11	10

*Former West Germany.

** Tie

Group Exercise
Looking into a Cultural Mirror

Objectives

1 To generate group discussion about the impact of societal culture on managerial style.

2 To increase your cultural awareness.

3 To discuss the idea of a distinct style of management in your chosen country.

4 To explore the pros and cons of the style of management in your chosen country.

Introduction

A time-tested creativity technique involves 'taking something familiar and making it strange'. This technique can yield useful insights by forcing us to take a close look at things we tend to take for granted. In the case of this group exercise, the focus of your attention will be mainstream cultural tendencies in your country (or any other country you or your instructor may select) and management. A 15-minute, small-group session will be followed by brief oral presentations and a general class discussion. Total time required is about 35 to 45 minutes.

Instructions

Your instructor will divide your class randomly into small groups of five to eight. Half the teams will be designated 'red' and the other half 'green'. Each team will assign someone the role of recorder-cum-presenter, examine the cultural traits listed below and develop a cultural profile of 'that particular country's management style'. Members of each red team will explain the positive implications of each trait in their cultural profile. Green team members will explain the negative implications of the traits in their profiles.

During the brief oral presentations by the various teams, the instructor may jot down on the board or flip chart a composite cultural profile of the managers of that country. A general class discussion of positive and negative implications will follow. Note: special effort should be made to solicit comments and observations from foreign students and students who have travelled or worked in other countries. Discussion needs to focus on the appropriateness or inappropriateness of the country's cultural style of management in other countries and cultures.

As 'seed' for group discussion, here is a list of cultural traits identified by researchers;** (feel free to supplement this short list, e.g. by the traits discussed in this chapter:

- Individualistic
- Independent
- Aggressive/assertive/blunt
- Competitive
- Informal
- Pragmatic/practical
- Impatient
- Materialistic
- Unemotional/rational/objective
- Hard working.

Questions for Discussion

1 Are you surprised by anything you have just heard? Explain.

2 Is there a distinct management style? Explain.

3 Can the management style be exported easily? If it needs to be modified, how?

4 What do managers need to do to be more effective at home and in foreign countries?

Part Two

2

Individual Behaviour
in Organisations

Chapter Five

Individual Differences: Personality, Attitudes, Abilities and Emotions

Character Assignation at Liverpool Victoria

Introverts and extraverts have such different training needs that Liverpool Victoria, a company that sells insurance and pension products, devised separate development programmes for them. Tony Miller, a former group training manager at Liverpool Victoria, and Adrian Furnham, professor of psychology at the London University, set up a study at the company's telephone call centre and discovered that personality crucially affects productivity, and therefore adapted the company's policies to match their findings. ▶

'Most companies have clear policies about selection and training, believing that they know what they are doing–what to select for, how to train and, equally important, how to manage their employees. But their confidence may be misplaced', says Tony Miller. 'Few managers have done the research to back up their intuitions or, indeed, their prejudices. Such work can be expensive and time-consuming but if you want to examine the effects of training, you need sound information about people's behaviour and performance.'

Doing applied research is a way of gaining competitive advantage, Miller and Furnham found in their study at Liverpool Victoria. Call centres are one of the fastest-growing industries in the UK, already employing more than one per cent of the working population. But there is significant evidence that they are experiencing serious problems in the recruitment, selection, motivation, productivity and retention of their employees. Companies that install the latest systems for handling telephone business can be seriously handicapped if they do not have properly trained, satisfied and confident staff.

Therefore, Miller and Furnham wanted more insight into the individual characteristics of the call centre employees. They looked at a number of personality factors, and matched these against people's performance. These personality factors were:

- Extraversion or sociability: Miller and Furnham thought that being an extravert could be a double-edged sword in telesales. Extraverts are more people-oriented. This is obviously desired but there are also sensation-seekers among them who are easily bored. The physical constraints of telesales might lead to greater productivity but also to greater absenteeism.
- Negative affectivity or neuroticism: unstable people tend to be more moody, have a lower job satisfaction and tend not to get on with their colleagues and supervisors.
- Learning style: This provides four measures of how people learn—people can be classified as activists, pragmatists, theorists and reflectors.

Performance was measured in two ways: firstly, by the researchers looking at ratings from supervisors and secondly, by measuring absenteeism caused by sickness.

'The results confirmed our prediction that extraversion is a mixed blessing for work in a call centre', Miller explains. 'The extraverts were absent more often but were given higher performance ratings. But they also received a lower developmental rating from their supervisors. It could be that the supervisors perceived extraverts as good "short-hire" staff who were too easily bored or ambitious for a long career in telesales. Introverts were seen as having more potential in the long term.'

The best and most consistent predictors of success in terms of both productivity and development were found to be the learning styles. Being a reflector—that is, thoughtful, thorough and methodical—was associated with poor performance, possibly because people with this learning style are averse to taking risks and tend to hold back from direct participation.

But being a theorist was positively related to telesales success. They tend to be logical, rational, disciplined and objective. It may be their low tolerance of uncertainty, ambiguity and disorder that makes them good sales staff.

'What we were able to show was that personality variables and learning styles do statistically predict productivity at work', says Adrian Furnham. 'We are the first to admit that these are not the only factors that lead to productivity but one should not overlook the potential benefits this study has offered to Liverpool Victoria in understanding individual differences of their staff.'

The results of the study were indeed successfully fed back into recruitment, training and motivational programmes at Liverpool Victoria. The company developed a clear picture of the type of personality that would be suited to working in a call centre. This gave its recruitment process a clear focus. For jobs on the sales side, the personality profile favoured extroverts, while introverts were the preferred character type for customer service posts.

The company's approach to staff training was then extensively modified, with different programmes developed for extraverts and introverts, although both types learned the same skills.

Extraverts need to be continually stimulated and respond better to imaging and activity-based training. So participation was actively ▶

encouraged in their development programmes, backed up by the use of picture-aided visual aids. Alternatively, introverts prefer to absorb the material by reading it, rather than making presentations and participating in group work. They also react better to text-based

For discussion
Do you think this type of extensive personality research will become common in European organizations? What are the possible benefits and drawbacks of surveying all employees like this?

What makes you *you*? What characteristics do you share with others? Which ones set you apart? Perhaps you have a dynamic personality and dress accordingly, while a low-key friend dresses conservatively and avoids crowds. People's attitudes, abilities, and emotions also vary. Some computer buffs would rather surf the Internet than eat; other people suffer from computer phobia. Sometimes students who skim their reading assignments at the last moment get higher grades than those who study for days. People standing patiently in a long queue watch an angry customer shout at a store clerk. One employee consistently does more than asked, while another equally skilled employee barely does the job. Thanks to a vast array of individual differences such as these, modern organizations have a rich and interesting human texture. On the other hand, individual differences make the manager's job endlessly challenging. In fact, according to research, 'variability among workers is substantial at all levels but increases dramatically with job complexity. In life insurance sales, for example, variability in performance is around six times as great as in routine clerical jobs.'[2]

Growing workforce diversity compels managers to view individual differences in a fresh new way. The case for this new perspective was presented in Britain's *Journal of Managerial Psychology*:

> *For many years businesses sought homogeneity—a work force that believed in, supported, and presented a particular image. The notion of the company man dressed for success in the banker's blue or corporation's grey flannel suit was* de riguer. *Those able to move into leadership positions succeeded to the extent they behaved and dressed according to a rather narrowly defined standard. To compete today, and in preparation for the work force of tomorrow, successful businesses and organizations are adapting to both internal and external changes. New operational styles, language, customs, values, and even dress, are a real part of this adaptation. We now hear leaders talking about 'valuing differences' and 'learning to manage diversity'.*[3]

So rather than limiting diversity, as in the past, today's managers need to better understand and accommodate employee diversity and individual differences.[4]

This chapter explores the following important dimensions of individual differences:

▼ **self-concept**

▼ **personality traits**

▼ **attitudes**

▼ **abilities**

▼ **emotions.**

Figure 5–1 is a conceptual model showing the relationship between self-concept (how you view yourself), personality (how you appear to others), and key forms of self-expression. Considered as an integrated package, these factors provide a foundation for better understanding each organizational contributor as a unique and special individual.

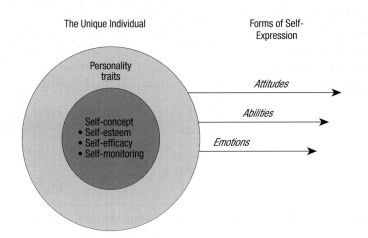

Figure 5–1
*A Conceptual Model
for the Study of
Individual
Differences in OB*

SELF-CONCEPT: THE I AND ME IN OB

Self is the core of one's conscious existence. Awareness of self is referred to as one's self-concept. Sociologist, Viktor Gecas, defines self-concept as 'the concept the individual has of himself as a physical, social, and spiritual or moral being.'[5] In other words, because you have a self-concept, you recognize yourself as a distinct human being. For example, consider how Richard Hunter, director of an Irish company, struggles to behave according to his self-concept and at the same time be a good boss.

> As a boss, 'away weekends' and Christmas lunches are the only times where you are allowed to be yourself. When I come into the office, I'm different from when I'm at home and I would like my employees to meet the Richard-at-home every now and then. Away weekends are perfect for this, but only as long as you make sure that, come Monday, it's back to work—you have to show that you are in charge of your chameleon nature. At a weekend, I'm quite happy to get a little tipsy with the rest of them but I have a policy of going to bed by 2 a.m. because that's when things start to get messy. If people are rowing drunkenly while you're in bed, it's not your responsibility.[6]

A self-concept would be impossible without the capacity to think. This brings us to the role of cognitions. Cognitions represent 'any knowledge, opinion or belief about the environment, about oneself or about one's behaviour'.[7] Among the many different types of cognitions, those involving anticipation, planning, goal setting, evaluating, and setting personal standards, are particularly relevant to OB.[8]

Several cognition-based topics are discussed in later chapters. Differing cognitive styles are introduced in this chapter. Cognitions play a central role in social perception, as will be discussed in Chapter 6. Also, as we will see in Chapters 7 and 8, modern motivation theories and techniques are powered by cognitions. Successful self-management, covered in Chapter 10, requires cognitive support.

Importantly, ideas of self and self-concept vary from one historical era to another, from one socio-economic class to another, and from culture to culture.[9] How well one detects and adjusts to different cultural notions of self can spell the difference between success and failure in international dealings.

For example, as detailed in the following International OB, Japanese−US communication and understanding is often hindered by significantly different degrees of self-disclosure. With a comparatively large public self, Americans pride themselves in being open, honest, candid and to the point [direct]. Meanwhile, Japanese people, who culturally discourage self-disclosure, typically view Americans as blunt, prying and insensitive to formalities. For their part, Americans tend to see Japanese as distant, cold and evasive.[10] One culture is not right and the other wrong. They are just different, and a key difference involves culturally rooted conceptions of self and self-disclosure.

Self-concept
person's self-perception as a physical, social, spiritual being

Cognitions
a person's knowledge, opinions or beliefs

Keeping this cultural qualification in mind, let us explore three topics invariably mentioned when behavioural scientists discuss self-concept. They are self-esteem, self-efficacy and self-monitoring. We also consider the ethical implications of organizational identification, a social aspect of self. Each of these areas deserves a closer look by those who want to better understand and effectively manage people at work.

International OB

http://japaneseculture.miningco.com

Culture Dictates the Degree of Self-Disclosure in Japan and the United States

Survey research in Japan and the United States uncovered the following *distinct contrasts* in Japanese versus American self-disclosure.

Japanese Public and Private Self

Private Self
Public Self

American Public and Private Self

Private Self
Public Self

Private self (the self not revealed to others)
Public self (the self made accessible to others)

- Americans disclosed nearly as much to strangers as the Japanese did to their own fathers.

- Americans reported two to three times greater physical contact with parents and twice greater contact with friends than the Japanese.

- The Japanese may be frightened at the prospect of being communicatively invaded (because of the unexpected spontaneity and bluntness of the American); the American is annoyed at the prospect of endless formalities and tangential replies.

- American emphasis on self-assertion and talkativeness cultivates a communicator who is highly self-oriented and expressive; the Japanese emphasis on 'reserve' and 'sensitivity' cultivates a communicator who is other-oriented [oriented toward the other person] and receptive.

Adapted from D C Barnlund, 'Public and Private Self in Communicating with Japan,' *Business Horizons*, March–April 1989, pp 32–40.

Self-Esteem: A Controversial Topic

Self-esteem
one's overall self-evaluation

Self-esteem is a belief about one's own self-worth based on an overall self-evaluation.[11] Self-esteem is measured by having survey respondents indicate their agreement or disagreement with both positive and negative statements. A positive statement on one general self-esteem survey is: 'I feel I am a person of worth, the equal of other people.'[12] Among the negative items is: 'I feel I do not have much to be proud of.'[13] Those who agree with the positive statements and disagree with the negative statements have high self-esteem. They see themselves as worthwhile, capable and acceptable. People with low self-esteem view themselves in negative terms. They do not feel good about themselves and are hampered by self-doubts.[14]

The Battle Over Self-Esteem

The subject of self-esteem has generated a good deal of controversy in recent years, particularly among educators and those seeking to help the disadvantaged.[15] While both sides generally agree that positive self-esteem is a good thing for students and youngsters, disagreement rages over how to improve self-esteem.

Feelings of self-esteem are, in fact, shaped by our circumstances and how others treat us. Researchers who surveyed 654 young adults (192 male, 462 female) over eight years found higher self-esteem among those in school or working full-time than among those with part-time jobs or unemployed.[16]

Surprising Research Insights

Is high self-esteem always a good thing? Research evidence provides both expected and surprising answers. A pair of recent studies confirmed that people with high self-esteem (HSE) handle failure better than those with low self-esteem (LSE). Specifically, when confronted with failure, HSEs drew upon their strengths and emphasized the positive whereas LSEs focused on their weaknesses and had primarily negative thoughts.[17] But in another study, HSEs tended to become egotistical and boastful when faced with pressure situations.[18] Other researchers found high levels of self-esteem associated with aggressive and even violent behaviour. Indeed, contrary to the common belief that low self-esteem and criminality go hand in hand, youth gang members and criminals often score highly on self-esteem and become violent when their inflated egos are threatened.[19] Our conclusion is that high self-esteem can be a good thing, but only if—like many other human characteristics such as creativity, intelligence and persistence—it is nurtured and channelled in constructive and ethical ways. Otherwise, it can become antisocial and destructive.[20]

Recently, the striking results of a thirty-year longitudinal study in Britain were presented. Leon Fernstein and his team, of the Centre for Economic Performance at the London School of Economics, interviewed the parents of all babies born in the UK in the first week of April 1970. The children were subsequently questioned at ages 5, 10, 16, 26 and again as they reached their 30th birthday in April 2000. Self-esteem was monitored at the age of 10 by asking the children a series of questions. Fernstein found a very close correlation between childhood self-esteem and adult success. According to Fernstein, 'there is now clear evidence that children with higher self-esteem at age 10 get as much of a kick to their adult earning power as those with equivalent higher maths or reading ability. Childhood self-esteem can overwhelm academic disadvantage or social deprivation in determining future earnings power.'[21]

Self-Esteem across Cultures

What are the cross-cultural implications for self-esteem, a concept that has been called uniquely Western? In a survey of 13,118 students from 31 countries worldwide, a moderate positive correlation was found between self-esteem and life satisfaction. But the relationship was stronger in individualistic cultures (such as the United States, Canada, New Zealand and The Netherlands) than in collectivist cultures (such as Korea, Kenya and Japan). The researchers concluded that individualistic cultures socialize people to focus more on themselves, while people in collectivist cultures 'are socialized to fit into the community and to do their duty. Thus, how a collectivist feels about himself or herself is less relevant to . . . . life satisfaction.'[22] Global managers need to remember to de-emphasize self-esteem when doing business in collectivist ('we') cultures, as opposed to emphasizing it in individualistic ('me') cultures.

Can General Self-Esteem be Improved?

The short answer is *yes*. More detailed answers come from research. A recent study led to this conclusion: 'Low self-esteem can be raised more by having the person think of *desirable* characteristics *possessed* rather than of undesirable characteristics from which he or she is free.'[23] This approach can help neutralize the self-defeating negative thoughts of LSEs, discussed earlier. (See our related discussions of the self-fulfilling prophecy in Chapter 6 and self-talk in Chapter 10.)

Organization-Based Self-Esteem

The self-esteem just discussed is a global belief about oneself. But what about self-esteem in organizations, a more restricted context of greater importance to managers? A model of organization-based self-esteem was developed and validated using seven studies involving 2,444 teachers, students, managers and employees. The researchers defined **organization-based self-esteem (OBSE)** as the 'self-perceived value that individuals have of themselves as organization members acting within an organizational context'.[24]

> **Organization-based self-esteem (OBSE)**
> *an organization member's self-perceived value*

Those scoring high on OBSE tend to view themselves as important, worthwhile, effectual and meaningful within the context of their employing organization. Take a moment to complete the brief OBSE questionnaire in the OB Exercise. This exercise will help you better understand the concept of organization-based self-esteem, as well as assessing the supportiveness of your work setting.

OB Exercise

How Strong is your OBSE?

Instructions

Relative to your present (or last) job, how strongly do you agree or disagree with each of the following statements?

	Strongly Disagree — Strongly Agree		Strongly Disagree — Strongly Agree
1 I count around here.	1–2–3–4–5	**6** I can make a difference around here.	1–2–3–4–5
2 I am taken seriously around here.	1–2–3–4–5	**7** I am valuable around here.	1–2–3–4–5
3 I am important around here.	1–2–3–4–5	**8** I am helpful around here.	1–2–3–4–5
4 I am trusted around here.	1–2–3–4–5	**9** I am efficient around here.	1–2–3–4–5
5 There is faith in me around here.	1–2–3–4–5	**10** I am co-operative around here.	1–2–3–4–5
	Total score = _____		Total score = _____

Arbitrary norms for comparison purposes are: Low OBSE = 10–20; Moderate OBSE = 21–39; High OBSE = 40–50.

Adapted from discussion in J L Pierce, D G Gardner, L L Cummings, and R B Dunham, 'Organization-Based Self-Esteem: Construct Definition, Measurement, and Validation,' *Academy of Management Journal*, September 1989, pp 622–48.

A basic model of OBSE is displayed in Figure 5–2. On the left side of the model are three primary determinants of organization-based self-esteem. OBSE tends to increase when employees believe their supervisors have a genuine concern for employees' welfare. Flexible, organic organization structures generate higher OBSE than do mechanistic (rigid bureaucratic) structures (the organic–mechanistic distinction is discussed in Chapter XX). Complex and challenging jobs foster higher OBSE than do simple, repetitive and boring jobs. Significantly, these same factors are also associated with greater task motivation.

Factors positively influenced by high OBSE and negatively impacted by low OBSE are listed in the right side of Figure 5–2. Intrinsic motivation refers to personal feelings of accomplishment. *Citizenship behaviour* involves doing things that are beneficial to the organization itself. The other consequences of OBSE are self-explanatory. In sum, active enhancement of organization-based self-esteem promises to build a very important cognitive bridge to greater productivity and satisfaction.[25]

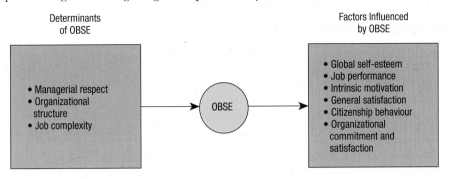

Figure 5-2

The Determinants and Consequences of Organization-Based Self-Esteem (OBSE)

Practical Tips for Building On-the-Job Self-Esteem

According to a study by the Society for Human Resource Management, managers can build employee self-esteem in four ways.

1 Be supportive by showing concern for personal problems, interests, status and contributions.

2 Offer work involving variety, autonomy, and challenges that suit the individual's values, skills and abilities.

3 Strive for management–employee cohesiveness and build trust. (Trust, an important teamwork element, is discussed in Chapter 13.)

4 Have faith in each employee's self-management ability (see Chapter 10). Reward each success.[26]

Self-Efficacy

Have you noticed how those who are confident about their ability tend to succeed, while those who are preoccupied with failing tend to fail? At the heart of this performance mismatch is a specific dimension of self-esteem called self-efficacy. Self-efficacy is a person's belief about his or her chances of successfully accomplishing a specific task. According to one OB writer, 'Self-efficacy arises from the gradual acquisition of complex cognitive, social, linguistic, and/or physical skills through experience.'[27] To gain a better understanding of what this concept entails, carefully read the following examples.

> According to the Briton, James Dyson, the founder of Dyson Appliances:
> *'The key to success is failure. Not other people's failure but how you respond to failure yourself. Everyone gets knocked back, no-one rises smoothly to the top without hindrance. The ones who succeed are the ones who say, right, let's give it another go. Who cares what others think? I believe in what I'm doing. I will never give up. Success is made up of 99 per cent failure. You galvanize yourself and you keep going.'*[28]

> In 1998, Lamin Jusu Jarka was a security officer for Barclays Bank in Freetown, Sierra Leone, when members of the Revolutionary United Front came to enforce their 'Operation No Living Thing'. They tried to take a 14-year-old girl but he helped her escape. He paid the price for his courage: they forced his arms against a mango tree and chopped of both his hands. Two years later, he gave a remarkable interview for the UK newspaper, The Independent:
> *'Do you want to see what I can do?' lively Jarka asked, holding up the two metal claws where his hands had once been. 'They thought by doing this they would make me helpless but I have learnt to do all kinds of chores again. They thought they would destroy my mind but I have learnt to write again. Watch.'*[29]

Self-efficacy
belief in one's ability to do a task

The relationship between self-efficacy and performance is a cyclical one. Efficacy → performance cycles can spiral upward toward success or downward toward failure.[30] Researchers have documented in naval cadets a strong linkage between high self-efficacy expectations and success in widely varied physical and mental tasks, anxiety reduction, addiction control, pain tolerance, illness recovery and avoidance of seasickness.[31] In contrast, those with low self-efficacy expectations tend to have low success rates. Chronically low self-efficacy is associated with a condition called **learned helplessness**, the severely debilitating belief that one has no control over one's environment.[32] Although self-efficacy sounds like some sort of mental magic, it operates in a very straightforward manner.

learned helplessness
debilitating lack of faith in one's ability to control the situation

What Are the Mechanisms of Self-Efficacy?

A basic model of self-efficacy is displayed in Figure 5–3. It draws upon the work of the US' Stanford University psychologist, Albert Bandura. Let us explore this model with a simple illustrative task. Imagine you have been told to prepare and deliver a 10-minute talk to an OB class of 50 students on the workings of the self-efficacy model in Figure 5–3. Your self-efficacy calculation would involve cognitive appraisal of the interaction between your perceived capability and the situational opportunities and obstacles.

As you begin to prepare for your presentation, the four sources of self-efficacy beliefs would come into play. Because prior experience is the most potent source, according to Bandura, it is listed first and connected to self-efficacy beliefs with a solid line.[33] Past success in public speaking would boost your self-efficacy. But bad experiences with delivering speeches would foster low self-efficacy. Regarding behaviour models as a source of self-efficacy beliefs, you would be influenced by the success or failure of your classmates in delivering similar talks. Their successes would tend to bolster you (or perhaps their failure would, if you were very competitive and had high self-esteem). Likewise, any supportive persuasion from your classmates that you will do a good job would enhance your self-efficacy. Physical and emotional factors might also affect your self-confidence. A sudden case of laryngitis or a bout of stage fright could cause your self-efficacy expectations to plunge. Your cognitive evaluation of the situation would then yield a self-efficacy belief—ranging from high to low expectations for success. Importantly, self-efficacy beliefs are not merely boastful statements based on bravado; they are deep convictions supported by experience.

Moving to the *behavioural patterns* portion of Figure 5–3, we see how self-efficacy beliefs are acted out. In short, if you have high self-efficacy about giving your 10-minute speech you will work harder, more creatively and longer when preparing for your talk than will your low self-efficacy classmates. The results would then take shape accordingly. People programme themselves for success or failure by enacting their self-efficacy expectations. Positive or negative results subsequently become feedback for one's base of personal experience. Bob Schmonsees, a US software entrepreneur, is an inspiring example of the successful route through Figure 5–3.

A contender in mixed-doubles tennis and a former football star, Mr Schmonsees was standing near a ski lift when an out-of-control skier rammed him. His legs were paralysed. He would spend the rest of his life in a wheelchair. Fortunately, he discovered a formula for his different world: figure out the new rules for any activity, then take as many small steps as necessary to master those rules. After learning the physics of a tennis swing on wheels and the geometry of playing a second bounce (standard rules), he became the world's top wheelchair player over 40.[34]

Figure 5-3 *A Model of How Self-Efficacy Beliefs Can Pave the Way for Success or Failure*

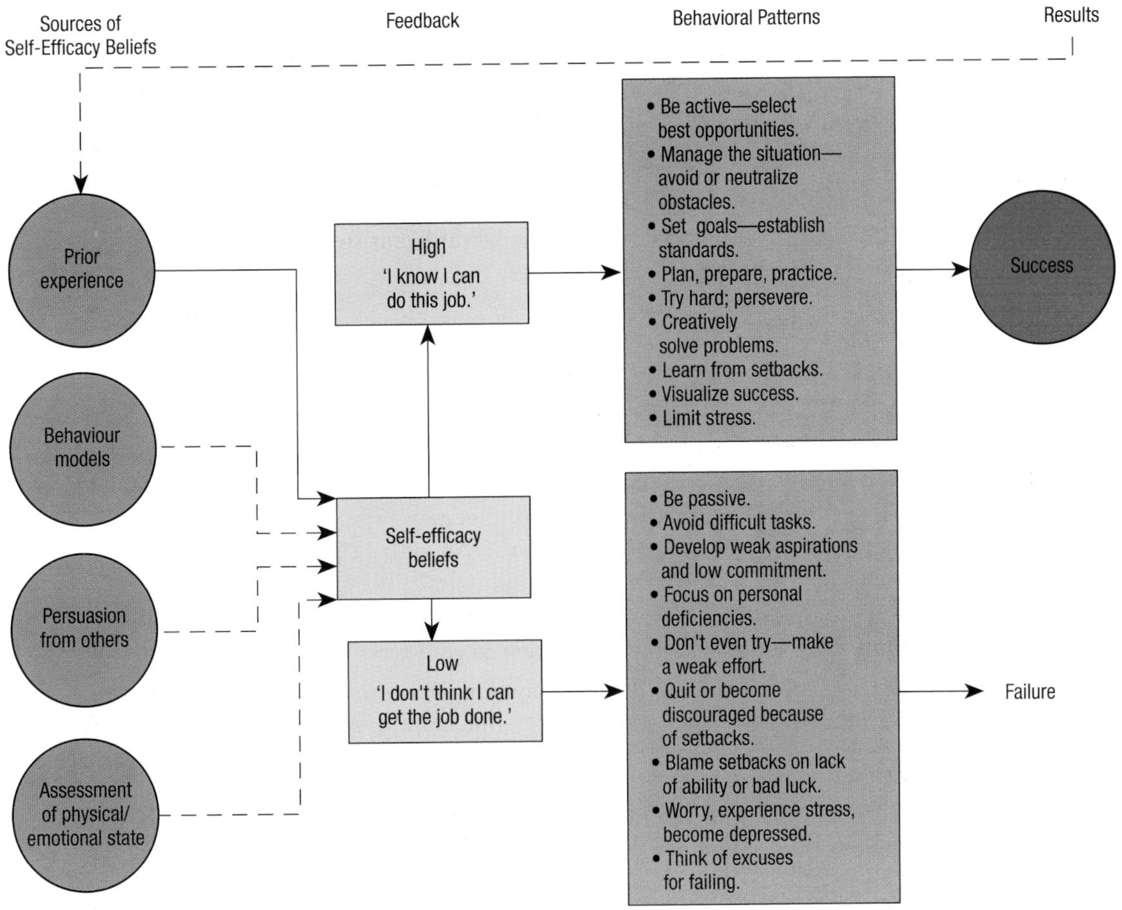

Source: Adapted from discussion in A Bandura, 'Regulation of Cognitive Processes through Perceived Self-Efficacy', *Developmental Psychology*, September 1989, pp 729–35: and R Wood and A Bandura, 'Social Cognitive Theory of Organizational Management,' *Academy of Managment Review*, July 1989, pp 361–84.

Self-Efficacy Implications for Managers

On-the-job research evidence encourages managers to nurture self-efficacy, both in themselves and in others. In fact, a recent meta-analysis encompassing 21,616 participants found a significant positive correlation between self-efficacy and job performance.[35] Self-efficacy requires constructive action in each of the following eight managerial areas.

1 *Recruiting/selection/job assignments.* Interview questions can be designed to probe job applicants' general self-efficacy as a basis for determining orientation and training needs. Pencil-and-paper tests for self-efficacy are not in an advanced stage of development and validation. Care needs to be taken not to hire solely on the basis of self-efficacy because studies have detected below-average self-esteem and self-efficacy among women and protected minorities.[36]

2 *Job design.* Complex, challenging and autonomous jobs tend to enhance perceived self-efficacy.[37] Boring, tedious jobs generally do the opposite.

3 *Training and development.* Employees' self-efficacy expectations for key tasks can be improved through guided experiences, mentoring and role modelling.[38]

4 *Self-management.* Systematic self-management training, as discussed in Chapter 10, involves enhancement of self-efficacy expectations.[39]

5 *Goal setting and quality improvement.* Goal difficulty needs to match the individual's perceived self-efficacy.[40] As self-efficacy and performance improve, goals and quality standards can be made more challenging.

6 *Coaching.* Those with low self-efficacy, and employees victimized by learned helplessness, need lots of constructive pointers and positive feedback.[41]

7 *Leadership.* The necessary leadership talent surfaces when top management gives high self-efficacy managers a chance to prove themselves under pressure.

8 *Rewards.* Small successes need to be rewarded as stepping-stones to a stronger self-image and greater achievements.

Self-Monitoring

Consider the following contrasting scenarios.

1 You are rushing to an important meeting when a co-worker pulls you aside and starts to discuss a personal problem. You want to break off the conversation, so you glance at your watch. He keeps talking. You say, 'I'm late for a big meeting.' He continues. You turn and start to walk away. The person keeps talking as if they never received any of your verbal and non-verbal signals that the conversation was over.

2 Same situation. Only this time, when you glance at your watch, the person immediately says, 'I know, you've got to go. Sorry. We'll talk later.'

In the first, all-too-familiar scenario, you are talking to a 'low self-monitor'. The second scenario involves a 'high self-monitor.' But more is involved here than an irritating situation. A significant and measurable individual difference in self-expression behaviour, called self-monitoring, is highlighted. **Self-monitoring** is the extent to which a person observes their own self-expressive behaviour and adapts it to the demands of the situation. Experts on the subject offer this explanation:

> **Self-monitoring**
> *observing one's own behaviour and adapting it to the situation*

Individuals high in self-monitoring are thought to regulate their expressive self-presentation for the sake of desired public appearances, and thus to be highly responsive to social and interpersonal cues of situationally appropriate performances. Individuals low in self-monitoring are thought to lack either the ability or the motivation to so regulate their expressive self-presentations. Their expressive behaviours, instead, are thought to functionally reflect their own enduring and momentary inner states, including their attitudes, traits and feelings.[42]

In organizational life, both high and low monitors are subject to criticism. High self-monitors are sometimes called *chameleons*, who readily adapt their self-presentation to their surroundings. Low self-monitors, on the other hand, are often criticized for being on their own planet and insensitive to others. Importantly, within an OB context, self-monitoring is like any other individual difference, not a matter of right or wrong or good versus bad but rather a source of diversity that needs to be adequately understood by present and future managers.

A Matter of Degree

Self-monitoring is not an either–or proposition. It is a matter of degree; a matter of being relatively high or low in terms of related patterns of self-expression. The following OB Exercise is designed to assess your self-monitoring tendencies. It can help you better understand your*self*. Take a short break from your reading to complete the 10-item survey. Does your score surprise you in any way? Are you unhappy with the way you present yourself to others? What are the ethical implications of your score (particularly with regard to items 9 and 10)?

OB Exercise

what are your self-monitoring tendencies?

Instructions

In an honest self-appraisal, mark each of the following statements as true (T) or false (F), and then consult the scoring key.

_____ 1 I reckon I put on a show to impress or entertain others.

_____ 2 In a group of people, I am rarely the centre of attention.

_____ 3 In different situations and with different people, I often act like very different people.

_____ 4 I would not change my opinions (or the way I do things) in order to please someone or win their favour.

_____ 5 I have considered being an entertainer.

_____ 6 I have trouble changing my behaviour to suit different people and different situations.

_____ 7 At a party I let others keep the jokes and stories going.

_____ 8 I feel a bit awkward in public and do not show up quite as well as I should.

_____ 9 I can look anyone in the eye and tell a lie with a straight face (if for the right reason).

_____ 10 I may deceive people by being friendly when I really dislike them.

Scoring Key

Score one point for each of the following answers:

1 T; 2 F; 3 T; 4 F; 5 T; 6 F; 7 F; 8 F; 9 T; 10 T

Score: _____

1–3 = Low self-monitoring

4–5 = Moderately low self-monitoring

6–7 = Moderately high self-monitoring

8–10 = High self-monitoring

SOURCE: Excerpted and adapted from M Snyder and S Gangestad, 'On the Nature of Self-Monitoring: Matters of Assessment, Matters of Validity,' *Journal of Personality and Social Psychology*, July 1986, p 137.

Research Findings and Practical Recommendations

According to field research, there is a positive relationship between high self-monitoring and career success. Among 139 American MBA graduates who were surveyed over five years, high self-monitors enjoyed more internal and external promotions than did their low self-monitoring classmates.[43] Another study of 147 managers and professionals found that high self-monitors had a better record of acquiring a mentor (someone to act as a personal career coach and professional sponsor).[44] These results mesh well with an earlier study that found managerial success (in terms of speed of promotions) tied to political savvy (knowing how to socialize, network, and engage in organizational politics).[45]

The foregoing evidence and practical experience leads us to make the following practical recommendations.

For high, moderate, and low self-monitors: Become more consciously aware of your self-image and how it affects others (the OB Exercise is a good start).[46]

For high self-monitors: Don't overdo it by turning from a successful chameleon into someone who is widely perceived as insincere, dishonest, phony and untrustworthy. You cannot be everything to everyone.

For low self-monitors: You can bend without breaking, so try to be a bit more accommodating while being true to your basic beliefs. Don't wear out your welcome when communicating. Practice reading and adjusting to non-verbal cues in various public situations. If your conversation partner is bored or distracted, stop–because they are not really listening.

Organizational Identification: A *Social* Aspect of Self-Concept with Ethical Implications

The dividing line between self and others is not a neat and precise one. A certain amount of blurring occurs, for example, when an employee comes to define himself or herself with a *specific* organization–a psychological process called *organizational identification*. According to an expert on this emerging OB topic, 'organizational identification occurs when one comes to integrate beliefs about one's organization into one's identity'.[47] People with a strong organizational identification are very concerned about their company's welfare; and regard their work as something central to their lives. For example, Richard Desmond, head of the–at that moment–troubled Daily Express newspaper in the UK, stated in an interview that 'The papers mean a lot to me and I'm passionate about their future. You know, my mum and my dad read the Express . . . .'[48] Organizational identification goes to the heart of organizational culture and socialization (recall our discussion in Chapter 3).

Organizational identification
organizational values or beliefs become part of one's self-identity

Managers put a good deal of emphasis today on issues of organizational mission, philosophy and values with the express intent of integrating the company into each employee's self-identity. Hopefully, as the logic goes, employees who identify closely with the organization will be more loyal, more committed and harder working.[49] As an extreme case in point, organizational identification among employees at Harley-Davidson's motorcycle factories is so strong many have had the company logo tattooed on their bodies.[50] Working at Harley is not just a job, it is a lifestyle. A company tattoo may be a bit extreme but the ethical implications of encouraging employees to identify closely with the organization are profound. As discussed in Chapter 1, the new employment contract calls for a *fair* exchange between employee and employer. Therefore, it is fine for employers to strive for greater organizational identification–as long as they nurture employees as valuable human resources and not treat them as expendable goods.

We now turn our attention to how the self is expressed through personality traits.

Personality: Dimensions, Insights and Issues

Individuals have their own way of thinking and acting, their own unique style or *personality*. **Personality** is defined as the combination of stable physical and mental characteristics that give the individual his or her identity.[51] These characteristics or traits–including how one looks, thinks, acts and feels–are the product of interacting genetic and environmental influences. In this section, we introduce the Big Five personality dimensions, issue some cautions about workplace personality testing, and examine an important personality factor called locus of control. Finally, as we enter the 21st century, we couldn't deny some recent findings on the link between personality and the new technologies.

Personality
stable physical and mental characteristics responsible for a person's identity

The Big Five Personality Dimensions

Long and confusing lists of personality dimensions have been distilled in recent years into the Big Five.[52] They are extraversion, agreeableness, conscientiousness, emotional stability, and openness to experience (see Table 5–1 for descriptions). Standardized personality tests determine how positively or negatively a person scores on each of the Big Five. For example, someone scoring negatively on extraversion would be an introverted person prone to shy and withdrawn behaviour.[53] Someone scoring negatively on emotional security would be nervous, tense, angry and worried. A person's scores on the Big Five reveal a personality profile as unique as his or her fingerprints. Yet one important question lingers: Are personality models ethnocentric or unique to the culture in which they were developed? At least as far as the Big Five model goes, recent cross-cultural research evidence points in the direction of 'no.'

Specifically, the Big Five personality structure held up very well in a study of men and women from Russia, Canada, Hong Kong, Poland, Germany and Finland.[54]

Personality Dimension	Characteristics of a Person Scoring Positively on the Dimension
1. Extraversion	Outgoing, talkative, sociable, assertive
2. Agreeableness	Trusting, good natured, co-operative, soft-hearted
3. Conscientiousness	Dependable, responsible, achievement-oriented, persistent
4. Emotional stability	Relaxed, secure, unworried
5. Openness to experience	Intellectual, imaginative, curious, broad-minded

Table 5–1

The Big Five Personality Dimensions

SOURCE: Adapted from M R Barrick and M K Mount, 'Autonomy as a Moderator of the Relationships between the Big Five Personality Dimensions and Job Performance', *Journal of Applied Psychology*, February 1993, pp 111–18.

Personality and Job Performance

Those interested in OB want to know the connection between the Big Five and job performance. Ideally, Big Five personality dimensions that correlate positively and strongly with job performance would be helpful in the selection, training and appraisal of employees. A meta-analysis, of 117 studies involving 23,994 participants from many professions, offers guidance.[55] Among the Big Five, *conscientiousness* had the strongest positive correlation with job performance and training performance. According to the researchers, 'those individuals who exhibit traits associated with a strong sense of purpose, obligation and persistence generally perform better than those who do not'.[56] Another expected finding is that extraversion (an outgoing personality) was associated with success for managers and salespeople. Also, extraversion was a stronger predictor of job performance than agreeableness, across all professions. The researchers concluded, 'It appears that being courteous, trusting, straightforward and soft-hearted has a smaller impact on job performance than being talkative, active and assertive.'

Issue: Is There an 'Ideal' Employee Personality Profile?

Given the complexity of today's work environments, the diversity of today's workforce, and recent research evidence,[57] the quest for an ideal employee personality profile is sheer folly. Just as one shoe does not fit all people, one personality profile does not fit all job situations.

Issue: What about Personality Testing in the Workplace?

Personality testing as a tool for making decisions about hiring, training and promotion is questionable for two main reasons. First is the issue of *predictive validity*. Can personality tests actually predict job performance? In the Big Five meta-analysis discussed earlier, conscientiousness may have been the best predictor of job performance but it was *not* a strong predictor. Moreover, the most widely used personality test, the Minnesota Multiphasic Personality Inventory (MMPI), does not directly measure conscientiousness. No surprise that the MMPI and other popular personality tests have, historically, been poor predictors of job performance.[58]

Second is the issue of *differential validity*, relative to race. Do personality tests measure whites and minority races differently? We still do not have a definitive answer to this important and difficult question. Respected Big Five researchers recently concluded, 'To date, the evidence indicates that differential validity is not typically associated with personality measures. Caution is required in interpreting this conclusion, however, in light of the small number of studies available.'[59] Meanwhile, personality testing remains a lightening rod for controversy in the workplace.

Table 5–2

Words of Caution about Personality Testing in the Workplace

- Rely on reputable, licensed psychologists for selecting and overseeing the administration, scoring and interpretation of personality and psychological tests.
- Do not make employment-related decisions strictly on the basis of personality test results. Supplement any personality test data with information from reference checks, personal interviews, ability tests and job performance records.
- Avoid hiring people on the basis of specified personality profiles. As a case in point, there is no distinct 'managerial personality'. One study found the combination of mental ability and personality to be responsible for only 21% of the variation in managerial success.*
- Regularly assess any possible adverse impact on women and minorities.
- Be wary of slickly packaged gimmicks claiming to accurately assess personalities. A prime example is *graphology*, whereby handwriting 'experts' infer personality traits and aptitudes from samples of one's penmanship. This European transplant has enjoyed zealous growth in the United States. But judging from research evidence, graphology is an inappropriate hiring tool and probably an open invitation to discrimination lawsuits. In a meta-analysis of 17 studies, 63 graphologists did a slightly *worse* job of predicting future performance than did a control group of 51 non-graphologists. Indeed, psychologists with no graphology experience consistently outperformed the graphologists.†
- The rapidly growing use of *integrity* tests to screen out dishonest job applicants seems to be justified by recent research evidence. Dishonest people reportedly have a general lack of conscientiousness that is difficult for them to fake, even on a written test.‡

SOURCES: *For details, see J S Schippmann and E P Prien, 'An Assessment of the Contributions of General Mental Ability and Personality Characteristics to Managerial Success', *Journal of Business and Psychology*, Summer 1989, pp 423–37; †Data from E Neter and G Ben-Shakhar, 'The Predictive Validity of Graphological Inferences: A Meta-Analytic Approach', *Personality and Individual Differences*, no. 7, 1989, pp 737–45; ‡See D S Ones, C Viswesvaran, and F L Schmidt, 'Comprehensive Meta-Analysis of Integrity Test Validities: Findings and Implications for Personnel Selection and Theories of Job Performance', *Journal of Applied Psychology*, August 1993, pp 679–703; and D S Ones and C Viswesvaran, 'Gender, Age, and Race Differences on Overt Integrity Tests: Results across Four Large-Scale Job Applicant Data Sets', *Journal of Applied Psychology*, February 1998, pp 35–42.

The practical tips in Table 5–2 can help managers avoid abuses when using personality and psychological testing for employment-related decisions.[60] Another alternative for employers is to eliminate personality testing altogether. The growing practice of job-related skills testing is another alternative to personality testing.[61]

Issue: Why Not Just Forget about Personality?

Personality testing problems and unethical applications do not automatically cancel out the underlying concepts. Present and future managers need to know about personality traits and characteristics, despite the controversy over personality testing. Rightly or wrongly, the term *personality* is routinely encountered both inside and outside the workplace.[62]

Knowledge of the Big Five encourages more precise understanding of the rich diversity among today's employees. Good management involves taking the time to get to know *each* employee's *unique combination* of personality, abilities and potential and to then create a productive and satisfying person-job fit.

Let us take a look at locus of control, another important job-related personality factor.

Locus of Control: Self or Environment?

Individuals vary in terms of how much personal responsibility they take for their behaviour and its consequences. Julian Rotter, a personality researcher, identified a dimension of personality he labelled *locus of control* to explain these differences. He proposed that people tend to attribute the causes of their behaviour primarily to either themselves or environmental factors.[63] This personality trait produces distinctly different behaviour patterns.

People who believe they control the events and consequences that affect their lives are said to possess an **internal locus of control**. For example, such a person tends to attribute positive outcomes, such as passing an exam, to her or his own abilities. Similarly, an 'internal' tends to blame negative events, such as failing an exam, on personal shortcomings—not studying hard enough, perhaps. Many entrepreneurs eventually succeed because their *internal* locus of control helps them overcome setbacks and disappointments. They see themselves as masters of their own fate and not simply lucky. But, as *Fortune's* Jaclyn Fierman humorously noted, luck is a matter of interpretation and not always a bad thing.

> **Internal locus of control**
> *attributing outcomes to one's own actions*

> For those of us who believe we are the masters of our fate, the captains of our soul, the notion that a career might hinge on random events is unthinkable. Self-made men and women are especially touchy on this subject. If they get all the breaks, it's because they're smarter and harder working than everyone else. If they know the right people, it's because they network the nights away. Luck? Many successful people think it diminishes them. Hard workers do get ahead, no doubt about it . . . . But then there are folks like Ringo Starr. One day he was an obscure drummer of limited talent from Liverpool; the next day he was a Beatle. Nobody demonstrates better than Ringo that true luck is accidental, not inevitable.[64]

On the other side of this personality dimension are those who believe their performance is the product of circumstances beyond their immediate control. These individuals are said to possess an external locus of control and tend to attribute outcomes to environmental causes, such as luck or fate. Unlike someone with an internal locus of control, an 'external' would attribute a pass in an exam to something external (an easy test or a good day) and attribute a failing grade to an unfair test or problems at home. A shortened version of an instrument Rotter developed to measure one's locus of control is presented in the next OB Exercise. Where is your locus of control: internal, external or a combination?

> **External locus of control**
> *attributing outcomes to circumstances beyond one's control*

Research Findings on Locus of Control

Researchers have found important behavioural differences between internals and externals.

▼ Internals display greater work motivation.

▼ Internals have stronger expectations that effort leads to performance.

▼ Internals exhibit higher performance on tasks involving learning or problem solving, when performance leads to valued rewards.

▼ There is a stronger relationship between job satisfaction and performance for internals than externals.

▼ Internals obtain higher salaries and larger salary increases than externals.

▼ Externals tend to be more anxious than internals.[65]

Implications of Locus of Control Differences for Managers

The preceding summary of research findings on locus of control has important implications for managing people at work. Let us examine two of them.

First, since internals have a tendency to believe they control the work environment through their behaviour, they will attempt to exert control over the work setting. This can be done by trying to influence work procedures, working conditions, task assignments or relationships with peers and supervisors. As these possibilities imply, internals may resist a manager's attempts to closely supervise their work. Therefore, management may want to place internals in jobs requiring high initiative and low compliance. Externals, on the other hand, might be more amenable to highly structured jobs requiring greater compliance. Direct participation can also bolster the attitudes and performance of externals. This conclusion comes from a field study of 85 computer system users in a wide variety of business and government organizations. Externals who had been significantly involved in designing their organization's computer information system had more favourable attitudes toward the system than their external-locus co-workers who had not participated.[66]

Second, locus of control has implications for reward systems. Given that internals have a greater belief that their effort leads to performance, internals would probably prefer, and respond more productively to, incentives such as merit pay or sales commissions.[67]

OB Exercise

Where is Your Locus of Control

Circle one letter for each pair of items, in accordance with your beliefs:

1   a   Many of the unhappy things in people's lives are partly due to bad luck.

   b   People's misfortunes result from the mistakes they make.

2   a   Unfortunately, an individual's worth often passes unrecognized no matter how hard he or she tries.

   b   In the long run, people get the respect they deserve.

3   a   Without the right breaks one cannot be an effective leader.

   b   Capable people who fail to become leaders have not taken advantage of their opportunities.

4   a   I have often found that what is going to happen will happen.

   b   Trusting to fate has never turned out as well for me as making a decision to take a definite course of action.

5   a   Most people don't realize the extent to which their lives are controlled by accidental happenings.

   b   There really is no such thing as 'luck.'

6   a   In the long run, the bad things that happen to us are balanced by the good ones.

   b   Most misfortunes are the result of lack of ability, ignorance, laziness, or all three.

7   a   Many times I feel I have little influence over the things that happen to me.

   b   It is impossible for me to believe that chance or luck plays an important role in my life.

Note: In determining your score, A = 0 and B = 1. Arbitrary norms for this shortened version are: External locus of control = 1–3; Balanced internal and external locus of control = 4; Internal locus of control = 5–7.

Excerpted from J B Rotter, 'Generalized Expectancies for Internal versus External Control of Reinforcement', ***Psychological Monographs,*** **vol 80 (Whole no. 609, 1966), pp 11–12. ©1966 by the American Psychological Association. Reprinted with permission.**

The Personality of the Emailer

In our fast changing world we increasingly rely on new technologies and communication tools to facilitate our work and our daily life. However, it has been said that the way people use these new technologies differs from person to person. A manager in a large company might use the Internet solely for business purposes and use short, formal messages. A 16-year-old school girl, on the other hand, might regard Internet as a way of keeping in touch with her friends. In this light, a study carried out in 1999 by the Dutch research agency, MarketResponse, described four different types of email users: the functionalist, the pleasure seeker, the process-controller and the adventurer.[68]

Functionalists need email for pure practical reasons. They only use email if it serves a useful purpose, and only send short and professional, businesslike messages. They like to keep their life simple and goal-oriented.

Pleasure seekers are receptive to new and pleasant things. They like contacts with other people and email is a possibility for them to maintain or expand these contacts. They prefer to add a personal touch to their messages, they write the way they talk. Sometimes they send an email just to let others know they're there or they send funny messages, jokes and cartoons. The pleasure seekers are the ones who make most extensive use of email, about six times a week.

Process controllers are rational and well-structured types who like to have things under control. For them, email is an tool that offers them precise control, because they can open and read their mail whenever they want. Through the tracking options they can also check whether the addressee has read his mail yet. They store their messages so as to always have 'proof'. Their mails are short, businesslike and in the style of a telegram.

Adventurers are continually seeking for things that bring excitement to their lives. For them, email is an exciting means of communication tied closely to the Internet. The Internet brings the entire world to within reach. The adventurer mails often. But he keeps his messages short, because a day has too few hours for him.

ATTITUDES AND BEHAVIOUR

Hardly a day goes by without the popular media reporting the results of another attitude survey. The idea is to take the pulse of public opinion. What do we think about euthanasia, the Euro, the refugee problem, legalization of soft-drugs or abortion? In the workplace, meanwhile, managers conduct attitude surveys to monitor such things as job and pay satisfaction.[69] All this attention to attitudes is based on the assumption that attitudes somehow influence behaviour such as voting for someone, working hard, or quitting one's job. In this section, we will examine the connection between attitudes and behaviour.

Attitudes versus Values

An **attitude** is defined as a 'learned predisposition to respond in a consistently favourable or unfavourable manner with respect to a given object.'[70] Attitudes affect behaviour at a different level than do values. While values represent global beliefs that influence behaviour across *all* situations, attitudes relate only to behaviour directed toward *specific* objects, persons or situations.[71] Values and attitudes are generally, though not always, in harmony. A manager who strongly values helpful behaviour may have a negative attitude towards helping an unethical co-worker.

Attitude
*learned
predispositions
towards a given
object*

How Stable Are Attitudes?

In one landmark study, researchers found the *job* attitudes of 5,000 middle-aged male employees to be very stable over a five-year period. Positive job attitudes remained positive; negative ones remained negative. Even those who changed jobs or occupations tended to maintain their prior job attitudes.[72] More recent research suggests the foregoing study may have overstated the stability of attitudes because it was restricted to a middle-aged sample. This time, researchers asked, 'What happens to attitudes over the entire span of adulthood?' *General* attitudes were found to be more susceptible to change during early and late adulthood than during middle adulthood. Three factors accounted for middle-age attitude stability:

▼ **greater personal certainty**

▼ **perceived abundance of knowledge**

▼ **a need for strong attitudes.**

Thus the conventional notion, that general attitudes become less likely to change as the person ages, was rejected. Elderly people, along with young adults, can and do change their general attitudes because they are more open and less self-assured.[73]

Because our cultural backgrounds and experiences vary, our attitudes and behaviour vary. Attitudes are translated into behaviour via behavioural intentions. Let us examine an established model of this important process.

Attitudes and Behavioural Intentions

Behavioural scientists, Martin Fishbein and Icek Ajzen, developed a comprehensive model of behavioural intentions used widely to explain attitude–behaviour relationships.[74] As depicted in Figure 5–4, an individual's intention to engage in a given behaviour is the best predictor of that behaviour. For example, the quickest and possibly most accurate way of determining whether an individual will quit his or her job, is to have an objective third party ask if he or she intends to quit. A meta-analysis of 34 studies of employee turnover, involving more than 83,000 employees, validated this direct approach. The researchers found stated behavioural intentions to be a better predictor of employee turnover than job satisfaction, satisfaction with the work itself or organizational commitment.[75]

Although asking about intentions enables one to predict who will quit, it does not help explain *why* an individual would want to quit. Thus, to better understand why employees exhibit certain behaviours, such as quitting their jobs, one needs to consider their relevant attitudes. As shown in Figure 5–4, behavioural intentions are

Figure 5–4 *A Model of Behavioural Intention*

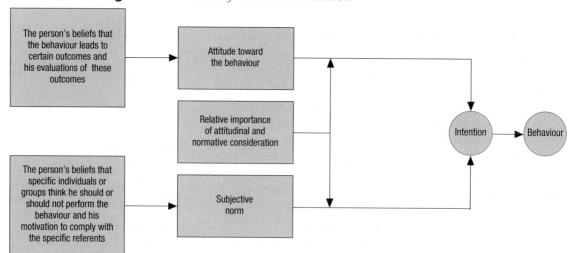

Note: Arrows indicate the direction of influence.

SOURCE: Icek Ajzen and Martin Fishbein, *Understanding Attitudes and Predicting Social Behaviour,* © 1980, p 8 Reprinted by permission of Prentice Hall, Upper Saddle River, NJ.

influenced both by one's attitude towards the behaviour; and by perceived norms about exhibiting that behaviour. In turn, attitudes and subjective norms are determined by personal beliefs.

Beliefs Influence Attitudes

A person's belief system is a mental representation of his or her relevant surroundings, complete with probable cause-and-effect relationships. Beliefs are the result of direct observation and inferences from previously learned relationships. For example, we tend to infer that a laughing co-worker is happy. In terms of the strength of the relationship between beliefs and attitudes, beliefs do not have equal impacts on attitudes. Research indicates that attitudes are based on salient or important beliefs that may change as relevant information is received. For example, your beliefs about the quality of a particular automobile may change after hearing the car has been recalled for defective brakes.

In Figure 5–4, you can see that an individual will have positive attitudes toward performing a behaviour when he or she believes that it is associated with positive outcomes. An individual is more likely to quit a job when he or she believes it will result in a better position and a reduction in job stress. In contrast, negative attitudes toward quitting will be formed when a person believes quitting leads to negative outcomes, such as the loss of money and status.

Beliefs Influence Subjective Norms

Subjective norms refer to perceived social pressure to perform a specific behaviour. As noted by Ajzen and Fishbein, 'Subjective norms are also a function of beliefs, but beliefs of a different kind, namely the person's beliefs that specific individuals or groups think he should or should not perform the behaviour.'[76] Subjective norms can exert a powerful influence on the behavioural intentions of those who are sensitive to the opinions of respected role models. This effect was observed in a laboratory study of students' intentions to apply for a job at companies that reportedly tested employees for drugs. The students generally had a negative attitude about companies that tested for drugs. But positive statements from influential persons about the need for drug testing tended to strengthen intentions to apply to companies engaged in drug testing.[77]

Thus, as shown in Figure 5–4, both attitudes and subjective norms shape behavioural intentions.

Attitudinal Research and Application

Research has demonstrated that Fishbein and Ajzen's model accurately predicted intentions to buy consumer products, have children, and choose a career versus become a homemaker. Weight loss intentions and behaviour, voting for political candidates and attending on-the-job training sessions have also been predicted successfully by the model.[78]

From a practical management standpoint, the behavioural intention model we have just reviewed has important implications. First, managers need to appreciate the dynamic relationships between beliefs, attitudes, subjective norms, and behavioural intentions when attempting to foster productive behaviour. Although attitudes are often resistant to change, they can be influenced *indirectly* through education and training experiences that change underlying beliefs. A case in point is a recent study documenting how men's beliefs about gender differences can be reduced by taking a women's studies course.[79] Another tactic involves redirecting subjective norms through clear and credible communication, organizational culture values and role models. Finally, regular employee-attitude surveys can let managers know whether their ideas and changes go with or against the grain of popular sentiment.[80]

ABILITIES AND PERFORMANCE

Individual differences in abilities and accompanying skills are a central concern for managers because nothing can be accomplished without appropriately skilled personnel. An **ability** represents a broad and stable characteristic responsible for a person's maximum—as opposed to typical—performance on mental and physical tasks. A **skill**, on the other hand, is the specific capacity to physically manipulate objects. Consider this difference as you imagine yourself being the only passenger on a small commuter plane in which the pilot has just passed out. As the plane nose-dives, your effort and abilities will not be enough to save yourself and the pilot if you do not possess flying skills. As shown in Figure 5–5, successful performance (be it landing a plane or performing any other job) depends on the right combination of effort, ability and skill.

Ability
stable characteristic responsible for a person's maximum physical or mental performance

Skill
specific capacity to manipulate objects

Abilities and skills are getting a good deal of attention in management circles these days. The more encompassing term *competencies* is typically used. Among the many desirable competencies are oral communication, initiative, decisiveness, tolerance, problem solving and adaptability. Importantly, our earlier cautions about on-the-job personality testing extend to ability, intelligence and competency testing and certification.

Before moving on, we need to say something about a modern-day threat to abilities, skills and general competence. That threat, according to public health officials, is *sleep deprivation*. If you are routinely short-changing your basic sleep needs, you are likely to be less effective and more stressed (see Chapter 17) than you should be.

The balance of this section explores important abilities and cognitive styles related to job performance.

Figure 5–5
Performance Depends on the Right Combination of Effort, Ability and Skill

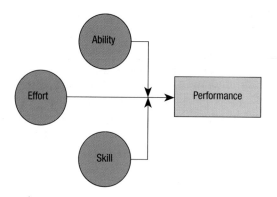

Intelligence and Cognitive Abilities

Intelligence
capacity for constructive thinking, reasoning, problem solving

Although experts do not agree on a specific definition, **intelligence** represents an individual's capacity for constructive thinking, reasoning and problem solving.[81] Historically, intelligence was believed to be an innate capacity, passed genetically from one generation to the next. Research since has shown, however, that intelligence (like personality) is also a function of environmental influences.[82] Organic factors have more recently been added to the formula as a result of mounting evidence of the connection between alcohol and drug abuse by pregnant women and intellectual development problems in their children.[83]

Researchers have produced some interesting findings about abilities and intelligence in recent years. A unique, five-year study documented the tendency of people to 'gravitate to jobs commensurate with their abilities'.[84] This prompts the vision of the job market acting as a giant sorting or sifting machine, with employees tumbling into various ability bins. Meanwhile, a steady and significant rise in average intelligence among those in developed countries has been observed over the last 70 years. Why?

Experts at a recent conference concluded, 'Some combination of better schooling, improved socio-economic status, healthier nutrition and a more technologically complex society, might account for the gains in IQ scores.'[85] So if you think you're smarter than your parents and your teachers, you're probably right!

Two Types of Ability

Human intelligence has been studied predominantly through the empirical approach. By examining the relationship between measures of mental abilities and behaviour, researchers have statistically isolated major components of intelligence. Using this empirical procedure, pioneering psychologist Charles Spearman proposed, in 1927, that all cognitive performance is determined by two types of abilities. The first can be characterized as a general mental ability required for *all* cognitive tasks. The second is unique to the task at hand.[86] For example, an individual's ability to complete crossword puzzles is a function of his or her broad mental abilities as well as the specific ability to perceive patterns in partially completed words.

Seven Major Mental Abilities

Through the years, much research has been devoted to developing and expanding Spearman's ideas on the relationship between cognitive abilities and intelligence. One research psychologist listed 120 distinct mental abilities. Table 5–3 contains definitions of the seven most frequently cited mental abilities. Of these seven, personnel selection researchers have found verbal ability, numerical ability, spatial ability, and inductive reasoning to be valid predictors of job performance for both minority and mainstream applicants.[87]

Table 5–3

Mental Abilities Underlying Performance

Ability	Description
1 Verbal comprehension	The ability to understand what words mean and to readily comprehend what is read
2 Word fluency	The ability to produce isolated words that fulfill specific symbolic or structural requirements
3 Numerical	The ability to make quick and accurate arithmetic computations such as adding and subtracting
4 Spatial	Being able to perceive spatial patterns and to visualize how geometric shapes would look if transformed in shape or position
5 Memory	Having good rote memory for paired words, symbols, lists of numbers or other associated items
6 Perceptual speed	The ability to perceive figures, identify similarities and differences, and carry out tasks involving visual perception
7 Inductive reasoning	The ability to reason from specifics to general conclusions

SOURCE: Adapted from M D Dunnette, 'Aptitudes, Abilities, and Skills', in *Handbook of Industrial and Organizational Psychology*, ed M D Dunnette (Skokie, IL: Rand McNally, 1976), pp 478–83.

What About Emotional Intelligence?

In 1995, Daniel Goleman, a psychologist turned journalist, created a stir in education and management circles with the publication of his book *Emotional Intelligence*. Hence, an obscure topic among psychologists became mainstream. In an interview, Jack Welch, former chief executive of US giant, General Electric, called it *'soft stuff with hard results'*.[88] According to Goleman, traditional models of intelligence (IQ) are too narrow. His approach to *emotional intelligence* includes

. . . abilities such as being able to motivate oneself and persist in the face of frustrations; to control impulse and delay gratification; to regulate one's moods and keep distress from swamping the ability to think; to empathize and to hope. Unlike IQ, with its nearly one-hundred-year history of research with hundreds of thousands of people, emotional intelligence is a new concept. No one can yet say exactly how much of the variability from person to person in life's course it accounts for. But what data exist suggest it can be as powerful, and at times more powerful, than IQ.[89]

Self-assessment instruments supposedly measuring emotional intelligence have appeared in the popular management literature. Sample questions include: 'I believe I can stay on top of tough situations',[90] and 'I am able to admit my own mistakes.'[91] Recent research, however, casts serious doubt on the reliability and validity of such instruments.[92] Even Goleman concedes, 'It's very tough to measure our own emotional intelligence, because most of us don't have a very clear sense of how we come across to other people . . . .'[93] Honest feedback from others is necessary. Still, the area of emotional intelligence is useful for lecturers and organizational trainers because, unlike IQ, social problem solving and the ability to control one's emotions can be taught and learned. Scores on emotional intelligence tests definitely should *not* be used for making hiring and promotion decisions until valid measuring tools are developed.

Jung's Cognitive Styles Typology

Cognitive style
a perceptual and judgemental tendency, according to Jung's typology

Within the context of Jung's theory, the term cognitive style refers to mental processes associated with how people perceive and make judgements from information. Although the landmark work on cognitive styles was completed in the 1920s by the noted Swiss psychoanalyst Carl Jung, his ideas did not catch on in the study of personality until the 1940s. That was when the mother–daughter team of Katharine C Briggs and Isabel Briggs Myers developed the Myers–Briggs Type Indicator (MBTI), an instrument for measuring Jung's cognitive styles. Today, the MBTI is a widely used (and abused) personal growth and development tool in further education and business.[94]

Four Different Cognitive Styles

According to Jung, two dimensions influence perception and two others affect individual judgement. Perception is based on either *sensation*, using one's physical senses to interpret situations, or *intuition*, relying on past experience. In turn, judgements are made by either *thinking* or *feeling*. Finally, Jung proposed that an individual's cognitive style is determined by the pairing of one's perception and judgement tendencies. The resulting four cognitive styles are as follows:

▼ **sensation/thinking (ST)**

▼ **intuition/thinking (NT)**

▼ **sensation/feeling (SF)**

▼ **intuition/feeling (NF)**

Characteristics of each style are presented in Figure 5–6.[95] (The Personal Awareness and Growth Exercise at the end of this chapter, patterned after the MBTI, will help you determine your cognitive style.)

An individual with an ST style uses senses for perception and rational thinking for judgement. The ST-style person uses facts and impersonal analysis and develops greater abilities in technical areas involving facts and objects. A successful engineer could be expected to exhibit this cognitive style. In contrast, a person with an NT style focuses on possibilities rather than facts and displays abilities in areas involving theoretical or technical development. This style would enhance the performance of a research scientist. Although an SF person is likely to be interested in gathering facts, he or she tends to treat others with personal warmth, sympathy, and friendliness. Successful counsellors or teachers probably use this style. Finally, an individual with an NF style tends to exhibit artistic flair while relying heavily on personal insights rather than objective facts (see Figure 5–6).

Figure 5–6 *People Have Different Cognitive Styles and Corresponding Characteristics*

	Decision Style			
	ST Sensation/Thinking	**NT** Intuition/Thinking	**SF** Sensation/Feeling	**NF** Intuition/Feeling
Focus of attention	Facts	Possibilities	Facts	Possibilities
Method of handling things	Impersonal analysis	Impersonal analysis	Personal warmth	Personal warmth
Tendency to become	Practical and matter-of-fact	Logical and ingenious	Sympathetic and friendly	Enthusiastic and insightful
Expression of abilities	Technical skills with facts and objects	Theoretical and technical developments	Practical help and services for people	Understanding and communicating with people
	Technician	Planner	Teacher	Artist
Representative occupation		Manager		

SOURCE: W Taggart and D Robey, 'Minds and Managers: On the Dual Nature of Human Information Processing and Management', *Academy of Management Review*, April 1981, p 190. Used with permission.

Practical Research Findings

If Jung's cognitive styles typology is valid, then individuals with different cognitive styles should seek different kinds of information when making a decision. A study of 50 MBA students found that those with different cognitive styles did in fact use qualitatively different information while working on a strategic planning problem.[96] Research has also shown that people with different cognitive styles prefer different careers. For example, people who rely on intuition prefer careers in psychology, advertising, teaching and the arts.

Findings have further shown that individuals who make judgements based on the 'thinking' approach have higher work motivation and quality of work life than those who take a 'feeling' approach. In addition, individuals with a sensation mode of perception have higher job satisfaction than those relying on intuition.[97] Small business owner and managers with a 'thinking' style made more money than their 'feeling' counterparts. But no correlation was found between the four Jungian styles and small business owner/manager success.[98] The following conclusion from a recent exhaustive review of management-oriented MBTI studies makes us cautious about these findings: 'It is clear that efforts to detect simplistic linkages between type preferences and managerial effectiveness have been disappointing. Indeed, given the mixed quality of research and the inconsistent findings, no definitive conclusions regarding these relationships can be drawn.'[99] On balance, we believe Jung's cognitive styles typology and the MBTI are useful for diversity training and management development purposes[100] but are inappropriate for making personnel decisions such as hiring and promoting.

EMOTIONS: AN EMERGING OB TOPIC

In the ideal world of management theory, employees pursue organizational goals in a logical and rational manner. Emotional behaviour seldom appears in the equation. Yet day-to-day organizational life shows us how prevalent and powerful emotions can be. Anger and jealousy, both potent emotions, often push aside logic and rationality in the workplace. Managers use fear and other emotions to both motivate and intimidate. Consider the following story.

> *Although I was a very competent trainer with several years of experience, every course I gave was highly critiqued by my boss. Time after time, verbal abuse would start and my feeling of well-being would evaporate in seconds to be replaced by humiliation and depression. He needed someone to humiliate and I was the usual target. There was no logical reason for his actions. He used me as a verbal punchbag for reasons best known to himself. Over a long time, I lost count of the number of highly personal and offensive remarks he made.*[101]

In this final section of the chapter, our examination of individual differences turns to defining emotions, reviewing a typology of 10 positive and negative emotions, and focusing on the management of anger—a potentially destructive and dangerous emotion.

Positive and Negative Emotions

Emotions
complex human reactions to personal achievements and setbacks that may be felt and displayed

Richard S Lazarus, a leading authority on the subject, defines **emotions** as 'complex, patterned, organismic reactions to how we think we are doing in our lifelong efforts to survive and flourish and to achieve what we wish for ourselves'.[102] The word *organismic* is appropriate because emotions involve the *whole* person—biological, psychological and social. Importantly, psychologists draw a distinction between *felt* and *displayed* emotions.[103] For example, referring back to our earlier discussion, Goleman would say a person with high emotional intelligence might feel angry (felt emotion) at a rude co-worker but not make a nasty remark in return (displayed emotion). As discussed in Chapter 17, emotions play roles in both causing and adapting to stress and its associated biological and psychological problems. The destructive effect of emotional behaviour on social relationships is all too obvious in daily life.

Lazarus's definition of emotions centres on a person's goals. Accordingly, his distinction between positive and negative emotions is goal oriented. Some emotions are triggered by frustration and failure when pursuing one's goals. Lazarus calls these *negative* emotions. They are said to be goal incongruent. For example, which of the six negative emotions in Figure 5–7 are you likely to experience if you fail the final exam in a required course? Failing the exam would be incongruent with your goal of graduating on time. On the other hand, which of the four *positive* emotions in Figure 5–7 would you probably experience if you graduated on time and with honours? The emotions you would experience in this situation are positive because they are congruent (or consistent) with an important lifetime goal.

The individual's goals, it is important to note, may or may not be socially acceptable. Thus, a positive emotion, such as love/affection, may be undesirable if associated with sexual harassment. Oppositely, slight pangs of guilt, anxiety and envy can motivate extra effort. On balance, the constructive or destructive nature of a particular emotion must be judged in terms of both its intensity and the person's relevant goal.

More Attention Needed

Emotional behaviour receives less than its fair share of attention in the general business and management literature. Often, emotions are mentioned only in passing or as a side issue. Other recent articles have mentioned how emotions can override reason, how leaders need to acknowledge and deal with both their own and others' emotions, and the role of fear in team-building activities.

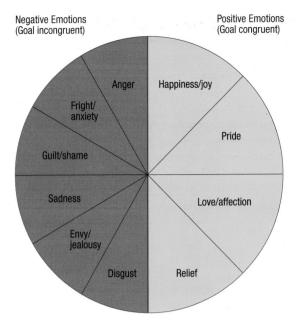

Figure 5-7

Positive and Negative Emotions

Source: Adapted from discussion in R S Lazarus, *Emotion and Adaptation* (New York: Oxford University Press, 1991), Chs 6, 7.

The OB research literature is even more sparse. Typically, emotional behaviour is not covered as a central variable but rather as a subfactor in discussions of organizational politics, conflict and stress. Here are some recent insights. According to a British organizational psychologist, we need to do a better job of dealing with emotions in career management programmes.[104] Under the new employment contract, job-hunting skills are not enough. Emotional skills are needed to handle frequent and often difficult career transitions. Two field studies, with nurses and accountants as subjects, found a strong linkage between the work group's collective mood and the individual's mood.[105] The bad news: Foul moods are contagious. But so are good moods. Go spread the cheer!

We look forward to more comprehensive OB research on the causes and consequences of emotional behaviour.

Managing Anger

Of all the emotions in Figure 5-7, anger is the one most likely to be downright dangerous. It deserves special attention. Unchecked anger could be a key contributing factor to what one team of researchers calls *organization-motivated aggression*.[105] Worse, uncontrolled anger is certainly a contributor to workplace violence. As awareness of workplace violence increases, employers are installing various security systems and training employees to avoid or diffuse incidents. The European Commission's definition of workplace violence includes 'incidents where persons are abused, threatened or assaulted in circumstances relating to their work, involving an explicit challenge to their safety, well-being and health'.[106] Anger-management training for all employees, based on the self-control tactics listed in Table 5-4, could make a positive contribution to reducing workplace violence and improving the general quality of work life. In summary, if the most troublesome emotion—anger—can be managed through learned self-control, then all the emotions can be managed. (See the behavioural self-management model and related techniques in Chapter 10.) Meantime, the workplace remains an emotionally charged environment where too much in the way of either positive or negative emotions is counter-productive.

Table 5–4

How to Manage Anger in Yourself and Others

Reducing Chronic Anger [in Yourself]	Responding to Angry Provocation
Guides for Action	**Guides for Action**
• Appreciate the potentially valuable lessons from anger	• Expect angry people to exaggerate
• Use mistakes and slights to learn	• Recognize the other's frustrations and pressures
• Recognize that you and others can do well enough without being perfect	• Use the provocation to develop your abilities
• Trust that most people want to be caring, helpful family members and colleagues	• Allow the other to let off steam
• Forgive others and yourself	• Begin to problem solve when the anger is at moderate levels
• Confront unrealistic, blame-oriented assumptions	• Congratulate yourself on turning an outburst into an opportunity to find solutions
• Adopt constructive, learning-oriented assumptions	• Share successes with partners
Pitfalls to Avoid	**Pitfalls to Avoid**
• Assume every slight is a painful wound.	• Take every word literally
• Equate not getting what you want with catastrophe	• Denounce the most extreme statements and ignore more moderate ones
• See every mistake and slip as a transgression that must be corrected immediately	• Doubt yourself because the other does
• Attack someone for your getting angry.	• Attack because you have been attacked
• Attack yourself for getting angry	• Forget the experience without learning from it
• Try to be and have things perfect	
• Suspect people's motives unless you have incontestable evidence that people can be trusted	
• Assume any attempt to change yourself is an admission of failure	
• Never forgive	

SOURCE: Reprinted with permission from D Tjosvold, *Learning to Manage Conflict: Getting People to Work Together Productively*, pp 127–29. Copyright © 1993 Dean Tjosvold. First published by Lexington Books. All rights reserved.

Summary of Key Concepts

1 Explain the nature and determinants of organization-based self-esteem.

Organization-based self-esteem (OBSE) is an employee's self-perceived value as an organizational member. People high in OBSE see themselves as important and meaningful within the organization. Three primary determinants of high OBSE are managerial respect and concern, flexible organization structure, and complex and challenging jobs.

2 Define self-efficacy, and explain its sources.

Self-efficacy involves one's belief about his/her ability to accomplish specific tasks. Those extremely low in self-efficacy suffer from learned helplessness. Four sources of self-efficacy beliefs are prior experience, behaviour models, persuasion from others, and assessment of one's physical and emotional states. High self-efficacy beliefs foster constructive and goal-oriented action, whereas low self-efficacy fosters passive, failure-prone activities and emotions.

3 Contrast high and low self-monitoring individuals and describe the resulting problems each may have.

A high self-monitor strives to make a good public impression by closely monitoring his or her behaviour and adapting it to the situation. Very high self-monitoring can create a 'chameleon' who is seen as insincere and dishonest. Low self-monitors do the opposite by acting out their momentary feelings, regardless of their surroundings. Very low self-monitoring can lead to a one-way communicator who seems to ignore verbal and non-verbal cues from others.

4 Identify and describe the Big Five personality dimensions, and specify which one is correlated most strongly with job performance.

The Big Five personality dimensions are extraversion (social and talkative), agreeableness (trusting and co-operative), conscientiousness (responsible and persistent), emotional stability (relaxed and unworried), and openness to experience (intellectual and curious). Conscientiousness is the best predictor of job performance.

5 Explain the difference between an internal and external locus of control.

People with an internal locus of control, such as entrepreneurs, believe they are masters of their own fate. Those with an external locus of control attribute their behaviour and its results to situational forces.

6 Explain how attitudes influence behaviour in terms of the Fishbein and Ajzen model of behavioural intentions.

According to Fishbein and Ajzen's model, beliefs about behaviour-outcome relationships and how one should act influence attitudes and subjective norms. Depending on their relative importance, attitudes and norms together foster a behavioural intention, the best predictor of actual behaviour.

7 Describe Carl Jung's cognitive styles typology.

By combining two dimensions of perception (sensation and intuition) with two dimensions of judgment (thinking and feeling), Carl Jung identified four cognitive styles. They are sensation/thinking (practical and matter-of-fact), intuition/thinking (logical and ingenious), sensation/feeling (sympathetic and friendly), and intuition/feeling (enthusiastic and insightful).

8 Distinguish between positive and negative emotions, and explain how they can be judged.

Positive emotions—happiness/joy, pride, love/affection and relief—are personal reactions to circumstances congruent with one's goals. Negative emotions—anger, fright/anxiety, guilt/shame, sadness, envy/jealousy and disgust—are personal reactions to circumstances incongruent with one's goals. Both types of emotions need to be judged in terms of intensity and the appropriateness of the person's relevant goal.

Discussion Questions

1 How should the reality of a more diverse workforce affect management's approach to dealing with individual differences?

2 What is your personal experience of organization-based self-esteem?

3 How is someone you know with low self-efficacy, relative to a specified task, 'programming themselves for failure?' What could be done to help that individual develop high self-efficacy?

4 What are the career implications of your self-monitoring score in the second OB Exercise?

5 Why is organizational identification both a good and bad thing in today's workplace?

6 On scales of Low = 1 to High = 10, how would you rate yourself on the Big Five personality dimensions? Is your personality profile suitable for a managerial position?

7 How would you respond to the following statement? 'Whenever possible, managers should hire people with an external locus of control.'

8 How would you respond to a manager who made this statement? 'I'm only interested in behaviour. I've never seen an attitude, so why be concerned with attitudes?'

9 According to Jung's typology, which cognitive style do you exhibit? How can you tell? Is it an advantage or a disadvantage?

10 What are your personal experiences of negative emotions being positive; and of positive emotions being negative?

Internet Exercise

Lots of interactive questionnaires can be found on the Internet to help you learn more about yourself. *Note:* These self-tests are for instructional and entertainment purposes only. They are not intended to replace rigorously validated and properly administered psychometric tests and should not be used to establish qualifications or make personnel decisions. Still, they can provide useful insights and stimulate discussion. The purpose of this exercise is to learn more about general intelligence (IQ) and emotional intelligence (EQ), two topics discussed in this chapter.

A Free Online Interactive Intelligence (IQ) Test

Go to Self Discovery Workshop's home page on the Internet (www.iqtest.com/welcometest.html). For instructive background, select and read the first two menu items, *What is an IQ score?* and *History of this intelligence test*. Then proceed to the third menu item, *Let me take this intelligence test now*. Follow the prompts. You will be given some instructions, a sample three-item pre-test, and then you will be asked to provide some personal data.

Note: As specified in the instructions, you do not have to fill out your details (name, address, etc.) to take the free IQ test. Simply skip ahead to the test, making sure to read the instructions very carefully because you will be given only 13 minutes to complete the 38 true/false test items. Only one run through the IQ test is appropriate if the results are to have any meaning at all. The test is scored automatically and you will be given both your IQ score and comparative norms. (*Note:* We recommend that you take this test when you are rested, refreshed and have a clear mind. Also,

www.iqtest.com/welcometest.html

people who do not respond well to time pressure may want to skip it to avoid unnecessary stress.)

A Free Online Emotional Intelligence (EQ) Test

Go to the Emotional Intelligence Services page of the HayGroup (**http://ei.haygroup.com**) and select *take an emotional intelligence quiz* in the left column. Fill in the short, 10-item questionnaire that appears on your screen. It's a very quick and easy test that is devised by Daniel Goleman himself. After completing the test, follow the prompt to submit your answers to automatic scoring. You may also want to check out the latest articles by EQ prominents, which you can click on the starting page.

Questions

1   Do you believe this sort of so-called pencil-and-paper psychological testing has any merit? Explain your rationale.

2   Could self-serving bias, discussed at the end of Chapter 6, influence the way people evaluate intelligence tests? Briefly, self-serving bias involves taking personal responsibility for your successes and blaming your failures on other factors. For example, 'I scored high, so I think it's a good test.' 'I scored low, so it's an unfair or invalid test.' Explain.

3   Do you agree with psychologist Daniel Goleman that EQ can be more important and more powerful than IQ? Explain.

Personal Awareness and Growth Exercise
What Is Your Cognitive Style?

Objectives

1 To identify your cognitive style, according to Carl Jung's typology.[107]

2 To consider the managerial implications of your cognitive style.

Instructions

Please respond to the 16 items below. There are no right or wrong answers. After you have completed all the items, refer to the scoring key, and follow its directions.

Questionnaire

Part I. Circle the response that comes closest to how you usually feel or act.

1 Are you more careful about:
   a people's feelings
   b their rights.
2 Do you usually get along better with:
   a imaginative people
   b realistic people.
3 Which of these two is the higher compliment:
   a a person has real feeling
   b a person is consistently reasonable.
4 In doing something with many other people, does it appeal more to you:
   a to do it in the accepted way
   b to invent a way of your own.
5 Do you get more annoyed at:
   a fancy theories
   b people who don't like theories.
6 It is higher praise to call someone:
   a a person of vision
   b a person of common sense.
7 Do you more often let:
   a your heart rule your head
   b your head rule your heart.
8 Do you think it is worse:
   a to show too much warmth
   b to be unsympathetic.
9 If you were a teacher, would you rather teach:
   a courses involving theory
   b fact courses.

Part II Which word in each of the following pairs appeals to you more? Circle **a** or **b**.

10 a compassion
b foresight
11 a justice
b mercy
12 a production
b design
13 a gentle
b firm
14 a uncritical
b critical
15 a literal
b figurative
16 a imaginative
b matter of fact.

Scoring Key

To categorize your responses to the questionnaire, count one point for each response on the following four scales, and total the number of points recorded in each column. Instructions for classifying your scores are indicated below.

SENSATION	INTUITION	THINKING	FEELING
2 B _____	2 A _____	1 B _____	1 A _____
4 A _____	4 B _____	3 B _____	3 A _____
5 A _____	5 B _____	7 B _____	7 A _____
6 B _____	6 A _____	8 A _____	8 B _____
9 B _____	9 A _____	10 B _____	10 A _____
12 A _____	12 B _____	11 A _____	11 B _____
15 A _____	15 B _____	13 B _____	13 A _____
16 B _____	16 A _____	14 B _____	14 A _____
Totals = _____	= _____	= _____	= _____

Classifying Total Scores

Write *intuitive* if your intuition score is equal to or greater than your sensation score.

Write *sensation* if sensation is greater than intuition.

Write *feeling* if feeling is greater than thinking.

Write *thinking* if thinking is greater than feeling.

When *thinking* equals feeling, you should write feeling if a male and thinking if a female.

Questions for discussion

1 What is your cognitive style?

Sensation/thinking (ST)

Intuition/thinking (NT)

Sensation/feeling (SF)

Intuition/feeling (NF)

2 Do you agree with this assessment? Why or why not?

3 Will your cognitive style, as determined in this exercise, help you achieve your career goal(s)?

4 Would your style be an asset or liability for a managerial position involving getting things done through others?

Group Exercise

Anger Control Role Play

Objectives

1 To demonstrate that emotions can be managed.

2 To develop your interpersonal skills for managing both your own and someone else's anger.

Introduction

Personal experience and research tells us that anger begets anger. People do not make their best decisions when angry. Angry outbursts often inflict unintentional interpersonal damage by triggering other emotions (such as disgust in observers and subsequent guilt and shame in the angry person). Effective managers know how to break the cycle of negative emotions by defusing anger in themselves and others. This is a role-playing exercise for groups of four. You will have a chance to play two different roles. All the roles are generic, so they can be played as either a woman or a man.

Instructions

Your instructor will divide the class into groups of four. Everyone should read all five roles described. Members of each foursome will decide among themselves who will play which roles. All told, you will participate in two rounds of role playing (each round lasting no longer than 8 minutes). In the first round, one person will play Role 1 and another will play Role 3; the remaining two group members will play Role 5. In the second round, those who played Role 5 in the first round will play Roles 2 and 4. The other two will switch to Role 5.

ROLE 1: THE ANGRY (OUT-OF-CONTROL) SHIFT SUPERVISOR

You work for a leading electronics company that makes computer chips and other computer-related equipment. Your factory is responsible for assembling and testing the company's most profitable line of computer microprocessors. Business has been good, so your factory is working three shifts. The day shift, which you are now on, is the most desirable one. The night shift, from 11 p.m. to 7:30 a.m. is the least desirable and least productive. In fact, the night shift is such a mess that your boss, the factory manager, wants you to move to the night shift next week. Your boss just broke this bad news as the two of you are having lunch in the company cafeteria. You are shocked and angered because you are one of the most senior and highly rated shift supervisors in the factory. Thanks to your leadership, your shift has broken all production records during the past year. As the divorced single parent of a 10-year-old child, the radical schedule change would be a major lifestyle burden. Questions swirl through your head. 'Why me?' 'What kind of reliable child-care will be available when I sleep during the day and work at night?' 'Why should I be "punished" for being a top supervisor?' 'Why don't they hire someone for the position?' Your boss asks what you think.

When playing this role, be as realistic as possible without getting so loud that you disrupt the other groups. Also, if anyone in your group would be offended by foul language, please refrain from cursing during your angry outburst.

ROLE 2: THE ANGRY (UNDER-CONTROL) SHIFT SUPERVISOR

Although you will use the same situation as in Role 1, this role will require you to read and act according to the tips for reducing chronic anger in the left side of Table 5–4. You have plenty of reason to be frustrated and angry, but you realize the importance of maintaining a good working relationship with the factory manager.

ROLE 3: THE (HARD-DRIVING) FACTORY MANAGER

You have a reputation for having a 'short fuse'. When someone gets angry with you, you attack. When playing this role, be as realistic as possible. Remember, you are responsible for the entire factory with its 1,200 employees and hundreds of millions of dollars of electronics products. A hiring freeze is in place, so you have to move one of your current supervisors. You have chosen your best supervisor because the night shift is your biggest threat to profitable operations. The night-shift supervisor gets a 10 per cent bonus. Ideally, the move will only be for six months.

ROLE 4: THE (MELLOW) FACTORY MANAGER

Although you will use the same general situation as in Role 3, this role will require you to read and act according to the tips for responding to angry provocation in the right side of Table 5–4. You have a reputation for being results-oriented but reasonable. You are good at taking a broad, strategic view of problems and are a good negotiator.

ROLE 5: SILENT OBSERVER

Follow the exchange between the shift supervisor and the factory manager without talking or getting actively involved. Jot down some notes (for later class discussion) as you observe whether or not the factory manager did a good job of managing the supervisor's anger.

Questions for Discussion

1   Why is uncontrolled anger a sure road to failure?

2   Is it possible to express anger without insulting others? Explain.

3   Which is more difficult, controlling anger in yourself or defusing someone else's anger? Why?

4   What useful lessons did you learn from this role-playing exercise?

Chapter Six

Social Perception and Attributions

Learning Objectives

When you finish studying the material in this chapter, you should be able to:

- Describe perception in terms of the social information processing model.

- Identify and briefly explain four managerial implications of social perception.

- Discuss stereotypes and the process of stereotype formation.

- Summarize the managerial challenges and recommendations of sex-role, age and race stereotypes.

- Discuss how the self-fulfilling prophecy is created and how it can be used to improve individual and group productivity.

- Explain, according to Kelley's model, how external and internal causal attributions are formulated.

- Review Weiner's model of attribution.

- Contrast the fundamental attribution bias and the self-serving bias.

Big Brother? No, it's just another day at the office

You have one colleague who embarrassingly burst into tears rather too often to your opinion. Another colleague withdraws from confrontation at every opportunity, something which you eventually find drives you crazy. And you're sick and tired of the good-looking smooth-talker from the accountancy department who tells tall tales and whose anti-gay talk the other day just confirmed everyone's suspicions that he might have something to hide. It's enough to make you think about giving in your notice. ▶

But these tiresome acquaintances are not in your workplace. They are appearing almost nightly on various channels throughout Europe—including the UK, Belgium, Holland, Switzerland, Italy and Spain—in Big Brother, the programme where 10 handsome young men and women have been locked up for two months in a house with one voted out each week.

When the show launched, critics assumed it would be sex appeal that guaranteed its audience. In fact, we have been compelled by seeing the chilling way in which a randomly-selected group of people sets about destroying one another under the gentle guise of mutual co-operation. Sound's familiar? It's probably a workplace near you.

The most frightening thing about the melodrama being played out in front of millions of people—and talked about by millions more than admit watching the programme—is its alarming similarity to the world in which we all live. Home, school, college and work are social environments in which we can often identify relatives, friends or colleagues whose apotheosis we now see on our television screens.

This is the 'ambulance effect', explains Professor Cary Cooper, one of Britain's leading specialists in work relationships. 'You see potential disaster and you want to look. The biggest similarity of all, that Big Brother possesses, is to a workplace. After all, they are working, even if they don't do much, and also they are very competitive.

'Work is just like a game; some people get promotion, some people get rejected and some people who don't get promoted will leave. We're learning from Big Brother who is perceived by others to be worthwhile and who will be retained.

'That's just like the office. People chat at the coffee machine and talk about other people and their relationships. They make assumptions about colleagues and bosses. They wonder how they can make themselves more popular. They spread gossip. But this programme actually allows you to hear the rumours firsthand.'

However, in the Big Brother house—like too many workplaces—there is a much more sinister objective lurking beneath much of the residents' conversational veneer. Each is jockeying for someone else to be ditched but at the same they want to be liked.

'Big Brother shows us an environment where people are uncomfortable with their roles', said Angela Ishmael of the Industrial Society. 'It's exactly what's happening in lots of workplaces. When managers aren't able to manage relationships in a team, team power takes over. It is a classic bullying scenario too, and it is becoming more and more common.'

'It's interesting how viewers form a certain picture of the people taking part in the programme. One person is marked as dishonest for not being open about plotting to get other people thrown out', said Ishmael. ' But he is quite genuine in terms of his feelings for his colleagues.'

'The simple truth is that he will look after himself more than everyone else. He's just more rehearsed that the rest of them at manipulating people. But another participant, who clearly isn't liked, will tell everyone exactly how he feels.'

'Even though that's quite aggressive, most people can identify with it. The sort of thing the second person will be accused of is not caring for other people's feelings. The sort of bullying the first one gets involved in is not as confrontational as the other approach but people do realize afterwards that they are being manipulated. That upsets them.'

'What the programme also picks up on vividly is an almost adolescent need for conformity', said Philip Hodson of the British Association for Counselling. 'It's that terrible fear of whether we're approved of, always worrying *does my bum look big in this?* So much of it is centred on trust, being liked and hanging up a positive picture of one's self. Do people say one thing to our face and another to our backs? Someone you think you trust is capable of damning you terribly.'

'At the heart of the programme is a focus on isolation', said Professor Cooper. 'This sort of environment is all about politics with a small "p", isolating certain people. They may be a threat to your promotion or they may be about to discover how incompetent you are. And you want to ensure their influence is minimal, so you spread rumours so that their position is undermined. Sometimes in this environment you will target someone by allying with a colleague, a third party, to put them down. That goes on in lots of organizations.

It may be to undermine them or perhaps just because you don't like them.'

'When we watch Big Brother we're learning lessons at an unconscious level for use in our workplace. Is it any wonder that we're all entranced?'[1]

In every social situation, we gather information on others. We form a certain picture of people based on the signals we receive from them. We encode and store this information and use it every time we interact with each other. In fact, we are constantly striving to make sense of our social surroundings, be it when watching a political conversation on TV or when having a romantic dinner.

The resulting knowledge influences our behaviour and helps us navigate our way through life. For example, think of the perceptual process that occurs when meeting someone for the first time. Your attention is drawn to the individual's physical appearance, mannerisms, actions and reactions to what you say and do. You ultimately arrive at conclusions based on your perceptions of this social interaction. The brown-haired, green-eyed individual turns out to be friendly and fond of outdoor activities. You further conclude that you like this person and then ask him or her to go to a concert, calling the person by the name you stored in memory.

This reciprocal process of perception, interpretation and behavioural response also applies at work. A field study illustrates this relationship. Researchers wanted to know whether employees' perceptions of how much an organization valued them affected their behaviour and attitudes. The researchers asked samples of high school teachers, brokerage-firm clerks, manufacturing workers, insurance representatives and police officers to indicate their perception of the extent to which their organization valued their contributions and their well-being. Employees who perceived that their organization cared about them reciprocated with reduced absenteeism, increased performance, innovation and positive work attitudes.[2] This study illustrates the importance of employees' perceptions. Also, many trainers in social skills increasingly emphasize the importance of perception in their seminars. For example, one trainer of the Dutch management consulting firm, Multiplus, recently stated the following.

> *Working with people requires both insight into others and into ourselves. If our self-concept doesn't match with the image others have of us, we can feel uncertain and conflicts can arise. By becoming conscious of what plays a role in our daily perceptions, we can appreciate the views of others. It is of great importance for everybody who has to work with people to learn the physiological, psychological and cultural factors that influence our perceptions and thereby limit our objectivity.*[3]

Perception is not only vital for managers; perception theories are also increasingly being applied in politics, the media, recruitment advertisements and so on. For example, the London-based Institution of Chemical Engineers, which was suffering from a serious drop in its student numbers, hoped that by invoking the names of famous 'chemical engineers' such as Cindy Crawford and the Swedish actor Dolph Lundgren, it could tempt young people to take up the subject. By coupling the names of celebrities to it, the Institution tried to turn 'chemical engineering' into something 'cool' and appealing. Instead of perceiving the subject as boring, people could now say: 'Why not? Cindy Crawford and Dolph Lundgren did it!'[4]

In this chapter, we focus on a social information processing model of perception; stereotypes; the self-fulfilling prophecy; and how causal attributions are used to interpret behaviour.

A SOCIAL INFORMATION PROCESSING MODEL OF PERCEPTION

Perception is a cognitive process that enables us to interpret and understand our surroundings. Recognition of objects is one of this process's major functions. For example, both people and animals recognize familiar objects in their environments. You would recognize a picture of your best friend; dogs and cats can recognize their food dishes or a favorite toy. Reading involves recognition of visual patterns representing letters in the alphabet. People must recognize objects to meaningfully interact with their environment. But since OB's principal focus is on people, the following discussion emphasizes *social* perception rather than object perception.

Perception
process of interpreting one's environment

The study of how people perceive one another has been labelled *social cognition* and *social information processing*. It is very different from the perception of objects.

> *Social cognition is the study of how people make sense of other people and themselves. It focuses on how ordinary people think about people and how they* think *they think about people . . . .*

> *Research on social cognition also goes beyond naive psychology. The study of social cognition entails a fine-grained analysis of how people think about themselves and others, and it leans heavily on the theory and methods of cognitive psychology.*[5]

Moreover, while general theories of perception date back many years, the study of social perception is relatively new, having originated in about 1976.

Four-Stage Sequence and a Working Example

Social perception involves a four-stage information processing sequence (hence, the label 'social information processing'). Figure 6–1 illustrates a basic social information processing model. Three of the stages in this model—selective attention/comprehension, encoding and simplification, and storage and retention—describe how specific social information is observed and stored in memory. The fourth and final stage, retrieval and response, involves turning mental representations into real-world judgements and decisions.

Keep the following everyday example in mind as we look at the four stages of social perception. Suppose you were thinking of taking a course in, say, personal finance. Three lecturers teach the same course, using different types of instruction and testing procedures. Through personal experience, you have come to prefer good lecturers who rely on the case method of instruction and essay tests. According to social perception theory, you would be most likely to arrive at a decision regarding which lecturer to select in the following way.

Stage 1: Selective Attention/Comprehension

People are constantly bombarded by physical and social stimuli in the environment. Since they do not have the mental capacity to fully comprehend all this information, they selectively perceive subsets of environmental stimuli. This is where attention plays a role. Attention is the process of becoming consciously aware of something or someone. Attention can be focused on information either from the environment or from memory. In respect of the latter, if you sometimes find yourself thinking about totally unrelated events or people while reading a textbook, your memory is the focus of your attention. Research has shown that people tend to pay attention to salient stimuli.

Attention
being consciously aware of something or someone

Figure 6-1 *Social Perception: A Social Information Processing Model*

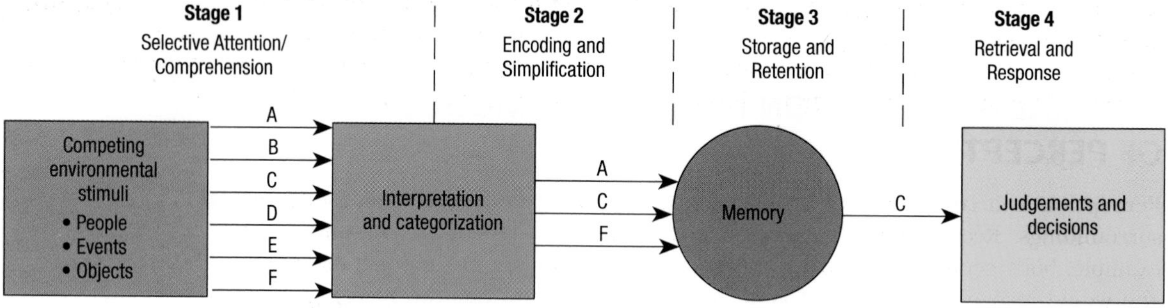

Stage 1	Stage 2	Stage 3	Stage 4
Selective Attention/ Comprehension	Encoding and Simplification	Storage and Retention	Retrieval and Response

Competing environmental stimuli
- People
- Events
- Objects

A
B
C
D
E
F

Interpretation and categorization

A
C
F

Memory

C

Judgements and decisions

Salient Stimuli

Something is *salient* when it stands out from its context. For example, Youko Ahola, a 130 kg Fin and the winner of the 'World's Strongest Man' competition in 1999, would certainly be salient in a women's aerobics class but not at the annual 'Viking Games' in Reykjavik. Social salience is determined by several factors, including being:

▼ **novel (the only person in a group of that race, gender, hair colour or age)**

▼ **bright (wearing a yellow shirt)**

▼ **unusual for that person (behaving in an unexpected way, such as a person with a fear of heights climbing a steep mountain)**

▼ **unusual for a person's social category (such as a company president driving a motorcycle to work)**

▼ **unusual for people in general (driving 30 km an hour in a 90 km an hour speed zone)**

▼ **extremely positive (a noted celebrity) or negative (the victim of a bad traffic accident)**

▼ **dominant in the visual field (sitting at the head of the table).[6]**

One's needs and goals often dictate which stimuli are salient. For a driver whose petrol gauge shows empty, a Shell or BP sign is more salient than a McDonald's or Pizza Hut sign. The reverse would be true for a hungry driver with a full petrol tank. Moreover, research shows that people have a tendency to pay more attention to negative than to positive information. This leads to a negativity bias.[7] This bias helps explain the 'gawking factor' that slows traffic to a crawl following a car accident.

Back to Our Example

You begin your search for the 'right' personal finance lecturer by asking friends who have taken classes from the lecturers. You also may interview the various lecturers who teach the class in order to gather still more relevant information. Returning to Figure 6–1, all the information you obtain represents competing environmental stimuli labelled A to F. Because you are concerned about the method of instruction (e.g., line A in Figure 6–1), testing procedures (e.g., line C), and past grade distributions (e.g., line F), information in those areas is particularly salient to you. Figure 6–1 shows that these three salient pieces of information are thus perceived. You can then proceed to the second stage of information processing. Meanwhile, competing stimuli represented by lines B, D and E in Figure 6–1 fail to get your attention and are discarded from further consideration.

Stage 2: Encoding and Simplification

Observed information is not stored in the memory in its original form. Encoding is required; raw information is interpreted or translated into mental representations. To accomplish this, perceivers assign pieces of information to cognitive categories. 'By *category* we mean a number of objects that are considered equivalent. Categories are generally designated by names, such as *dog, animal*.[8] People, events and objects are interpreted and evaluated by comparing their characteristics with information contained in a schema (or, if plural, schemata).

> **Cognitive Categories**
> *mental depositories for storing information*

Schemata

According to social information processing theory, a schema represents a person's mental picture or summary of a particular event or type of stimulus.[9] For example, your restaurant schema probably is quite similar to the description provided in Table 6–1.

> **Schema**
> *mental picture of an event or object*

Cognitive-category labels are needed to make schemata meaningful. The next OB Exercise illustrates this by asking you to rate the comprehensiveness of a schema both without and with its associated category label. Take a moment now to complete this exercise.

Encoding Outcomes

We use the encoding process to interpret and evaluate our environment. Interestingly, this process can result in differing interpretations and evaluations of the same person or event. The next International OB, for example, explains how countries with universalist and particularist cultures encode and interpret events in totally the opposite way to each other. Varying interpretations of what we observe occur for many reasons. First, people possess different information in the schemata used for interpretation. For instance, male CEOs and female executives disagree in their assessment of barriers preventing women from advancing to positions of corporate

Table 6–1

Restaurant Schema

Schema: Restaurant.

Characters: Customers, hostess, waiter, chef, cashier.

Scene 1: Entering.
    Customer goes into restaurant.
    Customer finds a place to sit.
        He may find it himself.
        He may be seated by a hostess.
            He asks the hostess for a table.
            She gives him permission to go to the table.

Scene 2: Ordering.
    Customer receives a menu.
    Customer reads it.
    Customer decides what to order.
    Waiter takes the order.
        Waiter sees the customer.
        Waiter goes to the customer.
        Customer orders what he wants.
    Chef cooks the meal.

Scene 3: Eating.
    After some time the waiter brings the meal from the chef.
    Customer eats the meal.

Scene 4: Exiting.
    Customer asks the waiter for the check.
    Waiter gives the check to the customer.
    Customer leaves a tip.
        The size of the tip depends on the goodness of the service.
    Customer pays the cashier.
    Customer leaves the restaurant.

SOURCE: From D. Rumelhart, *Introduction to Human Information Processing* (New York: John Wiley & Sons, Inc., 1977. Reprinted by permission of John Wiley & Sons, Inc.

leadership. Women and men also have different ideas about what types of behaviour constitute sexual harassment.[10] Second, our moods and emotions influence our focus of attention and evaluations.[11] Third, people tend to apply recently used cognitive categories during encoding. For example, you are more likely to interpret a neutral behaviour exhibited by a lecturer as positive if you were recently thinking about positive categories and events.[12] Fourth, individual differences influence encoding. Pessimistic or depressed individuals, for instance, tend to interpret their surroundings more negatively than optimistic and happy people.[13] The point is that we should not be surprised when people interpret and evaluate the same situation or event differently. Researchers are currently trying to identify the host of factors that influence the encoding process.

OB Exercise

Does a Schema Improve the Comprehension of Written Material?

Instructions

The purpose of this exercise is to demonstrate the role of schema in encoding. First read the passage shown below. Once done, rate the comprehensiveness of what you read using the scale provided. Next, examine the schema label presented in Reference 9 in the Notes section at the end of the book. With this label in mind, re-read the passage, and rate its comprehensiveness. Then think of an explanation of why your ratings changed. You will then have just experienced the impact of schema in encoding.

Read this Passage

The procedure is actually quite simple. First you arrange things into different groups. Of course, one pile may be sufficient depending on how much there is to do. If you have to go somewhere else due to lack of facilities, that is the next step; otherwise you are pretty well set. It is important not to overdo things. That is, it is better to do too few things at once than too many. In the short run this may not seem important but complications can easily arise. A mistake can be expensive as well. At first the whole procedure will seem complicated. Soon, however, it will become just another facet of life. It is difficult to foresee any end to the necessity for this task in the immediate future, but then one never can tell. After the procedure is completed, one arranges the materials into different groups again. Then they can be put into their appropriate places. Eventually they will be used once more, and the whole cycle will then have to be repeated. However, that is part of life.

Comprehensive Scale

Very Uncomprehensive	Neither	Very Comprehensive
	1 — 2 — 3 — 4 — 5	

J D Bransford and M K Johnson, 'Contextual Prerequisite for Understanding: Some Investigations of Comprehension and Recall', *Journal of Verbal Learning and Verbal Behavior*, December 1972, p 722. Reprinted with permission of Academic Press, Inc.

Back to Our Example

Having collected relevant information about the three personal finance lecturers and their approaches, you compare this information with other details contained in the schemata. This leads you to form an impression and evaluation of what it would be like to take a course with each lecturer. In turn, the relevant information contained on paths A, C and F in Figure 6–1 are passed along to the third stage of information processing.

Stage 3: Storage and Retention

This phase involves storage of information in long-term memory. Long-term memory is like an apartment complex consisting of separate units connected to one another. Although different people live in each apartment, they sometimes interact. In addition, large apartment complexes have different wings (such as A, B, and C). Long-term memory similarly consists of separate but related categories. Like the individual apartments inhabited by unique residents, the connected categories contain different types of information. Information also passes between these categories. Finally, long-term memory is made up of three compartments (or wings) containing categories of information about events, semantic materials, and people.[14]

Event Memory

This compartment is composed of categories containing information about both specific and general events. These memories describe appropriate sequences of events in well-known situations, such as going to a restaurant (refer back to Table 6–1), going on a job interview, to a food store or to a movie.

Semantic Memory

Semantic memory refers to general knowledge about the world. In so doing, it functions as a mental dictionary of concepts. Each concept contains a definition (such as a good leader) and associated traits (outgoing), emotional states (happy), physical characteristics (tall), and behaviours (works hard). Just as there are schemata for general events, concepts in semantic memory are stored as schemata. Given our previous discussion of managing diversity in Chapter 2, it should come as no surprise that there are cultural differences in the type of information stored in semantic memory.

International OB

Perception and Culture: Universalist (Rule-Based) versus Particularist (Relationship-Based) Cultures

There are two 'pure' yet alternative types of judgement. At one extreme, we encounter an obligation to adhere to standards which are universally agreed by the culture in which we live. 'Do not lie. Do not steal. Do unto others as you would have them do unto you' (the Golden Rule), and so on. At the other extreme, we encounter particular obligations to people we know. 'X is my dear friend, so obviously I would not lie to him or steal from him. It would hurt us both to show less than kindness to one another.'

Universalist, or rule-based, behaviour tends to be abstract. Try crossing the street when the light is red in a very rule-based society like Switzerland or Germany. Even if there is no traffic, you will still be frowned at. It also tends to imply equality in the sense that all individuals falling under the rule should be treated the same. But situations are ordered by categories. For example, if 'others' to whom you 'do unto' are not categorized as human, the rules may not apply. Finally, rule-based conduct has a tendency to resist exceptions that might weaken

that rule–there is a fear that once you start to make exceptions for illegal conduct the system will collapse.

Particularist judgements focus on the exceptional nature of present circumstances. This person is not a 'citizen' but my friend, brother, husband, child or person of unique importance to me, with special claims on my love or my hatred. I must therefore sustain, protect, or discount this person no matter what the rules say. [Particularist cultures are found in Russia, China, India and Mexico.]

Business people from both societies will tend to think each other corrupt. A universalist will say of particularists, 'they cannot be trusted; they will always help out their friends' and a particularist, conversely, will say of universalists, 'you cannot trust them; they would not even help a friend'.

In practice we use both kinds of judgement and in most of the situations we encounter, they reinforce each other. If an employee is harassed in the workplace we would

International OB

disapprove of this because 'harassment is immoral and against company rules' and/or because 'it was a terrible experience for Jennifer and really upset her'. The universalist's chief objection, though, would be at the breach of rules: 'employees should not have to deal with harassment in the workplace; it is wrong'. The

particularist is likely to be more disapproving of the fact that it caused distress to poor Jennifer.

Source: Excerpted from F Trompenars and C Hampden-Turner, *Riding the Waves of Culture* **(New York: McGraw-Hill, 1998), pp 31–32. © 1998. Reproduced with permission of the McGraw-Hill Companies.**

Person Memory

Categories within this compartment contain information about a single individual (your supervisor) or groups of people (managers).

Back to Our Example

As the time draws near for you to decide which personal finance lecturer to take, your schemata of them are stored in the three categories of long-term memory. These schemata are available for immediate comparison and/or retrieval.

Stage 4: Retrieval and Response

People retrieve information from memory when they make judgements and decisions. Our ultimate judgements and decisions are either based on the process of drawing on, interpreting, and integrating categorical information stored in long-term memory or on retrieving a summary judgement that was already made.[15]

Concluding our example, it is registration day and you have to choose which lecturer to take for personal finance. After retrieving from memory your schemata-based impressions of the three lecturers, you select a good one who uses the case method and gives essay tests (line C in Figure 6–1). In contrast, you may choose your preferred lecturer by simply recalling the decision you made two weeks ago.

Managerial Implications

Social cognition is the window through which we all observe, interpret and prepare our responses to people and events. A wide variety of managerial activities, organizational processes, and quality-of-life issues are thus affected by perception. Consider, for example, the following implications.

Hiring

Interviewers make hiring decisions based on their impression of how an applicant fits the perceived requirements of a job. Inaccurate impressions in either direction produce poor hiring decisions. Moreover, interviewers with racist or sexist schemata can undermine the accuracy and legality of hiring decisions. Those invalid schemata need to be confronted and improved through coaching and training. Failure to do so can lead to poor hiring decisions. For example, a study of 46 male and 66 female financial-institution managers revealed that their hiring decisions were biased by the physical attractiveness of applicants. More attractive men and women were hired over less attractive applicants with equal qualifications.[16] On the positive side, however, a recent study demonstrated that interviewer training can reduce the use of invalid schema. Training improved interviewers' ability to obtain high-quality, job-related information and to stay focused on the interview task. Trained interviewers provided more balanced judgements about applicants than did non-trained interviewers.[17] A Belgian study of 1,724 respondents on the perception of diversity in the workplace, revealed that people pretended to be rarely influenced by sex differences when hiring new employees. Age played a more important role: younger people preferred younger people, older respondents opted for their contemporaries. In traditional environments, people chose more traditionally: ethnic minorities and [known] homosexuals had less chance of being recruited.[18]

Performance Appraisal

Faulty schemata about what constitutes good as opposed to poor performance can lead to inaccurate performance appraisals, which erode work motivation, commitment and loyalty. For example, a recent study of 166 production employees indicated that they had greater trust in management when they perceived that the performance appraisal process provided accurate evaluations of their performance.[19] Therefore, it is important for managers to accurately identify the behavioural characteristics and results indicative of good performance at the beginning of a performance review cycle. These characteristics can then serve as the benchmarks for evaluating employee performance. The importance of using objective rather than subjective measures of employee performance was highlighted in a meta-analysis involving 50 studies and 8,341 individuals. Results revealed that objective and subjective measures of employee performance were only moderately related. The researchers concluded that objective and subjective measures of performance are not interchangeable.[20] Managers are thus advised to use more objectively based measures of performance—as much as possible— because subjective indicators are prone to bias and inaccuracy. In those cases where the job does not possess objective measures of performance, however, managers should still use subjective evaluations. Furthermore, because memory for specific instances of employee performance deteriorates over time, managers need a mechanism for accurately recalling employee behaviour.[21] Research reveals that individuals can be trained to be more accurate raters of performance.[22]

Leadership

Research demonstrates that employees' evaluations of leader effectiveness are influenced strongly by their schemata of good and poor leaders. A leader will have a difficult time influencing employees when he or she exhibits behaviours contained in employees' schemata of poor leaders. A team of researchers investigated the behaviours contained in our schemata of good and poor leaders. Good leaders were perceived as exhibiting the following behaviours:

▼ **assigning specific tasks to group members**
▼ **telling others that they had done well**
▼ **setting specific goals for the group**
▼ **letting other group members make decisions**
▼ **trying to get the group to work as a team**
▼ **maintaining definite standards of performance.**

In contrast, poor leaders were perceived as exhibiting the following behaviours:

▼ **telling others that they had performed poorly**
▼ **insisting on having their own way**
▼ **doing things without explaining themselves**
▼ **expressing worry over the group members' suggestions**
▼ **frequently changing plans**
▼ **letting the details of the task become overwhelming.** [23]

Communication

Managers need to remember that social perception is a screening process that can distort communication, both incoming and outgoing. Messages are interpreted and categorized according to schemata developed through past experiences and influenced by one's age, gender, and ethnic, geographic and cultural orientations. Effective communicators try to tailor their messages to the receiver's perceptual schemata. This requires well-developed listening and observation skills and cross-cultural sensitivity.

STEREOTYPES: PERCEPTIONS ABOUT GROUPS OF PEOPLE

While it is often true that beauty is in the eye of the beholder, perception does result in some predictable outcomes. Managers aware of the perception process and its outcomes enjoy a competitive edge. The Walt Disney Company, for instance, takes full advantage of perceptual tendencies to influence customers' reactions to waiting in long lines at its theme parks.

> In order to make the experience less psychologically wearing, the waiting times posted by each attraction are generously overestimated, so that one comes away mysteriously grateful for having hung around 20 minutes for a 58-second twirl in the Alice in Wonderland teacups. The lines [queues], moreover, are always moving, even if what looks like the end is actually the start of a second set of switchbacks leading to—oh, no!–a pre-ride waiting area. Those little tricks of the theme park mean a lot.[24]

Likewise, managers can use knowledge of perceptual outcomes to help them interact more effectively with employees. For example, Table 6–2 describes five common perceptual errors. Since these perceptual errors often distort the evaluation of job applicants and of employee performance, managers need to guard against them. This section examines one of the most important and potentially harmful perceptual outcomes associated with person perception: stereotypes. After exploring the process of stereotype formation and maintenance; we discuss stereotypes in relation to sex-roles, age, race, and disability; and then look at the managerial challenge to avoid stereotypical biases.

Stereotype Formation and Maintenance

Stereotype
beliefs about the characteristics of a group

'A **stereotype** is an individual's set of beliefs about the characteristics or attributes of a group.'[25] Stereotypes are not always negative. For example, the belief that engineers are good at maths is certainly part of a stereotype. Stereotypes may be accurate but very often this is not the case, as you can see in the following examples.

> Footage of aggressive English football fans at Euro 2000 would lead us to believe that they are uniquely chubby, balding and working class. This image is not accurate because plenty of football hooligans are educated, middle-class bankers or professionals, whose comfortable, rather dull lifestyles are supplemented by the occassional excesses at the football stadium. However, today's cameramen are still instructed by their editors only to film tattooed, beer-gutted, tonsured barbarians head-butting the French or pulverising the Portugese. This just adds to our perception that all the middle-class fans must be round the corner visiting a museum or tutting at the trouble over a cappucino.[26]

> Net users are frequently seen as nerds. However, recent research revealed that they are not sad and lonely misfits but actually visit and contact relatives and friends more frequently than those who live their lives offline. In a study, in which 3,500 adults were questioned, it was found that 72 per cent of Internet users had visited a relative or a friend in the last day. Only 61 per cent of those without an online account had done the same. Rather than breaking friendships, the Internet seems to promote them. Many people use the Internet to re-establish contact with friends they have lost touch with.[27]

In general, stereotypic characteristics are used to differentiate a particular group of people from other groups.[28] Consider walking into a business meeting with 10 people situated around a conference table. You notice a male at the head of the table and a woman seated immediately to his right, taking notes. Due to ingrained stereotypes, you might assume that the man is the top-ranking person in the room and the woman, his administrative assistant. This example highlights how people use stereotypes to interpret their environment and to make judgements about others.

Unfortunately, stereotypes can lead to poor decisions, can create barriers for women, older individuals, people of colour and people with disabilities, and can undermine loyalty and job satisfaction. For example, a recent study of 280 executives from minority groups revealed that 40 per cent believed they had been denied well-deserved promotions because of discrimination. Another sample of 2,958 workers indicated that women and coloured people perceived lower chances of advancement than whites. Finally, respondents who saw little opportunity for advancement tended to be less loyal, less committed, and less satisfied with their jobs.[29]

Table 6–2

Commonly Found Perceptual Errors

Perceptual Error	Description	Example
Halo	A rater forms a overall impression about an object and then uses that impression to bias ratings about the object.	Rating a professor high on the teaching dimensions of ability to motivate students, knowledge, and communication because we like him or her.
Leniency	A personal characteristic that leads an individual to consistently evaluate other people or objects in an extremely positive fashion.	Rating a professor high on all dimensions of performance regardless of his or her actual performance. The rater who hates to say negative things about others.
Central tendency	The tendency to avoid all extreme judgments and rate people and objects as average or neutral.	Rating a professor average on all dimensions of performance regardless of his or her actual performance.
Recency effects	The tendency to remember recent information. If the recent information is negative, the person or object is evaluated negatively.	Although a professor has given good lectures for 12 to 15 weeks, he or she is evaluated negatively because lectures over the last 3 weeks were done poorly.
Contrast effects	The tendency to evaluate people or objects by comparing them with characteristics of recently observed people or objects.	Rating a good professor as average because you compared his or her performance with three of the best professors you have ever had in college. You are currently taking courses from the three excellent professors.

Stereotyping is a four-step process. It begins by categorizing people into groups according to various criteria, such as gender, age, race, and occupation. Next, we infer that all people within a particular category possess the same traits or characteristics (such as all women are nurturing, older people have more job-related accidents, all blacks are good athletes, all lecturers are absent-minded). Then, we form expectations of others and interpret their behaviour according to our stereotypes. Finally, stereotypes are maintained by:

▼ overestimating the frequency of stereotypic behaviours exhibited by others

▼ incorrectly explaining expected and unexpected behaviours

▼ differentiating minority individuals from oneself.[30]

Although these steps are self-reinforcing, there are ways to break the chain of stereotyping.

Research shows that the use of stereotypes is influenced by the amount and type of information available to an individual and his or her motivation to accurately process information.[31] People are less apt to use stereotypes to judge others when they encounter salient information that is highly inconsistent with a stereotype. For instance, you are unlikely to assign stereotypic 'lecturer' traits to a new lecturer you have this term if he or she rides a Harley-Davidson, wears leather gear to lectures, and has a pierced nose. People also are less likely to rely on stereotypes when they are motivated to avoid using them. That is, accurate information-processing requires mental effort. Stereotyping is generally viewed as a less effort-inducing strategy for information processing. Let us now take a look at different types of stereotypes and consider additional methods for reducing their biasing effects.

Sex-Role Stereotypes

Sex-role stereotype
beliefs about appropriate roles for men and women

A **sex-role stereotype** is the belief that differing traits and abilities make men and women particularly well suited to different roles. For example, gender stereotypes view women as more expressive, less independent, more emotional, less logical, less quantitatively oriented and more participative than men. Men, on the other hand, are more often perceived as lacking interpersonal sensitivity and warmth, less expressive, less apt to ask for directions, more quantitatively oriented, and more autocratic and directive than women.[32]

Although research demonstrates that men and women do not systematically differ in the manner suggested by traditional stereotypes,[33] these stereotypes still persist. A study compared sex-role stereotypes held by men and women from five countries: China, Japan, Germany, the United Kingdom, and the United States. Males in all five countries perceived that successful managers possessed characteristics and traits more commonly ascribed to men in general than to women in general. Among the females, the same pattern of managerial sex typing was found in all countries except the United States. US females perceived that males and females were equally likely to possess traits necessary for managerial success.[34] Also of interest, research recently revealed that the old image of the 'dumb blonde' still remains entrenched. Tony Cassidy of Coventry University in the UK asked 120 students of both sexes to look at a photograph of a model and rate her intelligence, shyness, aggression, temperament and popularity. They were given one of four photos of the same woman, identical except for the hair colour: platinum blonde, natural blonde, brown haired or red haired. The platinum blonde was rated as significantly less intelligent than the others, and this was slightly more apparent when the viewers were men.[35]

The key question now becomes whether these stereotypes influence the hiring, evaluation and promotion of people at work. A meta-analysis of 19 studies comprising 1,842 individuals found no significant relationships between applicant gender and hiring recommendations.[36] A second meta-analysis of 24 experimental studies revealed that men and women received similar performance ratings for the same level of task performance. Stated differently, there was no pro-male bias. These experimental results were further supported in a field study of female and male lecturers.[37] Unfortunately, results pertaining to promotion decisions are not as promising. A field study of 682 employees in a multinational company revealed that gender was significantly related to ratings of promotion potential. Men received more favourable evaluations than women in spite of controlling for age, education, organizational tenure, salary grade and type of job.[38] Another recent study of 100 male and female army officers at the rank of captain unfortunately produced similar results. Men were consistently judged to be better leaders than women.[39] The existence of sex-role stereotypes may partially explain this finding.

Age Stereotypes

Age stereotypes reinforce age discrimination because of their negative orientation. In The Netherlands, a study carried out among 1,128 companies showed that applicants are mainly refused the position because of their age. This conclusion was confirmed by 75 per cent of the employers questioned.[40] For example, long-standing age stereotypes depict older workers as less satisfied, not as involved with their work, less motivated, not as committed, less productive than their younger co-workers and more apt to be absent from work. Older employees are also perceived as being more accident prone. As with sex-role stereotypes, these age stereotypes are more fiction than fact.

OB researcher, Susan Rhodes, sought to determine whether age stereotypes were supported by data from 185 different studies. She discovered that as age increases so too do employees' job satisfaction, job involvement, internal work motivation and organizational commitment. Moreover, older workers were not more accident prone.[41]

Results are not as clear-cut regarding job performance. A meta-analysis of 96 studies representing 38,983 people and a cross section of jobs, revealed that age and job performance were unrelated.[42] Some OB researchers, however, believe that this finding does not reflect the true relationship between age and performance. They propose that the relationship between age and performance changes as people grow older.[43] This idea was tested on data obtained from 24,219 individuals. In support of this hypothesis, results revealed that age was positively related to performance for younger employees (25 to 30 years of age) and then plateaued: Older employees were not less productive. Age and experience also predicted a better performance for more complex jobs than other jobs; and job experience had a stronger relationship with performance than age.[44] Another recent study examined memory, reasoning, spatial relations and dual tasking for 1,000 doctors, ages 25 to 92, and 600 other adults. The researchers concluded 'that a large proportion of older individuals scored as well or better on aptitude tests than those in the prime of life. We call these intellectually vigorous individuals "optimal agers".'[45]

What about turnover and absenteeism? A meta-analysis containing 29 samples and a total of 12,356 individuals revealed that age and turnover were negatively related. That is, older employees quit less often than younger employees. Similarly, another meta-analysis of 34 studies encompassing 7,772 workers indicated that age was inversely related to both voluntary (a day at the beach) and involuntary (sick day) absenteeism.[46] Contrary to stereotypes, older workers are ready and able to meet their job requirements. Moreover, results from the meta-analysis suggest managers should focus more attention on the turnover and absenteeism among younger workers than among older workers.

Race Stereotypes

There is not a large percentage of ethnic minority managers in Europe. Negative racial stereotypes are one of several potential explanations for this state of affairs. Consider women applicants who are also from a minority. There appears to be a stereotype that these 'minority women' are frequently hired to fulfill equal employment opportunity requirements.

Some research supports this experience. A recent study attempted to determine whether there was a relationship between being labelled an 'affirmative action' employee and perceptions of an employee's competence. Results both from an experiment using university students and a field test using 184 white men, supported the conclusion that a stigma of incompetence arises when people are hired for supposed 'affirmative action' reasons. Consider the case of Kate Redfern.

Kate Redfern, a white teacher, claims to have been sacked–along with three colleagues– from Peckham Rye primary school (UK) as part of an effort to impose race quotas aimed at giving blacks a third of all teaching jobs.[47]

Another study, covering 814 black managers and 814 white managers, examined the relationship of race to employee attitudes. The results demonstrated that blacks, when compared to whites, felt less accepted by their peers, perceived lower managerial discretion on their jobs, reached career plateaux more frequently, noted lower levels of career satisfaction and received lower performance ratings.[48] Negative findings like these prompted researchers to investigate whether race stereotypes actually bias performance ratings and hiring decisions. Given the increasing number of people of ethnic minorities that will enter the workforce over the next 10 years (remember our discussion in Chapter 2), employers should focus on nurturing and developing women and ethnic minorities as well as increasing managers' sensitivities to invalid racial stereotypes.

Managerial Challenges and Recommendations

The key managerial challenge is to make decisions that are blind to gender, age and race. To do so, organizations need first to educate themselves about the problem of stereotyping through employee training. The next step entails engaging in a broad effort to reduce stereotypes throughout the organization. The next International OB discusses how the Bank of Montreal tried to accomplish this recommendation. Social scientists believe that 'quality' interpersonal contact among mixed groups is the best way to reduce stereotypes because it provides people with more accurate data about the characteristics of other groups of people. As such, organizations should create opportunities for diverse employees to meet and work together in co-operative groups of equal status.

Another recommendation is for managers to identify valid individual differences (discussed in Chapter 5) that differentiate between successful and unsuccessful performers. As previously discussed, for instance, research reveals experience is a better predictor of performance than age. Research also shows that managers can be trained to use these valid criteria when hiring applicants and evaluating employee performance.[49]

Removing promotional barriers for men and women and for coloured people is another viable solution to alleviating the stereotyping problem. This can be accomplished by minimizing the differences in job experience across groups of people. Similar experience, coupled with the accurate evaluation of performance, helps managers to make decisions that are blind to gender, age, race and disability.

There are several recommendations that can be pursued based on the documented relationship between age and performance.

1　Because performance plateaus with age for non-complex jobs, organizations may use the variety of job design techniques discussed in Chapter 7 to increase employees' intrinsic motivation.

2　Organizations may need to consider using incentives to motivate employees to upgrade their skills and abilities. This will help avoid unnecessary plateaus.[50]

3　It may be advisable to hire older people in order to acquire their accumulated experience. This is especially useful for highly complex jobs. Moreover, hiring older workers is a good solution for reducing turnover, providing role models for younger employees, and coping with the current shortage of qualified entry-level workers.

A good example is the opening of a new store in Macclesfield, UK by B&Q, Britain's largest home-improvement chain.[51] The store was staffed entirely with workers aged 50 or older. Consider the results obtained from comparing the Macclesfield store with five B&Q stores with similar employment and sales levels.

- ▼ **Macclesfield was 18 per cent more profitable than the average of the five comparison B&Q stores.**
- ▼ **Employee turnover at Macclesfield was nearly six times lower than the average of the comparison stores.**
- ▼ **The older workers at Macclesfield were absent 39 per cent less than workers in the other stores.**
- ▼ **Leakage, which is the difference between stock expected in the store and stock actually in the store because of theft, damage and inventory not received, at Macclesfield is less than half the average of the five comparison stores.**
- ▼ **Extra training has not been required for older workers.**

It is important to obtain top management's commitment and support to eliminate the organizational practices that support or reinforce stereotyping and discriminatory decisions. Research clearly demonstrates that top management support is essential to successful implementation of the types of organizational changes being recommended.[52]

International OB

Bank of Montreal Proactively Reduces Stereotypes of Women

www.bmo.com

The Bank of Montreal found that stereotypes were the primary obstacle to women's advancement. In addition to the belief that mothers lack job commitment, the company found that many employees thought women didn't 'have the right stuff', or needed more education to qualify for top jobs. Personnel files, however, showed that women in lower-level jobs were better educated than their male peers and that more female employees than men at all levels got top-flight performance ratings.

The company followed up by improving career planning, broadening flexible scheduling, and

holding managers accountable for advancing women. Today, 19 per cent of Bank of Montreal's senior executives are women, up from 6 per cent in 1991. The company also monitors the rumour mill, most recently tackling employee talk that 'men are an endangered species around here'. Again, personnel files revealed men were receiving a fair number of promotions.

SOURCE: S Shellenbarger, 'Work & Family: Shedding Light on Women's Records Dispels Stereotypes', *The Wall Street Journal*, December 20, 1995, p B1.

SELF-FULFILLING PROPHECY: THE PYGMALION EFFECT

Historical roots of the self-fulfilling prophecy are found in Greek mythology. According to mythology, Pygmalion was a sculptor who hated women yet fell in love with an ivory statue he carved of a beautiful woman. He became so infatuated with the statue that he prayed to the goddess Aphrodite to bring her to life. The goddess heard his prayer, granted his wish, and Pygmalion's statue came to life. The essence of the **self-fulfilling prophecy**, or Pygmalion effect, is that people's expectations or beliefs determine their behaviour and performance, thus serving to make their expectations come true. In other words, we strive to validate our *perceptions* of reality, no matter how faulty they may be. Thus, the self-fulfilling prophecy is an important perceptual outcome we need to understand better.

Self-fulfilling prophecy
people's expectations determine behaviour and performance

Research and an Explanatory Model

The self-fulfilling prophecy was first demonstrated in an academic environment. After giving a bogus test of academic potential to students from grades 1 to 6, researchers informed teachers that certain students had high potential for achievement. In reality, students were randomly assigned to the 'high potential' and 'control' (normal potential) groups. Results showed that children designated as having high potential obtained significantly greater increases in both IQ scores and reading ability than did the control students.[53] The teachers of the supposedly high potential group got better results because their high expectations caused them to give harder assignments, more feedback, and more recognition of achievement. Students in the normal potential group did not excel because their teachers did not expect outstanding results.

Research has similarly shown that by raising instructors' and managers' expectations for individuals performing a wide variety of tasks, higher levels of achievement and productivity can be obtained.[54] Subjects in these field studies included airmen at the United States Air Force Academy Preparatory School, disadvantaged people in job-training programmes, electronics assemblers, trainees in a military command course, US naval personnel, and cadets in a naval officer course in the Israel Defense Forces. There is an interesting trend inherent in research supporting the Pygmalion effect. All studies exclusively involved men.

To overcome this limitation, a recent team of researchers conducted two experimental studies on samples of female and male cadets in the Israel Defense Forces. Results revealed that the Pygmalion effect was produced for both female and male cadets—but only when the leader was male. Female leaders did not produce a significant Pygmalion effect. This finding must be considered in the light of the fact that women were rated as better leaders than men in the Israel Defense Forces. The researchers concluded that the Pygmalion effect clearly works on both women and men when the leader is male but not when the leader is female.[55] Future research is obviously needed to uncover the cause of these gender-based differences.

Figure 6–2 presents a model of the self-fulfilling prophecy that helps explain these results. This model attempts to outline how supervisory expectations affect employee performance. As indicated, high supervisory expectation produces better leadership (linkage 1), which subsequently leads employees to develop higher self-expectations (linkage 2). Higher expectations motivate workers to exert more effort (linkage 3), ultimately increasing performance (linkage 4) and supervisory expectations (linkage 5). Successful performance also improves an employee's self-expectancy for achievement (linkage 6). A team of researchers recently coined the term the 'set-up-to-fail syndrome' to represent the negative side of the performance enhancing process depicted in Figure 6–2.[56] Let us consider how it works.

Say that an employee makes a mistake, such as losing notes during a meeting or exhibits poor performance on a task by turning in a report a day late. A manager then begins to wonder if this person has what it takes to be successful in the organization. This doubt leads the manager to watch this person more carefully. The employee, of course, notices this doubt and begins to sense a loss of trust. The suspect employee then responds in one of two ways. He or she may doubt his or her own judgement and competence. This in turn leads the individual to become more averse to taking risk and to decrease the amount of ideas and suggestions for the manager's critical review. The manager notices this behaviour and interprets it as an example of less initiative. Alternatively, the employee may do the opposite and take on more and more responsibility so that he or she can demonstrate his or her competence and worth. This is likely to cause the employee to fail on something, which in turn reinforces the manager's suspicions.[57] You can see that this process results in a destructive relationship that is fuelled by negative expectations. The point to remember is that the self-fulfilling prophecy works in both directions. The next section discusses ideas for enhancing the Pygmalion effect and reducing the set-up-to-fail syndrome.

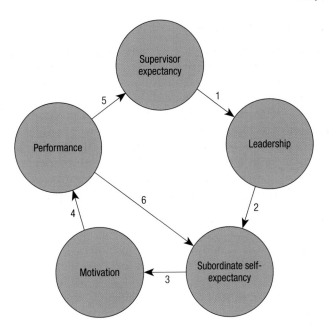

Figure 6–2
A Model of the Self-Fulfilling Prophecy

SOURCE: D Eden, 'Self-Fulfilling Prophecy as a Management Tool: Harnessing Pygmalion', *Academy of Management Review*, January 1984, p 67. Used with permission.

Putting the Self-Fulfilling Prophecy to Work

Largely due to the Pygmalion effect, managerial expectations powerfully influence employee behaviour and performance. Consequently, managers need to harness the Pygmalion effect by building a hierarchical framework that reinforces positive performance expectations throughout the organization.

Employees' self-expectations are the foundation of this framework. In turn, positive self-expectations improve interpersonal expectations by encouraging people to work toward common goals. This co-operation enhances group-level productivity and promotes positive performance expectations within the work group. At Microsoft Corporation, for example, employees routinely put in 75-hour weeks, especially when work groups are trying to meet shipment deadlines for new products. Because Microsoft is known for meeting its deadlines, positive group-level expectations help to create and reinforce an organizational culture of high expectancy of success. This process then makes people enthusiastic about working for the organization, thereby reducing turnover.[58]

As positive self-expectations are the foundation for creating an organization-wide Pygmalion effect, then let us consider how managers can create positive performance expectations. This task may be accomplished by using various combinations of the following.

1 Recognize that everyone has the potential to increase his or her performance.
2 Instil confidence in your staff.
3 Set high performance goals.
4 Positively reinforce employees for a job well done.
5 Provide constructive feedback when necessary.
6 Help employees rise through the organization.
7 Introduce new employees as if they have outstanding potential.
8 Become aware of your personal prejudices and any non-verbal messages that may discourage others.
9 Encourage employees to visualize the successful execution of tasks.
10 Help employees master key skills and tasks.[59]

CAUSAL ATTRIBUTIONS

Attribution theory is based on the premise that people attempt to infer causes for observed behaviour. Rightly or wrongly, we constantly formulate cause-and-effect explanations for our own and others' behaviour. Attributional statements such as the following are common: 'Joe drinks too much because he has no willpower; but I need a couple of drinks after work because I'm under a lot of pressure.' Formally defined, **causal attributions** are suspected or inferred causes of behaviour. Even though our causal attributions tend to be self-serving and are often invalid, it is important to understand how people formulate attributions because they profoundly affect organizational behaviour. For example, a supervisor who attributes an employee's poor performance to a lack of effort might reprimand that individual. However, training might be deemed necessary if the supervisor attributes the poor performance to a lack of ability.

Causal Attributions
suspected or inferred causes of behaviour

Generally speaking, people formulate causal attributions by considering the events preceding an observed behaviour. This section introduces and explores two different widely cited attribution models proposed by Harold Kelley and Bernard Weiner. Attributional tendencies, research and related managerial implications are also discussed.

Kelley's Model of Attribution

Current models of attribution, such as Kelley's, are based on the pioneering work of the late Fritz Heider. Heider, the founder of attribution theory, proposed that behaviour can be attributed either to **internal factors** within a person (such as ability) or to **external factors** within the environment (such as a difficult task). This line of thought parallels the idea of an internal versus external locus of control, as discussed in Chapter 5. Building on Heider's work, Kelley attempted to pinpoint major antecedents of internal and external attributions. Kelley hypothesized that people make causal attributions after gathering information about three dimensions of behaviour: consensus, distinctiveness and consistency.[60] These dimensions vary independently, thus forming various combinations and leading to differing attributions.

Internal factors
personal characteristics that cause behaviour

External factors
environmental characteristics that cause behaviour

Figure 6–3 presents performance charts showing low versus high consensus, distinctiveness, and consistency. These charts are now used to help develop a working knowledge of all three dimensions in Kelley's model.

Consensus involves a comparison of an individual's behaviour with that of his or her peers. There is high consensus when one acts like the rest of the group and low consensus when one acts differently. As shown in Figure 6–3, high consensus is indicated when persons A, B, C, D and E obtain similar levels of individual performance. In contrast, person C's performance is low in consensus because it significantly varies from the performance of persons A, B, D and E.

Distinctiveness is determined by comparing a person's behaviour on one task with his or her behaviour on other tasks. High distinctiveness means the individual has performed the task in question in a significantly different manner from the way he or she has performed other tasks. Low distinctiveness means stable performance or quality from one task to another. Figure 6–3 reveals that the employee's performance on task 4 is highly distinctive because it significantly varies from his or her performance on tasks 1, 2, 3 and 5.

Consistency is determined by judging if the individual's performance on a given task is consistent over time. High consistency implies that a person performs a certain task the same way, time after time. Unstable performance of a given task over time would mean low consistency. The downward spike in performance depicted in the consistency graph of Figure 6–3 represents low consistency. In this case, the employee's performance on a given task varied over time.

Figure 6–3

*Performance Charts Showing Low and High Consensus, Distinctiveness and
Consistency Information*

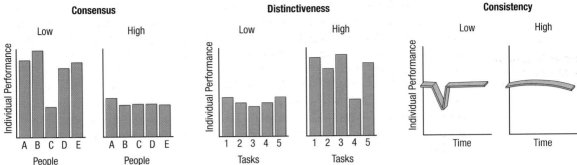

SOURCE: K A Brown, 'Explaining Group Poor Performance: An Attributional Analysis', *Academy of
Management Review*, January 1984, p 56. Used with permission.

It is important to remember that consensus relates to other *people*, distinctiveness relates
to other *tasks*, and consistency relates to *time*. The question now is: How does information
about these three dimensions of behaviour lead to internal or external attributions?

Kelley hypothesized that people attribute behaviour to *external* causes (environmental
factors) when they perceive high consensus, high distinctiveness and low consistency.
Internal attributions (personal factors) tend to be made when observed behaviour is
characterized by low consensus, low distinctiveness and high consistency. So, for
example, when all employees are performing poorly (high consensus), when the poor
performance occurs on only one of several tasks (high distinctiveness), and the poor
performance occurs during only one time period (low consistency), a supervisor will
probably attribute an employee's poor performance to an external source such as peer
pressure or an overly difficult task. In contrast, performance will be attributed to an
employee's personal characteristics (an internal attribution) when only the individual
in question is performing poorly (low consensus), when the inferior performance is
found across several tasks (low distinctiveness), and when the low performance has
persisted over time (high consistency). Many studies supported this predicted pattern
of attributions.[61]

Weiner's Model of Attribution

Bernard Weiner, a noted motivation theorist, developed an attribution model to
explain achievement behaviour and to predict subsequent changes in motivation and
performance. Figure 6–4 presents a modified version of his model. Weiner believes
that the attribution process begins after an individual performs a task. A person's
performance leads him or her to judge whether it was successful or unsuccessful. This
evaluation then produces a causal analysis to determine if the performance was due to
internal or external factors. Figure 6–4 shows that ability and effort are the primary
internal causes of performance and task difficulty; luck, and help from others, are the
key external causes. These attributions for success and failure then influence how
individuals feel about themselves.

For instance, a meta-analysis of 104 studies involving almost 15,000 individuals found
that people who attributed failure to their lack of ability (as opposed to bad luck)
experienced psychological depression. The exact opposite attributions (to good luck
rather than to high ability) tended to trigger depression in people experiencing positive
events. In short, perceived bad luck took the sting out of a negative outcome, but
perceived good luck reduced the joy associated with success.[62]

Returning to Figure 6–4, note that the psychological consequences can either increase or decrease depending on the causes of performance. For example, your self-esteem is likely to increase after achieving an 'A' in your next exam if you believe that your performance was due to your ability or effort. In contrast, this same grade can either increase or decrease your self-esteem if you believe that the test was easy. Finally, the feelings that people have about their past performance influences future performance. Figure 6–4 reveals that future performance is higher when individuals attribute success to internal causes and lower when failure is attributed to external factors. Future performance is more uncertain when individuals attribute either their success or failure to external causes.

In further support of Weiner's model, a study of 130 salesmen in the United Kingdom revealed that positive, internal attributions for success were associated with higher sales and performance ratings.[63] A second study examined the attributional processes of 126 employees who were made redundant by a plant closing. Practice was seen to be consistent with the model: the explanation for job loss was attributed to internal and stable causes; so the life satisfaction, self-esteem and expectations for re-employment, diminished. Furthermore, research also shows that when individuals attribute their success to internal rather than external factors, they have higher expectations for future success; report a greater desire for achievement; and set higher performance goals.[64]

Figure 6–4 *A Modified Version of Weiner's Attribution Model*

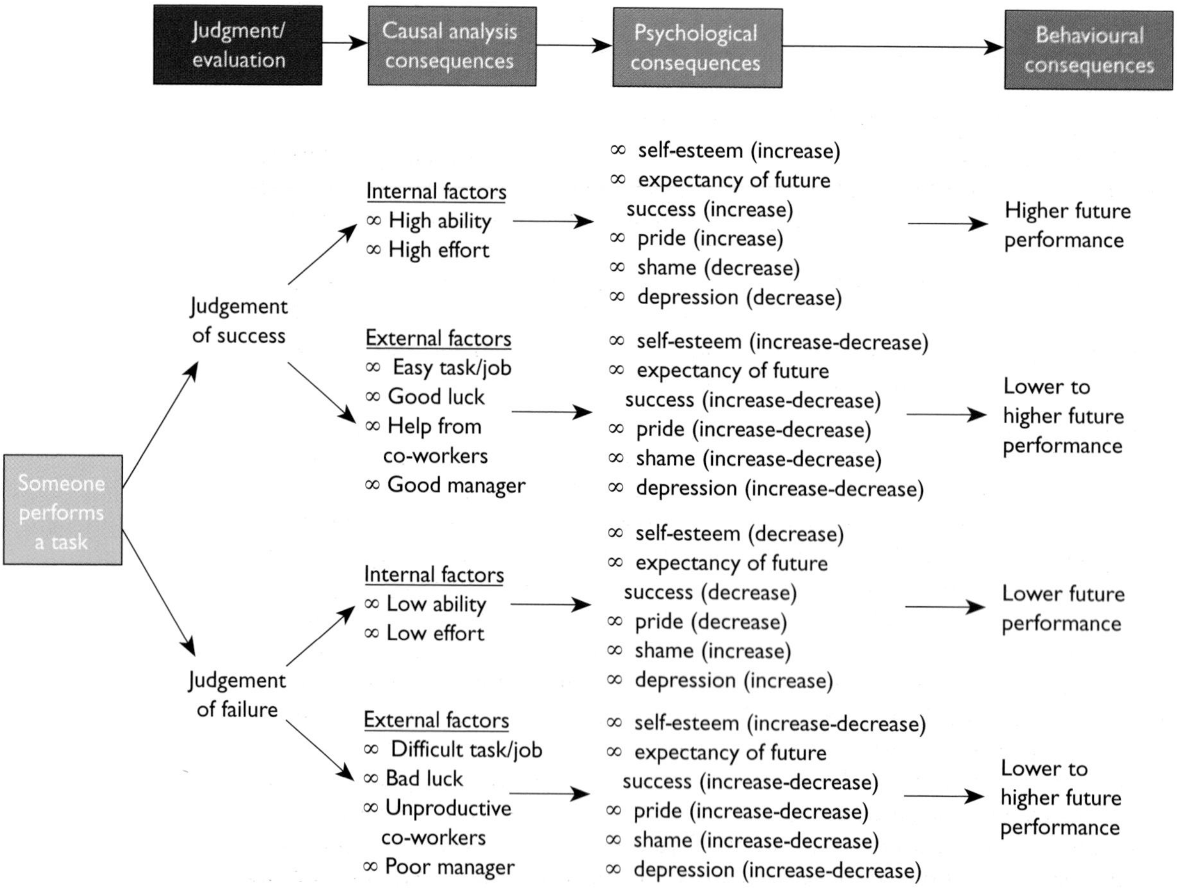

SOURCE: Based in part on B Weiner, 'An Attributional Theory of Achievement Motivation and Emotion', *Psychological Review*, October 1985, pp 548–73; and T S Bateman, G R Ferris and S Strasser, 'The "Why" behind Individual Work Performance', *Management Review*, October 1984, p 71.

Attributional Tendencies

Researchers have uncovered two attributional tendencies that distort one's interpretation of observed behaviour–fundamental attribution bias and self-serving bias.

Fundamental Attribution Bias

The **fundamental attribution bias** reflects one's tendency to attribute another person's behaviour to his or her personal characteristics, as opposed to situational factors. This bias causes perceivers to ignore important environmental forces that often significantly affect behaviour. For example, a study of 1,420 employees of a large utility company demonstrated that supervisors tended to make more internal attributions about worker accidents than did the workers. Interestingly, research also shows that people from Westernized cultures tend to exhibit the fundamental attribution bias more than do individuals from East Asia.[65]

> **Fundamental attribution bias**
> *ignoring environmental factors that affect behaviour*

Self-Serving Bias

The **self-serving bias** represents one's tendency to take more personal responsibility for success than for failure. Referring again to Figure 6–4, employees tend to attribute their successes to internal factors (high ability and/or hard work) and their failures to uncontrollable external factors (tough job, bad luck, unproductive co-workers or an unsympathetic boss).[66] This self-serving bias is evident in how students typically analyse their performance in exams. Grade 'A' students are likely to attribute their marks to high ability or hard work. Grade 'D' students, meanwhile, tend to pin the blame on factors like an unfair test, bad luck, or unclear lectures. Because of self-serving bias, it is very difficult to pin down personal responsibility for mistakes in today's complex organizations.

> **Self-serving bias**
> *taking more personal responsibility for succes than failure*

Managerial Application and Implications

Attribution models can be used to explain how managers handle poorly performing employees. One study revealed that managers gave employees more immediate, frequent and negative feedback when they attributed their performance to low effort. This reaction was even more pronounced when the manager's success was dependent on an employee's performance. A second study indicated that managers tended to transfer employees whose poor performance was attributed to a lack of ability. These same managers also decided to take no immediate action when poor performance was attributed to external factors beyond an individual's control.[67]

The preceding situations have several important implications for managers. First, managers tend to disproportionately attribute behaviour to *internal* causes.[68] This can result in inaccurate evaluations of performance, leading to reduced employee motivation. No one likes to be blamed for something caused by factors they perceive to be beyond their control. Further, because managers' responses to employee performance vary according to their attributions, attributional biases may lead to inappropriate managerial actions, including promotions, transfers, lay-offs, and so forth. This can dampen motivation and performance. Attributional training sessions for managers are in order. Basic attributional processes can be explained, and managers can be taught to detect and avoid attributional biases. Finally, an employee's attributions for his or her own performance have dramatic effects on subsequent motivation, performance and personal attitudes such as self-esteem. For instance, people tend to give up, develop lower expectations for future success, and experience decreased self-esteem when they attribute failure to a lack of ability. Fortunately, attributional retraining can improve both motivation and performance. Research shows that employees can be taught to attribute their failures to a lack of effort rather than to a lack of ability.[69] This attributional realignment paves the way for improved motivation and performance.

In summary, managers need to keep a finger on the pulse of employee attributions if they are to make full use of the motivation concepts in the next two chapters.

Summary of Key Concepts

1 Describe perception in terms of the social information processing model.

Perception is a mental and cognitive process that enables us to interpret and understand our surroundings. Social perception, also known as social cognition and social information processing, is a four-stage process. The four stages are selective attention/comprehension, encoding and simplification, storage and retention, and retrieval and response. During social cognition, salient stimuli are matched with schemata, assigned to cognitive categories, and stored in long-term memory for events, semantic materials, or people.

2 Identify and briefly explain four managerial implications of social perception.

Social perception affects hiring decisions, performance appraisals, leadership perceptions, and communication processes. Inaccurate schemata or racist and sexist schemata may be used to evaluate job applicants. Similarly, faulty schemata about what constitutes good versus poor performance can lead to inaccurate performance appraisals. Invalid schemata need to be identified and replaced with appropriate schemata through coaching and training. Further, managers are advised to use objective rather than subjective measures of performance. With respect to leadership, a leader will have a difficult time influencing employees when he or she exhibits behaviours contained in employees' schemata of poor leaders. Finally, communication is influenced by schemata used to interpret any message. Effective communicators try to tailor their messages to the receiver's perceptual schemata.

3 Discuss stereotypes and the process of stereotype formation.

Stereotypes represent grossly oversimplified beliefs or expectations about groups of people. Stereotyping is a four-step process that begins by categorizing people into groups according to various criteria. Next, we infer that all people within a particular group possess the same traits or characteristics. Then, we form expectations of others and interpret their behaviour according to our stereotypes. Finally, stereotypes are maintained by: overestimating the frequency of stereotypic behaviours exhibited by others; incorrectly explaining expected and unexpected behaviours; and differentiating minority individuals from oneself. The use of stereotypes is influenced by the amount and type of information available to an individual and his or her motivation to accurately process information.

4 Summarize the managerial challenges and recommendations of sex-role, age and race stereotypes.

The key managerial challenge is to make decisions that are blind to gender, age, race and disabilities. Training can be used to educate employees about the problem of stereotyping and to equip managers with the skills needed to handle unique situations associated with managing certain employees. Because mixed-group contact reduces stereotyping, organizations should create opportunities for diverse employees to meet and work together in co-operative groups of equal status. Hiring decisions should be based on valid individual differences. Managers can be trained to use valid criteria when evaluating employee performance. Minimizing differences in job opportunities and experiences across groups of people can help alleviate promotional barriers. Job design techniques can be used to reduce performance plateaus associated with age. Organizations may also need to use incentives to motivate employees to upgrade their skills and abilities, and hiring older workers has many potential organizational benefits. It is critical to obtain top management's commitment and support to eliminate stereotyping and discriminatory decisions.

5 Discuss how the self-fulfilling prophecy is created and how it can be used to improve individual and group productivity.

The self-fulfilling prophecy, also known as the Pygmalion effect, describes how people behave so their expectations come true. High managerial expectations foster high employee self-expectations. These, in turn, lead to greater effort and better performance, and yet higher expectations. Conversely, the set-up-to-fail syndrome represents the negative side of the self-fulfilling prophecy. Managers are encouraged to harness the Pygmalion effect by building a hierarchical framework that reinforces positive performance expectations throughout the organization.

6 Explain, according to Kelley's model, how external and internal causal attributions are formulated.

Attribution theory attempts to describe how people infer causes for observed behaviour. According to Kelley's model of causal attribution, external attributions tend to be made when consensus and distinctiveness are high and consistency is low. Internal (personal responsibility) attributions tend to be made when consensus and distinctiveness are low and consistency is high.

7 Review Weiner's model of attribution.

Weiner's model of attribution predicts achievement behaviour in terms of causal attributions. Attributions of ability, effort, task difficulty, luck, and help from others affect how individuals feel about themselves. In turn, these feelings directly influence subsequent achievement-related performance.

8 Contrast the fundamental attribution bias and the self-serving bias.

Fundamental attribution bias involves emphasizing personal factors more than situational factors while formulating causal attributions for the behaviour of others. Self-serving bias involves personalizing the causes of one's successes and externalizing the causes of one's failures.

Discussion Questions

1. Why is it important for managers to have a working knowledge of perception and attribution?

2. When you are sitting in your course group, what stimuli are salient? What is your schema for course group activity?

3. Have you ever been stereotyped by someone else? Discuss.

4. Which type of stereotype (sex-role, age, race) do you believe is more pervasive in organizations? Why?

5. What evidence of self-fulfilling prophecies have you seen lately?

6. How might your lecturer use the process outlined in Figure 6–2 to improve the overall performance of the students in your course group?

7. How would you formulate an attribution, according to Kelley's model, for the behaviour of a fellow student who starts arguing in class with your lecturer?

8. In what situations do you tend to attribute your successes/failures to luck? How well does Weiner's attributional model in Figure 6–4 explain your answers? Explain.

9. Are poor people victimized by a fundamental attribution bias? Explain.

10. What evidence of the self-serving bias have you observed lately?

Internet Exercise

www.adl.org

This chapter examined the process of stereotype formation and discussed stereotpyes pertaining to gender, age, race and disabilities. The purpose of this is to explore the issue of stereotypes in more detail. Go to the Internet home page for the Anti-Defamation League (ADL) at (www.adl.org), and browse through the different issues on extremism, anti-semitism, hate crimes and the holocaust. After reading these sections, select the option that provides information about the Anti Defamation League, 'about ADL'. There you will find historical information and some annual reports. Finally, conduct a search within the ADL's database on the terms *stereotypes* and *discrimination*.

Questions

1. Who founded the ADL? What is the purpose of the ADL and how has it evolved?

2. What are the differences between stereotypes, prejudice, discrimination, and scapegoating?

3. How prevalent are anti-Semitic views? Who is most likely to hold anti-Semitic views?

4. How can organizations reduce the use of stereotypes and discrimination at work?

Interpersonal Awareness Exercise
How Do Diversity Assumptions Influence Team Member Interactions?

Objectives

1. To identify diversity assumptions.

2. To consider how diversity assumptions affect team members' interactions.

Introduction

Assumptions can be so ingrained that we do not even know that we are using them. Negative assumptions can limit our relationships with others because they influence how we perceive and respond to those we encounter in our daily lives. This exercise is designed to help identify the assumptions that you have about groups of people. Although this exercise may make you uncomfortable because it asks you to identify stereotypical assumptions, it is a positive first step to facing and examining the assumptions we make about other people. This awareness can lead to positive behavioural change.

Instructions

Complete the diversity assumptions worksheet.[70] The first column contains various dimensions of diversity. For each dimension, the second column asks you to identify the assumptions held by the general public about people with this characteristic. Use the third column to determine how each assumption might limit team members' ability to effectively interact with each other. Finally, answer the questions for discussion.

Questions for Discussion

1. Where do our assumptions about others come from?

2. Is it possible to eliminate negative assumptions about others? How might this be done?

3. What most surprised you about your answers to the diversity assumption worksheet?

Diversity Assumption Worksheet

Dimension of Diversity	Assumption That Might Be Made	Affect on Team Members' Interactions
Age	Example: You can't teach an old dog new tricks. Older people are closed to new Example: Younger people haven't had the proper experience to come up with good solutions.	Example: Older people are considered to be resistant to change. Example: Input from younger employees is not solicited.
Ethnicity (e.g., Mexican)		
Gender		
Race		
Physical ability (e.g., hard of hearing)		
Sexual orientation		
Marital/parental status (e.g., single parent with children)		
Religion (e.g., Buddhist)		
Recreational habits (e.g., hikes on weekends)		
Educational background (e.g., college education)		
Work experience (e.g., union)		
Appearance (e.g., overweight)		
Geographic location (e.g., rural)		
Personal habits (e.g., smoking)		
Income (e.g., well-to-do)		

Group Exercise
Using Attribution Theory to Resolve Performance Problems

Objectives

1   To gain experience determining the causes of performance.
2   To decide on corrective action for employee performance.

Introduction

Attributions are typically made to internal and external factors. Perceivers arrive at their assessments by using various informational cues or antecedents. To determine the types of antecedents people use, we have developed a case containing various informational cues about an individual's performance. You will be asked to read the case and make attributions about the causes of performance. To assess the impact of attributions on managerial behaviour, you will also be asked to recommend corrective action.

Instructions

Presented below is a case study that depicts the performance of Mary Martin, a computer programmer. Please read the case and then identify the causes of her behaviour by answering the question following the case. After completing this task, decide on the appropriateness of various forms of corrective action. A list of potential recommendations has been drawn up. The list is divided into four categories. Read each action, and evaluate its appropriateness by using the scale provided. Next, compute a total score for each of the four categories.

Causes of Performance

To what extent was each of the following a cause of Mary's performance? Use the following scale:

Very Little				Very much
1 —— 2 —— 3 —— 4 —— 5				

a	High ability	1	2	3	4	5
b	Low ability	1	2	3	4	5
c	Low effort	1	2	3	4	5
d	Difficult job	1	2	3	4	5
e	Unproductive co-workers	1	2	3	4	5
f	Bad luck	1	2	3	4	5

THE CASE OF MARY MARTIN

Mary Martin, 30, received her baccalaureate degree in computer science from a reputable state school in the US Midwest. She also graduated with above-average grades. Mary is currently working in the computer support/analysis department as a programmer for a US-based firm. During the past year, Mary has missed 10 days of work. She seems unmotivated and rarely completes her assignments on time. Mary is usually given the harder programs to work on.

Past records indicate that Mary, on average, completes programs classified as 'routine' in about 45 hours. Her co-workers, on the other hand, complete these routine programs in an average of 32 hours. Further, Mary finishes programs considered 'major problems' in about 115 hours on average. Her co-workers, however, finish these same assignments, in an average of 100 hours. When Mary has worked in programming teams, her peer performance reviews are generally average to negative. Her male peers have noted she is not creative in attacking problems and she is difficult to work with.

The computer department recently sent a questionnaire to all users of its services to evaluate the usefulness and accuracy of data received. The results indicate many departments are not using computer output because they cannot understand the reports. It was also determined that the users of output generated from Mary's programs found the output chaotic and not useful for managerial decision making.[70]

Appropriateness of Corrective Action

Evaluate the following courses of action by using the scale below:

Very Inappropriate				Very Appropriate
1 —— 2 —— 3 —— 4 —— 5				

Coercive Actions

a	Reprimand Mary for her performance	1	2	3	4	5
b	Threaten to fire Mary if her performance does not improve	1	2	3	4	5

Change Job

c	Transfer Mary to another job	1	2	3	4	5
d	Demote Mary to a less demanding job	1	2	3	4	5

Non-Punitive Actions

e	Work with Mary to help her do the job better	1	2	3	4	5
f	Offer Mary encouragement to help her improve	1	2	3	4	5

No Immediate Actions

g	Do nothing	1	2	3	4	5
h	Promise Mary a pay raise if she improves	1	2	3	4	5

Compute a score for the four categories:[71]

Coercive actions = a + b =

Change job = c + d =

Non-punitive actions = e + f =

No immediate actions = g + h =

Questions for Discussion

1 How would you evaluate Mary's performance in terms of consensus, distinctiveness, and consistency?

2 Is Mary's performance due to internal or external causes?

3 What did you identify as the top two causes of Mary's performance? Are your choices consistent with Weiner's classification of internal and external factors? Explain.

4 Which of the four types of corrective action do you think is most appropriate? Explain. Can you identify any negative consequences of this choice?

Chapter Seven

Motivation through Needs, Job Design and Satisfaction

Learning Objectives

When you finish studying the material in this chapter, you should be able to:

- Define the term *motivation*.

- Discuss the job performance model of motivation.

- Review the historical roots of modern motivation theories.

- Contrast Maslow's and McClelland's need theories.

- Demonstrate your familiarity with scientific management, job enlargement, job rotation and job enrichment.

- Explain the practical significance of Herzberg's distinction between motivators and hygiene factors.

- Describe how internal work motivation is increased by using the job characteristics model.

- Discuss the causes and consequences of job satisfaction.

Ninety-five per cent of this man's staff say they love working for him. What's his secret?

Management, the Julian Richer way, is simple: make sure your staff are happy in order to give good customer service, increase turnover, reduce complaints, cut theft and absenteeism. 'You've got a good payback financially', adds Richer, the 38-year-old founder of the hi-fi chain Richer Sounds, 'plus the fact that you sleep better at night as a chief executive'. ▶

In the past few years, bosses at Sears, Halifax and Asda have hired Richer to help instigate some of his motivational schemes.

His methods of creating a happy workforce are numerous and legendary, including free access for staff to seven holiday homes in the UK and Paris (regardless of sales performance), trips on the Orient Express for staff who come up with good ideas, a fiver every month to each employee so they can go down to the pub and brainstorm, and the use of a Bentley or Jaguar for a month for the best performing shop.

A bit gimmicky perhaps? He laughs: 'I prefer the word innovative. Take the cars, my colleagues love them and the holiday homes are rarely empty. People may say that's a gimmick. But if they're used, they work, and people can say what the heck they like. 'Gimmicky' sounds like a cheap trick but I'm very sincere about my philosophy. You've got to keep the buzz going–and work at making it as much fun as possible. That's no gimmick!'

His indignation is perhaps justified. True, he has had several business failures, including a £400,000 stumble when he invested in a friends's keyboard shop. But Richer has been in 'the biz', as he calls it, for 19 years and his tiny hi-fi stores, splattered with Day-Glo labels in the cheaper ends of town, have achieved extraordinary sales per square foot, with his London Bridge shop boasting the highest sales density in the world. All this helped provide Richer with a mansion in Yorkshire and an annual salary of £650,000, as well as 27 hi-fi stores and the chairmanship of another 10 companies (of which he controls 9). His latest venture, buying into the ailing digital camera store, Tecno, with its 26 outlets, could finally see him heading a quoted company.

With all this in the bag, Richer really doesn't have anything to prove. What motivates him, he says, is a love of the job. If it was just for the money, he would have quit years ago. 'I don't want to sit on a beach all day', he insists. 'I love the biz, I really enjoy it.'

That enthusiasm and candour fired the imagination of Richer's fans, gained through his work in consulting. 'We saw someone with novel ideas who understood people', says John Lee, group personnel and services director at the Halifax bank. Lee may have recoiled when he saw Richer Sounds' cluttered shops but his confidence paid off as he watched Richer turn the bank's traditional, moribound Staff Suggestion Scheme on its head. We'd never have had the guts to do it without him', says Lee. 'He got senior managers to encourage their teams to come up with ideas, then set up a small team to handle them quickly. Everyone gets a reply signed by the chief executive or a director–the good ones have undoubtedly made or saved money. It's been phenomenal. With over 50,000 suggestions in less than two years from 37,000 staff, Lee is convinced he has the most succesful scheme in the country.

Richer also used this approach with supermarket chain Asda. 'I don't advise people because I need the money', Richer insists again. 'I do it because I enjoy working on a bigger stage. Working with Asda has been one of the most satisfying aspects of my career. Here were superstores with a middle-aged, unmotivated, part-time workforce sitting on the check-outs on paltry wages. To get 70,000 people doing something that originated from an idea of yours is phenomenally satisfying and motivating. It proved to me that the philosophy can be interpreted across the board.'

With the sales of his book, *The Richer Way*, already at 25,000 and conferences, videos and a recruitment service launched recently, Richer's ideas seem to be gaining ground all over Britain. As a result, in 1998, he launched Richer Consulting, dedicated to preaching his gospel. His hi-fi chain, Richer Sounds, will be lead now by David Robinson, who has worked for Richer since he was 16.[1]

For discussion
Why do you think the Richer Way has proven to be so effective?

Effective employee motivation and satisfaction has long been one of management's most difficult and important duties. Success in this endeavour is becoming more challenging in the light of organizational trends to downsize and re-engineer and the demands associated with managing a diverse workforce. Companies are using a wide range of techniques to keep their staff happy and motivated, ranging from classical measures such as job redesign and stimulating compensation schemes through to the 'gimmicks' Julian Richer used, as seen in the opening case study. It is said that companies not just want their employees to like their job, they want them to love their job. '*Contented cows give better milk*', write HR-specialists Richard Hadden and Bill Catlette.[2] As a result, some innovative companies nowadays increasingly experiment with alternative, creative ploys to create an overtly enthusiastic workforce. An executive cynically explains the rationale behind this trend: 'with the old techniques, we got their mind, now we've got their heart and soul too . . . .'[3] Consider the following examples.

> *Some Dotcom companies in London are trying to hang on to people by introducing supermarket-style reward points for good performance. These are accumulated and cashed in for benefits covering everything from paid sabbaticals to in-house yoga sessions.*[4]

> *At TBWA, a British advertising agency, staff can chill out in a leisure zone equipped with two Sony Playstation pods and all the latest games, video screens and a pool table.*[5]

> *Saloman Smith Barney has taken to providing gourmet meals, fresh underwear and free toothbrushes to staff working past 7 p.m.*[6]

Also, as we enter the 21st century, it is said that most employees have undergone thorough motivational changes. The researchers Ester, Halman and de Moor of the university of Tilburg in the Netherlands, for example, compared the motivation and values of modern day workers with those of previous generations, such as their parents and grandparents. They concluded that people nowadays want significantly more than just a high salary and good career prospects. They want to express autonomy, creativity and growth in their job. They rate meeting new challenges and finding self-expression higher than accruing status.[7]

All these changes and trends put together, impose great challenges for contemporary employers, who want to keep their people motivated. Accordingly, the purpose of this chapter, as well as the next, is to provide you with a foundation for understanding the complexities of employee motivation. Specifically, this chapter provides a definitional and theoretical foundation for the topic of motivation so that a rich variety of motivation theories and techniques can be introduced and discussed.

Coverage of employee motivation extends to Chapter X. After providing a conceptual model for understanding motivation, this chapter focuses on: need theories of motivation; an overview of job design methods used to motivate employees; a job characteristics approach to job design; and job satisfaction and work-family relationships. In the next chapter, attention turns to equity, expectancy, and goal-setting.

WHAT DOES MOTIVATION INVOLVE?

Motivation
psychological processes that arouse and direct goal-directed behaviour

The term **motivation** derives from the Latin word *movere*, meaning 'to move'. In the present context, motivation represents 'those psychological processes that cause the arousal, direction, and persistence of voluntary actions that are goal directed'.[8] Managers need to understand these psychological processes if they are to successfully guide employees toward accomplishing organizational objectives. This section therefore provides a conceptual framework for understanding motivation and examines the historical roots of motivational concepts.

A Job Performance Model of Motivation

Terence Mitchell, a well-known OB researcher, proposed a broad conceptual model that explains how motivation influences job behaviours and performance. This model, which is shown in Figure 7–1, integrates elements from several of the theories we discuss in this book. It identifies the causes and consequences of motivation.[9]

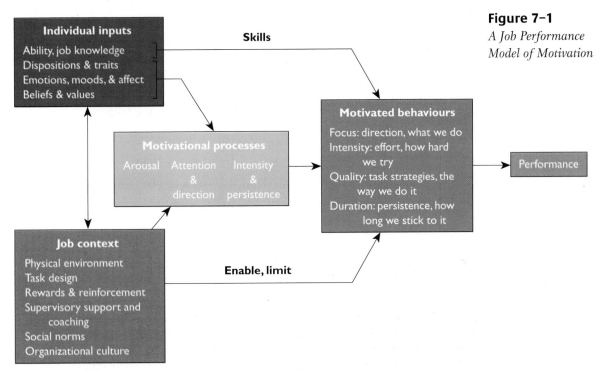

Figure 7–1

A Job Performance Model of Motivation

SOURCE: Adapted from T R Mitchell, 'Matching Motivational Strategies with Organizational Contexts,' in *Research in Organizational Behavior* (vol 19), eds L L Cummings and B M Staw (Greenwich, CT: JAI Press, 1997), p 63.

Figure 7–1 shows that individual inputs and job context are the two key categories of factors that influence motivation. As discussed in Chapter X, employees bring ability, job knowledge, dispositions and traits, emotions, moods, beliefs and values to the work setting. The job context includes the physical environment, the tasks one completes, the organization's approach to recognition and rewards, the adequacy of supervisory support and coaching, and the organization's culture (recall our discussion in Chapter 3). These two categories of factors influence each other as well as the motivational processes of arousal, direction and persistence. Consider the motivational implications associated with the job contexts in the following examples.

Workers at the British car constructor, Land Rover, used to call their filthy and musty workplace 'The Bat Cave'. But since Martin Burela was assigned as a new production manager, lots of things have changed. As he walks through the production hall, he looks at the floor and points at the bouncy 'anti-fatigue mats' he installed. He also renewed the assembly line and installed an air-conditioning machine. 'We want to impart our workers with a feeling of passion', Burela says, 'and that starts with tackling some fundamental aspects which impact on our employees, like we did with the bat cave'.[10]

The consulting agency Office Angels gave some companies the advise to install more 'professional' sounding job titles as a part of their culture. Filing clerks would prefer to be called 'data storage specialists', Tea ladies would want to be 'catering supervisors', dustmen 'disposal operators' and secretaries 'management assistants' or 'administration executives'. A survey by the agency revealed that 7 out of 10 workers would consider forgoing a pay rise if they were offered a more pompous job title instead. According to the consultants, new job titles can make people feel more valued and motivated, as well as more confident in social situations.[11]

Figure 7–1 further reveals that *motivated behaviours* are directly affected by an individual's ability and job knowledge (skills), motivation, and a combination of enabling and limiting job context factors. For instance, it would be difficult to persist on a project if you were working with defective raw materials or broken equipment. In contrast, motivated behaviours are likely to be enhanced when managers supply employees with adequate resources to get the job done and provide effective coaching. This coaching might entail furnishing employees with successful role models, showing employees how to complete complex tasks, and helping them maintain high self-efficacy and self-esteem (recall the discussion in Chapter 5). Performance is, in turn, influenced by motivated behaviour.

There are four important conclusions to remember about Figure 7–1.

First, motivation is different from behaviour. Motivation involves a host of psychological processes that culminate in an individual's desire and intentions to behave in a particular way. Behaviour reflects something that we can see or hear. The outcomes of motivation are generally assessed either in terms of the behaviours actually exhibited, the amount of effort exerted, or the choice of strategies used in order to complete a job or task. Actual effort or persistence are the most direct behavioural outcomes of motivation.

Second, behaviour is influenced by more than just motivation. Behaviour is affected by individual inputs, job context factors and motivation. For example, the amount of time you spend studying for your next exam (behaviour) is influenced by your motivation in combination with your ability and personal goals (individual inputs) and the quality of your lecture notes (enabling or limiting the job context variable). This example illustrates that behaviour is due to a combination of factors rather than simply to motivation alone.

Third, behaviour is different from performance. Performance represents an accumulation of behaviours that occur over time and across contexts and people. Performance also reflects an external standard that is typically set by the organization and assessed by an employee's manager. Consider the final grade a student might receive for accumulating a final course average of 88 per cent. While this average is based on behaviours exhibited over an entire class, the student's final grade or performance might range from an A to a B. The final grade depends on the specific lecturer's standards and the grade distribution of the class under consideration.

Fourth, motivation is a necessary but insufficient contributor to job performance. This conclusion reveals that performance problems are due to a combination of individual inputs, job context factors, motivation and appropriate motivated behaviours. Drawing a distinction between motivation and performance has its advantages. According to one motivation expert,

> *The implication is that there are probably some jobs for which trying to influence motivation will be irrelevant for performance. These circumstances can occur in a variety of ways. There may be situations in which ability factors or role expectation factors are simply more important than motivation. For example, the best predictor of high school grades, typically, is intellectual endowment not hours spent studying . . . . Another circumstance may occur in which performance is controlled by technological factors. For example, on an assembly line, given that minimally competent and attentive people are there to do the job, performance may not vary from individual to individual. Exerting effort may be irrelevant for performance. Managers are better able to identify and correct performance problems when they recognize that poor performance is not due solely to inadequate motivation. This awareness can foster better interpersonal relations in the workplace.*[12]

Historical Roots of Modern Motivation Theories

Five methods of explaining behaviour—needs, reinforcement, cognition, job characteristics, and feelings/emotions—underlie the evolution of modern theories of human motivation. As we proceed through this review, remember the objective of each alternative motivation theory is to explain and predict purposeful or goal-directed behaviour. As will become apparent, the differences between theoretical perspectives lie in the causal mechanisms used to explain behaviour.

Needs

Needs theories are based on the premise that individuals are motivated by unsatisfied needs. Dissatisfaction with your social life, for example, should motivate you to participate in more social activities. Henry Murray, a 1930's psychologist, was the first behavioural scientist to propose a list of needs thought to underlie goal-directed behaviour. From Murray's work sprang a wide variety of need theories, some of which remain influential today. Recognized need theories of motivation are explored in the next section of this chapter.

Reinforcement

Reinforcement theorists, such as Edward L Thorndike and B F Skinner, proposed that behaviour is controlled by its consequences, not by the result of hypothetical internal states such as instincts, drives or needs. This proposition is based on research data demonstrating that people repeat behaviours that are followed by favourable consequences and avoid behaviours that result in unfavourable consequences. Few would argue with the statement that organizational rewards have a motivational impact on job behaviour. However, behaviourists and cognitive theorists do disagree over the role, in motivation, of an individual's internal states and processes.

Cognitions

Uncomfortable with the idea that behaviour is shaped completely by environmental consequences, cognitive motivation theorists contend that behaviour is a function of beliefs, expectations, values, and other mental cognitions. Behaviour is therefore viewed as the result of rational and conscious choices among alternative courses of action. In Chapter 7, we discuss cognitive motivation theories involving equity, expectancies, and goal setting.

Job Characteristics

This theoretical approach is based on the idea that the task itself is the key to employee motivation. Specifically, a boring and monotonous job stifles motivation to perform well, whereas a challenging job enhances motivation. Three ingredients of a more challenging job are variety, autonomy and decision-making authority. Two popular ways of adding variety and challenge to routine jobs are job enrichment (or job redesign) and job rotation. These techniques are discussed later in this chapter.

Feelings/Emotions

This most recent addition to the evolution of motivation theory is based on the idea that workers are 'whole people' who pursue goals other than that of becoming a high performer.[13] For example, you may want to be a brilliant student, loving boyfriend or girlfriend, caring parent, good friend, responsible citizen or a happy person. Work motivation is thus thought to be a function of your feelings and emotions toward the multitude of interests and goals that you have. You are likely to study long and hard if your only interest in life is to enter graduate school and become a doctor. In contrast, a highly motivated lecturer is likely to stop lecturing and dismiss the students upon receiving a message that his or her child was seriously hurt in an accident.

A Motivational Puzzle

Motivation theory presents managers with a psychological puzzle composed of alternative explanations and recommendations. There is no single theory of motivation that is suitable for all situations. Rather, managers need to use a contingency framework to pick and choose the motivational techniques best suited to the people and situation involved.

The matrix in Figure 7–2 was created to help managers make these decisions. Because managers face a variety of motivational problems that can be solved with different theories of motivation, the matrix crosses outcomes of interest with six major motivation theories.[14] Entries in the matrix indicate which theories are best suited for explaining each outcome. For instance, each motivation theory can help managers determine how to increase employee effort. In contrast, need, equity and job characteristics theories are most helpful in developing programmes aimed at increasing employees' job satisfaction. Managers faced with high turnover are advised to use the reinforcement, equity, expectancy or job characteristics theory to correct the problem.

You will be better able to apply this matrix after reading the material in the rest of this chapter and in Chapters 8 and 10. This chapter covers theories related to needs and job characteristics; Chapter 8 focuses on equity, expectancy and goal setting; while reinforcement theory is reviewed in Chapter 10.

Figure 7–2 *Motivation Theories and Workplace Outcomes: A Contingency Approach*

Motivation Theories

Outcome of Interest	Need	Reinforcement	Equity	Expectancy	Goal Setting	Job Characteristics
• Choice to pursue a course of action				X		
• Effort	X	X	X	X	X	X
• Performance		X	X		X	X
• Satisfaction	X		X			X
• Absenteeism		X	X			X
• Turnover		X	X	X		X

SOURCE: Adapted and extended from F J Landy and W S Becker, 'Motivation Theory Reconsidered', in L L Cummings and B M Staw (eds), *Research in Organizational Behavior* (Greenwich, CT: JAI Press, 1987), vol 9, p 33.

NEED THEORIES OF MOTIVATION

Needs
physiological or psychological deficiencies that arouse behaviour

Need theories attempt to pinpoint internal factors that energize behaviour. **Needs** are physiological or psychological deficiencies that arouse behaviour. They can be strong or weak and are influenced by environmental factors. Thus, human needs vary over time and place. Two popular need theories are discussed in this section: Maslow's need hierarchy theory and McClelland's need theory.

Maslow's Need Hierarchy Theory

In 1943, psychologist Abraham Maslow published his now-famous need hierarchy theory of motivation. Although the theory was based on his clinical observation of a few neurotic individuals, it has subsequently been used to explain the entire spectrum of human behaviour. Maslow proposed that motivation is a function of five basic needs–physiological, safety, love, esteem and self-actualization (see Figure 7–3).

Maslow said these five need categories are arranged in a graduated hierarchy. In other words, he believed human needs generally emerge in a predictable stair-step fashion. Accordingly, once one's physiological needs are relatively satisfied, one's safety needs emerge, and so on up the need hierarchy, one step at a time. Once a need is satisfied it activates the next higher need in the hierarchy. This process continues until the need for self-actualization is activated.[15]

Figure 7–3 *Maslow's Need Hierarchy*

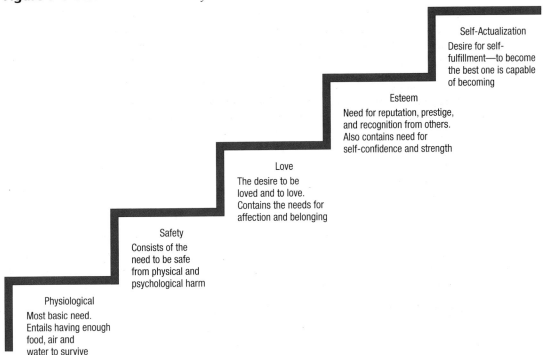

SOURCE: Adapted from descriptions provided by A H Maslow, 'A Theory of Human Motivation', *Psychological Review*, July 1943, pp 370–96.

Research Findings on Maslow's Theory

Research does not clearly support this theory because results from studies testing the need hierarchy are difficult to interpret. A well-known motivation scholar summarized the research evidence as follows.

> *On balance, Maslow's theory remains very popular among managers and students of organizational behaviour, although there are still very few studies that can legitimately confirm (or refute) it . . . . It may be that the dynamics implied by Maslow's theory of needs are too complex to be put into operation and confirmed by scientific research. If this is the case, we may never be able to determine how valid the theory is or, more precisely, which aspects of the theory are valid and which not.*[16]

Managerial Implications of Maslow's Theory

A satisfied need may lose its motivational potential. Therefore, managers are advised to motivate employees by devising programmes or practices aimed at satisfying emerging or unmet needs.

> *'You can't fascinate IT-professionals for very long by just offering a competitive salary', says a recruitment manager at the Real Software Group, one of Europe's leading software companies. 'You've got to beam out a certain dynamism and creativity through your company, and offer them a wide variety of future perspectives. We offer our IT'ers a technologically oriented career with four or five dimensions. They can fulfil the role of project manager, programmer, documentalist, implementator, end-users' coach, and so on. Those who had enough of a certain technology get the chance to re-educate themselves or concentrate on another technology. This is a much more powerful 'glue' than just offering high pay. Salary is a strong motivator on a short term base but, in the long run, we see that what drives IT-professionals the most is their love for a certain technology or scientific field.'*[17]

The same recommendation applies to the context of motivating customers to purchase specific products. The Ritz-Carlton, for example, believes that customer loyalty and satisfaction are based on satisfying customer needs. The organization attempts to motivate us to stay at its hotels by first gathering detailed information on customer preferences and needs from a variety of sources. This information is then entered into an on-line, nationwide computer system. The Ritz-Carlton then uses this information to satisfy customer needs.

> When a repeat customer calls the central reservations number to book a room, the agent can retrieve the individual's preference information directly from the on-line system. This information is sent to the specific Ritz location where the room is reserved. The hotel then outputs the data in a daily guest recognition and preference report, which is circulated to all staff. With this system, hotel staff can anticipate a particular guest's breakfast habits, newspaper choices and room preferences. The Ritz's employees are well trained to ensure they are able to respond to the customers' needs. A customer management system ensures that the first employee who becomes aware of a customer complaint becomes responsible for resolving the problem quickly and completely. Each employee can reverse a transaction of up to $2,000 without *prior approval—if necessary—to keep a customer satisfied.*[18]

McClelland's Need Theory

David McClelland has been studying the relationship between needs and behaviour since the late 1940s. Although he is mainly recognized for his research on the need for achievement, he also investigated the needs for affiliation and power. Before discussing each of these needs, let us consider the typical approach used to measure the strength of an individual's needs.

Measuring Strength of Need

The Thematic Apperception Test (TAT) is frequently used to measure an individual's motivation to satisfy various needs. In completing the TAT, people are asked to write stories about ambiguous pictures. These descriptions are then scored for the extent to which they contain achievement, power, and affiliation imagery. A meta-analysis of 105 studies demonstrated that the TAT is a valid measure of the need for achievement.[19]

Now, we would like you to examine the picture in the following OB Exercise and then write a brief description of what you think is happening to the people in the picture, then what you think will happen to them in the future. Once you have completed this, use the scoring guide to determine your need strength. What is your most important need?

OB Exercise

Assess Your Need Strength with a Thematic Apperception Test (TAT)

Instructions

The purpose of this exercise is to help you identify motivational themes expressed in the picture shown below. There are two steps. First, look at the picture briely (10 to 20 seconds), and write the story it suggests by answering the following questions:

- What is happening? Who are the people?
- What past events led to this situation?
- What is wanted by whom?
- What will happen? What will be done?

Next, score your story for achievement, power and affiliation motivation by using the scoring guide and scales shown below. Score the motives from 1 (low) to 5 (high). The scoring guide identifies the types of story descriptions/words that are indicative of high motives. Give yourself a low score if you fail to describe the story with words and phrases contained in the scoring guidelines. A moderate score indicates that you used some of the phrases identified in the scoring guide to describe your story. Do not read the scoring guidelines until you have written your story.

Scoring Guidelines

Score achievement motivation high if:

- A goal, objective or standard of excellence is mentioned.
- Words such as good, better or best are used to evaluate performance.
- Someone in your story is striving for a unique accomplishment.
- Reference is made to career status or being a success in life.

Score power motivation high if:

- There is emotional concern for influencing someone else.
- Someone is actively striving to gain or keep control over others by ordering, arguing, demanding, convincing, threatening or punishing.
- Clear reference is made to a superior–subordinate relationship and the superior is taking steps to gain or keep control over the subordinate.

Score affiliation motivation high if:

- Someone is concerned about establishing or maintaining a friendly relationship with another.
- Someone expresses the desire to be liked by someone else.
- There are references to family ties, friendly discussions, visits, reunions, parties or informal get-togethers.

LOW	MODERATE	HIGH

- Achievement motivation

    1———2———3———4———5

- Power motivation

    1———2———3———4———5

- Affiliation motivation

    1———2———3———4———5

The Need for Achievement

Achievement theories propose that motivation and performance vary according to the strength of one's need for achievement. For example, a field study of 222 life insurance brokers found a positive correlation between the number of policies sold and the brokers' need for achievement. McClelland's research supported an analogous relationship for societies as a whole. His results revealed that a country's level of economic development was positively related to its overall achievement motivation.[20]

The **need for achievement** is defined by the following desires.

Need for achievement
desire to accomplish something difficult

To accomplish something difficult. To master, manipulate or organize physical objects, human beings or ideas. To do this as rapidly and as independently as possible. To overcome obstacles and attain a high standard. To excel one's self. To rival and surpass others. To increase self-regard by the successful exercise of talent.[21]

This definition reveals that the need for achievement overlaps Maslow's higher order needs of esteem and self-actualization. Mr K Y Ho is a good example of someone with a high need for achievement (see the next International OB). Not only does Mr Ho display the need for achievement but his story highlights the point that achievement needs actually display themselves in all walks of life. One does not have to be a famous athlete, executive or personality to display high achievement. Let us now consider the characteristics of high achievers.

Characteristics of High Achievers

Achievement-motivated people share three common characteristics. One is a preference for working on tasks of *moderate* difficulty. For example, when high achievers are asked to stand wherever they like while tossing rings at a peg on the floor, they tend to stand about 10 to 20 feet from the peg. This distance presents the ring tosser with a challenging but not impossible task. People with a low need for achievement, in contrast, tend to either walk up to the peg and drop the rings on or gamble on a lucky shot from far away. The high achiever's preference for moderately difficult tasks reinforces achievement behaviour by reducing the frequency of failure and increasing the satisfaction associated with successfully completing challenging tasks.

Achievers also like situations in which their performance is due to their own efforts rather than to other factors, such as luck. A third identifying characteristic of high achievers is that they desire more feedback on their successes and failures than do low achievers.[22] Given these characteristics, McClelland proposed that high achievers are more likely to be successful entrepreneurs. A recent review of research on the 'entrepreneurial' personality supported this conclusion. Entrepreneurs were found to have a higher need for achievement than non-entrepreneurs.[23]

The Need for Affiliation

Researchers believe that people possess a basic desire to form and maintain a few lasting, positive and important interpersonal relationships. A recent summary of research supported this premise. In addition, the researchers noted that both psychological and physical health problems are higher among people who lack social attachments.[24] Just the same, not everyone has a high need to affiliate. People with a high **need for affiliation** prefer to spend more time maintaining social relationships, joining groups, and wanting to be loved. Individuals high in this need are not the most effective managers or leaders because they have a hard time making difficult decisions without worrying about being disliked.

Need for affiliation
desire to spend time in social relationships and activities

The Need for Power

The **need for power** reflects an individual's desire to influence, coach, teach, or encourage others to achieve. People with a high need for power like to work and are concerned with discipline and self-respect. There is a positive and negative side to this need. The negative face of power is characterized by an 'if I win, you lose' mentality. In contrast, people with a positive orientation to power focus on accomplishing group goals and helping employees obtain the feeling of competence. More is said about the two faces of power in Chapter 15.

Need for power
desire to influence, coach, teach or encourage others to achieve

Because effective managers must positively influence others, McClelland proposes that top managers should have a high need for power coupled with a low need for affiliation. He also believes that individuals with high achievement motivation are *not* best suited for top management positions. Several studies support these propositions.[25]

Managerial Implications

Given that adults can be trained to increase their achievement motivation,[26] organizations should consider the benefits of providing achievement training for employees. Moreover, the achievement, affiliation and power needs of individuals can be considered during the selection process in order to achieve better placement. For example, a study revealed that individuals' need for achievement affected their preference to work in different companies. People with a high need for achievement were more attracted to companies that had a pay-for-performance environment than were those with a low achievement motivation.[27] Finally, managers should create challenging task assignments or goals because the need for achievement is positively correlated with goal commitment, which, in turn, influences performance.[28] Moreover, challenging goals should be accompanied with a more autonomous work environment and employee empowerment to capitalize on the characteristics of high achievers.

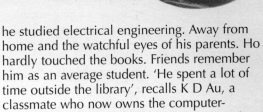

International OB

http://www.ati.com

K Y Ho Displays a High Need for Achievement

BusinessWeek

For K Y Ho, growing up in mainland China in the 1950s meant hunger and ragged clothes. To help out his mother, Ho, the youngest of three brothers and a sister, peddled vegetables from the family garden. His father, labouring in Hong Kong for most of Ho's childhood, sent back what he could. Later, after the family reunited in Hong Kong, life in a crammed one-room flat was scarcely better. Says Ho, 'We always worried about money, money, money.'

No longer. Now the 48-year-old Ho, living in Canada since 1983, is one of that country's most successful high-tech entrepreneurs. Today, Ho is worth about [US]$143 million, thanks to his 4.4 per cent stake in ATI Technologies Inc., which he started with two friends shortly after arriving in Canada. ATI makes graphics accelerators, the specialized 3-D chips that give popular video games such as Tomb Raider and Quake III their realistic look.

Despite his early poverty, Ho hails from a highly educated, upper-class family. His maternal grandfather was a prosperous landowner who fell on hard times after the Japanese invasion in 1937. His paternal grandfather was a book dealer and teacher. After the communists came to power in 1949, both grandparents lost most of their property. Ho's father, also a teacher, was unable to find work and left his wife and young children for a series of factory jobs in Hong Kong when Ho was still an infant. Twelve long years later, Ho and his mother joined Ho's father and an older brother. Ho's other brother and sister were forced by the government to stay behind.

Later, Ho earned a place at a top Taiwanese college, National Cheng Kung University, where

he studied electrical engineering. Away from home and the watchful eyes of his parents. Ho hardly touched the books. Friends remember him as an average student. 'He spent a lot of time outside the library', recalls K D Au, a classmate who now owns the computer-peripherals wholesaler, Althon Micro Inc., in Los Angeles, USA.

But once in the job market, Ho thrived. After graduating from university in 1974, he raced through several electronics-industry jobs at big-name corporations in Hong Kong, including Control Data Systems Inc. and Philips Electronics. Ho learned all about video games in 1981 when he went to work for Wong's Electronics Co. Ltd, a leading Hong Kong Manufacturer that dealt regularly with hotshot game makers Atari and Coleco. 'He learned everything very, very fast', recalls Benedict C M Wong, the company's president.

Affable and quick with a smile, Ho nonetheless often disagreed with his superiors. 'He's so straightforward that he could hardly get along with the boss', recalls Patrick Hung, a classmate who later worked with Ho at Wong's. In 1983, Ho left for Canada, where many Hong Kong Chinese went looking for a fresh start. Ho's first impression: 'A lot of open space and lots of opportunity.'

SOURCE: Excerpted from J Weber and A Reinhardt, 'From Rags to 3-D Chips', *Business Week*, June 21, 1999, pp 86, 90.

Entrepreneurs such as K Y Ho, co-founder of ATI Technologies Inc., tend to have a high need for achievement. Mr Ho's need for achievement certainly contributed to his rise from poverty in mainland China to one of Canada's most successful high-tech entrepreneurs.

HISTORICAL APPROACHES TO JOB DESIGN

Job design

changing the content and/or process of a specific job to increase job satisfaction and performance

Job design, also referred to as job redesign, 'refers to any set of activities that involves the alteration of specific jobs or interdependent systems of jobs with the intent of improving the quality of employee job experience and their on-the-job productivity'.[29] There are two very different routes, one traditional and one modern, that can be taken when deciding how to design jobs. Each is based on a different assumption about people.

The first route entails *fitting people to jobs*. It is based on the assumption that people will gradually adjust and adapt to any work situation. Thus, employee attitudes toward the job are ignored, and jobs are designed to produce maximum economic and technological efficiency. This approach uses the principles of scientific management and work simplification. In contrast, the second route involves *fitting jobs to people*. It assumes that people are underutilized at work and that they desire more challenges and responsibility. This philosophy is part of the driving force behind the widespread implementation of work teams. Also, consider how SCA Hygiene Products, a company based in Groningen, Holland, used the principle of fitting jobs to people as a motivational asset.

> *Production workers at SCA are given full authority over their own working hours. The many football fans in the company, for example, can choose freely whether they want to spend the evening watching the Champions League or work, as long as they fulfill the required number of working hours every week. The 550 employees who work at SCA can freely switch between [work] teams and shifts. Director Dick Heinen implemented this system as a one-year test to see how things turn out but the results already show very positive. 'We used to stick to a 5-shift system but teams are now allowed to set up their own working schedules', Heinen says. This flexibility is possible because every team controls one machine and each machine can operate independently of the others. And, indeed, it frequently happens that a team decides to work alternative hours to go watch an important match together. 'Of course, as a result, we had an overwhelming amount of football fans applying here lately', Heinen laughingly adds.*[30]

Apart from the approach used by SCA Hygiene Products, there are a number of methods of job design to be widely used in industry. The most common are scientific management, job enlargement, job rotation, job enrichment and job characteristics. The first four are discussed in the remainder of this section. The next section explores the job characteristics approach to job design.

Scientific Management

Developed by Frederick Taylor, scientific management relied on research and experimentation to determine the most efficient way to perform jobs. He used time and task studies to determine the most efficient and safe manner to perform a job. Jobs are highly specialized and standardized when they are designed according to the principles of scientific management. This technique was the impetus for the development of assembly line technology and is currently used in many manufacturing and production-oriented firms throughout the United States and western Europe.

Designing jobs according to the principles of scientific management has both positive and negative consequences. Positively, employee efficiency and productivity are increased. On the other hand, research reveals that simplified, repetitive jobs also lead to job dissatisfaction, poor mental health, higher levels of stress and a low sense of accomplishment and personal growth.[31] Further, the principles of scientific management do not apply to professional 'knowledge' workers; and they are not consistent with the trend to empower both employees and work teams. These negative consequences paved the way for the development of other job designs. Newer approaches attempt to design intrinsically satisfying jobs.

Job Enlargement

This technique was first used in the late 1940s in response to complaints about tedious and overspecialized jobs. **Job enlargement** involves putting more variety into a worker's job by combining specialized tasks of comparable difficulty. Some call this *horizontally loading* the job.

Proponents of job enlargement claim it can improve employee satisfaction, motivation and quality of production. Unfortunately, research reveals that job enlargement, by itself, does not have a significant and lasting positive impact on job performance. Researchers recommend using job enlargement as part of a broader approach that uses multiple job design techniques.[32]

> **Job enlargement**
> *putting more variety into one job*

Job Rotation

As with job enlargement, job rotation's purpose is to give employees greater variety in their work. **Job rotation** calls for moving employees from one specialized job to another. Rather than performing only one job, workers are trained and given the opportunity to perform two or more separate jobs on a rotating basis. By rotating employees from job to job, managers believe they can stimulate interest and motivation while providing employees with a broader perspective of the organization. Other proposed advantages of job rotation include increased worker flexibility and easier scheduling because employees are 'cross trained' to perform different jobs. In turn, this cross-training requires employees to learn new skills, which can assist them in upward or lateral mobility. Although some documented cases support the use of job rotation, the promised benefits associated with job rotation programmes have not been adequately researched.[33]

> **Job rotation**
> *moving employees from one specialized job to another*

Job Enrichment

Job enrichment is the practical application of Frederick Herzberg's motivator–hygiene theory of job satisfaction.[34] After reviewing the foundation of Herzberg's theory, we will discuss its application through job enrichment.

The Legacy of Herzberg's Motivator–Hygiene Theory

Herzberg's theory is based on a landmark study in which he interviewed 203 accountants and engineers. These interviews sought to determine the factors responsible for job satisfaction and dissatisfaction. Herzberg found separate and distinct clusters of factors associated with job satisfaction and dissatisfaction. Job satisfaction was more frequently associated with achievement, recognition, characteristics of the work, responsibility and advancement. These factors were all related to outcomes associated with the *content* of the task being performed. Herzberg labelled these factors **motivators** because each was associated with strong effort and good performance. He hypothesized that motivators cause a person to move from a state of no satisfaction to satisfaction (see Figure 7–4). Therefore, Herzberg's theory predicts managers can motivate individuals by incorporating 'motivators' into an individual's job.

> **Motivators**
> *job characteristics associated with job satisfaction*

Herzberg found job *dissatisfaction* to be associated primarily with factors in the work *context* or environment. Specifically, company policy and administration, technical supervision, salary, interpersonal relations with one's supervisor and working conditions were most frequently mentioned by employees expressing job dissatisfaction. Herzberg labelled this second cluster of factors **hygiene factors**. He further proposed that they were not motivational. At best, according to Herzberg's interpretation, an individual will experience no job dissatisfaction when he or she has no grievances about hygiene factors (refer to Figure 7–4).[35]

> **Hygiene factors**
> *job characteristics associated with dissatisfaction*

Figure 7–4

*Herzberg's
Motivator–Hygiene
Model*

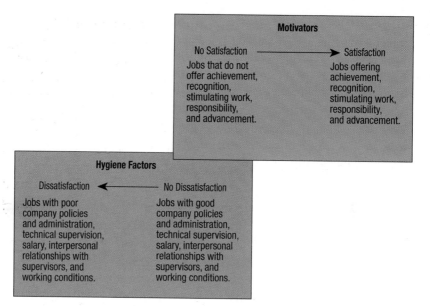

SOURCE: Adapted in part from D A Whitsett and E K Winslow, 'An Analysis of Studies Critical of the Motivator–Hygiene Theory', *Personnel Psychology*, Winter 1967, pp 391–415.

The Midway Zero

The key to adequately understanding Herzberg's motivator–hygiene theory is to recognize that he believes that satisfaction is not the opposite of dissatisfaction. Herzberg concludes that 'the opposite of job satisfaction is not job dissatisfaction, but rather no job satisfaction; and similarly, the opposite of job dissatisfaction is not job satisfaction, but no dissatisfaction'.[36] Herzberg thus asserts that the dissatisfaction–satisfaction continuum contains a zero point, midway between dissatisfaction and satisfaction, where neither are present. Conceivably, an organization member who has good supervision, pay and working conditions but a tedious and unchallenging task with little chance of advancement would be at the zero midpoint. That person would have no dissatisfaction (because of good hygiene factors) and no satisfaction (because of a lack of motivators). Consequently, Herzberg warns managers that it takes more than good pay and good working conditions to motivate today's employees. It takes an 'enriched job' that offers the individual opportunity for achievement and recognition, stimulation, responsibility and advancement. Unfortunately, a study of 600 managers and 900 workers indicated that organizations may not be heeding Herzberg's advice. Results revealed that only 33 per cent felt that their managers knew what motivated them, and 60 per cent concluded that they did not receive any sort of recognition or rewards for their work.[37]

Research on the Motivator–Hygiene Theory

Herzberg's theory generated a great deal of research and controversy. The controversy revolved around whether studies supporting the theory were flawed and thus invalid.[38] A motivation scholar attempted to sort out the controversy by concluding the following.

On balance, when we combine all of the evidence with all of the allegations that the theory has been misinterpreted, and that its major concepts have not been assessed properly, one is left, more than twenty years later, not really knowing whether to take the theory seriously, let alone whether it should be put into practice in organizational settings . . . . There is support for many of the implications the theory has for enriching jobs to make them more motivating. But the two-factor aspect of the theory—the feature that makes it unique—is not really a necessary element in the use of the theory for designing jobs, per se.[39]

Applying Herzberg's Model through Vertical Loading

Job enrichment is based on the application of Herzberg's ideas. Specifically, job enrichment entails modifying a job such that an employee has the opportunity to experience achievement, recognition, stimulating work, responsibility and advancement. These characteristics are incorporated into a job through vertical loading.

Job enrichment
text to go here?

Rather than giving employees additional tasks of similar difficulty (horizontal loading), *vertical loading* consists of giving workers more responsibility. In other words, employees take on chores normally performed by their supervisors. Managers are advised to follow seven principles when vertically loading jobs (see Table 7–1).

Principle	Motivators Involved
A. Removing some controls while retaining accountability	Responsibility and personal achievement
B. Increasing the accountability of individuals for their own work	Responsibility and recognition
C. Giving a person a complete natural unit of work (module, division, area, and so on)	Responsibility, achievement, and recognition
D. Granting additional authority to an employee in his activity; job freedom	Responsibility, achievement, and recognition
E. Making periodic reports directly available to the worker himself rather than to the supervisor	Internal recognition
F. Introducing new and more difficult tasks not previously handled	Growth and learning
G. Assigning individuals specific or specialized tasks, enabling them to become experts	Responsibility, growth, and advancement

Table 7–1
Principles of Vertically Loading a Job

SOURCE: Reprinted by permission of the *Harvard Business Review*. An exhibit from 'One More Time: How Do You Motivate Employees?' by F Herzberg (January/February 1968). Copyright © 1968 by the President and Fellows of Harvard College; all rights reserved.

JOB CHARACTERISTICS APPROACH TO JOB DESIGN

The job characteristics model is a more recent approach to job design. It is a direct offshoot of job enrichment and attempts to pinpoint those situations and those individuals for which job design is most effective. In this regard, the job characteristics model represents a contingency approach.

Overview of the Job Characteristics Model

Two OB researchers, J Richard Hackman and Greg Oldham, played a central role in developing the job characteristics approach. These researchers tried to determine how work can be structured so that employees are internally (or intrinsically) motivated. Internal motivation occurs when an individual is 'turned on to one's work because of the positive internal feelings that are generated by doing well, rather than by being dependent on external factors (such as incentive pay or compliments from the boss) for the motivation to work effectively.'[40]

Internal motivation
motivation caused by positive internal feelings

An example of a highly internally motivated person is Nathalie Vincke, who works at the emergency department of the Academic Hospital of Brussels.

'My working days are too short!' she says. 'Some young people might have a hard time finding a job in which they feel good, but in my case it certainly wasn't so. Everyday it is a pleasure to come to work, even if that means getting up really early. When I started here after I graduated from nursing school, I had the feeling that this was the moment when life really started. I have always wanted to become a nurse, ever since I was a

child. I can remember a teacher in secondary school warning me that I only saw the sunny side of it and that I'd also have to do the dirty jobs but that didn't deter me. On the contrary, I am really hooked on it now. To be able to help to the patients even more, I am continually learning new things. For example, I often visit the library to find more information on diseases. And I am studying an extra course on Thursday evenings.' Nathalie is also enthusiastic about the way new employees are introduced to the hospital. 'The hospital made great efforts to get us started', she says. 'When we arrived, there was a training course and a senior nurse was assigned to each of us as a mentor. Also, the team spirit is fantastic. If the atmosphere at work wasn't as good, nursing would sometimes seem an impossible task. But still, the feeling I get when I help a patient in a critical condition to pull through or to stabilize is indescribable.' [41]

These positive feelings power a self-perpetuating cycle of motivation. As shown in Figure 7–5, internal work motivation is determined by three psychological states. In turn, these psychological states are fostered by the presence of five core job dimensions. As you can see in Figure 7–5, the object of this approach is to promote high internal motivation by designing jobs that possess the five core job characteristics. Let us examine the major components of this model to see how it works.

Figure 7–5

The Job Characteristics Model

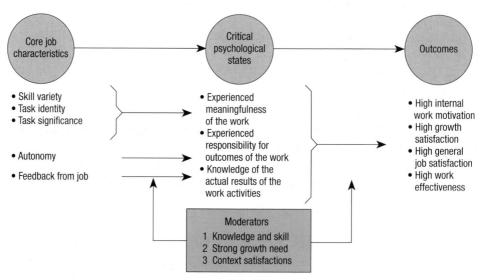

SOURCE: J R Hackman and G R Oldham, ***Work Redesign***, © 1980, Addison-Wesley Publishing Co., Reading, MA, p 90. Reprinted with permission.

Critical Psychological States

A group of management experts described the conditions under which individuals experienced the three critical psychological states as follows.

Experienced meaningfulness
feeling that one's job is important and worthwhile

Experienced responsibility
believing that one is accountable for work outcomes

Knowledge of results
feedback about work outcomes

1 **Experienced meaningfulness.** The individual must perceive her work as worthwhile or important by some system of value she accepts.

2 **Experienced responsibility.** He must believe that he personally is accountable for the outcomes of his efforts.

3 **Knowledge of results.** She must be able to determine, on some fairly regular basis, whether or not the outcomes of her work are satisfactory. [42]

These psychological states generate internal work motivation. Moreover, they encourage job satisfaction and perseverance because they are self-reinforcing. If one of the three psychological states is short-changed, motivation diminishes. Consider, for example, Joyce Roché's decision to quit her job as vice president of global marketing at Avon.

The decision to ditch a plum, top position in a major corporation where one is highly regarded might strike most people as insane. But Roché's decision grew out of her realization that despite the great title and income (she had a very-high salary with substantial bonus potential), her job did not hold the level of autonomy or responsibility she initially thought it had.[43]

Joyce Roché's internal motivation was diminished by not feeling the psychological state of 'experienced responsibility'.

Core Job Dimensions

In general terms, core job dimensions are common characteristics found to a varying degree in all jobs. Once again, five core job characteristics elicit the three psychological states (see Figure 7–5). Three of those job characteristics–skill variety, task identity and task significance–combine to determine experienced meaningfulness of work.

▼ *Skill variety.* The extent to which the job requires an individual to perform a variety of tasks that require him or her to use different skills and abilities.

▼ *Task identity.* The extent to which the job requires an individual to perform a whole or completely identifiable piece of work. In other words, task identity is high when a person works on a product or project from beginning to end and sees a tangible result.

▼ *Task significance.* The extent to which the job affects the lives of other people within or outside the organization.

Experienced responsibility is elicited by the job characteristic of autonomy; whereas knowledge of results is fostered by the job characteristic of feedback, and these are defined as follows.

▼ Autonomy: the extent to which the job enables an individual to experience freedom, independence, and discretion in both scheduling and determining the procedures used in completing the job.

▼ Feedback: the extent to which an individual receives direct and clear information about how effectively he or she is performing the job.[44]

Motivating Potential of a Job

Hackman and Oldham devised a tool for self-reporting in order to assess the extent to which a specific job possesses the five core job characteristics. With this tool, which is discussed in the next section, it is possible to calculate a motivating potential score for a job. The motivating potential score (MPS) is a summary index that represents the extent to which the job characteristics foster internal work motivation. Low scores indicate that an individual will not experience high internal work motivation from the job. Such a job is a prime candidate for job redesign. High scores reveal that the job is capable of stimulating internal motivation.

The MPS is computed as follows.

$$MPS = \frac{skill\ variety + task\ identity + task\ significance}{3} \times autonomy \times feedback$$

Judging from this equation, which core job characteristics do you think are relatively more important in determining the motivational potential of a job? Because autonomy and feedback are not divisible by another number, low amounts of autonomy and feedback have a greater chance of lowering MPS than the job characteristics of skill variety, task identity and task significance.

Does the Theory Work for Everyone?

As previously discussed, not all people may want enriched work. Hackman and Oldham incorporated this conclusion into their model by identifying three attributes that affect how individuals respond to jobs with a high MPS. These attributes are

Core job dimensions *job characteristics found to various degrees in all jobs*

Motivating potential score *the amount of internal work motivation associated with a specific job*

concerned with the individual's knowledge and skill, need for strong growth (representing the desire to grow and develop as an individual), and context satisfactions (see Figure 7-5). Context satisfactions represent the extent to which employees are satisfied with various aspects of their job, such as pay, co-workers and supervision.

Hackman and Oldham proposed that people will respond positively to jobs with a high MPS when they have:

▼ **the knowledge and skills necessary to do the job**

▼ **high growth needs**

▼ **an overall satisfaction with various aspects of the work context, such as pay and co-workers.**

Although these recommendations make sense, several studies did not support the moderating influence of an employee's growth needs and context satisfaction.[45] The model worked equally well for employees with high and low growth needs and context satisfaction. Future research needs to examine whether an employee's knowledge and skills are an important moderator of the model's effectiveness.

Applying the Job Characteristics Model

There are three major steps to follow when applying Hackman and Oldham's model. Since the model seeks to increase employee motivation and satisfaction, the first step consists of diagnosing the work environment to determine if a problem exists. Hackman and Oldham developed a self-report instrument for managers to use called the *job diagnostic survey* (JDS).

Diagnosis begins by determining whether motivation and satisfaction are lower than desired. If they are, a manager then assesses the MPS of the jobs being examined. National norms are used to determine whether the MPS is low or high.[46] National norms represent the average scores for the MPS and the individual job characteristics based on administering the JDS to numerous samples throughout the world. If the MPS is low, an attempt is made to determine which of the core job characteristics is causing the problem. If the MPS is high, managers need to look for other factors eroding motivation and satisfaction. (You can calculate your own MPS in the group exercise at the end of this chapter.) Potentially demotivating factors may be identified by considering other motivation theories discussed in this book.

Step two consists of determining whether job redesign is appropriate for a given group of employees. Job redesign is most likely to work in a participative environment in which employees have the necessary knowledge and skills.

In the third step, managers need to consider how to redesign the job. The focus of this effort is to increase those core job characteristics that are lower than national norms. Managers are advised to gain employees' input during this step.

Practical Implications of the Job Characteristics Model

Managers may want to use this model to increase employee job satisfaction. Research overwhelmingly demonstrates the existence of a moderately strong relationship between job characteristics and satisfaction.[47] A recent study of 459 employees from a glass manufacturing company also indirectly supported the job characteristics model. The company redesigned the work environment by increasing employees' autonomy and participation in decision-making and then measured employees' self-efficacy to carry out a broader and more proactive role 18 months later. Job redesign resulted in higher self-efficacy.[48]

Unfortunately, job redesign appears to reduce the quantity of output just as often as it has a positive impact. Caution and situational appropriateness are advised. For example, one study demonstrated that job redesign works better in less complex organizations (small plants or companies).[49]

Nonetheless, managers are likely to find noticeable increases in the quality of performance after a job redesign programme. Results from 21 experimental studies revealed that job redesign resulted in a median increase of 28 per cent in the quality of performance.[50] Moreover, two separate meta-analyses support the practice of using the job characteristics model to help managers reduce absenteeism and turnover;[51] and job characteristics were found to predict absenteeism over a six-year period. This latter result is very encouraging because it suggests that job redesign can have long-lasting positive effects on employee behaviour.

Job characteristics research also underscores an additional implication for companies undergoing re-engineering. Re-engineering potentially leads to negative work outcomes because it increases job characteristics beyond reasonable levels. This occurs for two reasons:

▼ **re-engineering requires employees to use a wider variety of skills to perform their jobs**
▼ **re-engineering typically results in downsizing and short-term periods of understaffing.**[52]

The unfortunate catch is that understaffing was found to produce lower levels of group performance, and jobs with either overly low or high levels of job characteristics were associated with higher stress.[53] Managers are advised to carefully consider the level of perceived job characteristics when implementing re-engineering initiatives.

In conclusion, managers need to realize that job redesign is not a panacea for all their employee satisfaction and motivation problems. To enhance their chances of success with this approach, managers need to remember that a change in one job or department can create problems of perceived inequity in related areas or systems within the organization. Managers need to take an open systems perspective when implementing job redesign, as was suggested by Hackman and Oldham when they wrote the following.

Our observations of work redesign programmes suggest that attempts to change jobs frequently run into—and sometimes get run over by—other organizational systems and practices, leading to a diminution (or even a reversal) of anticipated outcomes . . . .

The 'small change' effect, for example, often develops as managers begin to realize that radical changes in work design will necessitate major changes in other organizational systems as well.[54]

JOB SATISFACTION

An individual's work motivation is related to his or her job satisfaction. Motivation is not independent of an employee's work environment or personal life. For example, your desire to study for your next OB test is jointly affected by how much you like the course and the state of your health at the time you are studying. It is very hard to study when you have a bad cold or the flu. Because of these dynamic relationships, we conclude our discussion of motivation in this chapter by discussing the causes and consequences of job satisfaction. This information will increase your understanding of how to motivate others as well as yourself.

The Causes of Job Satisfaction

Job satisfaction is an affective or emotional response toward various facets of one's job. This definition means job satisfaction is not a unitary concept. Rather, a person can be relatively satisfied with one aspect of his or her job and dissatisfied with another. For example, researchers at Cornell University in the US developed the Job

Job satisfaction
an affective or emotional response to one's job

Descriptive Index (JDI) to assess one's satisfaction with the following job dimensions: work, pay, promotions, co-workers, and supervision.[55]

Researchers at the US University of Minnesota concluded that there are 20 different dimensions underlying job satisfaction. Selected Minnesota Satisfaction Questionnaire (MSQ) items–measuring satisfaction with recognition, compensation and supervision–are listed in the next OB Exercise. Please take a moment now to determine how satisfied you are with these three aspects of your present or most recent job, and then use the norms to compare your score.[56] How do you feel about your job?

OB Exercise

How Satisfied Are You with Your Present Job?

	VERY DISSATISFIED				VERY SATISFIED
1 The way I am noticed when I do a good job	1	2	3	4	5
2 The recognition I get for the work I do	1	2	3	4	5
3 The praise I get for doing a good job1	1	2	3	4	5
4 How my pay compares with that for similar jobs in other companies	1	2	3	4	5
5 My pay and the amount of work I do	1	2	3	4	5
6 How my pay compares with that of other workers	1	2	3	4	5
7 The way my boss handles employees	1	2	3	4	5
8 The way my boss takes care of complaints brought to him/her by employees	1	2	3	4	5
9 The personal relationship between my boss and his/her employees	1	2	3	4	5

Total score for satisfaction with recognition (add questions 1–3), compensation (add questions 4–6), and supervision (add questions 7–9). Comparative norms for each dimension of job satisfaction are: Total score of 3–6 = Low job satisfaction; 7–11 = Moderate satisfaction; 12 and above = High satisfaction.

SOURCE: Adapted from D J Weiss, R V Dawis, G W England, and L H Lofquist, *Manual for the Minnesota Satisfaction Questionnaire*, (Minneapolis: Industrial Relations Center, University of Minnesota, 1967). Used with permission.

Five predominant models of job satisfaction specify its causes. They are need fulfillment, discrepancy, value attainment, equity, and dispositional/genetic components. A brief review of these models will provide insight into the complexity of this seemingly simple concept.[57]

Need Fulfilment

These models propose that satisfaction is determined by the extent to which the characteristics of a job allow an individual to fulfil his or her needs. For example, a recent survey of 30 law firms revealed that 35 to 50 per cent of law-firm associates left their employers within three years of starting because the firms did not accommodate family needs. This example illustrates that unmet needs can affect both satisfaction and turnover.[58] Although these models generated a great degree of controversy, it is generally accepted that need fulfilment is correlated with job satisfaction.[59]

Discrepancies

These models propose that satisfaction is a result of met expectations. Met expectations represent the difference between what an individual expects to receive from a job, such as good pay and promotional opportunities, and what he or she actually receives. When expectations are greater than what is received, a person will be dissatisfied. In contrast, this model predicts the individual will be satisfied when he or she attains outcomes above and beyond expectations. A meta-analysis of 31 studies, which included 17,241 people, demonstrated that met expectations were significantly related to job satisfaction. [60]

Met expectations
the extent to which one receives what he or she expects from a job

Value Attainment

The idea underlying value attainment is that satisfaction results from the perception that a job allows for fulfilment of an individual's important work values.[61] In general, research consistently supports the prediction that value fulfilment is positively related to job satisfaction.[62] Managers can thus enhance employee satisfaction by structuring the work environment and its associated rewards and recognition to reinforce employees' values.

Value attainment
the extent to which a job allows fulfillment of one's work values

Equity

In this model, satisfaction is a function of how 'fairly' an individual is treated at work. Satisfaction results from one's perception that work outcomes, relative to inputs, compare favourably those of a significant other. A meta-analysis, involving data from 30 different organizations and 12,979 people, supported this model. Employees perceived fairness of pay and promotions were significantly correlated with job satisfaction.[63] Chapter 7 explores this promising model in more detail.

Dispositional/Genetic Components

Have you ever noticed that some of your co-workers or friends appear to be satisfied across a variety of job circumstances, whereas others always seem dissatisfied? This model of satisfaction attempts to explain this pattern.[64] Specifically, the dispositional/genetic model is based on the belief that job satisfaction is partly a function of both personal traits and genetic factors. As such, this model implies that stable individual differences are just as important in explaining job satisfaction as are characteristics of the work environment. Although only a few studies have tested these propositions, results support a positive, significant relationship between personal traits and job satisfaction over time periods ranging from 2 to 50 years.[65] Genetic factors were also found to significantly predict life satisfaction, well-being and general job satisfaction.[66] Additional research is needed to test this new model of job satisfaction.

The Consequences of Job Satisfaction

This area has significant managerial implications because thousands of studies have examined the relationship between job satisfaction and other organizational variables. Because it is impossible to examine them all, we will consider a subset of the more important variables from the standpoint of managerial relevance.

Table 7-2 summarizes the pattern of results. The relationship between job satisfaction and these other variables is either positive or negative. The strength of the relationship ranges from weak (very little relationship) to strong. Strong relationships imply that managers can significantly influence that particular variable by increasing job satisfaction. Let us now consider several of the key correlates of job satisfaction.

Motivation

A recent meta-analysis of nine studies and 2,237 workers revealed a significant positive relationship between motivation and job satisfaction. Because satisfaction with

Table 7–2

Correlates of Job Satisfaction

Variables Related with Satisfaction	Direction of Relationship	Strength of Relationship
Motivation	Positive	Moderate
Job involvement	Positive	Moderate
Organizational citizenship behavior	Positive	Moderate
Organizational commitment	Positive	Strong
Absenteeism	Negative	Weak
Tardiness	Negative	Weak
Turnover	Negative	Moderate
Heart disease	Negative	Moderate
Perceived stress	Negative	Strong
Pro-union voting	Negative	Moderate
Job performance	Positive	Weak
Life satisfaction	Positive	Moderate
Mental health	Positive	Moderate

supervision was also significantly correlated with motivation, managers are advised to consider how their behaviour affects employee satisfaction.[67] Managers can potentially enhance employees' motivation through various attempts to increase job satisfaction.

Job Involvement

Job involvement represents the extent to which an individual is personally involved with his or her work role. A meta-analysis involving 27,925 individuals from 87 different studies demonstrated that job involvement was moderately related with job satisfaction.[68] Managers are thus encouraged to foster satisfying work environments in order to fuel employees' job involvement.

Organizational Citizenship Behaviour

Organizational citizenship behaviours consist of employee behaviours that are beyond the call of duty. Examples include 'such gestures as constructive statements about the department, expression of personal interest in the work of others, suggestions for improvement, training new people, respect for the spirit as well as the letter of housekeeping rules, care for organizational property, and punctuality and attendance well beyond standard or enforceable levels'.[69] Managers would certainly like employees to exhibit these behaviours. A meta-analysis covering 6,746 people and 28 separate studies revealed a significant, and moderately positive, correlation between organizational citizenship behaviours and job satisfaction.[70] Moreover, additional research demonstrated that employees' citizenship behaviours were determined more by leadership and characteristics of the work environment than by an employee's personality.[71] It thus appears that managerial behaviour significantly influences an employee's willingness to exhibit citizenship behaviours. This relationship is important to recognize because organizational citizenship behaviours were positively correlated with performance ratings.[72]

Organizational Commitment

Organizational commitment reflects the extent to which an individual identifies with an organization and is committed to its goals. A meta-analysis of 68 studies and 35,282 individuals uncovered a significant and strong relationship between organizational commitment and satisfaction.[73] Managers are advised to increase job satisfaction in order to elicit higher levels of commitment. In turn, higher commitment can facilitate higher productivity.[74]

Absenteeism

Absenteeism is costly, and managers are constantly on the lookout for ways to reduce it. One recommendation has been to increase job satisfaction. If this is a valid recommendation, there should be a strong negative relationship (or negative correlation) between satisfaction and absenteeism. In other words, as satisfaction increases, absenteeism should decrease. A researcher investigated this prediction by synthesizing three separate meta-analyses containing a total of 74 studies. Results revealed a weak negative relationship between satisfaction and absenteeism.[75] It is unlikely, therefore, that managers will realize any significant decrease in absenteeism by increasing job satisfaction.

Turnover

Turnover is important to managers because it both disrupts organizational continuity and is very costly. A meta-analysis of 78 studies covering 27,543 people demonstrated a moderate negative relationship between satisfaction and turnover.[76] (See Table 7–2.) Given the strength of this relationship, managers would be well advised to try to reduce turnover by increasing employee job satisfaction.

Perceived Stress

Stress can have very negative effects on organizational behaviour and an individual's health. Stress is positively related to absenteeism, turnover, coronary heart disease, and viral infections.[77] Based on a meta-analysis of seven studies covering 2,659 individuals, Table 7–2 reveals that perceived stress has a strong, negative relationship with job satisfaction.[78] It is hoped that managers would attempt to reduce the negative effects of stress by improving job satisfaction.

Job Performance

One of the biggest controversies within organizational research centres on the relationship between satisfaction and job performance. Some, such as Herzberg, argue that satisfaction leads to higher performance while others contend that high performance leads to satisfaction. In an attempt to resolve this controversy, a meta-analysis accumulated results from 74 studies. Overall, the relationship between job satisfaction and job performance was examined for 12,192 people. It was discovered that there was a small positive relationship between satisfaction and performance.[79]

Researchers have identified two key reasons this result is misleading and understates the true relationship between satisfaction and performance.

First, job satisfaction is not expected, in theory, to have a strong influence on behaviour (such as performance and turnover). Rather, satisfaction is hypothesized to indirectly affect performance through an employee's intentions or effort.[80] Figure 7–1 shows this relationship. Returning to Figure 7–1, note how job satisfaction, which is represented by the term 'affect' in the individual input box, is at the far left of the model and that performance is on the far right. Performance is expected to be more strongly influenced by the boxes in-between individual inputs and performance, namely motivational processes and motivated behaviours. A recent meta-analysis supported this conclusion.[81]

The second reason revolves around the accuracy of measuring an individual's performance. If performance ratings do not reflect the actual interactions and interdependencies at work, weak meta-analytic results arise partially due to incomplete measures of individual-level performance.[82] Examining the relationship between aggregate measures of job satisfaction and organizational performance is one solution to this problem. In a recent study found a significant, positive correlation between organizational performance and employee satisfaction for data collected from 298 schools and 13,808 teachers.[83] Thus, it appears that managers can positively affect performance by increasing employee job satisfaction.

Summary of Key Concepts

1 Define the term motivation.

Motivation is defined as those psychological processes that cause the arousal, direction and persistence of voluntary, goal-oriented actions. Managers need to understand these psychological processes if they are to successfully guide employees toward accomplishing organizational objectives.

2 Discuss the job performance model of motivation.

Individual inputs and job context variables are the two key categories of factors that influence motivation. In turn, motivation leads to motivated behaviours, which then affect performance. The model highlights four key issues.

- Motivation is different from behaviour.
- Behaviour is influenced by more than just motivation.
- Behaviour is different from performance.
- Motivation is a necessary but insufficient contributor to job performance.

3 Review the historical roots of modern motivation theories.

Five ways of explaining behaviour—needs, reinforcement, cognition, job characteristics, and feelings/emotions—underlie the evolution of modern theories of human motivation. Some theories of motivation focus on internal energizers of behaviour such as needs, satisfaction, and feelings/emotions. Other motivation theories, which deal in terms of reinforcement, cognitions, and job characteristics, focus on more complex person-environment interactions. There is no single, universally accepted theory of motivation.

4 Contrast Maslow's and McClelland's need theories.

Two well-known need theories of motivation are Maslow's need hierarchy and McClelland's need theory. Maslow's notion of a graduated hierarchy of five levels of needs has not stood up well under research. McClelland believes that motivation and performance vary according to the strength of an individual's need for achievement. High achievers prefer moderate risks and situations where they can control their own destiny. Top managers should have a high need for power coupled with a low need for affiliation.

5 Demonstrate your familiarity with scientific management, job enlargement, job rotation and job enrichment.

Each of these techniques is used in the process of job design. Job design involves altering jobs with the intent of increasing employee job satisfaction and productivity. Scientific management designs jobs by using research and experimentation to identify the most efficient way to perform tasks. Jobs are horizontally loaded in job enlargement by giving workers more than one specialized task to complete. Job rotation increases workplace variety by moving employees from one specialized job to another. Job enrichment vertically loads a job by giving employees administrative duties normally performed by their superiors.

6 Explain the practical significance of Herzberg's distinction between motivators and hygiene factors.

Herzberg believes job satisfaction motivates better job performance. His *hygiene* factors, such as policies, supervision and salary, erase sources of dissatisfaction. On the other hand, his *motivators*, such as achievement, responsibility and recognition, foster job satisfaction. Although Herzberg's motivator–hygiene theory of job satisfaction has been criticized on methodological grounds, it has practical significance for job enrichment.

7 Describe how internal work motivation is increased by using the job characteristics model.

The psychological states of experienced meaningfulness, experienced responsibility, and knowledge of results, produce internal work motivation. These psychological states are fostered by the presence of five core job characteristics. People respond positively to jobs containing these core job characteristics when they have the knowledge and skills necessary to perform the job, high growth needs, and high context satisfactions.

8 Discuss the causes and consequences of job satisfaction.

Job satisfaction is an affective or emotional response toward various facets of one's job. Five models of job satisfaction specify its causes. They are need fulfilment, discrepancy, value attainment, equity, and trait/genetic components. Job satisfaction has been correlated with hundreds of consequences. Table 7–2 summarizes the pattern of results found for a subset of the more important variables.

Discussion Questions

1 Why should the average manager be well versed in the various motivation theories?

2 From a practical standpoint, what is a major drawback of theories of motivation based on internal factors such as needs, satisfaction and feelings/emotions?

3 Are you a high achiever? How can you tell? How will this help or hinder your path to top management?

4 How have hygiene factors and motivators affected your job satisfaction and performance?

5 How might the job characteristics model be used to increase your internal motivation to study?

6 Do you know anyone who would not respond positively to an enriched job? Describe this person.

7 Do you believe that job satisfaction is partly a function of both personal traits and genetic factors? Explain.

8 Do you think job satisfaction leads directly to better job performance? Explain.

9 What are the three most valuable lessons about employee motivation that you have learned from this

Internet Exercise

www.fed.org/library/index.html

This chapter discussed a variety of approaches for motivating employees. We noted that there is no 'one best theory' of motivation and that managers can use different theories to solve various types of performance problems. The purpose of this exercise is for you to identify motivational techniques or programmes that are being used by different companies. Begin by visiting the Web site for The Foundation for Enterprise Development at http://www.fed.org/library/index.html.

The Foundation is a non-profit organization that helps managers to implement equity-based compensation and broad-based participation programmes aimed at improving corporate performance. To begin your search, select the resource library and follow up by choosing to view the library by subject. You will be given a variety of categories to choose from. Use the categories of *case studies of private companies* or *case studies of public companies*, and then pick two companies that you would like to analyse.

Questions

1 In what ways are these companies using the theories and models discussed in this chapter?

2 To what extent is employee motivation related to these organizations' cultures?

3 What motivational methods are these companies using that were not discussed in this chapter?

Personal Awareness and Growth Exercise
What Is Your Work Ethic?

Objectives

1 To measure your work ethic.

2 To determine how well your work ethic score predicts your work habits.

Introduction

The work ethic reflects the extent to which an individual values work. A strong work ethic involves the belief that hard work is the key to success and happiness. In recent years, there has been concern that the work ethic is dead or dying. This worry is based on findings from observational studies and employee attitude surveys.

People differ in terms of how much they believe in the work ethic. These differences influence a variety of behavioural outcomes. What better way to gain insight into the work ethic than by measuring your own work ethic and seeing how well it predicts your everyday work habits?

Instructions

To assess your work ethic, complete the following eight-item instrument developed by a respected behavioural scientist.[85] Being honest with yourself, circle your responses on the rating scales following each of the eight items. There are no right or wrong answers. Add up your total score for the eight items, and record it in the space provided.

Following the work ethic scale is a short personal-work-habits questionnaire. Your responses to this questionnaire will help you determine whether your work ethic score is a good predictor of your work habits.

Work Ethic Scale

1 When the workday is finished, people should forget their jobs and enjoy themselves.

Agree completely 1–2–3–4–5 Disagree completely

2 Hard work does not make an individual a better person.

Agree completely 1–2–3–4–5 Disagree completely

3 The principal purpose of a job is to provide a person with the means for enjoying his or her free time.

Agree completely 1–2–3–4–5 Disagree completely

4 Wasting time is not as bad as wasting money.

Agree completely 1–2–3–4–5 Disagree completely

5 Whenever possible, a person should relax and accept life as it is, rather than always striving for unreachable goals.

Agree completely 1–2–3–4–5 Disagree completely

6 A person's worth should not be based on how well he or she performs a job.

Agree completely 1–2–3–4–5 Disagree completely

7 People who do things the easy way are the smart ones.

Agree completely 1–2–3–4–5 Disagree completely

8 If all other things are equal, it is better to have a job with little responsibility than one with a lot of responsibility.

Agree completely 1–2–3–4–5 Disagree completely

Total = _____

The higher your total score, the stronger your work ethic.

Personal Work Habits Questionnaire

1 How many unexcused absences from classes did you have last term?

_____absences

2 How many credit hours are you taking this term?

_____hours

3 What is your overall grade point average?

_____GPA

4 What percentage of your course expenses are you earning through full- or part-time employment?

_____%

5 In percentage terms, how much effort do you typically put forth into your studies and/or work?

Studies =_____%   Work = _____%

1 How strong is your work ethic?

Weak = 8–18 Moderate = 19–29 Strong = 30–40

2 How would you rate your work habits/results?

Below average_____ Average _____
Above average_____

3 How well does your work ethic score predict your work habits or work results?

Poorly_____ Moderately well_____ Very well_____

Group Exercise

Applying the Job Characteristics Model

Objectives

1 To assess the motivating potential score (MPS) of several jobs.

2 To determine which core job characteristics need to be changed for each job.

3 To explore how you might redesign one of the jobs.

Introduction

The first step in calculating the MPS of a job is to complete the job diagnostic survey (JDS). Since the JDS is a long questionnaire, we would like you to complete a subset of the instrument. This will enable you to calculate the MPS and to identify deficient job characteristics.

Instructions

Your instructor will divide the class into groups of four to six. Each group member will first assess the MPS of his or her current job and then will identify which core job characteristics need to be changed. Once each group member has completed these tasks, the group will identify the job with the lowest MPS and devise a plan for redesigning it. The following steps should be used.

First you should complete the 12 items from the JDS. For each item, indicate whether it is an accurate or inaccurate description of your current or most recent job by selecting one number from the scale provided. Write your response in the space provided next to each item. After completing the JDS, use the scoring key to compute a total score for each of the core job characteristics.

1 = Very inaccurate   5 = Slightly accurate

2 = Mostly inaccurate   6 = Mostly accurate

3 = Slightly inaccurate   7 = Very accurate

4 = Uncertain

_____ *1* Supervisors often let me know how well they think I am performing the job.

_____ *2* The job requires me to use a number of complex or high-level skills.

_____ *3* The job is arranged so that I have the chance to do an entire piece of work from beginning to end.

_____ *4* Just doing the work required by the job provides many chances for me to figure out how well I am doing.

_____ *5* The job is not simple and repetitive.

_____ *6* This job is one where a lot of other people can be affected by how well the work gets done.

_____ *7* The job does not deny me the chance to use my personal initiative or judgement in carrying out the work.

_____ *8* The job provides me with the chance to completely finish the pieces of work I begin.

_____ *9* The job itself provides plenty of clues about whether or not I am performing well.

_____ *10* The job gives me considerable opportunity for independence and freedom in how I do the work.

_____ *11* The job itself is very significant or important in the broader scheme of things.

_____ *12* The supervisors and co-workers on this job almost always give me 'feedback' about how well I am doing in my work.

Scoring Key

Compute the *average* of the two items that measure each job characteristic.

Skill variety (2 and 5) _____

Task identity (3 and 8) _____

Task significance (6 and 11) _____

Autonomy (7 and 10) _____

Feedback from job itself (4 and 9) _____

Feedback from others (1 and 12) _____

Now you are ready to calculate the MPS. First, you need to compute a total score for the *feedback* job characteristic. This is done by computing the average of the job characteristics entitled 'feedback from job itself' and 'feedback from others'. Second, use the MPS formula presented earlier in this chapter to calculate the MPS. Finally, use the JDS norms provided to interpret the relative status of the MPS and each individual job characteristic.[85]

Once all group members have finished these activities, convene as a group to complete the exercise. Each group member should present his or her results and interpretations of the strengths and deficiencies of the job characteristics. Next, pick the job within the group that has the lowest MPS. Prior to redesigning this job, however, each group member needs more background information. The individual who works in the lowest MPS job should thus provide a thorough description of the job, including its associated tasks, responsibilities and reporting relationships. A brief overview of the general working environment is also useful. With this information to hand, the group should now devise a detailed plan for how it would redesign the job.

Norms

	TYPE OF JOB			
	Professional/ Technical	Clerical	Sales	Service
Skill variety	5.4	4.0	4.8	5.0
Task identity	5.1	4.7	4.4	4.7
Task significance	5.6	5.3	5.5	5.7
Autonomy	5.4	4.5	4.8	5.0
Feedback from job itself	5.1	4.6	5.4	5.1
Feedback from others	4.2	4.0	3.6	3.8
MPS	154	106	146	152

Questions for discussion

1 Using the norms, which job characteristics are high, average, or low for the job being redesigned?

2 Which job characteristics did you change? Why?

3 How would you specifically redesign the job under consideration?

4 What would be the difficulties in implementing the job characteristics model in a large organization?

Chapter Eight

Motivation through Equity, Expectancy and Goal Setting

Learning Objectives

When you finish studying the material in this chapter, you should be able to:

- Discuss the role of perceived inequity in employee motivation.

- Explain the differences between distributive, procedural and interactional justice.

- Describe the practical lessons derived from equity theory.

- Explain Vroom's expectancy theory.

- Discuss Porter and Lawler's expectancy theory of motivation.

- Describe the practical implications of expectancy theory of motivation.

- Explain how goal setting motivates an individual.

- Identify five practical lessons to be learned from goal-setting research.

- Specify issues that should be addressed before implementing a motivational programme.

Nokia's Jorma Ollila wants to unwire the world

Even as dozens of other high-tech industry executives are obsessed with wiring the planet, Jorma Ollila, chairman and CEO of Finland's Nokia Corp., is equally intent on bringing people, words, data and the Internet together, anytime anywhere, without wires. Ollila, *Industry Week's* CEO of the Year (2000), calls it creating the Mobile Information Society. 'What the Mobile Information Society really achieves for us is that it helps us to increase our quality of life by making the ▶

most of our limited supply of time. It helps boost our efficiency. It allows us to do more. To achieve more. It empowers us to make more of ourselves,' he says. If that seems unabashedly ambitious for a former Citigroup Inc. banker, so be it.

Indeed, promoting a culture of risk-taking has been one of the major themes of Ollila's eight years as chief executive of Nokia, the world's largest mobile phone manufacturer. 'If you want to reach a certain goal, you have to allow for mistakes and learn from them. If you don't fail throughout your career at certain points, then you haven't stretched yourself properly. A challenge that is met too easily can hardly be called a challenge.' Therefore, at Nokia there is a palpable culture of tolerating mistakes and encouraging people to learn and develop. 'Every single appointment is a signal that this is the kind of thing we are encouraging–this is the kind of personality, behaviour and experience that we want to bring into this team', Ollila asserts.

For many years, Ollila has been playing a financially winning game but in 2000, however, Nokia picked up some financial static. For example, Nokia's share price fell about 25 per cent. And recently, in a cover story, Britain's *The Economist* magazine asserted that 'the sheer smartness of Mr. Ollila and his close-knit team of fellow Finns is now being tested more profoundly than at any time during the nineties'. Among the challenges: intense Japanese competition.

Ollila remains calm, however, as if some extra pressure makes him even more determined to attain his goal of an 'unwired world'. 'The stock market is what it is. You live with that', says Ollila. 'You just do the best you can on a daily basis, the right balance of short-term and long-term actions. That's the only attitude you can take to avoid losing sleep unnecessarily. It's no use bothering over things you have very little direct influence on anyway. You have to keep going.'

As for market competition, Ollila concedes nothing. 'I don't think there is any other company that is better placed than we are to tackle the next paradigm of software-intensive applications and services', he asserts. 'I don't think the Far Eastern companies have an edge. We do. We understand user needs, and we have the drive to do it.'

Since 1992, Nokia has had 15 significant market firsts. Characteristically, when Nokia announces a new model, the collective pronoun 'we' is used. All over Nokia, many people, including Ollila, talk of teams. 'Ollila has that ability to create teams around himself, where they discuss and brainstorm, and sort of converge to a certain view', notes Goran Lindahl, president and CEO of the Zürich-based ABB Ltd. 'But then', he says, identifying a critically important aspect of Ollila's management approach, 'he takes responsibility and says: "Oh . . . I see . . . Fine . . . . Now we do this." He apparently has a great talent for staying calm and motivating himself and his employees to go a step further each day: 'That's where we are, that's where we want to be, so let's do it . . .'.

Ollila believes that people at Nokia are empowered, able to speak their minds to him and everyone else in the company. 'That's extremely positive for the innovation of individuals and the organization', he says. 'But we are, at the same time, a very pragmatic organization', he stresses. 'We don't analyse problems to death. We're pretty determined about timelines [deadlines] and getting things done. Somebody has to take the responsibility and say, "O.K. this is it. That's what we're going to do." Otherwise you just have a lot of fun discussing things and nobody takes the ball and carries it. It's all very well passing it around in a circle. But somebody, at the right point in time, has to grab it and run. You can not keep a team motivated unless they know where they're going.'

One of Ollila's accomplishments at Nokia has been to make it possible for many people to grab opportunities and run with them. 'This is an organization where, if you want to prove yourself, if you want to develop yourself and grow towards your goals, we will give you the platform,' Ollila says. 'This is what we want to do—to create a platform that is attractive to young people, that is a little bit special in terms of a working environment. Getting results is always part of it. But providing the platform is fundamental.'[1]

For discussion
Striving towards one's goals is an essential part of Jorma Ollila's philosophy. Do you think managers can actually serve as a motivational example by setting challenging goals for themselves and beaming out a 'can do' mentality?

As seen in the opening case, the life of the Finn, Jorma Ollila, is clearly filled with a sense of purpose. He has a wide range of personal goals he wants to accomplish, from 'unwiring the world', as he describes it, through to maintaining a balanced life and forming a competent team.[2] As was the case with Nokia's Mr Olllila, it is the continuous striving for various goals that motivates people. In another context, a long-distance runner, for example, who wants to take part in the Rotterdam Marathon will train twice as hard as he would if he were not in a competition. And, even as soon as two weeks after the 2000 Olympics in Sidney, many athletes started their new training routines with the 2004 games in mind. The goal setting theory of motivation provides a good explanation for their behaviour.

This chapter explores three cognitive theories of work motivation: equity, expectancy and goal setting. Each theory is based on the premise that employees' cognitions are the key to understanding their motivation. To help you apply what you have learned, we conclude the chapter by highlighting the prerequisites of successful motivational programmes.

ADAM'S EQUITY THEORY OF MOTIVATION

Equity theory
holds that motivation is a function of fairness in social exchanges

Defined generally, equity theory is a model of motivation that explains how people strive for *fairness* and *justice* in social exchanges or give-and-take relationships. Equity theory is based on cognitive dissonance theory, developed by social psychologist Leon Festinger in the 1950s.[3]

According to Festinger's theory, people are motivated to maintain consistency between their cognitive beliefs and their behaviour. Perceived inconsistencies create cognitive dissonance (or psychological discomfort) which, in turn, motivates corrective action. For example, a cigarette smoker who sees a heavy-smoking relative die of lung cancer probably would be motivated to quit smoking if he or she attributes the death to smoking.

Accordingly, when victimized by unfair social exchanges, our resulting cognitive dissonance prompts us to correct the situation. Corrective action may range from a slight change in attitude or behaviour through to stealing or, in an extreme case, to trying to harm someone. For example, researchers have demonstrated that people attempt to 'get even' for perceived injustices by using either direct (e.g., theft or sabotage) or indirect (e.g., intentionally working slowly, giving a co-worker the silent treatment) retaliation.[4]

Psychologist J Stacy Adams pioneered the application of the equity principle to the workplace. Central to understanding Adams's equity theory of motivation is an awareness of key components of the individual–organization exchange relationship. This relationship is pivotal in the formation of employees' perceptions of equity and inequity.

The Individual–Organization Exchange Relationship

Adams points out that two primary components are involved in the employee–employer exchange, *inputs* and *outcomes*. An employee's inputs, for which he or she expects a just return, include education, experience, skills and effort. On the outcome side of the exchange, the organization provides such things as pay, fringe benefits and recognition. These outcomes vary widely, depending on one's organization and rank. Table 8–1 presents a list of on-the-job inputs and outcomes that employees consider when making equity comparisons.

Negative and Positive Inequity

At work, feelings of inequity revolve around a person's evaluation of whether he or she receives adequate rewards to compensate for his or her contributive inputs. People perform these evaluations by comparing the perceived fairness of their employment exchange to that of relevant others. This comparative process, which is based on an equity norm, was found to generalize across countries.[5] People tend to compare themselves to other individuals with whom they have close interpersonal ties, such as friends, and/or to similar others—such as people performing the same job or of the same gender or educational level—rather than dissimilar ones.[6]

Three different equity relationships are illustrated in Figure 8–1: equity, negative inequity, and positive inequity. Assume the two people in each of the equity relationships in Figure 8–1 have equivalent backgrounds (equal education, seniority and so forth) and perform identical tasks. Only their hourly pay rates differ. Equity exists for an individual when his or her ratio of perceived outcomes to inputs is equal to the ratio of outcomes to inputs for a relevant co-worker (see part A in Figure 8–1). Since equity is based on comparing *ratios* of outcomes to inputs, inequity will not necessarily be perceived just because someone else receives greater rewards. If the other person's additional outcomes are due to his or her greater inputs, a sense of equity may still exist. However, if the comparison person enjoys greater outcomes for similar inputs, **negative inequity** will be perceived (see part B in Figure 8–1). On the other hand, a person will experience **positive inequity** when his or her outcome to input ratio is greater than that of a relevant co-worker (see part C in Figure 8–1).

Negative equity
comparison in which another person receives greater outcomes for similar inputs

Positive equity
comparison in which another person receives lesser outcomes for similar inputs

Figure 8–1 *Negative and Positive Inequity*

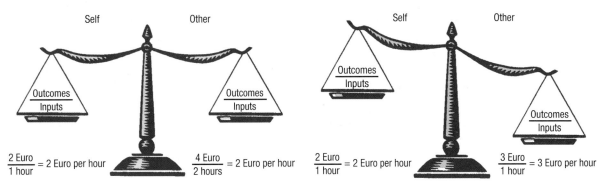

A. **An Equitable Situation** B. **Negative Inequity**

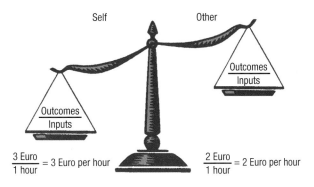

C. **Positive Inequity**

Let us consider the type of equity associated with the pay gap between chief executive officers and workers.

The pay gap between company directors and their employees is getting bigger, according to a report from the British union organization, the TUC. Directors of the UK's largest 500 firms are paid on average 18 times the amount their staff get. Moreover, when it comes to the top five companies, the top executives earned an

Table 8-1

Factors Considered When Making Equity Comparisons

Inputs	Outcomes
Time	Pay/bonuses
Education/training	Fringe benefits
Experience	Challenging assignments
Skills	Job security
Creativity	Career advancement/promotions
Seniority	Status symbols
Loyalty to organization	Pleasant/safe working environment
Age	Opportunity for personal growth/development
Personality traits	Supportive supervision
Effort expended	Recognition
Personal appearance	Participation in important decisions

SOURCE: Based in part on J S Adams, 'Toward an Understanding of Inequity', *Journal of Abnormal and Social Psychology*, November 1963, pp 422–36.

average of £1.5m (2.3m Euro) in 1999—up to 94 times more than those who work for them. This differential in pay rates—the widest in Europe—was described as 'staggering' by the TUC. The average salary for a chief executive in the largest 500 firms was £413,000 (653,000 Euro) in 1999, 18 times more than the workers who earned an average of £22,400 (35,398 Euro). When long-term incentives were added, top executives earned 26 times more than workers. That pay differential between top executives and average workers can be viewed in comparison to Sweden, where it was just seven to one and Germany, where it was eight to one. Despite government appeals for wage restraint, directors were awarding themselves ever bigger pay rises and perks.[7]

How do you think the typical employee would interpret this situation? Workers are likely to interpret this situation as negative inequity in spite of the increased stress and responsibility associated with being a CEO. Perceived inequity is often at the core of many actions undertaken to obtain pay rises. When asked by a reporter why he was striking, one worker cynically answered: 'Some people here are more equal than others . . .'.[8]

In contrast, Ruth Lee from the British Institute of Directors, defended the pay of top directors, which had to be high enough to stop executives being poached by even higher paying US firms. (In the United States, the bosses' pay was 27 times higher than that of the workers). She said that if companies paid below the market rate they faced losing their top talent—and all for failing to spend £100,000 (158,000 Euro) extra. 'For a multi-billion pound company that is absolutely nothing', she said.[9] (The next International OB highlights how compensation practices affect companies that have operations in both the United States and Europe, and those international companies wanting to hire American managers.)

Indeed, well-known CEOs such as Jack Welch, of General Electric, and Eastman Kodak's George Fisher, believe that compensation is fair. When *The Wall Street Journal* asked Welch about his $22 million (24.5 million Euro) compensation in 1995, he replied: 'This is a market. It's a free market and people have choices.' Similarly, George Fisher concluded, 'We all should be compensated based on competitive issues. If you want world-class leadership, you pay. The good news is that many CEOs are getting well compensated for really good performances.'[10] We wonder whether workers also believe that they are being well compensated for really good performances.

Perceived pay inequity can be devastating for one's motivation and performance at work. For example, British prisoners are said to receive inadequate health care because medical staff in the prison service are paid less than their counterparts in the National

Health Services (NHS). According to Sir David Ramsbotham, chief inspector of prisons, 'this pay inequality means that prison inmates get a worse standard of health care than they would in the community. Young offenders are particularly hard hit because they need good health if they are to develop properly and play a useful role in society on their release. But without pay levels on a par with those of the NHS, it is difficult for the prison service to attract staff with the same abilities.'[11]

International OB

www.alcatel.com

Pay Equity Is an International Issue

BusinessWeek

France's Alcatel learned a hard lesson last month in how costly it can be to keep up with US pay. It paid $350 million for Assured Access Technology Inc. in Milpitas, Calif., which provides plumbing for the Internet. Included in the price: $60 million to keep Assured's 55 engineers from bolting at the prospect of a low-paying French employer.

The Alcatel experience shows how pressure is mounting on Europeans to boost pay. Globalizing outfits such as Daimler-Chrysler and Deutsche Bank say they can't compete in the United States or hire top international people without offering US pay. But it's not just about grabbing talent abroad: Once companies do that, they find home-grown employees clamouring for more, too. Meanwhile, a new focus on shareholder interests is breaking down barriers to [between] stock options and incentive-pay packages.

To be sure, salaries in Europe remain below those in America. In Britain, for example, companies offer base salaries for chief executives from the United States that are 30 per cent more than their British counterparts get, according to consultants Monks Partnership. Bonuses for US executives are even more generous–twice the British level. The difference reflects a recognition by companies that, if they want to hire a top American manager, they have to pay a premium. That also explains why the CEO of drugmaker [pharmaceutical manufacturer] SmithKline Beecham Plc, Jan Leschly—a Dane who spent most of his career in the United States—just won a $143 million

package, Britain's highest ever. Still, shareholders remained conspicuously silent—which shows how perceptions have changed.

Elsewhere in egalitarian Europe, though, big pay remains controversial. When Finnish papers reported last spring that Chairman Jorma Ollila of Nokia Corp. had accumulated $15 million worth of company stock under an incentive pay program, it caused a scandal. Ollila's response: Nokia needed a stock-option program to attract top talent. 'It's no easy job recruiting people to live in Helsinki', he says.

When Daimler-Benz took over Chrysler Corp. last year; CEO Jürgen E Schrempp had to confront the fact that Chrysler CEO Robert Eaton—who earned over $11 million in 1997, including exercised options—appears to have made more than the rest of Daimler's management board members put together. Worse, Daimler had to pay $395 million— primarily in stock—to Chrysler's top 30 executives to cash out their options. Since cutting the pay of the Chrysler people would be tough, Daimler was forced to boost its own compensation. Deutsche Bank faces similar pressures. Burned by defections from its US operations last year, it agreed to pay $187 million to retain five top execs at Bankers Trust Co. after its takeover of the US bank is done. Not bad, considering CEO Rolf Breuer is estimated to make no more than about $1.5 million a year.

SOURCE: Excerpted from J Ewing, S Baker, W Echikson, and K Capell, 'Eager Europeans Press Their Noses to the Glass,' *Business Week*, April 19, 1999, p 91.

Dynamics of Perceived Inequity

Managers can derive practical benefits from Adams's equity theory by recognizing that:

▼ **negative inequity is less tolerable than positive inequity**

▼ **inequity can be reduced in a variety of ways.**

Thresholds of Inequity

People have a lower tolerance for negative inequity than they do for positive inequity. Those who are short-changed are more powerfully motivated to correct the situation than those who are excessively rewarded. For example, if you have ever been overworked and underpaid, you know how negative inequity can erode your job satisfaction and performance. Perhaps you put in less effort or quit the job to escape the negative inequity. Hence, it takes much more positive inequity than it does negative to produce the same degree of motivation. Moreover, a meta-analysis of 12,979 people demonstrated that males and females had equal reactions to negative inequity. There were no gender differences in response to perceived inequity.[12]

Reducing Inequity

Table 8–2 lists eight possible ways to reduce inequity. It is important to note that equity can be restored by altering one's equity ratios either behaviourally or cognitively, or both. Equity theorists propose that the many possible combinations of behavioural and cognitive adjustments are influenced by the following tendencies.

1 An individual will attempt to maximize the amount of positive outcomes he or she receives.

2 People resist increasing inputs when it requires substantial effort or costs.

3 People resist behavioural or cognitive changes in inputs important to their self-concept or self-esteem.

4 Rather than change cognitions about oneself, an individual is more likely to change cognitions about the comparison person's inputs and outcomes.

5 Leaving the field (quitting) is chosen only when severe inequity cannot be resolved through other methods.[13]

Table 8–2

Eight Ways to Reduce Inequity

Methods	Examples
1. Person can increase his or her inputs.	Work harder; attend school or a specialized training program.
2. Person can decrease his or her inputs.	Don't work as hard; take longer breaks.
3. Person can attempt to increase his or her outcomes.	Ask for a raise; ask for a new title; seek outside intervention.
4. Person can decrease his or her outcomes.	Ask for less pay.
5. Leave the field.	Absenteeism and turnover.
6. Person can psychologically distort his or her inputs and outcomes.	Convince self that certain inputs are not important; convince self that he or she has a boring and monotonous job.
7. Person can psychologically distort the inputs or outcomes of comparison other.	Conclude that other has more experience or works harder; conclude that other has a more important title.
8. Change comparison other.	Pick a new comparison person; compare self to previous job.

SOURCE: Adapted from J S Adams, 'Toward an Understanding of Inequity', *Journal of Abnormal and Social Psychology*, November 1963, pp 422–36.

Expanding the Concept of Equity

From the 1980s, researchers began to expand the role of equity theory to explain employee attitudes and behaviour. This led to a domain of research called *organizational justice*. Organizational justice reflects the extent to which people perceive that they are treated fairly at work. This, in turn, led to the identification of three different components of organizational justice: distributive, procedural and interactional. Distributive justice reflects the perceived fairness of how resources and rewards are distributed or allocated. Procedural justice is defined as the perceived fairness of the process and procedures used to make allocation decisions. Research shows that positive perceptions of distributive and procedural justice are enhanced by giving employees a 'voice' in decisions that affect them.[14] A voice represents the extent to which employees who are affected by a decision can present relevant information about the decision to others. A voice is analogous to asking employees for their input into the decision-making process.

The last justice component pertains to the interpersonal side of how employees are treated at work. Specifically, interactional justice 'refers to the interpersonal side of decision-making, specifically to the fairness of the decision-maker's behaviour in the process of making decisions. Those making decisions behave in an interactionally fair manner when they treat those affected by the decision properly and enact the decision policy or procedure properly.'[15] Fair interpersonal treatment necessitates that managers communicate truthfully and treat people with courtesy and respect. Fair enactment of procedures further requires that managers suppress personal biases, consistently apply decision-making criteria, provide timely feedback, and justify decisions.[16]

Distributive justice
the perceived fairness of how resources and rewards are distributed

Procedural justice
the perceived fairness of the process and procedures used to make allocation decisions

Interactional justice
the perceived fairness of the decision-maker's behaviour in the process of making decisions

Equity Research Findings

Different managerial insights have been gained from laboratory and field studies.

Insights from Laboratory Studies

The basic approach used in laboratory studies is to pay an experimental subject more (overpayment) or less (underpayment) than the standard rate for completing a task. People are paid on either an hourly or piece-rate basis. Research findings supported equity theory. Overpaid subjects on a piece-rate system lowered the quantity of their performance and increased the quality of their performance. In contrast, underpaid subjects increased the quantity and decreased the quality of their performance.[17] A study extended this stream of research by examining the effect of underpayment inequity on ethical behaviour. A total of 102 undergraduate students were either equitably paid or underpaid for performing a clerical task. Results indicated that underpaid students stole money to compensate for their negative inequity.[18]

Insights from Field Studies

Field studies of organizational justice are on the rise. Overall, results support predictions derived from equity theory. For example, perceptions of distributive justice and procedural justice were positively related to pay and benefit satisfaction, job satisfaction, organizational commitment, trust in management and commitment to support a decision;[19] and negatively associated with retaliatory behaviours, absenteeism, intentions to quit, and turnover.[20] It thus appears beneficial for managers to equitably distribute monetary rewards and promotions by using a fair and equitable decision-making process. Interactional justice was also positively correlated with job satisfaction and reactions to performance appraisals; and negatively related with work withdrawal and experiences of sexual harassment.[21] These findings further suggest that the perceived fairness of interpersonal interactions between employees and decision-makers can significantly influence important organizational outcomes.

Practical Lessons from Equity Theory

Equity theory has at least eight important practical implications. First, equity theory provides managers with yet another explanation of how beliefs and attitudes affect job performance. According to this line of thinking, the best way to manage job behaviour is to adequately understand underlying cognitive processes. Indeed, we are motivated powerfully to correct the situation when our ideas of fairness and justice are offended.

Second, research on equity theory emphasizes the need for managers to pay attention to employees' perceptions of what is fair and equitable. No matter how fair management thinks the organization's policies, procedures and reward systems are, each employee's *perception* of the equity of those factors is what counts. People respond negatively when they perceive organizational and interpersonal injustices. Managers are thus encouraged to make hiring and promotion decisions on merit-based, job-related information. Moreover, because justice perceptions are influenced by the extent to which managers explain their decisions, managers are encouraged to explain the rationale behind their decisions.[22]

Third, managers benefit by allowing employees to participate in making decisions about important work outcomes. For example, employees were more satisfied with their performance appraisals and resultant outcomes when they had a 'voice' during the appraisal review.[23]

Fourth, employees should be given the opportunity to appeal against decisions that affect their welfare. Being able to appeal against a decision promotes the belief that management treats employees fairly. In turn, perceptions of fair treatment promote job satisfaction and organizational commitment and help reduce absenteeism and turnover.

Fifth, employees are more likely to accept and support organizational change when they believe it is implemented fairly and when it produces equitable outcomes.[24]

Sixth, managers can promote co-operation and teamwork among group members by treating them equitably. Research reveals that people are just as concerned with fairness in group settings as they are with their own personal interests.[25]

Seventh, treating employees inequitably can lead to litigation and costly court settlements. Employees denied justice at work are more likely to turn to arbitration and the courts.[26]

Finally, managers need to pay attention to the organization's climate for justice. For example, an organization's climate for justice was found to significantly influence employees' job satisfaction.[27] Researchers also believe that a climate of justice can significantly influence the type of customer service provided by employees. In turn, this level of service is likely to influence customers' perceptions of 'fair service' and their subsequent loyalty and satisfaction.[28]

Managers can attempt to follow these practical implications by monitoring equity and justice perceptions through informal conversations, interviews, or attitude surveys. For example, researchers have developed and validated a host of surveys that can be used for this purpose. Please take a moment now to complete the next OB Exercise. It contains part of a survey that was developed to measure employees' perceptions of fair interpersonal treatment. If you perceive your work organization as interpersonally unfair, you are probably dissatisfied and have contemplated quitting. In contrast, your organizational loyalty and attachment are likely to be greater if you believe you are treated fairly at work.

OB Exercise

Measuring Perceived Fair Interpersonal Treatment

Instructions

Indicate the extent to which you agree or disagree with each of the following statements by considering what your organization is like most of the time. Then compare your overall score with the arbitrary norms that are presented.

	Strongly Disagree	Disagree	Neither	Agree	Strongly Agree
1 Employees are praised for good work	1	2	3	4	5
2 Supervisors do not yell at employees	1	2	3	4	5
3 Employees are trusted	1	2	3	4	5
4 Employees' complaints are dealt with effectively	1	2	3	4	5
5 Employees are treated with respect	1	2	3	4	5
6 Employees' questions and problems are responded to quickly	1	2	3	4	5
7 Employees are treated fairly	1	2	3	4	5
8 Employees' hard work is appreciated	1	2	3	4	5
9 Employees' suggestions are used	1	2	3	4	5
10 Employees are told the truth	1	2	3	4	5

Total score = _____

Arbitrary Norms

Very fair organization = 38–50

Moderately fair organization = 24–27

Unfair organization = 10–23

SOURCE: Adapted in part from M A Donovan, F Drasgow and L Munson, 'The Perceptions of Fair Interpersonal Treatment Scale: Development and Validation of a Measure of Interpersonal Treatment in the Workplace', *Journal of Applied Psychology*, October 1998, pp 683–92.

EXPECTANCY THEORY OF MOTIVATION

Expectancy theory holds that people are motivated to behave in ways that produce desired combinations of expected outcomes. Perception plays a central role in expectancy theory because it emphasizes cognitive ability to anticipate likely consequences of behaviour. Embedded in expectancy theory is the principle of hedonism. Hedonistic people strive to maximize their pleasure and minimize their pain. Generally, expectancy theory can be used to predict behaviour in any situation in which a choice between two or more alternatives must be made. For example, it can be used to predict whether to quit or stay at a job; whether to exert substantial or minimal effort at a task; and whether to major in management, computer science, accounting, marketing, psychology or communication.

> **Expectancy theory**
> *holds that people are motivated to behave in ways that produce valued outcomes*

This section introduces and explores two expectancy theories of motivation: Vroom's expectancy theory and Porter and Lawler's expectancy theory. Understanding these cognitive process theories can help managers develop organizational policies and practices that enhance rather than inhibit employee motivation.

Vroom's Expectancy Theory

Victor Vroom formulated a mathematical model of expectancy theory in his 1964 book *Work and Motivation*.[29] Vroom's theory has been summarized as follows.

> *The strength of a tendency to act in a certain way depends on the strength of an expectancy that the act will be followed by a given consequence (or outcome) and on the value or attractiveness of that consequence (or outcome) to the actor.*[30]

Motivation, according to Vroom, boils down to the decision of how much effort to exert in a specific task situation. This choice is based on a two-stage sequence of expectations (effort → performance and performance → outcome). First, motivation is affected by an individual's expectation that a certain level of effort will produce the intended performance goal. For example, if you do not believe increasing the amount of time you spend studying will significantly raise your marks in an exam, you will probably not study any harder than usual. Motivation is also influenced by the employee's perceived chances of getting various outcomes as a result of accomplishing his or her performance goal. Finally, individuals are motivated to the extent that they value the outcomes received.

Consider the motivation and behaviour of Hans Vermeulen. In 1993, Hans Vermeulen was expelled as a member of the Dutch Stock Exchange (AEX) by the disciplinary committee as a consequence of his misbehaviour in his trading activities. Many considered his punishment too light. At the end of 1993, he became managing director at Leemhuis & Van Loon, a Dutch company active on the Dutch Stock Exchange. In 1995, Vermeulen was again discredited for malversations but nothing happened. In 1997, he was at last arrested for committing fraud and for laundering practices.[31] Based on expectancy theory, we would expect Hans Vermeulen to continue his current behaviour because he values money and there are no major consequences for his questionable conduct.

Vroom used a mathematical equation to integrate these concepts into a predictive model of motivational force or strength. For our purposes, however, it is sufficient to define and explain the three key concepts within Vroom's model—expectancy, instrumentality and valence.

Expectancy

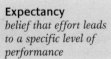

Expectancy
belief that effort leads to a specific level of performance

An **expectancy**, according to Vroom's terminology, represents an individual's belief that a particular degree of effort will be followed by a particular level of performance. In other words, it is an effort → performance expectation. Expectancies take the form of subjective probabilities. As you may recall from a course in statistics, probabilities range from zero to one. An expectancy of zero indicates effort has no anticipated impact on performance.

For example, suppose you do not know how to use a typewriter. No matter how much effort you exert, your perceived probability of typing 30 error-free words per minute are likely to be zero. An expectancy of 'one' suggests that performance is totally dependent on effort. If you decided to take a typing course as well as practice a couple of hours a day for a few weeks (high effort), you should be able to type 30 words per minute without any errors. In contrast, if you do not take a typing course and only practice an hour or two per week (low effort), there is a very low probability (say, a 20 per cent chance) of being able to type 30 words per minute without any errors.

The following factors influence an employee's expectancy perceptions:

- ▼ self-esteem
- ▼ self-efficacy
- ▼ previous success at the task
- ▼ help received from a supervisor and subordinates
- ▼ information necessary to complete the task
- ▼ good materials and equipment to work with.[32]

Instrumentality

An **instrumentality** is a performance → outcome perception. It represents a person's belief that a particular outcome is contingent on accomplishing a specific level of performance. Performance is instrumental when it leads to something else. For example, passing exams is instrumental to graduating from college.

Instrumentalities range from −1.0 to 1.0. An instrumentality of 1.0 indicates that attainment of a particular outcome is totally dependent on task performance. An instrumentality of zero indicates that there is no relationship between performance and outcome. For example, most companies link the number of vacation days to seniority, not job performance. Finally, an instrumentality of −1.0 reveals that high performance reduces the chance of obtaining an outcome while low performance increases the chance. For example, the more time you spend studying to get a high grade on an exam (high performance), the less time you will have for enjoying leisure activities. Similarly, as you lower the amount of time spent studying (low performance), you increase the amount of time that may be devoted to leisure activities.

The concept of instrumentality is applied very clearly in the concept of performance-related pay (PRP). In this system, an employee's pay varies with the amount and the quality of work he carries out. According to a survey by the British Institute of Personnel and Development, 59 per cent of British companies introduced some performance-related pay schemes between 1995 and 2000.[33] Advocates of this approach claim that variable pay schemes like PRP make employees better understand the connection between their performances and the rewards they receive.

> **Instrumentality**
> *a performance →*
> *outcome perception*

Valence

As Vroom used the term, **valence** refers to the positive or negative value people place on outcomes. Valence mirrors our personal preferences.[34] For example, most employees have a positive valence for receiving additional money or recognition. In contrast, job stress and redundancy would be likely to prove negatively valent for most individuals. In Vroom's expectancy model, *outcomes* refer to different consequences that are contingent on performance, such as pay, promotions or recognition. An outcome's valence depends on an individual's needs and can be measured for research purposes with scales ranging from a negative to a positive value. For example, an individual's valence toward more recognition can be assessed on a scale ranging from 22 (very undesirable) to 0 (neutral) to 12 (very desirable). One company who brought the principle of valence and personal preferences into practice is Laboratoires Boiron of Lyon, France.

> **Valence**
> *the value of a reward*
> *or outcome*

> *According to the company's HR manager, cash is rarely an effective employee retention tool but, when it's doled out to help employees achieve things they really value, it can create a powerful bond between workers and their company. Therefore, Laboratoires Boiron, a maker of homeopathic medicines, sets aside about 60,000 Euro a year to help employees realize their personal dreams. One warehouse worker got nine months off and 4,000 Euro to help finance a voyage around the world with her husband and two children. The company also gave about 4,500 Euro to a telephone order-taker to finance a sculpture and painting studio.*[35]

More commonly, many contemporary companies make use of alternative bonuses like extra holiday time. Holiday is the most popular employee incentive after cash.[36] According to the Briton, John Fisher, who runs The Motivation Consultancy, extra holidays need not cost the company that much and it can reduce absenteeism. 'However, the most effective is an incentive scheme where employees can choose between those options they value most', Fisher tells. 'For our clients, we often devise "all-in" incentive plans, including holiday time, private healthcare insurance, increased pension contributions and so on.'[37]

Vroom's Expectancy Theory in Action

Vroom's expectancy model of motivation can be used to analyse a real-life motivation programme. Consider the following performance problem described by Frederick W Smith, founder and chief executive officer of Federal Express Corporation.

> . . . we were having a large problem keeping things running on time. The airplanes would come in, and everything would get backed up. We tried every kind of control mechanism that you could think of, and none of them worked. Finally, it became obvious that the underlying problem was that it was in the interest of the employees at the cargo terminal—they were college kids, mostly—to run late, because it meant that they made more money. So what we did was give them all a minimum guarantee and say, 'Look, if you get through before a certain time, just go home, and you will have beat the system.' Well, it was unbelievable. I mean, in the space of about 45 days, the place was way ahead of schedule. And I don't even think it was a conscious thing on their part.[38]

How did Federal Express get its student cargo-handlers to switch from low effort to high effort? According to Vroom's model, the student workers originally exerted low effort because they were paid on the basis of time, not output. It was in their best interest to work slowly and accumulate as many hours as possible. By offering to let the student workers *go home early if and when they completed their assigned duties*, Federal Express prompted high effort. This new arrangement created two positively valued outcomes: guaranteed pay plus the opportunity to leave early. The motivation to exert high effort became greater than the motivation to exert low effort.

Judging from the impressive results, the student workers had both high effort → performance expectancies and positive performance → outcome instrumentalities. Moreover, the guaranteed pay and early departure opportunity evidently had strongly positive valences for the student workers.

Figure 8–2 *Porter and Lawler's Expectancy Model*

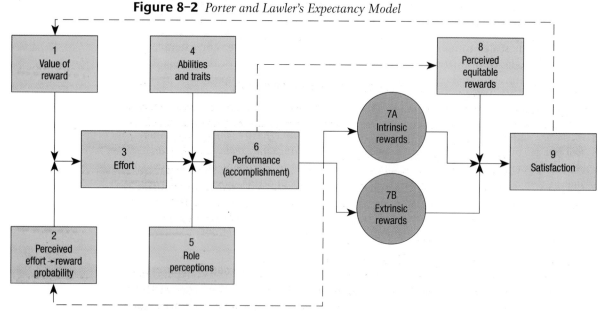

SOURCE: L W Porter and E E Lawler III, *Managerial Attitudes and Performance* (Homewood, IL: Richard D Irwin, 1968), p 165.

Porter and Lawler's Extension

Two OB researchers, Lyman Porter and Edward Lawler III, developed an expectancy model of motivation that extended Vroom's work. This model attempted to:

1 identify the source of people's valences and expectancies

2 link effort with performance and job satisfaction.

The model is presented in Figure 8–2.[39]

Predictors of Effort

Effort is a function of the perceived value of a reward (box 1 in Figure 8–2), which represents the reward's valence, and the perceived effort → reward probability (box 2, which reflects an expectancy). Employees should exhibit more effort when they believe they will receive valued rewards for task accomplishment.

Predictors of Performance

Performance is determined by more than effort. Figure 8–2 indicates that the relationship between effort and performance (boxes 3 and 6) is contingent on an employee's abilities and traits (box 4) and role perceptions (box 5). That is, employees with higher abilities attain higher performance for a given level of effort than employees with less ability. Similarly, effort results in higher performance when employees clearly understand, and are comfortable with, their roles. This occurs because effort is channelled into the most important job activities or tasks.

Predictors of Satisfaction

Employees receive both intrinsic (circle 7A in Figure 8–2) and extrinsic (circle 7B) rewards for performance. Intrinsic rewards are self-granted and consist of intangibles such as a sense of accomplishment and achievement. Extrinsic rewards are tangible outcomes such as pay and public recognition. In turn, job satisfaction is determined by employees' perceptions of the equity of the rewards received (box 8 in Figure 8–2). Employees are more satisfied when they feel equitably rewarded. Figure 8–2 further shows that job satisfaction affects employees' subsequent valence of rewards. Finally, employees' future effort → reward probabilities are influenced by past experience with performance and rewards.

Research on Expectancy Theory and Managerial Implications

Many researchers have tested expectancy theory. In support of the theory, a meta-analysis of 77 studies indicated that expectancy theory significantly predicted performance, effort, intentions, preferences, and choice.[40] Another summary of 16 studies revealed that expectancy theory correctly predicted occupational or organizational choice 63.4 per cent of the time; this was significantly better than chance predictions.[41] Further, components of expectancy theory accurately predicted task persistence, achievement, employment status of previously unemployed people, job satisfaction, decisions to retire (80 per cent accuracy), voting behaviour in union representation elections (over 75 per cent accuracy) and the frequency of drinking alcohol.[42]

Nonetheless, expectancy theory has been criticized for a variety of reasons. For example, the theory is difficult to test, and the measures used to assess expectancy, instrumentality, and valence have questionable validity.[43] In the final analysis, however, expectancy theory has important practical implications for individual managers and organizations as a whole (see Table 8–3).

Managers are advised to enhance effort → performance expectancies by helping employees accomplish their performance goals. Managers can do this by providing support and coaching and by increasing employees' self-efficacy. A management expert suggests that managers can effectively coach for success by:

1   establishing both individual and team goals

2   holding individuals and team members accountable for goals

3   showing employees how to complete difficult assignments and tasks

4   advising employees on how to overcome performance roadblocks

5   verbally expressing support

6   listening to employees and fostering two-way communication

7   sharing and recognizing progress.[44]

It also is important for managers to influence employees' instrumentalities and to monitor valences for various rewards. This raises the issue of whether organizations should use monetary rewards as the primary method to reinforce performance. Although money is certainly a positively valent reward for most people, there are three issues to consider when deciding on the relative balance between monetary and non-monetary rewards. First, some research shows that workers value interesting work and recognition more than money.[45] Second, extrinsic rewards can lose their motivating properties over time and may undermine intrinsic motivation.[46] This conclusion, however, must be balanced by the fact that performance is related to the receipt of financial incentives. A recent meta-analysis of 39 studies involving 2,773 people showed that financial incentives were positively related to performance quantity but not to performance quality. Another recent study showed that the promise of a financial reward increased children's creativity when they knew that there was an explicit positive relationship between creative performance and rewards.[47] Third, monetary rewards must be large enough to generate motivation. For example, Steven Kerr, chief learning officer at General Electric, estimates that monetary awards must be at least 12 to 15 per cent above employees' base pay to truly motivate people.[48] Unfortunately, this percentage is well above the typical salary increase received by employees.

In summary, there is no one best type of reward. Individual differences and need theories tell us that people are motivated by different rewards. Managers should therefore focus on linking employee performance to valued rewards, regardless of the type of reward used to enhance motivation.

There are four prerequisites to linking performance and rewards.

1   Managers need to develop and communicate performance standards to employees. For instance, a survey of 487 managers indicated that they were not held accountable for increasing quality. In turn, these managers did not set or enforce high performance standards among their employees.[49] Without question, increased motivation will not result in higher performance unless employees know how and where to direct their efforts.

2   Managers need valid and accurate performance ratings with which to compare employees. Inaccurate ratings create perceptions of inequity and thereby erode motivation.

3   Managers need to determine the relative mix of individual versus team contribution to performance and then reward accordingly. If an employee is truly an independent contributor, then recognition and rewards should be based solely on his or her performance. In contrast, many organizations believe that individual performance is partly due to team-level efforts and productivity. For example, team-based rewards among mid-sized and large US employers grew from 12 per cent in 1993 to 24 per cent in 1999.[50]

4   Managers should use the performance ratings to differentially allocate rewards among employees. That is, it is critical that managers allocate significantly different amounts of rewards for various levels of performance.

Implications for Managers	Implications for Organizations
Determine the outcomes employees value.	Reward people for desired performance, and do not keep pay decisions secret.
Identify good performance so appropriate behaviors can be rewarded.	Design challenging jobs.
Make sure employees can achieve targeted performance levels.	Tie some rewards to group accomplishments to build teamwork and encourage cooperation.
Link desired outcomes to targeted levels of performance.	Reward managers for creating, monitoring, and maintaining expectancies, instrumentalities, and outcomes that lead to high effort and goal attainment.
Make sure changes in outcomes are large enough to motivate high effort.	Monitor employee motivation through interviews or anonymous questionnaires.
Monitor the reward system for inequities.	Accommodate individual differences by building flexibility into the motivation program.

Table 8–3

Managerial and Organizational Implications of Expectancy Theory

MOTIVATION THROUGH GOAL SETTING

Regardless of the nature of their specific achievements, successful people tend to have one thing in common. Their lives are goal oriented. This is as true for politicians seeking votes as it is for rocket scientists probing outer space. In Lewis Carroll's delightful tale of *Alice's Adventures in Wonderland*, the smiling Cheshire cat advised the bewildered Alice, 'If you don't know where you're going, any road will take you there.' Goal-oriented managers tend to find the right road because they know where they are going. Within the context of employee motivation, this section explores the theory, research and practice of goal setting.

Goals: Definition and Background

Edwin Locke, a leading authority on goal setting, and his colleagues define a **goal** as 'what an individual is trying to accomplish; it is the object or aim of an action'.[51] Expanding this definition, they add the following.

> *The concept is similar in meaning to the concepts of purpose and intent . . . . Other frequently used concepts that are also similar in meaning to that of goal include performance standard (a measuring rod for evaluating performance), quota (a minimum amount of work or production), work norm (a standard of acceptable behaviour defined by a work group), task (a piece of work to be accomplished), objective (the ultimate aim of an action or series of actions), deadline (a time limit for completing a task), and budget (a spending goal or limit).*[52]

The motivational impact of performance goals and goal-based reward plans has been recognized for a long time. At the turn of the century, Frederick Taylor attempted to scientifically establish how much work of a specified quality an individual should be assigned each day. He proposed that bonuses be based on accomplishing those output standards. More recently, goal setting has been promoted through a widely used management technique called management by objectives (MBO).

Management by objectives is a management system that incorporates participation in decision-making, goal-setting and objective feedback.[53] A meta-analysis of MBO programmes showed productivity gains in 68 out of 70 different organizations. Specifically, results uncovered an average gain in productivity of 56 per cent when top-management commitment was high. The average gain was only 6 per cent when

Goal
what an individual is trying to accomplish

Management by objectives
management system incorporating participation in decision-making, goal-setting and feedback

commitment was low. A second meta-analysis of 18 studies further demonstrated that employees' job satisfaction was significantly related to top management's commitment to an MBO implementation.[54] These impressive results highlight the positive benefits of implementing MBO and setting goals. To further understand how MBO programmes can increase both productivity and satisfaction, let us examine the process by which goal setting works.

How Does Goal-Setting Work?

Despite abundant goal-setting research and practice, goal-setting theories are surprisingly scarce. An instructive model was formulated by Locke and his associates (see Figure 8–3). According to Locke's model, goal setting has four motivational mechanisms.

Figure 8–3

Locke's Model of Goal Setting

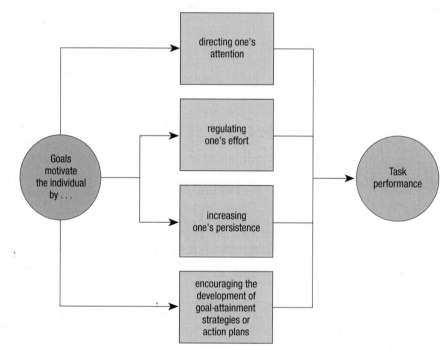

SOURCE: Adapted from *A Theory of Goal Setting & Task Performance* by Locke/Latham, © 1990. Adapted by permission of Prentice-Hall, Inc., Upper Saddle River, N.J. (Englewood Cliffs, NJ: Prentice-Hall, 1990). Reprinted by permission of Prentice-Hall, Inc.

Goals Direct Attention

Goals that are personally meaningful tend to focus one's attention on what is relevant and important. If, for example, you have a term project due in a few days, your thoughts tend to revolve around completing that project. Similarly, the members of a home appliance salesforce who are told they can win a trip to Hawaii for selling the most refrigerators will tend to steer customers toward the refrigerator display.

Goals Regulate Effort

Not only do goals make us selectively perceptive, they also motivate us to act. The instructor's deadline for turning in your term project would prompt you to complete it, as opposed to going out with friends, watching television or studying for another course. Generally, the level of effort expended is proportionate to the difficulty of the goal. Consider the motivation of Willy Ombelet, head of a fertility clinic in Brussels.

I want to mean something to our society, I want to make a difference to anonymous people who will never really know me. That's why I keep doing scientific work. A good scientist is like an artist. He creates, investigates and confirms. Those who haven't got this inside them, won't learn it either. For every patient, I try to find the best possible treatment. Actually, in everything I do, I'm looking for that little extra, for new things that demand from me a lot of time and effort. I have tried a bit of everything yet sometimes I have to learn things the hard way. But I keep going on. I have a feeling that I have to bring the world a message.[55]

Goals Increase Persistence

Within the context of goal setting, **persistence** represents the effort expended on a task over an extended period of time. It takes effort to run 100 metres; it takes persistence to run a 42-kilometre marathon. Persistent people tend to see obstacles as challenges to be overcome rather than as reasons to fail. A difficult goal that is important to an individual is a constant reminder to keep exerting effort in the appropriate direction. Astronaut Jim Lovell represents a great example of someone who persisted at his goals. Lovell commanded NASA's ill-fated Apollo 13 mission that almost did not return from deep space. Here's what Lovell had to say about his career during an interview.

> *When you look at the end result today, it's so easy to think that it was nothing but smooth sailing all the way. But perseverance was absolutely essential to getting where I am . . . . Not only did I fail to get into the Naval Academy the first time I tried–I barely made it as the first alternate the second time. Then to be the only one of 32 guys to flunk [fail] the physical for the Mercury Programme–you can imagine how that sets you back. But I persevered, and that's why I made it when I got the second shot.*
>
> *There are three traits that I think are absolutely essential to achieving success, and the first one is perseverance.* [56]

> **Persistence**
> *extent to which effort is expended on a task over time*

Goals Foster Strategies and Action Plans

If you are here and your goal is out there somewhere, you face the problem of getting from here to there. For example, the person who has resolved to lose 10 kilos must develop a plan for getting from 'here' (his or her present weight) to 'there' (10 kilos lighter). Goals can help because they encourage people to develop strategies and action plans that enable them to achieve their goals.[57] By virtue of setting a weight-reduction goal, the dieter may choose a strategy of exercising more, eating less, or some combination of the two.

Insights from Goal-Setting Research

Research has consistently supported goal setting as a motivational technique. Setting performance goals increases individual, group and organizational performance. Further, the positive effects of goal setting were not only found in the US but also elsewhere, in Australia, Canada, the Caribbean, England, Japan and west Germany. Goal setting works in different cultures. Reviews of the many goal-setting studies conducted over the last couple of decades have given managers the following five practical insights.

1 *Difficult goals lead to higher performance.* **Goal difficulty** reflects the amount of effort required to meet a goal. It is more difficult to sell nine cars a month than it is to sell three a month. A meta-analysis spanning 4,000 people and 65 separate studies revealed that goal difficulty was positively related to performance.[58] As illustrated in Figure 8–4, however, the positive relationship between goal difficulty and performance breaks down when goals are perceived to be impossible. Figure 8–4 reveals that performance goes up when employees are given hard goals as opposed to easy or moderate goals (section A). Performance then plateaus (section B) and drops (section C) as the difficulty of a goal goes from challenging to impossible.[59]

> **Goal difficulty**
> *the amount of effort required to meet a goal*

2 *Specific, difficult goals lead to higher performance for simple rather than complex tasks.* **Goal specificity** pertains to the quantifiability of a goal. For example, a goal of selling nine cars a month is more specific than telling a salesperson to do his or her best. In an early review of goal-setting research, 99 out of 110 studies (90 per cent) found that specific, hard goals led to better performance than did either easy, medium, do-your-best goals or none. This result was confirmed in a meta-analysis of 70 studies conducted between 1966 and 1984, involving 7,407 people.[60] In contrast to these positive effects, several recent studies demonstrated that setting specific, difficult goals leads to poorer performance under certain circumstances. For example, a meta-analysis of 125 studies indicated that goal-setting effects were strongest for easy tasks and weakest for complex tasks.[61] There are two explanations for this finding. First, employees are not likely to put forth increased effort to achieve complex goals unless they 'buy-into' or support them.[62] Thus, it is important for managers to obtain employee support for the goal-setting process. Second, novel and complex tasks take employees longer to complete. This occurs because employees spend more time thinking about how to approach and solve these tasks. In contrast, employees do not have to spend much time thinking about solutions for easy tasks. Specific, difficult goals thus impair performance on novel, complex tasks when employees do not have clear strategies for solving these types of problems. On a positive note, however, a recent study demonstrated that goal setting led to gradual improvements in performance on complex tasks when people were encouraged to explicitly solve the problem at hand.[63] Finally, positive effects of goal setting were also reduced when people worked on interdependent tasks.[64] Managers need to encourage co-operation and efficient work flow in these situations.

3 *Feedback enhances the effect of specific, difficult goals.* Feedback plays a key role in all of our lives. For example, consider the role of feedback in bowling. Imagine going to the bowling lanes only to find that someone had hung a sheet from the ceiling to the floor in front of the pins. How likely is it that you would reach your goal score or typical bowling average? Not likely, given your inability to see the pins. Regardless of your goal, you would have to guess where to throw your second ball if you did not get a strike on your first shot. The same principles apply at work. Feedback lets people know if they are headed toward their goals or if they are off course and need to redirect their efforts. Goals plus feedback is the recommended approach.[65] Goals inform people about performance standards and expectations so that they can channel their energies accordingly. In turn, feedback provides the information needed to adjust direction, effort and strategies for goal accomplishment.

4 *Participative goals, assigned goals and self-set goals are equally effective.* Both managers and researchers are interested in identifying the best way to set goals. Should goals be participatively set, assigned or set by the employee him- or herself? A summary of goal-setting research indicated that no single approach was consistently more effective than others in increasing performance.[66] Managers are advised to use a contingency approach by picking a method that seems best suited to the individual and situation at hand. For example, employees' preferences for participation should be considered. Some employees desire to participate in the process of setting goals, whereas others do not. Employees are also more likely to respond positively to the opportunity to participate in goal setting when they have greater task information, higher levels of experience and training, and greater levels of task involvement. Finally, a participative approach helps reduce employees' resistance to goal setting.

5 *Goal commitment and monetary incentives affect goal-setting outcomes.* **Goal commitment** is the extent to which an individual is personally committed to achieving a goal. In general, an individual is expected to persist in attempts to accomplish a goal when he or she is committed to it. Researchers believe that goal commitment moderates the relationship between the difficulty of a goal and performance. That is, difficult goals lead to higher performance only when employees are committed to their goals. Conversely, difficult goals are hypothesized to lead to lower performance when people are not committed to their goals. A meta-analysis of 21 studies based on 2,360 people supported these predictions.[67] Take a moment now to complete the goal commitment scale and the study habits questions contained in the following OB Exercise. Is your goal commitment related to the behaviours associated with your study habits? If not, what is the cause of the discrepancy?

Figure 8–4

Relationship between Goal Difficulty and Performance

A Performance of committed individuals with adequate ability
B Performance of committed individuals who are working at full capacity
C Performance of individuals who lack commitment to high goals

SOURCE: *A Theory of Goal Setting and Task Performance*, by Locke/Latham, © 1990. Adapted by permission of Prentice-Hall, Upper Saddle River, N.J. Reprinted by permission of Prentice-Hall, Inc., Englewood Cliffs, NJ.

OB Exercise

Is Your Commitment to Achieving Your Performance Goal for This Course Related to Your Behaviour?

Instructions

Begin by identifying your performance goal (desired grade) for this course. My desired grade is _____. Next, use the rating scale shown below to circle the answer that best represents how you feel about each of the following statements. After computing a total score for the goal commitment items, answer the questions related to your study habits for this course.

1 = Strongly disagree

2 = Disagree

3 = Neither agree nor disagree

4 = Agree

5 = Strongly agree

1	I am trying hard to reach my performance goal	1	2	3	4	5
2	I am exerting my maximum effort (100 per cent) in pursuit of my performance goal	1	2	3	4	5

3 I am committed to my performance goal	1	2	3	4	5
4 I am determined to reach my performance goal	1	2	3	4	5
5 I am enthusiastic about attempting to achieve my performance goal	1	2	3	4	5
6 I am striving to attain my performance goal	1	2	3	4	5

Total score _____

Arbitrary Norms:

Low goal commitment = 6–15

Moderate goal commitment = 15–23

High goal commitment = 24–30

Study Habits:

How many hours have you spent studying for this course? ____ hours

What is your grade at this point in the course? ____

How many times have you missed lectures? ____ absences

SOURCE: Items were adapted from those presented in R W Renn, C Danehower, P M Swiercz, and M L Icenogle, 'Further Examination of the Measurement Properties of Leifer & McGannon's (1986) Goal Acceptance and Goal Commitment Scales', *Journal of Occupational and Organizational Psychology,* **March 1999, pp 107–13.**

Like goal setting, the use of monetary incentives to motivate employees is seldom questioned. Unfortunately, recent research uncovered some negative consequences when goal achievement is linked to individual incentives. Case studies, for example, reveal that pay should not be linked to goal achievement unless the following are satisfied:

▼ **performance goals are under the employees' control**

▼ **goals are quantitative and measurable**

▼ **frequent, relatively large payments are made for performance achievement.**[68]

Goal-based incentive systems are more likely to produce undesirable effects if these three conditions are not satisfied.

Moreover, empirical studies demonstrated that goal-based bonus incentives produced higher commitment to easy goals and lower commitment to difficult goals. People were reluctant to commit to difficult goals that were tied to monetary incentives. People with high goal commitment also offered less help to their co-workers when they received goal-based bonus incentives to accomplish difficult individual goals. Individuals neglected aspects of the job that were not covered in the performance goals.[69] For example, a sales consultant who works for a national retail store and is paid an hourly rate plus a commission tied to achieving sales goals indicates that the salespeople who make the most sales and receive the greatest commissions are those who focus on their own self-interests. So, rather than engaging in behaviour that promotes outstanding customer service (such as keeping the salesfloor straightened up and clean, taking the time to ring up small cash sales, writing up sales for colleagues who are missing from the floor, following up with customers to ensure that they received their merchandise in a timely manner, and sending thank-you notes), these individuals focus on maximizing their personal monetary sales at the expense of customer service for the store at large. As another case in point, several studies revealed that quality suffered when employees were given quantity goals.[70]

These findings underscore some of the dangers of using goal-based incentives, particularly for employees in complex, interdependent jobs requiring co-operation. Managers need to consider the advantages, disadvantages, and dilemmas of goal-based incentives prior to their implementation.

Practical Application of Goal Setting

There are three general steps to follow when implementing a goal-setting programme. Serious deficiencies in one step cannot make up for strength in the other two. The three steps need to be implemented in a systematic fashion.

Step 1: Set Goals

A number of sources can be used as input during this goal-setting stage. Time and motion studies are one source. A second is the average past performance of job holders. Third, the employee and his or her manager may set the goal participatively, through give-and-take negotiation. Fourth, goals can be set by conducting external or internal benchmarking. Benchmarking is used when an organization wants to compare its performance or internal work processes with those of other organizations (external benchmarking) or other internal units, branches, departments or divisions within the organization (internal benchmarking).[71] For example, a company might set a goal to surpass the customer service levels or profits of a benchmarked competitor. Finally, the overall strategy of a company (such as becoming the lowest-cost producer) may affect the goals set by employees at various levels within the organization.

In accordance with available research evidence, goals should be 'SMART'. SMART is an acronym that stands for Specific, Measurable, Attainable, Results-oriented, and Time-bound. Table 8–4 contains a set of guidelines for writing SMART goals. There are two additional recommendations to consider when setting goals. First, for complex

Table 8–4

Guidelines for Writing SMART Goals

Specific	Goals should be stated in precise rather than vague terms. For example, a goal that provides for 20 hours of technical training for each employee is more specific than stating that a manager should send as many people as possible to training classes. Goals should be quantified when possible.
Measurable	A measurement device is needed to assess the extent to which a goal is accomplished. Goals thus need to be measurable. It also is critical to consider the quality aspect of the goal when establishing measurement criteria. For example, if the goal is to complete a managerial study of methods to increase productivity, one must consider how to measure the quality of this effort. Goals should not be set without considering the interplay between quantity and quality of output.
Attainable	Goals should be realistic, challenging, and attainable. Impossible goals reduce motivation because people do not like to fail. Remember, people have different levels of ability and skill.
Results oriented	Corporate goals should focus on desired end-results that support the organization's vision. In turn, an individual's goals should directly support the accomplishment of corporate goals. Activities support the achievement of goals and are outlined in action plans. To focus goals on desired end-results, goals should start with the word 'to,' followed by verbs such as complete, acquire, produce, increase, and decrease. Verbs such as develop, conduct, implement, or monitor imply activities and should not be used in a goal statement.
Time bound	Goals specify target dates for completion.

SOURCE: A J Kinicki, *Performance Management Systems*, (Superstition Mt., AZ: Kinicki and Associates Inc., 1992), pp 2–9. Reprinted with permission; all rights reserved.

tasks, managers should train employees in problem-solving techniques and encourage them to develop a performance action plan. Action plans specify the strategies or tactics to be used in order to accomplish a goal.

Second, because of individual differences (recall our discussion in Chapter 5), it may be necessary to establish different goals for employees performing the same job. For example, a study of 103 undergraduate business students revealed that individuals high in conscientiousness had higher motivation, greater goal commitment and obtained higher grades than students low in conscientiousness.[72] An individual's goal orientation is another important individual difference to consider when setting goals. There are two types of goal orientations: a learning one and a performance one. A team of researchers described the differences and implications for goal setting in the following way.

Individuals with a learning goal orientation are primarily concerned with developing their skills and ability. Given this focus, a difficult goal should be of interest because it provides a challenging opportunity that can lead to personal growth. In contrast, individuals with a performance goal orientation are concerned with obtaining positive evaluations about their ability. Given this focus, a difficult goal should be of lower interest because it provides a greater potential for failure. As goal difficulty increases, the probability of obtaining a positive evaluation through goal attainment decreases.[73]

A series of studies demonstrated that people set higher goals, exerted more effort and achieved higher performance when they possessed a learning orientation toward goal setting rather than a performance orientation.[74] In conclusion, therefore, managers should consider individual differences when setting goals.

Step 2: Promote Goal Commitment

Obtaining goal commitment is important because employees are more motivated to pursue goals they view as reasonable, obtainable and fair. Goal commitment may be increased by using one or more of the following techniques.

1 Provide an explanation for why the organization is implementing a goal-setting programme.

2 Present the corporate goals, and explain how and why an individual's personal goals support them.

3 Have employees establish their own goals and action plans. Encourage them to set challenging, stretching goals. Goals should not be impossible.

4 Train managers in how to conduct participative goal-setting sessions; and train employees in how to develop effective action plans.

5 Be supportive, and do not use goals to threaten employees.

6 Set goals that are under the employees' control and then provide them with the necessary resources

7 Provide monetary incentives or other rewards for accomplishing goals.

Step 3: Provide Support and Feedback

Step 3 calls for providing employees with the necessary support elements or resources to get the job done. This includes ensuring that each employee has the necessary abilities and information to reach his or her goals. As a pair of goal-setting experts succinctly stated, 'Motivation without knowledge is useless.'[75] Often training is required to help employees achieve difficult goals. Moreover, managers should pay attention to employees' perceptions of effort → performance expectancies, self-efficacy and the valence of rewards. Finally, as we discuss in detail in Chapter 9 employees should be provided with timely, specific feedback (knowledge of results) on how they are doing.

PUTTING MOTIVATIONAL THEORIES TO WORK

Successfully designing and implementing motivational programmes is not easy. Managers cannot simply take one of the theories discussed in this book and apply it word for word. Dynamics within organizations interfere with applying motivation theories in 'pure' form. According to management scholar Terence Mitchell, there are:

> . . . situations and settings that make it exceptionally difficult for a motivational system to work. These circumstances may involve the kinds of jobs or people present, the technology, the presence of a union, and so on. The factors that hinder the application of motivational theory have not been articulated either frequently or systematically.[76]

With Mitchell's cautionary statement in mind, this section uses Figure 7–1 in Chapter 7 to raise issues that need to be addressed before implementing a motivational programme. Our intent is not to discuss all relevant considerations but rather to highlight a few important ones.

Assuming a motivational programme is being considered to improve productivity, quality, or customer satisfaction, the first issue revolves around the difference between motivation and performance. As pointed out in Chapter 7, motivation and performance are not one and the same. Motivation is only one of several factors that influence performance. For example, poor performance may be more a function of outdated or inefficient materials and machinery, not having goals to direct one's attention, a monotonous job, feelings of inequity, a negative work environment characterized by political behaviour and conflict, poor supervisory support and coaching, or poor work flow. Motivation cannot make up for a deficient job context (see Figure 7–1).

Importantly, managers should not ignore the individual inputs identified in Figure 7–1. As discussed in this chapter as well as Chapters 5 and 7, individual differences are an important input that influence motivation and motivated behaviour. Managers are advised to develop employees so that they have the ability and job knowledge to effectively perform their jobs. In addition, attempts should be made to nurture positive employee characteristics, such as self-esteem, self-efficacy, positive emotions, a learning goal orientation and need for achievement.

Because motivation is goal directed, the process of developing and setting goals should be consistent with our previous discussion. Moreover, the method used to evaluate performance also needs to be considered. Without a valid performance appraisal system, it is difficult, if not impossible, to accurately distinguish good and poor performers. Managers need to keep in mind that both equity and expectancy theory suggest that employee motivation is crushed by inaccurate performance ratings. Inaccurate ratings also make it difficult to evaluate the effectiveness of any motivational programme, so it is beneficial for managers to assess the accuracy and validity of their appraisal systems.

In keeping with expectancy theory and the principles of behaviour modification as discussed in Chapter 10, managers should make rewards contingent on performance.[77] In doing so, it is important that managers consider the accuracy and fairness of the reward system. As discussed under expectancy theory, the promise of increased rewards will not prompt greater effort and good performance unless those rewards are clearly tied to performance and they are large enough to gain employees' interest or attention. Moreover, equity theory tells us that motivation is influenced by employee perceptions about the fairness of reward allocations. Motivation is decreased when employees believe rewards are inequitably allocated. Rewards also need to be integrated appropriately into the appraisal system. If performance is measured at the individual level, individual achievements need to be rewarded. On the other hand, when performance is the result of group effort, rewards should be allocated to the group.

Feedback should also be linked to performance. Feedback provides the information and direction needed to keep employees focused on relevant tasks, activities and goals. Managers should strive to provide specific, timely and accurate feedback to employees.

Finally, an organization's culture significantly influences employee motivation and behaviour. A positive self-enhancing culture is more likely to engender higher motivation and commitment than a culture dominated by suspicion, fault finding, and blame. We end this chapter with the following example from Disneyland Paris.

To improve motivation, morale and quality of service provided to visitors, France's Disneyland has launched 'Small World', named after one of its attractions:

the whole idea is to improve motivation through a process of decentralising power, cutting down hierarchy and creating internal competition between different parts of the park—although with certain limits. The park's operations will be split into 'small world' units of 30 to 50 staff, headed by a manager. Each will be given greater responsibility and flexibility than in the past to meet three goals: to achieve management targets, improve visitor satisfaction and get to know and motivate staff. Small world managers will receive up to 10 per cent of their salary in bonuses linked to performance. Other staff will receive non-financial rewards, including improved promotion prospects.[78]

Summary of Key Concepts

1 Discuss the role of perceived inequity in employee motivation.

Equity theory is a model of motivation that explains how people strive for fairness and justice in social exchanges. At work, feelings of inequity revolve around a person's evaluation of whether he or she receives adequate rewards to compensate for his or her contributive inputs. People perform these evaluations by comparing the perceived fairness of their employment exchange with that of relevant others. Perceived inequity creates motivation to restore equity.

2 Explain the differences between distributive, procedural and interactional justice.

Distributive, procedural and interactional justice are the three key components underlying organizational justice. Distributive justice reflects the perceived fairness of how resources and rewards are distributed. Procedural justice represents the perceived fairness of the process and procedures used to make allocation decisions. Interactional justice entails the perceived fairness of a decision-maker's behaviour in the process of decision-making.

3 Describe the practical lessons derived from equity theory.

Equity theory has at least eight practical implications. First, because people are motivated to resolve perceptions of inequity, managers should not discount employees' feelings and perceptions when trying to motivate workers. Second, managers should pay attention to employees' *perceptions* of what is fair and equitable. It is the employee's view of reality that counts when trying to motivate someone, according to equity theory. Third, employees should be given a voice in decisions that affect them. Fourth, employees should be given the opportunity to appeal against decisions that affect their welfare. Fifth, employees are more likely to accept and support organizational change when they believe it is implemented fairly and when it produces equitable outcomes. Sixth, managers can promote co-operation and teamwork among group members by treating them equitably. Seventh, treating employees inequitably can lead to litigation and costly court settlements. Finally, managers need to pay attention to the organization's climate for justice because it influences employee attitudes and behaviour.

4 Explain Vroom's expectancy theory.

Expectancy theory assumes motivation is determined by one's perceived chances of achieving valued outcomes. Vroom's expectancy model of motivation reveals how both the effort → performance expectancies and the performance → outcome instrumentalities will influence the degree of effort expended to achieve desired (positively valent) outcomes.

5 Discuss Porter and Lawler's expectancy theory of motivation.

Porter and Lawler developed a model of expectancy that enlarged upon the theory proposed by Vroom. This model specifies (a) the source of people's valences and expectancies and (b) the relationship between performance and satisfaction.

6 Describe the practical implications of expectancy theory of motivation.

Managers are advised to enhance effort→performance expectancies by helping employees accomplish their performance goals. With respect to instrumentalities and valences, managers should attempt to link employee performance and valued rewards. There are four prerequisites for linking performance and rewards, managers: need to develop and communicate performance standards to employees; need valid and accurate performance ratings; need to determine the relative mix of individual versus team contribution to performance and then reward accordingly; and, finally, managers should use performance ratings to differentially allocate rewards between employees.

7 Explain how goal setting motivates an individual.

Goal setting provides four motivational mechanisms, they: direct one's attention; regulate effort; increase persistence; and encourage development of goal-attainment strategies and action plans.

8 Identify five practical lessons to be learned from goal-setting research.

Difficult goals lead to higher performance than easy or moderate goals: goals should not be impossible to achieve. Specific, difficult goals lead to higher performance for simple rather than complex tasks. Third, feedback enhances the effect of specific, difficult goals. Fourth, participative goals, assigned goals, and self-set goals are equally effective. Fifth, goal commitment and monetary incentives affect goal-setting outcomes.

9 Specify issues that should be addressed before implementing a motivational programme.

Managers need to consider the variety of causes of poor performance and employee misbehaviour. Undesirable employee performance and behaviour may be due to a host of deficient individual inputs (such as ability, dispositions, emotions and beliefs) or job context factors (such as materials and machinery, job characteristics, reward systems, supervisory support and coaching, and social norms). The method used to evaluate both performance and the link between performance and rewards, must be examined. Performance must be accurately evaluated and rewards should be equitably distributed. Managers should also recognize that employee motivation and behaviour are influenced by organizational culture.

Discussion Questions

1 Have you experienced positive or negative inequity at work? Describe the circumstances in terms of the inputs and outcomes of the comparison person and yourself.

2 Could a manager's attempt to treat his or her employees equally lead to perceptions of inequity? Explain.

3 What work outcomes (refer to Table 8–1) are most important to you? Do you think different age groups value different outcomes? What are the implications for managers who seek to be equitable?

4 Relative to Table 8–2, what techniques have you relied on recently to reduce either positive or negative inequity?

5 What is your definition of studying hard? What is your expectancy for earning an A in the next exam in this course? What is the basis of this expectancy?

6 If someone who reported to you at work had a low expectancy for successful performance, what could you do to increase this?

7 Do goals play an important role in your life? Explain.

8 How would you respond to a manager who said, 'Goals must be participatively set?'

9 Goal-setting research suggests that people should be given difficult goals. How does this prescription mesh with expectancy theory? Explain.

10 How could a lecturer use equity, expectancy and goal-setting theory to motivate students?

Internet Exercise

www.ge.com/index.htm

This chapter discussed how employee motivation is influenced by goal setting and the relationship between performance and rewards. We also reviewed the variety of issues that managers should consider when implementing motivational programmes. The purpose of this exercise is for you to examine the motivational techniques used by the US' giant General Electric (GE). GE is one of the most successful companies in the world. The company is well known for establishing clear corporate goals and then creating the infrastructure (for example, rewards) to achieve them. Begin by visiting GE's home page at http://www.ge.com/index.htm. Begin your search by locating GE's corporate values and corporate goals. Then expand your search by looking for information that discusses the different incentives GE uses to motivate its employees.

Questions

1 How will the values influence goal-setting and motivation?

2 Based on the values and goals, what type of behaviour is the organization trying to motivate?

3 What rewards does GE use to reinforce desired behaviour and performance?

4 To what extent are GE's practices consistent with the material covered in this chapter?

Personal Awareness and Growth Exercise

What Outcomes Motivate Employees?

Objectives

1 To determine how accurately you perceive the outcomes that motivate non-managerial employees.

2 To examine the managerial implications of inaccurately assessing employee motivators.

Introduction

A thousand employees were given a list of 10 outcomes people want from their work. They were asked to rank these items from *most important* to *least important*.[79] We are going to ask you to estimate how you think these workers ranked the various outcomes. This will enable you to compare your perceptions with the average rankings documented by a researcher. The survey results are presented in End Note 80 at the end of this book. Please do not read them until indicated.

Instructions

Below is a list of 10 outcomes people want from their work. Read the list, and then rank each item according to how you think the typical non-managerial employee would rank them. Rank the outcomes from 1 to 10; where 1 = most important and 10 = least important. (Please do this now before reading the rest of these instructions.)

After you have completed your ranking, calculate the discrepancy between your perceptions and the actual results. Take the absolute value of the difference between your ranking and the actual ranking for each item, and then add them to get a total discrepancy score. For example, if you gave job security a ranking of 1, your discrepancy score would be 3 because the actual ranking was 4. The lower your discrepancy score, the more accurate your perception of the typical employee's needs. The actual rankings are shown in End Note 80. How do you believe the typical non-managerial employee would rank these outcomes?

_____ Full appreciation of work done

_____ Job security

_____ Good working conditions

_____ Feeling of being 'in on things' [involved]

_____ Good wages

_____ Tactful discipline

_____ Personal loyalty to employees

_____ Interesting work

_____ Sympathetic help with personal problems

_____ Promotion and growth in the organization

1 Were your perceptions accurate? Why were they or why not?

2 What would expectancy theory suggest you should do?

3 Based on the size of your discrepancy, what does the systems model of motivation and performance in Figure 8–5 suggest will happen to satisfaction and commitment?

4 Would you generalize the actual survey results to all non-managerial employees? Why would you or why not?

Group Exercise
The Case of the Missing Form

Objectives

1 To give you practice at diagnosing the causes of a performance problem by using the systems model of motivation and performance.

2 To apply one of the motivation models discussed in Chapters 7 and 8 in order to solve a performance problem.

Introduction

Managers frequently encounter performance problems. These problems might represent incidents such as missed deadlines, poor quality, inadequate levels of performance, excessive time off, cynical or negative behaviour, and lack of co-operation with team members. As we discussed in both this chapter and Chapter 7, motivation is only one factor in these types of performance problems. As such, managers must learn how to diagnose the cause(s) of performance problems prior to trying to solve them. The following case study provides you with this opportunity. After diagnosing the cause(s) of the performance problem, you will be asked to solve it. The models of motivation presented in Chapters 7 and 8 provide useful frameworks for generating solutions.

Instructions

Your instructor will divide the class into groups of four to six. You should first read the case provided. Once all group members are finished, meet as a group to discuss the case. Begin your discussion by brainstorming a list of potential causes of the performance problem. Use the systems model of motivation and performance shown in Figure 8--5 to conduct this brainstorming activity. Be sure to consider whether each and every input and transformational element are possible causes of the problem. Once the group has identified the causes of the performance problem, the group should answer the discussion questions that follow the case.

The Case of the Missing Form[81]

S	M	T	W	T	F	S		S	M	T	W	T	F	S
			MAY								JUNE			
			1	2	3	4								1
5	6	7	8	9	10	11		2	3	4	5	6	7	8
12	13	14	15	16	17	18		9	10	11	12	13	14	15
19	20	21	22	23	24	25		16	17	18	19	20	21	22
26	27	28	29	30	31			23	24	25	26	27	28	29
								30						

Ann Anders has been manager of Training and Development at TYCO Financial Services for three years. (Ann has been with TYCO for 21 years.) She has 10 professional-level trainers reporting to her.

Her boss, Joyce Davis, Director of Training, asked Ann to put together a new cost benefit analysis (CBA) package on a project Ann had completed. This had not been required of Ann by her previous boss; training had never been measured in terms of dollars and cents.

Joyce explained that she wanted Ann to document the savings that the Customer Dispute Resolution training programme had produced so she could share it with her peers in the other divisions of TYCO. She wanted to formalize the practice of preparing a CBA format because this was something no-one else had done. She directed Ann to do further research to validate the findings and put it into a form (Joyce's idea of a form was a page with lines and boxes). It was Wednesday, May 15th; Joyce was leaving for a meeting in New York at 8:00 a.m. on Monday, May 20th. She wanted to take this assignment with her. Joyce asked Ann to see her on Friday to report on her progress.

On Thursday, Ann had a meeting with the Performance Engineering department at TYCO and then described to Joyce a format they were currently using on their projects.

Ann agreed to apply that process to her training project. Joyce was pleased with the progress.

Ann returned to Joyce on Friday, May 17th, with the formula for the training CBA typed on a plain white page. Joyce acknowledged the work done to prepare the calculations and again asked if Ann could create a form. Joyce had to catch her plane first thing on Monday morning and knew she would not have time to review a second document. Joyce took the work Ann had completed, however, but decided to postpone presenting the idea until the next monthly meeting in June.

The following week, on May 27th, Joyce explained to Ann that there was not enough time to discuss her CBA at the meeting so she would do it next month instead. Joyce asked Ann for additional information that needed to be gathered to effectively document the project and set a new completion date of June 10th: only one week prior to the June 17th meeting.

Ann returned on June 10th with more calculations that were thoroughly documented. Joyce was happy to see the additional research. However, she was disappointed because the format had not yet been put into a professional 'form'. Joyce then took out a piece of paper and wrote the sections for Ann so she could better understand what she wanted.

Joyce felt confident that Ann understood what she wanted. Joyce, in order to give Ann the maximum time to get it right this time, said she needed the document no later than the end of Friday, June 14th.

On Friday June 14th, at the end of the day, Ann walked into Joyce's office proudly displaying the neatly typed document. However, there were no lines or boxes as you would see on a traditional business form. Joyce said 'This is not a form! I'll take it home over the weekend and bring you the changes on Monday morning, you can then fax the revised version to me at the meeting.'

Joyce then took 15 to 20 minutes on Sunday to draw out the lines and reformat the information for ease of reading and to create a professional image for the product. On Monday morning, Joyce stopped by and gave the changes to her secretary to finish. Ann faxed the changes. Joyce presented 'the form' at the meeting, and it had the positive impact she expected.

After the meeting, Joyce reflected on Ann's problem. After 21 years with the company and three years as a manager, why couldn't Ann create something as simple as a business form? Joyce is trying to determine the root cause(s) of Ann's poor performance.

Questions for Discussion

1   What are the causes of Ann's poor performance? Explain your rationale.

2   Based on the causes you identified, how would you keep the problem from happening again?

3   Which of the motivation models discussed in Chapters 7 and 8 are most relevant for solving this problem? Why?

4   How would you use the model identified in question 3 to improve Ann's future performance? Be sure to specifically discuss how you would apply the model.

9 Chapter Nine

Improving Job Performance with Feedback and Rewards

Feedback goes electronic

Receiving honest feedback from your boss, colleagues and subordinates can be uncomfortable. Receiving it electronically, and from colleagues who do not speak your native tongue, sounds potentially excruciating. Yet Alliance UniChem, the pan-European pharmaceuticals distribution group, has been putting its top managers through just such an experience for the past few months. ▶

The company, formed two years ago by the merger of Alliance Santé of France and UniChem of the UK, introduced an Internet-based feedback system as a way of fostering co-operation across its subsidiaries.

The group, which has 20,000 employees and had a reported turnover of £6.1bn ($9.1bn) in 1999, has expanded rapidly in Europe, adding pharmacies in the Netherlands and Switzerland to its operations in the UK, France, Italy, Spain, Portugal and the Czech Republic.

It commissioned Advanced Personnel Technology (APT), a UK company specialising in electronic feedback systems, to provide a common method for measuring employees' performance across the group.

To avoid linguistic misunderstandings, the system operates simultaneously in English, French, Italian, Portuguese and Spanish. Thus a manager in France can provide feedback in French on the performance of her Italian boss, who can then read it in Italian.

The system is a sophisticated electronic form of established 360° feedback. Employees first assess themselves using about 100 different statements of behaviour, such as 'takes the lead in uncertain situations' or 'creates an atmosphere of mutual trust at work'. They then invite their boss and six to eight peers and subordinates to assess them, via a secure Internet site. They can also ask external suppliers and customers for feedback.

Employees are scored according to how frequently or strongly they display the behaviour in question. The findings are presented graphically, starting with a summary of how they fare on eight 'core competences'. They can click on any individual result to obtain more detailed feedback, again receiving it in bar chart form.

The system, known as the Personal Development Planner, also provides advice on how to rectify weaknesses and an action plan into which the employee can cut and paste options for self-improvement.

Alliance UniChem decided to make the feedback confidential to the employee. 'The focus is on helping yourself,' says Simon Liebling, the German information technology director at the Moss Pharmacy subsidiary.

However, the data are being aggregated and will be presented to the company in January, providing it with a picture of management trends in different divisions and countries. It should be able to use these to identify training and recruitment needs.

As well as being multilingual, the system has other advantages over traditional paper-based assessment, says Graham Wharton, head of human resources at the group's UK distribution division. 'This is 21st-century stuff,' he says. 'It saves time and therefore costs. It greatly speeds up the processing of the data. With paper there's a risk you might lose it and it's difficult and unwieldy to cut and paste it in different ways.'

The system could eventually be used by all the group's employees. 'We couldn't do that very easily on paper. It would be fraught with human error.' But Mr Wharton warns that the ease of collecting, storing and analysing so much data could give greater weight to the findings than is justified. 'This is very much a snapshot. You shouldn't be using it as an absolute.'

There are potential dangers in how employees interpret the feedback. The bar-chart format gives a stark illustration of people's blind spots—where their positive or negative opinion of themselves is out of line with the views held by their colleagues. Those with a tendency to self-criticism will dwell on the negative scores. Self-satisfied types will do the opposite.

To help them interpret the data in a balanced way, Roger Edwards, an APT consultant, has been working through the feedback with each of the 55 senior managers. The crucial thing is to act on the results, he says. 'These can be quite sensitive issues for individuals to address. But if this [process] is not going to drive business performance and culture change, there's no point in doing it.'[1]

For discussion

What do you think are some possible advantages and drawbacks of using modern technology in employee feedback? Do you think traditional, face-to-face feedback can easily be replaced by virtual systems in the way that Alliance UniChem did?

Productivity and total quality experts tell us we need to work smarter, not harder. While it is true that a sound education and appropriate skills training are necessary if one is to work smarter, the process does not end there. Today's employees need instructive and supportive feedback as well as 'desired rewards' if they are to translate their knowledge into improved productivity and superior quality. Figure 9–1 illustrates a cycle of learning and development in which feedback enhances ability, encourages effort and acknowledges results. Rewards, meanwhile, motivate effort and compensate those for achieving results. Learning and personal development, according to the authors of the book, *Working Wisdom*, are the key to success at all levels:

> . . . *work can be an enriching experience, a way of developing mastery in the world, a source of valued relationships, and for some—however high-minded this may sound—a path to self-realization. Combining work and learning to promote personal development, as well as a profitable enterprise, is the key. As the pace of change quickens, individuals, companies and countries that fail to continually learn and adapt to change will be left behind.*[2]

It seems that more and more European organizations are formally installing feedback and appraisal procedures. According to the Dutch consultant Loek van den Broek, author of the book *Feedback as an Eye-Opener* this is a natural evolution. 'People want to know if they're doing well. It's just inherent in human nature. They also want to know what others think of them. Moreover, everybody is constantly looking for ways to improve his functioning. The opinion of other people is indispensable to this.'[3]

However, giving and receiving proper feedback is not as self-evident matter as may first appear. Winston Fletcher, communications director for FCB Europe has strikingly illustrated this.

> *I once asked the CEO of a large advertising agency whether or not he carried out formal appraisals or feedback sessions with his subordinates. 'Guys working for me know what I think of 'em,' he answered. 'If they don't, I make sure they soon stop working for me.'*
>
> *On another occasion one of the directors grumbled that he wasn't really enjoying his work because nobody ever really expressed their opinions. 'I don't pay you big money to enjoy yourself', the CEO answered. 'If you want to enjoy yourself working here, you should be paying me money.'*[4]

Properly administered feedback and rewards can guide, teach and motivate people in the direction of positive change. To illustrate this, scholars of the Copenhagen

Figure 9–1

Feedback and Rewards Are Important Links in the Job Performance Cycle

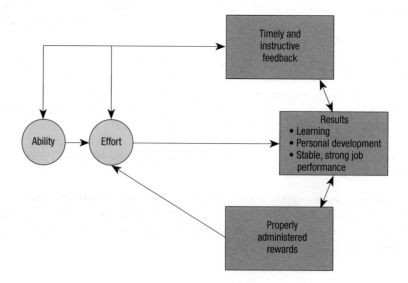

Business School recently examined the outcomes of the feedback process by questioning 115 employees and their supervisors in a large Danish bank. Results showed that people who perceived that they were receiving more feedback–both positive and negative–from their supervisors, rated themselves higher in performance and self-development.[5]

This chapter continues our discussion of individual behaviour by discussing the effect of feedback and rewards on behaviour and by incorporating those insights into what you have already learned about individual differences, perception and the various motivational tools, including goal setting.

UNDERSTANDING THE FEEDBACK PROCESS

Numerous surveys tell us employees have a hearty appetite for feedback.[6] So also do achievement-oriented students. Following a difficult exam, for instance, students want to know two things: how they did and how their peers did. By letting students know how their work relates to grades and competitive standards, an instructor's feedback permits the students to adjust their study habits in order to reach their goals. Likewise, managers in well-run organizations follow up goal setting with a feedback programme to provide a rational basis for adjustment and improvement. For instance, consider the following two diverse feedback examples.

IBM's Raleigh, USA, personal computer factory: 'Every day, managers see a fresh . . . number on their screens, telling them how many PCs have been shipped so far this year . . . every model is broken out [detailed] so managers can see what's moving and what's not.'[7]

A 55,000-employee copper mine in Zambia, Africa: 'As largely uneducated workers march into the front entrance, they can't help but spot a 50-foot-high scoreboard that lists monthly and year-to-date financials, from 'copper revenue' to 'corporate depreciation'.[8]

Although this sort of *open book management* is becoming popular, feedback too often gets short-changed. In fact, 'poor or insufficient feedback' was the leading cause of deficient performance in a survey of US and European companies.[9]

As the term is used here, **feedback** is objective information about individual or collective performance. Subjective assessments such as, 'You're doing a poor job', 'You're too lazy', or 'We really appreciate your hard work' do not qualify as objective feedback. But hard data such as units sold, days absent, amount of money saved, projects completed, customers satisfied, and products rejected are all suitable for objective feedback programmes. Management consultants Chip Bell and Ron Zemke offered the following perspective on feedback.

Feedback
objective information about performance

> *Feedback is, quite simply, any information that answers those 'How am I doing?' questions. Good feedback answers them truthfully and productively. It's information people can use either to confirm or correct their performance. Feedback comes in many forms and from a variety of sources. Some is easy to get and requires hardly any effort to understand. The charts and graphs tracking group and individual performance, that are fixtures in many workplaces, are an example of this variety. Performance feedback–the numerical type at least–is at the heart of most approaches to total quality management.*

> *Some feedback is less accessible. It's tucked away in the heads of customers and managers. But no matter how well-hidden the feedback, if people need it to keep their performance on track, we need to get it to them–preferably while it's still fresh enough to make an impact.*[10]

Two Functions of Feedback

Experts say feedback serves two functions for those who receive it, one is instructional and the other motivational. Feedback instructs when it clarifies roles or teaches new behaviour. For example, an assistant accountant might be advised to handle a certain entry as a capital item rather than as an expense item. On the other hand, feedback motivates when it serves as a reward or promises a reward.[11] Having the boss tell you that a gruelling project you worked on earlier has just been completed can be a rewarding piece of news. As documented in one study, the motivational function of feedback can be significantly enhanced by pairing specific, challenging goals with specific feedback about results.[12] We expand upon these two functions in this section by analysing a cognitive model of feedback and by reviewing the practical implications of recent feedback research.

A Cognitive-Processing Model of Performance Feedback

Giving and receiving feedback at work are popular ideas today. Conventional wisdom says the more feedback organizational members get, the better. An underlying assumption is that feedback works automatically. Managers simply need to be motivated to give it. According to a recent meta-analysis of 23,663 feedback incidents, however, feedback is far from automatically effective. While feedback did, in fact, have a generally positive impact on performance, performance actually *declined* in more than 38 per cent of the feedback incidents.[13]

These results are a stark caution light for those interested in improving job performance with feedback. Subjective feedback is easily contaminated by situational factors. Moreover, if objective feedback is to work as intended, managers need to understand the interaction between feedback recipients and their environment.[14] A more complete understanding of how employees cognitively or mentally process feedback is an important first step. This complex process is illustrated in Figure 9–2. Immediately obvious is the fact that feedback must successfully clear many hurdles if the desired behavioural outcomes are to be achieved. A lighthearted case in point is Scott Adams, the former telephone company employee who draws the popular cartoon strip, Dilbert. According to *The Wall Street Journal*.

> . . . he can thank feedback from his readers, who flooded him with comments—about 200 a day—after he published his email address in 1993. They persuaded him to concentrate on workplace issues, which had been a smaller part of the strip, and Dilbert's popularity soared. 'There was this huge vein of discontent and nobody was talking about it from the employees' perspective,' he says.

Thanks to his experiences in the trenches, and his email army, Mr Adams has become a walking database of workplace foibles and career frustrations.[15]

If you've ever had a good laugh at a Dilbert cartoon, you can thank the feedback process. Feedback—from customers in this case—was effective because cartoonist Adams not only wanted feedback, he actively sought it, and acted on it. A step-by-step exploration of the model in Figure 9–2 can help us better understand this sort of feedback-performance relationship.

Sources of Feedback

It almost goes without saying that employees receive objective feedback from others such as peers, supervisors, subordinates and outsiders. Perhaps less obvious is the fact that the task itself is a ready source of objective feedback.[16] Anyone who has spent hours on a 'quick' Internet search can appreciate the power of task-provided feedback. Similarly, skilled tasks such as computer programming or landing a jet provide a steady stream of feedback about how well or poorly one is doing. Although a third source of

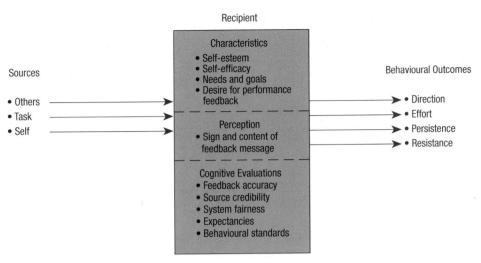

Figure 9–2

*A Cognitive–
Processing Model
of Feedback*

SOURCE: Based in part on discussion in M S Taylor, C D Fisher and D R Ilgen, 'Individuals' Reactions to Performance Feedback in Organizations: A Control Theory Perspective', in *Research in Personnel and Human Resources Management*, vol. 2, eds K M Rowland and G R Ferris (Greenwich CT: JAI Press, 1984), pp 81–124; and A N Kluger and A DeNisi, 'The Effects of Feedback Interventions on Permformance: A Historic Review, a Meta-Analysis, and a Preliminary Feedback Intervention Theory', *Psychological Bulletin*, March 1996, pp254–84.

feedback is oneself, self-serving bias and other perceptual problems can contaminate this source. Those high in self-confidence tend to rely on personal feedback more than those with low self-confidence. Although circumstances vary, an employee can be bombarded by feedback from all three sources simultaneously. This is where the 'gatekeeping functions' of perception and cognitive evaluation are needed to help sort things out.

The Recipient of Feedback

Listed in the centre portion of Figure 9–2 are three aspects of the recipient requiring our attention. They are the individual's characteristics, perceptions and cognitive evaluations. As mentioned earlier, each recipient variable is a hurdle that feedback must clear in order to be effective. Knowing about these recipient hurdles is therefore a big step in the right direction.

The Recipient's Characteristics

Personality characteristics such as self-esteem and self-efficacy can help or hinder one's readiness for feedback.[17] Those having low self-esteem and low self-efficacy generally do not actively seek feedback. Needs and goals also influence one's openness to feedback. In a laboratory study, Japanese psychology students who scored high on the need for achievement, responded more favourably to feedback than did their classmates who had a low need for achievement.[18] High self-monitors, those chameleon-like people we discussed in Chapter 5, are also more open to feedback because it helps them adapt their behaviour to the situation. Recall from Chapter 5 that high self-monitoring employees were found to be better at initiating relationships with mentors (who typically provide feedback).[19] Low self-monitoring people, ín contrast, are tuned into their own internal feelings more than they are to external cues.

Researchers have started to focus more directly on the recipient's actual desire for feedback, as opposed to indirectly on personality characteristics, needs and goals. Everyday experience tells us that not everyone really wants the performance feedback they supposedly seek. Restaurant servers who ask, 'How was everything?' while presenting the bill, are not usually interested in a detailed reply. A study of 498 supervisors yielded an instrument for measuring desire for performance feedback[20] (see the next OB Exercise for a shortened version). Such desire involves self-reliance (items 1–3), self-assessment ability (items 4–6), and a preference for external information (items 7–10). The general contingency approach to management would require different strategies for giving feedback to employees scoring low versus high on the OB Exercise.

OB Exercise

How Strong Is Your Desire for Performance Feedback?

Instructions

Circle one number to indicate the strength of your agreement or disagreement with each statement. Total your responses, and compare your score with our arbitrary norms.

DISAGREE   AGREE

1 As long as I think that I have done something well, I am not too concerned about how other people think I have done.   5 — 4 — 3 — 2 — 1

2 How other people view my work is not as important as how I view my own work.   5 — 4 — 3 — 2 — 1

3 It is usually better not to put much faith in what others say about your work, regardless of whether it is complimentary or not.   5 — 4 — 3 — 2 — 1

4 If I have done something well, I know it without other people telling me so.   5 — 4 — 3 — 2 — 1

5 I usually have a clear idea of what I am trying to do and how well I am proceeding toward my goal.   5 — 4 — 3 — 2 — 1

6 I find that I am usually a pretty good judge of my own performance.   5 — 4 — 3 — 2 — 1

7 It is very important to me to know what people think of my work.   5 — 4 — 3 — 2 — 1

8 It is a good idea to get someone to check your work before it's too late to make changes.   5 — 4 — 3 — 2 — 1

9 Even though I may think I have done a good job, I feel a lot more confident about it after someone else has told me so.   5 — 4 — 3 — 2 — 1

10 Since one cannot be objective about one's own performance, it is best to listen to the feedback provided by others.   5 — 4 — 3 — 2 — 1

Total score = _____

Arbitrary Norms

10–23 = Low desire for feedback
24–36 = Moderate desire for feedback
37–50 = High desire for feedback

SOURCE: Excerpted and adapted from D M Herold, C K Parsons and R B Rensvold, 'Individual Differences in the Generation and Processing of Performance Feedback', *Educational and Psychological Measurement*, February 1996, Table 1, p 9. Copyright; © 1996 by Sage Publications. Reprinted by permission of Sage Publications, Inc.

The Recipient's Perception of Feedback

The *sign* of feedback refers to whether it is positive or negative. Generally, people tend to perceive and recall positive feedback more accurately than they do negative feedback.[21] But feedback with a negative sign (such as being told your performance is below average) can have a *positive* motivational impact. In fact, in one study, those who were told they were below average on a creativity test subsequently outperformed those who were led to believe their results were above average. The subjects apparently took the negative feedback as a challenge and so then set and pursued higher goals. Those receiving positive feedback were apparently less motivated to do better.[22]

Nonetheless, feedback with a negative sign or threatening content needs to be administered carefully to avoid creating insecurity and defensiveness. Self-efficacy can also be damaged by negative feedback, as discovered in a pair of experiments with business students. The researchers concluded, 'To facilitate the development of strong efficacy beliefs, managers should be careful about the provision of negative feedback. Destructive criticism by managers which attributes the cause of poor performance to internal factors, reduces both the beliefs of self-efficacy and the self-set goals of recipients.'[23]

Also of interest, a recent British study into feedback at work showed that managers think they praise people more than they actually do, whereas employees report receiving five times more criticism than praise. According to the researchers, this gap between perception and reality is partly due to it being easy to forget to praise good work, whereas bawling someone out has an urgency to it. Another reason is that much positive feedback is followed by a 'but'. To tell an employee 'that was excellent but . . .' is basically a waste of praise: what is heard and remembered is the actual or implied criticism.[24]

The Recipient's Cognitive Evaluation of Feedback

Upon receiving feedback, people cognitively evaluate factors such as its accuracy, the credibility of the source, the fairness of the system (e.g., a performance appraisal system), their performance-reward expectancies, and the reasonableness of the standards. Any feedback that fails to clear one or more of these cognitive hurdles will be rejected or played down. Personal experience largely dictates how these factors are weighed. For instance, you would probably discount feedback from someone who exaggerates or from someone who performed poorly on the same task as the one you have just successfully completed. In view of the 'trust gap', discussed in Chapter 12, managerial credibility is an ethical matter of central importance today. According to the authors of the book *Credibility: How Leaders Gain and Lose It, Why People Demand It*, 'without a solid foundation of personal credibility, leaders can have no hope of enlisting others in a common vision'.[25] Managers who have proven untrustworthy and not credible have a hard time improving job performance through feedback.[26]

Feedback from a source who apparently shows favouritism or relies on unreasonable standards behaviour would be suspect.[27] Also, as predicted by expectancy motivation theory, feedback must foster high effort→performance expectancies and performance→reward instrumentalities if it is to motivate the desired behaviour. For example, many growing children have been cheated out of the rewards of athletic competition because they were told by respected adults that they were too small, too short, too slow, too clumsy and so forth. Feedback can have a profound and lasting impact on behaviour.

Behavioural Outcomes of Feedback

In Chapter 8, we discussed how goal setting gives behaviour direction, increases expended effort and fosters persistence. Because feedback is intimately related to the goal-setting process, it involves the same behavioural outcomes: direction, effort and persistence. However, while the fourth outcome of goal setting involves formulating goal-attainment strategies, the fourth possible outcome of feedback is *resistance*. Feedback schemes that either smack of manipulation or fail on one or more of the perceptual and cognitive evaluation tests just discussed, breed resistance.[28]

Practical Lessons from Feedback Research

After reviewing dozens of laboratory and field studies of feedback, a trio of OB researchers cited the following practical implications for managers.

▼ **The positive acceptance of feedback should not be treated as a given; feedback is often perceived wrongly or rejected. This is especially true in cross-cultural exchanges.**

▼ **Managers can enhance their credibility as sources of feedback by developing their expertise and creating a climate of trust.**

▼ **Negative feedback is typically perceived wrongly or rejected.**

▼ **Although very frequent feedback may erode one's sense of personal control and initiative, feedback is too *infrequent* in most workplaces.**

▼ **Feedback needs to be tailored to the recipient.**

▼ **While average and below-average performers need extrinsic rewards for performance, high performers respond to feedback that enhances their feelings of competence and personal control.[29]**

More recent research insights about feedback include the following.

▼ **Computer-based performance feedback leads to greater improvements in performance when it is received directly from the computer system rather than via an immediate supervisor.[30]**

▼ **Recipients of feedback perceive it to be more accurate when they actively participate in the feedback session than when they simply receive it passively.[31]**

▼ **Destructive criticism tends to cause conflict and reduce motivation.[32]**

▼ **'The higher one rises in an organization the less likely one is to receive quality feedback about job performance.'[33]**

Managers who act on these research implications and the warning signs in Table 9–1 can build credible and effective feedback systems.[34]

So far we have focused on traditional downward feedback. Let us now explore a couple of new and interesting approaches to feedback in the workplace.

NON-TRADITIONAL FEEDBACK: UPWARD AND 360-DEGREE

Traditional top-down feedback programmes have given way to some interesting variations in recent years. Two newer approaches, discussed in this section, are upward feedback and so-called 360-degree feedback. Aside from breaking away from a strict

Table 9–1

Six Common Trouble Signs for Organizational Feedback Systems

1. Feedback is used to punish, embarrass, or put down employees.
2. Those receiving the feedback see it as irrelevant to their work.
3. Feedback information is provided too late to do any good.
4. People receiving feedback believe it relates to matters beyond their control.
5. Employees complain about wasting too much time collecting and recording feedback data.
6. Feedback recipients complain about feedback being too complex or difficult to understand.

SOURCE: Adapted from C Bell and R Zemke, 'On-Target Feedback', *Training*, June 1992, pp 36–44.

superior-to-subordinate feedback loop, these newer approaches are different because they typically involve *multiple sources* of feedback. Instead of simply getting feedback from one boss, often during an annual performance appraisal, more and more managers are getting structured feedback from superiors, subordinates, peers, and even outsiders such as customers.

Non-traditional feedback is growing in popularity for at least six reasons.

1 Traditional performance appraisal systems have created widespread dissatisfaction.

2 Team-based organization structures are replacing traditional hierarchies. This trend requires managers to have good interpersonal skills that are best evaluated by team members.

3 Systems using 'multiple-raters' are said to make for more valid feedback than single-source rating.[35]

4 Advanced computer network technology (the Internet and company Intranets) now facilitates multiple-rater systems.[36]

5 Bottom-up feedback meshes nicely with the trend toward participative management and employee empowerment.

6 Co-workers and subordinates are said to know more about a manager's strengths and limitations than the boss.[37]

Together, these factors make a compelling case for looking at better ways to give and receive performance feedback.

Upward Feedback

Upward feedback stands the traditional approach on its head by having subordinates provide feedback on a manager's style and performance. This type of feedback is generally anonymous. Most students are familiar with upward feedback programmes from years of filling out anonymous lecturer evaluation surveys.

> **Upward feedback**
> *subordinates evaluate their boss*

Managers typically resist upward feedback programmes because they believe it erodes their authority. Other critics say anonymous upward feedback can become little more than a personality contest, or worse, the system can be manipulated by managers making promises or threats. What does the research literature tell us about upward feedback?

Research Insights

Three different studies, with diverse samples, have given us the following useful insights.

The question of whether upward feedback should be *anonymous* was addressed by a study at a large US insurance company. All told, 183 employees rated the skills and effectiveness of 38 managers. Managers who received anonymous upward feedback received *lower* ratings and liked the process *less* than did those receiving feedback from identifiable employees. This finding confirmed the criticism of the system which states that employees will tend to go easier on their boss when not protected by confidentiality.[38]

In another study, 83 supervisors were divided into three feedback groups:

▼ **Group 1: feedback from both superiors and subordinates**

▼ **Group 2: feedback from superiors only**

▼ **Group 3: feedback from subordinates only.**

Group 1 was most satisfied with the overall evaluation process and responded more positively to upward feedback. 'Group 3 expressed more concern that subordinate appraisals would undermine supervisors' authority and that supervisors would focus on pleasing subordinates.'[39]

In a field study of 238 corporate managers, upward feedback had a positive impact on the performance of low to moderate performers.[40]

General Recommendations for Using Upward Feedback

These research findings suggest the practical value of anonymous upward feedback used in combination with other sources of performance feedback and evaluation. Because of managerial resistance and potential manipulation, using upward feedback as the primary determinant for promotions and pay decisions is *not* recommended. Carefully collected upward feedback is useful for management development programmes.

360-Degree Feedback

The concept of giving a manager collective feedback from different levels and categories of co-workers is not new. Training and development specialists have used multi-rater, multilevel feedback for more than 20 years. As aggressively marketed 360-degree feedback software programmes became available in recent years, corporate use mushroomed. Whether 360-degree feedback goes down in history as just another passing fad or an established practice remains to be seen.[41] An unfortunate by-product of sudden popularity is that enthusiastic sellers of 360-degree feedback systems are more interested in advocacy than objective evaluation.[42] Importantly, our goal here is not to provide cookbook instructions in how to administer complex 360-degree reviews. Rather, our purpose is to see if the concept is sound and deserves managerial time and money.

360-degree feedback
comparison of anonymous feedback from one's superior, subordinates and peers, with one's self-perceptions

The concept of 360-degree feedback involves letting individuals compare their own perceived performance with that of behaviourally specific (and usually anonymous) performance information supplied by their manager, subordinates, and peers. Even outsiders may be involved in what is sometimes called full-circle feedback (see Figure 9–3). *Fortune* offered this humorous yet instructive explanation:

> *Here's how it works. Everyone from the office screwup [are obsequious] to your boss, including your crackerjack assistant and your rival across the hall, and now they will fill out lengthy, anonymous questionnaires about you. You'll complete one too. Are you crisp, clear and articulate? Abrasive? Spreading yourself too thin? Trustworthy? Off-the-cuff remarks may be gathered too. A week or two later you'll get the results, all crunched and graphed by a computer. Ideally, all this will be explained by someone from your Human Resources department or the company that handled the questionnaires, a person who can break bad news gently. You get to see how your opinion of yourself differs from those of the group of subordinates who participated, your peer group, and the boss.[43]*

The idea is to let the individual know how their behaviour affects others, with the goal of motivating change. In a 360-degree feedback programme, a given manager will play different roles, including focal person, superior, subordinate, and peer. Of course, the focal person role is played only once. The other roles are played in relation to other focal persons.[44] Looking at the practice of different companies, apparently 360-degree feedback can be used for a number of purposes. Consider the various applications in the following organizations.

The British Automobile Association worked out some new standards. With 360-degree feedback employees are now screened to see whether they meet these standards. Aside from their results, employees also receive a 'development guide', containing tips from supervisors, subordinates and colleagues to tackle certain weaknesses. This process is again guided by those who give the feedback. According to the company's HR manager, this system has been proven to be very effective. 'I see a lot of employees now who really place a high value on their evaluations and who do things in a different way now', he says.[45]

Baxter Healthcare uses a questionnaire to check whether employees are following the ethical values outlined by the company. Each individual obtains an evaluation containing the opinions of many people within the organisation on the degree to which he or she works according to the company's ethics.[46]

Avon Rubber Company uses 360-degree feedback as a teambuilding tool. Employees are evaluated by their fellow team members on aspects such as openness and co-operation and are given some useful behavioural remarks to improve their functioning within the team.[47]

The consultants of Coopers & Lybrandt are so competitive that they want to know where they stand in relation to each other. So 360-degree feedback is used.[48]

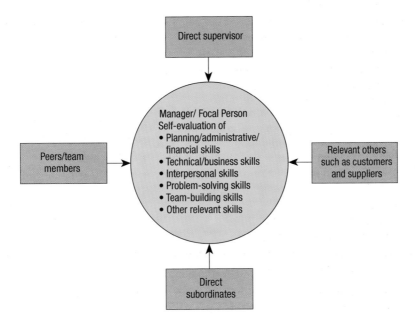

Figure 9–3

Sources and Types of Feedback in the 360-Degree Approach

Relevant Research Evidence

Because upward feedback is part of 360-degree feedback programmes, the evidence reviewed earlier applies here as well. As with upward feedback, the peer- and self-evaluations that are central to 360-degree feedback programmes, are also a significant affront to tradition. But advocates insist that co-workers and managers are appropriate performance evaluators because they are closest to the action. Generally, research builds a stronger case for peer appraisals than for self-appraisals.[49] Self-serving bias, as discussed in Chapter 6, is a problem.

Rigorous research evidence of 360-degree feedback programmes is scarce. A two-year study of 48 managers given 360-degree feedback led to these somewhat promising results. According to the researchers, 'The group as a whole developed its skills but there was substantial variability among individuals in how much change occurred.'[50] Thus, as with any feedback, individuals vary in their response to 360-degree feedback.

Practical Recommendations for 360-Degree Feedback Programmes

Our recommendations for upward feedback, *favouring* anonymity and *discouraging* linkage to pay and promotion decisions, also apply to 360-degree feedback programmes. According to one expert, *trust* is the issue.

Trust is at the core of using 360-degree feedback to enhance productivity. Trust determines how much an individual is willing to contribute for an employer. Using 360 [degree feedback] confidentially, for developmental purposes, builds trust; using it to trigger pay and personnel decisions puts trust at risk.[51]

We agree that 360-degree feedback has a place in the development of managerial skills, especially in today's team-based organizations. However, it is important to remember that this complex feedback process is only as strong as its various components:

▼ **process design and planning**

▼ **instrument development**

▼ **instrument design**

▼ **administration**

▼ **feedback processing and reporting**

▼ **action planning as a result of feedback.**[52]

It is not a quick-and-easy fix, as some advocates would have us believe.

Some Concluding Tips for Giving Good Feedback

Managers need to keep the following tips in mind when giving feedback.

▼ Relate feedback to existing performance *goals* and clear *expectations.*

▼ Give *specific* feedback tied to observable behaviour or measurable results.

▼ Channel feedback toward *key result* areas.

▼ Give feedback as *soon* as possible.[53]

▼ Give positive feedback for *improvement,* not just final results.

▼ Focus feedback on *performance,* not personalities.

▼ Base feedback on *accurate* and *credible* information.

ORGANIZATIONAL REWARD SYSTEMS

Rewards are an ever-present and always controversial feature of organizational life.[54] Some employees see their jobs as the source of a pay cheque and little else. Others derive great pleasure from their jobs and association with co-workers. Even volunteers who donate their time to charitable organizations, such as the Red Cross, walk away with rewards in the form of social recognition and the pride of having given unselfishly of their time. Hence, the subject of organizational rewards includes, but goes far beyond, monetary compensation.[55] This section examines key components of organizational reward systems to provide a conceptual background for discussing the timely topics of pay for performance and team-based pay.

Despite the fact that reward systems vary widely, it is possible to identify and interrelate some common components. The model in Figure 9–4 focuses on four important components, which we will now examine:

▼ **types of rewards**

▼ **reward norms**

▼ **distribution criteria**

▼ **desired outcomes.**

Types of Rewards

As well as the usual pay cheque, the variety and magnitude of organizational rewards boggles the mind—from subsidized day care to education subsidies to stock options, from boxes of chocolates to golf club membership. Consider the French example of Naf Naf's stock-option plan.

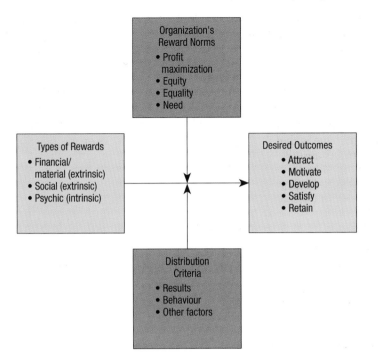

Figure 9–4

A General Model of Organizational Reward Systems

In order to reward employees and to establish their loyalty to the company, Naf Naf regularly offers stock-options to a selected number of employees, from packer to executive. Naf Naf's system is very innovative, as its 250 head-office and warehouse employees may receive stock-options, whereas most companies reserve this reward system for top-management.

Empoyees are nominated by their immediate superiors then the board of directors take the final decision. The chosen employees receive a document by post from Mr. Gérard Pariente, the company's CEO, giving all information on the use of stock options.

As Naf Naf is a young company, stock-options are an excellent way to directly individualise employees' salaries. 'The employees feel their efforts are recognised and they are proud to have contributed to the company's success', says Ms Gwenaëlle Duval, human resource manager.

Naf Naf's system is open to all head office and warehouse employees on condition that they have been in the company for the last six months. In time, Naf Naf wants to reach 90 per cent of its target group. In cases of professional misconduct or where an employee leaves the company within three years of receiving the stock-options, the options are withdrawn.[56]

In addition to the obvious pay and benefits, there are less obvious social and psychic rewards. Social rewards include praise and recognition from others both inside and outside the organization. Psychic rewards come from personal feelings of self-esteem, self-satisfaction and accomplishment.

An alternative typology for organizational rewards is the distinction between extrinsic and intrinsic rewards. Financial, material and social rewards qualify as **extrinsic rewards** because they come from the environment. Psychic rewards, however, are **intrinsic rewards** because they are self-granted. An employee who works to obtain extrinsic rewards, such as money or praise, is said to be extrinsically motivated. One who derives pleasure from the task itself or experiences a sense of competence or self-determination is said to be intrinsically motivated.[57] The relative importance of extrinsic and intrinsic rewards is a matter of culture and personal tastes (See the next International OB).

Extrinsic rewards
financial, material or social rewards from the environment

Intrinsic rewards
self-granted, psychic rewards

International OB

www.jnj.com

Foreign Employers Rely on Unique Extrinsic and Intrinsic Rewards in China

In spite of all the complications for foreign employers, one advantage they do have is that the Chinese like working for them because it gives the workers status. As one individual reported, 'work for a joint venture and I report to a foreign boss—this is cool.' Also, it usually means that they get to practise their English and learn about life and cultures outside China. I was told of good employees quitting when they had been assigned to a local Chinese boss.

For foreign firms, the other big attraction that can keep mainland Chinese anchored to the desk for some time is the chance to travel abroad, particularly for training. Although it is not always easy to get exit permits for people, at least for any length of time, it is an increasing trend. Typically, Chinese nationals are being trained in Singapore, Australia, New Zealand and the USA. The main advantage of training

employees abroad is that it buys some time, and companies usually link overseas development assignments to an agreement with individuals to stay with the company for two to three years after they return.

An example of this is Johnson & Johnson's executive MBA program with the University of Singapore. Twenty of its own staff and ten from its distributors take part in a three-year program that costs upwards of $20,000 per person. This kind of investment gives foreign companies a good reputation (which means local talent will be quick to join), and in China, good news travels fast around the cadre of highly qualified personnel.

SOURCE: Excerpted from M Johnson, 'Beyond Pay: What Rewards Work Best When Doing Business in China', *Compensation & Benefits Review*, November–December, 1998, p 54.

Organizational Reward Norms

As discussed in Chapter 8 under the heading of equity theory, the employer–employee linkage can be viewed as an exchange relationship. Employees exchange their time and talent for rewards. Ideally, four alternative norms dictate the nature of this exchange. In pure form, each would lead to a significantly different reward distribution system. These four norms: profit maximisation, equity, equality, and need, are defined as follows.

Profit maximization: The objective of each party is to maximize its net gain, regardless of how the other party fares. A profit-maximizing company would attempt to pay the least amount of wages for maximum effort. Conversely, a profit-maximizing employee would seek maximum rewards, regardless of the organization's financial well-being, and leave the organization for a better deal.

> **Reward equity norm**
> *rewards should be tied to contributions*

Equity: According to the reward equity norm, rewards should be allocated in proportion to contributions. Those who contribute the most should be rewarded the most. A cross-cultural study of American, Japanese and Korean college students led the researchers to conclude: 'Equity is probably a phenomenon common to most cultures, but its strength will vary.'[58] Basic principles of fairness and justice, evident in most cultures, drive the equity norm.

> **Reward equality norm**
> *everyone should get the same rewards*

Equality: The reward equality norm calls for rewarding all parties equally, regardless of their comparative contributions. Because absolute equality does not exist in today's hierarchical organizations, researchers recently explored the impact of pay inequality. They looked at pay dispersion (the pay gap between high-level and low-level employees). Result: the smaller the pay gap, the better the individual and organizational performance.[59] Thus, the outlandish compensation packages for many of today's top executives is not only a widely debated moral issue, it is a productivity issue as well.[60]

Need: This norm calls for distributing rewards according to employees' needs, rather than their contributions.[61]

A pair of researchers concluded, in the following paragraph, that these contradictory norms are typically intertwined.

> *We propose that employer–employee exchanges are governed by the contradictory norms of profit maximization, equity, equality and need. These norms can coexist; what varies is the extent to which the rules for correct application of a norm are clear and the relative emphasis different managements will give to certain norms in particular allocations.*[62]

Conflict and ethical debates often arise over the perceived fairness of reward allocations because of disagreement about reward norms.[63] Stockholders might prefer a profit-maximization norm, while technical specialists would like an equity norm, and unionised hourly workers would argue for a pay system based on equality. A reward norm anchored to need might prevail in a family-owned and -operated business. Effective reward systems are based on clear and consensual exchange norms.

Reward Distribution Criteria

According to one expert on organizational reward systems, there are three general criteria for the distribution of rewards.

1 *Performance: results.* Tangible outcomes such as individual, group or organization performance; quantity and quality of performance.

2 *Performance: actions and behaviours.* Such as teamwork, co-operation, risk taking, creativity.

3 *Non-performance considerations.* Customary or contractual, where the type of job, nature of the work, equity, tenure, level in the hierarchy and so forth, are rewarded.[64]

Desired Outcomes of the Reward System

As listed in Figure 9–4, a good reward system should attract talented people and motivate and satisfy them once they have joined the organization.[65] Further, a good reward system should foster personal growth and development and keep talented people from leaving.

Why Do Rewards Fail to Motivate?

Despite huge investments of time and money for organizational reward systems, often the desired motivational impact is not achieved. A management consultant/writer offered the following eight reasons.

1 Too much emphasis on monetary rewards.

2 Rewards lack an 'appreciation effect'.

3 Extensive benefits become entitlements.

4 Counter-productive behaviour is rewarded. (For example, a pizza delivery company related its rewards to the 'on time' performance of its drivers, only to discover that it was inadvertently rewarding reckless driving.[66])

5 Too long a delay between performance and rewards.

6 Too many one-size-fits-all rewards.

7 Use of one-shot rewards with a short-lived motivational impact.

8 Continued use of demotivating practices such as lay-offs, across-the-board pay rises and cuts, and excessive executive compensation.[67]

These stubborn problems have fostered a growing interest in more effective reward and compensation practices. Although we cannot engage in a comprehensive discussion of modern compensation practices in the rest of this chapter, a subject requiring an entire book,[68] we can explore general approaches to boosting the motivational impact of monetary rewards. This is where pay for performance—including profit sharing, gainsharing, and team-based pay—enters the picture.

PAY FOR PERFORMANCE

Our discussion of organizational rewards would not be complete without more closely considering the role of *money* (see the next OB Exercise). In today's workplace, despite lots of complaints about pay, money remains the central organizational reward. Consequently, we need to address this important underlying OB question: How can managers increase the incentive effect of monetary compensation? Managers who adequately comprehend this issue are in a better position to make decisions about specific compensation plans.

OB Exercise

What Are Your Attitudes toward Money? (Lessons from Your *Money Autobiography*)

Instructions

Take a few minutes to reflect on your life-long relationship with money. Does the topic of money trigger good or bad memories? Is money an emotional topic? What are your earliest memories of money? What 'messages' about money did you receive while growing up? How did your family handle discussions about money? Have your spent your money wisely or foolishly over the years? What are your expectations and plans for making, saving and investing money in the future?

Summarize these thoughts about money in a brief autobiographical narrative. The beauty of your prose is not as important as the content. *Note:* There are no right or wrong answers to the following questions, so express yourself freely and honestly. The idea is to appreciate how much your past experiences influence your present attitudes toward money, for better or for worse.

For Consideration and Discussion

1 Are you having trouble following out-of-date 'money rules'?

2 Is money a 'means' or an 'end' in your life?

3 Are your expectations about money realistic? Explain.

4 How will your attitude toward money help or hinder the pursuit of your career and/or life goals?

SOURCE: Adapted from discussion in P Kruger, 'Money – Is That What You Want?' *Fast Company*, May 1999, pp 48–50.

Pay for Performance: The Concept

Pay for performance
monetary incentives tied to one's results or accomplishments

Pay for performance is the popular term for monetary incentives linking at least some portion of the pay cheque directly to results or accomplishments. Many refer to it simply as *incentive pay*, while others call it *variable pay*.[69] The general idea behind pay-for-performance schemes—including, but not limited to, merit pay, bonuses and profit sharing—is to give employees an incentive for working harder or smarter. Pay for performance is something extra, that is, compensation above and beyond basic wages and salaries. Proponents of incentive compensation say something extra is needed because hourly wages and fixed salaries do little more than motivate people to show up at work and put in the required hours.[70] The most basic form of pay-for-performance is the traditional piece rate plan, whereby the employee is paid a specified amount of money for each unit of work. For example, a drill press operator gets 25 cents for every gasket drilled in four places. Sales commissions, whereby a salesperson receives a specified amount of money for each unit sold, is another longstanding example of pay for performance. Today's service economy is forcing management to creatively adapt, and to go beyond, piece rate and sales commission plans in order to accommodate greater emphasis on product and service quality, interdependence, and teamwork.

Preoccupation with the size of executive rewards seems to be a largely Anglo/American phenomenon; but the popularity of share options has spilled into France, where companies have been quick to spot their tax advantages. 'Options have become practically the most significant element of executive compensation', says Eduardo de Martino, a partner with accountants Arthur Andersen in Paris. 'You can't really recruit or retain a high-quality executive without them.'[71]

In the most other European countries, the culture of share options has yet to develop, although bonuses are commonplace. In Italy for instance—where the small and medium-sized enterprises which form the backbone of the Italian economy are not listed on the stock exchange—top Italian directors may receive up to 25 or 30 per cent of their renumeration in the form of cash bonuses.[72]

The fiercest debates about executive pay, however, are taking place in the USA and UK, both of which have highly developed stock markets and find that the influence of individual shareholders on company directors is relatively weak.

Consider the following example of Whirlpool's pay for performance system, which was gradually introduced from 1987 on.

True pay-for-performance became the foundation of the new system for all employee segments, along with a strong focus on shareholder value creation, including introduction of an all-employee stock option programme in November 1991. Even at the board level, Whirlpool substantially revamped the total compensation programme for directors, revising stock option grants so they are awarded only if the company achieves certain performance targets. At senior management levels, annual bonus opportunity shifted from 'unknown' to a clear 50 to 100 per cent of base, depending on achievement of targeted corporate and business-unit financial goals and individual performance. Long-term incentives shifted from occasional use of stock options to annual stock-options awards plus new plants that incorporated an equity focus.[73]

Pay for Performance: The Evidence

Does pay for performance work as promised? According to available expert opinion and research results, pay for performance too often falls short of its goal of improved job performance. 'Experts say that roughly half the incentive plans they see don't work, victims of poor design and administration.'[74] In fact, one recent study documented how incentive pay had a *negative* effect on the performance of 150,000 managers from 500 financially distressed companies.[75] A recent meta-analysis of 39 studies found only a modest positive correlation between financial incentives and performance *quantity* and no impact on performance *quality*.[76] Other researchers have found only a weak statistical link between large executive bonuses paid out in good years and subsequent improvement in corporate profitability.[77] Also, in a survey of small business owners, more than half said their commission plans failed to motivate extra effort from their salespeople.[78] Linking teachers' merit pay to student performance, an exciting school reform idea, turned out to be a big disappointment: 'The bottom line is that despite high hopes, none of the 13 districts studied was able to use teacher pay incentives to achieve significant, lasting gains in student performance.'[79]

Clearly, the pay-for-performance trend could stall if constructive steps are not taken. Could profit sharing and gainsharing help?

Profit Sharing versus Gainsharing

The terms *profit sharing* and *gainsharing* are sometimes used interchangeably. That is not only a conceptual mistake but also a major disservice to gainsharing. These two general approaches to pay for performance differ significantly in both method and results.

Profit Sharing

Profit sharing
portion of bottom-line economic profits given to employees

Most of today's corporate pay-for-performance plans are profit-sharing schemes. Profit sharing occurs when individual employees or work groups are granted a specified portion of any economic profits earned by the business as a whole. These internally distributed profits may be apportioned according to the equality or equity norms discussed earlier. Equity distributions supposedly occur when performance-appraisal results are used to gauge who gets how much in the way of merit pay or profit-sharing bonuses. Profit-sharing bonuses may be paid in cash, deferred until retirement or death, or in some combination of the two (see the top section of Table 9–2).

Table 9–2

Profit-Sharing and Gainsharing Plans

Types of Profit-Sharing Plans

Deferred plan—Credit individuals with periodic earnings, delaying actual distribution until their disability, retirement, or death.

Distribution plan—Fully distributes each period's earned benefits as soon as the profit-sharing pool can be calculated.

Combination plan—Allows employees to receive a portion of each period's earnings in cash, while the remainder awaits future distribution.

Types of Gainsharing Plans

Improshare plans—Based on employees' ability to complete assignments in less time than would be expected given the historical productivity base ratio. Work-hours saved are divided between the firm and plan participants according to a set percentage, such as 50 percent. Individuals receive a corresponding percentage increase in gross pay. Although no structural barriers exist, these plans generally do not provide formal participation in decision making.

Rucker plan—Generally limits decision-making participation to a single screening committee or the interface of a production and a screening committee. The Rucker formula assesses the relationship between the value added to produced goods as they pass through the manufacturing process and total labor costs. Unlike the typical Scanlon ratio, this formula enables workers to benefit from savings in production-related materials, supplies, and services. Bonuses result when the current ratio is better than that for the base period. A reserve pool is established to offset bad months. The reserves left over at the end of the year are paid out to employees as an additional bonus.

Scanlon plan—Uses a dual-committee system to foster companywide participation in decision making. Draws upon a historical productivity base ratio relating adjusted sales to total payroll. A bonus pool is created whenever actual output, as measured by adjusted sales, requires lower labor costs than would be expected using the base ratio. Each month, a percentage of the bonus pool is held in reserve to offset deficit months. The remaining funds are divided between the firm and employees. All of the retained funds remaining at year's end are proportionately shared by the parties.

SOURCE: 'Analyzing Group Incentive Plans', by Gary W Florkowski, January 1990. Reprinted with permission of *HRMagazine*, published by the Society for Human Resource Management, Alexandria, VA, USA.

Research carried out by the London School of Economics, based on information from more than 1,500 work places with more than 25 employees, observed that employee-involvement profit sharing and merit pay schemes were positively linked to productivity and job creation. Cash-based profit sharing schemes are linked to econmic outcomes, but not to better industrial relations. The authoritarian workplace—with hardly any employee involvement—has a positive impact on industrial relations (e.g. lower turnover and absenteeism) but a negative one on productivity.[80]

Gainsharing

Perhaps because it tends to be used in smaller companies with 500 or fewer employees, gainsharing is not as well known as profit sharing. 'Gainsharing involves a measurement of productivity combined with the calculation of a bonus designed to offer employees a mutual share of any increases in total organizational productivity. Usually all those responsible for the increase receive the bonus.'[81] Gainsharing has been around for more than a half century and typically goes by one of the following names: Improshare®, Rucker® plan or Scanlon plan (see the bottom section of Table 9–2 for details). Distinguishing characteristics of gainsharing include the following.

> **Gainsharing**
> *bonuses tied to measurable productivity increases*

▼ **An organizational culture based on workforce–management co-operation, trust, free-flowing information and extensive participation.**

▼ **Built-in employee involvement structures such as suggestion systems or quality circles.**

▼ **Precise measurement and tracking of cost and/or productivity data for comparison purposes.**

▼ **The sharing with managerial and non-managerial employees of the proceeds from any productivity gains.**[82]

Ideally, a self-perpetuating cycle develops. Communication and participation generate creative suggestions; which in turn foster productivity gains that yield bonuses; which then build motivation and trust.

How Do Profit Sharing and Gainsharing Measure Up?

Profound differences mark these two general approaches to pay for performance. Gainsharing, by definition, is anchored to hard productivity data; whereas profit sharing, generally-speaking, is more loosely linked to the results of performance appraisals. Thus profit-sharing determinations, like performance appraisals, are readily plagued by bias and incorrect perceptions. Another significant problem with profit sharing is that bottom-line profits are influenced by many factors beyond the average employee's control. Those factors include strategy, pricing, competition, and fluctuating interest rates, to name but a few. Profit sharing's principal weaknesses are effectively neutralized by gainsharing's major strength, namely a quantified performance-pay formula.

Critics of profit sharing admit it is generous to share the good times with employees; but they fear profit-sharing bonuses are perceived as a reward for past performance, not as an incentive to work harder in the future. Moreover, gainsharing rewards participation and teamwork while profit sharing generally does not. On the other hand, gainsharing formulas are complex and require extensive communication and training commitments.[83]

So, on balance, which is better? Judging by available research evidence, much of which is subjective, the vote goes to gainsharing. A study of 71 managers and professionals in a metals processing company found no significant correlation between individual performance and profit-sharing bonuses.[84] Another study of 1,746 manufacturing employees, at seven firms with Scanlon plans and two control firms without Scanlon plans, found higher job satisfaction and commitment among the Scanlon employees. Additionally, participation was a significantly stronger cultural norm in the Scanlon organizations. Scanlon participants quickly passed this norm on to new employees.[85] (Gainsharing seems to work best when it becomes embedded in the organization's culture.)[86] A study of four companies with Scanlon-type plans in force for four or more years, found positive results in terms of lower costs, improved quality, and improved health and safety conditions.[87]

Team-Based Pay

One clear trend in today's workplace is the move toward teams (see Chapter 12). There are permanent work teams and temporary project teams. There are cross-functional teams with specialists from different areas such as engineering, production, marketing and finance. There are self-managed teams, where employees take turns handling traditional managerial tasks including staffing, scheduling, training and recordkeeping. Most recently, there are *virtual* teams where people from different geographic locations collaborate via computer networks, often with little or no face-to-face contact. While the move toward team structure certainly is a promising one, there are many loose ends, a major one being how to reward team members and teamwork. Training magazine's Beverly Geber puts things into context by noting the following.

> It's a struggle trying to persuade many employees that working co-operatively with others is in their best interest. It's an epic battle teaching them how to collaborate, especially when it means they must resist a lifetime of seeking personal glory. And it's truly exasperating trying to get non-teamed parts of the organization, as well as customers and suppliers, to work harmoniously with the teams.

> Unfortunately, there's another bugaboo waiting just around the corner. It is the issue of compensation. To wit: now that people are working closely together to produce a product jointly, how do you pay them in a way that encourages collaboration and spurs the team to produce its utmost but does not ignore the individual's innate desire for personal recognition?[88]

Team-based pay
linking pay to teamwork behaviour and/or team results

Team-based pay is defined as incentive compensation that rewards individuals for teamwork and/or rewards teams for collective results. This definition highlights an important distinction between individual *behaviour* and team *results*. Stated another way, it takes team players to get team results. Any team-oriented pay plan that ignores this distinction will almost certainly fail.

Problems

The biggest single barrier to effective team-based pay is a cultural one, and is no more so than in such highly individualistic cultures as those of Britain, Sweden, Germany, the USA and Australia. Individual competition for pay and pay rises has long been the norm in these countries. Entrenched grading schemes in schools and colleges, focusing on individual competition and not group achievement, are a good preview for the traditional American and western European workplace. Team-based pay is a direct assault on the cultural tradition of putting the individual above the group.

Another culturally rooted problem is a general lack of teamwork skills. Members of high-performance teams are skilled communicators, conflict handlers, and negotiators; they are flexible, adaptable, and open to change. Employees accustomed to being paid for personal achievements tend to resent having their pay dependent upon others' performances and problems. The combination of poor interpersonal skills and an individualistic work ethic can breed conflict and excessive peer pressure.

Research Evidence

Research evidence to date is not encouraging. A recent comprehensive review of studies that examined team-based rewards in the workplace led to the conclusion: 'The field-based empirical evidence is limited and inconclusive.'[89]

Recommendations

The state of the art in team-based pay is very primitive. Given the many different types of teams, we can be certain there is no single best approach. However, based on anecdotal evidence from the general management literature and case studies,[90] we can make five recommendations.

▼ *Prepare employees* for team-based systems with as much interpersonal skills training as possible. This ongoing effort should include diversity training and skill training in communication, conflict resolution, trust building, group problem solving, and negotiating.

▼ *Establish teams* and get them running smoothly before introducing team-based pay incentives to avoid overload and frustration.

▼ Create a pay plan that *blends* individual achievement and team incentives.

▼ Begin by rewarding teamwork *behaviours* (such as mutual support, co-operation, and group problem solving), and then phase in pay incentives for team *results.*

▼ When paying for team results, make sure individual team members see a clear connection between their own work and team results. Compensation specialists call this a *clear line of sight.*

Making Pay for Performance Work

From a practical 'so what' perspective, the real issue is not profit-sharing versus gainsharing versus team-based pay. Rather, the issue is this: How can managers improve the motivational impact of their current pay-for-performance plan? The fact is, most such plans are not pure types. They are hybrids. They combine features of profit sharing, gainsharing and team approaches.[91] One option is to hire consultants to establish one of the trademarked gainsharing plans or the Scanlon plan. A second, more broadly applicable, option is to build the best characteristics of profit sharing, gainsharing, and team-pay plans into the organization's pay-for-performance plan. The following practical recommendations can help in this regard.

▼ Make pay for performance an integral part of the organization's basic strategy (e.g., pursuit of best-in-the-industry product or service quality).

▼ Base incentive determinations on objective performance data.

▼ Have all employees actively participate in the development, implementation and revision of the performance-pay formulae.

▼ Encourage two-way communication so problems with the pay-for-performance plan will be detected early.

▼ Build the pay-for-performance plan around participative structures such as suggestion systems or quality circles.

▼ Reward teamwork and co-operation whenever possible.

▼ Actively sell the plan to supervisors and middle managers who may view employee participation as a threat to their traditional notion of authority.

▼ If annual cash bonuses are granted, pay them in a lump sum to maximize their motivational impact.

▼ Remember that money motivates when it comes in significant amounts, not in hand-outs of loose change.

Summary of Key Concepts

1 *Specify the two basic functions of feedback and three sources of feedback.*

Feedback, in the form of objective information about performance, both instructs and motivates. According to the cognitive-processing model, individuals receive feedback from others, the task and from themselves.

2 *Discuss how the recipient's characteristics, perceptions and cognitive evaluations affect how the individual processes feedback.*

The recipient's openness to feedback is determined by their self-esteem, self-efficacy, needs and goals, and desire for feedback. The individual's perception determines whether feedback is viewed positively or negatively. Cognitively, the recipient will tend to act on feedback that is seen as accurate, from a credible source, based on a fair system, and tied to reasonable expectations and behavioural standards.

3 *List at least three practical lessons from feedback research.*

Feedback is not automatically accepted as intended, especially negative feedback. Managerial credibility can be enhanced through expertise and a climate of trust. Feedback must neither be too frequent nor too scarce and must be tailored to the individual. Feedback accessed directly from computers is effective. Active participation in the feedback session helps people perceive feedback as more accurate. The quality of feedback received decreases as one moves up the organizational hierarchy.

4 *Define upward feedback and 360-degree feedback, and summarize the general tips for giving good feedback.*

Lower-level employees provide upward feedback (usually anonymously) to their managers. A focal person receives 360-degree feedback from their subordinates, manager, peers and selected others such as customers or suppliers. Good feedback is tied to performance goals and clear expectations, linked with specific behaviour or results, reserved for key result areas, given as soon as possible, provided for improvement as well as for final results, focused on performance rather than on personalities, and based on accurate and credible information.

5 *Briefly explain the four different organizational reward norms.*

Maximizing individual gain is the object of the *profit maximization* reward norm. The *equity* norm calls for distributing rewards in proportion to contributions (those who contribute the most should earn the most). Everyone is rewarded equally when the *equality* reward norm is in force. The *need* reward norm involves distributing rewards based on employees' needs.

6 *Summarize the reasons rewards often fail to motivate employees.*

Reward systems can fail to motivate employees for these reasons: overemphasis on money, no appreciation effect, benefits become entitlements, wrong behaviour is rewarded, rewards are delayed too long, use of one-size-fits-all rewards, one-shot rewards with temporary impact, and demotivating practices such as lay-offs.

7 *Distinguish between profit sharing, gainsharing and team-based pay.*

Profit-sharing plans give employees a specified portion of the business's economic profits. Gainsharing ties bonuses to documented productivity increases. Team-based pay is incentive pay for engaging in teamwork *behaviours* and/or for team *results*.

8 *Discuss how managers can generally improve pay-for-performance plans.*

They need to be strategically anchored, based on quantified performance data, highly participative, actively sold to supervisors and middle managers, and teamwork oriented. Annual bonuses of significant size are helpful.

Discussion Questions

1 How can feedback and rewards combine to improve job performance?

2 How has feedback instructed and/or motivated you lately?

3 Relative to your course work, which of the three sources of feedback–others, task, self–has the greatest impact on your performance? If you have a job, which source of feedback is most potent in that situation?

4 Which of the five cognitive evaluation criteria for feedback–feedback accuracy, source credibility, system fairness, expectancies, behavioural standards–do you think ranks as most important? Explain.

5 What is the most valuable lesson feedback research teaches us? Explain.

6 How would you summarize the practical benefits and drawbacks of 360-degree feedback?

7 Which of the four organizational reward norms do you prefer? Why?

8 What is your personal experience with failed organizational reward systems and practices?

9 As a modern manager, which pay-for-performance approach do you like better: profit sharing, gainsharing, or team-based pay?

10 How would you respond to a manager who said, 'Employees cannot be motivated with money'?

Internet Exercise

www.panoramicfeedback.com

As discussed in this chapter, 360-degree feedback is getting a good deal of attention these days. Our purpose here is to introduce you to a sample 360-degree evaluation from an innovative Internet-based programme marketed by Panoramic Feedback. (Note: Our use of this sample is for instructional purposes only and does not constitute an endorsement of the programme, that may or may not suit your needs.)

Go to the Internet home page (www.panoramicfeedback.com), and select *Sample Questionnaire* from the main menu. The sample evaluation is for a hypothetical supervisor. For our purposes, substitute the name of your manager from your present or past job. The idea is to do an upward evaluation of someone you actually know. Read the brief background piece, and proceed to Part One of the Questionnaire. Read and follow the instructions for the eight performance dimensions. All responses you click and any comments you type into the two boxes in Part One will show up on your printed copy, if you choose to make one. Move to Part Two and type your personal evaluations of your manager in the box provided. These comments will also be on any printed copy you may make.

Questions

1 How would you rate the eight performance dimensions in this brief sample? Relevant? Important? Good basis for constructive feedback?

2 If you were to expand this evaluation, what other performance scales would you add?

3 Is this a fair evaluation, as far as it goes? Explain.

4 How comfortable would you be in evaluating the following people with this type of *anonymous* 360-degree instrument: your boss, peers, self, people reporting directly to you?

5 Would you like to be the focal person of a 360-degree review? Under what circumstances? Explain.

6 Results of anonymous 360-degree reviews should be used for which of the following purposes: promotions, pay rises, job assignments, feedback for personal growth and development? Explain.

Personal Awareness and Growth Exercise

What Kind of Feedback Are You Getting?

Objectives

1 To provide actual examples of on-the-job feedback from three primary sources: organization/supervisor, co-workers, and self/task.

2 To provide a handy instrument for evaluating the comparative strength of positive feedback from these three sources.

Introduction

A pair of researchers from Georgia Tech developed and tested a 63-item feedback questionnaire to demonstrate the importance of both the sign and content of feedback messages.[92] Although their instrument contains both positive and negative feedback items, we have extracted 18 positive items for this self-awareness exercise.

Instructions

Thinking of your current job (or your most recent job), circle one number for each of the 18 items. Alternatively, you could ask one or more employed individuals to complete the questionnaire for you. Once the questionnaire has been completed, calculate subtotal and total scores by adding the circled numbers. Then try to answer the discussion questions.

Instrument

How frequently do you experience each of the following outcomes in your present (or past) job?

ORGANIZATIONAL/SUPERVISORY FEEDBACK

	Rarely	Occasionally	Very Frequently
1 My supervisor complimenting me on something I have done.	1———2———3———4———5		
2 My supervisor increasing my responsibilities.	1———2———3———4———5		
3 The company expressing pleasure with my performance.	1———2———3———4———5		
4 The company giving me a pay rise.	1———2———3———4———5		
5 My supervisor recommending me for a promotion or pay rise.	1———2———3———4———5		
6 The company providing me with favourable data concerning my performance.	1———2———3———4———5		

Subscore = _____

CO-WORKER FEEDBACK	**SELF/TASK FEEDBACK**

7 My co-workers coming to me for advice. 1——2——3——4——5

8 My co-workers expressing approval of my work. 1——2——3——4——5

9 My co-workers liking to work with me. 1——2——3——4——5

10 My co-workers telling me that I am doing a good job. 1——2——3——4——5

11 My co-workers commenting favourably on something I have done. 1——2——3——4——5

12 Receiving a compliment from my co-workers. 1——2——3——4——5

Subscore = _____

13 Knowing that the way I go about my duties is superior to most. 1——2——3——4——5

14 Feeling I am accomplishing more than I used to. 1——2——3——4——5

15 Knowing that I can now perform or do things which previously were difficult for me. 1——2——3——4——5

16 Finding that I am satisfying my own standards for 'good work'. 1——2——3——4——5

17 Knowing that what I am doing 'feels right'.

18 Feeling confident of being able to handle all aspects of my job. 1——2——3——4——5

Subscore = _____

Total Score = _____

Questions for Discussion

1 Which items on this questionnaire would you rate as primarily instructional in function? Are all of the remaining items primarily motivational? Explain.

2 In terms of your own feedback profile, which of the three types is the strongest (has the highest subscore)? Which is the weakest (has the lowest subscore)? How well does your feedback profile explain your job performance and/or satisfaction?

3 How does your feedback profile measure up against those of the other students? (Arbitrary norms, for comparative purposes, are: Deficient feedback = 18–42; Moderate feedback = 43–65; Abundant feedback = 66–90.)

4 Which of the three sources of feedback is most critical to your successful job performance and/or job satisfaction? Explain.

Group Exercise

Rewards, Rewards, Rewards

Objectives

1 To tap the class's collective knowledge of organizational rewards.

2 To appreciate the vast array of potential rewards.

3 To contrast individual and group perceptions of rewards.

4 To practice your group creativity skills.

Introduction

Rewards are a centrepiece of organizational life. Both extrinsic and intrinsic rewards motivate us to join and continue contributing to organized effort. But not all rewards have the same impact on work motivation. Individuals have their own personal preferences for rewards. The best way to discover people's reward preferences is to ask them, both individually and collectively. This group brainstorming and class discussion exercise requires about 20 to 30 minutes.

Instructions

Your instructor will divide your class randomly into teams of five to eight people. Each team will go through the following four-step process.

1 Each team will have a six-minute brainstorming session, with one person acting as recorder. The objective of this brainstorming session is to list as many different organizational rewards as the group can think of. Your team might find it helpful to think of rewards by category (such as rewards arising from the work itself, those you can spend, those you eat and drink, feel, wear, share, cannot see, etc.). Remember, good brainstorming calls on you to withhold judgements about whether ideas are good or not. Quantity is what's wanted. Building upon other people's ideas is encouraged too.

2 Next, each individual will take four minutes to write down, in decreasing order of importance, 10 rewards they want from the job. *Note:* These are your *personal* preferences; your 'top 10' rewards that will motivate you to do your best.

3 Each team will then take five minutes to generate a list of 'today's 10 most powerful rewards'. List them in decreasing order of their power to motivate job performance. Voting may be necessary.

4 A general class discussion of the questions listed below will conclude the exercise.

Questions for Discussion

1 How did your personal 'top 10' list compare with your group's 'top 10' list? If there is a serious mismatch, how would it affect your motivation? (To promote discussion, the instructor may ask several volunteers to read their personal 'top 10' lists to the class.)

2 Which team had the most productive brainstorming session? (The instructor may request each team to read its brainstormed list of potential rewards and 'top 10' list to the class.)

3 Were you surprised to hear certain rewards getting so much attention? Why?

4 How can managers improve the incentive effect of the rewards most frequently mentioned in class?

5 What is the likely future of organizational reward plans? Which of today's compensation trends will probably thrive, and which are probably passing fads?

Chapter Ten

Behaviour Modification and Self-Management

Bad neighbours should be offered money for good behaviour

Nightmare neighbours who terrorise people on some of Britain's roughest and poorest estates should be offered cash and other benefits in return for good behaviour, say researchers. A report, by the Institute for Public Policy Research [IPPR], a centre-left think-tank, found threatening people with conviction and using the law to fight anti-social behaviour is not improving life on large housing estates for thousands of people. ▶

The study on the future of social housing found councils or housing associations which reward tenants with a yearly bonus for good behaviour, such as paying rent on time, looking after their garden and property or getting involved in community activities, have reduced late-night noise, anti-social behaviour and vandalism.

The researchers say other benefits that could be offered should include low-cost home insurance, discounts on household goods, or access to training and work opportunities. The proposals for new 'contracts' between landlords and tenants in social housing, to prevent anti-social behaviour, are the result of a year-long IPPR Forum on the Future of Social Housing.

The Forum, made up of Britain's leading housing experts, believes rewarding good behaviour by benefits and cash is the only way to improve the life chances of people in our most deprived neighbourhoods and ensure everyone has the bedrock of a decent home in a safe community.

'The government has been rightly congratulated for its major investment in public services but, without tackling the apartheid at the heart of the housing system, the money will alleviate some of the symptoms but may not tackle the root causes,' said Matthew Taylor, director of the IPPR. 'Housing is a significant factor in determining health, educational attainment, safety and security. As a society we pay hugely, and in many ways, for the failure in housing.'

Tom Manion, chief executive of Irwell Valley Housing Association, which has 6,500 properties, introduced a reward scheme for good tenant behaviour two years ago. 'A culture of non-payment of rent had built up on many estates, which led to a breakdown in community relations,' he said. 'The good-behaviour scheme has improved the situation. We now spend 27 per cent less on security–such as boarding up houses, burglar alarms and dealing with vandalism–than two years ago.'

Four out of five people who live in the housing association accommodation are members of the Irwell Valley Gold Service scheme, and receive an individual bonus of £52 a year, low-cost contents insurance, education grants and scholarships. Of those originally rejected from the scheme because they were not good tenants, 60 per cent have changed their behaviour to qualify within two years. Only one per cent of residents was removed from the scheme for breaking the good-behaviour contract.[1]

For discussion

Do you think this approach to behaviour modification is a good idea or are there better ways to handle 'bad neighbours'? Why?

Imagine you are the general manager of the public transportation authority in a large city and one of your main duties is overseeing the city's bus system. Over several years, you have noted, with growing concern, the increasing number and severity of bus accidents. In the face of mounting public and administrative pressure, it is clear that a workable accident-prevention programme must be enacted. Large pay raises for the bus drivers and other expensive options are impossible because of a tight city budget. Based on what you have read so far in Part Two of this book, about motivation, feedback and rewards, what remedial action do you propose? (Please take a moment now to jot down some ideas.)

Since these facts have been drawn from a real-life field study, we can see what happened.[2] Management tried to curb the accident rate with some typical programmes, including yearly safety awards, stiffer enforcement of a disciplinary code, complimentary coffee and doughnuts for drivers who had a day without an accident, and a comprehensive training programme. Despite these remedial actions, the accident rate kept climbing. Finally, management agreed to a behaviour modification experiment that directly attacked unsafe driver behaviour.

A hundred of the city's 425 drivers were randomly divided into four experimental teams of 25 each. The remaining drivers served as a control group. During an 18-week period, the drivers received daily feedback on their safety performance on a chart posted in their canteen. An accident-free day was noted on the chart with a green dot, while a driver involved in an accident found a red dot posted next to his or her name. At two-weekly intervals, members of the team with the best competitive safety record received their choice of incentives averaging 5 Euro in value (such as cash, free petrol, free bus passes). Teams that went an entire two-week period without an accident received double incentives.

Unlike previous interventions, the behaviour modification programme reduced the accident rate. Compared with the control group, the experimental group recorded a 25 per cent lower accident rate. During an 18-week period following termination of the incentive programme, the experimental group's accident rate remained a respectable 16 per cent better than the control group's. This indicated a positive, long-term effect. Moreover, the programme was cost effective. The incentives cost the organization 2,200 Euro while it realized a saving of 10,300 Euro in accident settlement expenses (a 1:4.6 cost/benefit ratio).

Why did this particular programme work, while earlier attempts failed? It worked because a specific behaviour (safe driving) was modified through *systematic* management of the drivers' work environment. If the posted feedback, team competition, and rewards had been implemented in traditional piecemeal fashion, they probably would have failed to reduce the accident rate. However, when combined in a co-ordinated and systematic fashion, these common techniques produced favourable results. Research in Finland has demonstrated that behaviour modification techniques reduced accidents by as much as 80 per cent.[3]

This chapter introduces two systematic ways to manage job *behaviour*: behaviour modification and behavioural self-management. Both areas have a common theoretical heritage, behaviourism. In the concluding section, we go beyond behaviourism to explore an array of useful techniques for self-improvement.

Behaviour modification

making specific behaviour occur more or less often by managing its cues and consequences

WHAT IS BEHAVIOUR MODIFICATION?

Behaviour modification (B Mod) involves making specific behaviour occur more or less often by systematically managing its cues and consequences. Workplace behaviour modification has been alternatively labelled *organizational behaviour modification* (OB Mod), *organizational behaviour management* and *performance management*.[4] The generic term *behaviour modification* is used here to avoid unnecessary confusion. B

Mod traces back to the work of two pioneering psychologists, E L Thorndike and B F Skinner.

Thorndike's Law of Effect

During the early 1900s, Edward L Thorndike observed in his psychology laboratory that a cat would behave randomly and wildly when placed in a small box with a secret trip lever that opened a door. However, once the cat accidentally tripped the lever and escaped, the animal would go straight to the lever when placed back in the box. Hence, Thorndike formulated his famous **Law of Effect**, which says *behaviour with favourable consequences tends to be repeated, while behaviour with unfavourable consequences tends to disappear*.[5] This was a dramatic departure from the prevailing notion a century ago that behaviour was the product of inborn instincts.

Law of Effect
behaviour with favourable consequences is repeated; behaviour with unfavourable consequences disappears

Skinner's Operant Conditioning Model

Skinner refined Thorndike's conclusion that behaviour is controlled by its consequences. Skinner's work became known as *behaviourism* because he dealt strictly with observable behaviour.[6] As a behaviourist, Skinner believed it was pointless to explain behaviour in terms of unobservable inner states such as needs, drives, attitudes or thought processes.[7] He similarly put little credence in the idea of self-determination.

In his 1938 classic, *The Behaviour of Organisms*, Skinner drew an important distinction between the two types of behaviour: respondent and operant behaviour.[8] He labelled unlearned reflexes or stimulus–response (S–R) connections **respondent behaviour**. This category of behaviour was said to describe a very small proportion of adult human behaviour. Examples of respondent behaviour would include shedding tears while peeling onions and withdrawing one's hand on reflexive from a hot cooker.[9]

Respondent behaviour
Skinner's term for unlearned stimulus–response reflexes

Skinner attached the label **operant behaviour** to behaviour that is learned when one 'operates on' the environment to produce desired consequences. Some call this the response–stimulus (R–S) model. Years of controlled experiments with pigeons in 'Skinner boxes' helped Skinner develop a sophisticated technology of behaviour control, or operant conditioning. For example, he taught pigeons how to pace figure-eights and how to bowl by reinforcing the underweight (and thus hungry) birds with food whenever they more closely approximated target behaviours. Skinner's work has significant implications for OB because the vast majority of organizational behaviour falls into the operant category.[10]

Operant behaviour
Skinner's term for learned, consequence-shaped behaviour

PRINCIPLES OF BEHAVIOUR MODIFICATION

Although B Mod interventions in the workplace often involve widely used techniques such as goal setting, feedback, and rewards, B Mod is unique in its adherence to Skinner's operant model of learning.[11] To review, operant theorists assume it is more productive to deal with observable behaviour and its environmental determinants than with personality traits, perception, or inferred internal causes of behaviour such as needs or cognitions. The purpose of this section is to introduce important concepts and terminology associated with B Mod. Subsequent sections explore the application and research of B Mod and some of the issues both for and against its practice.

Behavioural contingencies
antecedent → behaviour → consequence (A→B→C) relationships

A→B→C Contingencies

To adequately understand the operant learning process, one needs a working knowledge of **behavioural contingencies**, as characterized by the A→B→C model. The initials stand for Antecedent, Behaviour, Consequence. When person–environment interaction is reduced to A→B→C terms (as in Figure 10–1), a **functional analysis** has taken place.[12]

Functional analysis
reducing person-environment interaction to A→B→C terms

Within the context of B Mod, *contingency* means that the antecedent, behaviour and consequence in a given A→B→C relationship are connected in an 'if-then' fashion. If the antecedent is present, then the behaviour is more likely to be displayed. If the behaviour is displayed, then the consequence is experienced. Furthermore, as learned from Thorndike's Law of Effect, if the consequence is pleasing, the behaviour will be strengthened (meaning it will occur more often). According to a pair of writers, one a clinical psychologist and the other a manager the following arises.

> *Some contingencies occur automatically; others we set up by linking our behavior with the behavior of others in an attempt to design an environment that will best serve our purposes. Setting up a contingency involves designating behaviors and assigning consequences to follow. We design contingencies for children fairly simply ('If you finish your homework, I'll let you watch television'), but influencing the behavior of people in the workforce is more difficult. As a result, managers often fail to use contingencies to their full advantage.*[13]

Let us look more closely at antecedents, behaviour and consequences to fully understand A→B→C contingencies.

Figure 10-1 *Productive Job Behavior Requires Supportive Antecedents and Consequences*

Antecedent→	Behavior→	Consequence	Behaviour Outcome
Manager: 'I suppose you haven't finished the payroll report yet.'	*Payroll clerk:* 'No way! I'm behind schedule because the supervisors didn't submit their payroll data on time.'	*Manager:* 'I'm sure everyone will enjoy getting their pay late again!'	The payroll clerk continues to make excuses while missing important deadlines because of the manager's negative antecedents and sarcastic consequences.
Manager: 'How are you coming along on this week's payroll report?'	*Payroll clerk:* 'I'm a little behind schedule. But if I work during my lunch hour, I'll have it in on time.'	*Manager:* 'I appreciate the extra effort! How would you like to spend tomorrow working on that bonus-pay project you suggested last week?'	The payroll clerk continues to meet important deadlines because of the manager's non-threatening antecedents and rewarding consequences.

The Role of Antecedents

Unlike the 'S' in the reflexive stimulus–response (S–R) model, antecedents *cue* rather than cause behaviour. For example, in classic S–R fashion, a blistering hot piece of pizza *causes* you to quickly withdraw it from your mouth. In contrast, an amber traffic light *cues* rather than causes you to brake. Because many motorists press the accelerator when a green traffic light changes to amber, traffic signals have *probable* rather than *absolute* control over driving behaviour. Antecedents get the power to cue certain behaviours from their associated consequences. For instance, if you have just been booked for jumping [ignoring] a red light, you will probably brake when encountering the next few ambers.

Focusing on Behaviour

True to Skinnerian behaviourism, B Mod proponents emphasize the practical value of focusing on behaviour. They caution against references to unobservable psychological states and general personality traits when explaining job performance (e.g., see Table 10-1). Phil's behavioural descriptions (the italicized portions in the bottom half of the table) give him a solid foundation for modifying Joe's behavioural performance problems.

When managers focus exclusively on behaviour, without regard to personality traits or cognitive processes, their approach qualifies as radical behaviourism.[14] As one might suspect, this extreme perspective has stirred debate and controversy, complete with philosophical and ethical implications.

Table 10-1

Behaviourists Explain How Managers Should Describe Job Behaviour: A Brief Case Study

---

The Wrong Way: Subjective appraisal of the **person,** rather than objective information about **performance.**

Phil Oaks, the department manager, describes his subordinate, Joe Scott, as follows:

> Well, Joe is just not easy to get along with. He's so disagreeable and negative all the time. He's very aggressive and disruptive. When he's unhappy he just sulks a lot, and he daydreams. He's also insubordinate and doesn't follow the rules. I don't know if he's immature, not intelligent, or irrational. Overall, his motivation is very low. He lacks drive and is generally hostile. I suspect that there may be a home problem also.

The Right Way: Objective information about **observable performance behaviors,** rather than subjective appraisal of the person.

In contrast, if Phil had training in pinpointing behaviors, he might describe Joe as follows:

> Well, whenever Joe is given some direction, he responds by immediately *telling you why it can't be done.* He frequently *threatens* other employees and has even been in one or two *fights.* He *leaves his own work area to tell jokes* to other workers. Sometimes he just *sits in a corner,* or *stares out the window* for several minutes.
>
> He has violated several company rules such as *smoking in a nonsmoking zone, working without safety goggles,* and *parking in a fire lane.* He can't seem to tell *right-handed prints from left-handed prints.* Also, he *arrived late for work* 10 times in the last month, and *returned from his break* late on 12 occasions.

SOURCE: Performance descriptions excerpted from C C Manz and H P Sims, Jr., *SuperLeadership: Leading Others to Lead Themselves* (New York: Prentice-Hall, 1989), pp 66–67.

Contingent Consequences

Contingent consequences, according to Skinner's operant theory, control behaviour in four ways: positive reinforcement, negative reinforcement, punishment and extinction.[15] These contingent consequences are managed systematically in B Mod programmes. To avoid the all-too-common mislabelling of these consequences, let us review some formal definitions.

Positive Reinforcement Strengthens Behaviour

Positive reinforcement is the process of strengthening a behaviour by contingently presenting something pleasing. (Remember that a behaviour is strengthened when it increases in frequency and weakened when it decreases in frequency.) A young design engineer who works overtime because of praise and recognition from the boss is responding to positive reinforcement.[16] Similarly, people tend to return to restaurants where they are positively reinforced with good food and friendly, high-quality service.[17]

Positive reinforcement *making behaviour occur more often by contingently presenting something positive*

Negative Reinforcement Also Strengthens Behaviour

Negative reinforcement is the process of strengthening a behaviour by contingently withdrawing something displeasing. For example, an army sergeant who stops yelling when a recruit jumps out of bed has negatively reinforced that particular behaviour. Similarly, the behaviour of clamping our hands over our ears when watching a jumbo jet take off is negatively reinforced by relief from the noise. Negative reinforcement is often confused with punishment. But the two strategies have opposite effects on behaviour. Negative reinforcement, as the word *reinforcement* indicates, strengthens a behaviour because it provides relief from an unpleasant situation.

Negative reinforcement *making behaviour occur more often by contingently withdrawing something negative*

Punishment Weakens Behaviour

Punishment
making behaviour occur less often by contingently presenting something negative or withdrawing something positive

Punishment is the process of weakening behaviour through either the contingent presentation of something displeasing or the contingent withdrawal of something positive. A manager assigning a tardy employee to a dirty job exemplifies the first type of punishment. Docking a tardy employee's pay is an example of the second type of punishment, called 'response cost' punishment. Legal fines involve response cost punishment. Salespeople who must make up any cash register shortages out of their own pockets are being managed through response cost punishment. Ethical questions can and should be raised about this type of punishment.[18]

International OB

North Americans Modify Behavior with Classical Music!

Canada

Music can do magical things, especially in Canada. First there was the 7-Eleven store in British Columbia that piped Muzak into the parking lot to keep teenagers from loitering. Out blasted the Mantovani and the kids scattered, leaving only a wake of Slurpee cups. Now downtown businesses in Edmonton, Alberta, are playing Bach and Mozart in a city park to drive away drug dealers and their clients. Police say drug activity in the park has dropped dramatically since Johann and Wolfgang arrived.

United States

If you want to chase away local louts, don't call the cops. Buy some cheap speakers. Ever since the owners of a Stockton, California, bar began blaring classical CDs into the streets, drug-pushing loiterers have cleared out. 'We pretty much stick to the opera one,' says co-owner Jeri Foppiano of her fave: 'Masters of Opera'. 'It seems to work the best.' Some opera fans protest the use of their beloved music as a torture device.

SOURCE: 'Let's Split!' *Newsweek*, August 20, 1990, p 2, and 'Scare Tactics,' *Newsweek*, September 25, 1995, p 10.

Extinction Also Weakens Behaviour

Extinction
making behaviour occur less often by ignoring it or not reinforcing it

Extinction is the weakening of a behaviour by ignoring it or making sure it is not reinforced. Getting rid of a former boyfriend or girlfriend by refusing to answer their phone calls is an extinction strategy. A good analogy for extinction is to imagine what would happen to your houseplants if you stopped watering them. Like a plant without water, a behaviour without occasional reinforcement eventually dies. Although very different processes, both punishment and extinction have the same weakening effect on behaviour.

How to Properly Categorize Contingent Consequences

In B Mod, consequences are defined in terms of their demonstrated impact on behaviour (see Figure 10–2), not subjectively or by their intended impact. For example, notice how one expert in the field distinguishes between reinforcement and rewards.

> *Reinforcement is distinguished from reward in that a reward is something that is perceived to be desirable and is delivered to an individual after performance. An increase in pay, a promotion, and a comment on good work performance may all be rewards. But rewards are not necessarily reinforcers. Reinforcers are defined by the increase in the rate of behaviour.[19]*

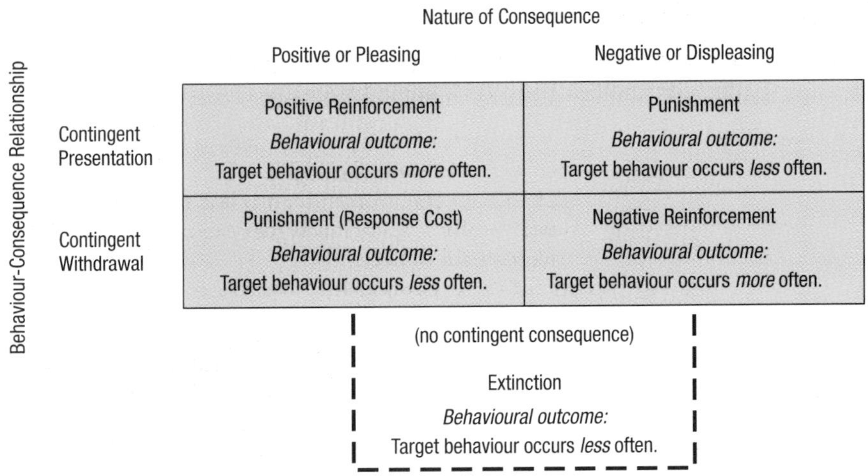

Figure 10–2

Contingent Consequences in Behaviour Modification

Nature of Consequence

	Positive or Pleasing	Negative or Displeasing
Contingent Presentation	Positive Reinforcement *Behavioural outcome:* Target behaviour occurs *more* often.	Punishment *Behavioural outcome:* Target behaviour occurs *less* often.
Contingent Withdrawal	Punishment (Response Cost) *Behavioural outcome:* Target behaviour occurs *less* often.	Negative Reinforcement *Behavioural outcome:* Target behaviour occurs *more* often.

Behaviour-Consequence Relationship

(no contingent consequence)

Extinction
Behavioural outcome:
Target behaviour occurs *less* often.

A promotion is both a reward and a positive reinforcer if the individual's performance subsequently improves.[20] On the other hand, *apparent* rewards may turn out to be the opposite.[21] For example, British Airways' decision to reform the way the airline rewards its most frequent flyers has brought about a storm of complaints, especially from some of BA's most regular—and important—customers. The passengers are unhappy about the new system that gives free short-haul flights to customers that have flown a certain number of kilometres. Under the former system, it was only the number of flights that counted, not the distance. Regular flyers to Paris now have to take up to four times more flights before they get the reward. On the other hand, the reward reform was installed after numerous complaints from people who regularly flew to distant locations... These passengers were not happy with the old system because it would have taken about 30 trips to Sydney for a passenger to qualify for a free journey to the same location. Under the BA's reformed system, only five such trips are needed . . .[22]

Contingent consequences are always categorized 'after the fact' by answering the following two questions:

▼ **Was something contingently presented or withdrawn?**

▼ **Did the target behaviour subsequently occur more or less often?**

Relying on what you have learned so far, can you figure out why BA's reward system actually turned out to be a punishment for a great deal of customers?

Schedules of Reinforcement

As just illustrated, contingent consequences are an important determinant of future behaviour. The *timing* of behavioural consequences can be even more important. Based on years of tedious laboratory experiments with pigeons in highly controlled environments, Skinner and his colleagues discovered distinct patterns of responding for various schedules of reinforcement.[23] Although some of their conclusions can be generalized to negative reinforcement, punishment and extinction, it is best to think only of positive reinforcement when discussing schedules.

Continuous Reinforcement

As indicated in Table 10–2, every instance of a target behaviour is reinforced when a **continuous reinforcement** (CRF) schedule is in effect. For instance, when your television set is operating properly, you are reinforced with a picture every time you turn it on (a CRF schedule). But, as with any CRF schedule of reinforcement, the behaviour of turning on the television will undergo rapid extinction if the set breaks

Continuous reinforcement
reinforcing every instance of a behaviour

Table 10-2 *Schedules of Reinforcement*

Schedule	Description	Probable Effects on Responding
Continuous (CRF)	Reinforcer follows every response.	Steady high rate of performance as long as reinforcement continues to follow every response. High frequency of reinforcement may lead to early satiation. Behavior weakens rapidly (undergoes extinction) when reinforcers are withheld. Appropriate for newly emitted, unstable, or low-frequency responses.
Intermittent	Reinforcer does not follow every response.	Capable of producing high frequencies of responding. Low frequency of reinforcement precludes early satiation. Appropriate for stable or high-frequency responses.
Fixed ratio (FR)	A fixed number of responses must be emitted before reinforcement occurs.	A fixed ratio of 1:1 (reinforcement occurs after every response); the same as a continuous schedule. Tends to produce a high rate of response, which is vigorous and steady.
Variable ratio (VR)	A varying or random number of responses must be emitted before reinforcement occurs.	Capable of producing a high rate of response, which is vigorous, steady, and resistant to extinction.
Fixed interval (FI)	The first response after a specific period of time has elapsed is reinforced.	Produces an uneven response pattern varying from a very slow, unenergetic response immediately following reinforcement to a very fast, vigorous response immediately preceding reinforcement.
Variable interval (VI)	The first response after varying or random periods of time have elapsed is reinforced.	Tends to produce a high rate of response, which is vigorous, steady, and resistant to extinction.

SOURCE: F Luthans and R Kreitner, *Organizational Behavior Modification and Beyond: An Operant and Social Learning Approach* (Glenview, IL: Scott, Foresman, 1985), p 58. Used with authors' permission.

Intermittent Reinforcement

Intermittent reinforcement
reinforcing some but not all instances of behaviour

Unlike CRF schedules, intermittent reinforcement involves reinforcement of some but not all instances of a target behaviour. Four subcategories of intermittent schedules, described in Table 10–2, are fixed and variable ratio schedules and fixed and variable interval schedules. Reinforcement in *ratio* schedules is contingent on the number of responses emitted. *Interval* reinforcement is tied to the passage of time. Some common examples of the four types of intermittent reinforcement are as follows.

▼ Fixed ratio: piece-rate pay; bonuses tied to the sale of a fixed number of units.

▼ Variable ratio: slot machines that pay out after a variable number of lever pulls; lotteries that pay out after the purchase of a variable number of tickets.

▼ Fixed interval: hourly pay; annual salary paid on a regular basis.

▼ Variable interval: random supervisory praise and 'pats on the back' for employees who have been doing a good job.

Scheduling is Critical

The schedule of reinforcement can more powerfully influence behaviour than the magnitude of reinforcement. Although this proposition grew out of experiments with pigeons, subsequent research in the workplace confirmed it. Consider, for example, a US field study of 12 unionized beaver trappers employed by a lumber company to keep the large rodents from eating newly planted tree seedlings.[24]

The beaver trappers were randomly divided into two groups that alternated weekly between two different bonus plans. Under the first bonus plan, each trapper earned his regular $7 an hour wage plus $1 for each beaver caught. Technically, this bonus was paid on a CRF schedule. The second plan involved the regular $7 an hour wage plus a one-in-four chance (determined by a roll of the dice) of receiving $4 for each beaver trapped. This second plan qualified as a variable ratio (VR-4) schedule. In the long run, both incentive plans averaged out to a $1-a-beaver bonus. Surprisingly, however, when the trappers were under the VR-4 schedule, they were 58 per cent more productive than under the CRF schedule, despite the fact that the net amount of pay averaged out the same for the two groups during the 12-week trapping season.

Work Organizations Typically Rely on the Weakest Schedule

Generally, variable ratio and variable interval schedules of reinforcement produce the strongest behaviour being one which is most resistant to extinction. As gamblers will attest, variable schedules hold the promise of reinforcement after the next target response. For example, the following drama at a Laughlin, Nevada, USA gambling casino is one more illustration of the potency of variable ratio reinforcement:

An elderly woman with a walker [Zimmer frame] had lost her grip on the slot
[machine] handle and had collapsed on the floor.
"Help," she cried weakly.
The woman at the machine next to her interrupted her play for a few seconds to try to
help her to her feet, but all around her the army of slot players continued feeding coins
to the machines. A security man arrived to soothe the woman and take her away.
"Thank you," she told him appreciatively.
"But don't forget my winnings." [25]

Organizations without at least some variable reinforcement are less likely to prompt this type of dedication to task. Despite the trend toward this sort of pay-for-performance, time-based pay schemes such as hourly wages and yearly salaries that rely on the weakest schedule of reinforcement (fixed interval) are still the rule in today's workplaces.

Behaviour Shaping

Have you ever wondered how trainers at aquarium parks manage to get bottle-nosed dolphins to do flips, killer whales to carry people on their backs, and seals to juggle balls? The results are seemingly magical. Actually, a mundane learning process called shaping is responsible for the animals' antics.

Two-ton killer whales, for example, have a big appetite, and they find buckets of fish very reinforcing. So if the trainer wants to ride a killer whale, he or she reinforces very basic behaviours that will eventually lead to the whale being ridden. The killer whale is contingently reinforced with a few fish for coming near the trainer, then for being touched, then for putting its nose in a harness, then for being straddled, and eventually for swimming with the trainer on its back. In effect, the trainer systematically raises the behavioural requirement for reinforcement. Thus, shaping is defined as the process of reinforcing closer and closer approximations to a target behaviour.

Shaping works very well with people, too, especially in training and quality programmes involving continuous improvement. Praise, recognition, and instructive and credible feedback cost managers little more than moments of their time.[26] Yet, when used in conjunction with a behaviour-shaping programme, these consequences can efficiently foster significant improvements in job performance.[27] The key to successful behaviour shaping lies in reducing a complex target behaviour to easily learned steps and then faithfully (and patiently) reinforcing any improvement.

Shaping
reinforcing closer and closer approximations to a target behaviour

A MODEL FOR MODIFYING JOB BEHAVIOUR

Someone once observed that children and pets are the world's best behaviour

Table 10-3

Ten Practical Tips for Shaping Job Behavior

1. *Accommodate the process of behavioral change.* Behaviors change in gradual stages, not in broad, sweeping motions.
2. *Define new behavior patterns specifically.* State what you wish to accomplish in explicit terms and in small amounts that can be easily grasped.
3. *Give individuals feedback on their performance.* A once-a-year performance appraisal is not sufficient.
4. *Reinforce behavior as quickly as possible.*
5. *Use powerful reinforcement.* To be effective, rewards must be important to the employee—not to the manager.
6. *Use a continuous reinforcement schedule.* New behaviors should be reinforced every time they occur. This reinforcement should continue until these behaviors become habitual.
7. *Use a variable reinforcement schedule for maintenance.* Even after behavior has become habitual, it still needs to be rewarded, though not necessarily every time it occurs.
8. *Reward teamwork—not competition.* Group goals and group rewards are one way to encourage cooperation in situations in which jobs and performance are interdependent.
9. *Make all rewards contingent on performance.*
10. *Never take good performance for granted.* Even superior performance, if left unrewarded, will eventually deteriorate.

SOURCE: Adapted from A T Hollingsworth and D Tanquay Hoyer, ' Supervisors Can Shape Behavior', *Personnel Journal*, May 1985, pp 86, 88.

modifiers. In fact, one of your authors responds obediently to his cats and jumps to satisfy contingencies arranged by them! Despite their ignorance of operant theory, children and pets are good behaviour modifiers because they: know precisely what behaviour they want to elicit; provide clear antecedents; and wield situationally appropriate and powerful contingent consequences. Let us learn from these 'masters' of behaviour modification and examine a four-step B Mod process for managing job behaviour[28] (see Figure 10-3). A review of practical implications follows.

Step 1: Identify Target Behaviour

Figure 10-3 *Modifying Work Place Behaviour*

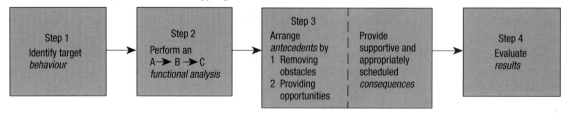

Managers who strictly follow the operant principle of focusing on observable behaviour rather than on inferred internal states, have two alternatives in step 1. They can pinpoint a *desirable* behaviour that occurs too *seldom* (such as contributing creative ideas at staff meetings), or they can focus on an *undesirable* behaviour that occurs too *often* (such as making disruptive comments at staff meetings).[29] Organizational behaviour modification proponents prefer the first alternative because it requires managers to see things in a positive, growth-oriented manner instead of in a negative, punitive manner. As a case in point, researchers have documented the benefits of 'well pay' versus the costs of traditional sick pay.[30] In short, every undesirable behaviour has a desirable opposite. Just a few of the many possible examples are: being absent/being on time, having an accident/working safely, remaining aloof/participating actively, procrastinating/completing assignments on time, competing destructively/being a team player.

Pointers for Identifying Behaviour

According to the former editor of the *Journal of Organizational Behaviour Management*, a journal devoted to the study of B Mod in the workplace, too many B Mod programmes focus on process (rule following) rather than on accomplishments. Thus, he offers the following three pointers for identifying target behaviours.

1   The primary focus should be on accomplishments or outcomes. These accomplishments should have significant organizational impact.

2   The targeting of process behaviours (rule adherence, etc.) should only occur when that behaviour can be functionally related to a significant organizational accomplishment.

3   There should be broad participation in the development of behavioural targets.[31]

These pointers are intended to prevent managers from falling victim to charges of unethical manipulation.

A Word of Caution about Shifting the Focus from Behaviour to Results

In laboratory settings or highly controlled situations such as lectures or machine shops, it is possible to directly observe and record the frequency of specific behaviours. Asking a question in a lecture, arriving late at work, and handing in an error-free report are all observable behavioural events. However, in today's complex organizations, it is not always possible (or desirable) to observe and record work behaviours firsthand. For example, top-level managers and technical specialists often spend time alone in closed offices. Field sales personnel and consultants also work 'out of sight.' When work behaviour cannot be monitored firsthand, the next-best alternative is to monitor results. Examples include number of units sold, number of customer complaints, degree of goal attainment, and percentage of projects completed. Managers who build contingencies around results need to keep in mind that those contingencies will be less precise than ones anchored to observable behavioural events.[32] For instance, the wrong person could be reinforced because organizational politicians sometimes take credit for others' results.

Step 2: Functionally Analyse the Situation

Any behaviours occurring on a regular basis necessarily have their own supportive cues and consequences. Thus, it is important for managers to identify existing A→B→C contingencies before trying to rearrange things. For example, it is important to know that a recently unco-operative employee is being pressured by co-workers to vote yes in an upcoming union certification election.

Step 3: Arrange Antecedents and Provide Consequences

In this third step, analysis gives way to action. An instructive way to discuss this step is to explore antecedent management and consequence management separately. In practice, though, antecedent and consequence management are closely intertwined.

Managing Antecedents

As specified in step 3 of Figure 10–3, antecedent management involves two basic strategies: removing obstacles; and/or providing opportunities. Some practical suggestions are listed in Table 10–4. Based on the discussion of goal setting in Chapter 8, the use of challenging objectives that specify what and when something is to be accomplished are probably the most potent antecedent management tool. For instance, supervisors in one study handed in their weekly reports more promptly when they were given specific target dates.[33]

By rearranging apparently insignificant antecedents, significant results can be achieved. Importantly, these must be *contingent* antecedents, as identified through an A→B→C functional analysis. For example, a telephone company was losing an estimated 270,000 Euro annually because its telephone installers were not reporting the installation of 'ceiling drops'. A ceiling drop involves installing extra wiring to compensate for a lowered ceiling. Despite comprehensive training on how to install and report ceiling drops, a large percentage of ceiling drops remained unreported and thus unbilled by the company. The following turn of events then took place.

> *A specialist in training design was called in to find out why the training had failed. She noted a curious thing. The form that the installers were required to fill out was extremely complicated and the part dealing with ceiling drops was even more complicated.*

> *One small change was made by adding a box where the installer could merely check 'ceiling drop installed'. Now the installer no longer had to fill out an extensive explanation of what took place in the house. Within one week after the change in the form, the number of ceiling drops reported and charged back to the customers had increased dramatically, far above what it was immediately after the training sessions.*[34]

Summarizing, from a B Mod perspective the telephone installers did not have an attitude or motivation problem. Nor did they have a knowledge deficiency requiring more training. They simply did not report ceiling drops because it was too complicated to do so. The streamlined reporting form presented the installers with an opportunity to behave properly, whereas the old form was an obstacle to good performance. In A→B→C terms, the streamlined reporting form became an antecedent that efficiently cured the desired behaviour.

Table 10–4

Paving the Way for Good Job Performance with Helpful Antecedents

Remove Obstacles	Provide Opportunities
Eliminate unrealistic plans, schedules, and deadlines.	Formulate difficult but attainable goals.
Identify and remedy skill deficiencies through training.	Provide clear instructions.
Eliminate confusing or contradictory rules.	Give friendly reminders, constructive suggestions, and helpful tips.
Avoid conflicting orders and priorities.	Ask nonthreatening questions about progress.
Remove distracting co-workers.	Display posters with helpful advice.
	Rely on easy-to-use forms.
	Build enthusiasm and commitment through participation and challenging work assignments.
	Promote personal growth and development through training.

Managing Consequences

Step 3 in Figure 10–3 calls for providing supportive and appropriately scheduled consequences. The following are six guidelines for successfully managing consequences during B Mod.

1 *Reinforce improvement not just final results.* Proper shaping cannot occur if the behavioural requirement for reinforcement is too demanding. Behaviour undergoes extinction when it is not shaped in achievable step-by-step increments.

2 *Fit the consequences to the behaviour.* A pair of B Mod scholars interpreted this guideline as follows.

Overrewarding a worker may make him feel guilty and certainly reinforces his current performance level. If the performance level is lower than that of others who get the same reward, he has no reason to increase his output. When a worker is underrewarded, he becomes angry with the system. His behaviour is being extinguished and the company may be forcing the good employee (underrewarded) to seek employment elsewhere while encouraging the poor employee (overrewarded) to stay on.[35]

Note how this recommendation is consistent with the discussion of equity theory in Chapter 8.

3 *Emphasize natural rewards over contrived rewards.* Natural rewards are potentially reinforcing consequences derived from day-to-day social and administrative interactions. Typical natural rewards include supervisory praise, assignment to favoured tasks, early time off with pay, flexible work schedules, and extended breaks. Contrived rewards include money and other tangible rewards. In relation to this distinction, it has been pointed out that:

> **Natural rewards**
> *normal social interactions such as praise or recognition*

Natural social rewards are potentially the most powerful and universally applicable reinforcers. In contrast to contrived rewards, they do not generally lead to satiation (people seldom get tired of compliments, attention or recognition) and can be administered on a very contingent basis.[36]

4 *Provide individuals with objective feedback whenever possible.* As discussed in Chapter 9, objective feedback can have a positive impact on future behaviour. This is particularly true when people have the opportunity to keep track of their own performance.[37] The three-way marriage of goal setting, objective feedback and positive reinforcement for improvement, can be fruitful indeed. For example, a field study of college hockey players demonstrated that a B Mod intervention of goal setting, feedback and praise increased the team's winning percentage by almost 100 per cent for two consecutive years.[38]

5 *Emphasize positive reinforcement; de-emphasize punishment.* Proponents of B Mod in the workplace, as mentioned earlier, recommend building up good behaviour with positive reinforcement instead of tearing down bad behaviour with punishment.[39] For instance, the authors of the best-seller, *The One Minute Manager*, told their readers to 'catch them doing something right!'[40] In other words, managers who focus on what's right with job performance unavoidably end up emphasizing positive reinforcement.

Regarding the use of punishment, operant researchers found it tends to suppress undesirable behaviour only temporarily while prompting emotional side effects. For example, a computer programmer who is reprimanded publicly for failing to 'debug' an important programme may get even with the boss by skillfully sabotaging another programme. Moreover, those punished come to fear and dislike the person administering the punishment.[41] Thus, it is unlikely that punitive managers can build the climate of trust so necessary for success in today's TQM-oriented organizations. For example, the 'giant retailer W T Grant, which went bankrupt in 1975, made it a practice to cut the tie of any sales manager who did not meet his quota.'[42] Constructive and positive feedback is a proven alternative to punishment (for example, see the next International OB).

6 *Schedule reinforcement appropriately.* Once again, immature behaviour requires the nurture of continuous reinforcement. Established or habitual behaviour, in contrast, can be maintained with fixed or variable schedules of intermittent reinforcement.

International OB

http://www.russiatoday.com

Organizational Behavior Modification (OB Mod) Successfully Exported to Russia

The Setting*

The study was conducted at the largest textile mill in Russia. The mill employed about 8,000 employees at the time of the study, late spring of 1990. This was after Gorbachev's perestroika (economic and political restructuring) had been implemented, but before the breakup of the Soviet Union. The factory is located in Tver (formerly Kalinin), about 96 miles northwest of Moscow.

The Intervention**

The supervisors were instructed on examples of specific functional and dysfunctional performance behaviors and were encouraged to ask clarifying questions. The researchers then instructed the supervisors to administer recognition and praise when workers performed the functional behaviors and to provide specific feedback to them about these behaviors. The supervisors were also instructed to give reminders and make corrections when they observed the dysfunctional behaviors but were specifically told not to give negative reprimands or punishment.

The Results*

First, the introduction of an OB Mod intervention led to an increase in functional behavior and a decrease in dysfunctional behavior among the [33] workers in this study. Second, the impact was more immediate and distinctive for eliminating undesired behaviors than for increasing desired behaviors. Third, both the functional and dysfunctional behaviors failed to reverse after the withdrawal of the intervention.

*Excerpted from D H B Welsh, F Luthans and S M Sommer, 'Organizational Behavior Modification Goes to Russia: Replicating an Experimental Analysis Across Cultures and Tasks', *Journal of Organizational Behavior Management*, no. 2, 1993, pp 15–35.

**Excerpted from D H B Welsh, F Luthans, and S M Sommer, 'Managing Russian Factory Workers: The Impact of US-Based Behavioral and Participative Techniques', *Academy of Management Journal*, February 1993, pp 58–79.

Step 4: Evaluate Results

B Mod intervention is effective if: a desirable target behaviour occurs more often; or an undesirable target behaviour occurs less often. Since *more* and *less* are relative terms, managers need a measurement tool that provides an objective basis for comparing pre-intervention with post-intervention data. This is where baseline data and behaviour charting can make a valuable contribution.

Baseline data
pre-intervention data collected by someone other than the target person

Baseline data are pre-intervention behavioural data collected without the target person's knowledge. This 'before' measure later provides a basis for assessing an intervention's effectiveness.

Behaviour chart
programme evaluation graph with baseline and intervention data

A behaviour chart is a B Mod programme evaluation tool that includes both pre-intervention baseline data and post-intervention data. The vertical axis of a behaviour chart can be expressed in terms of behaviour frequency, a percentage or results attained. A time dimension is typically found on the horizontal axis of a behaviour chart. When a goal is included, as shown in Figure 10–4, a behaviour chart quickly tells the individual where his or her performance has been, is, and should be. As the successful safety programme for bus drivers, discussed at the opening of this chapter illustrates, posted feedback can be a very effective management tool. Moreover, a behaviour chart provides an ongoing evaluation of a B Mod programme.

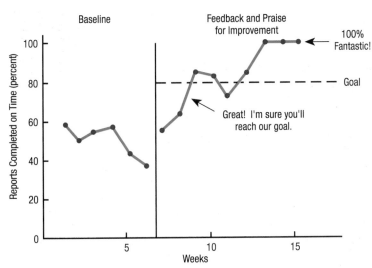

Figure 10–4

Behaviour Charts Help Evaluate B Mod Programs and Provide Feedback

SOURCE: 'Graping Employee Performance: An Effective Feedback Technique', by Rodney et al. Reprinted from *Supervisory Management*, December 1985, © 1985 American Management Association International. Reprinted by permission of the American Management Association International, New York, N.Y. All rights reserved. http://www.amanet.org

Some Practical Implications

Some believe B Mod does not belong in the workplace.[43] They see it as blatantly manipulative, demeaning and a threat to intrinsic motivation. Although even the severest critics admit it works, they rightly point out that workplace applications of B Mod have focused on superficial rule-following behaviour, such as getting to work on time. Indeed, B Mod is still in the transition phase from highly controlled and simple laboratory and clinical settings to loosely controlled and complex organizational settings.[44] A promising application of B Mod in recent years has been in the area of employee safety and accident prevention.[45] Research evidence is encouraging. According to a recent meta-analysis of 19 studies encompassing 2,818 subjects, OB Mod programmes were associated with a 17 per cent increase in job performance.[46] Despite the need for more B Mod research and application in complex organizations, some practical lessons have been learned already.

First, it is very difficult and maybe impossible to change organizational behaviour without systematically managing antecedents and contingent consequences. Second, even the best-intentioned reward system will fail if it does not include clear behaviour–consequence contingencies. Third, behaviour shaping is a valuable developmental technique. Fourth, goal setting, objective feedback, and positive reinforcement for improvement, when combined in systematic A→B→C fashion, are powerful management tools. Finally, because formal programme evaluation is fundamental to B Mod, those who use it in the workplace can be held accountable.

Why OB Mod is so Unpopular in Europe

Behavioural modification with its emphasis on 'rewards for good behaviour' seems to fit excellently with American values, such as individualism, competition, profit-orientation and so forth. European OB specialists, on the contrary, loathe behavioural modification for at least one of the following reasons[47]:

1 Europe has a strong humanistic tradition. 'Behaviour is shaped by its consequences' seems to deny that behaviour is shaped by free choice, intention and purposes. Employees do not have an array of behaviour at their disposal from which to choose. Rather, they are led into an increasingly narrow number of options, that is, the behaviours rewarded by management. This deprives

employees of their dignity and freedom of choice and is in fact the opposite of the notion of empowerment.[48] Skinner's most popular book on behaviourism bears the title *Beyond Freedom and Dignity*, as a kind of direct attack on European values.

2   Behavioural modification is overtly manipulative and its techniques can be so strong and effective that they arouse serious ethical questions. It is very easy for people to get addicted to gambling. Is it acceptable to use the same techniques as casinos do to 'motivate' employees? The ethical questions are described in Anthony Burgess's novel *A Clockwork Orange* where the leading character, Alex, is used as a guinea pig for an OB Mod experiment, loosing his free will. Can the use of techniques initially designed for the treatment of mental disorders be justified in the workplace? An alternative strategy to improve safety at the workplace is presented by Ricky Gilby, a specialist in this field of safety. According to her, accidents are multi-causal, and it only takes a trigger to make them happen. As an example, she takes the Zeebrugge example, the capsizing of the *Herald of Free Enterprise*, which was caused by a chain of events: the bosun being asleep, design failures, management failures, the culture of the owning company . . . . Instead of using the behaviour-based approach, she proposes the development of a positive 'safety culture'.[49]

3   Behavioural modification shifts the attention from intrinsic to extrinsic motivation. Why do we have to reinforce employees with extrinsic rewards for behaviour that should be intrinsically rewarded? This system may imply that management no longer seeks to enrich the tasks, that jobs that could have been made meaningful remain dull and monotone. Employees, on the other hand, may start to think that there is something wrong with their jobs, as management has to resort to rewards and punishments.

BEHAVIOURAL SELF-MANAGEMENT

Judging from the number of diet books appearing on best-seller lists each year, self-control seems to be in rather short supply. For example, musicians from the Royal College of London recently introduced the following high-tech form of self-control.

Twenty-two musicians have been trained how to improve their performance by learning to control their brain rythms using a computer game. They were taught how to access a relaxed brain state with a game that responded to the electrical activity in their heads. Professional musicians, asked to rate their performances after training, found that the quality of their music, emotional commitment and interpretive imagination all improved. To learn how to control their brain rythms, the musicians were shown a picture of a boat and asked to make it sail towards the horizon. This only happened when they achieved the desired brain state. 'First you try as hard as you can to make the boat move, and it just goes backwards,' John Gruzelier, professor of psychology at Imperial College Medical School, told the British Association's Festival of Science. 'Soon you learn to go with the flow, and let your brain do all the work for you. The idea is that having learned how to do this in the laboratory, you can turn it on anywhere. It would probably take 100 years to do it without the feedback.'[50]

Historically, when someone sought to wage the war of self-control, he or she was told to exercise willpower, be self-disciplined, resist temptation or seek divine guidance. Although well-intentioned, this advice gives the individual very little to go on relative to actually changing one's behaviour. Fortunately, behavioural scientists formulated step-by-step self-management models that have helped individuals conquer serious behavioural problems. Typical among these problems are alcohol and drug abuse, overeating, cigarette smoking, phobias, and antisocial behaviour. True to its interdisciplinary nature, the field of OB has recently translated self-management theory and techniques from the clinic to the workplace.

Formally defined, **behavioural self-management** (BSM) is the process of modifying one's own behaviour by systematically managing cues, cognitive processes and contingent consequences. The term *behavioural* signifies that BSM focuses primarily on modifying behaviour rather than on changing values, attitudes or personalities. At first glance, BSM appears to be little more than self-imposed B Mod. But BSM differs from B Mod in that cognitive processes are considered in BSM while they are ignored in B Mod. This adjustment reflects the influence of Albert Bandura's extension of operant theory into social learning theory.

Behavioural self-management
modifying one's own behaviour by managing cues, cognitive processes and consequences

In this section, we discuss Bandura's social learning theory, from which BSM has evolved. Next, a brief overview of the managerial context for BSM is presented. A social learning model of self-management is then introduced and explored, followed by some practical implications of relevant research findings.

Bandura's Social Learning Theory

Albert Bandura built on Skinner's work by initially demonstrating how people acquire new behaviour by imitating role models (called vicarious learning) and later exploring the cognitive processing of cues and consequences. (Recall our discussion of the Stanford psychologist's ideas about self-efficacy in Chapter 5.) Like Skinner's operant model, Bandura's approach makes observable behaviour the primary unit of analysis. Bandura also goes along with Skinner's contention that behaviour is controlled by environmental cues and consequences. However, Bandura has extended Skinner's operant model by emphasizing that cognitive or mental processes affect how one responds to surroundings. In short, Bandura considers factors *inside* the individual, whereas the operant model stays outside the person. This extension is called social learning theory.[51]

A Managerial Context for Behavioural Self-Management

OB scholars, Fred Luthans and Tim Davis, developed the managerial context for BSM as follows.

Research and writing in the management field have given a great deal of attention to managing societies, organizations, groups, and individuals. Strangely, almost no one has paid any attention to managing oneself more effectively. . . . Self-management seems to be a basic prerequisite for effective management of other people, groups, organizations, and societies.[52]

Moreover, some have wrapped BSM in ethical terms. 'Proponents of self-control contend that it is more ethically defensible than externally imposed behaviour control techniques when used for job enrichment, behaviour modification, management by objectives or organization development.'[53] Others have placed self-management within a managerial context by discussing it as a substitute for hierarchical leadership.[54] Behavioural self-management also meshes well with today's emphasis on empowerment, self-managed teams, self-directed learning and total quality management (TQM).[55] Remember that *everyone* is responsible for product and service quality in a TQM environment.

Social Learning Model of Self-Management

Bandura put self-management into a social learning context by noting the following.

[A] distinguishing feature of social learning theory is the prominent role it assigns to self-regulatory capacities. By arranging environmental inducements, generating cognitive supports, and producing consequences for their own actions people are able to exercise some measure of control over their own behaviour.[56]

In other words, to the extent that you can control your environment and your cognitive representations of your environment, you are the master of your own behaviour. The practical BSM model displayed in Figure 10−5 is derived from social learning theory. Reflecting Bandura's extension of Skinner's basic A→B→C model, the BSM model includes the person's psychological self. The two-headed arrows reflect Bandura's contention, discussed previously, that the individual has a degree of control over his or her own antecedent cues, behaviour and consequences. Each of the four major components of this BSM model requires a closer look. Since this is a behavioural model, let us begin our examination with the behaviour component in the centre of the triangle.[57]

Figure 10−5

A Social Learning Model of Self-Management

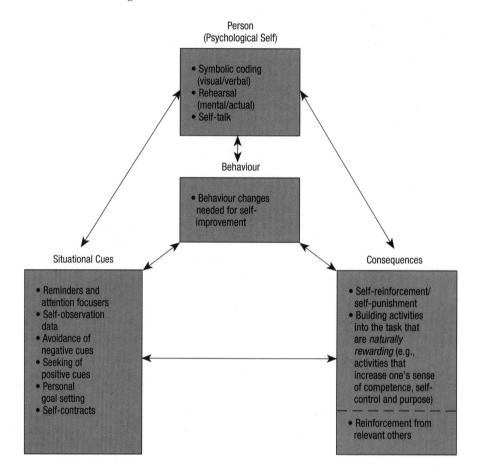

An Agenda for Self-Improvement

Self-improvement and self-development are more important than ever due to the *new employment contract* discussed in Chapter 1. Corporate hand-holding up each rung of a well-defined career ladder has become a thing of the past. Now, employees are told they 'own their own employability'. They must make the best of themselves and any opportunities that may come along. A brochure at Intel Corp., the computer-chip giant, tells employees: 'No one is more interested or qualified when it comes to evaluating your individual interests, values, skills and goals than you are.'[58] The new age of *career self-management* challenges you to do a better job of setting personal goals, having clear priorities, being well organized, skillfully managing your time, and developing a self-learning programme.[59]

Fortunately, Stephen R Covey, in his best-selling book *The 7 Habits of Highly Effective People*, has given managers a helpful agenda for improving themselves (see Table 10−5). Covey refers to the seven habits, practised by truly successful people, as 'principle-centred, character-based'.[60] The first step for those practicing BSM is to pick one or more of the seven habits that are personal trouble spots and translate them to specific behaviours. For example, 'think win/win' might remind a conflict-prone manager to practise co-operative teamwork behaviour with co-workers. Habit number five might prompt another manager to stop interrupting others during conversations.

As a procedural note, behaviour charts can be used in BSM to evaluate progress toward one's goals but baseline data, ideally, should be collected by someone else to ensure objectivity.[61]

Table 10–5

Covey's Seven Habits: An Agenda for Managerial Self-Improvement

1. *Be proactive.* Choose the right means and ends in life, and take personal responsibility for your actions. Make timely decisions and make positive progress.
2. *Begin with the end in mind.* When all is said and done, how do you want to be remembered? Be goal oriented.
3. *Put first things first.* Establish firm priorities that will help you accomplish your mission in life. Strike a balance between your daily work and your potential for future accomplishments.
4. *Think win/win.* Cooperatively seek creative and mutually beneficial solutions to problems and conflicts.
5. *Seek first to understand, then to be understood.* Strive hard to become a better listener.
6. *Synergize.* Because the whole is greater than the sum of its parts, you need to generate teamwork among individuals with unique abilities and potential. Value interpersonal differences.
7. *Sharpen the saw.* "This is the habit of self-renewal, which has four elements. The first is mental, which includes reading, visualizing, planning, and writing. The second is spiritual, which means value clarification and commitment, study, and meditation. Third is social/emotional, which involves service, empathy, synergy, and intrinsic security. Finally, the physical element includes exercise, nutrition, and stress management."

SOURCES: Adapted from discussion in S R Covey, *The 7 Habits of Highly Effective People* (New York: Simon & Schuster, 1989). Excerpt from 'Q & A with Stephen Covey', *Training*, December 1992, p 38.

Managing Situational Cues

When people try to give up a nagging habit such as smoking, the cards are stacked against them. Many people (friends who smoke) and situations (after dinner, when under stress at work, or when relaxing) serve as subtle yet powerful cues telling the individual to light up. If the behaviour is to be changed, the cues need to be rearranged so as to trigger the alternative behaviour. Six techniques for managing situational cues are listed in the left column of Figure 10–5.

Reminders and attention focusers do just that. For example, many students and managers cue themselves about deadlines and appointments with Post-It™ notes stuck all over their work areas, refrigerators and dashboards. Self-observation data, when compared against a goal or standard, can be a potent cue for improvement. Those who keep a weight chart near their bathroom scale will attest to the value of this tactic. Successful self-management calls for avoiding negative cues while seeking positive ones. Managers in the US-based Northwestern Mutual Life Insurance Company's new business department appreciate the value of avoiding negative cues 'On Wednesdays, the department shuts off all incoming calls, allowing workers to speed processing of new policies. On those days, the unit averages 23 per cent more policies than on other days.'[62]

Goals, as repeatedly mentioned in this text, are the touchstone of good management. So it is with challenging yet attainable personal goals and effective self-management. Goals simultaneously provide a target and a measuring stick of progress.[63] Finally, a self-contract is an 'if–then' agreement with oneself. For example, if you can define all the key terms in this chapter, then treat yourself to something special.

Arranging Cognitive Supports

This component makes BSM distinctly different from conventional behaviour modification. Referring to the *person* portion of the self-management model in Figure 10–5, the three cognitive supports for behaviour change are symbolic coding, rehearsal and self-talk. These amount to psychological, as opposed to environmental, cues. Yet, according to Bandura, they prompt appropriate behaviour in the same manner. Each requires a brief explanation.

Symbolic coding: From a social learning theory perspective, the human brain stores information in visual and verbal codes. For example, a sales manager could use the visual picture of a man chopping down a huge tree to remember Woodman, the name of a promising new client. In contrast, people commonly rely on acronyms to recall names, rules for behaviour, and other information. An acronym (or verbal code) that is often heard in managerial circles is the KISS principle, standing for 'Keep It Simple, Stupid.'

Rehearsal: While it is true that practise often makes perfect, one's chances of success can also be increased by the mental rehearsal of challenging tasks. Importantly, experts draw a clear distinction between systematic visualization of how one should proceed and daydreaming about success. Job-finding seminars are very popular on college campuses today because they typically involve both mental and actual rehearsals of tough job interviews. This sort of manufactured experience can build the confidence and self-efficacy necessary for real-world success.[64]

| **Self-talk** |
| *evaluating thoughts about oneself* |

Self-talk: According to an expert on the subject, 'self-talk is the set of evaluating thoughts that you give yourself about facts and events that happen to you'.[65] Personal experience tells us that self-talk tends to be a self-fulfilling prophecy. Negative self-talk tends to pave the way for failure, whereas positive self-talk often facilitates success. Replacing negative self-talk ('I'll never get a raise') with positive self-talk ('I deserve a raise and I'm going to get it') is fundamental to better self-management.[66] One business writer, while urging salespeople to be their own cheerleaders, offered the following advice for handling difficult situations.

> *Tell yourself there's a positive side to everything and train yourself to focus on it. At first your new self-talk will seem forced and unnatural, but stick with it. Use mental imagery to help you concentrate on the benefits of what you think is a bad situation. If you don't like cold calling, for example, think of how good you'll feel when you're finished, knowing you have a whole list of new selling opportunities. Forming a new habit isn't easy, but the effort will pay off.[67]*

Self-Reinforcement

The satisfaction of self-contracts and other personal achievements calls for self-reinforcement. According to Bandura, three criteria must be satisfied before self-reinforcement can occur.

1 The individual must have control over desired reinforcers.

2 Reinforcers must be self-administered on a conditional basis. Failure to meet the performance requirement must lead to self-denial.

3 Performance standards must be adopted to establish the quantity and quality of target behaviour required for self-reinforcement.[68]

In view of the following realities, self-reinforcement strategies need to be resourceful and creative.

> *Self-granted rewards can lead to self-improvement. But as failed dieters and smokers can attest, there are short-run as well as long-run influences on self-reinforcement. For the overeater, the immediate gratification of eating has more influence than the promise of a new wardrobe. The same sort of dilemma plagues procrastinators. Consequently, one needs to weave a powerful web of cues, cognitive supports, and*

internal and external consequences to win the tug-of-war with status-quo payoffs. Primarily because it is so easy to avoid, self-punishment tends to be ineffectual. As with managing the behaviour of others, positive instead of negative consequences are recommended for effective self-management.[69]

In addition, it helps to solicit positive reinforcement for self-improvement from supportive friends, co-workers and relatives.

Research and Managerial Implications

There is ample evidence that behavioural self-management works. For example, in one controlled study of 20 college students, 17 were able to successfully modify their own behaviour problems involving smoking, lack of assertiveness, poor study habits, over-eating, sloppy housekeeping, lack of exercise, and moodiness.[70] Research on self-monitoring, discussed in Chapter 5, may help explain why BSM works for some but not for others.[71] High self-monitors are likely to have an advantage over low self-monitors because they are more concerned about their social behaviour and tend to be more adaptable.

Because BSM has only recently been transplanted from clinical and classroom applications to the workplace, so job research evidence is limited. One pair of researchers reported successful BSM interventions in response to managerial problems, including those of over-dependence on the boss, ignoring paperwork, leaving the office without notifying anyone, and failing to fill out expense reports.[72] Also, absenteeism of unionized state government employees was significantly reduced with BSM training.[73] A survey of 36 organization development consultants found positive applications of mental imagery and visualization were used to solve organizational problems.[74] These preliminary studies need to be supplemented by research on how, why, and under what conditions, BSM does or does not work.[75] In the meantime, current and future managers can fine-tune their own behaviour by taking lessons from proven self-management techniques.

Summary of Key Concepts

1 State Thorndike's Law of Effect, and explain Skinner's distinction between respondent and operant behaviour.

According to Edward L Thorndike's Law of Effect, behaviour with favourable consequences tends to be repeated, while behaviour with unfavourable consequences tends to disappear. B F Skinner used the term *respondent behaviour* to describe unlearned stimulus–response reflexes. He applied the term *operant behaviour* to all behaviour learned through experience with environmental consequences.

2 Define the term behaviour modification, and explain the A→B→C model.

Behaviour modification (B Mod) is defined as the process of making specific behaviour occur more or less often by systematically managing (a) antecedent cues and (b) contingent consequences. B Mod involves managing person–environment interactions that can be functionally analysed into antecedent→ behaviour→ consequence (A→B→C) relationships. Antecedents cue rather than cause subsequent behaviour. Contingent consequences, in turn, either strengthen or weaken that behaviour.

3 Demonstrate your knowledge of positive reinforcement, negative reinforcement, punishment and extinction.

Positive and negative reinforcement are consequence management strategies that strengthen behaviour, whereas punishment and extinction weaken behaviour. These strategies need to be defined objectively in terms of their actual impact on behaviour frequency, not subjectively on the basis of intended impact.

4 Distinguish between continuous and intermittent schedules of reinforcement; and specify which schedules are most resistant to extinction.

Every instance of a behaviour is reinforced with a continuous reinforcement (CRF) schedule. Under intermittent reinforcement schedules–fixed and variable ratio or fixed and variable interval–some, rather than all, instances of a target behaviour are reinforced. Variable schedules produce the most extinction-resistant behaviour.

5 Demonstrate your knowledge of behaviour shaping.

Behaviour shaping occurs when closer and closer approximations of a target behaviour are reinforced. In effect, the standard for reinforcement is made more difficult as the individual learns. The process begins with continuous reinforcement, which gives way to intermittent reinforcement when the target behaviour becomes strong and habitual.

6 Identify and briefly explain each step in the four-step B Mod process.

Job behaviour can be modified with the following four-step model: identify target behaviour; functionally analyse the situation; arrange antecedents and provide consequences; and evaluate results. Behaviour charts, with baseline data for before-and-after comparison, are a practical way of evaluating the effectiveness of a B Mod programme.

7 Specify the six guidelines for managing consequences during B Mod.

(a) Reinforce improvement, not just final results. (b) Fit the consequences to the behaviour. (c) Emphasize natural rewards over contrived rewards. (d) Provide individuals with objective feedback whenever possible. (e) Emphasize positive reinforcement; de-emphasize punishment. (f) Schedule reinforcement appropriately.

8 Give three reasons why OB Mod is unpopular in Europe.

OB Mod is fundamentally opposed to the European humanistic, structuralistic and phenomenological management approach; OB Mod is overtly manipulative, which gives way to ethical questions; and OB Mod shifts the attention from intrinsic to extrinsic motivation.

9 Explain the social learning model of self-management.

Behaviour results from interaction between four components: situational cues; the person's psychological self; the person's behaviour; and consequences. Behaviour, such as Covey's seven habits of highly effective people, can be developed by relying on supportive cognitive processes such as mental rehearsal and self-talk. Carefully arranged cues and consequences also help in the self-improvement process.

Discussion Questions

1 What would an A→B→C functional analysis of you departing your residence *on time* for college or work look like? How about a functional analysis of your leaving late?

2 Why is the term *contingency* central to understanding the basics of B Mod?

3 What real-life examples of positive reinforcement, negative reinforcement, both forms of punishment, and extinction can you draw from your recent experience? Were these strategies appropriately or inappropriately used?

4 From a schedule of reinforcement perspective, why do people find gambling so addictive?

5 What sort of behaviour-shaping have you engaged in lately? Explain your success or failure.

6 With respect to the six guidelines for successfully managing consequences, which do you think ranks as the most important? Explain your rationale.

7 Why is valid baseline data essential in a B Mod programme?

8 What sort of luck have you had with self-management recently? Which of the self-management techniques discussed in this chapter would help you do better?

9 Do you agree with the assumption that managers need to do a good job with self-management before they can effectively manage others? Explain.

10 What importance would you attach to self-talk in self-management? Explain.

Internet Exercise

www.bfskinner.org

Biographical Information on B F Skinner

Even after his death, Skinner remains one of the most widely recognized and controversial people in the behavioural sciences. Whether or not you like his ideas about human behaviour, he was an intriguing man who led an interesting and unconventional life. See the B F Skinner Foundation Web site (www.bfskinner.org) and select 'About B F Skinner' to read about the many contributions of Skinner to the field of psychology. Also select 'publications' and 'media' for an interesting and instructive historical perspective. The subheading 'audio' contains some selected audio presentations given by B F Skinner.

Instructive Features on Self-Talk

www.accessyourpower.com/Positive.asp

As we discussed in this chapter, self-talk is a valuable tool in self-management programs. This website will help you to better understand this technique. Go to www.accessyourpower.com /Positive.asp and read the main text, containing some good examples of positive and negative self-talk. After reading this overview, go to the sections on "using your power", "understand your power" and "laws of the mind". If you practice any sports, you might also want to check the section on sports enhancement.

Questions

1 Do you believe in the power of self-talk? Explain.

2 How often do you use negative self-talk? Are you boxed in by it? Relative to what behaviours, characteristics or goals?

3 Do you already rely on positive self-talk? In what circumstances? Does it work?

4 How can you improve your self-talk strategies? Be specific regarding behaviours and situations.

Personal Awareness and Growth Exercise

How Are Your B Mod Skills?

Objectives

1 To better understand the principles of behaviour modification through firsthand experience.

2 To improve your own or someone else's behaviour by putting to use what you have learned in this chapter.

Introduction

Because the areas of B Mod and BSM are application oriented, they need to be put to practical use if they are to be fully appreciated. In a general sense, everyone is a behaviour modifier. Unfortunately, those without a working knowledge of behavioural principles tend to manage their own and others' behaviour rather haphazardly. They tend to unwittingly reinforce undesirable behaviour, put desirable behaviour in danger of extinction, and rely too heavily on punishment and negative reinforcement. This exercise is designed to help you become a more systematic manager of behaviour.

Instructions

Selecting the target behaviour of your choice, put the four-step behaviour modification model in Figure 10–3 into practice. The target may be your own behaviour (such as studying more, smoking fewer cigarettes, eating less or eating more nutritionally, or one of Covey's seven habits in Table 10–5) or someone else's (such as improving a roommate's housekeeping behaviour). Be sure to construct a behaviour chart (as in Figure 10–4) with the frequency of the target behaviour on the vertical axis and time on the horizontal. It is best to focus on a behaviour that occurs daily so a three- or four-day baseline period can be followed by a one- to two-week intervention period. Make sure you follow as many of the six consequence management guidelines as possible.

You will find it useful to perform an A→B→C functional analysis of the target behaviour to identify the relevant supporting (or hindering) cues and consequences. Then you will be in a position to set a reasonable goal and design an intervention strategy involving antecedent and consequence management. When planning a self-management intervention, give careful thought to how you can use cognitive supports. Make sure you use appropriate schedules of reinforcement.

Questions for Discussion

1 Did you target a specific behaviour (e.g., eating) or an outcome (e.g., pounds lost)? What was the advantage or disadvantage of monitoring that particular target?

2 How did your B Mod or BSM programme turn out? What did you do wrong? What did you do right?

3 How has this exercise increased your working knowledge of B Mod and/or BSM?

Group Exercise
A Human Resource Problem-Solving Team

Objectives

1   To continue developing your teamwork and group problem-solving skills.

2   To think creatively about solving common 'people problems'.

3   To put your knowledge of B Mod to work.

Introduction

People may be an organization's most important resource, but they also are the source of management's most vexing and troublesome problems. Deviant behaviour is wide ranging and managers need the skills to deal with it. This exercise introduces a useful typology of deviant behaviour as a stepping-stone toward developing B Mod interventions. A 30-minute small group session will be followed by brief oral reports to the entire class. The total time needed for this exercise is about 45 to 50 minutes.

Instructions

Your instructor will divide the class randomly into teams of five- to seven people. Each team will act as a human resource problem-solving team for a typical large organization. Step 1 for each team is to take five minutes to discuss the Typology of Deviant Workplace Behaviour provided and to brainstorm at least two additional deviant behaviours for each of the four categories. Step 2 calls for the group to select one behaviour from each of the four categories to serve as targets for behaviour modification. Step 3 involves developing a behaviour modification strategy for each of the four targeted deviant behaviours.

Tips: Be sure to rearrange antecedents and consequences for each target behaviour (making realistic assumptions about existing A→B→C relationships). Use behaviour charts whenever possible. Assign one team member the job of summarizing and reporting the team's B Mod strategies to the class.

Here are some things to keep in mind during step 3. Don't forget the common practice in B Mod of reinforcing a positive behaviour (e.g., good attendance) rather than punishing its reciprocal deviant behaviour (e.g., absenteeism). Of course, some of the deviant behaviours in the typology are so bad that termination of employment will be necessary. Your job as a human resource problem-solving team is to decide which behaviours warrant swift and sure punishment and which can be turned around with positive or negative reinforcement or extinction strategies.

Typology of Deviant Workplace Behaviour

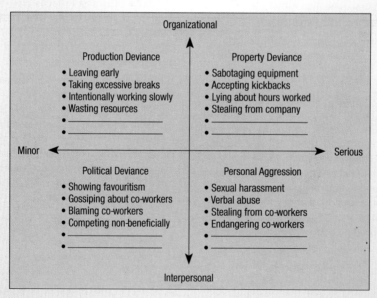

Questions for Discussion

1   Did your team do a good job of interpreting deviant behaviours as reinforceable productive behaviours (e.g., blaming co-workers versus owning up to one's mistakes)? Explain.

2   How difficult was it for your team to agree to fire someone for serious misconduct? Explain.

3   How realistic are the various B Mod strategies shared in class? Explain.

4   What situations were encountered where an approach other than B Mod would be best? Which approach?

Jeffrey believes that the most important factor in communicating effectively is knowing why you are doing your job. 'If you want to get your message across—whatever it is—it's essential to have a clear statement of intention in your head at all times. For me, it's to promote the Isle of Wight as a quality destination and support the tourism industry, and I keep that in mind whenever I'm dealing with someone.'

One moment she may be talking to a journalist from a national newspaper, the next to a local hotelier. 'It's important to deal with everyone in a similar way,' she believes, 'to return their calls immediately, answer queries or offer help. One of the most overlooked factors in effective communicating is listening—making sure you've really heard what they want and that you are responding to their needs.'

A large part of Jeffrey's role is ensuring people know what is happening on the island, much of which is done through press releases. 'When you're writing press releases you have to ensure everything is clear. There is an emphasis these days on using plain English, keeping things simple. It's also important to proof-read any document that is being sent out—if a release has mistakes or typing errors it creates a negative impression.'

There is more to successful communicating than simply making a succession of points. 'It's hugely important to have notes in front of you when you make a phone call so that you have all the information to hand, and know what points you need to make. But a call shouldn't be too formal—where possible it's good to try to form some sort of relationship with the person you're dealing with. If you are friendly and interested, people are far more receptive to what you have to say.'

A good phone manner, she believes, can make all the difference. 'I have been told that if you smile when you're on the phone people can sense it. Communicating is more than just passing on information. If you're upbeat and enthusiastic it tends to be infectious and people are generally more receptive to what you're saying.'

But things don't always go perfectly, and it's important to deal with problems or criticisms in the right way. 'If there is any negative feedback it's important to take in on board,' says Jeffrey. 'Getting defensive is pointless. You have to listen to what is said, think carefully about what sort of response to offer, and then come back with an explanation.'

The least effective way to communicate, she believes, is to be negative. 'Whether it's someone visiting the island, a local restaurant owner, or a TV crew wanting to come and film, I always tell them I can help. Even if I can't personally deal with their query, I can usually find someone who can, and that helps keep the lines of communication open. In my business I make it my policy never to say no.'[1]

For discussion

Sophie Jeffrey is undoubtedly an excellent communicator. What makes her so effective?

Management is communication. Every managerial function and activity involves some form of direct or indirect communication. Whether planning and organizing or directing and leading, managers find themselves communicating with and through others. Managerial decisions and organizational policies are ineffective unless they are understood by those responsible for enacting them. According to Brian Legget, a professor of management communication at the University of Navarra, Madrid, in today's consumer-driven business world a manager who cannot communicate is one who cannot truly be a leader.

For many people, the term manager is synonymous with leader: a person who, by word of mouth and/or personal example, markedly influences the behaviour, thoughts, and/or feelings of a significant number of people. Many of the best leaders have an almost magical ability to turn a phrase and are very articulate communicators.[2]

Linda Love of Pryor Resources, a company that gives communication seminars all over the world, takes a broader view and sees effective communication as vital to all our activities.

> *In everything you do you have to communicate effectively, whether it's going to the butcher or booking theatre tickets. You have to be able to ask for the things that you want, and understand the difference in your style of communication and other people's.*[3]

Management experts also note that effective communication is a cornerstone of ethical organizational behaviour.

> *Communication by top executives keeps the firm on its ethical course and top executives must ensure that the ethical climate is consistent with the company's overall objectives. Communication is important in providing guidance for ethical standards and activities that provide integration between the functional areas of the business. A vice president of marketing, for example, must communicate and work with regional sales managers and other marketing employees to make sure that all agree on what constitutes certain unethical activities such as bribery, price collusion and deceptive sales techniques. Top corporate executives must also communicate with managers at the operations level (in production, sales and finance, for example) and enforce overall ethical standards within the organization.*[4]

Moreover, effective communication is critical for both managerial and organizational success. For example, a study of 274 students revealed that the quality of student–faculty communication—in the instructor's office, informally on campus, or before and after class—was positively related to student motivation. Another study involving 65 savings and loan employees and 110 manufacturing employees revealed that employee satisfaction with organizational communication was positively and significantly correlated with both job satisfaction and performance.[5] Finally, a survey of 300 executives underscored the importance of communication. Results demonstrated that 71 per cent and 68 per cent of respondents, respectively, believed that written communication skills and interpersonal communication skills were critical competencies that needed enhancement via training. These executives believed the lack of communication skills had resulted in increased costs.[6]

This chapter will help you better understand how managers can both improve their communication skills and design more effective communication programmes. We will discuss: basic dimensions of the communication process, focusing on a perceptual process model and a contingency approach to selecting media; interpersonal communication; organizational communication patterns; and the dynamics of modern communications.

BASIC DIMENSIONS OF THE COMMUNICATION PROCESS

Communication is defined as 'the exchange of information between a sender and a receiver, and the inference (perception) of meaning between the individuals involved'.[7] Analysis of this exchange reveals that communication is a two-way process consisting of consecutively linked elements (see Figure 11–1). Managers who understand this process can analyse their own communication patterns as well as design communication programmes that fit organizational needs. This section reviews a perceptual process model of communication and discusses a contingency approach to choosing communication media.

Communication
interpersonal exchange of information and understanding

Figure 11–1 *A Perceptual Model of Communication*

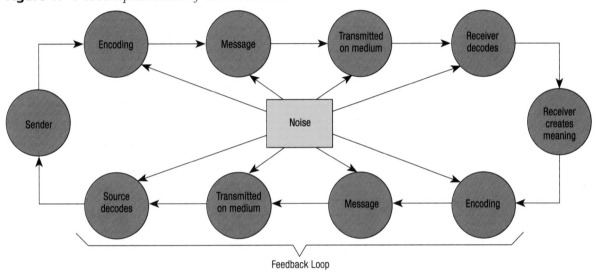

Feedback Loop

A Perceptual Process Model of Communication

Historically, the communication process has been described in terms of a *conduit* model. This traditional model depicts communication as a pipeline in which information and meaning are transferred from person to person. Recently, however, communication scholars have criticized the conduit model for being based on unrealistic assumptions. For example, the conduit model assumes communication transfers *intended meanings* from person to person.[8] If this assumption was true, miscommunication would not exist and there would be no need to worry about being misunderstood. We could simply say or write what we want and assume the listener or reader accurately understands our intended meaning.

As we all know, communicating is not that simple or clear-cut. Communication is fraught with miscommunication. In recognition of this, researchers have begun to examine communication as a form of social information processing (recall the discussion in Chapter XX) in which receivers interpret messages by cognitively processing information. This view led to development of a perceptual model of communication that depicts communication as a process in which receivers create meaning in their own minds. Let us briefly examine the elements of the perceptual process model shown in Figure 11–1.

Perceptual model of communication
consecutively linked elements within the communication process

Sender

The sender is an individual, group or organization that desires, or attempts, to communicate with a particular receiver. Receivers may be individuals, groups or organizations.

Encoding

Communication begins when a sender encodes an idea or thought. Encoding translates mental thoughts into a code or language that can be understood by others. Managers typically encode using words, numbers, gestures, non-verbal cues such as facial expressions, or pictures. Moreover, different methods of encoding can be used to portray similar ideas. The following short exercise highlights this point.

On a piece of paper, draw a picture of the area currently surrounding you. Now, write a verbal description of the same area. Does the pictorial encoding portray the same basic message as the verbal description? Which mode was harder to use and which more effective? Interestingly, a growing number of management consultants recommend using visual communication, such as drawings, to analyse and improve group interaction and problem solving and to reduce stress.

Also, as the possibilities of the Internet are increasing, email is expected to become more and more visual and vocal. Whereas email used to be the simplest part of the Internet user's experience, you can now expect to receive an increasing number of messages that arrive in HTML format—with photos, graphics, hypertext links to audio and video, and so forth–instead of bare text. The latest Internet trend is emails 'talking' to you. For example, Talksender is a free application that Web users can download to their PCs, and then use with a PC microphone to record up to 60 seconds of voice message. The message then gets emailed to the recipient. The recording plays when the email is opened.[9]

The Message

The output of encoding is a message. There are two important points to keep in mind about messages. First, they contain more than meets the eye. Messages may contain hidden agendas as well as trigger moods or emotional reactions. For example, comparisons of internal and external documents within the forest products industry, over a 10-year period, demonstrated that executives' private and public evaluative statements about events and situations were inconsistent. These executives apparently wanted to convey different messages to the public and to internal employees.[10] Duncan Green, who runs the testing department of a large internet service provider, knows all about these kind of difficulties.

'When I became the test manager I had to learn fast that your staff doesn't always tell you the whole truth,' he says, 'which can make things extremely complicated. I've had a member of my team, Jack, come and complain that someone wasn't pulling their weight on a project they had been given. When I investigated, it became clear that he had complained out of feelings of resentment that he hadn't been put onto the project himself.'[11]

The second point to consider about messages is that they need to match the medium used to transmit them. How would you evaluate the match between the message of letting someone know they have been laid off and the communication medium used in the following examples.

A man finds out he has been let go when a restaurant won't accept his company credit card. A woman manager gets the news via a note placed on her chair during lunch. Employees at a high-tech firm learn of their fate when their security codes no longer open the front door of their office building.[12]

These horrible mismatches reveal how thoughtless managers can be when they do not carefully consider the interplay between a message and the medium used to convey it. More is said about this issue in the next section.

Selecting a Medium

Managers can communicate through a variety of media. Potential media include face-to-face conversations, telephone calls, electronic mail, voice mail, videoconferencing, written memos or letters, photographs or drawings, meetings, bulletin boards, computer output, and charts or graphs. Choosing the appropriate media depends on many factors, including the nature of the message, its intended purpose, the type of audience, proximity to the audience, time horizon for disseminating the message and personal preferences, figure 11–2 shows the daily average number of messages sent and recieved by type of medium.

All media have advantages and disadvantages. Face-to-face conversations, for instance, are useful for communicating about sensitive or important issues and those requiring feedback and intensive interaction. Telephones are convenient, fast and private but non-verbal information is absent. Although writing memos or letters is time consuming, it is a good medium when it is difficult to meet, when formality and a written record are important, and when face-to-face interaction is not necessary to enhance understanding. More information about selecting the appropriate media is given later in this chapter.

Decoding

Decoding is the receiver's version of encoding. Decoding consists of translating verbal, oral, or visual aspects of a message into a form that can be interpreted. Receivers rely on social information-processing to determine the meaning of a message during decoding. Decoding is a key contributor to misunderstanding in interracial and intercultural communication because decoding by the receiver is subject to social values and cultural values that may not be understood by the sender. Also, the growing popularity of email has brought about what some people refer to as a new language, one which is not always easily decoded by those unfamiliar with it. The British consultancy firm, Pace Setter, calls it 'Weblish'.[13] It has only lower-case letters, no apostrophes or standard punctuation and no spelling rules, and many people use it all the time for emails.

'It all wouldn't bother me very much if it were confined to communication between nerds [boring computer know-alls] on the net', writes a cynical reporter in the *Sunday Times*, 'but it is already creeping into our everyday language. We'll all be nerds very soon, I guess. When I asked somebody to go for a drink after work, he mailed: 'sorry. can't. I'm on 24/7'. He seemed genuinely surprised when I asked him to explain. It turned out that he meant he was too busy, working '24 hours a day, 7 days a week'. There are many more such ugly examples: if you want to invite a couple for tea these days, you might mail: 'ru2up4T?' It seems that we will breed a generation of youngsters who will routinely write 'r' instead of 'are' and '2' instead of 'to' or 'too'.[14]

Creating Meaning

In contrast to the conduit model's assumption that meaning is directly transferred from sender to receiver, the perceptual model is based on the belief that a receiver creates the meaning of a message in his or her mind. Often, a receiver's interpretation of a message will differ from that intended by the sender. In turn, receivers act according to their own interpretations (not that of the communicator's). After considering this element of the communication process, a communication expert concluded the following.

> *Miscommunication and unintentional communication are to be expected, for they are the norm. Organizational communicators who [were to] take these ideas seriously would realize just how difficult successful communication truly is. Presumably, they would be conscious of the constant effort needed to communicate in ways most closely approximating their intentions . . . . Communication is fraught with unintentionality and, thereby, great difficulty for communicators.[15]*

Managers are encouraged to rely on *redundancy* of communication to reduce this unintentionality. This can be done by transmitting the message over multiple media.

For example, a production manager might follow up a phone conversation about a critical schedule change with a memo. According to Peter Honey, the British author of *Improve Your People Skills*, the easiest, but also the most neglected, way to avoid misunderstanding of a message is to ask questions.

'The business of testing understanding is integral to doing your job succesfully', he says. 'Meetings and conversations can go on for ages and its impossible to remember everything that's been said. It's always a good idea to ask for a recap or a summary, or for a clearer explanation. Asking questions is central to human nature but I think it gets knocked out of us in school—most of us can remember feeling foolish if we put our hand up to ask a question.' [16]

Feedback

The receiver's response to a message is the crux of the feedback loop. At this point in the communication process, the receiver becomes a sender. Specifically, the receiver encodes a response and then transmits it to the original sender. This new message is then decoded and interpreted. As you can see from this discussion, feedback is used as a comprehension check. It gives senders an idea of how accurately their message has been understood.

Noise

Noise
interference with the transmission and understanding of a message

Noise represents anything that interferes with the transmission and understanding of a message. It affects all linkages of the communication process. Noise includes factors such as a speech impairment, poor telephone connections, illegible handwriting, inaccurate statistics in a memo or report, poor hearing and eyesight, and physical distance between sender and receiver. Managers can improve communication by reducing noise.

Choosing Media: A Contingency Perspective

Survey results reported by the market research agency, Gallup, revealed that British employees send and receive an average of 169 emails a day.[17] In an American study, the majority of people surveyed noted that the number of messages sent and received has steadily increased from 1997 to today and that they felt overwhelmed by the high volume of information being transmitted.[18]

In a remarkable interview, Marc Van den Berghe, managing director of IBM Belgium, described what he calls his *communication consumption*.

Everyday I answer about 30 telephone calls. I receive between 80 and 110 emails a day. It takes me about two hours to go through them. Every day I attend about 5 to 10 meetings, and I shake at least 10 different hands, aside from those of my employees. I give about 24 internal and 10 external presentations a year. My cellular phone is kept in the car so that I can remain attainable constantly. I also use the Internet at home every evening to stay informed of current events. Finally, I'm a passionate user of videoconferencing and conference calls. [19]

How can managers help to reduce this information overload while also increasing communication effectiveness? One solution involves the effective selection of medium, suitable both for obtaining and disseminating information. If an inappropriate medium is used, managerial decisions may be based on inaccurate information or important messages may not reach the intended audience. Media selection therefore is a key component of communication effectiveness. This section explores a contingency model designed to help managers select communication media in a systematic and effective manner. Media selection in this model is based on the interaction between information richness and the complexity of the problem or situation at hand.

Figure 11-2 *Messages Sent and Received by Communication Medium*

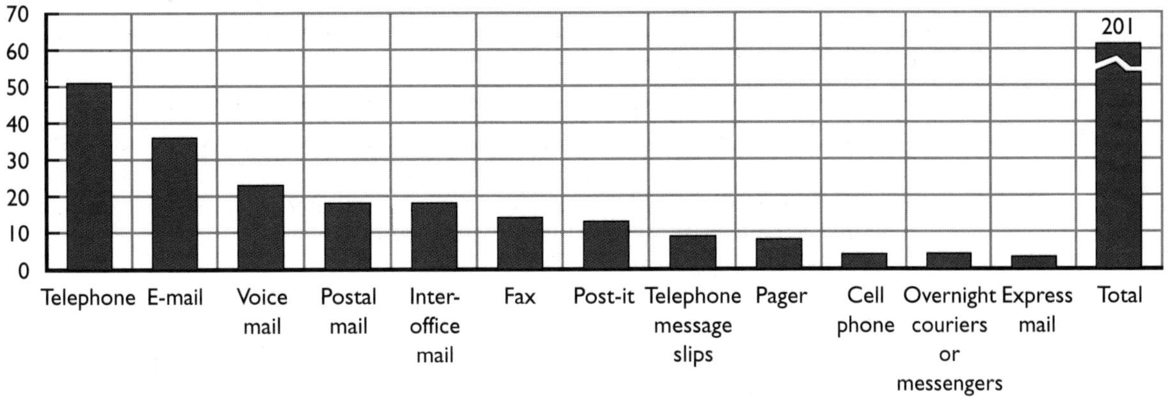

SOURCE: Clark, 'Managing the Mountain', *The Wall Street Journal*, June 21, 1999, p R4.

Information Richness

Organizational theorists Richard Daft and Robert Lengel define **information richness** in the following manner.

Richness is defined as the potential information-carrying capacity of data. If the communication of an item of data, such as a wink, provides substantial new understanding, it would be considered rich. If the datum provides little understanding, it would be low in richness.[20]

As this definition implies, alternative media possess levels of information richness that vary from high to low.

Information richness is determined by four factors:

▼ **feedback (ranging from immediate to very slow)**
▼ **channel (ranging from a combined visual and audio to limited visual)**
▼ **type of communication (personal versus impersonal)**
▼ **language source (body, natural or numeric).**

In Table 11-1, the information richness of five different media is categorized in terms of these four factors.

Face-to-face is the richest form of communication. It provides immediate feedback, which serves as a comprehension check. Moreover, it allows for the observation of

> **Information Richness**
> *information-carrying capacity of data*

Table 11-1 *Characteristics of Information Richness for Different Media*

Information Richness	Medium	Feedback	Channel	Type of Communication	Language Source
High	Face-to-face	Immediate	Visual, audio	Personal	Body, natural
↑	Telephone	Fast	Audio	Personal	Natural
	Personal written	Slow	Limited visual	Personal	Natural
	Formal written	Very slow	Limited visual	Impersonal	Natural
Low	Formal numeric	Very slow	Limited visual	Impersonal	Numeric

SOURCE: Adapted from R L Daft and R H Lengel, 'Information Richness: A New Approach to Managerial Behavior and Organization Design', in *Research in Organizational Behavior*, eds B M Staw and L L Cummings (Greenwich, CT: JAI Press, 1984), p 197.

multiple language cues, such as body language and tone of voice, over more than one channel. Although high in richness, the telephone is not as informative as the face-to-face medium. Formal numeric media such as quantitative computer printouts or video displays possess the lowest richness. Feedback is very slow, the channel involves only limited visual information, and the numeric information is impersonal.

Complexity of the Managerial Problem or Situation

Managers face problems and situations that range from low to high in complexity. Low-complexity situations are routine, predictable and are managed by using objective or standard procedures. Calculating an employee's pay is an example of low complexity. Highly complex situations, like a corporate reorganization, are ambiguous, unpredictable, hard to analyse and often emotion-laden. Managers spend considerably more time analysing these situations because they rely on more sources of information during their deliberations. There are no set solutions to complex problems or situations.

Contingency Recommendations

The contingency model for selecting media is graphically depicted in Figure 11–3. As shown, there are three zones of communication effectiveness. Effective communication occurs when the richness of the medium is matched appropriately with the complexity of the problem or situation. Media low in richness—formal numeric or formal written—are better suited to simple problems, while media high in richness—telephone or face-to-face—are appropriate for complex problems or situations. Consider, for example, how the Body Shop maintains communication with its many shops.

> *[Anita] Roddick, [the Body Shop's former head] constantly worked at communications within the company. Every shop had a bulletin board, a fax machine and a video player through which she bombarded staff with information.*[21]

Conversely, ineffective communication occurs when the medium is either too rich or insufficiently rich for the complexity of the problem or situation. Extending the preceding example, a district sales manager would fall into the *overload zone* if he or she communicated monthly sales reports through richer media. Conducting face-to-face meetings or telephoning each salesperson would provide excessive information and take more time than necessary to communicate monthly sales data. The

Figure 11–3

A Contingency Model for Selecting Communication Media

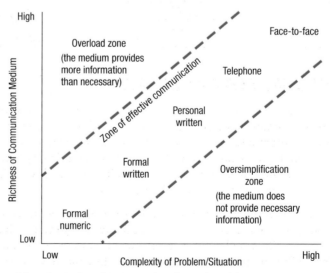

SOURCE: Adapted from R L Daft and R H Lengel, 'Information Richness: A New Approach to Managerial Behavior and Organization Design', in *Research in Organizational Behavior*, eds B M Staw and L L Cummings (Greenwich, CT: JAI Press, 1984), p 199. Used with permission.

oversimplification zone represents another ineffective choice of communication medium. In this situation, media with inadequate richness are used to communicate complicated problems. An example would be an executive who uses a letter or an email message to communicate news of a merger or a major reorganization. This choice of medium is ineffective because employees are likely to be nervous and concerned about how a merger or reorganization will affect their futures.

Research Evidence

The relationship between media richness and the complexity of the problem or situation has not been researched extensively as the underlying theory is relatively new. Available evidence indicates that managers used richer sources when confronted with ambiguous and complicated events, and miscommunication was increased when rich media were used to transmit information that was traditionally communicated through lean media.[22] Moreover, a meta-analysis of more than 40 studies revealed that media usage was significantly different in different organizational levels. Upper-level executives and managers spent more time in face-to-face meetings than did lower-level managers.[23] This finding is consistent with recommendations derived from the contingency model just discussed.

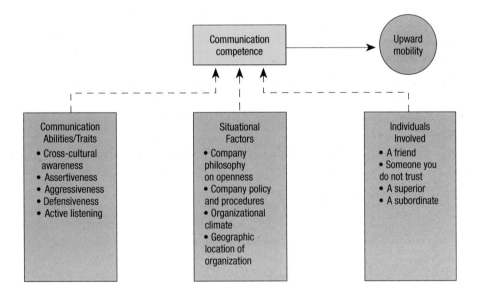

Figure 11–4

Communication Competence Affects Upward Mobility

INTERPERSONAL COMMUNICATION

The quality of interpersonal communication within an organization is very important. People with good communication skills have been found to help groups make better decisions and to be promoted more frequently than individuals with less developed abilities.[24] Although there is no universally accepted definition of communication competence, it is a performance-based index of an individual's ability to effectively use the appropriate communication behaviour in a given context.[25]

Communication competence is determined by three components: communication abilities and traits; situational factors; and the individuals involved in the interaction (see Figure 11–4). Cross-cultural awareness, for example, is an important communication ability or trait. As an example of this, the next International OB illustrates how a lack of cross-cultural awareness can have a negative effect on

Communication competence
ability to use the appropriate communication behaviour effectively in a given context

International OB

Cross-Cultural Awareness Affects Interpersonal Communication

John Gillespie—vice president of Clarke Consulting Group, based in Redwood City, California—recalls a meeting in Tokyo for which the Japanese participants had carefully arranged the room. When the American and European participants arrived, they rearranged the chairs to form a 'U'. The Japanese watched and said nothing. In the meeting, they also said nothing. Unwittingly, the Western participants had silenced their Japanese colleagues by assuming that the Western way was the only way.

Pacing is another factor influenced by culture. Westerners' typical 'do it now' approach can work against them in Asia . . . . In fact, Gillespie says that Asians say in confidential interviews that Americans interrupt and never listen.

'In Buddhist societies, silence is admired. In a Japanese context, when you finish saying something, you expect silence. In Asian cultures, too many words are considered suspicious.'

SOURCE: C C Hebard, 'Managing Effectively in Asia', *Training & Development*, April 1996, p 36.

Individuals involved in an interaction also affect communication competence. For example, people are likely to withhold information and react emotionally or defensively when interacting with someone they dislike or distrust. You can improve your communication competence through five communication styles under your control: assertiveness, aggressiveness, non-assertiveness, non-verbal communication and active listening. We conclude this section by discussing gender differences in communication.

Assertiveness, Aggressiveness and Non-Assertiveness

The American saying, 'You can attract more flies with honey than with vinegar', captures the difference between using an assertive communication style and an aggressive style. Research studies indicate that assertiveness is more effective than aggressiveness in both work-related and consumer contexts.[26] An **assertive style** is expressive and self-enhancing and is based on the 'ethical notion that it is not right or good to violate our own or others' basic human rights, such as the right to self-expression or the right to be treated with dignity and respect.'[27] In contrast, an **aggressive style** is expressive and self-enhancing and strives to take unfair advantage of others. A non-assertive style is characterized by timid and self-denying behaviour. **Non-assertiveness** is ineffective because it gives the other person an unfair advantage. For example, consider the assertive style of Sally Gordon, a personal assistant (PA) to Alexander van der Hooft, managing director of Pink Elephant UK, a company which supplies IT staff and services.

Assertive style
expressive and self-enhancing but does not take advantage of others

Aggressive style
expressive and self-enhancing but takes unfair advantage of others

Non-assertive style
timid and self-denying behaviour

'As a personal assistant, I have to fend off the queries and patter of numerous salespeople and headhunters [those actively seeking out potential staff] every day', she says. 'Everyone will try to speak to Alexander and a lot will try anything to get through to him, from saying they've spoken to him the previous day to telling me he'll be furious if I don't put them through'. Gordon believes that knowing how to be assertive without being aggressive is essential to her work. 'Everything to do with Alexander comes through me. I have to filter what's relevant', she says. 'I often get people from within the company ringing me to see if he is available, trying to see him as soon as possible. I have to judge when is a good time and often have to be quite firm with people, telling them things exactly as they are but in a polite manner. But it's external calls that cause the most problem. I've had people hang up on me or become rude or agresssive simply because I won't let them through to Alexander. The art is then to remain calm but at the same time display some authority. One of the best techniques is simply to keep on* *repeating the same phrase—I always say he is out of the office and that I can't put them through. People do tend to get quite shirty [agitated] and I think it's often based on snobbery—they can't believe that a PA is authorized to deal with them.'* [28]

Table 11–2 *Communication Styles*

Communication Style	Description	Nonverbal Behavior Pattern	Verbal Behavior Pattern
Assertive	Pushing hard without attacking; permits others to influence outcome; expressive and self-enhancing without intruding on others	Good eye contact Comfortable but firm posture Strong, steady, and audible voice Facial expressions matched to message Appropriately serious tone Selective interruptions to ensure understanding	Direct and unambiguous language No attributions or evaluations of other's behavior Use of 'I' statements and cooperative 'we' statements
Aggressive	Taking advantage of others; expressive and self-enhancing at other's expense	Glaring eye contact Moving or leaning too close Threatening gestures (pointed finger; clenched fist) Loud voice Frequent interruptions	Swear words and abusive language Attributions and evaluations of other's behavior Sexist or racist terms Explicit threats or put-downs
Nonassertive	Encouraging others to take advantage of us; inhibited; self-denying	Little eye contact Downward glances Slumped posture Constantly shifting weight Wringing hands Weak or whiny voice	Qualifiers ('maybe'; 'kind of') Fillers ('uh,' 'you know,' 'well') Negaters ('It's not really that important'; 'I'm not sure')

SOURCE: Adapted in part from J A Waters, 'Managerial Assertiveness', *Business Horizons*, September–October 1982, pp 24–29.

Managers may improve their communication competence by trying to be more assertive and less aggressive or non-assertive. This can be achieved by using the appropriate non-verbal and verbal behaviour listed in Table 11–2. For instance, managers should attempt to use the non-verbal behaviour of good eye contact; a strong, steady and audible voice; and selective interruptions. They should avoid non-verbal behaviour such as glaring or little eye contact; threatening gestures or slumped posture; and a weak or whiny voice. Appropriate verbal behaviour includes direct and unambiguous language and the use of 'I' messages instead of 'you' statements. For example, when you say, 'Mike, I was disappointed with your report because it contained typographical errors', rather than 'Mike, your report was poorly done', you reduce defensiveness. 'I' statements describe your feelings about someone's performance or behaviour instead of laying blame on the person.

Remember that non-verbal and verbal behaviour should complement and reinforce each other. James Waters, a communication expert, further recommends that assertiveness can be enhanced by using various combinations of the following assertiveness elements.

1 *Describe* the situation or the behaviour of people to which you are reacting.

2 *Express* your feelings, and/or *explain* what impact the other's behaviour has on you.

3 *Empathize* with the other person's position in the situation.

4 *Specify* what changes you would like to see in the situation or in another's behaviour, and offer to *negotiate* those changes with the other person.

5 *Indicate*, in a non-threatening way, the possible consequences that will follow if change does not occur.[29]

Waters offers managers the following situational advice when using the various assertiveness elements: *empathize and negotiate* with superiors or others on whom you are dependent; *specify* with friends and peers; and *describe* to strangers.

Sources of Non-Verbal Communication

Non-verbal communication is: 'Any message, sent or received independent of the written or spoken word . . . [It] includes such factors as use of time and space, distance between persons when conversing, use of colour, dress, walking behaviour, standing, positioning, seating arrangement, office locations and furnishing.'[30]

Communication experts estimate that non-verbal communication is responsible for up to 60 per cent of a message being communicated. It is therefore important to ensure that your non-verbal signals are consistent with your intended verbal messages. Inconsistencies create noise and promote miscommunication.[31]

Because of the prevalence of non-verbal communication and its significant impact on organizational behaviour (including but not limited to, perceptions of others, hiring decisions, work attitudes and turnover),[32] it is important that managers become consciously aware of the sources of non-verbal communication.

Body Movements and Gestures

Body movements (such as leaning forwards or backwards) and gestures (such as pointing) provide additional non-verbal information that can either enhance or detract from the communication process. A recent study, for example, showed that the use of appropriate hand gestures increased listeners' practical understanding of a message.[33] Open body positions such as leaning backward, communicate *immediacy*, a term used to represent openness, warmth, closeness and availability for communication. *Defensiveness* is communicated by gestures such as folding arms, crossing hands, and crossing one's legs.

Judith Hall, a communication researcher, conducted a meta-analysis of gender differences in body movements and gestures. Results revealed that women nodded their heads and moved their hands more than men. Leaning forward, large body shifts, and foot and leg movements were exhibited more frequently by men than women.[34] Although it is both easy and fun to interpret body movements and gestures, it is important to remember that body-language analysis is subjective, easily misinterpreted, and highly dependent on the context and cross-cultural differences.[35] Thus, managers need to be careful when trying to interpret body movements. Inaccurate interpretations can create additional 'noise' in the communication process.

Touch

Touching is another powerful non-verbal cue. People tend to touch those they like. A meta-analysis of gender differences in touching indicated that women do more touching during conversations than men.[36] Of particular note, however, is the fact that men and women interpret touching differently. Sexual harassment claims might be reduced by keeping this perceptual difference in mind.

Moreover, norms for touching vary significantly around the world. Consider the example of two males walking across campus holding hands. In the Middle East, this behaviour would be quite normal for males who are friends or who have great respect for each other. In contrast, this behaviour is not commonplace in other parts of the world. The next International OB presents cross-cultural norms for non-verbal behaviour, including touching, across Asia.

International OB

http://as.orientation.com

Norms for Touching Vary across Countries

China

- Hugging or taking someone's arm is considered inappropriate.

- Winking or beckoning with one's index finger is considered rude.

The Philippines

- Handshaking and a pat on the back are common greetings.

- Indonesia

- Handshaking and head nodding are customary greetings.

Japan

- Business cards are exchanged before bowing or handshaking.

- A weak handshake is common.

- Lengthy or frequent eye contact is considered impolite.

Malaysia

- It is considered impolite to touch someone casually, especially on the top of the head.

- It is best to use your right hand to eat and to touch people and things.

South Korea

- Men bow slightly and shake hands, sometimes with two hands; women refrain from shaking hands.

- It is considered polite to cover your mouth while laughing.

Thailand

- Public displays of temper or affection are frowned on.

- It is considered impolite to point at anything using your foot or to show the soles of your feet.

SOURCE: Guidelines taken from R E Axtell, *Gestures: The Do's and Taboos of Body Language Around the World* (New York: John Wiley & Sons, 1991)

Facial Expressions

Facial expressions convey a wealth of information. Smiling, for instance, typically represents warmth, happiness or friendship, whereas frowning conveys dissatisfaction or anger. Do you think these interpretations apply to different cross-cultural groups? If you said yes, it supports the view that there is a universal recognition of emotions from facial expressions. If you said no, this indicates you believe the relationship between facial expressions and emotions varies across cultures. A recent summary of relevant research revealed that the association between facial expressions and emotions varies across cultures.[37] A smile, for example, does not convey the same emotion in different countries. Therefore, managers need to be careful in interpreting facial expressions among diverse groups of employees.

Eye Contact

Eye contact is a strong non-verbal cue that serves four functions in communication. First, eye contact regulates the flow of communication by signalling the beginning and end of conversation. There is a tendency to look away from others when beginning to speak and to look at them when done. Second, gazing (as opposed to glaring) facilitates and monitors feedback because it reflects interest and attention. Third, eye contact conveys emotion. People tend to avoid eye contact when discussing bad news or providing negative feedback. Fourth, gazing relates to the type of relationship between communicators.

As is true for body movements, gestures and facial expressions, norms for eye contact vary across cultures. Westerners are taught at an early age to look at their parents when spoken to. In contrast, Asians are taught to avoid eye contact with a parent or superior in order to show obedience and subservience.[38] Once again, managers should be sensitive to different orientations toward maintaining eye contact with diverse employees.

Practical Tips

It is important to have good non-verbal communication skills in light of the fact that they are related to the development of positive interpersonal relationships.[39] A communication expert offers the following advice to improve non-verbal communication skills.

Positive non-verbal actions that help to communicate include:

▼ **maintaining eye contact**

▼ **occasionally nodding the head in agreement**

▼ **smiling and showing animation**

▼ **leaning toward the speaker**

▼ **speaking at a moderate rate, in a quiet, assuring tone.**

Whereas here are some actions to avoid:

▼ **looking away or turning away from the speaker**

▼ **closing your eyes**

▼ **using an unpleasant voice tone**

▼ **speaking too quickly or too slowly**

▼ **yawning excessively.**[40]

Practice these tips by turning the sound off while watching television and then trying to interpret emotions and interactions. Also helpful may be friends' honest feedback on your non-verbal communication style.

Active Listening

Some communication experts contend that listening is the key communication skill for employees involved in sales, customer service or management. In support of this conclusion, a study showed that listening effectiveness was positively associated with success in sales and obtaining managerial promotions.[41] Listening skills are particularly important for current and future managers because they spend a great deal of time listening to others. Estimates suggest that managers typically spend about 9 per cent of a working day reading, 16 writing, 30 talking and 45 listening.[42] Unfortunately, research evidence suggests that most people are not very good at listening. For example, communication experts estimate that people generally comprehend about 25 per cent of a typical verbal message. Interestingly, this problem is partly due to the fact that we can process information faster than most people talk. The average speaker communicates 125 words a minute while we can process 500 words a minute. Poor listeners use this information processing gap to daydream and think about other things, thereby missing important parts of what is being communicated.[43]

Listening involves much more than hearing a message. Hearing is merely the physical component of listening. **Listening** is the process of *actively* decoding and interpreting verbal messages. Listening requires cognitive attention and information processing; hearing does not. With these distinctions in mind, we will examine a model of listener comprehension, listening styles, and some practical advice for becoming a more effective listener.

Listening
actively decoding and interpreting verbal messages

Listener Comprehension Model

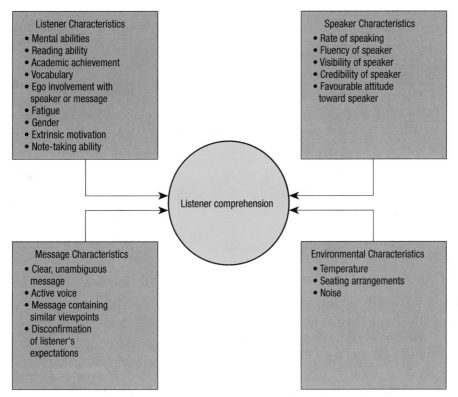

Figure 11–5
Listener Comprehensive Model

Listener Characteristics
• Mental abilities
• Reading ability
• Academic achievement
• Vocabulary
• Ego involvement with speaker or message
• Fatigue
• Gender
• Extrinsic motivation
• Note-taking ability

Speaker Characteristics
• Rate of speaking
• Fluency of speaker
• Visibility of speaker
• Credibility of speaker
• Favourable attitude toward speaker

Listener comprehension

Message Characteristics
• Clear, unambiguous message
• Active voice
• Message containing similar viewpoints
• Disconfirmation of listener's expectations

Environmental Characteristics
• Temperature
• Seating arrangements
• Noise

SOURCE: Adapted from discussion in K W Watson and L L Barker, 'Listening Behavior: Definition and Measurement', in *Communication Yearbook 8*, ed R N Bostrom (Beverly Hills, CA: Sage Publications, 1984), pp 178–97.

Listener comprehension represents the extent to which an individual can recall factual information and draw accurate conclusions and inferences from a verbal message. It is a function of listener, speaker, message and environmental characteristics (see Figure 11–5). Communication researchers Kittie Watson and Larry Barker conducted a global review of research into listening and arrived at the following conclusions. Listening comprehension is positively related to high mental and reading abilities, academic achievements, a large vocabulary, being 'ego-involved with the speaker', having energy, being female, having extrinsic motivation to pay attention and being able to take good notes. Speakers have a negative impact on listening comprehension when they talk too quickly or too slowly, possess disturbing accents or speech patterns, cannot be seen by the audience, lack credibility, or are disliked. In contrast, clear messages that are given in the active voice increase listening comprehension. The same is true of messages containing viewpoints similar to the listener's or those that disconfirm expectations. Finally, comfortable environmental characteristics and compact seating arrangements enhance listening comprehension.[44]

Listening Styles

A pair of communication experts identified three different listening styles.[45] Their research indicated that people prefer to hear information that is suited to their own listening style. People also tend to speak in a style that is consistent with their own listening style. Because inconsistent styles represent a barrier to effective listening, it is important for managers to understand and respond to the different listening styles. The three listening styles are based on results, reasons and processes.

Results-style listeners
interested in hearing the bottom line or result of a message

Results-style listeners don't like any beating around the bush. They are interested in hearing the 'bottom line' or result of the communication message first and then they like to ask questions. The following examples of behaviour identify a results-style listener:

▼ **They sound direct. Everything is explicit, so you never have to wonder. They may sound blunt or even rude sometimes.**

▼ **They are action oriented.**

▼ **They are oriented in the present.**

▼ **They love to solve problems. Because of their love of fixing things and their action orientation, they are usually good crisis managers.**

▼ **Their first interest is in the bottom line [final/financial outcome].**[46]

Reasons-style listeners
interested in hearing the rationale behind a message

Reasons-style listeners want to know the rationale for what someone is saying or proposing. They must be convinced about a point of view before accepting it. A reasons-style listener typically exhibits the following behaviour.

▼ **They are most concerned with whether or not a solution is practical, realistic, and reasonable for the situation.**

▼ **They weigh and balance everything . . . .**

▼ **If asked a direct question, they frequently answer, 'It depends'.**

▼ **They argue, out loud or internally.**

▼ **They expect people to present ideas in an organized way and have little tolerance, and no respect, for a 'disorderly' mind.**

▼ **Their first concern is 'Why?'** [47]

Process-style listeners
like to discuss issues in detail

Process-style listeners like to discuss issues in detail. They prefer to receive background information prior to having a thorough discussion and like to know why an issue is important in the first place. You can identify process-style listeners by watching for the following behaviour.

▼ **They are people oriented. They have a high concern for relationships, believing that people and relationships are the keys to long-term success.**

▼ **They like to know the whole story before making a decision.**

▼ **They have a high regard for quality and will hold out for a quality solution to a problem, even if it seems unrealistic to others.**

▼ **They are future oriented. They are not only concerned about the future but they predict what may happen as a result of decisions made today.**

▼ **They have ongoing conversations. They continue subjects from one conversation to the next.**

▼ **Their language and messages tend to be indirect. They imply rather than state the bottom line.**

▼ **Their primary concerns are 'How?' and ' What are the benefits?'** [48]

Managers can gain greater acceptance of their ideas and proposals by adapting the *form* and *content* of a message to fit a receiver's listening style.

1 For a results-style listener, for instance, the sender should present the bottom line at the beginning of the discussion.

2 Explain your rationale to a reasons-style listener.

3 For a process-style listener, describe the process and the benefits.

Becoming a More Effective Listener

In addition to following the preceding recommendations, you can improve your listening skills by avoiding the 10 habits of bad listeners while cultivating the 10 good listening habits (see Table 11–3). Stephen Covey, author of the bestseller *The 7 Habits of Highly*

Effective People, offers another good piece of advice about becoming a more effective listener. He concludes that we should 'seek first to understand, then to be understood'.[49] In conclusion, it takes awareness, effort and practice to improve one's listening comprehension. Listening is not a skill that will improve on its own. Is anyone listening?

Table 11–3 *The Keys to Effective Listening*

Keys to Effective Listening	The Bad Listener	The Good Listener
1. Capitalize on thought speed	Tends to daydream	Stays with the speaker, mentally summarizes the speaker, weighs evidence, and listens between the lines
2. Listen for ideas	Listens for facts	Listens for central or overall ideas
3. Find an area of interest	Tunes out dry speakers or subjects	Listens for any useful information
4. Judge content, not delivery	Tunes out dry or monotone speakers	Assesses content by listening to entire message before making judgments
5. Hold your fire	Gets too emotional or worked up by something said by the speaker and enters into an argument	Withholds judgment until comprehension is complete
6. Work at listening	Does not expend energy on listening	Gives the speaker full attention
7. Resist distractions	Is easily distracted	Fights distractions and concentrates on the speaker
8. Hear what is said	Shuts out or denies unfavorable information	Listens to both favorable and unfavorable information
9. Challenge yourself	Resists listening to presentations of difficult subject matter	Treats complex presentations as exercise for the mind
10. Use handouts, overheads, or other visual aids	Does not take notes or pay attention to visual aids	Takes notes as required and uses visual aids to enhance understanding of the presentation

SOURCES: Derived from N Skinner, 'Communication Skills', *Selling Power*, July/August 1999, pp 32–34; and G Manning, K Curtis and S McMillen, *Building the Human Side of Work Community* (Cincinnati, OH: Thomson Executive Press, 1996), pp 127–54.

ORGANIZATIONAL COMMUNICATION PATTERNS

Examining organizational communication patterns is a good way to identify factors contributing to effective and ineffective management. For example, research reveals that employees do not receive enough information from their immediate supervisors. It is therefore no surprise to learn that a lot of employees use unofficial, informal communication systems (the grapevine) as a source of information. This section promotes a working knowledge of three important communication patterns: hierarchical communication, the grapevine and communication distortion.

Hierarchical Communication

Hierarchical communication is defined as 'those exchanges of information and influence between organizational members, at least one of whom has formal authority (as defined by official organizational sources) to direct and evaluate the activities of other organizational members'.[50] This communication pattern involves information exchanged downward from manager to employee and upward from employee to manager. Managers provide five types of information through downward communication: job instructions, job rationale, organizational procedures and practices, feedback about performance, and indoctrination of goals. Employees,

Hierarchical communication
exchange of information between managers and employees

in turn, communicate information upward about themselves, co-workers and their problems, organizational practices and policies, and what needs to be done and how to do it. Timely and valid hierarchical communication can promote individual and organizational success. Managers are encouraged to foster two-way communication among all employees. Consider the two-way communication process in the following example.

> 'Striving to attain a mission is not just a matter for top management but one that everybody needs to be involved in', says Guy Strobbe of North Sea Petrochemicals. 'That's why management has to inform people and make it clear to them what they can contribute to the company goals. If there's a problem, those on the floor have to think it through to find a solution and then communicate it to the higher levels. We count on the 'learning ability' of every employee. Therefore, we try to bring about an open climate where everything can be spoken of freely, and where senior managers are easy to approach.' To enhance the flow of information, there are structured meetings at all levels: management teams, departmental meetings, shift-supervisor meetings...where the responsibility of each team is to run through the different aspects of a project. What is said at a senior level is then summarized and distributed so that lower level teams are informed of their conclusions. The management also convenes 'state of the company' quarterly meetings, to which all employees are invited. In these meetings, managers, production workers and occasionally external speakers present topics that are important to all employees: such as new trends in the sector, new training systems, and decisions made by management regarding safety. 'It is a forum where information and trends on various topics can be shared with the whole company', says Strobbe, who considers communication 'a building block of the company'.[51]

However, not every organization has as successful a communication programme as North Sea Petrochemicals. There are many companies where hierarchical communication turns out to be highly problematic. For instance, according to Angela Baron of the Institute of Personnel and Development, a surprising number of organizations fail to plan how they will tell staff about reorganizing. 'If a company plans to restructure, chances are that it won't tell the workers', she says. 'Many organizations don't keep staff informed but inevitably someone picks something up and rumours—and consequently stress and low morale—become rife. Even when there isn't harmful hearsay, sudden news of restructuring, without careful planning of how it will be communicated downwards, can leave employees feeling uninvolved and undervalued.[52]

To illustrate, Angela Baron tells the striking anecdote of the chief executive who, in an attempt to repair some of the damage that was already made by the lack of proper communication, organized an office party. 'Enjoy yourselves', he told employees during a brief speech at the start of the evening. 'And don't worry too much about the redundancies. We'll let you know about those at the next party.' To the chief's genuine surprise, his joke was met with silence.[53]

The Grapevine

Grapevine
unofficial communication system of the informal organization

The term *grapevine* originated from the US Civil War practice of stringing battlefield telegraph lines between trees. Today, the grapevine represents the unofficial communication system of the informal organization. Information travelling along the grapevine supplements official or formal channels of communication. Although the grapevine can be a source of inaccurate rumours, it functions positively as an early warning sign for organizational changes, a medium for creating organizational culture, a mechanism for fostering group cohesiveness and a way of informally bouncing ideas off others.[54] Evidence indicates that the grapevine is alive and well in today's workplace.

A national survey of the readers of *Industry Week*, a professional management magazine, revealed that employees used the grapevine as their most frequent source of information.[55] Contrary to general opinion, the grapevine is not necessarily counter-productive. Plugging into the grapevine can help employees, managers and organizations alike to achieve desired results.

> 'Having a brief chat when you're by the coffee machine or between meetings has always been an essential part of the daily grind [life] in any office. Now, though, employers are starting to accept that this kind of face-to-face communication is just as important as the more formal type you have with your superiors', states Bridget Hodd, an occupational psychologist at Development at Work, a British consulting organization, 'both go a long way to improve team-building, to get rid of conflict where necessary and improve staff morale.'[56]

To enhance your understanding of the grapevine, we will explore the patterns, research and managerial recommendations for monitoring this often misunderstood system of communication.

Grapevine Patterns

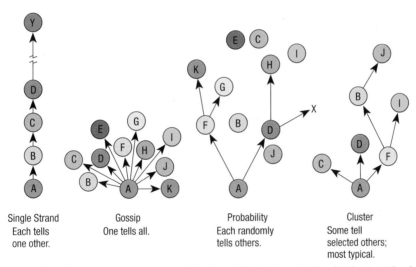

Figure 11–6
Grapevine Patterns

Single Strand
Each tells
one other.

Gossip
One tells all.

Probability
Each randomly
tells others.

Cluster
Some tell
selected others;
most typical.

SOURCE: K Davis and J W Newstrom, *Human Behavior at Work: Organizational Behavior*, 7th ed (New York: McGraw-Hill, 1985), p 317. Used with permission. Copyright © 1985. Reproduced with permission of the McGraw-Hill Companies.

Communication along the grapevine follows predictable patterns (see Figure 11–6). The most frequent pattern is not a single strand or gossip chain but a cluster.[57] Although the probability and cluster patterns look similar, the process by which information is passed is very different. People *randomly* gossip to others in a probability structure. For instance, Figure 11–6 shows that person A tells persons F and D a piece of information but ignores co-workers B and J. Person A may have done this simply because he or she ran into co-workers F and D in the corridor. In turn, persons F and D randomly discuss this information with others at work. In contrast, the cluster pattern is based on the idea that information is *selectively* passed from one person to another. People tend to selectively communicate because they know that certain individuals tend to leak or pass information to others, and they actually want the original piece of information to be spread around. For example, Figure 11–6 shows that person A selectively discusses a piece of information with three people, one of whom—person F—tells two others, and then one of those two—person B—tells another. Only certain individuals repeat what they hear when the probability or cluster patterns are operating. People who consistently pass along grapevine information to others are called **liaison individuals** or 'gossips'.

Liaison individuals
consistently pass grapevine information along to others

About 10 per cent of the employees on an average grapevine will be highly active participants. They serve as liaisons with the rest of the staff members who receive information but spread it to only a few other people. Usually these liaisons are friendly, outgoing people who are in positions that allow them to cross departmental lines. For example, secretaries tend to be liaisons because they can communicate with the top executive, the janitor and everyone in-between without raising eyebrows.[58]

Organizational moles
use the grapevine to enhance their power and status

Effective managers monitor the pulse of work groups by regularly communicating with known liaisons individuals. **Organizational moles**, however, use the grapevine for a different purpose. They obtain information, often negative, in order to enhance their power and status. They do this by secretly reporting their perceptions and hearsay about the difficulties, conflicts or failure of other employees to powerful members of management. This enables moles to divert attention away from themselves and to appear more competent than others. Management should attempt to create an open, trusting environment that discourages this behaviour because moles can destroy teamwork, create conflict and impair productivity.[59]

Research and Practical Implications

Although research activity on this topic has slowed in recent years, past research about the grapevine provided the following insights: it is faster than formal channels; it is about 75 per cent accurate; people rely on it when they are insecure, threatened or faced with organizational changes; and employees use the grapevine to acquire the majority of their workplace information.[60]

The key managerial recommendation is to *monitor* and *influence* the grapevine rather than attempt to control it. Effective managers accomplish this by openly sharing relevant information with employees. For example, managers can increase the amount of communication both by keeping in touch with liaison individuals and by making sure information travels to people 'isolated' from the formal communication system. Other ways of influencing and monitoring the grapevine is to provide it with advance notice of departmental or organizational changes, to carefully listen to employees' responses, and to selectively send information.

Many companies are actively trying to stimulate their informal communication dynamics. According to Bridget Hodd, we have started to lose the art of effective day-to-day contact since the advent of email and the ethos of working every minute of the day. Some organizations are so concerned that they are encouraging people to talk more. British supermarket chain Asda is just such an organization.

> *'We have made opportunities for people to break out of the "keep your head down, no time to chat" behaviour by creating situations, formal and informal, where they can talk freely and purposefully', explains Zaria Pinchbeck, who wears the title of Colleague Involvement Officer. Staff at Asda are encouraged to take more breaks and to go into five-minute informal huddles before or after shifts. Formal sessions have been set up too, in which managers listen to employees. 'Staff quickly related the improvements in communication to improvements in both their motivation and performance. Employee satisfaction levels increased by around 20 per cent', says Pinchbeck.*[61]

Communication Distortion between Managers and Employees

Communication distortion
purposely modifying the content of a message

Communication distortion occurs when an employee purposely modifies the content of a message, thereby reducing the accuracy of communication between managers and employees. Employees tend to engage in this practice because of workplace politics, a desire to manage impressions or fear of how a manager might respond to a message.[62] Communication experts point out the organizational problems caused by distortion.

Distortion is an important problem in organizations because modifications to messages cause misdirectives to be transmitted, non-directives to be issued, incorrect information to be passed on, and a variety of other problems related to both the quantity and quality of information.[63]

Knowledge of the antecedents or causes of communication distortion can help managers avoid or limit these problems.

Antecedents of Distortion

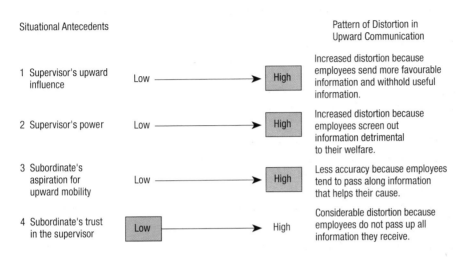

Situational Antecedents

Pattern of Distortion in Upward Communication

1 Supervisor's upward influence — Low → High — Increased distortion because employees send more favourable information and withhold useful information.

2 Supervisor's power — Low → High — Increased distortion because employees screen out information detrimental to their welfare.

3 Subordinate's aspiration for upward mobility — Low → High — Less accuracy because employees tend to pass along information that helps their cause.

4 Subordinate's trust in the supervisor — Low → High — Considerable distortion because employees do not pass up all information they receive.

Figure 11–7
Sources of Distortion in Upward Communication

SOURCE: Adapted in part from J Fulk and S Mani, 'Distortion of Communication in Hierarchical Relationships', in *Communication Yearbook 9*, ed M L McLaughlin (Beverly Hills, CA: Sage Publications, 1986).

Studies have identified four situational antecedents of distortion in upward communication (see Figure 11–7). Distortion tends to increase when supervisors have high upward influence or power. Employees also tend to modify or distort information when they aspire to move upward and when they do not trust their supervisors.[64] Mangers can reduce distortion in several ways, without having to reduce their upward influence or curb their subordinates' desire for upward mobility, by:

▼ reducing the emphasis on the power differential between themselves and their subordinates

▼ enhancing trust through a meaningful performance review process that rewards actual performance

▼ encouraging staff feedback by conducting smaller, more informal meetings

▼ establishing performance goals that encourage employees to focus on problems rather than personalities

▼ limiting distortion by encouraging dialogue between those with opposing viewpoints.

What Is Your Potential for Communication Distortion?

To assess the communication pattern between you and your immediate supervisor, please take a moment to complete the survey in the next OB Exercise. Think of your current (or last) job when responding to the various items. Once this is completed, check your responses to the first three statements to see whether they suggest low or high potential for distortion. Then compare this with your responses to the last three statements, which measure three outcomes of distortion.

OB Exercise

A Self-Assessment of Antecedents and Outcomes of Distortion in Upward Communication

Instructions

Circle your response to each question by using the following scale:

1 = Strongly disagree

2 = Disagree

3 = Neither agree nor disagree

4 = Agree

5 = Strongly agree

Supervisor's Upward Influence

In general, my immediate supervisor can have a big impact on my career in this organization.   1—2—3—4—5

Aspiration for Upward Mobility

It is very important for me to progress upward in this organization.   1—2—3—4—5

Supervisory Trust

I feel free to discuss the problems and difficulties of my job with my immediate supervisor without jeopardizing my position or having it count against me later.   1—2—3—4—5

Withholding Information

I provide my immediate supervisor with a small amount of the total information I receive at work.   1—2—3—4—5

Selective Disclosure

When transmitting information to my immediate supervisor, I often emphasize those aspects that make me look good.   1—2—3—4—5

Satisfaction with Communication

In general, I am satisfied with the pattern of communication between my supervisor and I.   1—2—3—4—5

Arbitrary Norms

Low = 1–2

Moderate = 3

High = 4–5

SOURCE: Adapted and excerpted in part from K H Roberts and C A O'Reilly III, 'Measuring Organizational Communication,' *Journal of Applied Psychology*, June 1974, p 323.

DYNAMICS OF MODERN COMMUNICATIONS

Effective communication is the cornerstone of survival in today's competitive business environment. This is particularly true for companies that operate or compete worldwide or those undertaking significant organizational change. Managers who use information technology effectively and are sensitive to various communication barriers are more likely to contribute to organizational success.

Communication in the Computerized Information Age

Organizations are increasingly using information technology as a lever to improve productivity and customer and employee satisfaction. In turn, communication patterns at work are radically changing. Consider how Patrick Braun, the German sales director for Cisco Systems' Benelux, Austria, eastern Europe and Middle Eastern regions, is using information technology to stay on top of his job.

I'm responsible for about 200 people in over 20 countries. Without the modern technical equipment it would be impossible to communicate with them fast and regularly. Since I'm travelling for about two-thirds of my working time, some instruments such as telephonic conference calls and videoconferencing are indispensable. Every Monday I talk to my senior managers for an hour-and-a-half while we're each in different regions of Europe. If I had to fly to each meeting I would lose a terrible amount of time. I mean, a single meeting in another country would take at least a day, even with the best flight schedule. I wouldn't be without my mobile phone either. Now I'm always attainable—not least now because now calls switch automatically between my office number, my mobile number and my voicemail. I also make use of the 'mobile office' concept: I can log in anytime and anywhere on the Cisco network, to read my mail or to get access to our Intranet. When I go to one of our offices in Norway or Switzerland, all I have to do is install my laptop. Our network is designed in a way that it recognizes me immediately and gives me direct access. Also, our administration system is almost paperless: all our documentation on customers is on CD-ROM. With all these technical aids, we are capable of operating our business with a relatively small group of people. If you were to take a look at our orderbook, you'd say we need at least another hundred people for Benelux alone. Finally, you must now think that I communicate only via the new technologies but the opposite is true: the time that I save by using mail, teleconferencing, etc. allows me to invest more in my personal contacts.[65]

Internet/Intranet/Extranet

The **Internet**, or more simply 'the Net' is more than a computer network. It is a *network of computer networks*. The Internet is a global network of independently operating but interconnected computers. It links more than 140,000 smaller networks in more than 200 countries. The Internet connects everything from supercomputers, to large mainframes housed in businesses, governments and universities, to the personal computers in our homes and offices. An **Intranet**, on the other hand, is nothing more than an organization's private Internet. Intranets also have *firewalls* that block outside Internet users from accessing internal information. This is done to protect the privacy and confidentiality of company documents. In the US, more than half the companies of 500 employees or more have corporate Intranets, according to Information Data Corporation.[66] In contrast to the internal focus of an Intranet, an **Extranet** is an extended Intranet in that it connects internal employees with selected customers, suppliers and other strategic partners. Ford Motor Company, for instance, has an Extranet that connects its dealers worldwide. Ford's Extranet was set up to help support the sales and servicing of cars and to enhance customer satisfaction.

The primary benefit of the Internet, Intranet and Extranet is that they can enhance the ability of employees to find, create, manage, and distribute information. The effectiveness of these 'Nets', however, depends on how organizations set up and manage their Intranet/Extranet and how employees use the acquired information—because information by itself cannot solve or do anything.[67] For example, communication effectiveness can actually decrease if a corporate Intranet becomes a dumping ground for disorganized information. In this case, employees will find themselves flailing in a sea of information.

Other reports detail stories of people spending hours 'surfing the Net' only to find themselves overwhelmed with information. Using the Internet can be very time consuming because the Internet is an unstructured repository of information that is becoming increasingly slow to access. Only the future will tell whether the Internet is more useful as a marketing and sales tool, a device to conduct personal transactions (such as banking or ordering books) or a management vehicle to enhance employee motivation and productivity.

Internet
a global network of computer networks

Intranet
an organization's private Internet

Extranet
connects internal employees with selected customers, suppliers and strategic partners

Electronic Mail

Electronic mail or email uses the Internet/Intranet to send computer-generated text and documents between people. Email is becoming a major communication medium because of four key benefits.[68]

1   Email reduces the cost of distributing information to a large number of employees.

2   Email is a tool for increasing teamwork. It enables employees to quickly send messages to colleagues on the next floor, in another building, or in another country. In support of this benefit, a study of 375 managers indicated they used email for three dominant reasons:

   (*a*) to keep others informed

   (*b*) to follow up an earlier communication

   (*c*) to communicate the same thing to many people.[69]

3   Email reduces the costs and time associated with print duplication and paper distribution.

4   Email fosters flexibility. This is particularly true for employees with a portable computer because they can log onto email whenever and wherever they want.

In spite of these positive benefits, there are three key drawbacks to consider. First, sending and receiving email can lead to a lot of wasted time and effort and it can distract employees from completing critical job duties. Information overload is the second drawback. People now tend to send more messages than ever, and there is a lot of 'spamming' going on: sending junk mail, bad jokes or irrelevant memos (such as email copies or 'cc'). Consider the frustration of Steven Roberts, a British freelance copywriter, when he came back to his office after a two week holiday.

A man walks into a bar . . . Why blondes are stupid . . . What a woman really means when she says . . . Has anybody seen my pen? This isn't my stream of consciousness, these are just some of the 328 unread messages I found in my inbox after my two weeks off. My heart sank as I scrolled down them: inane jokes, inane responses to inane jokes, inane responses to the responses . . . . Occasionally, there was something of import: a message from a client, a reminder that I have an appraisal next week. By the time I stored and deleted where appropriate, it was lunchtime. Then I started work, every thought interrupted by that familiar ping, as another email dropped into my inbox.[70]

Finally, preliminary evidence suggests that people are using electronic mail to communicate when they should be using other media. This practice can result in reduced communication effectiveness according to the contingency model of selecting medium that we discussed previously. A four-year study of communication patterns within a university supported this prediction. The increased use of electronic mail was associated with decreased face-to-face interactions and with a drop in the overall amount of organizational communication. Employees also expressed a feeling of being less connected and less cohesive as a department as the amount of emails increased.[71]

This interpersonal 'disconnection' may, indeed, be caused by the trend of replacing everyday face-to-face interactions with electronic messages. It is important to remember that employees' social needs are satisfied through the many different interpersonal interactions that occur at work. Steven Roberts again tells of his experiences in this matter.

'Recently', he says, 'I was working in the offices or a large television company. Nobody spoke to each other–virtually all information was communicated by email. Several times, I announced to my boss that I'd finished a job, only to be told to repeat this information by email and then to await my next instructions by email too. And my boss was sitting right next to me!'[72]

There are three additional issues to consider when using email. Firstly, email only works when the party with whom you wish to communicate also uses it. Email may not be a viable communication medium in all cases. Secondly, the speed of getting a response to an email message is dependent on how frequently the receiver examines his or her messages. It is important to consider this issue when picking a communication medium. Finally, many companies do not have policies for using email, which can lead to misuse and potential legal liability. Crédit Suisse, a Swiss bank, for instance, dismissed five employees after a routine audit of the firm's electronic mail system turned up lewd jokes and inappropriate messages that the individuals had been circulating inside and outside the firm.[73] Do not assume that your email messages are private and confidential. Organizations are advised to develop policies regarding the use of email.[74]

Videoconferencing

Videoconferencing, also known as teleconferencing, uses video and audio links along with computers to enable people who are located at different locations to see, hear and talk to each another. This enables people from many locations to conduct a meeting without having to travel. Videoconferencing thus can significantly reduce an organization's travel expenses. Many organizations set up special videoconferencing rooms or booths with specially equipped television cameras. More recent equipment enables people to attach small cameras and microphones to their desks or computer monitors. This enables employees to conduct long-distance meetings and training classes without leaving their office or cubicle. The use of videoconferencing is also growing within the executive search business.

Collaborative Computing

Collaborative computing entails using state-of-the-art computer software and hardware to help people *work together* better. They enable people to share information without the constraints of time and space. This is accomplished by using computer networks to provide a link—across a room or across the globe—between people. Collaborative applications include messaging and email systems, calendar management, videoconferencing, computer teleconferencing, electronic whiteboards, and the type of computer-aided decision-making systems discussed in Chapter 10.

Collaborative computing
using computer software and hardware to help people work together better

Organizations that use fully fledged collaborative systems have the ability to create virtual teams or to operate as a virtual organization. Virtual organizations are discussed in Chapter 12. You may recall that a 'virtual team' is a physically dispersed task group, it is also one that conducts its business using the type of information technology discussed here. Specifically, virtual teams tend to use Internet/Intranet systems, collaborative software systems and videoconferencing systems.[75] These real-time systems enable people to communicate with anyone at anytime.

It is important to keep in mind that modern-day information technology only enables people to interact virtually, it doesn't guarantee effective communications. Interestingly, there are a whole host of unique communication problems associated with using the information technology needed to 'operate virtually'.[76] For example, the Royal Bank of Scotland has used videoconferencing techniques since 1985, as face-to-face meetings have to take place every day and the participants are separated by 500 kilometres.

'Users at the bank have grown to live with it—it's very practical and we're hooked on the thing. We've expanded the initial service to include four suites here in Edinburgh, one in London and one in Manchester', says Mr James of the Edinburgh bank.'[77]

International OB

http://www.bangkokpost.net

Videoconferencing Leads to Increased Meetings and Costs in Thailand

Technology makes communication easier, especially across international borders, right? Not necessarily. Although Western companies are making major investments in technologies, designed to make their global communications more efficient, such tools are often underused and even counterproductive in cross-cultural business environments. You need to consider several factors before selecting which technology to use and in which context.

As for what can go wrong, consider the case of videoconferencing in Thailand. An American firm had invested in the installation of videoconferencing facilities in its Thailand subsidiary. In addition to enabling communication with other sites around the world, the new videoconferencing capability was intended to increase the productivity of the firm's local Thai employees. Many would have to spend an entire day travelling the crowded roads between the company's outlying factory to

attend a meeting at Bangkok headquarters. It was thought that videoconferencing would make such travel unnecessary. But things didn't quite turn out as planned. The Thais had trouble getting used to the new technology. The former managing director of the Thai subsidiary, a US expatriate, remembers ruefully, 'I soon found out that the local managers were conducting the videoconference for my benefit and then arranging to have a face-to-face meeting afterwards. They still wanted to be able to meet in person to gauge the reaction of others.'

So, instead of creating greater efficiency, the new videoconferencing facility resulted in additional meetings and extra costs.

SOURCE: Excerpt from E Gundling, 'How to Communicate', *Training and Development*, June 1999, p 28. Copyright June 1999, *Training and Development*, American Society for Training and Development. Reprinted with permission. All right reserved.

Telecommuting

Telecommuting
doing work that is generally performed in the office away from the office using different information technologies

Telecommuting, also known as teleworking, involves doing officework away from the office, using a variety of information technologies. Employees typically receive and send work from home using a phone, fax or a modem linking the home and office computers. Telecommuting is more common for jobs that involve computer work, writing, and phone or brain work that requires concentration and limited interruptions.[78] By midway through the nineties, 150,000 Germans, 560,000 Britons, 215,000 French and 80,000 Italians were already to be found teleworking. Today, the number of teleworkers in Europe counts for several million people.[79]

Proposed benefits of telecommuting include the following.

1 Reduction of capital costs.

2 Increased flexibility and autonomy for workers.

3 Competitive edge in recruitment.

4 Increased job satisfaction and lower turnover.

5 Increased productivity.

6 Additional sources of workers (such as prison inmates and the homebound disabled).

Employees like telecommuting because it helps resolve work–family conflicts. A study revealed that homeworkers at British Telecom coped better with the daily stresses of working than the office-bound operators.[80] Although telecommuting represents an attempt to accommodate employee needs and desires, it requires adjustments and is not for everybody. Many people thoroughly enjoy the social camaraderie that exists within an office setting. These individuals probably would not like to telecommute.

Others lack the self-motivation needed to work at home. Finally, organizations must be careful to implement telecommuting in a non-discriminatory manner. Organizations can easily and unknowingly violate one of several anti-discrimination laws.[81]

Barriers to Effective Communication

Communication noise is a barrier to effective communication because it interferes with the accurate transmission and reception of a message. Management awareness of these barriers is a good starting point to improve the communication process. There are four key barriers to effective communication: process, personal, physical and semantic barriers.

Process Barriers

Every element of the perceptual model of communication shown in Figure 11–1 is a potential process barrier. Consider the following examples.

1 *Sender barrier.* A customer gets incorrect information from a customer service agent because he or she was recently hired and lacks experience.

2 *Encoding barrier.* An employee for whom English is a second language has difficulty explaining why a delivery was late.

3 *Message barrier.* An employee misses a meeting for which he or she never received a confirmation memo.

4 *Medium barrier.* A salesperson gives up trying to make a sales call when the potential customer fails to return three previous phone calls.

5 *Decoding barrier.* An employee does not know how to respond to a manager's request to stop exhibiting 'passive aggressive' behaviour.

6 *Receiver barrier.* A student who is talking to a friend during a lecture asks the professor the same question as the one that has just been answered.

7 *Feedback barrier.* The non-verbal head-nodding of an interviewer leads an interviewee to think that he or she is answering questions well.

Barriers in any of these process elements can distort the transfer of meaning. Reducing these barriers is essential but difficult given the current diversity of the workforce.

Personal Barriers

There are many personal barriers to communication. We highlight eight of the more common ones. The first is our ability to communicate effectively. As highlighted throughout this chapter, people possess varying levels of communication skills. The second barrier is the way people process and interpret information. Chapter 6 highlighted the fact that people use different frames of reference and experiences to interpret the world around them. We also learned that people selectively attend to various stimuli. All told, these differences affect both what we say and what we think we hear. The third barrier is the level of interpersonal trust between people, which can either prevent or enable effective communication. Communication is more likely to be distorted when people do not trust each other. Stereotypes and prejudices are a fourth barrier. They can powerfully distort what we perceive about others. Our egos are a fifth barrier. Egos can cause political battles, turf wars, and the pursuit of power, credit and resources. Egos influence how people treat each other as well as our receptiveness to being influenced by others. The sixth barrier to communication, is that of poor listening skills.[82]

Carl Rogers, a renowned psychologist, identified the seventh and eighth barriers that interfere with interpersonal communication.[83] The seventh barrier is a natural tendency to evaluate or judge a sender's message. To highlight the natural tendency to evaluate, consider how you might respond to the statement 'I like the book you are reading.' What would you say? Your probable response is to approve or disapprove the statement. You may say, 'I agree, it's good,' or alternatively, 'I disagree, the book is boring.' The point is that we all tend to evaluate messages from our own point of view or frame of reference. The tendency to evaluate messages is greatest when one has strong feelings or emotions about the issue being discussed. The eighth personal barrier to effective communication is an inability to listen with understanding. Listening with understanding occurs when a receiver can 'see the expressed idea and attitude from the other person's point of view, to sense how it feels to him, to achieve his frame of reference in regard to the thing he is talking about'. Listening with understanding reduces defensiveness and improves accuracy in perceiving a message.

Physical Barriers

The distance between employees can interfere with effective communication. It is hard to understand someone who is speaking to you from 20 metres away. Work and office noise are additional barriers. Poor telephone lines or crashed computers represent physical barriers to effective IT communication.

In spite of the general acceptance of physical barriers, they can be reduced. Walls that are distracting or inhibiting can be torn down. It is important that managers attempt to manage these communication barriers by making the optimum choice of medium and so reduce the physical barriers.

Semantic Barriers

Semantics is the study of words. Semantic barriers show up as encoding and decoding errors because these phases of communication involve transmitting and receiving words and symbols. These barriers occur very easily. Consider the following statement: Crime is ubiquitous.

Do you understand this message? Even if you do, would it not be simpler to say that 'crime is all around us' or 'crime is everywhere'? Choosing our words more carefully is the easiest way to reduce semantic barriers. This barrier can also be decreased by attentiveness to mixed messages and cultural diversity. Mixed messages occur when a person's words imply one message while his or her actions or non-verbal cues suggest something different. Obviously, understanding is enhanced when a person's actions and non-verbal cues match the verbal message.

Summary of Key Concepts

1 Describe the perceptual process model of communication.

Communication is a process of consecutively linked elements. Historically, this process was described in terms of a conduit model. Criticisms of this model led to development of a perceptual process model of communication that depicts receivers as information processors who create the meaning of messages in their own mind. Because receivers' interpretations of messages often differ from those intended by senders, miscommunication is a common occurrence.

2 Explain the contingency approach to media selection.

Selecting media is a key component of communication effectiveness. Media selection is based on the interaction between the information richness of a medium and the complexity of the problem/situation at hand. Information richness ranges from low to high and is a function of four factors: speed of feedback, characteristics of the channel, type of communication, and language source. Problems/situations range from simple to complex. Effective communication occurs when the richness of the medium matches this complexity. Richer media need to be used as situations become more complex.

3 Contrast the communication styles of assertiveness, aggressiveness and non-assertiveness.

An assertive style is expressive and self-enhancing but does not violate others' basic human rights. In contrast, an aggressive style is expressive and self-enhancing but takes unfair advantage of others. A non-assertive style is characterized by timid and self-denying behaviour. An assertive communication style is more effective than either an aggressive or non-assertive style.

4 Discuss the primary sources of both non-verbal communication and listener comprehension.

There are several identifiable sources of non-verbal communication. Body movements and gestures, touch, facial expressions, and eye contact are important non-verbal cues. The interpretation of these non-verbal cues significantly varies across cultures. Listening is the process of actively decoding and interpreting verbal messages. Characteristics of the listener, speaker, message and environment influence listener comprehension.

5 Identify and give examples of the three different listening styles, and review the ten keys to effective listening.

Communication experts identified three unique types of listening styles. A results-style listener likes to hear the bottom line or result of a communication at the beginning of a conversation. Reasons-style listeners want to know the rationale for what someone is saying or proposing. Process-style listeners like to discuss issues in detail. Good listeners use the following ten listening habits: (a) capitalize on thought speed by staying with the speaker and listening between the lines (b) listen for ideas rather than facts (c) identify areas of interest between the speaker and listener (d) judge content and not delivery (e) do not judge until the speaker has completed his or her message (f) put energy and effort into listening (g) resist distractions (h) listen to both favourable and unfavourable information (i) read or listen to complex material to exercise the mind and (j) take notes when necessary and use visual aids to enhance understanding.

6 Discuss the patterns of hierarchical communication and the grapevine.

Hierarchical communication patterns describe exchanges of information between managers and the employees they supervise. Managers provide five types of downward communication: job instructions, job rationale, organizational procedures and practices, feedback about performance, and indoctrination of goals. Employees communicate information upward about themselves, co-workers and their problems, organizational practices and policies, and what needs to be done and how to do it. The grapevine is the unofficial communication system of the informal organization. Communication along the grapevine follows four predictable patterns: single strand, gossip, probability, and cluster. The cluster pattern is the most common.

7 Demonstrate your familiarity with four antecedents of communication distortion between managers and employees.

Communication distortion is a common problem that consists of modifying the content of a message. Employees distort upward communication when their supervisor has high upward influence or power. Distortion also increases when employees aspire to move upward and when they mistrust their supervisor.

8 Explain the information technology of Internet, Intranet, Extranet, email, videoconferencing and collaborative computing, then explain the related use of telecommuting.

The Internet is a global network of computer networks. An Intranet is an organization's private Internet. It contains a firewall that blocks outside Internet users from accessing private internal information. An Extranet connects an organization's internal employees with selected customers, suppliers, and strategic partners. The primary benefit of these 'nets' is that they can enhance the ability of employees to find, create, manage and distribute information. Email uses the Internet/Intranet/Extranet to send computer-generated text and documents between people. Videoconferencing uses video and audio links, along with computers, to enable people located at different sites to see, hear and talk to each other. Collaborative computing entails using state-of-the-art computer software and hardware to help people work together better. Information is shared across time and space by linking people via computer networks. Telecommuting involves doing work that is generally performed in the office away from the office using a variety of information technologies.

9 *Describe the process, personal, physical and semantic barriers to effective communication.*

Every element of the perceptual model of communication is a potential process barrier. There are eight personal barriers that commonly influence communication: (*a*) the ability to effectively communicate (*b*) the way people process and interpret information (*c*) the level of interpersonal trust between people (*d*) the existence of stereotypes and prejudices (*e*) the egos of the people communicating (*f*) the ability to listen (*g*) the natural tendency to evaluate or judge a sender's message and (*h*) the inability to listen with understanding. Physical barriers pertain to distance, physical objects, time, and work and office noise. Semantic barriers show up as encoding and decoding errors because these phases of communication involve transmitting and receiving words and symbols. Cultural diversity is a key contributor to semantic barriers.

Discussion Questions

1 Describe a situation where you had trouble decoding a message. What caused the problem?

2 What are some sources of noise that interfere with communication during a lecture, an encounter with a lecturer in his or her office, and a film?

3 Which of the three zones of communication in Figure 11–3 (overload, effective, oversimplification) do you think is most common in today's large organizations? What is your rationale?

4 Would you describe your prevailing communication style as assertive, aggressive, or non-assertive? How can you tell? Would your style help or hinder you as a manager?

5 Are you good at reading non-verbal communication? Give some examples.

6 What is your listening style? Give behavioural examples to support your assessment.

7 What is your personal experience of the grapevine? Do you see it as a positive or negative factor in the workplace? Explain.

8 Have you ever distorted upward communication? What was your reason? Was it related to one of the four antecedents of communication distortion? Explain.

9 Which barrier to effective communication is most difficult to reduce? Explain.

Internet Exercise

http://www.queendom.com

As covered in this chapter, communication styles vary from non-assertive to aggressive. We recommended that you strive to use an assertive style while avoiding the tendencies of being non-assertive or aggressive. In trying to be assertive, however, keep in mind that too much of a good thing is bad. That is, the use of an assertive style can become an aggressive one if taken too far.

A Free Self-Assessment Questionnaire for Assertiveness

The purpose of this exercise is to provide you with feedback on the extent to which you use an assertive communication style. Go to the Internet home page for Body-Mind QueenDom (www.queendom.com), and select the subheading *Tests* under the main menu heading *Interactive*. (*Note:* Our use of this questionnaire is for instructional purposes only and does not constitute an endorsement of any products that may or may not suit your needs. There is no obligation to buy anything.) At the *Tests* page, read the brief welcome statement about Queendom's psychological tests, and then scroll down to the category *Career*. Select the

Assertiveness Test, read the instructions, complete all 32 items, and click on the *score* button for automatic scoring. Read the interpretation of your results.

Questions

1 Possible scores on the self-assessment questionnaire range from 0 to 100. How did you score? Are you surprised by the results? Do you agree with the interpretation of your score?

2 Reviewing the questionnaire item by item, can you find aspects of communication in which you are either non-assertive or possibly too assertive? Do you think that your communication style can be improved by making adjustments within these areas of communication?

3 Based on the results of this questionnaire, develop an action plan for improving your communication style.

Personal Awareness and Growth Exercise
Assessing Your Listening Skills

Objectives

1 To assess your listening skills.

2 To develop a personal development plan aimed at increasing your listening skills.

Introduction

Listening is a critical component of effective communication. Unfortunately, research and case studies suggest that many of us are not very good at actively listening. This is particularly bad in light of the fact that managers spend more time listening than they do speaking or writing. This exercise provides you with the opportunity to assess your listening skills and develop a plan for improvement.

Instructions

The following statements reflect various habits we use when listening to others. For each statement, indicate the extent to which you agree or disagree with it by selecting one number from the scale provided. Circle your response for each statement. Remember, there are no right or wrong answers. After completing the survey, add up your total score for the 17 items and record it in the space provided.

Listening Skills Survey

1 = Strongly disagree

2 = Disagree

3 = Neither agree nor disagree

4 = Agree

5 = Strongly agree

1 I daydream or think about other things when listening to others. 1—2—3—4—5

2 I do not mentally summarize the ideas being communicated by a speaker. 1—2—3—4—5

3 I do not use a speaker's body language or tone of voice to help interpret what he or she is saying. 1—2—3—4—5

4 I listen more for facts than overall ideas during classroom lectures. 1—2—3—4—5

5 I tune out dry speakers. 1—2—3—4—5

6 I have a hard time paying attention to boring people. 1—2—3—4—5

7 I can tell whether someone has anything useful to say before he or she finishes communicating a message. 1—2—3—4—5

8 I stop listening to a speaker when I think he or she has nothing interesting to say. 1—2—3—4—5

9 I get emotional or upset when speakers make jokes about issues or things that are important to me. 1—2—3—4—5

10 I get angry or distracted when speakers use offensive words. 1—2—3—4—5

11 I do not expend a lot of energy when listening to others. 1—2—3—4—5

12 I pretend to pay attention to others even when I'm not really listening. 1—2—3—4—5

13 I get distracted when listening to others. 1—2—3—4—5

14 I deny or ignore information and comments that go against my thoughts and feelings. 1—2—3—4—5

15 I do not seek opportunities to challenge my listening skills. 1—2—3—4—5

16 I do not pay attention to the visual aids used during lectures. 1—2—3—4—5

17 I do not take notes on handouts when they are provided. 1—2—3—4—5

Total Score = _____

Preparing a Personal Development Plan

1 Use the following norms to evaluate your listening skills:

17–34 = Good listening skills

35–53 = Moderately good listening skills

54–85 = Poor listening skills.

How would you evaluate your listening skills?

2 Do you agree with the assessment of your listening skills? Why or why not?

3 The 17-item listening skills survey was developed to assess the extent to which you use the keys to effective listening presented in Table 11–2. Use Table 11–2 and the development plan format shown on the following page to prepare your development plan. First, identify the five statements from the listening skills survey that received your highest ratings–high ratings represent low skills. Record the survey numbers in the space provided in the development plan. Next, compare the content of these survey items to the descriptions of bad and good listeners shown in Table 11–2. This comparison will help you identify the keys to effective listening being measured by each survey item. Write down the keys to effective listening that correspond to each of the five items you want to improve. Finally, write down specific actions or behaviours that you can undertake to improve the listening skill being considered.

Development Plan

Survey Items	Key to Effective Listening I Want to Improve	Action Steps Required (What Do You Need to Do to Build Listening Skills for This Listening Characteristic?)

Group Exercise
Practising Different Styles of Communication

Objectives

1 To demonstrate the relative effectiveness of communicating assertively, aggressively, and non-assertively.

2 To give you hands-on experience with different styles of communication.

Introduction

Research shows that assertive communication is more effective than either an aggressive or non-assertive style. This role-playing exercise is designed to increase your ability to communicate assertively. Your task is to use different communication styles while attempting to resolve the work-related problems of a poor performer.

Instructions

Form a group of three and read the 'Poor Performer' and 'Store Manager' roles provided here. Then decide who will play the poor performer role, who the managerial role, and who the observer. The observer will be asked to provide feedback to the manager after each role play. When playing the managerial role, you should first attempt to resolve the problem by using an aggressive communication style. Attempt to achieve your objective by using the non-verbal and verbal behaviour patterns associated with the aggressive style shown in Table 11–2. Take about four to six minutes to act out the instructions. The observer should give feedback to the manager after completing the role play. The observer should comment on how the employee responded to the aggressive behaviours displayed by the manager.

After feedback is provided on the first role play, the person playing the manager should then try to resolve the problem with a non-assertive style. Observers once again should provide feedback. Finally, the manager should confront the problem with an assertive style. Once again, rely on the relevant non-verbal and verbal behaviour patterns presented in Table 11–2, and take four to six minutes to act out each scenario. Observers should try to provide detailed feedback on how effectively the manager exhibited non-verbal and verbal assertive behaviours. Be sure to provide positive and constructive feedback.

After completing these three role plays, switch roles: manager becomes observer, observer becomes poor performer, and poor performer becomes manager. When these role plays are completed, switch roles once again.

Role: Poor Performer

You sell shoes full-time for a national chain of shoe stores. Over the past month, you have been absent three times without giving your manager a reason. The quality of your work has been slipping. You have a lot of creative excuses when your boss tries to talk to you about your performance.

When playing this role, feel free to invent a personal problem that you may eventually want to share with your manager. However, make the manager dig for information about this problem. Otherwise, respond to your manager's comments as you would normally.

Role: Store Manager

You manage a store for a national chain of shoe stores. In the privacy of your office, you are talking to one of your salespeople who has had three unexcused absences from work during the last month. (This is excessive, according to company guidelines, and must be corrected.) The quality of the person's work has been slipping. Customers have complained that this person is rude and co-workers have told you this individual isn't carrying a fair share of the work. You are fairly sure this person has some sort of personal problem. You want to identify that problem and get him or her back on course.

Questions for Discussion

1 What drawbacks of the aggressive and non-assertive styles did you observe?

2 What were major advantages of the assertive style?

3 What were the most difficult aspects of trying to use an assertive style?

4 How important was non-verbal communication during the various role plays? Explain with examples.

Chapter Twelve

Teams and Teamwork

Learning Objectives

When you finish studying the material in this chapter, you should be able to:

- Describe the five stages in Tuckman's theory of group development.

- Identify and describe the four types of work teams.

- Explain the ecological model of work team effectiveness.

- Discuss why teams fail.

- Describe what is meant by the term *groupthink* and identify at least four of its symptoms.

- List at least three things managers can do to build trust.

- Distinguish two types of group cohesiveness and summarize the related research findings.

- Define quality circles, virtual teams and self-managed teams.

- Describe high-performance teams.

Teamwork is vital in battle of the elements

'Running a business is like sailing a yacht', says Ian Gordon-Cumming of British Telecommunications. 'It epitomises all the qualities required to compete in today's global marketplace: leadership, teamwork, innovation and competitiveness.' ▶

British Telecommunications, who organizes and sponsors the BT Global Challenge, a round-the-world sailing contest, believes this initiative will prove an innovative way of wooing customers by portraying the race as a metaphor for business. Also, as many of the participants are managers, another purpose of the race is to provide an excellent occasion to enhance one's people skills, skills which can be transferred into the workplace.

Since 1998, every year 12 skippers sail from Southampton in southern England intent on joining the exclusive club of those who have circled the world 'the wrong way'. Each will command a 72-foot, 42-tonne yacht and a 17-strong crew. All aim to finish first after the 45,000 km course, but the race requires more than navigation skills and an understanding of the sea. Apart from the skipper, all the crew members are amateurs, most never having sailed before. To cope with the challenge, skippers will have to draw on management and communication skills. 'The 12 competing yachts are identical. Winning will therefore solely depend on commitment, team dynamics and a uniting of cultural differences', says Gordon-Cumming.

Mr Hopkinson, who manages an IT team for Granada Media, says: 'the crew is 17 and at Granada, my team is the same. In both cases, my job is to persuade them to do things to achieve a common goal and make sure they work together. This won't be the easiest thing: the crew and the skippers face 160 days at sea. They will visit five continents, encountering the toughest ocean conditions one can think of. Nights will often be short on sleep and the weather a constant foe. There is also a high risk of injury. In the race, there will be great scope for disharmony and conflict.'

The skippers agree that establishing shared goals and fostering co-operation is an essential technique to counter friction on deck. 'You have to persuade your crew to buy into your goals. Every person on board has to be geared towards achieving them', says Hopkinson. The mutiny that occurred at the end of the first leg of the BT Global Challenge, aboard a boat ironically named 'Teamwork', shows the pressures that have to be contained.

One participant says: 'The 40-knot wind is clawing at you. Icy waves are slamming over your head. Beneath your feet, the bow of the boat is surging through 60 metres or more. You feel cold, exhausted, very frightened and wish you were somewhere else. But as you struggle to change the heavy sail, you have to keep going. The rest of the crew depend on you, particularly the person at your side.'

Many of the people in the race are attracted by the thrill of adventure. Others see it as a remarkable management-development course. 'You get a new focus and stop fussing about details when the next wave might kill you. When you go for a job interview, you can certainly demonstrate something a little different that lifts you above the crowd. Ocean racing turned me from a man into a manager', says Robin Knox-Johnston, who has participated in many races. 'It also has been a great lesson in the benefits of involving colleagues. I used to run my business treating staff as a means to an end. The race helped me to take on a broader perspective', he says.

'In an era where companies stress the importance of team building, such races can be an incomparable management-forcing house', says Anthony Lane, chairman of Time Management International, the consulting firm. 'This is one of the most accelerated personal-development courses you can possibly go on. Leadership and teamworking skills are right at the forefront–there is nowhere to hide. You can't get off a boat.'

Throughout the competition, representatives from 25 organizations will monitor the skippers' progress and draw management lessons from the race. There will also be business seminars at the seven ports where the challengers will dock.[1]

> **For discussion**
> Imagine that you were a participant in the BT Global Challenge. What to you are the most crucial characteristics your crew needs to succeed in the race, and how do you think these could be stimulated?

Teams and teamwork are popular terms in management circles these days. Cynics might dismiss teamwork as just another management fad or quick-fix gimmick. But a closer look reveals a more profound and durable trend. For instance, Manfred Kets de Vries, professor at Insead (one of Europe's leading business schools, based in Fontainbleau, France), has been searching for years for those key aspects that distinguish the best organizations from the others. He found some common traits at the heart of the most admired companies, and teamwork turned out to be a very important dominator.

Successful organizations are good at building teams and exploiting teamwork. People need to be able to work in teams, they need to subordinate their own agenda to the well-being of the group. Further, successful organizations foster diversity, which entails respect for the individual and makes group decision-making more creative. Such organizations also empower their employees. Decision-making is pushed to the lowest level at which a competent decision can be made, to the level of work groups and production teams. To foster such a process, managers should operate with minimal secrecy.[2]

The team approach to managing organizations is having diverse and substantial effects on individuals and organizations. In our contemporary organizations, people need a strong working knowledge of interpersonal behaviour and ability to consider how their behaviour impacts on others and how different people take on different roles in a team.[3] An ongoing study by the Centre for Creative Leadership (involving diverse samplings from France, Germany, Italy, Belgium, the United Kingdom, the United States and Spain) found four stumbling blocks that tend to derail executives' careers. These stumbling blocks are:

1   problems with interpersonal relationships
2   failure to meet business objectives
3   failure to change or adapt during a transition.[4]

Teams promise to be a cornerstone of progressive management for the foreseeable future. According to management expert Peter Drücker, tomorrow's organizations will be flatter, information based, and organized around teams.[5] This opinion was bolstered by a survey of human resource executives in which 44 per cent called for *more teamwork* when asked what change employees need to make to achieve current business goals.[6] This means virtually all employees will need to polish their team skills. According to some managers, even scientists and IT specialists, who are traditionally regarded as individualists and who rely mainly on technical skills to fulfil their jobs, will have to take on a broader role in the future.

Hardcore scientists and IT-specialists are frequently regarded as weirdos, dedicated 'lone wolfs', who are seemingly married to their research, their measuring equipment and their paradigms. 'This is probably the greatest cliché of the last few years', states an editorial article in the magazine Science Technology. *'In most cases, the modern scientist has become a "team-animal", who has to look beyond the limits of his own territory, otherwise his knowledge and career will fade very quickly. Renowned companies like Janssens Pharmaceuticals are now implementing cross-functional teamwork, even for their most specialised doctoral researchers.'*[7] *Marc Coninck, IT-manager at KBC Insurance agrees: 'The idea that a computer scientist is primary a technological whizz-kid is completely outdated. On the contrary, we increasingly have to act like people managers. Of course, you can try to fill in your function as chief of an IT-department from a purely technical perspective, but the core of our job is undoubtedly shifting to guiding people.'*[8]

Examples of the trend towards teams and teamwork abound. Consider the following sample of articles on global businesses.

▼ *Siemens, the German manufacturing company:* ' . . . a new generation of managers is fostering co-operation across the company: They are setting up teams to develop products and attack new markets. They are trying hiking expeditions and weekend workshops to spur ideas and new work methods.'[9]

▼ *Motorola's walkie-talkie plants in Penang, Malaysia, and Plantation, Florida:* 'The goal, pursued by Motorola worldwide, is to get employees at all levels to forget narrow job titles and work together in teams to identify and act on problems that hinder quality and productivity . . . . New applicants are screened on the basis of their attitude toward "teamwork".'[10]

▼ *Fiat's new car plant in Melfi, Italy:* 'Fiat slashed the layers between plant managers and workers and spent $64 million training its 7,000 workers and engineers to work in small teams. Now, the 31 independent teams—with 15 to 100 workers apiece—oversee car-assembly tasks from start to finish.[11]

▼ *Ford Motor Company's product-development Web site:* 'The Web brings 4,500 Ford engineers from labs in the United States, Germany and England together in cyberspace to collaborate on projects. The idea is to break down the barriers between regional operations so basic . . . components are designed once and used everywhere.'[12]

All of these huge global companies have staked their future competitiveness on teams and teamwork.

The emphasis in this chapter is on tapping the full and promising potential of work groups. We will: discuss how groups and teams develop; identify different types of work teams; introduce a model of team effectiveness; discuss some major threats to team effectiveness—such as *groupthink*; discuss keys to effective teamwork, such as trust; explore applications of the team concept; and review team-building techniques.

THE GROUP DEVELOPMENT PROCESS

Groups and teams in the workplace go through a maturation process, such as one would find in any life-cycle (e.g., humans, organizations or products). While there is general agreement among theorists that the group development process occurs in identifiable stages, they disagree about the exact number, sequence, length, and nature of those stages.[13] One frequently cited model is that proposed by educational psychologist Bruce W Tuckman in 1965. His original model involved only four stages (forming, storming, 'norming', and performing). The five-stage model in Figure 12–1 evolved when Tuckman and a doctoral student added 'adjourning' in 1977.[14] A word of caution is in order. Somewhat akin to Maslow's need hierarchy theory, Tuckman's theory has been repeated and taught so often and for so long that many have come to view it as documented fact, not merely a theory. Even today, it is good to remember Tuckman's own caution that his group development model was derived more from group therapy sessions than from everyday groups. Still, many in the OB field like Tuckman's five-stage model of group development because of its easy-to-remember labels and commonsense appeal.[15]

Five Stages

Let us briefly examine each of the five stages in Tuckman's model. Notice how, as shown in Figure 12–1, individuals give up a measure of their independence when they join and participate in a group. Also, the various stages are not necessarily of the same duration or intensity. For instance, the storming stage may be practically non-existent or painfully long, depending on the goal clarity and the commitment and maturity of the members. You can make this process come to life by relating the various stages to your own experience of work groups, committees, athletic teams, social or religious groups, or class project teams. Some group happenings, which surprised you when they occurred, may now make sense or strike you as inevitable when seen as part of a natural development process.

Stage 1: Forming

During this 'ice-breaking' stage, group members tend to be uncertain and anxious about such things as their roles, who is in charge, and the group's goals. Mutual trust is low and there is a good deal of holding back (waiting) to see who takes charge and how. If the formal leader (for example, a supervisor) does not assert his or her authority, an emergent leader will eventually step in to fulfil the group's need for leadership and direction. Leaders typically mistake this honeymoon period as a mandate for permanent control. But later problems may force a leadership change.

Stage 2: Storming

This is a time of testing. Individuals test the leader's policies and assumptions as they try to determine how they fit into the power structure.[16] Sub-groups take shape and subtle forms of rebellion, such as procrastination, occur. Many groups stall in stage 2 because power politics erupts into open rebellion.

Stage 3: Norming

Group cohesiveness
a 'we feeling' binding members of a group together

Groups that make it through stage 2 generally do so because a respected member, other than the leader, challenges the group to resolve its power struggles so something can be accomplished. Questions about authority and power are resolved through unemotional, pragmatic group discussion. A feeling of team spirit is experienced because members believe they have found their proper roles. **Group cohesiveness**, defined as the 'we feeling' that binds members of a group together, is the principal by-product of stage 3.[17]

Stage 4: Performing

Activity during this vital stage is focused on solving task problems. As members of a mature group, contributors get their work done without hampering others. There is a climate of open communication, strong co-operation and lots of helping behaviour. Conflicts and job-boundary disputes are handled constructively and efficiently. Cohesiveness and personal commitment to group goals help the group to achieve more than a single individual could. According to a pair of group development experts:

> . . . the group structure can become flexible and adjust to fit the requirements of the situation without causing problems for the members. Influence can shift depending on who has the particular expertise or skills required for the group task or activity. Sub-groups can work on special problems or sub-problems without posing threats to the authority or cohesiveness of the rest of the group.[18]

Stage 5: Adjourning

This is the stage where the team comes to an end. The work is done; it is time to move on to other things. Having worked so hard to get along and get something done, many members feel a compelling sense of loss. The return to independence can be eased by rituals celebrating 'the end' and 'new beginnings'. Parties, award ceremonies, graduations or mock funerals can provide the necessary punctuation at the end of a significant group project.

However, not all groups follow the complete route. For instance, some task groups get stuck in the early stages and never reach the performing stage. On the other hand, some groups and teams never adjourn, as in the following example.

> *17 former customer care employees of the travelling agency [travel agency] Leisureplanet decided to stay together when the company went bankrupt. Quite originally, they entered the labour market together, presenting themselves to potential employers as a team. 'It may sound a cliché', says one of the members, 'but through our work we have become true friends. Also, we know what we stand for and what we're worth. We decided that it*

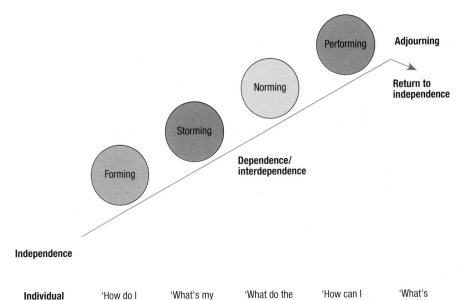

Figure 12–1

Tuckman's Five-Stage Theory of Group Development

Individual issues	'How do I fit in?'	'What's my role here?'	'What do the others expect me to do?'	'How can I best perform my role?'	'What's next?'

Individual issues	'How do I fit in?'	'What's my role here?'	'What do the others expect me to do?'	'How can I best perform my role?'	'What's next?'
Group issues	'Why are we here?'	'Why are we fighting over who is in charge and who does what ?'	'Can we agree on roles and work as a team?'	'Can we do the job properly?'	'Can we help members transition out?'

would be a pity to just end this co-operation and that's why we decided to . . . [hunt] for a new job together, looking for an employer who wants to hire us all as a team. This might sound crazy and naïve, but throughout the years we developed many valuable skills, so we thought: Why not? We have a lot to offer, more than each of us could do on his own.' The crew especially targets American companies who come to Europe to start a new filial [sister company or branch]. 'We can immediately fill in their entire call-centre, customer service or communication centre. We have all the assets required, and we certainly don't need no extra team-building, social skills or communication training.' As an . . . [application] letter, they designed a Web-site, and together they're good for five nationalities and a combined knowledge of ten languages.[19]

WORK TEAMS: TYPES AND EFFECTIVENESS

Jon R Katzenbach and Douglas K Smith, management consultants at McKinsey & Company, say it is a mistake to use the terms *group* and *team* interchangeably. After studying many different kinds of teams—from athletic to corporate to military—they concluded that successful teams tend to take on a life of their own. Katzenbach and Smith define a **team** as 'a small number of people with complementary skills who are committed to a common purpose, performance goals and approach for which they hold themselves mutually accountable'.[20] Relative to Tuckman's theory of group development—forming, storming, norming, performing and adjourning—teams are task groups that have matured to the *performing* stage (but not slipped into decay).

Because of conflicts over power and authority and unstable interpersonal relations, many work groups never qualify as a real team.[21] Katzenbach and Smith clarified the distinction this way: 'The essence of a team is common commitment. Without it, groups perform as individuals; with it, they become a powerful unit of collective performance.'[22] (See Table 12–1.)

Team
small group with complementary skills who hold themselves mutually accountable for common purpose, goals and approach

Table 12–1

The Evolution of a Team

A work group becomes a team when
1. *Leadership* becomes a shared activity.
2. *Accountability* shifts from strictly individual to both individual and collective.
3. The group develops its own *purpose* or mission.
4. *Problem solving* becomes a way of life, not a part-time activity.
5. *Effectiveness* is measured by the group's collective outcomes and products.

SOURCE: Condensed and adapted from J R Katzenbach and D K Smith, *The Wisdom of Teams: Creating the High-Performance Organization* (New York: HarperBusiness, 1999), p 214.

When Katzenbach and Smith refer to 'a small number of people' in their definition, they mean between 2 and 25 team members. Generally, they found effective teams to have fewer than ten members. This conclusion was echoed in a survey of 400 workplace team members in the United States and Canada: 'The average team consists of ten members. Eight is the most common size.'[23]

A General Typology of Work Teams

Work teams are created for various purposes and thus face different challenges. Managers can deal with those challenges more effectively when they understand how teams differ. A helpful way of sorting things out is to consider a typology of work teams developed by Eric Sundstrom and his colleagues.[24] Four general types of work teams listed in Table 12–2 are: advice, production, project, and action. Each of these labels identifies a basic purpose. For instance, advice teams tend to make recommendations for managerial decisions and seldom make final decisions themselves. In contrast, production and action teams actually carry out the decisions of the management.

Four key variables in Table 12–2 deal with technical specialization, co-ordination, work cycles, and outputs. Technical specialization is low when the team draws upon members' general experience and problem-solving ability. It is high when team members are required to apply technical skills acquired through higher education or extensive training. The degree of co-ordination with other work units is determined by the team's relative independence (low co-ordination) or interdependence (high co-ordination). Work cycles are the amount of time teams need to discharge their missions. The various outputs listed in Table 12–2 are intended to illustrate real-life effects. A closer look at each type of work team is required.[25]

Advice Teams

As their name implies, advice teams are created to broaden the information base for managerial decisions. Quality circles, discussed later, are a prime example because they facilitate suggestions for quality improvement from volunteer production or service workers. Advice teams tend to have a low degree of technical specialization. Likewise, co-ordination is low because advice teams generally work on their own. Ad hoc committees (e.g., the annual picnic committee) have shorter life cycles than standing committees (e.g., the grievance committee).

Production Teams

This second type of team is responsible for performing day-to-day operations. Minimal training for routine tasks accounts for the low degree of technical specialization. Generally, co-ordination is high, however, because work flows from one team to another. For example, track maintenance crews require fresh information from train crews about necessary repairs.

Table 12-2 *Four General Types of Work Teams and Their Outputs*

Types and Examples	Degree of Technical Specialization	Degree of Coordination with Other Work Units	Work Cycles	Typical Outputs
Advice Committees Review panels, boards Quality circles Employee involvement groups Advisory councils	Low	Low	Work cycles can be brief or long; one cycle can be team life span.	Decisions Selections Suggestions Proposals Recommendations
Production Assembly teams Manufacturing crews Mining teams Flight attendant crews Data processing groups Maintenance crews	Low	High	Work cycles typically repeated or continuous process; cycles often briefer than team life span.	Food, chemicals Components Assemblies Retail sales Customer service Equipment repairs
Project Research groups Planning teams Architect teams Engineering teams Development teams Task forces	High	Low (for traditional units) or High (for cross-functional units)	Work cycles typically differ for each new project; one cycle can be team life span.	Plans, designs Investigations Presentations Prototypes Reports, findings
Action Sports team Entertainment groups Expeditions Negotiating teams Surgery teams Cockpit crews Military platoons and squads	High	High	Brief performance events, often repeated under new conditions, requiring extended training and/or preparation.	Combat missions Expeditions Contracts, lawsuits Concerts Surgical operations Competitive events

SOURCE: Excerpted and adapted from E Sundstrom, K P De Meuse, and D Futrell, 'Work Teams', *American Psychologist*, February 1990, p 125.

Project Teams

Projects require creative problem-solving, often involving the application of specialized knowledge. For example, Boeing's new 777 jumbo jet was designed by project teams consisting of engineering, manufacturing, marketing, finance and customer service specialists. State-of-the-art computer modelling programmes allowed the teams to assemble three-dimensional computer models of the new aircraft. Design and assembly problems were ironed out during project team meetings before production workers started cutting any metal. Boeing's 777 design teams required a high degree of co-ordination between organizational sub-units because they were cross-functional.[26] A pharmaceutical research team of biochemists, on the other hand, would interact less with other work units because the projects are relatively self-contained.

The creation of a project team at Blue Circle, a British company, resulted in a totally new product on the European market. When Blue Circle introduced a standardized boiler for the European market, a design team was set up comprising British, French, German and Dutch specialists. Their task was to adapt to the huge variations in the different European housing, climate and plumbing demands. The team was based in the United Kingdom. English was the working language. The team's efforts finally resulted in a condensing boiler that could be used anywhere, not just in one particular country.[27]

Action Teams

This last type of team is best exemplified by sports teams, airline cockpit crews, hospital surgery teams, mountain-climbing expeditions, film crews, management and trade union negotiating committees, and police special intervention teams among others. A unique challenge for action teams is to exhibit peak performance on demand.

> *For example, teams at Stage Co—a company that delivers technical stage crew to summer festivals such as Glastonbury in the UK, the Roskilde-Festival in Denmark, the Werchter festival in Belgium and 'Rock am Ring' in Germany—need to combine high specialization with high co-ordination to ensure a good concert. Highly trained technicians build up the main stage, then they need to break it down immediately after the show, because the pieces are needed fast elsewhere, for the next festival. This requires immense speed and intense co-operation, so everybody in the crew needs to know exactly what to do. Moreover, co-ordination between the stage crew, the festival organizers, the sound engineers and the musicians has to be perfect. Also, some music groups bring their own crew along because of the specific needs of their performance, so a lot of topics have to be discussed with them too.[28]*

This four-way typology of work teams is dynamic and changing, not static. Some teams evolve from one type to another. Other teams represent a combination of types.

Work Team Effectiveness: An Ecological Model

The effectiveness of athletic teams is a straightforward matter of counting the competitions you win against those you loose. Things become more complicated, however, when the focus shifts to work teams in today's organizations.[29] Figure 12–2 lists two effectiveness criteria for work teams: performance and viability. According to Sundstrom and his colleagues: '*Performance* means acceptability of output to customers within or outside the organization who receive team products, services, information, decisions, or performance events (such as presentations or competitions).' While the foregoing relates to satisfying the needs and expectations of outsiders such as clients, customers, and fans, another team-effectiveness criterion arises. Namely, **team viability**, defined as team member satisfaction and continued willingness to contribute. Are the team members better or worse off for having contributed to the team effort? A work team is not truly effective if it gets the job done but self-destructs in the process or burns everyone out.

Team viability
team members satisfied and willing to contribute

Figure 12–2
An Ecological Model of Work Team Effectiveness

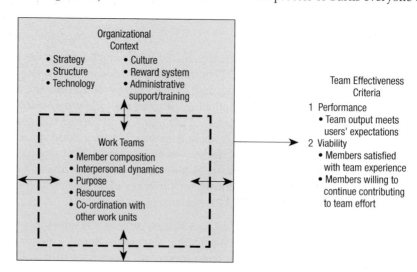

SOURCE: Adapted in part from E Sundstrom, K P De Meuse and D Futrell, 'Work Teams', *American Psychologist*, February 1990, pp 120–33.

Figure 12–2 is an *ecological* model because it portrays work teams within their organizational environment. In keeping with the true meaning of the word *ecology*—the study of interactions between organisms and their environments—this model emphasizes that work teams need an organizational life-support system. Six critical organizational context variables are listed in Figure 12–2. Work teams have a much greater chance of being effective if they are nurtured and helped by the organization. The team's purpose needs to be in concert with the organization's strategy. Similarly, team participation and autonomy require an organizational culture that values those processes. Team members also need appropriate technological tools and training. Teamwork needs to be reinforced by the organizational reward system. Such is not the case when pay and bonuses are tied solely to individual output.

Five important factors of the internal processes of work teams are listed in Figure 12–2. Contained in Table 12-3, is an expanded list of team characteristics which can prove useful in evaluating task teams both in college and at work.[30]

Table 12-3 *Characteristics of an Effective Team*

1. Clear purpose	The vision, mission, goal, or task of the team has been defined and is now accepted by everyone. There is an action plan.
2. Informality	The climate tends to be informal, comfortable, and relaxed. There are no obvious tensions or signs of boredom.
3. Participation	There is much discussion, and everyone is encouraged to participate.
4. Listening	The members use effective listening techniques such as questioning, paraphrasing, and summarizing to get out ideas.
5. Civilized disagreement	There is disagreement, but the team is comfortable with this and shows no signs of avoiding, smoothing over, or suppressing conflict.
6. Consensus decisions	For important decisions, the goal is substantial but not necessarily unanimous agreement through open discussion of everyone's ideas, avoidance of formal voting, or easy compromises.
7. Open communication	Team members feel free to express their feelings on the tasks as well as on the group's operation. There are few hidden agendas. Communication takes place outside of meetings.
8. Clear roles and work assignments	There are clear expectations about the roles played by each team member. When action is taken, clear assignments are made, accepted, and carried out. Work is fairly distributed among team members.
9. Shared leadership	While the team has a formal leader, leadership functions shift from time to time depending on the circumstances, the needs of the group, and the skills of the members. The formal leader models the appropriate behavior and helps establish positive norms.
10. External relations	The team spends time developing key outside relationships, mobilizing resources, and building credibility with important players in other parts of the organization.
11. Style diversity	The team has a broad spectrum of team-player types including members who emphasize attention to task, goal setting, focus on process, and questions about how the team is functioning.
12. Self-assessment	Periodically, the team stops to examine how well it is functioning and what may be interfering with its effectiveness.

SOURCE: G M Parker, *Team Players and Teamwork: The New Competitive Business Strategy* (San Francisco: Jossey-Bass, 1990), Table 2, p 33. Copyright © 1990 by Jossey-Bass Inc., Publishers. Reprinted by permission of John Wiley & Sons, Inc.

THREATS TO TEAM EFFECTIVENESS

Why Do Work Teams Fail? Pitfalls and Stumbling Blocks

Advocates of the team approach paint a very optimistic and bright picture. Yet there is a dark side to teams.[31] Teams have become a managerial panacea. They are used for problems where technological change, radical decisions or individual excellence would be a better solution. No wonder that at a seminar of senior managers held by Cranfield Management School, UK, two thirds of the participants expressed their disillusionment with the results of their teamworking initiatives. Also, research at Temple University, Florida, revealed that 80 to 90 per cent of teams had difficulties achieving their goals.[32] David Butcher of Cranfield presents the following viewpoint.

> *The root of the problem is that companies see teams as an end rather than a means, often setting them up where they are not required. In situations where their use is justified, their effectiveness is often stymied by managers who don't know how to handle them properly. Teams are over-hyped, overrated, but used in a wrong way. The paradox derives from the very 'diplomatic immunity' of teamwork: in many organizations it is so ingrained in management that it is impossible to attack, criticize or even discuss rationally.*[33]

When implemented unwisely, teamwork can turn into an organizational nightmare. For example, reflect on what probably happened at the European headquarters of Citrix Corporation in Shaffhausen, Switzerland, where a marketing executive quoted: 'Teamwork is a lot of people *doing what I say.*'[34] Although these words sound extreme, teams can and often do fail. The American team specialist Richard Whitely, speaks of a disease called *teamitis*.[35] Anyone contemplating the use of team structures in the workplace therefore needs a balanced perspective on their advantages and limitations. According to the British consultants Rob Yeung and Sebastian Bailey, in their daily work with various companies they encounter the following most frequently observed symptoms when implementing teamwork.[36]:

1 *Hidden agendas.* A belief that certain members of the team are secretly building their own empires or furthering their own careers rather than working for the good of the organizations.

   'Whenever I try to get my top executives together to wrestle with new challenges, invariably one or more of the division presidents will argue that they're aggressively dealing with the problem in their own units', says Richard, the chief executive of a large financial services firm. 'But these problems call for company-wide action, not piecemeal initiatives. Frankly, I think we're paying a big price for the autonomy we've granted senior executives. They're each running their own fiefdoms, unwilling to think about how they might disadvantage other departments. We can't get our act together.'[37]

2 *Lack of understanding.* Misconceptions about why the team has been brought together are common when a team is first formed.

3 *Lack of leadership.* The team leader does not have the skills required to manage the team effectively. Sometimes, it may be that no one member is recognized by all as the leader.

4 *Wrong mix of team members.* For example, there are 'creative types' who love to generate ideas but cannot focus on detail, while there are 'doers' who would rather not contribute to discussions and prefer to be given tasks to do. A team that is unevenly balanced could either generate ideas but fail to implement them, or alternatively, discover that it does not have any ideas to implement.

5 *Unhealthy team environment.* For example, the team is unable to cope under pressure as outlined in the following quote.

'The biggest pitfall in a team is not having issues raised early enough', says Gary Spellins, managing director of Lex Services, which delivers a range of outsourcing solutions to diverse companies. 'When you're working to tight deadlines, the earlier you put your hand up, the better, but very often team members are to afraid to take initiative and hope somebody else will ring the alarm bell. It's easier to add resources to fix a problem before a deadline than to rectify it after you've missed the deadline. In a team, you need to create an environment where there are no surprises.'[38]

If teams are to be effective, both management and team members must make a concerted effort to think and do things differently. Figure 12–3 presents a useful summary of various stumbling blocks and pitfalls, which managers and team members must bear in mind if they want to avoid the above problems.

Figure 12-3

Why Work Teams Fail

Mistakes typically made by management

- Teams cannot overcome weak strategies and poor business practices
- Hostile environment for teams (command-and-control culture; competitive/individual reward plans; management resistance)
- Teams adopted as a fad, a quick-fix; no long-term commitment
- Lessons from one team not transferred to others (limited experimentation with teams)
- Vague or conflicting team assignments
- Inadequate team skills training
- Poor staffing of teams
- Lack of trust

Unrealistic expectations resulting in frustration

Problems typically experienced by team members

- Team tries to do too much too soon
- Conflict over differences in personal work styles (and/or personality conflicts)
- Too much emphasis on results, not enough on team processes and group dynamics
- Unanticipated obstacle causes team to give up
- Resistance to doing things differently
- Poor interpersonal skills (aggressive rather than assertive communication, destructive conflict, win-lose negotiation)
- Poor interpersonal chemistry (loners, dominators, self-appointed experts do not fit in)
- Lack of trust

SOURCE: Adapted from discussion in S R Rayner, 'Team Traps: What They Are, How to Avoid Them', *National Productivity Review*, Summer 1996, pp 110–15; L Holpp and R Phillips, 'When Is a Team Its Own Worst Enemy?', *Training*, September 1995, pp 71–82; and B Richardson, 'Why Work Teams Flop–and What Can Be Done About It', *National Productivity Review*, Winter 1994/95, pp 9–13.

According to the centre of figure 12–3, the main threats to team effectiveness are unrealistic expectations leading to frustration. Frustration in turn, encourages people to abandon teams. Both managers and team members can be victimized by unrealistic expectations.[39]

On the left of figure 12–3 is a list of common management mistakes. These mistakes generally involve doing a poor job of creating a supportive environment for teams and teamwork. On the right of Figure 12–3 is a list of common problems for team members. Contrary to critics' Theory X contention that employees lack the motivation and creativity for real teamwork, it is common for teams to take on too much too quickly and to drive themselves too hard for fast results. Important group dynamics and team skills get lost in the rush for results. Consequently, team members' expectations need to be given a reality check by management and team members themselves. Also, teams need to be counselled against quitting when they run into an unanticipated obstacle. Failure is part of the learning process for teams, as it is elsewhere in life. Comprehensive training in interpersonal skills can prevent many common teamwork problems. Additional insights lie ahead as we will turn our attention, later in this chapter, to the subjects of co-operation, trust and cohesiveness.

But even when managers carefully staff and organize work teams and consider the above problems, team dynamics can still become erratic and out of control, because three psychological phenomena impose further threats. Some fundamental cognitive mistakes are said to stifle critical thinking or cause performance to deteriorate. These are: blind conformity, as reflected in the Asch Effect, 'groupthink' and social loafing.

The Asch Effect

Nearly 50 years ago, social psychologist Solomon Asch conducted a series of laboratory experiments that revealed a negative side of group dynamics.[40] Under the guise of a 'perception test', Asch had groups of seven to nine volunteer college students look at 12 pairs of cards such as the ones in Figure 12–4. The object was to identify the line that was the same length as the standard line. Each individual was told to announce his or her choice to the group. Since the differences among the comparison lines were obvious, there should have been unanimous agreement during each of the 12 rounds. But that was not the case.

Figure 12–4

The Asch Experiment

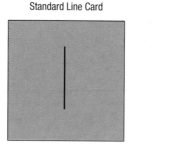

Standard Line Card   Comparison Lines Card

1   2   3

A Minority of One

All but one member of each group were Asch's confederates who agreed to systematically select the wrong line during seven of the rounds (the other five rounds were control rounds for comparison purposes). The remaining individual was the naive subject who was being tricked. Group pressure was created by having the naive subject in each group be among the last to announce his or her choice. Thirty-one subjects were tested. Asch's research question was: 'How often would the naive subjects conform to a majority opinion that was obviously wrong?'

Only 20 per cent of Asch's subjects remained entirely independent; 80 per cent yielded to the pressures of group opinion at least once! And 58 per cent knuckled under to the 'immoral majority' at least twice. Hence, the **Asch effect**, the distortion of individual judgement by a unanimous but incorrect opposition, was documented. (Do you ever turn your back on your better judgment by giving in to group pressure?)

Asch effect
giving in to a unanimous but wrong opposition

A Managerial Perspective

Asch's experiment has been widely replicated with mixed results. Both high and low degrees of blind conformity have been observed with various situations and subjects. Replications in Japan and Kuwait have demonstrated that the Asch effect is not unique to the United States.[41] A 1996 meta-analysis of 133 Asch-line experiments from 17 countries found a *decline* in conformity among US subjects since the 1950s.

Internationally, collectivist countries, where the group prevails over the individual, produced higher levels of conformity than individualistic countries.[42] The point here is not how great the Asch effect is in a given situation or culture, but rather that managers committed to ethical conduct need to be concerned whether the Asch effect is present. Even isolated instances of blind, unthinking conformity seriously threaten the effectiveness and integrity of work groups and organizations. Functional conflict and assertiveness can help employees respond appropriately when they find themselves facing an immoral majority. Also, ethical codes mentioning specific practices can provide support and guidance.

Groupthink

Why did President Lyndon B Johnson and his team of intelligent White House advisers make some very *unintelligent* decisions that escalated the Vietnam War? How is it possible that in 1995 Robert McNamara, US Secretary of Defense, had to admit, 'we were wrong, terribly wrong'?[43] Those fateful decisions were made despite obvious warning signs, including stronger than expected resistance from the North Vietnamese and withering support at home and abroad. Systematic analysis of the decision-making processes underlying the war in Vietnam and other US foreign policy fiascoes prompted Yale University's Irving Janis to coin the term **groupthink**.[44] Modern managers can all too easily become victims of groupthink, just like President Johnson's staff, if they passively ignore the danger.

Groupthink
Janis's term for a cohesive in-group's unwillingness to view alternatives realistically

Definition and Symptoms of Groupthink

Janis defines groupthink as 'a mode of thinking that people engage in when they are deeply involved in a cohesive in-group, when members' strivings for unanimity override their motivation to realistically appraise alternative courses of action.'[45] He adds, 'Groupthink refers to a deterioration of mental efficiency, reality testing and moral judgement that results from in-group pressures.'[46] Unlike Asch's subjects, who were strangers to each other, members of groups victimized by groupthink are friendly, tightly knit and cohesive. In short, policy- and decision-making groups can become so cohesive that strong-willed executives are able to gain unanimous support for poor decisions.

Figure 12–5 *Symptoms of Groupthink Lead to Defective Decision Making*

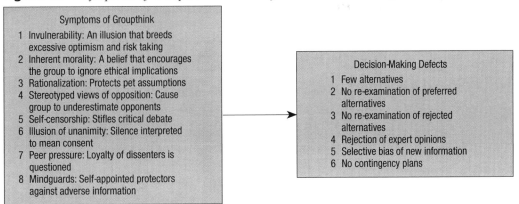

SOURCE: Symptoms adapted from I L Janis, *Groupthink*, 2nd ed (Boston: Houghton Mifflin, 1982), pp 174–75. Defects excerpted from G Moorhead, 'Groupthink: Hypothesis in Need of Testing', *Group & Organization Studies*, December 1982, p 434. Copyright © 1982 by Sage Publications. Reprinted by permission of Sage Publications, Inc.

Groupthink Research and Prevention

Laboratory studies using college students as subjects validate portions of Janis's groupthink concept. The following, in particular, has been found to be true.

▼ **Groups with a moderate amount of cohesiveness produce better decisions than those with low or high amounts.**

▼ **Highly cohesive groups victimized by groupthink make the poorest decisions, despite having considerable confidence in their decisions.**[47]

Janis believes prevention is better than cure when dealing with groupthink. He recommends the following preventive measures.

1　Each member of the group should be assigned the role of critical evaluator. This role involves actively voicing objections and doubts.

2　Top-level executives should not use policy committees to rubber-stamp decisions that have already been made.

3　Different groups with different leaders should explore the same policy questions.

4　Sub-group debates and outside experts should be used to introduce fresh perspectives.

5　Someone should be given the role of 'devil's advocate' (to express a contentious opinion in order to provoke debate) when discussing major alternatives. This person tries to uncover every conceivable negative factor.

6　Once a consensus has been reached, everyone should be encouraged to rethink their position to check for flaws.[48]

These anti-groupthink measures can help cohesive teams produce sound recommendations and decisions.

Social Loafing

Is group performance less than, equal to, or greater than the sum of its parts? Can three people, for example, working together accomplish less than, the same as, or more than they would working separately? An interesting study conducted more than a half century ago by a French agricultural engineer named Ringelmann found the answer to be 'less than'.[49] In a rope-pulling exercise, Ringelmann reportedly found that three people pulling together could achieve only two and a half times the average individual rate. Eight pullers achieved less than four times the individual rate. This tendency for individual effort to decline as group size increases has come to be called **social loafing**.[50] Let us briefly analyse this threat to team effectiveness and synergy with an eye toward avoiding it.

Social loafing
decrease in individual effort as group size increases

Social Loafing Theory and Research

Among the theoretical explanations for the social loafing effect are the following.

1　Equity of effort ('Everyone else is goofing off, so why shouldn't I?')

2　Loss of personal accountability ('I'm lost in the crowd, so who cares?')

3　Motivational loss due to the sharing of rewards ('Why should I work harder than the others when everyone gets the same reward?')

4　Co-ordination loss as more people perform the task ('We're getting in each other's way.')

Laboratory studies refined these theories by identifying situational factors that moderated the social loafing effect. Social loafing occurred when the following occurred.

▼ **The task was perceived to be unimportant, simple or uninteresting.**[51]

▼ **Group members thought their individual output was not identifiable.**[52]

▼ **Group members expected their co-workers to loaf.**[53]

But social loafing did *not* occur when group members in two laboratory studies expected to be evaluated.[54] Also, recent research suggests that self-reliant 'individualists' are more prone to social loafing than are group-oriented 'collectivists'. But individualists can be made more co-operative by keeping the group small and holding each member personally accountable for results.[55]

Practical Implications

These findings demonstrate that social loafing is not an inevitable part of group effort. Management can curb this threat to group effectiveness by making sure the task is challenging and perceived as important. Additionally, it is a good idea to hold group members personally accountable for identifiable portions of the group's task. One way to do this is with the *stepladder technique*, a group decision-making process that has proven effective in recent research (see Table 12–4). Compared to conventional groups, stepladder groups produced significantly better decisions in the same amount of time. 'Furthermore, stepladder groups' decisions surpassed the quality of their best individual members' decisions 56 per cent of the time. In contrast, conventional groups' decisions surpassed the quality of their best members' decisions only 13 per cent of the time.'[56] The stepladder technique could be a useful tool for organizations relying on self-managed or total quality management (TQM) teams.

Table 12–4

How to Avoid Social Loafing in Groups and Teams: The Stepladder Technique

The stepladder technique is intended to enhance group decision making by structuring the entry of group members into a core group. Increasing or decreasing the number of group members alters the number of steps. In a four-person group, the stepladder technique has three steps. Initially, two group members (the initial core group) work together on the problem at hand. Next, a third member joins the core group and presents his or her preliminary solutions for the same problem. The entering member's presentation is followed by a three-person discussion. Finally, the fourth group member joins the core group and presents his or her preliminary solutions. This is followed by a four-person discussion, which has as its goal the rendering of a final group decision.

The stepladder technique has four requirements. First, each group member must be given the group's task and sufficient time to think about the problem before entering the core group. Second, the entering member must present his or her preliminary solutions before hearing the core group's preliminary solutions. Third, with the entry of each additional member to the core group, sufficient time to discuss the problem is necessary. Fourth, a final decision must be purposely delayed until the group has been formed in its entirety.

SOURCE: Excerpted from S G Rogelberg, J L Barnes-Farrell, and C A Lowe, 'The Stepladder Technique: An Alternative Group Structure Facilitating Effective Group Decision Making,' *Journal of Applied Psychology*, October 1992, vol 77, p 731. Copyright © 1992 by the American Psychological Association. Reprinted with permission.

EFFECTIVE TEAMWORK THROUGH CO-OPERATION, TRUST AND COHESIVENESS

As competitive pressures intensify, experts say organizational success will depend increasingly on teamwork rather than individual stars. For instance, the Institute of Personnel and Development investigated seven European companies who were in the process of changing into what the researchers called 'lean and responsive organizations'. Teamwork and co-operation turned out to be the most important factors in this change process. A principal conclusion of the study was that employees have to work together and exchange experiences in order to succeed in the transformation process.[57] If this emphasis on teamwork has a familiar ring, it is because sports champions generally say they owe their success to it. Whether in the athletic arena or the world of business, three components of teamwork receiving the greatest attention are co-operation, trust, and cohesiveness. Let us explore the contributions each can make to effective teamwork.

Co-operation

Individuals are said to be co-operating when their efforts are systematically integrated to achieve a collective objective. The greater the integration, the greater the degree of co-operation.

As early as the 1940s, Morton Deutch showed how people's beliefs are related to their interdependence. When acting in co-operation with each other, they believe that goal attainment by other people will also foster their own goals. When in competition, however, people believe that goal attainment by others ('competitors') will diminish their own. 'When others fail I succeed.' Independent people see no relationship between their own results and the results of others.[58]

In practice, most team members find themselves in a 'mixed motive' situation. Just think of the footballer who is in a position to score, yet sees a teammate even better placed to score the winner. John Kay—the British strategy specialist—illustrates this with the following analysis of Liverpool Football Club.

> If we where to build a model of the game of football, it would recognize that every time a player has the ball he faces the alternative of shooting for goal or passing to a better placed player. If he passes to a player of similar calibre to himself, he will score fewer goals but the team will score more. If everyone in the team plays a passing game, every member of it can expect to score more goals than if their normal instinct is to shoot. That choice is repeated every few minutes in every match the team plays and there are two equilibria—a passing game or a shooting game. Liverpool is well known for its passing game. Many of its opponents adopt a more individualistic style.

> Liverpool illustrates the principal ways in which architecture can form the basis of a distinctive capability. The club has created an intangible asset—the organizational knowledge of the club—which, although it is derived from the contributions of the individual members, belongs to the firm and not to the individual members and cannot be appropriated by them. There are organizational routines—complex manoeuvres, perfected through repeated trial—in which each player fulfills his own role without needing or necessarily having, a picture of the whole. And there is the 'passing game', the co-operative ethic, in which the player's instinct is to maximize the number of goals the club scores rather than the number of goals he scores. Each of these sources of sporting success has it precise business analogies.[59]

However, it's not only managers and football trainers who have seen the benefits of co-operation. Many workers on the floor are delighted too by the team systems that are increasingly being implemented by Europe's largest companies. For instance, the following quote stems from an production worker at Philips.

> 'Today, the work isn't harder but it's completely different. Everybody now thinks ahead. Because everybody now works together and is kept informed, the work goes faster and more fluently. In the past, the only thing we thought about was women and booze. Today, working here is fun. Everybody is responsible. Everybody works in the same direction. Nowadays people don't mind staying a little later to solve a problem because they know why they're doing it. That's important.[60]

Co-operation versus Competition

A widely held assumption among American managers is that 'competition brings out the best in people'. From an economic viewpoint, business survival depends on staying ahead of the competition. But from an interpersonal viewpoint, critics contend competition has been overemphasized, primarily at the expense of co-operation.[61] Alfie Kohn is a strong advocate of greater emphasis on co-operation in our classrooms, offices and factories.

> My review of the evidence has convinced me that there are two . . . important reasons for competition's failure. First, success often depends on sharing resources efficiently,

and this is nearly impossible when people have to work against one another. Co-operation takes advantage of all the skills represented in a group as well as the mysterious process by which that group becomes more than the sum of its parts. By contrast, competition makes people suspicious and hostile toward one another and actively discourages this process . . . .

Second, competition generally does not promote excellence because trying to do well and trying to beat others simply are two different things. Consider a child in class, waving his arm wildly to attract the teacher's attention, crying, 'Oooh! Oooh! Pick me!' When he is finally recognized, he seems befuddled. 'Um, what was the question again?' he finally asks. His mind is focused on beating his classmates, not on the subject matter.[62]

Research Support for Co-operation

After conducting a meta-analysis of 122 studies encompassing a wide variety of subjects and settings, one team of researchers concluded the following.

1 Co-operation is superior to competition in promoting achievement and productivity.

2 Co-operation is superior to individualistic efforts in promoting achievement and productivity.

3 Co-operation *without* intergroup competition promotes higher achievement and productivity than co-operation *with* intergroup competition.[63]

Given the size and diversity of the research base, these findings strongly endorse co-operation in modern organizations. Co-operation can be encouraged by reward systems that reinforce teamwork as well as individual achievement.

Research suggests that managers can enhance equal employment opportunity and diversity programmes by encouraging *voluntary* helping behaviour in interracial work teams.[64] Accordingly, it is reasonable to conclude that voluntary helping behaviour could build co-operation in mixed-gender teams and groups as well. Remember Chapter 2 showed that 'diversity' should include more than just racial or gender differences. The Swedish-Swiss ABB group, for example, applied this idea when composing a team responsible for the design of a new factory.

'I put together a seven-member design team, composed of two workers from manufacturing, three from engineering, one from finance and myself. One team member was a female and one of the males was a person of colour. Their ages ranged from 23 to 49 years. Their company service ranged from 4 months to 12 years. They held [family] positions from [that of] a single mother to a father with teenage children. In short, they were a representative cross-section of business and modern lifestyles. Each member brought something unique to the team and each got something different from the experience', says B Randall Palef, ABB Switchgear Division's Human Resources Manager at the time of the project.[65]

Trust

These have not been good times for trust in the corporate world. Years of mergers, downsizings, lay-offs and redundancies, bloated executive bonuses and broken promises have left many employees justly cynical about trusting management. A survey of over 1,000 employees in six British companies concluded that trust is the missing factor: only 13 per cent think that the people they work with feel valued by the company; 9 per cent think that top management has a sincere interest in the welfare of its employees and hardly 8 per cent are convinced that management gives fair deals.[66] However, as an encouraging sign, an increasing amount of managers view trust as a key factor in doing business. One of them is Eduard Kint of the Swedish furniture company Kinnarps.

'A truly market-oriented team drives on trust', he says. 'From their first day off, I try to give my employees the feeling I trust them. I want them to decide autonomous and take initiative. This is not a kindergarten but a company of adults. I'm not here to control them all the time. Adults are to be treated as such. One exception aside, I have never regretted this mentality. I think, if you want to be an effective team, a high amount of trust is vital. That's why working here at Kinnarps has been summarized as 'freedom with the necessary responsibility', which has lead to enormous creativity and a fantastic team.'[67]

In this section, we examine the concept of trust and introduce six practical guidelines for building it.

A Cognitive Leap

Trust is defined as reciprocal faith in others' intentions and behaviour.[68] Experts on the subject explain the reciprocal (give-and-take) aspect of trust as follows.

When we see others acting in ways that imply that they trust us, we become more disposed to reciprocate by trusting in them more. Conversely, we come to distrust those whose actions appear to violate our trust or to distrust us.[69]

In short, we tend to give what we get: trust begets trust; distrust begets distrust. A newer model of organizational trust includes a personality trait called **propensity to trust**. The developers of the model explain it as follows.

Propensity might be thought of as the general willingness to trust others. Propensity will influence how much trust one has for a trustee prior to data on that particular party being available. People with different developmental experiences, personality types and cultural backgrounds vary in their propensity to trust . . . . An example of an extreme case of this is what is commonly called blind trust. *Some individuals can be observed to repeatedly trust in situations that most people would agree do not warrant trust. Conversely, others are unwilling to trust in most situations, regardless of circumstances that would support doing so.*[70]

What is your propensity to trust? How did you develop that personality trait? (See the trust questionnaire in the Personal Awareness and Growth Exercise at the end of this chapter.)

Trust involves 'a cognitive "leap" beyond the expectations that reason and experience alone would warrant'.[71] (see Figure 12–6). For example, suppose a member of a newly formed class project team works hard, based on the assumption that her teammates also are working hard. That assumption, on which her trust is based, is a cognitive leap that goes beyond her actual experience with her teammates. When you trust someone, you have *faith* in their good intentions. The act of trusting someone, however, carries with it the inherent risk of betrayal.[72] Progressive managers believe that the benefits of interpersonal trust far outweigh any risks of betrayed trust.

Figure 12–6

Interpersonal Trust Involves a Cognitive Leap

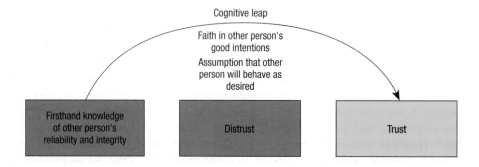

How to Build Trust

Management professor and consultant Fernando Bartolomé offers the following six guidelines for building and maintaining trust.

1 *Communication.* Keep team members and employees informed by explaining policies and decisions and providing accurate feedback. Be candid about one's own problems and limitations. Tell the truth.[73] As an example, according to Geoff Boisi, head of investment banking at Chase in London, the best way for someone to create a trusting, candid partnership, is to abandon the word 'I' and to plump for 'we' instead.

   'We have seen the light. We are never, ever going to use the first person singular again', he says. '"I" is weak . . . "We" hints at consensus and reflection. "I" is shot from the hip . . . "I" is asking for an argument . . . "We" is begging for agreement and trust. "We" means teamwork . . . "I" is a one-man band.' Boisi believes that these slight grammatical adjustments can really make a difference. 'It's simple but incredibly powerful', he says. 'I think this is an important tool that we should all incorporate in our daily lives.'[74]

2 *Support.* Be available and approachable. Provide help, advice, coaching, and support for team members' ideas.

3 *Respect.* Delegate real decision-making authority—it is the most important expression of managerial respect. Actively listening to the ideas of others is a close second. (Empowerment is not possible without trust.)[75]

4 *Fairness.* Be quick to give credit and recognition to those who deserve it. Make sure all performance appraisals and evaluations are objective and impartial.[76]

5 *Predictability.* As mentioned previously, be consistent and predictable in your daily affairs. Keep both expressed and implied promises.

6 *Competence.* Enhance your credibility by demonstrating good business sense, technical ability and professionalism.[77]

Trust needs to be earned; it cannot be demanded.

Cohesiveness

Cohesiveness is a process whereby 'a sense of 'we-ness' [togetherness] emerges to transcend individual differences and motives.'[78] Members of a cohesive group stick together. They are reluctant to leave the group. Cohesive group members stick together for one or both of the following reasons:

> ▼ they enjoy each others' company
> ▼ they need each other to accomplish a common goal.

Accordingly, two types of group cohesiveness, identified by sociologists, are socio-emotional cohesiveness and instrumental cohesiveness.[79]

Cohesiveness
a sense of 'we-ness' that helps group stick together

Socio-Emotional and Instrumental Cohesiveness

Socio-emotional cohesiveness is a sense of togetherness that develops when individuals derive emotional satisfaction from group participation. Most general discussions of group cohesiveness are limited to this type. However, from the standpoint of getting things accomplished in task groups and teams, we cannot afford to ignore instrumental cohesiveness. Instrumental cohesiveness is a sense of togetherness that develops when group members are mutually dependent on one another because they believe they could not achieve the group's goal by acting separately. A feeling of 'we' is *instrumental* to achieving the common goal. Team advocates generally assume both types of cohesiveness are essential to productive teamwork. But is this really true?

Socio-emotional cohesiveness
sense of togetherness based on emotional satisfaction

Instrumental cohesiveness
sense of togetherness based on the mutual dependency required to get the job done

Lessons from Group Cohesiveness Research

What is the connection between group cohesiveness and performance? A landmark meta-analysis of 49 studies involving 8,702 subjects provided the following insights.

▼ **There is a small but statistically significant cohesiveness→performance effect.**

▼ **The cohesiveness→performance effect was stronger for smaller and 'real' groups (as opposed to contrived groups in laboratory studies).**

▼ **The cohesiveness→performance effect becomes stronger as one moves from (real) civilian groups to military groups to sports teams.**

▼ **Commitment to the task at hand (meaning that the individual sees the performance standards as legitimate) has the most powerful impact on the cohesiveness→performance linkage.**

▼ **The performance→cohesiveness linkage is stronger than the cohesiveness→performance linkage. Thus, the tendency for success to bind group or team members together is greater than the tendency for closely knit groups to be more successful.**

▼ **Contrary to the popular view, cohesiveness is not 'a 'lubricant' that minimizes friction due to the human 'grit' in the system.'**[80]

▼ **All this evidence led the researchers to the practical conclusion that: 'Efforts to enhance group performance by fostering interpersonal attraction or 'pumping up' group pride are not likely to be effective.'**[81]

A second meta-analysis found no significant relationship between cohesiveness and the quality of group decisions. However, support was found for Janis's contention that *groupthink* tends to afflict cohesive in-groups with strong leadership. Groups whose members liked each other a great deal tended to make poorer quality decisions.[82]

Getting Some Positive Impact from Group Cohesiveness

Research tells us that group cohesiveness is no 'secret weapon' in the quest for improved group or team performance. The trick is to keep task groups small, make sure performance standards and goals are clear and accepted, achieve some early successes, and follow the tips in Table 12–5. A good example is Renault's restructured factory in Douai, France. A new production system was introduced for the construction of the Mégane, based on strong employee involvement. Those who were involved in the project from the beginning were responsible for the training of 200 colleagues, who, in turn, instructed their peers. This training system enhanced employee co-operation.[83]

Self-selected work teams (in which people pick their own teammates) and social events outside working hours can stimulate socio-emotional cohesiveness.[84] The fostering of socio-emotional cohesiveness needs to be balanced with instrumental cohesiveness. The latter can be encouraged by making sure everyone in the group recognizes and appreciates each member's vital contribution to the group goal. While balancing the two types of cohesiveness, managers need to remember that groupthink theory and research cautions against too much cohesiveness.

TEAMS IN ACTION: QUALITY CIRCLES, VIRTUAL TEAMS AND SELF-MANAGED TEAMS

All sorts of interesting approaches to teams and teamwork can be found in the workplace today. A great deal of experimentation is taking place as organizations struggle to become more flexible and responsive. New information technologies have spurred experimentation with team formats. This section profiles three different approaches to teams: quality circles, virtual teams, and self-managed teams. We have selected these particular types of teams for three reasons: they have recognizable labels; they have at least some research evidence; and they range from low to high degrees of empowerment.

Table 12–5

Steps Managers Can Take to Enhance the Two Types of Group Cohesiveness

Socio-Emotional Cohesiveness

Keep the group relatively small.

Strive for a favourable public image to increase the status and prestige of belonging.

Encourage interaction and cooperation.

Emphasize members' common characteristics and interests.

Point out environmental threats (e.g., competitors' achievements) to rally the group.

Instrumental Cohesiveness

Regularly update and clarify the group's goal(s).

Give every group member a vital 'piece of the action.'

Channel each group member's special talents toward the common goal(s).

Recognize and equitably reinforce every member's contributions.

Frequently remind group members they need each other to get the job done.

As indicated in Table 12–6, the three types of teams are distinct but not totally unique. Overlaps exist. For instance, computer-networked virtual teams may or may not have volunteer members and may or may not be self-managed. Another point of overlap involves the fifth variable in Table 12–6, that is, the relationship to organization structure. 'Quality circles' are called *parallel* structures because they exist outside normal channels of authority and communication.[85] Self-managed teams, on the other hand, are *integrated* into the basic organizational structure. Virtual teams vary in this regard, although they tend to be parallel because they are made up of functional specialists (engineers, accountants, marketers, etc.) who team up on temporary projects. Keeping these basic distinctions in mind, let us explore quality circles, virtual teams, and self-managed teams.

Table 12–6 *Basic Distinctions between Quality Circles, Virtual Teams and Self-Managed Teams*

	Quality Circles	Virtual Teams	Self-Managed Teams
Type of team (see Table 13–2)	Advice	Advice or project (usually project)	Production, project, or action
Type of empowerment (see Figure 16–2)	Consultation	Consultation, participation, or delegation	Delegation
Members	Production/service personnel	Managers and technical specialists	Production/service, technical specialists
Basis of membership	Voluntary	Assigned (some voluntary)	Assigned
Relationship to organization structure	Parallel	Parallel or integrated	Integrated
Amount of face-to-face communication	Strictly face to face	Periodic to none	Varies, depending on use of information technology

Quality Circles

Quality circles are small groups of people from the same work area who voluntarily get together to identify, analyse, and recommend solutions for problems related to quality, productivity, and cost reduction. Some prefer the term *quality control circles*. With an ideal size of 10 to 12 members, they typically meet for about an hour to an

Quality circles *small groups of volunteers who strive to solve quality-related problems*

hour-and-a-half at a time, on a regular basis. Some companies allow meetings during work hours, others encourage quality circles to meet after work on employees' time. Once a week or twice a month are common schedules. Management facilitates the quality circle programme through skills training and listening to periodic presentations of recommendations. Monetary rewards for suggestions tend to be the exception rather than the rule. Intrinsic motivation, derived from learning new skills and meaningful participation, is the primary reward for quality circle volunteers.

The Quality Circle Movement

American quality control experts helped introduce the basic idea of quality circles to Japanese industry soon after the Second World War. The idea eventually returned to the United States and became a fad during the 1970s and '80s. Proponents made zealous claims about how quality circles were the key to higher productivity, lower costs, employee development and improved job attitudes. At its zenith, during the mid-1980s, the quality circle movement claimed millions of employee participants around the world.[86] Hundreds of companies and government agencies adopted the idea under a variety of labels.[87] The dramatic growth of quality circles has been attributed to a desire to replicate Japan's industrial success; a penchant for business fads; and the relative ease of installing quality circles without restructuring the organization.[88] All too often, however, early enthusiasm gave way to disappointment, apathy and abandonment.[89]

But quality circles, if properly administered and supported by management, can be much more than a management fad seemingly past its prime. According to researchers Edward E Lawler and Susan A Mohrman, 'quality circles can be an important first step toward organizational effectiveness through employee involvement'.[90]

Insights from Field Research on Quality Circles

There is a body of objective field research on quality circles. Still, much of what we know comes from testimonials and case histories from managers and consultants who have a vested interest in demonstrating the technique's success. Although documented failures are scarce, one expert concluded that quality circles have failure rates of more than 60 per cent.[91] Poor implementation is probably more at fault than the concept itself.[92]

To date, field research on quality circles has been inconclusive. Lack of standardized variables is the main problem, as is typical when comparing the results of field studies.[93] Team participation programmes of all sizes and shapes have been called quality circles. Here's what we have learned to date. A case study of military and civilian personnel found a positive relationship between quality circle participation and desire to continue working for the organization. The observed effect on job performance was slight. A longitudinal study spanning 24 months revealed that quality circles had only a marginal impact on employee attitudes but had a positive impact on productivity. In a more recent study, utility company employees who participated in quality circles received significantly better job performance ratings and were promoted more frequently than non-participants. This suggests that quality circles live up to their billing as a good employee development technique.[94]

Overall, quality circles are a promising participative management tool, *if they are carefully implemented and supported by all levels of management.*

Virtual Teams

Virtual teams are a product of modern times. They take their name from *virtual reality* computer simulations, where 'it's almost like the real thing'. Thanks to evolving information technologies such as the Internet, email, videoconferencing, groupware and fax machines, you can be a member of a work team without really being there.[95] Traditional team meetings have a specific location. Team members are either physically present or absent. Virtual teams, in contrast, convene electronically with members reporting in from different locations, different organizations, and even different time zones (see the next International OB).

Because virtual teams are so new, there is no consensual definition. Our working definition of a **virtual team** is a physically dispersed task group that conducts its business through modern information technology.[96] Advocates say virtual teams are very flexible and efficient because they are driven by information and skills, not by time and location. People with the necessary information or skills can be team members, regardless of where or when they actually do their work. On the negative side, lack of face-to-face interaction can weaken trust, communication and accountability.

Virtual team
information technology allows group members in different locations to conduct business

Research Insights

As one might expect with a new and ill-defined area, research evidence to date is a bit sparse. Here is what we have learned so far from recent studies of computer-mediated groups.

▼ **Virtual groups formed over the Internet follow a group development process similar to that for face-to-face groups.**[97]

▼ **Internet chat rooms create more work and yield poorer decisions than face-to-face meetings and telephone conferences.**[98]

▼ **Successful use of groupware (software that facilitates interaction among virtual group members) requires training and hands-on experience.**[99]

▼ **Inspirational leadership has a positive impact on creativity in electronic brainstorming groups.**[100]

Practical Considerations

Virtual teams may be in fashion but they are not a cure-all. In fact, they may be a giant step backward for those not well-versed in modern information technology. Managers who rely on virtual teams agree on one point: *Meaningful face-to-face contact, especially during early phases of the group development process, is absolutely essential.* Virtual group members need 'faces' in their minds to go with names and electronic messages. Roy Harrison, training and development policy adviser at the Institute of Personnel and Development, states that the main question surrounding virtual teams is indeed how to encourage positive interaction without face-to-face contact. 'Technology allows people to get in touch but where do you get the 'soul' from?' he says.[101]

Additionally, virtual teams cannot succeed without some old-fashioned factors such as top-management support, hands-on training, a clear mission and specific objectives, effective leadership, and schedules and deadlines.[102]

International OB

http://www.shellglobalsolutions.com

A Virtual Shell Game for the Seven-Time-Zone Team

About the time the sun starts to go down in The Netherlands, Russ Conser's workday kicks into high gear. As a member of a team responsible for evaluating business opportunities for Shell Technology Ventures, a subsidiary of the oil giant Royal Dutch/Shell, Conser has been helping set up an office near The Hague. Thus far, much of his work has focused on hiring staff and figuring out the logistics of how to get the work done.

What often complicates Conser's day isn't so much the challenges that go along with opening a new office, it's keeping up with his team members—about half of whom are seven time zones away in Houston.

Conser and his colleagues rely heavily on E-mail and videoconferences to communicate with one another. But getting the right message to the right people on both sides of the Atlantic hasn't been easy. 'We routinely find out we're miscommunicating, that we forgot to inform a person in the loop that some people had different expectations as to what's going to happen,' he says.

The time difference adds another wrinkle. 'We have about a three-hour window each day when we can interact in real time,' he explains. Consequently, phone conversations often extend into the night, when the Houston staff is at the office. Other times, the team members in The Netherlands have to wait until the sun comes up in Houston to get information they need. 'When they get back to us, we've lost another day on the calendar,' says Conser, who has been in the Netherlands since August.

Conser isn't alone in his struggle to communicate with colleagues an ocean away. Rather, he is part of a growing community of people who work as members of 'virtual' teams, separated by time, distance, culture and organizational boundaries.

SOURCE: K Kiser, 'Working on World Time,' *Training*, March 1999, pp 29–30. Reprinted with permission from the March 1999 issue of *Training* magazine. Copyright © 1999, Lakewood Publications, Minneapolis, MN. All rights reserved. Not for resale.

Self-Managed Teams

Have you ever thought you could do a better job than your boss? Well, if the trend toward self-managed work teams continues to grow as predicted, you just may get your chance. Entrepreneurs and artisans often boast of not having a supervisor. The same generally cannot be said for employees working in organizational offices and factories. But things are changing. In fact, according to a British study published by the Industrial Society, 10 per cent of the 500 personnel managers polled, said that most teams in their organizations were self-managed. Nearly 40 per cent declared that their company operated at least some self-managed teams.[103] Consider, for example, the following situations.

The Body Shop experimented with an autonomous team existing of 30 full-time employees, all with equal status. Each member was paid the same salary. This group operated as a single self-managed team with the collective authority of a branch manager, rotating the four departmental teams and managerial responsibilities. Although some adjustments were carried out, the experiment was a great success.[104]

In an assignment for the European Foundation for Quality Management, the Belgian company Bekaert-Stanwick searched for a 'best practice' model to show how companies could use autonomous teams. At Bekaert-Stanwick, employees make decisions at the lowest level, at that of the production and assembly line workers. Teams of eight to ten people work in different shifts, aiming for faster and more qualitative production. Apart from the team leader, every member of the team is responsible for production, safety, communication, personnel problems and quality. Each team formulates its own mission, preferably as clear a one as possible. Within teams, everybody has his own responsibility, ranging from those of quality and safety to social activities. There's also a rotation system for the function of team leader.[105]

What Are Self-Managed Teams?

Something much more complex is involved than this apparently simple label suggests. The term *self-managed* does not mean simply turning workers loose to do their own thing. Indeed, as we will see, an organization embracing self-managed teams should be prepared to undergo revolutionary changes in management philosophy, structure, staffing and training practices, and reward systems. Moreover, the traditional notions of managerial authority and control are turned on their heads. Not surprisingly, many managers strongly resist giving up the reins of power to people they view as subordinates. They see self-managed teams as a threat to their job security.[106] Texas Instruments has constructively dealt with this problem at its Malaysian factory by making former production supervisors part of the all-important training function.

Self-managed teams are defined as groups of workers who are given 'administrative oversight' for their task domains. Administrative oversight involves delegating activities such as planning, scheduling, monitoring and staffing. These are chores normally performed by managers. In short, employees in these unique work groups act as their own supervisor.[107] Self-managed teams are variously referred to as semi-autonomous work groups, autonomous work groups or superteams.

A common feature of self-managed teams, particularly among those above the shop-floor or clerical level, is **cross-functionalism**.[108] In other words, specialists from different areas are put on the same team. Maxus Energy goes even further. This US oil company has built a cross-functional team that consists of different cultures, languages, locations and time zones.

> *To maximize oil and gas production, two Maxus groups formed a cross-functional, cross-cultural unit. Teaming up were Americans, Dutch, British and Indonesians. Some of these people believe in individualism, others believe in collectivism; some believe in equal opportunity based on achievement, others believe status is inherited. Politically, culturally and religiously this group is composed of disparate elements. Working together, the team not only stabilized production and avoided the expected 15 per cent reduction, but even leveled off production and helped the companies add oil reserves to their stock piles—an almost unprecedented achievement.*[109]

Among companies with self-managed teams, the most commonly delegated tasks are work scheduling and dealing directly with outside customers (see Table 12–7). The least common team chores are hiring and firing. Most of today's self-managed teams remain bunched at the shop-floor level in factory settings. Experts predict growth of the practice in the managerial ranks and in service operations.[110]

Percentage of Companies Saying Their Self-Managing Teams Perform These Traditional Management Functions by Themselves.	
Schedule work assignments	67%
Work with outside customers	67
Conduct training	59
Set production goals/quotas	56
Work with suppliers/vendors	44
Purchase equipment/services	43
Develop budgets	39
Do performance appraisals	36
Hire co-workers	33
Fire co-workers	14

SOURCE: Adapted from '1996 Industry Report: What Self-Managing Teams Manage', *Training*, October 1996, p 69.

Table 12–7
Survey Evidence: What Self-Managing Teams Manage

Sidebar definitions

Self-managed teams
groups of employees granted administrative oversight for their work

Cross-functionalism
team made up of technical specialists from different areas

Historical and Conceptual Roots of Self-Managed Teams

Self-managed teams are an offshoot of a combination of behavioural science and management practice.[111] Group dynamics research of variables, such as cohesiveness, initially paved the way. A later stimulus was the socio-technical systems approach in which first British, and then American researchers, tried to harmonize social and technical factors. Their goal was to increase productivity and the quality of employees' working lives simultaneously. More recently, the idea of self-managed teams has been given a strong boost by advocates of job design and participative management. The job characteristics model of Hackman and Oldham, for example, outlines in Chapter 7, showed that internal motivation, satisfaction and performance can be enhanced through five core job characteristics. In relation to members of self-managed teams, we can see that of those five core factors, increased *autonomy* is a major benefit. Autonomy itself comprises three types: method, scheduling and criteria (see the next OB Exercise on work group autonomy).

Members of self-managed teams score high on group autonomy. Autonomy empowers those who are ready and able to handle added responsibility. (So how did you score on the OB Exercise?) Finally, the social learning theory of self-management, as discussed in Chapter 10, has helped strengthen the case for self-managed teams.

OB Exercise

Measuring Work Group Autonomy

Instructions

Think of your current (or past) job and work groups. Characterize the group's situation by circling one number on the following scale for each statement. Add your responses for a total score.

Strongly Disagree					Strongly Agree
1 — 2 — 3 — 4 —	5 —	6 —	7		

Work Method Autonomy

1 My work group decides how to get the job done. _____

2 My work group determines what procedures to use. _____

3 My work group is free to choose its own methods when carrying out its work. _____

Work Scheduling Autonomy

4 My work group controls the scheduling of its work. _____

5 My work group determines how its work is sequenced. _____

6 My work group decides when to do certain activities. _____

Work Criteria Autonomy

7 My work group is allowed to modify the normal way it is evaluated so some of our activities are emphasized and some de-emphasized. _____

8 My work group is able to modify its objectives (what it is supposed to accomplish). _____

9 My work group has some control over what it is supposed to accomplish. _____

Total score =

Norms

9–26 = Low autonomy

27–45 = Moderate autonomy

46–63 = High autonomy

SOURCE: Adapted from an individual autonomy scale in J A Breaugh, 'The Work Autonomy Scales: Additional Validity Evidence', *Human Relations*, November 1989, pp 1033–1056.

The net result of this confluence is the continuum in Figure 12–7. The traditional clear-cut distinction between manager and managed is being blurred as non-managerial employees are delegated greater authority and granted increased autonomy. It is important to note, however, that self-managed teams do not eliminate the need for all managerial control (see the upper right-hand corner of Figure 12–7). Semi-autonomous work teams represent a balance between managerial and group control.[112]

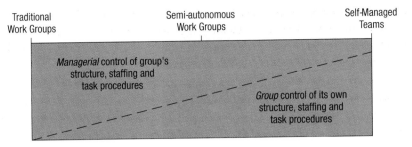

Figure 12–7

The Evolution of Self-Managed Work Teams

Are Self-Managed Teams Effective? Research Evidence

As with quality circles and virtual teams, much of what we know about self-managed teams comes from testimonials and case studies. Fortunately, a body of higher quality field research is slowly emerging. A review of three meta-analyses covering 70 individual studies concluded that self-managed teams had:

▼ **a positive impact on productivity**

▼ **a positive impact on specific attitudes relating to self-management (e.g., responsibility and control)**

▼ **no significant impact on general attitudes (e.g., job satisfaction and organizational commitment)**

▼ **no significant impact on absenteeism or turnover.**[113]

Although encouraging, these results do not qualify as a sweeping endorsement of self-managed teams. Nonetheless, experts say the trend toward self-managed work teams will continue upward. Managers need to be prepared for the resulting shift in organizational administration.

Setting the Stage for Self-Managed Teams

Experience shows that it is better to build a new production or service facility around self-managed teams than to attempt to convert an existing one. The former approach involves so-called 'greenfield sites'. Greenfield sites give management the advantage of selecting appropriate technology and carefully screening job applicants likely to be good team players.

But the fact is, most organizations are not afforded greenfield opportunities. They must settle for introducing self-managed teams into an existing organization structure.[114] This is where Lawler and Mohrman's transitional model is helpful (see Figure 12–8). Even though their model builds a bridge specifically from quality circles to team organization; their recommendations apply to the transition from any sort of organization structure to teams. As mentioned earlier, quality circles are a good stepping-stone from a non-participative organization to one driven by self-managed teams.

Making the Transition to Self-Managed Teams

Extensive *management training* and socialization are required to deeply embed Theory Y and participative management values into the organization's culture. It is necessary for this new logic to start with top management and filter down. Otherwise, resistance among middle- and lower-level managers will block the transition to teams.[115] Some turnover can be expected among managers who refuse to adjust to broader empowerment.

Both *technical and organizational* redesign are necessary for the transition to self-managed teams. The new teams may require special technology. Volvo's team-based car assembly plant, for example, relies on portable assembly platforms rather than traditional assembly lines. Structural redesign of the organization must take place because self-managed teams are an integral part of the organization, not patched onto it as in the case of quality circles.

Figure 12–8

Making the Transition between Quality Circles and Self-Managed Teams

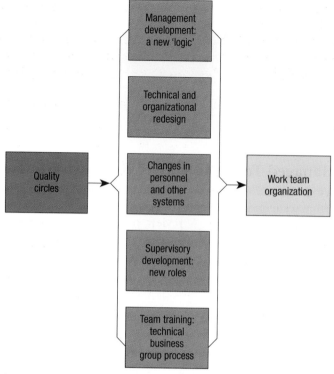

For example, in one of Texas Instruments' computer chip factories a hierarchy of teams operates within the traditional structure. Four levels of teams are responsible for different domains. Reporting to the steering team that deals with strategic issues are quality-improvement, corrective-action, and effectiveness teams. Texas Instrumens' quality-improvement and corrective-action teams are cross-functional teams; and are made up of middle managers and functional specialists such as accountants and engineers. Production workers make up the effectiveness teams. The corrective-action teams are unique because they are formed to deal with short-term problems and are disbanded when a solution is found. All the other teams are long-term assignments.[116]

In turn, systems for *personnel, goal setting and rewards* will need to be adapted to encourage the new self-managed teamwork. Staffing decisions may shift from management to team members who hire their own co-workers. A study of 60 self-managing teams involving 540 employees suggests how goal setting should be reoriented. Teams with highly *co-operative* goals functioned more smoothly and had better results than teams with competitive goals.[117] Accordingly, individual bonuses must give way to team bonuses. *Supervisory development workshops* are needed to teach managers to be facilitators rather than order givers.[118] Finally, extensive *team training* is required to help team members learn more about technical details, the business as a whole, and how to be team players. This is where team building enters the picture.

TEAM BUILDING

Team building
experiential learning aimed at better internal functioning of groups

Team building is a catch-all term for a whole host of techniques aimed at improving the internal functioning of work groups. Whether conducted by company trainers or outside consultants, team-building workshops strive for greater co-operation, better communication and less dysfunctional conflict. Experiential learning techniques such as interpersonal trust exercises, conflict-handling role play sessions and interactive games are common. For example, Germany's Opel uses Lego® blocks to teach its car workers the tight teamwork necessary for just-in-time production.[119] Meanwhile, Hamburg Mannheimer organized a three-day rafting in the French Alps: 15 staff who were performing well, went on an adventure survival-camp, including mountain climbing, bungee-jumping . . . .[120] And Insurance company Axa, sends her managers to a wine chateau in Bordeaux for management training, including team building activities in the form of role-play and simulations of business situations.[121]

Complete coverage of the many team-building techniques would require a separate book. Consequently, the scope of our current discussion is limited to the goal of team building and the day-to-day development of self-management skills. This foundation is intended to give you a basis for selecting appropriate team-building techniques from the many you are likely to encounter in the years ahead.[122]

The Goal of Team Building: High-Performance Teams

Team building allows team members to wrestle with simulated or real-life problems. Outcomes are then analysed by the group to determine what group processes need improvement. Learning stems from recognizing and addressing faulty group dynamics. Perhaps one sub-group withheld key information from another, thereby hampering group progress. With cross-cultural teams becoming commonplace in today's global economy, team building is more important than ever.[123] (see the next International OB).

International OB

http://www.onepine.demon.co.uk/people.htm

The Wild World of Cross-Cultural Team Building

Brussels–Anyone can talk about cultural differences. Fons Trompenaars tries to make his students feel them.

To do that, the Dutch leader of workshops on 'multicultural' management teaches his students (mostly executives) to play a game invented by one of his colleagues, L J P Brug. The object: building towers made of paper.

Mr Trompenaars, a 39-year-old former Royal Dutch/Shell executive, divides a group of several dozen Swedish managers into two groups. Four are designated as 'international experts' in building paper towers. Everyone else becomes a native of a make-believe village called Derdia.

'Your culture loves towers but doesn't know how to build them,' Mr Trompenaars tells the Derdians.

The experts are sent out of the room to learn to make paper towers and prepare to pass that skill on to Derdia. Meanwhile, Mr Trompenaars initiates the Swedes into the strange customs of Derdia.

Derdians' greetings involve kissing one another on the shoulder. Holding out a hand to someone means 'Please go away.' If they disagree, Derdians say 'Yes!' and nod their heads vigorously.

What's more, Derdian women have a taboo against using paper or scissors in the presence of men, while men would never use a pencil or a ruler in front of women.

The Swedes, reserved a moment ago, throw themselves into the task of acting like Derdians. They merrily tap one another, kiss shoulders and bray 'Yessss!'

Soon, two 'experts' are allowed back into the room for a brief study of Derdian culture. The Derdians flock to the experts and gleefully kiss their shoulders. The experts turn red. They seem lost already.

'Would you please sit?' asks Hans Olav Friberg, a young 'expert' who, back home in Sweden, works for a company that makes flooring.

'Yessss!' the Derdians say in a chorus. But they don't sit down.

'Who is in charge here?' Mr Friberg inquires. 'Yessss!' the Derdians reply.

Mr Friberg leaves the room to confer with his fellow experts. 'They didn't understand us,' he tells them. But fellow expert Hakan Kalmermo isn't about to be deterred by strange habits. He is taking charge. As he briskly practices making a paper tower, Mr Kalmermo says firmly to the other experts: 'The target is to have them produce one tower.'

The four experts carry paper and other supplies to the adjoining room, now known as Derdia. They begin to explain the process to the Derdians very slowly, as if speaking to small children. When one of the Derdians shows he understands the workings of a scissors, Mr Kalmermo exclaims: 'Good boy!'

Although Mr Kalmermo works hard at making himself clear, the Derdians' customs and taboos obstruct progress. The men won't use rulers as long as women are around but don't explain this behavior to the experts. The answer to every question seems to be 'yes.' At the end of 30 minutes, no tower has been completed.

The game is over; now comes the self-criticism. 'They treated us like idiots,' protests one of the Derdians.

The lessons are clear, but Mr Trompenaars drives them home: If you don't figure out basics of a foreign culture, you won't get much accomplished. And if your biases lead you to think of foreign ways as childish, the foreigners may well respond by acting childish.

Still, Mr Kalmermo, the take-charge expert, thinks his team was on the right track. 'If we'd had another hour,' he says, 'I think we would have had 15 towers built.'

SOURCE: B Hagerty, 'Learning to Turn the Other Shoulder', *The Wall Street Journal*, June 14, 1993, pp B1, B3. Reprinted by permission of *The Wall Street Journal* © 1993 Dow Jones & Company, Inc. All Rights Reserved Worldwide.

According to Richard Beckhard, a respected authority on organization development, the four purposes of team building are:

▼ **to set goals and/or priorities**

▼ **to analyse or allocate the way work is performed**

▼ **to examine the way a group is working and its processes (such as norms, decision making and communication)**

▼ **to examine relationships among the people doing the work.**[124]

A nationwide survey of team members from many organizations undertaken by Wilson Learning Corporation, provides a useful model or benchmark of what we should expect of teams. The researchers' question was simply: 'What is a high-performance team?'.[125] The respondents were asked to describe their peak experiences in work teams. Analysis of the survey results yielded the following eight attributes of high-performance teams.

1 *Participative leadership.* Creating an interdependency by empowering, freeing up, and serving others.

2 *Shared responsibility.* Establishing an environment in which all team members feel as responsible as the manager for the performance of the work unit.

3 *Aligned on purpose.* Having a sense of common purpose about why the team exists and the function it serves.

4 *Good communication.* Creating a climate of trust and open, honest communication.

5 *Future focused.* Seeing change as an opportunity for growth.

6 *Focused on task.* Keeping meetings focused on results.

7 *Creative talents.* Applying individual talents and creativity.

8 *Rapid response.* Identifying and acting on opportunities.[126]

These eight attributes effectively combine many of today's most progressive ideas on management,[127] among them being participation, empowerment, service ethic, individual responsibility and development, self-management, trust, active listening, and envisioning. But patience and diligence are also required. According to a manager familiar with work teams, 'high-performance teams may take three to five years to build.'[128] Let us keep this inspiring model of high-performance teams in mind as we conclude our discussion of team building.

Developing Team Members' Self-Management Skills

A promising dimension of team building has emerged in recent years. It is an extension of the behavioural self-management approach discussed in Chapter 10. Proponents call it **self-management leadership**, defined as the process of leading others to lead themselves. An underlying assumption is that self-managed teams are likely to fail if team members are not expressly taught to engage in self-management behaviours. This makes sense because it is unreasonable to expect employees who are accustomed to being managed and led to suddenly manage and lead themselves. Transition training is required, as discussed in the prior section. A key part of the transition to self-management involves *current managers* engaging in self-management leadership behaviours. This is team building in the fullest sense of the term.

> **Self-management leadership**
> *process of leading others to lead themselves*

Six aspects of self-management leadership behaviour were isolated in a field study of a manufacturing company organized around self-managed teams. The following leadership behaviour was observed.

1   *Encourages self-reinforcement* (e.g., getting team members to praise each other for good work and results).

2   *Encourages self-observation/evaluation* (e.g., teaching team members to judge how well they are doing).

3   *Encourages self-expectation* (e.g., encouraging team members to expect high performance from themselves and the team).

4   *Encourages self-goal-setting* (e.g., having the team set its own performance goals).

5   *Encourages rehearsal* (e.g., getting team members to think about and practice new tasks).

6   *Encourages self-criticism* (e.g., encouraging team members to be critical of their own poor performance).[129]

According to the researchers, Charles Manz and Henry Sims, this type of leadership is a dramatic departure from traditional practices such as giving orders and/or making sure everyone gets along. Empowerment, not domination, is the overriding goal.

Summary of Key Concepts

1   Describe the five stages in Tuckman's theory of group development.

The five stages in Tuckman's theory are *forming* (the group comes together), *storming* (members test the limits of each other), *norming* (questions of authority are resolved as the group becomes more cohesive), *performing* (effective communication and co-operation can help the group get things done), and *adjourning* (group members go their own way).

2   Identify and describe the four types of work teams.

Four general types of work teams are advice, production, project, and action teams. Each type has its characteristic degrees of specialization and co-ordination, work cycle, and outputs.

3   Explain the ecological model of work team effectiveness.

According to the ecological model, two effectiveness criteria for work teams are performance and viability. The performance criterion is met if the group satisfies its clients/customers. A work group is viable if its members are satisfied and continue contributing. An ecological perspective is appropriate because work groups require an organizational life-support system. For instance, group participation is enhanced by an organizational culture that values employee empowerment.

4   Discuss why teams fail.

Teams fail because unrealistic expectations cause frustration and failure. Common management mistakes include weak strategies, creating a hostile environment for teams, faddish use of teams, not learning from team experience, vague team assignments, poor team staffing, inadequate training and a lack of trust. Team members typically fail if they try too much too soon, experience conflict over differing work styles and personalities, ignore important group dynamics, resist change, exhibit poor interpersonal skills and chemistry, and display a lack of trust.

5   Describe what is meant by the term groupthink and identify at least four of its symptoms.

Groupthink plagues cohesive in-groups that shortchange moral judgement while putting too much emphasis on unanimity. Symptoms of groupthink include 'being invulnerable', inherent morality, rationalization, stereotyped views of opposition, self-censorship, illusion of unanimity, peer pressure and mindguards. Critical evaluators, outside expertise and devil's advocates are among the preventive measures recommended by Irving Janis, who coined the term groupthink.

6   List at least three things managers can do to build trust.

Six recommended ways to build trust are through communication, support, respect (especially delegation), fairness, predictability and competence.

7   Distinguish two types of group cohesiveness and summarize the research findings on it.

Cohesive groups have a shared sense of togetherness or a 'we' feeling. Socio-emotional cohesiveness involves emotional satisfaction. Instrumental cohesiveness involves goal-directed togetherness. There is a small but significant relationship between cohesiveness and performance. The effect is stronger for smaller groups. Commitment to task among group members strengthens the cohesiveness→performance linkage. Success can build group cohesiveness. Cohesiveness is not a cure-all for group problems. Too much cohesiveness can lead to groupthink.

8   Define quality circles, virtual teams and self-managed teams.

Quality circles are small groups of volunteers who meet regularly to solve quality-related problems in their work area. Virtual teams are physically dispersed work groups that conduct their business via modern information technologies such as the Internet, email and videoconferences. Self-managed teams are work groups that perform their own administrative chores such as planning, scheduling and staffing.

9   Describe high-performance teams.

Eight attributes of high-performance teams are (*a*) participative leadership (*b*) shared responsibility (*c*) aligned on purpose (*d*) high communication (*e*) future focused for growth (*f*) focused on task (*g*) creative talents applied and (*h*) rapid response.

Discussion Questions

1   Do you agree or disagree with Drucker's vision of more team-oriented organizations? Explain your assumptions and reasoning.

2   Which of the factors listed in Table 12–1 is most crucial to a successful team? Explain.

3   Why bother taking an ecological perspective of work team effectiveness?

4   In your personal friendships, how do you come to trust someone? How fragile is that trust? Explain.

5   Why is delegation so important to building organizational trust?

6   Why should a group leader strive for both socio-emotional and instrumental cohesiveness?

7   Are virtual teams likely to be just a passing fad? Why or why not?

8   Would you like to work on a self-managed team? Explain.

9   How would you respond to a manager who said, 'Why should I teach my people to manage themselves and work myself out of a job?'

10   Have you ever been a member of a high-performing team? If so, explain the circumstances and success factors.

Internet Exercise

A Free Self-Assessment Questionnaire for Social Skills

Social Skills are essential when working in teams. If you want to accomplish things with and through others, you simply cannot be effective if you are unable to interact skilfully in social settings. As with any skill development programme, you need to know *where you are* before constructing a learning agenda for *where you want to be.* Go to the Internet home page for Body-Mind QueenDom (www.queendom.com) and select the subheading "Tests" under the main menu heading "interactive". (Note: Our use of this questionnaire is for instructional purposes only and does not constitute an endorsement of any products that may or may not suit your needs. There is no obligation to buy anything.) At the "Tests" page, read the brief welcome statement about QueenDom's psychological tests, and then scroll down to the category "Relationships". Select the "Communication Skills Test", read the brief instructions, complete all 34 items, and click on the "score" button for automatic scoring. It is possible, if you choose, to print a personal copy of your completed questionnaire and results.

Questions:

1 Possible scores of the self-assessment questionnaire range from 0 to 100. How did you score? Are you pleasantly (or unpleasantly) surprised by your score?

2 What is your strongest social/communication skill?

3 Reviewing the questionnaire item by item, can you find obvious weak spots in your social/communication skills? For instance, are you a poor listener? Do you interrupt too often? Do you need to be more aware of others, both verbally and non-verbally? Do you have a hard time tuning into others' feelings or expressing your own feelings? How do you handle disagreement?

4 Based on the results of this questionnaire, what is your learning agenda for improving your social and communication skills. (Note: You will find lots of good ideas and practical tips throughout this text).

Personal Awareness and Growth Exercise

How Trusting Are You?

Objectives

1 To introduce you to different dimensions of interpersonal trust.

2 To measure your trust in another person.

3 To discuss the managerial implications of your propensity to trust.

Introduction

The trend toward more open and empowered organizations where teamwork and self-management are vital requires heightened interpersonal trust. Customers need to be able to trust organizations producing the goods and services they buy, managers need to trust non-managers to carry out the organization's mission, and team members need to trust each other in order to get the job done. As with any other interpersonal skill, we need to be able to measure and improve our ability to trust others. This exercise is a step in that direction.

Instructions[130]

Think of a specific individual who currently plays an important role in your life (e.g., present or future spouse, friend, supervisor, co-worker, team member, etc.), and rate his or her trustworthiness for each statement according to the following scale. Total your responses, and compare your score with the arbitrary norms provided.

Strongly Disagree									**Strongly Agree**
1 — 2 — 3 — 4 — 5 — 6 — 7 — 8 — 9 — 10									

Overall Trust	**Score**
1 I can expect this person to play fair.	_____
2 I can confide in this person and know she/he desires to listen.	_____
3 I can expect this person to tell me the truth.	_____
4 This person takes time to listen to my problems and worries.	_____

Emotional Trust

5 This person would never intentionally
misrepresent my point of view to
other people.   _____

6 I can confide in this person and know
that he/she will not discuss it with others.   _____

7 This person gives constructive and
caring responses to my problems.   _____

Reliableness

8 If this person promised to do me a favour,
she/he would carry out that promise.   _____

9 If I had an appointment with this person,
I could count on him/her showing up.   _____

10 I could lend this person money and count
on getting it back as soon as possible. _____

11 I do not need a back-up plan because
I know this person will come through
for me.   _____

Total score = _____

Trustworthiness Scale

63–88 = High (Trust is a precious thing.)

37–62 = Moderate (Be careful; get a rearview mirror.)

11–36 = Low (Lock up your valuables!)

Questions for Discussion

1 Which particular items in this trust questionnaire are
most central to your idea of trust? Why?

2 Does your score accurately depict the degree to which
you trust (or distrust) the target person?

3 Why do you trust (or distrust) this individual?

4 If you trust this person to a high degree, how hard was
it to build that trust? Explain. What would destroy that
trust?

5 Based on your responses to this questionnaire, how
would you rate your 'propensity to trust'? Low?
Moderate? High?

6 What are the managerial implications of your
propensity to trust?

Group Exercise
Student Team Development Project

Objectives

1 To help you understand the components of teamwork
better.

2 To give you a practical diagnostic tool to assess the
need for team building.

3 To give you a chance to evaluate and develop an
actual group/team.

Introduction

Student teams are very common in today's college
classrooms. They are an important part of the move toward
co-operative and experiential learning. In other words,
learning by doing. Group dynamics and teamwork are best
learned by doing. Unfortunately, many classroom teams
wallow in ambiguity, conflict and ineffectiveness. This team
development questionnaire can play an important role in the
life cycle of your classroom team or group. All members of
your team can complete this evaluation at one or more of the
following critical points in your team's life cycle: (1) when

the team reaches a crisis point and threatens to break up, (2)
about halfway through the life of the team, and (3) at the end
of the team's life cycle. Discussion of the results by all team
members can enhance the group's learning experience.

Instructions

Either at the prompting of your instructor or by group
consensus, decide at what point in your team's life cycle this
exercise should be completed. *Tip:* Have each team member
write their responses to the ten items on a sheet of paper with
no names attached. This will permit the calculation of a group
mean score for each item and for all ten items. Attention
should then turn to the discussion questions provided in order
to help any team development problems surface and to point
the way toward solutions.

(An alternative to these instructions is to evaluate a team or
work group you are associated with in your current job. You
may also draw from a group experience in a past job.)

Questionnaire[131]

1 To what extent do I feel a real part of the team?

5	4	3	2	1
Completely a part all the time.	A part most of the time.	On the edge– sometimes in, sometimes out.	Generally outside except for one or two short periods.	On the outside, not really a part of the team.

2 How safe is it in this team to be at ease and relaxed, and to be myself?

5	4	3	2	1
I feel perfectly safe to be myself; they won't hold mistakes against me.	I feel most people would accept me if I were completely myself, but there are some I am not sure about.	Generally one has to be careful what one says or does in this team.	I am quite fearful about being completely myself in this team.	I am not a fool; I would never be myself in this team.

3 To what extent do I feel 'under wraps', i.e., have private thoughts, unspoken reservations or unexpressed feelings and opinions which I have not felt comfortable bringing out into the open?

5	4	3	2	1
Almost completely under wraps.	Under wraps many times.	Slightly more free and expressive than under wraps.	Quite free and expressive much of the time.	Almost completely free and expressive.

4 How effective are we, in our team, in getting out and using the ideas, opinions and information of all team members in making decisions?

5	4	3	2	1
We don't really encourage everyone to share their ideas, opinions and information with the team when making decisions.	Only the ideas, opinions and information of a few members are really known and used in making decisions.	Sometimes we hear the views of most members before making decisions, and sometimes we disregard most members.	A few are sometimes hesitant about sharing their opinions but we generally have good participation in making decisions.	Everyone feels his or her ideas, opinions and information are given a fair hearing before decisions are made.

5 To what extent are the goals the team is working toward understood, and to what extent do they have meaning for you?

5	4	3	2	1
I feel extremely good about goals of our team.	I feel fairly good but some things are not too clear or meaningful.	A few things we are doing are clear and meaningful.	Much of the activity is not clear or meaningful to me.	I really do not understand or feel involved in the goals of the team.

6 How well does the team work at its tasks?

5	4	3	2	1
Coasts, loafs, makes no progress.	Makes a little progress but most members loaf.	Progress is slow; spurts of effective work.	Above average in progress and pace of work.	Works well; achieves definite progress.

7 Our planning and the way we operate as a team are largely influenced by:

5	4	3	2	1
One or two team members.	A clique.	Shifts from one person or clique to another.	Shared by most of the members but some are left out.	Shared by all members of the team.

8 What is the level of responsibility for work in our team?

5	4	3	2	1
Each person assumes personal responsibility for getting work done.	A majority of the members assume responsibility for getting work done.	About half assume responsibility; about half do not.	Only a few assume responsibility for getting work done.	Nobody (except perhaps one) really assumes responsibility for getting work done.

9   How are differences or conflicts handled in our team?

5	4	3	2	1
Differences or conflicts are denied, suppressed or avoided at all costs.	Differences or conflicts are recognized but remain mostly unresolved.	Differences or conflicts are recognized, and some attempts are made to work them through by some members, often outside the team meetings.	Differences and conflicts are recognized, and some attempts are made to deal with them in our team.	Differences and conflicts are recognized, and the team usually works through them satisfactorily.

10 How do people relate to the team leader, chairperson or 'boss'?

5	4	3	2	1
The leader dominates the team, and people are often fearful or passive.	The leader tends to control the team, although people generally agree with the leader's direction.	There is some give and take between the leader and the team members.	Team members relate easily to the leader and usually they are able to influence leader decisions.	Team members respect the leader but they work together as a unified team, with everyone participating and no one dominant.

Total score = _____

Questions for Discussion

1   Have any of the items on the questionnaire helped you to understand better why your team has had problems? What problems?

2   Based on Table 12–1, are you part of a group or team? Explain.

3   How do your responses to the items compare with the average responses from your group? What insights does this information provide?

4   Refer back to Tuckman's five-stage model of group development in Figure 12–1. Which stage is your team at? How can you tell?

5   If you are part way through your team's lifecycle, what steps does your team need to take to become more effective?

6   If this is the end of your team's lifecycle, what should your team have done differently?

7   What lasting lessons about teamwork have you learned from this exercise?

Chapter Thirteen

Managing Conflict and Negotiation

13

Learning Objectives

When you finish studying the material in this chapter, you should be able to:

- Define the term *conflict*, distinguish between functional and dysfunctional conflict, and identify three desired conflict outcomes.

- Define *personality conflicts* and explain how managers should handle them.

- Distinguish between instrumental and terminal values, identify three types of value conflict, and explain how value conflicts can be handled.

- Discuss the role of in-group thinking in conflict between groups and explain what management can do about these group conflicts.

- Discuss what can be done about cross-cultural conflict.

- Explain how managers can stimulate functional conflict and identify the five conflict-handling styles.

- Explain the nature and practical significance of conflict triangles.

- Explain the difference between distributive and integrative negotiation and discuss the concept of added-value negotiation.

A Vineyard's Bitter Fruit

Count Alexandre de Lur Saluces looks like the ultimate blueblood: dressed in jacket and tie, he strolls in front of his chateau, a pile dating back to the 15th century and topped by tidy stone turrets and parapets. Vines stretch down toward the Ciron River, a tributary of the broad Garonne. This is Chateau d'Yquem. Standing outside the village of Sauternes, 50 kilometers southeast of Bordeaux, the estate produces what could be the world's most famous wine–a luscious, opulently sweet white that, in some vintages, sells for thousands of dollars a bottle. ▶

The Lur Saluces family has put its name on this pale-gold nectar since 1593, always drawing it from grapes afflicted with *Botrytis cinerea*, or noble rot. The rot may be noble, but the vineyard itself has had an ignoble chapter in its recent history. Over the past decade, the tranquil-looking chateau was the scene of a struggle that pitted the power of French tradition against the raw force of the global marketplace. And the marketplace appears to have won.

Lur Saluces wanted to guard tradition by keeping d'Yquem under his own family's control. But many of his relatives and fellow shareholders, who rarely received any returns on their stakes, were angered by his imperious ways. After years of fighting, the count sold out last year to the giant Louis Vuitton Moet Hennessy (LVMH) conglomerate, owner of Moet & Chandon champagne, Louis Vuitton luggage, and the Givenchy and Dior fashion houses. The count, who once feared LVMH would devalue his family's wine by creating a d'Yquem perfume and d'Yquem fashion accessories, now works for his former enemy as a simple employee.

The bitter battle represents an all-too-common saga in the French countryside, particularly in the world of wine. Family-owned properties face a double whammy: high inheritance taxes plus the need for funds to modernize. Victorious corporations, meanwhile, confront other conflicting forces: tradition versus modernity, quantity versus quality. The twist is that corporations may end up being better guardians of French heritage than are impoverished, divided families. 'If we tried to leverage Chateau d'Yquem, we would risk destroying its mythical image,' says Pierre Gode, president of Louis Vuitton and No. 2 in the LVMH organization.

D'Yquem is indeed mythical–an exquisite and exceptional wine. When the 1855 Bordeaux classification was made, d'Yquem warranted a category of its own: premier cru superieur, or first great growth, surpassing premier cru, or first growth, which includes such illustrious names as Lafite- Rothschild and Latour.

Every year's production represents something of a miracle. Instead of waiting for the grapes merely to ripen, the masters of d'Yquem let the grapes shrivel and go nearly moldy. This noble rot concentrates flavour, producing the singular balance of sweetness and fruit for which d'Yquem is noted. Skilled workers harvest the crop grape by grape, returning to each vine up to 12 times over a month, waiting for the perfect moment to pluck. At d'Yquem, one vine yields a single glass.

Another thing d'Yquem yields in small amounts is money. When Lur Saluces took over in 1968, the chateau was producing an average of only 66,000 bottles a year; a good Bordeaux house such as Chateau Margaux makes 400,000. The next few years were marked by poor harvests. Then, the oil crisis slashed demand and prices plummeted. A bottle of d'Yquem back then sold for a mere 35 francs–about $5. Prices began to rise only in the 1980s.

By all accounts, Lur Saluces has done an admirable job of burnishing d'Yquem's luster. Tractors replaced horses, collapsing cellars were renovated, and unused acreage was planted. All this upped production in good years to 100,000 bottles. In such years, sales reach about $10 million. 'Alexandre Lur Saluces polished the finest diamond in the wine world,' says an admiring Count Xavier de Pontac, president of the Syndicat des Grands Crus Classes de Sauternes.

And the director lived a life appropriate for an ambassador of luxury. Under his aegis, dinners at d'Yquem became a celebration, with celebrities in attendance: Champagne as an aperitif, followed by first-growth red Bordeaux (he is particularly fond of Chateau Petrus), finished by an older d'Yquem and Havana cigars. You wouldn't know it by appearances, but Lur Saluces owned only 7% of the chateau, and his son, Bertrand, 2.2%. His older brother, Eugene, owned the largest chunk, 47%.

The rest of the property was split up over the generations among more than 40 other Lur Saluces and the related Hanguerlots. And therein lies the rub. Most small d'Yquem owners lived in Paris or other cities and most received little in the way of dividends. 'Many were struggling to pay the rents on their apartments,' says Bertrand Hanguerlot, a representative of the disenchanted family members. Even Eugene, the primary owner, hardly ever set foot on the property, living in relative squalor in Paris.

Not surprisingly, these silent shareholders seethed. They were scandalized when about $200,000 was spent for an ultramodern toilet. Lur Saluces never invited them to his fetes. He never gave them a bottle of d'Yquem, even though entire cases went to journalists–this writer not included–and Bordeaux officials. 'We were shut out of management,' complains Hanguerlot. Lur Saluces says he was just making necessary investments to safeguard the d'Yquem brand.

The open conflict began in 1992, when Lur Saluces tried to formalize his control so that he could pass the property on to his eldest son. The other shareholders, who by this time included the count's daughter and other son, went looking for a buyer. They persuaded Eugene to sell part of his holding, too. On Nov. 28, 1996, LVMH bought a 55% stake for about $100 million.

Lur Saluces went ballistic. He believed LVMH and its owner, Bernard Arnault, would ruin d'Yquem. Lur Saluces sued to stop the sale. 'Arnault wants to make perfume and call it d'Yquem,' he claimed at the time. 'For 30 years, I've fought against diluting the name of d'Yquem. Arnault buys brands and does just about anything with them.' The court battles in both Paris and Bordeaux stretched on for 30 months. Each time, Lur Saluces lost, although he won the PR skirmishes. Journalists, restaurateurs, and wine merchants all took his side, portraying capitalist greed as ready to destroy delicate French traditions.

By spring last year, both sides were ready to settle. Lur Saluces approached Arnault and said he was prepared to sell out—on certain conditions. (Neither Lur Saluces nor Arnault will discuss the negotiations.) The count wanted a premium on his shares. Although the return on LVMH's investment is a mere 2% a year, he insists that there is no desire to leverage the d'Yquem brand. 'We're not in this for cash flow or profitability but to develop our image of quality,' he says.

Lur Saluces agrees. After denouncing Arnault as the devil incarnate, he now praises him as d'Yquem's saviour. 'Arnault understands this is a jewel to be protected,' he says. 'I was wrong to suspect him.' He is not so tender about his own family: 'My family was motivated by childish jealousy,' he says.

And d'Yquem the wine? As extraordinary as ever. To finally celebrate the LVMH arrangement, Lur Saluces invited Arnault and Gode to lunch at d'Yquem last April. For dessert, he served an 1899. 'You could taste the entire century in your mouth,' recalls Gode. For less prestigious visitors–this writer not among them–a bottle of 1995 vintage is opened. Lur Saluces picks up his glass and sips. A smile comes over his previously impassive face. The pain from the long battle of Bordeaux finally dissolves.[1]

For discussion

Can you identify the basic dimensions in this conflict?

How would you handle this situation?

Your name is Annie and you are a product development manager for Amazon.de (Amazon Germany). While you were eating lunch today in your office, Sophie, a software project manager from an office nearby, asked if she could talk to you for a few minutes. You barely know Sophie and you have heard both good and bad things about her work habits. Although your mind was more on how to meet Friday's deadline than on lunch, you waved her in.

She proceeded to pour out her woes about how she was having an impossible time partnering Hans on a new special project. He is regarded as a top-notch software project manager but Sophie has found him to be ill-tempered and unco-operative. Sophie thought you and Hans were friends because she has seen the two of you talking in the cafeteria and parking lot. You told Sophie you have a good working relationship with Hans but that he's not really a friend. Still, Sophie pressed on. 'Would you straighten Hans out for me?' she asked. 'We've got to get moving on this special project.'

'Why this? Why now? Why me?!!' you thought as your eyes left Sophie and drifted back to your desk.

Write down some ideas about how to handle this all-too-common conflict situation. Set it aside. We'll revisit your recommendation later in the chapter. In the meantime, we need to explore the world of conflict. After discussing a modern view of conflict and four major types of conflict, we learn how to manage conflict both as a participant and as a third party. The related topic of negotiation is examined next. We conclude with a contingency approach to conflict management and negotiation.

CONFLICT: A MODERN PERSPECTIVE

Make no mistake about it. Conflict is an unavoidable aspect of modern life. These major trends conspire to make *organizational* conflict inevitable:

- ▼ **constant change**
- ▼ **greater employee diversity**
- ▼ **more teams (virtual and self-managed)**
- ▼ **less reliance on hierarchy**
- ▼ **more value-laden topics in the work place (environment, discrimination, work-family interface . . .)**
- ▼ **more dynamic careers (less loyalty)**
- ▼ **a global economy with increased cross-cultural dealings.**

Dean Tjosvold, now at HongKong university, notes that 'Change begets conflict, conflict begets change'[2] and challenges us to do better with the following sobering global perspective.

Learning to manage conflict is a critical investment in improving how we, our families, and our organizations adapt and take advantage of change. Managing conflicts well does not insulate us from change, nor does it mean that we will always come out on top or get all that we want. However, effective conflict management helps us keep in touch with new developments and create solutions appropriate for new threats and opportunities.

Much evidence shows we have often failed to manage our conflicts and respond to change effectively. High divorce rates, disheartening examples of sexual and physical abuse of children, the expensive failures of international joint ventures, and bloody ethnic violence have convinced many people that we do not have the abilities to cope with our complex interpersonal, organizational, and global conflicts.[3]

A comprehensive review of the conflict literature yielded this consensus definition: '**Conflict** is a process in which one party perceives that its interests are being opposed or negatively affected by another party.'[4] The word *perceives* reminds us that sources of conflict and issues can be real or imagined. The resulting conflict is the same. Conflict can escalate (strengthen) or de-escalate (weaken) over time. 'The conflict process unfolds in a context, and whenever conflict, escalated or not, occurs the disputants or third parties can attempt to manage it in some manner.'[5] Consequently, employees need to understand the dynamics of conflict and know how to handle it effectively (both as disputants and as third parties).

Conflict
one party perceives its interests are being opposed or set back by another party

A Conflict Continuum

Ideas about managing conflict underwent an interesting evolution during the 20th century. Initially, scientific management experts such as Frederick W Taylor believed all conflict ultimately threatened management's authority and thus had to be avoided or quickly resolved. Later, human relations theorists recognized the inevitability of conflict and advised managers to learn to live with it. Emphasis, however, remained on the resolution of the conflict whenever possible. From the 1970s, OB specialists began to realise that conflict had both positive and negative outcomes, depending on its nature and intensity. This perspective introduced the revolutionary idea that organizations could suffer from *too little* conflict. Figure 13–1 illustrates the relationship between conflict intensity and outcomes.

Figure 13–1

The Relationship between Conflict Intensity and Outcomes

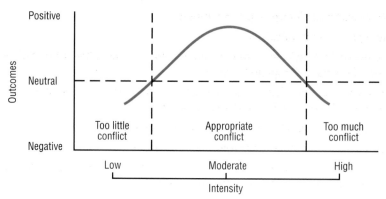

SOURCE: L D Brown, *Managing Conflict of Organizational Interfaces*, © 1986, Addison-Wesley Publishing Co., Inc., Reading, Massachusetts. Figure 1.1 on page 8. Reprinted with permission.

Work groups, departments or organizations that experience too little conflict tend to be plagued by apathy, lack of creativity, indecision and missed deadlines. Excessive conflict, on the other hand, can erode organizational performance because of political infighting, dissatisfaction, lack of teamwork, and turnover. Workplace aggression and violence can be manifestations of excessive conflict.[6] Appropriate types and levels of conflict energize people in constructive directions.[7]

Functional versus Dysfunctional Conflict

Functional conflict
serves organization's interests

Dysfunctional conflict
threatens organization's interests

The distinction between **functional conflict** and **dysfunctional conflict** pivots on whether the organization's interests are served. One conflict expert wrote the following.

Some [types of conflict] support the goals of the organization and improve performance; these are functional, constructive forms of conflict. They benefit or support the main purposes of the organization. Additionally, there are those types of conflict that hinder organizational performance; these are dysfunctional or destructive forms. They are undesirable and the manager should seek their eradication.[8]

Functional conflict is commonly referred to in management circles as constructive or co-operative conflict.[9]

Helmut Werner' performance is naturally of keen interest to his boss, Daimler Benz chief Jurgen E Schrempp. Daimler needs big profits from Mercedes as Schrempp expensively unwinds a failed diversification policy. But German business and auto [car] magazines regularly report stories of rows and back-stabbing that read like TV soap operas. Allegedly, Schrempp was leery of the Smart project and objected to building the A-Class in Brazil. Wrong, says Werner: There was lively debate about Smart, but Schrempp is on board. By another account, marketing czar Zetsche is Schrempp's spy to keep tabs on Werner. In reality, Werner got Zetsche his first big career break. Says an exasperated Werner: 'Nothing that is written about personal bitterness is true.' But he admits: 'We have controversial discussions. It is a very constructive conflict.'[10]

Antecedents of Conflict

Certain situations produce more conflict than others. By knowing the antecedents of conflict, managers are better able to anticipate conflict and take steps to resolve it if it becomes dysfunctional. Among the situations that tend to produce either functional or dysfunctional conflict are:

▼ **incompatible personalities or value systems**

▼ **overlapping or unclear job boundaries**

▼ **competition for limited resources**

▼ **interdepartment/intergroup competition**

▼ **inadequate communication**

▼ **interdependent tasks (e.g., one person cannot complete his or her assignment until others have completed their work)**

▼ **organizational complexity (conflict tends to increase as the number of hierarchical layers and specialized tasks increase)**

▼ **unreasonable or unclear policies, standards, or rules**

▼ **unreasonable deadlines or extreme time pressure**

▼ **collective decision making (the greater the number of people participating in a decision, the greater the potential for conflict)**

▼ **decision-making by consensus**

▼ **unmet expectations (employees who have unrealistic expectations about job assignments, pay, or promotions are more prone to conflict)**

▼ **unresolved or suppressed conflicts.**[11]

Proactive people carefully read these early warnings and take appropriate action. For example, group conflict can be reduced by making decisions on the basis of a majority vote rather than seeking a consensus.

Desired Conflict Outcomes

Within organizations, conflict management is more than simply a quest for agreement. If progress is to be made and dysfunctional conflict minimized, a broader agenda is in order. Tjosvold's co-operative conflict model calls for three desired outcomes.

1 *Agreement.* But at what cost? Equitable and fair agreements are best. An agreement that leaves one party feeling exploited or defeated will tend to breed resentment and subsequent conflict.

2 *Stronger relationships.* Good agreements enable conflicting parties to build bridges of goodwill and trust for future use. Moreover, conflicting parties who trust each other are more likely to keep their end of the bargain.

3 *Learning.* Functional conflict can promote greater self-awareness and creative problem solving. Like the practice of management itself, successful conflict handling is learned primarily by doing. Although knowledge of the concepts and techniques in this chapter is a necessary first step, there is no substitute for hands-on practice. In a contentious world, there are plenty of opportunities to practise conflict management.[12]

TYPES OF CONFLICT

Certain antecedents of conflict, highlighted earlier, deserve a closer look. This section probes the nature and organizational implications of four basic types of conflict: personality, value, intergroup, and cross-cultural. Our discussion of each type of conflict includes some practical tips and techniques.

Personality Conflict

We visited the topic of personalities in our discussion of diversity in Chapter 2, and again in Chapter 5 when we introduced the Big Five personality dimensions. Once again, your *personality* is the package of stable traits and characteristics creating your unique identity. Experts have the following to say on the subject.

Each of us has a unique way of interacting with others. Whether we are seen as charming, irritating, fascinating, non-descript, approachable, or intimidating depends in part on our personality, or what others might describe as our style.[13]

Please take a moment to refer back to the OB Exercise on page 35 in Chapter 2 titled 'Drawing Your Personality Profile.' If you have not completed the exercise yet, it would be instructive to do so now. How helpful is this contrast of profiles (for you and another person) for pinpointing specific sources of personality conflict? Given the many possible combinations of personality traits, it is clear why personality conflicts are inevitable. We define a **personality conflict** as interpersonal opposition based on personal dislike and disagreement.

Personality conflict
interpersonal opposition driven by personal dislike or disagreement

Workplace Incivility: The Seeds of Personality Conflict

Somewhat akin to physical pain, chronic personality conflicts often begin with seemingly insignificant irritations. For instance, an employee in a landscaped office can grow to deeply dislike someone who persistently whistles off-key while drumming their foot on the side of a filing cabinet. Sadly, grim little scenarios such as this are all too common today, given the steady erosion of civility in the workplace. Researchers recently noted how increased informality, pressure for results, and employee diversity have fostered an 'anything goes' atmosphere in today's workplaces. They view incivility as a self-perpetuating vicious cycle that can end in violence.[14]

Vicious cycles of incivility need to be avoided (or broken early) with an organizational culture that places a high value on respect for colleagues. This requires managers to act as caring and courteous role models. A positive spirit of co-operation, as opposed to one based on negativism and aggression, also helps. More specifically, constructive feedback or skillful behaviour modification, or both, can keep a single irritating behaviour from bringing about a full-blown personality conflict (or worse).

Dealing with Personality Conflicts

Personality conflicts are a potential minefield for managers. Let us examine the situation. Personality traits, by definition, are stable and resistant to change. Moreover, according to the American Psychiatric Association's *Diagnostic and Statistical Manual of Mental Disorders*, there are 410 psychological disorders that can and do show up in the workplace.[15] Also, sexual harassment and other forms of discrimination can grow out of apparent personality conflicts.[16] Finally, personality conflicts can spawn workplace aggression and violence.[17]

Table 13–1

How to Deal with Personality Conflicts

Tips for Employees Having a Personality Conflict	Tips for Third-Party Observers of a Personality Conflict	Tips for Managers Whose Employees Are Having a Personality Conflict
• Follow company policies for diversity, anti-discrimination, and sexual harassment.	• Follow company policies for diversity, anti-discrimination, and sexual harassment.	• Follow company policies for diversity, anti-discrimination, and sexual harassment.
• Communicate directly with the other person to resolve the perceived conflict (emphasize problem solving and common objectives, not personalities).	• Do not take sides in someone else's personality conflict.	• Investigate and document conflict.
• Avoid dragging co-workers into the conflict.	• Suggest the parties work things out themselves in a constructive and positive way.	• If appropriate, take corrective action (e.g., feedback or B Mod).
• If dysfunctional conflict persists, seek help from direct supervisors or human resource specialists.	• If dysfunctional conflict persists, refer the problem to parties' direct supervisors.	• If necessary, attempt informal dispute resolution.
		• Refer difficult conflicts to human resource specialists or hired counselors for formal resolution attempts and other interventions.

Traditionally, managers dealt with personality conflicts by either ignoring them or transferring one party. In view of the legal implications, just discussed, both of these options may be open invitations to take them to court for discrimination. Table 13–1 presents practical tips for both managers and non-managers who are involved in or affected by personality conflicts.

Value Conflict

In Chapter 3, we discussed organizational values, both espoused and enacted. We also looked at organizational value systems. Here, we look at instead at personal values and how they can trigger various forms of conflict.

According to Milton Rokeach, a pioneering values researcher, a value is 'an enduring belief that a specific mode of conduct or end-state of existence is personally or socially preferable to an opposite or converse mode of conduct or end-state of existence'.[18] An individual's value system is defined by Rokeach as an 'enduring organization of beliefs concerning preferable modes of conduct or end-states of existence along a continuum of relative importance.'[19] Lifelong behaviour patterns are dictated by values that are fairly well set by the time people are in their early teens. However, significant life-altering events–such as having a child, business failure, death of a loved one, going to war, or surviving a serious accident or disease–can reshape one's value system during adulthood.

Value (personal)
durable belief in a way of behaving or a preferred state of existence ('end-state')

Value system
the organization of one's belief about preferred ways of behaving and state ('end-state') of belief

Extensive research supports Rokeach's contention that differing value systems go a long way toward explaining individual differences in behaviour. Value → behaviour connections have been documented for a wide variety of behaviour, ranging from weight loss to shoppers' selections, from political party affiliation, religious involvement, to choice of degree course.[20] *Value conflict* can erupt when opposition is based on interpersonal differences in instrumental and terminal values.

Instrumental and Terminal Values

In line with his distinction between modes of conduct and states of existence ('end-states'), Rokeach distinguishes between instrumental values and terminal values. Instrumental values are alternative behaviour patterns or means by which we achieve desired ends. Sample instrumental values from Rokeach's original list of 18 are ambitious, honest, independent, loving and obedient.[21] Someone who ranks the instrumental value 'honest' highly, relative to the other instrumental values, is likely to be more honest than someone who gives it a low ranking.

Instrumental values
personally preferred ways of behaving

Highly ranked terminal values—such as a sense of accomplishment, happiness, pleasure, salvation, and wisdom—are desired states or life goals. Some would say terminal values are what life is all about. History is full of examples of people who were persecuted or put to death for their passionately held terminal values. Now let us turn our attention to three kinds of value conflict: inner (referred to in the US literature as intrapersonal), interpersonal, and individual–organization. The sources of conflict are, respectively, from inside the person, between people, and between the person and the organization.

Terminal values
personally preferred states of existence (or 'end-states')

An Inner Conflict of Values

Inner conflict and resultant stress are usually experienced when highly ranked instrumental and terminal values pull the individual in different directions. This is somewhat akin to role conflict, as discussed in Chapter 12. The main difference is locus of influence: Role conflict involves *outside* social expectations; inner (personal) value conflict involves *internal* priorities. For employees who want balance in their lives, a stressful conflict arises when one values, for example, 'being ambitious' (instrumental value) and 'ending up happy' (terminal value).

Interpersonal Value Conflict

This type of value conflict parallels personality conflict. Just as people have different styles that may or may not mesh, they also embrace unique combinations of instrumental and terminal values that inevitably spark disagreement.

Individual–Organization Value Conflict

As we saw in Chapter 3, companies actively seek to embed certain values into their corporate cultures. Conflict can occur when values espoused and enacted by the organization collide with employees' personal values.[22]

Like personalities, personal values are resistant to change.

Handling Value Conflicts through Values Clarification

For inner (personal) conflict, a Toronto management writer and consultant recommends getting out of what she calls 'the busyness trap' by asking the following questions.

▼ **Is your work really meeting your most important needs?**

▼ **Are you defining yourself purely in terms of your accomplishments?**

▼ **Why are you working so hard? To what personal ends?**

▼ **Are you making significant sacrifices in favour of your work?**

▼ **Is your work schedule affecting other people who are important in your life?**[23]

Yet another approach for dealing with all forms of value conflict is a career-counselling and team-building technique called *values clarification*. To gain useful hands-on experience, take a break from your reading and complete the next OB Exercise. (*Note:* Rokeach's original value survey with 18 instrumental and 18 terminal values is ideal for this exercise but the copyright holder does not permit mass reproduction.) The values listed in the OB Exercise, although not broken neatly into instrumental and terminal values, are a good substitute. Our main aim here is to get people to identify and talk about their personal values in order to establish common ground as a basis for teamwork, and conflict-avoidance and resolution.

OB Exercise
Personal Values Clarification

Instructions for Individuals Working Alone

Review the following list of 30 values and then rank your top 6 values (1 = most important; 6 = least important). What inner (personal) value conflicts can you detect? How can you resolve them? Which, if any, of your cherished values are likely to conflict with those deemed important by your family, friends, colleagues, and employer? What could be done to reduce this interpersonal and individual–organizational value conflict?

Instructions for Teams

Each team member should begin by ranking their top six personal values, as specified above. Appoint someone to record each team-member's top-ranked value on a flip chart or blackboard (no names attached). Then spend a few minutes discussing both differences and commonalities. Try to find common ground among seemingly different values. If your group is a task team, an additional step could be to derive four or more consensus values to guide the team's work. (Do not short-cut consensus seeking by voting.) How do your personal values align with your team-mates' values and the team's consensus values? What needs to be done to reduce actual or threatened value conflict?

_____ Responsibility (joint and/or individual)		_____ Accomplishments
_____ Involvement in decision-making		_____ Satisfying relationships
_____ Competence		_____ Creativity
_____ Meaning		_____ Self-worth
_____ Autonomy		_____ Self-expression
_____ Recognition		_____ Leadership opportunities
_____ Personal and professional growth		_____ Financial opportunities
_____ New and different experiences		_____ Diversity
_____ Collaboration on common tasks		_____ Career mobility
_____ Harmony or an absence of conflict		_____ A sense of belonging
_____ Competition		_____ Shared fun and experiences
_____ Meeting deadlines in a timely manner		_____ Peace and serenity
_____ A high standard of excellence		_____ Good health
_____ Status, position		_____ Loyalty
_____ Stimulation from challenge and change		_____ Duty to family
		_____ Other _____

SOURCE: List of values quoted from L Gardenswartz and A Rowe, *Diverse Teams at Work: Capitalizing on the Power of Diversity* (New York: McGraw-Hill, 1994), p 85, © 1994. Reproduced with permission of the McGraw-Hill Companies.

Intergroup Conflict

Conflict among work groups, teams and departments is a common threat to organizational competitiveness.

Siemens has also taken radical measures to force managers to adapt to the market's stern demands. The company called in its blue-ribbon customers. Engineers and managers alike were humbled as Opel, Ford, and Sony gave them an earful at three-day gripe sessions at Siemens' Bavarian hideaway. Alan Burton, Ford's European telecom manager, shocked one group by disclosing he had received competing bids from three Siemens divisions for the same tender.[24]

Managers who understand the mechanics of intergroup conflict are better equipped to face this sort of challenge.

In-Group Thinking: The Seeds of Intergroup Conflict

As we discussed in previous chapters, *cohesiveness*—a 'we feeling' binding group members together—can be a good or bad thing. A certain amount of cohesiveness can turn a group of individuals into a smooth-running team. Too much cohesiveness, however, can breed 'groupthink' because a desire to get along pushes aside critical thinking. The study of in-groups by small group researchers has revealed a whole package of changes associated with increased group cohesiveness.

▼ Members of in-groups view themselves as a collection of unique individuals, while they stereotype members of other groups as being 'all alike'.

▼ In-group members see themselves positively and as morally correct, while they view members of other groups negatively and as immoral.

▼ In-groups view outsiders as a threat.

▼ In-group members exaggerate the differences between their group and other groups. This typically involves a distorted perception of reality.[25]

Avid sports fans who simply can't imagine how someone could support the opposing team exemplify one form of in-group thinking. Also, this pattern of behaviour is a form of ethnocentrism, discussed as a cross-cultural barrier in Chapter 4. Reflect for a moment on evidence of in-group behaviour in your life. Does your circle of friends make fun of others because of their race, gender, nationality, sexual preference, diploma or occupation?

In-group thinking is one more fact of organizational life that virtually guarantees conflict. Although managers cannot eliminate in-group thinking they certainly should not ignore it when handling intergroup conflicts.

Research Lessons for Handling Intergroup Conflict

Sociologists have long recommended the contact hypothesis for reducing intergroup conflict. According to the *contact hypothesis*, the more the members of different groups interact, the less intergroup conflict they will experience. Those interested in improving race, international, and union–management relations typically encourage cross-group interaction. The hope is that *any* type of interaction, short of actual conflict, will reduce stereotyping and combat in-group thinking. But recent research has shown this approach to be naive and limited. For example, one recent study of 83 health centre employees (83 per cent female) probed the specific nature of intergroup relations and the following conclusion.

> *The number of negative relationships was significantly related to higher perceptions of intergroup conflict. Thus, it seems that negative relationships have a salience that overwhelms any possible positive effects from friendship links across groups.*[26]

International OB

http://www.british-airways.com

Breaking Barriers at British Airways

Who Marcia Bradley, 45, marketing manager, culture-change projects, British Airways.

What's Your Problem? 'We're quality fanatics. There's a "BA way", and there's a wrong way. But sometimes we go outside the company for ideas. How do I turn outsiders into insiders without compromising their ideas? How do I convince insiders to give outsiders a chance?'

Tell Me About It 'I'm part of a major initiative to rethink the experience of being at an airport. I work with lots of vendors and consultants. But we have such a strong way of doing things at BA that there's a tendency to keep outsiders at arm's length. We risk creating great proposals that collect dust—or rolling out initiatives that don't meet expectations. I need to show my BA colleagues and my outside colleagues what they can learn from each other.'

What's Your Solution? 'Total immersion. Before we even think about a proposal, we might spend three months introducing our partners to BA, and vice versa. We make sure that the consultants experience our product. We arrange for them to fly BA to meetings—both in Club

Class (first class) and in World Traveller (economy class). We ask for their impressions: How comfortable were the seats? How long did you wait at the counter? We open a dialogue about the company.

'Partners also meet key BA players—in structured get-to-know-you gatherings as well as for brainstorming. We even ask these partners to spend time with people with whom they won't be working. They visit departments; they drop in on meetings.

'Finally, they get a formal education in BA's values and in our brand integrity. It's part history lesson, part 'rules of the road' orientation. We cover everything from our principles of customer service to the choice of colors on our aircraft.

'The pay-off is huge. When it's time to sign off on budgets or to approve designs, we do it faster and more confidently.'

SOURCE: C Olofson, 'Let Outsiders In, Turn Your Insiders Out,' *Fast Company*, **March 1999, p 46.**

Friendships between groups are still desirable, as documented in many studies,[27] but negative interactions between the groups readily overpower them. Thus, *the first priority for people faced with intergroup conflict is to identify and root out specific negative linkages between groups*. A single personality conflict, for instance, may contaminate the entire intergroup experience. The same goes for an employee who voices negative opinions or spreads negative rumours about another group. Our updated contact model in Figure 13–2 is based on this and other recent research insights, such as the need to foster positive attitudes toward other groups.[28] Also, notice how conflict within the group and negative gossip from third parties are threats that need to be neutralized if intergroup conflict is to be minimized.

As demonstrated by British Airways in the next International OB, the quest for good relations between groups needs to be creative, systematic and relentless.

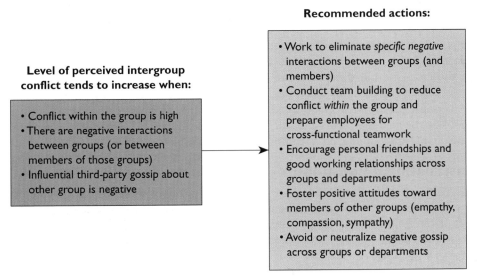

Recommended actions:

Figure 13–2

An Updated Contact Model for Minimizing Intergroup Conflict

Level of perceived intergroup conflict tends to increase when:

- Conflict within the group is high
- There are negative interactions between groups (or between members of those groups)
- Influential third-party gossip about other group is negative

- Work to eliminate *specific negative interactions* between groups (and members)
- Conduct team building to reduce conflict *within* the group and prepare employees for cross-functional teamwork
- Encourage personal friendships and good working relationships across groups and departments
- Foster positive attitudes toward members of other groups (empathy, compassion, sympathy)
- Avoid or neutralize negative gossip across groups or departments

SOURCE: Based on research evidence in G Labianca, D J Brass, and B Gray, 'Social Networks and Perceptions of Intergroup Conflict: The Role of Negative Relationships and Third Parties', *Academy of Management Journal*, February 1998, pp 55–67; C D Batson et al., 'Empathy and Attitudes: Can Feeling for a Member of a Stigmatized Group Improve Feelings toward the Group?' *Journal of Personality and Social Psychology*, January 1997, pp 105–18; and S C Wright et al., 'The Extended Contact Effect: Knowledge of Cross-Group Friendships and Prejudice', *Journal of Personality and Social Psychology*, July 1997, pp 73–90.

Cross-Cultural Conflict

Doing business with people from different cultures is commonplace in our global economy where cross-border mergers, joint ventures and alliances are the order of the day.[29] Because of differing assumptions about how to think and act, the potential for cross-cultural conflict is both immediate and huge.[30] Success or failure, when conducting business across cultures, often hinges on avoiding and minimizing actual or perceived conflict. For example, consider the following cultural mismatch.

Xenophobe's Guide to the Germans

I should have known what I was in for. As a student at the University of Hamburg in the late 1970s, I studied and worked in Germany for a year. But moving from Detroit to Bonn last fall [autumn] touched off a surprisingly robust resurgence of culture shock. Notwithstanding the mellowing effect of good German beer, which can be purchased from a vending machine in our office building, I find myself cursing my adopted home. At nearly every turn, I'm ensnared by Germany's vast bureaucracy. I hadn't been in Bonn for a week before Big Brother grabbed me by the lapels. German customs refused to hand over a few boxes of clothing until I had registered my whereabouts with city hall. I collected the appropriate residency form (in triplicate), had it filled out by a befuddled manager at the Hotel Domicil, where I was staying, and returned to city hall. A clerk stamped the forms with a vigorous flourish, telling me that I had two weeks to re-register when I moved. I chuckled to myself that such rules would last about two seconds in Detroit. Retailers often present a similar cold shoulder. For starters, German stores are almost never open. At least, not when normal working people from Detroit can shop. When I temporarily moved to a furnished apartment (I never registered; don't tell Big Brother), there was no soap. Tough luck, again. Even in cosmopolitan cities such as Berlin, Bonn and Munich, all stores must close at 6:30 p.m., except on Thursdays, when closing moves up to 8:30. And they generally close on Saturdays at 2 p.m. The next day after work, I searched in vain for soap at Kaufhof, a downtown department store. A gruff clerk told me to try toiletries, first floor. My heart sank: It was already past closing. Deodorant bar in hand, I approached the register, where the clerk demanded: 'Where did you come from?' I must have looked—or smelled—pitiful, since she sold me the soap.[31]

This is not a matter of who is right and who is wrong; rather it is a matter of accommodating cultural differences for a successful business transaction. Awareness of the cross-cultural differences we discussed in Chapters 3 and 4—individualism/collectivism, perceptions of time, interpersonal space, language, religion, and universalist/particularist (rule-based/relationship-based) cultures—is an important first step. Beyond that, cross-cultural conflict can be moderated by using international consultants and building cross-cultural relationships.

International Consultants

In response to broad demand, there is a growing army of management consultants specializing in cross-cultural relations. Competency and fees vary widely, of course. But a carefully selected cross-cultural consultant can be helpful, as the following illustration shows.

Last year, when electronics-maker Canon planned to set up a subsidiary in Dubai through its Netherlands division, it asked consultant Sahid Mirza of Glocom, based in Dubai, to find out how the two cultures would work together.

Mirza sent out the test questionnaires and got a sizeable response. 'The findings were somewhat surprising,' he recalls. 'We found that, at the bedrock level, there were relatively few differences. Many of the Arab businessmen came from former British colonies and viewed business in much the same way as the Dutch.'

But at the level of behaviour, there was a real conflict. 'The Dutch are blunt and honest in expression, and such expression is very offensive to Arab sensibilities.' Mirza offers the example of a Dutch executive who says something like, 'We can't meet the deadline.' Such a negative expression—true or not—would be gravely offensive to an Arab. As a result of Mirza's research, Canon did start the subsidiary in Dubai, but it trained both the Dutch and the Arab executives first.[32]

Consultants, too, can help untangle possible personality, value and group conflicts from those rooted in differing national cultures. Note: Although we have discussed these four basic types of conflict separately, usually they are encountered in complex, messy bundles.

Building Cross-Cultural Relationships to Avoid Dysfunctional Conflict

Rosalie L Tung's recent study of 409 expatriates from US and Canadian multinational firms, mentioned in Chapter 4, is very instructive.[33] Her survey sought to pinpoint success factors for the expatriates (14 per cent female) who were working in 51 different countries worldwide. Table 13–2 lists nine specific ways to facilitate interaction with host-country nationals as ranked, from most useful to least useful, by the respondents. Good listening skills topped the list, followed by sensitivity to others and co-operativeness rather than competitiveness. Some managers need to add self-management to the list of methods they use to minimize cross-cultural conflict.

Table 13-2
Ways to Build Cross-Cultural Relationships

Behavior	Rank
Be a good listener	1
Be sensitive to needs of others	2 >Tie
Be co-operative, rather than overly competitive	2
Advocate inclusive (participative) leadership	3
Compromise rather than dominate	4
Build rapport through conversations	5
Be compassionate and understanding	6
Avoid conflict by emphasizing harmony	7
Nurture others (develop and mentor)	8

SOURCE: Adapted from R L Tung, 'American Expatriates Abroad: From Neophytes to Cosmopolitans', ***Journal of World Business*****, Summer 1998, Table 6, p 136.**

MANAGING CONFLICT

As we have seen, conflict has many faces and is a constant challenge for managers who are responsible for reaching organizational goals. Our attention now turns to the active management of both functional and dysfunctional conflict. We discuss how to stimulate functional conflict, how to handle dysfunctional conflict, and how third parties can deal effectively with conflict. Relevant research lessons also are examined.

Stimulating Functional Conflict

Sometimes committees and decision-making groups become so bogged down in details and procedures that nothing substantive is accomplished. Carefully monitored functional conflict can help get the creative juices flowing once again. Managers basically have two options. They can fan the fires of naturally occurring conflict–but this approach can be unreliable and slow. Alternatively, managers can resort to programmed conflict.

Experts in the field define **programmed conflict** as 'conflict that raises different opinions *regardless of the personal feelings of the managers*.'[34] The trick is to get contributors to either defend or criticize ideas based on relevant facts rather than on the basis of personal preference or political interests. This requires disciplined role playing. Two programmed conflict techniques with proven track records are 'devil's advocacy' and the dialectic method. Let us explore these two ways of stimulating functional conflict.

Programmed conflict *encourages different opinions without protecting management's personal feelings*

Devil's Advocacy

This technique gets its name from a traditional practice within the Roman Catholic Church. When someone's name came before the College of Cardinals for elevation to sainthood, it was absolutely essential to ensure that he or she had a spotless record. Consequently, one individual was assigned the role of *devil's advocate* to uncover and air all possible objections to the person's canonization. In accordance with this practice, **devil's advocacy** in today's organizations involves assigning someone the role of critic.[35] Recall from Chapter 13, Irving Janis recommended the devil's advocate role for preventing 'groupthink'.

Devil's Advocacy *assigning someone the role of critic*

In the left half of Figure 13–3, note how devil's advocacy alters the usual decision-making process in steps 2 and 3. This approach to programmed conflict is intended to generate critical thinking and reality testing.[36] It is a good idea to rotate the job of devil's advocate so that a person or group does not develop a strictly negative reputation. Moreover, periodic devil's advocacy role-playing is good training for developing analytical and communication skills.

Figure 13–3

Techniques for Stimulating Functional Conflict: Devil's Advocacy and the Dialectic Method

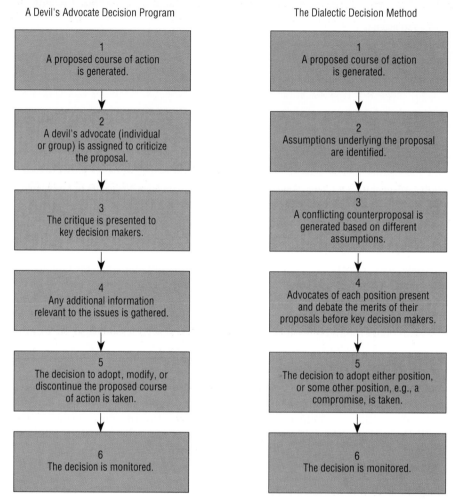

A Devil's Advocate Decision Program

The Dialectic Decision Method

SOURCE: R A Coslier and C R Schwenk, 'Agreement and Thinking Alike: Ingredients for Poor Decisions', *Academy of Management Executive*, February 1990, pp 72–73. Used with permission.

The Dialectic Method

Like devil's advocacy, the dialectic method is a time-honoured practice. This particular approach to programmed conflict traces back to the dialectic school of philosophy in ancient Greece. Plato and his followers attempted to synthesize truths by exploring opposite positions (called thesis and antithesis). Court procedures in many countries throughout the world rely on directly opposing points of view for determining guilt or innocence. Accordingly, today's **dialectic method** calls for managers to foster a structured debate of opposing viewpoints prior to making a decision.[37] Steps 3 and 4 in the right half of Figure 13–3 set the dialectic approach apart from the normal decision-making process.

A major drawback of the dialectic method is that 'winning the debate' may overshadow the issue at hand. Also, the dialectic method requires more skill, and hence training,

Dialectic method
fostering a debate of opposing viewpoints to better understand an issue

than devil's advocacy. With respect to the comparative effectiveness of these two approaches, however, a laboratory study ended in a draw. Compared with groups that strived to reach a consensus, decision-making groups using either devil's advocacy or the dialectic method yielded similarly better quality decisions.[38] But, in a more recent laboratory study, groups using devil's advocacy produced more potential solutions and made better recommendations for a case problem than did groups using the dialectic method.[39] In view of this mixed evidence, managers have some latitude in using either devil's advocacy or the dialectic method to pump creative life back into stalled deliberations. Personal preference and the role players' experience may well be deciding factors in choosing one approach over the other. The important thing is to actively stimulate functional conflict when necessary (such as when the risk of blind conformity or groupthink is high).

Alternative Styles for Handling Dysfunctional Conflict

People tend to handle negative conflict in patterned ways referred to as *styles*. Several conflict styles have been categorized over the years. According to the model of Afzalur Rahim's, conflict specialist, five different conflict-handling styles can be plotted on a 2 x 2 grid. High to low concern for *self* is found on the horizontal axis of the grid while low to high concern for *others* forms the vertical axis (see Figure 13–4). Various combinations of these variables produce the five different conflict-handling styles: integrating, obliging, dominating, avoiding, and compromising.[40] No style is best; each has strengths and limitations and is subject to situational constraints.

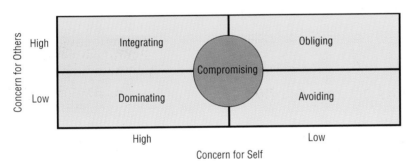

Figure 13–4

Five Conflict-Handling Styles

SOURCE: M A Rahim, 'A Strategy for Managing Conflict in Complex Organizations', *Human Relations,* January 1985, p 84. Used with permission of Plenum Publishing.

Integrating (Problem-Solving)

In this style, interested parties confront the issue and co-operatively identify the problem, generate and weigh alternative solutions, and select a solution. Integrating is appropriate for complex issues plagued by misunderstanding. However, it is inappropriate for resolving conflicts rooted in opposing value systems. Its primary strength is that it lasts longer because it deals with the underlying problem rather than merely the symptoms. The primary weakness of this style is that it is very time consuming.

Obliging (Smoothing)

'An obliging person neglects his or her own concern to satisfy the concern of the other party.'[41] This style, often called smoothing, involves playing down differences while emphasizing commonalities. Obliging may be an appropriate conflict-handling strategy when it is possible to eventually get something in return. But it is inappropriate for complex or worsening problems. Its primary strength is that it encourages co-operation. Its main weakness is that it's a temporary fix that fails to confront the underlying problem.

Dominating (Forcing)

High concern for self and low concern for others encourages 'I win, you lose' tactics. The other party's needs are largely ignored. This style is often called forcing because it relies on formal authority to force compliance. Dominating is appropriate when an unpopular solution must be implemented, the issue is minor or a deadline is near. It is inappropriate in an open and participative climate. Speed is its primary strength. The primary weakness of this domineering style is that it often breeds resentment.

Avoiding

This tactic may involve either passive withdrawal from the problem or active suppression of the issue. Avoidance is appropriate for trivial issues or when the costs of confrontation outweigh the benefits of resolving the conflict. It is inappropriate for difficult and worsening problems. The main strength of this style is that it buys time in unfolding or ambiguous situations (see the next International OB). The primary weakness is that the tactic provides a temporary fix that sidesteps the underlying problem.

Compromising

This is a give-and-take approach involving moderate concern for both self and others. Compromise is appropriate when parties have opposite goals or possess equal power. But compromise is inappropriate when overuse would lead to inconclusive action (e.g., failure to meet production deadlines). The primary strength of this tactic is that the democratic process has no losers; but it's a temporary fix that can stifle creative problem-solving.

International OB

http://www.escapeartist.com

Looking to Avoid Cross-Cultural Conflict

Katie Koehler, vice president of human resources for Marriott International's Caribbean and Latin American regions, got her foreign experience right after graduating from an executive MBA program, accepting an offer from Marriott to work in Mexico City in 1996.

Being a woman in a Latin culture posed some challenges. At a breakfast meeting, a top union leader told a crude joke in Spanish. 'I was being tested,' Ms Koehler says. 'Will I understand and how will I respond?' She responded with a stern look and a lifted eyebrow, subtly signalling that, while she didn't intend to make a scene that would embarrass him and abort their budding relationship, she didn't think the joke was funny. Her approach apparently worked, 'After that we had a good relationship,' she says.

SOURCE: Excerpted from H Lancaster, 'To Get Shipped Abroad, Women Must Overcome Prejudice at Home,' *The Wall Street Journal*, June 29 1999, p B1.

Third-Party Interventions

In a perfect world, people would creatively avoid conflict and handle actual conflicts directly and positively. Dream on! Organizational politics being what they are, we can find ourselves as unwilling (and often unready) third parties to someone else's conflict. Thus, a working knowledge of conflict triangles is essential to effective management today.

Conflict Triangles

Remember Annie, the *Amazon.de* manager at the start of this chapter? Her busy day was interrupted by her colleague Sophie's tale of a conflict situation. Sophie was recruiting Annie to help settle the situation. This is a classic **conflict triangle**. A conflict triangle 'occurs when two people are having a problem and, instead of addressing the problem directly with each other, one of them gets a third person involved'.[42] As will be discussed under the heading of organizational politics, in Chapter 15, employees tend to form political *coalitions* because there is power in numbers. In Annie's case, Sophie was engaged in a not-so-subtle attempt to gang up against her adversary, Hans. Moreover, Sophie was using Annie to vent her pent-up frustrations. This is a common and often very disruptive situation in today's organizations. The question is, what do you do?

Those finding themselves in conflict triangles have a wide range of options, according to experts on the subject. Figure 13–5 shows how responses can promote either functional or dysfunctional conflict. Preferred options 1 and 2, called *detriangling* in the Figure, find the third party channelling the disputants' energy in a direct and positive manner, toward each other. It is important to note that the third party avoids becoming part of a political coalition in options 1 and 2. Options 3 to 8 can be a slippery slope toward worsening the effect of the triangle. Also, political and ethical implications multiply as the third party progresses to option 3 and beyond.

Conflict triangle
conflicting parties involve a third person rather than dealing directly with each other

Detriangling
(least political; low risk of dysfunctional conflict)

More triangling
(most political; high risk of dysfunctional conflict)

1. Reroute complaints by coaching the sender to find ways to constructively bring up the matter with the receiver. Do not carry messages for the sender.
2. Facilitate a meeting with the sender and receiver to coach them to speak directly and constructively with each other.
3. Transmit verbatim messages with the sender's name included and coach the receiver on constructive ways to discuss the message with the sender.
4. Carry the message verbatim but protect the sender's name.
5. Soften the message to protect the sender.
6. Add your spin to the message to protect the sender.
7. Do nothing. The participants will triangle in someone else.
8. Do nothing and spread the gossip. You will triangle in others.

Figure 13–5

Third-Party Intervention Options for Handling Conflict Triangles

SOURCE: List of options excerpted from P Ruzich, 'Triangles: Tools for Untangling Interpersonal Messes', *HRMagazine*, July 1999, p 134. Reprinted with the permission of *HR Magazine* published by the Society for Human Resource Management, Alexandria, VA.

Practical Lessons from Conflict Research

Laboratory studies, relying on college students as subjects, uncovered the following insights about organizational conflict.

▼ **People with a high need for affiliation tended to rely on a smoothing (obliging) style while avoiding a forcing (dominating) style.**[43] **Thus, personality traits affect how people handle conflict.**

▼ **Disagreement expressed in an arrogant and demeaning manner produced significantly more negative effects than the same sort of disagreement expressed in a reasonable manner.**[44] **In other words,** *how* **you disagree with someone is very important in conflict situations.**

▼ **Threats and punishment, by one party in a disagreement, tended to produce intensifying threats and punishment from the other party.**[45] **In short, aggression breeds aggression.**

▼ **As conflict increased, group satisfaction decreased. An integrative style of handling conflict led to higher group satisfaction than did an avoidance style.**[46]

Field studies involving managers and real organizations have given us the following insights.

▼ Both conflict within and between departments decreased as goal difficulty and goal clarity increased. Thus, challenging and clear goals can defuse conflict.

▼ Higher levels of conflict tended to erode job satisfaction and internal (personal) work motivation.[47]

▼ Men and women at the same managerial level tended to handle conflict similarly. In short, there was no gender effect.[48]

▼ Conflict tended to move around the organization.[49] Thus, managers need to be alert to the fact that conflict often originates in one area or level and becomes evident somewhere else. Conflict needs to be traced back to its source if there is to be lasting improvement.

▼ Samples of Japanese, German and American managers who were presented with the same example of a conflict situation preferred different resolution techniques. Japanese and German managers did not share the Americans' enthusiasm for integrating the interests of all parties. The Japanese tended to look upward to management for direction, whereas the Germans were more bound by rules and regulations. In cross-cultural conflict resolution, there is no one best approach. Cultural-specific preferences need to be taken into consideration prior to beginning the conflict resolution process.[50]

NEGOTIATION

Negotiation
give-and-take process between conflicting interdependent parties

Formally defined, **negotiation** is a give-and-take decision-making process involving interdependent parties with different preferences.[51] Common examples include union–management negotiations over wages, hours and working conditions and negotiations between supply chain specialists and vendors involving price, delivery schedules and credit terms. Self-managed work teams with overlapping task boundaries also need to rely on negotiated agreements.[52] Negotiating skills are more important than ever today.[53]

Two Basic Types of Negotiation

Negotiation experts distinguish between two types of negotiation—*distributive* and *integrative*. The former, referred to in US books as 'fixed-pie' thinking, is explained in the following way.

> A distributive *negotiation usually involves a single issue—a 'fixed-pie'—in which one person gains at the expense of the other. For example, haggling over the price of a rug in a bazaar is a distributive negotiation. In most conflicts, however, more than one issue is at stake, and each party values the issues differently. The outcomes available are no longer a fixed-pie divided among all parties. An agreement can be found that is better for both parties than what they would have reached through distributive negotiation. This is an* integrative *negotiation.*
>
> *However, parties in a negotiation often don't find these beneficial trade-offs because* each *assumes* its interests *directly* conflict *with those of the other party. 'What is good for the other side must be bad for us' is a common and unfortunate perspective that most people have. This is the mind-set we call the* mythical *'fixed-pie.'*[54]

Distributive negotiation involves traditional win-lose thinking. Integrative negotiation calls for a progressive win-win strategy,[55] such as the one illustrated in Figure 13–6. In a laboratory study of joint venture negotiations, teams that were trained in integrative tactics achieved better outcomes for *both* sides than did untrained teams.[56] However, another study involving 700 employees from 11 cultures discovered the integrative (or problem-solving) approach to negotiation was *not* equally effective across cultures.[57] North American negotiators generally are too short-term oriented and poor relationship builders when negotiating in Asia, Latin America and the Middle East.[58]

Figure 13–6 *An Integrative Approach: Added-Value Negotiation*

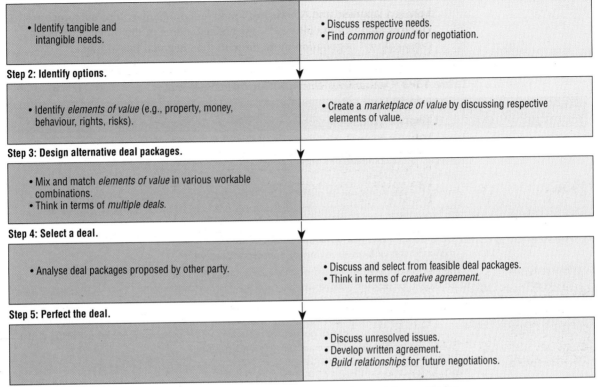

SOURCE: Adapted from K Albrecht and S Albrecht, 'Added Value Negotiation', *Training*, April 1993, pp 26–29.

Ethical Pitfalls in Negotiation

The success of integrative negotiation, such as added-value negotiation, hinges to a large extent on the *quality* of information exchanged, as researchers have recently documented.[59] Telling lies, hiding key facts, and engaging in the other potentially unethical tactics listed in Table 13–3 erode trust and goodwill, both of which are vital in win-win negotiations.[60] An awareness of these dirty tricks can keep those bargaining in good faith from being unfairly exploited.[61] Unethical negotiating tactics need to be pointed out in organizational codes of ethics.

Practical Lessons from Negotiation Research

Recent laboratory and field studies have yielded these insights.

▼ Negotiators with single issue (win–lose) expectations produced poor joint outcomes because they restricted and mismanaged information.[62]

▼ A meta-analysis of 62 studies found a *slight* tendency for women to negotiate more co-operatively than men. But when faced with a 'tit-for-tat' bargaining strategy (equivalent countermoves), women were significantly more competitive than men.[63]

▼ Personality characteristics can affect negotiating success. Negotiators who scored high on the Big Five personality dimensions of extraversion and agreeableness (refer back to Table 5–1) tended to do poorly with distributive (win–lose) negotiations.[64]

▼ Good and bad moods can have positive and negative effects, respectively, on negotiators' plans and outcomes.[65] So wait until both you and your boss are in a good mood before you ask for an increase in pay.

▼ Studies of negotiations between Japanese participants; between Americans; and between Japanese and Americans; found less productive joint outcomes across cultures than within cultures.[66] Less understanding of the other party makes cross-cultural negotiation more difficult than negotiations at home.

Table 13–3 *Questionable/Unethical Tactics in Negotiation*

Tactic	Description/Clarification/Range
Lies	Subject matter for lies can include limits, alternatives, the negotiator's intent, authority to bargain, other commitments, acceptability of the opponent's offers, time pressures, and available resources.
Puffery	Among the items that can be puffed up are the value of one's payoffs to the opponent, the negotiator's own alternatives, the costs of what one is giving up or is prepared to yield, importance of issues, and attributes of the products or services.
Deception	Acts and statements may include promises or threats, excessive initial demands, careless misstatements of facts, or asking for concessions not wanted.
Weakening the opponent	The negotiator here may cut off or eliminate some of the opponent's alternatives, blame the opponent for his own actions, use personally abrasive statements to or about the opponent, or undermine the opponent's alliances.
Strengthening one's own position	This tactic includes building one's own resources, including expertise, finances, and alliances. It also includes presentations of persuasive rationales to the opponent or third parties (e.g., the public, the media) or getting mandates for one's position.
Nondisclosure	Includes partial disclosure of facts, failure to disclose a hidden fact, failure to correct the opponents' misperceptions or ignorance, and concealment of the negotiator's own position or circumstances.
Information exploitation	Information provided by the opponent can be used to exploit his weaknesses, close off his alternatives, generate demands against him, or weaken his alliances.
Change of mind	Includes accepting offers one had claimed one would not accept, changing demands, withdrawing promised offers, and making threats one promised would not be made. Also includes the failure to behave as predicted.
Distraction	These acts or statements can be as simple as providing excessive information to the opponent, asking many questions, evading questions, or burying the issue. Or they can be more complex, such as feigning weakness in one area so that the opponent concentrates on it and ignores another.
Maximization	Includes demanding the opponent make concessions that result in the negotiator's gain and the opponent's equal or greater loss. Also entails converting a win-win situation into win-lose.

SOURCE: H J Reitz, J A Wall, Jr, and M S Love, 'Ethics in Negotiation: Oil and Water or Good Lubrication?' Reprinted with the permission of *Business Horizons*, May–June 1998, p 6. Copyright © 1998 by the Board of Trustees at Indiana University, Kelley School of Business.

CONFLICT MANAGEMENT AND NEGOTIATION: A CONTINGENCY APPROACH

Three realities dictate how organizational conflict should be managed. First, various types of conflict are inevitable because they are triggered by a wide variety of antecedents. Second, too little conflict may be as counter-productive as too much. Third, there is no single best way of avoiding or resolving conflict. Consequently, conflict specialists recommend a contingency approach to managing conflict. Antecedents of conflict and actual conflict need to be monitored. If signs of too little conflict such as apathy or lack of creativity appear, then functional conflict needs to be stimulated. This can be done by nurturing appropriate antecedents of conflict or programming conflict with techniques such as devil's advocacy and the dialectic method. On the other hand, when conflict becomes dysfunctional, the appropriate conflict-handling style needs to be enacted. Realistic training involving role playing can prepare managers to try alternative conflict styles.

Third-party interventions are necessary when conflicting parties are unwilling or unable to engage in conflict resolution or integrative negotiation. Integrative or added-value negotiation is most appropriate for handling conflict between groups and between organizations. The key is to get the conflicting parties to abandon traditional single issue (win-lose) thinking and their win-lose expectations.

Managers can prevent themselves from getting too deeply embroiled in conflict by applying four lessons from recent research: establish challenging and clear goals; disagree in a constructive and reasonable manner; do not get caught up in conflict triangles; and refuse to get caught in the aggression-breeds-aggression spiral.

Summary of Key Concepts

1 Define the term conflict, distinguish between functional and dysfunctional conflict, and identify three desired conflict outcomes.

Conflict is a process in which one party perceives that its interests are being opposed or negatively affected by another party. It is inevitable and not necessarily destructive. Too little conflict, as evidenced by apathy or lack of creativity, can be as great a problem as too much conflict. Functional conflict enhances organizational interests while dysfunctional conflict is counter-productive. Three desired conflict outcomes are agreement, stronger relationships and learning.

2 Define personality conflicts, and explain how managers should handle them.

Personality conflicts involve interpersonal opposition based on personal dislike or disagreement (or as an outgrowth of workplace incivility). Care needs to be taken with personality conflicts in the workplace because of the legal implications of discrimination and sexual harassment. Managers should investigate and document personality conflict, take corrective actions such as feedback, or behaviour modification if appropriate, or attempt informal dispute resolution. Difficult or persistent personality conflicts need to be referred to human resource specialists or counsellors.

3 Distinguish between instrumental and terminal values; identify three types of value conflict; and explain how value conflicts can be handled.

Instrumental values are enduring beliefs in ways of behaving (e.g., being honest or loving). Terminal values are enduring beliefs in desired states of existence, also known as end-states (e.g., accomplishment or happiness). Three types of value conflict are inner (personal), interpersonal, and individual-organization. *Values clarification*, whereby individuals or teams identify and compare their highly-ranked values, can establish common ground for building teamwork and resolving conflicts.

4 Discuss the role of in-group thinking in conflict between groups, and explain what management can do about this type of conflict.

Members of in-groups tend to see themselves as unique individuals who are more moral than outsiders, whom they view as a threat and stereotype as being all alike. In-group thinking is associated with ethnocentric behaviour. According to the updated contact model, managers first must strive to eliminate negative relationships between conflicting groups. Beyond that, they need to provide team building, encourage personal friendships across groups, foster positive attitudes about other groups, and minimize negative gossip about groups.

5 Discuss what can be done about cross-cultural conflict.

International consultants can prepare people from different cultures to work effectively together. Cross-cultural conflict can be minimized by having expatriates build strong cross-cultural relationships with their hosts (primarily by being good listeners, being sensitive to others, and being more co-operative than competitive).

6 Explain how managers can stimulate functional conflict; and identify the five conflict-handling styles.

There are many antecedents of conflict–including incompatible personalities, competition for limited resources, and unrealized expectations–that need to be monitored. Functional conflict can be stimulated by permitting antecedents of conflict to persist or by programming conflict during decision-making using devil's advocates or the dialectic method. The five conflict-handling styles are integrating (problem solving), obliging (smoothing), dominating (forcing), avoiding, and compromising. There is no best overall style.

7 Explain the nature and practical significance of conflict triangles.

A conflict triangle occurs when one member of a conflict seeks the help of a third party rather than facing the opponent directly. 'Detriangling' is advised, whereby the third-party redirects the disputants' energy toward each other in a positive and constructive manner.

8 Explain the difference between distributive and integrative negotiation, and discuss the concept of added-value negotiation.

Distributive negotiation involves single issue and win-lose thinking. Integrative negotiation is a win-win approach to better results for both parties. The five steps in added value negotiation are as follows: Step 1, clarify interests; Step 2, identify options; Step 3, design alternative deal packages; Step 4, select a deal; and Step 5, perfect the deal. Elements of value, multiple deals, and creative agreement are central to this approach.

Discussion Questions

1 What examples of functional and dysfunctional conflict have you observed lately?

2 Which of the antecedents of conflict do you think are most common (or most troublesome) in workplaces at present?

3 Have you ever been directly involved in a personality conflict? Explain. Was it handled well? Explain. What could have been done differently?

4 Does your personal value profile in the OB Exercise help explain any inner, interpersonal, or individual–organization value conflict you may have experienced? Explain.

5 How could in-group thinking affect the performance of a manager living and working in a foreign country?

6 Which of the five conflict-handling styles is your strongest (your weakest)? How can you improve your ability to handle conflict?

7 What is your personal experience of conflict triangles? Based on what you have learned in this chapter, do you think you could do a better job of handling conflict triangles in the future? Explain.

8 Which of the six ADR techniques appeals to you most? Why?

9 Had your concept of negotiation, prior to reading this chapter, been restricted to win-lose thinking? Explain.

10 How could added-value negotiation make your life a bit easier? Explain in terms of a specific problem, conflict or deadlock.

Internet Exercise

http://www.books.mcgraw-hill.com
http://www.pon.harvard.edu

A great deal of interesting and useful material about conflict and negotiation can be found on the Internet. This is a good thing because the more than six billion inhabitants of this planet have a lot to learn about getting along. The purpose of this exercise is to help develop your conflict-handling skills and broaden your understanding of negotiation.

An Exercise on Dealing with a Poor Working Relationship

McGraw-Hill, the publisher of this textbook, has an extensive on-line collection of free training games and exercises gleaned from McGraw-Hill publications. Start with the Internet home page www.books.mcgraw-hill.com, and select the main menu item *Education & Training*. (*Note:* Although this is a commercial Web site, you need not buy anything to complete this exercise.) On successive pages, select the following chain of items from the main menus: *Training McGraw-Hill, Trainer's Toolchest,* and *Free Training Games.* At the Free Training Games page, scroll down to the heading Conflict Resolution and select *Dialogue with an Imaginary Guru.* (*Note:* Although this exercise is intended to be administered to a group, you can work through it in your own.) Be sure to read the 'D.A.R.R.N.-It!' handout for Step 1. In Step 2, complete the

Dialogue handout. You probably will want to print personal copies of these handouts. Be creative and have fun when writing the dialogue with your imaginary guru.

Research Updates on Negotiation

Harvard Law School, in co-operation with other leading universities, hosts the Internet site 'Programme on Negotiation' (www.pon.harvard.edu). Select the heading *Publications* from the main menu. Next, click on *Negotiation Journal* and survey the brief article summaries from recent issues of that quarterly journal. Focus on topics and findings related to managing organizational behaviour.

Questions

1 If you completed the Imaginary Guru exercise, was it helpful to take a different perspective of your poor working relationship? Explain. How important is it to 'walk in the other person's shoes' (to view things from the other's perspective) when trying to avoid or resolve a conflict? Explain.

2 What new insights did you pick up from the *Negotiation Journal*? Explain.

Personal Awareness and Growth Exercise
What Is Your Primary Conflict-Handling Style?

Objectives

1 To continue building your self-awareness.

2 To assess your approach to conflict.

3 To provide a springboard for handling conflicts more effectively.

Introduction

Professor Afzalur Rahim, developer of the five-style conflict model in Figure xx, created an assessment instruction upon which the one in this exercise is based. The original instrument was validated thorugh a factor analysis of responses from 1,219 managers from across the United States.

Instructions

For each of the 15 items, indicate how often you rely on that tactic by circling the appropriate number. After you have responded to all 15 items, complete the scoring key below.

Conflict-Handling Tactics	Rarely				Always
1 I argue my case with my colleagues to show the merits of my position.	1 — 2 — 3 — 4 — 5				
2 I negotiate with my colleagues so that a compromise can be reached.	1 — 2 — 3 — 4 — 5				
3 I try to satisfy the expectations of my colleagues.	1 — 2 — 3 — 4 — 5				
4 I try to investigate an issue with my colleagues to find a solution acceptable to us.	1 — 2 — 3 — 4 — 5				
5 I am firm in pursuing my side of the issue.	1 — 2 — 3 — 4 — 5				

6 I attempt to avoid being 'put on the spot' and try to keep my conflict with my colleagues to myself. 1 — 2 — 3 — 4 — 5

7 I hold on to my solution to a problem. 1 — 2 — 3 — 4 — 5

8 I use 'give and take' so that a compromise can be made. 1 — 2 — 3 — 4 — 5

9 I exchange accurate information with my colleagues to solve a problem together. 1 — 2 — 3 — 4 — 5

10 I avoid open discussion of my differences with my colleagues. 1 — 2 — 3 — 4 — 5

11 I accommodate the wishes of my colleagues. 1 — 2 — 3 — 4 — 5

12 I try to bring all our concerns out in the open so that the issues can be resolved in the best possible way. 1 — 2 — 3 — 4 — 5

13 I propose a middle ground for breaking deadlocks. 1 — 2 — 3 — 4 — 5

14 I go along with the suggestions of my colleagues. 1 — 2 — 3 — 4 — 5

15 I try to keep my disagreements with my colleagues to myself in order to avoid hard feelings. 1 — 2 — 3 — 4 — 5

Scoring Key

Integrating		Obliging		Dominating	
Item	Score	Item	Score	Item	Score
4	_____	3	_____	1	_____
9	_____	11	_____	5	_____
12	_____	14	_____	7	_____

Total = _____   Total = _____   Total = _____

Avoiding		Compromising	
Item	Score	Item	Score
6	_____	2	_____
10	_____	8	_____
15	_____	13	_____
Total = _____		Total = _____	

Your primary conflict-handling style is: _____

(The category with the highest total.)

Your back-up conflict-handling style is: _____

(The category with the second highest total.)

Questions for Discussion

1 Are the results what you expected? Explain.

2 Is there a clear gap between your primary and back-up styles or did they score about the same? If they are about the same, does this suggest indecision about handling conflict on your part? Explain.

3 Will your primary conflict-handling style carry over well to many different situations? Explain.

4 What is your personal learning agenda for becoming a more effective conflict handler?

SOURCE: Adapted and excerpted in part from M A Rahim, 'A Measure of Styles of Handling Interpersonal Conflict', Academy of Management Journal, June 1983, pp 368–76.

Group Exercise
Bangkok Blowup (A Role-Playing Exercise)

Objectives

1 To further your knowledge of interpersonal conflict and conflict-handling styles.

2 To give you a firsthand opportunity to try the various styles of handling conflict.

Introduction

This is a role-playing exercise intended to develop your ability to handle conflict. There is no single best way to resolve the conflict in this exercise. One style might work for one person, while another gets the job done for someone else.

Instructions

Read the following short case, 'Can Larry Fit In?' Pair up with someone else and decide which of you will play the role of Larry and which will play the role of Melissa, the office manager. Pick up the action from where the case leaves off. Try to be realistic and true to the characters in the case. The manager is primarily responsible for resolving this conflict situation. Whoever plays Larry should resist any unreasonable requests or demands and co-operate with any personally workable solution. *Note:* To conserve time, try to resolve this situation in less than 15 minutes.

CASE: 'CAN LARRY FIT IN?';[67]

Melissa, Office Manager

You are the manager of an auditing team sent to Bangkok, Thailand, to represent a major international accounting firm headquartered in New York. You and Larry, one of your auditors, were sent to Bangkok to set up an auditing operation. Larry is about seven years older than you and has had five more years with the firm. Your relationship has become very strained since you were recently appointed as the office manager. You feel you were given the promotion because you have established an excellent working relationship with the Thai staff as well as a broad range of international clients. In contrast, Larry has told other members of the staff that your promotion simply reflects the firm's heavy emphasis on affirmative action. He has tried to isolate you from the all-male accounting staff by focusing discussions on sports, local night spots and so forth.

You are sitting in your office reading some complicated new reporting procedures that have just arrived from the home office. Your concentration is suddenly interrupted by a loud knock on your door. Without waiting for an invitation to enter, Larry bursts into your office. He is obviously very upset, and it is not difficult for you to surmise why he is in such a nasty mood.

You recently posted the audit assignments for the coming month, and you scheduled Larry for a job you knew he wouldn't like. Larry is one of your senior auditors, and the company norm is that they get the choice assignments. This particular job will require him to spend two weeks away from Bangkok in a remote town, working with a company whose records are notoriously messy.

Unfortunately, you have had to assign several of these less-desirable audits to Larry recently because you are short of personnel. But that's not the only reason. You have received several complaints from the junior staff (all Thais) recently that Larry treats them in a condescending manner. They feel he is always looking for an opportunity to boss them around, as if he were their supervisor instead of an experienced, supportive mentor. As a result, your whole operation works more smoothly when you can send Larry out of town on a solo project for several days. It keeps him from coming into your office and telling you how to do your job, and the morale of the rest of the auditing staff is significantly higher.

Larry slams the door and proceeds to express his anger over this assignment.

Larry, Senior Auditor

You are really annoyed! Melissa is deliberately trying to undermine your status in the office. She knows that the company norm is that senior auditors get the better jobs. You've paid your dues and now expect to be treated with respect. And this isn't the first time this has happened. Since she was made the office manager, she has tried to keep you out of the office as much as possible. It's as if she doesn't want her rival for leadership around the office. When you were asked to go to Bangkok, you assumed that you would be made the office manager because of your seniority in the firm. You are certain that the decision to pick Melissa is yet another indication of reverse discrimination against white males.

In staff meetings, Melissa has talked about the need to be sensitive to the feelings of the office staff as well as the clients in this multicultural setting. 'Who is she to preach about sensitivity! What about my feelings, for heaven's sake?' you wonder. This is nothing more than a straightforward power play. She is probably feeling insecure about being the only female accountant in the office and being promoted over someone with more experience. 'Sending me out of town,' you decide, 'is a clear case of "out of sight, out of mind".'

Well, it's not going to happen that easily. You are not going to let her treat you unfairly. It's time for a showdown. If she doesn't agree to change this assignment and apologize for the way she's been treating you, you're going to register a formal complaint with her boss in the New York office. You are prepared to submit your resignation if the situation doesn't improve.

Questions for Discussion

1 What antecedents of conflict appear to be present in this situation? What can be done about them?

2 Having heard how others handled this conflict, did one particular style seem to work better than the others?

Chapter Fourteen

Individual and Group Decision-Making

Flight simulators for management

Thor Sigvaldason is late. As part of a novel consulting cluster at PriceWaterhouseCoopers, he is supposed to be at an important client meeting at 10 a.m. But he has overslept for the session with a top executive of a department store.

When Sigvaldason finally arrives, 20 minutes late, his brown hair is still wet from a shower. He eases quietly into the room, watched only by his boss, K. Winslow Farrell Jr., 45, whose face doesn't hide his displeasure. ▷

Thor brings up on a computer screen what has taken the team 1,800 hours to construct. It shows awkward block-like figures roaming about a crude layout of a department store. They have created an elaborate computer model of a department store with hundreds of "synthetic" shoppers. The idea is to simulate how real shoppers actually operate in a store. If all goes well, the actions of those "adaptive agents" will so closely mimic human behaviour that managers for the first time will be able to use them to test the impact of their decisions before implementing them in the real world. Farrell sees it as the ultimate "flight simulator" for management. The system will allow the client to make risk-free decisions such as:

▼ **The number of salespeople needed in each store department to maximise profits,**

▼ **How to turn browsers into shoppers,**

▼ **Where to locate service desks and cash registers to increase sales.**

Farrell is trying to create a virtual world where executives can safely test hunches, run scenarios, and preview the impact of big and small decisions—all without major investments, public embarrassments, and competitive backfires.

And if you make a wrong decision in the model, you're only dealing with a synthetic public, not the real world.

For years, management has sought to harness the power of econometrics and technology. Operations research and linear programming, however, rarely won the attention of the CEO because they were so esoteric and difficult to grasp. Farrell's group is hoping that the ability to see decisions acted out on a computer screen will greatly help sell the idea in the executive suite. Others agree. "Management is numerically illiterate," insists Michael Schrage, a technology consultant and author. "Instead of selling equations, they are selling pretty pictures. Visualisation is the marriage of mathematics and marketing."

The potential is great. For a major entertainment company, his group has created 40,000 movie-going agents—cloned from a survey of actual movie-goers—to help executives determine the best way to market and distribute films. Farrell says that the model is up and working, forecasting first week box-office receipts at accuracy rates of more than 30% better than traditional forecasting methods that rely on historical records.

Like Sigvaldason, 31, whose forte is visualisation, many are unaccustomed to working in a corporate setting where they have to attend meetings on time, wear suits, and keep their hair neatly trimmed. Until several women joined the group, a couple of team members would show up for work in flannel shirts, jeans, and hiking boots, then strip in the lab to slip into suits for meetings.

In the windowless lab room, it's not unusual for profanity to be heard in an array of languages. The work is often long and tedious. Sometimes, team members toil until the wee hours of the morning to debug some software or meet a client deadline. Wei says his wife often scolds him for coming home late, and he wonders whether his nearly two-year-old son recognises him.

Still, it's easy to overlook things humans take for granted—and that may be the biggest hurdle Farrell faces in creating a practical management tool. In an early iteration of the model built for the entertainment company, almost all the agents rushed out to see a film in its first week. The reason: The consultants failed to account for whether the agents had enough leisure time to go to the cinema.

If Farrell's team can deliver on the promise of these new concepts, they will likely give birth to a new and powerful management tool that could change the way executives manage their companies. But they have many daunting hurdles to overcome—starting with the need to show up on time for those client presentations.[1]

For discussion
Do you think 'flight simulators for management' can improve decision-making?

Decision-making is one of the primary responsibilities of all employees. The quality of decisions made is important for two principal reasons. First, the quality of decisions directly affects career opportunities, rewards and job satisfaction. Second, decisions contribute to the success or failure of an organization.

Decision-making
identifying and choosing solutions that lead to a desired end result

Decision-making is a means to an end. It entails identifying and choosing alternative solutions that lead to a desired state of affairs. The process begins with a problem and ends when a solution has been chosen. To gain an understanding of how managers can make better decisions, this chapter focuses on: models of decision-making; the dynamics of decision-making; group decision-making; and creativity.

MODELS OF DECISION-MAKING

There are several models of decision-making. Each is based on a different set of assumptions and offers a unique insight into the decision-making process. This section reviews three key historical models of decision-making. They are:

▼ the rational model

▼ Simon's normative model

▼ the 'garbage can' model.

Each successive model assumes that the decision-making process is less and less rational. Let us begin with the most orderly or rational explanation of decision-making.

The Rational Model

Rational model
logical four-step approach to decision-making

The **rational model** proposes that people use a rational, four-step sequence when making decisions, that is, they identify the problem, generate alternative solutions, select a solution, and implement and evaluate the solution. According to this model, managers are entirely objective and possess complete information on which to make a decision. Despite criticism for being unrealistic, the rational model is instructive because it analytically breaks down the decision-making process and serves as a conceptual anchor for more recent models.[2] Let us now consider each of these four steps in detail.

Identifying the Problem

Problem
gap between an actual and desired situation

A **problem** exists when the actual situation and the desired situation differ. For example, a problem exists when you have to pay rent at the end of the month but don't have enough money. Your problem is not that you have to pay rent. Your problem is obtaining the necessary funds.

> *The challenge for post-communist Georgia, a nation of 5.4 million, is to turn its wine into a quality export that can compete with the table wines of Spain, Italy, and France and someday yield an award-winning vintage. But as I learned on a recent three-day visit, there's a long way to go before Georgia can consistently produce the rival of a typical Chianti, much less a noble St Emilion. The problem is an economy and political culture that are still dysfunctional 10 years after Soviet rule. The banking system barely works, depriving businesses of credit, and corruption is pervasive, with widespread counterfeiting of products including wine.[3]*

How do companies know when a problem exists or is going to in the near future? One expert proposed that managers use one of three methods to identify problems: historical cues, planning, and other people's perceptions.[4]

1 Using historical cues to identify problems assumes that the recent past is the best estimate of the future. Thus, managers rely on past experience to identify discrepancies (problems) from expected trends. For example, a sales manager may conclude that a problem exists because the first-quarter sales are less than they were a year ago. This method is prone to error because it is highly subjective.

2 A planning approach is more systematic and can lead to more accurate results. This method consists of using projections or imagined events (scenarios) to estimate what is expected to occur in the future. A time period of one or more years is generally used.

The **scenario technique** is used to identify future states, based on a given set of circumstances ('environmental conditions'). Once different scenarios are developed, companies devise alternative strategies to survive in the various circumstances. This process helps in the creation of contingency plans for far into the future. Companies such as Royal Dutch/Shell, IBM and Pfizer are increasingly using the scenario technique as a planning tool.[5]

> **Scenario technique**
> *speculative forecasting method*

3 A final approach to identifying problems is to rely on the perceptions of others. A restaurant manager may realize that his or her restaurant provides poor service when a large number of customers complain about how long it takes to receive food after placing an order. In other words, customers' comments signal that a problem exists. Interestingly, companies frequently compound their problems by ignoring customer complaints or feedback.

Generating Solutions

After identifying a problem, the next logical step is to generate alternative solutions. For repetitive and routine decisions, such as deciding when to send customers a bill, alternatives are readily available in the form of 'decision rules'. For example, a company might routinely bill customers three days after shipping a product. Where no decision rules exist, however, novel and unstructured decisions must be made. Managers must creatively generate alternative solutions. Managers can use a number of techniques to stimulate the necessary creativity and these are discussed later in this chapter.

Selecting a Solution

Ideally, decision makers want to choose the alternative with the greatest value. Decision theorists refer to this as maximizing the expected utility of an outcome. This is no easy task. First, assigning values to alternatives is complicated and prone to error. Not only are values subjective but they also vary according to the preferences of the decision maker.

Research demonstrates that people vary in their preferences for safety or risk when making decisions.[6] For example, a recent meta-analysis of 150 studies revealed that males displayed more risk-taking than females.[7] The second step in selecting a solution, that of evaluating alternatives, assumes that each can be judged according to set standards or criteria. This further assumes that: valid criteria exist, each alternative can be compared against these criteria, and that the decision maker actually uses the criteria. As you know from making your own key life decisions, people frequently violate these assumptions.

Implementing and Evaluating the Solution

Once a solution is chosen, it needs to be implemented. Before implementing a solution, though, managers need to do their homework. For example, three ineffective managerial tendencies have been observed frequently during the initial stages of implementation (see Table 14–1). Skilful managers try to avoid these tendencies. Table 14–1 indicates that to promote necessary understanding, acceptance and motivation, managers should involve implementers in the choice-making step.

Table 14-1 *Three Managerial Tendencies Reduce the Effectiveness of Implementation*

Managerial Tendency	Recommended Solution
The tendency not to ensure that people understand what needs to be done.	Involve the implementators in the choice-making step. When this is not possible, a strong and explicit attempt should be made to identify any misunderstanding, perhaps by having the implementor explain what he or she thinks needs to be done and why.
The tendency not to ensure the acceptance or motivation for what needs to be done.	Once again, involve the implementators in the choice-making step. Attempts should also be made to demonstrate the payoffs for effective implementation and to show how completion of various tasks will lead to successful implementation.
The tendency not to provide appropriate resources for what needs to be done.	Many implementations are less effective than they could be because adequate resources, such as time, staff, or information, were not provided. In particular, the allocations of such resources across departments and tasks are assumed to be appropriate because they were appropriate for implementing the previous plan. These assumptions should be checked.

SOURCE: Modified from G P Huber, *Managerial Decision Making* (Glenview, IL: Scott, Foresman, 1980), p 19.

After the solution is implemented, the evaluation phase assesses its effectiveness. If the solution is effective, it should reduce the difference between the actual and desired states that created the problem. If the gap is not closed, the implementation was not successful, and one of the following is true: either the problem was incorrectly identified, or the solution was inappropriate. If the implementation was, indeed, unsuccessful, management can return to the first step, that of problem identification. If the problem was correctly identified, then management should consider implementing one of the previously identified but untried solutions. This process can continue until all feasible solutions have been tried or the problem has changed.[8]

Summarizing the Rational Model

The rational model is based on the premise that, when managers make decisions, they are aiming to solve problems by producing the best possible solution, which is referred to in the literature as **optimizing**. This assumes that managers have:

Optimizing
choosing the best possible solution

▼ knowledge of all possible alternatives
▼ complete knowledge about the consequences that follow each alternative
▼ a well-organized and stable set of preferences for these consequences
▼ the computational ability to compare consequences and to determine which one is preferred.[9]

As noted by Herbert Simon, a decision theorist who in 1978 earned the Nobel Prize for his work on decision-making, 'The assumptions of perfect rationality are contrary to fact. It is not a question of approximation; they do not even remotely describe the processes that human beings use for making decisions in complex situations.'[10] Thus, the rational model is at best an instructional tool. Since decision makers do not follow these rational procedures, Simon proposed a normative model of decision-making.

Simon's Normative Model

Bounded rationality
constraints that restrict decision-making

This model attempts to identify the process that managers actually use when making decisions. The process is guided by a decision maker's bounded rationality. **Bounded rationality** represents the notion that decision makers are 'bounded' or restricted by a variety of constraints when making decisions. These constraints include any personal or environmental characteristics that reduce rational decision-making. Examples are the limited capacity of the human mind, problem complexity and uncertainty, amount and timeliness of information at hand, importance of the decision, and time demands.[11]

In contrast to the rational model, Simon's normative model suggests that decision-making is characterized by: limited information processing; the use of judgemental heuristics; and a process that involves 'satisficing' with something short of ideal. Each of these characteristics is now explored.

Limited Information Processing

Managers are limited by how much information they process because of bounded rationality. This results in the tendency to acquire manageable rather than optimal amounts of information. In turn, this practice makes it difficult for managers to identify all possible alternative solutions. In the long run, the constraints of bounded rationality cause decision makers to fail to evaluate all potential alternatives.

Judgemental Heuristics

Judgemental heuristics represent rules of thumb or shortcuts that people use to reduce information processing demands.[12] We use them automatically without being aware of it. The use of heuristics helps decision makers to reduce the uncertainty inherent within the decision-making process. Because these shortcuts represent knowledge gained from past experience, they can help decision makers evaluate current problems. They can, however, lead to systematic errors that erode the quality of decisions. There are two common categories of heuristics that are important to consider: the availability heuristic and the representativeness heuristic.

> **Judgement heuristic**
> *rules of thumb or shortcuts that people use to reduce information-processing demands*

The **availability heuristic** represents a decision maker's tendency to base decisions on information that is readily available in memory.[13] Information is more accessible in memory when it involves an event that recently occurred, when it is salient (such as a plane crash), and when it evokes strong emotions (such as a shooting incident). This heuristic is likely to cause people to overestimate the occurrence of unlikely events such as a plane crash or a shooting. This bias also is partially responsible for the recency effect discussed in Chapter 6. For example, a manager is more likely to give an employee a positive performance evaluation if the employee exhibited excellent performance over the last few months.

> **Availability heuristic**
> *tendency to base decisions on information readily available in memory*

The **representativeness heuristic** is used when people estimate the probability of an event occurring. It reflects the tendency to assess the likelihood of an event occurring based on one's impressions about similar occurrences. A manager, for example, may employ a graduate from a particular university because the past three people taken on from this university turned out to be good performers. In this case, the 'establishment attended' criterion is used to facilitate complex information processing associated with employment interviews. Unfortunately, this shortcut can result in a biased decision. Similarly, an individual may believe that he or she can master a new software package in a short period of time because he or she was previously able to learn how to use a different type of software quickly. This estimate may or may not be accurate. For example, it may take the individual a much longer period of time to learn the new software because it requires the person to learn a new programming language.

> **Prevalence (or representativeness) heuristic**
> *tendency to assess the likelihood of an event occurring based on impressions about similar occurrences*

Satisficing

People 'satisfice' because they do not have the time, information or ability to handle the complexity associated with following a rational process. This is not necessarily undesirable. **Satisficing** consists of choosing a solution that meets some minimum qualifications, one that is 'good enough'. It resolves problems by producing solutions that are satisfactory, as opposed to optimal. Finding a radio station to listen to in your car is a good example of this process. You cannot optimize your choice because it is impossible to listen to all stations at the same time. You thus stop searching for a station when you find one playing a song you like or do not mind hearing.

> **Satisficing**
> *choosing a solution that meets a minimum standard of acceptance*

The 'Garbage Can' Model

This approach, like Simon's normative model, came about as a response to the rational model's inability to explain how decisions are actually made. It assumes that organizational decision-making is a sloppy and haphazard process. This contrasts sharply with the rational model, which proposed that decision makers follow a sequential series of steps beginning with a problem and ending with a solution. According to the **'garbage can' model**, decisions result from a complex interaction between four independent streams of events: problems, solutions, participants, and choice opportunities.[14]

'Garbage can' model
holds that decision-making is sloppy and haphazard

The interaction of these events creates 'a collection of choices looking for problems, issues and feelings looking for decision situations in which they might be aired, solutions looking for issues to which they might be the answer, and decision makers looking for work.'[15] A similar type of process occurs in your dustbin. We randomly discard our rubbish and it gets thrown together based on chance interactions. Consider, for instance, going to your dustbin and noticing that the used coffee granules are stuck to banana peel. Can you explain how this might occur? The answer is simple: because they were thrown in at about the same time. Just like the process of mixing rubbish in a dustbin, the 'garbage can model' of decision-making assumes that decision-making does not follow an orderly series of steps. Rather, attractive solutions can get matched up with whatever handy problems exist at that time or people get assigned to projects because their work load is low at that moment. This model of decision-making thus attempts to explain how problems, solutions, participants, and choice opportunities interact and lead to a decision. After discussing the streams of events and how they interact, this section highlights managerial implications of this model.

Figure 14–1

'Garbage Can' Model of Organizational Decision-Making

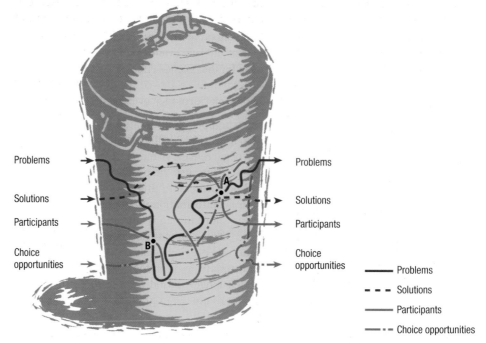

Streams of Events

The four streams of events—problems, solutions, participants, and choice opportunities—represent independent entities that flow in and out of organizational decision situations (see Figure 14–1). Because decisions are a function of the interaction between these independent events, the stages of problem identification and problem solution may be unrelated. For instance, a solution may be proposed for a problem that does not exist. This can be observed when students recommend that a test be curved, even though the average test score is a comparatively high 85 per cent. On the other hand, some problems are never solved. Each of the four events in the garbage can model deserves a closer look.

▼ *Problems.* As defined earlier, problems represent a gap between an actual situation and a desired condition. But problems are independent from alternatives and solutions. The problem may or may not lead to a solution.

▼ *Solutions.* Solutions are answers looking for questions. They represent ideas constantly flowing through an organization. Contrary to the classical model, however, solutions are used to formulate problems rather than vice versa. This is predicted to occur because managers often do not know what they want until they have some idea of what they can get.

▼ *Participants.* Participants are the organizational members who come and go throughout the organization. They bring different values, attitudes, and experiences to a decision-making situation. Time pressures limit the extent to which participants are involved in decision-making.

▼ *Choice opportunities.* Choice opportunities are occasions in which an organization is expected to make a decision. While some opportunities, such as hiring and promoting employees, occur regularly, others do not because they result from some type of crisis or unique situation.

Interactions between the Streams of Events

Because of the independent nature of the streams of events, they interact in a random fashion. This implies that decision-making is more a function of chance encounters than a rational process. Thus, the organization is characterized as a 'garbage can' (dustbin) in which problems, solutions, participants and choice opportunities are all mixed together (see Figure 14–1). Only when the four streams of events happen to connect, such as at point A in Figure 14–1, is a decision made. Because these connections randomly occur within the countless combinations of streams of events, decision quality generally depends on *timing*. (Some might use the term *luck*.) In other words, good decisions are made when these streams of events interact at the proper time. This explains why problems do not necessarily relate to solutions (point B in Figure 14–1) and why solutions do not always solve problems. In support of the model, one study indicated that decision-making in the textbook publishing industry conformed to it. Moreover, knowledge of the model helped the researchers to identify a variety of best-selling textbooks.[16]

Managerial Implications

This model of organizational decision-making has four practical implications.[17] The first of these is that many decisions will be made by oversight or the presence of a salient opportunity. Consider Coca-Cola Company's 1996 decision to hire a large cargo plane to take an 80-ton bottling line out to a new plant in Vladivostok, Russia.

Soda sales in Russia were booming. Rather than wait for a ship to deliver the parts for the new line in eastern Russia, Coca-Cola Co. snared an Antonov AN-124, with a cargo bay big enough to hold 10 elephants, to airlift the equipment. Company officials dubbed it the Siberian Express. 'We didn't want to lose any time,' Neville Isdell, then Coke's European chief, said at the time. 'Russia has a big thirst for Coca-Cola; our sales there have quadrupled since 1991.' Today, three years later, much of that demand seems to have evaporated almost as quickly as the company sought to fill it. With Russia's economy in shambles, Coke isn't on most Russian shopping lists.[18]

Coca-Cola's decision to use a cargo plane instead of a ship was based on the perceived opportunity to capture more of Russia's soft-drink market. Moreover, Coca-Cola would perhaps not have made the decision to invest in building bottling plants in

Russia had it foreseen the collapse of Russia's economy. Second, political motives frequently guide the process by which participants make decisions. Participants tend to make decisions that promise to increase their status. Third, the process is sensitive to load. That is, as the number of problems increases, relative to the amount of time available to solve them, problems are less likely to be solved. Finally, important problems are more likely to be solved than unimportant ones because they are more salient to organizational participants.[19]

Dynamics of Decision-making

Decision-making is part science and part art. Accordingly, this section examines three dynamics of decision-making—contingency considerations, decision-making styles, and the problem of escalation of commitment—that affect the 'science' component. An understanding of these dynamics can help managers make better decisions.

Selecting Solutions: A Contingency Perspective

The previous discussion of decision-making models noted that managers typically select solutions that will suffice. However, we did not probe how managers actually evaluate and select solutions. Let us explore the model in Figure 14–2 to better understand how individuals make decisions.

Strategies for Selecting a Solution

What procedures do decision makers use to evaluate the costs and benefits of alternative solutions? According to management experts Lee Roy Beach and Terence Mitchell, one of three approaches is used: aided-analytic, unaided-analytic, and non-analytic.[20] Decision makers systematically use tools such as mathematical equations, calculators, or computers to analyse and evaluate alternatives within an **aided-analytic** approach.

Aided-analytic
using tools to make decisions

Figure 14–2

A Contingency Model for Selecting a Solution

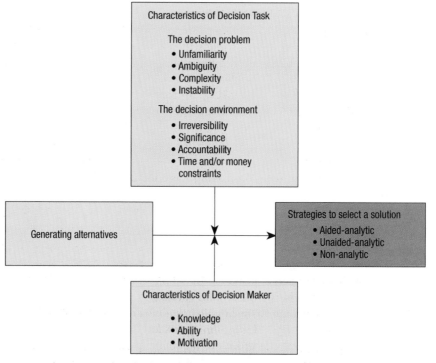

SOURCE: Based on L R Beach and T R Mitchell, 'A contingency Model for the Selection of Decision Strategies', *Academy of Management Review*, July 1978, pp 439–44.

Weather forecasters, astronomers and insurance analysts are good examples of people who make their decisions by using an aided-analytic strategy. This type of professional tends to make decisions by analyzing data with complex computer models.[21] In addition to using decision-making tools, organizations may create a decision-making team or hire consultants to conduct a formal study of the problem to hand.

In the high-tech world of aerospace manufacturing, where a few products can account for most of a factory's output, a bad production decision can cause trouble for years down the road.

The solution has been a cost-assessment system known as activity-based costing, or ABC. This analytical approach breaks down all activities in a manufacturing plant and determines the portion of overhead used to make each product. It's like splitting the bill at a restaurant, says Anthony A. Atkinson, a professor of accountancy at Canada's University of Waterloo. Where traditional accounting divides the bill evenly between all the diners, ABC determines who had the T-bone and who had the burger. Once an arcane research topic, this approach is now the focus of intense study by hundreds of manufacturers. Thanks to the falling cost of computing power, even small companies now have access to powerful ABC software tools.[22]

In contrast, decision makers rely on the confines of their minds when using an **unaided-analytic** strategy. In other words, the decision maker systematically compares alternatives, but the analysis is limited to evaluating information that can be directly processed in his or her head. Decision-making tools, such as a personal computer, are not used. Chess masters and counsellors use this strategy in the course of their work. Finally, a **non-analytic** strategy consists of using a simple rule formulated beforehand to make the decision. Examples are flipping a coin, habit, normal convention ('we've always done it that way'), using a conservative approach ('better safe than sorry') or following procedures offered in instruction manuals. Both the cost and level of sophistication decrease as one moves from an aided-analytic to a non-analytic strategy.

Unaided-analytic
analysis is limited to processing information in one's mind

Non-analytic
using rules, formulated beforehand, to make decisions

Determining which approach to use depends on two sets of contingency factors: the characteristics of the decision task and those of the decision maker (refer again to Figure 14-2).

Characteristics of the Decision Task

These characteristics reflect the demands and constraints a decision maker faces and comprise two components: those relating to the specific problem and those pertaining to the general decision environment. In general, the greater the demands and constraints encountered by a decision maker, the higher the probability that an aided-analytic approach will be used. This conclusion is consistent with results from two recent studies.

The first study comprised a series of experiments with undergraduate students. Findings revealed that the students made less consistent decisions in less predictable and unstable situations. Aided-analytic methods could have helped these individuals make more consistent decisions. The second study examined the strategic decision-making process within 24 organizations with annual sales ranging from US$1.5 million to more than $3 billion. Results demonstrated that more effective decisions were made by managers who collected information and used analytical techniques than by managers who did not.[23]

The environment also restricts the type of analysis used. For instance, a study of 75 MBA students revealed that they purchased and used less information for decision-making as the cost of information increased. In contrast, they purchased and used more information when they were rewarded for making good decisions. These results suggest that both the cost of information and one's accountability for a decision affect the type of analysis used to solve a problem.[24] Moreover, time constraints influence selection of a solution. Poorer decisions are bound to be made in the face of severe time pressure.

Characteristics of the Decision Maker

Chapter 5 highlighted a variety of individual differences that affect employee behaviour and performance. In the present context, an individual's knowledge, ability and motivation affect the type of analytical procedure used in coming to a decision. In general, research supports the prediction that aided-analytic strategies are more likely to be used by competent and motivated individuals.[25]

Table 14–2

Contingency Relationships in Decision Making

1. Analytic strategies are used when the decision problem is unfamiliar, ambiguous, complex, or unstable.
2. Nonanalytic methods are employed when the problem is familiar, straightforward, or stable.
3. Assuming there are no monetary or time constraints, analytic approaches are used when the solution is irreversible and significant and when the decision maker is accountable.
4. Nonanalytic strategies are used when the decision can be reversed and is not very significant or when the decision maker is not held accountable.
5. As the probability of making a correct decision goes down, analytic strategies are used.
6. As the probability of making a correct decision goes up, nonanalytic strategies are employed.
7. Time and money constraints automatically exclude some strategies from being used.
8. Analytic strategies are more frequently used by experienced and educated decision makers.
9. Nonanalytic approaches are used when the decision maker lacks knowledge, ability, or motivation to make a good decision.

SOURCE: Adapted from L R Beach and T R Mitchell, 'A Contingency Model for the Selection of Decision Strategies', *Academy of Management Review*, July 1978, pp 439–44.

Contingency Relationships

There are many ways in which characteristics of the task and the decision maker can interact to influence the strategy used to select a solution. In choosing a strategy, decision makers must make a compromise between their desire to make correct decisions and the amount of time and effort they put into the decision-making process. Table 14–2 lists contingency relationships that help reconcile these competing demands. As shown in this table, analytic strategies are more likely to be used when the problem is unfamiliar and irreversible. In contrast, non-analytic methods are employed on familiar problems or problems in which the decision can be reversed.

General Decision-Making Styles

The previous section stressed that individual differences or characteristics of a decision *maker* influence the decision-making process. This section expands on this discussion by focusing on how an individual's decision-making *style* affects his or her approach to decision-making.

Decision-making style
a combination of how individuals perceive and respond to information

A **decision-making style** reflects the combination of how an individual perceives and comprehends stimuli and the general manner in which he or she chooses to respond to it.[26] A team of researchers developed a model that is based on the idea that of decision-making styles vary along two different dimensions: value orientation and tolerance for ambiguity.[27] Value orientation reflects the extent to which an individual focuses either on task and technical concerns or people and social concerns when making decisions. Some people, for instance, are very task focused at work and do not pay much attention to people issues, whereas others are just the opposite. The second dimension pertains to a person's tolerance for ambiguity, that is, the extent to which a person needs structure or control in his or her life. Some people desire a lot of structure in their lives (a low tolerance for ambiguity) and find ambiguous situations stressful and psychologically uncomfortable. In contrast, others do not have a high need for structure and can thrive in uncertain situations (a high tolerance for ambiguity). Ambiguous situations can energize people with a high tolerance for ambiguity. When the dimensions of value orientation and tolerance for ambiguity are combined, they form four styles of decision-making (see Figure 14–3): directive, analytical, conceptual and behavioural.

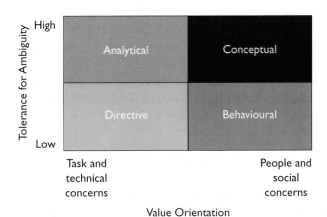

Figure 14–3
Decision-Making Styles

SOURCE: Based on discussion contained in A J Rowe and R O Mason, *Managing with Style: A Guide to Understanding, Assessing, and Improving Decision Making* (San Francisco: Jossey-Bass, 1987), pp 1–17.

Directive

People with a directive style have a low tolerance for ambiguity and are oriented toward task and technical concerns when making decisions. They are efficient, logical, practical and systematic in their approach to solving problems. People with this style are action oriented and decisive and like to focus on facts. In their pursuit of speed and results, however, these individuals tend to be autocratic, exercise power and control, and focus on the short run.

Analytical

This style has a much higher tolerance for ambiguity and is characterized by the tendency to analyse a situation too closely. People with this style like to consider more information and alternatives than do directives. Analytic individuals are careful decision makers who take longer than others to make decisions but who can, when necessary, respond well to new or uncertain situations. They can often be autocratic.

Conceptual

People with a conceptual style have a high tolerance for ambiguity and tend to focus on the people or social aspects of a work situation. They take a broad perspective to problem solving and like to consider many options and future possibilities. Conceptual types adopt a long-term perspective and rely on intuition and discussion with others to acquire information. They are willing to take risks and are good at finding creative solutions to problems. On the downside, however, a conceptual style can foster an idealistic and indecisive approach to decision-making.

Behavioural

Of the four styles, this is the one which focuses most on the people aspect of decisions. Individuals with this style work well with others and enjoy social interactions in which opinions are openly exchanged. Behavioural types are supportive, receptive to suggestions, show warmth, and prefer verbal to written information. Although they like to hold meetings, people with this style have a tendency to avoid conflict and to be too concerned about others. This can lead behavioural types to adopt a 'wishy-washy' approach to decision-making and to have a hard time saying *no* to others and to have difficulty making difficult decisions.

Research and Practical Implications

Research shows that very few people have only one dominant decision-making style. Rather, most managers have characteristics that fall into two or three styles. Studies also show that decision-making styles vary across occupations, job levels and countries.[28] You can use knowledge of decision-making styles in three ways.

First, knowledge of styles helps you to understand yourself. Awareness of your style assists you in identifying your strengths and weaknesses as a decision maker and facilitates the potential for self-improvement. (You can assess your decision-making style by completing the Personal Awareness and Growth Exercise located at the end of this chapter.)

Second, you can increase your ability to influence others by being aware of styles. For example, if you are dealing with an analytical person, you should provide as much

International OB

www.daewoo-auto.com

Daewoo Motor Company Falls Prey to Escalation of Commitment

Business Week logo to go here

Kim Woo Choong thought he'd scored quite a coup in 1993. That year, his Daewoo Motor Co. got the green light to assemble cars in Vietnam. Then the economy stalled, and demand for cars plunged by one-third, to just 5,200 units annually. Daewoo's sales shrivelled to 423 vehicles in 1998. Undaunted, Daewoo launched a new car, the Matiz, for $8,800. Sales in Vietnam may now double this year. But rivals doubt Daewoo's total $33 million investment is paying off. 'There's no way they could make money at this price,' says a foreign auto executive in Hanoi.

The Vietnam quagmire helps explain why Korea's Daewoo Group is in such a mess that creditors are now trying to force its breakup—and why it is negotiating with General Motors Corp. to sell pieces of its car company. From the United States to India, Chairman Kim is stumbling in his quest to build a car giant. In most places, the reasons are similar: plunging into dicey countries, selling at a loss to gain share, and refusing to retreat when the cause is hopeless.

Daewoo's Global Headaches

Korea	United States	Western Europe	India	Vietnam
Car sales plunged by 56% in 1998, to 234,000 units, as Daewoo was adding capacity.	The goal to sell 100,000 cars in its first year is unlikely to be met. Daewoo is offering steep rebates.	Sales have risen in Britain, Germany, and Italy. But analysts don't expect the gains to last.	Analysts estimate Daewoo is losing more than $30 million annually by offering $2,500 discounts.	Its hopes of hitting it big by arriving early have been dashed by rivals and a decline in demand.

SOURCE: Excerpted from J Veale, L Armstrong, and J Muller, 'How Daewoo Ran Itself Off the Road', *Business Week*, August 30, 1999, p 48.

information as possible to support your ideas. This same approach is more likely to frustrate a directive type.

Finally, knowledge of styles gives you an awareness of how people can take the same information and yet arrive at different decisions by using a variety of decision-making strategies. Different decision-making styles represent one likely source of interpersonal conflict at work (conflict was discussed in Chapter 13). It is important to conclude with the caveat that there is no one ideal decision-making style applicable to all situations.

Escalation of Commitment

Once a decision has been made, there can be a tendency to stick to that decision regardless. Escalation situations involve circumstances in which things have gone wrong but where the situation could possibly be turned around by investing additional time, money or effort.[29] The next International OB provides an example of escalation of commitment at Daewoo Motor Company.

Escalation of commitment refers to the tendency to stick to an ineffective course of action when it is unlikely that the bad situation can be reversed. Personal examples include investing more money into an old or broken car, waiting an extremely long time for a bus when you could have walked there just as easily, or trying to save a disruptive personal relationship that has lasted ten years. Case studies also indicate that escalation of commitment is partially responsible for some of the worst financial losses experienced by organizations. For example, from 1966 to 1989 the Long Island Lighting Company's investment in the Shoreham nuclear power plant in the US escalated from $65 million to $5 billion, despite a steady flow of negative feedback. The plant was never opened.[30]

Escalation of commitment
sticking to an ineffective course of action too long

OB Researchers Jerry Ross and Barry Staw identified four reasons for escalation of commitment (see Figure 14–4). They involve psychological and social determinants, organizational determinants, project characteristics, and contextual determinants.[31]

Figure 14–4 *A Model of Escalation of Commitment*

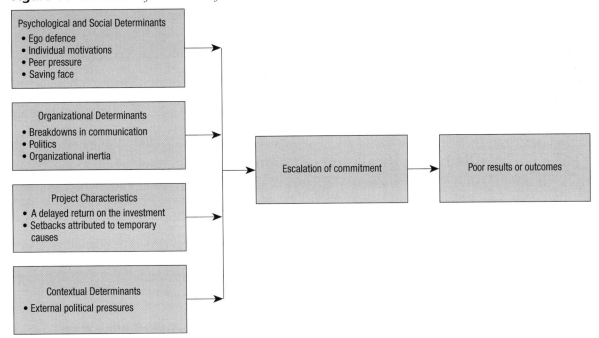

Psychological and Social Determinants
- Ego defence
- Individual motivations
- Peer pressure
- Saving face

Organizational Determinants
- Breakdowns in communication
- Politics
- Organizational inertia

Project Characteristics
- A delayed return on the investment
- Setbacks attributed to temporary causes

Contextual Determinants
- External political pressures

Escalation of commitment → Poor results or outcomes

SOURCE: Based on discussion in J Ross and B M Straw, 'Organizational Escalation and Exit: Lessons from the Shoreham Nuclear Power Plant', *Academy of Management Journal*, August 1993, pp 701–32.

Psychological and Social Determinants

Defence of one's ego and individual motivations are the key psychological contributors to escalation of commitment. Individuals continue to invest when the signs say otherwise—throw good money after bad—because they tend to bias facts so that they support previous decisions, take more risks when a decision is stated in negative terms (to recover losses) rather than positive ones (to achieve gains), and their ego becomes bound up with the project's success or failure. Because failure threatens an individual's self-esteem or ego, people tend to ignore negative signs and push on.[32]

Social pressures can make it difficult for a manager to reverse a course of action. For instance, peer pressure makes it difficult for an individual to drop a course of action when he or she publicly supported it in the past. Further, managers may continue to support bad decisions because they don't want their mistakes exposed to others. For example, a recent study involving 102 students working on a computer-simulated competition revealed that they engaged in less escalation of commitment when their performance was being monitored.[33]

Organizational Determinants

Factors arising from the organization itself, can cause it to maintain a bad course of action and these can include a breakdown in communication, workplace politics, and organizational inertia.

Project Characteristics

Project characteristics involve the objective features of a project. They have the greatest impact on escalation decisions. For example, because most projects do not reap benefits until some delayed time period, decision makers are motivated to stay with the project until the end. Thus, there is a tendency to attribute setbacks to temporary causes that are correctable with additional expenditures. Moreover, escalation is related to whether the project has clearly defined goals and whether people receive clear feedback about performance. A recent study, for instance, revealed that escalation was fueled by ambiguous performance feedback and the lack of performance standards.[34]

Contextual Determinants

This category of determinant of escalation refers to those causes arising from external political forces beyond an organization's control. For instance, the continuance of the previously discussed Shoreham nuclear power plant was partially influenced by pressures from other public utilities interested in nuclear power, representatives of the nuclear power industry, and people in the federal government pushing for the development of nuclear power.[35]

Reducing Escalation of Commitment

It is important to reduce escalation of commitment because it leads to poor decision-making for both individuals and groups.[36] Barry Staw and Jerry Ross, the researchers who originally identified the phenomenon of escalation, recommended several ways to reduce it.

▼ Set minimum targets for performance, and get decision makers to compare their performance with these targets.

▼ Have the initial and subsequent decisions about a project made by different individuals.

▼ Encourage decision makers to become less 'ego-involved' with a project.

▼ Provide more frequent feedback about project completion and costs.

▼ Reduce the risk or penalties of failure.

▼ Make decision makers aware of the costs of persistence.[37]

GROUP DECISION-MAKING

Groups such as committees, task forces, or review panels often play a key role in the decision-making process. Are two or more heads *always* better than one? Do all employees desire to have a say in the decision-making process? When and how should a manager use group decision-making? This section provides the background for answering these questions, essential for gaining maximum benefits from group decision-making. We discuss (1) advantages and disadvantages of group-aided decision-making, (2) participative management, (3) when to use groups in decision-making, and (4) group problem-solving techniques. A broader examination of group dynamics was provided in Chapter 12.

Table 14–3 *Advantages and Disadvantages of Group-Aided Decision Making*

Advantages	Disadvantages
1. *Greater pool of knowledge.* A group can bring much more information and experience to bear on a decision or problem than can an individual acting alone.	1. *Social pressure.* Unwillingness to 'rock the boat' and pressure to conform may combine to stifle the creativity of individual contributors.
2. *Different perspectives.* Individuals with varied experience and interests help the group see decision situations and problems from different angles.	2. *Domination by a vocal few.* Sometimes the quality of group action is reduced when the group gives in to those who talk the loudest and longest.
3. *Greater comprehension.* Those who personally experience the give-and-take of group discussion about alternative courses of action tend to understand the rationale behind the final decision.	3. *Logrolling.* Political wheeling and dealing can displace sound thinking when an individual's pet project or vested interest is at stake.
4. *Increased acceptance.* Those who play an active role in group decision making and problem solving tend to view the outcome as 'ours' rather than 'theirs.'	4. *Goal displacement.* Sometimes secondary considerations such as winning an argument, making a point, or getting back at a rival displace the primary task of making a sound decision or solving a problem.
5. *Training ground.* Less experienced participants in group action learn how to cope with group dynamics by actually being involved.	5. *'Groupthink.'* Sometimes cohesive 'in groups' let the desire for unanimity override sound judgment when generating and evaluating alternative courses of action. (Groupthink is discussed in Chapter 12.)

SOURCE: R Kreitner, *Management*, 7th ed (Boston: Houghton Mifflin, 1998), p 234.

Advantages and Disadvantages of Group-Aided Decision-making

Including groups in the decision-making process has both advantages and disadvantages (see Table 14–3). On the positive side, groups contain a greater pool of knowledge, provide more varied perspectives, create more comprehension of decisions, increase decision acceptance, and create a training ground for inexperienced employees. These advantages must be balanced, however, with the disadvantages listed in Table 14–3. In doing so, managers need to determine the extent to which the advantages and disadvantages apply to the situation in hand. The following three guidelines may then be applied to help decide whether groups should be included in the decision-making process.

1 If additional information would increase the quality of the decision, managers should involve those people who can provide the necessary information.

2 If acceptance is important, managers need to involve those individuals whose acceptance and commitment are important.

3 If peoples' skills can be developed through their participation, managers may want to involve those whose development is most important.[38]

Group versus Individual Performance

Before recommending that managers involve groups in decision-making, it is important to examine whether groups perform better or worse than individuals. After reviewing 61 years of relevant research, a decision-making expert concluded that 'Group performance was generally qualitatively and quantitatively superior to the performance of the average individual.'[39] Although subsequent research of small-group decision-making generally supported this conclusion, five important issues arose which are important to consider when using groups to make decisions.

1   Groups were less efficient than individuals. This suggests that time constraints are an important consideration in determining whether to involve groups in decision-making.

2   Groups were more confident about their judgements and choices than individuals. Because group confidence does not necessarily guarantee the quality of a decision, this overconfidence can fuel 'groupthink' and a resistance to considering alternative solutions proposed by outsiders.

3   Group size affected decision outcomes. Decision quality was negatively related to group size.[40]

4   Decision-making accuracy was higher both when groups knew a great deal about the issues at hand and group leaders possessed the ability to effectively evaluate the group members' opinions and judgements. Groups need to give more weight to relevant and accurate judgements while downplaying irrelevant or inaccurate judgements made by its members.[41]

5   The composition of a group affects its decision-making processes and ultimately performance. For example, groups of familiar people are more likely to make better decisions when members share a lot of unique information. In contrast, unacquainted group members should outperform groups of friends when most group members possess common knowledge.[42]

Additional research suggests that managers should use a contingency approach when determining whether to include others in the decision-making process. Let us now consider these contingency recommendations.

Practical Contingency Recommendations

If the decision occurs frequently, such as deciding on promotions or who qualifies for a loan, use groups as they tend to produce more consistent decisions than do individuals. Given time constraints, let the most competent individual, rather than a group, make the decision. In the face of 'environmental threats' such as time pressure and the potentially serious effect of a decision, groups use less information and fewer communication channels. This increases the probability of a bad decision.[43] This conclusion underscores a general recommendation that managers should keep in mind, not least because the quality of communication strongly affects a group's productivity. It is essential, therefore, to devise mechanisms to enhance the effectiveness of communication when dealing with complex tasks.

Participative Management

An organization needs to maximize its workers' potential if it wants to compete successfully in the global economy. As noted by Jack Welch, the former CEO of General Electric, 'Only the most productive companies are going to win. If you can't sell a top-quality product at the world's lowest price, you're going to be out of the game. In that environment, 6 per cent annual improvement in productivity may not be good enough anymore; you may need between 8 and 9 per cent.'[44] Participative management and employee empowerment, which was discussed in Chapter, are highly touted methods for meeting this productivity challenge. Interestingly, employees also seem to desire or recognize the need for participative management. A survey of 2,408 employees, for example, revealed that almost 66 per cent desired more influence or decision-making power in their jobs.[45]

Confusion exists about the exact meaning of participative management (PM). One management expert clarified this situation by defining participative management as the process whereby employees play a direct role in setting goals, making decisions, solving problems, and making changes in the organization. Without question, participative management entails much more than simply asking employees for their ideas or opinions.

Advocates of PM claim employee participation increases employee satisfaction, commitment and performance. To gain a greater understanding of how and when participative management works, we begin by discussing a model of participative management.

Participative management
involving employees in various forms of decision-making

A Model of Participative Management

Consistent with both Maslow's need theory and the job characteristics model of job design (see Chapter 7), participative management is predicted to increase motivation because it helps employees fulfil three basic needs: autonomy, meaningful work, and interpersonal contact. Satisfaction of these needs enhances feelings of acceptance and commitment, security, challenge, and satisfaction. In turn, these positive feelings are purported to lead to increased innovation and performance.[46]

Participative management does not work in all situations. Three factors influence the effectiveness of PM: the design of work, the level of trust between management and employees, and the employees' competence and readiness to participate. With respect to the design of work, individual participation is counter-productive when employees are highly dependent on each other, as on an assembly line. The problem with individual participation in this case is that employees generally do not have a broad understanding of the entire production process. Also, participative management is less likely to succeed when employees mistrust management. Finally, PM is more effective when employees are competent, prepared and interested in participating.[47]

Research and Practical Suggestions

Participative management can significantly increase employee job involvement, organizational commitment, creativity, and perceptions of procedural justice and personal control.[48] Two meta-analyses provide additional support for the value of participative management. Results from a meta-analysis involving 27 studies and 6,732 individuals revealed that employee participation in the performance appraisal process was positively related to an employee's satisfaction with his or her performance review, perceived value of the appraisal, motivation to improve performance following a performance review, and perceived fairness of the appraisal process.[49] A second meta-analysis of 86 studies involving 18,872 people further demonstrated that participation had a small but significant effect on job performance and a moderate link with job satisfaction.[50] This latter finding questions the widespread conclusion that participative management should be used to increase employee performance.

So what is a manager to do? We believe that PM is not a quick-fix solution for low productivity and motivation, as some enthusiastic supporters claim. Nonetheless, because participative management is effective in certain situations, managers can increase their chances of obtaining positive results by using, once again, a contingency approach.[51] For example, the effectiveness of participation depends on the type of interactions between managers and employees as they jointly solve problems. Effective participation requires a constructive interaction that fosters co-operation and respect, as opposed to competition and defensiveness.[52] Managers are advised not to use participative programmes when they are having destructive interactions with their employees.

Experiences of companies implementing participative management programmes suggest three additional practical recommendations. First, supervisors and middle managers tend to resist participative management because it reduces their power and authority. It is important to gain the support and commitment of employees who have managerial responsibility. Second, a longitudinal study of *Fortune* 1,000 firms in 1987, 1990 and 1993 indicated that employee involvement was more effective when it was implemented as part of a broader total quality management programme.[53] This study suggests that organizations should use participative management and employee involvement as vehicles to help them meet their strategic and operational goals as opposed to using these techniques as ends in themselves. Third, the process of implementing participative management must be monitored and managed by top management.[54]

When to Have Groups Participate in Decision-Making: The Vroom/Yetton/Jago Model

Victor Vroom and Philip Yetton developed a model in 1973 to help managers determine the degree of group involvement in the decision-making process. It was later expanded by Vroom and Arthur Jago.[55] The model is prescriptive in that it specifies decision-making styles that should be effective in different situations.

Vroom and Jago's model is represented as a decision tree. The manager's task is to move from left to right along the various branches of the tree. A specific decision-making style is prescribed at the end point of each branch. Before we apply the model, however, it is necessary to consider the different decision styles, from which managers ultimately choose, and an approach for diagnosing the problem situation.

Table 14–4

Management Decision Styles

AI	You solve the problem or make the decision yourself, using information available to you at that time.
AII	You obtain the necessary information from your subordinate(s), then decide on the solution to the problem yourself. You may or may not tell your subordinates what the problem is in getting the information from them. The role played by your subordinates in making the decision is clearly one of providing the necessary information to you rather than generating or evaluating solutions.
CI	You share the problem with relevant subordinates individually, getting their ideas and suggestions without bringing them together as a group. Then you make the decision that may or may not reflect your subordinates' influence.
CII	You share the problem with your subordinates as a group, collectively obtaining their ideas and suggestions. Then you make the decision that may or may not reflect your subordinates' influence.
GII	You share a problem with your subordinates as a group. Together you generate and evaluate alternatives and attempt to reach agreement (consensus) on a solution. Your role is much like that of a chairman. You do not try to influence the group to adopt 'your' solution, and you are willing to accept and implement any solution that has the support of the entire group.

SOURCE: 'A New Look at Managerial Decision Making' by V H Vroom. Reprinted from *Organizational Dynamics*, Spring 1973, p 67, © 1973 American Management Association International. Reprinted by permission of American Management Association International, New York, NY. All rights reserved. http://www.amanet.org.

Five Decision-Making Styles

Vroom and Yetton identified five distinct styles for making decisions. In Table 14–4, each style is represented by a letter. The letter indicates the basic thrust of the style. For example, A stands for *autocratic*, C for *consultative*, and G for *group*. There are several important issues to consider as one moves from an AI style to a GII style.

▼ The problem or decision is discussed with more people.

▼ Group involvement moves from merely providing data to recommending solutions.

▼ Group 'ownership' and commitment to the solution increases.

▼ As group commitment increases, so too does the time needed to arrive at a decision.

Style choice depends on the type of problem situation.

Matching the Situation to a Style

Vroom and Jago developed eight problem attributes that managers can use to diagnose a situation. They are shown at the top of the decision tree presented in Figure 14–5 and are expressed as questions. Answers to these questions lead managers along different branches, pointing the way to potentially effective decision-making styles.

Figure 14–5 *Vroom and Jago's Decision-Making Model*

QR	Quality Requirement	How important is the technical quality of this decision?
CR	Commitment Requirement	How important is subordinate commitment to the decision?
LI	Leader's Information	Do you have sufficient information to make a high-quality decision?
ST	Problem Structure	Is the problem well structured?
CP	Commitment Probability	If you were to make the decision by yourself, is it reasonably certain that your subordinate(s) would be committed to the decision?
GC	Goal Congruence	Do subordinates share the organizational goals to be attained in solving this problem?
CO	Subordinate Conflict	Is conflict among subordinates over preferred solutions likely?
SI	Subordinate Information	Do subordinates have sufficient information to make a high-quality decision?

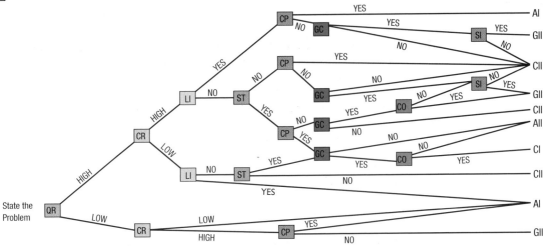

SOURCE: Reprinted from *The New Leadership: Managing Participation in Organizations* by Victor H Vroom and Arthur G Jago 1988, Englewood Cliffs, NJ: Prentice-Hall. © 1987 by V H Vroom and A G Jago. Used with permission of the authors.

Applying the Model

Because Vroom and Jago developed four decision trees, the first step is to choose one of the trees. Each tree represents a generic type of problem that managers frequently encounter. They are: an individual-level problem with time constraints; an individual-level problem in which the manager wants to develop an employee's decision-making abilities; a group-level problem in which the manager wants to develop employees' decision-making abilities; and a time-driven group problem.[56] Figure 14–5 illustrates this last option.

To use the model in Figure 14–5, start at the left and move toward the right by asking yourself the questions associated with each decision point encountered as represented by a box in the Figure. A decision-making style is prescribed at the end of each branch.

Let us pass a simple example through 'the tree' of Figure 14–5. Suppose you have to determine the work schedule for a group of part-time workers who report to you. The first question is 'How important is the technical quality of this decision?' It seems rather low. This leads us to the second question: 'How important is subordinate commitment to the decision?' Assuming acceptance is important, this takes us along the branch leading to the question about commitment probability (CP). If you were to make the decision by yourself, is it reasonably certain that your subordinates would be committed to the decision? A 'yes' answer suggests you should use an AI decision-making style (see Table 14–4) whereas a 'no' suggests a GII style. The Group Exercise at the end of this chapter provides you with an opportunity to apply this model. You will receive feedback on the accuracy of your analysis.

Research Insights and Managerial Implications

Very little research has tested the predictive accuracy of this model. Nonetheless, a study containing three different samples of managers supported the Vroom–Jago decision-making model. Decisions were more effective when managers used decision-making styles consistent with the model.[57] Managers are advised, therefore, to use different decision-making styles for different situations.

Also, the model can help managers to determine when, and to what extent, they should involve employees in decision-making. By simply being aware of the eight diagnostic questions, managers can enhance their ability to structure ambiguous problems. This should ultimately enhance the quality of managerial decisions.

Group Problem-Solving Techniques

Consensus
presenting opinions and gaining agreement to support a decision

Using groups to make decisions generally requires that they reach a consensus. According to a decision-making expert, a **consensus** 'is reached when all members can say they either agree with the decision or have had their "day in court" and were unable to convince the others of their viewpoint. In the final analysis, everyone agrees to support the outcome.'[58] This definition indicates that consensus does not require unanimous agreement because group members may still disagree with the final decision but are willing to work toward its success.

Groups can come across obstacles as they try to arrive at a consensus decision. For example, groups may not generate all the relevant alternatives to a problem because an individual dominates or intimidates other group members. This is can be either overt or subtle, or indeed both. For instance, group members who possess power and authority, such as a CEO, can be intimidating, regardless of interpersonal style, simply by being present in the room. Moreover, shyness inhibits the generation of alternatives. Shy or socially anxious individuals may withhold their input for fear of embarrassment or lack of confidence.[59] Satisficing (or sufficing) is another hurdle to effective group decision-making and is due to a group having limited time or information, or an inability to handle large amounts of information.[60] A management expert offered the following advice for successfully achieving consensus: groups should use active listening skills, involve as many members as possible, seek out the reasons behind arguments, and dig for the facts. At the same time, groups should not 'horse trade' (I'll support you on this decision because you supported me on the last one), vote or agree just to avoid upsetting the process.[61] Voting is not encouraged because it can split the group into winners and losers.

Decision-making experts have developed three group problem-solving techniques–brainstorming, the nominal group technique, and the Delphi technique– to reduce the above obstacles. Knowledge of these techniques can help current and future managers to use group-aided decision-making more effectively. Further, the advent of computer-aided decision-making enables managers to use these techniques to solve complex problems with large groups of people.

Brainstorming

Brainstorming was developed by A F Osborn, an advertising executive, to increase creativity.[62] **Brainstorming** is a technique used to help groups generate multiple ideas and alternatives for solving problems. It is effective because it helps reduce interference, during this early stage, from the critical and judgemental reactions of other group members.

Brainstorming
process to generate a quantity of ideas

When brainstorming, a group is convened, and the problem at hand is reviewed. Then individual members are asked to silently generate ideas, or alternatives, for solving the problem. Silent idea generation is recommended in preference to having group members randomly shout out their ideas because it leads to a greater number of unique ideas. Next, these ideas are solicited and written on a blackboard or flip chart. A recent study suggests that managers or team leaders may prefer to collect the brainstormed ideas anonymously. Results demonstrated that more controversial ideas and more useful ideas were generated by anonymous brainstorming groups.[63] Finally, a second session is used to check and evaluate the alternatives. Managers are advised to follow four rules for brainstorming:[64]

1 Stress quantity over quality. Managers should try to generate and write down as many ideas as possible. Encouraging quantity encourages people to think beyond their favourite (pet) ideas.

2 Freewheeling, as in 'thinking without the brakes on', should be encouraged; do not set limits. Group members are advised to offer any and all the ideas they have. The wilder and more outrageous, the better.

3 Suspend judgement. Don't criticize during the initial stage of idea generation. Phrases such as 'we've never done it that way,' 'it won't work,' 'it's too expensive,' and 'the boss will never agree,' should not be used.

4 Ignore seniority. People cannot think or suggest freely when they are trying to impress the boss or when office politics are involved. The facilitator of a brainstorming session should emphasize that everyone has the same rank. No one is given 'veto power' when brainstorming.

Brainstorming is an effective technique for generating new ideas and alternatives. It is not appropriate for evaluating alternatives or selecting solutions.

The Nominal Group Technique

The **nominal group technique** (NGT) helps groups not only generate ideas but also to evaluate and select solutions. NGT is a structured group meeting that adheres to the following format.[65]

Nominal group technique
process to generate ideas and evaluate solutions

A group is convened to discuss a particular problem or issue. After the problem is understood, individuals silently generate ideas in writing. Each individual, in turn, then offers one idea from his or her list. Ideas are recorded on a blackboard or flip chart; they are not discussed at this stage of the process. Once all ideas are elicited, the group discusses them. Anyone may criticize or defend any item. During this step, clarification is provided as well as general agreement or disagreement with the idea. The '30-second soap box' technique, which entails giving each participant a maximum of 30 seconds to argue for or against any of the ideas under consideration, can be used to facilitate this discussion.

Finally, group members vote anonymously for their top choices with weighted votes (e.g., 1st choice = 3 points; 2nd choice = 2 points; 3rd choice = 1 point). The group leader then adds the votes to determine the group's choice. Prior to making a final decision, the group may decide to discuss the top ranked items and conduct a second round of voting.

The nominal group technique reduces the obstacles to group decision-making by: separating brainstorming from evaluation; promoting balanced participation between group members; and incorporating mathematical voting techniques in order to reach consensus. NGT has been used successfully in many different decision-making situations.

The Delphi Technique

This problem-solving method was originally developed by the Rand Corporation for technological forecasting.[66] Now it is used as a multipurpose planning tool. The **Delphi technique** is a group process that, anonymously, generates ideas or judgements from physically dispersed experts. Unlike the NGT, experts' ideas are obtained from questionnaires or via the internet rather than by face-to-face group discussion.

Delphi technique
group process that anonymously generates ideas from physically dipersed experts

A manager begins the Delphi process by identifying the issue or issues to be investigated. For example, a manager might want to inquire about customer demand, customers' future preferences or the effect of locating a plant in a certain region of the country. Next, participants are identified and a questionnaire is developed. The questionnaire is sent to participants and returned to the manager. In today's computer-networked environments, this often means that the questionnaires are emailed to participants. The manager then summarizes the responses and sends feedback to the participants. At this stage, participants are asked to:

1 review the feedback
2 prioritize the issues being considered
3 return the survey within a specified time period.

This cycle repeats until the manager obtains the necessary information.

The Delphi technique is useful in instances when: face-to-face discussions are impractical; disagreements and conflict are likely to impair communication; certain individuals might severely dominate group discussion; or 'groupthink' is a probable outcome of the group process.[67]

Computer-Aided Decision-Making

The purpose of computer-aided decision-making is to reduce obstacles to consensus while collecting more information in a shorter period of time. There are two types of computer-aided decision-making systems: chauffeur-driven and group-driven.[68] Chauffeur-driven systems ask participants to answer predetermined questions on electronic keypads or dials. Live television audiences on quiz shows such as 'Who Wants to Be a Millionaire' are frequently polled for their answers using this system. The computer system tabulates participants' responses in a matter of seconds.

Group-driven meetings are conducted in special facilities equipped with individual computer workstations that are networked to each other. Instead of talking, participants type their input, ideas, comments, reactions, or evaluations on their keyboards. The input simultaneously appears on a large projector screen at the front of the room, thereby enabling all participants to see all the input. This computer-driven process reduces obstacles to consensus as the input is anonymous, everyone gets a chance to contribute, and no one can dominate the process. Research demonstrated that, for large groups of people, computer-aided decision-making produces a greater quality and quantity of ideas than either traditional brainstorming or the nominal group technique. There were no significant advantages to group-aided decision-making with smaller groups of four to six.[69] Moreover, a recent study demonstrated that computer-aided decision-making produced relatively more ideas as group size increased from 5 to 10 members. The positive benefits of larger groups, however, were more pronounced for heterogeneous as opposed to homogeneous groups.[70]

CREATIVITY

In the light of today's need for quick decisions, an organization's ability to stimulate the creativity and innovation of its employees is becoming increasingly important. Some organizations believe that creativity and innovation are the seeds of success.

An office is more than a place to house employees. These days, it's a place to seek the inspiration of an urban skyline or a peaceful sunset. Not to mention a place to shoot a few hoops, play some ping-pong, take a nap, sip an espresso—or build a little buzz. Today's small companies seek an environment that quickly communicates an image of success and creativity, one that wows potential clients, reassures investors, attracts hard-to-find recruits and helps employees forget how hard they're working. Achieving all that can mean going to extraordinary lengths. The firm of Thompson & Rose Architects pushes the process to the next level. In their architecture for the office of the future, everything is mutable. Nothing is fixed, not even the exterior skin of the office building, which changes with the weather—shading in summer, allowing more solar heating in the winter, permitting ambient light inside in all seasons.[71]

To gain further insight into managing the creative process, we begin by defining creativity and highlighting the stages underlying individual creativity. This section then presents a model of organizational creativity and innovation.

Definition and Stages

Although many definitions have been proposed, **creativity** is defined here as the process of using imagination and skill to develop a new or unique product, object, process or thought.[72] It can be as simple as locating a new place to hang your car keys to as complex as developing a pocket-size microcomputer. This definition highlights three broad types of creativity; creating something new (creation); combining or synthesizing things (synthesis); and improving or changing things (modification).

Creativity
process of developing something new or unique

Early approaches to explaining creativity were based on differences between the left and right hemispheres of the brain. Researchers thought the right-hand-side of the brain was responsible for creativity. More recently, however, researchers have questioned this explanation.

'The left brain/right brain dichotomy is simplified and misleading,' says Dr John C Mazziotta, a researcher at the University of California at Los Angeles School of Medicine. What scientists have found instead is that creativity is a feat of mental gymnastics engaging the conscious and subconscious parts of the brain. It draws on everything from knowledge, logic, imagination, and intuition to the ability to see connections and distinctions between ideas and things.[73]

Let us now examine the stages underlying the creativity process.

Researchers are not absolutely certain how creativity takes place. None-the-less, we do know that creativity involves 'making remote associations' between unconnected events, ideas, physical objects or information stored in memory (recall our discussion in Chapter 6). Consider how remote associations led to a creative idea that ultimately increased revenue for Japan Railways (JR) East, the largest rail carrier in the world.

While JR East was building a new bullet-train line, water began to cause problems in the tunnel being dug through Mount Tanigawa. As engineers drew up plans to drain it away, some of the workers had found a use for the water—they were drinking it. A maintenance worker, whose job was to check the safety of the tunneling equipment, thought it tasted so good that he proposed that JR East should bottle and market it as premium mineral water. This past year, 'Oshimizu' water generated some $60 million of sales for JR East.[74]

The maintenance worker obviously associated the tunnel water with bottled water, and this led to the idea of marketing the water as a commercial product. Figure 14–6 depicts five stages underlying the creative process.[75]

Figure 14–6 *Stages of the Creative Process*

The *preparation* stage reflects the notion that creativity starts from a base of knowledge. Experts suggest that creativity involves a convergence between tacit or implied knowledge and explicit knowledge. Notice how these two forms of knowledge converged to help create a new product at Matsushita Electric (see the next International OB).

International OB

www.matsushita-europe.com

Matsushita Electric Creates Breadmaker by Combining Tacit and Explicit Knowledge

In Japan, Matsushita Electric used to be known as *maneshita*, which means 'copycat.' Big and successful but not an innovator. That changed dramatically with the introduction of the Home Bakery, the first automatic breadmaker. A software engineer, a woman named Tanaka, recognized that with Westernization, the time had come for a breadmaker in Japan. But she knew almost nothing about baking. So she apprenticed herself to a master baker. He had all the knowledge at his fingertips, but it was very hard for him to verbalize. After watching him for two or three weeks, she went back to Matsushita to write up a set of specifications for the machine, translating his tacit knowledge into something explicit.

They made a prototype, but the bread tasted terrible. So Tanaka-san brought a group of her peers to observe the baker again. Finally, they realized that what the machine lacked was the twisting motion the baker used when kneading his dough. Incorporating that understanding enabled them to develop a hugely successful product.

The breadmaker changed the corporate culture at Matsushita. People in other divisions said, 'Why can't we do that?'

During the *concentration* stage, an individual focuses on the problem at hand. Interestingly, Japanese companies are noted for encouraging this stage as part of a quality improvement process—more so than Western companies. For example, the average number of suggestions per employee for improving quality and productivity is significantly lower in the typical western company than in comparable Japanese firms.[76]

Incubation is done unconsciously. During this stage, people engage in daily activities while their minds simultaneously mull over information and make remote associations. These associations, ultimately, are generated in the *illumination* stage. Finally, *verification* entails going through the entire process to verify, modify or try out the new idea.

Let us examine the stages of creativity to determine why Japanese organizations propose and implement more ideas than Western companies. To address this issue, a creativity expert visited and extensively interviewed employees from five major Japanese companies. He observed that Japanese firms have created a management infrastructure that encourages and reinforces creativity. People were taught to identify problems (discontents) on their first day of employment. In turn, these discontents were referred to as 'golden eggs' to reinforce the notion that it is good to identify problems.

These organizations also promoted the stages of incubation, illumination and verification through teamwork and incentives. For example, some companies posted the golden eggs on large wall posters in the work area; employees were then encouraged to interact with each other to execute the final three stages of the creative process. Employees eventually received monetary awards for any suggestions that passed all five phases of this process.[77] This research underscores the conclusion that creativity can be enhanced by effectively managing the creativity process. Hallmark cards does a good job of managing the creativity process:

It takes 740 creative people to produce 18,000 new Hallmark greeting cards each year. To manage that creative energy, CEO Irv Hockaday says, 'We have the largest creative staff in the world. If you mismanage, it's like a sack full of cats. You have to strike a balance between defining for them generally what you want and then giving them a lot of running room to try ways to respond to it. You don't overmanage, but you anchor them in well-articulated consumer needs. Then allow them exposure to all kinds of trends going on. We encourage them to travel and we support their traveling. They follow fashion trends, go to museums, look at what the automotive industry is doing in terms of design and colour pallets. We have a wonderful pastoral environment, a retreat where they can go and reflect.'[78]

A Model of Organizational Creativity and Innovation

Organizational creativity and innovation are relatively unexplored topics within the field of OB despite their importance for organizational success. Rather than focus on group and organizational creativity, researchers had previously examined the predictors of individual creativity. This final section examines a process model for understanding organizational creativity. Knowledge of its linkages can help you to facilitate and contribute to organizational creativity.

Figure 14–7 illustrates the process underlying organizational creativity and innovation. It shows that this creativity is directly influenced by organizational characteristics and the amount of creative behaviour that occurs within work groups. In turn, a group's creative behaviour is influenced both by the group's characteristics and the individuals' creative behaviour. This individual creative behaviour is, in turn, directly affected by a variety of individual characteristics. The double-headed arrows between individual and group characteristics and between group and organizational characteristics indicate that these all influence each other. Let us now consider the model's major components.

Individual Characteristics[79]

Creative people seem to 'march to the beat of a different drummer' by operating differently to others. They are highly motivated individuals who spend considerable time developing both tacit (implied) and explicit knowledge of their field of interest or occupation. But contrary to stereotypes, creative people are not necessarily geniuses or studious introverts. In addition, they are not *adaptors*. 'Adaptors are those who . . . prefer to resolve difficulties or make decisions in such a way as to have the least impact upon the assumptions, procedures, and values of the organization . . . .'[80] In contrast, creative individuals are dissatisfied with the status quo. They look for new and exciting solutions to problems. Because of this, creative organizational members can be perceived as disruptive and hard to get along with. Further, research indicates that male and female managers do not differ in levels of creativity. There are, however, a host of personality characteristics that are positively associated with creativity. These characteristics include, but are not limited to, those shown in Figure 14–7.

Figure 14–7

*A Model of
Organizational
Creativity and
Innovation*

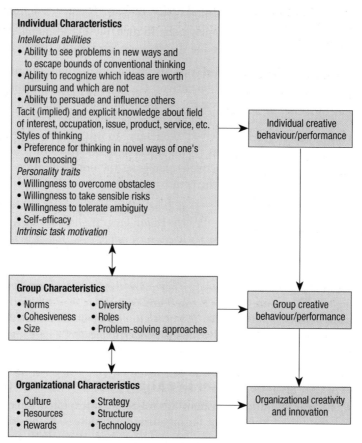

SOURCE: Based on discussion in R J Sternberg and R I Lubart, 'Investing in Creativity', American Psychologist, July 1996, pp 677–88; and R W Woodman, J E Sawyer and R W Griffin, 'Toward a Theory of Organizational Creativity', Academy of Management Review, April 1993.

The Post-it Notes story represents a good illustration of how the individual characteristics shown in Figure 14–7 promote creativity. Post-it Notes are a $200 million-a-year product for 3M Corporation.

The idea originated with Art Fry, a 3M employee who used bits of paper to mark hymns when he sat in his church choir. These markers kept falling out of the hymn books. He decided that he needed an adhesive-backed paper that would stick as long as necessary but could be removed easily. He soon found what he wanted in the 3M laboratory, and the Post-it Note was born. Fry saw the market potential of his invention, but others did not. Market-survey results were negative; major office-supply distributors were skeptical. So he began giving samples to 3M executives and their secretaries. Once they actually used the little pieces of adhesive paper, they were hooked. Having sold 3M on the project, Fry used the same approach with other executives throughout the United States.[81]

Notice how Fry had to influence others to try out his idea. Figure 14–7 shows that creative people have the ability to persuade and influence others.

Group Characteristics

Figure 14–7 also lists six characteristics that influence the level of creativity exhibited by a work group. In general, group creativity is fuelled by a cohesive environment that supports open interaction, diverse viewpoints and playful surroundings.[82] Kodak, for example, created a 'humour room' where employees can relax and have creative brainstorming sessions. The room contains joke books, videotapes of comedians, stress-reducing toys, and software for creative decision-making.[83] Structured problem-solving procedures, such as those previously discussed and supportive supervision, also enhance creativity.[84]

Organizational Characteristics

Research and corporate examples clearly support the importance of organizational characteristics in generating organizational creativity. Organizations such as Virgin, 3M, Microsoft, The Body Shop, and DuPont are all known as innovative companies that encourage creativity via the organizational characteristics shown in Figure 14–7. DuPont, for example, created the Center for Creativity and Innovation in 1991. Its mission is to encourage creativity throughout the organization.

Although the center is staffed by only three full-time employees, it has the support of 10 facilitators—creativity-training 'volunteers' who hold full-time DuPont jobs outside the center. In this way, DuPont conducts creativity training in-house. This has two important advantages: first, the company has fewer security concerns; and second, training costs are lower.

Top management support for the center is visible and continuous. A senior manager sponsors each creative problem-solving workshop and attends as a full participant, not just an observer. The company's support for creativity training is expressed by Edgar Woolard, chairman: 'We intend to provide hero status to those who show us how to get products to the marketplace more promptly and more creatively.'[85]

This example illustrates the point that organizational creativity requires resources, commitment and a reinforcing organizational culture. Table 14–5 presents a number of suggestions that may be used to help create this culture.

Develop an environment that supports creative behavior.
Try to avoid using an autocratic style of leadership.
Encourage employees to be more open to new ideas and experiences.
Keep in mind that people use different strategies, like walking around or listening to music, to foster their creativity.
Provide employees with stimulating work that creates a sense of personal growth.
Allow employees to have fun and play around.
Encourage an open environment that is free from defensive behavior.
Treat errors and mistakes as opportunities for learning.
Let employees occasionally try out their pet ideas. Provide a margin of error.
Avoid using a negative mind-set when an employee approaches you with a new idea.
Reward creative behavior.

Table 14–5

Suggestions for Improving Employee Creativity

SOURCE: Adapted from discussion in E Raudsepp, '101 Ways to Spark Your Employees' Creative Potential', *Office Administration and Automation*, September 1985, pp 38, 39–43, 56.

Summary of Key Concepts

1 Compare and contrast the rational model of decision-making, Simon's normative model, and the garbage can model.

The rational decision-making model consists of identifying the problem, generating alternative solutions, evaluating and selecting a solution, and implementing and evaluating the solution. Research indicates that decision makers do not follow the series of steps outlined in the rational model.

Simon's normative model is guided by a decision maker's bounded rationality. Bounded rationality means that decision makers are bounded or restricted by a variety of constraints when making decisions. The normative model suggests that decision-making is characterized by (a) limited information processing, (b) the use of judgemental heuristics, and (c) satisficing.

The 'garbage can' model of decision-making assumes that decision-making does not follow an orderly series of steps. In this process, decisions result from the interaction among four independent streams of events: problems, solutions, participants and choice opportunities.

2 Discuss the contingency relationships that influence the three primary strategies used to select solutions.

Decision makers use either an aided-analytic, unaided-analytic, or non-analytic strategy when selecting a solution. The choice of a strategy depends on the characteristics of the decision task and the characteristics of the decision maker. In general, the greater the demands and constraints faced by a decision maker, the higher the probability that an aided-analytic approach will be used. Aided-analytic strategies are more likely to be used by competent and motivated individuals. Ultimately, decision makers must compromise between their desire to make correct decisions and the amount of time and effort they can allow for the decision-making process.

3 Explain the model of decision-making styles.

The model of decision-making styles is based on the idea that styles vary along two different dimensions: value orientation and tolerance for ambiguity. When these two dimensions are combined, they form four styles of decision-making: directive, analytical, conceptual and behavioural. People with a directive style have a low tolerance for ambiguity and are oriented task itself and technical concerns. Analytics have a higher tolerance for ambiguity and are characterized by a tendency to overly analyse a situation. People with a conceptual style have a high threshold for ambiguity and tend to focus on the people or social aspects of a work situation. This behavioural style is the most people oriented of the four styles.

4 Describe the model of escalation of commitment.

Escalation of commitment refers to the tendency to stick to an ineffective course of action despite it being unlikely that a bad situation can be reversed. Psychological and social determinants, organizational determinants, project characteristics, and contextual determinants cause managers to exhibit this decision-making error.

5 Summarize the advantages and disadvantages of involving groups in the decision-making process.

Although research shows that groups typically outperform the average individual, there are five important issues to consider when using groups to make decisions: (a) groups are less efficient than individuals (b) a group's overconfidence can fuel groupthink (c) decision quality is negatively related to group size (d) groups are more accurate when they know a great deal about the issues at hand and when the leader possesses the ability to effectively evaluate the group members' opinions and judgements (e) the composition of a group affects its decision-making processes and performance. In the final analysis, managers are encouraged to use a contingency approach when determining whether to include others in the decision-making process.

6 Explain how participative management affects performance.

Participative management reflects the extent to which employees participate in setting goals, making decisions, solving problems, and making changes in the organization. Participative management is expected to increase motivation because it helps employees fulfil three basic needs: (a) autonomy, (b) meaningful work and (c) interpersonal contact. Participative management does not work in all situations. The design of work and the level of trust between management and employees influence the effectiveness of participative management.

7 Review Vroom and Jago's decision-making model.

Vroom, Yetton and Jago developed a model to help managers determine the extent to which they should include groups in the decision-making process. Through the use of decision trees, the model identifies appropriate decision-making styles for various types of managerial problems. The styles range from autocratic to highly participative.

8 Contrast brainstorming, the nominal group technique, the Delphi technique, and computer-aided decision-making.

Group problem-solving techniques facilitate better decision-making within groups. Brainstorming is used to help groups generate multiple ideas and alternatives for solving problems. The nominal group technique assists groups both to generate ideas and to evaluate and select solutions. The Delphi technique is a group process that anonymously generates ideas or judgements from physically dispersed experts. The purpose of computer-aided decision-making is to reduce the obstacles to consensus, while collecting more information in a shorter period of time.

9 Describe the stages of the creative process.

Creativity is defined as the process of using imagination and skill to develop a new or unique product, object, process or thought. It is not adequately explained by differences between the left and right hemispheres of the brain. There are five stages of the creative process: preparation, concentration, incubation, illumination and verification.

10 Explain the model of organizational creativity and innovation.

Organizational creativity is directly influenced by organizational characteristics and the creative behaviour that occurs within work groups. In turn, a group's creative behaviour is influenced by group characteristics and the individual creative behaviour and performance of its members. Individual creativity is directly affected by a variety of individual characteristics. Finally, individual, group and organizational characteristics all influence each other within this process.

Discussion Questions

1 What role do emotions play when a making decision?

2 Do you think people are rational when they make decisions? Under what circumstances would an individual tend to follow a rational process?

3 Describe a situation in which you 'satisficed' when making a decision. Why did you do this instead of optimizing the decision?

4 Do you think the 'garbage can' model is a realistic representation of organizational decision-making? Explain your rationale.

5 Why would decision-making styles be a source of interpersonal conflict?

6 Describe a situation in which you exhibited escalation of commitment. Why did you escalate a losing situation?

7 Do you prefer to solve problems in groups or by yourself? Why?

8 Given the intuitive appeal of participative management, why do you think it fails as often as it succeeds? Explain.

9 Do you think you are creative? Why or why not?

10 What advice would you offer a manager who was attempting to improve the creativity of his or her employees? Explain.

Internet Exercise

There are countless brainstorming sessions conducted by individuals and groups within organizations on a daily basis. We do not expect this trend to stop. To help you successfully set up and participate in a brainstorming session, this chapter provided a set of guidelines for conducting a brainstorming session. We did not, however, discuss different techniques that can be used to enhance individual and group creativity while brainstorming. The purpose of this exercise is for you to learn two techniques that can be used to enhance creative idea generation and to complete two creativity puzzles.

Begin the exercise by going to the following Internet site: www.brainstorming.co.uk. Then select their home page. Once at the home page, click on the option for *training on creative techniques*. After a brief discussion about creativity, you will be given the option to learn more about a variety of different techniques that can be used to enhance creativity. Choose any two techniques and then answer questions 1 and 2 below.

http://www.brainstorming.co.uk

Now return to the home page, and select the option for creativity puzzles. Follow the instructions and attempt to complete two puzzles. Don't peek at the answers until you have tried to finish the activity. Based on your experience with these creativity puzzles, answer questions 3, 4, and 5.

Questions

1 How might you use these techniques in a study group project?

2 Should different techniques be used in different situations? Explain.

3 To what extent were the puzzles hard to complete?

4 Why do these puzzles help people to think 'outside the box', i.e., creatively?

5 How might these puzzles be used during a brainstorming session?

Personal Awareness and Growth Exercise
What Is Your Decision-Making Style?

Objectives

1 To assess your decision-making style.

2 To consider the managerial implications of your decision-making style.

Introduction

Earlier in the chapter we discussed a model of decision-making styles that is based on the idea that styles vary along the dimensions of an individual's value orientation and tolerance for ambiguity. In turn, these dimensions combine to form four styles of decision-making (see Figures 14–3): directive, analytical, conceptual and behavioural. Alan Rowe, an OB researcher, developed an instrument called the Decision Style Inventory to measure these four styles. This exercise provides the opportunity for you to assess and interpret your decision-making style using this measurement device.

Instructions

The Decision Style Inventory consists of 20 questions, each with four responses.[88] You must consider each possible response to a question and then rank them according to how much you prefer each response. There are no right or wrong answers, so respond with what first comes to mind. Although many of the questions are based on how individuals make decisions at work, feel free to use your student role as a frame of reference to answer the questions. For each question, you have four responses, and each should be ranked either 1, 2, 4 or 8; with 8 being for the response that is most like you, 4 for the one moderately like you, 2 for slightly like you, and 1 for least like you. For instance, a question could be answered as follows: [8], [4], [2], [1]. Notice that each number was used only once to answer a question. Do not repeat any number when answering a given question. These numbers should be written in the blank column alongside each response.

Once all of the responses for the 20 questions have been ranked, total the scores in each of the four columns. The total score for column one represents your score for the directive style, column two your analytical style, column three your conceptual style, and column four your behavioural style.

Questions for Discussion

1 In terms of your decision-making profile, which of the four styles represents your decision-making style best (i.e., has the highest score)? Which is the least reflective of your style (has the lowest score)?

2 Do you agree with this assessment? Explain.

3 How do your scores compare with the following norms: directive (75), analytical (90), conceptual (80), and behavioural (55)? What do the differences between your scores and the survey norms suggest about your decision-making style?

4 What are the advantages and disadvantages of your decision-making profile?

5 Which of the other decision-making styles is most inconsistent with your style? How would this difference affect your ability to work with someone who has this style?

1 My prime objective in life is to:	have a position with status	be the best in whatever I do	be recognized for my work	feel secure in my job
2 I enjoy work that:	is clear and well defined	is varied and challenging	lets me act independently	involves people
3 I expect people to be:	productive	capable	committed	responsive
4 My work lets me:	get things done	find workable approaches	apply new ideas	be truly satisfied
5 I communicate best by:	talking with others	putting things in writing	being open with others	having a group meeting
6 My planning focuses on:	current problems	how best to meet goals	future opportunities	needs of people in the organization
7 I prefer to solve problems by:	applying rules	using careful analysis	being creative	relying on my feelings
8 I prefer information that is:	simple and direct	complete	broad and informative	easily understood
9 When I'm not sure what to do, I:	rely on my intuition	search for alternatives	try to find a compromise	avoid making a decision
10 Whenever possible, I avoid:	long debates	incomplete work	technical problems	conflict with others
11 I am really good at:	remembering details	finding answers	seeing many options	working with people
12 When time is important, I:	decide and act quickly	apply proven approaches	look for what will work	refuse to be pressurised
13 In social settings, I:	speak to many people	observe what others are doing	contribute to the conversation	want to be part of the discussion
14 I always remember:	people's names	places I have been	people's faces	people's personalities

15 I prefer jobs where I:	receive high rewards		have challenging assignments		can reach my personal goals		am accepted by the group	
16 I work best with people who are:	energetic and ambitious		very competent		open minded		polite and understanding	
17 When I am under stress, I:	speak quickly		try to concentrate on the problem		become frustrated		worry about what I should do	
18 Others consider me:	aggressive		disciplined		imaginative		supportive	
19 My decisions are generally:	realistic and direct		systematic and logical		broad and flexible		sensitive to the other's needs	
20 I dislike:	losing control		boring work		following rules		being rejected	
Total score								

SOURCE: © Alan J Rowe, Professor Emeritus. Revised 12/18/98. Reprinted by permission.

Group Exercise
Applying the Vroom/Yetton/Jago Decision-Making Model

Introduction

Vroom and Jago extended an earlier model, by Vroom and Yetton, to help managers determine the extent to which they should include groups in the decision-making process. To enhance your understanding of this model, we would like you to use it to analyze a brief case. You will be asked to read the case and use the information to determine an appropriate decision-making style. This will enable you to compare your solution with that recommended by Vroom and Jago. Their analysis is presented in End Note number 89 and you will be instructed when to examine it for feedback.

Instructions

Your instructor will divide the class into groups of four to six. Once the group is assembled, each member should read the case presented. It depicts a situation faced by the manufacturing manager of an electronics plant.[90] The group should then use Vroom and Jago's model (refer to Figure 14–5 and Table 14–4) to arrive at a solution. At this point, it might be helpful for the group to reread the material that explains how to apply the model. Keep in mind that you move toward a solution by asking yourself the questions (at the top of Figure 14–4) associated with each relevant decision point. After the group completes its analysis, compare your solution with the one offered by Vroom and Jago.

Leadership Case

You are a manufacturing manager in a large electronics plant. The company's management has recently installed new machines and put in a simplified work system but, to the surprise of everyone, yourself included, the expected increase in productivity has not been realized. In fact, production has begun to drop, quality has fallen off, and the number of employee separations has risen.

You do not believe that there is anything wrong with the machines. You have reports from other companies that are using them and they confirm this opinion. You have also had representatives from the firm that built the machines go over them, and they report that they are operating at peak efficiency.

You suspect that some parts of the new work system may be responsible for the change but this view is not widely shared among your immediate subordinates, who are four first-line supervisors, each in charge of a section, and your supply manager. The drop in production has been variously attributed to poor training of the operators, lack of an adequate system of financial incentives, and poor morale. Clearly, this is an issue about which there is considerable depth of feeling within individuals and potential disagreement among your subordinates.

This morning you received a phone call from your division manager. He had just received your production figures for the last six months and was calling to express his concern. He indicated that the problem was yours to solve in any way that you think best, but that he would like to know within a week what steps you plan to take.

You share your division manager's concern with the falling productivity and know that your staff are also concerned. The problem is to decide what steps to take to rectify the situation.

Questions for Discussion

1 What decision-making style from Table 14–4 do you recommend?

2 Did you arrive at the same solution as Vroom and Jago (their analysis is presented in End Note number 89)? If not, what do you think caused the difference?

3 Based on this experience, what problems would a manager encounter in trying to apply this model?

Part Four

Organizational Processes

Chapter Fifteen

Influence, Power and Politics

Learning Objectives

When you finish studying the material in this chapter, you should be able to:

- Explain the concept of mutuality of interest.

- Name at least three 'soft' and two 'hard' influence tactics, and summarize the practical lessons from influence research.

- Identify and briefly describe French and Raven's five bases of power and discuss the responsible use of power.

- Define the term *empowerment* and discuss the realities of open-book management.

- Explain why delegation is the highest form of empowerment and discuss the connections between delegation, trust and personal initiative.

- Define *organizational politics* and explain what triggers it.

- Distinguish between favourable and unfavourable impression management tactics.

- Explain how to manage organizational politics.

Managers are opting for the hands-off approach

How would you feel if you only ever saw your boss once a week—or even once a month? Philip Dray, director of advanced services at Energis, the power, telecoms and data solutions group, spends as many as three days a week working from home and manages 50 employees scattered around the UK. ▶

He spends one day a week travelling to meet staff at one of the regional offices in Birmingham, Leeds or Manchester. A second day will be spent travelling to meet one of the company's big corporate customers such as Sainsbury's, Boots or the Exchange Insurance Group.

Mr Dray is typical of a growing band of senior managers and directors who prefer the light touch to that of barking orders and peering over people's shoulders to check they are getting on with the job. So how does he manage? By email, by phone, by video-conferencing?

'It comes down to management style,' says Mr Dray. 'You need trust in working with people. How do I know they are doing a good job? I ask our customers—there is no more effective way.'

Of course, Mr Dray has an endless stream of management information at his fingertips, and prefers hot-desking with a laptop computer and mobile phone to working in one location. Not having an office, he maintains, gives him a more hands-on feel for the way the business is running. He says: 'Having a desk or an office creates barriers between me and the people I'm working with. This is a fast-moving business and we've got to be fast, too.'

According to the Institute of Personnel and Development (IPD), one in 20 of us now works remotely. Increasing numbers of UK industry staff are becoming much more flexible in terms of when and where they work. But the area where remote working or teleworking is being championed is in the IT and telecoms sectors, where even the most senior managers keep their fingers on the pulse via technology such as high-speed data transmission and Wap phones—mobile platforms providing instant access to the Internet.

Dr Monica Seeley, of Imperial College Management School and the author of *Using the PC to Boost Executive Performance*, believes remote management is fast becoming the accepted norm. 'Senior managers are finding IT a huge benefit,' she says. 'They can exchange a lot of information electronically and send each other 'what if' plans. Face-to-face meetings can then become a lot more productive.'

David West, a programme director at Unisys, manages 125 staff yet has no permanent office and is rarely in the same place for longer than a day at a time. He calls himself a remote manager.

This is not because he is unapproachable or uncontactable—a diary packed with meetings and a mobile phone at his side are evidence to the contrary—it is because he manages virtual teams.

Software consultants could be working away from home for as much as 80 per cent of the time, working with clients on solutions to their business needs. Besides trust, Mr West has a sophisticated computer management system that he can access remotely by linking his laptop to the company intranet or by using his data-enabled home phone.

In Unisys, technical support or sales staff might work in virtual teams, exchanging information by email, downloading data via the company intranet and then coming together at one of the drop-in business centres the company is building at its regional offices. These are places where the atmosphere is relaxed and informal and where people can plug in their phones and laptops and discuss the next project.

Team members would set targets and short-term aims and, when a project is over, hold a debriefing session to evaluate their performance. Staff are encouraged to make use of an online Career Fitness Check, a self-evaluation of training needs and career development. Mr West makes a point of travelling to regional offices regularly to meet staff and find out face to face what their concerns are and to offer support and encouragement.

He argues that he would be a far more remote person in the organization if he stayed put behind a desk in a London head office, and says: 'Empowerment goes all the way up and all the way down. It's very rare to see a senior manager in our kind of organization flying a desk more than one day a week.'

Architectural consultancy DEGW is involved in designing workplaces to meet the needs of more flexible managers. Partner John Worthington says: 'People are moving away from the concept of

For discussion
How can 'remote managers' like Philip Dray and David West still excerpt power and reflect authority on their employees?

419

At the very heart of interpersonal dealings in today's work organizations is a constant struggle between individual and collective interests. For example, Björn wants a pay increase but his company doesn't make enough money to both grant increases and pay minimum shareholder dividends. Preoccupation with self-interest is understandable. After all, each of us was born, not as a co-operative member of an organization but as an individual with instincts for self-preservation. It took socialization in family, school, religious, sports, recreation and employment settings to introduce us to the notion of mutuality of interest. Basically, **mutuality of interest** involves win–win situations in which one's self-interest is served by co-operating actively and creatively with potential adversaries. A pair of organization development consultants offered the following managerial perspective of mutuality of interest.

Mutuality of interest
balancing individual and organizational interests through win-win co-operation

> *Nothing is more important than this sense of mutuality to the effectiveness and quality of an organization's products and services. Management must strive to stimulate a strong sense of shared ownership in every employee, because otherwise an organization cannot do its best in the long run. Employees who identify their own personal self-interest with the quality of their organization's output understand mutuality and strive to maintain it in their jobs and work relations.*[2]

Figure 15–1 graphically portrays the constant dilemma between employees' self-interest and the organization's need for mutuality of interest. It also shows the linkage between this chapter—influence, power and politics—and other key topics in this book. Managers need a complete tool kit of techniques to guide diverse individuals—who are often powerfully motivated to put their own self-interests first—to pursue common objectives. At stake in this tug-of-war between individual and collective interests is no less than the ultimate survival of the organization.

Figure 15–1
The Constant Tug-of-War between Self-Interest and Mutuality of Interest Requires Managerial Action

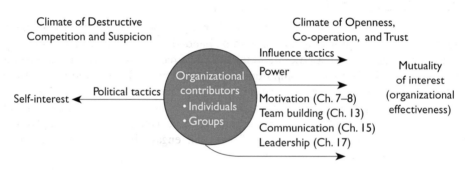

ORGANIZATIONAL INFLUENCE TACTICS: GETTING ONE'S WAY AT WORK

How do you get others to carry out your wishes? Do you simply tell them what to do? Or do you prefer a less direct approach, such as promising to return the favour? Whatever approach you use, the crux of the issue is *social influence*. A large measure of interpersonal interaction involves attempts to influence others, including parents, bosses, co-workers, spouses, teachers, friends and children. Even if managers do not expect to get dramatic results, they need to sharpen their influence skills. A good starting point is familiarity with the following research insights.

Nine Generic Influence Tactics

A particularly fruitful stream of research, initiated by David Kipnis and his colleagues in 1980, reveals how people influence each other in organizations. The Kipnis methodology involved asking employees how they managed to get their bosses, co-workers or subordinates to do what they wanted them to do.[3] Statistical refinements and replications by other researchers over a 13-year period eventually yielded nine influence tactics. The nine tactics, ranked in diminishing order of use in the workplace are as follows.

1   *Rational persuasion.* Trying to convince someone with reason, logic, or facts.

2   *Inspirational appeals.* Trying to build enthusiasm by appealing to others' emotions, ideals, or values.

3   *Consultation.* Getting others to participate in planning, making decisions, and changes.

4   *Ingratiation.* Getting someone in a good mood prior to making a request; being friendly, helpful and using praise or flattery.

5   *Personal appeals.* Referring to friendship and loyalty when making a request.

6   *Exchange.* Making express or implied promises and trading favours.

7   *Coalition tactics.* Getting others to support your effort to persuade someone.

8   *Pressure.* Demanding compliance or using intimidation or threats.

9   *Legitimating tactics.* Basing a request on one's authority or right, organizational rules or policies, or the express or implied support of superiors.[4]

These approaches can be considered generic influence tactics because they characterize social influence in all directions. Researchers have found this ranking to be fairly consistent regardless of whether the direction of influence is downward, upward or lateral.[5]

Some call the first five influence tactics—rational persuasion, inspirational appeals, consultation, ingratiation, and personal appeals—*soft* tactics because they are friendlier and not as coercive as the last four tactics. Exchange, coalition, pressure, and legitimating tactics are called *hard* tactics, therefore, because they involve more overt pressure.

Three Possible Influence Outcomes

Put yourself in this familiar situation. It's Wednesday and a big project you've been working on for your project team is due to be handed in on Friday. You're behind on the preparation of your computer graphics for your final report and presentation. You catch a friend who is great at computer graphics as they head out of the office at the end of the day. You try this *exchange tactic* to get your friend to help you out: 'I am way behind. I need your help. If you could come back in for two to three hours tonight and help me with these graphics, I'll complete those spreadsheets you've been complaining about.' According to researchers, your friend will engage in one of three possible responses to your use of influence tactic.

1   *Commitment.* Your friend enthusiastically agrees and will demonstrate initiative and persistence while completing the assignment.

2   *Compliance.* Your friend grudgingly complies and will need prodding to satisfy minimum requirements.

3   *Resistance.* Your friend will say no, make excuses, stall or put up an argument.[6]

The best outcome is commitment because the target person's intrinsic motivation will energize good performance. However, managers often have to settle for compliance in today's hectic workplace. Resistance means a failed influence attempt.

Practical Research Insights

Laboratory and field studies have taught us useful lessons about the relative effectiveness of influence tactics along with other instructive insights.

▼ **Commitment is more likely when people rely on consultation, strong rational persuasion, and inspirational appeals and *do not* rely on pressure and coalition tactics.[7] Interestingly, in one study, managers were not very effective at *downward* influence. They relied most heavily on inspiration (an effective tactic), ingratiation (a moderately effective tactic), and pressure (an ineffective tactic).[8]**

▼ A meta-analysis of 69 studies suggests ingratiation (making the boss feel good) can slightly improve your performance appraisal results and make your boss like you significantly more.[9]

▼ Commitment is more likely when the influence attempt involves something important and enjoyable and is based on a friendly relationship.[10]

▼ In a survey, 214 employed MBA students (55 per cent female) tended to perceive their superiors' 'soft' influence tactics as fair and 'hard' influence tactics as unfair. Unfair influence tactics were associated with greater resistance among employees.[11]

▼ Another study probed male–female differences in influencing work group members. Many studies have found women to be perceived as less competent and less influential in work groups than men. The researchers had male and female work group leaders engage in either task behaviour (demonstrating ability and task competence) or dominating behaviour (relying on threats). For both women and men, task behaviour was associated with perceived competence and effective influence. Dominating behaviour was not effective. The following conclusion by the researchers has important practical implications for all current and future managers who desire to influence others successfully: 'The display of task cues is an effective means to enhance one's status in groups and . . . the attempt to gain influence in task groups through dominance is an ineffective and poorly received strategy for both men and women.'[12]

▼ According to a recent study, a laugh can influence people more powerfully than speech, tapping into their subconscious and manipulating reactions. But although laughter is a strong persuasion tool, it is also uncontrolled, the survey found, suggesting that humans evolved the ability to laugh as a means of manipulating others but employ it unconsciously and instinctively. According to the researchers, 'we use laughter as a mechanism of social influence. We don't use it for the good of the social group. We use it for our own ends. It is one of the most powerful and least understood of all the social tools human beings possess.'[13]

▼ After reviewing relevant studies, a team of researchers concluded: 'Each tactic includes a broad variety of behaviour; when planning an influence attempt, it is important to consider not only what tactics to use but also what forms of each tactic are most appropriate for the situation.'[14]

▼ Interpersonal influence is bound by culture. The foregoing research evidence on influence tactics has a bias in favour of Europeans and North Americans. Much remains to be learned about how to influence others effectively (without unintended insult) in today's diverse workforce and cross-cultural economy.

How to Extend Your Influence by Forming Strategic Alliances

In their book, *Influence without Authority*, Allan R Cohen and David L Bradford extended the concept of corporate strategic alliances to interpersonal influence. Hardly a day goes by without another mention in the business press of a new strategic alliance between two global companies intent on staying competitive. These win–win relationships are based on complementary strengths. According to Cohen and Bradford, managers need to follow suit by forming some strategic alliances of their own with anyone who has a stake in their area. This is particularly true given today's rapid changes, cross-functional work teams, and diminished reliance on traditional authority structures.

While admitting the task is not an easy one, Cohen and Bradford recommend the following tips for dealing with potential allies.

1 *Mutual respect.* Assume they are competent and smart.

2 *Openness.* Talk straight to them. It isn't possible for any one person to know everything, so give them the information they need to know to help you better.

3 *Trust.* Assume that no one will take any action that is purposely intended to hurt another, so don't refrain from giving any information that the other could use, even if it doesn't help your immediate position.

4 *Mutual benefit.* Plan every strategy so that both parties win. If that doesn't happen over time, the alliance will break up. When dissolving a partnership becomes necessary as a last resort, try to do it in a clean way that minimizes residual anger. Some day, you may want a new alliance with that person.[15]

Certainly, these tactics involve taking some personal risks. But the effectiveness of interpersonal strategic alliances is anchored in the concept of reciprocity. '**Reciprocity** is the almost universal belief that people should be paid back for what they do—that one good (or bad) turn deserves another.'[16] In short, people tend to get what they give when attempting to influence others.

> **Reciprocity**
> *widespread belief that people should be given something in return for their positive or negative act*

By demonstrating the rich texture of social influence, the foregoing research evidence and practical advice whet our appetite for learning more about how today's managers can and do reconcile individual and organizational interests. Let us focus on social power.

SOCIAL POWER

The term *power* evokes mixed and often passionate reactions. Citing recent instances of government corruption and corporate misconduct, many observers view power as a sinister force. To these sceptics, Lord Acton's time-honoured statement that 'power corrupts and absolute power corrupts absolutely' is as true as ever. However, OB specialists remind us that, like it or not, power is a fact of life in modern organizations. One management writer looks at it in the following way.

> *Power must be used because managers must influence those they depend on. Power is crucial in the development of managers' self-confidence and willingness to support subordinates. From this perspective, power should be accepted as a natural part of any organization. Managers should recognize and develop their own power to co-ordinate and support the work of subordinates; it is powerlessness, not power, that undermines organizational effectiveness.*[17]

Thus, power is a necessary and generally positive force in organizations. As the term is used here, **social power** is defined as 'the ability to marshal the human, informational and material resources to get something done.'[18] Power is, however, a strong weapon, which can be used to get things done, as illustrated in the following example of pyramid sales.

> **Social power**
> *ability to get things done using human, informational and material resources*

> *In some form of Hollywood spectacle, Titan, a Hamburg-based company, tries to convince people to 'invest' 4,500 German marks. By recruiting three others to invest the same amount, you advance on the Titan 'ladder' and you are paid commission. All power lies in the hands of the fluent speaker on the podium, who uses all his ability to talk the audience into joining the system. According to one ex-distributor of Amway, a system equal to Titan, pyramid selling is based on pure indoctrination. Competition is stirred up through sophisticated systems of rewards and bonuses.*[19]

Dimensions of Power

While power may be an elusive concept to the casual observer, social scientists view power as having reasonably clear dimensions. Two dimensions of power that deserve our attention are (1) socialized versus personalized power and (2) the five bases of power.

Two Types of Power

Behavioural scientists such as David McClelland contend that one of the basic human needs is the need for power (referred to as 'n Pwr'). Because this need is learned and not innate, it has been studied extensively. Historically, the need for power was scored when subjects interpreted pictures, in Thematic Appreciation Tests (TAT), in terms of one person attempting to influence, convince, persuade or control another, as discussed in Chapter 7. More recently, however, researchers have drawn a distinction between **socialized power** and **personalized power**.

Socialized power
directed at helping others

> *There are two subscales or 'faces' in n Pwr. One face is termed 'socialized' (s Pwr) and is scored in the Thematic Apperception Test (TAT) as 'plans, self-doubts, mixed outcomes and concerns for others, . . .' while the second face is 'personalized' power (p Pwr), in which expressions of power for the sake of personal aggrandizement become paramount.*[20]

Personalized power
directed at helping oneself

This distinction between socialized and personalized power helps explain why power has a negative connotation for many people.[21] Managers and others who pursue personalized power for their own selfish ends give power a bad name. But a series of interviews with 25 American women elected to public office found a strong preference for socialized power. The following comments illustrate their desire to wield power effectively and ethically.

> ▼ 'Power in itself means nothing . . . .. I think power is the opportunity to really have an impact on your community.'
> ▼ 'My goal is to be a powerful advocate on the part of my constituents.'[22]

Five Bases of Power

A popular classification scheme for social power goes back 40 years to the work of John French and Bertram Raven. They proposed that power arises from five different bases: reward power, coercive power, legitimate power, expert power, and referent power.[23] Each involves a different approach to influencing others.

Reward power
obtaining compliance with promised or actual rewards

A manager has **reward power** to the extent that he or she obtains compliance by promising or granting rewards. Behaviour modification at work, for example, relies heavily on reward power.

Coercive power
obtaining compliance through threatened or actual punishment

Threats of punishment and actual punishment give an individual **coercive power**. A sales manager who threatens to fire any salesperson who uses a company car for family holidays is relying on coercive power.

Legitimate power
obtaining compliance through formal authority

Legitimate power is based on one's formal position or authority. Thus, individuals who obtain compliance primarily because of their formal authority to make decisions have legitimate power. Legitimate power may express itself in either a positive or negative manner. Positive legitimate power focuses constructively on job performance. Negative legitimate power tends to be threatening and demeaning to those under its influence, and is mainly used to inflate the ego of the person holding the power.

Expert power
obtaining compliance through one's knowledge or information

Valued knowledge or information gives an individual **expert power** over those who need such knowledge or information. The power of supervisors is enhanced because they know about work schedules and assignments before their employees do. Skilful use of expert power played a key role in the effectiveness of team leaders in a recent study of three teams of medics.[24] Knowledge *is* power in today's high-tech workplaces.

Referent power
obtaining compliance through charisma or personal attraction

Also called charisma, **referent power** comes into play when one's personality becomes the reason for compliance. Role models have referent power over those who identify closely with them.[25]

> *Shipley and Egan invested the relationship between brewers and their tenants in the UK. They concluded that brewers apply the wrong types of power in the wrong way and consequently these brewers generate too little co-operation and too much conflict.*

Most tenants are small independent business people contracted for a short period (three years). These short tenancy contracts give brewers substantial power to apply coercive power by threatening non-renewal. Conversely, tenants have little or no countervailing power. The results showed that tenants are not well motivated and it's concluded that this is because brewers use coercive power excessively and reward power insufficiently.[26]

To further your understanding of these five bases of power and to assess your self-perceived power, please take a moment to complete the questionnaire in the next OB Exercise. Think of your present job or your most recent job when responding to the various items. What is your power profile?

OB Exercise

What Is Your Self-Perceived Power?

Instructions

Score your various bases of power for your current (or former) job, using the following scale:

1 = Strongly disagree   2 = Disagree   3 = Slightly agree

4 = Agree   5 = Strongly agree

Reward Power Score =

1   I can reward individuals at lower levels.

2   My review actions affect the rewards gained at lower levels.

3   Based on my decisions, lower level personnel may receive a bonus.

Coercive Power Score =

1   I can punish employees at lower levels.

2   My work is a check on lower level employees.

3   My diligence reduces error.

Legitimate Power Score =

1   My position gives me a great deal of authority.

2   The decisions made at my level are of critical importance.

3   Employees look to me for guidance.

Expert Power Score =

1   I am an expert in this job.

2   My ability gives me an advantage in this job.

3   Given some time, I could improve the methods used on this job.

Referent Power Score =

1   I attempt to set a good example for other employees.

2   My personality allows me to work well in this job.

3   My fellow employees look to me as their informal leader.

Arbitrary norms for each of the five bases of power are:
3–6 = Weak power base;
7–11 = Moderate power base;
12–15 = Strong power base.

SOURCE: Adapted and excerpted in part from D L Dieterly and B Schneider, 'The Effect of Organizational Environment on Perceived Power and Climate: A Laboratory Study', *Organizational Behavior and Human Performance,* **June 1974, pp 316–37.**

Research Insights about Social Power

In one study, a sample of 94 male and 84 female non-managerial and professional employees completed TAT tests. The researchers found that the male and female employees had similar needs for power (n Pwr) and personalized power (p Pwr). But the women had a significantly higher need for socialized power (s Pwr) than did their male counterparts.[27] This bodes well for today's work organizations where women are playing an ever greater administrative role. Unfortunately, as women gain power in the workplace, greater tension between men and women has been observed. *Training* magazine offered the following perspective.

> *. . . observers view the tension between women and men in the workplace as a natural outcome of power inequities between the genders. Their argument is that men still have most of the power and are resisting any change as a way to protect their power base. [Consultant Susan L] Webb asserts that sexual harassment has far more to do with exercising power in an unhealthy way than with sexual attraction. Likewise, the glass ceiling, a metaphor for the barriers women face in climbing the corporate ladder to management and executive positions, is about power and access to power.*[28]

In the same context, a recent Swedish survey revealed that gender-differentiated access to power in organizations is essential to any explanation of women's relatively low wages. Moreover, women who work in organizations in which relatively many of the managers are men, have lower pay than do those women with similar qualifications and job demands who work in organizations with a stronger female representation in the power structure. According to the researchers, 'power relations are of crucial importance for understanding how gender inequalities in financial rewards are generated and sustained in the labor market'.[29] As an illustration, in the UK, female managers are on average paid 18 per cent less than their male counterparts.[30]

A reanalysis of 18 field studies, which measured French and Raven's five bases of power, uncovered 'severe methodological shortcomings'.[31] After correcting for these problems, the researchers identified the following relationships between power bases and work outcomes such as job performance, job satisfaction and turnover.

▼ **Expert and referent power had a generally positive impact.**

▼ **Reward and legitimate power had a slightly positive impact.**

▼ **Coercive power had a slightly negative impact.**

The same researcher, in a 1990 follow-up study involving 251 employed business seniors, looked at the relationship between influence styles and bases of power. This was a 'bottom-up study', that is, employee perceptions of managerial influence and power were examined. Rational persuasion was found to be a highly acceptable managerial influence tactic. Why? Because employees perceived it to be associated with the three bases of power they viewed positively: legitimate, expert and referent.[32]

In summary, expert and referent power appear to get the best *combination* of results and favourable reactions from lower-level employees.[33]

Using Power Responsibly and Ethically

As democracy continues to spread around the world, one reality stands out. Leaders who do not use their power responsibly risk losing it. This holds for corporations and non-profit organizations as well as for governments. A key to success in this regard is understanding the difference between commitment and mere compliance.

Responsible managers strive for socialized power while avoiding personalized power. In fact, in a recent survey, organizational commitment was higher among executives whose superiors exercised socialized power than among colleagues with 'power-hungry' bosses. The researchers used the appropriate terms *uplifting power* versus *dominating power*.[34]

How does this relate to the five bases of power? As with influence tactics, managerial power has three possible outcomes: commitment, compliance or resistance. Reward, coercive, and negative legitimate power tend to produce *compliance* (and sometimes, resistance). On the other hand, positive legitimate power, expert power, and referent power tend to foster *commitment*. Once again, commitment is superior to compliance because it is driven by internal or intrinsic motivation.[35]

Employees who merely comply require frequent 'jolts' of power from the boss to keep them headed in a productive direction. Committed employees tend to be self-starters who do not require close supervision—a key success factor in today's flatter, team-oriented organizations.

According to research cited earlier, expert and referent power have the greatest potential for improving job performance and satisfaction, and for reducing turnover. Formal education, training and self-development can build a manager's expert power. At the same time, one's referent power base can be strengthened by forming and developing strategic alliances (discussed earlier under the heading of influence tactics).

EMPOWERMENT: FROM POWER SHARING TO POWER DISTRIBUTION

An exciting trend, in today's organization, centres on giving employees a greater say in the workplace. This trend is referred to in many ways, including 'participative management' and 'open-book management'. Regardless of the label one prefers, it is all about empowerment. One management writer defines **empowerment** in terms of serving the customer.

Empowerment quite simply means granting supervisors or workers permission to give the customer priority over other issues in the operation. In practical terms, it relates to the resources, skill, time and support to become leaders rather than controllers or mindless robots.[36]

Engelbert Breuker, director of Penta Scope, a Dutch consulting agency, explains why his company became an 'empowered organization'.

> **Empowerment**
> *sharing varying degrees of power with lower-level employees to better serve the customer*

'Since 1997, Penta Scope has the form of a networked organization where empowerment is the basic philosophy. Most of our people were, as line managers, the victims of massive IT-changes occuring halfway through the nineties. Everybody thinks that changes are the result of technology, but it is in fact mostly people that take an important place in these processes. Empowerment then, supplies people with power, strength and energy to tackle these changes. In my vision, the most important thing is not human resource management, but human talent. As an employee in our organization, you are your own boss, your ambitions lie within the network and can be realised there. Those who have an idea, those who want to do something, must also be able to bring it into practice. Formerly, one person used to decide for everyone, now everyone can decide for themselves. In fact we turned our personnel management completely upside down.'[37]

No Information Sharing, No Empowerment

Open-book management breaks down the traditional organizational caste system made up of information 'haves' (managers) and information 'have-nots' (non-managers). Until now, managers were afraid to tell their employees about innovations, company finances, and strategic plans for fear of giving the advantage to unions and competitors. To varying extents, those threats still persist today. But, in the larger scheme of things, organizations with unified and adequately informed employees are now seen to have a significant competitive advantage.

One organization that makes extensive use of information-sharing initiatives as a basis for empowerment is British Petroleum. BP has a sustained effort underway to increase communication and 'knowledge flow' across the company. Group executives seek extensive employee input before decisions are made. To enhance things, a dedicated Intranet site provides employees with business information. Futhermore, a flat organizational structure—there is nothing between the 92 business units and the nine-member executive group to whom they report—makes it possible to engage more staff members.[38]

The problematic question then becomes: How much information sharing is enough (or too much)? As demonstrated in the large- and small-company case studies in Table 15–1, there is no exact answer. Empowering managers need to learn from experience, be careful in what they share, and let employees know when certain information requires secrecy. Make no mistake, however, empowerment through open-book management carries some risk of betrayal, like any act of trust. Advocates of empowerment believe the rewards (more teamwork and greater competitiveness) outweigh the risks.

Table 15-1 *How Much Information Should Be Shared? Two Cases*

Large Company
www.campbellsoup.com

When Ron Ferner first joined Campbell's Soup, in the 1960s, none of the company's executives believed in sharing any kind of information with anybody. By the time he retired, in 1996, Ferner and his colleagues had started sharing everything—goals, financials, product news—with employees.

"At first I was very skeptical about sharing information with employees, but now I'm a believer. I saw the power of the thing. But we always drew the line at salaries. And if we had a supersecret project that we were not sure we would actually launch, we may not have told. But everything else was fair game. Even with the hourly employees that ran the filling machines, putting soup in the cans, we shared the financials.

"At one point Campbell's had a philosophy of meeting with all employees every quarter. I had 1,800 people in my plant. It took three days to hold the meetings. It was quite a chore, but worth it. The employees got very comfortable. It was a real change from the old days, when we would stand behind a post and peek out to watch them work.

"That approach doesn't work overnight. If you don't talk to employees for 10 years and then show up and say that today we start talking, you'll be really disappointed. You have to pick where to draw the line very carefully. You're building trust and don't want to backtrack. It took us years to talk to employees and make them comfortable. Once they were, we started getting their ideas and finding out what the real problems were. A lot of things amazed us.

"One time a packaging team in Sacramento was having problems with boxes breaking. Some of us managers started talking to them about what the problems were and realized they really had a good handle on what was wrong. So we said "Why don't you guys call the supplier?" Then we called the supplier to tell them they would be hearing from our crew, and they said, "Why not have them talk directly to our hourly employees?"

"If the managers alone had tried to solve this problem, it would have gone on forever. Instead, we rented a van, sent our people over, and solved the whole thing. Afterward, we had a party. It gave the workers great confidence. That never would have happened in the days when Campbell's had a policy of not telling anybody anything that wasn't written down for them."

Small Company
www.sapient.com

Adjacency CEO Andrew Sather and his partner, Chris DeVore, figured that for their four-year-old [Internet service] company to become a powerhouse, they would have to tap into the entrepreneurial instincts of every staffer. That meant treating all employees as if they were partners. All were given equity stakes. "I tried to set up the kind of company where I'd like to work," Sather says.

Last year, Sather and DeVore gathered their 25 workers together every week to discuss the most intimate details of their company, including cash flow and potential customers. The partners could tell that workers appreciated the honest communication. At meetings, employees would pepper the partners with loads of questions. But it quickly became apparent that there were some things employees would rather not know. For instance, they didn't want to hear about Adjacency's close calls with missing payroll—not an uncommon syndrome in the entrepreneurial world, but one that employees find quite unnerving. "We overestimated our employees' desire to be entrepreneurs, and sometimes we scared them," Sather says.

Sather and DeVore also overestimated their staff's ability to keep secrets. Last summer they told employees about a huge, potentially lucrative deal with a hot new client. One worker left the meeting so pumped that he bragged to a friend at a competing company. Bad move. The "friend" relayed the news to his bosses, who promptly tried to persuade the coveted customer to dump Adjacency and go with them. "We almost lost the client," DeVore says. "The client was livid, and rightfully so."

The partners considered shutting down the flow of sales information but decided against it. Now they're careful to identify what information is top secret.

"We've learned to get a lot more explicit about how information can be used," Sather says. In fact, the partners still divulge just as much confidential information as they did before the incident, conveying to employees that they trust them more than ever. There is one topic though, that Sather and DeVore are careful to avoid: the nitty-gritty details of cash flow. "We've learned to filter some information that employees find disconcerting," Sather admits.

[Now that Adjacency has fully integrated its business with Sapient, an innovative E-services consultancy, it will be interesting to observe how much of its open-book management style persists.]

SOURCES: Thea Singer, 'Share It All with Employees, Soup to Nuts', *Inc.*, Tech 1999, No. 1, p 48; and S Greco and M Ballon, 'Too Hot To Handle', *Inc.*, February 1999, p 52.

A Matter of Degree

The concept of empowerment requires some adjustments in traditional thinking. First, power is not a 'zero-sum' situation where one person's gain is another's loss. Social power is unlimited. This requires win–win thinking. 'The more power you give away, the more you have,' it is said.[39] Authoritarian managers who view employee empowerment as a threat to their personal power are missing the point because of their win-lose thinking.[40]

The second adjustment to traditional thinking involves seeing empowerment as a matter of degree not as an all-or-nothing proposition.[41] Figure 15–2 illustrates how power can be shifted to the hands of non-managers step by step. The overriding goal is to increase productivity and competitiveness in leaner organizations. Each step in this evolution increases the power of organizational contributors who, traditionally, had little or no legitimate power.

Figure 15–2 *The Evolution of Power: From Domination to Delegation*

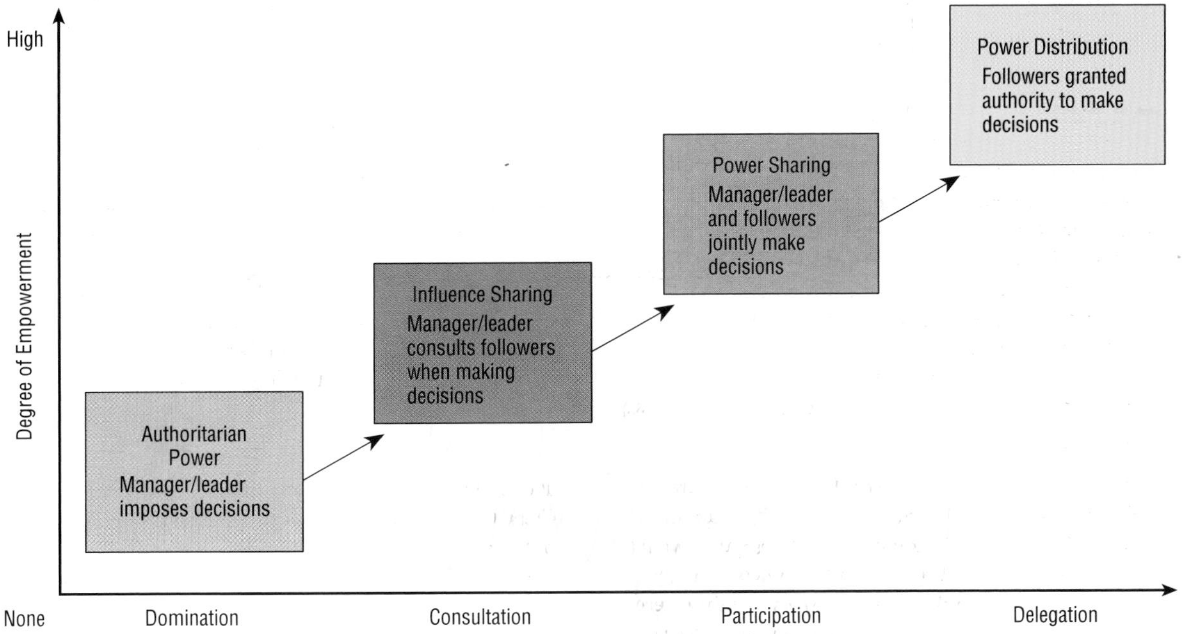

Delegation

The highest degree of empowerment is delegation. This amounts to *power distribution*. Delegation has long been the recommended way to lighten the busy manager's load while at the same time developing employees' abilities. Importantly, delegation gives non-managerial employees more than simply a voice in decisions. It empowers them to make their own decisions. A prime example of an entrepreneur that has discovered the benefits of delegation is Paul Bishop, founder of the British training company Winning Moves.

Delegation
granting decision-making authority to people at lower levels

'I used to be a genuine control freak. I was starting work at 5 a.m. and not getting back home until after my children had gone to bed—but I still had to examine every letter that left the office, and change something, even if the letter was perfect,' says Bishop. His company had grown rapidly, passing the 1 million turnover mark within three years. His diary was crammed, his desk overflowing, and there were never enough hours in the day to complete the many projects he started. He only realised there was a problem when his employees criticized communication within the company in a staff survey. 'I knew we wouldn't grow further unless I relaxed my grip on others,' he says. 'I had to learn to empower the people around me.' Bishop acted fast. He forced himself to 'butt out' of group meetings where he was answering questions on behalf of

others. He evolved a system whereby top-line goals for the company were set collectively but where responsibility for how best to achieve them was delegated to the individuals involved. It worked. Bishop is now getting home to see his kids and he is clearly pleased that his employees are keen to take on more responsibility and improve their skills and that they appear more motivated.[42]

Barriers to Delegation

Delegation is easy to talk about but many managers find it hard to actually do. A concerted effort to overcome the following common barriers to delegation needs to be made.

▼ Belief in the fallacy, 'If you want it done right, do it yourself.'

▼ Lack of confidence and trust in lower-level employees.

▼ Low self-confidence.

▼ Fear of being called lazy.

▼ Vague job definition.

▼ Fear of competition from those below.

▼ Reluctance to take the risks involved in depending on others.

▼ Lack of controls that provide early warning of problems with delegated duties.

▼ Poor example set by bosses who do not delegate.[43]

Delegation Research and Implications for Trust and Personal Initiative

Researchers at the State University of New York at Albany recently surveyed pairs of managers and employees, then did follow-up interviews with the managers about their delegation habits. Their results confirmed some important commonsense notions about delegation. Greater delegation was associated with the following factors.

1 A competent employee.

2 An employee who shared the manager's task objectives.

3 A manager who had a long-standing and positive relationship with the employee.

4 The lower-level person was also a supervisor.[44]

This delegation scenario boils down to one pivotal factor, *trust.*[45]

Managers prefer to delegate important tasks and decisions to the people they trust. As discussed in Chapter 13, it takes time and favourable experience to build trust. Of course, trust is fragile; it can be destroyed by a single remark, act or omission. Ironically, managers cannot learn to trust someone without, initially at least, running the risk of betrayal. This is why the empowerment evolution in Figure 15–2 represents a stairway to trust: consultation, participation and delegation. In other words, managers need to start small and work up the empowerment ladder. They need to delegate small tasks and decisions and scale up as competence, confidence and trust grow. Employees need to work on their side of the trust equation as well. One of the best ways to earn a manager's trust is to show *initiative* (see Figure 15–3). Researchers in the area offer the following instructive definition and characterization.

Personal initiative
going beyond formal job requirements and being an active self-starter

Personal initiative is a behaviour syndrome resulting in an individual taking an active and self-starting approach to work and going beyond what is formally required in a given job. More specifically, personal initiative is characterized by the following aspects: it is consistent with the organization's mission; has a long-term focus; is goal-directed and action-oriented; persistent in the face of barriers and setbacks; and self-starting and proactive.[46]

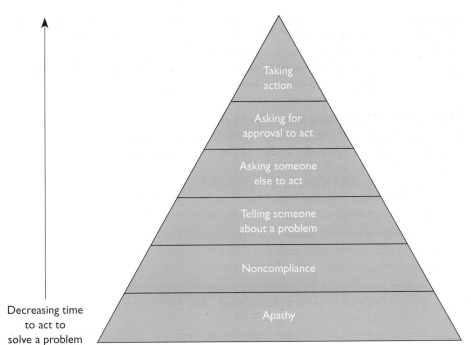

Figure 15–3
*Personal Initiative:
The Other Side of
Delegation*

Decreasing time
to act to
solve a problem

Tips for Personal Initiative and Taking Action

1 Go beyond the job
   • Do more than you're asked to do.
   • Identify and fix problems.
   • Help things move along quickly and smoothly.

2 Follow through on new ideas
   • Work on something original.
   • Improve upon your own and others' prior work.
   • Build support for your new ideas by showing how they can benefit the organization.

3 Don't be defeated by criticism; learn from it.
   • Actively seek input from others.
   • Improve your ideas from reactions, comments, and criticism.
   • Build bridges of support by incorporating others' ideas.

4 Look ahead (and around)
   • Plan for future projects.
   • Search for interesting projects and job opportunities within the organization.
   • Build your network to learn new things and find new opportunities.

SOURCES: Figure from A L Frohman, 'Igniting Organizational Change from Below: The Power of Personal Initiative', *Organizational Dynamics*, Winter 1997, p 46, © 1997 American Management Association International. Reprinted by permission of American Management Association International, New York, NY. All rights reserved. http://www.amanet.org. Tips adapted from R Kelley and J Caplan, 'How Bell Labs Create Star Performers', *Harvard Business Review*, July–August 1993, pp 128–39.

Empowerment: The Research Record and Practical Advice

Like other widely heralded techniques—such as TQM, 360-degree reviews, teams, and learning organizations—empowerment has its fair share of critics and suffers from unrealistic expectations.[47] Research results to date are mixed, with a recent positive uptrend.

▼ According to a field study of 26 insurance claims supervisors, employees who enjoyed a greater degree of delegation processed more insurance claims at lower cost.[48]

▼ A study of 297 service employees led the researchers to conclude: 'Empowerment may contribute to an employee's job satisfaction, but not as profoundly shape work effort and performance.'[49]

▼ A study of 24 growing companies by the Centre for Entreprise at Cambridge University in the UK, showed that delegation is fundamental to the expansion of a company. While the leaders of the companies examined were all highly motivated and ambitious, some achieved much faster and more consistent growth than others. These high achievers were characterised by their ability to recruit a team of senior managers at an early stage and by their willingness to cede a high degree of control and responsibility to them.[50]

▼ When the job performance of 81 empowered employees at the home office of a Canadian life insurance company was compared with a control group of 90 employees, the researchers found 'minimal support' for empowerment.[51]

▼ Factors associated with perceived empowerment were studied at a US hospital. Among 612 nurses, skilled professionals, and administrators (21 per cent of whom were male), higher perceived empowerment was associated with higher rank, longer tenure with the organization, approachable leaders, effective and worthwhile task groups, higher job satisfaction, and lower propensity to quit. No gender or race effects were found.[52]

We believe empowerment is very promising if managers go about it properly. Empowerment is a sweeping concept with many different definitions. Consequently, researchers use inconsistent measurements; and the cause–effect relationships are fuzzy. Managers committed to the idea of employee empowerment need to follow the path of continuous improvement, learning from their successes and failures. Eight years of research with 10 'empowered' companies led consultant W Alan Randolph to formulate the three-pronged empowerment plan shown in Figure 15–4. Notice how open-book management and active information sharing are needed to build the necessary foundation of trust. Beyond that, clear goals and lots of relevant training are needed. While noting that the empowerment process can take several years to unfold, Randolph offered the following perspective.

While the keys to empowerment may be easy to understand, they are hard to implement. It takes tremendous courage to start sharing sensitive information. It takes true strength to build more structure just at the point when people want more freedom of action. It takes real growth to allow teams to take over the management decision-making process. And above all, it takes perseverance to complete the empowerment process.[53]

ORGANIZATIONAL POLITICS AND IMPRESSION MANAGEMENT

Most students of OB find the study of organizational politics intriguing. Perhaps this topic owes its appeal to the antics of certain movies, picturing corporate villains who get their way by stepping on anyone and everyone. As we will see, however, organizational politics includes, but is not limited to, dirty dealing. Organizational politics is an ever-present and sometimes annoying feature of modern working life. For example, a recent survey showed that internal office politics are holding back the growth of the UK's electronic-economy. It was found that 25 per cent of IT directors believe politics is to blame for the brakes being put on e-business projects.[54] On the other hand, organizational politics is often a positive force in modern work organizations. Skillful and well-timed politics can help you get your point across, neutralize resistance to a key project, or get a choice job assignment. David Butcher,

Figure 15–4 *Randolph's Empowerment Model*

The Empowerment Plan

Share Information
- Share company performance information.
- Help people understand the business.
- Build trust through sharing sensitive information.
- Create self-monitoring possibilities.

Create Autonomy Through Structure	**Let Teams Become The Hierarchy**
• Create a clear vision and clarify the little pictures. • Clarify goals and roles collaboratively. • Create new decision-making rules that support empowerment. • Establish new empowering performance management processes. • Use heavy doses of training.	• Provide direction and training for new skills. • Provide encouragement and support for change. • Gradually have managers let go of control. • Work through the leadership vacuum stage. • Acknowledge the fear factor.

**Remember: Empowerment is not magic;
it consists of a few simple steps and a lot of persistence.**

SOURCE: 'Navigating the Journey to Empowerment', by W Alan Randolph. Reprinted from *Organizational Dynamics*, Spring 1995. © 1995 American Management Association International. Reprinted by permission of the American Management Association International. New York, NY. All rights reserved. http://www.amanet.org

who leads executive seminars on organizational politics at Cranfield Management School in the UK, puts things in perspective by observing the following.

> 'The idea that business and politics don't mix is one of management's most deeply ingrained myths. When people say of a corporation or a hospital that 'it's a very political organization', it's not meant as a compliment. In the same way, 'he or she plays politics' is a damning assessment of a person. But the ideal of a company as a politics-free zone is getting harder and harder to sustain. It was born of an era where rationality and control were the paramount values, and hierarchy and bureaucracy the logical management expression of them. Unfortunately, the world is no longer predictable and stable, but chaotic and volatile, so the simplistic vision of management as an exercise in machine-like rationality is no longer realistic. Large organizations are hotbeds of political intrigue. Senior managers have competing agendas. It was ever thus. Management works that way. If you ask managers what they do, they say that politics is part of their job. It's a purely notional view that says otherwise. It's time we recognise that fact. Once you accept that a company is a political system, you can begin to make things happen.'[55]

We explore this important and interesting area by: defining the term *organizational politics*; identifying three levels of political action; discussing eight specific political tactics; considering a related area called *impression management*; and examining relevant research and practical implications.

Definition and Domain of Organizational Politics

'Organizational politics involves intentional acts of influence to enhance or protect the self-interest of individuals or groups.'[56] An emphasis on *self-interest* distinguishes this form of social influence. Managers are endlessly challenged to achieve a workable balance between employees' self-interests and organizational interests, as discussed at the beginning of this chapter. When a proper balance exists, the pursuit of self-interest may serve the organization's interests. Political behaviour becomes a negative force when self-interests erode or defeat organizational interests. For example, researchers have documented the political tactic of filtering and distorting information flowing up to the boss. This self-serving practice put the reporting employees in the best possible light.[57]

Organizational politics
intentional enhancement of self-interest

Uncertainty Triggers Political Behaviour

Political manoeuvring is triggered primarily by uncertainty. The following five common sources of uncertainty within organizations.

1 Unclear objectives.

2 Vague performance measures.

3 Ill-defined decision processes.

4 Strong individual or group competition.[58]

5 Any type of change.

With regard to this last source of uncertainty, organization development specialist Anthony Raia noted, 'Whenever we attempt to change, the political subsystem becomes active. Vested interests are almost always at stake and the distribution of power is challenged.'[59]

Thus, we would expect a field sales representative, striving to achieve an assigned quota, to be less political than a management trainee working on a variety of projects. While some management trainees stake their career success on hard work, competence and a bit of luck, many do not. These people attempt to gain a competitive edge through some combination of the political tactics discussed below. Meanwhile, the salesperson's performance is measured in actual sales, not in terms of being friends with the boss or taking credit for others' work. Thus, the management trainee would tend to be more political than the field salesperson because of greater uncertainty about management's expectations. Because employees generally experience greater uncertainty during the earlier stages of their careers, it has also been found that junior employees are more political than more senior ones.[60]

Three Levels of Political Action

Although much political manoeuvring occurs at the individual level, it can also involve group or collective action. Figure 15–5 illustrates three different levels of political action: the individual, coalition, and network levels.[61] Each level has its distinguishing characteristics. At the individual level, personal self-interests are pursued by the individual. The political aspects of coalitions and networks are not so obvious, however.

Coalition
temporary groupings of people who actively pursue a single issue

People with a common interest can form a political **coalition**, which may or may not coincide with formal group membership. When the target issue is resolved (for example, when someone responsible for sexually harrassing a colleague is fired), the coalition disbands. Experts note that political coalitions have 'fuzzy boundaries,' meaning they are fluid in membership, flexible in structure, and temporary in duration.[62]

A third level of political action involves networks.[63] Unlike coalitions, which pivot on specific issues, networks are loose associations of individuals seeking social support for their general self-interests. Politically, networks are people oriented, while coalitions are issue oriented. Networks have broader and longer-term agendas than coalitions.

Figure 15–5

Levels of Political Action in Organizations

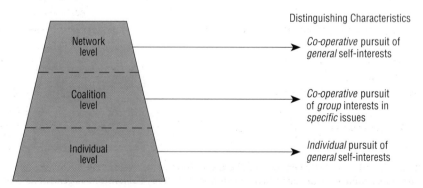

Distinguishing Characteristics

Network level — *Co-operative* pursuit of *general* self-interests

Coalition level — *Co-operative* pursuit of *group* interests in *specific* issues

Individual level — *Individual* pursuit of *general* self-interests

Political Tactics

Anyone who has worked in an organization has firsthand knowledge of blatant politicking. Blaming someone else for your mistake is an obvious political ploy. But other political tactics are more subtle. Researchers have identified a range of political behaviour.

One landmark study, involving in-depth interviews with 87 managers from 30 electronics companies in Southern California, identified eight political tactics. Top-, middle-, and low-level managers were represented about equally in the sample. According to the researchers: 'Respondents were asked to describe organizational political tactics and personal characteristics of effective political actors based upon their accumulated experience in *all* the organizations in which they had worked.'[64] Listed in descending order of occurrence, are the following eight political tactics that emerged.

1   Attacking or blaming others.
2   Using information as a political tool.
3   Creating a favourable image. (Also known as impression management.)[65]
4   Developing a base of support.
5   Praising others (ingratiation).
6   Forming power coalitions with strong allies.
7   Associating with influential people.
8   Creating obligations (reciprocity).

Table 15–2 describes these political tactics and indicates how often each reportedly was used by the interviewed managers.

Table 15–2 *Eight Common Political Tactics in Organizations*

Political Tactic	Percentage of Managers Mentioning Tactic	Brief Description of Tactic
1. Attacking or blaming others	54%	Used to avoid or minimize association with failure. Reactive when scapegoating is involved. Proactive when goal is to reduce competition for limited resources.
2. Using information as a political tool	54	Involves the purposeful withholding or distortion of information. Obscuring an unfavorable situation by overwhelming superiors with information.
3. Creating a favorable image (impression management)	53	Dressing/grooming for success. Adhering to organizational norms and drawing attention to one's successes and influence. Taking credit for others' accomplishments.
4. Developing a base of support	37	Getting prior support for a decision. Building others' commitment to a decision through participation.
5. Praising others (ingratiation)	25	Making influential people feel good ("apple polishing").
6. Forming power coalitions with strong allies	25	Teaming up with powerful people who can get results.
7. Associating with influential people	24	Building a support network both inside and outside the organization.
8. Creating obligations (reciprocity)	13	Creating social debts ("I did you a favor, so you owe me a favor").

SOURCE: Adapted from R W Allen, D L Madison, L W Porter, P A Renwick and B T Mayes, 'Organizational Politics: Tactics and Characteristics of Its Actors', *California Management Review*, Fall 1979, pp 77–83.

The researchers distinguished between reactive and proactive political tactics. Some of the tactics, such as scapegoating, were reactive because the intent was to defend one's self-interest. Other tactics, such as developing a base of support, were proactive because they sought to promote the individual's self-interest.

What is your attitude toward organizational politics? How often do you rely on the various tactics in Table 15–2? You can get a general indication of your political tendencies by comparing your behaviour with the characteristics in Table 15–3. Would you characterize yourself as politically naive, politically sensible or a political shark? How do you think others view your political actions? What are the career, friendship and ethical implications of your political tendencies?[66]

(For a more detailed analysis of your political tendencies, see the Personal Awareness and Growth Exercise at the end of this chapter.)

Table 15–3 *Are You Politically Naive, Politically Sensible or a Political Shark?*

Characteristics	Naive	Sensible	Sharks
Underlying attitude	Politics is unpleasant.	Politics is necessary.	Politics is an opportunity.
Intent	Avoid at all costs.	Further departmental goals.	Self-serving and predatory.
Techniques	Tell it like it is.	Network; expand connections; use system to give and receive favors.	Manipulate; use fraud and deceit when necessary.
Favorite tactics	None—the truth will win out.	Negotiate, bargain.	Bully; misuse information; cultivate and use 'friends' and other contacts.

SOURCE: Reprinted with permission from J K Pinto and O P Kharbanda, 'Lessons for an Accidental Profession', *Business Horizons*, March–April 1995, p 45. Copyright © 1998 by the Indiana University Board of Trustees at Indiana University, Kelley School of Business.

Impression Management

Impression management is defined as 'the process by which people attempt to control or manipulate the reactions of others to images of themselves or their ideas.'[67] This encompasses how one talks, behaves and looks. Most attempts at impression management are directed at making a *good* impression on relevant others. But, as we will see, some employees strive to make a *bad* impression. For purposes of conceptual clarity, we will focus on *upward* impression management (trying to impress one's immediate supervisor) because it is most relevant for managers. Still, it is good to remember that anyone can be the intended target of impression management. Parents, teachers, peers, employees and customers are all fair game when it comes to managing the impressions of others.

Impression management

getting others to see us in a certain manner

A Conceptual Crossroads

Impression management is an interesting conceptual crossroads involving self-monitoring, attribution theory and organizational politics.[68] Perhaps this explains why impression management has received active research attention in recent years. High self-monitoring employees ('chameleons' who adjust to their surroundings) are likely to be more inclined to engage in impression management than low self-monitors. Impression management also involves the systematic manipulation of attributions. For example, a bank president will look good if the board of directors is encouraged to attribute organizational successes to her efforts and attribute problems and failures to factors beyond her control. Impression management definitely fits into the realm of organizational politics because of an overriding focus on furthering one's self-interests.

Making a Good Impression

If you 'dress for success', project an upbeat attitude at all times, and avoid offending others, you are engaging in favourable impression management—particularly so if your motive is to improve your chances of getting what you want in life.[69] Former British Airways chairman, Lord King, admitted he had underestimated his casually dressed rival (Richard Branson, Virgin Atlantic chairman). 'If Branson had worn a pair of steel-rimmed shoes, a double-breasted suit and shaved off his beard, I would have taken him seriously. As it was, I couldn't. I underestimated him.'[70] On the lighter side, the trends towards more casual dress codes has working men and women rethinking what it means to dress for success. *Newsweek* recently framed the irony as follows.

> *Guys, it's your turn. As women are liberated from some of the meaner dictates of dress, men are losing a certain brand of fashion freedom. Sure, you may no longer have to wear a suit and tie to work. But there's the rub. With so many offices gone 'casual', the corporate uniform is gone. You have to consider not only when to dress up or down, but a whole new vocabulary of texture, pattern and fabric. And that mandate dreaded by some females of the species now applies to you too: accessorize! Can I wear a silk-crepe tie with denim? Bucks with dress pants?*[71]

No one ever said that impression management was easy!

A statistical factor analysis of the influence attempts reported by a sample of 84 bank employees (including 74 women) identified three categories of favourable upward impression management tactics.[72] As the next OB Exercise shows, favourable upward impression management tactics can be divided into three categories: *job-focused* (manipulating information about one's job performance), *supervisor-focused* (praising and doing favours for one's supervisor), and *self-focused* (presenting oneself as a polite and nice person). Take a short break from your studying to complete the OB Exercise.

How did you do on the OB Exercise? A moderate amount of upward impression management is a necessity for the average employee today. Too little, and busy managers are liable to overlook some of your valuable contributions when they make job assignment, pay, and promotion decisions. Too much, and you run the risk of being branded a 'flatterer,' a 'phoney,' and other unflattering things by your co-workers.[73] Excessive flattery and ingratiation can backfire by embarrassing the target person and damaging one's credibility. Also, the risk of unintended insult is very high when impression management tactics cross gender, racial, ethnic and cultural lines.[74] International management experts offer the following warning.

> *The impression management tactic is only as effective as its correlation to accepted norms about behavioural presentation. In other words, slapping a Japanese subordinate on the back with a rousing 'Good work, Hiro!' will not create the desired impression in Hiro's mind that the expatriate intended. In fact, the behaviour will likely create the opposite impression.*[75]

Making a Poor Impression

At first glance, the idea of consciously trying to make a bad impression in the workplace seems absurd. But an interesting new line of impression management research has uncovered both motives and tactics for making oneself look *bad*. In a survey of the work experiences of business students at a large US university, more than half 'reported witnessing a case of someone intentionally looking bad at work'.[76] Why? Four motives came out of the study.

1 *Avoidance:* Employee seeks to avoid additional work, stress, burnout, or an unwanted transfer or promotion.

2 *Obtain concrete rewards:* Employee seeks to obtain a pay increase or a desired transfer, promotion, or demotion.

3 *Exit:* Employee seeks to get laid off, fired or suspended, and perhaps also to collect unemployment or workers' compensation.

4 *Power:* Employee seeks to control, manipulate, intimidate or get revenge on others, or to make someone else look bad.[77]

Within the context of these motives, *unfavourable* upward impression management makes sense.

Five unfavourable upward impression management tactics identified by the researchers are as follows.

▼ *Decreasing performance:* **restricting productivity, making more mistakes than usual, lowering quality, neglecting tasks.**

▼ *Not working to potential:* **pretending ignorance, having unused capabilities.**

▼ *Withdrawing:* **being tardy, taking excessive breaks, faking illness.**

▼ *Displaying a bad attitude:* **complaining, getting upset and angry, acting strangely, not getting along with co-workers.**

▼ *Broadcasting limitations:* **letting co-workers know about one's physical problems and mistakes (both verbally and non-verbally).**[78]

Recommended ways to manage employees who try to make a bad impression can be found throughout this book. They include more challenging work, greater autonomy, better feedback, supportive leadership, clear and reasonable goals, and a less stressful work setting.[79]

OB Exercise

How Much Do You Rely on Upward Impression Management Tactics?

Instructions

Rate yourself on each item according to how you behave on your current (or most recent) job. Add your circled responses to calculate a total score. Compare your score with our arbitrary norms.

Job-Focused Tactics   **Rarely Very Often**

1 I exaggerate the value of my positive work results and make my supervisor aware of them.   1 – 2 – 3 – 4 – 5

2 I try to make my work appear better than it is.   1 – 2 – 3 – 4 – 5

3 I try to take responsibility for positive results, even when I'm not solely responsible for achieving them.   1 – 2 – 3 – 4 – 5

4 I try to make my negative results less severe than they initially appear, when informing my supervisor.   1 – 2 – 3 – 4 – 5

5 I arrive at work early and/or work late to show my supervisor I am a hard worker.   1 – 2 – 3 – 4 – 5

Supervisor-Focused Tactics

6 I show an interest in my supervisor's personal life.   1 – 2 – 3 – 4 – 5

7 I praise my supervisor about his/her accomplishments.   1 – 2 – 3 – 4 – 5

8 I do personal favours for my supervisor that I'm not required to do.   1 – 2 – 3 – 4 – 5

9 I compliment my supervisor on her/his dress or appearance.   1 – 2 – 3 – 4 – 5

10 I agree with my supervisor's major suggestions and ideas.   1 – 2 – 3 – 4 – 5

Self-Focused Tactics

11 I am very friendly and polite in the presence of my supervisor.   1 – 2 – 3 – 4 – 5

Research Evidence on Organizational Politics and Impression Management

Recent field research involving employees in real organizations rather than students in contrived laboratory settings, has yielded the following useful insights.

▼ **A study of 68 women and 84 men employed by five different service and industrial companies in the United States uncovered significant gender-based insights about organizational politics. In what might be termed the battle of the sexes . . . it was found that political behaviour was perceived more favourably when it was performed *against* a target of the *opposite* gender. Thus subjects of both sexes tend to relate to gender as a meaningful affiliation group. This finding presents a different picture from the one suggesting that women tend to accept male superiority at work and generally agree with sex stereotypes which are commonly discriminatory in nature.**[80]

▼ **Impression management attempts can either positively or negatively affect one's performance appraisal results.**[81] **The researchers in one study of 67 manager–employee pairs concluded that 'Subordinates who were friendly and reasonable were perceived as amiable, and favourably evaluated.'**[82] **However, subordinates who relied on ingratiation (making the boss feel good) did not get better performance appraisals.**[83]

Managing Organizational Politics

Organizational politics cannot be eliminated. A manager would be naive to expect such an outcome. But political manoeuvring can and should be managed to keep it constructive and within reasonable bounds. Harvard's Abraham Zaleznik put the issue this way: 'People can focus their attention on only so many things. The more it lands on politics, the less energy—emotional and intellectual—is available to attend to the problems that fall under the heading of real work.'[84]

An individual's degree of enthusiasm for using political tactics is a matter of personal values, ethics and temperament. People who are either strictly apolitical or highly political generally pay a price for their behaviour. The former may experience slow promotions and feel left out, while the latter may run the risk of being called self-serving and lose their credibility. People at both ends of the political spectrum may be considered poor team players. Normally, a moderate amount of prudent political behaviour is considered a survival tool in complex organizations. Experts remind us that:

. . . political behaviour has earned a bad name only because of its association with politicians. On its own, the use of power and other resources to obtain your objectives is not inherently unethical. It all depends on what the preferred objectives are.[85]

With this perspective in mind, the practical steps in Table 15–4 are recommended. Notice the importance of reducing uncertainty through standardized performance evaluations and clear performance–reward linkages.[86] Measurable objectives are management's first line of defense against negative expressions of organizational politics.[87]

Table 15–4

Some Practical Advice on Managing Organizational Politics

To Reduce System Uncertainty

Make clear what are the bases and processes for evaluation.

Differentiate rewards among high and low performers.

Make sure the rewards are as immediately and directly related to performance as possible.

To Reduce Competition

Try to minimize resource competition among managers.

Replace resource competition with externally oriented goals and objectives.

To Break Existing Political Fiefdoms

Where highly cohesive political empires exist, break them apart by removing or splitting the most dysfunctional subgroups.

If you are an executive, be keenly sensitive to managers whose mode of operation is the personalization of political patronage. First, approach these persons with a directive to "stop the political maneuvering." If it continues, remove them from the positions and, preferably, the company.

To Prevent Future Fiefdoms

Make one of the most important criteria for promotion an apolitical attitude that puts organizational ends ahead of personal power ends.

SOURCE: D R Beeman and T W Sharkey, 'The Use and Abuse of Corporate Politics'. Reprinted with permission of *Business Horizons*, March–April 1987, p 30. Copyright © 1987 by the Board of Trustees at Indiana University, Kelley School of Business.

Summary of Key Concepts

1 Explain the concept of mutuality of interest.

Managers are constantly challenged to foster mutuality of interest (a win-win situation) between individual and organizational interests. Organization members need to actively co-operate with actual and potential adversaries for the common good.

2 Name at least three 'soft' and two 'hard' influence tactics, and summarize the practical lessons from influence research.

Five soft influence tactics are rational persuasion, inspirational appeals, consultation, ingratiation, and personal appeals. They are more friendly and less coercive than the four hard influence tactics: exchange, coalition, pressure, and legitimating tactics. According to research, soft tactics are better for generating commitment and are perceived as more fair than hard tactics. Ingratiation—making the boss feel good through compliments and being helpful—can slightly improve performance appraisal results and make the boss like you a lot more. Influence through domination is a poor strategy for both men and women. Influence is a complicated and situational process that needs to be undertaken with care, especially across cultures.

3 Identify and briefly describe French and Raven's five bases of power and discuss the responsible use of power.

French and Raven's five bases of power are reward power (rewarding compliance), coercive power (punishing non-compliance), legitimate power (relying on formal authority), expert power (providing needed information), and referent power (relying on personal attraction). Responsible and ethical managers strive to use socialized power (primary concern is for others) rather than personalized power (primary concern for self). Research found higher organizational commitment among employees with bosses who used uplifting power than among those with power-hungry bosses who relied on dominating power.

4 Define the term empowerment, and discuss the realities of open-book management.

Empowerment involves sharing varying degrees of power and decision-making authority with lower-level employees to better serve the customer. Surveys indicate widespread use of open-book management, whereby managers share more information than usual about innovations, company finances, and strategy. This act of trust carries with it the risk of betrayal. But advocates of empowerment and open-book management say the promises of more teamwork and greater competitiveness outweigh the risks.

5 Explain why delegation is the highest form of empowerment, and discuss the connections between delegation, trust and personal initiative.

Delegation gives employees more than a participatory role in decision making. It allows them to make their *own* work-related decisions. Managers tend to delegate to employees they trust. Employees can get managers to trust them by demonstrating personal initiative (going beyond formal job requirements and being self-starters).

6 Define organizational politics, and explain what triggers it.

Organizational politics is defined as intentional acts of influence to enhance or protect the self-interests of individuals or groups. Uncertainty triggers most political activity in organizations. THis activity occurs at individual, coalition and network levels. Coalitions are informal, temporary and single-issue alliances.

7 Distinguish between favourable and unfavourable impression management tactics.

Favourable upward impression management can be job-focused (manipulating information about one's job performance), supervisor-focused (praising or doing favours for the boss), or self-focused (being polite and nice). Unfavourable upward impression management tactics include decreasing performance, not working to potential, withdrawing, displaying a bad attitude, and broadcasting one's limitations.

8 Explain how to manage organizational politics.

Since organizational politics cannot be eliminated, managers need to learn to deal with it. Uncertainty can be reduced by evaluating performance and linking rewards to performance. Measurable objectives are key. Participative management also helps.

Discussion Questions

1 Of the nine generic influence tactics, which do you use the most when dealing with friends, parents, your boss or your lecturers? Would other tactics be more effective?

2 Before reading this chapter, did the term *power* have a negative connotation for you? Do you view it differently now? Explain.

3 What base(s) of power do you rely on in your daily affairs? (Use the OB Exercise on page 425 to assess your power bases at work.) Do you handle power effectively and responsibly?

4 In your opinion, how much empowerment is 'too much' in today's workplace?

5 Will empowerment turn out to be just another management fad? Explain your rationale.

6 What are the main advantages and drawbacks of the trend toward increased delegation?

7 Why do you think organizational politics is triggered primarily by uncertainty?

8 What personal experiences have you had with coalitions? Explain any positive or negative outcomes.

9 According to the OB Exercise, how heavily do you rely on upward impression management tactics? What are the career implications of your approach to impression management?

10 How much impression management do you see in your department or workplace today? Citing specific examples, state whether the tactics are effective.

Internet Exercise

http://www.influenceatwork.com

Influence and political tactics are an inescapable part of modern organizational life, as discussed in this chapter. The purpose of this exercise is to broaden your understanding of organizational influence and politics and help you to deal with them effectively.

A Free Tutorial on Social Influence

Do you get the feeling advertisers, the media, politicians, salespeople, parents, teachers and friends sometimes try to 'trick' you by manipulating words and images in self-serving ways? According to Professor Robert B Cialdini and his colleague, consultant Kelton Rhoads, you are right to feel a bit put upon. After all, as their research has documented, each of us is the recipient (or victim) of countless social influence attempts during every waking hour. Their

fascinating Internet site (www.influenceatwork.com) provides an inside look at social influence so we will not be unfairly or unwittingly manipulated. At the home page, first choose the *academic path*. Arrived there, we recommend you start to click on the *What's Your Influence Quotient?* icon. The short quiz will get you thinking about the power and pervasiveness of social influence. Back at the *academic* home page, you might want to select the heading *The Authors* from the main menu, for relevant background. Returning once again to the home page, select *Introduction to Influence* from the main menu. All of the tutorial pieces are worth exploration but we especially recommend the first six categories, including the two on ethics. The '6 Principles' and collection of readings on 'Framing' are very interesting and instructive.

Personal Awareness and Growth Exercise
How Political Are You?

Objectives

1 To get to know yourself a little better.

2 To assess your political tendencies, within an organizational context.

3 To consider the career implications of your political tendencies.

Introduction

Organizational politics is an unavoidable feature of life in a modern organization. Your career success, job performance

and job satisfaction can hinge on your political skills. But it is important to realize that some political tactics can cause ethical problems.

Instructions

For each of the 10 statements, select the response that best characterizes your behaviour. You do not have to engage in the behaviour at all times to answer true.[88]

1 You should make others feel important through an open appreciation of their ideas and work. _____ True _____ False

2 Because people tend to judge you when they first meet you, always try to make a good first impression. _____ True _____ False

3 Try to let others do most of the talking, be sympathetic to their problems, and resist telling people that they are totally wrong. _____ True _____ False

4 Praise the good traits of the people you meet and always give people an opportunity to save face if they are wrong or make a mistake. _____ True _____ False

5 Spreading false rumours, planting misleading information and backstabbing (criticizing someone while feigning friendship) are necessary, if somewhat unpleasant, methods of dealing with your enemies. _____ True _____ False

6 Sometimes it is necessary to make promises that you know you will not or cannot keep. _____ True _____ False

7 It is important to get along with everybody, even those who are generally recognized as overly talkative, abrasive, or constant complainers. _____ True _____ False

8 It is vital to do favours for others so that you can call in these IOUs at times when they will do you the most good. _____ True _____ False

9 Be willing to compromise, particularly on issues that are minor to you, but important to others. _____ True _____ False

10 On controversial issues, it is important to delay or avoid your involvement if possible. _____ True _____ False

Scoring and Interpretation

The author of this quiz recommends the following scoring system:

A confirmed organizational politician will answer 'true' to all 10 questions. Organizational politicians with fundamental ethical standards will answer 'false' to Questions 5 and 6, which deal with deliberate lies and uncharitable behaviour. Individuals who regard manipulation, incomplete disclosure, and self-serving behaviour as unacceptable will answer 'false' to all or almost all of the questions.[89]

Questions for Discussion

1 Did this instrument accurately assess your tendencies toward organizational politics? Explain.

2 Do you think a confirmed organizational politician would answer this quiz honestly? Explain.

3 Will your political tendencies help or hinder your career? Explain.

4 Are there any potential ethical problems with any of your answers? Which ones?

5 How important is political behaviour for career success today? Explain, relative to the industry or organization you have in mind.

Group Exercise
You Make Me Feel So Good!

Objectives

1 To introduce a different type of impression management and sharpen your awareness of impression management.

2 To promote self-awareness and diversity awareness by comparing your perceptions and ethics with others.

Introduction

This is a group discussion exercise designed to enhance your understanding of impression management. Personal interpretations are involved, so there are no strictly right or wrong answers.

Researchers recently have explored beneficial impression management, the practice of helping friends and significant others look good. This new line of inquiry combines the established OB topics of social support (discussed relative to stress in Chapter 18) and impression management (discussed in this chapter). In this exercise, we explore the practical and ethical implications of 'strategically managing information to make your friends look good'. We also consider impression management in general.

Instructions

This is a two-stage exercise: a private note-taking part, followed by a group discussion.

Stage 1 (5 to 7 minutes): Read the two scenarios in the box below and then rate each one according to the following three scales.

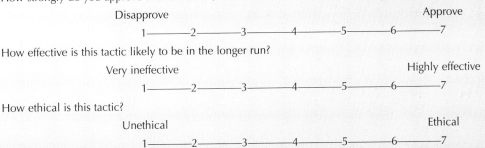

How strongly do you approve of this tactic? (Mark an 'X' for scenario I and an 'O' for scenario 2.)

Disapprove   Approve

1———2———3———4———5———6———7

How effective is this tactic likely to be in the longer run?

Very ineffective   Highly effective

1———2———3———4———5———6———7

How ethical is this tactic?

Unethical   Ethical

1———2———3———4———5———6———7

Scenarios[90]

1 A member of the school football team buoys the spirits of a teammate who misses the goal at a crucial moment in the match by emphasizing the latter's game-winning goal last week, and by noting that even the best footballers miss more times than they score. He may privately suspect his teammate has only mediocre talent but by putting his comments in a positive way and not sharing his doubts, he makes his teammate feel better, builds his confidence so he can face tomorrow's game in a more optimistic frame of mind, and boosts the teammate's image in fron of the other players who can hear the reassuring words.

2 At a party, a college student describes her roommate to a potential date she knows her friend finds extremely attractive. She stresses her friend's intelligence, attractiveness and common interests but fails to mention that her friend can also be quite arrogant.

Stage 2 (10 to 15 minutes): Join two or three others in a discussion group and compare scores for both scenarios.

Are there big differences of opinion or is there a general consensus? Next, briefly discuss these questions: How do *you* create a good first impression in *specific* situations? What goes through your mind when you see someone trying to create a good impression of themselves or on behalf of someone else? *Note:* Your tutor may ask you to pick a spokesperson to briefly report the results of your discussion to the group. If so, be sure to keep notes during the discussion.

Questions for Discussion

1 Is the whole practice of impression management a dishonest waste of time or does it have a proper place in society? Why?

2 In what situations can impression management attempts have the reverse effect to that intended?

3 How do you know someone has taken impression management too far?

4 How would you respond to a person who made the statement: 'I never engage in impression management'?

Chapter Sixteen

Leadership

Somebody has to take the lead

Thomas Middelhoff doesn't look up as his Gulfstream jet gains altitude over France's Côte d'Azur. He ignores views of the shimmering Mediterranean and the mist-shrouded Alpes-Maritimes. Instead, the chairman and CEO of Bertelsmann, the world's third-largest media company, is hunched over a pile of newspaper clippings, devouring the day's news from the ▶

446

entertainment and online world. And it has already been a long day. After waking at 5 a.m. in the rural German town of Gutersloh and taking a swim in his indoor pool, Middelhoff has hopped on a plane for Cannes to give a pep talk to top executives of BMG Entertainment, Bertelsmann's music division. Then it's back to the airport in a Mercedes whose chauffeur seems to be on loan from Formula One.

Twelve days later, Middelhoff is stepping out of a black stretch limo at New York's Essex House hotel. Waiting outside is the Internet's No. 1 bad boy, 20-year-old Shawn Fanning, the founder of Napster Inc., the 18-month-old Silicon Valley start-up that has turned the music industry on its head by creating software that allows people to trade music for free. The lanky German gets out of his limo, walks over to Fanning, rubs his close-cropped head, and hugs him like an old friend. Thirty minutes later, the pair walk into a press conference, where Middelhoff announces a deal that could help transform his once-sleepy publishing house into a powerhouse for the Internet Age. The irrepressible 47-year-old Middelhoff wants to convert Napster from a renegade, cash-starved outfit into the very center of on-line media distribution and e-commerce.

The deal is as bold, visionary, and complicated as anything to hit the industry in years. If Napster complies with this new plan, Middelhoff conceivably will rescue the concept of profitable intellectual property in the Information Age. The dark nightmare of the media industry has been that file-sharing would spread like wildfire in the networked world. First, file-sharers would download music without paying–as they have with Napster. But they wouldn't stop there. Soon any media product that could be digitized— novels, textbooks, magazines, maybe even movies—would lose all copyright protection and be swiped en masse by the denizens of the Net.

Middelhoff's answer: Recruit the thief to protect the jewels.

The Napster deal shows Bertelsmann can move fast. Middelhoff credits his chief of e-commerce, Andreas Schmidt, who worked on virtually nothing else for weeks, for landing the Napster deal. But Middelhoff also took part,

phoning counterparts at Napster in the middle of the night when a new idea hit him or spontaneously flying to New York to try to push the deal forward.

Middelhoff's sense of urgency is unmistakable. He isn't seeing much of his five children these days, or his renovated farm and its population of several dozen sheep, goats, and horses.

Middelhoff is girding his staff for a Net breakthrough. He has banned paper interoffice memos, accepting only emails. He personally answers about 130 a day. He ordered PCs for every employee to use at home. He has forbidden neckties at management board meetings.

Middelhoff is now trying to import some American energy to Gutersloh, where cows graze practically up to the wall of the low-rise Bertelsmann headquarters. Sometimes he wishes he had been born in freewheeling Silicon Valley rather than uptight Dusseldorf. 'Deep in my heart, I'm really American,' he says. Middelhoff spends close to half his time at Bertelsmann's New York headquarters in the heart of Times Square.

Middelhoff figures he started shedding his German identity on 2nd November, 1994. That was the day he met Steve Case. Back then, Middelhoff was Bertelsmann's head of corporate development. He arrived for a meeting with Case, thinking he would give the young American a lecture on the media business. He left blown away by Case's vision of an online media empire. Eventually, Bertelsmann's management board agreed to buy 5 per cent of AOL for $50 million. This prescient call boosted Middelhoff's ascension to the CEO slot by demonstrating to patriarch Mohn the power of the new medium. It showed 'he [could] provide the leadership necessary to bring Bertelsmann into the Internet Century,' recalls Case.[1]

> ### For discussion
> Is Thomas Middelhof a leader or a manager?

Someone once observed that a leader is a person who finds out which way the parade is going, jumps in front of it, and yells 'Follow me!' The plain fact is that this approach to leadership has little chance of working in today's rapidly changing world. Admired leaders, such as Nelson Mandela, Mahatma Ghandi, Body Shop's Anita Roddick, John Kennedy, and Virgin's Richard Branson, led people in bold new directions. They envisioned how things could be improved, rallied followers and refused to accept failure. In short, successful leaders are those individuals who can make a noticeable difference. But how much of a difference can leaders make in modern organizations?

OB researchers have discovered that leaders can make a difference. One study, for example, tracked the relationship between net profit and leadership in 167 companies from 13 industries. It also covered a time span of 20 years. Higher net profits were earned by companies with effective leaders.[2] Successful organizational change is highly dependent upon effective leadership throughout an organization. According to John Kotter, organizational change expert, successful organizational transformation requires 70 to 90 per cent leadership and 10 to 30 per cent management.[3] In a carefully controlled study of Icelandic fishing ships, it was found that differences in skippers accounted for a third to half the catch.[4] Leadership can make a difference.

On the other hand, subordinates are generally not very pleased with their leaders, as can be found in Table 16–1.

Table 16–1

What the Successful Business Leader Should Have and What He Really Has

	WHAT HE/SHE SHOULD HAVE	WHAT MY PRESENT CEO HAS
Able to build effective teams	96%	50%
Knows how to listen	93%	44%
Capable of making decisions on his own	87%	66%
Knows how to retain good people	86%	39%
Energetic	85%	62%
Innovative	83%	47%
Visionary	79%	45%
Has high ethical standards	76%	53%
Strong-willed	70%	65%
Charismatic	54%	34%
Motivated by power	35%	59%
Motivated by money	17%	40%
Ruthless	10%	28%
Paternalistic	6%	24%

SOURCE: 'Leadership', *Management Centre Europe*, 1988, p 11.

But even the research data are not very conclusive. Peter Wright, a British OB-specialist, offers the following view in his book on managerial leadership.

> *Most research findings, even when significant, account for a relatively small amount of the variance in subordinates' work performance and satisfaction. Similarly, there are a great many alternative approaches to leadership theory, the different theories within any one approach often contradict each other, and none is without flaws or limitations.[5]*

Leadership is culturally bound. Americans are the only people who talk so openly—sometimes obsessively—about the very notion of leadership. In America, leadership has become something of a cult concept. The French, tellingly, have no adequate word of their own for it. Germans have perfectly good words for leader and leadership; but Hitler rendered them politically incorrect (though Helmut Kohl has started occasionally to extol the virtues of *Führerschaft*). Mussolini similarly stigmatized the word *duce*.[6] The situation is even more extreme in The Netherlands or the Scandinavian countries, where leaders don't behave like leaders at all, at least not in the way described in American textbooks.[7]

An excellent example of informal leadership is the way Ingvar Kamprad managed IKEA, the world's largest home furnishing chain. The patriarchal way in which he treated his customers and staff reflected his philosophy of life. He is blessed with a genuine warmth and interest in people, which is undoubtedly one of the most important reasons for his success. Thanks to his influence, the company has an informal atmosphere which stresses simplicity. It is reflected in the neat but casual dress of the employees–jeans and sweaters–and in the relaxed office atmosphere where practically everyone sits in an open-plan office.[8]

This culturally bound phenomenon is not only restricted to charismatic leaders or to top management. The tendency to rely on supervision is clearly much stronger in English-speaking countries, especially in the US, than in other countries. Figure 16–1 gives a survey of the intensity of supervision in a number of European countries and in the US. Supervision varies from very low in Switzerland to very high in the US.

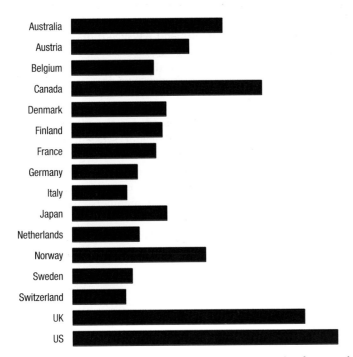

Figure 16–1

The Intensity of Supervision in 16 Countries

SOURCE: D Gordon, 'Boxes of Different Stripes: A Cross National Perspective on Monitoring and Supervision', *AEA Papers and Proceedings*, May 1994, p 376.

Concepts of leadership also differ between clusters of European countries. Northwestern European countries, and in particular the Nordic countries, score very highly on a dimension called 'interpersonal directness and proximity'. In these countries, successful business leaders are seen as enthusiastic, encouraging, sincere, informal, trustworthy and inspirational. In countries such as Georgia, Poland, Turkey and Slovenia, successful leaders are seen as self-interested, non-participative, asocial, very administrative, well organized, face-saving and indirect. The Germanic cluster (Germany, Austria, Switzerland) and the Czech Republic score very highly on the dimension called 'autonomy': successful leaders are seen as independent, autonomous, unique and even self-sacrificing. The Latin cluster (Portugal, Spain, Italy) is situated on the other end of this dimension: middle management in those countries see successful leaders as visionary, team integrators and status conscious.[9]

After formally defining the term *leadership*, this chapter focuses on the following areas: trait and behavioural approaches to leadership; alternative situational theories of leadership; charismatic leadership; and additional perspectives on leadership. Because there are so many different leadership theories within each of these areas, it is impossible to discuss them all.

WHAT DOES LEADERSHIP INVOLVE?

Because the topic of leadership has fascinated people for centuries, many definitions abound. This section presents a definition of leadership and highlights the similarities and differences between leading and managing.

What Is Leadership?

Disagreement about the definition of leadership stems from the fact that it involves a complex interaction between the leader, followers and situation. For example, some researchers define leadership in terms of personality and physical traits, while others believe leadership is represented by a set of prescribed behaviours. In contrast, other researchers believe that leadership is a temporary role that can be filled by anyone. There is a common thread, however, among the different definitions of leadership. The common thread is social influence.

Leadership
influencing employees to voluntarily pursue organizational goals

The succinct definition of **leadership** can be elaborated, for the purpose of this chapter, to 'a social influence process in which the leader seeks the voluntary participation of subordinates in an effort to reach organizational goals.'[10] An even more formal definition is given by the GLOBE research group as: 'the ability of an individual to influence, motivate and enable others to contribute toward the effectiveness and success of organizations of which they are members'.[11]

Figure 16–2 *A Conceptual Framework for Understanding Leadership*

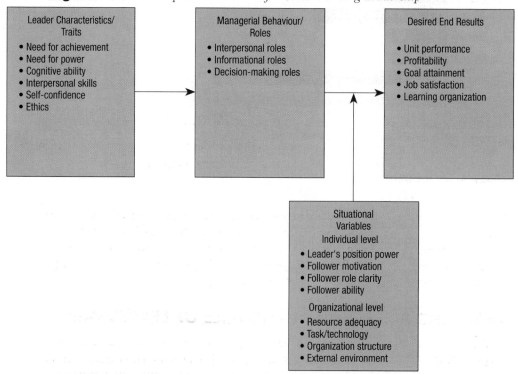

SOURCE: Adapted in part from G Yukl, 'Managerial Leadership: A Review of Theory and Research', *Journal of Management*, June 1989, p 274.

As you can see from this definition, leadership clearly entails more than wielding power and exercising authority, and is exhibited on different levels. At the individual level, for example, leadership involves mentoring, coaching, inspiring and motivating. Leaders build teams, create cohesion, and resolve conflicts at the group level. Finally, leaders build culture and create change at the organizational level.[12]

Figure 16–2 provides a conceptual framework for understanding leadership. It was created by integrating components of the different theories and models discussed in this chapter. Figure 16–2 indicates that certain leader characteristics or traits are the foundation of effective leadership. In turn, these characteristics affect an individual's ability to employ managerial behaviour and roles. Effective leadership also depends on various situational variables. These variables are important components of the contingency leadership theories discussed later in this chapter. Finally, leadership is results oriented.

Leading versus Managing

It is important to appreciate the difference between leadership and management in order to fully understand what leadership is all about. Bernard Bass, a leadership expert, concluded that 'Leaders manage and managers lead but the two activities are not synonymous.'[13] Bass tells us that although leadership and management overlap, each entails a unique set of activities or functions. Broadly speaking, managers typically perform functions associated with planning, investigating, organizing and control; while leaders deal with the interpersonal aspects of a manager's job. Leaders inspire others, provide emotional support and try to get employees to rally around a common goal. Leaders also play a key role in creating a vision and strategic plan for an organization. Managers, in turn, are charged with implementing the vision and strategic plan. Table 16–2 summarizes the key differences found between leaders and managers.[14]

Leaders	Managers
Innovate	Administer
Develop	Maintain
Inspire	Control
Long-term view	Short-term view
Ask what and why	Ask how and when
Originate	Initiate
Challenge the status quo	Accept the status quo
Do the right things	Do things right

Table 16–2
Differences between Leaders and Managers

SOURCE: Distinctions were taken from W G Bennis, *On Becoming a Leader* (Reading, MA: Addison-Wesley, 1989).

Distinctions between leading and managing highlight the point that leadership is not restricted to people in particular positions or roles. Anyone from the bottom to the top of an organization can be a leader. Many an informal leader has contributed to organizational effectiveness. Bennis characterized managers as people who *do things right* and leaders as individuals who *do the right things*.

TRAIT AND BEHAVIOURAL THEORIES OF LEADERSHIP

This section examines the two earliest approaches used to explain leadership. Trait theories focused on identifying the personal traits that differentiated leaders from followers. Behavioural theorists examined leadership from a different perspective. They tried to uncover the different kinds of leader behaviour that resulted in higher work group performance.

Trait Theory

At the turn of the 20th century, the prevailing belief was that leaders were born not made. Selected people were thought to possess inborn traits that made them successful leaders hence the idea of a **leader trait**.

Before the Second World War, hundreds of studies were conducted to pinpoint the traits of successful leaders. Dozens of leadership traits were identified. During the post-war period, however, enthusiasm was replaced by widespread criticism. Studies conducted by Ralph Stogdill in 1948 and by Richard Mann in 1959, which sought to summarize the impact of traits on leadership, caused the trait approach to fall into disfavour.

Leader trait
personal characteristic that differentiates a leader from a follower

Stogdill's and Mann's Findings

Based on his review, Stogdill concluded that five traits tended to differentiate leaders from average followers: (1) intelligence, (2) dominance, (3) self-confidence, (4) level of energy and activity, and (5) task-relevant knowledge.[15] Jack Welch, former chief executive officer of General Electric, was one of the most highly regarded managers in the world. Consider the leadership traits that he indicated he was looking for in his replacement during an interview with *Fortune*.

> 'Vision. Courage. The four E's: energy, ability to energize others, the edge to make tough decisions, and execution, which is key because you can't just decide but have got to follow up in 19 ways. Judgement. The self-confidence to always hire someone who's better than you. Are they growing things? Do they add new insights to the businesses they run? Do they like to nurture small businesses?'
>
> And one more: an insatiable appetite for accomplishment. Too many CEOs, Welch once said, believe that the high point comes the day they land the job. Not Welch, who says, 'I'm 63 and finally getting smart.'[16]

Although Welch was looking for some of the same traits as those identified by Ralph Stogdill, research revealed that these five traits did not accurately predict which individuals became leaders in organizations.

Mann's review was similarly disappointing for the trait theorists. Among the seven categories of personality traits he examined, Mann found intelligence was the best predictor of leadership. However, Mann warned that all observed positive relationships between traits and leadership were weak (correlations averaged about 0.15).[17]

Together, Stogdill's and Mann's findings nearly dealt a death blow to the trait approach. But now, decades later, leadership traits are once again receiving serious research attention.

Contemporary Trait Research

Two OB researchers concluded in 1983 that past trait data may have been incorrectly analysed. By applying modern statistical techniques to an old database, they demonstrated that the majority of a leader's behaviour could be attributed to stable underlying traits.[18] Unfortunately, their methodology did not specify which traits.

A 1986 meta-analysis by Robert Lord and his associates remedied this shortcoming. Based on a re-analysis of Mann's data and subsequent studies, Lord concluded that people have leadership *prototypes* that affect our perceptions of who is and who is not an effective leader. Your **leadership prototype** is a mental representation of the traits and behaviours that you believe are possessed by leaders. We thus tend to perceive that someone is a leader when he or she exhibits traits or types of behaviour that are consistent with our prototypes.[19] Lord's research demonstrated that people are perceived as being leaders when they exhibit the traits associated with intelligence, masculinity and dominance. A more recent study of 200 students also confirmed the

Leadership prototype
mental representation of the traits and behaviours possessed by leaders

idea that leadership prototypes influence leadership perceptions. Results revealed that perceptions of an individual as a leader were affected by that person's sex—males were perceived to be leaders more than females—and behavioural flexibility. People who were more behaviourally flexible were perceived to be more like a leader.[20]

Another pair of leadership researchers attempted to identify key leadership traits by asking the following open-ended question to more than 20,000 people around the world: 'What values (personal traits or characteristics) do you look for and admire in your superiors?' The top four traits included honesty, forward-looking, inspiring, and competent.[21] The researchers concluded that these four traits constitute a leader's credibility. This research suggests that people want their leaders to be credible and to have a sense of direction.

Gender and Leadership

The increase in the number of women in the workforce has generated much interest in understanding the similarities and differences between female and male leaders. Important issues concern whether women and men: assume varying leadership roles within work groups; use different leadership styles; are more or less effective in leadership roles; and whether there are situational differences that produce gender differences in leadership effectiveness. Three meta-analyses were conducted to summarize research pertaining to these issues.

The first meta-analysis demonstrated that men and women differed in the type of leadership roles they assumed within work groups. Men were seen as displaying more overall leadership and task leadership. In contrast, women were perceived as displaying more social leadership.[22] Results from the second meta-analysis revealed that leadership styles varied by gender. Women used a more democratic or participative style than men. Men employed a more autocratic and directive style than women.[23] Finally, a meta-analysis of more than 75 studies uncovered three key findings.

1 Female and male leaders were rated as equally effective. This is a very positive outcome because it suggests that despite barriers and possible negative stereotypes toward female leaders, female and male leaders were equally effective.

2 Men were rated as more effective leaders than women when their roles were defined in more masculine terms, and women were more effective than men in roles defined in less masculine terms.

3 Gender differences in leadership effectiveness were associated with the percentage of male leaders and male subordinates. Specifically, male leaders were seen as more effective than females when there was a greater percentage of male leaders and male subordinates. Interestingly, a similar positive bias in leadership effectiveness was not found for women.[24]

Research carried out in the UK by Hay Management Consultants on 15 male, 20 female and 191 male and female subordinates concluded the following.

The styles that female managers use are not working as effectively with their male subordinates. The men do not see female managers doing such things as giving clear directions, explaining decisions and monitoring task performance. The authoritative style is an effective and important one. If women are not seen as using it by men this may not only affect their team's effectiveness but could influence their visibility with colleagues and bosses.[25]

In contrast to these traits, the next International OB on outlines the relevant leadership traits of Russian leaders from the 1400s to the present day. As you can see, Russian organizations need to nurture and develop a similar but different set of leadership traits.

International OB

http://www.amcham.ru

Russian Leadership Traits in Three Eras

Leadership Trait	Traditional Russian Society (1400s to 1917)	The Red Executive (1917 to 1991)	The Market -Oriented Manager (1991 to present)
Leadership Motivation			
Power	Powerful autocrats	Centralized leadership stifled grass-roots democracy	Shared power and ownership
Responsibility	Centralization of responsibility	Micromanagers and macropuppets	Delegation and strategic decision making
Drive			
Achievement motivation	Don't rock the boat	Frustrated pawns	The sky's the limit
Ambition	Equal poverty for all	Service to party and collective good	Overcoming the sin of being a winner
Initiative	Look both ways	Meticulous rule following and behind-the-scenes finessing	Let's do business
Energy	Concentrated spasms of work	'8-hour day, '8 to 8, firefighting	8-day week, chasing opportunities
Tenacity	Life is a struggle	Struggling to accomplish the routine	Struggling to accomplish the new
Honesty and Integrity			
Dual ethical standard	Deception in dealings, loyalty in friendships	Two sets of books, personal integrity	Wild capitalism, personal trust
Using connections (*blat*)	Currying favour with landowners	Greasing the wheels of the state	Greasing palms, but learning to do business straight
Self-Confidence			
	From helplessness to bravado	From inferior quality to 'big is beautiful'	From cynicism to overpromising

SOURCE: S M Puffer, 'Understanding the Bear: A Portrait of Russian Business Leaders', *Academy of Management Executive*, February 1994, p 42. Used with permission.

Behavioural Styles Theory

This phase of leadership research began during the Second World War as part of an effort to develop better military leaders. It was a response to the seeming inability of trait theory to explain leadership effectiveness and to the human relations movement, an offshoot of the Hawthorne Studies. The thrust of early behavioural leadership theory was to focus on leader behaviour, instead of on personality traits. It was believed that leader behaviour directly affected the effectiveness of the work group. This led researchers to identify patterns of behaviour (called leadership styles) that enabled leaders to influence others effectively.

The Ohio State Studies

Researchers at Ohio State University began by generating a list of the types of behaviour exhibited by leaders. At one point, the list contained 1,800 statements describing nine categories. Ultimately, the Ohio State researchers concluded there were only two independent dimensions to describe the behaviour of a leader: consideration and initiating structure. **Consideration**, involving as it does a focus on a concern for group members' needs and desires, is well illustrated by the leadership style of Penny Hughes, former president of Coca-Cola Company Great Britain and Ireland.

> *According to a close colleague of hers: Penny is really excellent at establishing rapport with people and encouraging them to be more open, more challenging. To an unusual and refreshing degree she genuinely values people and is totally fair with them. She often walks around the office, sits on the back of a chair and shares a joke with us. There is always lots of laughter!* [26]

Initiating structure is leader behaviour that organizes and defines what group members should be doing to maximize output. These two dimensions of leader behaviour were oriented at right angles to yield four behavioural styles of leadership (see Figure 16–3).

Initially, it was hypothesized that a high-structure, high-consideration style would be the one best style of leadership. Over the years, the effectiveness of this 'style has been tested many times. Overall, results have been mixed. Researchers thus concluded that there is not one best style of leadership.[27] Rather, it is argued that effectiveness of a given leadership style depends on situational factors.

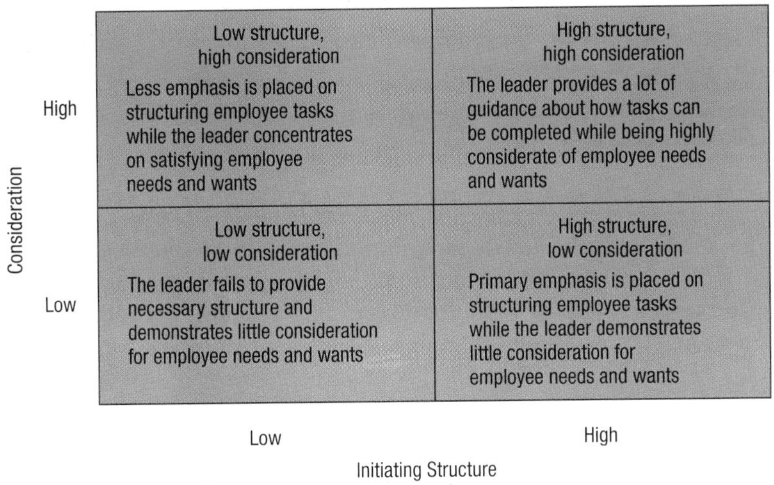

Consideration
creating mutual respect and trust between leader and followers

Initiating structure
organizing and defining what group members should be doing

Figure 16–3
Four Leadership Styles Derived from the Ohio State Studies

University of Michigan Studies

As in the Ohio State studies, this research sought to identify behavioural differences between effective and ineffective leaders. Researchers identified two different styles of leadership: one was centred on the employee, the other on the job. These behavioural styles parallel the consideration and initiating-structure styles identified by the Ohio State group. In summarizing the results of these studies, one management expert concluded that effective leaders:

▼ tend to have supportive or employee-centred relationships with employees

▼ use group rather than individual methods of supervision

▼ set high performance goals.[28]

Figure 16–4 *The Leadership Grid®*

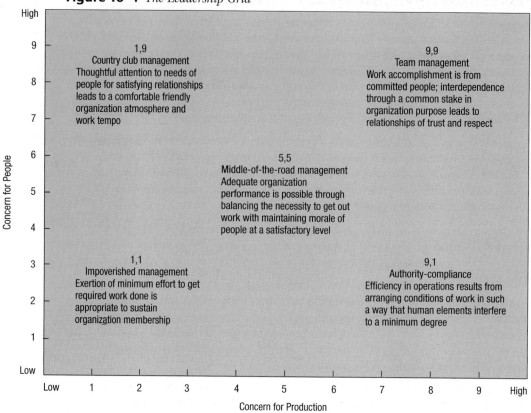

SOURCE: From *Leadership Dilemmas–Grid Solutions*, p 29 by Robert R Blake and Anne Adams McCanse. Copyright © 1991 by Robert R Blake and the estate of Jane S Mouton. Used with permission. All rights reserved.

Blake and Mouton's Managerial/Leadership Grid®

Perhaps the most widely known behavioural styles model of leadership is the Managerial Grid.® Behavioural scientists Robert Blake and Jane Srygley Mouton, developed and trademarked the highly controversial[29] grid. They use it to demonstrate that there *is* one best style of leadership. Blake and Mouton's Managerial Grid® (renamed the **Leadership Grid®** in 1991) is a matrix formed by the intersection of two dimensions of leader behaviour (see Figure 16–4). On the horizontal axis is 'concern for production'. 'Concern for people' is on the vertical axis.

Leadership Grid®
Represents four leadership styles found by crossing concern for production and concern for people

Blake and Mouton point out that 'the variables of the Managerial Grid® are *attitudinal* and *conceptual*, with *behaviour* descriptions derived from and connected with the thinking that lies behind action'.[30] In other words, concern for production and concern for people involve attitudes and patterns of thinking, as well as specific types of behaviour. By scaling each axis of the grid from 1 to 9, Blake and Mouton were able to plot five leadership styles. Because it emphasizes teamwork and interdependence, the 9,9 style is considered by Blake and Mouton to be the best, regardless of the situation.

In support of the 9,9 style, Blake and Mouton cite the results of a study in which 100 experienced managers were asked to select the best way of handling 12 managerial situations. Between 72 and 90 per cent of the managers selected the 9,9 style for each of the 12 situations.[31] Moreover, Blake and Mouton report, 'The 9,9, orientation . . . leads to productivity, satisfaction, creativity and health.'[32] Critics point out that Blake and Mouton's research may be self-serving. At issue is the grid's extensive use as a training and consulting tool for diagnosing and correcting organizational problems.

Behavioural Styles Theory in Perspective

By emphasizing the *behaviour* of leaders, something that is learned, the behavioural style approach makes it clear that leaders are made, not born. This is the opposite of the traditional assumption of the trait theorists. Given what we know about behaviour shaping and model-based training, the behaviour of a leader can be systematically improved and developed. Consider, for example, how Steve Sitek, director of performance development and training at Ernst and Young's Finance, Technology and Administration Division, is striving to grow and develop leadership talent within the organization.

> Sitek oversees a senior development programme that helps executives gain feedback on how they measure up against 11 critical leadership characteristics. Internal studies have shown a direct correlation between executive performance and the 11 characteristics, which include being innovative, excited, persuasive and strategic. In one-to-one encounters with superiors, managers discuss their assessments to identify characteristics that need strengthening and are charged with structuring their own development plans . . . . Managers are encouraged to work on the characteristics they need to grow incrementally over a multi-year period. Sitek produces specific training geared to each characteristic. 'I have a training programme for each one,' he says. 'For example, the No. 1 development gap that we discovered was the characteristic of persuasiveness. I offer a one-day programme on this characteristic.'[33]

Behavioural styles research also revealed that there is no one best style of leadership. The effectiveness of a particular leadership style depends on the situation at hand. For instance, employees prefer structure over consideration when faced with role ambiguity.[34] Finally, research also reveals that it is important to consider the difference between how frequently and how effectively managers exhibit various types of leadership behaviour. For example, a manager might ineffectively display a lot of considerate leader behaviours. Such a style is likely to frustrate employees and possibly result in lowered job satisfaction and performance. Because the frequency of exhibiting leadership behaviours is secondary in importance to effectiveness, managers are encouraged to concentrate on improving the *effective* execution of their leader behaviours.[35] Take a moment to complete the next OB Exercise on assessing leadership style.

OB Exercise

Assessing the Tutor's Leadership Style, Study Group Satisfaction and Student Role Clarity

Instructions

A team of researchers converted a set of leadership measures for application in a student setting. For each of the items shown here, use the following rating scale to circle the answer that best represents your feelings. Next, use the scoring key to calculate the scores for your tutor's (or lecture's) leadership style, your study group satisfaction and student role clarity.

1 = Strongly disagree

2 = Disagree

3 = Neither agree nor disagree

4 = Agree

5 = Strongly agree

1 My tutor behaves in a manner which is thoughtful of my personal needs.   1—2—3—4—5

2 My tutor maintains a friendly working relationship with me.   1—2—3—4—5

The exercise gives you the opportunity to test the behavioural styles theory by assessing your tutor's leadership style and your associated class satisfaction and role clarity. Are you satisfied with this class? If yes, the behavioural styles approach is supported if your tutor displayed both high consideration and initiating structure. In contrast, the behavioural style approach is not supported if you are satisfied with this class and your teacher exhibits something other than the standard high-high style. Do your results support the proposition that there is one best style of leadership? Are your results consistent with past research that showed leadership behaviour depends on the situation at hand? The answer is 'yes' if, when faced with high role ambiguity, you prefer initiating structure over consideration. The answer is also 'yes' if, when role ambiguity is low, you prefer consideration over structure. We now turn our attention to discussing alternative situational theories of leadership.

SITUATIONAL THEORIES

**Situational
theories**
*propose that leader
styles should match
the situation at hand*

Situational leadership theories came about as a result of an attempt to explain the inconsistent findings about traits and styles. **Situational theories** propose that the effectiveness of a particular style of leader behaviour depends on the situation. As situations change, different styles become appropriate. This directly challenges the idea of one best style of leadership. Let us closely examine three alternative situational theories of leadership.

Fiedler's Contingency Model

Fred Fiedler, an OB scholar, developed a situational model of leadership. It is the oldest and one of the most widely known models of leadership. Fiedler's model is based on the following assumption.

The performance of a leader depends on two interrelated factors: the degree to which the situation gives the leader control and influence—that is, the likelihood that [the leader] can successfully accomplish the job; and the leader's basic motivation—that is, whether [the leader's] self-esteem depends primarily on accomplishing the task or on having close supportive relations with others.[36]

With respect to a leader's basic motivation, Fiedler believes that leaders are either task motivated or relationship motivated. These basic motivations are similar to initiating structure/concern for production and consideration/concern for people. Consider the basic leadership motivation possessed by Cynthia Danaher, general manager of Hewlett-Packard's Medical Products Group.

Once a manager is in charge of thousands of employees, the ability to set the direction and delegate is more vital than team-building and coaching, she believes . . . . When Ms Danaher changed her top management team and restructured the Medical Products Group, moving out of slow-growth businesses to focus on more-profitable clinical equipment, she had to relinquish her need for approval. 'Change is painful, and someone has to be the bad guy,' she says. Suddenly employees she considered friends avoided her and told her she was ruining the group. 'I didn't use to be able to tolerate that, and I'd try to explain over and over why change had to occur,' she says. Over time, she has learned to simply 'charge ahead', accepting that not everyone will follow and that some won't survive.[37]

Clearly, Danaher has used a 'task motivated' style of leadership to create organizational change within Hewlett-Packard.

Fiedler's theory is also based on the premise that leaders have one dominant leadership style that is resistant to change. He suggests that leaders must learn to manipulate or influence the leadership situation in order to create a 'match' between their leadership style and the amount of control within the situation at hand. After discussing the components of situational control and the leadership matching process, we review relevant research and managerial implications.[38]

Situational Control

Situational control refers to the amount of control and influence the leader has in her or his immediate work environment. Situational control ranges from high to low. High control implies that the leader's decisions will produce predictable results because the leader has the ability to influence work outcomes. Low control implies that the leader's decisions may not influence work outcomes because the leader has very little influence. There are three dimensions of situational control: leader–member relations, task structure, and position power. These dimensions vary independently, forming eight combinations of situational control (see Figure 16–5).

The three dimensions of situational control are as follows.

▼ **Leader–member relations is the most important component of situational control. Good leader–member relations suggest that the leader can depend on the group, thus ensuring that the work group will try to meet the leader's goals and objectives.**

▼ **Task structure is the second most important component of situational control. A managerial job, for example, contains less structure than that of a bank teller. Because structured tasks have guidelines for how the job should be completed, the leader has more control and influence over employees performing such tasks.**

▼ **Position power, the final component, covers the leader's formal power to reward, punish or otherwise obtain compliance from employees.**[39]

Leader–member relations
extent to which leader has the support, loyalty and trust of work group

Task structure
amount of structure contained within work tasks

Position power
degree to which leader has formal power

Figure 16–5

*Representation of
Fiedler's Contingency
Model*

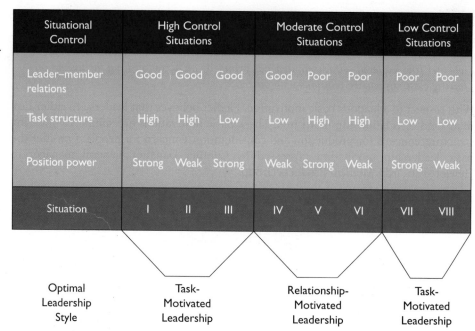

SOURCE: Adapted from F E Fiedler, 'Situational Control and a Dynamic Theory of Leadership', in *Managerial Control and Organizational Democracy*, eds B King, S Streufert and F E Fiedler (New York: John Wiley & Sons, 1978), P 114.

Linking Leadership Motivation and Situational Control

Fiedler's complete contingency model is presented in Figure 16–5. The last row under the Situational Control column shows that there are eight different leadership situations. Each situation represents a unique combination of leader–member relations, task structure, and position power. Situations I, II, and III represent high control situations. The Figure also shows that task-motivated leaders are expected to be the most effective in situations of high control. Under conditions of moderate control (situations IV, V, and VI), relationship-motivated leaders are thought to be the most effective. Finally, the results orientation of task-motivated leaders is predicted to be more effective under conditions of low control (situations VII and VIII).

Research and Managerial Implications

The overall accuracy of Fiedler's contingency model was tested by means of a meta-analysis of 35 studies containing 137 leader style–performance relations. The researchers found the following to be true.

1 The contingency theory was correctly deduced from studies on which it was based.

2 In laboratory studies testing the model, the theory was supported for all leadership situations except situation II.

3 In field studies testing the model, three of the eight situations (IV, V and VII) produced completely supportive results, while partial support was obtained for situations I, II, III, VI and VIII.

A more recent meta-analysis of data obtained from 1,282 groups also provided mixed support for the contingency model.[40] These findings suggest that Fiedler's model needs theoretical refinement.[41]

The major contribution of Fiedler's model is that it prompted others to examine the contingency nature of leadership. This research, in turn, reinforced the notion that there is no one best style of leadership. Leaders are advised to alter their task and relationship orientation to fit the demands of the situation at hand.

Path–Goal Theory

Path–goal theory is based on the expectancy theory of motivation discussed previously in Chapter 8. Expectancy theory proposes that motivation to exert effort increases as one's effort→performance→outcome expectations improve. Path–goal theory focuses on how leaders influence followers' expectations.

Robert House produced the path–goal theory of leadership. He proposed a model that describes how the contingent relationships between four leadership styles and various employee attitudes and behaviours influences expectancy perceptions. (see Figure 16–6).[42]

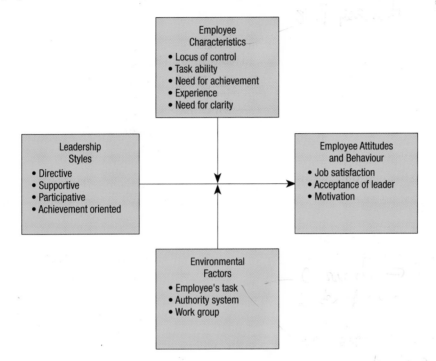

Figure 16–6

A General Representation of House's Path–Goal Theory

According to the path–goal model, behaviour of a leader is acceptable when employees view it as a source of satisfaction or as paving the way to future satisfaction. In addition, it is motivational to the extent that it clears the obstacles to goal accomplishment; provides the guidance and support needed by employees; and ties meaningful rewards to goal accomplishment. Because the model deals with pathways to goals and rewards, it is called the path–goal theory of leadership. House sees the leader's main job as helping employees to keep to the right paths to reach challenging goals and valued rewards.

Leadership Styles

House believes leaders can exhibit more than one leadership style. This contrasts with Fiedler, who proposes that leaders have only one dominant style. The four leadership styles identified by House are as follows.

▼ *Directive leadership.* Providing guidance to employees about what should be done and how to do it, scheduling work and maintaining standards of performance.

▼ *Supportive leadership.* Showing concern for the well-being and needs of employees, being friendly and approachable, and treating workers as equals.

▼ *Participative leadership.* Consulting with employees and seriously considering their ideas when making decisions.

▼ *Achievement-oriented leadership.* Encouraging employees to perform at their highest level by setting challenging goals, emphasizing excellence and demonstrating confidence in employee abilities.[43]

Research evidence supports the idea that leaders exhibit more than one leadership style.[44] Descriptions of business leaders reinforce these findings. Percy Barnevik, former ABB (Asea Brown Boveri) CEO, uses multiple leadership styles. When he introduced a matrix organization and seriously reduced staff numbers, he preferred to communicate directly with the 206,000 staff members: 'You cannot hide up there in an ivory tower. You have to be out there.' Although he prefers a persuasive approach when dealing with conflicts, he had to adopt a severe approach when he was faced with stubborn unions in the 1980s. It was only by issuing an ultimatum that Barnevik achieved the cuts he wanted.[45]

Contingency Factors

Contingency factors
situational variables that influence the appropriateness of a leadership style

Contingency factors affect expectancy or path–goal perceptions. This model has two groups of contingency variables (see Figure 16–6). They are employee characteristics and environmental factors. Five important employee characteristics are their locus of control, task ability, need for achievement, experience, and need for clarity. Three relevant environmental factors are the employee's task, authority system and work group. All these factors have the potential for hindering or motivating employees.

Research has focused on determining whether the various contingency factors influence the effectiveness of different leadership styles. A summary of this research revealed that only 138 of the 562 (25 per cent) contingency relationships tested actually confirmed the theory. Although these results were greater than chance, they provided limited support for the moderating relationships predicted by the path–goal theory. On the positive side, however, the results obtained–for the *task characteristics* of autonomy, variety and significance; and the *employee characteristics* of ability, experience, training and knowledge, professional orientation, indifference to organizational rewards, and need for independence–were partially consistent with the theory.[46]

Managerial Implications

There are two important managerial implications. First, leaders possess and use more than one style of leadership. Managers, therefore, should not be hesitant to try out new styles of behaviour when the situation calls for it. Second, a small set of task and employee characteristics are relevant contingency factors. Managers are encouraged to modify their leadership style to fit these various task and employee characteristics. For example, supportive and achievement leadership are more likely to be satisfying when employees have a lot of ability and experience.

Hersey and Blanchard's Situational Leadership Theory

Readiness
follower's ability and willingness to complete a task

Situational leadership theory (SLT) was developed by management writers Paul Hersey and Kenneth Blanchard.[47] According to their theory, effective leadership behaviour depends on the level of **readiness** of a leader's followers. Part of this readiness, willingness, is a combination of confidence, commitment and motivation.

The SLT model is summarized in Figure 16–7. The appropriate leadership style is found by cross-referencing follower readiness (which varies from low to high) with one of four leadership styles. The four leadership styles represent combinations of task and relationship-oriented leader behaviours (S_1 to S_4). Leaders are encouraged to use a 'telling style' (directive) for followers with low readiness. This style combines high task-oriented leader behaviours, such as providing instructions, with low relationship-oriented behaviours, such as close supervision (see Figure 16–7). As follower readiness increases, leaders are advised to gradually move from a telling to a selling style, then on to a participating and, ultimately, a delegating style. In the most recent description of this model, the four leadership styles depicted in Figure 16–7 are referred to as telling or directing (S_1), persuading or coaching (S_2), participating or supporting (S_3), and delegating (S_4).[48]

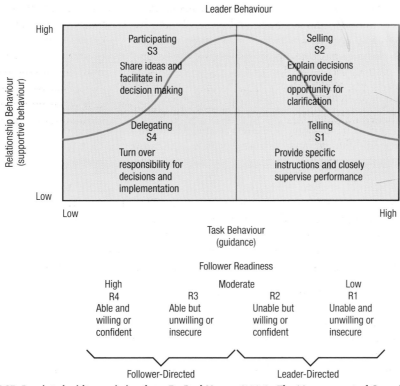

Figure 16–7
*Situational
Leadership Model*

SOURCE: Reprinted with permission from Dr Paul Hersey (1984). *The Management of Organizational Behavior: Utilizing Human Resources*, The Center for Leadership Studies, Escondido, CA. All rights reserved.

Although SLT is widely used as a training tool, it is not strongly supported by scientific research. For instance, leadership effectiveness was not attributable to the predicted interaction between follower readiness and leadership style in a study of 459 salespeople.[49] Moreover, a study of 303 teachers indicated that SLT was accurate only for employees with low readiness. This finding is consistent with a survey of 57 chief nurse executives in California. These executives did not delegate in accordance with SLT.[50] Finally, researchers have concluded that the self-assessment instrument used to measure leadership style and follower readiness is inaccurate and should be used with caution.[51] In summary, managers should exercise discretion when using prescriptions from SLT.

FROM TRANSACTIONAL TO CHARISMATIC LEADERSHIP

New perspectives of leadership theory have emerged in the past 15 years, variously referred to as 'charismatic', 'heroic', 'transformational' or 'visionary' leadership.[52] These competing but related perspectives have created confusion amongst researchers and practising managers. Fortunately, Robert House and Boas Shamir have given us a practical, integrated theory. It is referred to as that of *charismatic leadership*.

This section begins by highlighting the differences between transactional and charismatic leadership. We then discuss a model of the charismatic leadership process and its implications for research and management.

What Is the Difference between Transactional and Charismatic Leadership?

Most of the models and theories previously discussed earlier in this chapter represent **transactional leadership**. Leaders are seen as engaging in behaviours that maintain a quality interaction between themselves and followers. The two underlying

Transactional leadership
focuses on interpersonal interactions between managers and employees

characteristics of transactional leadership are that leaders use contingent rewards to motivate employees; and leaders exert corrective action only when subordinates fail to obtain performance goals.

Charismatic leadership

transforms employees to pursue organizational goals over self-interests

In contrast, **charismatic leadership** emphasizes 'symbolic leader behaviour, visionary and inspirational messages, non-verbal communication, appeal to ideological values, intellectual stimulation of followers by the leader, display of confidence in self and followers, and leader expectations for follower self-sacrifice and for performance beyond the call of duty.'[53] Charismatic leadership can produce significant organizational change and results because it 'transforms' employees to pursue organizational goals in lieu of self-interests. Richard Branson, chief operating officer of the Virgin group, is a good example of a charismatic leader.

> *Richard didn't breeze through school. It wasn't just a challenge for him, it was a nightmare. His dyslexia embarrassed him as he had to memorize and recite word for word in public. He was sure he did terribly on the standard IQ tests . . . these are tests that measure abilities where he is weak. In the end, it was the tests that failed. They totally missed his ability and passion for sports. They had no means to identify ambition, the fire inside that drives people to find a path to success that zigzags around the maze of standard doors that won't open. They never identified the most important talent of all. It's the ability to connect with people, mind to mind, soul to soul. It's that rare power to energize the ambitions of others so that they, too, rise to the level of their dreams.*[54]

Let us now examine how charismatic leadership transforms followers.

How Does Charismatic Leadership Transform Followers?

Charismatic leaders transform followers by creating changes in their goals, values, needs, beliefs and aspirations. They accomplish this transformation by appealing to followers' self-concepts—namely, their values and personal identity. Figure 16–8 presents a model of how charismatic leadership accomplishes this transformation process.

Figure 16–8 *A Charismatic Model of Leadership*

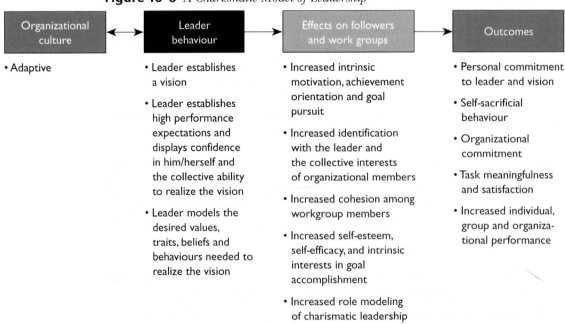

SOURCE: Based in part on D A Waldman and F J Yammarino, 'CEO Charismatic Leadership: Levels-of-Management and Levels-of-Analysis Effects', *Academy of Management Review*, April 1999, pp 266–85; and B Shamir, R J House and M B Arthur, 'The Motivational Effects of Charismatic Leadership: A Self-Concept Based Theory', *Organization Science*, November 1993, pp 577–94.

Figure 16–8 shows that organizational culture is a key precursor of charismatic leadership. You may recall from our discussion of organizational culture in Chapter 3 that long-term financial performance was highest for organizations with an adaptive culture. Organizations with adaptive cultures anticipate and adapt to environmental changes and focus on leadership that emphasizes the importance of service to customers, stockholders and employees. This type of management orientation involves the use of charismatic leadership.

Charismatic leaders first engage in three key sets of leader behaviour. If done effectively, this behaviour positively affects individual followers and their work groups. These positive effects, in turn, influence a variety of outcomes. Before discussing the model of charismatic leadership in more detail, it is important to note two general conclusions about charismatic leadership.[55] First, the two-headed arrow between organizational culture and leader behaviour in Figure 16–8 reveals that individuals with charismatic behavioural tendencies are able to influence culture. This implies that charismatic leadership reinforces the core values of an adaptive culture and helps to change the dysfunctional aspects of an organization's culture that develop over time. Second, charismatic leadership has an effect on multiple levels within an organization. For example, Figure 16–8 shows that charismatic leadership can positively influence individual outcomes (e.g., motivation), group outcomes (e.g., group cohesion), and organizational outcomes (e.g., financial performance). You can see that the potential for positive benefits from charismatic leadership is quite widespread.

Charismatic Leader Behaviour

The first set of charismatic leader behaviours involves establishing a common vision of the future. A vision is 'a realistic, credible, attractive future for your organization'.[56] According to Burt Nanus, a leadership expert, the 'right' vision unleashes human potential because it serves as a beacon of hope and common purpose. It does this by attracting commitment, energizing workers, creating meaning in employees' lives, establishing a standard of excellence, promoting high ideals, and bridging the gap between an organization's present problems and its future goals and aspirations.[57] In contrast, the 'wrong' vision can be very damaging to an organization. Consider what happened to Britain's Saatchi and Saatchi, once the world's most famous publicity agency.

> *Strengthened by successive successful publicity campaigns, including Margaret Thatcher's in the eighties, Maurice Saatchi's unrestrained ambition pulled down the entire business. Thanks to a positive evolution on the stock market, he suddenly had an enormous budget at his disposal which prompted him to buy publicity agencies, marketing companies, public relations agencies and publishing houses. He was game for anything. His wild buying binge led to pure megalomania as, in 1987, he decided to takeover Hill Samuel to be followed by one of Britain's biggest banks, the Midland Bank. Mismanagement and disorganization, followed by a crash resulted in the company's breakdown.[58]*

As you can see, Maurice Saatchi's vision produced disastrous results. This highlights the fact that charismatic leaders do more than simply establish a vision. They must also gain input from others in developing an effective implementation plan. For example, Johnson & Johnson obtained input about its vision and implementation plan by carrying out a survey amongst all its 80,000 employees.[59]

The second set of leader behaviours involves two key components.

▼ **Charismatic leaders set high performance expectations and standards because they know challenging, attainable goals lead to greater productivity.**

▼ **Charismatic leaders need to publicly express confidence in the followers' ability to meet high performance expectations. This is essential because employees are more likely to pursue difficult goals when they believe they can accomplish them.**

The third and final set of leader behaviours involves being a role model. Through their actions, charismatic leaders model the desired values, traits, beliefs and behaviours needed to realize the vision.

Motivational Mechanisms Underlying the Positive Effects of Charismatic Leadership

Charismatic leadership positively affects employee motivation (see Figure 16–8). One way in which this occurs is by increasing the intrinsic value of an employee's effort and goals. Leaders do this by emphasizing the symbolic value of effort; that is, charismatic leaders convey the message that effort reflects important organizational values and collective interests. Followers come to learn that their level of effort represents a moral statement. For example, high effort represents commitment to the organization's vision and values, whereas low effort reflects a lack of commitment.

Charismatic leadership also increases employees' effort→performance expectancies by positively contributing to followers' self-esteem and self-efficacy. Leaders increase the intrinsic value of goal accomplishment by explaining the organization's vision and goals in terms of the personal values they represent. This helps employees to connect personally with the organization's vision. Charismatic leaders further increase the meaningfulness of actions aimed toward goal accomplishment by showing how goals move the organization toward its positive vision, which then gives followers a sense of 'growth and development', both of which are important contributors to a positive self-concept.

Research and Managerial Implications

The charismatic model of leadership presented in Figure 16–8 was partially supported by previous research. A study of 50 field companies in the Israel Defence Forces revealed that charismatic leader behaviour was positively related to the followers' identification with and trust in the leader, motivation, self-sacrifice, identification with, and attachment to, the work group.[60]

A meta-analysis of 54 studies further indicated that charismatic leaders were viewed as more effective leaders by both supervisors and followers; and had followers who exerted more effort and reported higher levels of job satisfaction than non-charismatic leaders.[61]

Other studies showed that charismatic leadership was positively associated with followers' individual performance, job satisfaction and their satisfaction with the leader.[62] At the organizational level, a second meta-analysis demonstrated that this type of leadership was positively correlated with organizational measures of effectiveness.[63] Two additional studies demonstrated that both charismatic and transactional leadership were positively associated with a variety of important employee outcomes.[64] Finally, a study of 31 presidents of the United States indicated that charisma significantly predicted presidential performance.[65]

These results underscore four important managerial implications. First, the best leaders are not just charismatic, they are both transactional and charismatic. Leaders should attempt these two types of leadership while avoiding a 'laissez-faire' or 'wait-and-see' style. Laissez-faire leadership is the most ineffective leadership style.[66]

Second, charismatic leadership is not applicable to all organizational situations. According to a team of experts, charismatic leadership is most likely to be effective in the following instances.

▼ **The situation offers opportunities for 'moral' involvement.**

▼ **Performance goals cannot be easily established and measured.**

▼ **Extrinsic rewards cannot be clearly linked to individual performance.**

▼ **There are few situational cues or constraints to guide behaviour.**

▼ **Exceptional effort, behaviour, sacrifices and performance are required of both leaders and followers.**[67]

Third, employees at any level in an organization can be trained to be more transactional and charismatic.[68] This reinforces the organizational value of developing and offering a combination of transactional and charismatic leadership training for all employees. Fourth, charismatic leaders can be ethical or unethical. Whereas ethical charismatic leaders enable employees to enhance their self-concepts, unethical ones select or produce obedient, dependent and compliant followers.[69] Top management can create and maintain ethical charismatic leadership by:

▼ **creating and enforcing a clearly stated code of ethics**

▼ **recruiting, selecting and promoting people with high morals and standards**

▼ **developing performance expectations around the treatment of employees; these expectations can then be assessed in the performance appraisal process**

▼ **training employees to value diversity**

▼ **identifying, rewarding and publicly praising employees who exemplify high moral conduct.**[70]

ADDITIONAL PERSPECTIVES ON LEADERSHIP

This section examines four additional approaches to leadership: substitutes for leadership, servant leadership, *superleadership* and coaching.

Substitutes for Leadership

Virtually all leadership theories assume that some sort of formal leadership is necessary, whatever the circumstances. But this basic assumption is questioned by this model of leadership. Specifically, some OB scholars propose that there are a variety of situational variables that can act as **substitutes for leadership**.[71] These substitutes can thus increase or diminish a leader's ability to influence the work group. For example, leader behaviour that initiates structure would tend to be resisted by independent-minded employees with high ability and vast experience. Consequently, such employees would be guided more by their own initiative than by managerial directives.

> **Substitutes for leadership**
> *situational variables that can substitue for, neutralize or enhance the effects of leadership*

Kerr and Jermier's Substitutes for Leadership Model

According to Steven Kerr and John Jermier, the OB researchers who developed this model, the key to improving leadership effectiveness is to identify the substitutes for leadership (see Table 16–3). Characteristics of the subordinate, the task, and the organization can act as substitutes for traditional hierarchical leadership. Further, different characteristics are predicted to negate different types of leader behaviour.

For example, tasks that provide feedback concerning accomplishment, such as taking a test, tend to negate task-oriented but not relationship-oriented leader behaviour (see Table 16–3). Although the list in Table 16–3 is not all-inclusive, it shows that there are more substitutes for task-oriented leadership than for relationship-oriented leadership.

Research and Managerial Implications

Two different approaches have been used to test this model. The first is based on the idea that substitutes for leadership are contingency variables that moderate the relationship between leader behaviour and employee attitudes and behaviour.[72] A recent summary of this research revealed that only 318 of the 3,741 (9 per cent) contingency relationships tested supported the model.[73] This demonstrates that substitutes for leadership do not moderate the effect of a leader's behaviour as suggested by Steve Kerr and John Jermier. The second approach to test the substitutes model examined whether substitutes for leadership have a direct effect on employee attitudes and behaviours. A recent meta-analysis of 36 different samples revealed that the combination of substitute variables and leader behaviours significantly explained

Table 16-3

Substitutes for Leadership

Characteristic	Relationship-Oriented or Considerate Leader Behaviour Is Unnecessary	Task-Oriented or Initiating Structure Leader Behaviour Is Unnecessary
Of the Subordinate		
1 Ability, experience, training, knowledge		X
2 Need for independence	X	X
3 'Professional' orientation	X	X
4 Indifference toward organizational rewards	X	X
Of the Task		
5 Unambiguous and routine		X
6 Methodologically invariant		X
7 Provides its own feedback concerning accomplishment		X
8 Intrinsically satisfying	X	
Of the Organization		
9 Formalization (explicit plans, goals and areas of responsibility)		X
10 Inflexibility (rigid, unbending rules and procedures)		X
11 Highly specified and active advisory and staff functions		X
12 Closely knit, cohesive work groups	X	X
13 Organizational rewards not within the leader's control	X	X
14 Spatial distance between superior and subordinates	X	X

SOURCE: Adapted from S Kerr and J M Jermier, 'Substitutes for Leadership: Their Meaning and Measurement', *Organizational Behavior and Human Performance*, December 1978, pp 375–403.

a variety of employee attitudes and behaviours. Interestingly, the substitutes for leadership were more important than leader behaviours in accounting for employee attitudes and behaviours.[74]

The key implication is that managers should be attentive to the substitutes listed in Table 16–3 because they directly influence employee attitudes and performance. Managers can positively influence the substitutes through employee selection, job design, work group assignments, and the design of organizational processes and systems.[75]

Servant-Leadership

Servant-leadership is more a philosophy of managing than a testable theory. The term *servant-leadership* was coined by Robert Greenleaf in 1970. Greenleaf believes that great leaders act as servants, putting the needs of others, including employees, customers and community, as their first priority. Servant-leadership focuses on increased service to others rather than to oneself.[76] Servant-leadership is not a quick-fix approach to leadership. Rather, it is a long-term, transformational approach to life and work. Table 16–4 presents 10 characteristics possessed by servant-leaders. One can hardly go wrong by trying to adopt these characteristics.

Servant-leadership
focuses on increased service to others rather than to oneself

Table 16–4 *Characteristics of the Servant-Leader*

Servant-Leadership Characteristics	Description
1. Listening	Servant-leaders focus on listening to identify and clarify the needs and desires of a group.
2. Empathy	Servant-leaders try to empathize with others' feelings and emotions. An individual's good intentions are assumed even when he or she performs poorly.
3. Healing	Servant-leaders strive to make themselves and others whole in the face of failure or suffering.
4. Awareness	Servant-leaders are very self-aware of their strengths and limitations.
5. Persuasion	Servant-leaders rely more on persuasion than positional authority when making decisions and trying to influence others.
6. Conceptualization	Servant leaders take the time and effort to develop broader based conceptual thinking. Servant-leaders seek an appropriate balance between a short-term, day-to-day focus and a long-term, conceptual orientation.
7. Foresight	Servant-leaders have the ability to foresee future outcomes associated with a current course of action or situation.
8. Stewardship	Servant-leaders assume that they are stewards of the people and resources they manage.
9. Commitment to the growth of people	Servant-leaders are committed to people beyond their immediate work role. They commit to fostering an environment that encourages personal, professional, and spiritual growth.
10. Building community	Servant-leaders strive to create a sense of community both within and outside the work organization.

SOURCE: These characteristics and descriptions were derived from L C Spears, 'Introduction: Servant-Leadership and the Greenleaf Legacy', in *Reflections on Leadership: How Robert K Greenleaf's Theory of Servant-Leadership Influenced Today's Top Management Thinkers*, ed L C Spears (New York: John Wiley & Sons, 1995), pp 1–14.

Superleadership

The approach to leadership of a superleader, leading others to lead themselves, has already been discussed in relation to developing team members' self-management skills in Chapter 12. We briefly highlight it again because superleadership is as relevant within teams as it is to any general leadership situation. Superleaders empower followers by acting as a teacher and coach rather than as a dictator and autocrat. The need for this form of leadership is underscored by a survey of 1,046 Americans. Results demonstrated that only 38 per cent of the respondents had ever had an effective coach or mentor.[77]

Superleader *someone who leads others to lead themselves*

Productive thinking is the cornerstone of superleadership. Specifically, managers are encouraged to teach followers how to engage in productive thinking.[78] This is expected to increase employees' feelings of personal control and intrinsic motivation. Superleadership has the potential to free up a manager's time because employees are encouraged to manage themselves. Future research is needed to test the validity of recommendations derived from this new approach to leadership.

Coaching

Modern management thinking is no longer characterized by dominant and authoritarian leadership but by coaching.[79] A good coach is able to offer commitment and support, build skills and teams, and to focus on results.

Commitment

The professional managers directs from a distance, whereas a coach acts directly with his players. A coach is present on the field, to support his team. He is present at the moment of action, which he experiences actively. He is not engrossed in files or participating in long-lasting meetings. Action happens in the field. A real coach is not afraid 'to put his shoulder to the wheel' and help when it's needed. The rational, cool and distant manager has to make place for the enthusiastic coach, who trusts his subordinates and knows them personally. He is conscious of their weaknesses and is capable of getting the best out of them. Day after day, he tries to improve his staff's performance and possibilities.

Skill building

The coach invests much effort in his employees' skill building. He is aware of the fact that they are the driving force of his organization. He will see to it that they improve their professional skills, can organize their work themselves, and are directed towards a common goal.

Support

The coach will principally support his team to enable it to show results.

Team builder

The coach is a team builder, he brings people together with different skills, interests and backgrounds to create a solid team. A struggle for power and political conflict has to be replaced by mutual respect. The coach is successful in transforming internal into external competition, directed towards the real competitors.

Result-oriented

The coach's efforts are not aimed at creating a cozy environment, he wants to see results.

Summary of Key Concepts

1 Define the term leadership, and explain the difference between leading versus managing.

Leadership is defined as a process of social influence in which the leader tries to obtain the voluntary participation of employees in an effort to reach organizational objectives. Leadership entails more than having authority and power. Although leadership and management overlap, each entails a unique set of activities or functions. Managers typically perform functions associated with planning, investigating, organizing, and control; while leaders deal with the interpersonal aspects of a manager's job. Table 16–2 summarizes the differences between leading and managing.

2 Review trait theory research and discuss the idea of one best style of leadership, using the Ohio State studies and the Leadership Grid® as points of reference.

Previous leadership research did not support the notion that effective leaders possessed unique traits to those of their followers. However, teams of researchers analysed this historical data again, this time using modern-day statistical procedures. Results revealed that individuals tend to be perceived as leaders when they possess one or more of the following traits: intelligence, dominance, and masculinity. A recent study further demonstrated that employees value credible leaders. Credible leaders are honest, forward-looking, inspiring and competent. Research also examined the relationship between gender and leadership. Results demonstrated that: men and women differed in the type of leadership roles they assume; leadership styles varied by gender; and gender differences in ratings of leadership effectiveness were associated with the percentage of male leaders and male subordinates. The Ohio State studies revealed that there were two key independent dimensions of leadership behaviour: consideration and initiating structure. Authors of the Leadership Grid® proposed that leaders should adopt a style that demonstrates high concern for production and people. Research did not support the premise that there is one best style of leadership.

3 Explain, according to Fiedler's contingency model, how leadership style interacts with situational control.

Fiedler believes the effectiveness of a leader depends on an appropriate match between leadership style and situational control. Leaders are either task motivated or relationship motivated. Situation control is composed of leader–member relations, task structure and position power. Task-motivated leaders are effective under situations of both high and low control. Relationship-motivated leaders are more effective when they have moderate situational control.

4 Discuss House's path–goal theory and Hersey and Blanchard's situational leadership theory.

According to path–goal theory, leaders can alternate between exhibiting directive, supportive, participative and achievement-oriented styles of leadership. The effectiveness of these styles depends on various employee characteristics and environmental factors. Path–goal theory has received limited support from research. There are two important managerial implications: (a) leaders possess and use more than one style of leadership, and (b) managers are advised to modify their leadership style to fit a small subset of task and employee characteristics. According to situational leadership theory (SLT), effective leader behaviour depends on the readiness level of a leader's followers. As follower readiness increases, leaders are advised to gradually move from a telling to a selling to a participating and, finally, to a delegating style. Research does not support SLT.

5 Define and differentiate between transactional and charismatic leadership.

There is an important difference between transactional and charismatic leadership. Transactional leaders focus on the interpersonal transactions between managers and employees. Charismatic leaders motivate employees to pursue organizational goals above their own self-interests. Both forms of leadership are important for organizational success.

6 Explain how charismatic leadership transforms followers and work groups.

Organizational culture is a key precursor of charismatic leadership, which is composed of three sets of leader behaviour. These sets, in turn, positively affect followers' and work groups' goals, values, beliefs, aspirations and motivation. These positive effects are then associated with a host of preferred outcomes.

7 Summarize the managerial implications of charismatic leadership.

There are four managerial implications: (a) The best leaders are both transactional and charismatic. (b) Charismatic leadership is not applicable to all organizational situations. (c) Employees at any level in an organization can be trained to be more transactional and charismatic. (d) Top management needs to promote and reinforce ethical charismatic leadership because charismatic leaders can be ethical or unethical.

8 Describe the substitutes for leadership and explain how they substitute for, neutralize, or enhance the effects of leadership.

There are 14 substitutes for leadership (see Table 16–3) that can substitute for, neutralize or enhance the effects of leadership. These substitutes contain characteristics of the subordinates, the task and the organization. Research shows that substitutes directly influence employee attitudes and performance.

9 Describe what is meant by superleadership.

A superleader is someone who leads others to lead themselves. Superleaders empower followers by acting as a teacher and coach rather than a dictator and autocrat.

10 Describe servant-leadership and coaching.

Servant-leadership is more a philosophy than a testable theory. It is based on the premise that great leaders act as servants, putting the needs of others, including employees, customers, and community, as their first priority. A superleader is someone who leads others to lead themselves. Superleaders empower followers by acting as a teacher and coach rather than as a dictator and autocrat. A good coach has the following characteristics: commitment, support, an ability to build skills and teams, and to focus on results.

Discussion Questions

1 Is everyone cut out to be a leader? Explain.

2 Has your college education helped you to develop any of the traits that characterize leaders?

3 Should organizations change anything in response to research pertaining to gender and leadership? If yes, describe your recommendations.

4 What leadership traits and behavioural styles are possessed by your prime minister?

5 Does it make more sense to change a person's leadership style or the situation? How would Fred Fiedler and Robert House answer this question?

6 Describe how a lecturer might use House's path–goal theory to clarify student's path–goal perceptions.

7 Identify three charismatic leaders and describe their leadership traits and behavioural styles.

8 Have you ever worked for a charismatic leader? Describe how he or she transformed followers.

9 Have you ever been a member of an in-group or out-group? For either situation, describe the pattern of interaction between you and your manager.

10 In your view, which leadership theory has the greatest practical application? Why?

Internet Exercise

http://www.leader-values.com

The topic of leadership has been important since the dawn of time. History is filled with examples of great leaders such as Mohandas ('Mahatma') Gandhi, Martin Luther King and Winston Churchill. These leaders are most likely to have possessed some of the leadership traits discussed in this chapter, and they probably used a situational approach to lead their followers. The purpose of this exercise is for you to evaluate the leadership styles of an historical figure.

Go to the Internet home page for Leadership Values (**www.leader-values.com**), and select the subheading *4 E's* on the left of the screen. This section provides an overview of leadership and suggests four essential traits and behaviours that are exhibited by leaders: to envision, enable, empower and energize. After reading this material, go back to the home page, and select the subheading *Historical Leaders* from the list on the lefthand side of the

page. Next, choose one of the leaders from the list of historical figures, and read the description about his or her leadership style. You may want to print all the material you read thus far from this web page to help you answer the following questions.

Questions

1 Describe the 4 E's of leadership.

2 To what extent do the 4 E's overlap with the theories and models of leadership discussed in this chapter?

3 Using any of the theories or models discussed in this chapter, how would you describe the leadership style of the historical figure you investigated?

4 Was this leader successful in using the 4 E's of leadership? Describe how he or she used the 4 E's.

Personal Awareness and Growth Exercise

How Ready Are You to Assume the Leadership Role?

Objectives

1 To assess your readiness for the leadership role.

2 To consider the implications of the gap between your career goals and your readiness to lead.

Introduction

Leaders assume multiple roles. Roles represent the expectations that others have of occupants of a position. It is important for potential leaders to consider whether they are ready for the leadership role because mismatches in expectations or skills can derail a leader's effectiveness. This exercise assesses your readiness to assume the leadership role.[80]

Instructions

For each statement, indicate the extent to which you agree or disagree with it by selecting one number from the scale provided. Circle your response for each statement.

Remember, there are no right or wrong answers. After completing the survey, add your total score for the 20 items, then record it in the space provided.

1 = Strongly disagree

2 = Disagree

3 = Neither agree nor disagree

4 = Agree

5 = Strongly agree

1 It is enjoyable having people rely on me for ideas and suggestions. 1—2—3—4—5

2 It would be accurate to say that I have inspired other people. 1—2—3—4—5

3 It's a good practice to ask people provocative questions about their work. 1—2—3—4—5

4 It's easy for me to compliment others. 1—2—3—4—5

5 I like to cheer people up even when my own spirits are down. 1—2—3—4—5

6 What my team accomplishes is more important than my personal glory. 1—2—3—4—5

7 Many people imitate my ideas. 1—2—3—4—5

8 Building team spirit is important to me. 1—2—3—4—5

9 I would enjoy coaching other members of the team. 1—2—3—4—5

10 It is important to me to recognize others for their accomplishments. 1—2—3—4—5

11 I would enjoy entertaining visitors to my firm even if it interfered with my completing a report. 1—2—3—4—5

12 It would be fun for me to represent my team at gatherings outside our department. 1—2—3—4—5

13 The problems of my teammates are my problems too. 1—2—3—4—5

14 Resolving conflict is an activity I enjoy. 1—2—3—4—5

15 I would co-operate with another unit in the organization even if I disagreed with the position taken by its members. 1—2—3—4—5

16 I am an idea generator on the job. 1—2—3—4—5

17 It's fun for me to bargain whenever I have the opportunity. 1—2—3—4—5

18 Team members listen to me when I speak. 1—2—3—4—5

19 People have asked me to assume the leadership of an activity several times in my life. 1—2—3—4—5

20 I've always been a convincing person. 1—2—3—4—5

Total score: _____

Norms for Interpreting the Total Score[80]

90–100	=	High readiness for the leadership role
60–89	=	Moderate readiness for the leadership role
40–59	=	Some uneasiness with the leadership role
39 or less	=	Low readiness for the leadership role

Questions for Discussion

1 Do you agree with the interpretation of your readiness to assume the leadership role? Explain why or why not.

2 If you scored below 60 and desire to become a leader, what might you do to increase your readiness to lead? To answer this question, we suggest that you study the statements carefully–particularly those with low responses–to determine how you might change either an attitude or a behaviour so that you can realistically answer more questions with a response of 'agree' or 'strongly agree'.

3 How might this evaluation instrument help you to become a more effective leader?

Group Exercise
Exhibiting Leadership within the Context of Running a Meeting[81]

Objectives

1 To consider the types of problems that can occur when running a meeting.

2 To identify the types of leadership behaviour that can be used to handle problems that occur in meetings.

Introduction

Managers often find themselves playing the role of formal or informal leader when participating in a planned meeting (e.g., committees, work groups, task forces, etc.). As a leader, individuals must often handle a number of interpersonal situations that have the potential of reducing the group's productivity. For example, if an individual has important information that is not shared with the group, the meeting will be less productive. Similarly, two or more individuals who engage in conversational asides could disrupt the normal functioning of the group. Finally, the group's productivity will also be threatened by two or more individuals who argue or engage in personal attacks on one another during a meeting. This exercise is designed to help you practice some of the behavior necessary to overcome these problems and at the same time share in the responsibility of leading a productive group[82]

Instructions

Your tutor will divide the class into groups of four to six. Once the group is assembled, briefly summarize the types of problems that can occur when running a meeting–start with the material presented in the preceding introduction. Write your final list on a piece of paper. Next, for each problem on the group's list, the group should brainstorm a list of appropriate leader behaviors that can be used to handle the problem. Use the guidelines for brainstorming discussed in Chapter 14. Try to arrive at an agreed list.

Questions for Discussion

1 What type of problems that occur during meetings is most difficult to handle? Explain.

2 Are there any particular leader behaviors that can be used to solve multiple problems during meetings? Discuss your rationale.

3 Was there a lot of agreement about which leader behaviours were useful for dealing with specific problems encountered in meetings? Explain.

Chapter Seventeen

Managing Occupational Stress

It's all down to me...

'My workload is relentless—that's not an unfair description. I have peaks and troughs, but there's no such thing as a clear desk at the end of the day. I am a personal assistant to the chairman of an investment trust, who also has philanthropic, artistic and community commitments outside his main corporate job. It's all work: whether it's the dry cleaner or the executive jet, it's all down to me. ▶

I start between 9 and 9.30 a.m. Lunch more often than not is a sandwich at my desk, and I get away between 6 and 7 p.m., sometimes taking work home because I can't find a quiet moment during the day. Trying to reconcile the credit card statements is difficult if you are constantly interrupted.

A lot of my time is spent organizing things, thinking "If he's going to be at that meeting, I need to organize this, and he'll have to go from that to the next meeting, so I need to remind him that when he does that he needs to do this." It's about thinking things through and organizing as much of his life as possible.

As a secretary, by definition it's my job to take on the stress of other people's jobs. It goes without saying that secretaries are less in control of their workloads and experience a lot of stress of their own. Some bosses may tell their secretary what needs doing, and leave them to get on with it uninterrupted. But in busy offices that's the last thing that happens. It's a constant case of "Can you just . . . ."

That's what creates most stress: not being in control of one's own day. I come in thinking, 'I must work on the New York trip', but my boss has worked on his own at home the night before and what I had planned to do is put on the back burner. And while that happens the email's going, and colleagues need things. The frustration comes from knowing that you should have planned the New York trip today and you haven't got round to it.

I have been with the company for 18 years and with my boss for 17, and life has definitely got busier in that time. I think it's just a question of pace. Thirty years ago letters came in and people dictated replies, and if you were lucky they were turned around in three or four days. Now everything has to be done very quickly. Also there's the globalization factor: if you have the misfortune to be working in London and dealing a lot with the west coast of America or even New York, you can't ring them in the morning. You have to stay late. It's the same thing with Europe in the morning. If people know they can snatch you early they will. There's no hiding place.

I try to keep my sense of humour, and a sense of balance and perspective. You need to be able to switch off otherwise you can easily get into waking up at night thinking, 'I didn't give him that memo . . .'. I also write everything down. Post-it notes, that's what has saved us–you wonder what we did before we had them!

One of the things that adds to the stress is if you are part of a bigger team and you have to rely on others to do certain things. But you have to be flexible and understand that they have their own priorities and difficulties. The pressure starts to build up because of interruptions and this element of firefighting, rather than a quietly organized work process.'[1]

For discussion

How do you respond to an intense workload, for example, during an examination period? What do you do to cope with it?

As this opening case suggests, life in the 21st century can be hectic and stressful. Students must cope with tests, projects and increasing competition when looking for a job after graduation. Married couples must wrestle with the demands of managing careers and a family. Single parents encounter similar pressures. Stress at work is also on the rise, as many workers today find themselves in a devastating spiral of overload, conflict, tension and burn-out, or as a reporter for the *Guardian* observed.

When asking somebody 'How's it going?' he or she'll probably tell you something like this: 'Oh, you know, a bit stressed', or maybe: 'OK. Exhausted, but OK.' Stressed, manic, unbelievably busy, crazy, shattered, absolutely frantic, seconds away from meltdown— these are now standard answers to any enquiry about your wellbeing.[2]

According to a study from the International Labour Organization, more than 10 million Europeans get ill because of stress every year. The costs of this 'stress epidemic' are huge: it is estimated that in the European Union an average of 3 to 4 per cent of gross national product is spent on mental health problems.[3]

For example, in the UK, a country known for its 'long-hours culture', 3 in 10 workers have mental health problems and 15 to 30 per cent suffer from anxiety and depression. In Finland, more than half of the workforce is blighted with stress-related symptoms, 7 per cent are 'severely burnt out' and the country suffers from a high suicide rate. In Germany, almost 10 per cent of early retirements are caused by depression and over 80 million working days are lost every year due to stress.[4] In Japan, a new term has been added to the dictionaries: *Karoshi*, meaning 'dead from overwork'.[5] It is not surprising, therefore, that a spokesman of the ILO stated: 'Today, the workers of the world are united in just one thing, that is: record levels of stress.'[6]

The biggest contributor to work stress arises from fundamental changes that have been made in many organizations. As a result of increased competition, employees are being asked to deliver a better quality and a greater quantity of work in less time with fewer resources. Second, technological advancements make it harder for employees to completely disconnect from the office. Pagers, fax machines, email and cellular phones make it easy to disrupt our free time while at home or on holiday. Finally, the dynamics of modern life make it difficult to balance the demands of work and home. Research demonstrates that work stress spills over into one's personal life and vice versa.[7]

Although stress cannot be completely eliminated, it can be reduced and managed. With this end in mind, this chapter looks at the sources of stress, examines stressors and burn-out, highlights four moderators of occupational stress and explores a variety of stress-reduction techniques.

SOURCES OF STRESS

We all experience stress on a daily basis. Although stress is caused by many factors, researchers conclude that stress triggers one of two basic reactions: active fighting or passive flight (running away or acceptance), the so-called **fight-or-flight response**.[8] Physiologically, this stress response is a biochemical 'top gear' involving hormonal changes that mobilize the body for extraordinary demands. Imagine how our prehistoric ancestors responded to the stress associated with a charging saber-toothed tiger. To avoid being eaten, they could stand their ground and fight the beast or run away. In either case, their bodies would have been energized by an identical hormonal change, involving the release of adrenaline into the bloodstream.

Fight-or-flight response
to either confront stressors or try to avoid them

In our contemporary society, this fight-or-flight system still has a very visible consequence in the way we handle stress. Psychotherapist, Bob Vansant, gives us the following explanation.

'In our world there are only two different types of people,' he says. 'On the one hand you have the maniacs with their cellular phones and portables close at range, the so-

called workaholics who are always in gear. On the other hand, you have the depressive people who can't keep up with the pace any more and try to hide themselves away as a sort of silent protest against our manic lifestyle.'[9]

In today's hectic, urbanized and industrialized society, charging beasts have been replaced by problems such as deadlines, role conflict and ambiguity, financial responsibilities, information overload, technology, traffic congestion, noise and air pollution, family problems and work overload. As with our ancestors, our response to stress may or may not trigger negative side effects, including headaches, ulcers, insomnia, heart attacks, high blood pressure and strokes. The same stress response that helped our prehistoric ancestors survive has too often become a factor that seriously impairs our daily lives. Consider the following two examples.

At the age of 35, Carolyn Draper's life went on hold. She was in a highly stressful job, teaching in a tough inner-city secondary school in Sheffield. She dreaded going to work and every day she came home and collapsed into a chair with exhaustion. Her limbs ached, she began to get headaches and she finally succumbed to a nasty bout of flu. 'From that day on my life was never really the same', Carolyn says. 'I felt so shattered that I was going to bed really early but waking up feeling even more tired than ever. When I told my superiors, they said I was feeling depressed and that two weeks of counselling would have me feeling as right as rain. I burst into tears. I began to think I was going round the bend.'[10]

Adrenaline surges through Christine Peters's veins. The information-systems supervisor is frazzled from her day-long battle with computer flare-ups and system crashes. Desperate for a moment of peace, Peters ducks into a washroom. She leans against the cool wall and breathes deep, trying to meditate. Her trance is shattered by a knock on the door. The computers have crashed again . . . .[11]

Because stress and its consequences are manageable, it is important for managers to learn as much as they can about occupational stress. This section provides a conceptual foundation by defining stress, presenting a model of occupational stress, and highlighting related organizational costs.

Defining Stress

To an orchestra violinist, stress may stem from giving a solo performance before a large audience. While heat, smoke and flames may represent stress to a firefighter, delivering a speech or presenting a lecture may be stressful for those who are shy. In short, stress means different things to different people. Managers need a working definition.

Formally defined, **stress** is 'an adaptive response, mediated by individual characteristics and/or psychological processes, that is a consequence of any external action, situation or event that places special physical and/or psychological demands upon a person'.[12] This definition is not as difficult as it seems when we reduce it to three interrelated dimensions of stress: environmental demands, referred to as stressors; that produce an adaptive response; that is influenced by individual differences.

Stress
behavioural, physical or psychological response to stressors

Hans Selye, considered the father of the modern concept of stress, pioneered the distinction between stressors and the stress response. Moreover, Selye emphasized that both positive and negative events can trigger an identical stress response, which can be either beneficial or harmful. He referred to stress that is positive or produces a positive outcome as 'eustress'. For example, an employee who has to make a presentation to a large audience can feel extra pressure but the fact that he or she likes to do presentations very much, will make him or her experience the pressure in a positive way—as very motivating and challenging—rather than in a negative way.[13] Selye also noted that:

Eustress
stress that is good or produces a positive outcome

▼ stress is not merely nervous tension

▼ stress can have positive consequences

▼ stress is not something to be avoided

▼ the complete absence of stress is death.[14]

Selye was right in pointing to the positive aspects of stress. All learning implies at least a moderate amount of stress. Regular exposure to a manageable amount of stress keeps us fit; too little stress makes us bored. But on the other hand, the same employee who really loved doing presentations will get fed up by them when he has to work out and prepare lots of labour-intensive, time-consuming presentations over a short period. He won't have the time to recover between the presentations and his regular tasks will keep on stacking up. If this situation continues, he might become very strained and exhausted.[15] So, although a moderate amount of stress seems to be beneficial, excessive stress proves to be very detrimental. What conditions cause excessive stress and how can it be alleviated or even eliminated?

A model of occupational stress

Figure 17–1 presents an instructive model of occupational stress. The model shows that four types of stressors lead to perceived stress which, in turn, produces a variety of outcomes. The model also specifies several individual differences that *moderate* the stressor–stress–outcome relationship. A moderator is a variable that causes the relationship between two variables–such as stress and outcomes–to be stronger for some people and weaker for others.

For example, a study of 256 employees in a business office of a large retail organization investigated whether allowing workers to use personal-stereo headsets influenced the relationship between job characteristics and a variety of work outcomes. Results revealed that employees who used stereo headsets had shown significant improvement in their performance, turnover intentions, job satisfaction and mood. Use of personal-stereo headsets moderated the effects of stress.[16]

Stressors

Stressors are a prerequisite for stress. Figure 18–1 shows the four major types of stressors: individual, group, organizational and those outside the organisation (extraorganizational). The most common examples of stressors are job demands, work overload, role conflict, role ambiguity, everyday hassles, perceived control over events occurring in the work environment, and job characteristics.[17]

Stressors
environmental factors that produce stress

Individual-level stressors are those directly associated with a person's work responsibilities. During the last few decades, a vast amount of research has been undertaken to determine the effect of these stressors. Some examples are listed below.

A study of 771 US workers and a total of 2,642 employees from Canada, the United Kingdom and Germany revealed that the increasing amount of time people spend sending and receiving messages was a stressor at work. US workers sent and received the most messages. Forty-five per cent of the US workers further indicated that they felt hassled or bothered by interruptions at work: they were interrupted at least six times an hour.[18]

In another study, among German blue collar workers, it was found that subjects experiencing high efforts and low reward conditions and subjects who had few possibilities to exert control in their job, had higher risks of coronary heart diseases than their counterparts in less adverse psychosocial environments.[19] A later study, among working men in Stockholm, also confirmed that decision latitude could influence the risk of coronary problems such as infarctions.[20]

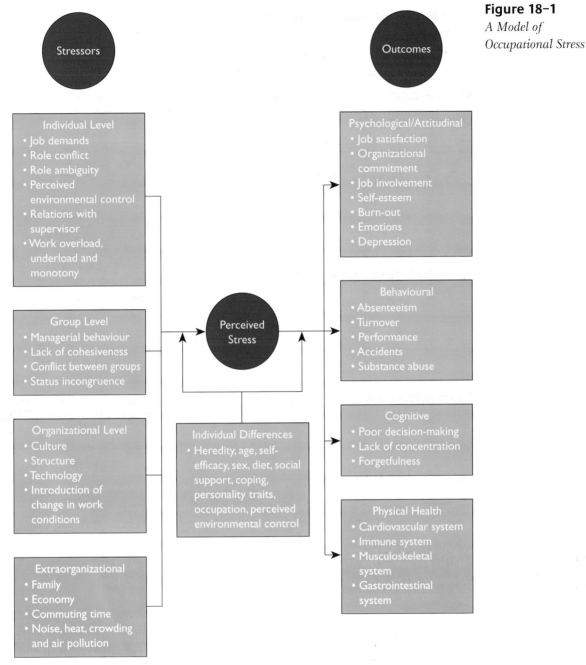

Figure 18–1
*A Model of
Occupational Stress*

SOURCES: Adapted from M Koslowsky, *Modeling the Stress-Strain Relationship in Work Settings* (New York: Routledge, 1998); and M T Matteson and J M Ivancevich, 'Organizational Stressors and Heart Disease: A Research Model', *Academy of Management Review*, July 1979, p 350.

With respect to job demands and workload, another survey of 700 people across the United States indicated that each respondent had someone they cared about who worked too hard. More than 22 per cent blamed a demanding supervisor for the fact that his or her spouse was a workaholic. Managers can help to reduce these stressors by providing direction and support and also by allocating work assignments more equitably within the work unit.[21]

Finally, it is important to manage the individual-level stressor of job security as it is associated with increased job satisfaction, organization commitment and performance, and it is decreasing. A recent longitudinal study in Finland, for instance, examined antecedents and outcomes of job insecurity. It was found that, if the organization was in a negative economic situation or there was a perceived probability that negative changes would occur over the next three years and employees were experiencing feelings of low self-esteem; then it was possible to predict that worries about job losses would be held by all. This insecurity led to a higher job exhaustion and higher absence-rates later on. The researchers concluded, therefore, that by preventing the experience of job insecurity, employers can promote employees' well-being at work.[22]

Group-level stressors are caused by group dynamics (recall our discussion in Chapter 12) and managerial behaviour. Managers create stress for employees by:

▼ **exhibiting inconsistent behaviour**

▼ **failing to provide support**

▼ **showing lack of concern**

▼ **providing inadequate direction**

▼ **creating a high-productivity environment**

▼ **focusing on negatives while ignoring good performance.**

The experience of sexual harassment represents another group-level stressor. Studies show that such experiences are negatively associated with work, supervision and promotion satisfaction while being positively related to ambiguity, conflict and stress.[23]

Organizational stressors also affect large numbers of employees. Organizational culture, which was discussed in Chapter 3 is a prime example. For instance, a high-pressure environment that places chronic work demands on employees fuels the stress response.[24] A sales manager who was taken over by the competitive atmosphere and the 'dog eat dog' culture in his company explains the situation.

> *At a given moment, I had become the sort of person who ate lunch with a fork in one hand and a phone in the other. When we got close to a deadline, I would apologize for visiting the toilet at work. Sometimes I was so afraid of going home that I left my jacket on the back of my chair, hoping the boss would think I've just nipped out for a cigarette.*[25]

Technological stressors. The increased use of information technology is another source of organizational stress. One manager describes a typical working day as follows.

> *I get to the office in the morning, and I've got 20 voice mail messages, 30 emails, and a stack of paper in the fax machine . . . by the time I get through checking my voice mail, there are 40 emails, and four more faxes. It's a never-ending cycle. You could spend your entire workday communicating.*[26]

Also, some people are technophobic. Dell Computer, for example, called 2,000 people and found out that 55 per cent of them were anxious and fearful about using computer-related technology.[27] In this light, psychologists have identified the archetypal affliction of the new millennium: 'Computer Failure Syndrome'. Cary Cooper, a renowned professor of organizational psychology at the University of Manchester, found in a survey of office workers that no less than one in eight sometimes found IT failure more stressful than the breakdown of a relationship. Cooper commented, 'What this survey shows is that we have become more and more dependent on this funny machine in front of us. As a result, people get hysterical when a computer breaks down. But actually, the fact that some find a computer breakdown more stressful than the end of a relationship is really pretty sad. Moreover, it's pathetic.'[28]

On the flip side, other people are so drawn to the use of email and the Internet that they developed an addiction called Internet Addiction Disorder.[29] Finally, the office design and general office environment are important organizational-level stressors. Research demonstrates that poor lighting, loud noise, improper placement of furniture, and a dirty or smelly environment create stress.[30] Managers are advised to monitor and eliminate these stressors.

Extraorganizational stressors are those caused by factors outside the organization. For instance, conflicts associated with balancing one's career and family life are stressful, as is shown in the following examples.

Londoner Matthew Wright would like to see more of his daughters—Olivia (seven) and Alexandra (four)—but work gets in the way. The 36-year-old managing director for Europe of head-hunters Russel Reynolds Associates squeezes his personal life in around long hours and foreign travel—he often spends two or three nights a week away from home. 'I only spend around 15 minutes with my children on weekdays', he admits. Even when working in London, his journey begins while the children are still asleep. Getting home at a reasonable time may well mean taking work home with him. 'I aim to get home in time to put them to bed', he says. Weekends on the other hand are 'exclusively for friends and family—apart from the odd Saturday morning flight back from the US'.[31]

'I saw the opportunities and I went for them. I didn't have the time for a family', says Stephanie Murdoch, 35. She chose work over motherhood shortly after joining insurance company JLT Group Services as a claims processor. Twelve years later, she is the managing director. The most stressful part of her life, she says, is 'maintaining the balance between work and home'. Left to my own devices I am the kind of person who puts everything into their job. The pressure turns me on.' She is married to a 'house-husband' who stopped work when Stephanie's job took them from Worcester to London. Now he provides regular 'reality-checks' if she is in danger of letting work take over. 'We do have rows about my work. I am not the easiest person to live with', she says.[32]

From these examples, it is clear that work often interferes with family life but the following results from two British studies are nevertheless pretty remarkable: in a survey by *Management Today*, it was found that 25 per cent of British workers find that stress continuously messes up their sex life.[33] A similar study undertaken by the company *Seven Seas* found that 65 per cent of those questioned in the UK claimed that their sexual performance was sometimes affected by stress, and one-third said their lives were so stressed that they had thought of work while having sex. A total of 89 per cent of men and women blamed work for not having enough time to meet the opposite sex.[34]

Organizations can help employees to cope with work–family balance issues by providing them with flexible schedules and cafeteria benefits. Socioeconomic status is another stressor to be found outside the organisation (an extraorganizational stressor). Stress is higher for people with lower 'socioeconomic status', that is, a combination of lower economic status (as measured by income), social status (as assessed by education level) and work status (as indexed by occupation). These stressors are likely to become more important in the future.

Perceived Stress

Perceived stress represents an individual's overall perception about how various stressors are affecting her or his life. The perception of stressors is an important component within the stress process because people interpret the same stressors differently.[35] For example, some individuals perceive unemployment as a positive, liberating experience, whereas others perceive it as a negative, debilitating one.[36]

Outcomes

Theorists contend that stress has psychological/attitudinal, behavioural, cognitive, and physical health consequences. A large body of research supports the theory that perceived stress has a negative effect of on many aspects of our lives. Stress was negatively related to job satisfaction, organizational commitment, positive emotions, and performance, whilst being positively correlated with burn-out and staff turnover.[37] For example, a recent survey of 750 workers over the age of 18, revealed that one in six reported being so angered by a co-worker that he or she felt like hitting the person. The greatest amount of pent-up anger was experienced by workers under the age of 35 and those in clerical, office and sales jobs.[38] Research also provides ample evidence to support the conclusion that stress negatively affects our physical health. Stress contributes to the following health problems: a lowered ability to ward off illness and infection, high blood pressure, coronary heart disease, tension headaches, back pain, diarrhea, and constipation.[39]

Individual Differences

People do not experience the same level of stress or exhibit similar outcomes for a given type of stressor. For example, the type of stressors experienced at work varied by occupation and gender. The stressor of low control (over one's job tasks) was higher in lower-level clerical jobs than professional occupations, while interpersonal conflict was a greater source of stress for women than men.[40] Perceived control was also a significant moderator of the stress process. People perceived lower levels of stress, and experienced more favorable consequences from stress, when they believed they could exert control over the stressors affecting their lives.[41]

In support of this finding, another study showed that employees had more negative physiological responses to perceived stress when they worked on an assembly line than in a more flexible work organization.[42] Assembly-line technology allows employees much less control than other organizational arrangements. Finally, the personality trait of chronic hostility or cynicism was also a significant moderator of the stress process. Research demonstrated that people who were chronically angry, suspicious, or mistrustful were twice as likely to have coronary artery blockages. We can all protect our hearts by learning to avoid these tendencies.[43]

In summary, even though researchers have been able to identify several important moderators, a large gap still exists in identifying relevant individual differences. For example, there are many people who never seem to get stressed, although they work very hard:

'I've never really felt under stress or overworked', says Tom Kok, a Dutch entrepreneur who has never worked less than a 60-hour-week in the past few years. 'But there have been some moments when I could very easily have been. Yet I also think I know how it feels to be overstressed: you get up in the morning and at first you think 'let's get started' but a few seconds later you break down. But one way or another, these things don't affect me very much. I think I have a healthy capacity to just shrug my shoulders and say 'So what . . . ?' I like to put things in perspective.'[44]

IMPORTANT STRESSORS AND STRESS OUTCOMES

As we have seen, stressors trigger stress which, in turn, leads to a variety of outcomes. This section explores an important category of extraorganizational stressors: that of stressful life events. Burn-out, another especially troublesome stress-related outcome, is also examined.

Stressful Life Events

Events such as experiencing the death of a family member, being assaulted, moving home, ending an intimate relationship, being seriously ill or taking a big test can create stress. These events are stressful because they involve significant changes that require adaptation and often social readjustment. These stressful life events, which are not work-related, have been the most extensively investigated extraorganizational stressors.

Stressful life events
life events that disrupt daily routines and social relationships

Thomas Holmes and Richard Rahe conducted pioneering research on the relationship between stressful life events and subsequent illness. During their research, they developed a widely used questionnaire to assess life stress.[45]

OB Exercise

The Revised Social Readjustment Rating Scale

Instructions

Place a check mark next to each of the events you experienced within the past year. Then add the life change units associated with the various events to derive your total life stress score.

Life Event	Life Change Unit
____ Death of spouse/mate	87
____ Death of close family member	79
____ Major injury/illness to self	78
____ Detention in prison or other institution	76
____ Major injury/illness to close family member	72
____ Foreclosure on loan/mortgage	71
____ Divorce	71
____ Being a victim of crime	70
____ Being the victim of police brutality	69
____ Infidelity	69
____ Experiencing domestic violence/sexual abuse	69
____ Separation or reconciliation with spouse/mate	66
____ Being fired/laid-off/unemployed	64
____ Experiencing financial problems/difficulties	62
____ Death of close friend	61
____ Surviving a disaster	59
____ Becoming a single parent	59
____ Assuming responsibility for sick or elderly loved one	56
____ Loss of, or major reduction in, health insurance/benefits	56
____ Self/close family member being arrested for breaking the law	56
____ Major disagreements over child support/custody/visiting rights	53
____ Experiencing/involved in a car accident	53
____ Being disciplined at work/demoted	53
____ Dealing with unwanted pregnancy	51
____ Adult child moving in with parent/parent moving in with adult child	50
____ Child develops behaviour or learning problem	49
____ Experiencing employment discrimination/sexual harassment	48
____ Attempting to modify addictive behaviour of self	47
____ Discovering/attempting to modify addictive behaviour of close family member	46
____ Employer reorganization/downsizing	45
____ Dealing with infertility/miscarriage	44
____ Getting married/remarried	43
____ Changing employers/careers	43
____ Failure to obtain/qualify for a mortgage	42
____ Pregnancy of self/spouse/mate	41
____ Experiencing discrimination/harassment outside the workplace	39
____ Release from prison	39
____ Spouse/mate begins/ceases work outside the home	38
____ Major disagreement with boss/co-worker	37
____ Change in residence	35
____ Finding appropriate child care/day care	34
____ Experiencing a large, unexpected monetary gain	33
____ Changing positions (transfer, promotion)	33
____ Gaining a new family member	33
____ Changing work responsibilities	32
____ Child leaving home	30
____ Obtaining a home mortgage	30
____ Obtaining a major loan other than home mortgage	30
____ Retirement	28
____ Beginning/ceasing formal education	26
____ Being booked for breaking the law	22

Total score _____

Interpretation Norms

Less than 150	= Odds are you will experience good health next year
150–300	= 50% chance of illness next year
Greater than 300	= 70% chance of illness next year

SOURCE: C J Hobson, J Kamen, J Szostek, C M Nethercut, J W Tiedmann and S Wojnarowicz, 'Stressful Life Events: A Revision and Update of the Social Readjustment Rating Scale', *International Journal of Stress Management*, January 1998, pp 7–8.

Assessing Stressful Life Events

The *Social Readjustment Rating Scale* developed by Holmes and Rahe has been the dominant method for assessing an individual's cumulative stressful life events for the past 30 years. The rating instrument was recently updated and revised by a group of researchers in order to modernize the list of stressors and to overcome some technical problems with the survey. As shown in the OB Exercise, page 483, the new rating scale consists of 51 life events. Each event has a corresponding value, called a life change unit, representing the degree of social readjustment necessary to cope with the event. The larger the value, the more stressful the event. These values were obtained from a national sample of 3,122 people who evaluated the stressfulness of each event.[46] (Please take a moment to complete the social readjustment rating scale and to calculate your total life stress score.)

Research revealed a positive relationship between the total score on the original social readjustment rating scale and subsequent illness. The interpretative norms reveal that low scores are associated with good health, and larger scores are related to increased chances of experiencing illness. A word of caution is in order, however. If you scored over 150, don't head for a sterile cocoon. High scores on the social readjustment rating scale do not guarantee you will become ill. Rather, a high score simply increases one's statistical risk of illness.[47]

Research and Practical Implications

Numerous studies have examined the relationship between life stress on the one hand and illness and job performance on the other. Subjects with higher scores on the social readjustment rating scale had significantly more problems with chronic headaches, sudden cardiac death, pregnancy and birth complications, tuberculosis, diabetes, anxiety, depression and a host of minor physical ailments. Meanwhile, psychosocial problems and academic and work performance declined as scores on the social readjustment rating scale increased.[48]

Negative (as opposed to positive) personal life changes were associated with greater susceptibility to colds, job stress and psychological distress, and also lower levels of job satisfaction and organizational commitment.[49]

Finally, recent studies revealed that women rated the life events contained in the social readjustment rating scale as more stressful than men. Results also showed that there were no meaningful differences in life event ratings between various age groups and income levels.[50] The key implication is that employee illness and job performance are affected by extraorganizational stressors, particularly those that are negative and uncontrollable. Because employees do not leave their personal problems at the office door or factory gate, management needs to be aware of external sources of employee stress or, as Cary Cooper argues, 'Employers have a duty of care in respect of how they manage not only their equipment or physical environment but also their people, including their workload, their hours of work and perhaps their careers.'[51]

Once identified, alternative work schedules, training programmes, and counselling can be used to help employees cope with these stressors. This may not only reduce the costs associated with illnesses and absenteeism but may also lead to positive work attitudes, better job performance and reduced staff turnover. For example, consider the views of the following managers, who actively try to make sure that their policies fit the needs of their employees.

Mireille Jacquemyn, HR-manager of the Antwerp Zoo, is responsible for a lot of employees. She tries to find rapid and practical solutions to their day-to-day problems. For example, her employees are free to work as much and whenever they want to. Further on, she organizes extra childcare for their children, an interesting option for employees who work at times when most childcare services fail, as is sometimes the case during weekends and public holidays.

Rozemarijn Laureyssens, medical director at Dupont de Nemours, tries to feel for the individual needs of all employees by implementing a range of flexibility systems. For example, employees can benefit from part-time working, job-sharing, compressed workweeks, working at home, flextime, . . . Moreover, all employees can take six-months leave without pay for social reasons.[52]

(The 'compressed workweeks' mentioned above, refer to completing the same number of required hours in fewer than the traditional 5-day working week, by working more hours per day. Usually, the 40-hour working week is scheduled over four 10-hour days, thereby allowing for an extra day off.) In addition, by acknowledging that work outcomes are affected by extraorganizational stressors, managers may avoid the trap of automatically attributing poor performance to low motivation or lack of ability. Such awareness is likely to engender positive reactions from employees and lead to resolution of problems, not just symptoms. For individuals with a high score on the social readjustment rating scale, it would be best to defer controllable stressors, such as moving or buying a new car, until things settle down.

Burn-out

Burn-out is a stress-induced problem common among members of 'helping' professions such as teaching, social work, human resources, nursing, and law enforcement. It does not involve a specific feeling, attitude or physiological outcome anchored to a specific point in time. Rather, **burn-out** is a condition that occurs over time. Dr Graham Lucas, psychiatrist at the Cromwell and Priory Hospitals in London, refers to the phenomenon as 'the catastrophic consequence of long-lasting, relentless stress'.[53] Consider the symptoms, causes and consequences of burn-out in the following two examples.

Burn-out
a condition of emotional exhaustion and negative attitudes

Sandy Wilson, a consultant with many years of experience, felt frustrated, tense and washed-out. He was 49 years old and had the knowledge to tackle any problem but he didn't have the courage any more. He took less physical exercise, drank a lot and neglected the relationship with his son. He only saw himself doing the same exhausting work for years to come. 'I've lost my spirit. I have no more will to fight', he told his wife.[54]

'In my case, burn-out came up very slowly and gradually', says A. B., who would like to remain anonymous. 'I've worked as a nurse for over twenty years. I was always prepared to engage in additional training and education, including weekend or evening-courses. And I never complained when I had to work overtime. But if you never get a pat on the back from the top, or if the management team gives very few stimuli to keep pace with recent developments, the motivation drops. In the long run there are no more challenges left.'[55]

You can see that burn-out has a devastating impact on employee well-being. Typical characteristics are withdrawal, fatigue and less job involvement, the latter being mainly noticed in those who are normally highly involved. If you can answer 'yes' to several of the following questions, you're probably heading for, or already suffering from, a major burn-out.

▼ Do you experience your work as an unbearable burden?

▼ Are you constantly worrying about your work?

▼ Do you consider every assignment an awful job?

▼ Are you constantly feeling empty and indifferent?

▼ Do you have to drag yourself out of your bed every morning?

▼ Is 'job satisfaction' a term you've only ever heard of (not experienced)?

▼ Can you hardly ever laugh at work?

▼ Do you find your colleagues immensely irritating?[56]

Of course, everyone has a bad day from time to time but people who suffer from burn-out are constantly feeling unhappy at work.

Table 17–1

Attitudinal Characteristics of Burnout

Attitude	Description
Fatalism	A feeling that you lack control over your work.
Boredom	A lack of interest in doing your job.
Discontent	A sense of being unhappy with your job.
Cynicism	A tendency to undervalue the content of your job and the rewards received.
Inadequacy	A feeling of not being able to meet your objectives.
Failure	A tendency to discredit your performance and conclude that you are ineffective.
Overwork	A feeling of having too much to do and not enough time to complete it.
Nastiness	A tendency to be rude or unpleasant to your co-workers.
Dissatisfaction	A feeling that you are not being justly rewarded for your efforts.
Escape	A desire to give up and get away from it all.

SOURCE: Adapted from D P Rogers, 'Helping Employees Cope with Burnout', *Business,* October–December 1984, p 4.

Table 17–1 describes 10 attitudinal characteristics of burn-out. Experts say a substantial number of people suffer from this problem. For example, a national study of 28,000 Americans indicated that more than 50 per cent were 'burned out'.[57] A study of 1,800 software professionals, from 19 German and Swiss companies, revealed a positive association between measures of burn-out (especially lack of identification) with job stressors and a lack of positive features in the work situation (such as control at work, complexity at work and openness to criticism within the team). These results imply that burn-out is not limited to people working in the helping professions. To promote better understanding of this important outcome of stress, we turn our attention to a model of the burn-out process and highlight relevant research and techniques for its prevention.[58]

Figure 17–2

A Model of Burn-out

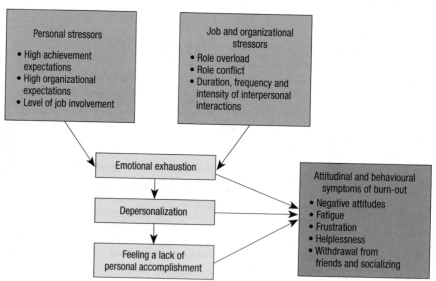

SOURCE: Based in part on C L Cordes and T W Dougherty, 'A Review and an Integration of Research on Job Burnout', *Academy of Management Review,* October 1993, p 641.

A Model of Burn-out

A model of burn-out is presented in Figure 17–2. The fundamental premise underlying the model is that burn-out develops in phases. The three key phases are emotional exhaustion, depersonalization, and feeling a lack of personal accomplishment.[59] As shown in Figure 17–2, emotional exhaustion is due to a combination of personal stressors and job and organizational stressors.[60] People who expect a lot from themselves and the organizations in which they work tend to create more internal stress, which, in turn, leads to emotional exhaustion. Similarly, emotional exhaustion is fuelled by having too much work to do, by role conflict, and by the type of interpersonal interactions encountered at work. Frequent, intense face-to-face interactions that are emotionally charged are associated with higher levels of emotional exhaustion. Over time, emotional exhaustion leads to depersonalization, which is a state of psychologically withdrawing from one's job. This ultimately results in a feeling of being unappreciated, ineffective or inadequate. The additive effect of these three phases is a host of negative attitudinal and behavioural outcomes. Consider the following case.

A vice president of a large corporation who hadn't received an expected promotion left his company to become the head of a smaller, family-owned business, which was floundering and needed his skills. Although he had jumped at the opportunity to rescue the small company, once there he discovered an unimaginable morass of difficulties, among them continual conflicts within the family. He felt he could not leave but neither could he succeed. Trapped in a kind of psychological quicksand, he worked days, nights and weekends for months in an attempt to pull himself free. His wife protested, to no avail. Finally, he was hospitalized for exhaustion.[61]

Research Findings and Prevention

A meta-analysis of 61 studies covering several thousand people uncovered three important conclusions.[62] First, burn-out was positively related to job stressors and turnover intentions and negatively associated with the receipt of supportive resources (e.g., social support and team cohesion), job enhancement opportunities, performance-contingent rewards, organizational commitment, and job satisfaction. Second, the different phases of burn-out, as shown in Figure 17–2, obtained differential relationships with a variety of behavioural and attitudinal symptoms of burn-out. This supports the idea that burn-out develops in phases. Nonetheless, researchers do not yet agree completely on the order of these phases.[63] Finally, burn-out was more strongly related to employees' work demands than it was to the resources people received at work. This suggests that organizations should be particularly sensitive to employees' workloads. The next International OB discusses how Zeneca Pharmaceuticals, which is located in the United Kingdom, tried to adhere to this recommendation.

International OB

How Zeneca Helps Employees Manage their Workloads

Zeneca's highly developed employee assistance programme is one of a small number in Britain that specifically aims to tackle stress at its source. Somewhere in the mid-1990s, the pharmaceutical firm set up a specialist team to give advice and training on how to balance the needs of the workplace with the pressures of everyday life.

Zeneca's Counselling and Life Management team, shortened to CALM, runs workshops and other events where employees can pick up tips on caring for elderly relatives, coping with marital break-ups, handling financial pressures and other matters that lead to stress. An assessment of mental health is part of the employees' medical screening.

More than 5,500 employees, who work either at Zeneca's UK headquarters near Macclesfield, Cheshire or at other centres around the country, can contact the CALM-team by telephone or request a face-to-face meeting. Earlier an entire manufacturing team, including managers and support staff, attended a three-hour workshop on balanced living.

International OB
(continued)

'What we are broadly telling people is that there are various arenas in their lives, including their family, social life, and intellectual and cultural aspects,' Richard Heron, medical officer at Zeneca, explains. 'It is important that they pay attention to all of them, because they all play their part in creating the whole person.'

Zeneca has been offering employee counselling for a long time, but it is only since setting up the CALM-programme that the company has made a real attempt to tackle the causes of stress at work, as well as treating the symptoms. For example, the company also decided to use its appraisal system to review workload and draft individual development plans, so that staff would have opportunities to develop knowledge and skills to match the demands of their jobs.

Pivotal to the success of these efforts to prevent excessive pressure on employees, was a letter from the company's chief executive urging managers to keep track of individual's workloads, set staff reasonable timescales, and make sure that they had 'enough free time for outside pursuits'.

SOURCE: N Merrick, 'Getting to grips', *People Management*, December 10, 1998 and A Arkin, 'HSE guide helps stress victims claim damages', *People Management*, June 15, 1996.

Buffers
resources or administrative changes that reduce burn-out

Removing personal, job and organizational stressors is the most straightforward way to prevent burn-out. Managers can also reduce burn-out by buffering its effects. Potential **buffers** include extra staff or equipment at peak work periods, support from top management, increased freedom to make decisions, recognition for accomplishments, time off for personal development or rest, and equitable rewards. Decreasing the quantity and increasing the *quality* of communications is another possible buffer. Finally, managers can change the content of an individual's job by adding or eliminating responsibilities, increasing the amount of participation in decision-making, altering the pattern of interpersonal contacts, or assigning the person to a new position.[64]

Both Deloitte & Touche and Ernst & Young have implemented some of these recommendations.

Deloitte & Touche is implementing a policy on some projects that curbs their consultants' travel time. Instead of spending five days a week at a client's offices, consultants spend three nights and four days, fly home and work a fifth day in their home cities. That means 'you can plan your life and be home for a real weekend,' says Malva Rabinowitz, a Deloitte managing director. Most clients 'recognize it's a good thing' when they see the policy in action.

Similarly, Ernst & Young is involving clients on some consulting projects in setting up a 'team calendar' that integrates team members' work and personal commitments, says Bob Forbes, an Ernst partner. While client needs still come first, the calendar puts people's off-the-job lives on the radar screen. Ernst & Young has a committee monitoring accountants' workloads. It helps burn-out candidates shift clients or schedule vacations.[65]

There also are two long-term strategies for reducing burn-out that are increasingly being used by companies. Apple Computer, American Express, IBM, McDonald's Corporation, and Intel, for instance, use sabbaticals to replenish employees' energy and desire to work. These programmes allow employees to take a designated amount of time off from work after being employed a certain number of years. Companies in Canada, Australia and Israel also use sabbaticals to prevent stress and burn-out, whereas Europe does not have a sabbatical culture. In The Netherlands, the organization Stichting Sabbatical Leave argues that a sabbatical leave should be a right for every employee. When a number of large Dutch companies such as PTT telecom, Randstad and KLM were asked if they were planning to introduce sabbatical leaves in the future, they did not seem to be very enthusiastic.[66]

An employee retreat is the second long-term strategy. Retreats entail sending employees to an offsite location for three to five days. While there, everyone can relax, reflect or engage in team and relationship building activities. This is precisely what Pricewaterhouse is doing to help its employees cope with work stress: PricewaterhouseCoopers has a two-day stress survival clinic where participants meet with a physician, nutritionist, and psychiatrist. The retreat, held in such locations as Toronto and Captiva Island, Florida, includes Mediterranean-style cuisine served in candlelight dining rooms and time to focus on coping better with pressure.[67]

MODERATORS OF OCCUPATIONAL STRESS

Moderators, as mentioned earlier, are variables that cause the relationship between stressors, perceived stress and outcomes to be weaker for some people and stronger for others. Managers with a working knowledge of important stress moderators can confront employee stress in the following ways.

1 Awareness of moderators helps identify those most likely to experience stress and its negative outcomes. Then stress-reduction programmes can be formulated for high-risk employees.

2 Moderators, in and of themselves, suggest possible solutions for reducing the negative outcomes of occupational stress.

Keeping these objectives in mind, we will examine four important moderators: social support, coping, hardiness and 'Type A behaviour'.

Social Support

Talking to a friend or getting together with 'mates' can be comforting during times of fear, stress or loneliness. For a variety of reasons, meaningful social relationships help people do a better job of handling stress. **Social support** is measured in terms of both the quantity and quality of an individual's social relationships. Figure 17–3 illustrates the mechanisms of social support.

Social support
amount of helpfulness derived from social relationships

A Model of Social Support

As Figure 17–3 shows, one's support network must be perceived before it can be used. Support networks evolve from any or all of five sources: cultural norms, social institutions, companies, groups, or individuals. For example, there is more cultural emphasis on caring for the elderly in Japan than in Europe. Japanese culture is thus a strong source of social support for older Japanese people. Alternatively, individuals may fall back on social institutions such as Social Security or the Red Cross, religious groups, or family and friends for support. In turn, these various sources provide four types of support.

▼ *Esteem support.* Providing information that a person is accepted and respected despite any problems or inadequacies.

▼ *Informational support.* Providing help in defining, understanding and coping with problems.

▼ *Social companionship.* Spending time with others in leisure and recreational activities.

▼ *Instrumental support.* Providing financial aid, material resources or necessary services.[68]

Figure 17–3

A Flow Model of the Mechanisms of Social Support

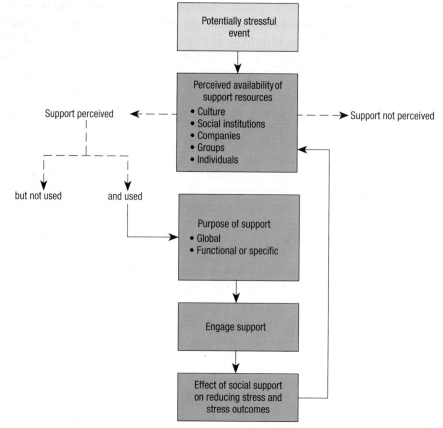

SOURCES: Portions adapted from S Cohen and T A Wills, 'Stress, Social Support, and the Buffering Hypothesis', *Psychological Bulletin*, September 1985, pp 310–57; and J G Bruhn and B U Philips, 'Measuring Social Support: A Synthesis of Current Approaches', *Journal of Behavioral Medicine*, June 1984, pp 151–69.

If social support is perceived as available, an individual then decides whether to use it.[69] Generally, social support is used either as a global or a functional support but in some cases it is used as both. **Global social support** is very broad in scope, coming as it does from four sources, and is applicable to any situation at any time. **Functional social support** is narrower and, if relied on in the wrong situation, can be unhelpful.

For example, if you crashed your new car, a good insurance (instrumental support) would be a better buffer than sympathy from a bartender. On the other hand, social companionship would be more helpful than instrumental support in coping with loneliness. After social support is engaged for one or both of these purposes, its effectiveness can be determined. If consolation or relief is not experienced, it may be that the type of support was inappropriate. The feedback loop in Figure 17–3, from effect of social support back to perceived availability, reflects the need to fall back on other sources of support when necessary.

Research Findings and Managerial Lessons

Research shows that global social support is negatively related to physiological processes and mortality. In other words, people with low social support tend to have poorer cardiovascular and immune system functioning and tend to die earlier than those with strong social support networks.[70] Further, global support protects against the perception of stress, depression, psychological illness, pregnancy complications, anxiety, loneliness, high blood pressure, and a variety of other ailments.

Global social support

the total amount of social support available

Functional social support

support sources that buffer stress in specific situations

In contrast, negative social support, which amounts to someone undermining another person, negatively affects one's mental health.[71] We would all be well advised to avoid people who try to undermine us. Moreover, there is no clear pattern of results regarding the buffering effects of both global and functional social support.[72] It appears that social support sometimes serves as a buffer against stress but we do not know precisely when or why so additional research is needed. Finally, as suggested in Figure 17–3, global social support is positively related to the availability of support resources; that is, people who interact with a greater number of friends, family or co-workers have a wider base of social support from which to draw during stressful periods.[73]

One practical recommendation is to keep employees informed about external and internal social support systems. Internally, managers can use esteem and informational support while administering daily feedback and coaching. Further, participative management programmes and company-sponsored activities that make employees feel they are an important part of an 'extended family' can be rich sources of social support. Employees need time and energy to adequately maintain their social relationships. If organizational demands are excessive, employees' social relationships and support networks will suffer, resulting in stress-related illness and decreased performance. Also, the positive effects of social support are enhanced when functional support is targeted precisely.

Coping

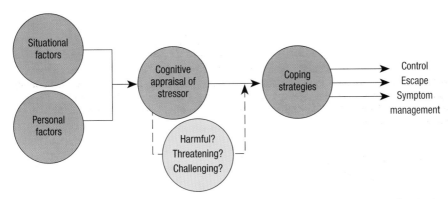

Figure 17–4
A Model of the Coping Process

SOURCE: Based in part on R S Lazarus and S Folkman, 'Coping and Adaptation', in *Handbook of Behavioral Medicine*, ed W D Gentry (New York: The Guilford Press, 1984), pp 282–325.

Coping is 'the process of managing demands (external or internal) that are appraised as taxing or exceeding the resources of the person'.[74] Because effective coping helps reduce the impact of stressors and stress, your personal life and managerial skills can be enhanced by better understanding this process. Figure 17–4 depicts an instructive model of coping.

Coping
process of managing stress

The coping process has three major components: situational and personal factors; cognitive appraisals of the stressor; and coping strategies. As shown in Figure 17–4, both situational and personal factors influence the appraisal of stressors. In turn, appraisal directly influences the choice of coping strategies. Each of the major components of this model deserves a closer look.

Situational and Personal Factors

Situational factors are environmental characteristics that affect how people interpret (appraise) stressors. For example, the ambiguity of a situation—such as walking down a dark street at night in an unfamiliar area—makes it difficult to determine whether a potentially dangerous situation exists. Ambiguity creates differences in how people appraise and subsequently cope with stressors. Other situational factors are the frequency of exposure to a stressor and social support networks.

Personal factors are personality traits and personal resources that affect the appraisal of stressors. For instance, because being tired or sick can distort the interpretation of stressors, an extremely tired individual may appraise an innocent question as a threat or challenge. Traits such as locus of control, self-esteem, optimism, self-efficacy (recall our discussion in Chapter 5), and work experience were also found to affect the appraisal of stressors.[75]

Cognitive Appraisal of Stressors

Cognitive appraisal reflects an individual's overall perception or evaluation of a situation or stressor. Cognitive appraisal results in a categorization of the situation or stressor as either harmful, threatening or challenging. It is important to understand the differences between these appraisals because they influence how people cope. '*Harm* (including loss) represents damage already done; *threat* involves the potential for harm; and *challenge* means the potential for significant gain under difficult odds.'[76] Coping with harm usually entails undoing or reinterpreting something that occurred in the past because the damage is already done. In contrast, threatening situations engage anticipatory coping. That is, people cope with threat by preparing for harm that may occur in the future. Challenge also activates anticipatory coping. In contrast with threat, an appraisal of challenge results in coping that focuses on what can be gained rather than what may be lost.

Coping Strategies

Coping strategies are characterized by the specific behaviours and cognitions used to cope with a situation. People use a combination of three approaches to cope with stressors and stress (see Figure 17–4).

Control strategy
coping strategy that directly confronts or solves problems

The first, called a **control strategy** has a 'take-charge' tone. For example, so-called 'downshifting', where someone moves to a less stressful job, is a possible coping strategy to gain more flexibility in your life. Consider the story of Krysia Devreux-Bletek, managing director of the Brussels software-company Ecsem.

'*We worked our brains out during the week. We drove thousands of kilometres a year. Over the weekends we were busy rebuilding, painting or wallpapering as if we wanted some kind of a palace. We bought ourselves a large freezer, a microwave and tons of vitamin tablets in order to keep going. After a while we started feeling guilty: we hardly had any time to see our kids grow up, and many friends who were in the same situation were divorced. Fortunately we worked in a super-booming sector, people admired us for what we were doing, we had lots of contacts and so we went even further and started our own business . . . . So, in addition to our relentless workload we took on an extra burden: financial risk. We never really slept well and now we know why. But the job was unbelievably fascinating and challenging, so we went all out for it. Dinners with friends or family? No time. Sport? No time. Just sitting around and do nothing for a moment? Nonsense. All at once, we finally got our senses back: our quality of life increased visibly when my husband took a sideways step and started working at home. At that time, our choice wasn't socially acceptable. Other couples faced a dilemma: her or me? They saw it as a sacrifice but to us it was an obvious decision. We've lost our feelings of guilt, the freezer is almost empty and we're enjoying playing sport together again . . . .*'[77]

Escape strategy
coping strategy that avoids or ignores stressors and problems

An **escape strategy** amounts to the opposite of tackling the problem head-on. Individuals use this strategy when they passively accept stressful situations or avoid them by failing to confront the cause of stress (an obnoxious co-worker, for instance).

Symptom management strategy
coping strategy that focuses on reducing the symptoms of stress

Finally, a **symptom management strategy** uses methods such as relaxation, meditation, medication, and exercise.

Research Findings and Managerial Recommendations

As suggested by the model in Figure 17–4, an individual's appraisal of a stressor correlates with the choice of a coping strategy.[78] In further support of the coping model, personal factors, appraisal and coping all significantly predicted psychological symptoms of stress. Nonetheless, research has not clearly identified which type of coping strategy–control, escape or symptom management–is most effective. It appears that the best coping strategy depends on the situation at hand.[79] Escaping stress—by going on vacation, for example—is sometimes better than confronting a stressor with a control-oriented coping strategy. Researchers are currently trying to determine these contingency relationships.

The preceding results suggest that employees should be taught a contingency approach to coping with organizational stressors. This might begin by helping employees to identify those stressors that they perceive as harmful or threatening. Training or managerial support can then be used to help employees manage and possibly eliminate the most serious stressors. The final section of this chapter describes specific techniques for that purpose.

Hardiness

Suzanne Kobasa, a behavioural scientist, identified a collection of personality characteristics, referred to as hardiness. These involve the ability to, perceptually or behaviourally, transform negative stressors into positive challenges. Hardiness embraces the personality dimensions of commitment, locus of control and challenge.[80]

Hardiness
personality characteristic that neutralizes stress

Personality Characteristics of Hardiness

Commitment reflects the extent to which an individual is involved in whatever he or she is doing. Committed people have a sense of purpose and do not give up under pressure because they tend to 'invest themselves' in the situation. The extent of commitment, however, is culturally determined, observes Cary Cooper: 'A UK manager who takes work home is said to be committed to his job. A German manager who does the same would be thought of as incompetent, because part of his job as a manager is to manage time.'[81]

As discussed in Chapter 5, individuals with an *internal locus of control* believe they can influence the events that affect their lives. People possessing this trait are more likely to foresee stressful events, thereby reducing their exposure to anxiety-producing situations. Moreover, their perception of being in control leads them to use proactive coping strategies.

Challenge is represented by the belief that change is a normal part of life. Hence, change is seen as an opportunity for growth and development rather than a threat to security.

Hardiness Research and Application

A five-year study of 259 managers from a public utility revealed that hardiness—commitment, locus of control and challenge—reduced the probability of illness following exposure to stress.[82] The three components of hardiness were also found to directly influence how 276 members of the Israeli Defence Forces appraised stressors and ultimately coped with them. Hardy individuals interpreted stressors less negatively and were more likely to use control strategies than less hardy people.[83] Furthermore, additional research demonstrated that hardy individuals displayed lower stress, burn-out, and psychological distress and experienced higher job satisfaction than their less hardy counterparts.[84] Finally, a study of 73 pregnant women revealed that hardy women had fewer problems during labour and more positive perceptions of their infants than less hardy women.[85]

One practical offshoot of this research is organizational training and development programmes that strengthen the characteristics of commitment, personal control and challenge. Because of cost limitations, it is necessary to target key employees or those most susceptible to stress (such as air traffic controllers). The hardiness concept also meshes nicely with job design. Enriched jobs are likely to fuel the hardiness components of commitment and challenge. A final application of the hardiness concept is as a diagnostic tool. Employees getting low scores on hardiness tests would be good candidates for stress-reduction programmes.

Type A Behaviour Pattern

Cardiovascular disease is the leading cause of death among adults in western industrialized countries. Because 'Type A behaviour' was linked to cardiovascular disease, researchers devoted significant effort in identifying Type A characteristics and the situations that elicit this behaviour pattern.

Type A Behaviour Defined

Type A behaviour syndrome
aggressively involved in a chronic, determined struggle to accomplish more in less time

Meyer Friedman and Ray Rosenman, the cardiologists who isolated the **Type A syndrome** in the 1950s, gave us the following explanation of the behaviour.

Type A behaviour pattern is an action–emotion complex that can be observed in any person who is aggressively involved in a chronic, incessant struggle to achieve more and more in less and less time, and if required to do so, against the opposing efforts of other things or persons. It is not a psychosis or a complex of worries or fears or phobias or obsessions but a socially acceptable–indeed often praised–form of conflict. People possessing this pattern are also quite prone to exhibiting a free-floating but extraordinarily well-rationalized hostility. As might be expected, this behaviour pattern has degrees of intensity.[86]

Because Type A behaviour is a matter of degree, it is measured on a continuum. This continuum has the hurried, competitive Type A behaviour pattern at one end and the more relaxed Type B behaviour at the other. Take a moment to complete the Type A survey contained in the next OB Exercise. This exercise will help you better understand the characteristics of the Type A behaviour pattern. Where do you fall on the Type A continuum?

OB Exercise

Where Are You on the Type A–B Behaviour Continuum?

Instructions
For each question, indicate the extent to which each statement is true of you.

	Not At All True of Me	Neither Very True Nor Very Untrue of Me	Very True of Me
1 I have given up before I'm absolutely sure that I'm licked (defeated).	1—2—3—4—5		
2 Sometimes I feel that I shouldn't be working so hard but something drives me on.	1—2—3—4—5		

3 I thrive on challenging situations. The more challenges I have, the better. 1—2—3—4—5

4 In comparison to most people I know, I'm very involved in my work. 1—2—3—4—5

5 It seems as if I need 30 hours a day to finish all the things I'm faced with. 1—2—3—4—5

6 In general, I approach my work more seriously than most people I know. 1—2—3—4—5

7 I guess there are some people
   who can be nonchalant
   about their work, but I'm
   not one of them.   1—2—3—4—5

8 My achievements are
   considered to be significantly
   higher than those of most
   people I know.   1—2—3—4—5

9 I've often been asked to be
   an manager of some group
   or groups.   1—2—3—4—5

Total score = _____

Arbitrary Norms

Type B	= 9–22
Balanced Type A and Type B	= 23–35
Type A	= 36–45

Source: Taken from R D Caplan, S Cobb, J R P French, Jr., R Van Harrison and S R Pinneau, Jr., *Job Demands and Worker Health* (New Publication No. [NIOSH] 75–160), (Washington, DC: US Department of Health, Education and Welfare, 1975), pp 253–54.

Table 17–2

Type A Characteristics

1. Hurried speech; explosive accentuation of key words.
2. Tendency to walk, move, and eat rapidly.
3. Constant impatience with the rate at which most events take place (e.g., irritation with slow-moving traffic and slow-talking and slow-to-act people).
4. Strong preference for thinking of or doing two or more things at once (e.g., reading this text and doing something else at the same time).
5. Tendency to turn conversations around to personally meaningful subjects or themes.
6. Tendency to interrupt while others are speaking to make your point or to complete their train of thought in your own words.
7. Guilt feelings during periods of relaxation or leisure time.
8. Tendency to be oblivious to surroundings during daily activities.
9. Greater concern for things worth *having* than with things worth being.
10. Tendency to schedule more and more in less and less time; a chronic sense of time urgency.
11. Feelings of competition rather than compassion when faced with another Type A person.
12. Development of nervous tics or characteristic gestures.
13. A firm belief that success is due to the ability to get things done faster than the other guy.
14. A tendency to view and evaluate personal activities and the activities of other people in terms of "numbers" (e.g., number of meetings attended, telephone calls made, visitors received).

SOURCE: Adapted from M Friedman and R H Rosenman, *Type A Behavior and Your Heart* (Greenwich, CT: Fawcett Publications, 1974), pp 100–2.

Type A Characteristics

While labelling Type A behaviour as 'hurry sickness', Friedman and Rosenman noted that Type A individuals frequently tend to exhibit most of the behaviour listed in Table 17–2. In high-pressure, achievement-oriented schools and work environments, Type A behaviour is unwittingly cultivated and even admired.

The next section highlights the advantages and disadvantages of being Type A.

Type A Research and Management Implications

OB research has demonstrated that Type A employees tend to be more productive than their Type B co-workers. For instance, Type A behaviour yielded a significant positive correlation with the average grades of 766 students, the quantity and o of 278 university lecturers' performances, and the sales performance of 222 life-insurance brokers.[87] On the other hand, Type A behaviour is associated with some negative consequences.

A meta-analysis of 99 studies revealed that Type A individuals had higher heart rates, diastolic blood pressure, and systolic blood pressure than Type B people. Type A people also showed greater cardiovascular activity when they encountered any of the following situations:

1 receipt of positive or negative feedback

2 receipt of verbal harassment or criticism

3 tasks requiring mental as opposed to physical work.[88]

Unfortunately for Type A individuals, these situations are frequently experienced at work. A second meta-analysis of 83 studies further demonstrated that the hard-driving and competitive aspects of Type A are related to coronary heart disease but that the speed, impatience and job involvement aspects are not. This meta-analysis also showed that feelings of anger, hostility and aggression were more strongly related to heart disease than was Type A behaviour.[89]

Researchers have now developed stress-reduction techniques to help Type A people to pace themselves more realistically and achieve better balance in their lives; they are discussed in the next section of this chapter. Management can help Type A people, however, by not overloading them with work despite their apparent eagerness to take an ever-increasing load. Managers need to actively help, rather than unthinkingly exploit, Type A individuals.

STRESS-REDUCTION TECHNIQUES

All told, it is estimated that almost 85 per cent of all illness and injury is the result of lifeystyle choices.[90] Therefore, it's not surprising that, increasingly, organizations are implementing a variety of stress-reduction programmes to help employees cope with modern-day stress. Consider the following example of Scient, an IT-company who actively tries to create a chilled atmosphere and a play-like culture to cope with the many pressures of everyday work.

'Dot-com consultancy is a high stress, long-hours occupation but you would not think it from the mellow, "take-it-easy" atmosphere of this workplace', says Tony O'Connell. He is one of the two "morale officers" in the company, charged with keeping the troops happy. 'Fun is part of our deal,' he says, 'otherwise our employees probably wouldn't last very long.' At Scient, IT-professionals whizz around on aluminium mini-scooters, riding past desks decorated with inflatable plastic aliens and Yogi Bears. Consultants hold discussion groups seated comfortably on colourful leather sofas and armchairs. Next door to the snooker room is the company snack bar, where staff can raid a chilled soft drinks cabinet and toast bagels in the microwave. Cream cheese and smoked salmon is in the fridge. Every day is dress-down Friday at Scient and in a break-out room, named after one of the staff's favourite local pubs, a group of young consultants attends a seminar on customer care. Scient is a young, fast-growing global company with a lot of blue chip clients but the key to its success in this competitive marketplace is its new take on human resources: the creation of a new post, the morale officer. 'I'm here to take the temperature, to act as a sounding board for employees with problems. I'm also a social secretary but most importantly: I'm here to spread fun. People who enjoy themselves can cope with the pressures better. That's why I ordered the mini scooters and the plastic aliens. I'm also organizing a movie night and a summer picnic. And those three cans of spray hair colouring you see on my desk are left over from the England versus Germany match in Euro 2000, when live pictures where projected on to a wall at Scient's offices and there was a bet with Scient's Munich office.'[91]

Although this example is pretty striking, stress prevention programmes in the UK tend to be confined to large organizations employing in excess of 500 employees. However, a number of government initiatives have been introduced within the European Union, including collaborative research programmes, new working regulations and published guidelines to help organizations reduce workplace stress, and the formation of a Europe-wide Health and Safety Agency in Bilbao, Spain.[92]

Stress intervention can focus on the individual, the organization (as in the above example) or on the interface between individual and organization (for example, through participation).

There are many different individual stress-reduction techniques available. The four most frequently used approaches are muscle relaxation, biofeedback, meditation, and cognitive restructuring. Each method involves somewhat different ways of coping with stress (see Table 17–3). Most workplace stress initiatives focus on individual stress management training and not on reducing the sources of organizational stress, for example by redesigning tasks. The different stress reduction therapies that are available can be classified as somatic, cognitive or behavioural. Some techniques deal almost exclusive with the bodily, somatic aspects, while others concentrate on cognitive restructuring, a third group concentrates on so-called coping behaviour.

Table 17–3

Stress-Reduction Techniques

Technique	Descriptions	Assessment
Muscle relaxation	Uses slow deep breathing and systematic muscle tension reduction.	Inexpensive and easy to use; may require a trained professional to implement.
Biofeedback	A machine is used to train people to detect muscular tension; muscle relaxation is then used to alleviate this symptom of stress.	Expensive due to costs of equipment; however, equipment can be used to evaluate effectiveness of other stress-reduction programs.
Meditation	The relaxation response is activated by redirecting one's thoughts away from oneself; a four-step procedure is used.	Least expensive, simple to implement, and can be practiced almost anywhere.
Cognitive restructuring	Irrational or maladaptive thoughts are identified and replaced with those that are rational or logical.	Expensive because it requires a trained psychologist or counselor.
Holistic wellness	A broad, interdisciplinary approach that goes beyond stress reduction by advocating that people strive for personal wellness in all aspects of their lives.	Involves inexpensive but often behaviorally difficult lifestyle changes.

Muscle Relaxation

The common denominators of various muscle relaxation techniques are slow and deep breathing and a conscious effort to relieve muscle tension. Among the variety of techniques available, the most frequently used is probably 'progressive relaxation'. It consists of repeatedly tensing and relaxing muscles beginning at the feet and progressing to the face. Relaxation is achieved by concentrating on the warmth and calmness associated with relaxed muscles. Take a few moments now to try this technique by carrying out the following.

While sitting in a chair, start by taking slow, deep breaths. Inhale through your nose and exhale through your mouth. Continue until you feel calm. Begin progressive relaxation by pointing your toes toward the ceiling for 10 seconds. Concentrate on the tension within your calves and feet. Now return your toes to a normal position and focus on the relaxed state of your legs and feet. (Your goal is to experience this feeling all over your body.) Tense and relax your feet for 10 seconds one more time. Moving to your calves, and continuing all the way to the muscles in your face, tense one major muscle at a time for 10 seconds, and then let it relax. Do this twice for each muscle before moving to another one. You should feel totally relaxed upon completing this routine.

Biofeedback

A biofeedback machine is used to train people to detect and control stress-related symptoms such as tense muscles and elevated blood pressure. The machine translates unconscious bodily signs into a recognizable cue (flashing light or beeper). Muscle relaxation and meditative techniques are then used to alleviate the underlying stress. The person learns to recognize bodily tension without the aid of the machine. In turn, according to the advocates of biofeedback, this awareness helps the person proactively cope with stress. Research supports the positive benefits of biofeedback. Biofeedback was found to significantly improve psychological and physiological changes, including increased problem-solving abilities.[93]

Meditation

Relaxation response
state of peacefulness

Meditation activates a relaxation response by redirecting one's thoughts away from oneself. The **relaxation response** is the physiological and psychological opposite of the fight-or-flight stress response. Importantly, however, the relaxation response must be learned and consciously activated, whereas the stress response is automatically engaged. Herbert Benson, a Harvard medical doctor, analysed many meditation programmes and derived a four-step relaxation response. The four steps are:

1 Find a quiet environment.
2 Use a mental device such as a peaceful word or pleasant image to shift the mind from externally oriented thoughts.
3 Disregard distracting thoughts by relying on a passive attitude.
4 Assume a comfortable position, preferably sitting erect in order to avoid undue muscular tension or going to sleep.

Benson emphasizes that the most important factor is a passive attitude.[94] Maximum benefits are supposedly obtained by following this procedure once or twice a day for 10 to 20 minutes, preferably just before breakfast and dinner. People following this advice experienced favourable reductions in blood pressure and anxiety levels and slept better.[95] For example, a recent study of 36 men and women between the ages of 55 and 85 showed that blood pressure significantly dropped from 145/94 to 135/88 after using transcendental meditation for three months.[96]

Cognitive Restructuring

A two-step procedure is followed. First, irrational or maladaptive thought processes that create stress are identified. For example, Type A individuals may believe they must be successful at everything they do. The second step consists of replacing these irrational thoughts with more rational or reasonable ones. Perceived failure would create stress for the Type A person. Cognitive restucturing would alleviate stress by encouraging the person to adopt a more reasonable belief about the outcomes associated with failure. For instance, the person might be encouraged to adopt the belief that isolated failure does not mean he or she is a bad person or a loser. Research revealed that stress symptoms were reduced when people jointly used cognitive restructuring and meditation.[97]

Effectiveness of Stress-Reduction Techniques

Two teams of OB researchers reviewed the research on stress management intervention. Although much of the published research is methodologically weak, results offer preliminary support for the conclusion that muscle relaxation, biofeedback, meditation, and cognitive restructuring all help employees cope with occupational stress.[98]

Some researchers advise organizations not to implement these stress-reduction programmes despite their positive outcomes. They rationalize that these techniques relieve *symptoms* of stress rather than eliminate the stressors themselves.[99] Thus, they conclude that organizations are using a 'Band-Aid' approach to stress reduction. A holistic approach has subsequently been offered as a more proactive and enduring solution.

A Holistic Wellness Model

A **holistic wellness approach** encompasses and goes beyond stress reduction by advocating that individuals strive for 'a harmonious and productive balance of physical, mental, and social well-being brought about by the acceptance of one's personal responsibility for developing and adhering to a health promotion programme.'[100] The following five dimensions of a holistic wellness approach.

> **Holistic wellness approach**
> *advocates personal responsibility for reducing stressors and stress*

1 *Personal responsibility.* Take responsibility for your own wellbeing (e.g., quit smoking, moderate your intake of alcohol, wear your seat belt). A study of 4,400 people revealed that continuous smoking throughout one's life reduces life expectancy by 18 years.[101]

2 *Nutritional awareness.* Because we are what we eat, try to increase your consumption of foods that are high in fibre, vitamins and nutrients—such as fresh fruit and vegetables, poultry and fish—while decreasing those high in sugar and fat.

3 *Stress reduction and relaxation.* Use the techniques just discussed to relax and reduce the symptoms of stress.

4 *Physical fitness.* Exercise to maintain strength, flexibility, endurance and a healthy body weight. A recent review of employee fitness programmes indicated that they were a cost-effective way of reducing medical costs, absenteeism, turnover and occupational injuries. Fitness programmes were also positively linked with job performance and job satisfaction.[102]

5 *Environmental sensitivity.* Be aware of your environment and try to identify the stressors that are causing your stress. A control strategy might be useful to eliminate stressors.

Pfizer Incorporated, a research-based health care company, is a good example of a company that supports a holistic wellness approach for its employees. The company instituted a model approach called Pfizer's Programmes for Integrating Total Health (PFIT):

Every employee is eligible to join PFIT, which is subsidized by Pfizer and requires minimal monthly payments from employees. Each new member is required to undergo a series of medical assessments: a maximal stress test, body fat analysis and a full physical exam, including blood analysis. Tests are performed at Pfizer's on-site medical facility by a registered nurse and internist/cardiologist. These assessments are used as a tool to determine cardiovascular risk factors and the current fitness levels of prospective members. The results are evaluated by the medical and fitness staff. After reviewing the tests, a fitness staff member gives the new participant an exercise orientation. During the orientation, the staff member and the participant discuss the results of the medical and nutritional assessment, identify cardiovascular risk factors, and develop a personalized exercise programme that is based on these results and the individual's goals. Members are assessed annually or biannually, depending on age and medical history . . . .

The physical therapy programme employs a licensed physical therapist and certified athletic trainer. If an employee is in need of physical therapy, he or she provides Pfizer with a prescription for therapy, and the physical therapy is provided on-site. An annual health promotion calendar is designed to offer all employees (members and non-members) monthly programme options, which include screenings, lectures, seminars and intervention programmes. Some examples of the intervention programmes include high blood pressure and cholesterol intervention, smoking cessation, diabetes control, stress management, nutrition education and cancer screenings.[103]

Pfizer has found that PFIT is an attractive benefit for potential employees and that it has helped to retain valuable employees.

In conclusion, advocates say that both your personal and professional life can be enriched by adopting a holistic approach to wellness.

Summary of Key Concepts

1 Define the term stress.

Stress is an adaptive reaction to environmental demands or stressors that triggers a fight-or-flight response. This response creates hormonal changes that mobilize the body for extraordinary demands.

2 Describe the model of occupational stress.

Perceived stress is caused by four sets of stressors: individual level, group level, organizational level, and extraorganizational. In turn, perceived stress has psychological/attitudinal, behavioural, cognitive, and physical health outcomes. Several individual differences moderate relationships between stressors, perceived stress and outcomes.

3 Discuss four reasons why it is important for managers to understand the causes and consequences of stress.

First, from a quality-of-working life perspective, workers are more satisfied when they are not under a lot of stress. Second, a moral imperative suggests that managers should reduce stress because it leads to negative outcomes. The third reason relates to the significant economic costs associated with stress. Finally, because stress-related illnesses may be covered under worker's compensation laws, employers can be sued for exposing employees to undue stress.

4 Explain how stressful life events create stress.

Stressful life events are changes that disrupt an individual's lifestyle and social relationships. Holmes and Rahe developed the Social Readjustment Rating Scale to assess an individual's cumulative stressful life events. A positive relationship exists between the scores on the social readjustment rating scale and illness. Uncontrollable events that are negative create the most stress.

5 Review the model of burn-out, then highlight the managerial solutions for reducing it.

Burn-out develops in phases. The three key phases are emotional exhaustion, depersonalization, and feeling a lack of personal accomplishment. Emotional exhaustion, the first phase, is due to a combination of personal stressors and job and organizational stressors. The total effect of the burn-out phases is a host of negative attitudinal and behavioural outcomes. Managers can reduce burn-out by buffering its effects; potential buffers include extra staff or equipment, support from top management, increased freedom to make decisions, recognition of accomplishments, time off, equitable rewards and increased communication from management. Managers can also change the content of an individual's job or assign the person to a new position. Sabbaticals and employee retreats are also used to reduce burn-out.

6 Explain the mechanisms of social support.

Social support, an important moderator of relationships between stressors, stress and outcomes, represents the amount of perceived helpfulness derived from social relationships. Cultural norms, social institutions, companies, groups and individuals are all sources of social support. These sources provide four types of support: esteem, informational, social companionship and instrumental.

7 Describe the coping process.

Coping is the management of stressors and stress. Coping is directly affected by the cognitive appraisal of stressors which, in turn, is influenced by situational and personal factors. People cope by using control, escape or symptom management strategies. Because research has not identified the most effective method of coping, a contingency approach to coping is recommended.

8 Discuss the personality characteristic of hardiness.

Hardiness is a collection of personality characteristics that neutralizes stress. It includes the characteristics of commitment, locus of control, and challenge. Research has demonstrated that hardy individuals respond less negatively to stressors and stress than less hardy people. Less hardy employees would be good candidates for stress-reduction programmes.

9 Discuss the Type A behaviour pattern and its management implications.

The Type A behaviour pattern is characterized by someone who is aggressively involved in a chronic, determined struggle to accomplish more and more in less and less time. Type B is the opposite of Type A. Although there are several positive outcomes associated with being Type A, Type A behaviour is positively correlated with coronary heart disease. Management can help Type A individuals by not overloading them with work despite their apparent eagerness to take on an ever-increasing work load.

10 Contrast the four dominant stress-reduction techniques.

Muscle relaxation, biofeedback, meditation, and cognitive restructuring are predominant stress-reduction techniques. Slow and deep breathing and a conscious effort to relieve muscle tension are common denominators of muscle relaxation. Biofeedback relies on a machine to train people to detect bodily signs of stress. This awareness facilitates proactive coping with stressors. Meditation activates the relaxation response by redirecting one's thoughts away from oneself. Cognitive restructuring entails identifying irrational or maladaptive thoughts and replacing them with rational or logical thoughts.

Discussion Questions

1 What are the key stressors encountered by students? Which ones are under their control?

2 Describe the behavioural and physiological symptoms you have observed in others when they are under stress.

3 Why do uncontrollable events lead to more stress than controllable events?

4 Why would people in the helping professions become burned out more readily than people in other occupations?

5 Do you think your lecturers are likely to become burned out? Explain your rationale.

6 Which of the five sources of social support is most likely to provide individuals with social support? Explain.

7 Why would people have difficulty using a control strategy to cope with the aftermath of a natural disaster like an earthquake or flood?

8 How can someone increase their hardiness and reduce their Type A behaviour?

9 Have you used any of the stress-reduction techniques? Evaluate their effectiveness.

10 What is the most valuable lesson you learned from this chapter? Explain.

Internet Exercise

http://www.queendom.com

We highlighted in this chapter how people cope with stress by using a variety of control, escape, and symptom management strategies. Your ability to effectively cope with perceived stress is very important because ineffective coping can make a stressful situation even worse.

A Free Self-Assessment Questionnaire to Measure Your Coping Skills

The purpose of this exercise is to provide you with feedback on how well you cope with perceived stress. Go to the Internet home page for Body-Mind QueenDom (**www.queendom.com**), and click the main menu heading *Tests & Profiles*. Read the brief welcome statement about Queendom's psychological tests and then choose the category for *Personality*. Now scroll down and select the *Coping Skills* test, read the instructions, complete all items, and click on the *score* button for automatic scoring. (*Note:* Our use of this questionnaire is for instructional purposes only and does not constitute an endorsement of any products that may or may not suit your needs. There is no obligation to buy anything.) You will receive an overall coping skills score as well as scores for seven coping sub-dimension scores: reactivity to stress, ability to assess situations, self-reliance, resourcefulness, adaptability and flexibility, proactive attitudes, and ability to relax. You can print a personal copy of the interpretation of your results for use when answering the following questions.

Questions

Possible scores for overall coping skills range from 0 (extremely poor coping skills) to 100 (extremely good coping skills).

1 How did you score? Are you surprised by the results?

2 How did you score on the coping skills sub-dimensions of reactivity to stress, ability to assess situations, self-reliance, resourcefulness, adaptability and flexibility, proactive attitudes, and ability to relax? Do you agree with the interpretation of your scores?

3 Based on the interpretation of your results, what can you do to improve your coping skills? How might you also reduce your level of perceived stress?

Personal Awareness and Growth Exercise
Are You Burned Out?

Objectives

1 To determine the extent to which you are burned out.

2 To determine if your burn-out scores are predictive of burn-out outcomes.

3 To identify specific stressors that affect your level of burn-out.

Introduction

An OB researcher named Christina Maslach developed a self-report scale measuring burn-out. This scale assesses burn-out in terms of three phases: depersonalisation, personal accomplishment and emotional exhaustion. To determine if you suffer from burn-out in any of these phases, we would like you to complete an abbreviated version of this scale. Moreover, because burn-out has been found to influence a variety of behavioural outcomes, we also want to determine how well burn-out predicts three important outcomes.

Instructions

To assess your level of burn-out, complete the following 18 statements development by Maslach.[89] Each item probes how frequently you experience a particular feeling or attitude. If you are currently working, use your job as the frame of reference for responding to each statement. If you are a full-time student, use your role as a student as your frame of reference. After you have completed the 18 items, refer to the scoring key and following its directions. Remember, there are no right or wrong answers. Indicate your answer for each statement by circling one number from the following scale.

1 = A few times a year

2 = Monthly

3 = A few times a month

4 = Every week

5 = A few times a week

6 = Every day

Burn-out Inventory

1 I've become more callous towards people since I took this job. 1—2—3—4—5—6

2 I worry that this job is hardening me emotionally 1—2—3—4—5—6

3 I don't really care what happens to some of the people who need my help. 1—2—3—4—5—6

4 I feel that people who need my help blame me for some of their problems. 1—2—3—4—5—6

5 I deal very effectively with the problems of those people who need my help. 1—2—3—4—5—6

6 I feel I'm positively influencing other people's lives through my work. 1—2—3—4—5—6

7 I feel very energetic. 1—2—3—4—5—6

8 I can easily create a relaxed atmosphere with those people who need my help. 1—2—3—4—5—6

9 I feel exhilarated after working closely with those who need my help. 1—2—3—4—5—6

10 I have accomplished many worthwhile things in the job. 1—2—3—4—5—6

11 In my work, I deal with emotional problems very calmly. 1—2—3—4—5—6

12 I feel emotionally drained from my work. 1—2—3—4—5—6

13 I feel used up at the end of the working day. 1—2—3—4—5—6

14 I feel fatigued when I get up in the morning. 1—2—3—4—5—6

15 I feel frustrated by my job. 1—2—3—4—5—6

16 I feel I'm working too hard at my job. 1—2—3—4—5—6

17 Working with people directly puts too much stress on me. 1—2—3—4—5—6

18 I feel like I'm at the end of my tether. 1—2—3—4—5—6

Scoring

Compute the average of those items measuring each phase of burn-out.

Depersonalization (questions 1–4) _____

Personal accomplishment (questions 5–11) _____

Emotional exhaustion (questions 12–18) _____

Assessing Burn-out Outcomes

1 How many times were you absent from work over the last three months (indicate the number of absences from your course last term if using the student role)?

_____ absences

2 How satisfied are you with your job (or role as a student)? Circle one.

Very
dissatisfied Dissatisfied Neutral Satisfied Very satisfied

3 Do you have trouble sleeping? Circle one.

Yes No

Questions for Discussion

1 To what extent are you burned out in terms of depersonalisation and emotional exhaustion?

Low = 1–2.99; Moderate = 3–4.99; High = 5 or above

2 To what extent are you burned out in terms of personal accomplishment?

Low = 5 or above; Moderate = 3–4.99; High = 1–2.99

3 How well do your burn-out scores predict your burn-out outcomes?

4 Do your burn-out scores suggest that burn-out follows a sequence going from depersonalisation, to feeling a lack of personal accomplishment, to emotional exhaustion? Explain.

5 Which of the unique burn-out stressors illustrated in Figure 17–2 are affecting your level of burn-out?

Group Exercise
Reducing the Stressors in Your Environment

Objectives

1 To identify the stressors in your environment.

2 To evaluate the extent to which each stressor is a source of stress.

3 To develop a plan for reducing the impact of stressors in your environment.

Introduction

Stressors are environmental factors that produce stress. They are prerequisites to experiencing the symptoms of stress. As previously discussed in this chapter, people do not appraise stressors in the same way. For instance, having to complete a challenging assignment may be motivational for one person and threatening to another. This exercise was designed to give you the opportunity to identify the stressors in your environment; to evaluate the extent to which these stressors create stress in your life; and to develop a plan for reducing the negative effects of these stressors.

Instructions

Your tutor will divide the class into groups of four to six. Once the group is assembled, the group should brainstorm and record a list of stressors that they believe exist in their environments. Use the guidelines for brainstorming discussed in Chapter 14. After recording all the brainstormed ideas on a piece of paper, remove redundancies and combine like items so that the group has a final list of unique stressors. Next, each group member should individually determine the extent to which each stressor is a source of stress in his or her life. For the purpose of this exercise, stress is defined as existing whenever you experience feelings of pressure, strain or emotional upset. The stress evaluation is done by first indicating the frequency with which each stressor is a source of stress to you. Use the six-point rating scale provided. Once everyone has completed their individual ratings, combine the numerical judgements to get an average stress score for each stressor. Next, identify the five stressors with the highest average stress ratings. Finally, the group should develop a plan for coping with each of these five stressors. Try to make your recommendations as specific as possible.

Rating Scale

Answer the following question for each stressor: To what extent is the stressor a source of stress?

1 = Never

2 = Rarely

3 = Occasionally

4 = Often

5 = Usually

6 = Always

Questions for Discussion

1 Are you surprised by the type of stressors that were rated as creating the most stress in your lives? Explain.

2 Did group members tend to agree or disagree when evaluating the extent to which the various stressors created stress in their lives? What is the source of the different appraisals?

3 Which form of coping did your plans include most, control or escape-oriented strategies? Explain.

Chapter Eighteen

Organizational Effectiveness and Design

Learning Objectives

When you finish studying the material in this chapter, you should be able to:

○ Describe the four characteristics common to all organizations and explain the difference between closed and open systems.

○ Contrast the following organizational metaphors: military/mechanical, biological, and cognitive systems.

○ Describe the ecosystem model of organizations and define the term *postmodern organization*.

○ Describe the four generic organizational effectiveness criteria and discuss how managers can prevent organizational decline.

○ Explain what the contingency approach to organization design involves.

○ Describe the relationship between differentiation and integration in effective organizations.

○ Discuss Burns and Stalker's findings regarding mechanistic and organic organizations.

○ Define and briefly explain the practical significance of centralization and decentralization.

○ Discuss the effective management of organizational size.

○ Describe horizontal, hourglass and virtual organizations.

Moving at the speed of Dell

On a foggy January morning at Dell Computer Corporation's headquarters in Round Rock, Texas, a receptionist boots up 10 computers that line two sides of the lobby in building RR3. The computers operate a number of programmes but default to Dell's home page, which is also available through the Internet. ▶

Among other functions, the page allows applicants who come by in person to view job listings, and directly create and submit résumés into a database that any Dell hiring manager can access.

It's a small innovation, perhaps, but one that helps Dell hire the 100 employees per week it needs to sustain its growth.

The company's growth, however, forces its human resources staff to constantly raise the bar by which it measures success. The challenges HR faces include selecting and developing a workforce that can meet constantly changing requirements without losing Dell's market and customer focus or its culture.

Here's how they do it.

Dell's Cell Division

To prevent its growth from spinning out of control, Dell uses a strategy that splits off business segments once they reach a certain threshold. Managers take charge of these smaller pieces of the business and attempt to grow them to the point where they can be split again–much in the way that a cell divides over and over to grow a human body.

Steve Price, vice president of human resources for Dell's Public and Americas International Group (PAI), gives the following example to show how the process works. 'Our education market is comprised of a higher education component and a school component. Today, that operates as an education business segment. But now it's gotten so big that we're going to split it and have a business segment called Higher Ed and a business segment called School.'

The decision to segment is not based on size or number of employees, says Price, but—at least in part—on whether the division has grown to a particular financial measure or threshold. The company couples that measure with anticipated market opportunity; and with the projected profits Dell might reap by focusing on that market opportunity; to arrive at a decision to segment. For example, the threshold number is driving the education split but the company 'also saw that it needed to approach these two groups differently', says Price.

Seeking People Who Seek Change

To make this segmentation strategy work, Dell actively seeks and cultivates a certain type of employee mind-set.

For example, potential employees are told early on that their former titles may not correlate exactly with positions at Dell because the company structure is relatively flat. 'We have to strip the paradigm that titles and levels mean anything,' says Price. 'People have to park their egos at the door.'

Furthermore, Dell's employees have to move away from the paradigm that more means better. 'It's just the reverse,' says Price. 'When we take half of what you have away from you and tell you to go rebuild it, that's a sign of success.' Dell's compensation strategy carefully backs up this unique measure of success by rewarding managers who grow the business to the point that segmentation is required.

Such efforts at developing the proper employee mind-set appear to be paying off. Dell employees, according to the company's HR professionals, welcome segmentation.

'There's an excitement about segmentation,' says Jim Koster, director of HR for customer service, 'because it creates opportunity.' When he was on the sales side, he remembers employees asking him 'We've reached X—when do we split?'

Erik Dithmer, senior manager of operations for Dell Plus, says that 'When someone says, "Now I don't want you to report metrics for education–I want you to report metrics for higher ed and school," everybody does that with a smile on their faces. They're saying "Ah! That's good!" '

That attitude is important because segmentation can occur rapidly at Dell. Dithmer notes that education's anticipated segmentation was preceded a year ago by a segmentation from state and local education. 'For a lot of people, this has been the second segmentation within nine or 10 months,' he says.

Other organizations may be able to duplicate this exuberant approach to change, but Dell appears to have an advantage that companies in other industries may not. That's because Dell mirrors the high-tech industry as a whole, where a fast pace and constant change are the norm.

'We typically attract people for whom change is not a problem,' says Koster. 'In fact, most people here thrive on it.' Koster believes there may come a time when HR has to slow down the process a little bit, 'to make sure that everything splits as it should'.[1]

> ### For discussion
> Is Dell Computer likely to be an effective company 10 years from now? Why or why not?

Virtually every aspect of life is affected at least indirectly by some type of organization.[2] We look to organizations to feed, clothe, house, educate and employ us. Organizations attend to our needs for entertainment, police and fire protection, insurance, recreation, national security, transportation, news and information, legal assistance and health care. Many of these organizations seek a profit, others do not. Some are extremely large, others are tiny family-run operations. Despite this mind-boggling diversity, modern organizations have one basic thing in common. They are the primary context for *organizational* behaviour. In a manner of speaking, organizations are the chessboard upon which the game of organizational behaviour is played. Therefore, present and future managers need a working knowledge of modern organizations to improve their chances of making the right moves when managing people at work.

This chapter explores the effectiveness, design and future of today's organizations. We begin by defining the term *organization*, discussing important dimensions of organization charts, and tracing the evolution of basic organizational models. Our attention then turns to criteria for assessing organizational effectiveness, with an eye toward avoiding organizational decline. Next, we discuss the contingency approach to organizational design. We conclude with a preview of tomorrow's organizations. Our overriding challenge is to build organizations capable of thriving in an environment characterized by rapid change and relentless global competition.

DEFINING AND CHARTING ORGANIZATIONS

As a necessary springboard for this chapter, we need to formally define the term *organization* and clarify the meaning of organization charts.

What Is an Organization?

Organization
system of consciously co-ordinated activities of two or more people

According to Chester I Barnard's classic definition, an organization is 'a system of consciously co-ordinated activities or forces of two or more persons'.[3] Embodied in the *conscious co-ordination* aspect of this definition are four common facors in all organizations: co-ordination of effort, a common goal, division of labour and a hierarchy of authority[4] (see Figure 18–1). Organization theorists refer to these factors as the organization's *structure*.[5]

Figure 18–1

Four Characteristics Common to All Organizations

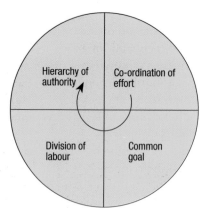

Co-ordination of effort is achieved through formulation and enforcement of policies, rules and regulations. Division of labour occurs when the common goal is pursued by individuals performing separate but related tasks. The hierarchy of authority, also called the chain of command, is a control mechanism dedicated to making sure the right people do the right things at the right time. Historically, managers have maintained the integrity of the hierarchy of authority by adhering to the **unity of command principle**. Without this, the argument goes, inefficiency would prevail because of conflicting orders and lack of personal accountability.[6] (Indeed, these are problems for those more fluid and flexible organizations that are based on innovations such as cross-functional and self-managed teams.) Managers in the hierarchy of authority also administer rewards and punishments. When the four factors in Figure 18–1 operate in concert, the dynamic entity called an organization exists.

> **Unity of command principle**
> *each employee should report to a single manager*

Organization Charts

An **organization chart**, to the casual observer, looks like a family tree—a pattern of boxes and lines posted on workplace walls. Within each box one usually finds the names and titles of current position holders. To organization theorists, however, organization charts reveal much more. The partial organization chart in Figure 18–2 reveals four basic dimensions of organizational structure:

> **Organization chart**
> *graphic illustration showing chain of formal authority and division of labour*

▼ **hierarchy of authority (who reports to whom)**

▼ **division of labour**

▼ **spans of control**

▼ **line and staff positions.**

Figure 18–2 *Sample Organization Chart for a US Hospital (executive and director levels only)*

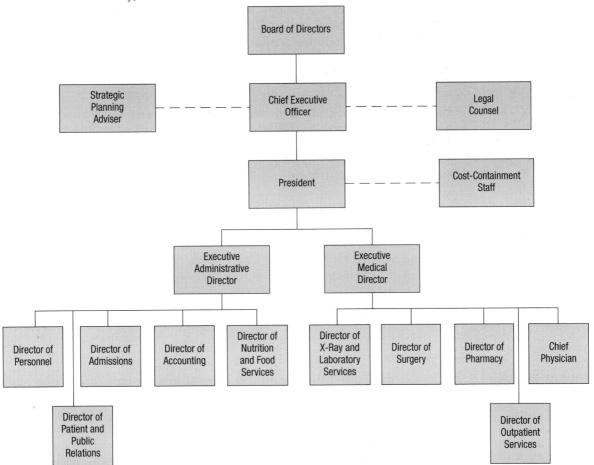

Hierarchy of Authority

As Figure 18–2 illustrates, there is an unmistakable hierarchy of authority.[7] Working from bottom to top, the 10 directors report to the two executive directors who report to the president who reports to the chief executive officer. Ultimately, the chief executive officer answers to the hospital's board of directors. The chart in Figure 18–2 shows strict unity of command up and down the line. A formal hierarchy of authority also delineates the official communication network.

Division of Labour

In addition to showing the chain of command, the sample organization chart indicates extensive division of labour. Immediately below the hospital's president, one executive director is responsible for general administration while another is responsible for medical affairs. Each of these two specialties is further subdivided as indicated by the next layer of positions. At each successively lower level in the organization, jobs become more specialized.

Spans of Control

Span of control
the number of people reporting directly to a given manager

The span of control refers to the number of people reporting directly to a given manager.[8] Spans of control can range from narrow to wide. For example, the president in Figure 18–2 has a narrow span of control of two. (Usually, staff assistants are not included in a manager's span of control.) The executive administrative director in Figure 18–2 has a wider span of control of five. Spans of control exceeding 30 can be found in assembly-line operations where machine-paced and repetitive work substitutes for close supervision. Historically, spans of five to six were considered best. Despite years of debate, organization theorists have not arrived at a consensus regarding the ideal span of control.

Generally, the narrower the span of control, the closer the supervision and the higher the administrative costs as a result of a higher manager-to-worker ratio. Recent emphasis on leanness and administrative efficiency dictates spans of control as wide as possible but guarding against inadequate supervision and lack of co-ordination. Wider spans also complement the trend toward greater worker autonomy and empowerment.

Line and Staff Positions

Staff personnel
provide research, advice and recommendations to line managers

Line managers
have authority to make organizational decisions

The organization chart in Figure 18–2 also distinguishes between line and staff positions. Line managers such as the president, the two executive directors, and the various directors occupy formal decision-making positions within the chain of command. Line positions are usually connected by solid lines on organization charts. Dotted lines indicate staff relationships. Staff personnel provide research, advice and recommendations to their line managers, who have the authority to make decisions. For example, the cost-containment specialists in the sample organization chart merely advise the president on relevant matters. Apart from supervising the work of their own staff assistants, they have no line authority over other organizational members. Modern trends, such as cross-functional teams and re-engineering, are blurring the distinction between line and staff positions.

According to a study of 207 police officers in Israel, line personnel exhibited greater job commitment than did their staff counterparts.[9] This result was anticipated because the line managers' decision-making authority empowered them and gave them comparatively more control over their work situations.

THE EVOLUTION OF ORGANIZATIONAL METAPHORS

The complexity of modern organizations makes them somewhat difficult to describe. Consequently, organization theorists have resorted to the use of metaphors.[10]

A *metaphor* is a figure of speech that characterizes one object in terms of another object. Good metaphors help us comprehend complicated things by describing them in everyday terms. For example, consider the following metaphor envisioning the modern organization as an orchestra.

> *The system can be thought of as a large modern orchestra with a number of professionals playing quite different instruments and performing separate—and often very difficult—tasks. Each instrumentalist, like so many in large organizations, is indeed a specialist in a particular field whose work must be integrated with the work of others to make up the whole.*

> *The manager's job is more than what the concert-goer sees. It includes planning the performance, helping to select those numbers that the orchestra can best perform, presiding at rehearsals, and doing many of the things that are required to make the final concert notable. The manager's contribution is much more than being the one with the baton, and what the audience sees should be understood in that context.*[11]

OB scholar, Kim Cameron, sums up the value of organizational metaphors as follows: 'Each time a new metaphor is used, certain aspects of organizational phenomena are uncovered that were not evident with other metaphors. In fact, the usefulness of metaphors lies in their possession of some degree of falsehood so that new images and associations emerge.'[12] With the orchestra metaphor, for instance, one could come away with an exaggerated picture of harmony in large and complex organizations. On the other hand, it realistically encourages us to view managers as facilitators rather than absolute dictators.

Four organizational metaphors that have evolved over the years characterize organizations alternatively as military/mechanical systems, biological systems, cognitive systems, and ecosystem participants. These four metaphors can be plotted on a continuum ranging from simple closed systems to complex open systems (see Table 18–1). We need to clarify the important distinction between closed and open systems before exploring the metaphors.

Table 18–1 *Four Contrasting Organizational Metaphors*

	CLOSED SYSTEMS		OPEN SYSTEMS	
	Military/Mechanical Model (Bureaucracy)	Biological Model (Resource Transformation System)	Cognitive Model (Interpretation and Meaning System)	Ecosystem Model (Life and Death Struggle in Organizational Communities)
Metaphorical comparison	Precision military unit/well-oiled machine	Human body	Human mind	Natural ecosystems; Darwin's theory of natural selection (survival of the fittest)
Assumption about organization's environment	Predictable (controllable impacts)	Uncertain (filled with surprises)	Uncertain and ambiguous	Primary determinant of success/failure
Organization's primary goal	Maximum economic efficiency through rigorous planning and control	Survival through adaptation to environmental constraints and opportunities	Growth and survival through environmental scanning, interpretation, and learning	Growth and survival through opportunistic cooperation and competition

Closed versus Open Systems

Closed system
a relatively self-sufficient entity

Open system
organism that must constantly interact with its environment to survive

The distinction between a closed system and an open system is a matter of degree. Because every worldly system is partly closed and partly open, the key question is: How great a role does the environment play in the functioning of the system? For instance, a battery-powered clock is a relatively closed system. Once the battery is inserted, the clock performs its time-keeping function hour after hour until the battery goes dead. The human body, on the other hand, is a highly open system because it requires a constant supply of life-sustaining oxygen from the environment. Nutrients are also imported from the environment. Open systems are capable of self-correction, adaptation and growth, thanks to characteristics such as homeostasis and feedback control.

The traditional military/mechanical metaphor is a closed system model because it largely ignores environmental influences. It gives the impression that organizations are self-sufficient entities. Conversely, the biological, cognitive and ecosystem metaphors emphasize interaction between organizations and their environments. These newer models are based on open-system assumptions. A closer look at the four organizational metaphors reveals instructive insights about organizations and how they work. Each perspective offers something useful.

Organizations as Military/Mechanical Bureaucracies

A major by-product of the Industrial Revolution was the factory system of production. People left their farms and cottage industries to operate steam-powered machines in centralized factories. The social unit of production evolved from the family to formally managed organizations encompassing hundreds or even thousands of people. Managers sought to maximize the economic efficiency of large factories and offices by structuring them according to military principles. At the turn of the 20th century, a German sociologist, Max Weber, formulated what he termed the most rationally efficient form of organization.[13] He patterned his ideal organization after the vaunted Prussian army and called it bureaucracy.

Bureaucracy
Max Weber's idea of the most rationally efficient form of organization

Weber's Bureaucracy

According to Weber's theory, the following four factors should make bureaucracies the epitome of efficiency.

1 Division of labour (people become proficient when they perform standardized tasks over and over again).
2 A hierarchy of authority (a formal chain of command ensures co-ordination and accountability).
3 A framework of rules (carefully formulated and strictly enforced rules ensure predictable behaviour).
4 Administrative impersonality (personnel decisions such as hiring and promoting should be based on competence not favouritism).[14]

How Bureaucracy Became a Synonym for Inefficiency

All organizations possess varying degrees of the four characteristics listed above. Thus, every organization is a bureaucracy to some extent. In terms of the ideal metaphor, a bureaucracy should run like a well-oiled machine and its members should perform with the precision of a polished military unit. But practical and ethical problems arise when bureaucratic characteristics become extreme or dysfunctional. For example, extreme expressions of specialization, rule following and impersonality can cause a bureaucrat to treat a client as a number rather than as a person.[15]

Weber would probably be surprised and dismayed that his model of rational efficiency has become a synonym for inefficiency.[16] Today, bureaucracy stands for being put on hold, waiting in queues, and getting shuffled from one office to the next. (See the next

International OB.) This irony can be explained largely by the fact that organizations with excessive or dysfunctional bureaucratic tendencies become rigid, inflexible and resistant to environmental demands and influences. Jack Welch, General Electric's former legendary CEO, told *Fortune* magazine about his 'tough love' approach to battling bureaucracy.

Giving people self-confidence is by far the most important thing that I can do. Because then they will act. I tell people, if this place is stifling you, shake it, shake it, break it. Check the system, because it wants to be a bureaucracy. And if it doesn't work, get the hell out. If GE can't give you what you want, go get it somewhere else.[17]

International OB

http://www.idsc.gov.eg.

The Mugama: Egypt's Bureaucratic Legacy

Cairo – In Egypt the bureaucracy is not just an engine of policy or even a state of mind. It is a semicircular concrete behemoth in the center of this city's central square.

In this towering edifice—the Mugama ('Uniting') Central Government Complex— office opens onto office, crumbling stairway onto stairway, and the circular corridors that wheel 14 stories high around a dusky inner courtyard seem to have no end.

The Mugama holds 20,000 public employees in 1,400 rooms. It is headquarters to 14 government departments. So deep is its reach into the everyday life of Cairenes that most adult city dwellers will find themselves forced to visit it several times a year. Upward of 45,000 people pass through its portals each day.

Perhaps unrivalled anywhere in the world as a symbol of government dithering and public despair, it is at once the most feared and hated structure in Egypt and the evolutionary product of millennia of bureaucracy on the shores of the Nile.

Twelve hapless clients of the Mugama have hurled themselves from its broken windows or from the soaring circular balconies that ring the central lobby up to the 13th floor dome. A generation of Arab social engineers, who threw off a monarchy and seized Egypt in the name of its poor and unrepresented, planted their dreams in the Mugama's corridors and largely watched them die there.

'The Mugama is to Egypt generally a symbol of 4,000 years of bureaucracy and for the average Egyptian, it means all that is negative about the bureaucracy routine, slow paperwork, complicated paperwork, a lot of signatures,

impersonality. It is a Kafka building,' said political sociologist Saad Eddin Ibrahim.

'You enter there, you can get the job done—the same job—in five minutes, in five days, in five months or five years,' Ibrahim said. 'You can never predict what might happen to you in that building. Anybody who has dealt with that building for whatever reason knows the uncertainty of his affairs there.'

In Egypt, the legacy of bureaucracy dates back to the time of the pharaohs. Temple walls and statues depict countless scribes, papyrus and pen in hand, taking down for the files of posterity everything from the deeds of the Pharaoh to the tax man's inventory. Subsequent French, Turkish and British occupiers refined Egyptian red tape to a fine art.

Today, it takes 11 different permits for a foreign resident to buy an apartment in downtown Cairo. A bride wishing to join her husband working abroad in the Persian Gulf region must get stamps and signatures from the Foreign Ministry, the Ministry of Justice, the prosecutor general, the local court in her district, and the regional court, a process that one Cairo newspaper referred to as 'legalized torture'.

One young physician recently left the Mugama in tears after three days of trying to resign from her government job.

'They told me finally it would be easier if I just took a long sick leave,' she said with a sigh. 'But I'm leaving the country for a year!'

SOURCE: 'Woe Awaits in Tower of Babble' by Kimberly Murphy, published May 24, 1993. Copyright, 1993, Los Angeles Times. Reprinted by permission.

Organizations as Biological Systems

Drawing upon the field of general systems theory that emerged during the 1950s,[18] organization theorists suggested a more dynamic model for modern organizations. As noted in Table 18–1, this metaphor likens organizations to the human body. Hence, it has been labelled the biological model. In his often-cited organization theory text, *Organizations in Action*, James D Thompson explained the biological model of organizations in the following terms.

> *Approached as a natural system, the complex organization is a set of interdependent parts which together make up a whole because each contributes something and receives something from the whole, which in turn is interdependent with some larger environment. Survival of the system is taken to be the goal, and the parts and their relationships presumably are determined through evolutionary processes.*
>
> *Central to the natural-system approach is the concept of homeostasis, or self-stabilization, which spontaneously, or naturally, governs the necessary relationships among parts and activities and thereby keeps the system viable in the face of disturbances stemming from the environment.*[19]

Unlike the traditional military/mechanical theorists who downplayed the environment, advocates of the biological model stress organization–environment interaction. As Figure 18–3 illustrates, the biological model characterizes the organization as an open system that transforms inputs into various outputs. The outer boundary of the organization is permeable. People, information, capital, and goods and services move back and forth across this boundary. Moreover, each of the five organizational

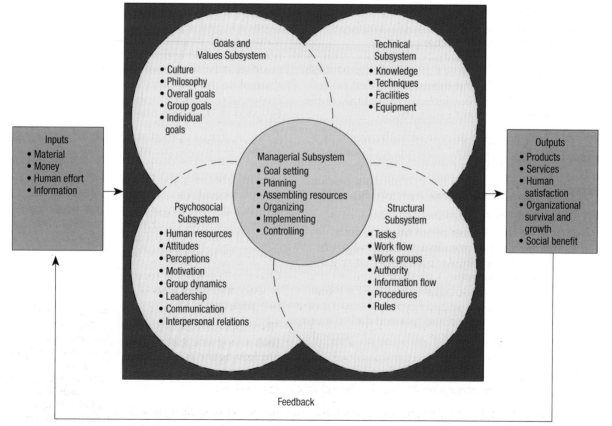

Figure 18–3 *The Organization as an Open System: The Biological Model*

SOURCE: This model is a combination of Figures 5–2 and 5–3 in F E Kast and J E Rosenzweig, *Organization and Management: A Systems and Contingency Approach*, 4th ed (New York: McGraw-Hill, 1986), pp 112, 114. Copyright © 1986. Reproduced with permission of the McGraw-Hill Companies.

subsystems—goals and values, technical, psychosocial, structural, and managerial—is dependent on the others. Feedback about such things as sales and customer satisfaction or dissatisfaction enables the organization to self-adjust and survive despite uncertainty and change.[20] In effect, the organization is alive.

Organizations as Cognitive Systems

A more recent metaphor characterizes organizations in terms of mental functions. Respected organization theorists Richard Daft and Karl Weick, offer the following explanation.

This perspective represents a move away from mechanical and biological metaphors of organizations. Organizations are more than transformation processes or control systems. To survive, organizations must have mechanisms to interpret ambiguous events and to provide meaning and direction for participants. Organizations are meaning systems, and this distinguishes them from lower-level systems.

Almost all outcomes in terms of organization structure and design, whether caused by the environment, technology or size, depend on the interpretation of problems or opportunities by key decision makers. Once interpretation occurs, the organization can formulate a response.[21]

This interpretation process, carried out at the top-management or strategic level, leads to organizational *learning* and adaptation.

In fact, the concept of the *learning organization*,[22] discussed in detail in Chapter 19, is very popular in management circles these days. Motorola Inc. is an excellent case in point. The giant manufacturer of electronics equipment and communications gear has a strong reputation for product quality that its executives fear will not be enough to compete globally during the next decade. While working hard to maintain its lead in quality, Motorola now seeks to become a learning organization that is creative, adaptive and responsive to change.

To develop those attributes, Motorola is gearing up a new campaign built around lifelong learning. Under a programme conceived by [former chairman] Robert W Galvin . . . Motorola will dramatically increase training of all employees, from the factory floor to the corner office. The goal is a workforce that is disciplined yet free-thinking. The initiative will aim to inculcate them with company procedures so they're a well-oiled machine but also to develop the knowledge and independent-mindedness that Motorola will need to conquer rapidly changing technologies and markets.[23]

Organizations as Ecosystem Participants

Managers have long joked about organizational life being a 'jungle' where it is 'dog eat dog'. According to the newest organizational metaphor, it is indeed a jungle out there. Organizational ecology parallels the study of earth's natural ecosystems. Ecologists are interested in the interaction between an organism and its environment. For instance, consider the fate of birds of prey in recent years. The pesticide DDT in the food chain caused these magnificent birds to lay eggs with shells too thin to make it through the incubation period. Thanks largely to the banning of DDT in some countries, the birds of prey are making a strong comeback[24] So too, according to this metaphor, do organizations live or die depending on the health and supportiveness of their environment. A recent review of the field produced this definition: '**Organizational ecologists** seek to explain how social, economic and political conditions affect the relative abundance and diversity of organizations and attempt to account for their changing composition.'[25]

Thus, organizational ecologists study organizational foundings, failures, changes and interrelationships within the context of environmental factors. They talk in terms of *populations* (groups of similar organizations) and *communities* (networks of differing organizations).

Organizational ecologists
those who study the effect of environmental factors on organizational success/failure and interrelationships among populations and communities of organizations

Inherent in the ecological metaphor, as indicated in Table 18–1, is Darwin's theory of natural selection. In the natural world, the fittest members of each species survive because in their particular environment they come out the strongest. James F Moore, in his best-selling book, *The Death of Competition: Leadership and Strategy in the Age of Business Ecosystems*, offers the following example.

> *Take the caribou and the wolf. The wolf culls the weaker caribou, which strengthens the herd. But with a stronger herd, it is imperative for wolves to evolve and become stronger themselves to succeed. And so the pattern is not simply competition or co-operation, but 'co-evolution'. Over time, as co-evolution proceeds, the whole system becomes more hardy.*[26]

Moving from the natural world to organizations, Moore goes on to explain the following.

> *Business ecosystems span a variety of industries. The companies within them co-evolve capabilities around the innovation and* work co-operatively and competitively *to support new products, satisfy customer needs and incorporate the next round of innovation. Microsoft, for example, anchors an ecosystem that traverses at least four major industries: personal computers, consumer electronics, information and communications. Centred on innovation in microprocessing, the Microsoft ecosystem encompasses an extended web of suppliers including Intel and Hewlett-Packard and myriad customers across market segments.*

> *. . . shaping cohesive strategy in the new order starts by defining an* opportunity environment. *Within such an environment, strategy-making revolves around devising novel ways to seize opportunities and create viable networks with other business ecosystems.*[27]

Organizational Metaphors in Perspective (toward Postmodern Organizations)

In newly industrialized nations with poorly educated workers, like most countries in the early 1900s, the military/mechanical approach was widely applicable. Narrowly defined jobs, military-like discipline and strict chains of command enabled factory and office managers to control their employees and meet production quotas. As things grew more complex, however, the military/mechanical model was found lacking. Thanks to modern open-system thinking, we now see organizations as more than internally focused control mechanisms.

A useful model of modern organizations emerges when we integrate the biological, cognitive and ecological metaphors. Conceptually, the organization's *body* and *head* need to be connected. One cannot function without the other. Managers of today's productive organizations are responsible for transforming factors of production into the necessary goods and services (the body). Yet they can remain competitive only if they wisely *interpret* environmental opportunities and obstacles (the head). Another job for the thinking/learning organization, according to the ecological model, is to 'co-evolve' with other organizations through balanced competition and co-operation.

Postmodern organizations
flexible organizations that are decentralized, computer linked and less hierarchical than bureaucracies

This sort of open-system thinking has turned managers away from rigid bureaucracies and toward what organization theorists call postmodern organizations, and to less emphasis on hierarchy (more emphasis on empowerment and teamwork).[28]

ORGANIZATIONAL EFFECTIVENESS (AND THE THREAT OF DECLINE)

How effective are you? If someone asked you this apparently simple question, you would likely ask for clarification before answering. For instance, you might want to know if they were referring to your average marks, annual income, actual accomplishments, ability to get along with others, public service or perhaps something else entirely. So it is with modern organizations. Effectiveness criteria abound.

Assessing organizational effectiveness is an important topic for an array of people, including managers, stockholders, government agencies, and OB specialists. The purpose of this section is to introduce a widely applicable and useful model of organizational effectiveness; we will also deal with the problem of organizational decline.

Generic Organizational-Effectiveness Criteria

A good way to understand this complex subject better is to consider four generic approaches to assessing an organization's effectiveness (see Figure 18–4). These effectiveness criteria apply equally well to large or small and profit or not-for-profit organizations. Moreover, as denoted by the overlapping circles in Figure 18–4, the four effectiveness criteria can be used in various combinations. The key thing to remember is 'no single approach to the evaluation of effectiveness is appropriate in all circumstances or for all organization types'.[29] What do Coca-Cola and France Télécom, for example, have in common, other than being large profit-seeking corporations? Because a multidimensional approach is required, we need to look more closely at each of the four generic effectiveness criteria.

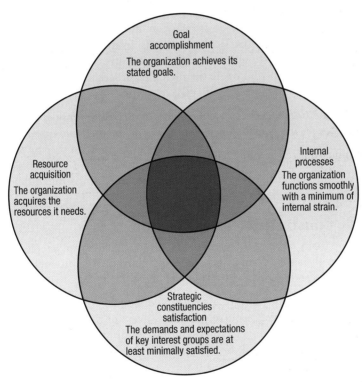

Figure 18–4

Four ways to Assess Organizational Effectiveness

SOURCE: Adapted from discussion in K Cameron, 'Critical Questions in Assessing Organizational Effectiveness', *Organizational Dynamics*, Autumn 1980, pp 66–80; and K S Cameron, 'Effectiveness as Paradox: Consensus and Conflict in Conceptions of Organizational Effectiveness', *Management Science*, May 1986, pp 539–53.

Goal Accomplishment

Goal accomplishment is the most widely used effectiveness criterion for organizations. Key organizational results or outputs are compared with previously stated goals or objectives. Deviations, either plus or minus, require corrective action. This is simply an organizational variation of the personal goal-setting process discussed in Chapter 8. Effectiveness, relative to the criterion of goal accomplishment, is gauged by how well the organization meets or exceeds its goals.[30]

Productivity improvement, involving the relationship between inputs and outputs, is a common organization-level goal.[31] Additionally, goals may be set for organizational efforts such as minority recruiting, pollution prevention and quality improvement. Given today's competitive pressures and e-commerce revolution, *innovation* and *speed* are very important organizational goals worthy of measurement and monitoring.[32] Toyota gave us a powerful indicator of where things are going in this regard. The Japanese auto maker announced it could custom-build a car in just five days! A customer's new Toyota would roll off the Ontario, Canada, assembly line just five days after the order was placed. A 30-day lag was the industry standard at the time.[33]

Resource Acquisition

This second criterion relates to inputs rather than outputs. An organization is deemed effective in this regard if it acquires necessary factors of production such as raw materials, labour, capital, and managerial and technical expertise. Organizations such as MSF (Médecins sans Frontières, also known as Doctors without Borders) also have to judge their effectiveness in terms of how much money they raise from donations.

Internal Processes

Some refer to this third effectiveness criterion as the 'healthy systems' approach. An organization is said to be a healthy system if information flows smoothly and if employee loyalty, commitment, job satisfaction and trust prevail. Goals may be set for any of these internal processes. Healthy systems, from a behavioural standpoint, tend to have a minimum of dysfunctional conflict and destructive political manoeuvring. M Scott Peck, the physician who wrote the highly regarded book, *The Road Less Travelled*, characterizes healthy organizations in ethical terms.

> *A healthy organization, Peck says, is one that has a genuine sense of community: It's a place where people are emotionally present with one another, and aren't afraid to talk about fears and disappointments—because that's what allows us to care for one another. It's a place where there is authentic communication, a willingness to be vulnerable, a commitment to speaking frankly and respectfully—and a commitment not to walk away when the going gets tough.*[34]

Strategic Constituencies Satisfaction

Organizations both depend on people and affect the lives of people. Consequently, many consider the satisfaction of key interested parties to be an important criterion of organizational effectiveness.

Strategic constituency
any group of people with a stake in the organization's operation or success

A **strategic constituency** is any group of individuals who have some stake in the organization—for example, resource providers, users of the organization's products or services, producers of the organization's output, groups whose co-operation is essential for the organization's survival, or those whose lives are significantly affected by the organization.[35]

Strategic constituencies (or stakeholders) generally have competing or conflicting interests.[36] For instance, shareholders who want higher dividends and consumers who seek lower prices would most likely disagree with a union's demand for a wage increase. Strategic constituents or stakeholders can be identified systematically through a **stakeholder audit**[37] (see the example in Figure 18–5). Conflicting interests and relative satisfaction among the listed stakeholders can then be dealt with.

Stakeholder audit
systematic identification of all parties likely to be affected by the organization

A never-ending challenge for management is to strike a workable balance between strategic constituencies so as to achieve at least minimal satisfaction on all fronts. McDonald's is an interesting and compelling case in point. After the smoke had cleared from the riots in south central Los Angeles in April 1992, observers were amazed to find *every* McDonald's restaurant in the area untouched by arsonists. But that outcome was not surprising to McDonald's.

Figure 18-5

A Sample US Stakeholder Audit Identifying Strategic Constituencies

For Edward H Rensi, president and CEO of McDonald's USA, the explanation of what happened, or didn't happen, in South Central LA was simple: 'Our businesses there are owned by African-American entrepreneurs who hired African-American managers who hired African-American employees who served everybody in the community, whether they be Korean, African American, or Caucasian.'[38]

Multiple Effectiveness Criteria: Some Practical Guidelines

Experts on the subject recommend a multidimensional approach to assessing the effectiveness of modern organizations. This means no single criterion is appropriate for all stages of the organization's life cycle. Nor will a single criterion satisfy competing stakeholders. Well-managed organizations mix and match effectiveness criteria to fit the unique requirements of the situation.[39] Managers need to identify and seek input from strategic constituencies. This information, when merged with the organization's stated mission and philosophy, enables management to derive an appropriate *combination* of effectiveness criteria. The following guidelines are helpful in this regard.

▼ *The goal accomplishment approach* **is appropriate when 'goals are clear, consensual, time-bounded, measurable'.**[40]

▼ *The resource acquisition approach* **is appropriate when inputs have a traceable effect on results or output. For example, the amount of money the American Red Cross receives through donations dictates the level of services provided.**

▼ *The internal processes approach* **is appropriate when organizational performance is strongly influenced by specific processes (e.g., cross-functional teamwork).**

▼ *The strategic constituencies approach* **is appropriate when powerful stakeholders can significantly benefit or harm the organization.**[41]

Keeping these basic concepts of organizational effectiveness in mind, we turn our attention to preventing organizational decline.

The Ever-Present Threat of Organizational Decline

If you think failure is scary, try success. Time after time, big companies such as Fiat, Apple Computers, Marks & Spencer, C&A, IBM, and Boeing have stumbled badly after periods of great success. Donald N Sull, a strategy professor at the London Business School, recently framed the situation as follows.

One of the most common business phenomena is also one of the most perplexing: when successful companies face big changes in their environment, they often fail to respond effectively. Unable to defend themselves against competitors armed with new products, technologies or strategies, they watch their sales and profits erode, their best people leave and their stock valuations tumble. Some ultimately manage to recover—usually after painful rounds of downsizing and restructuring—but many don't.[42]

Organizational decline
decrease in organization's resource base (money, customers, talent, innovations)

Researchers call this downward spiral organizational decline and define it as 'a decrease in an organization's resource base'.[43] The term *resource* is used very broadly in this context, encompassing money, talent, customers, and innovative ideas and products. Managers seeking to maintain organizational effectiveness need to be alert to the problem because experts tell us 'decline is almost unavoidable unless deliberate steps are taken to prevent it'.[44] The first key step is to recognize the early warning signs of organizational decline.

Early-Warning Signs of Decline

There are 14 early warning signs of organizational decline.

1 Excess personnel.

2 Tolerance of incompetence.

3 Cumbersome administrative procedures.

4 Disproportionate staff power (e.g., technical staff specialists politically overpower line managers, whom they view as unsophisticated and too conventional).

5 Replacement of substance with form (e.g., the planning process becomes more important than the results achieved).

6 Scarcity of clear goals and decision benchmarks.

7 Fear of embarrassment and conflict (e.g., formerly successful executives may resist new ideas for fear of revealing past mistakes).

8 Loss of effective communication.

9 Outdated organizational structure.[45]

10 Increased scapegoating by leaders.

11 Resistance to change.

12 Low morale.

13 Special interest groups are more vocal.

14 Decreased innovation.[46]

Managers who monitor these early warning signs of organizational decline are better able to reorganize in a timely and effective manner.[47] However, recent research has uncovered a troublesome tendency for inaccurate perception among entrenched top management teams. In companies where there had been little if any turnover among top executives, there was a tendency to attribute organizational problems to *external* causes (such as competition, the government, technology shifts). In contrast, *internal* attributions tended to be made by top management teams with *many* new members. Thus, proverbial 'new blood' at the top appears to be a good insurance policy against inaccurately perceiving the early-warning signs of organizational decline.[48]

Preventing Organizational Decline

The time to start doing something about organizational decline is when everything is going *right*. For it is during periods of high success that the seeds of decline are sown.[49] *Complacency* is the number one threat because it breeds overconfidence and inattentiveness.[50]

On a mild fall day in Paris two years ago, Alcatel Chairman Serge Tchuruk received a shrill wake-up call from Silicon Valley. Tchuruk had been busy selling money-losing divisions of the giant phone-gear manufacturer and carving out layers of bureaucracy—turning Alcatel around the old-fashioned way. But in its 102-year history, Alcatel had never faced a New World phenomenon like Cisco Systems Inc. The Silicon Valley hotshot had been racing around the Continent, gobbling up contracts at Alcatel's expense—and was so successful that on that September afternoon, Tchuruk had to issue a warning that earnings would not meet expectations. Investors, led by American fund managers, responded with a vengeance, driving Alcatel shares down by 38 per cent.

That hurt. But it also helped shake things up at Alcatel. After the plunge, Tchuruk kick-started an effort to remodel Alcatel after the Silicon Valley rivals that were stealing its business. Over the next 18 months, he went on a high-tech buying spree, gobbling up a half-dozen North American companies for $11.3 billion. He shifted entire divisions across the Atlantic, and named the American head of his U.S. unit, Krish Prabhu, president and heir to Alcatel's top job. He even instituted stock options, long taboo in egalitarian France. Now, looking out his window at the grey rooftops of Paris, Tchuruk muses: 'We're not really a French company anymore.' [51]

THE CONTINGENCY APPROACH TO ORGANIZATION DESIGN

According to the contingency approach to organization design, organizations tend to be more effective when they are structured to fit the demands of the situation.[52] A contingency approach can be put into practice by first assessing the degree of environmental uncertainty.[53] Next, the contingency model calls for using various organization design configurations to achieve an effective organization–environment fit. This section presents an environmental uncertainty model along with two classic contingency design studies.

> **Contingency approach to organization design**
> *creating an effective organization–environment fit*

Assessing Environmental Uncertainty

Robert Duncan proposed a two-dimensional model for classifying environmental demands on the organization (see Figure 18–6). On the horizontal axis is the simple→complex dimension. This dimension 'focuses on whether the factors in the environment considered for decision-making are few in number and similar or many in number and different'.[54] On the vertical axis of Duncan's model is the static→dynamic dimension. 'The static–dynamic dimension of the environment is concerned with whether the factors of the environment remain the same over time or change.'[55] When combined, these two dimensions characterize four situations that represent increasing uncertainty for organizations. According to Duncan, the complex–dynamic situation of highest uncertainty is the most common organizational environment today.

Amid these fast-paced times, nothing stands still. Not even in the simple–static quadrant. For example, during the first 94 years of the history of the Coca-Cola Company (to 1980), only one soft drink bore the company's name. Just six years later, Coke had its famous name on seven soft drinks, including Coca-Cola Classic, Coke and Cherry Coke. Despite operating in an environment characterized as simple and static, the Coca-Cola Company has had to become a more risk-taking, entrepreneurial company.[56] This means organizations facing moderate to high uncertainty (quadrants 3 and 4 in Figure 18–6) have to be highly flexible, responsive and adaptive today.[57] Contingency organization design is more important than ever because it helps managers to structure their organizations to fit the key situational factors discussed next.

Figure 18-6 *A Four-Way Classification of Organizational Environments*

	Simple	Complex
Static	**Low perceived uncertainty** • Small number of factors and components in the environment • Factors and components are somewhat similar to one another • Factors and components remain basically the same and are not changing • Example: Soft drink industry 1	**Moderately low perceived uncertainty** • Large number of factors and components in the environment • Factors and components are not similar to one another • Factors and components remain basically the same • Example: Food products 2

Dynamic	3
	Moderately high perceived uncertainty
	• Small number of factors and components in the environment
	• Factors and components are somewhat similar to one another
	• Factors and components of the environment are in continual process of change
	• Example: Fast-food industry
		4
		High perceived uncertainty
		• Large number of factors and components in the environment
		• Factors and components are not similar to one another
		• Factors and components of environment are in a continual process of change
		• Examples: Commercial airline industry
		    Telephone communications
		    (AT&T)

SOURCE: 'What Is the Right Organization Structure? Decision Tree Analysis Provides the Answer', by Robert Duncan. *Organizational Dynamics*, Winter 1979, © 1979, American Management Association International. Reprinted by permission of American Management Association International, New York, NY. All rights reserved. http://www.amanet.org.

Differentiation and Integration: The Lawrence and Lorsch Study

In their classic text, *Organization and Environment*, Harvard researchers Paul Lawrence and Jay Lorsch explained how two structural forces simultaneously fragment the organization and bind it together. They cautioned that an imbalance between these two forces—labelled *differentiation* and *integration*—could hinder organizational effectiveness.

Differentiation Splits the Organization Apart

Differentiation
division of labour and specialization that cause people to think and act differently

A behavioural outcome of **differentiation** is that technical specialists, such as computer programmers, tend to think and act differently to specialists in, say, accounting or marketing. Excessive differentiation can cause the organization to become entrenched in miscommunication, conflict and politics. Thus, differentiation needs to be offset by an opposing structural force to ensure the necessary *co-ordination*. This is where integration enters the picture (see Figure 18–7).

Integration Binds the Organization Together

Integration
co-operation among specialists to achieve common goals

According to the Lawrence and Lorsch model, **integration** can be achieved through various combinations of the following six mechanisms:

▼ **a formal hierarchy**

▼ **standardized policies, rules and procedures**

▼ **departmentalization**

▼ **committees and cross-functional teams**

▼ **human relations training**

▼ **individuals and groups acting as liaisons between specialists.**

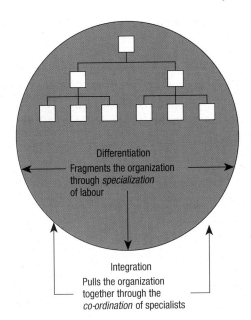

Figure 18-7

Differentiation and Integration are Opposing Structural Forces

Achieving the Proper Balance

When Lawrence and Lorsch studied successful and unsuccessful companies in three industries, they concluded the following: *As environmental complexity increased, successful organizations exhibited higher degrees of both differentiation and integration.* In other words, an effective balance was achieved. Unsuccessful organizations, in contrast, tended to suffer from an imbalance of too much differentiation and not enough offsetting integration. Managers need to fight this tendency if their growing and increasingly differentiated organizations are to be co-ordinated.

Lawrence and Lorsch also discovered that 'the more differentiated an organization, the more difficult it is to achieve integration'.[58] Managers of today's complex organizations need to strive constantly and creatively to achieve greater integration.[59] For example, how does 3M Company, with its dozens of autonomous divisions and more than 60,000 products, maintain its competitive edge in technology? Among other things, 3M makes sure its technical specialists interact with one another frequently so that cross-fertilization of ideas takes place. Art Fry, credited with inventing the now ubiquitous Post-it Notes, actually owes much of his success to colleague Spencer Silver, an engineer down the hall who created an apparently useless semi-adhesive.

If Fry and Silver had worked in a company without a strong commitment to integration, we probably would not now have Post-it Notes. 3M does not leave this sort of cross-fertilization to chance. It organizes for integration with such things as a Technology Council that regularly convenes researchers from various divisions and an annual science fair at which 3M scientists enthusiastically hawk their new ideas, not to customers, but to each other![60]

Mechanistic versus Organic Organizations

A second landmark contingency design study was reported by a pair of British behavioural scientists, Tom Burns and G M Stalker. In the course of their research, they drew a very instructive distinction between what they called mechanistic and organic organizations. Mechanistic organizations are rigid bureaucracies with strict rules, narrowly defined tasks, and top-down communication. For example, when *Business Week* correspondent Kathleen Deveny spent a day working in a McDonald's restaurant, she found a very mechanistic organization.

> **Mechanistic organizations**
> *rigid, command-and-control bureaucracies*

Here every job is broken down into the smallest of steps, and the whole process is automated . . . .

Anyone could do this, I think. But McDonald's restaurants operate like Swiss watches, and the minute I step behind the counter I am a loose part in the works . . . .

I bag French fries for a few minutes, but I'm much too slow. Worse, I can't seem to keep my station clean enough. Failing at French fries is a fluke, I tell myself . . . .

I try to move faster, but my co-workers are playing at 45 rpm, and I'm stuck at $33\frac{1}{3}$.[61]

This sort of mechanistic structure is necessary at McDonald's because of the competitive need for uniform product quality, speedy service and cleanliness. In contrast, organic organizations are flexible networks of multitalented individuals who perform a variety of tasks.[62]

> **Organic organizations**
> *fluid and flexible network of multitalented people.*

Meta4's name isn't the only clever thing about the seven-year-old software startup. Most of its 550 employees are whiz-kid programmers in their late 20s. Sales doubled last year, and 20 per cent of them are exports. Founder Juan Moran, 39, has banned paper communication at Meta4, insisting on email for speed and efficiency. And he recruits new talent for his fast-growing workforce over the Internet. 'In a knowledge-based economy, we can compete very well,' says Moran, who has introduced stock options for employees. The latest high-tech success story in Silicon Valley or Seattle? No, Meta4 is just outside Madrid—and a prime example of how Spain is racing ahead of European neighbors that are used to thinking of it mainly as a vacation mecca. Government-led labor reforms are creating a flexible workforce. And a new generation of managers is promoting innovation and developing intellectual capital.[63]

A Matter of Degree

Importantly, as illustrated in Table 18–2, each of the mechanistic–organic characteristics is a matter of degree. Organizations tend to be relatively mechanistic or relatively organic. Pure types are rare because divisions, departments or units in the same organization may be more or less mechanistic or organic. From an employee's standpoint, which organization structure would you prefer?

Different Approaches to Decision-making

There tends to be centralized decision-making in mechanistic organizations and decentralized decision-making in organic organizations. Generally, centralized organizations are more tightly controlled while decentralized organizations are more adaptive to changing situations.[64] Each has its appropriate use.

> **Centralized decision-making**
> *top managers make all key decisions*

> **Decentralized decision-making**
> *lower-level managers are empowered to make important decisions*

Experts on the subject warn against extremes of centralization or decentralization. The challenge is to achieve a workable balance between the two extremes. A management consultant put it as follows.

The modern organization in transition will recognize the pull of two polarities: a need for greater centralization to create low-cost shared resources; and, a need to improve market responsiveness with greater decentralization. Today's winning organizations are the ones that can handle the paradox and tensions of both pulls. These are the firms that analyse the optimum organizational solution in each particular circumstance, without prejudice for one type of organization over another. The result is, almost invariably, a messy mixture of decentralized units sharing cost-effective centralized resources.[65]

Centralization and decentralization are not an *either–or* proposition; they are an *and–also* balancing act.

Relevant Research Findings

When they classified a sample of actual companies as either mechanistic or organic, Burns and Stalker discovered one type was not superior to the other. Each type had its

Table 18-2 *Characteristics of Mechanistic and Organic Organizations*

Characteristic	Mechanistic Organization		Organic Organization
1. Task definition and knowledge required	Narrow; technical	→	Broad; general
2. Linkage between individual's contribution and organization's purpose	Vague or indirect	→	Clear or direct
3. Task flexibility	Rigid; routine	→	Flexible; varied
4. Specification of techniques, obligations, and rights	Specific	→	General
5. Degree of hierarchical control	High	→	Low (self-control emphasized)
6. Primary communication pattern	Top-down	→	Lateral (between peers)
7. Primary decision-making style	Authoritarian	→	Democratic; participative
8. Emphasis on obedience and loyalty	High	→	Low

SOURCE: Adapted from discussion in T Burns and G M Stalker, *The Management of Innovation* (London: Tavistock, 1961), pp 119–25.

appropriate place, depending on the environment. When the environment was relatively *stable and certain*, the successful organizations tended to be *mechanistic*. *Organic* organizations tended to be the successful ones when the environment was *unstable and uncertain*.[66]

In a more recent study of 103 department managers from eight manufacturing firms and two aerospace organizations, managerial skill was found to have a greater impact, on an overall measure of department effectiveness, in organic departments than in mechanistic departments. This led the researchers to recommend the following contingencies for management staffing and training.

If we have two units, one organic and one mechanistic, and two potential applicants differing in overall managerial ability, we might want to assign the more competent to the organic unit since in that situation there are few structural aids available to the manager in performing required responsibilities. It is also possible that managerial training is especially needed by managers being groomed to take over units that are more organic in structure.[67]

Another interesting finding comes from a study of 42 voluntary church organizations. As the organizations became more mechanistic (more bureaucratic) the intrinsic motivation of their members decreased. Mechanistic organizations apparently undermined the volunteers' sense of freedom and self-determination. Additionally, the researchers believe their findings help to explain why bureaucracy tends to feed on itself: 'A mechanistic organizational structure may breed the need for a more extremely mechanistic system because of the reduction in intrinsically motivated behaviour.'[68] Thus, bureaucracy begets greater bureaucracy.

Most recently, field research in two factories, one mechanistic and the other organic, found expected communication patterns. Command-and-control (downward) communication characterized the mechanistic factory. Consultative or participative (two-way) communication prevailed in the organic factory.[69]

Both Mechanistic and Organic Structures Are Needed

Although achievement-oriented students of OB typically express a distaste for mechanistic organizations, not all organizations or subunits can or should be organic. For example, as mentioned earlier, McDonald's could not achieve its admired quality and service standards without extremely mechanistic restaurant operations. Imagine the food and service you would get if McDonald's employees used their own favourite way of doing things and worked at their own pace! On the other hand, mechanistic structure alienates some employees because it erodes their sense of self-control.

THREE IMPORTANT CONTINGENCY VARIABLES: TECHNOLOGY, SIZE AND STRATEGIC CHOICE

Both the contingency theories examined above have one important thing in common. Each is based on an 'environmental imperative,' meaning the environment is said to be the primary determinant of effective organizational structure. Other organization theorists disagree. They contend that factors such as the organization's core technology, size and corporate strategy hold the key to organizational structure. This section examines the significance of these three additional contingency variables.

The Effect of Technology on Structure (Woodward and Beyond)

Joan Woodward proposed a technological imperative in 1965 after studying 100 small manufacturing firms in southern England. She found distinctly different structural patterns for effective and ineffective companies based on technologies of low, medium or high complexity. Effective organizations with either low- or high-complexity technology tended to have an organic structure. Effective organizations based on a technology of medium complexity tended to have a mechanistic structure. Woodward concluded that technology was the overriding determinant of organizational structure.[70]

Since Woodward's landmark work, many studies of the relationship between technology and structure have been conducted. Unfortunately, disagreement and confusion have prevailed. For example, a comprehensive review of 50 studies conducted between 1965 and 1980 found six technology concepts and 140 technology-structure relationships.[71] A statistical analysis of those studies prompted the following conclusions.

▼ **The more the technology requires *interdependence* between individuals and/or groups, the greater the need for integration (co-ordination).**

▼ **'As technology moves from routine to non-routine, subunits adopt less formalized and [less] centralized structures.'**[72]

Additional insights can be expected in this area as researchers co-ordinate their definitions of technology and refine their methodologies.[73]

Organizational Size and Performance

Size is an important structural variable subject to two schools of thought. According to the first school, economists have long extolled the virtues of economies of scale. This approach, often called the 'bigger is better' model, assumes the per-unit cost of production decreases as the organization grows. In effect, bigger is said to be more efficient. For example, on an annual basis, Daimler-Chrysler can supposedly produce its 100,000th car less expensively than its 10th.

The second school of thought pivots on the law of diminishing returns. Called the 'small is beautiful' model,[74] this approach contends that oversized organizations and subunits tend to be plagued by costly behavioural problems. Large and impersonal organizations are said to breed apathy and alienation, with resulting problems such as staff turnover and absenteeism. Two strong advocates of this second approach are the authors of the popular book *In Search of Excellence*.

In the excellent companies, small in almost every case is beautiful. The small facility turns out to be the most efficient; its turned-on, motivated, highly productive worker, in communication (and competition) with his peers, outproduces the worker in the big facilities time and again. It holds for plants, for project teams, for divisions—for the entire company.[75]

Is Complexity the Issue? (A Case against Mergers?)

Recent research suggests that when designing their organizations, managers should follow a middle ground between 'bigger is better' and 'small is beautiful' because both models have been oversold. Indeed, a newer perspective says *complexity*, not size, is the central issue.[76] British management teacher and writer Charles Handy recently offered the following instructive perspective.

Growth does not have to mean more of the same. It can mean better rather than bigger. It can mean leaner or deeper, both of which might improve rather than expand the current position. Businesses can grow more profitable by becoming better, or leaner, or deeper, more concentrated, without growing bigger. Bigness, in both business and life, can lead to a lack of focus, too much complexity and, in the end, too wide a spread to control. We have to know when big is big enough.[77]

We do not have a definite answer to the question of how big is too big, but the excessive complexity argument is compelling. This argument may also help explain why many mergers have been disappointing in recent years. According to *Business Week*, the 'historic surge of consolidations and combinations is occurring in the face of strong evidence that mergers and acquisitions, at least over the past 35 years or so, have hurt more than helped companies and shareholders.'[78]

Research Insights

Researchers measure the size of organizations and organizational subunits in different ways. Some focus on financial indicators such as total sales or total asset value. Others look at the number of employees, transactions (such as the number of students in a school district) or capacity (such as the number of beds in a hospital). A meta-analysis of 31 studies conducted between 1931 and 1985 that related organizational size to performance found the following.[79]

▼ **Larger organizations (in terms of assets) tended to be more productive (in terms of sales and profits).**

▼ **There were 'no positive relationships between organizational size and efficiency, suggesting the absence of net economy of scale effects'.[80]**

▼ **There were zero to slightly negative relationships between *subunit* size and productivity and efficiency.**

▼ **A more recent study examined the relationship between organizational size and employee turnover over a period of 65 months. Turnover was unrelated to organizational size.[81]**

Table 18–3

Organizational Size: Management Consultants Address the Question of 'How Big Is Too Big?'

Peter F Drucker, well-known management consultant:
> The real growth and innovation in this country has been in medium-size companies that employ between 200 and 4,000 workers. If you are in a small company, you are running all out. You have neither the time nor the energy to devote to anything but yesterday's crisis.
>
> A medium-sized company has the resources to devote to new products and markets, and it's still small enough to be flexible and move fast. And these companies now have what they once lacked—they've learned how to manage.

Thomas J Peters and Robert H Waterman, Jr, best-selling authors and management consultants:
> A rule of thumb starts to emerge. We find that the lion's share of the top performers keep their division size between $50 and $100 million, with a maximum of 1,000 or so employees each. Moreover, they grant their divisions extraordinary independence—and give them the functions and resources to exploit.

SOURCES: Excerpted from J A Byrne, 'Advice from the Dr. Spock of Business', *Business Week*, September 28, 1987, p 61; and T J Peters and R H Waterman, Jr, *In Search of Excellence* (New York: Harper & Row, 1982), pp 272–73.

Striving for Small Units in Big Organizations

In summary, bigger is not necessarily better and small is not necessarily beautiful.[82] Hard-and-fast numbers regarding exactly how big is 'too big' or how small is 'too small' are difficult to come by. Management consultants offer some rough estimates (see Table 18–3). Until better evidence is available, the best that managers can do is monitor the productivity, quality and efficiency of divisions, departments and profit centres. Unwieldy and overly complex units need to be promptly broken into ones of more manageable size. The trick is to *create smallness within bigness*.[83]

Strategic Choice and Organizational Structure

In 1972, British sociologist John Child rejected the environmental imperative approach to organizational structure. He proposed a strategic choice model based on behavioural rather than rational economic principles.[84] Child believed structure resulted from a political process involving organizational power holders. According to the strategic choice model that has evolved from Child's work,[85] an organization's structure is determined largely by a dominant coalition of top-management strategists.[86]

Figure 18–8 *The Relationship between Strategic Choice and Organizational Structure*

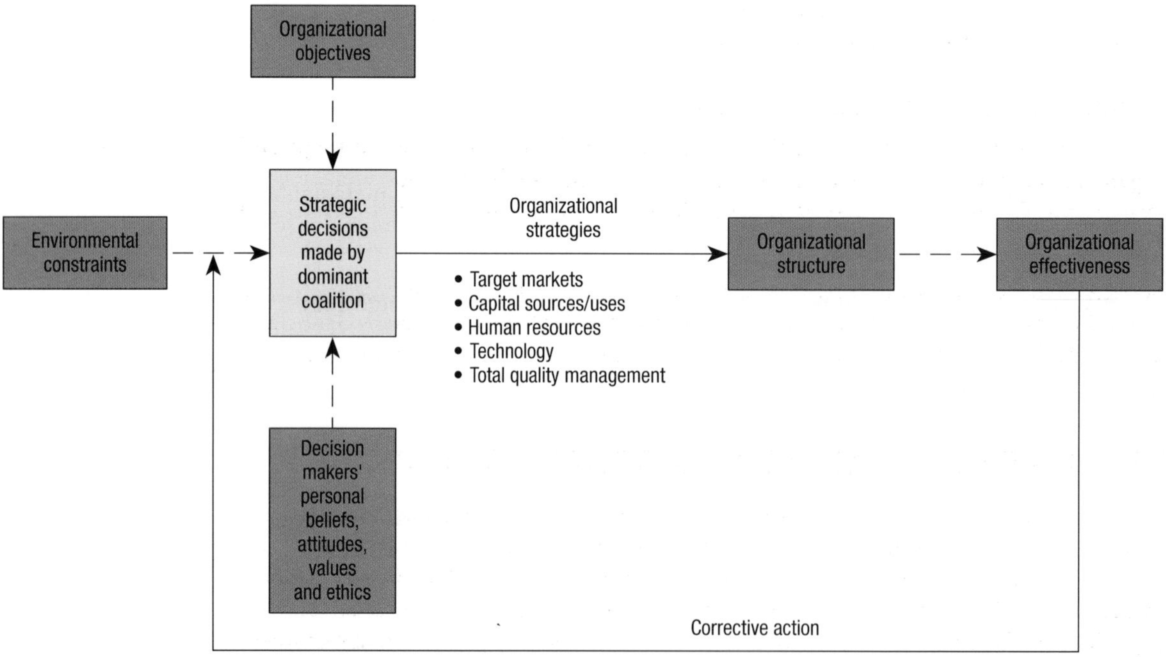

A Strategic Choice Model

As Figure 18–8 illustrates, specific strategic choices or decisions reflect how the dominant coalition perceives environmental constraints and the organization's objectives. These strategic choices are tempered by the decision makers' personal beliefs, attitudes, values, and ethics.[87] For example, consider this unusual relationship between top management's ethics and corporate strategy, as reported in the following extract from *Business Ethics* magazine.

> As a manufacturer and retailer of outdoor clothing and equipment, it's natural for Patagonia to be concerned about the environment. But as a for-profit business, it's also natural for the company to feel a need to look at its bottom line.
>
> Patagonia has found a way to do both, and to turn upside down traditional concepts of how companies grow in the bargain.

The company first warned its customers of the impending change in its [1992] fall/winter catalog . . . . 'We are limiting Patagonia's growth with the eventual goal of halting growth altogether. We dropped 30 per cent of our clothing line . . . .

'What does this mean to you? Well, last fall you had a choice of five ski pants; now you may choose between two. Two styles of ski pants are all anyone needs.'

And . . . [the 1993] catalog featured the following message: 'At Patagonia, as a company, and as individuals, we sometimes find the array of choices dizzying. But the choices must be faced, resolved soberly, and judicious action taken. To fully include environmental concerns in our ordinary work is to give something back to the planet that sustains us, and that we have taxed so heavily. It's a complex process, but the simplest of gifts.'

To that end, say Patagonia spokespeople Lu Setnicksa and Mike Harrelson, the company has embarked on an aggressive effort to examine everything from the materials it uses to produce its products, to which products it actually makes, to what kind of paper it uses in its copying machines.[88]

So far, a more efficient Patagonia has enjoyed increased profits, despite a decrease in sales revenue. Directing our attention once again to Figure 18–8, the organization is structured to accommodate its mix of strategies. Ultimately, corrective action is taken if organizational effectiveness criteria are not met.

Research and Practical Lessons

In a study of 97 small and mid-size companies in Quebec, Canada, strategy and organizational structure were found to be highly interdependent. Strategy influenced structure and structure influenced strategy. This was particularly true for larger, more innovative, and more successful firms.[89]

Strategic choice theory and research teaches managers at least two practical lessons. First, the environment is just one of many determinants of structure. Second, like any other administrative process, organization design is subject to the interplays of personal power and politics.

THE SHAPE OF TOMORROW'S ORGANIZATIONS

Organizations are basically tools invented to get things done through collective action. As any carpenter or plumber knows, different jobs require different tools. So it is with organizations. When the situation changes significantly, according to contingency thinking, a different type of organization may be appropriate. The need for new organizations is greater than ever today because managers face revolutionary changes.

What sorts of organization will prosper in the age of the Internet and e-commerce? Will they be adaptations of the traditional pyramid-shaped organization? Or will they be radically different? Let us put our imaginations to work by envisioning the shape of tomorrow's organizations.

New-Style versus Old-Style Organizations

Organization theorists Jay R Galbraith and Edward E Lawler III have called for a 'new logic of organizing.'[90] They recommend a whole new set of adjectives to describe organizations (see Table 18–4). Traditional pyramid-shaped organizations, conforming to the old-style pattern, tend to be too slow and inflexible today. Leaner, more organic organizations are needed to accommodate today's strategic balancing act between cost, quality, and speed. They are customer focused, dedicated to continuous improvement and learning, and structured around teams. These qualities, along with computerized information technology, hopefully enable big organizations to mimic the speed and flexibility of small organizations.

Table 18-4

Profiles of the New-Style and Old-Style Organizations

New	Old
Dynamic, learning	Stable
Information rich	Information is scarce
Global	Local
Small and large	Large
Product/customer oriented	Functional
Skills oriented	Job oriented
Team oriented	Individual oriented
Involvement oriented	Command/control oriented
Lateral/networked	Hierarchical
Customer oriented	Job requirements oriented

SOURCE: J R Galbraith and E E Lawler III, 'Effective Organizations: Using the New Logic of Organizing', p 298 in *Organizing for the Future: The New Logic for Managing Complex Organizations*, eds J R Galbraith, E E Lawler III and Associates. Copyright 1993 Jossey-Bass Inc. Publishers. Reprinted by permission of Jossey-Bass, Inc., a subsidiary of John Wiley & Sons, Inc.

Three New Organizational Patterns

Figure 18–9 illustrates three radical departures from the traditional pyramid-shaped organization. Each is the logical result of various trends that are evident today. In other words, we have exaggerated these new organizations for instructional purposes. You are likely to encounter various combinations of these pure types in the years ahead. Let us imagine life in the organizations of tomorrow. (Please note that these characterizations are not intended to be final answers. We simply seek to stimulate thoughtful debate.)

Figure 18-9

The Shape of Tomorrow's Organizations

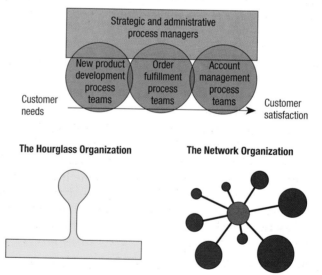

Horizontal Organizations

Despite the fact that *re-engineering* became synonymous with huge redundancies and has been called a passing fad, it is likely to have a lasting effect on organization design. Namely, it helped refine the concept of a horizontally oriented organization. Unlike traditional, vertically oriented organizations with functional units such as production, marketing and finance, horizontal organizations are flat and built around core processes aimed at satisfying customers.

Rather than focusing single-mindedly on financial objectives or functional goals, the horizontal organization emphasizes customer satisfaction. Work is simplified and hierarchy flattened by combining related tasks—for example, an account-management process that subsumes the sales, billing, and service functions—and eliminating work that does not add value. Information zips along an internal superhighway: The knowledge worker analyses it, and technology moves it quickly across the corporation instead of up and down, speeding up and improving decision-making.

Okay, so some of this is derivative; the obsession with process, for example, dates back to Total Quality Management. Part of the beauty of the horizontal corporation is that it distills much of what we know about what works in managing today. Its advocates call it an actionable model—jargon for a plan you can work with—that allows companies to use ideas like teams, supplier-customer integration, and empowerment in ways that reinforce each other. A key virtue is that the horizontal corporation is the kind of company a customer would design. In most cases, a horizontal organization requires some employees to be organized functionally where their expertise is considered critical, as in human resources or finance. But those departments are often pared down and judiciously melded into a design where the real authority runs along process lines.[91]

What will it be like to work in a horizontal organization?[92] It will be a lot more interesting than traditional bureaucracies with their functional ghettos. Most employees will be close to the customer (both internal and external)–asking questions, getting feedback, and jointly solving problems. Constant challenges will come from being on cross-functional teams where co-workers with different technical specialties work side-by-side on projects. Sometimes people will find themselves dividing their time between several projects. Blurred and conflicting lines of authority will break the traditional unity-of-command principle. Project goals and deadlines will tend to replace the traditional supervisor role. Training in both technical and teamwork skills will be a top priority. Multiskilled employees at all levels will find themselves working on different teams and various projects during the year. Paradoxically, self-starters and team players will thrive. Because of the flatness of the organization, lateral transfers will be more common than traditional vertical promotions. This will be a source of discontent for many of those who want to move upward. Constant change will take its toll in terms of interpersonal conflict, personal stress and burn-out. Skill-based pay will supplement pay-for-performance.

Hourglass Organizations

This pattern gets its name from the organization's pinched middle. Thanks to modern information technology, a relatively small executive group will be able to co-ordinate the efforts of numerous operating personnel who make goods or render services.[93] Multiple and broad layers of middle managers who served as conduits for information in old-style organizations will be unnecessary in hourglass organizations. Competition for promotions among operating personnel will be intense because of the restricted hierarchy. Lateral transfers will be more common. Management will compensate for the lack of promotion opportunities with job rotation, skill training and pay-for-performance.

What few middle managers there are will be cross-functional problem-solvers who also possess a number of technical skills. The potential for alienation between the executive elite and those at the base of the hourglass will be great, thus giving trade unions an excellent growth opportunity.

Virtual Organizations

Like virtual teams, discussed in Chapter 12, modern information technology allows people in virtual organizations to get something accomplished despite being geographically dispersed.[94] Instead of relying heavily on face-to-face meetings, as before, members of virtual organizations send email and voice-mail messages, exchange project information over the Internet, and convene videoconferences with far-flung participants. In addition, cellular phones have made the dream of 'doing business from the beach' a reality!

This disconnection between work and location is causing managers to question traditional assumptions about centralized offices and factories. Why keep offices for people who are never there because they are out finding and helping customers? Why have a factory when it is less expensive to contract out the work? Indeed, many so-called virtual organizations are really a *network* of several individuals or organizations hooked together contractually and electronically. A prime example is the Australian company OnLine English (www.oleng.com.au).

How does an academic from a non-English speaking background, wishing to publish in an English language international journal, find a service to edit his or her English? Ideally, they would have immediate access to a native speaker specialist editor with high level qualifications in their particular field. OnLine English (OLE) was designed as a virtual organization to address this need. Now, researchers based anywhere on the globe have immediate access to a team of specialist editors.

Highly skilled editors with PhDs, who are keen to work at short notice with rapid turnaround times, are rare. Using the Internet, OLE has been able to recruit from the whole of Australia to form a lively network of 30+ such individuals. Running a highly responsive service 24 hours a day, 365 days a year, once required large infrastructure costs. OLE has minimized such costs by creating a virtual infrastructure, co-ordinated from several home offices. Delivering a service with every document team-checked plus quality control and negotiation with the client once required considerable time and face-to-face meetings. OLE has developed online protocols with feedback procedures and quality control that enable consultants living thousands of kilometres apart to collaborate closely and rapidly. On any job, each team member sees exactly what other team members are contributing. Constant improvement and common standards are achieved through every job being incrementally checked and improved. These outcomes are jointly managed. The team operates within a clear framework. All communication is moderated by the manager. There is no off-task chatter. OLE believes that it has maximized the efficiency of the input of high level skills by team members. Those who like to work flexibly and intensively find this an attractive work environment. The outcome is that the customer benefits from having his or her manuscript rapidly edited into English ready for international publication. The fact that the service was delivered by an editing team in another part of the world, with most of the team never meeting face-to-face, is irrelevant. What is important to the client is the quality of the service delivery and of the product.

Here is how we envision life in the emerging virtual organizations and organizational networks. Things will be very interesting and profitable for the elite core of entrepreneurs and engineers who hit on the right business formula. Turnover among the financial and information 'have nots'—data entry, customer service, and production employees—will be high because of glaring inequities and limited opportunities for personal fulfillment and growth. Telecommuters who work from home will feel liberated and empowered (and sometimes lonely).

Commitment, trust and loyalty could erode badly if managers do not heed this caution by Charles Handy, the British management expert quoted earlier. According to Handy: 'A shared commitment still requires personal contact to make the commitment feel real. *Paradoxically, the more virtual an organization becomes the more its people need to meet in person.'*[95]

Independent contractors, both individuals and organizations, will participate in many different organizational networks and thus have diluted loyalty to any single one. Substandard working conditions and low pay at some smaller contractors will make them little more than Internet-age sweat shops. Companies living from one contract to another will offer little in the way of job security and benefits. Opportunities to start new businesses will be numerous but prolonged success could prove elusive at Internet speed.

The only certainty about tomorrow's organizations is they will produce a lot of surprises. Only flexible, adaptable people who see problems as opportunities, are self-starters capable of teamwork, and are committed to life-long learning will be able to handle whatever comes their way.

Summary of Key Concepts

1 Describe the four characteristics common to all organizations and explain the difference between closed and open systems.

They are co-ordination of effort (achieved through policies and rules), a common goal (a collective purpose), division of labour (people performing separate but related tasks), and a hierarchy of authority (the chain of command). Closed systems, such as a battery-powered clock, are relatively self-sufficient. Open systems, such as the human body, are highly dependent on the environment for survival. Organizations are said to be open systems.

2 Contrast the following organizational metaphors: military/mechanical, biological, and cognitive systems.

According to the military/mechanical model, a relatively closed system perspective, the organization seeks to maximize economic efficiency in a predictable environment. The biological metaphor views the organization as a living organism striving to survive in an uncertain environment. In terms of the cognitive metaphor, an organization is like the human mind, capable of interpreting and learning from uncertain and ambiguous situations.

3 Describe the ecosystem model of organizations and define the term postmodern organization.

Organizations are characterized as being in a life-and-death struggle for survival in an environment that presents opportunities to both compete and co-operate. Strategic emphasis needs to be on building co-operative relationships and exploiting opportunities within diverse organizational communities. The postmodern organization is decentralized, computer networked and less hierarchical than traditional organizations.

4 Describe the four generic organizational effectiveness criteria and discuss how managers can prevent organizational decline.

They are goal accomplishment (satisfying stated objectives), resource acquisition (gathering the necessary productive inputs), internal processes (building and maintaining healthy organizational systems), and strategic constituencies satisfaction (achieving at least minimal satisfaction for all key stakeholders). Because complacency is the leading cause of organizational decline, managers need to create a culture of continuous improvement. Decline automatically follows periods of great success if preventative steps are not taken to avoid the erosion of organizational resources (money, customers, talent, and innovative ideas).

5 Explain what the contingency approach to organization design involves.

The contingency approach to organization design calls for fitting the organization to the demands of the situation. Environmental uncertainty can be assessed in terms of various combinations of two dimensions: (a) simple or complex and (b) static or dynamic.

6 Describe the relationship between differentiation and integration in effective organizations.

Harvard researchers Lawrence and Lorsch found that successful organizations achieved a proper balance between the two opposing structural forces of differentiation and integration. Differentiation forces the organization apart. Through a variety of mechanisms—including hierarchy, rules, teams, and liaisons—integration draws the organization together.

7 Discuss Burns and Stalker's findings regarding mechanistic and organic organizations.

British researchers Burns and Stalker found that mechanistic (bureaucratic, centralized) organizations tended to be effective in stable situations. In unstable situations, organic (flexible, decentralized) organizations were more effective. These findings underscored the need for a contingency approach to organization design.

8 Define and briefly explain the practical significance of centralization and decentralization.

Because key decisions are made at the top of centralized organizations, they tend to be tightly controlled. In decentralized organizations, employees at lower levels are empowered to make important decisions. Contingency design calls for a proper balance.

9 Discuss the effective management of organizational size.

Regarding the optimum size for organizations, the challenge for today's managers is to achieve smallness within bigness by keeping subunits at a manageable size.

10 Describe horizontal, hourglass, and virtual organizations.

Horizontal organizations are flat structures built around core processes aimed at identifying and satisfying customer needs. Cross-functional teams and empowerment are central to horizontal organizations. Hourglass organizations have a small executive level, a short and narrow middle-management level (because information technology links the top and bottom levels), and a broad base of operating personnel. Virtual organizations are normally families of interdependent companies. They are contractual and fluid in nature.

Discussion Questions

1 How many organizations directly affect your life today? List as many as you can.

2 What would an organization chart of your current (or last) place of employment look like? Does the chart you have drawn reveal the hierarchy (chain of command), division of labour, span of control, and line–staff distinctions? Does it reveal anything else? Explain.

3 Why is it appropriate to view modern organizations as open systems?

4 How would you respond to a manager who claimed the only way to measure a business's effectiveness is in terms of how much profit it makes?

5 Why is it important to focus on the role of complacency in organizational decline?

6 Briefly, what does contingency organization design entail?

7 What is wrong with an organization having too much differentiation and too little integration?

8 If organic organizations are popular with most employees, why can't all organizations be structured in an organic fashion?

9 How can you tell if an organization (or subunit) is too big?

10 Which of the three new organizational configurations is likely to be most prevalent in 10 to 15 years from now? Why?

Internet Exercise

http://www.fortune.com

There is no single way to measure organizational effectiveness, as discussed in this chapter. Different stakeholders want organizations to do different and often conflicting things. The purpose of this exercise is to introduce alternative effectiveness criteria and to assess real companies with them.

Each year, *Fortune* magazine publishes a ranking of the World's Most Admired Companies. Some might pass this off as simply a corporate image popularity contest. But we view it as much more. *Fortune* applies a set of eight attributes that could arguably be called effectiveness criteria. You can judge for yourself by going to *Fortune's* Internet site (**www.fortune.com**) and clicking *view all fortune lists* on the left of the screen. Then scroll down the centre of this page, and select the heading *World's Most*

Admired Companies. Start with the category *All Industries.* You may then want to rank them according to your employer's industry or other industries of particular interest.

Questions

1 Do you agree that the eight attributes are really organizational effectiveness criteria? Explain. What others would you add to the list? Which would you remove from the list?

2 How did you rank each of the eight attributes?

3 Are you surprised by the top-ranked company (or companies) in the All Industries ranking? Explain.

4 Do you admire the top-ranked company? Why or why not?

Personal Awareness and Growth Exercise
Organization Design Field Study

Objectives

1 To get out into the field and talk to a practising manager about organizational structure.

2 To increase your understanding of the important distinction between mechanistic and organic organizations.

3 To broaden your knowledge of contingency design, in terms of organization–environment fit.

Introduction

A good way to test the validity of what you have just read about organization design is to interview a practising manager. (*Note:* If you are a manager, simply complete the questionnaire yourself.)

Instructions

Your objective is to interview a manager about aspects of organizational structure, environmental uncertainty and organizational effectiveness. A manager is defined as anyone who supervises other people in an organizational setting. The

organization may be small or large and for-profit or not-for-profit. Higher-level managers are preferred but middle managers and first-line supervisors are acceptable. If you interview a lower-level manager, be sure to remind him or her that you want a description of the overall organization, not just an isolated subunit. Your interview will centre on the adaptation of Table 18–2, as discussed below.

When conducting your interview, be sure to explain to the manager what you are trying to accomplish. But assure the manager that his or her name will not be mentioned in lecture or group discussions or any written projects. Try to take brief notes during the interview for later reference.

Questionnaire

The following questionnaire, adapted from Table 18–2, will help you determine if the manager's organization is relatively mechanistic or relatively organic in structure. *Note:* For items 1 and 2 on the following questionnaire, ask the manager to respond in terms of the average non-managerial employee. (Circle one number for each item.)

Characteristics

1	Task definition and knowledge required	Narrow; technical	1—2—3—4—5—6—7	Broad; general
2	Link between individual's contribution and organization purpose	Vague or indirect	1—2—3—4—5—6—7	Clear or direct
3	Task flexibility	Rigid; routine	1—2—3—4—5—6—7	Flexible; varied
4	Specification of techniques, obligations and rights	Specific	1—2—3—4—5—6—7	General
5	Degree of hierarchical control	High	1—2—3—4—5—6—7	Low (self-control emphasized)
6	Primary communication pattern	Top-down	1—2—3—4—5—6—7	Lateral (between peers)
7	Primary decision-making style	Authoritarian	1—2—3—4—5—6—7	Democratic; participative
8	Emphasis on obedience and loyalty	High	1—2—3—4—5—6—7	Low

Total score = ———

Additional Question about the Organization's Environment

This organization faces an environment that is (circle one number):

Stable and certain		Unstable and uncertain
	1—2—3—4—5—6—7—8—9—10	

Additional Questions about the Organization's Effectiveness

1 Profitability (if a profit-seeking business):

Low   1—2—3—4—5—6—7—8—9—10   High

2 Degree of organization goal accomplishment:

Low   1—2—3—4—5—6—7—8—9—10   High

3 Customer or client satisfaction:

Low   1—2—3—4—5—6—7—8—9—10   High

4 Employee satisfaction:

Low   1—2—3—4—5—6—7—8—9—10   High

Total effectiveness score = ———

(Add responses from above)

Questions for Discussion

1 Using the following norms, was the manager's organization relatively mechanistic or organic?

8–24 = Relatively mechanistic

25–39 = Mixed

40–56 = Relatively organic

2 In terms of Burns and Stalker's contingency theory, does the manager's organization seem to fit its environment? Explain.

3 Does the organization's degree of effectiveness reflect how well it fits its environment? Explain.

Group Exercise
Stakeholder Audit Team

Objectives

1 To continue developing your group interaction and teamwork skills.

2 To engage in open-system thinking.

3 To conduct a stakeholder audit and thus more fully appreciate the competing demands placed on today's managers.

4 To establish priorities and consider trade-offs for modern managers.

Introduction

According to open-system models of organizations, environmental factors—social, political, legal, technological and economic—greatly affect what managers can and cannot do. This exercise gives you an opportunity to engage in open-system thinking within a team setting. It requires a team meeting of about 20 to 25 minutes followed by a general class discussion for 10 to 15 minutes. Total time required for this exercise is about 30 to 40 minutes.

Instructions

Your instructor will randomly assign you to teams with five to eight members each. Choose one team member to act as recordkeeper and spokesperson. Either at your instructor's prompting or as a team, choose one of the following three options.

1 Identify an organization that is familiar to everyone in your team (it can be a local business, your college or university, or a well-known organization such as McDonald's, Royal Dutch Shell or British Airways.

2 Select an organization from any of the opening case studies following each chapter in this book.

Next do a *stakeholder audit* for the organization in question. This will require a team brainstorming session followed by brief discussion. Your team will need to make reasonable assumptions about the circumstances surrounding your target organization.

Finally, your team should select the three (or more) *high-priority* stakeholders on your team's list. Rank them number one, number two, and so on. (*Tip:* A top-priority stakeholder is one with the greatest short-term impact on the success or failure of your target organization.) Be prepared to explain to the entire class your rationale for selecting each high-priority stakeholder.

1 How does this exercise foster open-system thinking? Give examples.

2 Did this exercise broaden your awareness of the complexity of modern organizational environments? Explain.

3 Why do managers need clear priorities when it comes to dealing with organizational stakeholders?

4 How many *trade-offs* (meaning one party gains at another's expense) can you detect in your team's list of stakeholders? Specify them.

5 Does your experience with doing a stakeholder audit strengthen or weaken the validity of the ecosystem model of organizations? Explain.

6 How difficult was it for your team to complete this assignment? Explain.

Chapter Nineteen

Managing Change in Learning Organizations

How Gerhard Schulmeyer Changed the Culture at Siemens Nixdorf

In 1994 Siemens Nixdorf Informationssysteme (SNI) was a serious loss-maker: it is now the largest European player in data processing and the continent's number two in software, services and mainframes, with global sales of DM15bn. The programme, which put the company into profit within its initial two-year time-frame, is now in its fourth and ongoing stage, in which employees take responsibility for improving their business processes, effectively implementing their own re-engineering, ▶

538

and share their knowledge and ideas on the corporate intranet.

When Schulmeyer came to SNI late in the summer of 1994, after a career spent largely in the USA with Motorola and ABB, he found a demoralized PC-to-IT services group. The merger of Siemens and Nixdorf had left a divided culture and mounting losses despite a restructuring programme, which had slashed the workforce from 52,000 to 39,000, and several attempts to improve the company's alignment with its customers. Schulmeyer set out to introduce a fast-moving, entrepreneurial, Silicon Valley culture into what he calls the 'hard-wired, bolted-to-the-floor' values of German industry. The company would be rebuilt around customer-focused processes and *quickly*: what would normally take a year would be accomplished in a quarter of the time.

Schulmeyer knew that if processes were re-engineered before a thorough change of culture, the programme often withered at the roots. So he put the culture change first and this meant 'mobilizing' all the employees behind it, a process to which he allocated six months. In the three months before officially taking over at SNI and launching the change initiative in October 1994, Schulmeyer had spent most of his time meeting employees—around 9,000 of them, plus key customers—and frankly discussing the measures that were needed to dig the company out of its loss-making hole and the behavioural changes required to accomplish it.

Changing Values and Behaviour Patterns
The first priority was to get people behaving in new ways. Schulmeyer understood that it is easier for people to act their way into a new culture and, in an interview in 1995 reviewing the first year's progress, said: 'What numerous attempts that have gone wrong have shown us, is that it is not possible to change the processes in an organization without first changing and evolving . . . the underlying values behind all of the actions and the resulting behaviour patterns.'

The dynamic behind Schulmeyer's programme undeniably sprang from the huge voluntary creative and emotional support he managed to generate despite the financial plight of the company and worries over job security. People responded immediately with analyses of what had gone wrong—lack of communication was a leading candidate—and ideas for change.

'Usually 80 per cent of the problems of a company are known to the people who work there but they don't have the chance to do anything about them', Schulmeyer observed during the first year.

He was rarely seen without a sheaf of charts in his hands and for those early meetings with employees he carried with him the Schedule for Change, which was divided into quarters for the first year, running to the end of 1995. Two were allocated to culture change, one of which overlapped with 'baselining'-a critical exercise in which lines of business outlined their core competencies and options for future business. The third was devoted to SNI 'visioning' and partly to re-aligning and the fourth to budgeting and re-structuring. 'People usually talk about time spans of five years for a culture change', he remarked early in the process. 'It may take us five years but we have to gain the feeling that time is so valuable that we have to work and measure ourselves in much shorter slots.' The Schedule for Change was posted up all over the company to impart a sense of urgency.

Identifying Change Agents and Opinion Leaders
Schulmeyer began the process of mobilization with just three managers—from Human Resources, Corporate Communications and Corporate Strategy—tasking them to recruit like-minded change agents. The three soon turned into 30, who spent three intensive days discussing feedback from the new CEO's talks and identifying an agenda for action.

This agenda produced a 19-point programme for action in three main categories:

▼ *behavioural changes* among managers and employees in order to achieve dramatic performance improvements

▼ *changing work systems* to engender a culture of operational excellence

▼ *changing processes* to focus on, and interface with, the customer and to ensure a culture of customer excellence.

The number one problem perceived by employees was communication, with managers often keen to present a better picture to their senior managers than reality justified. The task of communicating the agenda to 36,000 employees around the world was a severe logistical challenge. The mechanism chosen was a series of large, corporate-wide, four-day events built around interactive workshops. They all took place in Hanover, each addressing a particular set of issues representing milestones in the transformation process, and became known as Hanover One, Two, Three and Four.

To lead the issues debate at Hanover One, which took place in December 1994 and represented 'the voice of the employee', the core change activators identified 300 further 'opinion leaders' who were considered highly motivated and capable of leading change in the workplace. They were joined at Hanover by 75 top managers and 30 workshop facilitators.

Out of the 19-point agenda came 60 agreed issues for action, which were carried back into the business. Project leaders built teams which started small but grew and developed their own databases. A striking example was the four-person team tasked with developing an inventory of corporate best practice in software and services. This originally consisted of four people from four nationalities: on return from Hanover it acquired six more people. Within three months it had developed a PC-based database, and was working with all 25 SNI regional managers to harvest best-practice information and share it with employees throughout the world.

The action teams displayed their achievements on exhibition stalls at a Results Fair in May 1995, held in Munich. More than 12,000 attended the two-day event. One notable result was the work of a team in SNI Greece which had taken on the task of re-engineering SNI's order-to-cash process and managed to slash its cycle time by half. About ten of the 60 actions resulted in company-wide initiatives, while 40 produced local business benefits. Only ten had no effect other than providing experience in culture-change projects.[1]

For discussion
Which were the most important contributions to successful change at SNI?

Increased competition and startling breakthroughs in information technology are forcing companies to change the way they do business. Customers are demanding greater value and lower prices. The rate of organizational and societal change is clearly accelerating. For example, a survey of 750 corporations revealed that all of them were involved in at least one organizational change programme. Another survey of 259 executives indicated that 84 per cent had one change initiative under way, while nearly 50 per cent were implementing three or more change programmes.[2]

A large consultancy firm, A T Kearny, asked senior executives in 294 medium and large European companies to rate their change programmes: 20 per cent were considered a success; 63 per cent had made some temporary improvement but failed to sustain it; and 17 per cent had achieved no improvement at all.[3]

Companies no longer have a choice—they must change to survive. Unfortunately, it is not easy to successfully implement organizational change. People frequently resist organizational change even when it is occurring for good reason. Many changes ultimately fail because companies do not properly understand that what is happening underneath, in the ways of working, is more important than the gains in short-term productivity. Management Consultant Peter Scott-Morgan calls these 'the unwritten rules'. These rules are in themselves logical and only by understanding their logic will companies be able to confront deep-seated resistance to change. Deep behavioural change is needed to create a culture of ongoing change.[4] Peter Senge, a well-known expert on the topic of organizational change, made the following comment about organizational change during an interview with *Fast Company* magazine.

When I look at efforts to create change in big companies over the past 10 years, I have to say that there's enough evidence of success to say that change is possible–and enough evidence of failure to say that it isn't likely.[5]

If Senge is correct, then it is all the more important for current and future managers to learn how they can successfully implement organizational change. This final chapter was written to help navigate the journey of change.

Specifically, we discuss the forces that create the need for organization change, models of planned change, resistance to change, and how to create a 'learning organization'.

FORCES OF CHANGE

How do organizations know when they should change? What cues should an organization look for? Although there are no clear-cut answers to these questions, the 'cues' that signal the need for change are found by monitoring the forces for change.

Organizations encounter many different forces for change. These forces come from sources outside the organization and from internal sources. This section examines the forces that create the need for change. Awareness of these forces can help managers determine when they should consider implementing an organizational change. The external and internal forces for change are presented in Figure 19–1.

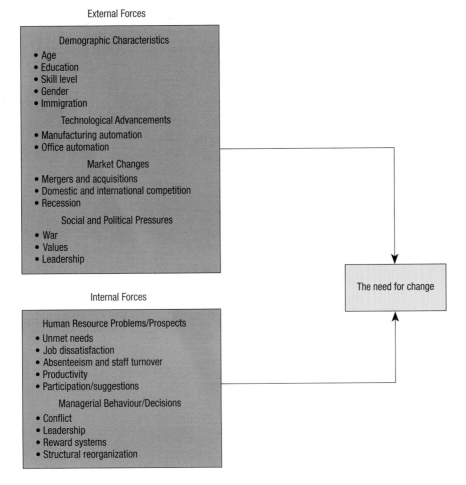

Figure 19–1

The External and Internal Forces for Change

External Forces

As **external forces for change** have global effects, they may cause an organization to question the essence of what business it is in and the process by which products and services are produced. There are four key external forces for change: demographic characteristics, technological advancements, market changes, and social and political pressures. Each is now discussed.

> **External forces for change**
> *originate outside the organization*

Demographic Characteristics

Chapter 2 provided a detailed discussion of the demographic changes occurring in the European workforce. Two key trends identified in this discussion were that: the workforce is more diverse; and there is a business imperative to effectively manage diversity. Organizations need to effectively manage diversity if they are to receive maximum contribution and commitment from employees.

Technological Advancements

Both manufacturing and service organizations are increasingly using technology as a means to improve productivity and market competitiveness. Manufacturing companies, for instance, have automated their operations with robotics; computerized numerical control (CNC), which is used for metal cutting operations; and computer-aided design (CAD). CAD is a computerized process for draughting and designing the engineering of products. Companies also use computer-integrated manufacturing (CIM). This highly technical process attempts to integrate product design with product planning, control and operations. In contrast to these manufacturing technologies, the service sector is using office automation. Office automation consists of a host of computerized technologies that are used to obtain, store, analyse, retrieve and communicate information.

The development and use of information technology is probably one of the biggest forces for change. Organizations, both large and small, private and public, for profit and not-for-profit, all must adapt to using a host of information technologies. Consider how the Virgin group is using the Internet to obtain more customers.

Richard C N Branson has made a career of confounding his critics. His Virgin Group Ltd spans 170 businesses, from airlines and railroads to music stores and condoms. So when the British tycoon moves online, one shouldn't expect just digital music and virtual airline reservations. Try some 5,500 London households paying gas and electric bills online through Virgin's Web site since July. An additional 2,000 Brits tooling around in cars they bought on the Net, thanks to a new Virgin service launched a month earlier. Then there are the nearly 2 million people in the country booking train tickets through Virgin–and 1 million using the Web to tap Virgin's help in managing $4 billion in assets, including insurance, mortgage, and investment funds. And don't forget the $58,000 worth of wine they're buying online from Branson each week.[6]

Experts believe that e-business will continue to create evolutionary changes in organizations throughout the world. Organizations are encouraged to join the e-volution! Most experts agree that the dot.com hype, where small companies could become very successful within only a few short months, really never existed. The major change is the way established companies use new technology.

Market Changes

The emergence of a global economy is forcing companies to change the way they do business. For example, many Japanese companies are having to discontinue their jobs-for-life philosophy because of increased international competition (see the next International OB).

Companies all over the word are forging new partnerships and alliances with their suppliers and potential competitors.

It was almost like the dramatic final act of a play but without the main character. As the top brass of General Motors Corp. and Turin-based Fiat gathered in the Italian company's auditorium to announce their broad strategic alliance, the key player who signed off the deal wasn't even there. Gianni Agnelli, the 79-year-old patriarch of Europe's most powerful industrial dynasty, was up in his fourth-floor office suite taping an interview for Italian television. He would leave it to others to announce the fate of the car company his grandfather and namesake had founded 101 years ago.[7]

This example highlights that organizations must learn how to create collaborative win-win relationships with other organizations if they are to survive in the worldwide restructuring of alliances and partnerships.

International OB

Japanese Firms Discontinue the Jobs-for-Life Philosophy

Sony President Nobuyuki Idei must think he's in Silicon Valley. How does he rev up his staff and boost flagging profits? By tossing the whole organization chart in the air, pulling vagrant subsidiaries back into the parent company, and committing to scrapping 20 per cent of his factories by 2003 while escorting some 17,000 workers to the door.

Idei's mid-March restructuring proposal dashes most hopes in Japan that the country's jobs-for-life policy would survive the recession. Facing

hefty losses this month a fiscal year, companies ha each other to announce re ...gs. NEC Corp. plans to slash 15,000 jobs worldwide over three years. Parts-maker Omron Corp.'s payroll will shrink by 2,000. And it's not just high tech. In a bid for public funds, Japan's top 15 banks have agreed to axe almost 20,000 jobs by 2004.

SOURCE: Exerpted from I M Kunii, E Thornton and J. Rae-Dupree, 'Sony's Shake Up', *Business Week*, March 22, 1999, p 52.

Social and Political Pressures

These forces are created by social and political events. For example, tobacco companies are experiencing a lot of pressure to alter the way they market their products. This pressure is being exerted through legislative bodies. Political events can create substantial change. For instance, the collapse of the Berlin Wall and communism in Russia created many new business opportunities. Although it is difficult for organizations to predict changes in political forces, many organizations hire lobbyists and consultants to help them detect and respond to social and political changes.

Internal Forces

Internal forces for change may be subtle, such as low job satisfaction, or they can manifest themselves in outward signs, such as low productivity and conflict. Internal forces for change come from human resource problems, and from managerial behaviour and decisions.

Internal forces for change
originate inside the organization

Human Resource Problems and Prospects

These problems stem from employee perceptions of how they are treated at work and the match between individual and organization needs and desires. Chapter 7 highlighted the relationship between an employee's unmet needs and job dissatisfaction. Dissatisfaction is a symptom of an underlying employee problem that should be addressed. Unusual or high levels of absenteeism and staff turnover also represent forces for change. Organizations might respond to these problems by using the various approaches to job design discussed in Chapter 7, by reducing employees' role conflict, overload and ambiguity and also by removing the different stressors discussed in Chapter 17. Prospects for positive change stem from employee participation and suggestions.

Managerial Behaviour and Decisions

Excessive interpersonal conflict between managers and their subordinates is a sign that change is needed. Both the manager and the employee may need interpersonal skills training or the two individuals may simply need to be separated. For example, one of the parties might be transferred to a new department. Inappropriate behaviour shown by leaders, such as inadequate direction or support, may require a change in the response to these human resource problems. As discussed in Chapter 16, leadership training is one potential solution for this problem. Inequitable reward systems—recall our discussion in Chapter 8—and the type of structural reorganizations discussed in Chapter 18, are additional forces for change.

MODELS AND DYNAMICS OF PLANNED CHANGE

Western managers are criticized for emphasizing short-term, quick-fix solutions to organizational problems. When applied to organizational change, this approach is doomed from the start. Quick-fix solutions do not really solve underlying problems, nor do they have much staying power. Therefore, researchers and managers alike have tried to identify effective ways to manage the change process. This section sheds light on their insights. After discussing different types of organizational change, we review Lewin's change model, a systems model of change, Kotter's eight-stages for leading organizational change, and organizational development.

Types of Change

A useful three-way typology of change is displayed in Figure 19–2.[8] This typology is generic because it relates to all sorts of change, including both administrative and technological changes. Adaptive change is lowest in complexity, cost and uncertainty. It involves repeating the implementation of a change in the same organizational unit later on or imitating a change that was implemented by a different unit. For example, an adaptive change for a department store would be to rely on 12-hour days during the annual inventory week. The store's accounting department could imitate the same change in work hours during end of year accounting. Adaptive changes are not particularly threatening to employees because they are familiar.

Figure 19–2

A Generic Typology of Organizational Change

Innovative changes fall midway on the continuum of complexity, cost and uncertainty. An experiment with flexible work schedules by a farm supply warehouse qualifies as an innovative change if it entails modifying the way other firms in the industry already use it. Unfamiliarity, and hence greater uncertainty, make fear of change a problem with innovative changes.

At the high end of the continuum of complexity, cost and uncertainty are the radically innovative changes. Changes of this sort are the most difficult to implement and tend to be the most threatening to managerial confidence and employee job security.[9] They can tear the fabric of an organization's culture. Resistance to change tends to increase as changes go from adaptive to innovative to radically innovative.

Lewin's Change Model

Most theories of organizational change originated from the landmark work of social psychologist Kurt Lewin. Lewin developed a three-stage model of planned change which explained how to initiate, manage and stabilize the change process.[10] The three stages are 'unfreezing', changing and refreezing. (*Unfreezing* is the accepted term for this OB process, instead of the more usual terms for unfreezing, i.e. *thawing* or *defrosting*.) Before reviewing each stage, it is important to highlight the assumptions that underlie this model.[11]

1 The change process involves learning something new, as well as discontinuing some current attitudes, behaviour and organizational practices.

2 Change will not occur unless there is motivation to change. This is often the most difficult part of the change process.

3 People are the hub of all organizational changes. Any change, whether in terms of structure, group process, reward systems or job design, requires individuals to change.

4 Resistance to change is found even when the goals of change are highly desirable.

5 Effective change requires reinforcing new types of behaviour, attitudes and organizational practices.

Let us now consider the three stages of change.

Unfreezing

The focus of this stage is to create the motivation to change. In so doing, individuals are encouraged to replace old behaviours and attitudes with those desired by management. Managers can begin the the unfreezing process by disconfirming the usefulness or appropriateness of employees' present behaviours or attitudes. In other words, employees need to become dissatisfied with the old way of doing things.

Benchmarking is a technique that can be used to help unfreeze an organization. Benchmarking 'describes the overall process by which a company compares its performance with that of other companies, then learns how the strongest-performing companies achieve their results.'[12] For example, one company discovered through benchmarking that their costs to develop a computer system were twice as high as the best companies in the industry, and the time it took to get a new product to market was four times longer than the benchmarked organizations. These data were ultimately used to unfreeze employees' attitudes and motivate people to change the organization's internal processes in order to remain competitive.[13] Managers also need to devise ways to reduce the barriers to change during this stage.

Benchmarking
process by which a company compares its performance with that of high-performing organizations

Changing

Because change involves learning, this stage entails providing employees with new information, new behavioural models or new ways of looking at things. The purpose is to help employees learn new concepts or points of view. Role models, mentors, experts, benchmarking results and training are all useful mechanisms to facilitate change. Experts recommend that it is best to convey the idea that change is a continuous learning process rather than a one-off event.

Refreezing

Change is stabilized during refreezing by helping employees to integrate the changed behaviour or attitude into their normal way of doing things. This is accomplished by first giving employees the chance to exhibit the new types of behaviour or attitudes. Once exhibited, positive reinforcement is used (recall our discussion in Chapter 10). Additional coaching and modelling are used at this point to reinforce the stability of the change.[14]

A Systems Model of Change

A systems approach takes a 'big picture' perspective of organizational change. It is based on the notion that any change, no matter how large or small, has a cascading or knock-on effect throughout an organization. For example, promoting an individual to a new work group affects the group dynamics in both the old and new groups. Similarly, creating project or work teams may necessitate the revamping of compensation practices. These examples illustrate that change creates additional change. Today's solutions are tomorrow's problems. A systems model of change offers managers a framework for understanding the broad complexities of organizational change.[15] The three main components of a systems model are inputs, target elements of change, and outputs (see Figure 19–3).

Figure 19–3 *A Systems Model of Change*

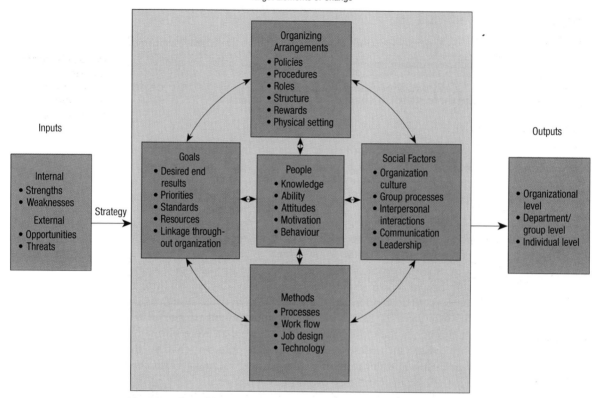

SOURCE: Adapted from D R Fuqua and D J Kurpius, 'Conceptual Models in Organizational Consultation', *Journal of Counseling & Development*, July/August 1993, pp 602–18; and D A Nadler and M L Tushman, 'Organizational Frame Bending: Principles for Managing Reorientation', *Academy of Management Executive*, August 1989, pp 194–203.

Inputs

All organizational changes should be consistent with an organization's mission, vision, and resulting strategic plan. A **mission statement** represents the 'reason' an organization exists. In Chapter 3 we defined an organization's *vision* as a long-term goal that describes 'what' an organization wants to become. Consider how the difference between mission and vision affects organizational change. Your university probably has a mission to educate people. This mission does not necessarily imply anything about change. It simply defines the university's overall purpose. In contrast, the university may have a vision to be recognized as the 'best' university in the country. This vision requires the organization to benchmark itself against other world-class universities and to create plans for achieving the vision. Philips Design for example, was trying to transform itself in order to accomplish the following vision: Philips Design has to create value for Philips' customers, shareholders and society through a new design concept called 'High Design'. This concept is characterized by a structured work process, joint efforts of different disciplines and, above all, an orientation towards people as end-users of products and services.

Mission statement
summarizes 'why' an organization exists

While vision statements point the way, strategic plans contain the detail needed to create organizational change.

Strategic plans are based on considering an organization's strengths and weaknesses relative to its environmental opportunities and threats. This comparison results in developing an organizational strategy to attain desired outputs such as profits, customer satisfaction, quality, adequate return on investment, and acceptable levels of staff turnover and employee commitment (see Figure 19–3). In summary, organizations tend to commit resources to counter-productive or conflicting activities when organizational changes are not consistent with its strategic plan.

Strategic plan
a long-term plan outlining actions needed to achieve planned results

Target Elements of Change

As shown in Figure 19–3, change can be directed at realigning organizing arrangements, social factors, methods, goals or people.[16] The choice of **target elements of change**, therefore, is based on the strategy being pursued or the organizational problem at hand. Consider the cultural change the British Ministry of Defence targeted in the following example.

Target elements of change
components of an organization that may be changed

> *Changing an organization's culture is always a difficult task but at the Ministry of Defence the process is that much tougher. When the procurement team of this ministry had to introduce a more entrepreneurial culture, the change process made managers rethink many of the accepted norms of their office, many of which have been inherited from the armed forces. There is an unwritten rule, for example, that people shouldn't speak directly to individuals who are more than two grades above them. The general belief, therefore, is that middle managers take the credit for any improvements suggested lower down the ranks, and that senior managers are out of touch.[17]*

There are two additional points to note about the systems model shown in Figure 19–3. First, the double-headed arrows among the target elements of change indicate that a change in one organizational component affects the others. Second, people are the hub of all change. Change will not succeed unless individuals embrace it in one way or another.

Outputs

Outputs represent the desired end results of a change. Once again, these end results should be consistent with an organization's strategic plan. Figure 19–3 indicates that change may be directed at the organizational level, department or group level or the individual level. The process of change is more complicated and difficult to manage when it is targeted at the organizational level, as it is more likely to affect *multiple* target elements of change (as shown in the model).

Kotter's Eight Steps for Leading Organizational Change

John Kotter, an expert in leadership and change management, believes that organizational change typically fails because senior management commits one or more of the following errors.[18]

1 Failure to establish a sense of urgency about the need for change.

2 Failure to create a powerful-enough guiding coalition that is responsible for leading and managing the change process.

3 Failure to establish a vision that guides the change process.

4 Failure to effectively communicate the new vision.

5 Failure to remove obstacles that impede the accomplishment of the new vision.

6 Failure to systematically plan for and create short-term wins. Short-term wins represent the achievement of important results or goals.

7 Declaration of victory too soon. This derails the long-term changes in infrastructure that are frequently needed to achieve a vision.

8 Failure to anchor the changes in the organization's culture. It takes years for long-term changes to become embedded within an organization's culture.

Kotter recommends that organizations should follow eight sequential steps to overcome these problems (see Table 19–1).

Table 19–1 *Sequential Steps to Leading Organizational Change*

Step	Description
1. Establish a sense of urgency	Unfreeze the organization by creating a compelling reason for why change is needed.
2. Create the guiding coalition	Create a cross-functional, cross-level group of people with enough power to lead the change.
3. Develop a vision and strategy	Create a vision and strategic plan to guide the change process.
4. Communicate the change vision	Create and implement a communication strategy that consistently communicates the new vision and strategic plan.
5. Empower broad-based action	Eliminate barriers to change, and use target elements of change to transform the organization. Encourage risk taking and creative problem solving.
6. Generate short-term wins	Plan for and create short-term "wins" or improvements. Recognize and reward people who contribute to the wins.
7. Consolidate gains and produce more change	The guiding coalition uses credibility from short-term wins to create more change. Additional people are brought into the change process as change cascades throughout the organization. Attempts are made to reinvigorate the change process.
8. Anchor new approaches in the culture	Reinforce the changes by highlighting connections between new behaviors and processes and organizational success. Develop methods to ensure leadership development and succession.

SOURCE: The steps were developed by J P Kotter, *Leading Change* (Boston: Harvard Business School Press, 1996).

Each of the steps shown in Table 19–1 is associated with one of the fundamental errors just discussed. These steps also subsume Lewin's model of change. The first four steps represent Lewin's 'unfreezing' stage. Steps 5, 6 and 7 represent 'changing', and step 8 corresponds to 'refreezing.' The value of Kotter's steps is that it provides specific recommendations about the types of behaviour that managers need to exhibit to successfully lead organizational change. It is important to remember that Kotter's research reveals that it is ineffective to skip steps and that successful organizational change is 70 to 90 per cent leadership and only 10 to 30 per cent management. Senior managers are thus advised to focus on leading rather than managing change.[19]

Organization Development

Organization development (OD) is an applied field of study and practice. A pair of OD experts defined **organization development** as follows.

> *Organization development is concerned with helping managers to plan change in organizing and managing people that will develop the requisite commitment, co-ordination and competence. Its purpose is to enhance both the effectiveness of organizations and the well-being of their members through planned interventions in the organization's human processes, structures and systems, using knowledge of behavioural science and its intervention methods.[20]*

These OD techniques or interventions apply to each of the change models discussed in this section. For example, OD is used during Lewin's 'changing' stage. It is also used to identify and implement targeted elements of change within the 'systems model of change'. Finally, OD might be used during Kotter's steps 1, 3, 5, 6 and 7. In this section,

Organization development
a set of techniques or tools that are used to implement organizational change

we briefly review the four identifying characteristics of OD and its research and practical implications.[21]

OD Involves Profound Change

Change agents using OD generally desire deep and long-lasting improvement. OD consultant Warner Burke, for example, who strives for fundamental *cultural* change, wrote: 'By fundamental change, as opposed to fixing a problem or improving a procedure, I mean that some significant aspect of an organization's culture will never be the same.'[22]

OD Is Value-Loaded

Owing to the fact that OD is partly rooted in humanistic psychology, many OD consultants carry certain values or biases into the client organization. They prefer co-operation over conflict, self-control over institutional control, and democratic and participative management over autocratic management. In addition to OD being driven by a consultant's values, some OD practitioners now believe that there is a broader 'value perspective' that should underlie any organizational change. Specifically, OD should always be customer focused. This approach implies that organizational interventions should be aimed at helping to satisfy customers' needs and thereby provide enhanced value to an organization's products and services. Consider the case of B&O.

On October 29, 1993, the chairman of the board of Bang & Olufsen (B&O) could, for the first time after years of losses, predict a profit of 126 million Danish kroner (DKK) for the financial year 1993–4. The company's share price had risen spectacularly, from DKK 325 in 1990–91 to DKK 1,450 in 1994–5. These figures indicated a dramatic turnaround of a long-tottering company.

B&O was the crown jewel of Danish industry, the exclusive producer of high-tech, high-fidelity audio-visual systems and other related products. Since its beginning, the company had been at the forefront of design innovation, a philosophy promoted by the two founders of the company. However, that original philosophy stressing product design—which had earned the company much acclaim—carried within it the seeds of failure. The sanctity of the design function came to reign over everything else, particularly cost and customer considerations. Saying 'no' to a new product from the design department was taboo, an action that would not even occur to anyone hoping to stay for long in the organization. Unfortunately, even though the company won one design prize after another, financially it was anything but a winner. The balance sheet had been tottering in and out of the red for 22 years, an unheard-of period of time. As the present CEO, Anders Knutsen, said during a presentation to a group of his key people, while recalling the situation, 'Bang & Olufsen was not interested in making money; it was interested only in winning prizes.'

Despite the dismal financial figures, not many at B&O seemed to be seriously worried. Most employees were used to the fact that the company was not making a profit, but they never had serious doubts about its survival. Employment security had always been an implicit part of their contract. If ever a doubt surfaced in anybody's mind about the company's future, top management's strong and confident statements reassured them. In the words of the present CEO, 'Every year when we had some problems, it was not our fault. It was the outside world that was so evil to poor Bang & Olufsen.'

Finally, when it became clear that the accounting period of 1990–91 would bring a deficit of 135.5 million DKK, the company's dismal situation could no longer be ignored. The Supervisory Board decided to pull the plug, replacing the CEO who for 10 years had been allowed to run the company at his own discretion, with Anders Knutsen. Knutsen had learned the business of B&O by starting out as a brand manager and working his way through different positions in production and product development until finally ending up as technical director.

His first step was an analysis of the company's cultural values, prepared by B&O's top executives, which centred around an intensive evaluation of the company's critical situation. In particular, the way in which the process of new-product acceptance was treated as sacrosanct was placed under the microscope.

What followed was, as one B&O employee described it, 'an atmosphere of chaos and upheaval'. People were shocked and disoriented, uncertain how the future–theirs and the company's–would look. The shock therapy seemed to achieve the desired effect, however. Participants, trying to impose order on the prevailing chaos, threw themselves wholeheartedly into the activities of the seminar. Despite the risks, they experienced for the first time the power to do something about their own company. They were asked to engage in a strategic dialogue with top management to help restructure and refocus the company. Participating in the design for the future made for motivation, commitment, and a sense of ownership. No longer was job security the main pillar of the contract. Instead, that pillar had become accountability and performance.

The distance between top management and the shop floor was cut by reducing the overall number of executives and by slashing two management layers entirely; a total of 712 people were dismissed. As accountability was pushed deep down the lines, employees were expected to develop a sense of ownership and personal responsibility for the company.

To internationalize the company, a new International Sales and Marketing Head Office was opened in Brussels. Product acceptance–the old Achilles' heel of the company (previously almost everything submitted by product design was accepted– became much more selective. This proved to be the most disturbing 'culture shock' experienced during the transformation, as it clearly signalled management's intent to change the company.

After a 2-year period, B&O moved from a deficit that seriously threatened the existence of the company to a surplus that exceeded all expectations. The first part of the change process had come to a successful end.[23]

OD Is a Cycle of Diagnosis and Prescription

OD theorists and practitioners have long adhered to a medical model of organization. Like medical doctors, internal and external OD consultants approach the 'sick' organization, 'diagnose' its ills, 'prescribe' and implement an intervention and 'monitor' progress.[24]

OD Is Process-Oriented

Ideally, OD consultants focus on the form and not the content of behavioural and administrative dealings. For example, product design engineers and market researchers might be coached on how to communicate more effectively with one another without the consultant knowing the technical details of their conversations. In addition to communication, OD specialists focus on other processes, including those of solving problems, making decisions, handling conflict, trust, sharing power and developing careers.

OD Research and Practical Implications

Before discussing OD research, it is important to note that many of the topics contained in this book are used during OD interventions. For example, role analysis, which was discussed in Chapter 12, is used to enhance co-operation between work group members by getting them to discuss their mutual expectations. Team building is also commonly used to improve the functioning of work groups and was reviewed in Chapter 13. OD research, therefore, has practical implications for a variety of OB applications. OD-related interventions produced the following insights.

▼ **A meta-analysis of 18 studies indicated that employee satisfaction with change was higher when top management was highly committed to the change effort.**[25]

▼ A meta-analysis of 52 studies provided support for the systems model of organizational change. Specifically, varying one target element of change created changes in other target elements. Also, there was a positive relationship between individual behaviour change and organizational-level change.[26]

▼ A meta-analysis of 126 studies demonstrated that multifaceted interventions, using more than one OD technique, were more effective in changing job attitudes and work attitudes than interventions that relied on only one human-process or technostructural approach.[27]

There are three practical implications to be derived from this research. First, planned organization change works. However, management and change agents are advised to rely on multifaceted interventions. As indicated elsewhere in this book, goal setting, feedback, recognition and rewards, training, participation, and challenging job design have good track records for improving performance and satisfaction. Second, change programmes are more successful when they are geared toward meeting both short- and long-term results. Managers should not engage in organizational change for the sake of it. Change efforts should produce positive results.[28] Finally, organizational change is more likely to succeed when top management is truly committed to the change process and the desired goals of the change programme. This is particularly true when organizations pursue large-scale transformation.[29]

UNDERSTANDING AND MANAGING RESISTANCE TO CHANGE

We are all creatures of habit. It is generally difficult for people to try new ways of doing things. It is precisely because of this basic human characteristic that most employees do not have enthusiasm for change in the workplace. Rare is the manager who does not have several stories about carefully cultivated changes that 'died on the vine' because of resistance to change. It is important for managers to learn to manage resistance because failed change efforts are costly. Costs include decreased employee loyalty, lowered probability of achieving corporate goals, a waste of money and resources, and difficulty in fixing the failed change effort. This section examines employee resistance to change, relevant research and practical ways of dealing with the problem.

Why People Resist Change in the Workplace

No matter how technically or administratively perfect a proposed change may be, people make or break it. Individual and group behaviour following an organizational change can take many forms (see Figure 19–4). The extremes range from acceptance to active resistance to change. Many targets or victims of change are cynical about its motives, relevance and processes. Cynicism about organizational change combines pessimism about the likelihood of successful change with blame; with those responsible for change being seen as incompetent, uncaring or simply lazy.[30] A change management programme in a large Spanish savings bank was intended to facilitate changes in managers' values, competences and practices by providing them with relevant feedback from subordinates. However, the change programmes was perceived as political and part of a power game, causing negative emotional reactions such as fear, suspicion and discomfort.[31]

> **Resistance to change**
> *emotional/behavioural response to real or imagined work changes*

Figure 19–4 shows that resistance can be as subtle as passive resignation and as overt as deliberate sabotage. Managers need to learn to recognize the manifestations of resistance, both in themselves and others, if they want to be more effective in creating and supporting change. For example, managers can use the list in Figure 19–4 to prepare answers and tactics to combat the various forms of resistance.

Now that we have examined the manifestations of resistance to change, let us consider the reasons employees resist change in the first place. Ten of the leading reasons are listed here.[32]

Figure 19–4

The Continuum of
Resistance to Change

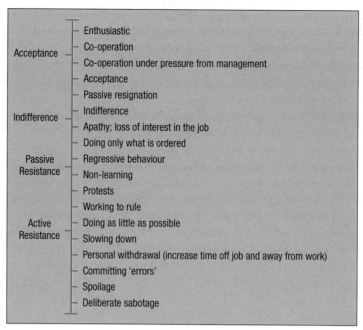

Acceptance
— Enthusiastic
— Co-operation
— Co-operation under pressure from management
— Acceptance

Indifference
— Passive resignation
— Indifference
— Apathy; loss of interest in the job
— Doing only what is ordered

Passive
Resistance
— Regressive behaviour
— Non-learning
— Protests
— Working to rule

Active
Resistance
— Doing as little as possible
— Slowing down
— Personal withdrawal (increase time off job and away from work)
— Committing 'errors'
— Spoilage
— Deliberate sabotage

SOURCE: A S Judson, *Changing Behavior in Organizations: Minimizing Resistance to Change* (Cambridge, MA: Basil Blackwell, Inc., 1991, p 48. Used with permission.

1   *An individual's predisposition toward change.* This predisposition is highly personal and deeply ingrained. It is an offshoot of how one learns to handle change and ambiguity as a child. Consider the hypothetical examples of Sandy and Carl. Sandy's parents were patient, flexible, and understanding. From the time Sandy was weaned, she was taught that there were positive compensations for the loss of immediate gratification. She learned that love and approval were associated with making changes. In contrast, Carl's parents were unreasonable, unyielding and forced him to comply with their wishes. They forced him to take piano lessons even though he hated them. Changes were demands for compliance. This taught Carl to be distrustful and suspicious of change. These learned predispositions ultimately affect how Sandy and Carl handle change as adults.[33] Dell Computer Corporation recognizes how important an individual's predisposition toward change can be and tries to hire people with positive predispositions.

> . . . Dell actively seeks and cultivates a certain type of employee mind-set. For example, potential employees are told early on that their former titles may not correlate exactly with positions at Dell because the company structure is relatively flat. 'We have to strip the paradigm that titles and levels mean anything,' says Price [Steve Price is vice president of human resources for Dell's Public and Americas International Group]. 'People have to park their egos at the door. Furthermore, Dell's employees have to move away from the paradigm that more means better. 'It's just the reverse,' says Price. 'When we take half of what you have away from you and tell you to go rebuild it, that's a sign of success.' . . . 'We typically attract people for whom change is not a problem,' says Koster
> [Jim Koster is director of human resources for customer service].[34]

2   *Surprise and fear of the unknown.* When innovative or radically different changes are introduced without warning, affected employees become fearful of the implications. Rumours from the grapevine fill the void created by a lack of official announcements. Harvard University's Rosabeth Moss Kanter recommends appointing a transition manager charged with keeping all relevant parties adequately informed.[35]

3 *Climate of mistrust.* Trust, as discussed in chapter 12, involves reciprocal faith in others' intentions and behaviour. Mutual mistrust can doom an otherwise well-conceived change to failure. Mistrust encourages secrecy, which begets deeper mistrust. Managers who trust their employees make the change process an open, honest and participative affair. Employees who, in turn, trust management are more willing to expend extra effort and take chances with something different.

4 *Fear of failure.* Intimidating changes to a job can cause employees to doubt their capabilities. Self-doubt erodes self-confidence and cripples personal growth and development.

5 *Loss of status or job security.* Administrative and technological changes that threaten to alter power bases or eliminate jobs generally trigger strong resistance. For example, most corporate restructuring involves the elimination of managerial jobs. One should not be surprised when middle managers resist restructuring and participative management programmes that reduce their authority and status.

6 *Peer pressure.* Someone who is not directly affected by a change may actively resist it to protect the interests of his or her friends and co-workers.

   The 'pockets of good practice' approach calls for change to be led and inspired by a small cadre of individuals from within the business.

   One of the UK's major timber and builder's merchants, Jewson, is already seeing significant improvements in profitability and productivity through nurturing 'pockets' in its branch network. Individual branch managers had always been encouraged to try out new ideas at a local level. Peter Hindle, Managing Director, Operations, explains: 'When I visited our branches I saw different ideas and different aspects of good practice but no one was talking to each other. I found myself like the Pied Piper, spending all my time telling branch managers about the good things that I'd seen going on in other places.' Peter's vision was to create a pocket made up of the most successful branch managers, who would learn from each other and share ideas. From this he hopes that a model of best practice for branch management would emerge. He started the initiative by getting the top 30 branch managers together for two days every month. The meetings were, deliberately, set up not as traditional training sessions but as forums for stimulating new ideas and sharing experiences. Flexible working, annualized-hours contracts, better product training and improved transport efficiency are just some of the benefits that have resulted.[36]

7 *Disruption of cultural traditions or group relationships.* Whenever individuals are transferred, promoted or reassigned, cultural and group dynamics are thrown into disequilibrium.

8 *Personality conflicts.* Just as a friend can get away with telling us something we would resent hearing from an adversary, the personalities of change agents can breed resistance.

9 *Lack of tact or poor timing.* Undue resistance can occur because changes are introduced in an insensitive manner or at an awkward time.

10 *Non-reinforcing reward systems.* Individuals resist when they do not foresee positive rewards for changing. For example, an employee is unlikely to support a change that is perceived as requiring him or her to work longer and under more pressure.

Research on Resistance to Change

In a recent survey among 90 British managers (almost half of whom were working in the public sector), the following themes emerged.

   ▼ **Continuing change is much higher on the agenda than managing discrete projects**

   ▼ **There is evidence of 'initiative fatigue' (most people want to see the pace of change relaxed for a while), information overload and even cynicism.**

▼ Major concerns exist over the lack of effective stress management.

▼ Negotiating, persuading and influencing skills are critical.

▼ Fear of the unknown is a major source of resistance to change but commitment to communication is instrumental rather than value-driven.

▼ A third of the managers enjoy the politics game, a third do not and a third are neutral.[37]

The classic study of resistance to change was reported in 1948 by Lester Coch and John R P French. They observed the introduction of a new work procedure in a garment factory. The change was introduced in three different ways to separate groups of workers. In the 'no participation' group, the garment makers were simply told about the new procedure. Members of a second group, called the 'representative' group, were introduced to the change by a trained co-worker. Employees in the 'total participation' group learned of the new work procedure through a graphic presentation of its cost-saving potential. Mixed results were recorded for the representative group. The no participation and total participation groups, meanwhile, went in opposite directions. Output dropped sharply for the no participation group, while grievances and staff turnover climbed. After a small dip in performance, the total participation group achieved record-high output levels while experiencing no staff turnover.[38] Since the Coch and French study, participation has been the recommended approach for overcoming resistance to change.[39]

Empirical research uncovered five additional personal characteristics related to resistance to change. A recent study of 514 employees from six organizations headquartered in four different continents (North America, Europe, Asia and Australia) revealed that personal dispositions pertaining to having a 'positive self-concept' and 'tolerance for risk' were positively related to coping with change. That is, people with a positive self-concept and a tolerance for risk handled organizational change better than those without these dispositions.[40]

A second study also found that high self-efficacy and an internal locus of control were negatively associated with resistance to change.[41] Finally, a study of 305 college students and 15 university staff members revealed that attitudes toward a specific change were positively related to the respondents' general attitudes toward change and content within their 'change schema' (you may recall from Chapter 6 that a change schema relates to various perceptions, thoughts and feelings that people have when they encounter organizational change).[42]

The preceding research is based on the assumption that individuals directly or consciously resist change. Some experts contend that this is not the case. Rather, there is a growing belief that resistance to change represents, instead, the employees' responses to obstacles in the organization that *prevent* them from changing.[43] For example, John Kotter, the researcher who developed the eight steps for leading organizational change discussed earlier in this chapter, studied more than 100 companies and concluded that employees generally wanted to change but were unable to do so because of obstacles that prevented execution. He noted that obstacles in the organization's structure or in a 'performance appraisal system [that] makes people choose between the new vision and their own self-interests' impeded change more than an individual's direct resistance.[44] This new perspective implies that a systems model, such as that shown in Figure 19–3 should be used to determine the causes of failed change. Such an approach would be most likely reveal that ineffective organizational change is due to faulty organizational processes and systems rather than to employees' direct resistance.[45] In conclusion, a systems perspective suggests that people do not resist change, per se, but rather that individual's 'anti-change' behaviour and attitudes are caused by obstacles within the work environment.

Alternative Strategies for Overcoming Resistance to Change

Before recommending specific approaches for overcoming resistance, there are four key conclusions that should be kept in mind. First, an organization must be ready for change.

Boehringer Ingelheim, a German pharmaceuticals manufacturer of more than 100 years'
standing, is one of the few remaining privately owned companies in the pharmaceutical
industry. Until the 1980s, its culture reflected a traditional, hierarchical management
structure and a strong paternalistic value system. At its UK subsidiary, management
identified some of the natural risk-takers who could become role models for other
employees. After looking for volunteers they ended up with a network comprising one
change agent for every 50 employees. This network provided the crucial element of
bottom-up and sideways-driven change facilitation to complement the more traditional
top-down directives.[46]

Just as a table must be set before you can eat, so must an organization be ready for
change before it can be effective.[47] The next OB Exercise contains a survey that
assesses an organization's readiness for change. Use the survey to evaluate a company
that you worked for or are familiar with that undertook to change. To what extent was
the company ready for change and how did this relate, in turn, to the success of the
effort to change?

OB Exercise
Assessing an Organization's Readiness for Change

Instructions
Circle the number that best represents your opinions about the company being evaluated.

3 = Yes

2 = Somewhat

1 = No

1 Is the change effort being
sponsored by a senior-level
executive (MD, CEO, COO)? 3—2—1

2 Are all levels of management
committed to the change? 3—2—1

3 Does the organization culture
encourage risk taking? 3—2—1

4 Does the organization culture
encourage and reward continuous
improvement? 3—2—1

5 Has senior management clearly
articulated the need for change? 3—2—1

6 Has senior management presented
a clear vision of a positive future? 3—2—1

7 Does the organization use
specific measures to assess
business performance? 3—2—1

8 Does the change effort support
other major activities going on
in the organization? 3—2—1

9 Has the organization benchmarked
itself against world-class companies? 3—2—1

10 Do all employees understand the
customers' needs? 3—2—1

11 Does the organization reward
individuals and/or teams for being
innovative and for looking for root
causes of organizational problems? 3—2—1

12 Is the organization flexible and
co-operative? 3—2—1

13 Does management effectively
communicate with all levels of
the organization? 3—2—1

14 Has the organization
successfully implemented other
change programmes? 3—2—1

15 Do employees take personal
responsibility for their behaviour? 3—2—1

16 Does the organization make
decisions quickly? 3—2—1

Total score: _____

Arbitrary Norms
40–48 = High readiness for change

24–39 = Moderate readiness for change

16–23 = Low readiness for change

**SOURCE: Based on the discussion contained in T A Stewart, 'Rate Your Readiness to Change', *Fortune*,
February 7, 1994, pp 106–10.**

Second, organizational change is less successful when top management fails to keep employees informed about the process of change. Third, do not assume that people are resisting change consciously. Managers are encouraged to use a systems model of change to identify the obstacles that are affecting the implementation process. Fourth, employees' perceptions or interpretations of a change affect resistance significantly. Employees are less likely to resist when they perceive that the benefits of a change overshadow the personal costs. As a minimum therefore, managers are advised to:

▼ **provide as much information as possible to employees about the change**

▼ **inform employees about the reasons/rationale for the change**

▼ **conduct meetings to address employees' questions regarding the change**

▼ **provide employees with the opportunity to discuss how the proposed change might affect them.**[48]

These recommendations underscore the importance of communicating with employees throughout the process of change.

In addition to communication, employee participation in the change process is another generic approach for reducing resistance. Consider how George Bauer, president of the US affiliate of Mercedes-Benz Credit Corp., used participation and employee involvement to re-engineer operations and downsize the workforce.

The first step is delegating re-engineering efforts to those who know best where to cut: the people actually doing the work. The second step is comforting them with a guarantee: anyone bold enough to eliminate his own job will receive a new job—and probably a better one—helping to create new growth.

So to the shock (and scepticism) of his superiors in Stuttgard, Mr Bauer delegated the problem of streamlining to groups of employees and managers, partly in the cold calculation that a grassroots effort would help workers 'buy in' and partly in the sincere belief that the best ideas would come from outside the executive suite.

The outcome shook the operation to its core. Managers proposed reducing or even wiping out their own departments through automation or restructuring. Four entire layers of management vanished. Employees were assigned to functional teams with almost complete authority to execute decisions.[49]

Bauer's radical approach to change management resulted in a 31 per cent increase in assets between 1992 and 1995 and a 19 per cent increase in staff. JD Power & Associates also rated Mercedes-Benz Credit as number one or customer satisfaction among all the import captive-finance companies in 1995.[50] In spite of positive results like those found by Bauer, organizational change experts have nonetheless criticized the tendency to treat participation as a cure-all for resistance to change. They prefer a contingency approach because resistance can take many forms and, furthermore, because situational factors vary (see Table 19–2). Participation + Involvement does, as shown in Table 19–2, have its place, but it takes time that is not always available. Also indicated in the Table is how each of the other five methods has its own situational niche, advantages and drawbacks. In short, there is no universal strategy for overcoming resistance to change. Managers need a complete repertoire of change strategies.[51]

CREATING A LEARNING ORGANIZATION

Organizations are finding that yesterday's competitive advantage is becoming the minimum entrance requirement for staying in business. This puts tremendous pressure on organizations to learn how best to improve and stay ahead of competitors. In fact, both researchers and practising managers agree that an organization's ability to learn is a key strategic weapon.[52] Hence, it is important for organizations to enhance and nurture their ability to learn.

Table 19–2 *Six Strategies for Overcoming Resistance to Change*

Approach	Commonly Used in Situations	Advantages	Drawbacks
Education + Communication	Where there is a lack of information or inaccurate information and analysis.	Once persuaded, people will often help with the implementation of the change.	Can be very time consuming if lots of people are involved.
Participation + Involvement	Where the initiators do not have all the information they need to design the change and where others have considerable power to resist.	People who participate will be committed to implementing change, and any relevant information they have will be integrated into the change plan.	Can be very time consuming if participators design an inappropriate change.
Facilitation + Support	Where people are resisting because of adjustment problems.	No other approach works as well with adjustment problems.	Can be time consuming, expensive, and still fail.
Negotiation + Agreement	Where someone or some group will clearly lose out in a change and where that group has considerable power to resist.	Sometimes it is a relatively easy way to avoid major resistance.	Can be too expensive in many cases if it alerts others to negotiate for compliance.
Manipulation + Co-optation	Where other tactics will not work or are too expensive.	It can be a relatively quick and inexpensive solution to resistance problems.	Can lead to future problems if people feel manipulated.
Explicit + Implicit coercion	Where speed is essential and where the change initiators possess considerable power.	It is speedy and can overcome any kind of resistance.	Can be risky if it leaves people mad at the initiators.

SOURCE: Reprinted by permission of the *Harvard Business Review*. An exhibit from 'Choosing Strategies for Change' by J P Kotter and L A Schlesinger (March/April 1979). Copyright © 1979 by the President and Fellows of Harvard College; all rights reserved.

So how do organizations create a learning organization? It is not easy! To help clarify what this process entails, this section begins by defining a learning organization. We then present a model of how to build an organization's learning capability and discuss some reasons why organizations naturally resist learning. The chapter concludes by reviewing new roles and skills required of leaders aiming to create a learning organization and several management practices that must be unlearned.

Defining a Learning Organization

Peter Senge, a professor at the Massachusetts Institute of Technology, popularized the term *learning organization* in his best-selling book entitled *The Fifth Discipline*. He described a learning organization as 'a group of people working together to collectively enhance their capacities to create results that they truly care about.'[53] A practical interpretation of these ideas results in the following definition. A learning organization is one that proactively creates, acquires, and transfers knowledge and that changes its behaviour on the basis of new knowledge and insights.[54]

By breaking this definition into its three component parts, we can clearly see the characteristics of a learning organization.

Learning organization
proactively creates, acquires and transfers knowledge throughout the organization and changes its behaviour on the basis of new knowledge and insights

1 New ideas are a prerequisite for learning. Learning organizations actively try to infuse their organizations with new ideas and information. They do this by constantly scanning their external environments, hiring new talent and expertise when needed, and by devoting significant resources to training and developing their employees.

2 New knowledge must be transferred throughout the organization. Learning organizations strive to reduce structural, process and interpersonal barriers to the sharing of information, ideas and knowledge among organizational members.

3 Behaviour must change as a result of new knowledge. Learning organizations are results oriented. They foster an environment in which employees are encouraged to use new types of behaviour and operational processes to achieve corporate goals.[55]

Building an Organization's Learning Capability

Learning capabilities
the set of core competencies and internal processes that enable an organization to adapt to its environment

Figure 19–5 presents a model of how organizations build and enhance their learning capability. **Learning capabilities** represent the set of core competencies, which are defined as the special knowledge, skills and technological know-how that differentiate an organization from its competitors, and processes that enable an organization to adapt to its environment.[56] The general idea underlying Figure 19–5 is that learning capabilities are the fuel for organizational success. Just like petrol enables a car's engine to perform, learning capabilities equip an organization to perform—to foresee and respond to internal and external changes. This ability, in turn, increases the chances of satisfying customers and boosting sales and profitability.[57] Let us now consider the two major contributors to an organization's learning capability: facilitating factors and learning mode.

Figure 19–5

Building an Organization's Learning Capability

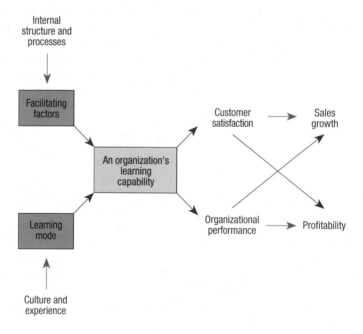

Facilitating Factors

Facilitating factors represent 'the internal structure and processes that affect how easy or hard it is for learning to occur and the amount of effective learning that takes place.'[58] Table 19–3 contains a list of 10 key facilitating factors. Keep in mind as you read them that these factors can either enable or impede an organization's ability to respond to its environment. Consider, for example, the 'concern for measurement' factor. A survey of 203 executives compared companies that did and did not focus on measurement-management. Results revealed that those companies who focused on

Table 19-3 *Factors That Facilitate Organizational Learning Capabilities*

1. Scanning imperative	Interest in external happenings and in the nature of one's environment. Valuing the processes of awareness and data generation. Curious about what is "out there" as opposed to "in here."
2. Performance gap	Shared perception of a gap between actual and desired state of performance. Disconfirming feedback interrupts a string of successes. Performance shortfalls are seen as opportunities for learning.
3. Concern for measurement	Spend considerable effort in defining and measuring key factors when venturing into new areas; strive for specific, quantifiable measures; discourse over metrics is seen as a learning activity.
4. Experimental mindset	Support for trying new things; curiosity about how things work; ability to "play" with things. Small failures are encouraged, not punished. See changes in work processes, policies, and structures as a continuous series of graded tryouts.
5. Climate of openness	Accessibility of information; relatively open boundaries. Opportunities to observe others; problems/errors are shared, not hidden; debate and conflict are acceptable.
6. Continuous education	Ongoing commitment to education at all levels; support for growth and development of members.
7. Operational variety	Variety exists in response modes, procedures, systems; significant diversity in personnel. Pluralistic rather than monolithic definition of valued internal capabilities.
8. Multiple advocates	Top-down and bottom-up initiatives are possible; multiple advocates and gatekeepers exist.
9. Involved leadership	Leadership at significant levels articulates vision and is very actively engaged in its actualization; takes ongoing steps to implement vision; "hands-on" involvement in educational and other implementation steps.
10. Systems perspective	Strong focus on how parts of the organization are interdependent; seek optimization of organizational goals at the highest levels; see problems and solutions in terms of systemic relationships.

SOURCE: Reprinted by permission of Sage Publications Ltd from B Moingeon and A Edmondson, in *Organizational Learning and Competitive Advantage*, (Thousand Oaks, CA: Sage,© 1996), p 43.

measurement-management were identified as industry leaders, had financial performance that put them in the top third of their industry, and were more successful at implementing and managing major change initiatives.[59] This study suggests that concern for measurement enhanced these organizations' learning capabilities. Ernst & Young is a good example of a company that used several of the listed facilitating factors to increase its learning capability.

Ernst & Young figures that its knowledge falls into three categories of 'content'. The first is benchmark data—studies, surveys, industry facts, and figures. 'Each year we buy about $30 million of this stuff in the United States alone, so that's valuable right there,' says Peetz [John Peetz is the chief knowledge officer]. 'The second content is point-to-point knowledge, which is people sharing what they know. And finally, we've got expert knowledge, or the best people in a given area who know how to solve specific problems.' To tie this together, Ernest & Young created 'power packs,' or databases on specific business areas that employees load into laptops. These packs also contain contact information for the firm's network of subject experts. If a consultant runs into *a glitch in a supply-chain management proposal, for example, he or she can instantly find and get help from Ernst & Young's most experienced supply-chain master.*[60]

Learning Mode

Learning modes, as shown in Figure 19–5, are directly influenced by an organization's culture and experience or past history. Consider how the culture at Siemens Power Transmission and Distribution affected its learning modes.

Concerned that the company cafeteria was becoming a place for inappropriate socializing, management had walled off part of the room, believing that decreasing the cafeteria's size would make it less convenient for workers to linger there. 'It was exactly the wrong thing to do,' says training director Barry Blystone. As it turned out, workers were using the cafeteria as a de facto meeting place where they could gather in a corner to discuss work issues (along with all the other things managers assumed they were talking about—cars, families, sports, etc.) . . . . 'By shrinking the size of the cafeteria, we're taking important space and time away from an informal learning opportunity,' Blystone says. Ironically, the company used the walled-off space for a conference room—one where meetings had to be scheduled in advance.[61]

This example illustrates at least two things: firstly, how Siemen's suspicious and low trusting culture detracted from the spontaneous learning that is critical within learning organizations, and secondly, when we reflect on the opening case study, how difficult it is for a large organization to share best practices.

OB researcher, Danny Miller, reviewed the literature on organizational learning and identified six dominant modes of learning.[62]

1 *Analytic learning.* Learning occurs through systematic gathering of internal and external information. Information tends to be quantitative and analysed by means of formal systems. The emphasis is on using deductive logic to analyse objective data numerically.

2 *Synthetic learning.* Synthetic learning is more intuitive and generic than the analytic mode. It emphasizes the synthesis of large amounts of complex information by using systems thinking. That is, employees try to identify interrelationships between issues, problems and opportunities.

3 *Experimental learning.* This mode is a rational methodological approach that is based on conducting small experiments and monitoring the results.

4 *Interactive learning.* This mode involves learning-by-doing. Rather than using systematic methodological procedures, learning occurs primarily through the exchange of information. Learning is more intuitive and inductive.

5 *Structural learning.* This mode is a methodological approach that is based on the use of organizational routines. These organizational routines represent standardized processes and procedures that specify how to carry out tasks and roles. People learn from routines because they direct attention, institutionalize standards and create consistent vocabularies.

6 *Institutional learning.* This mode represents an inductive process by which organizations share and model values, beliefs and practices either from their external environments or from senior executives. Employees learn by observing environmental examples or senior executives. Socialization and mentoring play a significant role in institutional learning.

How Facilitating Factors and Learning Modes Produce Learning Capability

Researchers suspect there is some type of optimal matching between the facilitating factors and learning modes that affect learning capability.[63] For example, the facilitating factor of an 'experimental mindset' should enhance the learning capability of a company that predominately uses the 'experimental learning' mode. In contrast, the inconsistency between an 'experimental mindset' and a 'structural learning' mode would be more likely to impede organizational learning. Because the concept of a learning organization is very new to the field of OB, we really do not know how the facilitating factors combine with learning modes to influence an organization's learning capability. Future empirical research is needed to examine this issue. Nonetheless, we do know that an organization's learning capability is an important contributor to organizational effectiveness.[64] Managers are thus advised to develop, nurture and reinforce their organizations' learning capabilities.

Consider once more the example of Ernst & Young.

> *Some firms* are *learning. Among them is Ernst & Young, the accountancy group, which has taken a lesson from the higher groves of academe. Like Oxbridge and Ivy League professors, its senior people are offered sabbaticals. Mark Jenner, learning and development manager in the consultancy-services division, says: 'We compete on ideas, so we need to allow people creative white space. A sabbatical allows them to recharge their batteries, top-up their knowledge and generate intellectual capital that we can use. It is also a way of retaining people. Consultants tell us that working on a long-term engagement is quite tough, and at the end many think, "Do I stay for the next one or leave?"'*

> *Andrew Holmes, a managing consultant, was chosen for a six-week sabbatical at Henley Management College, to work on his theory that sales could be improved if the firms' backgrounds and culture were taken into account more. He says: 'I have seen things go fundamentally wrong so many times because people behave in a way that is at odds with a company's culture.'*[65]

Let us now consider the reasons for organizations, unfortunately, having a natural tendency to resist learning.

Organizations Naturally Resist Learning

You may be wondering why any rational person or organization would resist learning. It just does not make sense. Well, organizations do not consciously resist learning. They do it because of three fundamental problems that plague society at large: focusing on fragmentation rather than systems, emphasizing competition over collaboration, and a tendency to be reactive rather than proactive.[66] Overcoming these problems requires a fundamental shift in how we view the world.

Focusing on Fragmentation Rather than Systems

Fragmentation involves the tendency to break down a problem, project or process into smaller pieces. For example, as students you are taught to memorize isolated facts, study abstract theories, and learn ideas and concepts that bear no resemblance to your personal life experiences. This reinforces the use of an analytic strategy that entails solving complex problems by studying the components rather than the whole. Unfortunately, modern-day problems such as runaway health care costs and crime prevention cannot be solved with piecemeal linear approaches.

In organizations, fragmentation creates functional 'walls' or 'silos' that separate people into independent groups. In turn, this results in creating specialists who work within specific functional areas. It also generates internal fiefdoms that battle over power, resources, and control. Learning, sharing, co-operation, and collaboration are ultimately lost on the battlefield.

Emphasizing Competition over Collaboration

Competition is a dominant societal and management **paradigm**. Although nothing is intrinsically wrong with competition, this paradigm results in employees competing with the very people with whom they need to collaborate for success. Moreover, it creates an

Paradigm
a generally accepted way of viewing the world

overemphasis on looking good rather than being good, which prohibits learning because people become reluctant to admit when they do not know something. This is especially true of leaders. In turn, employees hesitate to accept tasks or assignments that they are not good at. Finally, competition produces a fixation on short-term measurable results rather than on long-term solutions to the root causes of problems.

Being Reactive Rather than Creative and Proactive

People are accustomed to changing only when they need to because life is less stressful and frustrating when we stay within our comfort zones. This contrasts with the fundamental catalyst of real learning. The drive to learn is fuelled by personal interest, curiosity, aspiration, imagination, experimentation and risk taking. The problem is that all of us have been conditioned to respond and react to others' directions and approval. This undermines the intrinsic drive to learn. When this tendency is coupled with management by fear, intimidation and crisis, people not only resist learning, they become paralyzed by the fear of taking risks.

EFFECTIVE LEADERSHIP IS THE SOLUTION

There is hope! Effective leadership chisels away at these natural tendencies and paves the way for organizational learning. Leaders can create an organizational culture that promotes systems thinking over fragmentation; collaboration and co-operation over competition; and innovation and proaction over reactivity. Leaders must, however, adopt new roles and associated activities to create a learning organization.

Specifically, leaders perform three key functions in building a learning organization: building a commitment to learning; working to *generate* ideas with impact; and working to *generalize* ideas with impact.[67] Table 19–4 contains a list of leadership activities needed to support each role.

Table 19–4 *Leadership Roles and Activities for Building a Learning Organization*

Leadership Activities	Role 1: Build a Commitment to Learning	Role 2: Work to Generate Ideas with Impact	Role 3: Work to Generalize Ideas with Impact
Make learning a component of the vision and strategic objectives	X		
Invest in learning	X		
Publicly promote the value of learning	X		
Measure, benchmark, and track learning	X		
Create rewards and symbols of learning	X		
Implement continuous improvement programs		X	
Increase employee competence through training, or buy talent from outside the organization		X	
Experiment with new ideas, processes, and structural arrangements		X	
Go outside the organization to identify world-class ideas and processes		X	
Identify mental models of organizational processes		X	
Instill systems thinking throughout the organization		X	
Create an infrastructure that moves ideas across organizational boundaries			X
Rotate employees across functional and divisional boundaries			X

SOURCE: Based in part on D Ulrich, T Jick and M Von Glinow, 'High-Impact Learning: Building and Diffusing Learning Capability', *Organizational Dynamics*, Autumn 1993, pp 52–66.

Building a Commitment to Learning

Leaders need to instill an intellectual and emotional commitment to learning by using the ideas shown in Table 19–4. For example, Harley Davidson has identified 'intellectual curiosity' as one of its core corporate values. Leaders can promote the value of learning by modelling the desired attitudes and behaviours. They can attend seminars as presenters or participants, share effective managerial practices with peers, and disseminate readings, videos and other educational materials. Leaders also need to invest the financial resources needed to create a learning infrastructure. Consider the experience of the World Bank.

The World Bank devotes approximately 4 per cent of its administrative budget to knowledge management. According to Stephen Denning, programme director of knowledge management, this percentage is at the lower end of corporate spending but represents a significant amount for his non-profit organization. Senior leaders lend support to the initiative and provide the resources each of the bank's 20 sectors need to form local partnerships, provide ad hoc advice, and disseminate knowledge.[68]

Working to *Generate* Ideas with Impact

Ideas with impact are those that add value to one or more of an organization's three key stakeholders: employees, customers and shareholders. The leadership activities shown in Table 19–4 reveal six ways to generate ideas with impact.

Working to *Generalize* Ideas with Impact

Leaders must make a concerted effort to reduce interpersonal, group and organizational barriers to learning. This can be done by creating a learning infrastructure. This is a large-scale effort that includes the following activities:

- ▼ **measuring and rewarding learning**
- ▼ **increasing open and honest dialogue between organizational members**
- ▼ **reducing conflict**
- ▼ **increasing horizontal and vertical communication**
- ▼ **promoting teamwork**
- ▼ **rewarding risk taking and innovation**
- ▼ **reducing the fear of failure**
- ▼ **increasing the sharing of successes, failures and best practices across organizational members**
- ▼ **reducing stressors and frustration**
- ▼ **reducing internal competition**
- ▼ **increasing co-operation and collaboration**
- ▼ **creating a psychologically safe and comforting environment.[69]**

Unlearning the Organization

In addition to implementing the ideas listed in Table 19–4, organizations must concurrently 'forget' or 'unlearn' organizational practices and paradigms that made them successful. Quite simply, traditional organizations and the associated organizational behaviours they created have outlived their usefulness. Management must seriously question and challenge the ways of thinking that worked in the past if they want to create a learning organization.[70] For example, the old management paradigm of planning, organizing and controling might be replaced with one of vision, values and empowerment. The time has come for management and employees to think as owners, not as 'us' and 'them' adversaries.

Let us close our study of organizational behaviour by considering a mission statement that promotes this new managerial paradigm.

This is a company of owners, of partners, of businesspeople. We are in business together. Our economic figures—which is to say, our jobs and our financial security—depend not on management's generosity ('them') or on the strength of a union ('us') but on our collective success in the marketplace. We will share in the rewards just as—by definition—we share in the risks.

No one in this company is just an employee. People have different jobs, different salaries, different levels of authority. But all workers will see the same basic information and will have a voice in matters affecting them. And it will be everyone's responsibility to understand how the business operates, to keep track of its results, and to make decisions that contribute to its success in the marketplace.[71]

Summary of Key Concepts

1 Discuss the external and internal forces that create the need for organizational change.

Organizations encounter both external and internal forces for change. There are four key external forces for change: demographic characteristics, technological advancements, market changes, and social and political pressures. Internal forces for change come from both human resource problems and managerial behaviour/decisions.

2 Describe Lewin's change model and the systems model of change.

Lewin developed a three-stage model of planned change that explained how to initiate, manage, and stabilize the change process. The three states were *unfreezing*, which entails creating the motivation to change, *changing*, and stabilizing change through *refreezing*. A systems model of change takes a big picture perspective of change. It focuses on the interaction among the key components of change. The three main components of change are inputs, target elements of change, and outputs. The target elements of change represent the components of an organization that may be changed. They include organizing arrangements, social factors, methods, goals and people.

3 Discuss Kotter's eight steps for leading organizational change.

John Kotter believes that organizational change fails as a result of one or more of eight common errors. He proposed eight steps that organizations should follow to overcome these errors. The eight steps are as follows: (*a*) establish a sense of urgency, (*b*) create the guiding coalition, (*c*) develop a vision and strategy, (*d*) communicate the change vision, (*e*) empower broad-based action, (*f*) generate short-term wins, (*g*) consolidate gains and produce more change, (*h*) anchor new approaches in the culture.

4 Demonstrate your familiarity with the four identifying characteristics of organization development (OD).

The identifying characteristics of OD are that it: involves profound change; is value loaded; is a cycle of diagnosis and prescription; and is process oriented.

5 Discuss the 10 reasons employees resist change.

Resistance to change is an emotional/behavioural response to real or imagined threats to an established work routine. Ten reasons employees resist change are (*a*) an individual's predisposition toward change, (*b*) surprise and fear of the unknown, (*c*) climate of mistrust, (*d*) fear of failure, (*e*) loss of status or job security, (*f*) peer pressure, (*g*) disruption of cultural traditions and/or group relationships, (*h*) personality conflicts, (*i*) lack of tact or poor timing (*j*) non-reinforcing reward systems.

6 Identify alternative strategies for overcoming resistance to change.

Organizations must be ready for change. Assuming an organization is ready for change, the alternative strategies for overcoming resistance to change are education + communication, participation + involvement, facilitation + support, negotiation + agreement, manipulation + co-optation, and explicit + implicit coercion. Each has its situational appropriateness, and advantages and drawbacks.

7 Define a learning organization.

A learning organization is one that proactively creates, acquires and transfers knowledge and changes its behaviour on the basis of new knowledge and insights.

8 Discuss the process by which organizations build their learning capabilities.

Learning capabilities represent the set of core competencies and processes that enable an organization to adapt to its environment. Learning capabilities are directly affected by organizational facilitating factors and learning modes. Facilitating factors constitute the internal structure and processes that either encourage or impede learning within an organization. Learning modes represent the various ways by which organizations attempt to create and maximize their learning. Researchers believe that there is some type of optimal matching between the facilitating factors and learning modes that affects learning capability.

9 Review the reasons for organizations naturally resisting learning.

There are three underlying reasons. The first involves the tendency to focus on fragmentation rather than systems. Fragmentation involves the tendency to break down a problem, project or process into smaller pieces. It reinforces a linear analytic strategy that examines components rather than the whole. A dominant management paradigm that emphasizes competition over collaboration is the second reason. The third reason organizations naturally resist learning is that people have a tendency to be reactive rather than creative and proactive. This tendency stems from the fact that all of us have been conditioned to respond and react to others' directions and approval.

10 Discuss the role of leadership in creating a learning organization.

Leaders perform three key functions in building a learning organization: building a commitment to learning; working to generate ideas with impact; and working to generalize ideas with impact. There are 13 different leadership activities needed to support each role (see Table 19–4).

Discussion Questions

1 Which of the external forces for change do you believe will prompt the greatest change between now and the year 2010?

2 Have you worked in an organization where internal forces created change? Describe the situation and the resulting change.

3 How would you respond to a manager who made the following statement? 'Unfreezing is not important, employees will follow my directives.'

4 What are some useful methods that can be used to refreeze an organizational change?

5 Have you ever observed the systems model of change in action? Explain what occurred.

6 Have you ever resisted a change at work? Explain the circumstances and your thinking at the time.

7 Which source of resistance to change do you think is the most common? Which is the most difficult for management to deal with?

8 Does the company you work for act like a learning organization? Explain your rationale.

9 Which of the three reasons for organizations' natural resistance to learning is the most powerful? Explain.

Internet Exercise

http://www.sei.cmu.edu

In this chapter we reviewed several models of organizational change. Because these models are based on different sets of assumptions, each one offers managers a unique set of recommendations for how organizational change should be implemented. We also discussed a variety of recommendations for how managers might better implement organizational change. The purpose of this exercise is for you to expand your knowledge about how organizations should implement organizational change by considering recommendations provided by The Software Engineering Institute (SEI). The SEI is a federally funded research and development centre sponsored by the US Department of Defense. This organization focuses on assisting organizations to improve the process of software engineering. In so doing, the SEI has learned much about how to implement organizational change. Go to the Internet home page for the SEI (**http://www.sei.cmu.edu**),

and select the *search* option. This will enable you to search the SEI's database on selected topics. Search on the keyword *organizational change*. Use the sources identified through this search to answer the following questions.

Questions

1 What are the key elements of organizational change? How do these compare to the components contained in the systems model of organizational change presented in Figure 19–3?

2 What specific recommendations does the SEI offer for managing organizational change?

3 What roles do change agents, sponsors, champions and participants play in the process of implementing organizational change?

Personal Awareness and Growth Exercise
Applying the Systems Model of Change

Objectives

1 To help you understand the diagnosis step of planned organizational change.

2 To give you a practical diagnostic tool to assess which target elements of change in Figure 19–3 should be changed during a change process.

Introduction

Diagnosis is the first step in planned organizational change. It is used to identify past or current organizational problems that inhibit organizational effectiveness. As indicated in Figure 19–3, there are five organizational areas in which to look for problems: organizing arrangements, social factors, methods, goals, and people. In this exercise, you will be asked to complete a brief survey assessing these five areas of an organization.

Instructions

If you currently have a full- or part-time job, think of your organization and describe it by circling an appropriate response for each of the following 18 statements. Calculate a total score for each diagnostic area. Then connect the set of points for your organization in a vertical profile. If you are not currently employed, describe the last organization

you worked for. If you have never worked, use your current university or college as your frame of reference.

After completing the survey, think of an 'ideal' organization: an organization that you believe would be most effective. How do you believe this organization would stand in terms of the five diagnostic areas? We would like you to assess this organization with the same diagnostic survey. Circle your responses with a different colour or mark. Then vertically connect the set of points for your 'ideal' organization. Calculate a total score for each diagnostic area.

Organizational Diagnostic Survey

1 = Strongly disagree

2 = Disagree

3 = Neutral

4 = Agree

5 = Strongly agree

Organizing Arrangements

1 The company has the right recognition and rewards in place to support its vision and strategies.   1—2—3—4—5

2 The organizational structure facilitates goal accomplishment.   1—2—3—4—5

3 Organizational policies and
procedures are administered fairly.   1—2—3—4—5

Total Organizing Arrangements score = _____ _____

Social Factors

4 The culture promotes adaptability
and flexibility.   1—2—3—4—5

5 Interpersonal and group conflict
are handled in a positive manner.   1—2—3—4—5

6 Horizontal and vertical
communication is effective.   1—2—3—4—5

7 Leaders are good role models and
decision makers.   1—2—3—4—5

Total Social Factors score = _____ _____

Methods

8 The work flow promotes higher
quality and quantity of performance.   1—2—3—4—5

9 Technology is effectively utilized.   1—2—3—4—5

10 People focus on solving the cause of
problems rather than the symptoms.   1—2—3—4—5

Total Methods score = _____ _____

Goals

11 I am aware of the organization's vision
and strategic goals.   1—2—3—4—5

12 I have all the tools and resources
I need to do my job.   1—2—3—4—5

13 Corporate goals are cascaded down
the organization.   1—2—3—4—5

14 I am evaluated against specific
standards of performance.   1—2—3—4—5

Total Goals score = _____ _____

People

15 This organization inspires the very best
in me in the way of job performance. 1—2—3—4—5

16 I understand my job duties and
responsibilities.   1—2—3—4—5

17 I like working in this company.   1—2—3—4—5

18 People are motivated to do the
best job they can.   1—2—3—4—5

Total People score = _____ _____

Questions for Discussion

1 Based on your evaluation of your current organization, which diagnostic area(s) is most in need of change?

2 Based on a comparison of your current and ideal organizations, which diagnostic area(s) is most in need of change? If your answer is different from the first question, explain the difference.

3 What sort of intervention would be appropriate for your work group or organization? Give details.

Group Exercise
Creating Personal Change through Force-Field Analysis

Objectives

1 To apply force-field analysis to a behaviour or situation you would like to change.

2 To receive feedback on your strategies for bringing about change.

Introduction

The theory of force-field analysis is based on the premise that people resist change because of counteracting positive and negative forces. Positive forces for change are called *thrusters*. They propel people to accept change and modify their behaviour. In contrast, *counterthrusters* or *resistors* are negative forces that motivate an individual to maintain the status quo. People frequently fail to change because they experience equal amounts of positive and negative forces to change.

Force-field analysis is a technique used to facilitate change by first identifying the thrusters and resistors that exist in a specific situation. To minimize resistance to change, it is generally recommended to first reduce or remove the negative forces to change. Removing counterthrusters should create increased pressure for an individual to change in the desired direction. Managers can also further increase motivation to change by following up the

reduction of resistors with an increase in the number of positive thrusters of change.

Instructions

Your tutor will pair you up with another student. The two of you will serve as a team that evaluates the completeness of each other's force-field analysis and recommendations. Once the team is assembled, each individual should independently complete the Force-Field Analysis Form presented after these instructions. Once both of you complete this activity, one team member should present results from steps 2 to 5 from the five-step Force-Field Analysis Form. The partner should then evaluate the results by considering the following questions with his or her team member.

1 Are there any additional thrusters and counterthrusters that should be listed? Add them to the list.

2 Do you agree with the 'strength' evaluations of thrusters and counterthrusters in step 4? Ask your partner to share his or her rationale for the ratings. Modify the ratings as needed.

3 Examine the specific recommendations for change listed in step 5, and evaluate whether you think they will produce the desired changes. Be sure to consider whether the focal person has the ability to eliminate, reduce or increase each thruster and counterthruster that forms the basis of a specific recommendation. Are there any alternative strategies you can think of?

4 What is your overall evaluation of your partner's intervention strategy?

FORCE-FIELD ANALYSIS FORM[72]

Step 1

In the space provided, please identify a number of personal problems you would like to solve or aspects of your life you would like to change. Be as imaginative as possible. You are not limited to academic situations. For example, you may want to consider your work environment if you are currently employed, family situation, interpersonal relationships, club situations and so forth. It is important that you select some aspects of your life that you would like to change but until now have made no effort to.

Step 2

Review in your mind the problems or aspects listed in step 1. Now select one that you would really like to change and which you believe lends itself easily to force-field analysis. Select one that you will feel comfortable talking about to other people.

Step 3

On the form following step 4, indicate existing forces that are pushing you in the direction of change. Thrusters may be forces internal to yourself (pride, regret, fear) or they may be external to yourself (friends, the boss, a lecturer). Also list existing forces that are preventing you from changing. Again, the counterthruster may be internal to yourself (uncertainty, fear) or external (poor instruction, limited resources, lack of support mechanisms).

Step 4

In the space to the right of your list of thrusters and counterthrusters indicate their relative strength. For consistency, use a scale of 1 to 10, with 1 indicating a weak force and 10 indicating a high force.

Thrusters	Strength
_____	_____
_____	_____
_____	_____
_____	_____
_____	_____
_____	_____

Counterthrusters	Strength
_____	_____
_____	_____
_____	_____
_____	_____
_____	_____
_____	_____

Step 5

Analyze your thrusters and counterthrusters, and develop a strategy for bringing about the desired change. Remember that it is possible to produce the desired result by strengthening existing thrusters, introducing new thrusters, weakening or removing counterthrusters, or some combination of these. Consider the impact of your change strategy on the system's internal stress (i.e., on yourself and others), the likelihood of success, the availability of resources, and the long-term consequences of planned changes. Be prepared to discuss your recommendations with the partner in your group.

_____
_____
_____
_____
_____
_____
_____

Questions for Discussion

1 What was your reaction to doing a force-field analysis? Was it insightful and helpful?

2 Was it valuable to receive feedback about your force-field analysis from a partner? Explain.

3 How would you assess the probability of effectively implementing your recommendations?

Notes

Chapter 1

[1] C Cooper, 'Management blasted at nuclear plant', *People Management,* March 16, 2000.

[2] P Whiteley, 'Five steps to added value', *The Times*, October 19, 2000.

[3] Adapted and translated from D Sheff, 'Richard Branson: je mensen zijn belangrijkst', *Vacature*, June 28, 1997.

[4] Scott Adams, *The Dilbert Principle* (New York: HarperBusiness, 1996), p 51. Also see A Bryant, 'Make That Mr. Dilbert', *Newsweek*, March 22, 1999, pp 46–47.

[5] J Pfeffer and J F Veiga, 'Putting People First for Organizational Success', *Academy of Management Executive*, May 1999, p 37.

[6] Adapted and translated from K Weytjens, 'Fiere en geëngageerde werknemers', *Vacature*, May 1, 1999.

[7] J West and M Patterson, 'Profitable personnel', *People Management*, January 8, 1998.

[8] Adapted from J Pfeffer and J F Veiga, see ibid.

[9] See the brief report on lay-offs in the United States in G Koretz, 'Quick to Fire and Quick to Hire', *Business Week*, May 31, 1999, p 34. For the case against lay-offs, see J R Morris, W F Cascio and C E Young, 'Downsizing After All These Years: Questions and Answers About Who Did It, How Many Did It, and Who Benefited from It', *Organizational Dynamics*, Winter 1999, pp 78–87.

[10] Data from Pfeffer and Veiga, 'Putting People First for Organizational Success', p 47.

[11] H Mintzberg, 'The Manager's Job: Folklore and Fact', *Harvard Business Review*, July–August 1975, p 61. For an alternative perspective, see R J Samuelson, 'Why I Am Not a Manager', *Newsweek*, March 22, 1999, p 47.

[12] See, for example, H Mintzberg, 'Managerial Work: Analysis from Observation', *Management Science*, October 1971, pp B97–B110; and F Luthans, 'Successful vs. Effective Real Managers', *Academy of Management Executive*, May 1988, pp 127–32. For an instructive critique of the structured observation method, see M J Martinko and W L Gardner, 'Beyond Structured Observation: Methodological Issues and New Directions', *Academy of Management Review*, October 1985, pp 676–95. Also see N Fondas, 'A Behavioral Job Description for Managers', *Organizational Dynamics*, Summer 1992, pp 47–58.

[13] See L B Kurke and H E Aldrich, 'Mintzberg Was Right!: A Replication and Extension of *The Nature of Managerial Work*', *Management Science*, August 1983, pp 975–84.

[14] For example, see A I Kraut, P R Pedigo, D D McKenna and M D Dunnette, 'The Role of the Manager: What's Really Important in Different Management Jobs', *Academy of Management Executive*, November 1989, pp 286–93; J C McCune, 'Brave New World', *Management Review*, October 1997, pp 11–14; and N H Woodward, 'The Coming of the X Managers', *HR Magazine*, March 1999, pp 74–80.

[15] Validation studies can be found in E Van Velsor and J B Leslie, *Feedback to Managers, Volume II: A Review and Comparison of Sixteen Multi-Rater Feedback Instruments* (Greensboro, NC: Center for Creative Leadership, 1991); and F Shipper, 'A Study of the Psychometric Properties of the Managerial Skill Scales of the Survey of Management Practices', *Educational and Psychological Measurement*, June 1995, pp 468–79.

[16] For example, see S B Parry, 'Just What Is a Competency? (And Why Should You Care?)' *Training*, June 1998, pp 58–64.

[17] See F Shipper, 'Mastery and Frequency of Managerial Behaviors Relative to Sub-Unit Effectiveness', *Human Relations*, April 1991, pp 371–88.

[18] Ibid.

[19] Data from F Shipper, 'A Study of Managerial Skills of Women and Men and Their Impact on Employees' Attitudes and Career Success in a Nontraditional Organization', paper presented at the Academy of Management Meeting, August 1994, Dallas, Texas.

The same outcome for on-the-job studies is reported in A H Eagly and B T Johnson, 'Gender and Leadership Style: A Meta-Analysis', *Psychological Bulletin*, September 1990, pp 233–56.

[20] For instance, see J B Rosener, 'Ways Women Lead', *Harvard Business Review*, November–December 1990, pp 119–25; and C Lee, 'The Feminization of Management', *Training*, November 1994, pp 25–31.

[21] See, for example, N Munk, 'The New Organization Man', *Fortune*, March 16, 1998, pp 62–74; D T Hall and J E Moss, 'The New Protean Career Contract: Helping Organizations and Employees Adapt', *Organizational Dynamics*, Winter 1998, pp 22–37; N Munk, 'Finished at Forty', *Fortune*, February 1, 1999, pp 50–66; and B E Bellesi, 'The Changing American Workforce', *Management Review*, March 1999, p 9. For a collection of eight articles on the related topic of psychological contracts, see the special issue of *Journal of Organizational Behavior*, 1998.

[22] J M Hiltrop, 'The changing psychological contract: the human resource challenge for the 90's', *European Management Journal*, vol. 13 no. 3, 1995, pp 286–94.

[23] Drawn from W J Byron, 'Coming to Terms with the New Corporate Contract', *Business Horizons*, January–February 1995, pp 8–15.

[24] D Jones, 'Low employment makes employers less picky', *USA Today*, July 15, 1996.

[25] K R Brousseau and M J Driver, 'Career pandemonium: realigning organizations and individuals', *Academy of Management Executive*, vol. 10 issue 4, 1996, pp 52–66.

[26] See T J Tetenbaum, 'Shifting Paradigms: From Newton to Chaos', *Organizational Dynamics*, Spring 1998, pp 21–32; and R W Oliver, *The Shape of Things to Come* (New York: McGraw-Hill, 1999).

[27] Essential sources on re-engineering are M Hammer and J Champy, *Reengineering the Corporation: A Manifesto for Business Revolution* (New York: HarperCollins, 1993); and J Champy, *Reengineering Management: The Mandate for New Leadership* (New York: HarperCollins, 1995). Also see 'Anything Worth Doing Is Worth Doing from Scratch', *Inc.*, May 18, 1999 (20th Anniversary Issue), pp 51–52.

[28] For thoughtful discussion, see G G Dess, A M A Rasheed, K J McLaughlin and R L Priem, 'The New Corporate Architecture', *Academy of Management Executive*, August 1995, pp 7–20.

[29] See, for example, 'The Dreaded "E Word" ', *Training*, September 1998, p 19; K Dover, 'Avoiding Empowerment Traps', *Management Review*, January 1999, pp 51–55; and G B Weathersby, 'Management May Never Be the Same', *Management Review*, February 1999, p 5. A brief case study of empowerment in action can be found in C Dahle, 'Big Learning, Fast Futures', *Fast Company*, June 1999, pp 46, 48.

[30] See J B Miner, 'The Validity and Usefulness of Theories in an Emerging Organizational Science', *Academy of Management Review*, April 1984, pp 296–306.

[31] G W Dauphinais and C Price, 'The CEO as psychologist', *Management Review*, September 1998. ©1998 American Management Association. Published by American Management Association International, New York, NY. Used with permission of the publisher. All rights reserved. http://www.amanet.org.

[32] B S Lawrence, 'Historical Perspective: Using the Past to Study the Present', *Academy of Management Review*, April 1984, p 307.

[33] Evidence indicating that the original conclusions of the famous Hawthorne studies were unjustified may be found in R G Greenwood, A A Bolton and R A Greenwood, 'Hawthorne a Half Century Later: Relay Assembly Participants Remember', *Journal of Management*, Fall–Winter 1983, pp 217–31; and R H Franke and J D Kaul, 'The Hawthorne Experiments: First Statistical Interpretation', *American Sociological Review*, October 1978, pp 623–43. For a positive interpretation of the Hawthorne studies, see J A Sonnenfeld, 'Shedding Light on the

Hawthorne Studies', *Journal of Occupational Behaviour*, April 1985, pp 111–30.

[34] See M Parker Follett, *Freedom and Coordination* (London: Management Publications Trust, 1949).

[35] See D McGregor, *The Human Side of Enterprise* (New York: McGraw-Hill, 1960).

[36] R McHenry, 'Spuring Stuff', *People Management*, July 24, 1997.

[37] F van de Looy and J Benders, 'Not just money: quality of working life as employment strategy', *Health Manpower Management*, vol. 21 no. 3, 1995.

[38] Translated from J Kerkhofs, *De Europeanen en hun Waarden*, (Leuven: Davidsfonds, 1997).

[39] Ibid.

[40] EFQM, Brussels Representatives Office, Avenue des Pléiadies 15, B-1200 Brussels.

[41] Data from 'Workplace trends', *Training*, October 1995.

[42] M Sashkin and K J Kiser, *Putting total quality management to work*, (San Francisco: Berret-Koehler, 1993).

[43] R J Schonberger, 'Total Quality Management Cuts a Broad Swath—Through Manufacturing and Beyond', *Organizational Dynamics*, Spring 1992, p 18. Also see K Y Kim, J G Miller and J Heineke, 'Mastering the Quality Staircase, Step by Step', *Business Horizons*, January–February 1997, pp 17–21; R Bell and B Keys, 'A Conversation with Curt W Reimann on the Background and Future of the Baldrige Award', *Organizational Dynamics*, Spring 1998, pp 51–61; and B Kasanoff, 'Are You Ready for Mass Customization?' *Training*, May 1998, pp 70–78.

[44] See R K Reger, L T Gustafson, S M Demarie and J V Mullane, 'Reframing the Organization: Why Implementing Total Quality Is Easier Said than Done', *Academy of Management Review*, July 1994, pp 565–84.

[45] Deming's landmark work is W E Deming, *Out of the Crisis* (Cambridge, MA: MIT, 1986).

[46] See M Trumbull, 'What Is Total Quality Management?' *The Christian Science Monitor*, May 3, 1993, p 12; and J Hillkirk, 'World-Famous Quality Expert Dead at 93', *USA Today*, December 21, 1993, pp 1B–2B.

[47] Based on discussion in M Walton, *Deming Management at Work* (New York: Putnam/Perigee, 1990).

[48] Ibid., p 20.

[49] Adapted from D E Bowen and E E Lawler III, 'Total Quality-Oriented Human Resources Management', *Organizational Dynamics*, Spring 1992, pp 29–41.

[50] See T F Rienzo, 'Planning Deming Management for Service Organizations', *Business Horizons*, May–June 1993, pp 19–29. Also see M R Yilmaz and S Chatterjee, 'Deming and the Quality of Software Development', *Business Horizons*, November–December 1997, pp 51–58.

[51] For example, see J Shea and D Gobeli, 'TQM: The Experiences of Ten Small Businesses', *Business Horizons*, January–February 1995, pp 71–77; T L Zeller and D M Gillis, 'Achieving Market Excellence through Quality: The Case of Ford Motor Company', *Business Horizons*, May–June 1995, pp 23–31; and P McLagan and C Nel, 'A New Leadership Style for Genuine Total Quality', *Journal for Quality and Participation*, June 1996, pp 14–16.

[52] H L Tosi, Jr., and J W Slocum, Jr., 'Contingency Theory: Some Suggested Directions', *Journal of Management*, Spring 1984, p 9.

[53] For empirical evidence in a cross-cultural study, see D I Jung and B J Avolio, 'Effects of Leadership Style and Followers' Cultural Orientation on Performance in Groups and Individual Task Conditions', *Academy of Management Journal*, April 1999, pp 208–18.

[54] Adapted and translated from A van Bergen, '*Ethiek als richtsnoer: ABN laat zijn personeel open kaart spelen*', Gids voor Personeelsmanagement, vol. 78 issue 9, 1999.

[55] L Wah, 'Lies in the Executive Wing', *Management Review*, May 1999, p 9.

[56] S Hoare, 'Employees seduced by companies with principles', *The Times*, September 7, 2000.

[57] Excerpted from L Grensing-Pophal, 'Walking the Tightrope, Balancing Risks & Gains', *HRMagazine*, October 1998, p 112.

[58] See C Gilligan, 'In a Different Voice: Women's Conceptions of Self and Morality', *Harvard Educational Review*, November 1977, pp 481–517; and C Gilligan, *In a Different Voice: Psychological Theory and Women's Development* (Cambridge, MA: Harvard University Press, 1982).

[59] T Dickson, 'Management: crime busters on the board – spotting financial fraud is part of the non-executive's role', *The Financial Times*, May 17, 1995, p15

[60] Based on R B Morgan, 'Self- and Co-worker Perceptions of ethics and their relationship to leadership and salary', *Academy of Management Journal*, February 1993, pp 200–214.

[61] A new model of ethical behavior that is based on the interaction between person and situation factors is proposed by D J Brass, K D Butterfield and B C Skaggs, 'Relationships and Unethical Behavior: A Social Network Perspective', The *Academy of Management Review*, January 1998, pp 14–31.

[62] See Ch. 6 in K Hodgson, *A Rock and a Hard Place: How to Make Ethical Business Decisions When the Choices Are Tough* (New York: AMACOM, 1992), pp 66–77.

[63] Adapted from W E Stead, D L Worrell and J Garner Stead, 'An Integrative Model for Understanding and Managing Ethical Behavior in Business Organizations', *Journal of Business Ethics*, March 1990, pp 233–42.

[64] For an excellent review of integrity testing, see D S Ones and C Viswesvaran, 'Integrity Testing in Organizations', in *Dysfunctional Behavior in Organizations: Violent and Deviant Behavior*, eds R W Griffin *et al.* (Stamford, CT: JAI Press, 1998), pp 243–76.

[65] See 'Open Business Is Good for Business', *People Management*, January 1996, pp 24–27.

[66] B Briner, 'Feeling for the facts', *People Management*, January 9, 1997.

[67] See R L Daft, 'Learning the Craft of Organizational Research', *Academy of Management Review*, October 1983, pp 539–46.

[68] See K E Weick, 'Theory Construction as Disciplined Imagination', *Academy of Management Review*, October 1989, pp 516–31. Also see D A Whetten's article in the same issue, pp 490–95.

[69] Theory-focused versus problem-focused research is discussed in K E Weick, 'Agenda Setting in Organizational Behavior: A Theory-Focused Approach', *Journal of Management Inquiry*, September 1992, pp 171–82. Also see K J Klein, H Tosi and A A Cannella, Jr, 'Multilevel Theory Building: Benefits, Barriers, and New Developments', *Academy of Management Review*, April 1999, pp 243–48. (Note: The special forum on multilevel theory building in the April 1999 issue of *Academy of Management Review* includes an additional five articles.)

[70] For instance, see M R Buckley, G R Ferris, H J Bernardin and M G Harvey, 'The Disconnect between the Science and Practice of Management', *Business Horizons*, March–April 1998, pp 31–38.

[71] Complete discussion of this technique can be found in J E Hunter, F L Schmidt and G B Jackson, *Meta-Analysis. Cumulating Research Findings across Studies* (Beverly Hills, CA: Sage Publications, 1982); and J E Hunter and F L Schmidt, *Methods of Meta-Analysis: Correcting Error and Bias in Research Findings* (Newbury Park, CA: Sage Publications, 1990). Also see R Hutter Epstein, 'The Number-Crunchers Drugmakers Fear and Love', *Business Week*, August 22, 1994, pp 70–71.

[72] Limitations of meta-analysis technique are discussed in P Bobko and E F Stone-Romero, 'Meta-Analysis May Be Another Useful Tool, But It Is Not a Panacea', in *Research in Personnel and Human Resources Management*, vol. 16, ed G R Ferris (Stamford, CT: JAI Press, 1998), pp 359–97.

[73] For an interesting debate about the use of students as subjects, see J Greenberg, 'The College Sophomore as Guinea Pig: Setting the Record Straight', *Academy of Management Review*, January 1987, pp 157–59; and M E Gordon, L A Slade and N Schmitt, 'Student Guinea Pigs: Porcine Predictors and Particularistic Phenomena', *Academy of Management Review*, January 1987, pp 160–63.

[74] Good discussions of case studies can be found in A S Lee, 'Case Studies as Natural Experiments', *Human Relations*, February 1989, pp 117–37; and K M Eisenhardt, 'Building

Theories from Case Study Research', *Academy of Management Review*, October 1989, pp 532–50. The case survey technique is discussed in R Larsson, 'Case Survey Methodology: Analysis of Patterns across Case Studies', *Academy of Management Journal*, December 1993, pp 1515–46.

[75] Based on discussion found in J M Beyer and H M Trice, 'The Utilization Process: A Conceptual Framework and Synthesis of Empirical Findings', *Administrative Science Quarterly*, December 1982, pp 591–622.

[76] See J J Martocchio, 'Age-Related Differences in Employee Absenteeism: A Meta-Analysis', *Psychology & Aging*, December 1989, pp 409–14.

[77] For complete details, see G Hofstede, 'The cultural relativity of organizational practices and theories', *Journal of International Business Studies*, Fall 1983. For related discussion, see G Hofstede, 'Cultural constraints in management theories', Academy of Management, February 1993.

[78] C Schneider and J L Barsoux, *Managing across cultures*, (London: Prentice-Hall, 1997).

[79] These research results are discussed in detail in J B Miner and N R Smith, 'Decline and Stabilization of Managerial Motivation Over a 20-Year Period', *Journal of Applied Psychology*, June 1982, pp 297–305.

[80] See J B Miner, J M Wachtel and B Ebrahimi, 'The Managerial Motivation of Potential Managers in the United States and Other Countries of the World: Implications for National Competitiveness and the Productivity Problem', in *Advances in International Comparative Management*, vol. 4, ed B Prasad (Greenwich, CT: JAI Press, 1989), pp 147–70; and J B Miner, C C Chen and K C Yu, 'Theory Testing under Adverse Conditions: Motivation to Manage in the People's Republic of China', *Journal of Applied Psychology*, June 1991, pp 343–49.

[81] See J B Miner, B Ebrahimi and J M Wachtel, 'How Deficiencies in Motivation to Manage Contribute to the United States' Competitiveness Problem (and What Can Be Done about It)', *Human Resource Management*, Fall 1995, pp 363–87.

[82] Based on K M Bartol and D C Martin, 'Managerial Motivation among MBA Students: A Longitudinal Assessment', *Journal of Occupational Psychology*, March 1987, pp 1–12.

Chapter 2

[1] 'BAOBAB Catering wins an award for promoting equal opportunities', *EU Networks on Integration of Refugees*, August 2000, pp 12–13.

[2] B Clement, 'Racism hot line exposes threats, abuse and violence in workplaces', *The Independent*, 26 July 2000.

[3] Adapted and translated from D Hooghiemstra, 'Billenknijpers op het bureau', *NRC Handelsblad*, 31 January 1998, p 39.

[4] Based on D Campbell, 'Shunned Met Officer Takes Pill Overdose', *The Guardian*, January 7, 1995, p 5.

[5] Based on M Darch, 'Go Back and Make Coffee, Woman Pilot Told; Sandra Valentine', *The Times*, January 13, 1995, p 7.

[6] E Rana, 'Top firms fail ethnic minorities', *People Management*, 17 February 2000, pp 20–21.

[7] Adapted and translated from Y W M Benschop, B C T van den Berg and F van Winden, 'Personeelsmanagement in revisie. Omgaan met diversiteit in Nederland', *M&O*, March/April 1999, pp 7–19.

[8] This discussion is based on material in R R Thomas, Jr, *Redefining Diversity* (New York: AMACOM, 1996), pp 4–9.

[9] The following discussion is based on L Gardenswartz and A Rowe, *Diverse Teams at Work* (New York: McGraw-Hill, 1994), pp 31–57.

[10] This distinction is made by M Loden, *Implementing Diversity* (Chicago: Irwin, 1996).

[11] H Collingwood, 'Who Handles a Diverse Work Force Best?' *Working Women*, February 1996, p 25.

[12] Adapted and translated from E Rosenberg, 'Ik neem mijn personeel serieus', *NRC Handelsblad*, 28 October 1999.

[13] See M Minchan, 'Islam's Growth Affects Workplace Policies', *HRMagazine*, November 1998, p 216.

[14] J Hodges-Aeberhard', Affirmative action in employment: recent court approaches to a difficult concept', *International Labour Review*, 1999, pp 247–272.

[15] E Rana, 'EU laws on discrimination "will place onus on firms"', *People Management*, 2 March 2000, p 14.

[16] J Hodges-Aeberhard, op. cit.

[17] See R R Thomas, Jr, 'From Affirmative Action to Affirming Diversity', *Harvard Business Review*, March–April 1990, pp 107–17.

[18] Opposition to affirmative action was investigated by J Swim and D Miller, 'White Guilt: Its Antecedents and Consequences for Attitudes toward Affirmative Action', *Personality and Social Psychology Bulletin*, April 1999, pp 500–14; and J D Leck, D M Saunders and M Charbonneau, 'Affirmative Action Programs: An Organizational Justice Perspective', *Journal of Organizational Behavior*, January 1996, pp 79–89.

[19] For a thorough review of relevant research, see M E Heilman, 'Affirmative Action: Some Unintended Consequences for Working Women', in *Research in Organizational Behavior*, vol. 16, eds B M Staw and L L Cummings (Greenwich, CT: JAI Press, 1994), pp 125–69.

[20] Results from this study can be found in M E Heilman, W S Battle, C E Keller and R A Lee, 'Type of Affirmative Action Policy: A Determinant of Reactions to Sex-Based Preferential Selection?' *Journal of Applied Psychology*, April 1998, pp 190–205.

[21] See J Hodges-Aeberhard, op cit, and S Overell, 'ECJ takes negative view of positive disrimination', *People Management*, November 2, 1995, pp 13–14.

[22] L Dickens, 'Beyond the Business Case: a three-pronged approach to equality action', *Human Resource Management Journal*, 1999, (9)1, pp 9–19.

[23] Valuing diversity is discussed by R R Thomas, Jr, *Beyond Race and Gender* (New York: American Management Association, 1991).

[24] Different types of diversity training programmes are discussed in P L Nemetz and S L Christensen, 'The Challenge of Cultural Diversity: Harnessing a Diversity of Views to Understand Multiculturalism', *Academy of Management Review*, April 1996, pp 434–62.

[25] M Nelen, 'Diversiteitsmanagement met worklife balans', *Human Resources Magazine*, July 1999, pp 36–39.

[26] E Rana, 'CPS creates equality post to tackle racist culture', *People Management*, 25 May 2000, p 9.

[27] A M Morrison, *The New Leaders: Guidelines on Leadership Diversity in America* (San Francisco: Jossey-Bass, 1992), p 78.

[28] J Walsh, 'Private Companies equally guilty', *People Management*, 3 February 2000, p 11.

[29] D Hargreaves, 'Immigration: rocky road from control to management', *The Financial Times*, 12 October 2000, p 4.

[30] *Employment in Europe* 1999, (European Commission, 1999), p 7.

[31] Ibid, p 31.

[32] S Frank, 'On a wavelength with the Danes', *The Financial Times*, 23 October 2000, p 1.

[33] J Burns, 'Gender pay gap persists', *The Financial Times*, 15 September 2000.

[34] L Saigol, 'Being the Wrong Sex in the City: Attitudes to women in London's financial centre are improving gradually, but it can still be a difficult and even hostile working environment', *The Financial Times*, 5 August 2000.

[35] J Guyon, 'The Global Glass Ceiling', *Fortune*, 10 December 1998, p 102.

[36] J Welch, 'Climate of fear and sexism blocks path to City women', *People Management*, March 25, 1999, p 12.

[37] J Guyon, 'The Global Glass Ceiling', *Fortune*, 10 December 1998.

[38] Translated from I Froyen, 'Glazen plafond bestaat nog', *Jobat*, 16–22 September 2000, p 9.

[39] Adapted and translated from 'Steeds meer vrije beroepen', *Management Vandaag*, January 2000, p 11.

[40] G Shaw, 'Gaining from Diversity. Europe Moves Ahead', *Diversity Factor*, Fall 1998, pp 16–18.

[41] Adapted and translated from 'Aantal allochtonen in 2020 verdubbeld', *NRC Handelsblad*, 17 January 1997, p 2.

[42] E Rana, 'Construction employers vow to put house in order', *People Management*, 20 May 1999, p 11.

[43] See Y F Niemann and J F Dovidio, 'Relationship of Solo Status, Academic Rank, and Perceived Distinctiveness to Job Satisfaction of Racial/Ethnic Minorities', *Journal of Applied*

Psychology, February 1998, pp 55–71; J I Sanchez and P Brock, 'Outcomes of Perceived Discrimination among Hispanic Employees: Is Diversity Management a Luxury or a Necessity?' *Academy of Management Journal*, June 1996, pp 704–19; and T H Cox, Jr, and J A Finley, 'An Analysis of Work Specialization and Organization Level as Dimensions of Workforce Diversity', in *Diversity in Organizations*, eds M M Chemers, S Oskamp and M A Costanzo (Thousand Oaks, CA: Sage Publications, 1995), pp 62–88.

44 C Cooper, 'Coca-Cola loses its perfect harmony', *People Management*, 22 June 2000, p 16.

45 C Cooper, 'The Met fails inspection on race and recruitment', *People Management*, 20 January 2000, p 11.

46 D Hargreaves, 'Immigration: rocky road from control to management', *The Financial Times*, October 12, 2000, p 4.

47 G Shaw, 'Gaining from Diversity. Europe moves ahead', *Diversity Factor*, Fall 1998, pp 16–18.

48 A Pike, 'Enterprise: Time well spent in public appointments', *The Financial Times*, 24 August 2000.

49 A Pike, ibid.

50 C Mahony, 'Livingstone's equality policies under spotlight', *People Management*, 20 July 2000, p 15.

51 *Employment in Europe 1999*, (European Commission, 1999).

52 J Lamb, 'Age code needs legal backing', *People Management*, 16 March 2000, p 10.

53 V Pawsey, 'Youth fail prey to ageism', *People Management*, 6 July 2000, p 9.

54 A Maitland, 'Ageism "rife" in IT Industry despite severe skill shortages', *The Financial Times*, 16 October 2000, p 10.

55 J Welch, 'Older workers excluded as Eastern Europe modernises', *People Management*, 15 July 1999, p 17.

56 R Johnson, 'Equal opportunities slips down the list of priorities', *People Management*, 3 June 1999, p 22

57 K Hilpern, 'Disabled but not unfit', *The Independent*, 8 October 2000.

58 S Liff, 'Diversity and equal opportunities: room for a constructive compromise?' *Human Resource Management Journal*, (9)1, pp 65–75.

59 E Deeks, 'High-profile pair to lift diversity at Ford', *People Management*, 14 September 2000, p 6.

60 S Vinnicombe and H Harris, 'A gender hidden', *People Management*, 6 January 2000, p 28.

61 W R Thompson, 'Diversity among managers translates into profitability', *HRMagazine*, April 1999, p 10.

62 For research into TMT demographics, see K Y Williams, 'Demography and diversity in organisations: a review of 100 years of research' in *Research in Organizational Behavior*, vol. 20, eds B M Staw and L L Cummings (Greenwich, CT; JAI Press, 1998), p 77–140.

63 See R Moss-Kanter, *The Change Masters* (New York: Simon and Schuster, 1983); and L K Larkey, 'Toward a Theory of Communicative Interactions in Culturally Diverse Workgroups', *Academy of Management Review*, April 1996, pp 463–91.

64 See Williams, 'Demography and Diversity in Organizations: A Review of 100 Years of Research'.

65 S Liff, op cit.

66 Williams, op cit.

67 See W E Watson, K Kumar and L K Michaelson, 'Cultural Diversity's Impact on Interaction Process and Performance: Comparing Homogeneous and Diverse Task Groups', *Academy of Management Journal*, June 1993, pp 590–602; and V I Sessa and S E Jackson, 'Diversity in Decision-Making Teams: All Differences Are Not Created Equal', in *Diversity in Organizations*, eds M M Chemers, S Oskamp and M A Costanzo (Thousand Oaks, CA: Sage Publications, 1995), pp 133–56.

68 The relationship between conflict and stages of group development is discussed by D C Lau and J K Murnighan, 'Demographic Diversity and Faultlines: The Compositional Dynamics of Organizational Groups', *Academy of Management Review*, April 1998, pp 325–40.

69 See J A Chatman, J T Polzer, S G Barsade and M A Neale, 'Being Different Yet Feeling Similar: The Influence of Demographic Composition and Organizational Culture on Work Processes and Outcomes', *Administrative Science Quarterly*,

December 1998, pp 749–80; and D A Harrison, K H Price and M P Bell, 'Beyond Relational Demography: Time and the Effects of Surface- and Deep-Level Diversity on Work Group Cohesion', *Academy of Management Journal*, February 1998, pp 96–107.

70 These barriers were taken from discussions in Loden, *Implementing Diversity*; E E Spragins, 'Benchmark: The Diverse Work Force', *Inc.*, January 1993, p 33; and Morrison, *The New Leaders: Guidelines on Leadership Diversity in America*.

71 For a discussion of ethnocentrism, see M Kiselica, 'Confronting My Own Ethnocentrism and Racism: A Process of Pain and Growth', *Journal of Counseling & Development*, Winter 1999, pp 14–17; and S Perreult and R Y Bourhis, 'Ethnocentrism, Social Identification, and Discrimination', *Personality & Social Psychology Bulletin*, January 1999, pp 92–103.

72 See the related discussion in G R Ferris, D D Frink, D P S Bhawuk and D C Gilmore, 'Reactions of Diverse Groups to Politics in the Workplace', *Journal of Management*, 1996, pp 23–44.

73 This discussion is based on Thomas, *Redefining Diversity*.

74 Adapted and translated from B Debeuckelaere, 'Geef wat meer kleur aan je bedrijf', *Vacature*, 14 August 1999, p 1.

75 For complete details and results from this study, see Morrison, *The New Leaders: Guidelines on Leadership Diversity in America*.

76 'Balancing Act', *The Financial Times*, 9 May 2000.

77 'NHS Trust wins Parents at Work award', *People Management*, ???

78 A Iziren, 'Age concerns', *People Management*, 20 May 1999, pp 50–52.

79 R Johnson, 'Family Values', *People Management*, 11 March 1999, p 46.

80 B Debeuckelaere, 'M/V biedt aan: vakantie te koop', *Vacature.com*, 3 March 2000.

81 Adapted and translated from J Chorus, 'Wedijver boven de wieg', *NRC Handelsblad*, 17 August 1996, p 3.

82 Empirical support is provided by H Ibarra, 'Race, Opportunity, and Diversity of Social Circles in Managerial Networks', *Academy of Management Journal*, June 1995, pp 673–703; and P J Ohlott, M N Ruderman and C D McCauley, 'Gender Differences in Managers' Developmental Job Experiences', *Academy of Management Journal*, February 1994, pp 46–67.

83 E Deeks, 'High-profile pair to lift diversity at Ford', *People Management*, January 6, 2000, p 28.

84 Excerpted from M Adams, 'Building a Rainbow, One Stripe at a Time', *HRMagazine*, August 1998, p 73.

85 This exercise was modified from Gardenswartz and Rowe, *Diverse Teams at Work* (New York: McGraw-Hill, 1994), pp 60–61.

Chapter 3

1 Adapted and translated from I Froyen, 'DNA van bedrijf herschreven', *Jobat*, September 30, 2000, p 1.

2 For a comprehensive review of recent research, see D R Denison, 'What IS the Difference between Organizational Culture and Organizational Climate? A Native's Point of View on a Decade of Paradigm Wars', *Academy of Management Review*, July 1996, pp 619–54.

3 E H Schein, 'Culture: The Missing Concept in Organization Studies', *Administrative Science Quarterly*, June 1996, p 236.

4 This discussion is based on E H Schein, *Organizational Culture and Leadership*, 2nd ed (San Francisco: Jossey-Bass, 1992), pp 16–48.

5 P Freedman, 'Don't call me sir, I'm chief lizard wrangler', *The Sunday Times*, March 19, 2000.

6 Adapted and translated from K Weytjens, 'Koerier als visitekaartje', *Vacature*, October 24, 1998.

7 S H Schwartz, 'Universals in the Content and Structure of Values: Theoretical Advances and Empirical Tests in 20 Countries', in *Advances in Experimental Social Psychology*, ed M P Zanna (New York: Academic Press, 1992), p 4.

8 The discussion between espoused and enacted values is based on Schein, *Organizational Culture and Leadership*.

9 Adapted and translated from J Schuddinck, 'Finse Finesse',

Vacature, November 3, 2000 and A Nelissen and K Bosmans, 'Wie kan spreken is een potentiële klant', *Vacature*, February 25, 2000. Both reproduced with permission.

[10] G Jones, 'Look after your heart', *People Management*, July 29, 1999, p 27.

[11] Results can be found in S Clarke, 'Perceptions of Organizational Safety: Implications for the Development of Safety Culture', *Journal of Organizational Behavior*, March 1999, pp 185–98.

[12] J Schuddinck, op. cit.

[13] See Schwartz, 'Universals in the Content and Structure of Values: Theoretical Advances and Empirical Tests in 20 Countries'.

[14] Excerpted from S L Payne, 'Recognizing and Reducing Transcultural Ethical Tension', *The Academy of Management Executive*, August 1998, p 84.

[15] This typology and related discussion was derived from B Kabanoff and J Holt, 'Changes in the Espoused Values of Australian Organizations 1986–1990', *Journal of Organizational Behavior*, May 1996, pp 201–19.

[16] For an example of profiling organizational values see T J Kalliath, A C Bluedorn and D F Gillespie, 'A Confirmatory Factor Analyses of the Competing Values Instrument', *Educational and Psychological Measurement*, February 1999, pp 143–58.

[17] See T J Galpin, *The Human Side of Change* (San Francisco: Jossey-Bass, 1996); and J Kotter, *Leading Change* (Boston: Harvard Business School Press, 1996).

[18] Results can be found in Kabanoff and Holt, 'Changes in the Espoused Values of Australian Organizations 1986–1990'.

[19] Adapted from L Smircich, 'Concepts of Culture and Organizational Analysis', *Administrative Science Quarterly*, September 1983, pp 339–58.

[20] J M Higgins, 'Innovate or Evaporate: Seven Secrets of Innovative Corporations', *The Futurist*, September–October 1995, p 45.

[21] Anfuso, '3M's Staffing Strategy Promotes Productivity and Pride', p 28.

[22] Branch, 'The 100 Best Companies to Work for in America', p 144.

[23] See A Xenikou and A Furnham, 'A Correlated and Factor Analytic Study of Four Questionnaire Measures of Organizational Culture', *Human Relations*, March 1996, pp 349–71; and Denison, 'What IS the Difference between Organizational Culture and Organizational Climate? A Native's Point of View on a Decade of Paradigm Wars'.

[24] The validity of these cultural types was investigated and supported in R A Cooke and J L Szumal, 'Measuring Normative Beliefs and Shared Behavioral Expectations in Organizations: The Reliability and Validity of the Organizational Culture Inventory', *Psychological Reports*, June 1993, pp 1299–1330.

[25] Adapted and Translated from 'Menselijk Gezicht', *Vacature*, October 26, 2000. Reproduced with permission.

[26] Excerpted from G Jones, 'Cultural Evolution', *People Management*, October 29, 1998 and G Jones and R Goffee, *The Character of a Corporation*, (Harper Collins, 1998). Reproduced with permission.

[27] Results can be found in J P Kotter and J L Heskett, *Corporate Culture and Performance* (New York: The Free Press, 1992); and D R Denison and A K Mishra, 'Toward a Theory of Organizational Culture and Effectiveness', *Organization Science*, March–April 1995, pp 204–23.

[28] See S Tully, 'Northwest and KLM: The Alliance from Hell', *Fortune*, June 24, 1996, pp 64–72; and J Marren, *Mergers & Acquisitions: A Valuation Handbook* (Homewood, IL: Business One Irwin, 1993).

[29] The success rate of mergers is discussed in R J Grossman, 'Irreconcilable Differences', *HRMagazine*, April 1999, pp 42–48.

[30] Results can be found in Cooke and Szumal, 'Measuring Normative Beliefs and Shared Behavioral Expectations in Organizations: The Reliability and Validity of the Organizational Culture Inventory'.

[31] Supportive findings are discussed by C Vandenberghe, 'Organizational Culture, Person-Culture Fit, and Turnover: A Replication in the Health Care Industry', *Journal of Organizational Behavior*, March 1999, pp 175–84; S G Harris and K W Mossholder, 'The Affective Implications of Perceived Congruence with Culture Dimensions during Organizational Transformation', *Journal of Management*, 1996, pp 527–48; and B Schneider, H W Goldstein and D B Smith, 'The ASA Framework: An Update', *Personnel Psychology*, Winter 1995, pp 747–73.

[32] Results can be found in S Zamanou and S R Glaser, 'Moving Toward Participation and Involvement', *Group & Organization Management*, December 1994, pp 475–502.

[33] The relationship between organizational change and culture is discussed by J Silvester, N R Anderson and F Patterson, 'Organizational Culture Change: An Inter-Group Attributional Analysis', *Journal of Occupational and Organizational Psychology*, March 1999, pp 1–23; and T E Vollman, *The Transformation Imperative: Achieving Market Dominance through Radical Change* (Boston, MA: Harvard Business School Press, 1996).

[34] The IBM example was taken from J A Byrne, 'Strategic Planning', *Business Week*, August 26, 1996, pp 46–52.

[35] This perspective was promoted by Deal and Kennedy, *Corporate Cultures: The Rites and Rituals of Corporate Life*.

[36] This perspective is discussed in 'The Culture Wars', *Inc.*, May 15, 1999, pp 107–8.

[37] R H Kilman, M J Saxton and R Serpa, *Gaining Control of the Corporate Culture* (San Francisco: Jossey-Bass, 1986), p 356.

[38] Results from this study can be found in Kotter and Heskett, *Corporate Culture and Performance*.

[39] K Bemowski, 'Leaders on Leadership', *Quality Progress*, January 1996, p 43.

[40] B Domaine, 'Corporate Citizenship', *Fortune*, January 29, 1990, pp 50–54.

[41] The mechanisms were based on material contained in E H Schein, 'The Role of the Founder in Creating Organizational Culture', *Organizational Dynamics*, Summer 1983, pp 13–28.

[42] *The Philips Way. Our Values*.

[43] Excerpted from M Apgar IV, 'The Alternative Workplace: Changing Where and How People Work', *Harvard Business Review*, May–June 1998, p 123.

[44] G Jones, '*Look after your heart*', op.cit.

[45] Adapted and translated from: 'Goede ideeën brengen op', *Talent*, September 20, 1996, p 1–3.

[46] J Van Maanen, 'Breaking In: Socialization to Work', *Handbook of Work, Organization, and Society*, ed R Dubin (Chicago: Rand-McNally, 1976), p 67.

[47] L Adent Hoecklin, *Managing cultural changes for competitive advantage*, (London: The Economist Intelligence Unit, 1993).

[48] Adapted and translated from 'Meer dan klaarstomen voor gebruik', *Gids voor Personeelsmanagement*, vol. 75 issue 5, 2000.

[49] For an instructive capsule summary of the five different organizational socialization models, see J P Wanous, A E Reichers and S D Malik, 'Organizational Socialization and Group Development: Toward an Integrative Perspective', *Academy of Management Review*, October 1984, pp 670–83, Table 1. Also see D C Feldman, *Managing Careers in Organizations* (Glenview, IL: Scott, Foresman, 1988), Ch. 5.

[50] Supportive results can be found in P W Hom, R W Griffeth, L E Palich and J S Bracker, 'Revisiting Met Expectations as a Reason Why Realistic Job Previews Work', *Personnel Psychology*, Spring 1999, pp 97–112.

[51] Adapted and translated from J Schuddinck, 'Hightechbedrijf op de versiertoer', *Vacature*, March 3, 2000. Reproduced with permission.

[52] J Van Maanen, 'People Processing: Strategies of Organizational Socialization', *Organizational Dynamics*, Summer 1978, p 21.

[53] For a thorough review of socialization research, see T N Bauer, E W Morrison and R R Callister, 'Organizational Socialization: A Review and Directions for Future Research', *Research in Personnel and Human Resources Management*, vol. 16 (Stamford, CT: JAI Press, 1998), pp 149–214.

[54] Results can be found in B E Ashforth, A M Saks and R T Lee, 'Socialization and Newcomer Adjustment: The Role of Organizational Context', *Human Relations*, July 1998,

pp 897–926; and B E Ashforth and A M Saks, 'Socialization Tactics: Longitudinal Effects on Newcomer Adjustment', *Academy of Management Journal*, February 1996, pp 149–78.
55 Results from two separate studies can be found in E W Morrison, 'Longitudinal Study of the Effects of Information Seeking', *Journal of Applied Psychology*, April 1993, pp 173–83; and E W Morrison, 'Newcomer Information Seeking: Exploring Types, Modes, Sources and Outcomes', *Academy of Management Journal*, June 1993, pp 557–89.
56 See T N Bauer and S G Green, 'Testing the Combined Effects of Newcomer Information Seeking and Manager Behavior on Socialization', *Journal of Applied Psychology*, February 1998, pp 72–83.
57 See Bauer, Morrison and Callister, 'Organizational Socialization: A Review and Directions for Future Research.'
58 See A M Saks and B E Ashforth, 'Proactive Socialization and Behavioral Self-Management', *Journal of Vocational Behavior*, June 1996, pp 301–23.
59 For a thorough review of research on the socialization of diverse employees with disabilities see A Colella, 'Organizational Socialization of Newcomers with Disabilities: A Framework for Future Research', in *Research in Personnel and Human Resources Management*, ed G R Ferris (Greenwich, CT: JAI Press, 1996), pp 351–417.
60 See K E Kram, 'Phases of the Mentor Relationship', *Academy of Management Journal*, December 1983, pp 608–25.
61 K Hilpern, 'The Office Godfather', *The Guardian*, May 17, 1999.
62 H Lancaster, 'Managing Your Career: It's Harder, but You Still Can Rise Up from the Mail Room', *The Wall Street Journal*, June 18, 1996, p B1.
63 See S Seibert, 'The Effectiveness of Facilitated Mentoring: A Longitudinal Quasi-Experiment', *Journal of Vocational Behavior*, June 1999, pp 483–502; and T A Scandura, 'Dysfunctional Mentoring Relationships and Outcomes', *Journal of Management*, 1998, pp 449–67.
64 Results can be found in G F Dreher and T H Cox, Jr, 'Race, Gender, and Opportunity: A Study of Compensation Attainment and the Establishment of Mentoring Relationships', *Journal of Applied Psychology*, June 1996, pp 297–308.
65 Results from this study can be found in G F Dreher and J A Chargois, 'Gender, Mentoring Experiences, and Salary Attainment among Graduates of an Historically Black University', *Journal of Vocational Behavior*, December 1998, pp 401–16.
66 See S G Green and T N Bauer, 'Supervisory Mentoring by Advisers: Relationships with Doctoral Student Potential, Productivity, and Commitment', *Personnel Psychology*, Autumn 1995, pp 537–61; and
67 See R M O'Neill, S Horton and J F Crosby, 'Gender Issues in Developmental Relationships', in *Mentoring Dilemmas: Developmental Relationships within Multicultural Organizations. Applied Social Research*, eds A J Murrell *et al.* (Mahwah, NJ: Lawrence Erlbaum Associates, 1999), pp 63–80; and B R Ragins, 'Diversity, Power, and Mentorship in Organizations', in *Diversity in Organizations: New Perspectives for a Changing Workplace*, eds M M Chemers, S Oskamp and M A Costanzo (Thousand Oaks, CA: Sage, 1995), pp 91–132.
68 See Dreher and Cox, 'Race, Gender, and Opportunity: A Study of Compensation Attainment and the Establishment of Mentoring Relationships.'
69 See B J Tepper, 'Upward Maintenance Tactics in Supervisory Mentoring and Nonmentoring Relationships', *Academy of Management Journal*, August 1995, pp 1191–1205; A Vincent and J Seymour, 'Profile of Women Mentors: A National Survey', *SAM Advanced Management Journal*, Spring 1995, pp 4–10; and V A Parker and K E Kram, 'Women Mentoring Women: Creating Conditions for Connection', *Business Horizons*, March–April 1993, pp 42–51.
70 For a discussion of the practical guidelines for implementing mentoring programs see K Tyler, 'Mentoring Programs Link Employees and Experienced Execs', *HRMagazine*, April 1998, pp 99–103.
71 This exercise was adapted from R Pascale, 'The Paradox of Corporate Culture: Reconciling Ourselves to Socialization', University of California, pp 26–41.

Chapter 4

1 Adapted from D McGinn and S Theil, 'Hands on the Wheel', *Newsweek*, April 12, 1999, pp 49–52. For more, see B Vlasic and B Stertz, Taken for a Ride: How Daimler-Benz Drove Off With Chrysler, (William Morrow & Co., 2000)
2 Adapted and translated from D Pinedo, 'Vroeger Was de Wereld Veel Overzichtelijker', *NRC Handelsblad*, February 18, 2000, p 31.
3 J Fenby, 'Make That Foreign Posting Your Ticket to the Boardroom', *Management Today*, July 2000, pp 48–53.
4 G Dutton, 'Building a Global Brain', *Management Review*, May 1999, p 35.
5 Based on M Mabry, 'Pin a Label on a Manager—And Watch What Happens', *Newsweek*, May 14, 1990, p 43.
6 Adapted and translated from F Vuga, 'In een Moskee trek je je schoenen uit', *Knack*, December 16, 1987, pp 41–44.
7 Adapted from J Mole, *Mind Your Manners* (London: Nicholas Brealey Publishing, 1995).
8 M Mabry, op cit.
9 F Vuga, op cit.
10 J Mole, op cit.
11 E H Schein, *Organizational Culture and Leadership* (San Francisco: Jossey-Bass, 1985), p 9. Also see H H Baligh, 'Components of Culture: Nature, Interconnections, and Relevance to the Decisions on the Organization Structure', *Management Science*, January 1994, pp 14–27.
12 For instructive discussion, see J S Black, H B Gregersen, and M E Mendenhall, *Global Assignments: Successfully Expatriating and Repatriating International Managers* (San Francisco: Jossey-Bass, 1992), Ch. 2.
13 F Trompenaars and C Hampden-Turner, *Riding the Waves of Culture: Understanding Cultural Diversity in Global Business*, 2nd ed (New York: McGraw-Hill, 1998), pp 6–7.
14 'How Cultures Collide', *Psychology Today*, July 1976, p 69.
15 Adapted from Ian Bickerton, 'Interview: Lucas Brenninkmeijer', *The Financial Times*, October 28, 2000.
16 See M Mendenhall, 'A Painless Approach to Integrating "International" into OB, HRM, and Management Courses', *Organizational Behavior Teaching Review*, no. 3 (1988–89), pp 23–27.
17 See C L Sharma, 'Ethnicity, National Integration, and Education in the Union of Soviet Socialist Republics', *The Journal of East and West Studies*, October 1989, pp 75–93; and R Brady and P Galuszka, 'Shattered Dreams', *Business Week*, February 11, 1991, pp 38–42.
18 J Main, 'How to Go Global—And Why', *Fortune*, August 28, 1989, p 73.
19 An excellent contrast between French and American values can be found in C Gouttefarde, 'American Values in the French Workplace', *Business Horizons*, March–April 1996, pp 60–69.
20 Tony Major, 'Avoid merger most horrid', *The Financial Times*, September 19, 2000.
21 See G A Sumner, *Folkways* (New York: Ginn, 1906). Also see J G Weber, 'The Nature of Ethnocentric Attribution Bias: Ingroup Protection or Enhancement?' *Journal of Experimental Social Psychology*, September 1994, pp 482–504.
22 D A Heenan and H V Perlmutter, *Multinational Organization Development* (Reading, MA: Addison-Wesley, 1979), p 17.
23 J McClenahen, 'CEO of the year', *Industry Week*, November 15, 1999, pp 42–46.
24 Data from R Kopp, 'International Human Resource Policies and Practices in Japanese, European, and United States Multinationals', *Human Resource Management*, Winter 1994, pp 581–99.
25 J Fenby, op. cit.
26 See 'How Cultures Collide', pp 66–74, 97; and M Munter, 'Cross-Cultural Communication for Managers', *Business Horizons*, May–June 1993, pp 69–78.
27 D C Barnlund, 'Public and Private Self in Communicating with Japan', *Business Horizons*, March–April 1989, p 38.
28 See E W K Tsang, 'Can *Guanxi* Be a Source of Sustained Competitive Advantage for Doing Business in China?' *Academy of Management Executive*, May 1998, pp 64–73.
29 Y Richmond, *From Da to Yes. Understanding the Europeans*

(Yarmouth: Intercultural Press, 1995).

30 The concept of 'face' and good tips on saving face in Far East Asia are presented in J A Reeder, 'When West Meets East: Cultural Aspects of Doing Business in Asia', *Business Horizons*, January–February 1987, pp 69–74. Also see B Stout, 'Interviewing in Japan', *HRMagazine*, June 1998, pp 71–77; and J A Quelch and C M Dinh-Tan, 'Country Managers in Transitional Economies: The Case of Vietnam', *Business Horizons*, July–August 1998, pp 34–40.

31 The German management style is discussed in R Stewart, 'German Management: A Challenge to Anglo-American Managerial Assumptions', *Business Horizons*, May–June 1996, pp 52–54.

32 M Cleasby, 'Managing Global Contact', *British Journal of Administrative Management*, March/April 2000, pp 4–6.

33 R Hill, *We Europeans* (Brussels: Europublications, 1995)

34 Richmond, op. cit.

35 Based on J. Mole, op. cit.

36 See D Stauffer, 'No Need for Inter-American Culture Clash', *Management Review*, January 1998, p 8; J Scarborough, 'Comparing Chinese and Western Cultural Roots: Why "East Is East and ..." ', *Business Horizons*, November–December 1998, pp 15–24; and C B Meek, '*Ganbatte*: Understanding the Japanese Employee', *Business Horizons*, January–February 1999, pp 27–36.

37 This list is based on E T Hall, 'The Silent Language in Overseas Business', *Harvard Business Review*, May–June 1960, pp 87–96; and R Knotts, 'Cross-Cultural Management: Transformations and Adaptations', *Business Horizons*, January–February 1989, pp 29–33; and Trompenaars and Hampden-Turner, *Riding the Waves of Culture: Understanding Cultural Diversity in Global Business*.

38 A discussion of Japanese stereotypes in America can be found in L Smith, 'Fear and Loathing of Japan', *Fortune*, February 26, 1990, pp 50–57. Diversity in so-called Eastern Bloc countries in Central and Eastern Europe is discussed in F Luthans, R R Patrick and B C Luthans, 'Doing Business in Central and Eastern Europe: Political, Economic, and Cultural Diversity', *Business Horizons*, September–October 1995, pp 9–16. See Also R Khol, 'The Stereotypes about Germans and Americans are wrong', *Machine Design*, June 18, 1998.

39 M Cleasby, op. cit.

40 Based on discussion in P R Harris and R T Moran, *Managing Cultural Differences*, 3rd ed (Houston: Gulf Publishing, 1991) p 12. Also see 'Workers' Attitudes Similar Worldwide', *HRMagazine*, December 1998, pp 28–30; and C Comeau-Kirschner, 'It's a Small World', *Management Review*, March 1999, p 8.

41 Data from Trompenaars and Hampden-Turner, *Riding the Waves of Culture: Understanding Cultural Diversity in Global Business*, Ch. 5. For relevant research evidence, see Y A Fijneman, M E Willemsen and Y H Poortinga, 'Individualism–Collectivism: An Empirical Study of a Conceptual Issue', *Journal of Cross-Cultural Psychology*, July 1996, pp 381–402; D I Jung and B J Avolio, 'Effects of Leadership Style and Followers' Cultural Orientation on Performance in Groups and Individual Task Conditions', *Academy of Management Journal*, April 1999, pp 208–18; T M Singelis, M H Bond, W F Sharkey and C S Y Lai, 'Unpacking Culture's Influence on Self-Esteem and Embarrassability: The Role of Self-Construals', *Journal of Cross-Cultural Psychology*, May 1999, pp 315–41; and M J Bresnahan, R Ohashi, W Y Liu, R Nebashi and C Liao, 'A Comparison of Response Styles in Singapore and Taiwan', *Journal of Cross-Cultural Psychology*, May 1999, pp 342–58.

42 As quoted in E E Schultz, 'Scudder Brings Lessons to Navajo, Gets Some of Its Own', *The Wall Street Journal*, April 29, 1999, p C12.

43 Trompenaars and Hampden-Turner, *Riding the Waves of Culture: Understanding Cultural Diversity in Global Business*, p 56.

44 See, for example, N R Mack, 'Taking Apart the Ticking of Time', *The Christian Science Monitor*, August 29, 1991, p 17.

45 For a comprehensive treatment of time, see J E McGrath and J R Kelly, *Time and Human Interaction: Toward a Social Psychology of Time* (New York: The Guilford Press, 1986). Also

see L A Manrai and A K Manrai, 'Effects of Cultural-Context, Gender, and Acculturation on Perceptions of Work versus Social/Leisure Time Usage', *Journal of Business Research*, February 1995, pp 115–28.

46 A good discussion of doing business in Mexico is G K Stephens and C R Greer, 'Doing Business in Mexico: Understanding Cultural Differences', *Organizational Dynamics*, Summer 1995, pp 39–55.

47 R W Moore, 'Time, Culture, and Comparative Management: A Review and Future Direction', in *Advances in International Comparative Management*, vol. 5, ed S B Prasad (Greenwich, CT: JAI Press, 1990), pp 7–8.

48 See A C Bluedorn, C F Kaufman and P M Lane, 'How Many Things Do You Like to Do at Once? An Introduction to Monochronic and Polychronic Time', *Academy of Management Executive*, November 1992, pp 17–26.

49 'Multitasking' term drawn from S McCartney, 'The Breaking Point: Multitasking Technology Can Raise Stress and Cripple Productivity', *The Arizona Republic*, May 21, 1995, p D10.

50 see R Hill, op.cit and also Mole, op cit. p 59

51 O Port, 'You May Have To Reset This Watch—In a Million Years', *Business Week*, August 30, 1993, p 65.

52 See E T Hall, *The Hidden Dimension* (Garden City, NY: Doubleday, 1966).

53 Adapted from 'How Cultures Collide', p 72.

54 R Hill, op. cit. p 53

55 D Raybeck and D Herrmann, 'A Cross-Cultural Examination of Semantic Relations', *Journal of Cross-Cultural Psychology*, December 1990, p 470.

56 Based on V Houlder, 'Management: cultural exchanges.', *Financial Times*, April 5, 1995, p 19

57 G A Michaelson, 'Global Gold', *Success*, March 1996, p 16.

58 Translation services are discussed in D Pianko, 'Smooth Translations', *Management Review*, July 1996, p 10; and R Ganzel, 'Universal Translator? Not Quite', *Training*, April 1999, pp 22–24.

59 Based on J Bloom, 'Mind Your Language', *Management Today*, August 1998, pp 72–74.

60 V Houlder, 'Culture Shock for Executives', *The Financial Times*, April 5 1995, p. 19.

61 R Breedveld, 'Zoeken naar één van jullie: multicultureel personeelsbeleid', *Gids voor Personeelsmanagement*, vol. 78 issue 7/8 1999, pp 75–77.

62 Adapted and translated from F Bieckman, 'NL-GB liefdeslessen: Britten en Nederlanders werken veel maar moeizaam samen', *Management Team*, February 26 1999, pp 21–24.

63 P R Harris and R T Moran, *Managing Cultural Differences*, 4th ed, (Gulf Publishing Company) p 23.

64 N J Adler, *International Dimensions of Organizational Behavior*, 2nd ed (Boston: PWS-Kent, 1991), p 10. Also see P C Earley and H Singh, 'International and Intercultural Management Research: What's Next?' *Academy of Management Journal*, April 1995, pp 327–40; M B Teagarden *et al.*, 'Toward a Theory of Comparative Management Research: An Idiographic Case Study of the Best International Human Resources Management Project', *Academy of Management Journal*, October 1995, pp 1261–87; M H Segall, W J Lonner and J W Berry, 'Cross-Cultural Psychology as a Scholarly Discipline: On the Flowering of Culture in Behavioral Research', *American Psychologist*, October 1998, pp 1101–10; and M Easterby-Smith and D Malina, 'Cross-Cultural Collaborative Research: Toward Reflexivity', *Academy of Management Journal*, February 1999, pp 76–86.

65 For complete details, see G Hofstede, *Culture's Consequences: International Differences in Work-Related Values*, abridged ed (Newbury Park, CA: Sage Publications, 1984); G Hofstede, 'The Interaction between National and Organizational Value Systems', *Journal of Management Studies*, July 1985, pp 347–57; and G Hofstede, 'Management Scientists Are Human', *Management Science*, January 1994, pp 4–13. Also see V J Shackleton and A H Ali, 'Work-Related Values of Managers: A Test of the Hofstede Model', *Journal of Cross-Cultural Psychology*, March 1990, pp 109–18; R Hodgetts, 'A Conversation with Geert Hofstede', *Organizational Dynamics*, Spring 1993, pp 53–61; and

P B Smith, S Dugan and F Trompenaars, 'National Culture and the Values of Organizational Employees: A Dimensional Analysis Across 43 Nations', *Journal of Cross-Cultural Psychology*, March 1996, pp 231–64.

[66] See G Hofstede and M H Bond, 'Hofstede's Culture Dimensions: An Independent Validation Using Rokeach's Value Survey', *Journal of Cross-Cultural Psychology*, December 1984, pp 417–33. A recent study using the Chinese Value Survey (CVS) is reported in D A Ralston, D J Gustafson, P M Elsass, F Cheung and R H Terpstra, 'Eastern Values: A Comparison of Managers in the United States, Hong Kong, and the People's Republic of China', *Journal of Applied Psychology*, October 1992, pp 664–71.

[67] G Hofstede, 'Cultural Constraints in Management Theories', *Academy of Management Executive*, February 1993, p 90.

[68] See Y Paik and J H D Sohn, 'Confucius in Mexico: Korean MNCs and the Maquiladoras', *Business Horizons*, November–December 1998, pp 25–33.

[69] For complete details, see G Hofstede and M H Bond, 'The Confucius Connection: From Cultural Roots to Economic Growth', *Organizational Dynamics*, Spring 1988, pp 4–21.

[70] See P M Rosenzweig, 'When Can Management Science Research Be Generalized Internationally?' *Management Science*, January 1994, pp 28–39.

[71] A follow-up study is J P Johnson and T Lenartowicz, 'Culture, Freedom and Economic Growth: Do Cultural Values Explain Economic Growth?' *Journal of World Business*, Winter 1998, pp 332–56.

[72] Based on Trompenaars, *Riding the Waves of Culture* (London: Economist Books, 1994).

[73] S Brittan: 'Economic Viewpoint: the follies of the macho manager', *The Financial Times*, December 22, 1994, p 14.

[74] See C A Rodrigues, 'The Situation and National Culture as Contingencies for Leadership Behavior: Two Conceptual Models', in *Advances in International Comparative Management*, vol. 5, ed S B Prasad (Greenwich, CT: JAI Press, 1990), pp 51–68. For a study that found consistent perception of six leadership styles across four countries (Norway, United States, Sweden and Australia), see C B Gibson and G A Marcoulides, 'The Invariance of Leadership Styles across Four Countries', *Journal of Managerial Issues*, Summer 1995, pp 176–93.

[75] For details, see D H B Welsh, F Luthans and S M Sommer, 'Managing Russian Factory Workers: The Impact of US-Based Behavioral and Participative Techniques', *Academy of Management Journal*, February 1993, pp 58–79. Also see F Luthans, S J Peterson and E Ibrayeva, 'The Potential for the "Dark Side" of Leadership in Post-Communist Countries', *Journal of World Business*, Summer 1998, pp 185–201.

[76] P Kuchinke, 'Leadership and Culture: work related values and leadership styles among one company's U.S. and German telecommunication employees', *Human Resource Development Quarterly*, vol. 10 issue 2, 1999, pp 135–54.

[77] B Vlasic and B Stertz, 'Taken for a Ride: How Daimler-Benz Drove Off With Chrysler', 2000, William Morrow & Co.

[78] P Koopman, D Den Hertog, E Konrad *et al.*, 'National culture and leadership profiles in Europe: some results from the GLOBE study', *European Journal of Work and Organizational Psychology*, vol. 8 issue 4, 1999, pp 503–520.

[79] Anonymous, 'Foreign staff key to global future for BA', *People Management*, April 16, 1998, pp 21–22.

[80] Adapted and translated from G Bollen and B Debeuckelare, 'De euronomaden: Europese elite maakt carrière over de grenzen heen', *Vacature*, December 3, 1999.

[81] G Bollen and B Debeuckelare, op. cit.

[82] J S Black and H B Gregersen, 'The Right Way to Manage Expats', *Harvard Business Review*, March–April 1999, p 53. A more optimistic picture is presented in R L Tung, 'American Expatriates Abroad: From Neophytes to Cosmopolitans', *Journal of World Business*, Summer 1998, pp 125–44.

[83] Adapted from R L Tung, 'Expatriate Assignments: Enhancing Success and Minimizing Failure', *Academy of Management Executive*, May 1987, pp 117–26.

[84] S Dallas, 'Rule No. 1: Don't Diss the Locals', *Business Week*, May 15, 1995, p 8.

[85] Translated from S Jacobus, 'Femme Globale', *Management Team*, September 22, 1995, pp 111–14.

[86] Data from B Hagerty, 'Trainers Help Expatriate Employees Build Bridges to Different Cultures', *The Wall Street Journal*, June 14, 1993, pp B1, B3. Also see A Weiss, 'Global Doesn't Mean "Foreign" Anymore', *Training*, July 1998, pp 50–55; and G Dutton, 'Do You Think Globally?' *Management Review*, February 1999, p 6.

[87] C M Farkas and P De Backer, 'There Are Only Five Ways to Lead', *Fortune*, January 15, 1996, p 111. The shortage of global managers is discussed in L K Stroh and P M Caligiuri, 'Increasing Global Competitiveness through Effective People Management', *Journal of World Business*, Spring 1998, pp 1–16.

[88] An excellent reference book in this area is Black, Gregersen and Mendenhall, *Global Assignments: Successfully Expatriating and Repatriating International Managers*. Also see K Roberts, E E Kossek and C Ozeki, 'Managing the Global Workforce: Challenges and Strategies', *Academy of Management Executive*, November 1998, pp 93–106.

[89] Ibid., p 97.

[90] J S Lublin, 'Younger managers learn global skills', *The Wall Street Journal*, March 31, 1992, p B1.

[91] Adapted and translated from J Kroon, 'Leven in het land van de handkus', *NRC Handelsblad*, February 18, 1999.

[92] See Harris and Moran, *Managing Cultural Differences*, pp 223–28; M Shilling, 'Avoid Expatriate Culture Shock', *HRMagazine*, July 1993, pp 58–63; and D Stamps, 'Welcome to America: Watch Out for Culture Shock', *Training*, November 1996, pp 22–30.

[93] S Mackesy, 'I'm greedy therefore I am', *The Independent*, September 10, 2000.

[94] See H H Nguyen, L A Messe and G E Stollak, 'Toward a More Complex Understanding of Acculturation and Adjustment', *Journal of Cross-Cultural Psychology*, January 1999, pp 5–31.

[95] Adapted and transalated from M Haenen, 'Duimendraaien onder een palmboom', *NRC Handelsblad*, September 7, 1996, p 3.

[96] 'The fading charms of foreign fields', *Management Today*, August 1994, pp 49–51.

[97] See Black, Gregersen and Mendenhall, *Global Assignments: Successfully Expatriating and Repatriating International Managers*, p 227. Also see H B Gregersen, 'Commitments to a Parent Company and a Local Work Unit During Repatriation', *Personnel Psychology*, Spring 1992, pp 29–54; and H B Gregersen and J S Black, 'Multiple Commitments upon Repatriation: The Japanese Experience', *Journal of Management*, no. 2, 1996, pp 209–29.

[98] Ibid., pp 226–27.

[99] See J R Engen, 'Coming Home', *Training*, March 1995, pp 37–40; and L K Stroh, H B Gregersen and J S Black, 'Closing the Gap: Expectations versus Reality among Repatriates', *Journal of World Business*, Summer 1998, pp 111–24.

[100] This list of work goals is quoted from I Harpaz, 'The Importance of Work Goals: An International Perspective', *Journal of International Business Studies*, First Quarter 1990, p 79.

[101] Adapted from a seven-country summary in ibid., Table 2, p 81.

[102] See A Nimgade, 'American Management as Viewed by International Professionals', *Business Horizons*, November–December 1989, pp 98–105; R Calori and B Dufour, 'Management European Style', *Academy of Management Executive*, August 1995, pp 61–71; and W A Hubiak and S J O'Donnell, 'Do Americans Have Their Minds Set Against TQM?' *National Productivity Review*, Summer 1996, pp 19–32.

Chapter 5

[1] T Miller and A Furnham, 'Character assignation', *People Management*, April 2, 1998.

[2] D Seligman, 'The Trouble with Buyouts', *Fortune*, November 30, 1992, p 125.

[3] S I Cheldelin and L A Foritano, 'Psychometrics: Their Use in Organisation Development', *Journal of Managerial Psychology*, no. 4, 1989, p 21.

[4] See 'A Market Solution for Diversity?' *Training*, June 1998, p 14; R W Thompson, 'Diversity among Managers Translates into Profitability', *HRMagazine*, April 1999, p 10; J Crockett, 'DIVERSITY as a Business Strategy', *Management Review*, May 1999, p 62; and P Dass and B Parker, 'Strategies for Managing Human Resource Diversity: From Resistance to Learning', *Academy of Management Executive*, May 1999, pp 68–80.

[5] V Gecas, 'The Self-Concept', in *Annual Review of Sociology*, eds R H Turner and J F Short, Jr. (Palo Alto, CA: Annual Reviews Inc., 1982), vol. 8, p 3. Also see A P Brief and R J Aldag, 'The "Self" in Work Organizations: A Conceptual Review', *Academy of Management Review*, January 1981, pp 75–88; J J Sullivan, 'Self Theories and Employee Motivation', *Journal of Management*, June 1989, pp 345–63; P Cushman, 'Why the Self Is Empty', *American Psychologist*, May 1990, pp 599–611; and L Gaertner, C Sedikides and K Graetz, 'In Search of Self-Definition: Motivational Primacy of the Individual Self, Motivational Primacy of the Collective Self, or Contextual Primacy?' *Journal of Personality and Social Psychology*, January 1999, pp 5–18.

[6] C Williams, 'Tricks of the trade', *The Guardian*, October 18, 2000.

[7] L Festinger, *A Theory of Cognitive Dissonance* (Stanford, CA: Stanford University Press, 1957), p 3.

[8] See J Holt and D M Keats, 'Work Cognitions in Multicultural Interaction', *Journal of Cross-Cultural Psychology*, December 1992, pp 421–43.

[9] A Canadian versus Japanese comparison of self-concept can be found in J D Campbell, P D Trapnell, S J Heine, I M Katz, L F Lavallee and D R Lehman, 'Self-Concept Clarity: Measurement, Personality Correlates, and Cultural Boundaries', *Journal of Personality and Social Psychology*, January 1996, pp 141–56.

[10] See D C Barnlund, 'Public and Private Self in Communicating with Japan', *Business Horizons*, March–April 1989, pp 32–40; and the section on 'Doing Business with Japan' in P R Harris and R T Moran, *Managing Cultural Differences*, 4th ed (Houston: Gulf Publishing, 1996), pp 267–76.

[11] Based in part on a definition found in Gecas, 'The Self-Concept.' Also see N Branden, *Self-Esteem at Work: How Confident People Make Powerful Companies* (San Francisco: Jossey-Bass, 1998).

[12] H W Marsh, 'Positive and Negative Global Self-Esteem: A Substantively Meaningful Distinction or Artifacts?' *Journal of Personality and Social Psychology*, April 1996, p 819.

[13] Ibid.

[14] For related research, see R C Liden, L Martin and C K Parsons, 'Interviewer and Applicant Behaviors in Employment Interviews', *Academy of Management Journal*, April 1993, pp 372–86; M B Setterlund and P M Niedenthal, ' "Who Am I? Why Am I Here?": Self-Esteem, Self-Clarity, and Prototype Matching', *Journal of Personality and Social Psychology*, October 1993, pp 769–80; and G J Pool, W Wood and K Leck, 'The Self-Esteem Motive in Social Influence: Agreement with Valued Majorities and Disagreement with Derogated Minorities', *Journal of Personality and Social Psychology*, October 1998, pp 967–75.

[15] See S J Rowley, R M Sellers, T M Chavous and M A Smith, 'The Relationship between Racial Identity and Self-Esteem in African American College and High School Students', *Journal of Personality and Social Psychology*, March 1998, pp 715–24.

[16] See J A Stein, M D Newcomb and P M Bentler, 'The Relative Influence on Vocational Behavior and Family Involvement on Self-Esteem: Longitudinal Analyses of Young Adult Women and Men', *Journal of Vocational Behavior*, June 1990, pp 320–38.

[17] Based on P G Dodgson and J V Wood, 'Self-Esteem and the Cognitive Accessibility of Strengths and Weaknesses after Failure', *Journal of Personality and Social Psychology*, July 1998, pp 178–97.

[18] Details may be found in B R Schlenker, M F Weigold and J R Hallam, 'Self-Serving Attributions in Social Context: Effects of Self-Esteem and Social Pressure', *Journal of Personality and Social Psychology*, May 1990, pp 855–63.

[19] See R F Baumeister, L Smart and J M Boden, 'Relation of Threatened Egotism to Violence and Aggression: The Dark Side of High Self-Esteem', *Psychological Review*, January 1996, pp 5–33; and D Seligman, 'Down with Esteem', *Fortune*, April 29, 1996, pp 211–14.

[20] For related reading, see M Kaeter, 'False Identities', *Business Ethics*, March–April 1994, p 46.

[21] T Apter, 'Confidence Tricks', *The Guardian*, September 27, 2000.

[22] E Diener and M Diener, 'Cross-Cultural Correlates of Life Satisfaction and Self-Esteem', *Journal of Personality and Social Psychology*, April 1995, p 662. For cross-cultural evidence of a similar psychological process for self-esteem, see T M Singelis, M H Bond, W F Sharkey and C S Y Lai, 'Unpackaging Culture's Influence on Self-Esteem and Embarrassability', *Journal of Cross-Cultural Psychology*, May 1999, pp 315–41.

[23] W J McGuire and C V McGuire, 'Enhancing Self-Esteem by Directed-Thinking Tasks: Cognitive and Affective Positivity Asymmetries', *Journal of Personality and Social Psychology*, June 1996, p 1124.

[24] J L Pierce, D G Gardner, L L Cummings and R B Dunham, 'Organization-Based Self-Esteem: Construct Definition, Measurement, and Validation', *Academy of Management Journal*, September 1989, p 625. Also see J L Pierce, D G Gardner, R B Dunham and L L Cummings, 'Moderation by Organization-Based Self-Esteem of Role Condition-Employee Response Relationships', *Academy of Management Journal*, April 1993, pp 271–88.

[25] Practical steps are discussed in M Kaeter, 'Basic Self-Esteem', *Training*, August 1993, pp 31–35. Also see G Koretz, 'The Vital Role of Self-Esteem', *Business Week*, February 2, 1998, p 26; and T A Judge, E A Locke, C C Durham and A N Kluger, 'Dispositional Effects on Job and Life Satisfaction: The Role of Core Evaluations', *Journal of Applied Psychology*, February 1998, pp 17–34.

[26] Adapted from discussion in J K Matejka and R J Dunsing, 'Great Expectations', *Management World*, January 1987, pp 16–17. Also see P Pascarella, 'It All Begins with Self-Esteem', *Management Review*, February 1999, pp 60–61.

[27] M E Gist, 'Self-Efficacy: Implications for Organizational Behavior and Human Resource Management', *Academy of Management Review*, July 1987, p 472. Also see A Bandura, 'Self-Efficacy: Toward a Unifying Theory of Behavioral Change', *Psychological Review*, March 1977, pp 191–215; and M E Gist and T R Mitchell, 'Self-Efficacy: A Theoretical Analysis of Its Determinants and Malleability', *Academy of Management Review*, April 1992, pp 183–211.

[28] A Davidson, 'The Andrew Davidson interview: James Dyson', *Management Today*, July 1999.

[29] K Sengupta, 'With two metal claws and a will to live, a father learns to sign his name with pride', *The Independent*, June 1, 2000.

[30] Based on D H Lindsley, D A Brass and J B Thomas, 'Efficacy-Performance Spirals: A Multilevel Perspective', *Academy of Management Review*, July 1995, pp 645–78.

[31] See, for example, V Gecas, 'The Social Psychology of Self-Efficacy', in *Annual Review of Sociology*, eds W R Scott and J Blake (Palo Alto, CA: Annual Reviews, Inc., 1989), vol. 15, pp 291–316; C K Stevens, A G Bavetta and M E Gist, 'Gender Differences in the Acquisition of Salary Negotiation Skills: The Role of Goals, Self-Efficacy, and Perceived Control', *Journal of Applied Psychology*, October 1993, pp 723–35; and D Eden and Y Zuk, 'Seasickness as a Self-Fulfilling Prophecy: Raising Self-Efficacy to Boost Performance at Sea', *Journal of Applied Psychology*, October 1995, pp 628–35.

[32] For more on learned helplessness, see Gecas, 'The Social Psychology of Self-Efficacy'; M J Martinko and W L Gardner, 'Learned Helplessness: An Alternative Explanation for Performance Deficits', *Academy of Management Review*, April 1982, pp 195–204; and C R Campbell and M J Martinko, 'An Integrative Attributional Perspective of Empowerment and Learned Helplessness: A Multimethod Field Study', *Journal of*

Management, no. 2, 1998, pp 173–200.

[33] Research on this connection is reported in R B Rubin, M M Martin, S S Bruning and D E Powers, 'Test of a Self-Efficacy Model of Interpersonal Communication Competence', *Communication Quarterly*, Spring 1993, pp 210–20.

[34] Excerpted from T Petzinger Jr, 'Bob Schmonsees Has a Tool for Better Sales, and It Ignores Excuses', *The Wall Street Journal*, March 26, 1999, p B1.

[35] Data from A D Stajkovic and F Luthans, 'Self-Efficacy and Work-Related Performance: A Meta-Analysis', *Psychological Bulletin*, September 1998, pp 240–61.

[36] Based in part on discussion in Gecas, 'The Social Psychology of Self-Efficacy.'

[37] See S K Parker, 'Enhancing Role Breadth Self-Efficacy: The Roles of Job Enrichment and Other Organizational Interventions', *Journal of Applied Psychology*, December 1998, pp 835–52.

[38] The positive relationship between self-efficacy and readiness for retraining is documented in L A Hill and J Elias, 'Retraining Midcareer Managers: Career History and Self-Efficacy Beliefs', *Human Resource Management*, Summer 1990, pp 197–217. Also see A M Saks, 'Longitudinal Field Investigation of the Moderating and Mediating Effects of Self-Efficacy on the Relationship between Training and Newcomer Adjustment', *Journal of Applied Psychology*, April 1995, pp 211–25.

[39] See A D Stajkovic and Fred Luthans, 'Social Cognitive Theory and Self-Efficacy: Going Beyond Traditional Motivational and Behavioral Approaches', *Organizational Dynamics*, Spring 1998, pp 62–74.

[40] See P C Earley and T R Lituchy, 'Delineating Goal and Efficacy Effects: A Test of Three Models', *Journal of Applied Psychology*, February 1991, pp 81–98.

[41] See W S Silver, T R Mitchell and M E Gist, 'Response to Successful and Unsuccessful Performance: The Moderating Effect of Self-Efficacy on the Relationship between Performance and Attributions', *Organizational Behavior and Human Decision Processes*, June 1995, pp 286–99; R Zemke, 'The Corporate Coach', *Training*, December 1996, pp 24–28; and J P Masciarelli, 'Less Lonely at the Top', *Management Review*, April 1999, pp 58–61.

[42] M Snyder and S Gangestad, 'On the Nature of Self-Monitoring: Matters of Assessment, Matters of Validity', *Journal of Personality and Social Psychology*, July 1986, p 125.

[43] Data from M Kilduff and D V Day, 'Do Chameleons Get Ahead? The Effects of Self-Monitoring on Managerial Careers', *Academy of Management Journal*, August 1994, pp 1047–60.

[44] Data from D B Turban and T W Dougherty, 'Role of Protege Personality in Receipt of Mentoring and Career Success', *Academy of Management Journal*, June 1994, pp 688–702.

[45] See F Luthans, 'Successful vs. Effective Managers', *Academy of Management Executive*, May 1988, pp 127–32.

[46] For related research evidence on self-silencing, see L V Gratch, M E Bassett and S L Attra, 'The Relationship of Gender and Ethnicity to Self-Silencing and Depression among College Students', *Psychology of Women Quarterly*, December 1995, pp 509–15. Also see W G Graziano and W H M Bryant, 'Self-Monitoring and the Self-Attribution of Positive Emotions', *Journal of Personality and Social Psychology*, January 1998, pp 250–61.

[47] M G Pratt, 'To Be or Not to Be? Central Questions in Organizational Identification', in *Identity in Organizations*, eds D A Whetten and P C Godfrey (Thousand Oaks, CA: Sage Publications, 1998), p 172. Also see S Albert, B E Ashforth and J E Dutton, 'Organizational Identity and Identification: Charting New Waters and Building New Bridges', *Academy of Management Review*, January 2000, pp 13–17.

[48] C Jones, 'Richard Desmond: express route to respectability', *BBC News*, November 25, 2000.

[49] See G Dessler, 'How to Earn Your Employees' Commitment', *Academy of Management Executive*, May 1999, pp 58–67.

[50] For more, see B Filipczak, 'The Soul of the Hog', *Training*, February 1996, pp 38–42.

[51] For evidence of the stability of adult personality dimensions, see R R McCrae, 'Moderated Analyses of Longitudinal Personality Stability', *Journal of Personality and Social Psychology*, September 1993, pp 577–85. Adult personality changes are documented in L Kaufman Cartwright and P Wink, 'Personality Change in Women Physicians from Medical Student to Mid-40s', *Psychology of Women Quarterly*, June 1994, pp 291–308. Also see L Pulkkinen, M Ohranen and A Tolvanen, 'Personality Antecedents of Career Orientation and Stability among Women Compared to Men', *Journal of Vocational Behavior*, February 1999, pp 37–58.

[52] The landmark report is J M Digman, 'Personality Structure: Emergence of the Five-Factor Model', *Annual Review of Psychology*, vol. 41, 1990, pp 417–40. Also see M R Barrick and M K Mount, 'Autonomy as a Moderator of the Relationships between the Big Five Personality Dimensions and Job Performance', *Journal of Applied Psychology*, February 1993, pp 111–18; J A Johnson and F Ostendorf, 'Clarification of the Five-Factor Model with the Abridged Big Five Dimensional Circumplex', *Journal of Personality and Social Psychology*, September 1993, pp 563–76; and M Zuckerman, D M Kuhlman, J Joireman, P Teta and M Kraft, 'A Comparison of Three Structural Models for Personality: The Big Three, the Big Five, and the Alternative Five', *Journal of Personality and Social Psychology*, October 1993, pp 757–68.

[53] For a review of research on the relationship between introversion–extroversion, motivation and performance, see M S Humphreys and W Revelle, 'Personality, Motivation and Performance: A Theory of the Relationship between Individual Differences and Information Processing', *Psychological Review*, April 1984, pp 153–84. Also see D F Caldwell and J M Burger, 'Personality Characteristics of Job Applicants and Success in Screening Interviews', *Personnel Psychology*, Spring 1998, pp 119–36; J B Asendorpf and S Wilpers, 'Personality Effects on Social Relationships', *Journal of Personality and Social Psychology*, June 1998, pp 1531–44; K M DeNeve and H Cooper, 'The Happy Personality: A Meta-Analysis of 137 Personality Traits and Subjective Well-Being', *Psychological Bulletin*, September 1998, pp 197–229; and D P Skarlicki, R Folger and P Tesluk, 'Personality as a Moderator in the Relationship between Fairness and Retaliation', *Academy of Management Journal*, February 1999, pp 100–108.

[54] Data from S V Paunonen *et al.*, 'The Structure of Personality in Six Cultures', *Journal of Cross-Cultural Psychology*, May 1996, pp 339–53. Also see M S Katigbak, A T Church and T X Akamine, 'Cross-Cultural Generalizability of Personality Dimensions: Relating Indigenous and Imported Dimensions in Two Cultures', *Journal of Personality and Social Psychology*, January 1996, pp 99–114; V Benet-Martinez and O P John, '*Los Cinco Grandes* Across Cultures and Ethnic Groups: Multitrait Multimethod Analyses of the Big Five in Spanish and English', *Journal of Personality and Social Psychology*, September 1998, pp 729–750; and G Saucier and F Ostendorf, 'Hierarchical Subcomponents of the Big Five Personality Factors: A Cross-Language Replication', *Journal of Personality and Social Psychology*, April 1999, pp 613–27.

[55] See M R Barrick and M K Mount, 'The Big Five Personality Dimensions and Job Performance: A Meta-Analysis', *Personnel Psychology*, Spring 1991, pp 1–26. Also see R P Tett, D N Jackson and M Rothstein, 'Personality Measures as Predictors of Job Performance: A Meta-Analytic Review', *Personnel Psychology*, Winter 1991, pp 703–42.

[56] Barrick and Mount, 'The Big Five Personality Dimensions and Job Performance: A Meta-Analysis', p 18. See O Behling, 'Employee Selection: Will Intelligence and Conscientiousness Do the Job?' *Academy of Management Executive*, February 1998, pp 77–86.

[57] See S B Gustafson and M D Mumford, 'Personal Style and Person-Environment Fit: A Pattern Approach', *Journal of Vocational Behavior*, April 1995, pp 163–88.

[58] See discussion in Barrick and Mount, 'The Big Five Personality Dimensions and Job Performance: A Meta-Analysis', pp 21–22. Also see J M Cortina, M L Doherty, N Schmitt, G Kaufman and R G Smith, 'The "Big Five" Personality Factors in the IPI and MMPI: Predictors of Police Performance', *Personnel Psychology*, Spring 1992, pp 119–40; M J Schmit and A

M Ryan, 'The Big Five' in Personnel Selection: Factor Structure in Applicant and Nonapplicant Populations', *Journal of Applied Psychology*, December 1993, pp 966–74; and C Caggiano, 'Psychopath', *Inc.*, July 1998, pp 77–85.

59 M K Mount and M R Barrick, 'The Big Five Personality Dimensions: Implications for Research and Practice in Human Resources Management', in *Research in Personnel and Human Resources Management*, ed G R Ferris (Greenwich, CT: JAI Press, 1995), vol. 13, p 189. See J M Collins and D H Gleaves, 'Race, Job Applicants, and the Five-Factor Model of Personality: Implications for Black Psychology, Industrial/Organizational Psychology, and the Five-Factor Theory', *Journal of Applied Psychology*, August 1998, pp 531–44.

60 Other sources relating to Table 5–2 are 'Testing ... Testing', *Training*, September 1998, p 14; and B Leonard, 'Reading Employees', *HRMagazine*, April 1999, pp 67–73.

61 See C M Solomon, 'Testing at Odds with Diversity Efforts?' *Personnel Journal*, April 1996, pp 131–40; and J C McCune, 'Testing, Testing 1-2-3', *Management Review*, January 1996, pp 50–52.

62 For example, see J C Connor, 'The Paranoid Personality at Work', *HRMagazine*, March 1999, pp 120–26; and 'Your Sleep Has a Personality', *Management Review*, May 1999, p 9.

63 For an instructive update, see J B Rotter, 'Internal versus External Control of Reinforcement: A Case History of a Variable', *American Psychologist*, April 1990, pp 489–93. A critical review of locus of control and a call for a meta-analysis can be found in R W Renn and R J Vandenberg, 'Differences in Employee Attitudes and Behaviors Based on Rotter's (1966) Internal-External Locus of Control: Are They All Valid?' *Human Relations*, November 1991, p 1161–77.

64 J Fierman, 'What's Luck Got to Do with It?' *Fortune*, October 16, 1995, p 149.

65 For an overall review of research on locus of control, see P E Spector, 'Behavior in Organizations as a Function of Employee's Locus of Control', *Psychological Bulletin*, May 1982, pp 482–97; the relationship between locus of control and performance and satisfaction is examined in D R Norris and R E Niebuhr, 'Attributional Influences on the Job Performance–Job Satisfaction Relationship', *Academy of Management Journal*, June 1984, pp 424–31; salary differences between internals and externals were examined by P C Nystrom, "Managers' Salaries and Their Beliefs about Reinforcement Control", *The Journal of Social Psychology*, August 1983, pp 291–92.

66 See S R Hawk, 'Locus of Control and Computer Attitude: The Effect of User Involvement', *Computers in Human Behavior*, no. 3, 1989, pp 199–206. Also see A S Phillips and A G Bedeian, 'Leader-Follower Exchange Quality: The Role of Personal and Interpersonal Attributes', *Academy of Management Journal*, August 1994, pp 990–1001.

67 These recommendations are from Spector, 'Behavior in Organizations as a Function of Employee's Locus of Control.'

68 Adapted and translated from H Peverelli, 'De psychologie van het e-mailen', *Psychologie Magazine*, October 2000 and Anonymous, 'E-mailgedrag Nederlanders', http://www.marketresponse.nl/email/dutch.htm

69 See 'What Men Think About', *Training*, March 1995, p 14; and P Cappelli, 'Is the "Skills Gap" Really about Attitudes?' *California Management Review*, Summer 1995, pp 108–24.

70 M Fishbein and I Ajzen, *Belief, Attitude, Intention and Behavior: An Introduction to Theory and Research* (Reading, MA: Addison-Wesley Publishing, 1975), p 6. For more, see D Andrich and I M Styles, 'The Structural Relationship between Attitude and Behavior Statements from the Unfolding Perspective', *Psychological Methods*, December 1998, pp 454–69; A P Brief, *Attitudes In and Around Organizations* (Thousand Oaks, CA: Sage Publications, 1998); and 'Tips to Pick the Best Employee', *Business Week*, March 1, 1999, p 24.

71 For a discussion of the difference between values and attitudes, see B W Becker and P E Connor, 'Changing American Values—Debunking the Myth', *Business*, January–March 1985, pp 56–59.

72 See B M Staw and J Ross, 'Stability in the Midst of Change:

A Dispositional Approach to Job Attitudes', *Journal of Applied Psychology*, August 1985, pp 469–80. Also see J Schaubroeck, D C Ganster and B Kemmerer, 'Does Trait Affect Promote Job Attitude Stability?' *Journal of Organizational Behavior*, March 1996, pp 191–96.

73 Data from P S Visser and J A Krosnick, 'Development of Attitude Strength Over the Life Cycle: Surge and Decline', *Journal of Personality and Social Psychology*, December 1998, pp 1389–1410.

74 For a brief overview and update of the model, see M Fishbein and M Stasson, 'The Role of Desires, Self-Predictions, and Perceived Control in the Prediction of Training Session Attendance', *Journal of Applied Social Psychology*, February 1990, pp 173–98. Alternative models are discussed in M Sverke and S Kuruvilla, 'A New Conceptualization of Union Commitment: Development and Test of an Integrated Theory', *Journal of Organizational Behavior*, Special Issue, 1995, pp 505–32; and R C Thompson and J G Hunt, 'Inside the Black Box of Alpha, Beta and Gamma Change: Using a Cognitive-Processing Model to Assess Attitude Structure', *Academy of Management Review*, July 1996, pp 655–90.

75 See R P Steel and N K Ovalle II, 'A Review and Meta-Analysis of Research on the Relationship between Behavioral Intentions and Employee Turnover', *Journal of Applied Psychology*, November 1984, pp 673–86. Also see J A Ouellette and W Wood, 'Habit and Intention in Everyday Life: The Multiple Processes by Which Past Behavior Predicts Future Behavior', *Psychological Bulletin*, July 1998, pp 54–74; and 'Worker Retention Presents Challenge to US Employers', *HRMagazine*, September 1998, p 22.

76 I Ajzen and M Fishbein, *Understanding Attitudes and Predicting Social Behavior* (Englewood Cliffs, NJ: Prentice-Hall, 1980), p 7. Also see J Barling, K E Dupre, and C G Hepburn, 'Effects of Parents' Job Insecurity on Children's Work Beliefs and Attitudes', *Journal of Applied Psychology*, February 1998, pp 112–18; and J W Dean, Jr, P Brandes and R Dharwadkar, 'Organizational Cynicism', *Academy of Management Review*, April 1998, pp 341–52.

77 Drawn from J M Grant and T S Bateman, 'An Experimental Test of the Impact of Drug-Testing Programs on Potential Job Applicants' Attitudes and Intentions', *Journal of Applied Psychology*, April 1990, pp 127–31.

78 For an overall review of attitude formation research, see Ajzen and Fishbein, *Understanding Attitudes and Predicting Social Behavior*. Also see S Chaiken and C Stangor, 'Attitudes and Attitude Change', in *Annual Review of Psychology*, eds M R Rosenzweig and L W Porter (Palo Alto, CA: Annual Reviews, 1987), pp 575–630; and Fishbein and Stasson, 'The Role of Desires, Self-Predictions, and Perceived Control in the Prediction of Training Session Attendance.'

79 See P W Hom and C L Hulin, 'A Competitive Test of the Prediction of Reenlistment by Several Models', *Journal of Applied Psychology*, February 1981, pp 23–39. Also see P R Warshaw, R Calantone and M Joyce, 'A Field Study Application of the Fishbein and Ajzen Intention Model', *The Journal of Social Psychology*, February 1986, pp 135–365.

80 Based on evidence in C J Thomsen, A M Basu and M Tippens Reinitz, 'Effects of Women's Studies Courses on Gender-Related Attitudes of Women and Men', *Psychology of Women Quarterly*, September 1995, pp 419–26.

81 For interesting reading on intelligence, see E Cose, 'Teaching Kids to Be Smart', *Newsweek*, August 21, 1995, pp 58–60; A Farnham, 'Are You Smart Enough to Keep Your Job?' *Fortune*, January 15, 1996, pp 34–48; D Stamps, 'Are We Smart Enough for Our Jobs?' *Training*, April 1996, pp 44–50; K S Peterson, 'Do New Definitions of Smart Dilute Meaning?' *USA Today*, February 18, 1997, pp 1D–2D; and J R Flynn, 'Searching for Justice: The Discovery of IQ Gains Over Time', *American Psychologist*, January 1999, pp 5–20.

82 For an excellent update on intelligence, including definitional distinctions and a historical perspective of the IQ controversy, see R A Weinberg, 'Intelligence and IQ', *American Psychologist*, February 1989, pp 98–104.

83 Ibid.

[84] S L Wilk, L Burris Desmarais and P R Sackett, 'Gravitation to Jobs Commensurate with Ability: Longitudinal and Cross-Sectional Tests', *Journal of Applied Psychology*, February 1995, p 79.

[85] B Azar, 'People Are Becoming Smarter—Why?' *APA Monitor*, June 1996, p 20. Also see '"Average" Intelligence Higher than It Used to Be', *USA Today*, February 18, 1997, p 6D.

[86] For related research, see M J Ree and J A Earles, 'Predicting Training Success: Not Much More Than g', *Personnel Psychology*, Summer 1991, pp 321–32.

[87] See F L Schmidt and J E Hunter, 'Employment Testing: Old Theories and New Research Findings', *American Psychologist*, October 1981, p 1128. Also see Y Ganzach, 'Intelligence and Job Satisfaction', *Academy of Management Journal*, October 1998, pp 526–39.

[88] R Cooper, 'Sentimental Value', *People Management*, April 2, 1998.

[89] D Goleman, *Emotional Intelligence* (New York: Bantam Books, 1995), p 34. For more, see Q N Huy, 'Emotional Capability, Emotional Intelligence, and Radical Change', *Academy of Management Review*, April 1999, pp 325–45.

[90] M N Martinez, 'The Smarts That Count', *HRMagazine*, November 1997, pp 72–78.

[91] 'What's Your EQ at Work?' *Fortune*, October 26, 1998, p 298.

[92] Based on M Davies, L Stankov and R D Roberts, 'Emotional Intelligence: In Search of an Elusive Construct', *Journal of Personality and Social Psychology*, October 1998, pp 989–1015.

[93] A Fisher, 'Success Secret: A High Emotional IQ', *Fortune*, October 26, 1998, p 294.

[94] See I Briggs Myers (with P B Myers), *Gifts Differing* (Palo Alto, CA: Consulting Psychologists Press, 1980). Mentions of the MBTI can be found in B O'Reilly, 'Does Your Fund Manager Play the Piano?' *Fortune*, December 29, 1997, pp 139–44; T A Stewart, 'Escape from the Cult of Personality Tests', *Fortune*, March 16, 1998, p 80; J T Adams III, 'What's Your Type?' *HRMagazine*, June 1999, p 8; and T Petzinger Jr, 'With the Stakes High, a Lucent Duo Conquers Distance and Culture', *The Wall Street Journal*, April 23, 1999, p B1.

[95] For a complete discussion of each cognitive style, see J W Slocum, Jr, and D Hellriegel, 'A Look at How Managers' Minds Work', *Business Horizons*, July–August 1983, pp 58–68; and W Taggart and D Robey, 'Minds and Managers: On the Dual Nature of Human Information Processing and Management', *Academy of Management Review*, April 1981, pp 187–95. Also see M Wood Daudelin, 'Learning from Experience through Reflection', *Organizational Dynamics*, Winter 1996, pp 36–48.

[96] See B K Blaylock and L P Rees, 'Cognitive Style and the Usefulness of Information', *Decision Sciences*, Winter 1984, pp 74–91.

[97] Additional material on cognitive styles may be found in F A Gul, 'The Joint and Moderating Role of Personality and Cognitive Style on Decision Making', *The Accounting Review*, April 1984, pp 264–77; B H Kleiner, 'The Interrelationship of Jungian Modes of Mental Functioning with Organizational Factors: Implications for Management Development', *Human Relations*, November 1983, pp 997–1012; and J L McKenney and P G W Keen, 'How Managers' Minds Work', *Harvard Business Review*, May–June 1974, pp 79–90.

[98] See G H Rice, Jr, and D P Lindecamp, 'Personality Types and Business Success of Small Retailers', *Journal of Occupational Psychology*, June 1989, pp 177–82.

[99] W L Gardner and M J Martinko, 'Using the Myers-Briggs Type Indicator to Study Managers: A Literature Review and Research Agenda', *Journal of Management*, no. 1, 1996, p 77.

[100] For example, see F Ramsoomair, 'Relating Theoretical Concepts to Life in the Classroom: Applying the Myers-Briggs Type Indicator', *Journal of Management Education*, February 1994, pp 111–16. For related material, see S Shapiro and M T Spence, 'Managerial Intuition: A Conceptual and Operational Framework', *Business Horizons*, January–February 1997, pp 63–68.

[101] R Powell, 'Put bullies on the spot – intimidation in the workplace can no longer be tolerated, writes Rick Powell', *Scotland on Sunday*, November 12, 1995.

[102] R S Lazarus, *Emotion and Adaptation* (New York: Oxford University Press, 1991), p 6. Also see, Goleman, *Emotional Intelligence*, pp 289–90; and J A Russell and L F Barrett, 'Core Affect, Prototypical Emotional Episodes, and Other Things Called *Emotion*: Dissecting the Elephant', *Journal of Personality and Social Psychology*, May 1999, pp 805–19.

[103] Based on discussion in R D Arvey, G L Renz and T W Watson, 'Emotionality and Job Performance: Implications for Personnel Selection', in *Research in Personnel and Human Resources Management*, vol. 16, ed G R Ferris (Stamford, CT: JAI Press, 1998), pp 103–47. Also see L A King, 'Ambivalence Over Emotional Expression and Reading Emotions', *Journal of Personality and Social Psychology*, March 1998, pp 753–62.

[104] Based on J M Kidd, 'Emotion: An Absent Presence in Career Theory', *Journal of Vocational Behavior*, June 1998, pp 275–88.

[105] Drawn from P Totterdell, S Kellett, K Teuchmann and R B Briner, 'Evidence of Mood Linkage in Work Groups', *Journal of Personality and Social Psychology*, June 1998, pp 1504–15.

[106] E Davies, 'How violence at work can hit employers hard', *People Management*, September 12, 1996.

[107] The questionnaire and scoring key are excerpted from J W Slocum and D Hellriegel, 'A look at how managers minds work', *Business Horizons*, July-August 1983, pp 58–68.

Chapter 6

[1] B Summerskill, 'Big Brother? No, it's just another day at the office', *The Guardian*, August 13, 2000. Reproduced with permission.

[2] Details may be found in R Eisenberger, P Fasolo and V Davis-LaMastro, 'Perceived Organizational Support and Employee Diligence, Commitment, and Innovation', *Journal of Applied Psychology*, February 1990, pp 51–59.

[3] Adapted and translated from anonymous, 'Perceptie', see http://www.multiplus.nl/comm.htm .

[4] M McMahon, 'Cool Chemists', *The Times*, September 14, 2000.

[5] S T Fiske and S E Taylor, *Social Cognition*, 2nd ed (Reading, MA: Addison-Wesley Publishing, 1991), pp 1–2.

[6] Adapted from discussion in Fiske and Taylor, *Social Cognition*, 2nd ed, pp 247–50.

[7] The negativity bias was examined and supported by O Ybarra and W G Stephan, 'Misanthropic Person Memory', *Journal of Personality and Social Psychology*, April 1996, pp 691–700; and Y Ganzach, 'Negativity (and Positivity) in Performance Evaluation: Three Field Studies', *Journal of Applied Psychology*, August 1995, pp 491–99.

[8] E Rosch, C B Mervis, W D Gray, D M Johnson and P Boyes-Braem, 'Basic Objects in Natural Categories', *Cognitive Psychology*, July 1976, p 383.

[9] Washing clothes.

[10] See B R Ragins, B Townsend and M Mattis, 'Gender Gap in the Executive Suite: CEOs and Female Executives Report on Breaking the Glass Ceiling', *The Academy of Management Executive*, February 1998, pp 28–42; and P A Giuffre and C L Williams, 'Boundary Lines: Labeling Sexual Harassment in Restaurants', *Gender and Society*, September 1994, pp 378–401.

[11] See J P Forgas, 'On Being Happy and Mistaken: Mood Effects on the Fundamental Attribution Error', *Journal of Personality and Social Psychology*, August 1998, 318–31; and A Varma, A S DeNisi and L H Peters, 'Interpersonal Affect and Performance Appraisal: A Field Study', *Personnel Psychology*, Summer 1996, pp 341–60.

[12] See I Ajzen and J Sexton, 'Depth of Processing, Belief Congruence, and Attitude-Behavior Correspondence', in *Dual-Process Theories in Social Psychology*, eds S Chaiken and Y Trope (New York: The Guilford Press, 1999), pp 117–38; and A J Kinicki, P W Hom, M R Trost and K J Wade, 'Effects of Category Prototypes on Performance-Rating Accuracy', *Journal of Applied Psychology*, June 1995, pp 354–70.

[13] The relationship between depression and information processing is discussed by A Zelli and K A Dodge, 'Personality Development from the Bottom Up', in *The Coherence of Personality*, eds D Cervone and Y Shoda (New York: The Guilford Press, 1999), pp 94–126.

[14] For a thorough discussion about the structure and organization of memory, see L R Squire, B Knowlton and G Musen, 'The Structure and Organization of Memory', in *Annual Review of Psychology*, eds L W Porter and M R Rosenzweig (Palo Alto, CA: Annual Reviews Inc., 1993), vol. 44, pp 453–95.

[15] A thorough discussion of the reasoning process used to make judgements and decisions is provided by S A Sloman, 'The Empirical Case for Two Systems of Reasoning', *Psychological Bulletin*, January 1996, pp 3–22.

[16] Results can be found in C M Marlowe, S L Schneider and C E Nelson, 'Gender and Attractiveness Biases in Hiring Decisions: Are More Experienced Managers Less Biased?' *Journal of Applied Psychology*, February 1996, pp 11–21.

[17] Details of this study can be found in C K Stevens, 'Antecedents of Interview Interactions, Interviewers' Ratings, and Applicants' Reactions', *Personnel Psychology*, Spring 1998, pp 55–85.

[18] Adapted and translated from M Buelens, F Debussche and K Vanderheyden, *Mensen en Verscheidenheid* (Brussels: Vacature, 1997).

[19] See R C Mayer and J H Davis, 'The Effect of the Performance Appraisal System on Trust for Management: A Field Quasi-Experiment', *Journal of Applied Psychology*, February 1999, pp 123–36.

[20] Results can be found in W H Bommer, J L Johnson, G A Rich, P M Podsakoff and S B Mackenzie, 'On the Interchangeability of Objective and Subjective Measures of Employee Performance: A Meta-Analysis', *Personnel Psychology*, Autumn 1995, pp 587–605.

[21] See J I Sanchez and P D L Torre, 'A Second Look at the Relationship between Rating and Behavioral Accuracy in Performance Appraisal', *Journal of Applied Psychology*, February 1996, pp 3–10; and Kinicki, Hom, Trost and Wade, 'Effects of Category Prototypes on Performance-Rating Accuracy.'

[22] The effectiveness of rater training was supported by D V Day and L M Sulsky, 'Effects of Frame-of-Reference Training and Information Configuration on Memory Organization and Rating Accuracy', *Journal of Applied Psychology*, February 1995, pp 158–67.

[23] Results can be found in J S Phillips and R G Lord, 'Schematic Information Processing and Perceptions of Leadership in Problem-Solving Groups', *Journal of Applied Psychology*, August 1982, pp 486–92.

[24] C Leerhsen, 'How Disney Does It', *Newsweek*, April 3, 1989, p 52.

[25] C M Judd and B Park, 'Definition and Assessment of Accuracy in Social Stereotypes', *Psychological Review*, January 1993, p 110.

[26] J Brand, 'You can always spot a wife beater by the charm offensive', *The Independent*, July 2, 2000.

[27] M Ward, 'Net users are not nerds', *BBC News*, May 11, 2000.

[28] For a thorough discussion of stereotype accuracy, see M C Ashton and V M Esses, 'Stereotype Accuracy: Estimating the Academic Performance of Ethnic Groups', *Personality and Social Psychology Bulletin*, February 1999, pp 225–36.

[29] See C Comeau-Kirschner, 'Navigating the Roadblocks', *Management Review*, May 1999, p 8; and S Shellenbarger, 'Work-Force Study Finds Loyalty Is Weak, Division of Race and Gender Are Deep', *The Wall Street Journal*, September 3, 1993, pp B1, B9.

[30] The process of stereotype formation and maintenance is discussed by S T Fiske, M Lin and S L Neuberg, 'The Continuum Model: Ten Years Later', in *Dual-Process Theories in Social Psychology*, eds S Chaiken and Y Trope (New York: The Guilford Press, 1999) pp 231–54.

[31] This discussion is based on material presented in G V Bodenhausen, C N Macrae and J W Sherman, 'On the Dialectics of Discrimination', in *Dual-Process Theories in Social Psychology*, eds S Chaiken and Y Trope (New York: The Guilford Press, 1999) pp 271–90.

[32] See A H Eagly, S J Karu and B T Johnson, 'Gender and Leadership Style among School Principals: A Meta-Analysis', *Educational Administration Quarterly*, February 1992, pp 76–102; and I K Broverman, S Raymond Vogel,

D M Broverman, F E Clarkson and P S Rosenkrantz, 'Sex-Role Stereotypes: A Current Appraisal', *Journal of Social Issues*, 1972, p 75.

[33] See B P Allen, 'Gender Stereotypes Are Not Accurate: A Replication of Martin (1987) Using Diagnostic vs. Self-Report and Behavioral Criteria', *Sex Roles*, May 1995, pp 583–600.

[34] Results can be found in V E Schein, R Mueller, T Lituchy and J Liu, 'Think Manager—Think Male: A Global Phenomenon?' *Journal of Organizational Behavior*, January 1996, pp 33–41.

[35] S Bosseley, 'Gentlemen prefer blonde stereotypes', *The Guardian*, April 10, 1999.

[36] See J D Olian, D P Schwab and Y Haberfeld, 'The Impact of Applicant Gender Compared to Qualifications on Hiring Recommendations: A Meta-Analysis of Experimental Studies', *Organizational Behavior and Human Decision Processes*, April 1988, pp 180–95.

[37] Results from the meta-analyses are discussed in K P Carson, C L Sutton and P D Corner, 'Gender Bias in Performance Appraisals: A Meta-Analysis', paper presented at the 49th Annual Academy of Management Meeting, Washington, DC: 1989. Results from the field study can be found in T J Maurer and M A Taylor, 'Is Sex by Itself Enough? An Exploration of Gender Bias Issues in Performance Appraisal', *Organizational Behavior and Human Decision Processes*, November 1994, pp 231–51.

[38] See J Landau, 'The Relationship of Race and Gender to Managers' Ratings of Promotion Potential', *Journal of Organizational Behavior*, July 1995, pp 391–400.

[39] Results from this study can be found in M Biernat, C S Crandall, L V Young, D Kobrynowicz and S M Halpin, 'All That You Can Be: Stereotyping of Self and Others in a Military Context', *Journal of Personality and Social Psychology*, August 1998, pp 301–317.

[40] Based on and translated from 'Leeftijd sollicitant geeft de doorslag', *NRC Handelsblad*, May 7, 1997.

[41] For a complete review, see S R Rhodes, 'Age-Related Differences in Work Attitudes and Behavior: A Review and Conceptual Analysis', *Psychological Bulletin*, March 1983, pp 328–67. Supporting evidence was also provided by G Burkins, 'Work Week: A Special News Report about Life on the Job—and Trends Taking Shape There', *The Wall Street Journal*, May 5, 1996, p A1.

[42] See G M McEvoy, 'Cumulative Evidence of the Relationship between Employee Age and Job Performance', *Journal of Applied Psychology*, February 1989, pp 11–17.

[43] A thorough discussion of the relationship between age and performance is contained in D A Waldman and B J Avolio, 'Aging and Work Performance in Perspective: Contextual and Developmental Considerations', in *Research in Personnel and Human Resources Management*, ed G R Ferris (Greenwich, CT: JAI Press, 1993), vol. 11, pp 133–62.

[44] For details, see B J Avolio, D A Waldman and M A McDaniel, 'Age and Work Performance in Nonmanagerial Jobs: The Effects of Experience and Occupational Type', *Academy of Management Journal*, June 1990, pp 407–22.

[45] D H Powell, 'Aging Baby Boomers: Stretching Your Workforce Options', *HRMagazine*, July 1998, p 83.

[46] See P W Hom and R W Griffeth, *Employee Turnover* (Cincinnati, OH: SouthWestern, 1995), pp 35–50; and J J Martocchio, 'Age-Related Differences in Employee Absenteeism: A Meta-Analysis', *Psychology and Aging*, December 1989, pp 409–14.

[47] Based on L Lightfoot, 'Sacked white teacher claims race bias', *Sunday Times*, July 10, 1994.

[48] Details of the study on race and attitudes may be found in J H Greenhaus, S Parasuraman and W M Wormley, 'Effects of Race on Organizational Experiences, Job Performance Evaluations, and Career Outcomes', *Academy of Management Journal*, March 1990, pp 64–86.

[49] Supporting studies were conducted by A J Kinicki, C A Lockwood, P W Hom and R W Griffeth, 'Interviewer Predictions of Applicant Qualifications and Interviewer Validity', *Journal of Applied Psychology*, October 1990,

pp 477–86; and Day and Sulsky, 'Effects of Frame-of-Reference Training and Information Configuration on Memory Organization and Rating Accuracy'.

50 Skill based pay is discussed by T P Flannery, D A Hofrichter and P E Platten in People, *Performance, and Pay: Dynamic Compensation for Changing Organizations* (New York: The Free Press, 1996).

51 'Studies refute myths about older workers', *Society for Human Resource Management/ HR News*, July 1991.

52 Research is reviewed by R Rodgers, J E Hunter and D L Rogers, 'Influence of Top Management Commitment on Management Program Success', *Journal of Applied Psychology*, February 1993, pp 151–55.

53 The background and results for this study are presented in R Rosenthal and L Jacobson, *Pygmalion in the Classroom: Teacher Expectation and Pupils' Intellectual Development* (New York: Holt, Rinehart & Winston, 1968).

54 See D Eden and Y Zuk, 'Seasickness as a Self-Fulfilling Prophecy: Raising Self-Efficacy to Boost Performance at Sea', *Journal of Applied Psychology*, October 1995, pp 628–35. For a thorough review of research on the Pygmalion effect, see D Eden, *Pygmalion in Management: Productivity as a Self-Fulfilling Prophecy* (Lexington, MA: Lexington Books, 1990), Ch. 2.

55 This study was conducted by T Dvir, D Eden and M L Banjo, 'Self-Fulfilling Prophecy and Gender: Can Women Be Pygmalion and Galatea?' *Journal of Applied Psychology*, April 1995, pp 253–70.

56 See J-F Manzoni and J-L Barsoux, 'The Set-up-to-Fail Syndrome', *Harvard Business Review*, March–April 1998, pp 101–13.

57 This example was based on ibid; and 'Living Down to Expectations', *Training*, July 1998, p 15.

58 The role of positive expectations at Microsoft is discussed by S Hamm and O Port, 'The Mother of All Software Projects', *Business Week*, February 22, 1999, pp 69, 72.

59 These recommendations were adapted from J Keller, 'Have Faith—In You', *Selling Power*, June 1996, pp 84, 86; and R W Goddard, 'The Pygmalion Effect', *Personnel Journal*, June 1985, p 10.

60 Kelley's model is discussed in detail in H H Kelley, 'The Processes of Causal Attribution', *American Psychologist*, February 1973, pp 107–28.

61 For examples, see J Susskind, K Maurer, V Thakkar, D L Hamilton and J W Sherman, 'Perceiving Individuals and Groups: Expectancies, Dispositional Inferences, and Causal Attributions', *Journal of Personality and Social Psychology*, February 1999, pp 181–91; and J McClure, 'Discounting Causes of Behavior: Are Two Reasons Better than One?' *Journal of Personality and Social Psychology*, January 1998, pp 7–20.

62 See P D Sweeney, K Anderson and S Bailey, 'Attributional Style in Depression: A Meta-Analytic Review', *Journal of Personality and Social Psychology*, May 1986, pp 974–91.

63 Results can be found in P J Corr and J A Gray, 'Attributional Style as a Personality Factor in Insurance Sales Performance in the UK', *Journal of Occupational Psychology*, March 1996, pp 83–87.

64 Supportive results can be found in J Silvester, N R Anderson and F Patterson, 'Organizational Culture Change: An Inter-Group Attributional Analysis', *Journal of Occupational and Organizational Psychology*, March 1999, pp 1–23; J Greenberg, 'Forgive Me, I'm New: Three Experimental Demonstrations of the Effects of Attempts to Excuse Poor Performance', *Organizational Behavior and Human Decision Processes*, May 1996, pp 165–78; and G E Prussia, A J Kinicki and J S Bracker, 'Psychological and Behavioral Consequences of Job Loss: A Covariance Structure Analysis Using Weiner's (1985) Attribution Model', *Journal of Applied Psychology*, June 1993, pp 382–94.

65 Results from these studies can be found in D A Hofmann and A Stetzer, 'The Role of Safety Climate and Communication in Accident Interpretation: Implications for Learning from Negative Events', *Academy of Management Journal*, December 1998, pp 644–57; and I Choi, R E Nisbett and A Norenzayan,

'Causal Attribution Across Cultures: Variation and Universality', *Psychological Bulletin*, January 1999, pp 47–63.

66 The effect of the self-serving bias was tested and supported by P E De Michele, B Gansneder and G B Solomon, 'Success and Failure Attributions of Wrestlers: Further Evidence of the Self-Serving Bias', *Journal of Sport Behavior*, August 1998, pp 242–55; and C Sedikides, W K Campbell, G D Reeder and A J Elliot, 'The Self-Serving Bias in Relational Context', *Journal of Personality and Social Psychology*, February 1998, pp 378–86.

67 Details may be found in S E Moss and M J Martinko, 'The Effects of Performance Attributions and Outcome Dependence on Leader Feedback Behavior Following Poor Subordinate Performance', *Journal of Organizational Behavior*, May 1998, pp 259–74; and E C Pence, W C Pendelton, G H Dobbins and J A Sgro, 'Effects of Causal Explanations and Sex Variables on Recommendations for Corrective Actions Following Employee Failure', *Organizational Behavior and Human Performance*, April 1982, pp 227–40.

68 See D Konst, R Vonk and R V D Vlist, 'Inferences about Causes and Consequences of Behavior of Leaders and Subordinates', *Journal of Organizational Behavior*, March 1999, pp 261–71.

69 See M Miserandino, 'Attributional Retraining as a Method of Improving Athletic Performance', *Journal of Sport Behavior*, August 1998, pp 286–97; and F Forsterling, 'Attributional Retraining: A Review', *Psychological Bulletin*, November 1985, pp 496–512.

70 This exercise was modified from one contained in L Gardenwartz and A Rowe, *Diverse Teams at Work* (New York: McGraw-Hill, 1994), p 169.

71 The worksheet was adapted from ibid, p 169.

Chapter 7

1 S Beenstock, '95 per cent of this man's staff say they love working for him. What's his secret?', *Management Today*, April 1998.

2 Adapted and translated from G Bollen, 'Tevreden koeien geven betere melk', *Vacature*, February 25, 2000.

3 K Hilpern, 'Put a little spirit into your work', *The Guardian*, October 30, 2000.

4 A Chaudhuri, 'Perk Practice', *The Guardian*, August 30, 2000.

5 Ibid.

6 Ibid.

7 P Ester, L Halman and De Moor, *The Individualizing Society: value change in Europe and North America* (Tilburg: University Press, 1994).

8 T R Mitchell, 'Motivation: New Direction for Theory, Research, and Practice', *Academy of Management Review*, January 1982, p 81.

9 This discussion is based on T R Mitchell, 'Matching Motivational Strategies with Organizational Contexts', in *Research in Organizational Behavior* (vol. 19), eds L L Cummings and B M Staw (Greenwich, CT: JAI Press, 1997), pp 57–149.

10 T Burt, 'Land Rover unleashes its creativity', *The Financial Times*, October 28, 2000.

11 J Ezard, 'Seven out of ten office staff prefer grander job title to pay rise', *The Guardian*, April 18, 2000.

12 Mitchell, 'Motivation: New Direction for Theory, Research, and Practice', p 83.

13 The effects of feelings and emotions on work motivation are discussed by J M George and A P Brief, 'Motivational Agendas in the Workplace: The Effects of Feelings on Focus of Attention and Work Motivation', in *Research in Organizational Behavior*, eds B M Staw and L L Cummings (Greenwich, CT: JAI Press, 1996), vol. 18, pp 75–109.

14 For a complete discussion of the organizational criterion of interest to managers and researchers, see J T Austin and P Villanova, 'The Criterion Problem: 1917–1992', *Journal of Applied Psychology*, December 1992, pp 836–74.

15 For a complete description of Maslow's theory, see A H Maslow, 'A Theory of Human Motivation', *Psychological Review*, July 1943, pp 370–96.

16 C C Pinder, *Work Motivation: Theory, Issues, and Applications*

(Glenview, IL: Scott, Foresman, 1984), p 52.

[17] Adapted and translated from F Van der Auwera, 'Loon is maar een magere motivator', *Vacature*, July 12, 1999.

[18] Excerpted from W Band, 'Targeting Quality Efforts to Build Customer Loyalty', *The Quality Observer*, December 1995, p 34.

[19] Results can be found in W D Spangler, 'Validity of Questionnaire and TAT Measures of Need for Achievement: Two Meta-Analyses', *Psychological Bulletin*, July 1992, pp 140–54.

[20] Results can be found in S D Bluen, J Barling and W Burns, 'Predicting Sales Performance, Job Satisfaction, and Depression by Using the Achievement Strivings and Impatience–Irritability Dimensions of Type A Behavior', *Journal of Applied Psychology*, April 1990, pp 212–16; and D C McClelland, *The Achieving Society* (New York: Free Press, 1961).

[21] H A Murray, *Explorations in Personality* (New York: John Wiley & Sons, 1983), p 164.

[22] Recent studies of achievement motivation can be found in H Grant and C S Dweck, 'A Goal Analysis of Personality and Personality Coherence', in *The Coherence of Personality*, eds D Cervone and Y Shoda (New York: The Guilford Press, 1999), pp 345–71; and D Y Dai, S M Moon and J F Feldhusen, 'Achievement Motivation and Gifted Students: A Social Cognitive Perspective', *Educational Psychologist*, Spring/Summer 1998, pp 45–63.

[23] See K G Shaver, 'The Entrepreneurial Personality Myth', *Business and Economic Review*, April/June 1995, pp 20–23.

[24] Research on the affiliative motive can be found in S C O'Connor and L K Rosenblood, 'Affiliation Motivation in Everyday Experience: A Theoretical Comparison', *Journal of Personality and Social Psychology*, March 1996, pp 513–22; and R F Baumeister and M R Leary, 'The Need to Belong: Desire for Interpersonal Attachments as a Fundamental Human Motivation', *Psychological Bulletin*, May 1995, pp 497–529.

[25] See the following series of research reports: D K McNeese-Smith, 'The Relationship between Managerial Motivation, Leadership, Nurse Outcomes and Patient Satisfaction', *Journal of Organizational Behavior*, March 1999, pp 243–59; A M Harrell and M J Stahl, 'A Behavioral Decision Theory Approach for Measuring McClelland's Trichotomy of Needs', *Journal of Applied Psychology*, April 1981, pp 242–47; and M J Stahl, 'Achievement, Power and Managerial Motivation: Selecting Managerial Talent with the Job Choice Exercise', *Personnel Psychology*, Winter 1983, pp 775–89.

[26] For a review of the foundation of achievement motivation training, see D C McClelland, 'Toward a Theory of Motive Acquisition', *American Psychologist*, May 1965, pp 321–33. Evidence for the validity of motivation training can be found in H Heckhausen and S Krug, 'Motive Modification', in *Motivation and Society*, ed A J Stewart (San Francisco: Jossey-Bass, 1982).

[27] Results can be found in D B Turban and T L Keon, 'Organizational Attractiveness: An Interactionist Perspective', *Journal of Applied Psychology*, April 1993, pp 184–93.

[28] See D Steele Johnson and R Perlow, 'The Impact of Need for Achievement Components on Goal Commitment and Performance', *Journal of Applied Social Psychology*, November 1992, pp 1711–20.

[29] J L Bowditch and A F Buono, *A Primer on Organizational Behavior* (New York: John Wiley & Sons, 1985), p 210.

[30] Adapted and translated from anonymous, 'Werknemers kiezen zelf voor avondje voetbal of werken', *Nieuwsbank Persberichtenarchief*, March 24, 2000, www.nieuwsbank.nl

[31] Supporting results can be found in B Melin, U Lundberg, J Söderlund and M Granqvist, 'Psychological and Physiological Stress Reactions of Male and Female Assembly Workers: A Comparison between Two Different Forms of Work Organization', *Journal of Organizational Behavior*, January 1999, pp 47–61; and S Melamed, I Ben-Avi, J Luz and M S Green, 'Objective and Subjective Work Monotony: Effects on Job Satisfaction, Psychological Distress and Absenteeism in Blue-Collar Workers', *Journal of Applied Psychology*, February 1995, pp 29–42.

[32] This type of programme was developed and tested by M A Campion and C L McClelland, 'Follow-Up and Extension of the Interdisciplinary Costs and Benefits of Enlarged Jobs', *Journal of Applied Psychology*, June 1993, pp 339–51.

[33] An empirical test of the relationship between job rotation and career-related outcomes was conducted by M A Campion, L Cheraskin and M J Stevens, 'Career-Related Antecedents and Outcomes of Job Rotation', *Academy of Management Journal*, December 1994, pp 1518–42.

[34] See F Herzberg, B Mausner and B B Snyderman, *The Motivation to Work* (New York: John Wiley & Sons, 1959).

[35] Two tests of Herzberg's theory can be found in I O Adigun and G M Stephenson, 'Sources of Job Motivation and Satisfaction among British and Nigerian Employees', *The Journal of Social Psychology*, June 1992, pp 369–76; and E A Maidani, 'Comparative Study of Herzberg's Two-Factor Theory of Job Satisfaction Among Public and Private Sectors', *Public Personnel Management*, Winter 1991, pp 441–48.

[36] F Herzberg, 'One More Time: How Do You Motivate Employees?' *Harvard Business Review*, January/February 1968, p 56.

[37] Results are presented in 'Are Your Staffers Happy? They're in the Minority', *Supervisory Management*, March 1996, p 11.

[38] Both sides of the Herzberg controversy are discussed by N King, 'Clarification and Evaluation of the Two-Factor Theory of Job Satisfaction', *Psychological Bulletin*, July 1970, pp 18–31; and B Grigaliunas and Y Weiner, 'Has the Research Challenge to Motivation–Hygiene Theory Been Conclusive? An Analysis of Critical Studies', *Human Relations*, December 1974, pp 839–71.

[39] Pinder, *Work Motivation: Theory, Issues, and Applications*, p 28.

[40] J R Hackman, G R Oldham, R Janson and K Purdy, 'A New Strategy for Job Enrichment', *California Management Review*, Summer 1975, p 58.

[41] Adapted and translated from M Teugels, 'Mensen helpen, daar ga ik graag hard tegenaan', *Vacature*, March 7, 1998.

[42] J R Hackman and G R Oldham, p 58. (Emphasis added.)

[43] C V Clarke, 'Be All You Can Be!' *Black Enterprise*, February 1996, pp 72–73.

[44] Definitions of the job characteristics were adapted from J R Hackman and G R Oldham, 'Motivation through the Design of Work: Test of a Theory', *Organizational Behavior and Human Performance*, August 1976, pp 250–79.

[45] A review of this research can be found in M L Ambrose and C T Kulik, 'Old Friends, New Faces: Motivation Research in the 1990s', *Journal of Management*, 1999, pp 231–92.

[46] The complete JDS and norms for the MPS are presented in J R Hackman and G R Oldham, *Work Redesign* (Reading, MA: Addison-Wesley Publishing, 1980). Studies that revised the JDS were conducted by J L Cordery and P P Sevastos, 'Responses to the Original and Revised Job Diagnostic Survey: Is Education a Factor in Responses to Negatively Worded Items?' *Journal of Applied Psychology*, February 1993, pp 141–43; and J R Idaszak and F Drasgow, 'A Revision of the Job Diagnostic Survey: Elimination of a Measurement Artifact', *Journal of Applied Psychology*, February 1987, pp 69–74.

[47] See M L Ambrose and C T Kulik, 'Old Friends, New Faces: Motivation Research in the 1990s'; C Wong, C Hui and K S Law, 'A Longitudinal Study of the Job Perception–Job Satisfaction Relationship: A Test of the Three Alternative Specifications', *Journal of Occupational and Organizational Psychology*, June 1998, pp 127–46; and T Loher, R A Noe, N L Moeller and M P Fitzgerald, 'A Meta-Analysis of the Relation of Job Characteristics to Job Satisfaction', *Journal of Applied Psychology*, May 1985, pp 280–89.

[48] Results can be found in S K Parker, 'Enhancing Role Breadth Self-Efficacy: The Roles of Job Enrichment and Other Organizational Interventions', *Journal of Applied Psychology*, December 1998, pp 835–52.

[49] Results can be found in M R Kelley, 'New Process Technology, Job Design, and Work Organization: A Contingency Model', *American Sociological Review*, April 1990, pp 191–208.

[50] Productivity studies are reviewed in R E Kopelman, *Managing Productivity in Organizations* (New York: McGraw-Hill, 1986).

Notes

[51] Absenteeism results are discussed in Y Fried and G R Ferris, 'The Validity of the Job Characteristics Model: A Review and Meta-Analysis', *Personnel Psychology*, Summer 1987, pp 287–322; and J R Rentsch and R P Steel, 'Testing the Durability of Job Characteristics as Predictors of Absenteeism Over a Six-Year Period', *Personnel Psychology*, Spring 1998, pp 165–90. The turnover meta-analysis was conducted by G M McEvoy and W F Cascio, 'Strategies for Reducing Turnover: A Meta-Analysis', *Journal of Applied Psychology*, May 1985, pp 342–53.

[52] A thorough discussion of re-engineering and associated outcomes can be found in J Champy, *Reengineering Management: The Mandate for New Leadership* (New York: Harper Business, 1995); and M Hammer and J Champy, *Reengineering the Corporation: A Manifesto for Business Revolution* (New York: Harper Business, 1993).

[53] See J D Jonge and W B Schaufeli, 'Job Characteristics and Employee Well-Being: A Test of Warr's Vitamin Model in Health Care Workers Using Structural Equation Modelling', *Journal of Organizational Behavior*, July 1998, pp 387–407; and D C Ganster and D J Dwyer, 'The Effects of Understaffing on Individual and Group Performance in Professional and Trade Occupations', *Journal of Management*, 1995, pp 175–90.

[54] G R Oldham and J R Hackman, 'Work Design in the Organizational Context', in *Research in Organizational Behavior*, eds B M Staw and L L Cummings (Greenwich, CT: JAI Press, 1980), pp 248–49.

[55] For a review of the development of the JDI, see P C Smith, L M Kendall and C L Hulin, *The Measurement of Satisfaction in Work and Retirement* (Skokie, IL: Rand McNally, 1969).

[56] For norms on the MSQ, see D J Weiss, R V Dawis, G W England and L H Lofquist, *Manual for the Minnesota Satisfaction Questionnaire* (Minneapolis: Industrial Relations Center, University of Minnesota, 1967).

[57] For a review of these models, see A P Brief, *Attitudes In and Around Organizations* (Thousand Oaks, CA: Sage Publications, 1998).

[58] See A R Karr, 'Work Week: A Special News Report about Life on the Job—And Trends Taking Shape There', *The Wall Street Journal*, June 29, 1999, p A1.

[59] For a review of need satisfaction models, see E F Stone, 'A Critical Analysis of Social Information Processing Models of Job Perceptions and Job Attitudes', in *Job Satisfaction: How People Feel about Their Jobs and How It Affects Their Performance*, eds C J Cranny, P Cain Smith and E F Stone (New York: Lexington Books, 1992), pp 21–52.

[60] See J P Wanous, T D Poland, S L Premack and K S Davis, 'The Effects of Met Expectations on Newcomer Attitudes and Behaviors: A Review and Meta-Analysis', *Journal of Applied Psychology*, June 1992, pp 288–97; and P W Hom, R W Griffeth, L E Palich and J S Bracker, 'Revisiting Met Expectations as a Reason Why Realistic Job Previews Work', *Personnel Psychology*, Spring 1999, pp 97–112.

[61] A complete description of this model is provided by E A Locke, 'Job Satisfaction', in *Social Psychology and Organizational Behavior*, eds M Gruneberg and T Wall (New York: John Wiley & Sons, 1984).

[62] For a test of the value fulfillment value, see W A Hochwarter, P L Perrewe, G R Ferris and R A Brymer, 'Job Satisfaction and Performance: The Moderating Effects of Value Attainment and Affective Disposition', *Journal of Vocational Behavior*, April 1999, pp 296–313.

[63] Results from the meta-analysis can be found in L A Witt and L G Nye, 'Gender and the Relationship between Perceived Fairness of Pay or Promotion and Job Satisfaction', *Journal of Applied Psychology*, December 1992, pp 910–17.

[64] A thorough discussion of this model is provided by T A Judge, E A Locke and C C Durham, 'The Dispositional Causes of Job Satisfaction: A Core Evaluations Approach', in *Research in Organizational Behavior* (vol. 19), eds L L Cummings and B M Staw (Greenwich, CT: JAI Press, 1997), pp 151–88.

[65] Supportive results can be found in H M Weiss, J P Nicholas and C S Daus, 'An Examination of the Joint Effects of Affective Experiences and Job Beliefs on Job Satisfaction and Variances in Affective Experiences Over Time', *Organizational Behavior and Human Decision Processes*, April 1999, pp 1–24; J D Shaw, M K Duffy, G D Jenkins, Jr, and N Gupta, 'Positive and Negative Affect, Signal Sensitivity, and Pay Satisfaction', *Journal of Management*, 1999, pp 189–206; R P Steel and J R Rentsch, 'The Dispositional Model of Job Attitudes Revisited: Findings of a 10-Year Study', *Journal of Applied Psychology*, December 1997, pp 873–79; and B M Staw and J Ross, 'Stability in the Midst of Change: A Dispositional Approach to Job Attitudes', *Journal of Applied Psychology*, August 1985, pp 469–80.

[66] See E Diener and C Diener, 'Most People Are Happy', *Psychological Science*, May 1996, pp 181–85; D Lykken and A Tellegen, 'Happiness Is a Stochastic Phenomenon', *Psychological Science*, May 1996, pp 186–89; and R D Arvey, T J Bouchard, Jr, N L Segal and L M Abraham, 'Job Satisfaction: Environmental and Genetic Components', *Journal of Applied Psychology*, April 1989, pp 187–92.

[67] Results can be found in A J Kinicki, F M McKee-Ryan, C A Schriesheim and K P Carson, 'Assessing the Construct Validity of the Job Descriptive Index (JDI): A Review and Analysis', 2000, manuscript submitted for publication.

[68] See S P Brown, 'A Meta-Analysis and Review of Organizational Research on Job Involvement', *Psychological Bulletin*, September 1996, pp 235–55.

[69] D W Organ, 'The Motivational Basis of Organizational Citizenship Behavior', in *Research in Organizational Behavior*, eds B M Staw and L L Cummings (Greenwich, CT: JAI Press, 1990), p 46.

[70] See D W Organ and K Ryan, 'A Meta-Analytic Review of Attitudinal and Dispositional Predictors of Organizational Citizenship Behavior', *Personnel Psychology*, Winter 1995, pp 775–802.

[71] Supportive results can be found in M A Konovsky and D W Organ, 'Dispositional and Contextual Determinants of Organizational Citizenship Behavior', *Journal of Organizational Behavior*, May 1996, pp 253–66; and P M Podsakoff, S B MacKenzie and W H Bommer, 'Transformational Leader Behaviors and Substitutes for Leadership as Determinants of Employee Satisfaction, Commitment, Trust, and Organizational Citizenship Behaviors', *Journal of Management*, pp 259–98.

[72] See T D Allen and M C Rush, 'The Effects of Organizational Citizenship Behavior on Performance Judgments: A Field Study and a Laboratory Experiment', *Journal of Applied Psychology*, April 1998, pp 247–60.

[73] See R P Tett and J P Meyer, 'Job Satisfaction, Organizational Commitment, Turnover Intention, and Turnover: Path Analysis Based on Meta-Analytic Findings', *Personnel Psychology*, Summer 1993, pp 259–93.

[74] See J E Mathieu and D Zajac, 'A Review and Meta-Analysis of the Antecedents, Correlates, and Consequences of Organizational Commitment', *Psychological Bulletin*, September 1990, pp 171–94.

[75] See R D Hackett, 'Work Attitudes and Employee Absenteeism: A Synthesis of the Literature', *Journal of Occupational Psychology*, 1989, pp 235–48.

[76] The results can be found in P W Hom and R W Griffeth, *Employee Turnover* (Cincinnati, OH: SouthWestern, 1995), pp 35–50.

[77] See ibid; and C Kalb and A Rogers, 'Stress', *Newsweek*, June 14, 1999, pp 56–63.

[78] Results can be found in M A Blegen, 'Nurses' Job Satisfaction: A Meta-Analysis of Related Variables', *Nursing Research*, January/February 1993, pp 36–41.

[79] The relationship between performance and satisfaction was reviewed by M T Iaffaldano and P M Muchinsky, 'Job Satisfaction and Job Performance: A Meta-Analysis', *Psychological Bulletin*, March 1985, pp 251–73.

[80] The relationship between satisfaction and performance is discussed by P C Smith and C Cranny, 'Psychology of Men at Work', *Annual Review of Psychology*, 1968, pp 467–96; and R A Katzell, D E Thompson and R A Guzzo, 'How Job Satisfaction and Job Performance Are and Are Not Linked', in *Job Satisfaction: How People Feel about Their Jobs and How It Affects Their Performance*, eds C J Cranny, P Cain Smith and

E F Stone (New York: Lexington Books, 1992), pp 195–217.

[81] See Kinicki, McKee-Ryan, Schriesheim and Carson, 'Assessing the Construct Validity of the Job Descriptive Index (JDI): A Review and Analysis.'

[82] These issues are discussed by C Ostroff, 'The Relationship between Satisfaction, Attitudes, and Performance: An Organizational Level Analysis', *Journal of Applied Psychology*, December 1992, pp 963–74.

[83] Ibid.

[84] Adapted from M R Blood, 'Work Values and Job Satisfaction', *Journal of Applied Psychology*, December 1969, pp 456–59.

[85] The JDS and its norms were adapted from Hackman and Oldham, *Work Redesign*, pp 280–81, 317.

Chapter 8

[1] J S McClenahen, 'CEO of the year: Nokia's Jorma Ollila wants to unwire the world', *Industry Week*, November 20, 2000.

[2] Ibid.

[3] See L Festinger, *A Theory of Cognitive Dissonance* (Stanford, CA: Stanford University Press, 1957).

[4] Retaliation in response to perceived injustice was investigated by D P Skarlicki and R Folger, 'Retaliation in the Workplace: The Roles of Distributive, Procedural, and Interactional Justice', *Journal of Applied Psychology*, June 1997, pp 434–43.

[5] The generalizability of the equity norm was examined by J K Giacobbe-Miller, D J Miller and V I Victorov, 'A Comparison of Russian and U.S. Pay Allocation Decisions, Distributive Justice Judgments, and Productivity Under Different Payment Conditions', *Personnel Psychology*, Spring 1998, pp 137–63.

[6] The choice of a comparison person is discussed by P P Shah, 'Who Are Employees' Social Referents? Using a Network Perspective to Determine Referent Others', *Academy of Management Journal*, June 1998, pp 249–68; and J Greenberg and C L McCarty, 'Comparable Worth: A Matter of Justice', in *Research in Personnel and Human Resources Management*, eds G R Ferris and K M Rowland (Greenwich, CT: JAI Press, Inc., 1990), vol. 8, pp 265–303.

[7] 'UK pay gap widens', *BBC Online News*, November 24, 1999.

[8] L Brooks, 'Some are more equal than others', *The Guardian*, November 11, 1999.

[9] 'UK pay gap widens', *BBC Online News*, November 24, 1999.

[10] C Duff, 'Top Executives Ponder High Pay, Decide They're Worth Every Cent', *The Wall Street Journal*, May 13, 1996, p B1.

[11] 'Prison health care failing', *BBC Online News*, October 28, 1998, www.news.bbc.co.uk

[12] See C Lee and J-L Farh, 'The Effects of Gender in Organizational Justice Perception', *Journal of Organizational Behavior*, January 1999, pp 133–43; and L A Witt and L G Nye, 'Gender and the Relationship between Perceived Fairness of Pay or Promotion and Job Satisfaction', *Journal of Applied Psychology*, December 1992, pp 910–17.

[13] Adapted from a discussion in R L Opsahl and M Dunette, 'The role of financial compensation in industrial motivation', *Psychological Bulletin*, August 1966, pp 94–118.

[14] Supportive results can be found in D P Skarlicki, J H Ellard and B R C Kelln, 'Third-Party Perceptions of a Layoff: Procedural, Derogation, and Retributive Aspects of Justice', *Journal of Applied Psychology*, February 1998, pp 119–27; and V Scarpello and F F Jones, 'Why Justice Matters in Compensation Decision Making', *Journal of Organizational Behavior*, May 1996, pp 285–99.

[15] M A Korsgaard, L Roberson and R D Rymph, 'What Motivates Fairness? The Role of Subordinate Assertive Behavior on Manager's Interactional Fairness', *Journal of Applied Psychology*, October 1998, p 731.

[16] Ibid, pp 731–44.

[17] Results can be found in R W Griffeth, R P Vecchio and J W Logan, Jr, 'Equity Theory and Interpersonal Attraction', *Journal of Applied Psychology*, June 1989, pp 394–401; and R P Vecchio, 'Predicting Worker Performance in Inequitable Settings', *Academy of Management Review*, January 1982, pp 103–10.

[18] See J Greenberg, 'Stealing in the Name of Justice:

Informational and Interpersonal Moderators of Theft Reactions to Underpayment Inequity', *Organizational Behavior and Human Decision Process*, February 1993, pp 81–103.

[19] See M L Ambrose and C T Kulik, 'Old Friends, New Faces: Motivation Research in the 1990s', *Journal of Management*, 1999, pp 231–92; and J H Dulebohn and J J Martocchio, 'Employee Perceptions of the Fairness of Work Group Incentive Pay Plans', *Journal of Management*, 1998, pp 469–88.

[20] Supporting studies were conducted by D P Skarlicki, R Folger and P Tesluk, 'Personality as a Moderator in the Relationship between Fairness and Retaliation', *Academy of Management Journal*, February 1999, pp 100–8; and Skarlicki and Folger, 'Retaliation in the Workplace: The Roles of Distributive, Procedural, and Interactional Justice'.

[21] Results can be found in M A Korsgaard, L Roberson and R D Rymph, 'What Motivates Fairness? The Role of Subordinates Assertive Behavior on Managers' Interactional Fairness'; and M A Donovan, F Drasgow and L J Munson, 'The Perceptions of Fair Interpersonal Treatment Scale: Development and Validation of a Measure of Interpersonal Treatment in the Workplace', *Journal of Applied Psychology*, October 1998, pp 683–92.

[22] See C R Wanberg, L W Bunce and M B Gavin, 'Perceived Fairness of Layoffs among Individuals Who Have Been Laid Off: A Longitudinal Study', *Personnel Psychology*, Spring 1999, pp 59–84.

[23] See Korsgaard, Roberson and Rymph, 'What Motivates Fairness? The Role of Subordinates Assertive Behavior on Managers' Interactional Fairness.'

[24] The role of equity in organizational change is thoroughly discussed by A T Cobb, R Folger and K Wooten, 'The Role Justice Plays in Organizational Change', *Public Administration Quarterly*, Summer 1995, pp 135–51.

[25] A comparison of individual and group perceptions of justice was conducted by E A Lind, L Kray and L Thompson, 'The Social Comparison of Injustice: Fairness Judgments in Response to Own and Others' Unfair Treatment by Authorities', *Organizational Behavior and Human Decision Processes*, July 1998, pp 1–22.

[26] The legal issues of pay equity and employment at-will are discussed by M Adams, 'Fair and Square', *HRMagazine*, May 1999, pp 38–44; and B B Dunford and D J Devine, 'Employment At-Will and Employee Discharge: A Justice Perspective on Legal Action Following Termination', *Personnel Psychology*, Winter 1998, pp 903–34.

[27] Results can be found in K W Mossholder, N Bennett and C L Martin, 'A Multilevel Analysis of Procedural Justice Context', *Journal of Organizational Behavior*, March 1998, pp 131–41.

[28] The relationship between organizational justice and customer service is discussed by D E Bowen, S W Gilliland and R Folger, 'HRM Service Fairness: How Being Fair with Employees Spills Over to Customers', *Organizational Dynamics*, Winter 1999, pp 7–23.

[29] For a complete discussion of Vroom's theory, see V H Vroom, *Work and Motivation* (New York: John Wiley & Sons, 1964).

[30] E E Lawler III, *Motivation in Work Organizations* (Belmont, CA: Wadsworth, 1973), p 45.

[31] Based on and translated from 'Amsterdamse beurs geschokt door grootscheeps fraude onderzoek', *Financieel Economische Tijd*, October 28, 1997, p7.

[32] See J Chowdhury, 'The Motivational Impact of Sales Quotas on Effort', *Journal of Marketing Research*, February 1993, pp 28–41; and C C Pinder, *Work Motivation* (Glenview, IL: Scott, Foresman, 1984), Ch. 7.

[33] Adapted and translated from 'Managers vallen voor prestatieloon', *Vacature*, March 3, 1998.

[34] The measurement and importance of valence was investigated by N T Feather, 'Values, Valences, and Choice: The Influence of Values on the Perceived Attractiveness and Choice of Alternatives', *Journal of Personality and Social Psychology*, June 1995, pp 1135–51; and A Pecotich and G A Churchill, Jr, 'An Examination of the Anticipated-Satisfaction Importance Valence Controversy', *Organizational Behavior and Human

Performance, April 1981, pp 213–26.
[35] P Nolan, 'Make a wish', *Potentials*, October 2000.
[36] S Trelford, 'Choice rewards', *Marketing Week*, June 24, 1999.
[37] Ibid.
[38] Excerpted from 'Federal Express's Fred Smith', *Inc.*, October 1986, p 38.
[39] For a thorough discussion of the model, see L W Porter and E E Lawler III, *Managerial Attitudes and Performance* (Homewood, IL: Richard D. Irwin, 1968).
[40] Results can be found in W van Eerde and H Thierry, 'Vroom's Expectancy Models and Work-Related Criteria: A Meta-Analysis', *Journal of Applied Psychology*, October 1996, pp 575–86.
[41] See J P Wanous, T L Keon and J C Latack, 'Expectancy Theory and Occupational/Organizational Choices: A Review and Test', *Organizational Behavior and Human Performance*, August 1983, pp 66–86.
[42] These results are based on T K DeBacker and R M Nelson, 'Variations on an Expectancy-Value Model of Motivation in Science', *Contemporary Educational Psychology*, April 1999, pp 71–94; R M Lynd-Stevenson, 'Expectancy-Value Theory and Predicting Future Employment Status in the Young Unemployed', *Journal of Occupational and Organizational Psychology*, March 1999, pp 101–6; E D Pulakos and N Schmitt, 'A Longitudinal Study of a Valence Model Approach for the Prediction of Job Satisfaction of New Employees', *Journal of Applied Psychology*, May 1983, pp 307–12; A J Kinicki, 'Predicting Occupational Role Choices for Involuntary Job Loss', *Journal of Vocational Behavior*, October 1989, pp 204–18; T A DeCotiis and J-Y LeLouarn, 'A Predictive Study of Voting Behavior in a Representation Election Using Union Instrumentality and Work Perceptions', *Organizational Behavior and Human Performance*, February 1981, pp 103–18; P W Hom, 'Expectancy Prediction of Reenlistment in the National Guard', *Journal of Vocational Behavior*, April 1980, pp 235–48; D F Parker and L Dyer, 'Expectancy Theory as a Within-Person Behavioral Choice Model: An Empirical Test of Some Conceptual and Methodological Refinements', *Organizational Behavior and Human Performance*, October 1976, pp 97–117; and A W Stacy, K F Widaman and G A Marlatt, 'Expectancy Models of Alcohol Use', *Journal of Personality and Social Psychology*, May 1990, pp 918–28.
[43] For reviews of the criticisms of expectancy theory, see F J Landy and W S Becker, 'Motivation Theory Reconsidered', in *Research in Organizational Behavior*, vol. 9, eds L L Cummings and B M Staw (Greenwich, CT: JAI Press, 1987), pp 1–38; and T R Mitchell, 'Expectancy Models of Job Satisfaction, Occupational Preference and Effort: A Theoretical, Methodological, and Empirical Appraisal', *Psychological Bulletin*, December 1974, pp 1053–77.
[44] Components of coaching are discussed by M Fleschner, 'The Winning Season: How Legendary Wrestling Coach Dan Gable Built Championships to Last', *Selling Power*, April 1998, pp 14, 16; and S R Levine, 'Performance Coaching: Great Coaching Skills Help Build a Team of Champions', *Selling Power*, July/August 1996, p 46.
[45] Supportive results are presented in L Morris, 'Employees Not Encouraged to Go Extra Mile', *Training & Development*, April 1996, pp 59–60; and 'Crossed Wires on Employee Motivation', *Training & Development*, July 1995, pp 59–60.
[46] See D R Spitzer, 'Power Rewards: Rewards That Really Motivate', *Management Review*, May 1996, pp 45–50; and A Kohn, *Punished by Rewards: The Trouble with Gold Stars, Incentive Plans, A's, Praise, and Other Bribes* (Boston: Houghton Mifflin Company, 1993).
[47] Results from these studies can be found in G D Jenkins, Jr, A Mitra, N Gupta and J D Shaw, 'Are Financial Incentives Related to Performance? A Meta-Analytic Review of Empirical Research', *Journal of Applied Psychology*, October 1998, pp 777–87; and R Eisenberger, S Armeli and J Pretz, 'Can the Promise of Reward Increase Creativity?' *Journal of Personality and Social Psychology*, March 1998, pp 704–14.
[48] See S Kerr, 'Organizational Rewards: Practical, Cost-Neutral Alternatives That You May Know, But Don't Practice',

Organizational Dynamics, Summer 1999, pp 61–70.
[49] P Ancona, 'Nice Bosses Often Don't Get Quality They Want', *The Arizona Daily Star*, February 8, 1993, p 9.
[50] See L Wah, 'Rewarding Efficient Teamwork', *Management Review*, February 1999, p 7.
[51] E A Locke, K N Shaw, L M Saari and G P Latham, 'Goal Setting and Task Performance: 1969–1980', *Psychological Bulletin*, July 1981, p 126.
[52] Ibid.
[53] A thorough discussion of MBO is provided by P F Drucker, *The Practice of Management* (New York: Harper, 1954); and P F Drucker, 'What Results Should You Expect? A User's Guide to MBO', *Public Administration Review*, January/February 1976, pp 12–19.
[54] Results from both studies can be found in R Rodgers and J E Hunter, 'Impact of Management by Objectives on Organizational Productivity', *Journal of Applied Psychology*, April 1991, pp 322–36; and R Rodgers, J E Hunter and D L Rogers, 'Influence of Top Management Commitment on Management Program Success', *Journal of Applied Psychology*, February 1993, pp 151–55.
[55] Adapted and translated from 'De Dokter', *Vacature*, March 17, 2000.
[56] M Fleschner, 'How high can you fly', *Selling Power*, November/December 1995, p 15.
[57] Project planning is discussed by T D Conkright, 'So You're Going to Manage a Project ...', *Training*, January 1998, pp 62–67.
[58] Results can be found in P M Wright, 'Operationalization of Goal Difficulty as a Moderator of the Goal Difficulty-Performance Relationship', *Journal of Applied Psychology*, June 1990, pp 227–34.
[59] This linear relationship was not supported by P M Wright, J R Hollenbeck, S Wolf and G C McMahan, 'The Effects of Varying Goal Difficulty Operationalizations on Goal Setting Outcomes and Processes', *Organizational Behavior and Human Decision Processes*, January 1995, pp 28–43.
[60] See Locke, Shaw, Saari and Latham, 'Goal Setting and Task Performance: 1969–1980'; and A J Mento, R P Steel and R J Karren, 'A Meta-Analytic Study of the Effects of Goal Setting on Task Performance: 1966–1984', *Organizational Behavior and Human Decision Processes*, February 1987, pp 52–83.
[61] Results from the meta-analysis can be found in R E Wood, A J Mento and E A Locke, 'Task Complexity as a Moderator of Goal Effects: A Meta-Analysis', *Journal of Applied Psychology*, August 1987, pp 416–25.
[62] See the related discussion in L A King, 'Personal Goals and Personal Agency: Linking Everyday Goals to Future Images of the Self', in *Personal Control in Action: Cognitive and Motivational Mechanisms*, eds M Kofta, G Weary and G Sedek (New York: Plenum Press, 1998), pp 109–28.
[63] See R P DeShon and R A Alexander, 'Goal Setting Effects on Implicit and Explicit Learning of Complex Tasks', *Organizational Behavior and Human Decision Processes*, January 1996, pp 18–36.
[64] Results can be found in K H Doerr, T R Mitchell, T D Klastorin and K A Brown, 'Impact of Material Flow Policies and Goals on Job Outcomes', *Journal of Applied Psychology*, April 1996, pp 142–52.
[65] Supportive results can be found in K L Langeland, C M Johnson and T C Mawhinney, 'Improving Staff Performance in a Community Mental Health Setting: Job Analysis, Training, Goal Setting, Feedback, and Years of Data', *Journal of Organizational Behavior Management*, 1998, pp 21–43; and L A Wilk, 'The Effects of Feedback and Goal Setting on the Productivity and Satisfaction of University Admissions Staff', *Journal of Organizational Behavior Management*, 1998, pp 45–68.
[66] See E A Locke and G P Latham, *A Theory of Goal Setting & Task Performance* (Englewood Cliffs, NJ: Prentice-Hall, 1990).
[67] See J J Donovan and D J Radosevich, 'The Moderating Role of Goal Commitment on the Goal Difficulty-Performance Relationship: A Meta-Analytic Review and Critical Reanalysis', *Journal of Applied Psychology*, April 1998, pp 308–15.
[68] See the related discussion in T P Flannery, D A Hofrichter

and P E Platten, *People, Performance, & Pay* (New York: The Free Press, 1996).

69 See R Ganzel, 'What's Wrong with Pay for Performance?' *Training*, December 1998, pp 34–40; and P M Wright, J M George, S R Farnsworth and G C McMahan, 'Productivity and Extra-Role Behavior: The Effects of Goals and Incentives on Spontaneous Helping', *Journal of Applied Psychology*, June 1993, pp 374–81.

70 Supporting results can be found in S W Gilliland and R S Landis, 'Quality and Quantity Goals in a Complex Decision Task: Strategies and Outcomes', *Journal of Applied Psychology*, October 1992, pp 672–81.

71 The benefits of benchmarking were examined by L Mann, D Samson and D Dow, 'A Field Experiment on the Effects of Benchmarking and Goal Setting on Company Sales Performance', *Journal of Management*, 1998, pp 73–96.

72 See J A Colquitt and M J Simmering, 'Conscientiousness, Goal Orientation, and Motivation to Learn During the Learning Process: A Longitudinal Study', *Journal of Applied Psychology*, August 1998, pp 654–65.

73 D VandeWalle, S P Brown, W L Cron and J W Slocum, Jr, 'The Influence of Goal Orientation and Self-Regulated Tactics on Sales Performance: A Longitudinal Field Test', *Journal of Applied Psychology*, April 1999, p 250.

74 See Ibid, pp 249–59; and H Grant and C S Dweck, 'A Goal Analysis of Personality and Personality Choice', in *The Coherence of Personality: Social-Cognitive Bases of Consistency, Variability, and Organization*, eds D Cervone and Y Shoda (New York: The Guilford Press, 1999), pp 345–71.

75 E A Locke and G P Latham, *Goal Setting: A Motivational Technique That Works!* (Englewood Cliffs, NJ: Prentice-Hall, 1984), p 79.

76 T R Mitchell, 'Motivation: New Directions for Theory, Research, and Practice', *Academy of Management Review*, January 1982, p 81.

77 This conclusion is consistent with research summarized in F Luthans and A D Stajkovic, 'Reinforce for Performance: The Need to Go Beyond Pay and Even Rewards', *The Academy of Management Executive*, May 1999, pp 49–57.

78 A Jack, 'Big Stackes in a small world – Andrew Jack looks at the latest attempt to improve performance at EuroDisney', *The Financial Times*, January 13, 1995, p 12.

79 Results from this study are reported in K A Kovach, 'What motivates Employees? Workers and supervisors give different answers', *Business Horizons*, September–October 1987, pp 58–65.

80 Actual survey rankings are as follows: (1) interesting work, (2) full appreciation of work done, (3) feeling of being in on things, (4) job security, (5) good wages, (6) promotion and growth in the organization, (7) good working conditions, (8) personal loyalty to employees, (9) tactful discipline, and (10) sympathetic help with personal problems.

81 A Kinicki, 'The Case of the Missing Form', *Performance Management Systems* (Kinicki and Associates, Inc.: 1992) pp 3–35.

Chapter 9

1 A Maitland, 'Feedback goes electronic', *The Financial Times*, January 4, 2001.

2 R Aubrey and P M Cohen, *Working Wisdom: Timeless Skills and Vanguard Strategies for Learning Organizations* (San Francisco: Jossey-Bass, 1995), p 4.

3 Adapted and translated from Loek Van Den Broek, '360°-feedback: waarom nu?', *Gids voor Personeelsmanagement*, vol. 78 no. 10, 1999.

4 W Fletcher, 'Sitting in Judgment of Others', *Management Today*, August 2000.

5 M London, H H Larsen and L N Thisted, 'Relationships between feedback and self-development', *Group & Organization Management*, vol. 24 no. 1, March 1999.

6 For instance, see 'Worker Retention Presents Challenge to U.S. Employers', *HRMagazine*, September 1998, p 22; L Wah, 'An Ounce of Prevention', *Management Review*, October 1998, p 9; and S Armour, 'Cash or Critiques: Which Is Best?' *USA Today*, December 16, 1998, p 6B.

7 I Sager, 'The Man Who's Rebooting IBM's PC Business', *Business Week*, July 24, 1995, p 70.

8 J A Byrne, 'Management Meccas', *Business Week*, September 18, 1995, p 128.

9 Data from M Hequet, 'Giving Feedback', *Training*, September 1994, pp 72–77.

10 C Bell and R Zemke, 'On-Target Feedback', *Training*, June 1992, p 36.

11 Both the definition of feedback and the functions of feedback are based on discussion in D R Ilgen, C D Fisher and M S Taylor, 'Consequences of Individual Feedback on Behavior in Organizations', *Journal of Applied Psychology*, August 1979, pp 349–71; and R E Kopelman, *Managing Productivity in Organizations: A Practical People-Oriented Perspective* (New York: McGraw-Hill, 1986), p 175.

12 See P C Earley, G B Northcraft, C Lee and T R Lituchy, 'Impact of Process and Outcome Feedback on the Relation of Goal Setting to Task Performance', *Academy of Management Journal*, March 1990, pp 87–105.

13 Data from A N Kluger and A DeNisi, 'The Effects of Feedback Interventions on Performance: A Historical Review, a Meta-Analysis, and a Preliminary Feedback Intervention Theory', *Psychological Bulletin*, March 1996, pp 254–84.

14 See D M Herold and D B Fedor, 'Individuals' Interaction with Their Feedback Environment: The Role of Domain-Specific Individual Differences', in *Research in Personnel and Human Resources Management*, vol. 16, ed G R Ferris (Stamford, CT: JAI Press, 1998), pp 215–54.

15 H Lancaster, 'Scott Adams Offers Valuable Lessons from Life with Dilbert', *The Wall Street Journal*, August 8, 1995, p B1.

16 For relevant research, see J S Goodman, 'The Interactive Effects of Task and External Feedback on Practice Performance and Learning', *Organizational Behavior and Human Decision Processes*, December 1998, pp 223–52.

17 See P E Levy, M D Albright, B D Cawley and J R Williams, 'Situational and Individual Determinants of Feedback Seeking: A Closer Look at the Process', *Organizational Behavior and Human Decision Processes*, April 1995, pp 23–37; M R Leary, E S Tambor, S K Terdal and D L Downs, 'Self-Esteem as an Interpersonal Monitor: The Sociometer Hypothesis', *Journal of Personality and Social Psychology*, June 1995, pp 518–30; and M A Quinones, 'Pretraining Context Effects: Training Assignment as Feedback', *Journal of Applied Psychology*, April 1995, pp 226–38.

18 See T Matsui, A Okkada and T Kakuyama, 'Influence of Achievement Need on Goal Setting, Performance, and Feedback Effectiveness', *Journal of Applied Psychology*, October 1982, pp 645–48.

19 See D B Turban and T W Dougherty, 'Role of Protégé Personality in Receipt of Mentoring and Career Success', *Academy of Management Journal*, June 1994, pp 688–702. Also see M E Burkhardt, 'Social Interaction Effects Following a Technological Change: A Longitudinal Investigation', *Academy of Management Journal*, August 1994, pp 869–98.

20 See D M Herold, C K Parsons and R B Rensvold, 'Individual Differences in the Generation and Processing of Performance Feedback', *Educational and Psychological Measurement*, February 1996, pp 5–25.

21 See B D Bannister, 'Performance Outcome Feedback and Attributional Feedback: Interactive Effects on Recipient Responses', *Journal of Applied Psychology*, May 1986, pp 203–10.

22 For complete details, see P M Podsakoff and J-L Farh, 'Effects of Feedback Sign and Credibility on Goal Setting and Task Performance', *Organizational Behavior and Human Decision Processes*, August 1989, pp 45–67. Also see S J Ashford and A S Tsui, 'Self-Regulation for Managerial Effectiveness: The Role of Active Feedback Seeking', *Academy of Management Journal*, June 1991, pp 251–80.

23 W S Silver, T R Mitchell and M E Gist, 'Responses to Successful and Unsuccessful Performance: The Moderating Effect of Self-Efficacy on the Relationship between Performance and Attributions', *Organizational Behavior and Human Decision Processes*, June 1995, p 297. Also see

T A Louie, 'Decision Makers' Hindsight Bias after Receiving Favorable and Unfavorable Feedback', *Journal of Applied Psychology*, February 1999, pp 29–41.

24 I Krechowiecka, 'Help: why is there always a but?', *The Guardian*, June 24, 2000.

25 J M Kouzes and B Z Posner, *Credibility: How Leaders Gain and Lose It, Why People Demand It* (San Francisco: Jossey-Bass, 1993), p 25.

26 See J McCune, 'That Elusive Thing Called Trust', *Management Review*, July–August 1998, pp 10–16; K van den Bos, H A M Wilke and E A Lind, ' When Do We Need Procedural Fairness? The Role of Trust in Authority', *Journal of Personality and Social Psychology*, December 1998, pp 1449–58; O Harari, 'The TRUST Factor', *Management Review*, January 1999, pp 28–31; and A C Wicks, S L Berman and T M Jones, 'The Structure of Optimal Trust: Moral and Strategic Implications', *Academy of Management Review*, January 1999, pp 99–116.

27 See S E Moss and M J Martinko, 'The Effects of Performance Attributions and Outcome Dependence on Leader Feedback Behavior Following Poor Subordinate Performance', *Journal of Organizational Behavior*, May 1998, pp 259–74.

28 See S H Barr and E J Conlon, 'Effects of Distribution of Feedback in Work Groups', *Academy of Management Journal*, June 1994, pp 641–55.

29 Based on discussion in Ilgen, Fisher and Taylor, 'Consequences of Individual Feedback on Behavior in Organizations', pp 367–68. Also see A M O'Leary-Kelly, 'The Influence of Group Feedback on Individual Group Member Response', in *Research in Personnel and Human Resources Management*, vol. 16, ed G R Ferris (Stamford, CT: JAI Press, 1998), pp 255–94.

30 See P C Earley, 'Computer-Generated Performance Feedback in the Magazine-Subscription Industry', *Organizational Behavior and Human Decision Processes*, February 1988, pp 50–64.

31 See M De Gregorio and C D Fisher, 'Providing Performance Feedback: Reactions to Alternate Methods', *Journal of Management*, December 1988, pp 605–16.

32 For details, see R A Baron, 'Countering the Effects of Destructive Criticism: The Relative Efficacy of Four Interventions', *Journal of Applied Psychology*, June 1990, pp 235–45. Also see M L Smith, 'Give Feedback, Not Criticism', *Supervisory Management*, February 1993, p 4.

33 C O Longenecker and D A Gioia, 'The Executive Appraisal Paradox', *Academy of Management Executive*, May 1992, p 18. Also see 'It's Still Lonely at the Top', *Training*, April 1993, p 8.

34 Practical tips for giving feedback can be found in E Van Velsor and S J Wall, 'How to Choose a Feedback Instrument', *Training*, March 1992, pp 47–52; T Lammers, 'The Effective Employee-Feedback System', *Inc.*, February 1993, pp 109–11; L Smith, 'The Executive's New Coach', *Fortune*, December 27, 1993, pp 126–34; and M Hequet, 'Giving Good Feedback', *Training*, September 1994, pp 72–77.

35 See M R Edwards, A J Ewen and W A Verdini, 'Fair Performance Management and Pay Practices for Diverse Work Forces: The Promise of Multisource Assessment', *ACA Journal*, Spring 1995, pp 50–63.

36 See G D Huet-Cox, T M Nielsen and E Sundstrom, 'Get the Most from 360-Degree Feedback: Put It on the Internet', *HRMagazine*, May 1999, pp 92–103.

37 This list is based in part on discussion in H J Bernardin, 'Subordinate Appraisal: A Valuable Source of Information about Managers', *Human Resource Management*, Fall 1986, pp 421–39.

38 Data from D Antonioni, 'The Effects of Feedback Accountability on Upward Appraisal Ratings', *Personnel Psychology*, Summer 1994, pp 349–56.

39 H J Bernardin, S A Dahmus and G Redmon, 'Attitudes of First-Line Supervisors toward Subordinate Appraisals', *Human Resource Management*, Summer/Fall 1993, p 315.

40 Data from J W Smither, M London, N L Vasilopoulos, R R Reilly, R E Millsap and N Salvemini, 'An Examination of the Effects of an Upward Feedback Program over Time', *Personnel Psychology*, Spring 1995, pp 1–34.

41 See S Haworth, 'The Dark Side of Multi-Rater Assessments', *HRMagazine*, May 1998, pp 106–14; and D A Waldman, L E Atwater and D Antonioni, 'Has 360 Degree Feedback Gone Amok?' *Academy of Management Executive*, May 1998, pp 86–94.

42 For example, see R Hoffman, 'Ten Reasons You Should Be Using 360-Degree Feedback', *HRMagazine*, April 1995, pp 82–85; '360-Degree Feedback: Will The Circle Be Broken?' *Training*, October 1996, pp 24–25; R Lepsinger and A D Lucia, '360° Feedback and Performance Appraisal', *Training*, September 1997, pp 62–70; and K M Nowack, J Hartley and W Bradley, 'How to Evaluate Your 360 Feedback Efforts', *Training & Development*, April 1999, pp 48–53.

43 B O'Reilly, '360 Feedback Can Change Your Life', *Fortune*, October 17, 1994, p 93.

44 For a comprehensive overview of 360-degree feedback, see W W Tornow and M London, *Maximizing the Value of 360-Degree Feedback* (San Francisco: Jossey-Bass, 1998).

45 Adapted and translated from anonymous, 'Het oordeel van iedereen rondom je', *HRM Magazine*, September 1, 1997.

46 Ibid.

47 Ibid.

48 Ibid.

49 See M M Harris and J Schaubroeck, 'A Meta-Analysis of Self-Supervisor, Self-Peer, and Peer-Supervisor Ratings', *Personnel Psychology*, Spring 1988, pp 43–62, and J Lane and P Herriot, 'Self-Ratings, Supervisor Ratings, Positions and Performance', *Journal of Occupational Psychology*, March 1990, pp 77–88. Also see J R Williams and P E Levy, 'The Effects of Perceived System Knowledge on the Agreement between Self-Ratings and Supervisor Ratings', *Personnel Psychology*, Winter 1992, pp 835–47; R F Martell and M R Borg, 'A Comparison of the Behavioral Rating Accuracy of Groups and Individuals', *Journal of Applied Psychology*, February 1993, pp 43–50; J D Makiney and P E Levy, 'The Influence of Self-Ratings versus Peer Ratings on Supervisors' Performance Judgments', *Organizational Behavior and Human Decision Processes*, June 1998, pp 212–28; and G W Cheung, 'Multifaceted Conceptions of Self-Other Ratings Disagreement', *Personnel Psychology*, Spring 1999, pp 1–36.

50 Fisher Hazucha, S A Hezlett and R J Schneider, 'The Impact of 360-Degree Feedback on Managerial Skills Development', *Human Resource Management*, Summer/Fall 1993, p 42. Also see M K Mount, T A Judge, S E Scullen, M R Sytsma and S A Hezlett, 'Trait, Rater and Level Effects in 360-Degree Performance Ratings', *Personnel Psychology*, Autumn 1998, pp 557–76.

51 D E Coates, 'Don't Tie 360 Feedback to Pay', *Training*, September 1998, pp 68–78.

52 List quoted from D W Bracken, 'Straight Talk about Multirater Feedback', *Training & Development*, September 1994, p 46. Also see D Antonioni, 'Designing an Effective 360-Degree Appraisal Feedback Process', *Organizational Dynamics*, Autumn 1996, pp 24–38.

53 For supporting evidence of employees' desire for prompt feedback, see D H Reid and M B Parsons, 'A Comparison of Staff Acceptability of Immediate versus Delayed Verbal Feedback in Staff Training', *Journal of Organizational Behavior Management*, no. 2, 1996, pp 35–47.

54 See B Filipczak, 'Can't Buy Me Love', *Training*, January 1996, pp 29–34; and S Kerr, 'Risky Business: The New Pay Game', *Fortune*, July 22, 1996, pp 94–95.

55 Strategic models of pay and rewards are discussed in C Joinson, 'Pay Attention to Pay Cycles', *HRMagazine*, November 1998, pp 71–78; M Bloom and G T Milkovich, 'A SHRM Perspective on International Compensation and Reward Systems', in *Research in Personnel and Human Resources Management*, supplement 4, ed G R Ferris (Stamford, CT: JAI Press, 1999), pp 283–303; and J Dolmat-Connell, 'Developing a Reward Strategy That Delivers Shareholder and Employee Value', *Compensation & Benefits Review*, March–April 1999, pp 46–53.

56 Based on and translated from V Giolito, 'Naf Naf étend aux non-cadres le régime des stock option', *L'essentiel du management*, August 1995, p 46.

57 For complete discussions, see A P Brief and R J Aldag, 'The Intrinsic-Extrinsic Dichotomy: Toward Conceptual Clarity', *Academy of Management Review*, July 1977, pp 496–500; and E L Deci, *Intrinsic Motivation* (New York: Plenum Press, 1975), Ch. 2.

58 See K I Kim, H-J Park and N Suzuki, 'Reward Allocations in the United States, Japan, and Korea: A Comparison of Individualistic and Collectivistic Cultures', *Academy of Management Journal*, March 1990, pp 188–98. Also see C C Chen, J R Meindl and H Hui, 'Deciding on Equity or Parity: A Test of Situational, Cultural, and Individual Factors', *Journal of Organizational Behavior*, March 1998, pp 115–29.

59 Based on M Bloom, 'The Performance Effects of Pay Dispersion on Individuals and Organizations', *Academy of Management Journal*, February 1999, pp 25–40.

60 Good discussions can be found in W Grossman and R E Hoskisson, 'CEO Pay at the Crossroads of Wall Street and Main: Toward the Strategic Design of Executive Compensation', *Academy of Management Executive*, February 1998, pp 43–57; J Kahn, 'A CEO Cuts His Own Pay', *Fortune*, October 26, 1998, pp 56, 60, 64; and A Rappaport, 'New Thinking on How to Link Executive Pay with Performance', *Harvard Business Review*, March–April 1999, pp 91–101.

61 List adapted from J L Pearce and R H Peters, 'A Contradictory Norms View of Employer–Employee Exchange', *Journal of Management*, Spring 1985, pp 19–30.

62 Ibid., p 25.

63 See D B McFarlin and P D Sweeney, 'Distributive and Procedural Justice as Predictors of Satisfaction with Personal and Organizational Outcomes', *Academy of Management Journal*, August 1992, pp 626–37.

64 M Von Glinow, 'Reward Strategies for Attracting, Evaluating, and Retaining Professionals', *Human Resource Management*, Summer 1985, p 193.

65 Six reward system objectives are discussed in E E Lawler III, 'The New Pay: A Strategic Approach', *Compensation & Benefits Review*, July–August 1995, pp 14–22.

66 D R Spitzer, 'Power Rewards: Rewards That Really Motivate', *Management Review*, May 1996, p 47. Also see S Kerr, 'An Academy Classic: On the Folly of Rewarding A, while Hoping for B', *Academy of Management Executive*, February 1995, pp 7–14.

67 List adapted from discussion in Spitzer, 'Power Rewards: Rewards that Really Motivate', pp 45–50. Also see R Eisenberger and J Cameron, 'Detrimental Effects of Reward: Reality or Myth?' *American Psychologist*, November 1996, pp 1153–66.

68 See, for example, T P Flannery, D A Hofrichter and P E Platten, *People, Performance, and Pay: Dynamic Compensation for Changing Organizations* (New York: The Free Press, 1996).

69 See S T Johnson, 'Plan Your Organization's Reward Strategy through Pay-for-Performance Dynamics', *Compensation & Benefits Review*, May–June 1998, pp 67–72; D Barksdale, 'Leading Employees through the Variable Pay Jungle', *HRMagazine*, July 1998, pp 111–18; R P Semler, 'Making a Difference: Developing Management Incentives That Drive Results', *Compensation & Benefits Review*, July–August 1998, pp 41–48; R Ganzel, 'What's Wrong with Pay for Performance?' *Training*, December 1998, pp 34–40; and R Plachy and S Plachy, 'Rewarding Employees Who Truly Make a Difference', *Compensation & Benefits Review*, May–June 1999, pp 34–39.

70 For both sides of the 'Does money motivate?' debate, see N Gupta and J D Shaw, 'Let the Evidence Speak: Financial Incentives Are Effective!!' *Compensation & Benefits Review*, March–April 1998, pp 26, 28–32; A Kohn, 'Challenging Behaviorist Dogma: Myths about Money and Motivation', *Compensation & Benefits Review*, March–April 1998, pp 27, 33–37; and B Ettorre, 'Is Salary a Motivator?' *Management Review*, January 1999, p 8.

71 H Gleckman, 'bonus-pay: buzzword or bonanza?', *Business Week*, November 14, 1994.

72 Ibid.

73 'How four companies are redefining the employment relationship through innovative changes in compensation and benefits, case studies: Whirlpool, Nike, Salamon and PSEG', *Compensation and Benefits Review*, January–February 1995, pp 71–80.

74 Data from N J Perry, 'Here Come Richer, Riskier Pay Plans', *Fortune*, December 19, 1988, p 51. Also see W Zellner, 'Trickle-Down Is Trickling Down at Work', *Business Week*, March 18, 1996, p 34.

75 Data from M Bloom and G T Milkovich, 'Relationships among Risk, Incentive Pay, and Organizational Performance', *Academy of Management Journal*, June 1998, pp 283–97.

76 For details, see G D Jenkins, Jr, N Gupta, A Mitra and J D Shaw, 'Are Financial Incentives Related to Performance? A Meta-Analytic Review of Empirical Research', *Journal of Applied Psychology*, October 1998, pp 777–87.

77 See M J Mandel, 'Those Fat Bonuses Don't Seem to Boost Performance', *Business Week*, January 8, 1990, p 26.

78 Based on discussion in R Ricklefs, 'Whither the Payoff on Sales Commissions?' *The Wall Street Journal*, June 6, 1990, p B1.

79 G Koretz, 'Bad Marks for Pay-by-Results', *Business Week*, September 4, 1995, p 28.

80 S Fernie and D Metcalf, *Participation, Contingent Pay, Representation and Workplace Performance: Evidence from Great Britain* (London: Centre for Economic Performance, 1995).

81 B Graham-Moore, 'Review of the Literature', in *Gainsharing*, eds B Graham-Moore and T L Ross (Washington, DC: The Bureau of National Affairs, 1990), p 20 (Emphasis added).

82 Ibid., based largely on pp 3–4. Also see J G Belcher, Jr, 'Gainsharing and Variable Pay: The State of the Art', *Compensation & Benefits Review*, May–June 1994, pp 50–60; and T M Welbourne and L R Gomez Mejia, 'Gainsharing: A Critical Review and a Future Research Agenda', *Journal of Management*, no. 3, 1995, pp 559–609.

83 For gainsharing success factors and problems, see D O Kim, 'Factors Influencing Organizational Performance in Gainsharing Programs', *Industrial Relations*, April 1996, pp 227–44; D Collins, 'Death of a Gainsharing Plan: Power Politics and Participatory Management', *Organizational Dynamics*, Summer 1995, pp 23–38; and D Collins, 'Case Study: 15 Lessons Learned from the Death of a Gainsharing Plan', *Compensation & Benefits Review*, March–April 1996, pp 31–40.

84 For details, see S E Markham, 'Pay-for-Performance Dilemma Revisited: Empirical Example of the Importance of Group Effects', *Journal of Applied Psychology*, May 1988, pp 172–80.

85 Data from K I Miller, 'Cultural and Role-Based Predictors of Organizational Participation and Allocation Preferences', *Communication Research*, December 1988, pp 699–725.

86 Gainsharing studies are reviewed in W Imberman, 'Gainsharing: A Lemon or Lemonade?' *Business Horizons*, January–February 1996, pp 36–40. Also see T M Welbourne, D B Balkin and L R Gomez Mejia, 'Gainsharing and Mutual Monitoring: A Combined Agency-Organizational Justice Interpretation', *Academy of Management Journal*, June 1995, pp 881–99.

87 Data from D Collins, 'How and Why Participatory Management Improves a Company's Social Performance', *Business & Society*, June 1996, pp 176–210.

88 B Geber, 'The Bugaboo of Team Pay', *Training*, August 1995, pp 25–26. Also see E Neuborne, Companies Save, But Workers Pay', *USA Today*, February 25, 1997, pp 1B–2B.

89 J S Dematteo, L T Eby and E Sundstrom, 'Team-Based Rewards: Current Empirical Evidence and Directions for Future Research', in *Research in Organizational Behavior*, vol. 20, eds B M Staw and L L Cummings (Greenwich, CT: JAI Press, 1998), p 152.

90 For example, see R Sisco, 'Put Your Money Where Your Teams Are', *Training*, July 1992, pp 41–45; J L Morris, 'Bonus Dollars for Team Players', *HRMagazine*, February 1995, pp 76–83; W J Timmins, 'Team-Based Compensation at Recently Reengineered Zeneca Ag Products', *Employment Relations Today*, Summer 1995, pp 43–51; R L Heneman and C von Hippel, 'Balancing Group and Individual Rewards: Rewarding Individual Contributions to the Team', *Compensation & Benefits Review*, July–August 1995, pp 63–68; and A Muoio, 'At SEI,

Teamwork Pays', *Fast Company*, April 1999, p 186.

[91] See D O'Neill, 'Blending the Best of Profit Sharing and Gainsharing, *HRMagazine*, March 1994, pp 66–70.

[92] This exercise is adapted from material in D M Herold and C K Parsons, 'Assessing the Feedback Environment in Work Organizations: Development of the Job Feedback Survey', *Journal of Applied Psychology*, May 1985, pp 290–305.

Chapter 10

[1] C Norton, 'Bad neighbours should be offered money for good behaviour', *The Independent*, July 26, 2000. Reproduced with permission.

[2] Complete details of this field study may be found in R S Haynes, R C Pine and H G Fitch, 'Reducing Accident Rates with Organizational Behavior Modification', *Academy of Management Journal*, June 1982, pp 407–16. A related study in The Netherlands is reported in S Siero, M Boon, G Kok and F Siero, 'Modification of Driving Behavior in a Large Transport Organization: A Field Experiment', *Journal of Applied Psychology*, June 1989, pp 417–23.

[3] J Saari, 'When does behaviour modification prevent accidents', *Leadership and Organization Development Journal*, vol. 15, 1994, pp 11–15.

[4] For a good background article on performance management, see G Rummler, 'In Search of the Holy Performance Grail', *Training & Development*, April 1996, pp 26–32.

[5] See E L Thorndike, *Educational Psychology: The Psychology of Learning, Vol. II* (New York: Columbia University Teachers College, 1913).

[6] Discussion of an early behaviourist who influenced Skinner's work can be found in P J Kreshel, 'John B Watson at J Walter Thompson: The Legitimation of "Science" in Advertising', *Journal of Advertising*, no. 2, 1990, pp 49–59. Recent discussions involving behaviourism include M R Ruiz, 'B F Skinner's Radical Behaviorism: Historical Misconstructions and Grounds for Feminist Reconstructions', *Psychology of Women Quarterly*, June 1995, pp 161–79; J A Nevin, 'Behavioral Economics and Behavioral Momentum', *Journal of the Experimental Analysis of Behavior*, November 1995, pp 385–95; and H Rachlin, 'Can We Leave Cognition to Cognitive Psychologists? Comments on an Article by George Loewenstein', *Organizational Behavior and Human Decision Processes*, March 1996, pp 296–99.

[7] For recent discussion, see J W Donahoe, 'The Unconventional Wisdom of B F Skinner: The Analysis–Interpretation Distinction', *Journal of the Experimental Analysis of Behavior*, September 1993, pp 453–56.

[8] See B F Skinner, *The Behavior of Organisms* (New York: Appleton-Century-Crofts, 1938).

[9] For modern approaches to respondent behaviour, see B Azar, 'Classical Conditioning Could Link Disorders and Brain Dysfunction, Researchers Suggest', *APA Monitor*, March 1999, p 17.

[10] For interesting discussions of Skinner and one of his students, see M B Gilbert and T F Gilbert, 'What Skinner Gave Us', *Training*, September 1991, pp 42–48; and 'HRD Pioneer Gilbert Leaves a Pervasive Legacy', *Training*, January 1996, p 14.

[11] For an instructive overview of learning, see G S Odiorne, 'Four Magic Moments in Changing Behavior', *Training*, June 1991, pp 43–46.

[12] Complete discussion of the A→B→C model may be found in F Luthans and R Kreitner, *Organizational Behavior Modification and Beyond: An Operant and Social Learning Approach* (Glenview, IL: Scott, Foresman, 1985), pp 46–49.

[13] D H Ruben and M J Ruben, 'Behavioral Principles on the Job: Control or Manipulation?' *Personnel*, May 1985, p 61.

[14] See P A Lamal, 'The Continuing Mischaracterization of Radical Behaviorism', *American Psychologist*, January 1990, p 71.

[15] See Luthans and Kreitner, *Organizational Behavior Modification and Beyond*, pp 49–56.

[16] The effect of praise is explored in C M Mueller and C S Dweck, 'Praise for Intelligence Can Undermine Children's Motivation and Performance', *Journal of Personality and Social Psychology*, July 1998, pp 33–52.

[17] See D H B Welsh, D J Bernstein and F Luthans, 'Application of the Premack Principle of Reinforcement to the Quality Performance of Service Employees', *Journal of Organizational Behavior Management*, no. 1, 1992, pp 9–32.

[18] Research on punishment is reported in B P Niehoff, R J Paul and J F S Bunch, 'The Social Effects of Punishment Events: The Influence of Violator Past Performance Record and Severity of the Punishment on Observers' Justice Perceptions and Attitudes', *Journal of Organizational Behavior*, November 1998, pp 589–602.

[19] L M Miller, *Behavior Management: The New Science of Managing People at Work* (New York: John Wiley & Sons, 1978), p 106.

[20] For a unique psychobiological interpretation of reinforcement, see N M White and P M Milner, 'The Psychobiology of Reinforcers', *Annual Review of Psychology*, vol. 43, 1992, pp 443–71.

[21] A useful resource on rewards is B Nelson, *1001 Ways to Reward Employees* (New York: Workman Publishing, 1994).

[22] D Gledhill, 'BA runs into air miles squall', *The Independent*, January 21, 2001.

[23] See C B Ferster and B F Skinner, *Schedules of Reinforcement* (New York: Appleton-Century-Crofts, 1957).

[24] See L M Saari and G P Latham, 'Employee Reactions to Continuous and Variable Ratio Reinforcement Schedules Involving a Monetary Incentive', *Journal of Applied Psychology*, August 1982, pp 506–8.

[25] P Brinkley-Rogers and R Collier, 'Along the Colorado, the Money's Flowing', *The Arizona Republic*, March 4, 1990, p A12.

[26] The topic of managerial credibility is covered in J M Kouzes and B Z Posner, *Credibility* (San Francisco: Jossey-Bass, 1993).

[27] See, for example, J C Bruening, 'Shaping Workers' Attitudes toward Safety', *Occupational Hazards*, March 1990, pp 49–51.

[28] An alternative five-step model—pinpoint, record, involve, coach, evaluate—may be found in K Blanchard and R Lorber, *Putting the One Minute Manager to Work* (New York: Berkley Books, 1984), p 58. Also see the model in F Luthans and A D Stajkovic, 'Reinforce for Performance: The Need to Go Beyond Pay and Even Rewards', *Academy of Management Executive*, May 1999, p 53.

[29] For related reading, see L J Rifkind and L F Harper, 'Conflict Management Strategies for the Equal Opportunity Difficult Person in the Sexually Harassing Workplace', *Public Personnel Management*, Fall 1994, pp 487–500.

[30] For example, see 'High-Risk Employees Often Require Coaxing to Watch Their Health', *The Wall Street Journal*, September 24, 1996, p A1; and P Brotherton, 'Paybacks Are Healthy', *HRMagazine*, August 1998, pp 2–6.

[31] L W Frederiksen, 'The Selection of Targets for Organizational Interventions', *Journal of Organizational Behavior Management*, no. 4, 1981–1982, p 4. Also see M E Furman, 'Reverse the 80-20 Rule', *Management Review*, January 1997, pp 18–21.

[32] For related discussion, see W Wilhelm, 'Changing Corporate Culture—or Corporate Behavior? How to Change Your Company', *Academy of Management Executive*, November 1992, pp 72–77.

[33] See J Conrin, 'A Comparison of Two Types of Antecedent Control over Supervisory Behavior', *Journal of Organizational Behavior Management*, Fall–Winter 1982, pp 37–47. For a report of the positive impact of antecedents on consumer behaviour, see M J Martinko, J D White and B Hassell, 'An Operant Analysis of Prompting in a Sales Environment', *Journal of Organizational Behavior Management*, no. 1, 1989, pp 93–107. Antecedent control of safety behaviour is reported in F M Streff, M J Kalsher and E S Geller, 'Developing Efficient Workplace Safety Programs: Observations of Response Covariation', *Journal of Organizational Behavior Management*, no. 2, 1993, pp 3–14.

[34] T K Connellan, *How to improve human performance: behaviourism in business and industry* (New York: Harper & Row, 1978), p 27. Effective antecedent control is reported in G Koretz, 'No smoking is working', *Business Week*, July 8, 1996, p 24.

[35] W C Hamner and E P Hamner, 'Behavior Modification on the Bottom Line', *Organizational Dynamics*, Spring 1976, p 8.

36 Luthans and Kreitner, *Organizational Behavior Modification and Beyond*, p 128. Incentive programmes are assessed in B Filipczak, 'Why No One Likes Your Incentive Program', *Training*, August 1993, pp 19–25; and A Kohn, 'Why Incentive Plans Cannot Work', *Harvard Business Review*, September–October 1993, pp 54–63.

37 See 'At Emery Air Freight: Positive Reinforcement Boosts Performance', *Organizational Dynamics*, Winter 1973, pp 41–50.

38 See D C Anderson, C R Crowell, M Doman and G S Howard, 'Performance Posting, Goal Setting, and Activity-Contingent Praise as Applied to a University Hockey Team', *Journal of Applied Psychology*, February 1988, pp 87–95.

39 An alternative perspective of punishment is presented in L Klebe Trevino, 'The Social Effects of Punishment in Organizations: A Justice Perspective', *Academy of Management Review*, October 1992, pp 647–76.

40 K Blanchard and S Johnson, *The One Minute Manager* (New York: Berkley Books, 1982), p 39. Interestingly, managers were given this identical bit of advice, 'Catch them doing something right!' five years earlier in R Kreitner, 'People Are Systems, Too: Filling the Feedback Vacuum', *Business Horizons*, November 1977, pp 54–58.

41 For a review of this research, see Luthans and Kreitner, *Organizational Behavior Modification and Beyond*, pp 139–44. An alternative view of the benefits of punishment is discussed in R D Arvey and J M Ivancevich, 'Punishment in Organizations: A Review, Propositions, and Research Suggestions', *Academy of Management Review*, January 1980, pp 123–32. Also see L E Atwater, S D Dionne, J F Camobreco, B J Avolio and A Lau, 'Individual Attributes and Leadership Style: Predicting the Use of Punishment and Its Effects', *Journal of Organizational Behavior*, November 1998, pp 559–76.

42 S Narod, 'Off-Beat Company Customs', *Dun's Business Month*, November 1984, p 66.

43 For example, see F L Fry, 'Operant Conditioning in Organizational Settings: Of Mice or Men?' *Personnel*, July–August 1974, pp 17–24; and E A Locke, 'The Myths of Behavior Mod in Organizations', *Academy of Management Review*, 1977, pp 543–53.

44 Evidence of constructive applications of B Mod in the workplace can be found in K O'Hara, C M Johnson and T A Beehr, 'Organizational Behavior Management in the Private Sector: A Review of Empirical Research and Recommendations for Further Investigation', *Academy of Management Review*, October 1985, pp 848–64. Also see additional issues of *Journal of Organizational Behavior Management*, particularly the special issue: 'Promoting Excellence through Performance Management', *Journal of Organizational Behavior Management*, no. 1, 1990; and W C Byham and A Pescuric, 'Behavior Modeling at the Teachable Moment', *Training*, December 1996, pp 50–56.

45 See R A Reber, J A Wallin and D L Duhon, 'Preventing Occupational Injuries through Performance Management', *Public Personnel Management*, Summer 1993, pp 301–11; R Ceniceros, 'Safety Rewards Can Lead to Real Change', *Business Insurance*, May 1, 1995, p 21; M A Hofmann, 'Behavior Modification at Work', *Business Insurance*, April 29, 1996, p 18; and M Z Kay, 'Achieving That 'EVEREST Feeling'', *Management Review*, April 1999, p 13. Related research is reported in S Clarke, 'Perceptions of Organizational Safety: Implications for the Development of Safety Culture', *Journal of Organizational Behavior*, March 1999, pp 185–98.

46 Data from A D Stajkovic and F Luthans, 'A Meta-Analysis of the Effects of Organizational Behavior Modification on Task Performance, 1975–95', *Academy of Management Journal*, October 1997, pp 1122–49. A brief summary of this study is reported in C Comeau-Kirschner, 'Improving Productivity Doesn't Cost a Dime', *Management Review*, January 1999, p 7.

47 Most European textbooks do not devote much attention to the subject [for an exception see J Arnold, C L Cooper and I T Robertson, *Work Psychology* (London: Pitman Publishing, 1995)] and even the reasons why European OB specialists do not like OB mod are not well documented.

48 R Gilby, 'Bogus behavior', *The Safety and Health Practitioner*, August 1996, pp 13–15.

49 Gilby, op. cit., p 13.

50 Helen Briggs, 'Brain control improves the music', *BBC News Online*, http://news.bbc.co.uk

51 See A Bandura, *Social Learning Theory* (Englewood Cliffs, NJ: Prentice-Hall, 1977). A further refinement is reported in A D Stajkovic and F Luthans, 'Social Cognitive Theory and Self-Efficacy: Going Beyond Traditional Motivational and Behavioral Approaches', *Organizational Dynamics*, Spring 1998, pp 62–74. Also see M Uhl-Bien and G B Graen, 'Individual Self-Management: Analysis of Professionals' Self-Managing Activities in Functional and Cross-Functional Work Teams', *Academy of Management Journal*, June 1998, pp 340–50.

52 F Luthans and T R V Davis, 'Behavioral Self-Management—The Missing Link in Managerial Effectiveness', *Organizational Dynamics*, Summer 1979, p 43.

53 Luthans and Kreitner, *Organizational Behavior Modification and Beyond*, p 158.

54 See, for example, C C Manz and H P Sims, Jr, 'Self-Management as a Substitute for Leadership: A Social Learning Theory Perspective', *Academy of Management Review*, July 1980, pp 361–67; C C Manz, *The Art of Self-Leadership* (Englewood Cliffs, NJ: Prentice-Hall, 1983); C C Manz, 'Self-Leadership: Toward an Expanded Theory of Self-Influence Processes in Organizations', *Academy of Management Review*, July 1986, pp 585–600; and C C Manz and H P Sims, Jr, *SuperLeadership: Leading Others to Lead Themselves* (New York: Prentice-Hall, 1989). An application of the social learning model is discussed in A M O'Leary-Kelly, R W Griffin and D J Glew, 'Organization-Motivated Aggression: A Research Framework', *Academy of Management Review*, January 1996, pp 225–53.

55 For example, see R Kelley and J Caplan, 'How Bell Labs Creates Star Performers', *Harvard Business Review*, July–August 1993, pp 128–39; E E Lawler III, 'Total Quality Management and Employee Involvement: Are They Compatible?' *Academy of Management Executive*, February 1994, pp 68–76; M J Stevens and M A Campion, 'The Knowledge, Skill, and Ability Requirements for Teamwork: Implications for Human Resource Management', *Journal of Management*, Summer 1994, pp 503–30; P F Drucker, 'Managing Oneself', *Harvard Business Review*, March–April 1998, pp 65–74; R Zemke, 'In Search of Self-Directed Learners', *Training*, May 1998, pp 60–68; and G Sexton, 'Invisible Assets', *Training*, June 1999, p 88.

56 Bandura, *Social Learning Theory*, p 13.

57 For related research, see M Castaneda, T A Kolenko and R J Aldag, 'Self-Management Perceptions and Practices: A Structural Equations Analysis', *Journal of Organizational Behavior*, January 1999, pp 101–20.

58 'Career Self-Management', *Industry Week*, September 5, 1994, p 36.

59 For more, see H Lancaster, 'Is Your Messy Desk a Sign You're Busy or Just Disorganized?' *The Wall Street Journal*, January 30, 1996, p B1; S Shellenbarger, 'Good Time-Managers Try Not to Manage All of Their Time', *The Wall Street Journal*, October 9, 1996, p B1; P Buhler, 'Time Management Is Really Self-Management', *Supervision*, March 1996, pp 24–26; H Lancaster, 'Procrastinators: Mend Your Ways Before Your Job Stalls', *The Wall Street Journal*, May 7, 1996, p B1; M O'Brien, 'Personal Mastery: The New Executive Curriculum', *Training*, July 1996, p 82; B Moses, 'The Busyness Trap', *Training*, November 1998, pp 38–42; and D J Abernathy, 'A Get-Real Guide to Time Management', *Training & Development*, June 1999, pp 22–26.

60 S R Covey, *The 7 Habits of Highly Effective People* (New York: Simon & Schuster, 1989), p 42. Also see J Hillkirk, 'Golden Rules Promoted for Work Success', *USA Today*, August 20, 1993, pp 1B–2B; L Bongiorno, 'Corporate America, Dr. Feelgood Will See You Now', *Business Week*, December 6, 1993, p 52; T K Smith, 'What's So Effective About Stephen Covey?' *Fortune*, December 12, 1994, pp 116–26; and E Brown, 'Stephen Covey's New One-Day Seminar', *Fortune*, February 1, 1999, pp 138–40.

61 Self-observation distortion is explored in S D Gosling, O P John, K H Craik and R W Robins, 'Do People Know How They Behave? Self-Reported Act Frequencies Compared with On-Line Codings by Observers', *Journal of Personality and Social*

Psychology, May 1998, pp 1337–49.

62 'Labor Letter: A Special News Report on People and their Jobs in Offices, Fields, and Factories', *The Wall Street Journal*, October 15, 1985, p 1.

63 Helpful instructions on formulating career goals may be found in D Heide and E N Kushell, 'I Can Improve My Management Skills by: _____ ', *Personnel Journal*, June 1984, pp 52–54. Also see B Farber, 'A Winning Attitude', *Selling Power*, April 1996, pp 70–71. Related research is reported in D VandeWalle, S P Brown, W L Cron and J W Slocum, Jr, 'The Influence of Goal Orientation and Self-Regulation Tactics on Sales Performance: A Longitudinal Field Test', *Journal of Applied Psychology*, April 1999, pp 249–59.

64 For excellent tips on self-management, see C P Neck, 'Managing Your Mind', *Internal Auditor*, June 1996, pp 60–63.

65 C Zastrow, *Talk to Yourself: Using the Power of Self-Talk* (Englewood Cliffs, NJ: Prentice-Hall, 1979), p 60. Also see Manz and Sims, *SuperLeadership*, pp 41–43; and C C Manz and C P Neck, 'Inner Leadership: Creating Productive Thought Patterns', *Academy of Management Executive*, August 1991, pp 87–95.

66 See C C Manz and C P Neck, 'Inner Leadership: Creating Productive Thought Patterns', pp 87–95. Also see C N Macrae, G V Bodenhausen and A B Milne, 'Saying No to Unwanted Thoughts: Self-Focus and the Regulation of Mental Life', *Journal of Personality and Social Psychology*, March 1998, pp 578–89.

67 E Franz, 'Private Pep Talk', *Selling Power*, May 1996, p 81.

68 Drawn from discussion in A Bandura, 'Self-Reinforcement: Theoretical and Methodological Considerations', *Behaviorism*, Fall 1976, pp 135–55.

69 R Kreitner and F Luthans, 'A Social Learning Approach to Behavioral Management: Radical Behaviorists "Mellowing Out"', *Organizational Dynamics*, Autumn 1984, p 63.

70 See R F Rakos and M V Grodek, 'An Empirical Evaluation of a Behavioral Self-Management Course in a College Setting', *Teaching of Psychology*, October 1984, pp 157–62.

71 S J Zaccaro, R J Foti and D A Kenny, 'Self-Monitoring and Trait-Based Variance in Leadership: An Investigation of Leader Flexibility across Multiple Group Situations', *Journal of Applied Psychology*, April 1991, p 309.

72 Luthans and Davis, 'Behavioral Self-Management—The Missing Link in Managerial Effectiveness', pp 52–59.

73 Results are presented in C A Frayne and G P Latham, 'Application of Social Learning Theory to Employee Self-Management of Attendance', *Journal of Applied Psychology*, August 1987, pp 387–92. Follow-up data are presented in G P Latham and C A Frayne, 'Self-Management Training for Increasing Job Attendance: A Follow-Up and a Replication', *Journal of Applied Psychology*, June 1989, pp 411–16.

74 See M A Howe, 'Using Imagery to Facilitate Organizational Development and Change', *Group & Organizational Studies*, March 1989, pp 70–82.

75 See C A Frayne and J M Geringer, 'Self-Management Training for Joint Venture General Managers', *Human Resource Planning*, no. 4, 1992, pp 69–85.

76 S L Robinson and R J Bennett, 'A Typology of Deviant Workplace Behaviors: A Multidimensional Scaling Study', *Academy of Management Journal*, April 1995, p 565.

Chapter 11

1 A Thorpe, 'The Office Gossip', *The Guardian*, May 15, 2000. Reproduced with permission.

2 B Legget, 'Getting the sound to match the vision', *The Guardian*, August 12, 2000.

3 I Labon, 'How I learnt to stop worrying and love the phone', *The Sunday Times*, May 7, 2000.

4 O C Ferrell and John Fraedrich, *Business Ethics: Ethical Decision Making and Cases* (Boston: Houghton Mifflin, 1991), p 143.

5 See M A Jaasma and R J Koper, 'The Relationship of Student-Faculty Out-of-Class Communication to Instructor Immediacy and Trust and to Student Motivation', *Communication Education*, January 1999, pp 41–47; and P G Clampitt and

C W Downs, 'Employee Perceptions of the Relationship between Communication and Productivity: A Field Study', *Journal of Business Communication*, 1993, pp 5–28.

6 Results can be found in D Fenn, 'Benchmark: What Drives the Skills Gap?' *Inc.*, May 1996, p 111.

7 J L Bowditch and A F Buono, *A Primer on Organizational Behavior*, 4th ed (New York: John Wiley & Sons, 1997), p 120.

8 For a review of these criticisms see L L Putnam, N Phillips and P Chapman, 'Metaphors of Communication and Organization', in *Handbook of Organization Studies*, eds S R Clegg, C Hardy and W R Nord (London: Sage Publications, 1996), pp 375–408.

9 S Outling, 'Why is my mail talking to me?', *The Guardian*, Monday April 7, 2000.

10 Results of this study can be found in C M Fiol, 'Corporate Communications: Comparing Executives' Private and Public Statements', *Academy of Management Journal*, April 1995, pp 522–36.

11 A Thorpe, 'How to ... avoid misunderstandings', *The Guardian*, November 4, 2000.

12 L Labich, 'How to Fire People and Still Sleep at Night', *Fortune*, June 10, 1996, p 65.

13 J Humphrys, 'Hell is other people talking webspeak on mobile phones', *The Sunday Times*, August 27, 2000.

14 Ibid.

15 S R Axley, 'Managerial and Organizational Communication in Terms of the Conduit Metaphor', *Academy of Management Review*, July 1984, pp 428–37.

16 A Thorpe, 'How to ... avoid misunderstandings', *The Guardian*, November 4, 2000.

17 Adapted and translated from anonymous, '169 berichten per dag', *Vacature*, July 28, 1998.

18 Results can be found in D Clark, 'Managing the Mountain', *The Wall Street Journal*, June 21, 1999, p R4.

19 Adapted and translated from J Schuddinck, 'Interactiviteit zonder grenzen', *Vacature*, January 28, 2000.

20 R L Daft and R H Lengel, 'Information Richness: A New Approach to Managerial Behavior and Organizational Design', in *Research in Organizational Behavior*, eds B M Staw and L L Cummings (Greenwich, CT: JAI Press, 1984), p 196.

21 C A Bartlett, L Elderkin, K McQuade and M Hart, 'The Body Shop International', in: R D Buzzell, J A Quelch and C A Bartlett, *Global Marketing Management: cases and readings* (Reading: Addison-West Publishing Company), p 619.

22 See V Anand, C C Manz and W H Glick, 'An Organizational Memory Approach to Information Management', *Academy of Management Review*, October 1998, pp 796–809; J Webster and L K Trevino, 'Rational and Social Theories as Complementary Explanations of Communications Media Choices: Two Policy-Capturing Studies', *Academy of Management Journal*, December 1995, pp 1544–72, and J Fulk, 'Social Construction of Communication Technology', *Academy of Management Journal*, October 1993, pp 921–50.

23 See R E Rice and D E Shook, 'Relationships of Job Categories and Organizational Levels to Use of Communication Channels, Including Electronic Mail: A Meta-Analysis and Extension', *Journal of Management Studies*, March 1990, pp 195–229.

24 Results can be found in B Davenport Sypher and T E Zorn, Jr, 'Communication-Related Abilities and Upward Mobility: A Longitudinal Investigation', *Human Communication Research*, Spring 1986, pp 420–31.

25 Communication competence is discussed by J S Hinton and M W Kramer, 'The Impact of Self-Directed Videotape Feedback on Students' Self-Reported Levels of Communication Competence and Apprehension', *Communication Education*, April 1998, pp 151–61; and L J Carrell and S C Willmington, 'The Relationship between Self-Report Measures of Communication Apprehension and Trained Observers' Ratings of Communication Competence', *Communication Reports*, Winter 1998, pp 87–95.

26 See E Raudsepp, 'Are You Properly Assertive?' *Supervision*, June 1992, pp 17–18; and D A Infante and W I Gorden, 'Superiors' Argumentativeness and Verbal Aggressiveness as Predictors of Subordinates' Satisfaction', *Human*

Communication Research, Fall 1985, pp 117–25.

27 J A Waters, 'Managerial Assertiveness', *Business Horizons*, September–October 1982, p 25.

28 A Thorpe, 'The Office Gossip', *The Guardian*, July 24, 2000.

29 J A Waters, p 27.

30 W D St. John, 'You Are What You Communicate', *Personnel Journal*, October 1985, p 40.

31 The importance of non-verbal communication is discussed by L K Guerrero and J A DeVito, *The Nonverbal Communication Reader: Classic and Contemporary Readings*, 2nd ed (Prospect Heights, IL: Waveland Press, 1999).

32 The effect of non-verbal cues on hiring decisions was examined by G E Wright and K D Multon, 'Employer's Perceptions of Nonverbal Communication in Job Interviews for Persons with Physical Disabilities', *Journal of Vocational Behavior*, October 1995, pp 214–27; and R C Liden, C L Martin and C K Parsons, 'Interviewer and Applicant Behaviors in Employment Interviews', *Academy of Management Journal*, April 1993, pp 372–86.

33 Results can be found in S D Kelly, D J Barr, R B Church and K Lynch, 'Offering a Hand to Pragmatic Understanding: The Role of Speech and Gesture in Comprehension and Memory', *Journal of Memory and Language*, May 1999, pp 577–92.

34 Related research is summarized by J A Hall, 'Male and Female Nonverbal Behavior', in *Multichannel Integrations of Nonverbal Behavior*, eds A W Siegman and S Feldstein (Hillsdale, NJ: Lawrence Erlbaum, 1985), pp 195–226.

35 A thorough discussion of cross-cultural differences is provided by R E Axtell, *Gestures: The Do's and Taboos of Body Language Around the World* (New York: John Wiley & Sons, 1991). Problems with body language analysis are also discussed by C L Karrass, 'Body Language: Beware the Hype', *Traffic Management*, January 1992, p 27; and M Everett and B Wiesendanger, 'What Does Body Language Really Say?' *Sales & Marketing Management*, April 1992, p 40.

36 Results can be found in Hall, 'Male and Female Nonverbal Behavior'.

37 See J A Russell, 'Facial Expressions of Emotion: What Lies Beyond Minimal Universality?' *Psychological Bulletin*, November 1995, pp 379–91.

38 Norms for cross-cultural eye contact are discussed by C Engholm, *When Business East Meets Business West: The Guide to Practice and Protocol in the Pacific Rim* (New York: John Wiley & Sons, 1991).

39 Results can be found in J S Carton, E A Kessler and C L Pape, 'Nonverbal Decoding Skills and Relationship Well-Being in Adults', *Journal of Nonverbal Behavior*, Spring 1999, pp 91–100.

40 St. John, 'You Are What You Communicate', p 43.

41 See D Ray, 'Are You Listening?' *Selling Power*, June 1999, pp 28–30; and P Meyer, 'So You Want the President's Job', *Business Horizons*, January–February 1998, pp 2–6.

42 Estimates are provided in both J Hart Seibert, 'Listening in the Organizational Context', in *Listening Behavior: Measurement and Application*, ed R N Bostrom (New York: The Guilford Press, 1990), pp 119–27; and D W Caudill and R M Donaldson, 'Effective Listening Tips for Managers', *Administrative Management*, September 1986, pp 22–23.

43 See C G Pearce, 'How Effective Are We as Listeners?' *Training & Development*, April 1993, pp 79–80; and G Manning, K Curtis and S McMillen, *Building Community: The Human Side of Work* (Cincinnati, OH: Thomson Executive Press, 1996), pp 127–54.

44 For a summary of supporting research, see K W Watson and L L Barker, 'Listening Behavior: Definition and Measurement', in *Communication Yearbook 8*, ed R N Bostrom (Beverly Hills, CA: Sage Publications, 1984); and L B Comer and T Drollinger, 'Active Empathetic Listening and Selling Success: A Conceptual Framework', *Journal of Personal Selling & Sales Management*, Winter 1999, pp 15–29.

45 For a thorough discussion of the different listening styles, see R T Bennett and R V Wood, 'Effective Communication via Listening Styles', *Business*, April–June 1989, pp 45–48.

46 Ibid., p 46.

47 Ibid., p 47.

48 Ibid., p 46.

49 See S R Covey, *The 7 Habits of Highly Effective People* (New York: Simon & Schuster, 1989).

50 C Redding, *Communication within the Organization: An Interpretive Review of Theory and Research* (New York: Industrial Communication Council, 1972).

51 Adapted and translated from L De Smet, 'Communicatie is mortel van het bedrijf', *Vacature*, September 1, 1996. Reproduced with permission.

52 K Hilpern, 'Hang on – that's my job', *The Guardian*, February 14, 2000.

53 Ibid.

54 Organizational benefits of the grapevine are discussed by T Galpin, 'Pruning the Grapevine', *Training & Development*, April 1995, pp 28–32; and J Smythe, 'Harvesting the Office Grapevine', *People Management*, September 1995, pp 24–27.

55 Results can be found in S J Modic, 'Grapevine Rated Most Believable', *Industry Week*, May 15, 1989, pp 11, 14.

56 Anonymous, 'Why it's good to talk', *The Guardian*, April 12, 1999.

57 See K Davis, 'Management Communication and the Grapevine', *Harvard Business Review*, September–October 1953, pp 43–49.

58 H B Vickery III, 'Tapping into the Employee Grapevine', *Association Management*, January 1984, pp 59–60.

59 A thorough discussion of organizational moles is provided by J G Bruhn and A P Chesney, 'Organizational Moles: Information Control and the Acquisition of Power and Status', *Health Care Supervisor*, September 1995, pp 24–31.

60 Earlier research is discussed by Davis, 'Management Communication and the Grapevine'; and R Rowan, 'Where Did *That* Rumor Come From?' *Fortune*, August 13, 1979, pp 130–31, 134, 137. The most recent research is discussed by S M Crampton, J W Hodge and J M Mishra, 'The Informal Communication Network: Factors Influencing Grapevine Activity', *Public Personnel Management*, Winter 1998; 'Pruning the Company Grapevine', *Supervision*, September 1986, p 11; and R Half, 'Managing Your Career: "How Can I Stop the Gossip?"' *Management Accounting*, September 1987, p 27.

61 Anonymous, 'Why it's good to talk', *The Guardian*, April 12, 1999.

62 For a thorough discussion of communication distortion, see E W Larson and J B King, 'The Systematic Distortion of Information: An Ongoing Challenge to Management', *Organizational Dynamics*, Winter 1996, pp 49–61.

63 J Fulk and S Mani, 'Distortion of Communication in Hierarchical Relationships', in *Communication Yearbook 9*, ed M L McLaughlin (Beverly Hills, CA: Sage Publications, 1986), p 483.

64 For a review of this research, see ibid., pp 483–510.

65 Adapted and translated from F Van der Auwera, 'Nieuwe technologie maakt managers mobiel', *Vacature*, May 31, 1997.

66 Results were reported in A Petersen, 'A Fine Line: Companies Face a Delicate Task When It Comes to Deciding What to Put on Their Intranets: How Much Is Too Much?' *The Wall Street Journal*, June 21, 1999, p R8.

67 This conclusion is discussed by O Edwards, 'Inflammation Highway', *Forbes*, February 26, 1996, p 120.

68 The benefits of using email were derived from a discussion in R F Federico and J M Bowley, 'The Great E-Mail Debate', *HRMagazine*, January 1996, pp 67–72.

69 Results can be found in M L Markus, 'Electronic Mail as the Medium of Managerial Choice', *Organization Science*, November 1994, pp 502–27.

70 H Freeman, 'Caught up in the communication loop', *The Guardian*, September 30, 2000.

71 Results can be found in M S Thompson and M S Feldman, 'Electronic Mail and Organizational Communication: Does Saying "Hi" Really Matter', *Organization Science*, November–December 1998, pp 685–98.

72 H Freeman, op. cit.

73 M Bender, 'CSFB fires for dirty jokes on e-mail system', *Investment Dealers Digest*, vol. 63, no. 36, pp 8–10.

[74] See the discussion in B Fryer, 'E-Mail: Backbone of the Info Age or Smoking Gun?' *Your Company*, July/August 1999, pp 73–76.

[75] The types of information technology used by virtual teams is discussed by A M Townsend, S M DeMarie and A R Hendrickson, 'Virtual Teams: Technology and the Workplace of the Future', *Academy of Management Executive*, August 1998, pp 17–29.

[76] Challenges associated with virtual operations are discussed by S O'Mahony and S R Barley, 'Do Digital Telecommunications Affect Work and Organization? The State of Our Knowledge', in *Research in Organizational Behavior*, vol. 21, eds R I Sutton and B M Staw (Stamford, CT: JAI Press, 1999), pp 125–61; and C Grove and W Hallowell, 'Spinning Your Wheels? Successful Global Teams Know How to Gain Traction', *HRMagazine*, April 1998, pp 25–28.

[77] M Demsey, 'Scottish pace-setter – for a decade, the Royal Bank has pioneered in video', *The Financial Times*, November 1, 1995.

[78] Excerpted from K Kiser, 'Working on World Time', *Training*, March 1999, p 29.

[79] L Vervenne, 'Tele-flexibiliteit', *Belgian Business and Industry*, November 3, 1994.

[80] D Panucci, 'Remote Control', *Management Today*, April 1995, pp 78–80.

[81] Supporting evidence is presented S Fister, 'A Lure for Labor', *Training*, February 1999, pp 56–62; M Apgar, IV, 'The Alternative Workplace: Changing Where and How People Work', *Harvard Business Review*, May–June 1998, pp 121–36; and C Hymowitz, 'Remote Managers Find Ways to Narrow the Distance Gap', *The Wall Street Journal*, April 6, 1999, p B1.

[82] The preceding barriers are discussed by J P Scully, 'People: The Imperfect Communicators', *Quality Progress*, April 1995, pp 37–39.

[83] For a thorough discussion of these barriers, see C R Rogers and F J Roethlisberger, 'Barriers and Gateways to Communication', *Harvard Business Review*, July–August 1952, pp 46–52.

Chapter 12

[1] Based on C Cameron, 'Teamwork is vital in battle of the elements', *Financial Times*, January 27, 2000; Anonymous, 'Running a business is like sailing a yacht', *Business Day* (South Africa), August 31, 2000 and R Eglin, 'Ocean racing turns men into managers', *The Sunday Times*, October 15, 2000.

[2] M Kets de Vries, 'Mastering management: trust is at the core of corporate values', *The Financial Times*, October 2, 2000.

[3] See, for example, J P Masciarelli, 'Are you managing your relationships?', *Management Review*, April 1998, pp 41–45

[4] E Van Velsor and J Brittain Leslie, 'Why executives derail: perspectives across time and culture', *Academy of Management Executive*, November 1995, p 62.

[5] See P F Drucker, 'The Coming of the New Organization', *Harvard Business Review*, January–February 1988, pp 45–53.

[6] Data from 'HR Data Files', *HRMagazine*, June 1995, p 65.

[7] Adapted and translated from F Van der Auwera, 'Teambeesten', *Vacature*, June 12, 1999.

[8] Adapted and translated from F Van der Auwera, 'Wij zijn vooral evenwichtskunstenaars', *Vacature*, October 10, 1998. Reproduced with permission.

[9] K Lowry Miller, 'Siemens Shapes Up', *Business Week*, May 1, 1995, p 52.

[10] P Engardio and G DeGeorge, 'Importing Enthusiasm', *Business Week*, 1994 Special Issue: 21st Century Capitalism, p 122.

[11] J Rossant, 'The Man Who's Driving Fiat Like a Ferrari', *Business Week*, January 23, 1995, p 82.

[12] S Hamm and M Stepanek, 'From Reengineering to E-Engineering', *Business Week* E.BIZ, March 22, 1999.

[13] See B W Tuckman, 'Developmental sequence in small groups', *Psychological Bulletin*, June 1965, pp 384–99; and B W Tuckaman and M A C Jensen, 'Stages of small group development revisited', *Group & Organization Studies*,

December 1977, pp 419–27. An instructive adaptation of the Tuckman model can be found in L Holpp, 'If empowerment is so good, why does it hurt?', *Training*, March 1995, p 56.

[14] Alternative group development models are discussed in L N Jewell and H J Reitz, *Group Effectiveness in Organizations* (Glenview, IL: Scott, Foresman, 1981), pp 15–20; and R S Wellins, W C Byham and J M Wilson, *Empowered Teams: Creating Self-Directed Work Groups That Improve Quality, Productivity, and Participation* (San Francisco: Jossey-Bass, 1991).

[15] Practical advice on handling a dominating group member can be found in M Finley, 'Belling the Bully', *HRMagazine*, March 1992, pp 82–86.

[16] Jewell and Reitz, op. cit., p 19.

[17] D Davies and B C Kuypers, 'Group Development and Interpersonal Feedback', *Group & Organizational Studies*, June 1985, p 194.

[18] Ibid., pp 184–208.

[19] Adapted and translated from M Vandersmissen, 'Als collega's vrienden worden', *De Standaard*, September 21, 2000.

[20] J R Katzenbach and D K Smith, *The Wisdom of Teams: Creating the High-Performance Organization* (New York: HarperBusiness, 1999), p 45.

[21] See L G Bolman and T E Deal, 'What Makes a Team Work?' *Organizational Dynamics*, Autumn 1992, pp 34–44.

[22] J R Katzenbach and D K Smith, 'The Discipline of Teams', *Harvard Business Review*, March–April 1993, p 112.

[23] 'A Team's-Eye View of Teams', *Training*, November 1995, p 16.

[24] See E Sundstrom, K P DeMeuse and D Futrell, 'Work Teams', *American Psychologist*, February 1990, pp 120–33.

[25] For an alternative typology of teams, see S G Cohen, 'New Approaches to Teams and Teamwork', in *Organizing for the Future: The New Logic for Managing Complex Organizations*, eds J R Galbraith, E E Lawler III and Associates (San Francisco: Jossey-Bass, 1993), Ch. 8, pp 194–226.

[26] For a good update, see A Reinhardt and S Browder, 'Boeing', *Business Week*, September 30, 1996, pp 119–25. Also see G Van der Vegt, B Emans and E Van de Vliert, 'Effects of Interdependencies in Project Teams', *The Journal of Social Psychology*, April 1999, pp 202–14.

[27] Based on P Marsh: 'Management down in the boiler room – Peter Marsch explains how Blue Circle developed a standardised product for the European market.', *The Financial Times*, August 21, 1995, p 8.

[28] Descriptions of action teams can be found in D Field, 'Air and Ground Crews Team to Turn around Flights', *USA Today*, March 17, 1998, p 10E; and K S Peterson, 'Minding the Patient: Teams Listen to Hearts, Minds', *USA Today*, November 9, 1998, p 6D. Also see A B Drexler and R Forrester, 'Interdependence: The Crux of Teamwork', *HRMagazine*, September 1998, pp 52–62.

[29] An instructive overview of group effectiveness models can be found in P S Goodman, E Ravlin and M Schminke, 'Understanding Groups in Organizations', in *Research in Organizational Behavior*, eds L L Cummings and B M Staw (Greenwich, CT: JAI Press, 1987), vol. 9, pp 121–73. Also see D Dunphy and B Bryant, 'Teams: Panaceas or Prescriptions for Improved Performance?' *Human Relations*, May 1996, pp 677–99; and G A Neuman and J Wright, 'Team Effectiveness: Beyond Skills and Cognitive Ability', *Journal of Applied Psychology*, June 1999, pp 376–89.

[30] Other team criteria are discussed in N R Anderson and M A West, 'Measuring Climate for Work Group Innovation: Development and Validation of the Team Climate Inventory', *Journal of Organizational Behavior*, May 1998, pp 235–58; and M J Stevens and M A Campion, 'Staffing Work Teams: Development and Validation of a Selection Test for Teamwork Settings', *Journal of Management*, no. 2, 1999, pp 207–28.

[31] For example, see S R Rayner, 'Team Traps: What They Are, How to Avoid Them', *National Productivity Review*, Summer 1996, pp 101–15; P W Mulvey, J F Veiga and P M Elsass, 'When Teammates Raise a White Flag', *Academy of Management Executive*, February 1996, pp 40–49; L Holpp and R Phillips,

'When Is a Team Its Own Worst Enemy?' *Training*, September 1995, pp 71–82; B Richardson, 'Why Work Teams Flop—and What Can Be Done about It', *National Productivity Review*, Winter 1994/95, pp 9–13; and B Dumaine, 'The Trouble with Teams', *Fortune*, September 5, 1994, pp 86–92.

32 D Butcher and C Bailey, 'Crewed Awakenings', *People Management*, August 3, 2000.

33 D Butcher and C Bailey, ibid.

34 Anonymous, 'Managerial wisdom: Real-life Dilberts – did managers really say that?', *The Guardian*, September 28, 1999.

35 Adapted R Whitely & Diane Hessan, *De klant als de kern van de zaak', Vijf strategieën voor klantgerichte groei'*, (Amsterdam/Antwerpen: Contact Business Bibliotheek, 1997).

36 R Yeung and S Bailey, 'Get it together', *Accountancy*, June 1999.

37 D Hambrick 'Mastering Management: putting the team back into top management', *The Financial Times*, October 9, 2000.

38 R Yeung and S Bailey, op. cit.

39 Team problems are revealed in L Holpp, 'The Betrayal of the American Work Team', *Training*, May 1996, pp 38–42; S Wetlaufer, 'The Team That Wasn't', *Harvard Business Review*, November–December 1994, pp 22–38; 'More Trouble with Teams', *Training*, October 1996, p 21; and E Neuborne, 'Companies Save, But Workers Pay', *USA Today*, February 25, 1997, pp 1B–2B.

40 For additional information, see S E Asch, *Social Psychology* (Englewood Cliffs, NJ: Prentice-Hall, 1952), Ch. 16.

41 See T P Williams and S Sogon, 'Group Composition and Conforming Behavior in Japanese Students', *Japanese Psychological Research*, no. 4, 1984, pp 231–34; and T Amir, 'The Asch Conformity Effect: A Study in Kuwait', *Social Behavior and Personality*, no. 2, 1984, pp 187–90.

42 Data from R Bond and P B Smith, 'Culture and Conformity: A Meta-Analysis of Studies Using Asch's (1952b, 1956) Line Judgment Task', *Psychological Bulletin*, January 1996, pp 111–37.

43 R McNamara, *In retrospect: The Tragedy and Lessons of Vietnam* (New York: Times Books, 1995).

44 For a comprehensive update on groupthink, see the entire February–March 1998 issue of *Organizational Behavior and Human Decision Processes* (12 articles).

45 I L Janis, *Groupthink*, 2nd ed (Boston: Houghton Mifflin, 1982), p 9. Alternative models are discussed in K Granstrom and D Stiwne, 'A Bipolar Model of Groupthink: An Expansion of Janis's Concept', *Small Group Research*, February 1998, pp 32–56; and A R Flippen, 'Understanding Groupthink From a Self-Regulatory Perspective', *Small Group Research*, April 1999, pp 139–65.

46 Ibid. For an alternative model, see R J Aldag and S Riggs Fuller, 'Beyond Fiasco: A Reappraisal of the Groupthink Phenomenon and a New Model of Group Decision Processes', *Psychological Bulletin*, May 1993, pp 533–52. Also see A A Mohamed and F A Wiebe, 'Toward a Process Theory of Groupthink', *Small Group Research*, August 1996, pp 416–30.

47 Details of this study may be found in M R Callaway and J K Esser, 'Groupthink: Effects of Cohesiveness and Problem-Solving Procedures on Group Decision Making', *Social Behavior and Personality*, no. 2, 1984, pp 157–64. Also see C R Leana, 'A Partial Test of Janis's Groupthink Model: Effects of Group Cohesiveness and Leader-Behavior on Defective Decision Making', *Journal of Management*, Spring 1985, pp 5–17; and G Moorhead and J R Montanari, 'An Empirical Investigation of the Groupthink Phenomenon', *Human Relations*, May 1986, pp 399–410. A more modest indirect effect is reported in J N Choi and M U Kim, 'The Organizational Application of Groupthink and Its Limitations in Organizations', *Journal of Applied Psychology*, April 1999, pp 297–306.

48 Adapted from discussion in Janis, *Groupthink*, Ch. 11.

49 Based on discussion in B Latane, K Williams and S Harkins, 'Many Hands Make Light the Work: The Causes and Consequences of Social Loafing', *Journal of Personality and Social Psychology*, June 1979, pp 822–32; and D A Kravitz and B Martin, 'Ringelmann Rediscovered: The Original Article', *Journal of Personality and Social Psychology*, May 1986, pp 936–41.

50 See J A Shepperd, 'Productivity Loss in Performance Groups: A Motivation Analysis', *Psychological Bulletin*, no. 1, 1993, pp 67–81; R E Kidwell, Jr, and N Bennett, 'Employee Propensity to Withhold Effort: A Conceptual Model to Intersect Three Avenues of Research', *Academy of Management Review*, July 1993, pp 429–56; and S J Karau and K D Williams, 'Social Loafing: Meta-Analytic Review and Theoretical Integration', *Journal of Personality and Social Psychology*, October 1993, pp 681–706.

51 See S J Zaccaro, 'Social Loafing: The Role of Task Attractiveness', *Personality and Social Psychology Bulletin*, March 1984, pp 99–106; J M Jackson and K D Williams, 'Social Loafing on Difficult Tasks: Working Collectively Can Improve Performance', *Journal of Personality and Social Psychology*, October 1985, pp 937–42; and J M George, 'Extrinsic and Intrinsic Origins of Perceived Social Loafing in Organizations', *Academy of Management Journal*, March 1992, pp 191–202.

52 For complete details, see K Williams, S Harkins and B Latane, 'Identifiability as a Deterrent to Social Loafing: Two Cheering Experiments', *Journal of Personality and Social Psychology*, February 1981, pp 303–11.

53 See J M Jackson and S G Harkins, 'Equity in Effort: An Explanation of the Social Loafing Effect', *Journal of Personality and Social Psychology*, November 1985, pp 1199–1206.

54 Both studies are reported in S G Harkins and K Szymanski, 'Social Loafing and Group Evaluation', *Journal of Personality and Social Psychology*, June 1989, pp 934–41.

55 Data from J A Wagner III, 'Studies of Individualism-Collectivism: Effects on Cooperation in Groups', *Academy of Management Journal*, February 1995, pp 152–72. Also see P W Mulvey and H J Klein, 'The Impact of Perceived Loafing and Collective Efficacy on Group Goal Processes and Group Performance', *Organizational Behavior and Human Decision Processes*, April 1998, pp 62–87; and P W Mulvey, L Bowes-Sperry and H J Klein, 'The Effects of Perceived Loafing and Defensive Impression Management on Group Effectiveness', *Small Group Research*, June 1998, pp 394–415.

56 S G Rogelberg, J L Barnes-Farrell and C A Lowe, 'The Stepladder Technique: An Alternative Group Structure Facilitating Effective Group Decision Making', *Journal of Applied Psychology*, October 1992, p 730.

57 Adapted and translated from Anonymous, 'Zuinige manier van werken', *Vacature*, January 25, 1999.

58 M Deutsch, *The resolution of conflict* (New Haven, CT: Yale University Press, 1973)

59 J Kay, *Foundations of corporate success*, (New York: Oxford University Press, 1993), pp 70–71.

60 Adapted and translated from Anonymous, 'Het teamwork groeide van onderuit', *Vacature*, October 3, 1998.

61 See J T Delaney, 'Workplace Cooperation: Current Problems, New Approaches', *Journal of Labor Research*, Winter 1996, pp 45–61; H Mintzberg, D Dougherty, J Jorgensen and F Westley, 'Some Surprising Things about Collaboration—Knowing How People Connect Makes It Work Better', *Organizational Dynamics*, Spring 1996, pp 60–71; R Crow, 'Institutionalized Competition and Its Effects on Teamwork', *Journal for Quality and Participation*, June 1995, pp 46–54; K G Smith, S J Carroll and S J Ashford, 'Intra- and Interorganizational Cooperation: Toward a Research Agenda', *Academy of Management Journal*, February 1995, pp 7–23; M E Haskins, J Liedtka and J Rosenblum, 'Beyond Teams: Toward an Ethic of Collaboration', *Organizational Dynamics*, Spring 1998, pp 34–50; and C C Chen, X P Chen and J R Meindl, 'How Can Cooperation Be Fostered? The Cultural Effects of Individualism-Collectivism', *Academy of Management Review*, April 1998, pp 285–304.

62 A Kohn, 'How to Succeed without Even Vying', *Psychology Today*, September 1986, pp 27–28. Sports psychologists discuss 'co-operative competition' in S Sleek, 'Competition: Who's the Real Opponent?' *APA Monitor*, July 1996, p 8.

63 D W Johnson, G Maruyama, R Johnson, D Nelson and L Skon, 'Effects of Cooperative, Competitive, and Individualistic Goal Structures on Achievement: A Meta-Analysis', *Psychological Bulletin*, January 1981, pp 56–57. An alternative interpretation of the foregoing study that emphasizes the influence of situational factors can be found in J L Cotton and M S Cook, 'Meta-Analysis and the Effects of Various Reward Systems: Some Different Conclusions from Johnson et al.', *Psychological Bulletin*, July 1982, pp 176–83. Also see A E Ortiz, D W Johnson and R T Johnson, 'The Effect of Positive Goal and Resource Interdependence on Individual Performance', *The Journal of Social Psychology*, April 1996, pp 243–49; and S L Gaertner, J F Dovidio, M C Rust, J A Nier, B S Banker, C M Ward, G R Mottola and M Houlette, 'Reducing Intergroup Bias: Elements of Intergroup Cooperation', *Journal of Personality and Social Psychology*, March 1999, pp 388–402.

64 S W Cook and M Pelfrey, 'Reactions to Being Helped in Cooperating Interracial Groups: A Context Effect', *Journal of Personality and Social Psychology*, November 1985, p 1243. Also see W E Watson, L Johnson and D Merritt, 'Team Orientation, Self-Orientation, and Diversity in Task Groups', *Group & Organization Management*, June 1998, pp 161–88.

65 B Randall Palef, 'The team and me: reflections of a design group', *Personnel Journal*, February 1994, p 8.

66 Cruise and R O'Brien, 'Is trust a calculable asset in the firm?', *Business Strategy Review*, Winter 1995, pp 39–54.

67 Adapted and translated from Anonymous, 'Een team draait op vertrouwen', *Vacature*, August 23, 1997.

68 Also see D M Rousseau, S B Sitkin, R S Burt and C Camerer, 'Not So Different After All: A Cross-Discipline View of Trust', *Academy of Management Review*, July 1998, pp 393–404; and A C Wicks, S L Berman and T M Jones, 'The Structure of Optimal Trust: Moral and Strategic Implications', *Academy of Management Review*, January 1999, pp 99–116.

69 J D Lewis and A Weigert, 'Trust as a Social Reality', *Social Forces*, June 1985, p 971. Trust is examined as an *indirect* factor in K T Dirks, 'The Effects of Interpersonal Trust on Work Group Performance', *Journal of Applied Psychology*, June 1999, pp 445–55.

70 R C Mayer, J H Davis and F D Schoorman, 'An Integrative Model of Organizational Trust', *Academy of Management Review*, July 1995, p 715.

71 Lewis and Weigert, 'Trust as a Social Reality', p 970. Also see S G Goto, 'To Trust or Not to Trust: Situational and Dispositional Determinants', *Social Behavior and Personality*, no. 2, 1996, pp 119–32; T Tyler, P Degoey and H Smith, 'Understanding Why the Justice of Group Procedures Matters: A Test of the Psychological Dynamics of the Group-Value Model', *Journal of Personality and Social Psychology*, May 1996, pp 913–30; S C Currall and T A Judge, 'Measuring Trust between Organizational Boundary Role Persons', *Organizational Behavior and Human Decision Processes*, November 1995, pp 151–70; L T Hosmer, 'Trust: The Connecting Link between Organizational Theory and Philosophical Ethics', *Academy of Management Review*, April 1995, pp 379–403; and D J McAllister, 'Affect- and Cognition-Based Trust as Foundations for Interpersonal Cooperation in Organizations', *Academy of Management Journal*, February 1995, pp 24–59.

72 For an interesting trust exercise, see G Thompson and P F Pearce, 'The Team-Trust Game', *Training & Development Journal*, May 1992, pp 42–43.

73 For interesting new theory and research on telling lies, see B M DePaulo, D A Kashy, S E Kirkendol, M M Wyer and J A Epstein, 'Lying in Everyday Life', *Journal of Personality and Social Psychology*, May 1996, pp 979–95; and D A Kashy and B M DePaulo, 'Who Lies?' *Journal of Personality and Social Psychology*, May 1996, pp 1037–51.

74 L Kellaway, 'Wellcome to the world of we', *The Financial Times*, September 11, 2000.

75 For support, see G M Spreitzer and A K Mishra, 'Giving Up Control without Losing Control: Trust and Its Substitutes' Effects on Managers' Involving Employees in Decision Making', *Group & Organization Management*, June 1999, pp 155–87.

76 For more on fairness, see K Seiders and L L Berry, 'Service Fairness: What It Is and Why It Matters', *Academy of Management Executive*, May 1998, pp 8–20.

77 Adapted from F Bartolomé, 'Nobody Trusts the Boss Completely—Now What?' *Harvard Business Review*, March–April

1989, pp 135–42. Also see P Chattopadhyay, 'Beyond Direct and Symmetrical Effects: The Influence of Demographic Dissimilarity on Organizational Citizenship Behavior', *Academy of Management Journal*, June 1999, pp 273–87.

78 W Foster Owen, 'Metaphor Analysis of Cohesiveness in Small Discussion Groups', *Small Group Behavior*, August 1985, p 416. Also see J Keyton and J Springston, 'Redefining Cohesiveness in Groups', *Small Group Research*, May 1990, pp 234–54.

79 This distinction is based on discussion in A Tziner, 'Differential Effects of Group Cohesiveness Types: A Clarifying Overview', *Social Behavior and Personality*, no. 2, 1982, pp 227–39.

80 B Mullen and C Copper, 'The Relation between Group Cohesiveness and Performance: An Integration', *Psychological Bulletin*, March 1994, p 224.

81 Ibid. Additional research evidence is reported in T Kozakaï, S Moscovici and B Personnaz, 'Contrary Effects of Group Cohesiveness in Minority Influence: Intergroup Categorization of the Source and Levels of Influence', *European Journal of Social Psychology*, November–December 1994, pp 713–18; and J Henderson, A E Bourgeois, A LeUnes and M C Meyers, 'Group Cohesiveness, Mood Disturbance, and Stress in Female Basketball Players', *Small Group Research*, April 1998, pp 212–25.

82 Based on B Mullen, T Anthony, E Salas and J E Driskell, 'Group Cohesiveness and Quality of Decision Making: An Integration of Tests of the Groupthink Hypothesis', *Small Group Research*, May 1994, pp 189–204.

83 Translated and adapted from Ph Tranchart, 'Révolution culturelle chez Renault', *Entreprises Formation*, December 1995, pp 10–11.

84 See, for example, P Jin, 'Work Motivation and Productivity in Voluntarily Formed Work Teams: A Field Study in China', *Organizational Behavior and Human Decision Processes*, 1993, pp 133–55. The related topic of commitment is discussed in B Fehr, 'Laypeople's Conceptions of Commitment', *Journal of Personality and Social Psychology*, January 1999, pp 90–103.

85 Based on discussion in E E Lawler III and S A Mohrman, 'Quality Circles: After the Honeymoon', *Organizational Dynamics*, Spring 1987, pp 42–54.

86 For a report on 8,000 quality circles in Mexico, see R Carvajal, 'Its Own Reward', *Business Mexico*, Special Edition 1996, pp 26–28.

87 The historical development of quality circles is discussed by C Stohl, 'Bridging the Parallel Organization: A Study of Quality Circle Effectiveness', in *Organizational Communication*, ed M L McLaughlin (Beverly Hills, CA: Sage Publications, 1987), pp 416–30; T Li-Ping Tang, P Smith Tollison and H D Whiteside, 'The Effect of Quality Circle Initiation on Motivation to Attend Quality Circle Meetings and on Task Performance', *Personnel Psychology*, Winter 1987, pp 799–814; and N Kano, 'A Perspective on Quality Activities in American Firms', *California Management Review*, Spring 1993, pp 12–31. Also see the discussion of quality circles in J B Keys, L T Denton and T R Miller, 'The Japanese Management Theory Jungle—Revisited', *Journal of Management*, Summer 1994, pp 373–402.

88 Based on discussion in K Buch and R Spangler, 'The Effects of Quality Circles on Performance and Promotions', *Human Relations*, June 1990, pp 573–82.

89 See G R Ferris and J A Wagner III, 'Quality Circles in the United States: A Conceptual Reevaluation', *The Journal of Applied Behavioral Science*, no. 2, 1985, pp 155–67.

90 Lawler and Mohrman, 'Quality Circles: After the Honeymoon', p 43. Also see E E Lawler III, 'Total Quality Management and Employee Involvement: Are They Compatible?' *Academy of Management Executive*, February 1994, pp 68–76.

91 See M L Marks, 'The Question of Quality Circles', *Psychology Today*, March 1986, pp 36–38, 42, 44, 46.

92 See A K Naj, 'Some Manufacturers Drop Effort to Adopt Japanese Techniques', *The Wall Street Journal*, May 7, 1993, p A1.

93 See E E Adam, Jr, 'Quality Circle Performance', *Journal of*

Management, March 1991, pp 25–39.

94 See R P Steel and R F Lloyd, 'Cognitive, Affective, and Behavioral Outcomes of Participation in Quality Circles: Conceptual and Empirical Findings', *The Journal of Applied Behavioral Science*, no. 1, 1988, pp 1–17; M L Marks, P H Mirvis, E J Hackett and J F Grady, Jr, 'Employee Participation in a Quality Circle Program: Impact on Quality of Work Life, Productivity, and Absenteeism', *Journal of Applied Psychology*, February 1986, pp 61–69; and Buch and Spangler, 'The Effects of Quality Circles on Performance and Promotions.' Additional research is reported in T Li-Ping Tang, P Smith Tollison and H D Whiteside, 'Differences between Active and Inactive Quality Circles in Attendance and Performance', *Public Personnel Management*, Winter 1993, pp 579–90; and C Doucouliagos, 'Worker Participation and Productivity in Labor-Managed and Participatory Capitalist Firms: A Meta-Analysis', *Industrial and Labor Relations Review*, October 1995, pp 58–77.

95 See K Kiser, 'Tools for Teaming', *Training*, March 1999, pp 32–33.

96 See A M Townsend, S M DeMarie and A R Hendrickson, 'Virtual Teams: Technology and the Workplace of the Future', *Academy of Management Executive*, August 1998, pp 17–29.

97 Based on P Bordia, N DiFonzo and A Chang, 'Rumor as Group Problem Solving: Development Patterns in Informal Computer-Mediated Groups', *Small Group Research*, February 1999, pp 8–28.

98 See K A Graetz, E S Boyle, C E Kimble, P Thompson and J L Garloch, 'Information Sharing in Face-to-Face, Teleconferencing, and Electronic Chat Groups', *Small Group Research*, December 1998, pp 714–43.

99 Based on F Niederman and R J Volkema, 'The Effects of Facilitator Characteristics on Meeting Preparation, Set Up, and Implementation', *Small Group Research*, June 1999, pp 330–60.

100 Based on J J Sosik, B J Avolio and S S Kahai, 'Inspiring Group Creativity: Comparing Anonymous and Identified Electronic Brainstorming', *Small Group Research*, February 1998, pp 3–31.

101 N Merrick, 'Remote Control', *People Management*, September 26, 1996.

102 For practical tips, see K Kiser, 'Building a Virtual Team', *Training*, March 1999, p 34.

103 L Wood, 'Increase in self-managed teams', *The Financial Times*, June 26, 1995, p 11.

104 'Industrial relations services, autonomy in store: self-management at the Body Shop, *Industrial Relations Review and Report*, 583, June 1993.

105 Adapted and translated from Anonymous, 'Beslissen op het laagste niveau', *Vacature*, August 1, 1998.

106 See M Moravec, O J Johannessen and T A Hjelmas, 'The Well-Managed SMT', *Management Review*, June 1998, pp 56–58; and 'Case Study in C-Sharp Minor', *Training*, October 1998, p 21.

107 For example, see M Selz, 'Testing Self-Managed Teams, Entrepreneur Hopes to Lose Job', *The Wall Street Journal*, January 11, 1994, pp B1–B2. Also see 'Even in Self-Managed Teams There Has to Be a Leader', *Supervisory Management*, December 1994, pp 7–8.

108 See D R Denison, S L Hart and J A Kahn, 'From Chimneys to Cross-Functional Teams: Developing and Validating a Diagnostic Model', *Academy of Management Journal*, August 1996, pp 1005–23. Cross-functional teams are discussed in D Lei, J W Slocum and R A Pitts, 'Designing Organizations for Competitive Advantage: The Power of Unlearning and Learning', *Organizational Dynamics*, Winter 1999, pp 24–38.

109 Based on C M Solomon, 'Global teams: the ultimate collaboration', *Personnel Journal*, September 1995, pp 49–58.

110 See P S Goodman, R Devadas and T L Griffith Hughson, 'Groups and Productivity: Analyzing the Effectiveness of Self-Managing Teams', in *Productivity in Organizations*, eds J P Campbell, R J Campbell and Associates (San Francisco: Jossey-Bass, 1988), pp 295–327.

111 Good background discussions can be found in work cited in note 73 and in C Lee, 'Beyond Teamwork', *Training*, June 1990, pp 25–32. Also see S G Cohen, G E Ledford, Jr, and G M Spreitzer, 'A Predictive Model of Self-Managing Work Team Effectiveness', *Human Relations*, May 1996, pp 643–76.

112 For an instructive continuum of work team autonomy, see R D Banker, J M Field, R G Schroeder and K K Sinha, 'Impact of Work Teams on Manufacturing Performance: A Longitudinal Field Study', *Academy of Management Journal*, August 1996, pp 867–90.

113 Drawn from Goodman, Devadas and Hughson, 'Groups and Productivity: Analyzing the Effectiveness of Self-Managing Teams'. Also see E F Rogers, W Metlay, I T Kaplan and T Shapiro, 'Self-Managing Work Teams: Do They Really Work?' *Human Resource Planning*, no. 2, 1995, pp 53–57; and V U Druskat and S B Wolff, 'Effects and Timing of Developmental Peer Appraisals in Self-Managing Work Groups', *Journal of Applied Psychology*, February 1999, pp 58–74.

114 For useful tips, see L Holpp, 'Five Ways to Sink Self-Managed Teams', *Training*, September 1993, pp 38–42.

115 See B Dumaine, 'The New Non-Manager Managers', *Fortune*, February 22, 1993, pp 80–84. Also see 'Easing the Fear of Self-Directed Teams', *Training*, August 1993, pp 14, 55–56.

116 See Dumaine, 'Who Needs a Boss?' pp 55, 58; and J Hillkirk, 'Self-Directed Work Teams Give TI Lift', *USA Today*, December 20, 1993, p 8B. A good contingency model for empowering teams is presented in R C Liden, S J Wayne and L Bradway, 'Connections Make the Difference', *HRMagazine*, February 1996, pp 73–79.

117 Data from S Alper, D Tjosvold and K S Law, 'Interdependence and Controversy in Group Decision Making: Antecedents to Effective Self-Managing Teams', *Organizational Behavior and Human Decision Processes*, April 1998, pp 33–52.

118 For an instructive case study on this topic, see C C Manz, D E Keating and A Donnellon, 'Preparing for an Organizational Change to Employee Self-Management: The Managerial Transition', *Organizational Dynamics*, Autumn 1990, pp 15–26. Also see B L Kirkman and B Rosen, 'Beyond Self-Management: Antecedents and Consequences of Team Empowerment', *Academy of Management Journal*, February 1999, pp 58–74.

119 Based on K Lowry Miller, 'GM's German Lessons', *Business Week*, December 20, 1993, pp 67–68.

120 Adapted and translated from anonymous, 'Voorbeelden van teambuilding', *Vacature*, March 10, 2000.

121 Ibid.

122 An excellent resource is W G Dyer, *Team Building: Current Issues and New Alternatives*, 3rd ed (Reading, MA: Addison-Wesley, 1995). Also see G L Stewart, C C Manz and H P Sims, Jr, *Team Work and Group Dynamics* (New York: Wiley, 1999).

123 See A B Hollingshead, 'Group and Individual Training: Impact of Practice on Performance', *Small Group Research*, April 1998, pp 254–80; and L McDermott, B Waite and N Brawley, 'Putting Together a World-Class Team', *Training & Development*, January 1999, pp 47–51.

124 R Beckhard, 'Optimizing team building efforts', *Journal of Contemporary Business*, Summer 1972, p 24.

125 S Bucholz and T Roth, *Creating the High-Performance Team* (New York: John Wiley & Sons, 1987), p xi.

126 Ibid., p 14. Also see S A Wheelan, D Murphy, E Tsumura and S F Kline, 'Member Perceptions of Internal Group Dynamics and Productivity', *Small Group Research*, June 1998, pp 371–93; M F R Kets De Vries, 'High-Performance Teams: Lessons from the Pygmies', *Organizational Dynamics*, Winter 1999, pp 66–77; G Buzaglo and S A Wheelan, 'Facilitating Work Team Effectiveness: Case Studies from Central America', *Small Group Research*, February 1999, pp 108–29; K Maani and C Benton, 'Rapid Team Learning: Lessons from Team New Zealand America's Cup Campaign', *Organizational Dynamics*, Spring 1999, pp 48–62; J Lipman-Blumen and H J Leavitt, 'Hot Groups "With Attitude": A New Organizational State of Mind', *Organizational Dynamics*, Spring 1999, pp 63–73; and M J Waller, 'The Timing of Adaptive Group Responses to Nonroutine Events', *Academy of Management Journal*, April 1999, pp 127–37.

[127] P King, 'What Makes Teamwork Work?' *Psychology Today*, December 1989, p 17. A critical view of teams is presented in C Casey, ' "Come, Join Our Family": Discipline and Integration in Corporate Organizational Culture', *Human Relations*, February 1999, pp 155–78.

[128] Adapted from C C Manz and H P Sims, Jr, 'Leading Workers to Lead Themselves: The External Leadership of Self-Managing Work Teams', *Administrative Science Quarterly*, March 1987, pp 106–29. Also see C C Manz, 'Beyond Self-Managing Work Teams: Toward Self-Leading Teams in the Workplace', in *Research in Organizational Change and Development*, vol. 4, eds R W Woodman and W A Pasmore (Greenwich, CT: JAI Press, 1990), pp 273–99; C C Manz, 'Self-Leading Work Teams: Moving Beyond Self-Management Myths', *Human Relations*, no. 11, 1992, pp 1119–40; C C Manz, *Mastering Self-Leadership: Empowering Yourself for Personal Excellence* (Englewood Cliffs, NJ: Prentice-Hall, 1992); M Uhl-Bien and G B Graen, 'Individual Self-Management: Analysis of "Professional" Self-Managing Activities in Functional and Cross-Functional Work Teams', *Academy of Management Journal*, June 1998, pp 340–50; G E Prussia, J S Anderson and C C Manz, 'Self-Leadership and Performance Outcomes: The Mediating Influence of Self-Efficacy', *Journal of Organizational Behavior*, September 1998, pp 523–38; and P Troiano, 'Nice Guys Finish First', *Management Review*, December 1998, p 8.

[129] Questionnaire items adapted from C Johnson-George and W C Swap, 'Measurement of Specific Interpersonal Trust: Construction and Validation of a Scale to Assess Trust in a Specific Other', *Journal of Personality and Social Psychology*, December 1982, pp 1306–17; and D J McAllister, 'Affect- and Cognition-Based Trust as Foundations for Interpersonal Cooperation in Organizations', *Academy of Management Journal*, February 1995, pp 24–59.

[130] Ten questionnaire items excerpted from W G Dyer, *Team Building: Current Issues and New Alternatives*, 3rd ed (Reading, MA: Addison-Wesley, 1995), pp 96–99.

Chapter 13

[1] Adapted from W Echikson, 'A Vineyard's Bitter Fruit', *Business Week*, November 13, 2000.

[2] D Tjosvold, *Learning to Manage Conflict: Getting People to Work Together Productively* (New York: Lexington Books, 1993), p xi.

[3] Ibid., pp xi–xii.

[4] J A Wall, Jr, and R Robert Callister, 'Conflict and Its Management', *Journal of Management*, no. 3, 1995, p 517.

[5] Ibid., p 544.

[6] See A M O'Leary-Kelly, R W Griffin and D J Glew, 'Organization-Motivated Aggression: A Research Framework', *Academy of Management Review*, January 1996, pp 225–53; and D Bencivenga, 'Dealing with the Dark Side', *HRMagazine*, January 1999, pp 50–58.

[7] See S Alper, D Tjosvold and K S Law, 'Interdependence and Controversy in Group Decision Making: Antecedents to Effective Self-Managing Teams', *Organizational Behavior and Human Decision Processes*, April 1998, pp 33–52.

[8] S P Robbins, ' "Conflict Management" and "Conflict Resolution" Are Not Synonymous Terms', *California Management Review*, Winter 1978, p 70.

[9] Co-operative conflict is discussed in Tjosvold, *Learning to Manage Conflict: Getting People to Work Together Productively*. Also see A C Amason, 'Distinguishing the Effects of Functional and Dysfunctional Conflict on Strategic Decision Making: Resolving a Paradox for Top Management Teams', *Academy of Management Journal*, February 1996, pp 123–48.

[10] Adapted from J Templeman, B Vlasic and C Power, 'The New Mercedes', *Business Week*, August 26, 1996.

[11] Adapted in part from discussion in A C Filley, *Interpersonal Conflict Resolution* (Glenview, IL: Scott, Foresman, 1975), pp 9–12; and B Fortado, 'The Accumulation of Grievance Conflict', *Journal of Management Inquiry*, December 1992, pp 288–303. Also see D Tjosvold and M Poon, 'Dealing with Scarce Resources: Open-Minded Interaction for Resolving Budget Conflicts', *Group & Organization Management*, September 1998, pp 237–55.

[12] Adapted from discussion in Tjosvold, *Learning to Manage Conflict: Getting People to Work Together Productively*, pp 12–13.

[13] L Gardenswartz and A Rowe, *Diverse Teams at Work: Capitalizing on the Power of Diversity* (New York: McGraw-Hill, 1994), p 32.

[14] See L M Andersson and C M Pearson, 'Tit for Tat? The Spiraling Effect of Incivility in the Workplace', *Academy of Management Review*, July 1999, pp 452–71; and C Lee, 'The Death of Civility', *Training*, July 1999, pp 24–30.

[15] Data from D Stamps, 'Yes, Your Boss Is Crazy', *Training*, July 1998, pp 35–39. Also see L Huggler, 'Companies on the Couch', *HRMagazine*, November 1997, pp 80–84; and J C Connor, 'The Paranoid Personality at Work', *HRMagazine*, March 1999, pp 120–26.

[16] See J Muller, 'Keeping an Investigation on the Right Track', *Business Week*, July 5, 1999, p 84.

[17] See Bencivenga, 'Dealing with the Dark Side'; and C Lee, 'Tips for Surviving Rude Encounters', *Training*, July 1999, p 29.

[18] M Rokeach, *The Nature of Values* (New York: Free Press, 1973), p 5. Also see J Cathcart, 'Searching for the Hot Button— What *Really* Motivates People?' *Canadian Manager*, Summer 1999, pp 12–13, 30.

[19] Ibid.

[20] See S H Schwartz and W Bilsky, 'Toward a Theory of the Universal Content and Structure of Values: Extensions and Cross-Cultural Replications', *Journal of Personality and Social Psychology*, May 1990, pp 878–91. For other values-related research, see M G Martinsons and A B Martinsons, 'Conquering Cultural Constraints to Cultivate Chinese Management Creativity and Innovation', *Journal of Management Development*, no. 9, 1996, pp 18–35; G R Maio and J M Olson, 'Values as Truisms: Evidence and Implications', *Journal of Personality and Social Psychology*, February 1998, pp 294–311; B M Meglino and E C Ravlin, 'Individual Values in Organizations: Concepts, Controversies, and Research', *Journal of Management*, no. 3, 1998, pp 351–89; L A King and C K Napa, 'What Makes a Life Good?' *Journal of Personality and Social Psychology*, July 1998, pp 156–65; and R A Rodriguez, 'Challenging Demographic Reductionism: A Pilot Study Investigating Diversity in Group Composition', *Small Group Research*, December 1998, pp 744–59.

[21] See M Rokeach, *Beliefs, Attitudes, and Values* (San Francisco: Jossey-Bass, 1968).

[22] For example, see T Petzinger Jr, 'New Business Leaders Find Greater Profit Mixing Work, Caring', *The Wall Street Journal*, April 2, 1999, p B1; and J L Seglin, 'It's Not That Easy Going Green', *Inc.*, May 1999, pp 28–32.

[23] B Moses, 'The Busyness Trap', *Training*, November 1998, p 42.

[24] P Schinzler, 'Offices that spark creativity', *Business Week*, August 28, 2000.

[25] Based on discussion in G Labianca, D J Brass and B Gray, 'Social Networks and Perceptions of Intergroup Conflict: The Role of Negative Relationships and Third Parties', *Academy of Management Journal*, February 1998, pp 55–67. Also see N Ellemers, R Spears and B Doosje, 'Sticking Together or Falling Apart: In-Group Identification as a Psychological Determinant of Group Commitment versus Individual Mobility', *Journal of Personality and Social Psychology*, March 1997, pp 617–26; C S Ryan and L M Bogart, 'Development of New Group Members' In-Group and Out-Group Stereotypes: Changes in Perceived Group Variability and Ethnocentrism', *Journal of Personality and Social Psychology*, October 1997, pp 719–32; H Rothgerber, 'External Intergroup Threat as an Antecedent to Perceptions of In-Group and Out-Group Homogeneity', *Journal of Personality and Social Psychology*, December 1997, pp 1206–12; H Rothgerber and S Worchel, 'The View from Below: Intergroup Relations from the Perspective of the Disadvantaged Group', *Journal of Personality and Social Psychology*, December 1997, pp 1191–1205; and J Duckitt and T Mphuthing, 'Group Identification and Intergroup Attitudes: A Longitudinal Analysis in South Africa', *Journal of Personality and Social Psychology*, January 1998, pp 80–85.

26 Labianca, Brass and Gray, 'Social Networks and Perceptions of Intergroup Conflict: The Role of Negative Relationships and Third Parties', p 63 (Emphasis added).

27 For example, see S C Wright, A Aron, T McLaughlin-Volpe and S A Ropp, 'The Extended Contact Effect: Knowledge of Cross-Group Friendships and Prejudice', *Journal of Personality and Social Psychology*, July 1997, pp 73–90.

28 See C D Batson, M P Polycarpou, E Harmon-Jones, H J Imhoff, E C Mitchener, L L Bednar, T R Klein and L Highberger, 'Empathy and Attitudes: Can Feeling for a Member of a Stigmatized Group Improve Feelings toward the Group?' *Journal of Personality and Social Psychology*, January 1997, pp 105–18.

29 For example, see A B Sim and Y Ali, 'Performance of International Joint Ventures from Developing and Developed Countries: An Empirical Study in a Developing Country Context', *Journal of World Business*, Winter 1998, pp 357–77; A Parkhe, 'Building Trust in International Alliances', *Journal of World Business*, Winter 1998, pp 417–37; B Kogut, 'What Makes a Company Global?' *Harvard Business Review*, January–February 1999, pp 165–70; and D Cyr, 'High Tech, High Impact: Creating Canada's Competitive Advantage through Technology Alliances', *Academy of Management Executive*, May 1999, pp 17–26.

30 For example, see A S Hubbard, 'Cultural and Status Differences in Intergroup Conflict Resolution: A Longitudinal Study of a Middle East Dialogue Group in the United States', *Human Relations*, March 1999, pp 303–26; and S Rosenbush, 'Global One Rift Looms', *USA Today*, July 15, 1999, p 3B.

31 D Woodruff, 'Frowns, Fees and Forms', *Business Week*, February 5, 1996.

32 Reprinted from A Rosenbaum, 'Testing Cultural Waters', *Management Review*, July–August 1999, p 43.

33 See R L Tung, 'American Expatriates Abroad: From Neophytes to Cosmopolitans', *Journal of World Business*, Summer 1998, pp 125–44.

34 R A Cosier and C R Schwenk, 'Agreement and Thinking Alike: Ingredients for Poor Decisions', *Academy of Management Executive*, February 1990, p 71. Also see J P Kotter, 'Kill Complacency', *Fortune*, August 5, 1996, pp 168–70; and S Caudron, 'Keeping Team Conflict Alive', *Training & Development*, September 1998, pp 48–52.

35 For example, see 'Facilitators as Devil's Advocates', *Training*, September 1993, p 10. Also see K L Woodward, 'Sainthood for a Pope?' *Newsweek*, June 21, 1999, p 65.

36 Good background reading on devil's advocacy can be found in C R Schwenk, 'Devil's Advocacy in Managerial Decision Making', *Journal of Management Studies*, April 1984, pp 153–68.

37 See G Katzenstein, 'The Debate on Structured Debate: Toward a Unified Theory', *Organizational Behavior and Human Decision Processes*, June 1996, pp 316–32.

38 See D M Schweiger, W R Sandberg and P L Rechner, 'Experiential Effects of Dialectical Inquiry, Devil's Advocacy, and Consensus Approaches to Strategic Decision Making', *Academy of Management Journal*, December 1989, pp 745–72.

39 See J S Valacich and C Schwenk, 'Devil's Advocacy and Dialectical Inquiry Effects on Face-to-Face and Computer-Mediated Group Decision Making', *Organizational Behavior and Human Decision Processes*, August 1995, pp 158–73.

40 A recent statistical validation for this model can be found in M A Rahim and N R Magner, 'Confirmatory Factor Analysis of the Styles of Handling Interpersonal Conflict: First-Order Factor Model and Its Invariance Across Groups', *Journal of Applied Psychology*, February 1995, pp 122–32.

41 M A Rahim, 'A Strategy for Managing Conflict in Complex Organizations', *Human Relations*, January 1985, p 84.

42 P Ruzich, 'Triangles: Tools for Untangling Interpersonal Messes', *HRMagazine*, July 1999, p 129.

43 See R E Jones and B H Melcher, 'Personality and the Preference for Modes of Conflict Resolution', *Human Relations*, August 1982, pp 649–58.

44 See R A Baron, 'Reducing Organizational Conflict: An Incompatible Response Approach', *Journal of Applied Psychology*, May 1984, pp 272–79.

45 See G A Youngs, Jr, 'Patterns of Threat and Punishment Reciprocity in a Conflict Setting', *Journal of Personality and Social Psychology*, September 1986, pp 541–46.

46 For more details, see V D Wall, Jr, and L L Nolan, 'Small Group Conflict: A Look at Equity, Satisfaction and Styles of Conflict Management', *Small Group Behavior*, May 1987, pp 188–211. Also see S M Farmer and J Roth, 'Conflict-Handling Behavior in Work Groups: Effects of Group Structure, Decision Processes, and Time', *Small Group Research*, December 1998, pp 669–713.

47 See M E Schnake and D S Cochran, 'Effect of Two Goal-Setting Dimensions on Perceived Intraorganizational Conflict', *Group & Organization Studies*, June 1985, pp 168–83. Also see O Janssen, E Van De Vliert, and C Veenstra, 'How Task and Person Conflict Shape the Role of Positive Interdependence in Management Teams', *Journal of Management*, no. 2, 1999, pp 117–42.

48 Drawn from L H Chusmir and J Mills, 'Gender Differences in Conflict Resolution Styles of Managers: At Work and at Home', *Sex Roles*, February 1989, pp 149–63.

49 See K K Smith, 'The Movement of Conflict in Organizations: The Joint Dynamics of Splitting and Triangulation', *Administrative Science Quarterly*, March 1989, pp 1–20. Also see J B Olson-Buchanan, F Drasgow, P J Moberg, A D Mead, P A Keenan and M A Donovan, 'Interactive Video Assessment of Conflict Resolution Skills', *Personnel Psychology*, Spring 1998, pp 1–24; and D E Conlon and D P Sullivan, 'Examining the Actions of Organizations in Conflict: Evidence from the Delaware Court of Chancery', *Academy of Management Journal*, June 1999, pp 319–29.

50 Based on C Tinsley, 'Models of Conflict Resolution in Japanese, German, and American Cultures', *Journal of Applied Psychology*, April 1998, pp 316–23; and S M Adams, 'Settling Cross-Cultural Disagreements Begins with "Where" Not "How"', *Academy of Management Executive*, February 1999, pp 109–10. Also see K Ohbuchi, O Fukushima and J T Tedeschi, 'Cultural Values in Conflict Management: Goal Orientation, Goal Attainment, and Tactical Decision', *Journal of Cross-Cultural Psychology*, January 1999, pp 51–71; and R Cropanzano, H Aguinis, M Schminke and D L Denham, 'Disputant Reactions to Managerial Conflict Resolution Tactics: A Comparison among Argentina, The Dominican Republic, Mexico, and the United States', *Group & Organization Management*, June 1999, pp 124–54.

51 Based on a definition in M A Neale and M H Bazerman, 'Negotiating Rationally: The Power and Impact of the Negotiator's Frame', *Academy of Management Executive*, August 1992, pp 42–51.

52 See L Thompson, E Peterson and S E Brodt, 'Team Negotiation: An Examination of Integrative and Distributive Bargaining', *Journal of Personality and Social Psychology*, January 1996, pp 66–78.

53 See D A Whetten and K S Cameron, *Developing Management Skills*, 3rd ed (New York: HarperCollins, 1995), pp 425–30. Also see C Joinson, 'Talking Dollars: How to Negotiate Salaries with New Hires', *HRMagazine*, July 1998, pp 73–78; 'Negotiation Is Not War', *Fortune*, October 12, 1998, pp 160–64; A Davis, 'For Dueling Lawyers, the Internet Is Unlikely Referee', *The Wall Street Journal*, May 12, 1999, pp B1, B4; and R Shell, 'Negotiator, Know Thyself', *Inc.*, May 1999, pp 106–7.

54 M H Bazerman and M A Neale, *Negotiating Rationally* (New York: The Free Press, 1992), p 16. Also see J F Brett, G B Northcraft and R L Pinkley, 'Stairways to Heaven: An Interlocking Self-Regulation Model of Negotiation', *Academy of Management Review*, July 1999, pp 435–51.

55 Good win-win negotiation strategies can be found in R R Reck and B G Long, *The Win-Win Negotiator: How to Negotiate Favorable Agreements That Last* (New York: Pocket Books, 1987); R Fisher and W Ury, *Getting to YES: Negotiating Agreement without Giving In* (Boston: Houghton Mifflin, 1981); and R Fisher and D Ertel, *Getting Ready to Negotiate: The Getting to YES Workbook* (New York: Penguin Books, 1995).

56 See L R Weingart, E B Hyder and M J Prietula, 'Knowledge Matters: The Effect of Tactical Descriptions on Negotiation Behavior and Outcome', *Journal of Personality and Social Psychology*, June 1996, pp 1205–17.

57 Data from J L Graham, A T Mintu and W Rodgers, 'Explorations of Negotiation Behaviors in Ten Foreign Cultures Using a Model Developed in the United States', *Management Science*, January 1994, pp 72–95.

58 For practical advice, see K Kelley Reardon and R E Spekman, 'Starting Out Right: Negotiation Lessons for Domestic and Cross-Cultural Business Alliances', *Business Horizons*, January–February 1994, pp 71–79.

59 For supporting evidence, see J K Butler, Jr, 'Trust Expectations, Information Sharing, Climate of Trust, and Negotiation Effectiveness and Efficiency', *Group & Organization Management*, June 1999, pp 217–38.

60 See H J Reitz, J A Wall, Jr, and M S Love, 'Ethics in Negotiation: Oil and Water or Good Lubrication?' *Business Horizons*, May–June 1998, pp 5–14.

61 For related research, see A E Tenbrunsel, 'Misrepresentation and Expectations of Misrepresentation in an Ethical Dilemma: The Role of Incentives and Temptation', *Academy of Management Journal*, June 1998, pp 330–39.

62 Based on R L Pinkley, T L Griffith and G B Northcraft, '"Fixed Pie" a la Mode: Information Availability, Information Processing, and the Negotiation of Suboptimal Agreements', *Organizational Behavior and Human Decision Processes*, April 1995, pp 101–12.

63 Based on A E Walters, A F Stuhlmacher and L L Meyer, 'Gender and Negotiator Competitiveness: A Meta-Analysis', *Organizational Behavior and Human Decision Processes*, October 1998, pp 1–29.

64 Based on B Barry and R A Friedman, 'Bargainer Characteristics in Distributive and Integrative Negotiation', *Journal of Personality and Social Psychology*, February 1998, pp 345–59. Also see C K W De Dreu, E Giebels and E Van de Vliert, 'Social Motives and Trust in Integrative Negotiation: The Disruptive Effects of Punitive Capability', *Journal of Applied Psychology*, June 1998, pp 408–22.

65 For more, see J P Forgas, 'On Feeling Good and Getting Your Way: Mood Effects on Negotiator Cognition and Bargaining Strategies', *Journal of Personality and Social Psychology*, March 1998, pp 565–77.

66 Drawn from J M Brett and T Okumura, 'Inter- and Intracultural Negotiation: US and Japanese Negotiators', *Academy of Management Journal*, October 1998, pp 495–510. For more negotiation research findings, see G B Northcraft, J N Preston, M A Neale, P H Kim and M C Thomas-Hunt, 'Non-Linear Preference Functions and Negotiated Outcomes', *Organizational Behavior and Human Decision Processes*, January 1998, pp 54–75; J T Polzer, E A Mannix and M A Neale, 'Interest Alignment and Coalitions in Multiparty Negotiation', *Academy of Management Journal*, February 1998, pp 42–54; J M Brett, D L Shapiro and A L Lytle, 'Breaking the Bonds of Reciprocity in Negotiations', *Academy of Management Journal*, August 1998, pp 410–24; W P Bottom, 'Negotiator Risk: Sources of Uncertainty and the Impact of Reference Points on Negotiated Agreements', *Organizational Behavior and Human Decision Processes*, November 1998, pp 89–112; and D A Moore, T R Kurtzberg and L L Thompson, 'Long and Short Routes to Success in Electronically Mediated Negotiations: Group Affiliations and Good Vibrations', *Organizational Behavior and Human Decision Processes*, January 1999, pp 22–43.

67 The complete instrument may be found in M A Rahim, 'A Measure of Styles of Handling Interpersonal Conflict', *Academy of Management Journal*, June 1983, pp 368–76. A validation study of Rahim's instrument may be found in E Van De Vliert and B Kabanoff, 'Toward Theory-Based Measures of Conflict Management', *Academy of Management Journal*, March 1990, pp 199–209.

68 D A Whetten and K S Cameron, *Developing Management Skills*, (Scott, Foresman and Company 1984).

Chapter 14

1 Business Week: September 21, 1998. Reproduced with permission.

2 For a review of research on rational decision making, see K E Stanovich, *Who Is Rational?* (Mahwah, NJ: Lawrence Erlbaum, 1999), pp 1–31.

3 P Starobin, 'A wine region waiting to ripen', *Business Week*, February 19, 2001.

4 See W F Pounds, 'The Process of Problem Finding', *Industrial Management Review*, Fall 1969, pp 1–19.

5 Scenario planning is discussed by C M Perrottet, 'Scenarios for the Future', *Management Review*, January 1996, pp 43–46.

6 See B A Melers, A Schwartz and A D J Cooke, 'Judgment and Decision Making', in *Annual Review of Psychology*, eds J T Spence, J M Darley and D J Foss (Palo Alto, CA: Annual Reviews, 1998), pp 447–77; and E U Webber, C K Hsee and J Sokolowska, 'What Folklore Tells Us about Risk and Risk Taking: Cross-Cultural Comparisons of American, German, and Chinese Proverbs', *Organizational Behavior and Human Decision Processes*, August 1998, pp 170–86.

7 Results can be found in J P Byrnes, D C Miller and W D Schafer, 'Gender Differences in Risk Taking: A Meta-Analysis', *Psychological Bulletin*, May 1999, pp 367–83.

8 The implementation process and its relationship to decision outcomes is discussed by S J Miller, D J Hickson and D C Wilson, 'Decision-Making in Organizations', in *Handbook of Organization Studies*, eds S R Clegg, C Hardy and W R Nord (London: Sage Publications, 1996), pp 293–312.

9 For a review of these assumptions, see H A Simon, 'A Behavioral Model of Rational Choice', *The Quarterly Journal of Economics*, February 1955, pp 99–118.

10 H A Simon, 'Rational Decision Making in Business Organizations', *The American Economic Review*, September 1979, p 510.

11 For a complete discussion of bounded rationality, see H A Simon, *Administrative Behavior*, 2nd ed (New York: Free Press, 1957); J G March and H A Simon, *Organizations* (New York: John Wiley, 1958); H A Simon, 'Altruism and Economics', *American Economic Review*, May 1993, pp 156–61; and R Nagel, 'A Survey on Experimental Beauty Contest Games: Bounded Rationality and Learning', in *Games and Human Behavior*, eds D V Budescu, I Erev and R Zwick (Mahwah, NJ: 1999), pp 105–42.

12 Biases associated with using shortcuts in decision making are discussed by A Tversky and D Kahneman, 'Judgment under Uncertainty: Heuristics and Biases', *Science*, September 1974, pp 1124–31; and D Stahlberg, F Eller, A Maass and D Frey, 'We Knew It All Along: Hindsight Bias in Groups', *Organizational Behavior and Human Decision Processes*, July 1995, pp 46–58.

13 For a recent study of the availability heuristic, see L A Vaughn, 'Effects of Uncertainty on Use of the Availability of Heuristic for Self-Efficacy Judgments', *European Journal of Social Psychology*, March–May 1999, pp 407–10.

14 The model is discussed in detail in M D Cohen, J G March and J P Olsen, 'A Garbage Can Model of Organizational Choice', *Administrative Science Quarterly*, March 1971, pp 1–25; and P L Koopman, J W Broekhuijsen and A F M Wierdsma, 'Complex-Decision Making in Organizations', in *Handbook of Work and Organizational Psychology*, 2nd ed, eds P J D Drenth and J Thierry (Hove, England: 1998), pp 357–86.

15 Cohen, March and Olsen, 'A Garbage Can Model of Organizational Choice', p 2.

16 Results can be found in B Levitt and C Nass, 'The Lid on the Garbage Can: Institutional Constraints on Decision Making in the Technical Core of College-Text Publishers', *Administrative Science Quarterly*, June 1989, pp 190–207.

17 This discussion is based on material presented by J G March and R Weissinger-Baylon, *Ambiguity and Command* (Marshfield, MA: Pitman Publishing, 1986), pp 11–35.

18 Excerpted from N Deogun, 'Burst Bubbles: Aggressive Push Abroad Dilutes Coke's Strength as Big Markets Stumble', *The Wall Street Journal*, February 8, 1999, p A1.

19 Simulated tests of the garbage can model were conducted by M Masuch and P LaPotin, 'Beyond Garbage Cans: An A1 Model of Organizational Choice', *Administrative Science Quarterly*, March 1989, pp 38–67; and M B Mandell, 'The Consequences of Improving Dissemination in Garbage-Can Decision Processes', *Knowledge: Creation, Diffusion, Utilization*, March 1988, pp 343–61.

20 For a complete discussion, see L R Beach and T R Mitchell, 'A Contingency Model for the Selection of Decision Strategies', *Academy of Management Review*, July 1978, pp 439–44.

21 See B Azar, 'Why Experts Often Disagree', *APA Monitor*, May 1999, p 13.

22 H Filman, 'Manufacturing Masters its ABCs', *Business Week*, August 7, 2000.

23 Results can be found in N Harvey, 'Why Are Judgments Less Consistent in Less Predictable Task Situations?' *Organizational Behavior and Human Decision Processes*, September 1995, pp 247–63; and J W Dean, Jr, and M P Sharfman, 'Does Decision Process Matter? A Study of Strategic Decision-Making Effectiveness', *Academy of Management Journal*, April 1996, pp 368–96.

24 Results from this study can be found in S W Gilliland, N Schmitt and L Wood, 'Cost-Benefit Determinants of Decision Process and Accuracy', *Organizational Behavior and Human Decision Processes*, November 1993, pp 308–30.

25 See P E Johnson, S Grazioio, K Jamal and I A Zualkernan, 'Success and Failure in Expert Reasoning', *Organizational Behavior and Human Decision Processes*, November 1992, pp 173–203.

26 This definition was derived from A J Rowe and R O Mason, *Managing with Style: A Guide to Understanding, Assessing and Improving Decision Making* (San Francisco: Jossey-Bass, 1987).

27 The discussion of styles was based on material contained in ibid.

28 Ibid; and M J Dollinger and W Danis, 'Preferred Decision-Making Styles: A Cross-Cultural Comparison', *Psychological Reports*, 1998, pp 755–61.

29 A thorough discussion of escalation situations can be found in B M Staw and J Ross, 'Behavior in Escalation Situations: Antecedents, Prototypes, and Solutions', in *Research in Organizational Behavior*, vol. 9, eds L L Cummings and B M Staw (Greenwich, CT: JAI Press, 1987), pp 39–78.

30 The details of this case are discussed in J Ross and B M Staw, 'Organizational Escalation and Exit: Lessons from the Shoreham Nuclear Power Plant', *Academy of Management Journal*, August 1993, pp 701–32.

31 Ibid.

32 Psychological determinants of escalation are discussed by J H Hammond, R L Keeney and H Raiffa, 'The Hidden Traps in Decision Making', *Harvard Business Review*, September–October 1998; and J Brockner, 'The Escalation of Commitment to a Failing Course of Action: Toward Theoretical Progress', *Academy of Management Review*, January 1992, pp 39–61.

33 Results can be found in S L Kirby and M A Davis, 'A Study of Escalating Commitment in Principal-Agent Relationships: Effects of Monitoring and Personal Responsibility', *Journal of Applied Psychology*, April 1998, pp 206–17.

34 See D A Hantula and J L D Bragger, 'The Effects of Feedback Equivocality on Escalation of Commitment: An Empirical Investigation of Decision Dilemma Theory', *Journal of Applied Social Psychology*, February 1999, pp 424–44; and H Garland, C A Sandefur and A C Rogers, 'De-Escalation of Commitment in Oil Exploration: When Sunk Costs and Negative Feedback Coincide', *Journal of Applied Psychology*, December 1990, pp 721–27.

35 See Ross and Staw, 'Organizational Escalation and Exit: Lessons from the Shoreham Nuclear Power Plant.'

36 Escalation among individuals and groups was examined by J Schaubroeck and E Davis, 'Prospect Theory Predictions When Escalation Is Not the Only Chance to Recover Sunk Costs', *Organizational Behavior and Human Decision Processes*, January 1994, pp 59–82; and G Whyte, 'Escalating Commitment in Individual and Group Decision Making: A Prospect Theory

Approach', *Organizational Behavior and Human Decision Processes*, April 1993, pp 430–55.

37 See Staw and Ross, 'Behavior in Escalation Situations: Antecedents, Prototypes, and Solutions'; and W S Silver and T R Mitchell, 'The Status Quo Tendency in Decision Making', *Organizational Dynamics*, Spring 1990, pp 34–36.

38 These guidelines were derived from G P Huber, *Managerial Decision Making* (Glenview, IL: Scott, Foresman, 1980), p 149.

39 G W Hill, 'Group versus Individual Performance: Are N 1 1 Heads Better than One?' *Psychological Bulletin*, May 1982, p 535.

40 These conclusions were based on the following studies: J H Davis, 'Some Compelling Intuitions about Group Consensus Decisions, Theoretical and Empirical Research, and Interpersonal Aggregation Phenomena: Selected Examples, 1950–1990', *Organizational Behavior and Human Decision Processes*, June 1992, pp 3–38; and J A Sniezek, 'Groups Under Uncertainty: An Examination of Confidence in Group Decision Making', *Organizational Behavior and Human Decision Processes*, June 1992, pp 124–55.

41 Supporting results can be found in J Hedlund, D R Ilgen and J R Hollenbeck, 'Decision Accuracy in Computer-Mediated versus Face-to-Face Decision-Making Teams', *Organizational Behavior and Human Decision Processes*, October 1998, pp 30–47; and J R Hollenbeck, D R Ilgen, D J Sego, J Hedlund, D A Major and J Phillips, 'Multilevel Theory of Team Decision Making: Decision Performance in Teams Incorporating Distributed Expertise', *Journal of Applied Psychology*, April 1995, pp 292–316.

42 See J R Winquist and J R Larson, Jr, 'Information Pooling: When It Impacts Group Decision Making', *Journal of Personality and Social Psychology*, February 1998, pp 371–77; and D H Gruenfeld, E A Mannix, K Y Williams and M A Neale, 'Group Composition and Decision Making: How Member Familiarity and Information Distribution Affect Process and Performance', *Organizational Behavior and Human Decision Processes*, July 1996, pp 1–15.

43 See D L Gladstein and N P Reilly, 'Group Decision Making under Threat: The Tycoon Game', *Academy of Management Journal*, September 1985, pp 613–27.

44 'Jack Welch's Lessons for Success', *Fortune*, January 25, 1993, p 86.

45 Results are presented in J T Delaney, 'Workplace Cooperation: Current Problems, New Approaches', *Journal of Labor Research*, Winter 1996, pp 45–61.

46 For an extended discussion of this model, see M Sashkin, 'Participative Management Is an Ethical Imperative', *Organizational Dynamics*, Spring 1984, pp 4–22.

47 See G Yukl and P P Fu, 'Determinants of Delegation and Consultation by Managers', *Journal of Organizational Behavior*, March 1999, pp 219–32.

48 Supporting results can be found in J Hunton, T W Hall and K H Price, 'The Value of Voice in Participative Decision Making', *Journal of Applied Psychology*, October 1998, pp 788–97; C R Leana, R S Ahlbrandt and A J Murrell, 'The Effects of Employee Involvement Programs on Unionized Workers' Attitudes, Perceptions, and Preferences in Decision Making', *Academy of Management Journal*, October 1992, pp 861–73; and D Plunkett, 'The Creative Organization: An Empirical Investigation of the Importance of Participation in Decision Making', *The Journal of Creative Behavior*, Second Quarter 1990, pp 140–48.

49 Results can be found in B D Cawley, L M Keeping and P E Levy, 'Participation in the Performance Appraisal Process and Employee Reactions: A Meta-Analytic Review of Field Investigations', *Journal of Applied Psychology*, August 1998, pp 615–33.

50 Results are contained in J A Wagner III, C R Leana, E A Locke and D M Schweiger, 'Cognitive and Motivational Frameworks in US Research on Participation: A Meta-Analysis of Primary Effects', *Journal of Organizational Behavior*, 1997, pp 49–65.

51 See E A Locke, D M Schweiger and G R Latham, 'Participation in Decision Making: When Should It Be Used?'

Organizational Dynamics, Winter 1986, pp 65–79.

[52] A thorough discussion of this issue is provided by W A Randolph, 'Navigating the Journey to Empowerment', *Organizational Dynamics*, Spring 1995, pp 19–32.

[53] Results can be found in S A Mohrman, E E Lawler III and G E Ledford, Jr, 'Organizational Effectiveness and the Impact of Employee Involvement and TQM Programs: Do Employee Involvement and TQM Programs Work?' *Journal for Quality and Participation*, January/February 1996, pp 6–10.

[54] See R Rodgers, J E Hunter and D L Rogers, 'Influence of Top Management Commitment on Management Program Success', *Journal of Applied Psychology*, February 1993, pp 151–55.

[55] See V H Vroom and P W Yetton, *Leadership and Decision Making* (Pittsburgh, PA: University of Pittsburgh Press, 1973); and V H Vroom and A G Jago, *The New Leadership: Managing Participation in Organizations* (Englewood Cliffs, NJ: Prentice-Hall, 1988), p 184.

[56] For a complete discussion of these decision trees, see Vroom and Jago, *The New Leadership: Managing Participation in Organizations*.

[57] See R H G Field and J P Andrews, 'Testing the Incremental Validity of the Vroom-Jago versus Vroom-Yetton Models of Participation in Decision Making', *Journal of Behavioral Decision Making*, December 1998, pp 251–61.

[58] G M Parker, *Team Players and Teamwork: The New Competitive Business Strategy* (San Francisco, CA: Jossey-Bass, 1990).

[59] Results can be found in L M Camacho and P B Paulus, 'The Role of Social Anxiousness in Group Brainstorming', *Journal of Personality and Social Psychology*, June 1995, pp 1071–80.

[60] Methods for increasing group consensus were investigated by R L Priem, D A Harrison and N K Muir, 'Structured Conflict and Consensus Outcomes in Group Decision Making', *Journal of Management*, 1995, pp 691–710.

[61] These recommendations were obtained from Parker, *Team Players and Teamwork: The New Competitive Business Strategy*.

[62] See A F Osborn, *Applied Imagination: Principles and Procedures of Creative Thinking*, 3rd ed (New York: Scribners, 1979).

[63] See W H Cooper, R Brent Gallupe, S Pollard and J Cadsby, 'Some Liberating Effects of Anonymous Electronic Brainstorming', *Small Group Research*, April 1998, pp 147–78; and P B Paulus, T S Larey and A H Ortega, 'Performance and Perceptions of Brainstormers in an Organizational Setting', *Basic and Applied Social Psychology*, August 1995, pp 249–65.

[64] These recommendations were derived from C Caggiano, 'The Right Way to Brainstorm', *Inc*, July 1999, p 94; and G McGartland, 'How to Generate More Ideas in Brainstorming Sessions', *Selling Power*, July/August 1999, p 46.

[65] See J G Lloyd, S Fowell and J G Bligh, 'The Use of the Nominal Group Technique as an Evaluative Tool in Medical Undergraduate Education', *Medical Education*, January 1999, pp 8–13; and A L Delbecq, A H Van de Ven and D H Gustafson, *Group Techniques for Program Planning: A Guide to Nominal Group and Delphi Processes* (Glenview, IL: Scott, Foresman, 1975).

[66] See N C Dalkey, D L Rourke, R Lewis and D Snyder, *Studies in the Quality of Life: Delphi and Decision Making* (Lexington, MA: Lexington Books: D C Heath and Co, 1972).

[67] Benefits of the Delphi technique are discussed by N I Whitman, 'The Committee Meeting Alternative: Using the Delphi Technique', *Journal of Nursing Administration*, July/August 1990, pp 30–36.

[68] A thorough description of computer-aided decision-making systems is provided by M C Er and A C Ng, 'The Anonymity and Proximity Factors in Group Decision Support Systems', *Decision Support Systems*, May 1995, pp 75–83; and A LaPlante, 'Brainstorming', *Forbes*, October 25, 1993, pp 45–61.

[69] Results can be found in J S Valacich and C Schwenk, 'Devil's Advocacy and Dialectical Inquiry Effects on Face-to-Face and Computer-Mediated Group Decision Making', *Organizational Behavior and Human Decision Processes*, August 1995, pp 158–73; R B Gallupe, W H Cooper, M Grise and L M Bastianutti, 'Blocking Electronic Brainstorms', *Journal of*

Applied Psychology, February 1994, pp 77–86; and A R Dennis and J S Valacich, 'Computer Brainstorms: More Heads Are Better than One', *Journal of Applied Psychology*, August 1993, pp 531–37.

[70] This study was conducted by J S Valacich, B C Wheeler, B E Mennecke, R Wachter, 'The Effects of Numerical and Logical Group Size on Computer-Mediated Idea Generation', *Organizational Behavior and Human Decision Processes*, June 1995, pp 318–29.

[71] P Schinzler, 'Offices that spark creativity', *Business Week*, August 28, 2000.

[72] This definition was adapted from one provided by R K Scott, 'Creative Employees: A Challenge to Managers', *Journal of Creative Behavior*, First Quarter, 1995, pp 64–71.

[73] E T Smith, 'Are You Creative?' *Business Week*, September 30, 1985, pp 81–82. For a review of research about the left and right hemispheres of the brain, see T Hines, 'Left Brain/Right Brain Mythology and Implications for Management and Training', *Academy of Management Review*, October 1987, pp 600–6.

[74] Excerpted from S Stern, 'How Companies Can Be More Creative', *HRMagazine*, April 1998, p 59.

[75] These stages are thoroughly discussed by E Glassman, 'Creative Problem Solving', *Supervisory Management*, January 1989, pp 21–26.

[76] Details of this study can be found in M Basadur, 'Managing Creativity: A Japanese Model', *Academy of Management Executive*, May 1992, pp 29–42.

[77] Ibid.

[78] 'Caring Enough', *Selling Power*, June 1999, p 18.

[79] This discussion is based on research reviewed in M A Collins and T M Amabile, 'Motivation and Creativity', in *Handbook of Creativity*, eds R J Sternberg (Cambridge, UK: Cambridge University Press, 1999), pp 297–311; G J Feist, 'A Meta-Analysis of Personality in Scientific and Artistic Creativity', *Personality and Social Psychology Review*, 1998, pp 290–309; and R W Woodman, J E Sawyer and R W Griffin, 'Toward a Theory of Organizational Creativity', *Academy of Management Review*, April 1993, pp 292–321.

[80] T A Matherly and R E Goldsmith, 'The Two Faces of Creativity', *Business Horizons*, September–October 1985, p 9.

[81] Higgins, 'Innovate or Evaporate: Seven Secrets of Innovative Corporations', p 46.

[82] See the related discussion in T M Amabile, 'How to Kill Creativity', *Harvard Business Review*, September–October 1998, pp 77–87.

[83] See S Caudron, 'Humor Is Healthy in the Workplace', *Personnel Journal*, June 1992, pp 63–66.

[84] See T DeSalvo, 'Unleash the Creativity in Your Organization', *HRMagazine*, June 1999, pp 154–64; and G R Oldham and A Cummings, 'Employee Creativity: Personal and Contextual Factors at Work', *Academy of Management Journal*, June 1996, pp 607–34.

[85] L K Gundry, J R Kickul and C W Prather, 'Building the Creative Organization', *Organizational Dynamics*, Spring 1994, p 32.

[86] The survey and detailed norms can be found in A J Rowe and R O Mason, *Managing with Style: A Guide to Understanding, Assessing, and Improving Decision Making* (San Francisco: Jossey-Bass, 1987).

[87] V H Vroom, 'A New Look at Managerial Decision Making', *Organizational Dynamics*, Spring 1973, p 72.

[88] Vroom and Jago's Analysis and Solution:
Question:
(QR: quality requirement) 5 Critical/high importance
(CR: commitment requirement) 5 High importance
(LI: leader's information) 5 Probably no
(ST: problem structure) 5 No
(CP: commitment probability) 5 Probably no
(GC: goal congruence) 5 Probably yes
(CO: subordinate conflict) 5 Not a consideration for this problem.
(SI: subordinate information) 5 Maybe [but probably not]
Decision-making style 5 CII

Chapter 15

[1] S Hoare, 'Managers are opting for the hands-off approach', *The Times*, May 25, 2000. Reproduced with permission.

[2] H Malcolm and C Sokoloff, 'Values, Human Relations, and Organization Development', in *The Emerging Practice of Organizational Development*, eds W Sikes, A Drexler and J Gant (San Diego: University Associates, 1989), p 64.

[3] See D Kipnis, S M Schmidt and I Wilkinson, 'Intraorganizational Influence Tactics: Explorations in Getting One's Way', *Journal of Applied Psychology*, August 1980, pp 440–52. Also see C A Schriesheim and T R Hinkin, 'Influence Tactics Used by Subordinates: A Theoretical and Empirical Analysis and Refinement of the Kipnis, Schmidt and Wilkinson Subscales', *Journal of Applied Psychology*, June 1990, pp 246–57; and G Yukl and C M Falbe, 'Influence Tactics and Objectives in Upward, Downward and Lateral Influence Attempts', *Journal of Applied Psychology*, April 1990, pp 132–40.

[4] Based on Table 1 in G Yukl, C M Falbe and J Y Youn, 'Patterns of Influence Behavior for Managers', *Group & Organization Management*, March 1993, pp 5–28. An additional influence tactic is presented in B P Davis and E S Knowles, 'A Disrupt-then-Reframe Technique of Social Influence', *Journal of Personality and Social Psychology*, February 1999, pp 192–99.

[5] For related reading, see M Lippitt, 'How to Influence Leaders', *Training & Development*, March 1999, pp 18–22; and L Schlesinger, 'I've Got Three Words for You: Suck It Up', *Fast Company*, April 1999, p 104.

[6] Based on discussion in G Yukl, H Kim and C M Falbe, 'Antecedents of Influence Outcomes', *Journal of Applied Psychology*, June 1996, pp 309–17.

[7] Data from ibid.

[8] Data from G Yukl and J B Tracey, 'Consequences of Influence Tactics Used with Subordinates, Peers, and the Boss', *Journal of Applied Psychology*, August 1992, pp 525–35. Also see C M Falbe and G Yukl, 'Consequences for Managers of Using Single Influence Tactics and Combinations of Tactics', *Academy of Management Journal*, August 1992, pp 638–52.

[9] Data from R A Gordon, 'Impact of Ingratiation on Judgments and Evaluations: A Meta-Analytic Investigation', *Journal of Personality and Social Psychology*, July 1996, pp 54–70. Also see S J Wayne, R C Liden and R T Sparrowe, 'Developing Leader-Member Exchanges', *American Behavioral Scientist*, March 1994, pp 697–714; A Oldenburg, 'These Days, Hostile Is Fitting for Takeovers Only', *USA Today*, July 22, 1996, pp 8B, 10B; and J H Dulebohn and G R Ferris, 'The Role of Influence Tactics in Perceptions of Performance Evaluations' Fairness', *Academy of Management Journal*, June 1999, pp 288–303.

[10] Data from Yukl, Kim and Falbe, 'Antecedents of Influence Outcomes'.

[11] Data from B J Tepper, R J Eisenbach, S L Kirby and P W Potter, 'Test of a Justice-Based Model of Subordinates' Resistance to Downward Influence Attempts', *Group & Organization Management*, June 1998, pp 144–60.

[12] J E Driskell, B Olmstead and E Salas, 'Task Cues, Dominance Cues, and Influence in Task Groups', *Journal of Applied Psychology*, February 1993, p 51. No gender bias was found in H Aguinis and S K R Adams, 'Social-Role versus Structural Models of Gender and Influence Use in Organizations: A Strong Inference Approach', *Group & Organization Management*, December 1998, pp 414–46.

[13] A Hill, 'If you want to get ahead, get a laugh', *The Observer*, August 20, 2000.

[14] Yukl, Falbe and Youn, 'Patterns of Influence Behavior for Managers', p 27.

[15] J James, 'Working at self-control', *The Guardian*, July 24, 2000.

[16] A R Cohen and D L Bradford, *Influence without Authority* (New York: John Wiley & Sons, 1990), p 28. Another excellent source on this subject is R B Cialdini, *Influence* (New York: William Morrow, 1984).

[17] D Tjosvold, 'The Dynamics of Positive Power', *Training and Development Journal*, June 1984, p 72. Also see T A Stewart, 'Get with the New Power Game', *Fortune*, January 13, 1997, pp 58–62.

[18] M W McCall, Jr, *Power, Influence, and Authority: The Hazards of Carrying a Sword*, Technical Report No. 10 (Greensboro, NC: Center for Creative Leadership, 1978), p 5. For an excellent update on power, see E P Hollander and L R Offermann, 'Power and Leadership in Organizations', *American Psychologist*, February 1990, pp 179–89. Also see E Lesly, 'Manager See, Manager Do', *Business Week*, April 3, 1995, pp 90–91. Also see R Greene, *The 48 Laws of Power* (New York: Viking, 1998).

[19] Based on and translated from M Hensen, 'De polonaise van het grote geld', *De Standaard*, January 20–21, 1996.

[20] L H Chusmir, 'Personalized versus Socialized Power Needs among Working Women and Men', *Human Relations*, February 1986, p 149.

[21] See B Lloyd, 'The Paradox of Power', *The Futurist*, May–June 1996, p 60.

[22] D W Cantor and T Bernay, *Women in Power: The Secrets of Leadership* (Boston: Houghton Mifflin, 1992), p 40; and K Morris, 'Trouble in Toyland', *Business Week*, March 15, 1999, p 40.

[23] See J R P French and B Raven, 'The Bases of Social Power', in *Studies in Social Power*, ed D Cartwright (Ann Arbor: University of Michigan Press, 1959), pp 150–67. Also see J M Whitmeyer, 'Interest-Network Structures in Exchange Networks', *Sociological Perspectives*, Spring 1999, pp 23–47.

[24] Data from J R Larson, Jr, C Christensen, A S Abbott and T M Franz, 'Diagnosing Groups: Charting the Flow of Information in Medical Decision-Making Teams', *Journal of Personality and Social Psychology*, August 1996, pp 315–30.

[25] See D A Morand, 'Forms of Address and Status Leveling in Organizations', *Business Horizons*, November–December 1995, pp 34–39; and H Lancaster, 'A Father's Character, Not His Success, Shapes Kids' Careers', *The Wall Street Journal*, February 27, 1996, p B1.

[26] D Shipley and C Egan, 'Power, conflict and co-operation in brewer-tenant distribution channels', *International Journal of Service Industry Management*, vol. 3 no. 4, 1992, pp 44-62.

[27] Details may be found in Chusmir, 'Personalized versus Socialized Power Needs among Working Women and Men', pp 149–59. For a review of research on individual differences in the need for power, see R J House, 'Power and Personality in Complex Organizations', in *Research in Organizational Behavior*, ed B M Staw and L L Cummings (Greenwich, CT: JAI Press, 1988), pp 305–57.

[28] B Filipczak, 'Is It Getting Chilly in Here?' *Training*, February 1994, p 27.

[29] M Hultin and R Szulkin, 'Wages and unequal access to organizational power: an empirical test of gender discrimination', *Administrative Science Quarterly*, September 1999.

[30] M Woolf, 'Women given boost to end the pay gap', *The Independent*, December 12, 2000.

[31] P M Podsakoff and C A Schriesheim, 'Field Studies of French and Raven's Bases of Power: Critique, Reanalysis, and Suggestions for Future Research', *Psychological Bulletin*, May 1985, p 388. Also see M A Rahim and G F Buntzman, 'Supervisory Power Bases, Styles of Handling Conflict with Subordinates, and Subordinate Compliance and Satisfaction', *Journal of Psychology*, March 1989, pp 195–210; D Tjosvold, 'Power and Social Context in Superior-Subordinate Interaction', *Organizational Behavior and Human Decision Processes*, June 1985, pp 281–93; and C A Schriesheim, T R Hinkin and P M Podsakoff, 'Can Ipsative and Single-Item Measures Produce Erroneous Results in Field Studies of French and Raven's (1950) Five Bases of Power? An Empirical Investigation', *Journal of Applied Psychology*, February 1991, pp 106–14.

[32] See T R Hinkin and C A Schriesheim, 'Relationships between Subordinate Perceptions and Supervisor Influence Tactics and Attributed Bases of Supervisory Power', *Human Relations*, March 1990, pp 221–37. Also see D J Brass and M E Burkhardt, 'Potential Power and Power Use: An Investigation of Structure and Behavior', *Academy of Management Journal*, June 1993, pp 441–70; and K W Mossholder, N Bennett, E R Kemery and M A Wesolowski, 'Relationships between Bases of Power and

Work Reactions: The Mediational Role of Procedural Justice', *Journal of Management*, no. 4, 1998, pp 533–52.

[33] See H E Baker III, ' "Wax On—Wax Off": French and Raven at the Movies', *Journal of Management Education*, November 1993, pp 517–19.

[34] Based on P A Wilson, 'The Effects of Politics and Power on the Organizational Commitment of Federal Executives', *Journal of Management*, Spring 1995, pp 101–18. For related research, see J B Arthur, 'Effects of Human Resource Systems on Manufacturing Performance and Turnover', *Academy of Management Journal*, June 1994, pp 670–87.

[35] For related research, see L G Pelletier and R J Vallerand, 'Supervisors' Beliefs and Subordinates' Intrinsic Motivation: A Behavioral Confirmation Analysis', *Journal of Personality and Social Psychology*, August 1996, pp 331–40.

[36] J Macdonald, 'The Dreaded "E Word"', *Training*, September 1998, p 19. Also see R C Liden and S Arad, 'A Power Perspective of Empowerment and Work Groups: Implications for Human Resources Management Research', in *Research in Personnel and Human Resources Management*, vol. 14, ed G R Ferris (Greenwich, CT: JAI Press, 1996), pp 205–51.

[37] Adapated and translated from M Knapen, 'Het nieuwe delegeren', *Management Team*, September 11, 1998.

[38] S Caudron, 'The only way to stay ahead', *Industry Week*, August 17, 1998.

[39] L Shaper Walters, 'A Leader Redefines Management', *The Christian Science Monitor*, September 22, 1992, p 14.

[40] For related discussion, see M M Broadwell, 'Why Command & Control Won't Go Away', *Training*, September 1995, pp 62–68; R E Quinn and G M Spreitzer, 'The Road to Empowerment: Seven Questions Every Leader Should Consider', *Organizational Dynamics*, Autumn 1997, pp 37–49; and I Cunningham and L Honold, 'Everyone Can Be a Coach', *HRMagazine*, June 1998, pp 63–66.

[41] See R C Ford and M D Fottler, 'Empowerment: A Matter of Degree', *Academy of Management Executive*, August 1995, pp 21–31.

[42] S Gracie, 'Delegate, don't abdicate', *Management Today*, March 1999.

[43] Robert Kreitner, *Management*, 7th ed (Boston: Houghton Mifflin, 1998), p 306. Also see K Dover, 'Avoiding Empowerment Traps', *Management Review*, January 1999, pp 51–55.

[44] Drawn from G Yukl and P P Fu, 'Determinants of Delegation and Consultation by Managers', *Journal of Organizational Behavior*, March 1999, pp 219–32. Also see C A Schriesheim, L L Neider and T A Scandura, 'Delegation and Leader-Member Exchange: Main Effects, Moderators, and Measurement Issues', *Academy of Management Journal*, June 1998, pp 298–318.

[45] See G M Spreitzer and A K Mishra, 'Giving Up without Losing Control: Trust and Its Substitutes' Effects on Managers' Involving Employees in Decision Making', *Group & Organization Management*, June 1999, pp 155–87.

[46] M Frese, W Kring, A Soose and J Zempel, 'Personal Initiative at Work: Differences between East and West Germany', *Academy of Management Journal*, February 1996, p 38. (Emphasis added.)

[47] See J A Belasco and R C Stayer, 'Why Empowerment Doesn't Empower: The Bankruptcy of Current Paradigms', *Business Horizons*, March–April 1994, pp 29–41.

[48] For complete details, see C R Leana, 'Power Relinquishment versus Power Sharing: Theoretical Clarification and Empirical Comparison of Delegation and Participation', *Journal of Applied Psychology*, May 1987, pp 228–33.

[49] M D Fulford and C A Enz, 'The Impact of Empowerment on Service Employees', *Journal of Managerial Issues*, Summer 1995, p 172.

[50] M Jansen, 'Delegation is the key to effective growth', *The Times*, October 26, 1999.

[51] Data from A J H Thorlakson and R P Murray, 'An Empirical Study of Empowerment in the Workplace', *Group & Organization Management*, March 1996, pp 67–83.

[52] Data from C S Koberg, R W Boss, J C Senjem and

E A Goodman, 'Antecedents and Outcomes of Empowerment: Empirical Evidence from the Health Care Industry', *Group & Organization Management*, March 1999, pp 71–91. Also see K Aquino, S L Grover, M Bradfield and D G Allen, 'The Effects of Negative Affectivity, Hierarchical Status, and Self-Determination on Workplace Victimization', *Academy of Management Journal*, June 1999, pp 260–72.

[53] W A Randolph, 'Navigating the Journey to Empowerment', *Organizational Dynamics*, Spring 1995, p 31.

[54] C Hirst, 'Boardroom battles slow e-business advance', *The Independent*, December 3, 2000.

[55] Adapted from S Caulkin, 'Political? Be proud of it', *The Observer*, September 3, 2000 and D Dearlove, 'Power games play off', *The Times*, November 11, 1999.

[56] R W Allen, D L Madison, L W Porter, P A Renwick and B T Mayes, 'Organizational Politics: Tactics and Characteristics of Its Actors', *California Management Review*, Fall 1979, p 77. Also see K M Kacmar and G R Ferris, 'Politics at Work: Sharpening the Focus of Political Behavior in Organizations', *Business Horizons*, July–August 1993, pp 70–74. A comprehensive update can be found in K M Kacmar and R A Baron, 'Organizational Politics: The State of the Field, Links to Related Processes, and an Agenda for Future Research', in *Research in Personnel and Human Resources Management*, vol. 17, ed G R Ferris (Stamford, CT: JAI Press, 1999), pp 1–39.

[57] See P M Fandt and G R Ferris, 'The Management of Information and Impressions: When Employees Behave Opportunistically', *Organizational Behavior and Human Decision Processes*, February 1990, pp 140–58.

[58] First four based on discussion in D R Beeman and T W Sharkey, 'The Use and Abuse of Corporate Politics', *Business Horizons*, March–April 1987, pp 26–30.

[59] A Raia, 'Power, Politics, and the Human Resource Professional', *Human Resource Planning*, no. 4, 1985, p 203.

[60] A J DuBrin, 'Career Maturity, Organizational Rank, and Political Behavioral Tendencies: A Correlational Analysis of Organizational Politics and Career Experience', *Psychological Reports*, October 1988, p 535.

[61] This three-level distinction comes from A T Cobb, 'Political Diagnosis: Applications in Organizational Development', *Academy of Management Review*, July 1986, pp 482–96.

[62] An excellent historical and theoretical perspective of coalitions can be found in W B Stevenson, J L Pearce and L W Porter, 'The Concept of "Coalition" in Organization Theory and Research', *Academy of Management Review*, April 1985, pp 256–68.

[63] See K G Provan and J G Sebastian, 'Networks within Networks: Service Link Overlap, Organizational Cliques, and Network Effectiveness', *Academy of Management Journal*, August 1998, pp 453–63.

[64] Allen, Madison, Porter, Renwick and Mayes, 'Organizational Politics: Tactics and Characteristics of Its Actors', p 77.

[65] See W L Gardner III, 'Lessons in Organizational Dramaturgy: The Art of Impression Management', *Organizational Dynamics*, Summer 1992, pp 33–46.

[66] For more on political behaviour, see A Nierenberg, 'Masterful Networking', *Training & Development*, February 1999, pp 51–53.

[67] A Rao, S M Schmidt and L H Murray, 'Upward Impression Management: Goals, Influence Strategies, and Consequences', *Human Relations*, February 1995, p 147.

[68] See P M Fandt and G R Ferris, 'The Management of Information and Impressions: When Employees Behave Opportunistically', *Organizational Behavior and Human Decision Processes*, February 1990, pp 140–58; W L Gardner and B J Avolio, 'The Charismatic Relationship: A Dramaturgical Perspective', *Academy of Management Review*, January 1998, pp 32–58; L Wah, 'Managing—Manipulating?—Your Reputation', *Management Review*, October 1998, pp 46–50; and M C Bolino, 'Citizenship and Impression Management: Good Soldiers or Good Actors?' *Academy of Management Review*, January 1999, pp 82–98.

[69] For related research, see M G Pratt and A Rafaeli, 'Organizational Dress as a Symbol of Multilayered Social

Identities', *Academy of Management Journal*, August 1997, pp 862–98.

70 A Arkin, 'Tailoring clothes to suit the image', *People Management*, August 24, 1995.

71 J Solomon, 'Why worry about pleat pull and sloppy socks?', *Newsweek*, September 30, 1996.

72 See S J Wayne and G R Ferris, 'Influence Tactics, Affect, and Exchange Quality in Supervisor-Subordinate Interactions: A Laboratory Experiment and Field Study', *Journal of Applied Psychology*, October 1990, pp 487–99. For another version, see Table 1 (p 246) in S J Wayne and R C Liden, 'Effects of Impression Management on Performance Ratings: A Longitudinal Study', *Academy of Management Journal*, February 1995, pp 232–60.

73 See R Vonk, 'The Slime Effect: Suspicion and Dislike of Likeable Behavior toward Superiors', *Journal of Personality and Social Psychology*, April 1998, pp 849–64; and M Wells, 'How to Schmooze Like the Best of Them', *USA Today*, May 18, 1999, p 14E.

74 See P Rosenfeld, R A Giacalone and C A Riordan, 'Impression Management Theory and Diversity: Lessons for Organizational Behavior', *American Behavioral Scientist*, March 1994, pp 601–04; R A Giacalone and J W Beard, 'Impression Management, Diversity, and International Management', *American Behavioral Scientist*, March 1994, pp 621–36; and A Montagliani and R A Giacalone, 'Impression Management and Cross-Cultural Adaptation', *The Journal of Social Psychology*, October 1998, pp 598–608.

75 M E Mendenhall and C Wiley, 'Strangers in a Strange Land: The Relationship between Expatriate Adjustment and Impression Management', *American Behavioral Scientist*, March 1994, pp 605–20.

76 T E Becker and S L Martin, 'Trying to Look Bad at Work: Methods and Motives for Managing Poor Impressions in Organizations', *Academy of Management Journal*, February 1995, p 191.

77 Ibid., p 181.

78 Adapted from ibid., pp 180–81.

79 Based on discussion in ibid., pp 192–93.

80 A Drory and D Beaty, 'Gender Differences in the Perception of Organizational Influence Tactics', *Journal of Organizational Behavior*, May 1991, pp 256–57. Also see L A Rudman, 'Self-Promotion as a Risk Factor for Women: The Costs and Benefits of Counterstereotypical Impression Management', *Journal of Personality and Social Psychology*, March 1998, pp 629–45; and J Tata, 'The Influence of Gender on the Use and Effectiveness of Managerial Accounts', *Group & Organization Management*, September 1998, pp 267–88.

81 See S J Wayne and R C Liden, 'Effects of Impression Management on Performance Ratings: A Longitudinal Study', *Academy of Management Journal*, February 1995, pp 232–60.

82 Rao, Schmidt and Murray, 'Upward Impression Management: Goals, Influence Strategies, and Consequences', p 165.

83 Also see A Tziner, G P Latham, B S Price and R Haccoun, 'Development and Validation of a Questionnaire for Measuring Perceived Political Considerations in Performance Appraisal', *Journal of Organizational Behavior*, March 1996, pp 179–90.

84 A Zaleznik, 'Real Work', *Harvard Business Review*, January–February 1989, p 60.

85 C M Koen, Jr, and S M Crow, 'Human Relations and Political Skills', *HR Focus*, December 1995, p 11.

86 For more on workplace politics, see 'Smart Workplace Politics', *Supervisory Management*, September 1994, pp 11–12; J A Byrne, 'How to Succeed: Same Game, Different Decade', *Business Week*, April 17, 1995, p 48; and M Moats Kennedy, 'Political Mistakes of the Newly Promoted', *Across the Board*, October 1995, pp 53–54.

87 See L A Witt, 'Enhancing Organizational Goal Congruence: A Solution to Organizational Politics', *Journal of Applied Psychology*, August 1998, pp 666–74.

88 Ten quiz items quoted from J F Byrnes, 'Connecting Organizational Politics and Conflict Resolution', *Personnel Administrator*, June 1986, p 49.

89 Scoring system quoted from ibid.

90 B R Schlenker and T W Britt, 'Beneficial Impression Management: Strategically Controlling Information to Help Friends', *Journal of Personality and Social Psychology*, April 1999, p 559.

Chapter 16

1 Adapted from 'Somebody has to take the lead', *Businessweek*, November 13, 2000.

2 See S Lieberson and J F O'Connor, 'Leadership and Organizational Performance: A Study of Large Corporations', *American Sociological Review*, April 1972, pp 117–30.

3 The role of leadership within organizational change is discussed by O Harari, 'Why Do Leaders Avoid Change', *Management Review*, March 1999, pp 35–38; and J P Lotter, *Leading Change* (Boston: Harvard Business School Press, 1996).

4 T Thorlindson, *The Skipper Effect in Icelandic Herring Fishing* (Reykjavik: University of Iceland, 1987) in M Smith and C Cooper, 'Leadership and stress', *Leadership and Organization Development Journal*, vol. 15 no. 2, 1994, pp 3–7.

5 P Wright, *Managerial Leadership*, (London: Routledge, 1996)

6 The American Survey, *The Economist*, December 9, 1995, pp 53–54.

7 In the UK, John Adair has become very popular as an expert on leadership training. See a.o. J Adair, *Effective Leadership*, (London: Pan Books, 1988).

8 Based on C A Bartlett and A Nanda, 'Ingvar Kamprad and Ikea', in: R Buzzell, J Quelch and C Bartlett, *Global Marketing Management: cases and readings*, (Reading: Addison-Wesley Publishing Company), pp 69–95; and B Ernström, 'The Well Tempered Viking', *Scanorama*, June 1989, pp 64–72.

9 R J House, N S Wright and R N Aditiya, 'Cross-cultural research on organizational leadership: a critical analysis and a proposed theory', in: P C Earley and M Erez, *New perspectives in international industrial organizational psychology*, pp 535–625, (San Francisco, CA: New Lexington).

10 C A Schriesheim, J M Tolliver and O C Behling, 'Leadership Theory: Some Implications for Managers', *MSU Business Topics*, Summer 1978, p 35.

11 R J House, N S Wright and R N Aditiya, op. cit.

12 See H Mintzberg, 'Covert Leadership: Notes on Managing Professionals', *Harvard Business Review*, November–December 1998, pp 140–47.

13 B M Bass, *Bass & Stogdill's Handbook of Leadership: Theory, Research, and Managerial Applications*, 3rd ed, (New York: Free Press, 1990), p 383.

14 For a thorough discussion about the differences between leading and managing, see G Weathersby, 'Leading vs. Management', *Management Review*, March 1999, p 5; R J House and R N Aditya, 'The Social Scientific Study of Leadership: Quo Vadis?' *Journal of Management*, pp 409–73; and A Zalesnik, 'Managers and Leaders: Are They Different?' *Harvard Business Review*, May–June 1977, pp 67–78.

15 For complete details, see R M Stogdill, 'Personal Factors Associated with Leadership: A Survey of the Literature', *Journal of Psychology*, 1948, pp 35–71; and R M Stogdill, *Handbook of Leadership* (New York: Free Press, 1974).

16 Excerpted from T A Stewart, 'The Contest for Welch's Throne Begins: Who Will Run GE?' *Fortune*, January 11, 1999, p 27.

17 See R D Mann, 'A Review of the Relationships between Personality and Performance in Small Groups', *Psychological Bulletin*, July 1959, pp 241–70.

18 See D A Kenny and S J Zaccaro, 'An Estimate of Variance Due to Traits in Leadership', *Journal of Applied Psychology*, November 1983, pp 678–85. Results from a more recent verification can be found in S J Zaccaro, R J Foti and D A Kenny, 'Self-Monitoring and Trait-Based Variance in Leadership: An Investigation of Leader Flexibility across Multiple Group Situations', *Journal of Applied Psychology*, April 1991, pp 308–15.

19 See A J Kinicki, P W Hom, M R Trost and K J Wade, 'Effects of Category Prototypes on Performance-Rating Accuracy', *Journal of Applied Psychology*, June 1995, pp 354–70; J S Phillips and R G Lord, 'Schematic Information Processing and Perceptions of Leadership in Problem-Solving Groups', *Journal of Applied Psychology*, August 1982, pp 486–92; and R J Foti, S L Fraser and R G Lord, 'Effects of Leadership Labels and Prototypes on Perceptions of Political Leaders', *Journal of Applied Psychology*, June 1982, pp 326–33.

[20] See R J Hall, J W Workman and C A Marchioro, 'Sex, Task, and Behavioral Flexibility Effects on Leadership Perceptions', *Organizational Behavior and Human Decision Processes*, April 1998, pp 1–32; and R G Lord, C L De Vader and G M Alliger, 'A Meta-Analysis of the Relation between Personality Traits and Leadership Perceptions: An Application of Validity Generalization Procedures', *Journal of Applied Psychology*, August 1986, p 407.

[21] Results can be found in J M Kouzes and B Z Posner, *The Leadership Challenge* (San Francisco: Jossey-Bass, 1995).

[22] Gender and the emergence of leaders was examined in A H Eagly and S J Karau, 'Gender and the Emergence of Leaders: A Meta-Analysis', *Journal of Personality and Social Psychology*, May 1991, pp 685–710; and R K Shelly and P T Munroe, 'Do Women Engage in Less Task Behavior Than Men?' *Sociological Perspectives*, Spring 1999, pp 49–67.

[23] See A H Eagly, S J Karau and B T Johnson, 'Gender and Leadership Style among School Principals: A Meta-Analysis', *Educational Administration Quarterly*, February 1992, pp 76–102.

[24] Results can be found in A H Eagly, S J Karau and M G Makhijani, 'Gender and the Effectiveness of Leaders: A Meta-Analysis', *Psychological Bulletin*, January 1995, pp 125–45.

[25] Hay Management Consultants

[26] R Tait, op. cit., p 21.

[27] This research is summarized and critiqued by E A Fleishman, 'Consideration and Structure: Another Look at Their Role in Leadership Research', in *Leadership: The Multiple-Level Approaches*, eds F Dansereau and F J Yammarino (Stamford, CT: JAI Press, 1998), pp 51–60; and Bass, *Bass & Stogdill's Handbook of Leadership: Theory, Research, and Managerial Applications*, Ch. 24.

[28] See V H Vroom, 'Leadership', in *Handbook of Industrial and Organizational Psychology*, ed M D Dunnette (Chicago: Rand McNally, 1976).

[29] Even the way Blake and Mouton cite research that contradicts their theory as supportive is sometimes highly questionable.

[30] R R Blake and J S Mouton, 'A Comparative Analysis of Situationalism and 9,9 Management by Principle', *Organizational Dynamics*, Spring 1982, p 23.

[31] Ibid., pp 28–29. Also see R R Blake and J S Mouton, 'Management by Grid Principles or Situationalism: Which?' *Group & Organization Studies*, December 1981, pp 439–55.

[32] Ibid., p 21.

[33] Excerpted from R J Grossman, 'Heirs Unapparent', *HRMagazine*, February 1999, p 39.

[34] See Bass, *Bass & Stogdill's Handbook of Leadership: Theory, Research, and Managerial Applications*, Ch. 20–25.

[35] The relationships between the frequency and mastery of leader behaviour and various outcomes were investigated in F Shipper and C S White, 'Mastery, Frequency, and Interaction of Managerial Behaviors Relative to Subunit Effectiveness', *Human Relations*, January 1999, pp 49–66.

[36] F E Fiedler, 'Job Engineering for Effective Leadership: A New Approach', *Management Review*, September 1977, p 29.

[37] Excerpted from C Hymowitz, 'In the Lead: How Cynthia Danaher Learned to Stop Sharing and Start Leading', *The Wall Street Journal*, March 16, 1999, p B1.

[38] For more on this theory, see F E Fiedler, 'A Contingency Model of Leadership Effectiveness', in *Advances in Experimental Social Psychology*, vol. 1, ed L Berkowitz (New York: Academic Press, 1964); F E Fiedler, *A Theory of Leadership Effectiveness* (New York: McGraw-Hill, 1967).

[39] Additional information on situational control is contained in F E Fiedler, 'The Leadership Situation and the Black Box in Contingency Theories', in *Leadership Theory and Research: Perspectives and Directions*, eds M M Chemers and R Ayman (New York: Academic Press, 1993), pp 2–28.

[40] See L H Peters, D D Hartke and J T Pohlmann, 'Fiedler's Contingency Theory of Leadership: An Application of the Meta-Analyses Procedures of Schmidt and Hunter', *Psychological Bulletin*, March 1985, pp 274–85. The meta-analysis was conducted by C A Schriesheim, B J Tepper and L A Tetrault, 'Least Preferred Co-Worker Score, Situational Control, and Leadership Effectiveness: A Meta-Analysis of Contingency Model Performance Predictions', *Journal of Applied Psychology*, August 1994, pp 561–73.

[41] A recent review of the contingency theory and suggestions for future theoretical development is provided by R Ayman, M M Chemers and F Fiedler, 'The Contingency Model of Leadership Effectiveness: Its Levels of Analysis', in *Leadership: The Multiple-Level Approaches*, eds Dansereau and Yammarino, pp 73–94; and R P Vecchio, 'Some Continuing Challenges for the Contingency Model of Leadership', in *Leadership: The Multiple-Level Approaches*, eds Dansereau and Yammarino, pp 115–24.

[42] For more detail on this theory, see R J House, 'A Path–Goal Theory of Leader Effectiveness', *Administrative Science Quarterly*, September 1971, pp 321–38.

[43] Adapted from R J House and T R Mitchell, 'Path–Goal Theory of Leadership', *Journal of Contemporary Business*, Autumn 1974, p 83.

[44] See R Hooijberg, 'A Multidirectional Approach toward Leadership: An Extension of the Concept of Behavioral Complexity', *Human Relations*, July 1996, pp 917–46.

[45] Based on A Bronw, 'Top of the Bosses', *International Management*, April 1994, pp 26–31.

[46] Results can be found in P M Podsakoff, S B MacKenzie, M Ahearne and W H Bommer, 'Searching for a Needle in a Haystack: Trying to Identify the Illusive Moderators of Leadership Behaviors', *Journal of Management*, 1995, pp 422–70.

[47] A thorough discussion of this theory is provided by P Hersey and K H Blanchard, *Management of Organizational Behavior: Utilizing Human Resources*, 5th ed (Englewood Cliffs, NJ: Prentice-Hall, 1988).

[48] A comparison of the original theory and its latent version is provided by P Hersey and K Blanchard, 'Great Ideas Revisited', *Training & Development*, January 1996, pp 42–47.

[49] Results can be found in J R Goodson, G W McGee and J F Cashman, 'Situational Leadership Theory', *Group & Organization Studies*, December 1989, pp 446–61.

[50] The first study was conducted by R P Vecchio, 'Situational Leadership Theory: An Examination of a Prescriptive Theory', *Journal of Applied Psychology*, August 1987, pp 444–51. Results from the study of nurse executives can be found in C Adams, 'Leadership Behavior of Chief Nurse Executives', *Nursing Management*, August 1990, pp 36–39.

[51] See D C Lueder, 'Don't Be Misled by LEAD', *Journal of Applied Behavioral Science*, May 1985, pp 143–54; and C L Graeff, 'The Situational Leadership Theory: A Critical View', *Academy of Management Review*, April 1983, pp 285–91.

[52] For details on these different theories, see J McGregor Burns, *Leadership* (New York: Harper & Row, 1978); N M Tichy and M A Devanna, *The Transformational Leader* (New York: John Wiley & Sons, 1986); J M Kouzes and B Z Posner, *The Leadership Challenge: How to Get Extraordinary Things Done in Organizations* (San Francisco: Jossey-Bass, 1990); B Bass and B J Avolio, 'Transformational Leadership: A Response to Critiques', in *Leadership Theory and Research: Perspectives and Directions*, eds M M Chemers and R Ayman (New York: Academic Press, 1993), pp 49–80; B Nanus, *Visionary Leadership* (San Francisco: Jossey-Bass, 1992); and B Shamir, R J House and M B Arthur, 'The Motivational Effects of Charismatic Leadership: A Self-Concept Based Theory', *Organization Science*, November 1993, pp 577–94.

[53] Shamir, House and Arthur, 'The Motivational Effects of Charismatic Leadership: A Self-Concept Based Theory', p 578.

[54] see http://www.execpc.com/~shepler/branson

[55] This discussion is based on D A Waldman and F J Yammarino, 'CEO Charismatic Leadership: Levels-of-Management and Levels-of-Analysis Effects', *Academy of Management Review*, April 1999, pp 266–85.

[56] Nanus, *Visionary Leadership*, p 8.

57 See Ibid; and W L Gardner and B J Avolio, 'The Charismatic Relationship: A Dramaturgical Perspective', *Academy of Management Review*, January 1998, pp 32–58.

58 Based on and translated from J Grobben, 'Tien voor twee', *Knack*, February 2, 1995, pp 40-42.

59 See G Fuchsberg, 'Visioning Missions Becomes Its Own Mission', *The Wall Street Journal*, January 7, 1994, p B1.

60 Results can be found in B Shamir, E Zakay, E Breinin and M Popper, 'Correlates of Charismatic Leader Behavior in Military Units: Subordinates' Attitudes, Unit Characteristics, and Superiors' Appraisals of Leader Performance', *Academy of Management Journal*, August 1998, pp 387–409.

61 Results can be obtained from T G DeGroot, D S Kiker and T C Cross, 'A Meta-Analysis to Review the Consequences of Charismatic Leadership', paper presented at the annual meeting of the Academy of Management, Cincinnati, Ohio, 1996.

62 Supporting research can be found in R Pillai and J R Meindl, 'Context and Charisma: A 'Meso' Level Examination of the Relationship of Organic Structure, Collectivism, and Crisis to Charismatic Leadership', *Journal of Management*, 1998, 643–71; and J C Wofford, V L Goodwin and J L Whittington, 'A Field Study of a Cognitive Approach to Understanding Transformational and Transactional Leadership', *Leadership Quarterly*, 1998, pp 55–84.

63 See K B Lowe, K G Kroeck and N Sivasubramaniam, 'Effectiveness Correlates of Transformational and Transactional Leadership: A Meta-Analytic Review of the MLQ Literature', *Leadership Quarterly*, 1996, pp 385–425.

64 See D I Jung and B J Avolio, 'Effects of Leadership Style and Followers' Cultural Orientation on Performance in Group and Individual Task Conditions', *Academy of Management Journal*, April 1999, pp 208–18; and A J Dubinsky, F J Yammarino, M A Jolson and W D Spangler, 'Transformational Leadership: An Initial Investigation in Sales Management', *Journal of Personal Selling & Sales Management*, Spring 1995, pp 17–31.

65 Results can be found in R J House, W D Spangler and J Woycke, 'Personality and Charisma in the US Presidency: A Psychological Theory of Leader Effectiveness', *Administrative Science Quarterly*, September 1991, pp 364–96.

66 See B M Bass, 'Does the Transactional-Transformational Leadership Paradigm Transcend Organizational and National Boundaries?' *American Psychologist*, February 1997, pp 130–39.

67 See B Shankar Pawar and K K Eastman, 'The Nature and Implications of Contextual Influences on Transformational Leadership: A Conceptual Examination', *Academy of Management Review*, January 1997, pp 80–109; and P Sellers, 'What Exactly Is Charisma?' *Fortune*, January 15, 1996, pp 68–75.

68 Supporting research is summarized by Bass and Avolio, 'Transformation Leadership: A Response to Critiques', pp 49–80. The effectiveness of leadership training is discussed by J Huey, 'The Leadership Industry', *Fortune*, February 21, 1994, pp 54–56.

69 The ethics of charismatic leadership is discussed by D Sankowsky, 'The Charismatic Leader as Narcissist: Understanding the Abuse of Power', *Organizational Dynamics*, Spring 1995, pp 57–71.

70 These recommendations were derived from J M Howell and B J Avolio, 'The Ethics of Charismatic Leadership: Submission or Liberation', *The Executive*, May 1992, pp 43–54.

71 For an expanded discussion of this model, see S Kerr and J Jermier, 'Substitutes for Leadership: Their Meaning and Measurement', *Organizational Behavior and Human Performance*, December 1978, pp 375–403.

72 See J P Howell, P W Dorfman and S Kerr, 'Moderator Variables in Leadership Research', *Academy of Management Review*, January 1986, pp 88–102.

73 Results can be found in Podsakoff, MacKenzie, Ahearne and Bommer, 'Searching for a Needle in a Haystack: Trying to Identify the Illusive Moderators of Leadership Behaviors'.

74 For details of this study, see P M Podsakoff, S B MacKenzie and W H Bommer, 'Meta-Analysis of the Relationship between Kerr and Jermier's Substitutes for Leadership and Employee Job Attitudes, Role Perceptions, and Performance', *Journal of Applied Psychology*, August 1996, pp 380–99.

75 See the related discussion in J P Howell, D E Bowen, P W Dorfman, S Kerr and P M Podsakoff, 'Substitutes for Leadership: Effective Alternatives to Ineffective Leadership', in Leadership: *Understanding the Dynamics of Power and Influence in Organizations*, ed R P Vecchio (Notre Dame, IN: University of Notre Dame Press, 1997), pp 381–95.

76 An overall summary of servant leadership is provided by L C Spears, *Reflections on Leadership: How Robert K Greenleaf's Theory of Servant-Leadership Influenced Today's Top Management Thinkers* (New York: John Wiley & Sons, 1995).

77 See E McShulskis, 'HRM Update: Coaching Helps, But Is Not Often Used', *HRMagazine*, March 1966, pp 15–16; and L McDermott, 'Wanted: Chief Executive Coach', *Training & Development*, May 1996, pp 67–70.

78 For a discussion of superleadership, see C C Manz and H P Sims, Jr, 'SuperLeadership: Beyond the Myth of Heroic Leadership', in *Leadership: Understanding the Dynamics of Power and Influence in Organizations*, ed Vecchio, pp 411–28; and C C Manz and H P Sims, Jr, *Superleadership: Leading Others to Lead Themselves* (New York: Berkley Books, 1989).

79 Based on T Peters and N Austin, *A Passion for Excellence* (Glasgow: Collins, 1985); C D Orth, H E Wilkinson and R C Benfari, 'The Manager's Role as Coach and Mentor', *Organizational Dynamics*, 1987, vol. 15, no. 4, pp 66–74; R D Evered and J C Selman, 'Coaching and the Art of Management', *Organizational Dynamics*, 1989, vol. 18, pp 16–32.

80 The scale used to assess readiness to assume the leadership role was taken from A J DuBrin, *Leadership: Research Findings, Practice, and Skills* (Boston: Houghton Mifflin Company, 1995), pp 10–11.

81 This exercise was based on one contained in L W Mealiea, *Skills for Managers in Organizations* (Burr Ridge, IL: Irwin, 1994), pp 96–97.

82 The introduction was quoted from ibid., p 96.

Chapter 17

1 Excerpted from E Addley, 'It's all down to me', *The Guardian*, May 8, 2000. Reproduced with permission.

2 S Watson, 'Of course I'm stressed out – I'm important!', *The Guardian*, April 7, 2000.

3 F Williams, 'ILO warns of epidemic of stress', *The Financial Times*, October 10, 2000, p 8.

4 A Osborn, 'Workplace blues leave employers in the red', *The Guardian*, October 12, 2000.

5 M Coles, 'Managers tire of only living to work', *The Sunday Times*, July 30, 2000.

6 F Williams, op. cit.

7 See L Grunberg, S Moore and E S Greenberg, 'Work Stress and Problem Alcohol Behavior: A Test of the Spillover Model', *Journal of Organizational Behavior*, September 1998, pp 487–502.

8 The stress response is thoroughly discussed in H Selye, *Stress without Distress* (New York: J. B. Lippincott, 1974).

9 Adapted and translated from M Teugels, 'Manisch levensritme leidt tot depressies', *Vacature*, February 20, 1999.

10 L Bestic, 'Tired? Ignore it at your peril', *The Independent*, February 24, 2000.

11 J Amparano, 'On-Job Stress Is Making Workers Sick', *The Arizona Republic*, August 4, 1996, pp A1, A12.

12 J M Ivancevich and M T Matteson, *Stress and Work: A Managerial Perspective* (Glenview, IL: Scott, Foresman, 1980), pp 8–9.

13 Adapted and translated from A Giegas, 'Dossier: Stress', *Vacature*, published online only: http://www.vacature.com/scripts/indexpage.asp?headingID=1103 , 2000

14 See Selye, *Stress without distress*.

15 A Giegas, op. cit.

16 This study was conducted by G R Oldham, A Cummings, L J Mischel, J M Schmidtke, J Zhou, 'Listen While You Work? Quasi-Experimental Relations between Personal-Stereo Headset Use and Employee Work Responses', *Journal of Applied Psychology*, October 1995, pp 547–64.

[17] See J D Jonge, G J P Van Breikelen, J A Landeweerd and F J N Nijhuis, 'Comparing Group and Individual Level Assessments of Job Characteristics in Testing the Job Demand-Control Model: A Multilevel Approach', *Human Relations*, January 1999, pp 95–122; and J Schaubroeck and L S Fink, 'Facilitating and Inhibiting Effects of Job Control and Social Support on Stress Outcomes and Role Behavior: A Contingency Model', *Journal of Organizational Behavior*, March 1998, pp 167–95.

[18] Results from these studies are reported in C Frankie, 'Americans Tops in Work Messages', *The Arizona Republic*, October 3, 1999, p A29; and A R Karr, 'Work Week: A Special News Report About Life on the Job—And Trends Taking Shape There', *The Wall Street Journal*, February 9, 1999, p A1.

[19] H Bosma, R Peter and J Siegrist, 'Two alternative job stress models and the risk of coronary heart disease', *American Journal of Public Health*, vol. 88 no. 1, January 1998, pp 68–74.

[20] T Theorell et al, 'Decision Latitude, Job Strain and Mycardial Infarction: a study of working men in Stockholm.', *American Journal of Public Health*, March 1998, vol. 88 no.3, March 1998, pp 382–88.

[21] C Frankie, op. cit.

[22] U Kinnunen, S Mauno, S Nätti and M Happonen, 'Perceived Job Insecurity: a longitudinal study among Finnish employees', *European Journal of Work and Organizational Psychology*, vol. 8 issue 2, 1999, pp 243–60.

[23] Supportive results can be found in V J Magley, C L Hulin, L F Fitzgerald and M DeNardo, 'Outcomes of Self-Labeling Sexual Harassment', *Journal of Applied Psychology*, June 1999, pp 390–402; and L F Fitzgerald, F Drasgow, C L Hulin, M J Gelfand and V J Magley, 'Antecedents and Consequences of Sexual Harassment in Organizations: A Test of an Integrated Model', *Journal of Applied Psychology*, August 1997, pp 578–89.

[24] The relationship between chronic work demands and stress was investigated by J Schaubroeck and D C Ganster, 'Chronic Demands and Responsivity to Challenge', *Journal of Applied Psychology*, February 1993, pp 73–85.

[25] C Midgley, 'Make this the week that you reclaim your life', *The Times*, May 8, 2000.

[26] Excerpted from R Ganzel, 'Feeling Squeezed by Technology?' *Training*, April 1998, p 62.

[27] Ibid, pp 62–70.

[28] R Mendick, 'Better a broken heart than a frozen screen', *The Independent*, September 3, 2000.

[29] R Ganzel, op. cit.

[30] See G Stern, 'Take a Bite, Do Some Work, Take a Bite', *The Wall Street Journal*, January 17, 1994, pp B1, B2; R F Bettendorf, 'Curing the New Ills of Technology: Proper Ergonomics Can Reduce Cumulative Trauma Disorders among Employees', *HRMagazine*, March 1990, pp 35–36, 80; and S Overman, 'Prescriptions for a Healthier Office', *HRMagazine*, February 1990, pp 30–34.

[31] E Davis, 'Does your life work?' *Management Today*, August 1999, pp 48–55.

[32] E Davis, op. cit.

[33] Anonymous, 'Het Britse Seksleven is in gevaar', *Vacature*, December 3, 1999.

[34] Anonymous, 'Stress causes one-third to think about work while having sex', *The Guardian*, November 5, 1999.

[35] See R Lazarus, *Stress and Emotion: A New Synthesis* (New York: Springer Publishing, 1999).

[36] Research on job loss is summarized by K A Hanisch, 'Job Loss and Unemployment Research from 1994 to 1998: A Review and Recommendations for Research and Intervention', *Journal of Vocational Behavior*, October 1999, pp 188–220.

[37] Supportive results can be found in A A Grandey and R Cropanzano, 'The Conservation of Resources Model Applied to Work–Family Conflict and Strain', *Journal of Vocational Behavior*, April 1999, pp 350–70; J R Edwards and N P Rothbard, 'Work and Family Stress and Well-Being: An Examination of Person–Environment Fit in the Work and Family Domains', *Organizational Behavior and Human Decision Processes*, February 1999, pp 85–129; and A J Kinicki, F M McKee and K J Wade, 'Annual Review, 1991–1995;

Occupational Health', *Journal of Vocational Behavior*, October 1996, pp 190–220.

[38] Results from this study were reported in 'Poll: 1 in 6 Workers Want to Hit Someone', *The Arizona Republic*, September 6, 1999, p A11.

[39] Reviews of this research can be found in R S DeFrank and J M Ivancevich, 'Stress on the Job: An Executive Update', *Academy of Management Executive*, August 1998, pp 55–66; and M Koslowsky, *Modeling the Stress–Strain Relationship in Work Settings* (New York: Routledge, 1998).

[40] Results can be found in L Narayanan, S Menon and P E Spector, 'Stress in the Workplace: A Comparison of Gender and Occupations', *Journal of Organizational Behavior*, 1999, pp 63–73.

[41] See M E Lachman and S L Weaver, 'The Sense of Control as a Moderator of Social Class Differences in Health and Well-Being', *Journal of Personality and Social Psychology*, March 1998, pp 763–73.

[42] These findings are reported in B Melin, U Lundberg, J Soderlund and M Granqvist, 'Psychological and Physiological Stress Reactions of Male and Female Assembly Workers: A Comparison between Two Different Forms of Work Organization', *Journal of Organizational Behavior*, January 1999, pp 47–61.

[43] Research on chronic hostility is discussed by 'Healthy Lives: A New View of Stress', *University of California, Berkeley Wellness Letter*, June 1990, pp 4–5. Also see R S Jorgensen, B T Johnson, M E Kolodziej and G E Schreer, 'Elevated Blood Pressure and Personality: A Meta-Analytic Review', *Psychological Bulletin*, September 1996, pp 293–320.

[44] P De Winter, 'Dat meldt zich maar ziek !' *Management Team*, May 19, 2000, pp 90–101.

[45] This landmark study was conducted by T H Holmes and R H Rahe, 'The Social Readjustment Rating Scale', *Journal of Psychosomatic Research*, August 1967, pp 213–18.

[46] The rating scale was recently revised by C J Hobson, J Kamen, J Szostek, C M Nethercut, J W Tiedmann and S Wojnarowicz, 'Stressful Life Events: A Revision and Update of the Social Readjustment Rating Scale', *International Journal of Stress Management*, January 1998, pp 1–23.

[47] Normative predictions are discussed in O Behling and A L Darrow, 'Managing Work-Related Stress', in *Modules in Management*, eds J E Rosenzweig and F E Kast (Chicago: Science Research Associates, 1984).

[48] This research is discussed by K S Kendler, L M Karkowski and C A Prescott, 'Causal Relationship between Stressful Life Events and the Onset of Major Depression', *American Journal of Psychiatry*, June 1999, pp 837–48; C Segrin, 'Social Skills, Stressful Life Events, and the Development of Psychosocial Problems', *Journal of Social and Clinical Psychology*, Spring 1999, pp 14–34; and R S Bhagat, 'Effects of Stressful Life Events on Individual Performance Effectiveness and Work Adjustment Processes within Organizational Settings: A Research Model', *Academy of Management Review*, October 1983, pp 660–71.

[49] See D R Pillow, A J Zautra and I Sandler, 'Major Life Events and Minor Stressors: Identifying Mediational Links in the Stress Process', *Journal of Personality and Social Psychology*, February 1996, pp 381–94; R C Barnett, S W Raudenbush, R T Brennan, J H Pleck and N L Marshall, 'Change in Job and Marital Experiences and Change in Psychological Distress: A Longitudinal Study of Dual-Earner Couples', *Journal of Personality and Social Psychology*, November 1995, pp 839–50; and S Cohen, D A J Tyrell and A P Smith, 'Negative Life Events, Perceived Stress, Negative Affect, and Susceptibility to the Common Cold', *Journal of Personality and Social Psychology*, January 1993, pp 131–40.

[50] See Hobson, Kamen, Szostek, Nethercut, Tiedmann and Wojnarowicz, 'Stressful Life Events: A Revision and Update of the Social Readjustment Rating Scale', pp 1–23; and R H Rahe, 'Life Changes Scaling: Other Results; Gender Differences', *International Journal of Stress Management*, October 1998, pp 249–50.

[51] S Cartwright, 'Taking the Pulse of Executive Health in the

U.K.', *The Academy of Management Executive*', vol. 14, no. 2, 2000, pp 16–24.

52 Adapted and translated from M Teugels, 'Leg je mensen in de watten', *Vacature*, October 10, 2000.

53 A Maitland, 'Management burnout: anxiety, depression and stress at work can end in personal catastrophe', *The Financial Times*, November 20, 1998.

54 A Maitland, op. cit.

55 Adapted and translated from M Teugels, 'Het burnout-fenomeen', *Vacature*, May 9, 2000.

56 Adapted and translated from A Giegas, 'Dossier Burnout', *Vacature*, published only on the website, url: http://www.vacature.com/scripts/indexpage.asp?headingID=1477 , 2000

57 Results are presented in T D Schellhardt, 'Off the Track: Is Your Job Going Nowhere? That May Be Natural, but It Doesn't Have to Be Permanent', *The Wall Street Journal* (Eastern Edition), February 26, 1996, p R4.

58 S Sonnentag, F C Brodbeck, T Heinbokel and W Stolte, 'Stressor–burnout relationship on software development teams', *Journal of Occupational and Organizational Psychology*, vol. 67, pp 327–341.

59 The phases are thoroughly discussed by C Maslach, *Burnout: The Cost of Caring* (Englewood Cliffs, NJ: Prentice-Hall, 1982).

60 The discussion of the model is based on C L Cordes and T W Dougherty, 'A Review and Integration of Research on Job Burnout', *Academy of Management Review*, October 1993, pp 621–56.

61 H Levinson, 'When Executives Burn Out', *Harvard Business Review*, July–August 1996, p 153.

62 Results and conclusions can be found in R T Lee and B E Ashforth, 'A Meta-Analytic Examination of the Correlates of the Three Dimensions of Burnout', *Journal of Applied Psychology*, April 1996, pp 123–33.

63 See Ibid; E Babakus, D W Cravens, M Johnston and W C Moncrief, 'The Role of Emotional Exhaustion in Sales Force Attitude and Behavior Relationships', *Journal of the Academy of Marketing Science*, 1999, pp 58–70; and R D Iverson, M Olekalns and P J Erwin, 'Affectivity, Organizational Stressors, and Absenteeism: A Causal Model of Burnout and Its Consequences', *Journal of Vocational Behavior*, February 1998, pp 1–23.

64 Recommendations for reducing burnout are discussed by J E Moore, 'Are You Burning Out Valuable Resources', *HRMagazine*, January 1999, pp 93–97; and L Grensing-Pophal, 'Recognizing and Conquering On-the-Job Burnout: HR, Heal Thyself', *HRMagazine*, March 1999, pp 82–88.

65 Excerpted from S Shellenbarger, 'Work & Family: Three Myths That Make Managers Push Staff to the Edge of Burnout', *The Wall Street Journal*, March 17, 1999, p B1.

66 Based on and translated from E Verdegaal, 'Sabbatical Leave: Prima, maar niet in de tijd van de baas', *Management Team*, November 17, 1995, pp 111–114.

67 S Armour, 'Employers Urge Workers to Chill Out Before Burning Out', *USA Today*, June 22, 1999, p 5B.

68 Types of support are discussed in S Cohen and T A Wills, 'Stress, Social Support, and the Buffering Hypothesis', *Psychological Bulletin*, September 1985, pp 310–57.

69 The perceived availability and helpfulness of social support was discussed by B P Buunk, J D Jonge, J F Ybema and C J D Wolff, 'Psychosocial Aspects of Occupational Stress', in *Handbook of Work and Organizational Psychology*, 2nd ed, P J D Drenth, H Thierry and C J D Wolff (New York: Psychology Press, 1998), pp 145–82.

70 See B N Uchino, J T Cacioppo and J K Kiecolt-Glaser, 'The Relationship between Social Support and Physiological Processes: A Review with Emphasis on Underlying Mechanisms and Implications for Health', *Psychological Bulletin*, May 1996, pp 488–531; and H Benson and M Stark, *Timeless Healing: The Power and Biology of Belief* (New York: Scribner, 1996).

71 Supporting results can be found in C J Holahan, R H Moos, C K Holahan and R C Cronkite, 'Resource Loss, Resource Gain, and Depressive Symptoms: A 10-Year Model', *Journal of Personality and Social Psychology*, September 1999, pp 620–29;

D S Carlson and P L Perrewe, 'The Role of Social Support in the Stressor–Strain Relationship: An Examination of Work–Family Conflict', *Journal of Management*, 1999, pp 513–40; and M H Davis, M M Morris and L A Kraus, 'Relationship-Specific and Global Perceptions of Social Support: Associations with Well-Being and Attachment', *Journal of Personality and Social Psychology*, February 1998, pp 468–81.

72 See S Aryee, V Luk, A Leung and S Lo, 'Role Stressors, Interrole Conflict, and Well-Being: The Moderating Influence of Spousal Support and Coping Behaviors among Employed Parents in Hong Kong', *Journal of Vocational Behavior*, April 1999, pp 259–78; and C Viswesvaran, J I Sanchez and J Fisher, 'The Role of Social Support in the Process of Work Stress: A Meta-Analysis', *Journal of Vocational Behavior*, April 1999, pp 314–34.

73 For details, see B P Buunk, B J Doosje, L G J M Jans and L E M Hopstaken, 'Perceived Reciprocity, Social Support, and Stress at Work: The Role of Exchange and Communal Orientation', *Journal of Personality and Social Psychology*, October 1993, pp 801–11; and C E Cutrona, 'Objective Determinants of Perceived Social Support', *Journal of Personality and Social Psychology*, February 1986, pp 349–55.

74 R S Lazarus and S Folkman, 'Coping and Adaptation', in *Handbook of Behavioral Medicine*, ed W D Gentry (New York: The Guilford Press, 1984), p 283.

75 The antecedents of appraisal were investigated by G J Fogarty, M A Machin, M J Albion, L F Sutherland, G I Lalor and S Revitt, 'Predicting Occupational Strain and Job Satisfaction: The Role of Stress, Coping, Personality, and Affectivity Variables', *Journal of Vocational Behavior*, June 1999, pp 429–52; E C Chang, 'Dispositional Optimism and Primary and Secondary Appraisal of a Stressor: Controlling Influences and Relations to Coping and Psychological and Physical Adjustment', *Journal of Personality and Social Psychology*, April 1998, pp 1109–20; and J C Holder and A Vaux, 'African American Professionals: Coping with Occupational Stress in Predominantly White Work Environments', *Journal of Vocational Behavior*, December 1988, pp 315–33.

76 Lazarus and Folkman, 'Coping and Adaptation', p 289.

77 Adapted and Translated from K Devreux-Bletek, 'Schat, vergeet niet je multi-vitamine preparaat te nemen', *Vacature*, April 4, 2000. Reproduced with permission.

78 See C R Leana, D C Feldman and G Y Tan, 'Predictors of Coping Behavior after a Layoff', *Journal of Organizational Behavior*, 1998, pp 85–97; and B Major, C Richards, M L Cooper, C Cozzarelli and J Zubek, 'Personal Resilience, Cognitive Appraisals, and Coping: An Integrative Model of Adjustment to Abortion', *Journal of Personality and Social Psychology*, March 1998, pp 735–52.

79 See results presented in M A Gowan, C M Riordan and R D Gatewood, 'Test of a Model of Coping with Involuntary Job Loss Following a Company Closing', *Journal of Applied Psychology*, February 1999, pp 75–86; and T M Begley, 'Coping Strategies as Predictors of Employee Distress and Turnover after an Organizational Consolidation: A Longitudinal Analysis', *Journal of Occupational and Organizational Psychology*, December 1998, pp 305–29.

80 This pioneering research is presented in S C Kobasa, 'Stressful Life Events, Personality, and Health: An Inquiry into Hardiness', *Journal of Personality and Social Psychology*, January 1979, pp 1–11.

81 'Burning the midnight oil', *Management Today*, February 1995, pp 11–12.

82 See S C Kobasa, S R Maddi and S Kahn, 'Hardiness and Health: A Prospective Study', *Journal of Personality and Social Psychology*, January 1982, pp 168–77.

83 Results can be found in V Florian, M Mikulincer and O Taubman, 'Does Hardiness Contribute to Mental Health during a Stressful Real-Life Situation? The Roles of Appraisal and Coping', *Journal of Personality and Social Psychology*, April 1995, pp 687–95; and K L Horner, 'Individuality in Vulnerability: Influences on Physical Health', *Journal of Health Psychology*, January 1998, pp 71–85.

84 See C Robitschek and S Kashubeck, 'A Structural Model of

Parental Alcoholism, Family Functioning, and Psychological Health: The Mediating Effects of Hardiness and Personal Growth Orientation', *Journal of Counseling Psychology*, April 1999, pp 159–72; and 'Basic Behavioral Science Research for Mental Health', *American Psychologist*, January 1996, pp 22–28.
[85] B Priel, N Gonik and B Rabinowitz, 'Appraisals of Childbirth Experience and Newborn Characteristics: The Role of Hardiness and Affect', *Journal of Personality*, September 1993, pp 299–315.
[86] M Friedman and R H Rosenman, *Type A Behavior and Your Heart* (Greenwich, CT: Fawcett Publications, 1974), p 84. (Bold typeface added.)
[87] See C Lee, L F Jamieson and P C Earley, 'Beliefs and Fears and Type A Behavior: Implications for Academic Performance and Psychiatric Health Disorder Symptoms', *Journal of Organizational Behavior*, March 1996, pp 151–77; S D Bluen, J Barling and W Burns, 'Predicting Sales Performance, Job Satisfaction, and Depression by Using the Achievement Strivings and Impatience–Irritability Dimensions of Type A Behavior', *Journal of Applied Psychology*, April 1990, pp 212–16; and M S Taylor, E A Locke, C Lee and M E Gist, 'Type A Behavior and Faculty Research Productivity: What Are the Mechanisms?' *Organizational Behavior and Human Performance*, December 1984, pp 402–18.
[88] Results from the meta-analysis are contained in S A Lyness, 'Predictors of Differences between Type A and B Individuals in Heart Rate and Blood Pressure Reactivity', *Psychological Bulletin*, September 1993, pp 266–95.
[89] See S Booth-Kewley and H S Friedman, 'Psychological Predictors of Heart Disease: A Quantitative Review' *Psychological Bulletin*, May 1987, pp 343–62. More recent results can be found in T Q Miller, T W Smith, C W Turner, M L Guijarro and A J Hallet, 'A Meta-Analytic Review of Research on Hostility and Physical Health', *Psychological Bulletin*, March 1996, pp 322–48.
[90] See J Rothman, 'Wellness and Fitness Programs', in *Sourcebook of Occupational Rehabilitation*, ed P M King (New York: Plenum Press, 1998), pp 127–44; and S Shellenbarger, 'Work & Family: Rising Before Dawn, Are You Getting Ahead or Just Getting Tired?' *The Wall Street Journal*, February 17, 1999, p B1.
[91] S Hoare, 'Where fun is part of the deal', *The Times*, September 7, 2000.
[92] S Cartwright, op. cit.
[93] Supportive results can be found in W E Holden, M M Deichmann and J D Levy, 'Empirically Supported Treatments in Pediatric Psychology: Recurrent Pediatric Headache', *Journal of Pediatric Psychology*, April 1999, pp 91–109; and V Barcia, P Maria, J Sanz and F J Labrador, 'Psychological Changes Accompanying and Mediating Stress-Management Training for Essential Hypertension.' *Applied Psychophysiology and Biofeedback*, September 1998, pp 159–78.
[94] See H Benson, *The Relaxation Response* (New York: William Morrow and Co., 1975).
[95] Research pertaining to meditation is discussed by A G Marlatt and J L Kristeller, 'Mindfulness and Mediation', in *Integrating Spirituality Into Treatment: Resources for Practitioners*, ed W R Miller (Washington, DC: American Psychological Association, 1999), pp 67–84; and H Benson and M Stark, *Timeless Healing* (New York: Scribner, 1996).
[96] Results are presented in 'Your Blood Pressure: Think It Down', *Cooking Light*, October 1996, p 24.
[97] See M W Otto, 'Cognitive Behavioral Therapy for Social Anxiety Disorder: Model, Methods, and Outcome', *Journal of Clinical Psychiatry*, 1999, pp 14–19.
[98] See S Reynolds, E Taylor and D A Shapiro, 'Session Impact in Stress Management Training', *Journal of Occupational Psychology*, June 1993, pp 99–113; and J M Ivancevich, M T Matteson, S M Freedman and J S Phillips, 'Worksite Stress Management Interventions', *American Psychologist*, February 1990, pp 252–61.
[99] An evaluation of stress-reduction programmes is conducted by P A Landsbergis and E Vivona-Vaughan, 'Evaluation of an Occupational Stress Intervention in a Public Agency', *Journal of Organizational Behavior*, January 1996, pp 29–48; and D C

Ganster, B T Mayes, W E Sime and G D Tharp, 'Managing Organizational Stress: A Field Experiment', *Journal of Applied Psychology*, October 1982, pp 533–42.
[100] R Kreitner, 'Personal Wellness: It's Just Good Business', *Business Horizons*, May–June 1982, p 28.
[101] Results are presented in 'The 18-Year Gap', *University of California, Berkeley Wellness Letter*, January 1991, p 2.
[102] A thorough review of this research is provided by D L Gebhardt and C E Crump, 'Employee Fitness and Wellness Programs in the Workplace', *American Psychologist*, February 1990, pp 262–72. Also see A J Daley and G Parfitt, 'Good Health—Is It Worth It? Mood States, Physical Well-Being, Job Satisfaction and Absenteeism in Members and Non-Members of a British Corporate Health and Fitness Club', *Journal of Occupational and Organizational Psychology*, June 1996, pp 121–34.
[103] Excerpted from Rothman, 'Wellness and Fitness Programs', in P M King (ed.) *Sourcebook of Occupational Rehabilitation* (New York: Plenum Press, 1998), pp 140, 141, 143.
[104] Adapted from C Maslach and S E Jackson, 'The Measurement of Experienced Burnout', *Journal of Occupational Behavior*, April 1981, pp 99–113.

Chapter 18

[1] Excerpted from C Joinson, 'Moving at the Speed of Dell', *HRMagazine*, April 1999, pp 51–52. Also see J W Gurley, 'A Dell for Every Industry', *Fortune*, October 12, 1998, pp 167–72.
[2] See P F Drucker, 'The New Society of Organizations', *Harvard Business Review*, September–October 1992, pp 95–104; J R Galbraith, E E Lawler III, and Associates, eds, *Organizing for the Future: The New Logic for Managing Complex Organizations*, (San Francisco: Jossey-Bass, 1993); and R W Oliver, *The Shape of Things to Come: Seven Imperatives for Winning in the New World of Business* (New York: McGraw-Hill, 1999).
[3] C I Barnard, *The Functions of the Executive* (Cambridge, MA: Harvard University Press, 1938), p 73. Also see M C Suchman, 'Managing Legitimacy: Strategic and Institutional Approaches', *Academy of Management Review*, July 1995, pp 571–610.
[4] Drawn from E H Schein, *Organizational Psychology*, 3rd ed (Englewood Cliffs, NJ: Prentice-Hall, 1980), pp 12–15.
[5] For interesting and instructive insights about organization structure, see G Morgan, *Images of Organization* (Newbury Park, CA: Sage, 1986); G Morgan, *Creative Organization Theory: A Resource Book* (Newbury Park, CA: Sage, 1989); G Hofstede, 'An American in Paris: The Influence of Nationality on Organization Theories', *Organization Studies*, no. 3, 1996, pp 525–37; and J G March, 'Continuity and Change in Theories of Organizational Action', *Administrative Science Quarterly*, June 1996, pp 278–87.
[6] For related research, see S Finkelstein and R A D'Aveni, 'CEO Duality as a Double-Edged Sword: How Boards of Directors Balance Entrenchment Avoidance and Unity of Command', *Academy of Management Journal*, October 1994, pp 1079–1108.
[7] For an interesting historical perspective of hierarchy, see P Miller and T O'Leary, 'Hierarchies and American Ideals, 1900–1940', *Academy of Management Review*, April 1989, pp 250–65.
[8] For an excellent overview of the span of control concept, see D D Van Fleet and A G Bedeian, 'A History of the Span of Management', *Academy of Management Review*, July 1977, pp 356–72. Also see E E Lawler III and J R Galbraith, 'New Roles for the Staff: Strategic Support and Service', in *Organizing for the Future: The New Logic for Managing Complex Organizations*, eds J R Galbraith, E E Lawler III, and Associates (San Francisco: Jossey-Bass, 1993), pp 65–83.
[9] M Koslowsky, 'Staff/Line Distinctions in Job and Organizational Commitment', *Journal of Occupational Psychology*, June 1990, pp 167–73.
[10] See, for example, R J Marshak, 'Managing the Metaphors of Change', *Organizational Dynamics*, Summer 1993, pp 44–56; R Garud and S Kotha, 'Using the Brain as a Metaphor to Model Flexible Production Systems', *Academy of Management Review*, October 1994, pp 671–98; and R W Keidel, 'Rethinking Organizational Design', *Academy of Management Executive*,

November 1994, pp 12–30.

11 D S Brown, 'Managers' New Job Is Concert Building', *HRMagazine*, September 1990, p 42.

12 K S Cameron, 'Effectiveness as Paradox: Consensus and Conflict in Conceptions of Organizational Effectiveness', *Management Science*, May 1986, pp 540–41. Also see S Sackmann, 'The Role of Metaphors in Organization Transformation', *Human Relations*, June 1989, pp 463–84; and H Tsoukas, 'The Missing Link: A Transformational View of Metaphors in Organizational Science', *Academy of Management Review*, July 1991, pp 566–85.

13 See W R Scott, 'The Mandate Is Still Being Honored: In Defense of Weber's Disciples', *Administrative Science Quarterly*, March 1996, pp 163–71.

14 Based on M Weber, *The Theory of Social and Economic Organization*, translated by A M Henderson and T Parsons (New York: Oxford University Press, 1947). An instructive analysis of the mistranslation of Weber's work may be found in R M Weiss, 'Weber on Bureaucracy: Management Consultant or Political Theorist?' *Academy of Management Review*, April 1983, pp 242–48.

15 For a critical appraisal of bureaucracy, see R P Hummel, *The Bureaucratic Experience*, 3rd ed (New York: St. Martin's Press, 1987). The positive side of bureaucracy is presented in C T Goodsell, *The Case for Bureaucracy: A Public Administration Polemic* (Chatham, NJ: Chatham House Publishers, 1983).

16 See G Pinchot and E Pinchot, 'Beyond Bureaucracy', *Business Ethics*, March–April 1994, pp 26–29; and O Harari, 'Let the Computers Be the Bureaucrats', *Management Review*, September 1996, pp 57–60.

17 J Huey and G Colvin, 'The Jack and Herb Show', *Fortune*, January 11, 1999, p 164.

18 A management-oriented discussion of general systems theory—an interdisciplinary attempt to integrate the various fragmented sciences—may be found in K E Boulding, 'General Systems Theory—The Skeleton of Science', *Management Science*, April 1956, pp 197–208.

19 J D Thompson, *Organizations in Action* (New York: McGraw-Hill, 1967), pp 6–7. Also see A C Bluedorn, 'The Thompson Interdependence Demonstration', *Journal of Management Education*, November 1993, pp 505–09.

20 For more on this subject, see V-W Mitchell, 'Organizational Homoeostasis: A Role for Internal Marketing', *Management Decision*, no. 2, 1992, pp 3–7. Biological metaphors are explored in T Petzinger Jr, 'A New Model for the Nature of Business: It's Alive!' *The Wall Street Journal*, February 26, 1999, pp B1, B4; and T Petzinger Jr, 'Two Doctors Give New Meaning to Taking Your Business to Heart', *The Wall Street Journal*, April 30, 1999, p B1.

21 R L Daft and K E Weick, 'Toward a Model of Organizations as Interpretation Systems', *Academy of Management Review*, April 1984, p 293.

22 For good background reading, see the entire Autumn 1998 issue of *Organizational Dynamics*; D Lei, J W Slocum and R A Pitts, 'Designing Organizations for Competitive Advantage: The Power of Unlearning and Learning', *Organizational Dynamics*, Winter 1999, pp 24–38; L Baird, P Holland and S Deacon, 'Learning from Action: Imbedding More Learning into the Performance Fast Enough to Make a Difference', *Organizational Dynamics*, Spring 1999, pp 19–32; 'Leading-Edge Learning: Two Views', *Training & Development*, March 1999, pp 40–42; and A M Webber, 'Learning for a Change', *Fast Company*, May 1999, pp 178–88.

23 K Kelly, 'Motorola: Training for the Millennium', *Business Week*, March 28, 1994, p 158. For updates, see R O Crockett, 'How Motorola Lost Its Way', *Business Week*, May 4, 1998, pp 140–48; and R O Crockett, 'Motorola: Slow and Steady Isn't Winning Any Races', *Business Week*, August 10, 1998, pp 62, 64.

24 See J F Moore, *The Death of Competition: Leadership and Strategy in the Age of Business Ecosystems* (New York: HarperBusiness, 1996), pp 153–54; and 'Falcon May Be Taken Off Endangered List', *USA Today*, August 25, 1998, p 3A.

25 J A C Baum, 'Organizational Ecology', in *Handbook of Organization Studies*, eds S R Clegg, C Hardy and W R Nord (Thousand Oaks, CA: Sage Publications, 1996), p 77. (Emphasis added.) Also see C S Hunt and H E Aldrich, 'The Second Ecology: Creation and Evolution of Organizational Communities', in *Research in Organizational Behavior*, vol. 20, eds B M Staw and L L Cummings (Greenwich, CT: JAI Press, 1998), pp 267–301; and W Tsai and S Ghoshal, 'Social Capital and Value Creation: The Role of Intrafirm Networks', *Academy of Management Journal*, August 1998, pp 464–76.

26 Moore, *The Death of Competition*, pp 11–12.

27 Ibid., pp 15–16. (Emphasis added.) For updates, see D Kirkpatrick, 'Is the PC Dead? Not Even Close', *Fortune*, December 21, 1998, pp 211–14; D B Yoffie and M A Cusumano, 'Judo Strategy: The Competitive Dynamics of Internet Time', *Harvard Business Review*, January–February 1999, pp 71–81; B Gates, 'Why the PC Will Not Die', *Newsweek*, May 31, 1999, p 64; and J Dreyfuss, 'Death to the Personal Computer', *Fortune*, July 19, 1999, p 138[N].

28 Based on discussion in S R Clegg and C Hardy, 'Introduction: Organizations, Organization and Organizing', in *Handbook of Organization Studies*, eds S R Clegg, C Hardy and W R Nord (Thousand Oaks, CA: Sage Publications, 1996), pp 1–28. Also see B Ettorre, 'A Conversation with Charles Handy: On the Future of Work and an End to the "Century of the Organization"', *Organizational Dynamics*, Summer 1996, pp 15–26.

29 K Cameron, 'Critical Questions in Assessing Organizational Effectiveness', *Organizational Dynamics*, Autumn 1980, p 70. Also see J Pfeffer, 'When It Comes to "Best Practices"—Why Do Smart Organizations Occasionally Do Dumb Things?' *Organizational Dynamics*, Summer 1996, pp 33–44; G N Powell, 'Reinforcing and Extending Today's Organizations: The Simultaneous Pursuit of Person-Organization Fit and Diversity', *Organizational Dynamics*, Winter 1998, pp 50–61; R C Vergin and M W Qoronfleh, 'Corporate Reputation and the Stock Market', *Business Horizons*, January–February 1998, pp 19–26; K Gawande and T Wheeler, 'Measures of Effectiveness for Governmental Organizations', *Management Science*, January 1999, pp 42–58; and E V McIntyre, 'Accounting Choices and EVA', *Business Horizons*, January–February 1999, pp 66–72.

30 See B Wysocki Jr, 'Rethinking a Quaint Idea: Profits', *The Wall Street Journal*, May 19, 1999, pp B1, B6; and J Collins, 'Turning Goals into Results: The Power of Catalytic Mechanisms', *Harvard Business Review*, July–August 1999, pp 71–82.

31 See, for example, R O Brinkerhoff and D E Dressler, *Productivity Measurement: A Guide for Managers and Evaluators* (Newbury Park, CA: Sage Publications, 1990); J McCune, 'The Productivity Paradox', *Management Review*, March 1998, pp 38–40; and R J Samuelson, 'Cheerleaders vs. The Grumps', *Newsweek*, July 26, 1999, p 78.

32 See A Reinhardt, 'Log On, Link Up, Save Big', *Business Week*, June 22, 1998, pp 132–38; and R W Oliver, 'Happy 150th Birthday, Electronic Commerce!' *Management Review*, July–August 1999, pp 12–13.

33 Data from M Maynard, 'Toyota Promises Custom Order in 5 Days', *USA Today*, August 6, 1999, p 1B.

34 'Interview: M Scott Peck', *Business Ethics*, March–April 1994, p 17.

35 Cameron, 'Critical Questions in Assessing Organizational Effectiveness', p 67. Also see W Buxton, 'Growth from Top to Bottom', *Management Review*, July–August 1999, p 11.

36 See R K Mitchell, B R Agle and D J Wood, 'Toward a Theory of Stakeholder Identification and Salience: Defining the Principle of Who and What Really Counts', *Academy of Management Review*, October 1997, pp 853–96; W Beaver, 'Is the Stakeholder Model Dead?' *Business Horizons*, March–April 1999, pp 8–12; J Frooman, 'Stakeholder Influence Strategies', *Academy of Management Review*, April 1999, pp 191–205; and T M Jones and A C Wicks, 'Convergent Stakeholder Theory', *Academy of Management Review*, April 1999, pp 206–21.

37 See N C Roberts and P J King, 'The Stakeholder Audit Goes Public', *Organizational Dynamics*, Winter 1989, pp 63–79; and I Henriques and P Sadorsky, 'The Relationship between Environmental Commitment and Managerial Perceptions of Stakeholder Importance', *Academy of Management Journal*,

Notes

February 1999, pp 87–99.

38 E M Reingold, 'America's Hamburger Helper', *Time*, June 29, 1992, p 66.

39 See C Ostroff and N Schmitt, 'Configurations of Organizational Effectiveness and Efficiency', *Academy of Management Journal*, December 1993, pp 1345–61.

40 K S Cameron, 'Effectiveness as Paradox: Consensus and Conflict in Conceptions of Organizational Effectiveness', *Management Science*, May 1986, p 542.

41 Alternative effectiveness criteria are discussed in ibid.; A G Bedeian, 'Organization Theory: Current Controversies, Issues, and Directions', in *International Review of Industrial and Organizational Psychology*, eds C L Cooper and I T Robertson (New York: John Wiley & Sons, 1987), pp 1–33; and M Keeley, 'Impartiality and Participant-Interest Theories of Organizational Effectiveness', *Administrative Science Quarterly*, March 1984, pp 1–25.

42 D N Sull, 'Why Good Companies Go Bad', *Harvard Business Review*, July–August 1999, pp 42–52. Also see H B Cohen, 'The Performance Paradox', *Academy of Management Executive*, August 1998, pp 30–40.

43 M A Mone, W McKinley and V L Barker III, 'Organizational Decline and Innovation: A Contingency Framework', *Academy of Management Review*, January 1998, p 117.

44 P Lorange and R T Nelson, 'How to Recognize—and Avoid—Organizational Decline', *Sloan Management Review*, Spring 1987, p 47.

45 Excerpted from ibid., pp 43–45. Also see E E Lawler III and J R Galbraith, 'Avoiding the Corporate Dinosaur Syndrome', *Organizational Dynamics*, Autumn 1994, pp 5–17; and K Labich, 'Why Companies Fail', *Fortune*, November 14, 1994, pp 52–68.

46 For details, see K S Cameron, M U Kim and D A Whetten, 'Organizational Effects of Decline and Turbulence', *Administrative Science Quarterly*, June 1987, pp 222–40. Also see A G Bedeian and A A Armenakis, 'The Cesspool Syndrome: How Dreck Floats to the Top of Declining Organizations', *Academy of Management Executive*, February 1998, pp 58–63.

47 Twelve dysfunctional consequences of decline are discussed and empirically tested in K S Cameron, D A Whetten and M U Kim, 'Organizational Dysfunctions of Decline', *Academy of Management Journal*, March 1987, pp 126–38. Also see D K Hurst, *Crisis and Renewal: Meeting the Challenge of Organizational Change* (Boston: Harvard Business School Press, 1995).

48 Data from V L Barker III and P W Patterson, Jr, 'Top Management Team Tenure and Top Manager Causal Attributions at Declining Firms Attempting Turnarounds', *Group & Organization Management*, September 1996, pp 304–36. Stories of organizational decline can be found in G Colvin, 'How Rubbermaid Managed to Fail', *Fortune*, November 23, 1998, pp 32–33; W C Symonds, 'Paddling Harder at L L Bean', *Business Week*, December 7, 1998, pp 72, 75; J Weiner, 'How Nordictrack Lost Its Footing', *Business Week*, December 14, 1998, p 138; 'The Apple Story', p 38 in J Pfeffer and J F Veiga, 'Putting People First for Organizational Success', *Academy of Management Executive*, May 1999, pp 37–48; and R A Melcher, 'I'm Working My Tail Off to Fix It', *Business Week*, August 16, 1999, pp 72, 74.

49 For related reading, see C R Eitel, 'The Ten Disciplines of Business Turnaround', *Management Review*, December 1998, p 13; J R Morris, W F Cascio and C E Young, 'Downsizing After All These Years: Questions and Answers about Who Did It, How Many Did It, and Who Benefited from It', *Organizational Dynamics*, Winter 1999, pp 78–87; and S Kuczynski, 'Help! I Shrunk the Company!' *HRMagazine*, June 1999, pp 40–45.

50 A culture of 'entitlement' also hastens organizational decline. See J M Bardwick, *Danger in the Comfort Zone: From Boardroom to Mailroom—How to Break the Entitlement Habit That's Killing American Business* (New York: AMACOM, 1991). Also see D W Organ, 'Argue with Success', *Business Horizons*, November–December 1995, pp 1–2; and J P Kotter, 'Kill Complacency', *Fortune*, August 5, 1996, pp 168–70.

51 S Baker, 'Silicon D-Day: To survive in the Internet era, Europe's tech titans are learning to do business Valley-style', *Business Week*, October 23, 2000.

52 For updates, see J M Pennings, 'Structural Contingency Theory: A Reappraisal', *Research in Organizational Behavior* (Greenwich, CT: JAI Press, 1992), vol. 14, pp 267–309; A D Meyer, A S Tsui and C R Hinings, 'Configurational Approaches to Organizational Analysis', *Academy of Management Journal*, December 1993, pp 1175–95; and D H Doty, W H Glick and G P Huber, 'Fit, Equifinality, and Organizational Effectiveness: A Test of Two Configurational Theories', *Academy of Management Journal*, December 1993, pp 1196–1250.

53 An interesting distinction between three types of environmental uncertainty can be found in F J Milliken, 'Three Types of Perceived Uncertainty about the Environment: State, Effect, and Response Uncertainty', *Academy of Management Review*, January 1987, pp 133–43.

54 R Duncan, 'What Is the Right Organization Structure?' *Organizational Dynamics*, Winter 1979, p 63.

55 Ibid.

56 See P Sellers, 'Crunch Time for Coke', *Fortune*, July 19, 1999, pp 72–78.

57 See T J Tetenbaum, 'Shifting Paradigms: From Newton to Chaos', *Organizational Dynamics*, Spring 1998, pp 21–32; W Miller, 'Building the Ultimate Resource', *Management Review*, January 1999, pp 42–45; D P Ellerman, 'Global Institutions: Transforming International Development Agencies into Learning Organizations', *Academy of Management Executive*, February 1999, pp 25–35; and K Maani and C Benton, 'Rapid Team Learning: Lessons from Team New Zealand America's Cup Campaign', *Organizational Dynamics*, Spring 1999, pp 48–62.

58 P R Lawrence and J W Lorsch, *Organization and Environment* (Homewood, IL: Richard D Irwin, 1967), p 157.

59 Pooled, sequential, and reciprocal integration are discussed in J W Lorsch, 'Organization Design: A Situational Perspective', *Organizational Dynamics*, Autumn 1977, pp 2–14. Also see J E Ettlie and E M Reza, 'Organizational Integration and Process Innovation', *Academy of Management Journal*, October 1992, pp 795–827; and A L Patti and J P Gilbert, 'Collocating New Product Development Teams: Why, When, Where, and How?' *Business Horizons*, November–December 1997, pp 59–64.

60 See B Dumaine, 'Ability to Innovate', *Fortune*, January 29, 1990, pp 43, 46. For good reading on innovation and technology, see O Port, 'Getting to "Eureka!"' *Business Week*, November 10, 1997, pp 72–75; J W Gurley, 'Got a Good Idea? Better Think Twice', *Fortune*, December 7, 1998, pp 215–16; J C McCune, 'The Technology Treadmill', *Management Review*, December 1998, pp 10–12; and L Yates and P Skarzynski, 'How Do Companies Get to the Future First?' *Management Review*, January 1999, pp 16–22.

61 K Deveny, 'Bag Those Fries, Squirt That Ketchup, Fry That Fish', *Business Week*, October 13, 1986, p 86.

62 See D A Morand, 'The Role of Behavioral Formality and Informality in the Enactment of Bureaucratic versus Organic Organizations', *Academy of Management Review*, October 1995, pp 831–72.

63 G Edmondson, M Popper and A Robinson, 'Spain's success: no longer a Latin laggard, the country's economy is fast becoming one of Europe's healthiest', *Business Week*, August 3, 1998.

64 See G P Huber, C C Miller and W H Glick, 'Developing More Encompassing Theories about Organizations: The Centralization–Effectiveness Relationship as an Example', *Organization Science*, no. 1, 1990, pp 11–40; and C Handy, 'Balancing Corporate Power: A New Federalist Paper', *Harvard Business Review*, November–December 1992, pp 59–72. Also see W R Pape, 'Divide and Conquer', *Inc. Technology*, no. 2, 1996, pp 25–27; and J Schmidt, 'Breaking Down Fiefdoms', *Management Review*, January 1997, pp 45–49.

65 P Kaestle, 'A New Rationale for Organizational Structure', *Planning Review*, July–August 1990, p 22.

66 Details of this study can be found in T Burns and

G M Stalker, *The Management of Innovation* (London: Tavistock, 1961).

67 D J Gillen and S J Carroll, 'Relationship of Managerial Ability to Unit Effectiveness in More Organic versus More Mechanistic Departments', *Journal of Management Studies*, November 1985, pp 674–75.

68 J D Sherman and H L Smith, 'The Influence of Organizational Structure on Intrinsic versus Extrinsic Motivation', *Academy of Management Journal*, December 1984, p 883.

69 See J A Courtright, G T Fairhurst and L E Rogers, 'Interaction Patterns in Organic and Mechanistic Systems', *Academy of Management Journal*, December 1989, pp 773–802.

70 See J Woodward, *Industrial Organization: Theory and Practice* (London: Oxford University Press, 1965); and P D Collins and F Hull, 'Technology and Span of Control: Woodward Revisited', *Journal of Management Studies*, March 1986, pp 143–64.

71 See L W Fry, 'Technology-Structure Research: Three Critical Issues', *Academy of Management Journal*, September 1982, pp 532–52.

72 Ibid., p 548. Also see R Reese, 'Redesigning for Dial Tone: A Socio-Technical Systems Case Study', *Organizational Dynamics*, Autumn 1995, pp 80–90.

73 For example, see C C Miller, W H Glick, Y-D Wang and G P Huber, 'Understanding Technology-Structure Relationships: Theory Development and Meta-Analytic Theory Testing', *Academy of Management Journal*, June 1991, pp 370–99; and K H Roberts and M Grabowski, 'Organizations, Technology and Structuring', in *Handbook of Organization Studies*, eds S R Clegg, C Hardy and W R Nord (Thousand Oaks, CA: Sage Publications, 1996), pp 409–23.

74 The phrase 'small is beautiful' was coined by the late British economist E F Schumacher. See E F Schumacher, *Small Is Beautiful: Economics As If People Mattered* (New York: Harper & Row, 1973).

75 T J Peters and R H Waterman, Jr, *In Search of Excellence* (New York: Harper & Row, 1982), p 321. Also see T Peters, 'Rethinking Scale', *California Management Review*, Fall 1992, pp 7–29.

76 See, for example, W McKinley, 'Decreasing Organizational Size: To Untangle or Not to Untangle?' *Academy of Management Review*, January 1992, pp 112–23; W Zellner, 'Go-Go Goliaths', *Business Week*, February 13, 1995, pp 64–70; T Brown, 'Manage "BIG!"' *Management Review*, May 1996, pp 12–17; and E Shapiro, 'Power, Not Size, Counts', *Management Review*, September 1996, p 61.

77 C Handy, *The Hungry Spirit* (New York: Broadway Books, 1998), pp 107–8. Also see C Handy, 'The Doctrine of Enough', *Management Review*, June 1998, pp 52–54.

78 P L Zweig, 'The Case against Mergers', *Business Week*, October 30, 1995, p 122. Also see O Harari, 'Too Big for Your Own Good?' *Management Review*, November 1998, pp 30–32; G Colvin, 'The Year of the Mega Merger', *Fortune*, January 11, 1999, pp 62–64; A Taylor III, 'More Mergers. Dumb Idea.' *Fortune*, February 15, 1999, pp 26–27; P Troiano, 'Mergers: Good or Bad?' *Management Review*, April 1999, p 9; and R J Grossman, 'Irreconcilable Differences', *HRMagazine*, April 1999, pp 42–48.

79 R Z Gooding and J A Wagner III, 'A Meta-Analytic Review of the Relationship between Size and Performance: The Productivity and Efficiency of Organizations and Their Subunits', *Administrative Science Quarterly*, December 1985, pp 462–81.

80 Ibid., p 477.

81 Results are presented in P G Benson, T L Dickinson and C O Neidt, 'The Relationship between Organizational Size and Turnover: A Longitudinal Investigation', *Human Relations*, January 1987, pp 15–30. Also see M Yasai-Ardekani, 'Effects of Environmental Scarcity and Munificence on the Relationship of Context to Organizational Structure', *Academy of Management Journal*, March 1989, pp 131–56.

82 See E E Lawler III, 'Rethinking Organization Size', *Organizational Dynamics*, Autumn 1997, pp 24–35; O Harari, 'Honey, I Shrunk the Company!' *Management Review*,

December 1998, pp 39–41; and J C McCune, 'Stuck in the Middle?' *Management Review*, February 1999, pp 44–49.

83 See V Sathe, 'Fostering Entrepreneurship in the Large, Diversified Firm', *Organizational Dynamics*, Summer 1989, pp 20–32; J R Galbraith and E E Lawler III, 'Effective Organizations: Using the New Logic of Organizing', in *Organizing for the Future: The New Logic for Managing Complex Organizations*, eds J R Galbraith, E E Lawler III, and Associates (San Francisco: Jossey-Bass, 1993), pp 290–92; and J Kim, 'Welch Thinks Small, Acts Big', *USA Today*, February 26, 1993, p 2B.

84 See J Child, 'Organizational Structure, Environment and Performance: The Role of Strategic Choice', *Sociology*, January 1972, pp 1–22.

85 See J Galbraith, *Organization Design* (Reading, MA: Addison-Wesley Publishing, 1977); J R Montanari, 'Managerial Discretion: An Expanded Model of Organization Choice', *Academy of Management Review*, April 1978, pp 231–41; and H R Bobbitt, Jr, and J D Ford, 'Decision-Maker Choice as a Determinant of Organizational Structure', *Academy of Management Review*, January 1980, pp 13–23.

86 For an alternative model of strategy making, see S L Hart, 'An Integrative Framework for Strategy-Making Processes', *Academy of Management Review*, April 1992, pp 327–51. Also see F E Harrison and M A Pelletier, 'A Typology of Strategic Choice', *Technological Forecasting and Social Change*, November 1993, pp 245–63; H Mintzberg, 'The Rise and Fall of Strategic Planning', *Harvard Business Review*, January–February 1994, pp 107–14; M Valle, 'Buy High, Sell Low: Why CEOs Kiss Toads, and How Shareholders Get Warts', *Academy of Management Executive*, May 1998, pp 97–98; G R Weaver, L K Trevino and P L Cochran, 'Corporate Ethics Programs as Control Systems: Influences of Executive Commitment and Environmental Factors', *Academy of Management Journal*, February 1999, pp 41–57; and C McDermott and K K Boyer, 'Strategic Consensus: Marching to the Beat of a Different Drummer?' *Business Horizons*, July–August 1999, pp 21–28.

87 See A Bhide, 'How Entrepreneurs Craft Strategies That Work', *Harvard Business Review*, March–April 1994, pp 150–61; and J W Dean, Jr, and M P Sharfman, 'Does Decision Process Matter? A Study of Strategic Decision-Making Effectiveness', *Academy of Management Journal*, April 1996, pp 368–96; R L Osborne, 'Strategic Values: The Corporate Performance Engine', *Business Horizons*, September–October 1996, pp 41–47; and B Ettorre, 'When Patience Is a Corporate Virtue', *Management Review*, November 1996, pp 28–32.

88 S Perlstein, 'Less Is More', *Business Ethics*, September–October 1993, p 15.

89 Details may be found in D Miller, 'Strategy Making and Structure: Analysis and Implications for Performance', *Academy of Management Journal*, March 1987, pp 7–32. For more, see T L Amburgey and T Dacin, 'As the Left Foot Follows the Right? The Dynamics of Strategic and Structural Change', *Academy of Management Journal*, December 1994, pp 1427–52; and M W Peng and P S Heath, 'The Growth of the Firm in Planned Economies in Transition: Institutions, Organizations, and Strategic Choice', *Academy of Management Review*, April 1996, pp 492–528.

90 See Galbraith and Lawler, 'Effective Organizations: Using the New Logic of Organizing', pp 285–99.

91 R Jacob, 'The Struggle to Create an Organization for the 21st Century', *Fortune*, April 3, 1995, pp 91–92.

92 See S Sonnesyn Brooks, 'Managing a Horizontal Revolution', *HRMagazine*, June 1995, pp 52–58; and M Hequet, 'Flat and Happy', *Training*, April 1995, pp 29–34.

93 For related discussion, see B Filipczak, 'The Ripple Effect of Computer Networking', *Training*, March 1994, pp 40–47.

94 See O Harari, 'Transform Your Organization into a Web of Relationships', *Management Review*, January 1998, pp 21–24; R J Alford, 'Going Virtual, Getting Real', *Training & Development*, January 1999, pp 34–44; S Greco, 'Go Right to the Outsource', *Inc.*, February 1999, p 39; M Minehan, 'Forecasting Future Trends for the Workplace', *HRMagazine*, February 1999, p 176; and W B Werther, Jr, 'Structure-Driven Strategy and Virtual Organization Design', *Business Horizons*, March–April 1999, pp 13–18.

[95] Adapted from personal communication.

[96] Handy, *The Hungry Spirit*, p 186. (Emphasis added.)

Chapter 19

[1] C Kennedy, 'The Roadmap to success: how Gerard Schulmeyer changed the culture at Siemens Nixdorf', *Long Range Planning*, vol. 31 no. 2, pp 262–71, 1998. ©1998, with permission from Elsevier science.

[2] These statistics were taken from J A Lopez, 'Corporate Change: You Can Count on It', *The Arizona Republic*, March 3, 1996, pp D1, D3; and J J Laabs, 'Expert Advice on How to Move Forward with Change', *Personnel Journal*, July 1996, pp 54–63.

[3] M Coles, 'Consultants learn to achieve results', *The Sunday Times*, August 6, 2000.

[4] P Scott Morgan, *The Unwritten Rules of the Game*, (New York: McGraw-Hill, 1994).

[5] A M Webber, 'Learning for a Change', *Fast Company*, May 1999, p 180.

[6] K Capell, 'Virgin takes E-wing', *Business Week*, January 22, 2001.

[7] J Rossant, 'Fiat-GM: the Agnellis Face Reality', *Business Week*, March 27, 2000.

[8] This three-way typology of change was adapted from discussion in P C Nutt, 'Tactics of Implementation', *Academy of Management Journal*, June 1986, pp 230–61.

[9] Types of organizational change are discussed by K E Weick and R E Quinn, 'Organizational Change and Development', in *Annual Review of Psychology*, eds J T Spence, J M Darley and D J Foss (Palo Alto, CA: Annual Reviews, 1999), vol. 50, pp 361–86.

[10] For a thorough discussion of the model, see K Lewin, *Field Theory in Social Science* (New York: Harper & Row, 1951).

[11] These assumptions are discussed in E H Schein, *Organizational Psychology*, 3rd ed (Englewood Cliffs, NJ: Prentice-Hall, 1980).

[12] C Goldwasser, 'Benchmarking: People Make the Process', *Management Review*, June 1995, p 40.

[13] Benchmark data for 'America's Best Plants' can be found in J H Sheridan, 'Lessons from the Best', *Industry Week*, February 1996, pp 13–20.

[14] Top management's role in implementing change according to Lewin's model is discussed by E H Schein, 'The Role of the CEO in the Management of Change: The Case of Information Technology', in *Transforming Organizations*, eds T A Kochan and M Useem (New York: Oxford University Press, 1992), pp 80–95.

[15] Systems models of change are discussed by D W Haines, 'Letting "The System" Do the Work', *Journal of Applied Behavioral Science*, September 1999, pp 306–24; and D A Nadler and M L Tushman, 'Strategic Imperatives and Core Competencies for the 21st Century', *Organizational Dynamics*, Summer 1999, pp 45–59.

[16] A thorough discussion of the target elements of change can be found in M Beer and B Spector, 'Organizational Diagnosis: Its Role in Organizational Learning', *Journal of Counseling & Development*, July/August 1993, pp 642–50; and P Dainty, 'Organizational Change: A Strategy for Successful Implementation', *Journal of Business and Psychology*, Summer 1990, pp 463–81.

[17] D Littlefield, 'The Big Push', *People Management*, July 6, 2000.

[18] These errors are discussed by J P Kotter, 'Leading Change: The Eight Steps to Transformation' in *The Leader's Change Handbook*, eds J A Conger, G M Spreitzer and E E Lawler III (San Francisco, CA: 1999) pp 87–99.

[19] The type of leadership needed during organizational change is discussed by J P Kotter, *Leading Change* (Boston: Harvard Business School Press, 1996); and B Ettorre, 'Making Change', *Management Review*, January 1996, pp 13–18.

[20] M Beer and E Walton, 'Developing the Competitive Organization: Interventions and Strategies', *American Psychologist*, February 1990, p 154.

[21] An historical overview of the field of OD can be found in N A M Worren, K Ruddle and K Moore, 'From Organizational Development to Change Management', *Journal of Applied Behavioral Science*, September 1999, pp 273–86; and A H Church, J Waaclawski and W Siegal, 'Will the Real OD Practitioner Please Stand Up? A Call for Change in the Field', *Organization Development Journal*, Summer 1999, pp 49–59.

[22] W W Burke, *Organization Development: A Normative View* (Reading, MA: Addison-Wesley Publishing, 1987), p 9.

[23] M F Kets De Vries & K Balazs, 'Transforming the mind-set of the organization: a clinical perspective', *Administration & Society*, Jan 99, vol. 30 no. 6, pp 640–75.

[24] An example of using employee surveys to conduct OD is provided by B Schneider, S D Ashworth, A C Higgs and L Carr, 'Design, Validity, and Use of Strategically Focused Employee Attitude Surveys', *Personnel Psychology*, Autumn 1996, pp 695–705.

[25] See R Rodgers, J E Hunter and D L Rogers, 'Influence of Top Management Commitment on Management Program Success', *Journal of Applied Psychology*, February 1993, pp 151–55.

[26] Results can be found in P J Robertson, D R Roberts and J I Porras, 'Dynamics of Planned Organizational Change: Assessing Empirical Support for a Theoretical Model', *Academy of Management Journal*, June 1993, pp 619–34.

[27] Results from the meta-analysis can be found in G A Neuman, J E Edwards and N S Raju, 'Organizational Development Interventions: A Meta-Analysis of Their Effects on Satisfaction and Other Attitudes', *Personnel Psychology*, Autumn 1989, pp 461–90.

[28] The importance of results-oriented change efforts is discussed by R J Schaffer and H A Thomson, 'Successful Change Programs Begin with Results', *Harvard Business Review*, January–February 1992, pp 80–89.

[29] See the related discussion in D M Schneider and C Goldwasser, 'Be a Model Leader of Change: Here's How to Get the Results You Want from the Change You're Leading', *Management Review*, March 1998, pp 41–45.

[30] J P Wanous, A E Reichers & J T Austin, 'Cynicism about organizational change. Measurements, antecedents and correlates', *Group & Organization Management*, vol. 25, no. 2, June 2000, pp 132–53.

[31] J M Peiro, V Gonzalez-Roma and J Canero, 'Survey Feedback as a tool changing managerial culture: focusing on users' interpretations – a case study, *European Journal of Work and Organizational Psychology*, 1999, vol. 8 no. 4, pp 537–50.

[32] Adapted in part from B W Armentrout, 'Have Your Plans for Change Had a Change of Plan?' *HRFOCUS*, January 1996, p 19; and A S Judson, *Changing Behavior in Organizations: Minimizing Resistance to Change* (Cambridge, MA: Blackwell, Inc., 1991).

[33] See 'Vulnerability and Resilience', *American Psychologist*, January 1996, pp 22–28.

[34] Excerpted from C Joinson, 'Moving at the Speed of Dell', *HRMagazine*, April 1999, p 52.

[35] See R Moss Kanter, 'Managing Traumatic Change: Avoiding the "Unlucky 13"', *Management Review*, May 1987, pp 23–24.

[36] D Butcher and S Atkinson, 'Upwardly mobilised', *People Management*, January 14, 1999.

[37] D Buchanan, T Claydon and M Doyle. 'Organisation development and change: the legacy of the nineties', *Human Resource Management Journal*, vol. 9 no. 2, 1999.

[38] See L Coch and J R P French, Jr, 'Overcoming Resistance to Change', *Human Relations*, 1948, pp 512–32.

[39] For a thorough review of the role of participation in organizational change, see W A Pasmore and M R Fagans, 'Participation, Individual Development, and Organizational Change: A Review and Synthesis', *Journal of Management*, June 1992, pp 375–97.

[40] Results from this study can be found in T A Judge, C J Thoresen, V Pucik and T W Welbourne, 'Managerial Coping with Organizational Change: A Dispositional Perspective', *Journal of Applied Psychology*, February 1999, pp 107–22.

[41] L Morris, 'Research Capsules', *Training & Development*, April

1992, pp 74–76; and T Hill, N D Smith and M F Mann, 'Role of Efficacy Expectations in Predicting the Decision to Use Advanced Technologies: The Case of Computers', *Journal of Applied Psychology*, May 1987, pp 307–14.

42 Results can be found in C-M Lau and R W Woodman, 'Understanding Organizational Change: A Schematic Perspective', *Academy of Management Journal*, April 1995, pp 537–54.

43 See the related discussion in E B Dent and S G Goldberg, 'Challenging "Resistance to Change"', *Journal of Applied Behavioral Science*, March 1999, pp 25–41.

44 J P Kotter, 'Leading Change: Why Transformation Efforts Fail', *Harvard Business Review*, 1995, p 64.

45 See Dent and Goldberg, 'Challenging "Resistance to Change"', J Krantz, 'Comment on "Challenging Resistance to Change"', *Journal of Applied Behavioral Science*, March 1999, pp 42–44; and E B Dent and S G Goldberg, ' "Resistance to Change": A Limiting Perspective', *Journal of Applied Behavioral Science*, March 1999, pp 45–47.

46 G Tregunno, 'Changing routes at Boehringer Ingelheim', *People Management*, April 8, 1999.

47 Readiness for change is discussed by B Trahant and W W Burke, 'Traveling through Transitions', *Training & Development*, February 1996, pp 37–41.

48 For a discussion of how managers can reduce resistance to change by providing different explanations for an organizational change, see D M Rousseau and S A Tijoriwala, 'What's a Good Reason to Change? Motivated Reasoning and Social Accounts in Promoting Organizational Change', *Journal of Applied Psychology*, August 1999, pp 514–28.

49 T Petzinger, Jr, 'The Front Lines: Georg Bauer Put Burden of Downsizing into Employees' Hands', *The Wall Street Journal*, May 10, 1996, p B1.

50 Ibid.

51 Additional strategies for managing resistance are discussed by T J Galpin, *The Human Side of Change: A Practical Guide to Organizational Redesign* (San Francisco: Jossey-Bass, 1996); and D May and M Kettelhut, 'Managing Human Issues in Reengineering Projects', *Journal of Systems Management*, January/February 1996, pp 4–11.

52 See L Baird, P Holland and S Deacon, 'Learning from Action: Imbedding More Learning into the Performance Fast Enough to Make a Difference', *Organizational Dynamics*, Spring 1999, pp 19–32; and K Kuwada, 'Strategic Learning: The Continuous Side of Discontinuous Strategic Change', *Organization Science*, November–December 1998, pp 719–36.

53 R M Fulmer and J B Keys, 'A Conversation with Peter Senge: New Development in Organizational Learning', *Organizational Dynamics*, Autumn 1998, p 35.

54 This definition was based on D A Garvin, 'Building a Learning Organization', *Harvard Business Review*, July/August 1993, pp 78–91.

55 Organizational learning is discussed by K Maani and C Benton, 'Rapid Team Learning: Lessons from Team New Zealand America's Cup Campaign', *Organizational Dynamics*, Spring 1999, pp 48–62; and A Edmondson and B Moingeon, 'From Organizational Learning to the Learning Organization', *Management Learning*, 1998, pp 5–20.

56 A discussion of learning capabilities and core competencies is provided by W Miller, 'Building the Ultimate Resource', *Management Review*, January 1999, pp 42–45; and C Long and M Vickers-Koch, 'Using Core Capabilities to Create Competitive Advantage', *Organizational Dynamics*, Summer 1995, pp 7–22.

57 The relationship between organizational learning and various effectiveness criteria is discussed by S F Slater and J C Narver, 'Market Orientation and the Learning Organization', *Journal of Marketing*, July 1995, pp 63–74.

58 A J DiBella, E C Nevis and J M Gould, 'Organizational Learning Style as a Core Capability', in *Organizational Learning and Competitive Advantage*, eds B Moingeon and A Edmondson (Thousand Oaks, CA: Sage, 1996), pp 41–42.

59 Details of this study can be found in J H Lingle and W A Schiemann, 'From Balanced Scorecard to Strategic Gauges: Is Measurement Worth It?' *American Management Association*, March 1996, pp 56–61.

60 Excerpted from J Stuller, 'Chief of Corporate Smarts', *Training*, April 1998, p 32.

61 Excerpted from Stamps, 'Learning Ecologies', p 35.

62 This discussion and definitions are based on D Miller, 'A Preliminary Typology of Organizational Learning: Synthesizing the Literature', *Journal of Management*, 1996, pp 485–505.

63 See the related discussion in DiBella, Nevis and Gould, 'Organizational Learning Style as a Core Capability'.

64 See D Collis, 'Organizational Capability as a Source of Profit', in *Organizational Learning and Competitive Advantage*, eds B Moingeon and A Edmondson (Thousand Oaks, CA: Sage, 1996), pp 139–63.

65 M Coles, 'Creativity breaks refresh executives', *The Sunday Times*, March 12, 2000.

66 This discussion is based on material presented in P Senge, *The Dance of Change: The Challenges to Sustaining Momentum in Learning Organizations* (New York: Doubleday, 1999); and J B Keys, R M Fulmer and S A Stumpf, 'Microworlds and Simuworlds: Practice Fields for the Learning Organization', *Organizational Dynamics*, Spring 1996, pp 36–49.

67 The role of leadership in building a learning organization is discussed by M Beer, 'Leading Learning and Learning to Lead', in *The Leader's Change Handbook*, eds J A Conger, G M Spreitzer and E E Lawler III (San Francisco, CA: Jossey-Bass, 1999), pp 127–61; and Senge, *The Dance of Change: The Challenges to Sustaining Momentum in Learning Organizations*.

68 Excerpted from L Wah, 'Making Knowledge Stick', *Management Review*, May 1999, p 27.

69 See N A Wishart, J J Elam, D Robey, 'Redrawing the Portrait of a Learning Organization: Inside Knight-Ridder, Inc.', *Academy of Management Executive*, February 1996, pp 7–20; C Argyris, 'Good Communication That Blocks Learning', *Harvard Business Review*, July–August 1994, pp 77–85; and D A Garvin, 'Building a Learning Organization', *Harvard Business Review*, July–August 1993, pp 78–91.

70 See the related discussion in D Lei, J W Slocum and R A Pitts, 'Designing Organizations for Competitive Advantage: The Power of Unlearning and Learning', *Organizational Dynamics*, Winter 1999, pp 24–38.

71 J Case, 'A Company of Businesspeople', *Inc.*, April 1993, p 86.

72 Based on a group exercise in L W Mealiea, *Skills for Managers in Organizations* (Burr Ridge, IL: Irwin, 1994), pp 198–201.

73 The force-field analysis form was quoted directly from ibid, pp 199, 201.

Glossary

Ability *stable characteristic responsible for a person's maximum physical or mental performance*

Accountability practices *Focus on treating diverse employees fairly*

Adaptive perspective *assumes that adaptive cultures enhance a firm's financial performance*

Affirmative action *focuses on achieving equality of opportunity in an organization*

Aggressive style *expressive and self-enhancing but takes unfair advantage of others*

Aided-analytic *using tools to make decisions*

Asch effect *giving in to a unanimous but wrong opposition*

Assertive style *expressive and self-enhancing but does not take advantage of others*

Attention *Being consciously aware of something or someone*

Attitude *learned predispositions towards a given object*

Availability heuristic *tendency to base decisions on information readily available in memory*

Baseline data *pre-intervention data collected by someone other than the target person*

Behavioural contingencies *antecedent → behaviour → consequence (A→B→C) relationships*

Behaviour chart *programme evaluation graph with baseline and intervention data*

Behaviour modification *making specific behaviour occur more or less often by managing its cues and consequences*

Behavioural self-management *modifying one's own behaviour by managing cues, cognitive processes and consequences*

Benchmarking *process by which a company compares its performance with that of high-performing organizations*

Bounded rationality *constraints that restrict decision-making*

Brainstorming *process to generate a quantity of ideas*

Buffers *resources or administrative changes that reduce burn-out*

Bureaucracy *Max Weber's idea of the most rationally efficient form of organization*

Burn-out *a condition of emotional exhaustion and negative attitudes*

Case study *in-depth study of a single person, group or organization*

Casual attributions *suspected or inferred causes of behaviour*

Centralized decision-making *top managers make all key decisions*

Charismatic leadership *transforms employees to pursue organizational goals over self-interests*

Closed system *a relatively self-sufficient entity*

Coalition *temporary groupings of people who actively pursue a single issue*

Coercive power *obtaining compliance through threatened or actual punishment*

Cognitions *a person's knowledge, opinions or beliefs*

Cognitive categories *mental depositories for storing information*

Cognitive style *a perceptual and judgemental tendency, according to Jung's typology*

Cohesiveness *a sense of 'we-ness' that helps group stick together*

Collaborative computing *using computer software and hardware to help people work together better*

Collectivist culture *personal goals less important than community goals and interests*

Communication *interpersonal exchange of information and understanding*

Communication competence *ability to use the appropriate communication behaviour effectively in a given context*

Communication distortion *purposely modifying the content of a message*

Conflict *one party perceives its interests are being opposed or set back by another party*

Conflict triangle *conflicting parties involve a third person rather than dealing directly with each other*

Consensus *presenting opinions and gaining agreement to support a decision*

Consideration *creating mutual respect and trust between leader and followers*

Contingency approach *using management tools and techniques in a situationally appropriate manner; avoiding the one-best-way mentality*

Contingency approach to organization design *creating an effective organization–environment fit*

Contingency factors *situational variables that influence the appropriateness of a leadership style*

Continuous reinforcement *reinforcing every instance of a behaviour*

Control strategy *coping strategy that directly confronts or solves problems*

Coping *process of managing stress*

Core job dimensions *job characteristics found to various degrees in all jobs*

Creativity *process of developing something new or unique*

Cross-cultural management *understanding and teaching behavioural patterns in different cultures*

Cross-cultural training *structured experiences to help people adjust to a new culture or country*

Cross-functionalism *team made up of technical specialists from different areas*

Culture *socially derived, taken-for-granted assumptions about how to think and act*

culture shock *anxiety and doubt caused by an overload of new expectations and cues*

Decentralized decision-making *lower-level managers are empowered to make important decisions*

Decision-making *identifying and choosing solutions that lead to a desired end result*

Decision-making style *a combination of how individuals perceive and respond to information*

Delegation *granting decision-making authority to people at lower levels*

Delphi technique *group process that anonymously generates ideas from physically dipersed experts*

Development practices *Focus on preparing diverse employees for greater responsibility and advancement.*

Devil's Advocacy *assigning someone the role of critic*

Dialectic method *fostering a debate of opposing viewpoints to better understand an issue*

Differentiation *division of labour and specialization that cause people to think and act differently*

Distributive justice *the perceived fairness of how resources and rewards are distributed*

Diversity *the host of individual differences that makes people different from, and similar to, each other*

Dysfunctional conflict *threatens organization's interests*

Electronic mail *uses the Internet/Intranet to send computer-generated text and documents*

Empowerment *sharing varying degrees of power with lower-level employees to better serve the customer*

Emotions *complex human reactions to personal achievements and setbacks that may be felt and displayed*

Enacted values *the values and norms that are exhibited by employees*

Equity theory *holds that motivation is a function of fairness in social exchanges*

Escalation of commitment *sticking to an ineffective course of action too long*

Escape strategy *coping strategy that avoids or ignores stressors and problems*

Espoused values *the stated values and norms preferred by an organization*

Ethics *study of moral issues and choices*

Ethnocentrism *belief that one's native country, culture, language and behaviour are superior*

Eustress *stress that is good or produces a positive outcome*

Expatriate *anyone living or working in a foreign country*

Expectancy *belief that effort leads to a specific level of performance*

Expectancy theory *holds that people are motivated to behave in ways that produce valued outcomes*

Experienced meaningfulness *feeling that one's job is important and worthwhile*

Experienced responsibility *believing that one is accountable for work outcomes*

Expert power *obtaining compliance through one's knowledge or information*

External factors *environmental characteristics that cause behaviour*

External forces for change *originate outside the organization*

External locus of control *attributing outcomes to circumstances beyond one's control*

Extinction *making behaviour occur less often by ignoring it or not reinforcing it*

Extranet *connects internal employees with selected customers, suppliers and strategic partners*

Extrinsic rewards *financial, material or social rewards from the environment*

Feedback *objective information about performance*

Field study *examination of variables in real-life settings*

Fight-or-flight response *to either confront stressors or try to avoid them*

Fit perspective *assumes that culture must align with its business or strategic context*

Functional analysis *reducing person-environment interaction to $A \rightarrow B \rightarrow C$ terms*

Functional conflict *serves organization's interests*

Functional social support *support sources that buffer stress in specific situations*

Fundamental attribution bias *ignoring environmental factors that affect behaviour*

Gainsharing *bonuses tied to measurable productivity increases*

'Garbage can' model *holds that decision-making is sloppy and haphazard*

Glass ceiling *invisible barrier blocking women and minorities from top management positions*

Global social support *the total amount of social support available*

Goal *what an individual is trying to accomplish*

Goal commitment *amount of commitment to achieving a goal*

Goal difficulty *the amount of effort required to meet a goal*

Goal specificity *quantifiability of a goal*

Grapevine *unofficial communication system of the informal organization*

Group cohesiveness *a 'we feeling' binding members of a group together*

Groupthink *Janis's term for a cohesive in-group's unwillingness to view alternatives realistically*

Hardiness *personality characteristic that neutralizes stress*

High-context cultures *primary meaning derived from non-verbal situational cues*

Hierarchical communication *xchange of information between managers and employees*

Holistic wellness approach *advocates personal responsibility for reducing stressors and stress*

Hygiene factors *job characteristics associated with dissatisfaction*

Impression management *getting others to see us in a certain manner*

Individualistic culture *primary emphasis on personal freedom and choice*

Information Richness *information-carrying capacity of data*

Initiating structure *organizing and defining what group members should be doing*

Instrumental cohesiveness *sense of togetherness based on the mutual dependency required to get the job done*

Instrumentality *a performance $\rightarrow$ outcome perception*

Instrumental values *personally preferred ways of behaving*

Integration *co-operation among specialists to achieve common goals*

Intelligence *capacity for constructive thinking, reasoning, problem solving*

Interactional justice *the perceived fairness of the decision-maker's behaviour in the process of making decisions*

Intermittent reinforcement *reinforcing some but not all instances of behaviour*

Internal factors *personal characteristics that cause behaviour*

Internal forces for change *originate inside the organization*

Internal locus of control *attributing outcomes to one's own actions*

Internal motivation *motivation caused by positive internal feelings*

Internet *a global network of computer networks*

Intranet *an organization's private Internet*

Intrinsic rewards *self-granted, psychic rewards*

Job design *changing the content and/or process of a specific job to increase job satisfaction and performance*

Job enlargement *putting more variety into one job*

Job enrichment *text to go here?*

Job rotation *moving employees from one specialized job to another*

Job satisfaction *an affective or emotional response to one's job*

Judgement heuristic *rules of thumb or shortcuts that people use to reduce information-processing demands*

Knowledge of results *feedback about work outcomes*

Laboratory study *manipulation and measurement of variables in contrived situations*

Law of Effect *behaviour with favourable consequences is repeated; behaviour with unfavourable consequences disappears*

Leader-member relations *extent to which leader has the support, loyalty and trust of work group*

Leadership *influencing employees to voluntarily pursue organizational goals*

Leadership Grid® *Represents four leadership styles found by crossing concern for production and concern for people*

Leadership prototype *mental representation of the traits and behaviours possessed by leaders*

Leader trait *personal characteristic that differentiates a leader from a follower*

learned helplessness *debilitating lack of faith in one's ability to control the situation*

Learning capabilities *the set of core competencies and internal processes that enable an organization to adapt to its environment*

Learning modes *the various ways in which organizations attempt to create and maximize their learning*

Learning organization *proactively creates, acquires and transfers knowledge throughout the organization and changes its behaviour on the basis of new knowledge and insights*

Legitimate power *obtaining compliance through formal authority*

Liaison individuals *consistently pass grapevine information along to others*

Line managers *have authority to make organizational decisions*

Listening *actively decoding and interpreting verbal messages*

Low context cultures *primary meaning derived from written and spoken words*

Management *process of working with and through others to achieve organizational objectives efficiently and ethically*

Management by objectives *management system incorporating participation in decision-making, goal-setting and feedback*

Managing diversity *creating organizational changes that enable all people to perform up to their maximum potential*

Mechanistic organizations *rigid, command-and-control bureaucracies*

Mentoring *process of forming and maintaining developmental relationships between a mentor and a junior person*

Meta-analysis *pools the results of many studies through statistical procedure*

Met expectations *the extent to which one receives what he or she expects from a job*

Mission statement *summarizes 'why' an organization exists*

Monochronic time *preference for doing one thing at a time because time is limited, precisely segmented and schedule driven*

Motivating potential score *the amount of internal work motivation associated with a specific job*

Motivation *psychological processes that arouse and direct goal-directed behaviour*

Motivators *job characteristics associated with job satisfaction*

Mutuality of interest *balancing individual and organizational interests through win-win co-operation*

Natural rewards *normal social interactions such as praise or recognition*

Needs *physiological or psychological deficiencies that arouse behaviour*

Need for achievement *desire to accomplish something difficult*

Need for affiliation *desire to spend time in social relationships and activities*

Need for power *desire to influence, coach, teach or encourage others to achieve*

Negative equity *comparison in which another person receives greater outcomes for similar inputs*

Negative reinforcement *making behaviour occur more often by contingently withdrawing something negative*

Negotiation *give-and-take process between conflicting interdependent parties*

Noise *interference with the transmission and understanding of a message*

Nominal group technique *process to generate ideas and evaluate solutions*

Non-analytic *using rules, formulated beforehand, to make decisions*

Non-assertive style *timid and self-denying behaviour*

Non-verbal communication *messages sent that are neither written nor spoken*

Normative beliefs *thoughts and beliefs about expected behaviour and modes of conduct*

Open system *organism that must constantly interact with its environment to survive*

Operant behaviour *Skinner's term for learned, consequence-shaped behaviour*

Optimizing *choosing the best possible solution*

Organic organizations *fluid and flexible network of multitalented people.*

Organization *system of consciously co-ordinated activities of two or more people*

Organizational behaviour *interdisciplinary field dedicated to better understanding of management of people at work*

Organizational culture *shared values and beliefs that underlie a company's identity*

Organizational decline *decrease in organization's resource base (money, customers, talent, innovations)*

Organization development *a set of techniques or tools that are used to implement organizational change*

Organizational ecologists *those who study the effect of environmental factors on organizational success/failure and interrelationships among populations and communities of organizations*

Organizational identification *organizational values or beliefs become part of one's self-identity*

Organizational moles *use the grapevine to enhance their power and status*

Organizational politics *intentional enhancement of self-interest*

Organizational Socialization *process by which employees learn an organization's values, norms and required behaviours*

Organization-based self-esteem (OBSE) *an organization member's self-perceived value*

Organization chart *graphic illustration showing chain of formal authority and division of labour*

Paradigm *a generally accepted way of viewing the world*

Participative management *involving employees in various forms of decision-making*

Pay for performance *monetary incentives tied to one's results or accomplishments*

Perception *process of interpreting one's environment*

Perceptual model of communication *consecutively linked elements within the communication process*

Persistence *extent to which effort is expended on a task over time*

Personal initiative *going beyond formal job requirements and being an active self-starter*

Personality *stable physical and mental characteristics responsible for a person's identity*

Personality conflict *interpersonal opposition driven by personal dislike or disagreement*

Personalized power *directed at helping oneself*

Polychronic time *preference for doing more than one thing at a time because time is flexible and multidimensional*

Position power *degree to which leader has formal power*

Positive equity *comparison in which another person receives lesser outcomes for similar inputs*

Positive reinforcement *making behaviour occur more often by contingently presenting something positive*

Postmodern organizations *flexible organizations that are decentralized, computer linked and less hierarchical than bureaucracies*

Prevalence (or representativeness) heuristic *tendency to assess the likelihood of an event occurring based on impressions about similar occurrences*

Problem *gap between an actual and desired situation*

Procedural justice *the perceived fairness of the process and procedures used to make allocation decisions*

Process-style listeners *likes to discuss issues in detail*

Profit sharing *portion of bottom-line economic profits given to employees*

Programmed conflict *encourages different opinions without protecting management's personal feelings*

Propensity to trust *a personality trait involving one's general willingness to trust others*

Proxemics *Hall's term for the cultural expectations about interpersonal space*

Psychological contract *can be defined as the written and implied expectations between employer and employee*

Punishment *making behaviour occur less often by contingently presenting something negative or withdrawing something positive*

Quality circles *small groups of volunteers who strive to solve quality-related problems*

Rational model *logical four-step approach to decision-making*

Readiness *follower's ability and willingness to complete a task*

Realistic job preview *presents both positive and negative aspects of a job*

Reality shock *a newcomer's feeling of surprise after experiencing unexpected situations or events*

Reasons-style listeners *interested in hearing the rationale behind a message*

Reciprocity *widespread belief that people should be given something in return for their positive or negative act*

Recruitment practices *attempts to attract qualified, diverse employees at all levels*

Referent power *obtaining compliance through charisma or personal attraction*

Relaxation response *state of peacefulness*

Resistance to change *emotional/behavioural response to real or imagined work changes*

Respondent behaviour *Skinner's term for unlearned stimulus– response reflexes*

Results-style listeners *interested in hearing the bottom line or result of a message*

Reward equality norm *everyone should get the same rewards*

Reward equity norm *rewards should be tied to contributions*

Reward power *obtaining compliance with promised or actual rewards*

Sample survey *questionnaire responses from a sample of people*

Satisficing *choosing a solution that meets a minimum standard of acceptance*

Scenario technique *speculative forecasting method*

Schema *mental picture of an event or object*

Self-concept *person's self-perception as a physical, social, spiritual being*

Self-efficacy *belief in one's ability to do a task*

Self-esteem *one's overall self-evaluation*

Self-fulfilling prophecy *people's expectations determine behaviour and performance*

Self-managed teams *groups of employees granted administrative oversight for their work*

Self-management leadership *process of leading others to lead themselves*

Self-monitoring *observing one's own behaviour and adapting it to the situation*

Sex-role stereotype *beliefs about appropriate roles for men and women*

Self-serving bias *taking more personal responsibility for succes than failure*

Self-talk *evaluating thoughts about oneself*

Servant-leadership *focuses on increased service to others rather than to oneself*

Shaping *reinforcing closer and closer approximations to a target behaviour*

Situational theories *propose that leader styles should match the situation at hand*

Skill *specific capacity to manipulate objects*

Socialized power *directed at helping others*

Social loafing *decrease in individual effort as group size increases*

Social power *ability to get things done using human, informational and material resources*

Social support *amount of helpfulness derived from social relationships*

Socio-emotional cohesiveness *sense of togetherness based on emotional satisfaction*

Span of control *the number of people reporting directly to a given manager*

Staff personnel *provide research, advice and recommendations to line managers*

Stakeholder audit *systematic identification of all parties likely to be affected by the organization*

Stereotype *beliefs about the characteristics of a group*

Strategic constituency *any group of people with a stake in the organization's operation or success*

Strategic plan *a long-term plan outlining actions needed to achieve planned results*

Strength perspective *assumes that the strength of corporate culture is related to a firm's financial performance*

Stress *behavioural, physical or psychological response to stressors*

Stressful life events *life events that disrupt daily routines and social relationships*

Stressors *environmental factors that produce stress*

Substitutes for leadership *situational variables that can substitue for, neutralize or enhance the effects of leadership*

Superleader *someone who leads others to lead themselves*

Symptom management strategy *coping strategy that focuses on reducing the symptoms of stress*

Target elements of change *components of an organization that may be changed*

Task structure *amount of structure contained within work tasks*

Team *small group with complementary skills who hold themselves mutually accountable for common purpose, goals and approach*

Team-based pay *linking pay to teamwork behaviour and/or team results*

Team building *experiential learning aimed at better internal functioning of groups*

Team viability *team members satisfied and willing to contribute*

Telecommuting *doing work that is generally performed in the office away from the office using different information technologies*

Terminal values *personally preferred states of existence (or 'end-states')*

Theory *a story defining key terms, providing a conceptual framework and explaining why something occurs*

Theory Y *McGregor's modern and positive assumptions about employees being responsible and creative*

Total quality management *an organizational culture dedicated to training, continuous improvement and customer satisfaction*

Transactional leadership *focuses on interpersonal interactions between managers and employees*

Trust *reciprocal faith in other's intentions and behaviour*

Type A behaviour syndrome *aggressively involved in a chronic, determined struggle to accomplish more in less time*

Unaided-analytic *analysis is limited to processing information in one's mind*

Unity of command principle *each employee should report to a single manager*

Upward feedback *subordinates evaluate their boss*

Valence *the value of a reward or outcome*

Value attainment *the extent to which a job allows fulfillment of one's work values*

Value (personal) *durable belief in a way of behaving or a preferred state of existence ('end-state')*

Values *enduring belief in a mode of conduct or end-state*

Value system
the organization of one's belief about preferred ways of behaving and state ('end-state') of belief

Value system *pattern of values within an organization*

Valuing diversity *text to go here?*

Virtual team *information technology allows group members in different locations to conduct business*

Vision *long-term goal describing what an organization wants to become*

Workforce demographics *statistical profiles of adult workers*

360-degree feedback *comparison of anonymous feedback from one's superior, subordinates and peers, with one's self-perceptions*

Indexes

Name

COMPANY

SUBJECT

3197723S